To Peter Hennessy
with the kindest regards
Henry Mayhew [?]
July 1995

GW00762996

THE WHITEHALL COMPANION 1995-96

THE WHITEHALL COMPANION 1995-96

Foreword by Richard Mottram

Permanent Secretary, Ministry of Defence

DPR

Editor: Hilary Muggridge

Assistant Editor: Clare McVey

Production Editor: Isobel Smythe-Wood

Editorial: Diana LeCore, Valerie Passmore

Published by DPR Publishing Limited
33 John Street
London WC1N 2AT England

Chairman: Lord Holme of Cheltenham

First published in 1995

ISBN 1 872110 86 X

Typeset by Method Limited, Epping, Essex

Printed in the United Kingdom by Redwood Books, Trowbridge, Wiltshire

CONTENTS

FOREWORD

Last July the government published the White Paper *The Civil Service, Continuity and Change*, the first government document since the Fulton Report, more than 25 years ago, to address the role and future of the civil service as a whole. Following an important report by the Treasury and Civil Service Committee on *The Role of the Civil Service* and a further Command Paper, a clear way ahead has been established, built on continuity in the values of a permanent, politically-impartial civil service and the need for further change to improve performance.

Both the government and the select committee have reasserted the importance of the values on which the British civil service has been based for 100 years and more: integrity, objectivity, political impartiality, selection and promotion on merit, and accountability through ministers to Parliament.

At the same time the civil service must embrace all that is best in modern management practice. The change element includes more delegation of responsibility – for organisational structures, pay, grading, efficiency – to departments and agencies within tightly-controlled running costs; and the creation from next April of a new wider senior civil service including all agency chief executives.

"Whitehall" houses some of the nerve-centre of government and tends to be used as a symbol and a label for the whole civil service. But it is sometimes overlooked that only some 10 per cent of civil servants are engaged in classic Whitehall functions – policy making, resource allocation, legislation, regulation and so on. The vast majority of the staff and the resources are devoted to executive activities of many kinds, spread right across the whole country. Eighty per cent of the civil service now works outside London.

Within the next year or so, three-quarters of the total civil service will be working in "Next Steps" executive agencies. The nature of the work at senior levels in the service, and the mix of people performing it, are changing too. And the service is seeking to be more responsive to the needs of its users – whether individuals or organisations – and to be more open. The last year has seen the introduction of a Code of Practice on Access to Government Information, with independent review by the Parliamentary Ombudsman of disputes about the provision of government information.

Change on this scale is difficult enough for insiders to keep up with. But the civil service exists not for itself but for the benefit of the population as a whole, and they need help to find their way around its emerging structures. A quick glance at the biographies of individual civil servants – and of their military and diplomatic service colleagues – shows too the breadth of talent and diversity of backgrounds and experience on which the Government can call. I therefore very much welcome the publication on an annual basis of *The Whitehall Companion*, a guide to a "village" and to a potentially strange and diverse jungle whose inhabitants offer, we hope, an increasingly friendly and helpful face.

Richard Mottram
Permanent Secretary,
Ministry of Defence

Acknowledgements

We are grateful for the continuing support and encouragement of Sir Robin Butler, Secretary of the Cabinet Office and Head of the Home Civil Service, and Sir John Coles, Head of the Diplomatic Service.

Once again we should like to thank for their help and advice the many patient and long-suffering civil servants and officials in the parliamentary offices, government departments, next steps agencies and other bodies which go to make up this directory, in particular Alastair Howie from the Cabinet Office.

Our thanks also to all those who agreed to appear in the biographies section of the book, our unflagging and hardworking editorial team listed earlier, and finally to our indefatigable typesetters.

INTRODUCTION

The 1995–96 edition of *The Whitehall Companion* contains the following changes:

● The Security and Intelligence Services entry (see government departments' section) has been expanded to include the following:

- The Intelligence and Security Committee (the committee of MPs and peers which scrutinises the work of MI5, MI6 and GCHQ);
- Details of the staff counsellor for the security and intelligence services;
- Details of the two bodies investigating complaints from the public about the security and intelligence services: the Intelligence Services Tribunal and the Security Service Tribunal, can be found in the regulatory organisations' section.

● The ten Government Offices for the Regions now have a separate entry under the government departments' section as well as a brief entry in their "home" departments: Employment, Environment, Trade and Industry and Transport.

ABOUT THIS BOOK

This is the fourth edition of *The Whitehall Companion*, published by DPR Publishing, which brings together the biographies of senior civil servants and other top people in Whitehall and its environs, with the structure and functions of government departments, next steps agencies and various regulatory and public bodies.

Last minute changes are included in the Addenda. In the event of a government reshuffle subscribers will be sent, gratis, a list of the new ministers, their advisers and their parliamentary private secretaries and any changes in responsibility.

Biographies

The biographical section runs first and each entry contains some of or all the following information:

- Name, present job and grade (where known/if applicable) printed in bold type at the beginning of each entry
- Career details and information on any current non-Whitehall positions
- Some personal details: education, professional qualifications, honours and decorations, marriage, children and recreations
- Office addresses and fax numbers

There are biographies of:

- Top civil servants in government departments
- Chief executives and other senior staff in the government's 'next steps' executive agencies
- Senior people in the 103 selected regulatory organisations and other public bodies
- Ministers' advisers
- Staff in the No 10 Policy Unit

Civil servants included in this section are mainly grades 1–4 but, occasionally, grades 5–6 where the person concerned runs a next steps executive agency.

We have not included the biographies of ministers which can be found in the current edition of Dod's Parliamentary Companion.

Institutions

Parliamentary Offices

This section comprises the parliamentary offices (House of Commons, Lords, National Audit Office, Northern Ireland Audit Office) which are organised as follows:

Introduction

- Where relevant, when the office was founded
- Status
- Organisation
- Responsibilities
- Number of staff

Officials

- Addresses, telephone and, where relevant, fax numbers
- Listing of senior officials

Overview
– A brief overview of the work of the office, which indicates visually the management structure which links senior officials with other staff

Officials and their Offices
– Visual presentation of all the different sections within the offices showing the management structure, top officials, senior staff, the departments with which they deal, and the work they do

Government Departments

This section covers government departments. The entries are organised alphabetically as follows:

Introduction
– Date founded
– Number and rank of ministers
– To which minister responsible if a non-ministerial department
– Responsibilities
– Number of staff
– Names and numbers of executive agencies sponsored by that department

Ministers
– Main address, telephone and fax numbers of departments
– Ministers, their special advisers, parliamentary private secretaries and private secretaries
– House of Lords' spokesmen

Ministers' Responsibilities
– Detailed list of each minister's responsibilities

Departmental Overview
– A brief overview of the department's work which indicates visually the management structure which links ministers to civil servants to divisions within each department.

Civil Servants and Department
– Visual presentation of all the different sections within a department showing the management structure including top officials, senior staff (grades 1/2 down to grades 5/6), the divisions with which they deal and the work those divisions do.

Addresses/telephone/fax numbers
– Details of the department's subsidiary addresses, telephone and, where appropriate, fax numbers

'Next Steps' Executive Agencies

Details of the government's 108 'next steps' executive agencies in alphabetical order of agency. At the beginning of the section is a listing of all the agencies, plus the 65 candidates being considered for agency status

Each entry consists of:
– Name, address, telephone and fax numbers
– Senior staff
– Responsibilities
– Number of staff
– Sponsoring department
– Date launched

Regulatory Organisations and Public Bodies

A selection of 103 regulatory and public bodies including, for example, OFTEL, the Office of Telecommunications, the Monopolies and Mergers Commission, the Parliamentary Ombudsmen and the Independent Television Commission. At the beginning of this section is a complete list of all the organisations included. The alphabetical entries are organised as follows:
- Name, address, telephone and fax numbers
- Senior officials/staff
- Responsibilities
- Date founded

Abbreviations

A complete list of abbreviations of honours and decorations, academic and professional qualifications, parliamentary offices, government departments, next steps agencies and other organisations.

This list should be used in conjunction with the name index (see below).

Indexes

– A name index listing each person mentioned in the Companion, the department/agency/organisation with which they are associated, and where in the book they can be located. The relevant department/agency/organisation is represented by an acronym, the explanation of which can be found in the Abbreviations section.
– A general purpose index which includes the names of all the departments and organisations covered in the Companion

Civil Service Grading

Home Civil Service

0	**Head of the Home Civil Service**	
1	**Permanent Secretary**	Permanent head of a government department or (Grade 1A) head of distinct and major areas of policy within departments
1A	**2nd Permanent Secretary**	
2	**Deputy Secretary**	Heads of small departments or large executive agencies*. Heads of professions or substantial areas of policy within departments
3	**Under Secretary**	Comparable to board members in major companies. Most common level for holders of non-executive directorships
4		Generally senior professional civil servants
5	**Assistant Secretary**	Heads of discrete areas of policy

6 Senior Principal	In major executive areas** may command large regions with up to 30 local offices
7 Principal	In headquarters offices heads of smallest units of command reporting to grade 5 In executive areas heads of larger local offices
Higher Executive Officer Development (HEOD) **Administration Trainee (AT)**	Fast stream entry points to civil service for graduates or serving civil servants with two years service
Senior Executive Officer (SEO)	In headquarters offices may be either heads of smaller branches or deputise for grade 7 heads of larger branches. In executive areas heads of small local offices or second tier of management in large offices. SEOs often manage over 100 staff
Higher Executive Officer HEO	In headquarters offices HEOs often work directly to grade 7s, helping formulate and amend policy, prepare briefings, and represent their branches at meetings In executive areas HEOs have substantial management reponsibilities or deal with complex casework or a mixture of the two
Executive Officer (EO)	A major recruitment grade. In headquarters offices EOs help formulate and amend policy, prepare first drafts of briefings, gather and analyse information, and manage support staff. They normally work to an HEO In executive areas, EOs manage large numbers of clerical staff (AOs and AAs) where these are the working grades, or carry out relatively complex casework
Administrative Officer (AO) **Administrative Assistant (AA)**	These grades carry out the more routine casework, data processing and provide clerical support to more senior staff

* Executive Agencies are headed up at levels appropriate to the size and responsibilities of the agency. The major agencies are now in the process of assuming responsibility for designing their own grading systems, which means they will not necessarily fit in with the system described above.

** Executive areas of government, which include Next Steps agencies, are responsible for providing public services, such as paying sickness benefits and pensions, collecting taxes and national insurance contributions, running employment services, and providing services to industry and agriculture.

Diplomatic Service

The Diplomatic Service operates a different system of grading, details of which are given below.

PUS	No grade 1s in FCO
Senior grades 1 – 5	*Specialist/support staff:* Chief Economic Adviser
4	Conference Interpreter; Legal Counsellor *Specialist/support staff:* Senior Economic Adviser
5S	Senior Principal; Research Officer; Senior Assistant Legal Officer *Specialist/support staff:* Accountant
5	Principal; Research Officer; Assistant Legal Officer *Specialist/support staff:* Senior Investigating Officer; Economic Adviser; Accountant
6	*Specialist/support staff:* includes librarians, translators, information and field investigating officers and senior professional and technology officers
7D	Senior Research Officer *Specialist/support staff:* Senior Economic Assistant
7M	*Specialist/support staff:* includes librarians, translators, lecturers, information and field investigating officers and higher professional and technology officers, mapping and charting officers
8	Research Officer *Specialist/support staff:* Economic Assistant
9 **S1**	junior executive staff; senior secretarial staff
10 **S2**	clerks; personal secretaries
S3C	secretarial staff

Below is an abbreviated guide to the equivalent Home Civil Service and Diplomatic Service grades

Home Civil Service	**Diplomatic Service**
1	Permanent Under Secretary
2 – 4	Senior grades 1 – 5

5	DS 4
6	DS 5S
7	DS 5
SEO	DS 6
HEO(D)	DS 7D
HEO	DS 7M
AT	DS 8
EO	DS 9/S1
AO	DS 10/S2
AA	—
Clerical	DS S3C

ADDENDA

Government reshuffle

In the event of a government reshuffle subscribers to *The Whitehall Companion* will be sent, gratis, an updated listing of government ministers, their advisers and, where known, their parliamentary private secretaries.

Home Office: HM Inspectorate of Prisons

His Honour Judge Stephen Tumim, HM Chief Inspector of Prisons, England and Wales is to step down in November 1995. No replacement has yet been announced.

Prime Minister's Office: No 10 Policy Unit

The names and portfolios of the new members of the Prime Minister's Policy Unit are included in the Institutions section of *The Whitehall Companion*, although the newer members were appointed too late for their biographies to be included in this edition. **Nicholas True** has now left the Policy Unit.

Social Security

Sir Michael Partridge, Permanent Secretary at Social Security, is retiring in September 1995. He is being replaced by **Mrs Ann Bowtwell**, currently a Deputy Secretary in the department.

Regulatory Organisations: Local Government Commission for England

Bob Chilton, Director of Local Government Studies at the Audit Commission, has been seconded to be the new Chief Executive of the Local Government Commission for England, replacing **Martin Easteal**. Mr Chilton's twelve-month appointment began in June 1995.

Office of Fair Trading

Jeffrey Preston, currently Deputy Director-General of the Office of Fair Trading has become Acting Director-General following the resignation of Sir Bryan Carsberg from that post.

Office of the NI Parliamentary Commissioner for Administration; Office of the NI Commissioner for Complaints

Mrs Jill McIvor, is retiring in January 1996 as Ombudsman of both the Office of the Northern Ireland Parliamentary Commissioner for Administration and the Office of the Northern Ireland Commissioner for Complaints. No replacement has yet been announced.

Biographies

A-Z

A

ADAMS, DONALD WATSON Chief Crown Prosecutor, Humber, Crown Prosecution Service Grade: 4

Career: solicitor; Crown Prosecution Service: chief crown prosecutor, Humber 1993-

Date of birth: 5 April 1935 *Education/professional qualifications:* Kingswood School, Bath; Leeds University, law (LLB) *Marital status:* married Helga Stoxreiter 1971; 2 daughters *Recreations:* music, theatre

D W Adams Esq, Chief Crown Prosecutor, Humber, Crown Prosecution Service, Belgrave House, 47 Bank Street, Sheffield S1 2EH
Telephone: 01142 731261 *Fax:* 01142 762468

ADAMS, GORDON DUDLEY Secretary of the Commission for Local Administration in England (Local Government Ombudsman)

Career: hospital secretary various London hospitals 1962-68; deputy house governor Hammersmith hospital 1968-74; district administrator (DA) North Hammersmith health district 1974-76; Bromley health authority 1976-87: area administrator 1976-82, DA 1982-86, director of planning 1986-87; secretary of Commission for Local Administration in England 1987-

Date of birth: 28 July 1934 *Education/professional qualifications:* Bristol Grammar School; King's College, London, classics (BA 1956); AKC, MHSM, DipHSM *Marital status:* married Esther Jean 1992; 1 daughter *Recreations:* music, photography, DIY

Gordon D Adams Esq, Secretary of the Commission for Local Administration in England, 21 Queen Anne's Gate, London SW1H 9BU
Telephone: 0171-915 3210 *Fax:* 0171-233 0396

ADAMS, KEITH Special Adviser to Secretary of State for the Environment

Career: political secretary to John Selwyn Gummer; research assistant to Michael Marshall MP; special adviser to Mr Gummer as Minister for Agriculture, Fisheries and Food 1990-93, Secretary of State for Environment 1993-

Keith Adams Esq, Special Adviser, Department of the Environment, 2 Marsham Street, London SW1P 3EB *Telephone:* 0171-276 3511

ADDISON, MARK ERIC Director, Safety Policy Division, Health and Safety Executive Grade: 3

Career: British Airways 1973-74; student 1974-78; Department of Employment/Employment Department Group 1978-: Health and Safety Executive (HSE) and Manpower Services Commission 1978-82; private secretary (PS) to parliamentary under secretary 1982-83, principal training policy 1983-85; PS to prime minister 1985-88; London regional director Training Agency/Training, Enterprise and Education Directorate 1988-91; under secretary, director finance and resource management, resources and strategy directorate 1991-94; director safety policy division HSE 1994-

Date of birth: 22 January 1951 *Education/professional qualifications:* Marlborough College; St John's College, Cambridge, engineering (BA 1972, MA); City University, management science (MSc 1973); Imperial College,

London, industrial sociology (PhD and DIC 1979) *Marital status:* married Lucy Booth 1987

Mark E Addison, Under Secretary, Health and Safety Executive, Rose Court, 2 Southwark Bridge, London SE1 9HS *Telephone:* 0171-717 6203 *Fax:* 0171-717 6190

ADYE, Sir JOHN ANTHONY Director, Government Communications Headquarters (GCHQ)

Career: Government Communications Headquarters 1962-: second permanent secretary 1992-

Date of birth: 24 October 1939

Sir John Adye KCMG, Director, Government Communications Headquarters, Priors Road, Cheltenham, Gloucester GL52 5AJ *Telephone:* 01242 221491

AINSCOW, ROBERT MORRISON Deputy Secretary, Overseas Development Administration Grade: 2

Career: government of Rhodesia and Nyasaland 1957-61; UN secretariat 1961-65, 1966-68; Department of Economic Affairs 1965-66; Ministry of Overseas Development/Overseas Development Administration 1968-: economic adviser (EA) 1968-70; EA 1970-76; head South Asia department 1976-79; under secretary and principal finance officer 1979-86: chairman OECD development assistance committee working party on financial aspects of development assistance 1982-86; deputy secretary 1986-

Date of birth: 3 June 1936 *Education/professional qualifications:* Salford Grammar School; Liverpool University, economics (BA Econ 1957) *Honours, decorations:* CB 1989 *Marital status:* married Faye Bider 1965; 1 daughter, 1 son

Robert M Ainscow Esq CB, Deputy Secretary, Overseas Development Administration, 94 Victoria Street, London SW1E 5JL *Telephone:* 0171-917 0480 *Fax:* 0171-917 0651

ALCOCK, Air Chief Marshal Sir (ROBERT JAMES) MICHAEL Air Officer Commanding-in-Chief Logistics, Air Member for Logistics Command and Chief Engineer (RAF)

Career: Royal Air Force (RAF) 1958-: junior engineering appointments 1958-70; personal staff officer to director-general (DG) engineering (RAF) 1970-72; officer commanding (OC) engineering wing RAF Coningsby 1972-74; OC 23 maintenance unit RAF Aldergrove 1975-77; group captain plans HQ support command 1977-79; director of ground training Ministry of Defence (MoD) 1979-81; deputy commandant RAF staff college, Bracknell 1981-84; DG communications/information systems and organisation 1985-88; air officer (AO) engineering and supply HQ Strike Command 1988-91; MoD 1991-; chief of logistics support and chief engineer (CE) (RAF) 1991-93; air member (AM) for supply and organisation 1993-94; AO commanding-in-chief Logistics Command, AM for logistics and CE 1994-

Date of birth: 11 July 1936 *Education/professional qualifications:* Victoria College, Jersey; Royal Aircraft Establishment (CEng; FIMechE; FRAeS); RAF College Cranwell, air warfare course 1974; Royal College of Defence Studies 1984 *Honours, decorations:* CB 1989, KBE 1992 *Recreations:* golf

Air Chief Marshal Sir Michael Alcock KBE CB, Air Officer Commanding-in-Chief Logistics Command, RAF Brampton, Huntingdon, Cambridgeshire *Telephone and Fax:* 01480 52151

ALDER, ROY KENNETH **Executive Support, Medicines Control Agency (Executive Agency)** Grade: 4

Career: Department of Health [and Social Security] 1968-90: head of accommodation, purchasing and office services 1986-90; business manager (Executive Support) Medicines Control Agency 1990-

Date of birth: 6 November 1945 *Education/professional qualifications:* Magdalen College School, Brackley, Northamptonshire; Pembroke College, Oxford, history (BA 1967, MA) *Marital status:* married Hilary 1971; 2 daughters *Recreations:* running, skiing

Roy K Alder Esq, Business Manager, Medicines Control Agency, Market Towers, 1 Nine Elms Lane, London SW8 5NQ *Telephone:* 0171-273 0600 *Fax:* 0171-273 0548

ALDERSON, MATTI **Director-General, Advertising Standards Authority**

Career: legal executive Scottish law practices 1970-72; assistant to director Poster Bureau 1972-74, Royds Advertising 1974-75; Advertising Standards Authority (independent control non-broadcast advertising) 1975-: executive and secretary health and nutrition committee 1975-80, manager advertising practice committee 1980-89, deputy director 1989-90, deputy director-general 1990, director-general 1990- *Current non-Whitehall posts:* secretary Committee of Advertising Practice 1990-; member European Advertising Standards Alliance board 1991-; member editorial board Journal of Financial Regulation and Compliance

Date of birth: 20 December 1951 *Education/professional qualifications:* Bearsden Academy, Strathclyde; Open University, arts (BA 1994); FRSA 1993; FCAM 1993 *Marital status:* married Alan 1970 *Publications:* various papers on UK and European advertising control *Clubs:* Arts *Recreations:* design and architecture, travel, reading, driving

Mrs Matti Alderson, Director-General, Advertising Standards Authority, 2 Torrington Place, London WC1E 7HW *Telephone:* 0171-580 5555 *Fax:* 0171-631 3051

ALEXANDER, ROBERT SCOTT (Lord Alexander of Weedon) **Deputy Chairman, Securities and Investments Board**

Career: chairman general council of the Bar 1985-86, Panel on Takeovers and Mergers 1987-89, National Westminster Bank 1989-; deputy chairman Securities and Investments Board (regulation financial services industry) 1994- *Current non-Whitehall posts:* non-executive director RTZ Corporation 1991-

Date of birth: 5 September 1936 *Education/professional qualifications:* Brighton College; King's College, Cambridge, English and law (BA, MA 1959) *Honours, decorations:* QC 1973 *Marital status:* married Marie Anderson 1985; 2 sons, 1 daughter *Clubs:* Garrick *Recreations:* theatre, tennis, gardening

Lord Alexander of Weedon, Deputy Chairman, Securities and Investments Board, Gavrelle House, 2-14 Bunhill Row, London EC1Y 8RA *Telephone:* 0171-638 1240 *Fax:* 0171-382 5900

ALLAN, ALEX(ANDER) CLAUD STUART **Principal Private Secretary to Prime Minister** Grade: 3

Career: HM Customs and Excise 1973-76; HM Treasury 1976-: principal private secretary (PPS) to Chancellor of Exchequer 1986-89; under secretary: international finance 1989-90, general expenditure policy 1990-92; PPS to Prime Minister 1992-

Date of birth: 9 February 1951 *Education/professional qualifications:* Harrow School; Clare College, Cambridge, mathematics (BA 1972); University College, London, statistics (MSc 1973) *Marital status:* married Katie Clemson 1978 *Clubs:* Royal Ocean Racing *Recreations:* Grateful Dead music, sailing, computers, bridge

Alex Allan Esq, Principal Private Secretary to the Prime Minister, 10 Downing Street, London SW1A 2AA *Telephone and Fax:* 0171-930 4433

ALLAN, RICHARD **Head of Urban and Local Transport Directorate, Department of Transport** Grade: 3

Career: assistant principal/principal Department of [Trade and] Industry 1970-79; first secretary civil aviation and shipping Washington DC embassy 1980-84; Department of Transport 1984-: assistant secretary 1984-88, principal private secretary to secretaries of state 1985-87, under secretary 1988-: seconded to British Rail 1988-90, director of personnel 1990-94, head of urban and local transport directorate 1994-

Date of birth: 28 February 1948 *Education/professional qualifications:* Bolton School; Balliol College, Oxford, modern history (BA 1969, MA) *Marital status:* married Katharine Mary Tait 1975; 1 daughter, 1 son *Recreations:* choral singing, walking, theatre

Richard Allan Esq, Under Secretary, Department of Transport, 2 Marsham Street, London SW1P 3EB *Telephone:* 0171-276 5020 *Fax:* 0171-276 5815

ALLEN, (PHILIP) RICHARD HERNAMAN **Under Secretary, Division A, Department of Social Security** Grade: 3

Career: HM Customs and Excise (C&E) 1970-73; assistant private secretary to Paymaster General HM Treasury 1973-74, to Chancellor of Duchy of Lancaster, Cabinet Office 1974-75; C&E 1975-94: principal 1975-84, assistant secretary 1984-90, commissioner and director internal taxes directorate 1990-91, commissioner and director organisation 1991-94; under secretary division A (sick/disabled/maternity benefits, disability unit) Department of Social Security 1994-

Date of birth: 26 January 1949 *Education/professional qualifications:* Loughborough Grammar School; Merton College, Oxford, modern history (BA 1970) *Marital status:* married Vanessa Lampard 1970; 2 daughters *Recreations:* music, badminton, gardening, beer spotting, keep fit

Richard Allen Esq, Under Secretary, Department of Social Security, The Adelphi, 1-11 John Adam Street, London WC2N 6HT
Telephone: 0171-962 8000

ALLISON, RODERICK STUART **Chief Executive, Offshore Safety Division, Health and Safety Executive** Grade: 3

Career: Department of Employment 1959-89; Health and Safety Executive 1989-: director special hazards division 1989-92, safety policy division 1992-93, offshore safety division 1993; chief executive 1994-

Date of birth: 28 November 1936 *Education/professional qualifications:* Manchester Grammar School; Balliol College, Oxford, literae humaniores (MA) *Marital status:* married Anne Sergeant 1968; 1 son, 1 daughter *Recreations:* music, sailing, reading

Roderick Allison Esq, Chief Executive, Offshore Safety Division, Health and Safety Executive, Baynards House, 1 Chepstow Place, Westbourne Grove, London W2 4TF *Telephone:* 0171-717 6701

ALLNUTT, DENIS EDWIN Head of Analytical Services Branch, Department for Education Grade: 3

Career: statistician Ministry of Housing and Local Government, Departments of Environment (DoE) and Transport 1967-82; chief statistician (CS) (employment) Department of Employment 1982-88; CS (housing) DoE 1988-90; head of analytical services branch (economic, operational research and statistical work) Department of/for Education [and Science] 1990-

Date of birth: 17 May 1946 *Education/professional qualifications:* Hampton School, Middlesex; Birmingham University, mathematical statistics (BSc 1967) *Marital status:* married Patricia 1968; 1 son, 1 daughter

Denis E Allnutt Esq, Head of Analytical Services Branch, Department for Education, Sanctuary Buildings, Great Smith Street, London SW1P 3BT *Telephone:* 0171-925 5400 *Fax:* 0171-925 6986

ALLUM, A R Accountancy Adviser, Central Services Directorate, Department of Transport Grade: 4

A R Allum Esq, Accountancy Adviser, Central Services Directorate, Department of Transport, 2 Marsham Street, London SW1P 3EB *Telephone:* 0171-276 5072 *Fax:* 0171-276 5074

ALTOBELL, PAUL Chief Executive, Defence Analytical Services Agency (Executive Agency) Grade: 4

Career: new product development quality control Gillette Industries 1960-69; management consultant 1969-71; statistician/chief statistician Ministry of Defence (MoD) 1971-86; head of statistician group management unit Cabinet Office/Central Statistical Office 1986-91; chief executive Defence Analytical Services Agency (management information and services to MoD) 1992-

Date of birth: 26 April 1939 *Education/professional qualifications:* Gateway School, Leicester; Central London Polytechnic, statistics (CStats 1968); Webster University, USA, business management (MA); MIPM 1988 *Marital status:* married Celia De Val; 1 son, 1 daughter *Recreations:* pre-1939 detective fiction, sport

Paul Altobell Esq, Chief Executive, Defence Analytical Services Agency, Northumberland House, Northumberland Avenue, London WC2N 5BP *Telephone:* 0171-218 0872 *Fax:* 0171-218 5203

Parliamentary Offices

see page 347

AMANN, Professor RONALD Chief Executive and Deputy Chairman, Economic and Social Research Council Grade: 2

Career: consultant Organisation for Economic Co-operation and Development 1965-66; Birmingham University 1966-94: Centre for Russian and East European Studies 1966-89: Soviet science policy lecturer 1968-83, director 1983-89, Soviet politics professor 1986-89; commerce and social science dean 1989-91; pro-vice-chancellor 1991-94; chief executive and deputy chair Economic and Social Research Council 1994- *Current non-Whitehall posts:* non-executive director Birmingham City Hospital NHS Trust 1993-

Date of birth: 21 August 1943 *Education/professional qualifications:* Heaton Grammar School, Newcastle-upon-Tyne; Birmingham University: philosophy and social science (BSocSc 1964), Soviet politics/political science (MSocSc 1967), Soviet science policy (PhD 1976) *Marital status:* married Susan Frances 1965; 2 sons, 1 daughter *Publications:* Science Policy in the USSR (OECD, Paris 1969); The Technological Level of Soviet Industry (Yale University Press 1977); Industrial Innovation in the Soviet Union (Yale University Press 1982); Technical Progress and Soviet Economic Development (Blackwell 1986) *Clubs:* Athenaeum *Recreations:* modern jazz, walking

Professor Ronald Amann, Chief Executive, Economic and Social Research Council, Polaris House, North Star Avenue, Swindon, Wiltshire SN2 1UJ
Telephone: 01793 413004 *Fax:* 01793 413002

ANDERSON, DAVID HEYWOOD Second Legal Adviser, Foreign and Commonwealth Office Senior grade

Career: HM Diplomatic Service 1960-: assistant legal adviser (LA) Foreign and Commonwealth Office (FCO) 1966-69; LA Bonn embassy 1969-72; legal counsellor (LC) FCO 1972-79, 1982-87; LA UK mission to UN, New York 1979-82; FCO 1987-: deputy LA 1987-89, second LA (advice on international, EC and English law, particularly law of the sea) 1989-

Date of birth: 14 September 1937 *Education/professional qualifications:* King James' Grammar School, Almondbury; Leeds University, law (LLB 1958); London School of Economics, law (LLM 1960); Gray's Inn (barrister 1963) *Honours, decorations:* CMG 1982 *Marital status:* married Jennifer Ratcliffe 1961; 1 son, 1 daughter *Publications:* co-author International Maritime Boundaries (American Society of International Law 1993) *Recreations:* gardening, music

David H Anderson Esq CMG, Second Legal Adviser, Foreign and Commonwealth Office, King Charles Street, London SW1A 2AH
Telephone: 0171-270 3043 *Fax:* 0171-270 2767

ANDERSON, GAVIN ALAN Head of Division, Social Work Services Group, Scottish Office Home and Health Department Grade: 4

Career: research architect Edinburgh University 1966-73; Scottish Development Department 1973-85: architect 1973-76, principal architect 1976-85; Scottish Office Home and Health Department 1985-: assistant secretary 1985-90; director of strategic management, deputy chief executive NHS in Scotland 1990-93; head of division 2, social work services group (community care, voluntary sector) 1993-

Date of birth: 5 July 1939 *Education/professional qualifications:* Edinburgh College of Art, architecture (Dip Arch 1965); Edinburgh University, architecture (MPhil 1977) *Marital status:* married Margaret Clarke 1965; 1 son, 1 daughter *Recreations:* music, art, reading, walking

Gavin A Anderson Esq, Social Work Services Group, Scottish Office Home and Health Department, 43 Jeffrey Street, Edinburgh EH1 1DG
Telephone: 0131-244 5452 *Fax:* 0131-244 5514

ARCHER, PETER KINGSLEY (The Rt Hon The Lord Archer of Sandwell) Chairman, Council on Tribunals

Career: barrister 1953; Labour MP for Rowley Regis and Tipton 1966-74, for Warley West 1974-92: chief opposition spokesman on legal affairs 1981-82, on trade 1982-83, on Northern Ireland 1983-87; chairman Amnesty International 1971-74; Solicitor General 1974-79; recorder Crown Court 1980-; chairman Council on Tribunals (supervision tribunals and enquiries; advice on new tribunals and appeals procedures) 1992- *Current non-Whitehall posts:* House of Lords opposition spokesman on foreign affairs

Date of birth: 20 November 1926 *Education/professional qualifications:* Wednesbury High School, Staffordshire; London University, law (LLB 1943); London School of Economics, law (LLM 1950); University College, London, philosophy (BA 1952) *Honours, decorations:* QC 1971; PC 1976; baron 1992 *Marital status:* married Margaret Irene Smith 1954; 1 son *Publications:* The Queen's Courts (Penguin 1954); Communism and the Law (Bodley Head 1963); Freedom at Stake (Bodley Head 1966) *Recreations:* music, talking, writing

The Rt Hon The Lord Archer of Sandwell QC, Chairman, Council on Tribunals, 22 Kingsway, London WC2B 6LE *Telephone:* 0171-936 7045 *Fax:* 0171-936 7044

ARMSTRONG, REID TOTTENHAM Secretary and Chief Executive, Police Authority for Northern Ireland Grade: 3

Career: journalist Belfast News Letter 1957-64; head of information Pigs Marketing Board Northern Ireland (NI) 1964-72; Police Authority for NI 1972-: head of information, assistant secretary, secretary and chief executive 1991-

Date of birth: 13 February 1935 *Education/professional qualifications:* Glasgow Academy; Campbell College, Belfast; Queen's University, Belfast, economics (BSc Econ 1957) *Marital status:* married Rosemary Ann 1962; 2 sons (1 deceased) *Clubs:* Ulster Reform *Recreations:* golf, gardening, travel

Reid T Armstrong Esq, Secretary and Chief Executive, Police Authority for Northern Ireland, River House, 48 High Street, Belfast BT1 2DR
Telephone: 01232 230111 *Fax:* 01232 245098

ASHKEN, KENNETH RICHARD Director (Policy), Crown Prosecution Service Grade: 3

Career: Office of Director of Public Prosecutions 1972-86; Crown Prosecution Service 1986-: head of policy and information division 1986-90, director policy and communications group 1990-92, director (policy) 1992-

Date of birth: 13 June 1945 *Education/professional qualifications:* Whitgift School, Croydon; London School of Economics, law (LLB 1966); solicitor 1972; Cambridge Institute of Criminology (DipCrim

1967) *Marital status:* separated; 2 sons, 2 daughters *Clubs:* Royal Automobile *Recreations:* mountain biking

K R Ashken Esq, Director (Policy), Crown Prosecution Service, 50 Ludgate Hill, London EC4M 7JJ
Telephone: 0171-273 8124 *Fax:* 0171-329 8167

ASHMORE, GILLIAN Regional Director, Government Office for the South East Grade: 3

Career: Departments of the Environment, Transport, Employment, Trade and Industry 1971-: regional director government office for the south east 1994-

Date of birth: 14 October 1949 *Education/professional qualifications:* Walthamstow Hall School, Sevenoaks; Winchester County High School for Girls; Cambridge University, history (BA 1971) *Marital status:* married Frederick Scott 1971; 2 daughters, 2 sons *Recreations:* children, travel, novels, dancing, dreaming

Gillian Ashmore, Regional Director, Government Office for the South East, Charles House, 375 Kensington High Street, London W14 8QH
Telephone: 0171-605 9095 *Fax:* 0171-605 9133

ATWOOD, BARRY THOMAS Principal Assistant Solicitor, Ministry of Agriculture, Fisheries and Food Grade: 3

Career: solicitor 1961-66; Ministry of Agriculture, Fisheries and Food 1966-: conveyancing 1966-70, food legislation 1970-77, Common Agricultural Policy 1977-82; European Court of Justice litigation 1982-86, agricultural commodities and food safety bill 1986-89; principal assistant solicitor (under secretary) legal group B 1989-92, legal group A (legislation and advisory work) 1992-

Date of birth: 25 February 1940 *Education/professional qualifications:* Bristol Grammar School; Bristol University, law (LLB 1960); Law Society (solicitor 1965) *Marital status:* married Jennifer Ann Burgess 1965; 2 sons *Recreations:* family, music, swimming, walking, France

Barry T Atwood Esq, Principal Assistant Solicitor, Ministry of Agriculture, Fisheries and Food, 55 Whitehall, London SW1H 2AE
Telephone: 0171-270 8339 *Fax:* 0171-270 8166

AUSTIN, Air Marshal Sir ROGER MARK Controller Aircraft, Procurement Executive, Ministry of Defence

Career: Royal Air Force (RAF): pilot 1960-72; Army Staff College 1973; officer commanding (OC) 233 (Harrier) operational conversion unit 1974-77; Ministry of Defence (MoD) staff post 1977; personal staff officer to air officer commanding-in-chief Strike Command 1978-80; OC RAF Chivenor 1980-82; group captain operations HQ Strike Command 1982-84; director of operational requirements (air) 2 MoD 1984-85; Royal College of Defence Studies 1986; air officer in charge central tactics and trials organisation 1987; director general aircraft 1 MoD Procurement Executive (PE) 1987-89; air officer commanding and commandant RAF College Cranwell 1989-92; MoD 1992-: deputy chief of defence staff (systems) 1992-94; controller aircraft PE 1994-

Date of birth: 9 March 1940 *Education/professional qualifications:* King Alfred's Grammar School, Wantage *Honours, decorations:* AFC 1973; FRAeS 1991; KCB 1992 *Recreations:* walking, transport systems

Air Marshal Sir Roger Austin KCB AFC, Controller Aircraft, Procurement Executive, Ministry of Defence, Whitehall, London SW1A 2HB *Telephone:* 0171-218 7813 *Fax:* 0171-218 3849

AVERY, JOHN ERNEST Deputy Parliamentary Commissioner for Administration [Ombudsman] Grade: 3

Career: patent examiner Board of Trade 1964-72; Office of Fair Trading 1972-76; Department of [Trade and] Industry 1976-89: assistant secretary chemicals, textiles and paper division 1980-85, telecommunications division 1985-89; Office of Parliamentary Commissioner for Administration (investigation of alleged government maladministration) 1989-: director of investigations 1989-90, deputy parliamentary commissioner 1990-

Date of birth: 18 April 1940 *Education/professional qualifications:* Plymouth College; Leeds University, gas engineering (BSc 1962); Gray's Inn (barrister 1971) *Marital status:* married Anna Beatrice Meddings 1966; 2 daughters *Recreations:* squash, theatre

John E Avery Esq, Deputy Parliamentary Commissioner, Office of the Parliamentary Commissioner for Administration, Church House, Great Smith Street, London SW1P 3BW *Telephone:* 0171-276 2089 *Fax:* 0171-276 2104

AYLWARD, Dr MANSEL Principal Medical Adviser and Business Development Director, Social Security Benefits Agency Grade: 4

Career: chairman and chief executive Simbec Research Ltd 1974-84; Department of [Health and] Social Security (DSS) 1985-: medical officer (MO) Wales and West region 1985-88; senior MO DSS HQ medical division 1988-91; Social Security Benefits Agency 1991-: principal MO 1991-93, principal medical adviser and business development director 1993- *Current non-Whitehall posts:* medical adviser and director Women's Health Concern 1979-

Date of birth: 29 November 1942 *Education/professional qualifications:* Cyfarthfa Castle Grammar School, Merthyr Tydfil; Royal London Hospital Medical College, physiology (BSc 1965), medicine (MB BS 1967); FFPM RCP 1991 *Marital status:* married Angela Bridget Besley 1963; 1 son, 1 daughter *Publications:* The Disability Handbook (HMSO 1992); Management of Menopause and Postmenopausal Years (MTP 1979) *Clubs:* Royal Society of Medicine *Recreations:* military history, theatre, outdoors, swimming

Dr Mansel Aylward, Principal Medical Adviser, Social Security Benefits Agency Medical Services, Department of Social Security, The Adelphi, 1-11 John Adam Street, London WC2N 6HT *Telephone:* 0171-962 8082 *Fax:* 0171-962 8785

B

BACON, (JENNIFER) JENNY HELEN   Director-General, Health and Safety Executive

Career: assistant principal Ministry of Labour/Department of Employment (DEmp) 1967-71; DEmp 1971-78: private secretary (PS) to secretary of state (SoS) 1971-72; principal health and safety law 1972-74, industrial relations law 1974-76, management review 1976-77; principal PS to SoS 1977-78; assistant secretary training services Manpower Services Commission (MSC) 1978-80, machinery of government Civil Service Department 1981-82; under secretary, adult training director MSC 1982-86; school curriculum and assessment Department of Education and Science 1986-89; DEmp 1989-92: principal finance officer 1989-91; director of resources and strategy 1991-92; Health and Safety Executive 1992-: deputy director-general, policy 1992-95, director-general 1995- *Current non-Whitehall posts:* visiting fellow Nuffield College, Oxford 1989-; member Sheffield Development Corporation 1992-

Date of birth: 16 April 1945 *Education/professional qualifications:* Bedales, Petersfield; New Hall, Cambridge, archaeology and anthropology part 1, history part 2 (BA 1967) *Marital status:* single *Recreations:* walking, travel, classical music – especially opera

Miss Jenny Bacon, Director-General, Health and Safety Executive, Rose Court, 2 Southwark Bridge, London SE1 9HS *Telephone:* 0171-717 6633 *Fax:* 0171-717 6616

BAHL, KAMLESH   Chairwoman, Equal Opportunities Commission

Career: solicitor, London 1978-91; legal adviser British Steel Corporation 1981-84; solicitor Texaco Ltd 1984-87; Data Logic Ltd 1987-: company secretary and legal services manager 1989-93, legal consultant 1993-; chairwoman Equal Opportunities Ltd 1993- *Current non-Whitehall posts:* member Law Society council 1990-, Council of Justice 1993-, diplomatic appeal board, Foreign and Commonwealth Office 1993-, council National Association of Health Authorities and Trusts 1993-

Date of birth: 28 May 1956 *Education/professional qualifications:* Minchenden School, London; Birmingham University, law (LLB 1977) *Marital status:* married Dr Nitin Lakhani 1986 *Publications:* Managing Legal Practice in Business (1989) *Clubs:* Royal Society of Arts, Law Society *Recreations:* swimming, dancing, travel, theatre

Ms Kamlesh Bahl, Chairwoman, Equal Opportunities Commission, Overseas House, Quay Street, Manchester M3 3HN
Telephone: 0161-833 9244 *Fax:* 0161-832 8816

BAINES, PRISCILLA JEAN   Deputy Librarian, House of Commons   Grade: 4

Career: House of Commons Library 1968-: research division 1968-91; head of parliamentary division 1991-93; deputy librarian (including establishments officer duties) 1993-

Date of birth: 5 October 1942 *Education/professional qualifications:* Girls' Grammar School, Tonbridge; Somerville College, Oxford, agriculture (BA 1963); Linacre College, agricultural history, economics (BLitt 1969) *Marital status:* single *Publications:* contributions to various books by the Study of Parliament Group *Recreations:* cooking, opera-going, reading, travel

Miss Priscilla J Baines, Deputy Librarian, House of Commons, London SW1A 0AA *Telephone:* 0171-219 6179 *Fax:* 0171-219 2518

BAIRD, Air Vice-Marshal JOHN ALEXANDER Director-General Medical Services, Royal Air Force, Ministry of Defence

Career: Royal Air Force (RAF) medical service 1963-: command flight medical officer HQ Strike Command (STC) 1980-83; RAF medical directorate Ministry of Defence 1983-86; officer commanding RAF hospital, Ely 1987-88; principal medical officer HQ RAF Germany 1988-91, HQ STC 1991-94; director-general 1994-

Date of birth: 25 July 1937 *Education/professional qualifications:* Merchiston Castle School, Edinburgh; Edinburgh University, medicine (MB ChB 1961) *Honours, decorations:* DAvMed 1968, MRAes 1982, QHP 1991; FFOM 1994 *Recreations:* ornithology, cricket, music

Air Vice-Marshal John A Baird QHP, Director-General Medical Services Royal Air Force, HQ Personnel and Training Command, RAF Innsworth, Gloucester GL3 1EZ *Telephone:* 01452 712612 *Fax:* 01452 510841

BAKER, K B Assistant Chief Veterinary Officer, Ministry of Agriculture, Fisheries and Food Grade: 4

K B Baker Esq, Assistant Chief Veterinary Officer, Ministry of Agriculture, Fisheries and Food, Government Buildings, Hook Rise South, Tolworth, Surbiton, Surrey KT6 7NF *Telephone:* 0181-330 8304

BAKER, MARTYN MURRAY Under Secretary, Exports to Asia, Africa and Australasia, Department of Trade and Industry Grade: 3

Career: Ministry of Aviation (MAv) 1965-67; assistant private secretary (PS) to minister of state Ministry of Technology (MTech) 1968-69; PS to parliamentary under secretaries MTech, MAv and Department of Trade [and Industry] (DT[I]) 1969-71; DT[I] 1971-78: principal 1971-78: principal PS to Secretary of State for Trade 1977-78; assistant secretary 1978-86: civil aviation and shipping counsellor Washington DC embassy 1978-82; DTI 1982-: air division 1982-85, projects and export policy division 1985-86, under secretary (US) 1986-: north west regional director 1986-88, director enterprise and deregulation unit 1988-90, US overseas trade division 1990-93, exports to Asia, Africa and Australasia 1993-

Date of birth: 10 March 1944 *Education/professional qualifications:* Dulwich College, London; Pembroke College, Oxford, modern history (BA 1965, MA) *Honours, decorations:* FRSA 1988 *Marital status:* married Rosemary Caroline Holdich 1970

Martyn M Baker Esq, Under Secretary, Department of Trade and Industry, Kingsgate House, 66-74 Victoria Street, London SW1E 6SW *Telephone:* 0171-215 5345 *Fax:* 0171-931 0397

BALDWIN, Air Vice-Marshal NIGEL BRUCE Assistant Chief of Defence Staff (Overseas), Ministry of Defence

Career: Royal Air Force (RAF) 1962-: pilot/ADC 1963-73; student staff college 1973-74; staff officer HQ Strike Command (HQSTC) 1975-76; officer commanding 50 squadron Vulcans 1977-79; student Maxwell air force base, USA/faculty instructor air command and staff college 1980-82; station commander RAF Wyton 1983-85; assistant director defence policy Ministry of Defence (MoD)

1987-88; air commodore plans HQSTC 1989-92; assistant chief of defence staff, overseas (outside Europe) MoD 1993-

Date of birth: 20 September 1941 *Education/professional qualifications:* Peter Symond's School, Winchester; RAF College, Cranwell (commission 1962); RAF Staff College 1974; US Air War College 1980; US National Defense University international fellow 1986 *Honours, decorations:* CBE 1992 *Recreations:* hillwalking, music, military history

Air Vice-Marshal Nigel Baldwin CBE, Assistant Chief of Defence Staff, Ministry of Defence, Whitehall, London SW1A 2HB *Telephone:* 0171-218 7170 *Fax:* 0171-218 9737

BALLANTINE, (DAVID) GRANT Directing Actuary, Public Service Pensions, Government Actuary's Department Grade: 3

Career: assistant vice-president American Insurance Group 1968-73; Government Actuary's Department 1973-: actuary 1973-82, chief actuary 1983-90, directing actuary pension directorate (public sector pensions) 1991-

Date of birth: 24 March 1941 *Education/professional qualifications:* Daniel Stewart's College, Edinburgh; Edinburgh University, mathematics (BSc 1963); FFA 1968 *Marital status:* married Marjorie Campbell Brown 1969; 1 daughter, 1 son *Recreations:* hill-walking, politics

D Grant Ballantine Esq, Directing Actuary, Government Actuary's Department, 22 Kingsway, London WC2B 6LE *Telephone:* 0171-242 6828 *Fax:* 0171-831 6653

BALLARD, JOHN FREDERICK Director, Town and Country Planning Directorate, Department of the Environment Grade: 3

Career: academic registrar's department, Surrey University 1965-69; assistant principal Ministry of Transport 1969-72; principal Department of the Environment (DoE) 1972-76; HM Treasury 1976; assistant secretary, secretary Top Salaries Review Body and Police Negotiating Board 1978-79; DoE 1979-92: principal private secretary to secretary of state 1983-85; under secretary and regional director DoE and Department of Transport Yorkshire and Humberside region 1986-90; director housing associations and the private sector 1990-92; director Maxwell Pensions Unit, Department of Social Security 1992-93; director town and country planning directorate DoE 1993- *Current non-Whitehall posts:* associate special trustee Great Ormond Street Children's Hospital 1992-; trustee Maxwell Pensions Unit 1993-

Date of birth: 8 August 1943 *Education/professional qualifications:* Roundhay Grammar School, Leeds; Ifield Grammar School, W Sussex; Southampton University (BA); Exeter University (CertEd) *Marital status:* married 1976; separated 1986; 2 daughters, 1 son *Recreations:* squash, singing, reading

John F Ballard Esq, Director, Planning Directorate, Department of the Environment, 2 Marsham Street, London SW1P 3EB *Telephone:* 0171-276 3854 *Fax:* 0171-276 6344

BALMER, COLIN VICTOR Assistant Under Secretary, Management Strategy, Ministry of Defence Grade: 3

Career: Ministry of Defence (MOD) 1963-: assistant principal 1970-73: assistant private secretary (sc PS) to minister of state 1972-73, PS to under secretary for RAF 1973; principal MOD 1973-77; principal Cabinet Office 1977-79; PS to minister of state Foreign and Commonwealth Office 1980-82: first secretary UK delegation to NATO 1982-84; assistant secretary MOD 1984-89; minister Washington DC embassy 1990-92; assistant under secretary management strategy/financial management 1992-

Date of birth: 22 August 1946 *Education/professional qualifications:* Liverpool Institute *Recreations:* golf, tennis, bridge, music

Colin V Balmer Esq, Assistant Under Secretary, Ministry of Defence, Main Building, Whitehall, London SW1A 2HB *Telephone:* 0171-218 6188 *Fax:* 0171-218 1885

BARCLAY, KENNETH FORSYTH Secretary, Scottish Law Commission Grade: 5

Career: solicitor 1960-71; principal solicitor Cumbernauld Development Corporation 1971-73; senior legal assistant Scottish Office 1973-87: legal secretary Royal Commission on Legal Services in Scotland 1977-83; secretary (chief administrator) Scottish Law Commission 1987-

Date of birth: 1 February 1938 *Education/professional qualifications:* Woodside Senior Secondary School, Glasgow; Glasgow University, law (BL 1960) *Marital status:* married Jean Broom Curwen 1967; 1 daughter, 1 son *Recreations:* golf, reading

Kenneth F Barclay Esq, Secretary, Scottish Law Commission, 140 Causewayside, Edinburgh EH9 1PR *Telephone:* 0131-668 2131 *Fax:* 0131-662 4900

BARNES, CHRISTOPHER JOHN ANDREW Director of Establishments, Ministry of Agriculture, Fisheries and Food Grade: 3

Career: Ministry of Agriculture, Fisheries and Food 1962-: chief regional officer Nottingham and Reading 1980-83; head of personnel and research and development requirements divisions 1983-90; under secretary arable crops and alcoholic drinks/horticulture 1990-95; director of establishments 1995- *Current non-Whitehall posts:* member CSMAA management committee 1992-

Date of birth: 11 October 1944 *Education/professional qualifications:* London School of Economics, government (BScEcon) *Marital status:* married Carolyn Johnston 1978, divorced 1990; Susan Bird 1990; 4 sons (2 from first marriage) *Recreations:* off-road vehicles, country living, France

Christopher J A Barnes Esq, Under Secretary, Ministry of Agriculture, Fisheries and Food, Whitehall Place, London SW1A 2HH *Telephone:* 0171-270 8139 *Fax:* 0171-270 8186

BARNES, JACK HENRY Under Secretary, Industry and International Division, Department of Health Grade: 3

Career: Department of Health [and Social Security] 1983-: deputy chief inspector social services inspectorate 1983-88; deputy chief scientist/director of research management 1988-91; under secretary services development division, health care directorate, NHS Management Executive 1991-95; head of industry and international division 1995-

Date of birth: 11 December 1943 *Education/professional qualifications:* Hatfield School, Hertfordshire; Sussex University, history (BA 1966); London School of Economics, social administration (MSc 1968) *Marital status:* married Nicola 1966; 2 daughters

Jack H Barnes Esq, Head of Industry and International Division, Department of Health, Richmond House, 79 Whitehall, London SW1A 2NS *Telephone:* 0171-210 3000

BARNES, MICHAEL CECIL JOHN Legal Services Ombudsman Grade: 3

Career: advertising and marketing 1957-66; Labour MP for Brentford and Chiswick 1966-74; member National Consumer Council 1975-80; chairman Electricity Consumers' Council 1977-83; member Advertising Standards Authority 1979-85; director United Kingdom Immigrants Advisory Service 1984-90; lay member investigation committee Solicitors' Complaints Bureau 1987-90; legal services ombudsman (investigation of complaints against solicitors, barristers and licensed conveyors and their professional bodies) 1991-

Date of birth: 22 September 1932 *Education/professional qualifications:* Malvern College; Corpus Christi College, Oxford, classical mods and greats (BA, MA 1957) *Marital status:* married Anne Mason 1962; 1 son, 1 daughter *Recreations:* walking, swimming, dogs

Michael C J Barnes Esq, Legal Services Ombudsman, 22 Oxford Court, Manchester M2 3WQ *Telephone:* 0161-236 9532 *Fax:* 0161-236 2651

BARNES, PETER **Special Adviser to Secretary of State for Social Security**

Career: HM Treasury 1984-90: private secretary to economic secretary 1986-88; consultant Boston Consulting Group 1990-93; special adviser to Peter Lilley Secretary of State for Social Security 1993- *Education/professional qualifications:* Magdalen College, Oxford, philosophy, politics and economics (BA 1984); Stanford Business School, USA, business administration (MBA 1990)

Peter Barnes Esq, Special Adviser, Department of Social Security, Richmond House, 79 Whitehall, London SW1A 2NS *Telephone:* 0171-210 5481 *Fax:* 0171-839 1285

BARNETT, JOEL (The Rt Hon Lord BARNETT) **Chairman of the Council, Building Societies Ombudsman**

Career: senior partner accountants firm 1956-74, 1979-80; MP for Heywood and Royton 1964-83: chief secretary to Treasury 1974-79: cabinet minister 1977-79; vice-chairman board of governors BBC 1986-93, chairman Building Societies Ombudsman Council 1986- *Current non-Whitehall posts:* trustee Victoria and Albert Museum 1985-; chairman British Screen Finance Ltd 1986-, Educational Broadcasting Services Trust Ltd, Mansfield 2010; member international advisory board Unisys Ltd; trustee Open University 1994-

Date of birth: 14 October 1923 *Education/professional qualifications:* Jewish School and Central High School, Manchester; accountancy; ACCA 1956, FCCA *Honours, decorations:* PC 1975; baron 1983 *Marital status:* married Lilian Stella Goldstone 1949; 1 daughter *Publications:* Inside the Treasury (Andre Deutsch 1981) *Recreations:* theatre, sport, hiking

The Rt Hon The Lord Barnett, Chairman of the Council, Building Societies Ombudsman, Grosvenor Gardens House, 35-37 Grosvenor Gardens, London SW1X 7AW *Telephone:* 0171-931 0444 *Fax:* 0171-931 8485

BARTON, ALAN BURNELL **Under Secretary, Finance Division, Department of Health** Grade: 3

Career: operational research National Coal Board 1966-73; Department of Health [and Social Security] 1973-: principal 1973-78; assistant secretary 1979-90; director medical devices directorate 1990-93; under secretary finance division 1993-

Date of birth: 2 May 1943 *Education/professional qualifications:* Glyn Grammar School, Ewell, Surrey; Bristol University, chemistry (BSc 1965) *Marital status:* married Jirina Klapstova 1969; 1 daughter, 1 son *Recreations:* jazz, theatre, country houses

Alan B Barton Esq, Under Secretary, Department of Health, Richmond House, 79 Whitehall, London SW1A 2NS *Telephone:* 0171-210 4907 *Fax:* 0171-210 5722

BASSINGTHWAITE, Judge KEITH President Tribunal Service

Career: crown court recorder 1987-91; circuit judge 1991-; chairman industrial tribunals London central and south 1984-91; president Independent Tribunal Service (supervision social security, medical, vaccine damage, disability and child support appeal tribunals) 1995-

Date of birth: 19 January 1943 *Education/professional qualifications:* solicitor 1967

His Honour Judge Bassingthwaite, President, Independent Tribunal Service, City Gate House, 39-45 Finsbury Square, London EC2A 1PX *Telephone:* 0171-814 6500

BATES, JOHN GERALD HIGGS Principal Assistant Solicitor, Inland Revenue Grade: 3

Career: barrister 1962-66; solicitor's office Inland Revenue 1966-: legal assistant (LA) 1966-69, senior LA 1969-84; assistant solicitor (AS) 1984-90, principal AS 1990-

Date of birth: 28 July 1936 *Education/professional qualifications:* St Catharine's College, Cambridge (BA 1958); Harvard Law School, USA (LLM 1962); Middle Temple (barrister) *Marital status:* married Antoinette Lotery 1971 (died 1984); Alba Whicher 1992; 2 sons from previous marriage *Recreations:* music, food, wine

John G H Bates Esq, Principal Assistant Solicitor, Inland Revenue, Somerset House, London WC2R 1LB *Telephone:* 0171-438 6228 *Fax:* 0171-438 6246

BATTERSBY, EDWARD IAN Chief Actuary, Public Sector Pensions Division, Government Actuary's Department Grade: 4

E I Battersby Esq, Chief Actuary, Public Sector Pensions Division, Government Actuary's Department, 22 Kingsway, London WC2B 6LE *Telephone:* 0171-242 6828 *Fax:* 0171-831 6653

BATTISCOMBE, CHRISTOPHER CHARLES RICHARD Assistant Under Secretary, Public Departments, Foreign and Commonwealth Office Grade: 3

Career: HM Diplomatic Service: Middle East Centre for Arabic Studies 1963-65; 3rd, later 2nd secretary (SS) Kuwait 1965-68; SS Foreign and Commonwealth Office, London (FCO) 1968-69; assistant private secretary to Chancellor of Duchy of Lancaster 1969-71; first secretary UN delegation to OECD, Paris 1971-74, UK mission to UN, New York 1974-78, FCO 1978-81; commercial counsellor Cairo 1981-84, Paris 1984-86; counsellor FCO 1986-90; ambassador to Algeria 1990-94; assistant under secretary public departments directorate (cultural relations, information, news, consular, nationality, migration, parliamentary relations) FCO 1994-

Date of birth: 27 April 1940 *Education/professional qualifications:* Wellington College; New College, Oxford, mods and greats (BA 1963) *Honours, decorations:* CMG 1992 *Marital status:* married Brigid Melita Theresa Lunn 1972; 1 daughter, 1 son *Clubs:* Kandahar *Recreations:* tennis, skiing, golf

Christopher C R Battiscombe Esq CMG, Assistant Under Secretary, Foreign and Commonwealth Office, Old Admiralty Building, Whitehall, London SW1A 2AF *Telephone:* 0171-210 6349

BATTISHILL, Sir ANTHONY MICHAEL WILLIAM Chairman, Inland Revenue Grade: 1

Career: assistant principal (AP) stamps and taxes division Inland Revenue (IR) 1960-63; AP, private secretary (PS) to Financial Secretary HM Treasury (HMT) 1963-65; IR 1965-76: principal, stamps and taxes division 1965-70, assistant secretary (AS) personal taxation division 1970-76; AS Central Policy Review Staff Cabinet Office 1976-77; HMT 1977-82: AS, principal PS to Chancellor of Exchequer 1977-80, under secretary (US) fiscal policy group 1980-82; US business taxation division IR 1982-83; US central unit HMT

1983-85; IR 1985-: deputy chairman 1985-86, chairman 1986- *Current non-Whitehall posts:* member London School of Economics court of governors 1987-

Date of birth: 5 July 1937 *Education/professional qualifications:* Taunton School; Hele's School, Exeter; London School of Economics (BScEcon 1958) *Honours, decorations:* KCB 1989 *Marital status:* married Heather Frances Lawes 1961; 1 daughter *Recreations:* gardening, old maps

Sir Anthony Battishill KCB, Chairman, Inland Revenue, Somerset House, London WC2R 1LB *Telephone:* 0171-438 7711 *Fax:* 0171-438 6494

BATTLE, DENNIS FRANK ORLANDO Commissioner; Principal Establishment Officer; Director of Personnel and Finance, HM Customs and Excise Grade: 3

Career: HM Customs and Excise (C&E) 1962-67; National Board for Prices and Incomes 1967-72; Civil Service College 1972-75; C&E 1975-: assistant secretary 1985-90, commissioner and director of personnel 1990-, director of finance and principal establishments and finance officer 1994-

Date of birth: 17 December 1942 *Education/professional qualifications:* Bedford Modern School *Marital status:* married Sandra Moule 1965; 1 son, 1 daughter

Dennis Battle Esq, Commissioner, HM Customs and Excise, New King's Beam House, 22 Upper Ground, London SE1 9PJ *Telephone:* 0171-620 1313 *Fax:* 0171-865 5662

BAYLISS, VALERIE JUNE Under Secretary, Director, Youth and Education Policy, Employment Department Group Grade: 3

Career: Department of Employment 1968-: head job centre national policy 1978-82; head youth training scheme policy 1982-85; director of field operations 1985-87, of resources and personnel 1987-90; under secretary, director of education programmes 1991-93, of youth and education policy 1993- *Current non-Whitehall posts:* member Sheffield University Council; director Sheffield University Management School; member Rural Buildings Preservation Trust

Date of birth: 10 June 1944 *Education/professional qualifications:* Wallington County Grammar School for Girls; University of Wales, history (BA 1965, MA 1967); London School of Economics *Honours, decorations:* FRSA *Marital status:* married Derek 1971; 1 son *Recreations:* walking, reading, music

Ms Valerie J Bayliss, Director, Youth and Education Policy, Employment Department Group, Moorfoot, Sheffield S1 4PQ *Telephone:* 01142 594573 *Fax:* 01142 594746

BEAMISH, DAVID RICHARD Clerk of the Journals, House of Lords Grade: 4

Career: House of Lords (HoL) 1974-: senior clerk 1979-87: seconded as private secretary to leader of HoL and government chief whip 1983-86; chief clerk Committee Office 1987-88; establishment officer 1988-93; clerk of the journals (journal, information, printed paper and computer offices; clerk to procedure committee) 1993-

Date of birth: 20 August 1952 *Education/professional qualifications:* Marlborough College; St John's College, Cambridge, law (BA 1973, MA, LLM 1974) *Marital status:* married Philippa Tudor 1989; 1 daughter *Publications:* co-editor The House of Lords at Work (OUP 1993)

David R Beamish Esq, Clerk of the Journals, House of Lords, London SW1A 0PW *Telephone:* 0171-219 3187

BEAN, DAVID L S **South East Regional Controller, Inland Revenue** Grade: 4

Career: Inland Revenue 1955-: south east regional controller

Date of birth: 22 July 1938 *Marital status:* married; 2 sons, 1 daughter

D L S Bean Esq, Regional Controller, Inland Revenue, Albion House, Chertsey Road, Woking, Surrey GU21 1BT *Telephone:* 01483 723322 *Fax:* 01483 724910

BEARDSALL, E G **Director, Corporate Services, HM Land Registry (Executive Agency)** Grade: 4

E G Beardsall Esq, Director, Corporate Services, HM Land Registry, Lincoln's Inn Fields, London WC2A 3PH *Telephone:* 0171-917 8888 *Fax:* 0171-955 0110

BEATTIE, ANTHONY **Director and Chief Executive, Natural Resources Institute (Executive Agency)** Grade: 3

Career: economic planning division Malawi government 1966-69; Overseas Development Administration 1969-: director and chief executive Natural Resources Institute 1990-

Date of birth: 17 April 1944 *Education/professional qualifications:* Stationers' Company's School, London; Trinity College, Cambridge, economics (BA 1966, MA) *Marital status:* married Janet Frances Dring 1973; 1 son *Recreations:* music, countryside, border terriers

Anthony Beattie Esq, Director and Chief Executive, Natural Resources Institute, Central Avenue, Chatham Maritime, Kent ME4 4TB *Telephone:* 01634 880088 *Fax:* 01634 880066

BEAVER, WENDY MARGARET **Chief Actuary, Government Actuary's Department** Grade: 4

Career: actuarial analyst Royal Life Insurance Group 1980-83; actuarial and employee benefits consultant The Wyatt Company 1983-88, Towers Perrin 1988-92; Government Actuary's Department 1992-: actuary 1992-94, chief actuary pensions policy, demography and statistics division 1994-

Date of birth: 22 February 1960 *Education/professional qualifications:* High School for Girls, Southport; Sheffield University, mathematics (BSc 1980); FIA 1988 *Marital status:* married Brendan Gibney 1985; 2 sons *Recreations:* family, working out, entertaining

Ms Wendy Beaver, Chief Actuary, Government Actuary's Department, 22 Kingsway, London WC2B 6LE *Telephone:* 0171-242 6828 *Fax:* 0171-831 6653

BEETON, DAVID CHRISTOPHER **Chief Executive, Historic Royal Palaces (Executive Agency)** Grade: 3

Career: chief executive Bath City Council 1973-85; secretary National Trust 1985-89; chief executive Historic Royal Palaces (Hampton Court Palace, Tower of London, Banqueting House, Kensington Palace, Kew Palace) 1989- *Current non-Whitehall posts:* director London Tourist Board

Date of birth: 25 August 1939 *Education/professional qualifications:* Ipswich School; King's College, London, law (LLB 1961) *Marital status:* married Elizabeth Brenda Lomax 1968; 2 sons *Recreations:* classical music and opera, theatre, traditional cookery

David C Beeton Esq, Chief Executive, Historic Royal Palaces, Hampton Court Palace, East Molesey, Surrey KT8 9AU *Telephone:* 0181-781 9751 *Fax:* 0181-781 9754

BELFALL, DAVID J Under Secretary, Health Policy and Public Health, Scottish Office Home and Health Department Grade: 3

Career: Home Office 1969-88: private secretary to permanent under secretary 1973-74; Scottish Office Home and Health Department 1988-: under secretary emergency services 1988-91, health policy and public health directorate 1991-

Date of birth: 26 April 1947 *Education/professional qualifications:* Colchester Royal Grammar School; St John's College, Cambridge (BA) *Marital status:* married; 1 son, 1 daughter *Recreations:* squash, badminton

D J Belfall Esq, Under Secretary, Health Policy and Public Health Directorate, Scottish Office Home and Health Department, St Andrew's House, Edinburgh EH1 3DE *Telephone:* 0131-556 8400

BELL, DAVID JOHN Commissioner of Valuation and Chief Executive, Valuation and Lands Agency (NI) (Executive Agency) Grade: 3

Career: Department of Environment Northern Ireland 1973-84: divisional estates surveyor Land Service 1973-80, chief lands officer 1982-84; Valuation and Lands Office/Agency (valuation for rates assessment) 1984-: assistant commissioner 1984-87; deputy commissioner 1987-88, commissioner of valuation 1988-, chief executive 1993-

Date of birth: 17 March 1938 *Education/professional qualifications:* Regent House, Newtownards, County Down; FRICS 1981, IRRV 1990

David J Bell Esq, Commissioner of Valuation and Chief Executive, Valuation and Lands Agency, Queen's Court, 56-66 Upper Queen Street, Belfast BT1 6FD *Telephone:* 01232 439303 *Fax:* 01232 235897

BELL, MICHAEL JOHN VINCENT Deputy Chief of Defence Procurement (Support) Procurement Executive, Ministry of Defence Grade: 2

Career: research associate Institute for Strategic Studies 1964-65; Ministry of Defence 1965-: assistant principal 1965-69, principal 1969-75, assistant secretary 1975-82; seconded to HM Treasury 1977-79; assistant under secretary (resources and programmes) 1982-84; director general of management audit 1984-86; assistant secretary general for defence planning and policy NATO 1986-88; deputy under secretary finance 1988-92, procurement executive 1992-

Date of birth: 9 September 1941 *Education/professional qualifications:* Winchester College; Magdalen College, Oxford, literae humaniores (BA 1963) *Honours, decorations:* CB 1992 *Recreations:* motorcycling, military history

Michael J V Bell Esq CB, Deputy Chief, Defence Procurement, Procurement Executive, Ministry of Defence, Main Building, Whitehall, London SW1A 2HB *Telephone:* 0171-218 3213 *Fax:* 0171-218 7425

BELLAMY, Dr J D F Principal Medical Officer, Health Promotion Division, Health and Social Services Group, Department of Health Grade: 4

Dr J D F Bellamy, Principal Medical Officer, Health Promotion Division, Department of Health, Wellington House, 133-135 Waterloo Road, London SE1 8UG *Telephone:* 0171-972 4710

BELSTEAD, JOHN JULIAN GANZONI (The Rt Hon The Lord Belstead) Chairman, Parole Board for England and Wales

Career: JP for Ipswich 1962-; parliamentary under secretary Department of Education and Science 1970-73, Northern Ireland Office 1973-74, Home Office 1979-83; chairman Public Schools Governing Bodies Association 1974-79; minister of state Foreign and Commonwealth Office 1982-83, Ministry of Agriculture, Fisheries and Food 1983-87, Department of Environment 1987-88; House of Lords 1983-90: deputy leader 1983-88, leader and Lord Privy Seal 1988-90; Paymaster General and deputy to secretary of state for Northern Ireland 1990-92; chairman Parole Board for England and Wales 1992- *Current non-Whitehall posts:* Lord Lieutenant of Suffolk

Date of birth: 30 September 1932 *Education/professional qualifications:* Eton College; Christ Church, Oxford, history (BA 1955, MA) *Honours, decorations:* PC 1983 *Marital status:* single *Clubs:* Vincent's, Oxford; Boodles; MCC; All England Lawn Tennis *Recreations:* tennis, sailing, golf

The Rt Hon The Lord Belstead, Chairman, Parole Board for England and Wales, Abell House, John Islip Street, London SW1P 4LH *Telephone:* 0171-217 5690 *Fax:* 0171-217 5677

BENDER, BRIAN GEOFFREY Head of European Secretariat, Cabinet Office Grade: 2

Career: private secretary to secretary of state Department of Trade 1976-77; 1st secretary trade policy UK permanent representation to EC (UKPR), Brussels 1977-82; principal minerals and metals division Department of Trade and Industry (DTI) 1982-84; industry and energy counsellor UKPR 1985-89; under secretary European secretariat Cabinet Office (co-ordination of UK EC policy) 1990-93; regional development (and inward investment) division DTI 1993-94; deputy secretary, head of European secretariat Cabinet Office 1994-

Date of birth: 25 February 1949 *Education/professional qualifications:* Greenford County Grammar School, Middlesex; Imperial College, London, physics (BSc 1970, PhD 1973) *Marital status:* married Penelope Clark 1974; 1 daughter, 1 son *Recreations:* family, theatre

Brian G Bender Esq, Deputy Secretary, Cabinet Office, 70 Whitehall, London SW1A 2AS *Telephone:* 0171-270 0044 *Fax:* 0171-270 0112

BENNETT, ANDREW JOHN Chief Natural Resources Adviser, Overseas Development Administration Grade: 3

Career: VSO agricultural science lecturer, Kenya 1965-66; agricultural research officer, St Vincent government 1967-69; student 1969-70; maize agronomist, Malawi government 1971-75; chief research officer, Sudan government 1976-80; Overseas Development Administration 1980-: agricultural adviser 1980-83, natural resources adviser SE Asia development division 1983-85, head of British development division in Pacific 1985-87, under secretary and chief natural resources adviser 1987- *Current non-Whitehall posts:* nominated council member Royal Agricultural Society of England 1988-

Date of birth: 25 April 1942 *Education/professional qualifications:* St Edward's School, Oxford; University of Wales, agricultural chemistry (BSc 1965); University of West Indies, tropical agriculture (DTA 1967); Reading University, crop protection (MSc 1970) *Marital status:* single *Recreations:* walking, gardening

Andrew J Bennett Esq, Chief Natural Resources Adviser, Overseas Development Administration, 94 Victoria Street, London SW1 *Telephone:* 0171-917 0513 *Fax:* 0171-917 0679

BENNETT, Dr SETON JOHN **Chief Executive, National Weights and Measures Laboratory (Executive Agency)** Grade: 5

Career: research and development National Physical Laboratory 1967-85; National Weights and Measures Laboratory 1985-: deputy director 1985-90, chief executive 1990-

Date of birth: 10 July 1945 *Education/professional qualifications:* Queen Elizabeth's Grammar School, Barnet; Oriel College, Oxford, physics (BA 1967, MA); Imperial College, London, applied optics (PhD 1973) *Marital status:* married Lesley Joan Downs 1966; 2 sons *Recreations:* reading, theatre, travel

Dr Seton J Bennett, Chief Executive, National Weights and Measures Laboratory, Teddington, Middlesex TW11 0JZ *Telephone:* 0181-943 7211 *Fax:* 0181-943 7200

BENSON, Sir CHRISTOPHER **Chairman, Funding Agency for Schools**

Career: chartered surveyor and agricultural auctioneer 1953-64; director Arndale Developments Ltd 1965-69; chairman Dolphin Developments 1969-71; Law Land Co Ltd 1972-93: assistant managing director (MD) 1972-74, MD 1976-88, chairman 1988-93; director House of Fraser plc 1982-86; chairman LDDC 1984-88; chairman Reedpack Ltd 1989-90; underwriting member of Lloyd's 1979-; president British Property Federation 1981-83; chairman Civic Trust 1985-90; chairman Property Advisory Group Department of Environment 1988-90; chairman Funding Agency for Schools 1994- *Current non-Whitehall posts:* member council CBI 1990-; vice-president Cancer Relief Macmillan Fund 1991-, Royal Society of Arts 1992-; chairman Housing Corporation 1990-, Sun Alliance Group 1993-, Costain plc 1993-

Date of birth: 20 July 1933 *Education/professional qualifications:* Worcester Cathedral Kings School; Thames Nautical Training College, HMS Worcester *Honours, decorations:* KCB 1988 *Marital status:* married Margaret Josephine 1960;; 2 sons *Clubs:* Garrick, RAC, MCC *Recreations:* farming, aviation, opera, ballet

Sir Christopher Benson, Chairman, Funding Agency for Schools, Albion Wharf, 25 Skeldergate, York YO1 2XL *Telephone:* 01904 661604 *Fax:* 01904 661684

BERMAN, Sir FRANKLIN DELOW **Legal Adviser, Foreign and Commonwealth Office** Grade: DS2

Career: HM Diplomatic Service 1965-: assistant legal adviser (LA) Foreign and Commonwealth Office, London (FCO) 1965-71; LA British military government Berlin 1971-72, Bonn embassy 1972-74; legal counsellor (LC), London 1974-82; LA UK mission to UN, New York 1982-85; FCO 1985-: LC 1985-88; deputy LA 1988-91, LA1991- *Current non-Whitehall posts:* staff tribunal International Oil Pollution Compensation Fund 1986-; board of governors Institute of Advanced Legal Studies, London University 1992-; management council British Institute of International and Comparative Law 1992-; council British branch International Law Association 1993-; trustee Edward Fry Memorial Library 1992-; staff appeals board Western European Union 1994-

Date of birth: 23 December 1939 *Education/professional qualifications:* Rondebosch Boys' High School, Cape Town, South Africa (SA); Cape Town University, SA, mathematics (BA 1959), statistics (BSc 1960); Wadham College, Oxford, law (BA 1963, MA); Nuffield College, Oxford, public international law; Middle Temple (barrister 1967) *Honours, decorations:* CMG 1988; QC 1992; KCMG 1994 *Marital status:* married Christine Mary Lawler 1964; 2 sons, triplet daughters *Publications:* legal articles and reviews *Clubs:* United Oxford and Cambridge University *Recreations:* reading, walking, choral singing, gardening

Sir Franklin Berman KCMG QC, Legal Adviser, Foreign and Commonwealth Office, King Charles Street, London SW1A 2AH *Telephone:* 0171-270 3000 *Fax:* 0171-270 2767

BETTS, CHARLES VALENTINE Director-General Submarines, Procurement Executive, Ministry of Defence Grade: 3

Career: assistant constructor Ministry of Defence (MoD) Navy 1966-71; naval architecture lecturer University College, London (UCL) 1971-74; constructor HM Dockyard Portsmouth 1974-77, MoD Bath 1977-79; chief constructor MoD Bath 1979-83, MoD London 1983-85; professor of naval architecture UCL 1985-89; MoD Bath 1989-: director surface ships B 1989-92; assistant under secretary, director-general surface ships 1992-94; director-general submarines 1994- *Current non-Whitehall posts:* head Royal Corps of Naval Constructors 1992-

Date of birth: 10 January 1942 *Education/professional qualifications:* Ryde School, Isle of Wight; Merchant Taylors School, Liverpool; St Catharine's College, Cambridge, mechanical sciences (BA 1963, MA); Royal Naval College, Greenwich, naval architecture (RCNC 1966); UCL, naval architecture (MPhil 1975); CEng 1968; FRINA 1981; FEng 1991 *Honours, decorations:* FRSA *Publications:* co-author The Marine Technology Reference Book (Butterworth Scientific 1990) *Recreations:* sailing, music

Charles V Betts Esq, Director-General Submarines, Procurement Executive, Ministry of Defence, Foxhill, Bath BA1 5AB *Telephone:* 01225 882374 *Fax:* 01225 883599

BEVAN, NICOLAS Speaker's Secretary, House of Commons Grade: 5

Career: Ministry of Defence (MoD) 1964-73: assistant principal 1964, principal 1969, private secretary to chief of the air staff 1970-73; Cabinet Office (CO) 1973-75; MoD 1975-92: assistant secretary 1976; Royal College of Defence Studies 1981; assistant under secretary general finance, defence staff, commitments 1985-92; CO 1992-93; speaker's secretary House of Commons 1993-

Date of birth: 8 March 1942 *Education/professional qualifications:* Westminster School; Corpus Christi College, Oxford, literae humaniores (BA 1964, MA) *Honours, decorations:* CB 1991 *Marital status:* married (Helen) Christine Berry 1982 *Recreations:* gardening

Nicolas Bevan Esq CB, Speaker's Secretary, House of Commons, London SW1A 0AA *Telephone:* 0171-219 4111 *Fax:* 0171-219 6901

BEVERIDGE, CRAWFORD WILLIAM Chief Executive, Scottish Enterprise

Career: Hewlett Packard 1968-77; European personnel director Digital 1977-82; vice-president (VP) human resources Analog Devices 1982-85; VP corporate resources Sun Microsystems 1985-90; chief executive Scottish Enterprise (economy and skills development, environment improvement) 1991- *Current non-Whitehall posts:* chairman Scottish Development Finance 1991-; director United States Smaller Investment Trust plc 1991-; Autodesk 1993-

Date of birth: 3 November 1945 *Education/professional qualifications:* Edinburgh University, social science (BSc 1968); Bradford University, industrial administration (MSc 1969) *Marital status:* married Marguerite DeVoe 1977; 1 son, 1 daughter *Recreations:* music, cooking, paperweights

Crawford W Beveridge Esq, Chief Executive, Scottish Enterprise, 120 Bothwell Street, Glasgow G2 7JP *Telephone:* 0141-248 2700 *Fax:* 0141-221 2250

BEVERIDGE, W T **HM Deputy Senior Chief Inspector, HM Inspectorate of Schools, Scottish Office Education Department** Grade: 4

W T Beveridge Esq, HM Deputy Senior Chief Inspector of Schools, Education Department, Education Department, Scottish Office, New St Andrew's House, Edinburgh EH1 3TG *Telephone:* 0131-244 4548

BICHAN, Dr H ROY **Deputy Chairman, Welsh Development Agency**

Career: Robertson Group 1968-94: chief executive, executive chairman -1991, non-executive deputy chairman 1991-94; president Institute of Mining and Metallurgy 1988-89; chairman Confederation of British Industry North Wales 1990-92, Wales 1993-; deputy chairman Welsh Development Agency 1993- *Current non-Whitehall posts:* director Alchema Ltd 1992-; chairman Confederation of British Industry (Wales) 1994-

Date of birth: 5 November 1941 *Education/professional qualifications:* Aberdeen University, geology (BSc 1964); Leeds University, African geology (PhD 1967) *Marital status:* married Fiona Keay 1966; 2 daughters, 1 son *Recreations:* golf, gardening

Dr H Roy Bichan, Deputy Chairman, Welsh Development Agency, Pearl House, Greyfriars Road, Cardiff CF1 3XX; WDA, Unit 7, St Asaph Business Park, Glascoed Road, Clwyd LL17 0LS *Telephone:* 01222 828675; 01745 586234 *Fax:* 01222 345730; 01745 586259

BICHARD, MICHAEL **Permanent Secretary, Employment Department Group** Grade: 1 *(from August 1995)*

Career: chief executive London Borough of Brent 1980-86, Gloucestershire County Council 1986-90; chief executive Social Security Benefits Agency 1990-95; permanent secretary Employment Department Group 1995- *Current non-Whitehall posts:* trustee Public Management Foundation; committee member Prince's Trust Volunteers

Date of birth: 31 January 1947 *Education/professional qualifications:* Manchester University, law (LLB); solicitor 1971; Birmingham University, social science (MSocSci 1974) *Marital status:* married Christine; 1 son, 2 daughters *Recreations:* music, food, walking, sport

Michael Bichard Esq, Permanent Secretary, Employment Department Group, Caxton House, Tothill Street, London SW1H 9NF *Telephone:* 0171-273 5826

BICKERSTAFF, MOLLIE **Director of Purchasing, Audit Commission**

Career: Coopers and Lybrand chartered accountants 1973-93: partner 1983-93; director of purchasing (audit appointment and quality control) Audit Commission (external audit local government and NHS) 1994-

Date of birth: 23 October 1949 *Education/professional qualifications:* Carolan Grammar School, Belfast; Queen's University, Belfast, applied mathematics (BSc 1970); Somerville College, Oxford, theoretical physics (MSc 1973) *Marital status:* divorced

Ms Mollie Bickerstaff, Director of Purchasing, Audit Commission, 1 Vincent Square, London SW1P 2PN *Telephone:* 0171-828 1212 *Fax:* 0171-396 1369

Government Departments

see page 372

BIGGART, (THOMAS) NORMAN Chairman, Scottish Committee, Council on Tribunals

Career: naval national service 1954-56; solicitor: partner in private practice 1959-95; Law Society of Scotland: council member 1977-86, vice-president 1981-82, president 1982-83; chairman Scottish committee Council on Tribunals 1990- *Current non-Whitehall posts:* director Clydesdale Bank 1985-, Independent Insurance Group 1986-, Beechwood Glasgow 1989-: chairman 1989-; trustee Scottish Civic Trust 1989-

Date of birth: 24 January 1930 *Education/professional qualifications:* Morrisons Academy, Crieff; Glasgow University, law (MA 1951, LLB 1954) *Honours, decorations:* CBE 1984 *Marital status:* married Eileen Gemmell 1956; 1 son, 1 daughter *Clubs:* Western, Glasgow *Recreations:* golf, hillwalking

T Norman Biggart Esq CBE, Chairman, Scottish Committee, Council on Tribunals, 20 Walker Street, Edinburgh EH3 7HR
Telephone: 0131-220 1236 *Fax:* 0131-225 4271

BILLINGTON, (BRIAN JOHN) BILL Director, Network Management and Maintenance Directorate, Highways Agency (Executive Agency) Grade: 3

Career: statistician Ministry of Power/Department of Energy 1969-74; Department of Transport 1974-: chief statistician 1974-81; assistant secretary 1981-91; under secretary, director network management and maintenance (motorways and trunk roads) 1991-94; Highways Agency 1994-: director central services management 1994-95; Network Management and Maintenance Directorate 1995-

Date of birth: 25 February 1939 *Education/professional qualifications:* Slough Grammar School; Regent Street Polytechnic, London, statistics (BSc Econ 1966); London School of Economics, statistics (MSc 1968) *Marital status:* married Gillian Elizabeth Annis 1965; 2 daughters

Bill Billington Esq, Under Secretary, Highways Agency, St Christopher House, Southwark Street, London SE1 0TE *Telephone:* 0171-928 3666

BIRD, RICHARD Director of Personnel, Department of Transport Grade: 3

Career: Department of Environment 1971-75: assistant private secretary (PS) to minister for planning and local government 1974-75; Department of Transport (DTp) 1976-92: principal 1976-78; seconded to Foreign Office as first secretary UK permanent representation to EC, Brussels 1978-82; principal PS to secretary of state 1982-83; assistant secretary 1983-90: Driver and Vehicle Licensing Centre 1983-88; under secretary (US), head of road and vehicle safety directorate 1990-92; US domestic policy and legislation secretariat Cabinet Office 1992-94; director of personnel DTp 1994-

Date of birth: 12 February 1950 *Education/professional qualifications:* King's School, Canterbury; Magdalen College, Oxford, history (BA 1971) *Marital status:* married Penelope Anne Frudd 1973; 1 son, 1 daughter *Recreations:* choral singing, summer sports

Richard Bird Esq, Under Secretary, Department of Transport, Lambeth Bridge House, London SE1 7SB
Telephone: 0171-238 4449 *Fax:* 0171-238 5215

BLACKWELL, NORMAN ROY Head of Prime Minister's Policy Unit Grade: 1A

Career: partner McKinsey & Company management consultants 1978-86, 1988-95; member Prime Minister's Policy Unit 1986-87; strategic planning manager Plessey Company 1976-78; head of Prime Minister's Policy Unit 1995-

Date of birth: 29 July 1952 *Education/professional qualifications:* Latymer Upper School, London; Trinity College, Cambridge, natural sciences (BA 1973); Pennsylvania University, USA: business administration (MBA 1975), finance and economics (MA 1975, PhD 1976) *Marital status:* married Brenda 1974 *Clubs:* Carlton, Royal Automobile *Recreations:* music, walking

Dr Norman R Blackwell, Head of Prime Minister's Policy Unit, 10 Downing Street, London SW1A 2AA *Telephone:* 0171-270 3000

BLUNT, CRISPIN JEREMY RUPERT Special Adviser to Secretary of State for Defence

Career: army service 1979-90; student/self-employed 1990-92; political consultant 1993; special adviser to Malcolm Rifkind, Secretary of State for Defence 1993-

Date of birth: 15 July 1960 *Education/professional qualifications:* Wellington College, Berkshire; Durham University, politics (BA 1984); Cranfield Institute of Technology, business administration (MBA 1991) *Recreations:* cricket

Crispin J R Blunt Esq, Special Adviser, Ministry of Defence, Main Building, Whitehall, London SW1A 2HB *Telephone:* 0171-218 2911 *Fax:* 0171-218 7140

BLYTH, Sir JAMES Chairman, Prime Minister's Citizen's Charter Advisory Panel

Career: Mobil Oil 1963-69; General Foods 1969-71; Mars 1971-74; director and general manager Lucas Batteries 1974-77, Lucas Aerospace 1977-81, director Joseph Lucas 1977-81; head of defence sales Ministry of Defence 1981-85; managing director Plessey Electronic Systems 1985-86, Plessey 1986-87; chairman Prime Minister's Citizen's Charter Advisory Panel 1990- *Current non-Whitehall posts:* chief executive Boots 1987-; deputy chairman British Aerospace 1994-

Date of birth: 8 May 1940 *Education/professional qualifications:* Spiers School, Glasgow; Glasgow University, history (MA 1963) *Honours, decorations:* Kt 1985 *Marital status:* married Pamela Campbell-Dixon 1967; 1 daughter, 1 son (deceased) *Clubs:* Royal Automobile, Queen's, East India *Recreations:* skiing, tennis, paintings, theatre

Sir James Blyth, Chairman, Citizen's Charter Advisory Panel, Cabinet Office, Horse Guards Road, London SW1P 3AL *Telephone:* 0171-270 6425 *Fax:* 0171-270 5824

BLYTHE, MARK ANDREW Principal Assistant Solicitor, Treasury Advisory Division, Treasury Solicitor's Department Grade: 2

Career: barrister in private practice 1967-77; legal consultant New York 1978-80; Treasury Solicitor's Department 1981-: assistant solicitor European division 1986-89; principal assistant solicitor Treasury advisory division 1989-

Date of birth: 4 September 1943 *Education/professional qualifications:* University College, Oxford, law (BCL, MA); barrister (Inner Temple 1966); attorney (New York bar 1980) *Marital status:* married; 1 daughter, 2 sons *Recreations:* getting out of London

Mark A Blythe Esq, Principal Assistant Solicitor, Treasury Solicitor's Department, Queen Anne's Chambers, 28 Broadway, London, SW1H 9JS *Telephone:* 0171-210 3000

BOE, NORMAN WALLACE Deputy Solicitor to Secretary of State, Scottish Office Grade: 3

Career: legal assistant, Menzies and White 1967-70; Scottish Office 1970-: deputy solicitor 1987-

Date of birth: 30 August 1943 *Education/professional qualifications:* Edinburgh University (LLB 1965)

Marital status: married Margaret Irene McKenzie 1968; 1 son, 1 daughter *Clubs:* Edinburgh University Staff *Recreations:* golf, walking dog

Norman W Boe Esq, Deputy Solicitor, Scottish Office, New St Andrew's House, Edinburgh EH1 3TE *Telephone:* 0131-244 4884 *Fax:* 0131-244 4704

BOEUF, PETER Chief Crown Prosecutor, South West, Crown Prosecution Service Grade: 4

Career: Crown Prosecution Service 1986-: chief crown prosecutor Dorset/Hampshire 1986-93, South West 1993-

Date of birth: 22 August 1947 *Education/professional qualifications:* Salford Grammar School; London University, law (external LLB 1968); solicitor 1972 *Marital status:* married Kay Veronica Russell 1976; one son, one daughter *Clubs:* Civil Service *Recreations:* running, canoeing, listening to classical music, singing English folk music

Peter Boeuf Esq, Chief Crown Prosecutor, South West, Crown Prosecution Service, Hawkins House, Pynes Hill, Rydon Lane, Exeter, Devon EX2 5SS *Telephone:* 01392 422555 *Fax:* 01392 422111

BOLLAND, MARK WILLIAM Director, Press Complaints Commission

Career: public affairs executive, Canada 1985-87; marketing IBM (UK) 1987-88; adviser to director-general Advertising Standards Authority 1988-91; Press Complaints Commission 1991-: executive assistant to chairman 1991-92, director/chief executive 1992-

Date of birth: 10 April 1966 *Education/professional qualifications:* King's Manor School, Middlesbrough; York University, chemistry (BSc 1985) *Marital status:* single *Recreations:* theatre, opera, walking, talking

Mark W Bolland Esq, Director, Press Complaints Commission, 1 Salisbury Square, London EC4Y 8AE *Telephone:* 0171-353 1248 *Fax:* 0171-353 8355

BOND, Dr KEVIN PATRICK Director of Operations, National Rivers Authority Grade: 3

Career: police service 1972-90; National Rivers Authority 1990-: Anglian regional general manager 1990-91, director of operations 1991-

Date of birth: 17 August 1950 *Education/professional qualifications:* Cardinal Newman Secondary Modern School, Birmingham; Liverpool University, politics, philosophy, history (BA 1972); Michigan State University, USA, criminal justice management (MSc 1980); Aston Business School, business studies/cybernetics (PhD 1989); FIWM *Marital status:* married Susan Hansor 1972; 2 sons, 1 daughter *Recreations:* jogging, cycling

Dr Kevin P Bond, Director of Operations, National Rivers Authority, Rivers House, Waterside Drive, Aztec West, Almondsbury, Bristol BS12 4UD *Telephone:* 01179 624407 *Fax:* 01179 202547

BOOKER, (GORDON) ALAN Deputy Director-General, Office of Water Services Grade: 3

Career: Sheffield Water 1960-65; Birmingham Water 1965-70; West Glamorgan Water 1970-74; operations manager Welsh Water 1974-80; chief executive East Worcestershire Water Company 1980-89; managing director Biwater Supply Ltd 1987-90, Bournemouth and West Hampshire Water Companies 1989-90; deputy director-general Office of Water Services (economic regulation of the water industry in England and Wales) 1990-

Date of birth: 17 February 1938 *Education/professional qualifications:* Dronfield Grammar School; Sheffield University, mining engineering (BEng 1960); MICE 1963; FIWEM 1966 *Marital status:* married Anne Christine Pike 1957; 2 sons, 1 daughter *Recreations:* walking, painting

G Alan Booker Esq, Deputy Director-General, Office of Water Services, 7 Hill Street, Birmingham B5 4UA *Telephone:* 0121-625 1304 *Fax:* 0121-625 1311

BORRETT, NEIL EDGAR Director, Property Holdings, Department of the Environment Grade: 3

Career: director, managing director, partner commercial property companies 1963-90; director Property Holdings, Department of Environment (management of government office estate) 1990-

Date of birth: 10 March 1940 *Education/professional qualifications:* Dartford Grammar School; College of Estate Management (RICS 1968, FRICS) *Marital status:* married Jane Chapman 1965; 2 daughters *Recreations:* golf, boating

Neil E Borrett Esq, Director, Property Holdings, Department of the Environment, St Christopher House, Southwark Street, London SE1 0TE *Telephone:* 0171-921 4584 *Fax:* 0171-921 4877

BOUCHIER, Professor IAN ARTHUR DENNIS Chief Scientist, Scottish Office Home and Health Department Grade: 2

Career: clinical and academic posts 1955-65; senior lecturer/reader in medicine London University 1965-73; professor of medicine Dundee University 1973-86, Edinburgh University 1986-; chief scientist (health research) Scottish Office Home and Health Department 1992-

Date of birth: 7 September 1932 *Education/professional qualifications:* Rondesbosch Boys' High School, Cape Town, South Africa; Cape Town University, SA, medicine (MBChB 1954, MD 1960) *Honours, decorations:* CBE 1990; FRCP 1970; FRCPE 1973; FRSE 1985; FIBiol 1988; FRSA 1991; FFPHM 1992 *Marital status:* married Patricia Norma Henshilwood 1959; 2 sons *Publications:* 19 including Clinical Skills (W B Saunders 1976); Gastroenterology: Clinical Science and Practice (2nd ed W B Saunders 1993); Davidson's Principles and Practice of Medicine (17th ed Churchill Livingston 1994) *Clubs:* New *Recreations:* hillwalking, music, history of whaling

Professor Ian A D Bouchier, Chief Scientist, Scottish Home and Health Department, St Andrew's House, Regent Road, Edinburgh EH1 3DG *Telephone:* 0131-244 2769 *Fax:* 0131-244 2683

BOURDILLON, Dr PETER JOHN Head of Specialist Clinical Services Division, Department of Health Grade: 3

Career: junior medical posts at London hospitals, cardiologist 1966-74; Department of Health [and Social Security] 1975-: medical office (MO) 1975-82; senior MO 1982-91; senior principal MO 1991-: head of medical manpower and education division, health care directorate NHS Management Executive 1991-93; head of health care (medical division) 1993-95, of specialist clinical services 1995- *Current non-Whitehall posts:* consultant clinical cardiovascular physiologist Hammersmith and Queen Charlotte's Special Health Authority 1975-; honorary senior lecturer Royal Postgraduate Medical School 1979-

Date of birth: 10 July 1941 *Education/professional qualifications:* Rugby School; Middlesex Hospital Medical School (MB, BS 1965); FRCP 1983 *Marital status:* married Catriona 1964; 2 daughters, 1 son *Clubs:* Royal Society of Medicine *Recreations:* golf, skiing, computer programming

Dr Peter J Bourdillon, Head of Specialist Services Division, Department of Health, Wellington House, 133-155 Waterloo Road, London SE1 8UG *Telephone:* 0171-972 4339 *Fax:* 0171-972 4340

BOURN, Sir JOHN BRYANT Comptroller and Auditor General, National Audit Office Grade: 1

Career: Air Ministry 1956-63; HM Treasury 1963-64; private secretary to permanent under secretary Ministry of Defence (MoD) 1964-69; assistant secretary (AS), director of programmes Civil Service College 1969-72; AS MoD 1972-74; assistant under secretary Northern Ireland Office (NIO) 1974-77, MoD 1977-82; deputy under secretary NIO 1982-85, MoD defence procurement executive 1985-88; comptroller and auditor general National Audit Office (examination accounts of government departments, certain public bodies and international organisations) 1988- *Current non-Whitehall posts:* visiting professor London School of Economics 1983-

Date of birth: 21 February 1934 *Education/professional qualifications:* Southgate County Grammar School; London School of Economics (BScEcon 1954, PhD 1958) *Honours, decorations:* CB 1986, KCB 1991 *Marital status:* married Ardita Fleming 1959; 1 daughter, 1 son *Publications:* Management in Central and Local Government (Pitman 1979) *Recreations:* swimming, squash

Sir John Bourn KCB, Comptroller and Auditor General, National Audit Office, 157-159 Buckingham Palace Road, London SW1W 9SP *Telephone:* 0171-798 7777 *Fax:* 0171-233 6163

BOVEY, PHILIP HENRY Head of Solicitor's Division D, Department of Trade and Industry Grade: 3

Career: third secretary Foreign and Commonwealth Office 1970-71; solicitor Slaughter and May 1972-75; Department of Trade and Industry (DTI) 1976; Cabinet Office 1977-78; under secretary DTI 1979-: company, insurance, insolvency and securities law 1985-91; head of Solicitor's Division D (competition, international trade, consumers, establishments and deregulation) 1991-

Date of birth: 11 July 1948 *Education/professional qualifications:* Rugby School; Peterhouse, Cambridge, history (BA 1970, MA); solicitor *Marital status:* married Jenet Alison McTear 1974; one daughter, one son *Recreations:* photography

Philip H Bovey Esq, Under Secretary, Department of Trade and Industry, 10-18 Victoria Street, London SW1H 0NN *Telephone:* 0171-215 3452 *Fax:* 0171-215 3249

BOWEN, D Director General of Marketing, Defence Export Services, Ministry of Defence Grade: 3

D Bowen Esq, Director General, Marketing, Defence Export Services, Ministry of Defence, Main Building, Whitehall, London SW1A 2HB *Telephone:* 0171-218 9000

BOWMAN, (EDWIN) GEOFFREY Parliamentary Counsel, Parliamentary Counsel Office Grade: 2

Career: Chancery bar 1969-71; Parliamentary Counsel Office (drafting government bills) 1971-: deputy parliamentary counsel 1981-84; parliamentary counsel 1984-

Date of birth: 27 January 1946 *Education/professional qualifications:* Trinity College, Cambridge (senior scholar), law (MA, LLM); barrister, Lincoln's Inn (Cassel scholar) *Honours, decorations:* CB 1991 *Marital status:* married Carol Margaret Ogilvie 1969; 2 sons, 1 daughter *Publications:* The Elements of Conveyancing (with E L G Tyler) (1972) *Clubs:* Les Amis du Basson Français, Paris *Recreations:* music (bassoon), history

Geoffrey Bowman Esq CB, Parliamentary Counsel, Parliamentary Counsel Office, 36 Whitehall, London SW1A 2AY *Telephone:* 0171-210 6620

BOWTELL, ANN ELIZABETH Deputy Secretary (until September 1995) and then Permanent Secretary, Department of Social Security Grade: 2

Career: National Assistance Board 1960-67; Department of Health [and Social Security] (DH[SS]) 1967-93: assistant secretary 1973-80, under secretary 1980-86; deputy secretary DS DSS 1986-90; DH 1990-93; first civil service commissioner Cabinet Office 1993-95; DSS 1995-: DS 1995, permanent secretary September 1995- *Current non-Whitehall posts:* member degree-awarding sub-committee Higher Education Quality Council; member advisory group Middlesex University Business School; member management committee Civil Service Medical Aid Association 1994-

Date of birth: 25 April 1938 *Education/professional qualifications:* Kendrick Girls' School, Reading; Girton College, Cambridge, economics (BA 1960) *Honours, decorations:* CB 1989 *Marital status:* married Michael John 1961; 2 daughters, 2 sons *Recreations:* walking, birdwatching

Mrs Ann E Bowtell CB, Deputy Secretary (until September 1995) and then Permanent Secretary, Department of Social Security, Richmond House, 79 Whitehall, London SW1A 2NS *Telephone:* 0171-210 5983 *Fax:* 0171-210 5523

BOYCE, Admiral Sir MICHAEL CECIL Second Sea Lord and Commander-in-Chief, Naval Home Command Ministry of Defence

Career: Royal Navy 1961-: flag officer surface flotilla 1992-95; Second Sea Lord and commander-in-chief Naval Home Command Ministry of Defence 1995-

Date of birth: 2 April 1943

Admiral Sir Michael Boyce OBE, Second Sea Lord and Commander-in-Chief, Naval Home Command, Victory Building, HM Naval Base, Portsmouth, Hampshire PO1 3LS *Telephone:* 01705 727001

BOYCE, Dr (WILLIAM) JONATHAN Director, Health Studies, Audit Commission

Career: house officer Radcliffe Infirmary, Oxford 1976; field medical officer eastern Sudan refugee project 1977; (senior) registrar community medicine NE Thames and Oxford health authority 1979-85; district medical officer and director of planning and information Northampton health authority 1985-87; medical manager PPP Ltd 1988-89; director health studies (NHS and personal social services) Audit Commission (external audit local government and NHS) 1994- *Current non-Whitehall posts:* member council Zoological Society of London

Date of birth: 21 March 1950 *Education/professional qualifications:* Merchant Taylors' School; Merton College, Oxford, philosophy, politics and economics (BA, MA 1973), medicine (BM BCh 1975, DM 1987); MRCP 1979; FFPHM 1993 *Marital status:* married Theresa Marteau; 2 daughters, 1 son *Recreations:* wine

Dr W J Boyce, Acting Director Health Studies, Audit Commission, 1 Vincent Square, London SW1P 2PN *Telephone:* 0171-828 1212 *Fax:* 0171-976 6187

BOYD, JOHN MACINNES HM Chief Inspector of Constabulary for Scotland, Scottish Office Home and Health Department

Career: police service 1956-: Paisley 1956-67, Renfrew and Bute Constabulary 1967-75; Strathclyde Police 1975-84: assistant chief constable 1979-84; chief constable Dumfries and Galloway Constabulary 1984-89; police inspectorate Scottish Office Home and Health Department 1989-: chief inspector for Scotland 1993-

Date of birth: 14 October 1933 *Education/professional qualifications:* Oban High School *Honours, decorations:* QPM 1984; CBE 1990 *Marital status:* married Sheila MacSporran 1957; 2 sons *Recreations:* golf, gardening, reading

John M Boyd Esq CBE, QPM, HM Chief Inspector, HM Inspectorate of Constabulary for Scotland, 2 Greenside Lane, Edinburgh EH1 3AH *Telephone:* 0131-244 4510 *Fax:* 0131-244 5616

BOYD-CARPENTER, Lieutenant General The Hon Sir THOMAS PATRICK JOHN Deputy Chief of Defence Staff (Programmes and Personnel), Ministry of Defence

Career: army service 1956-: Army Staff College staff 1975-77; defence fellowship Aberdeen University 1978; commanding officer 1st battalion Scots Guards 1979-81; colonel tactical doctrine arms executive Ministry of Defence (MoD) 1981-82; commander 24 Infantry Brigade 1983-85; director of defence policy MoD 1985-87; chief of staff British Army of the Rhine 1988-89; MoD 1989-: assistant chief of defence staff (programmes) 1989-92, deputy chief of defence staff (programmes and personnel) 1992-

Date of birth: 16 June 1938 *Education/professional qualifications:* Stowe School *Honours, decorations:* MBE 1973, KBE 1992 *Publications:* Conventional Deterrence: into the 1990s (Macmillan 1989) *Recreations:* walking, reading, gardening

Lieutenant General The Hon Sir Thomas Boyd-Carpenter KBE, Deputy Chief of Defence Staff, Ministry of Defence, Whitehall, London SW1A 2HB *Telephone:* 0171-218 9000 *Fax:* 0171-218 3660

BOYLE, Major-General A H Director-General Command and Control Communications and Information Systems (Army) and Signal Officer-in-Chief (Army), Ministry of Defence

Major-General A H Boyle, Signal Officer-in-Chief (Army), Ministry of Defence, Main Building, Whitehall, London SW1A 2HB *Telephone:* 0171-218 9000

Regulatory Organisations and Public Bodies

see page 1013

BOYS, PENELOPE ANN Head of Personnel, Department of Trade and Industry Grade: 3

Career: assistant principal Ministry of Power 1969-71; private secretary to minister without portfolio 1972-73; Department of Energy (DEn) 1973-85: principal 1973-81, seconded to British National Oil Corporation 1978-80, head of international unit 1981-85; head of social services and territorial (group 2) HM Treasury 1985-87; director of personnel DEn 1987-89; deputy director-general Office of Electricity Regulation 1989-93; head of personnel Department of Trade and Industry 1993-

Date of birth: 11 June 1947 *Education/professional qualifications:* Guildford County School *Marital status:* married David Charles Henshaw Wright 1977 *Recreations:* music, theatre, cooking, horse-racing

Miss Penelope A Boys, Head of Personnel, Department of Trade and Industry, 1 Palace Street, London SW1E 5HE *Telephone:* 0171-238 2909 *Fax:* 0171-238 2953

BOYS SMITH, STEPHEN WYNN Deputy Under Secretary, Police Department, Home Office Grade: 2

Career: Home Office (HO) 1968-77; central policy review staff Cabinet Office 1977-79; HO 1979-81; Northern Ireland Office 1981-84; HO 1984-92: assistant under secretary police department 1989-92; under secretary pay group HM Treasury 1992-95; deputy under secretary police department Home Office 1995-

Date of birth: 4 May 1946 *Education/professional qualifications:* St John's College, Cambridge, history (BA 1967, MA); University of British Columbia, Canada, history (MA 1969) *Marital status:* married Linda Price 1971; 1 son, 1 daughter *Recreations:* gardening, reading

Stephen W Boys Smith Esq, Deputy Under Secretary, Home Office, 50 Queen Anne's Gate, London SW1H 9AT *Telephone:* 0171-273 3601 *Fax:* 0171-273 3420

BRACK, RODNEY LEE Chief Executive, Horserace Betting Levy Board

Career: chartered accountant 1963-68; finance manager Daily Mirror Group 1969-75; managing director EMI Ltd leisure division 1976-81; finance director Metropole Group Ltd leisure division 1981-84; Horserace Betting Levy Board 1985-: financial controller/deputy chief executive 1985-92, chief executive 1993-

Date of birth: 16 August 1945 *Education/professional qualifications:* Whitgift School, Croydon; FCA 1978 *Marital status:* married Marilyn Carol Martin 1973; 2 sons, 1 daughter *Clubs:* Royal Automobile *Recreations:* racing, cricket, theatre

Rodney L Brack Esq, Chief Executive, Horserace Betting Levy Board, 52 Grosvenor Gardens, London SW1W 0AU *Telephone:* 0171-333 0043 *Fax:* 0171-333 0041

BRADLEY, ROBIN METCALFE Chief Executive, Marine Safety Agency (Executive Agency) Grade: 4

Career: naval service 1959-92: production director Portsmouth dockyard 1983-86; superintendent ships, ship refitting directorate-general Ministry of Defence 1986-89; chief executive Royal Naval Engineering School 1989-92; surveyor general (marine safety and pollution prevention) Department of Transport 1993-94; chief executive Marine Safety Agency 1994-

Date of birth: 23 November 1940 *Education/professional qualifications:* Pangbourne College, Berkshire; Royal Naval Engineering College, mechanical engineering (IMechE degree exemption 1965); MIMechE, CEng 1972; EurIng 1993 *Marital status:* married Judy Sweet 1969; 2 daughters, 1 son *Clubs:* Royal Naval Golf Society, Royal Naval Sailing Association *Recreations:* sailing, golf, squash

Robin M Bradley Esq, Chief Executive, Marine Safety Agency, Spring Place, Commercial Road, Southampton SO15 1EG *Telephone:* 01703 329103 *Fax:* 01703 329105

BREARLEY, CHRISTOPHER JOHN SCOTT Deputy Secretary, Local Government and Planning, Department of the Environment Grade: 2

Career: assistant principal Ministry of Transport 1966-70: private secretary (PS) to permanent secretary 1969-70; principal Department of Environment (DoE) 1970-73; secretary Review of Development Control 1973-74; PS to Cabinet Secretary, Cabinet Office (CO) 1974-76; DoE 1977-83: assistant secretary 1977-81, director Scottish services, Property Services Agency 1981-83; under secretary CO 1983-85; DoE 1985-: director of local government finance 1985-88, of planning and development control 1988-90; deputy secretary local government group 1990- and planning 1994- *Current non-Whitehall posts:* governor and trustee Watford Boys' Grammar School 1988-; member board Public Finance Foundation 1990-

Date of birth: 25 May 1943 *Education/professional qualifications:* King Edward VII School, Sheffield; Trinity College, Oxford, philosophy, politics and economics (BA 1964, MA); philosophy (BPhil 1966) *Honours, decorations:* CB *Marital status:* married Rosemary Stockbridge 1971; 2 sons *Clubs:* New, Edinburgh *Recreations:* crosswords, walking

Christopher J S Brearley Esq CB, Deputy Secretary, Department of the Environment, 2 Marsham Street, London, SW1P 3EB *Telephone:* 0171-276 3479 *Fax:* 0171-276 4612

BRENDISH, CLAYTON Ministers' Adviser on Agencies, Office of Public Service and Science

Clayton Brendish Esq, Minister's Adviser on Agencies, Office of Public Service and Science, 70 Whitehall, London SW1A 2AS *Telephone:* 0171-270 3000

BRERETON, DON(ALD) Under Secretary, Social Security Policy Group, Department of Social Security Grade: 3

Career: VSO service 1963-64; Ministry of Health/Department of Health and Social Security 1968-89: assistant principal 1968-70; assistant private secretary (PS) to secretary of state (SoS) 1971-72; PS to permanent secretary 1972-73; principal, health services planning and policy 1973-79; PS to SoS for social services 1979-82; head of policy strategy unit 1982-84; secretary to housing benefit review team 1984-85; assistant secretary, housing benefit 1985-89; under secretary, head of Prime Minister's Efficiency Unit 1989-93, division E (national insurance, state pensions, unemployment benefit) social security policy group, Department of Social Security 1993-

Date of birth: 18 July 1945 *Education/professional qualifications:* Plymouth College; Plymouth Technical College; Newcastle University, politics and social administration (BA 1968) *Marital status:* married Mary Frances Turley 1969; 2 daughters, 1 son *Recreations:* squash, holidays, books, bridge, gardening

Don Brereton Esq, Under Secretary, Department of Social Security, The Adelphi, 1-11 John Adam Street, London WC2N 6HT
Telephone: 0171-962 8870 *Fax:* 0171-962 8867

BRETHERTON, JAMES RUSSELL Secretary, UK Atomic Energy Authority; Director, Property Management and Services UKAE Government Division

Career: Ministries of Fuel and Power, Technology/Department of Trade and Industry 1966-76; Department of Energy (DEn) 1976-86: principal private secretary to secretary of state for energy 1976-78; assistant secretary international policy division 1978-79; head of oil industry division International Energy Agency, Paris 1980-82; assistant secretary atomic energy division DEn 1983-86; United Kingdom Atomic Energy Authority (UKAEA) 1986-: principal finance and programmes officer 1986-90; AEA Technology (UKAEA trading arm) 1990-94: secretary 1990-, commercial and planning director 1990-94; property management and services director UKAEA government division 1994- *Current non-Whitehall posts:* non-executive director UK Nirex Ltd 1990-

Date of birth: 28 March 1943 *Education/professional qualifications:* King's School, Canterbury; Wadham College, Oxford, history (BA 1965, MA) *Marital status:* married Harriet Grace Drew 1968; 2 sons *Recreations:* gardening, swimming, walking, music, bassoon playing

James R Bretherton Esq, Secretary, UKAEA, 329 Harwell, Didcot, Oxfordshire OX11 0RA *Telephone:* 01235 432654 *Fax:* 01235 433288

BRINDLEY, JOHN Administrator, South Eastern Circuit, Court Service (Executive Agency) Grade: 3

Career: Lord Chancellor's Department 1971-:/Court Service 1995-: court business officer, Birmingham 1971-72; criminal business division 1972-76; head of HQ personnel branch 1976-81; courts administrator, Exeter 1981-87; head of court service management group 1987-92, of court service business group 1992-94; administrator south eastern circuit (management area's high, crown and county courts' business) 1995-

Date of birth: 25 September 1937 *Education/professional qualifications:* Leek Grammar School, Staffordshire *Marital status:* married Judith Sherratt 1960; 1 daughter *Recreations:* hockey, amateur dramatics

John Brindley Esq, Circuit Administrator, South Eastern Circuit Office, New Cavendish House, Maltravers Street, London WC2R 3EU
Telephone: 0171-936 7234 *Fax:* 0171-936 7230

BRITTAN, DIANA (Lady Brittan) Deputy Chairwoman, Equal Opportunities Commission

Diana Brittan, Deputy Chairwoman, Equal Opportunities Commission, Overseas House, Quay Street, Manchester M3 3HN *Telephone:* 0161-833 9244

BRITTON, ANDREW JAMES CHRISTIE Member, Forecasting Panel, HM Treasury

Career: HM Treasury (HMT) 1966-73; Department of Health and Social Security 1973-75; HMT 1975-78; London Business School 1978-79; under secretary HMT 1980-82; director National Institute of Economic and Social Research 1982-; member forecasting panel HMT 1992-

Date of birth: 1 December 1940 *Education/professional qualifications:* Royal Grammar School, Newcastle-upon-Tyne; Oriel College, Oxford, modern history (BA 1962); London School of Economics (MScEcon 1968) *Marital status:* married Pamela Anne Sutcliffe 1963; 3 daughters *Publications:* Macroeconomic Policy in Britain 1974-87 (Cambridge University Press 1991)

Andrew J C Britton Esq, Member, HM Treasury Forecasting Panel, c/o National Institute of Economic and Social Research, 2 Dean Trench Street, London SW1P 3HE *Telephone:* 0171-222 7665
Fax: 0171-222 1435

BRITTON, PAUL JOHN JAMES Director of Local Government Finance Policy, Department of the Environment Grade: 3

Career: Department of Environment (DoE) 1971-75; private secretary (PS) to chief executive Property Services Agency 1975-77; principal DoE/Transport 1977-83; DoE 1983-: PS to minister for housing and construction 1983-85; assistant secretary 1985-91; director of local government finance policy 1991-, under secretary 1992-

Date of birth: 17 April 1949 *Education/professional qualifications:* Clifton College, Bristol; Magdalene College, Cambridge, history (BA 1971, MA) *Marital status:* married Pauline Bruce 1972; 1 son, 1 daughter *Recreations:* architectural history, topography, photography

Paul J J Britton Esq, Under Secretary, Department of the Environment, 2 Marsham Street, London SW1P 3EB *Telephone:* 0171-276 3162
Fax: 0171-276 3089

BRITTON, RUPERT JOHN Secretary and Legal Adviser, Civil Aviation Authority

Career: articled clerk/assistant solicitor Greater London Council 1967-74; chief solicitor Mid-Bedfordshire district council 1974-77; assistant city solicitor Corporation of London 1977-80; Civil Aviation Authority 1980-: deputy legal adviser 1980-94, secretary and legal adviser 1994- *Current non-Whitehall posts:* company secretary Highlands and Islands Airports Ltd 1986-

Date of birth: 24 May 1945 *Education/professional qualifications:* Bedford School; Lincoln College, Oxford, law (BA 1967, MA); solicitor 1971 *Marital status:* married Jacquelynn Forster 1970; 2 sons, 1 daughter *Recreations:* naval history, Americana, swimming

Rupert J Britton, Secretary and Legal Adviser, Civil Aviation Authority, 45-59 Kingsway, London WC2B 6TE *Telephone:* 0171-832 5794
Fax: 0171-832 5429

BRODIE, ROBERT **Solicitor to Secretary of State for Scotland** Grade: 2

Career: legal assistant (LA) Scottish Law Commission 1965-70; senior LA Scottish Office (SO) 1970-74; deputy director Scottish Courts Administration 1975-82; SO 1982-: assistant solicitor 1982-84, deputy solicitor 1984-87, solicitor to secretary of state 1987-

Date of birth: 9 April 1938 *Education/professional qualifications:* Morgan Academy, Dundee; St Andrew's University, arts (MA 1959), law (LLB 1962) *Honours, decorations:* CB 1990 *Marital status:* married Jean Margaret McDonald 1970; 2 daughter, 2 sons *Recreations:* hill walking, music

Robert Brodie Esq CB, Solicitor to Secretary of State, Scottish Office, New St Andrew's House, Edinburgh EH1 3TE *Telephone:* 0131-244 5247 *Fax:* 0131-244 4704

BROOKE, Sir HENRY (The Hon Mr Justice Brooke) **Chairman, Law Commission**

Career: barrister 1963-88: junior counsel to crown, common law 1978-81, counsel to Sizewell B inquiry 1983-85; high court judge Queen's Bench division 1988-; chairman Law Commission (for simplifying and making legal processes cheaper) 1993-

Date of birth: 19 July 1936 *Education/professional qualifications:* Marlborough College; Balliol College, Oxford, literae humaniores (BA 1961, MA) *Honours, decorations:* QC 1981; Kt 1988 *Marital status:* married Bridget Mary Kalaugher 1966; 3 sons, 1 daughter

The Hon Mr Justice Brooke, Chairman, Law Commission, Conquest House, 37-38 John Street, Theobalds Road, London WC1N 2BQ
Telephone: 0171-411 1249 *Fax:* 0171-411 1297

BROOM, ALISON **Special Adviser to Secretary of State for Employment**

Ms Alison Broom, Special Adviser, Employment Department Group, Caxton House, Tothill Street, London SW1H 9NF *Telephone:* 0171-273 3000

BROWN, Sir (AUSTEN) PATRICK **Permanent Secretary, Department of Transport** Grade: 1

Career: executive Carreras Ltd 1961-69; management consultant Urwick Orr and Partners 1969-72; Department of the Environment (DoE) 1972-76; assistant secretary (AS) Property Services Agency (PSA) 1976-80; Department of Transport (DTp) 1980-88: AS 1980-83, under secretary 1983-88; deputy secretary DoE 1988-90; second permanent secretary and chief executive PSA services 1990-91; permanent secretary DTp 1991-

Date of birth: 14 April 1940 *Education/professional qualifications:* Royal Grammar School, Newcastle-upon-Tyne; School of Slavonic and East European Studies, London University, Russian (BA 1961) *Honours, decorations:* KCB 1994 *Marital status:* married Mary Bulger 1966; 1 daughter

Sir Patrick Brown KCB, Permanent Secretary, Department of Transport, 2 Marsham Street, London SW1P 3EB *Telephone:* 0171-276 0830
Fax: 0171-276 5139

BROWN, (HAROLD) VIVIAN BIGLEY Head of Small Firms and Business Link Division, Department of Trade and Industry Grade: 3

Career: Ministry of Technology/Department of Trade and Industry (DTI) 1970-86: private secretary to permanent secretary 1972-74: principal 1974-80: seconded as commercial first secretary Jedda embassy 1975-79; assistant secretary 1980-86, under secretary 1986-: head of science and technology assessment office Cabinet Office 1986-89; DTI 1989-: head of competition policy division 1989-91, of investigations (into commercial and financial malpractice) division 1991-92, of deregulation unit 1992-94, of small firms and business link division 1994-

Date of birth: 20 August 1945 *Education/professional qualifications:* Leeds Grammar School; St John's College, Oxford, oriental studies (BA 1967); St Cross College, Oxford, Islamic philosophy (BPhil 1969) *Marital status:* married Jean Josephine Bowyer 1970; 2 sons *Publications:* Islamic Philosophy and the Classical Tradition (1972) *Recreations:* piano, cycling

H V B Brown Esq, Under Secretary, Small Firms and Business Link Division, Department of Trade and Industry, Kingsgate House, 66-74 Victoria Street, London SW1E 6SW *Telephone:* 0171-215 2780 *Fax:* 0171-215 2773

BROWN, MARTIN Director, Central Operations, HM Customs and Excise Grade: 3

Career: HM Customs and Excise 1971-: various posts including head of anti-smuggling division, of excise duties on tobacco oil and gambling, of customs at Manchester airport, private secretary to Financial Secretary to the Treasury; director customs 1993-94, central operations 1994-

Date of birth: 26 January 1949 *Education/professional qualifications:* Bolton School; New College, Oxford, French and Italian (BA, MA) *Marital status:* married Frances Leithead 1971; 2 sons

Martin Brown Esq, Director, Central Operations, HM Customs and Excise, Queen's Dock, Liverpool L74 4AA *Telephone:* 0151-703 8111 *Fax:* 0151-703 8115

BROWN, (ROBERT) BOB BURNETT Under Secretary, Division D, Department of Social Security Grade: 3

Career: Department of [Health and] Social Security (D[H]SS) 1967-83: principal 1971-79, assistant secretary (AS) 1979-83; AS Cabinet Office/Treasury 1983-87; D[H]SS 1987-: under secretary corporate management division 1989-93, division D (income support, housing benefit) 1993-

Date of birth: 10 August 1942 *Education/professional qualifications:* Kirkcaldy High School; Edinburgh University, chemistry (BSc 1963) *Marital status:* married Anne Boschetti 1971 *Publications:* Government Purchasing (HMSO 1984) *Recreations:* football, jazz, Greece

Bob B Brown Esq, Under Secretary, Department of Social Security, Adelphi, 1-11 John Adam Street, London WC2N 6HT *Telephone:* 0171-962 8338 *Fax:* 0171-962 8359

BROWN, SARAH ELIZABETH Head of Companies Division, Department of Trade and Industry Grade: 3

Career: assistant principal Board of Trade 1965-70; principal Department of Trade and Industry (DTI) 1970-78; secretary Crown Agents Tribunal 1978-82; DTI 1982-: assistant secretary personnel management division 1982-84, financial services division 1985-86; under secretary 1986-: head of companies division 1986-91, of enterprise initiative division 1991-92, of small firms division 1992, of small firms and enterprise initiative divisions 1992-93, of small firms and business link division 1993-94, of companies division 1994-

Date of birth: 30 December 1943 *Education/professional qualifications:* St Paul's Girls' School, London; Newnham College, Cambridge, natural sciences (BA 1962) *Marital status:* married Philip Anthony Russell 1976 *Clubs:* United Oxford and Cambridge University, Royal Society of Arts *Recreations:* gardening, walking, travel

Mrs Sarah E Brown, Under Secretary, Department of Trade and Industry, 10-18 Victoria Street, London SW1H 0NN *Telephone:* 0171-215 3190 *Fax:* 0171-215 3245

BROWN, Sir SIMON DENIS (The Rt Hon Lord Justice Brown) President, Security Service Tribunal and Intelligence Services Tribunal

Career: army national service 1955-57; barrister 1961-: recorder 1979-84, first junior treasury counsel, common law 1979-84, high court judge 1984-92; Lord Justice of Appeal 1992-; president Security Service Tribunal (investigation public complaints against security service) 1989-, Intelligence Services Tribunal 1994-

Date of birth: 9 April 1937 *Education/professional qualifications:* Stowe School; Worcester College, Oxford, law; Middle Temple (barrister 1961) *Honours, decorations:* Kt 1984 *Marital status:* married Jennifer Buddicom 1963; 2 sons, 1 daughter *Recreations:* golf, skiing, theatre, fishing, reading

The Rt Hon Lord Justice Brown, President, Security Service Tribunal, PO Box 18, London SE1 0TZ; Intelligence Services Tribunal, PO Box 4823, London SW1A 9XD
Telephone: 0171-273 3357 (SST); 0171-273 4383 (IST)

BRUCE, GEOFF(REY) KEITH Chief Executive, Pesticides Safety Directorate (Executive Agency) Grade: 4

Career: Ministry of Agriculture, Fisheries and Food 1962-: private secretary to permanent secretary 1971-72; parliamentary secretary 1972-73; principal policy branches 1973-81: seconded to Civil Service selection board 1976-77; head of agricultural resources policy division 1981-85, of research and development division 1985-87; eastern regional director 1987-91; Pesticides Safety Division/Directorate 1991-: head 1991-92, chief executive 1992-

Date of birth: 10 July 1944 *Education/professional qualifications:* George Stephenson Grammar School, Newcastle-upon-Tyne *Marital status:* married Pamela Mary Thompson 1967; 2 sons *Recreations:* birdwatching, book collecting, walking

Geoff K Bruce Esq, Chief Executive, Pesticides Safety Directorate, Mallard House, Kings Pool, 3 Peasholme Green, York YO1 2PX
Telephone: 01904 455922 *Fax:* 01904 455733

BRUMMELL, D Solicitor, Litigation Division, Treasury Solicitor's Department Grade: 4

D Brummell Esq, Solicitor (Management), Litigation Division, Treasury Solicitor's Department, Queen Anne's Chambers, 28 Broadway, London SW1H 9JS *Telephone:* 0171-210 3034

BUCK, MARCUS Chief Executive, Queen Elizabeth II Conference Centre (Executive Agency) Grade: 5

Career: BOAC/British Airways; chief executive Queen Elizabeth II conference centre (for national and international government meetings) 1992- *Current non-Whitehall posts:* chairman Congress London; member London First/London Visitors council

Date of birth: 26 December 1938 *Education/professional qualifications:* Cheltenham Grammar School; Western Ontario University, Canada, marketing management; British Transport Staff College; FCIT, MBIM, MInstAM, MInstD, FRSA *Marital status:* married Elizabeth Mary Croser 1966; 1 son, 1 daughter *Clubs:* Oriental, Athaenium, Melbourne *Recreations:* rugby, archaeology, violin playing, sketching

Marcus Buck Esq, Chief Executive, Queen Elizabeth II Conference Centre, Broad Sanctuary, London SW1P 3EE *Telephone:* 0171-798 4061 *Fax:* 0171-798 4200

BUCKS, Rear Admiral Archdeacon MICHAEL Chaplain of the Fleet, Director-General Naval Chaplaincy Services, Ministry of Defence

Career: curate; naval service: HMSs Victory 1969, Eagle 1970, Raleigh 1970, Albion 1971, Neptune 1972-74; Mauritius 1974-76; HMS Fearless 1976; Royal Naval Engineering College, Manadon 1977-81; exchange US Navy 1981-83; staff chaplain Ministry of Defence 1983-86; Portsmouth naval base 1986-90; HMS Warrior, staff chaplain fleet 1990-93; chaplain of the fleet, director general naval chaplaincy services 1993-

Date of birth: 2 June 1940 *Education/professional qualifications:* Rossall School; King's College, London (BD, AKC) *Honours, decorations:* QHC *Recreations:* steam and model railways; country walking, organs and organ music, painting

Rear Admiral Archdeacon M W Bucks QHC, Chaplain of the Fleet, Ministry of Defence, Victory Building, HM Naval Base, Portsmouth PO1 3LS *Telephone:* 01705 727900 *Fax:* 01705 727112

BUDD, ALAN PETER Director, Macroeconomic Policy and Prospects Directorate, HM Treasury Grade: 1A

Career: economics lecturer Southampton University 1966-70; HM Treasury (HMT) 1970-74: economic adviser, senior economic adviser 1970-74; London Business School 1974-88: senior research fellow 1974-80, economics professor and director Centre for Economic Forecasting 1980-88; economic adviser Barclays Bank 1988-91; HMT 1991-: chief economic adviser and head of government economic service 1991-95, director macroeconomic policy and prospects directorate 1995- *Current non-Whitehall posts:* special trustee Middlesex Hospital 1988-; governor London School of Economics 1994-

Date of birth: 16 November 1937 *Education/professional qualifications:* Oundle; London School of Economics, economics (BScEcon 1963); Churchill College, Cambridge, economics (PhD 1970) *Marital status:* married Susan Millott 1964; 3 sons *Publications:* The Politics of Economic Planning (Fontana 1978) *Clubs:* Reform *Recreations:* music, gardening, reading

Alan P Budd Esq, Director, Macroeconomic Policy and Prospects Directorate, HM Treasury, Parliament Street, London SW1P 3AG *Telephone:* 0171-270 5203 *Fax:* 0171-270 4836

BULL, M P Chief Nursing Officer, Nursing Division, Welsh Office

Miss M P Bull OBE, Chief Nursing Officer, Welsh Office, Cathays Park, Cardiff CF1 3NQ *Telephone:* 01222 823469

BUNYAN, PETER JOHN Chief Scientific Adviser, Ministry of Agriculture, Fisheries and Food Grade: 2

Career: research associate King's College, London 1960-62, University College, London 1962-63; Ministry of Agriculture, Fisheries and Food 1963-: senior scientific officer (SO) infestation control laboratory 1963-69, principal SO pest infestation control laboratory 1969-73, senior principal SO pest control chemistry department 1973-80; assistant secretary, head of food science division 1980-84; under secretary Agricultural Development and Advisory Service (ADAS) 1984-91: head of agricultural science service, director research and development service 1987-90, director-general 1990-91; chief scientific adviser 1991-

Date of birth: 13 January 1936 *Education/professional qualifications:* Raynes Park County Grammar School, Merton; University College, Durham, chemistry (BSc 1957); King's College, London, organic chemistry (PhD 1960); University College, Durham, ecotoxicology (DSc 1982) *Marital status:* married June Rose Child 1961; 2 sons *Publications:* numerous scientific articles *Clubs:* Farmers' *Recreations:* gardening, jogging, music

Dr Peter J Bunyan, Chief Scientific Adviser, Ministry of Agriculture, Fisheries and Food, Nobel House, 17 Smith Square, London SW1P 3JR *Telephone:* 0171-238 5958 *Fax:* 0171-238 5959

BURDEN, Major General DAVID LESLIE Director-General Army Manning and Recruiting, Ministry of Defence

Career: army service 1964-: service in UK, Europe, Near and Far East: chief personnel and logistics UN force in Cyprus 1981-83; assistant chief of staff (ACOS) British forces Hong Kong 1985-87; ACOS BAOR 1989-91; Ministry of Defence 1992-: director-general of resettlement 1992, of logistic support (army) 1992-95, of army manning and recruiting 1995-

Date of birth: 14 July 1943 *Education/professional qualifications:* Portsmouth Grammar School; Staff College, Camberley; National Defence College; Royal College of Defence Studies *Honours, decorations:* CBE 1988 *Recreations:* sports, especially cricket, golf

Major General David L Burden CBE, Director-General Logistic Support (Army), HQ QMG, Portway, Monxton Road, Andover, Hampshire SP11 8HT *Telephone:* 01264 382111 *Fax:* 01264 382106

BURKE, (DAVID THOMAS) TOM Special Adviser to Secretary of State for the Environment

Career: non-executive director Earth Resources Research 1975-88; executive director Friends of the Earth 1975-79; member Waste Management Advisory Council 1976-80; policy adviser European Environmental Bureau (EEB) 1978-88; director Green Alliance 1982-91; honorary visiting fellow Manchester Business School 1984-86; member executive committee National Council of Voluntary Organisations 1984-89; director Sustainability Ltd 1987-89; member executive committee EEB 1985-91; council member Royal Society of Arts 1990-92; special adviser to Secretaries of State for the Environment Michael Heseltine and Michael Howard 1991- *Current non-Whitehall posts:* visiting fellow Cranfield School of Management 1991-; senior visiting fellow Manchester Business School; member overseas advisory committee Save the Children Fund 1992-

Date of birth: 5 January 1947 *Education/professional qualifications:* St Boniface's College, Plymouth; Liverpool University, philosophy (BA 1969) *Marital status:* single *Publications:* co-author Ethics, Environment and the Company (IBE 1990); Green Pages (RKP 1988); The Green Capitalists (Gollancz 1987) *Clubs:* Reform *Recreations:* bird-watching, photography, walking

Tom Burke Esq, Special Adviser, Department of the Environment, 2 Marsham Street, London SW1P 3EB *Telephone:* 0171-276 4299 *Fax:* 0171-276 3269

BURNS, IAN MORGAN Deputy Secretary, Policy Group, Lord Chancellor's Department *(from August 1995)* Grade: 2

Career: estate duty office Inland Revenue 1960-65; Home Office (HO) 1965-72: assistant principal 1965-69, principal 1969-72; Northern Ireland Office (NIO) 1972-76: principal 1972-74, assistant secretary (AS) 1974-76; AS HO 1977-79; assistant under secretary (US) NIO 1979-84; US Department of Health and Social Security 1985-86; deputy US 1987-: NIO 1987-90; head of police department HO 1990-95; deputy secretary policy group Lord Chancellor's Department 1995-

Date of birth: 3 June 1939 *Education/professional qualifications:* Bootham School, York; King's College, London, law (LLB 1963, LLM 1965) *Honours, decorations:* CB 1990 *Marital status:* married Susan Rebecca Wheeler 1965; 2 daughters *Clubs:* Royal Commonwealth Society *Recreations:* adventurous gardening

Ian M Burns Esq CB, Deputy Secretary, Lord Chancellor's Department, Trevelyan House, Great Peter Street, London SW1P 2BY *Telephone:* 0171-210 8719 *Fax:* 0171-210 8752

BURNS, Sir TERENCE Permanent Secretary, HM Treasury Grade: 1

Career: London Business School (LBS) 1965-79: research 1965-70, economics lecturer 1970-74, senior lecturer 1974-79: director LBS centre for economic forecasting 1976-79, professor of economics 1979; HM Treasury 1980-: chief economic adviser and head of government economic service 1980-91, permanent secretary 1991- *Current non-Whitehall posts:* vice-president Society of Business Economists 1985-; fellow London Business School 1988-; visiting fellow Nuffield College, Oxford 1989-; vice-president Royal Economic Society 1992-; companion Institute of Management

Date of birth: 13 March 1944 *Education/professional qualifications:* Houghton-le-Spring Grammar School; Manchester University, economics (BA 1965) *Honours, decorations:* Kt 1983 *Marital status:* married Anne Elizabeth Powell 1969; 1 son, 2 daughters *Publications:* "The UK Government's Financial Strategy" in Keynes and Economic Policy: The Relevance of the General Theory After 50 Years (Macmillan 1988) *Clubs:* Reform, Ealing Golf *Recreations:* music, golf, soccer spectator

Sir Terence Burns, Permanent Secretary, HM Treasury, Parliament Street, London SW1P 3AG *Telephone:* 0171-270 4360 *Fax:* 0171-270 4384

BURR, TIM(OTHY) JOHN Assistant Auditor General, National Audit Office Grade: 3

Career: HM Treasury 1968-94: assistant secretary 1985-90: head of education division 1985-88, employment division 1988-90; under secretary 1990-: seconded to economic secretariat Cabinet Office 1990-92; Treasury Officer of Accounts 1993-94; assistant auditor general National Audit Office 1994-

Date of birth: 31 March 1950 *Education/professional qualifications:* Dulwich College, London *Marital status:* married Gillian Croot 1975; 2 sons

T J Burr Esq, Assistant Auditor General, National Audit Office, 157-197 Buckingham Palace Road, London SW1W 9SP *Telephone:* 0171-798 7391 *Fax:* 0171-931 8303

BURROUGHS, Dr WILLIAM JAMES Head of International Relations Unit, Department of Health Grade: 4

Career: scientific officer (SO)/senior SO National Physical Laboratory 1964-71; scientific attache Washington DC embassy 1971-74; Department of Energy 1974-87: principal private secretary to secretary of state 1978-80; assistant secretary (AS) EC energy policy 1980-81, research and development strategy 1981-84, personnel management 1984-87; Department of Health [and Social Security] 1987-: AS alcohol, drug and smoking policy 1987-91; director of research management 1991-93; head of international relations unit 1993-

Date of birth: 11 May 1942 *Education/professional qualifications:* Royal Grammar School, Guildford; St Edmund Hall, Oxford, physics (BA 1964); Birkbeck College, London, infra-red physics (MSc 1967); King's College, London, atmospheric physics (PhD 1970) *Marital status:* married Suzanne Bradbury 1968; 1 son, 1 daughter *Publications:* Lasers (Priory Press 1976); Understanding Lasers (Longman 1982); Lasers: the Inside Story (Collins 1984); Watching the World's Weather (Cambridge University Press [CUP] 1991); Weather Cycles: Real or Imaginary? (CUP 1992) *Recreations:* squash, skiing, gardening, writing

Dr William J Burroughs, Head of International Relations Unit, Department of Health, Richmond House, Whitehall, London SW1A 2NA
Telephone: 0171-210 5332 *Fax:* 0171-210 4860

BURROWS, Professor ANDREW STEPHEN Commissioner, Law Commission

Career: law lecturer Manchester University 1981-86, and fellow Lady Margaret Hall, Oxford 1986-94; English law professor University College, London 1994-; commissioner Law Commission (law reform and revision) 1994-

Date of birth: 17 April 1957 *Education/professional qualifications:* Prescot Grammar School; Brasenose College, Oxford, law (BA 1978, MA, BCL 1979); Harvard Law School, USA, law (LLM 1980) *Marital status:* married Rachel Jane 1982; 3 sons *Publications:* Remedies for Torts and Breach of Contract (2nd edition Butterworths 1994); The Law of Restitution (Butterworths 1993) *Recreations:* sport, mountain walking

Professor Andrew S Burrows, Commissioner, Law Commission, Conquest House, 37-38 John Street, Theobalds Road, London WC1N 2BQ *Telephone:* 0171-411 1216 *Fax:* 0171-411 1297

BURTON, Major-General E F G Assistant Chief of Defence Staff, Operational Requirements (Land Systems), Ministry of Defence

Major-General E F G Burton, Assistant Chief of Defence Staff, Ministry of Defence, Main Building, Whitehall, London SW1A 2HB *Telephone:* 0171-218 9000

BUSH, GEOFFREY HUBERT Director-General, Inland Revenue Grade: 2

Career: Inland Revenue 1959-: assistant secretary 1984-86; assistant director operations 1986-88; director of central division 1988-90, of information technology 1990-93, of special projects 1993-94; director general (principal establishments officer) 1994-

Date of birth: 5 April 1942 *Education/professional qualifications:* Cotham Grammar School, Bristol *Marital status:* married Sylvia Mary Squibb 1965; 1 son, 1 daughter *Recreations:* country pursuits

Geoffrey H Bush Esq, Director-General, Inland Revenue, Somerset House, Strand, London WC2R 1LB
Telephone: 0171-438 6543 *Fax:* 0171-438 6937

BUTCHER, MICHAEL JAMES CHARLES Secretary, Accounting Standards Board

Career: Central Electricity Generating Board 1963-66; Home Office 1966-83: assistant private secretary to Home Secretary 1972-74, head of magistrates' courts division 1979-81, leader of prisons resource control review 1982-83, Department of [Trade and] Industry 1983-93: head of accounting and audit policy, companies division 1987-93; secretary Accounting Standards Board 1993-

Date of birth: 16 January 1942 *Education/professional qualifications:* Dulwich College, London; King's College, Cambridge, history (BA 1963, MA) *Marital status:* married Doris Isobel Randewich 1970; 2 sons *Recreations:* music, gardening

Michael J C Butcher Esq, Secretary, Accounting Standards Board, Holborn Hall, 100 Gray's Inn Road, London WC1X 8AL *Telephone:* 0171-404 8818 *Fax:* 0171-404 4497

BUTLER, (ANTHONY) TONY JOHN Director of Services, HM Prison Service (Executive Agency) Grade: 3

Career: Cambridge-Columbia fellow Columbia Law School, New York, USA 1968-69; Home Office 1969-: assistant principal 1969-74: police and criminal departments 1969-72, private secretary (PS) to minister of state 1972-74; principal 1974-80: general department, sex discrimination and race relations legislation units and broadcasting department 1974-79; PS to secretary of state 1979-80; assistant secretary, broadcasting, finance and prison departments 1980-88; assistant under secretary, seconded to Department of Environment as director Inner Cities 1988-90; principal finance officer 1990; HM Prison Service 1990-: director of personnel and finance 1990-93, of personnel and services 1993-94, of personnel 1994-95, of services 1995- *Current non-Whitehall posts:* chairman University College, Oxford Old Members' Trust 1991-

Date of birth: 30 January 1945 *Education/professional qualifications:* Maidstone Boys' Grammar School; University College, Oxford, history (BA 1967, MA); Institute of Criminology, Cambridge (DipCrim 1968); FIPM 1994 *Marital status:* married Margaret Ann Randon 1967; 1 daughter, 1 son *Recreations:* music

A J Butler Esq, Director of Services, HM Prison Service, Cleland House, Page Street, London SW1P 4LN *Telephone:* 0171-217 6203 *Fax:* 0171-217 6746

BUTLER, (CHRISTOPHER) DAVID Director, Department for National Savings *(until the end of 1995)* Grade: 2

Career: HM Treasury (HMT) 1964-70; Committee to Review National Savings 1970-72; HMT 1978-82; Central Computer and Telecoms Agency 1982-85; HMT 1985-89; Department for National Savings 1989-: deputy director 1989-91, director 1991- *Current non-Whitehall posts:* director Sadlers Wells Theatre Board

Date of birth: 27 May 1942 *Education/professional qualifications:* Christ's Hospital, Horsham; Jesus College, Oxford, history (BA 1964) *Marital status:* married Helen Christine Cornwell 1967; 2 *Recreations:* ballet, opera, reading, family

David Butler, Director, Department for National Savings, Charles House, 375 Kensington High St, London W14 8SD *Telephone:* 0171-605 9469 *Fax:* 0171-605 9481

BUTLER, Sir (FREDERICK EDWARD) ROBIN Secretary of the Cabinet and Head of the Home Civil Service Grade: 0

Career: HM Treasury (HMT) 1964-70: private secretary (PS) to financial secretary 1964-65, secretary to budget committee 1965-69; founder member Central Policy Review Staff, Cabinet Office 1971-72; PS to prime minister (PM) 1972-75; HMT 1975-82: head of financial information systems team 1975-77, of general expenditure policy group 1977-80, principal establishment and finance officer 1980-82; principal PS to PM 1982-85; second permanent secretary, public expenditure HMT 1985-87; secretary of the Cabinet and head of home civil service 1988-

Date of birth: 3 January 1938 *Education/professional qualifications:* Harrow School; University College, Oxford, mods and greats (BA 1961) *Honours, decorations:* CVO 1986, KCB 1988; GCB 1992 *Marital status:* married Gillian Lois Galley 1962; 2 daughters, 1 son *Clubs:* Anglo-Belgian, Athenaeum, Brooks's, United Oxford and Cambridge University *Recreations:* competitive games, opera

Sir Robin Butler GCB CVO, Secretary of the Cabinet and Head of the Home Civil Service, Cabinet Office, 70 Whitehall, London SW1A 2AS *Telephone:* 0171-270 3000 *Fax:* 0171-270 0208

BUTLER, ROSEMARY Director of Statistics, Department of Health Grade: 3

Career: Central Statistical Office 1967-73; Department of Employment 1973-80: senior assistant statistician/statistician Unit for Manpower Studies 1973-77, statistician 1977-80; Ministry of Defence 1980-85: statistician 1980-83, chief statistician (CS) 1983-85; CS HM Treasury 1985-89; assistant secretary Department of Social Security 1989-91; under secretary, director of statistics Department of Health 1991-

Date of birth: 15 July 1946 *Education/professional qualifications:* Maynard School, Exeter; London School of Economics, computational methods (BScEcon 1967) *Marital status:* married Anthony David 1971 *Recreations:* theatre, music, birdwatching

Mrs Rosemary Butler, Under Secretary, Department of Health, Skipton House, Elephant and Castle, London SE1 6LW *Telephone:* 0171-972 5362 *Fax:* 0171-972 5660

BUTLER-SLOSS, The Rt Hon Dame (ANNE) ELIZABETH OLDFIELD (The Rt Hon Lady Justice Butler-Sloss) Alternative Chairman, Security Commission

Career: practising barrister 1955-70; registrar principal registry family division (FD) 1970-79; high court judge FD 1979-88; chairman Cleveland child abuse inquiry 1987-88; Court of Appeal 1988-; alternative chairman Security Commission (investigation of security breaches) 1993-

Date of birth: 10 August 1933 *Education/professional qualifications:* Wycombe Abbey School *Honours, decorations:* DBE 1979; PC 1988 *Marital status:* married Joseph 1958; 1 daughter, 2 sons *Clubs:* Lansdowne; Royal Society of Medicine

The Rt Hon Dame Elizabeth Butler-Sloss, Alternative Chairman, Security Commission, c/o Cabinet Office, Whitehall, London SW1A 2AS *Telephone:* 0171-270 0170 *Fax:* 0171-270 0623

Parliamentary Offices

see page 347

BUTT, GEOFFREY FRANK Under Secretary (Legal), Solicitor's Office, Inland Revenue Grade: 3

Career: HM Customs and Excise 1971-93: legal assistant 1971-74, senior legal assistant 1974-82, assistant solicitor 1982-86, under secretary (legal) (USL) 1986-93; USL (personal tax, rating, international, double and oil tax) Inland Revenue 1993-

Date of birth: 5 May 1943 *Education/professional qualifications:* Royal Masonic School, Bushey, Hertfordshire; Reading University, English literature (BA 1965); law (solicitor 1970) *Marital status:* married Lee Anne Davey 1972; 2 sons, 1 daughter *Recreations:* classical music and art, reading, gardening

Geoffrey F Butt Esq, Under Secretary, Inland Revenue, Somerset House, Strand, London WC2R 1LB *Telephone:* 0171-438 7262 *Fax:* 0171-438 6246

BYATT, IAN Director-General, Office of Water Services

Career: economics lecturer Durham University 1955-62; economic consultant HM Treasury (HMT) 1962-64; economics lecturer London School of Economics 1964-67; senior economic adviser Department of Education and Science 1967-69; director of economics and statistics Ministry of Housing and Local Government 1970-72; director of economics Department of Environment 1970-78; HMT 1972-89: director of public sector economic unit 1972-78, deputy chief economic adviser 1978-89; director-general Office of Water Services (economic regulation of water industry in England and Wales) 1989-

Date of birth: 11 March 1932 *Education/professional qualifications:* Kirkham Grammar School, Lancashire; St Edmund Hall, Oxford, philosophy, politics and economics (BA 1955); Nuffield College, Oxford, economic history (DPhil 1962); Harvard University, USA, economics *Marital status:* married A S Drabble 1959 (divorced); 1 daughter, 1 son (deceased) *Publications:* British Electrical Industry 1875-1914 (OUP 1979) *Clubs:* United Oxford and Cambridge University *Recreations:* painting

Ian Byatt Esq, Director-General, Office of Water Services, 7 Hill Street, Birmingham B5 4UA *Telephone:* 0121-625 1350 *Fax:* 0121-625 1348

C

CADELL, PATRICK MOUBRAY Keeper of the Records of Scotland, Scottish Record Office (Executive Agency) Grade: 5

Career: British Museum 1964-68: assistant keeper (AK) department of manuscripts 1966-68; National Library of Scotland department of manuscripts 1968-90: AK 1968-83, keeper 1983-90; Scottish Record Office: Keeper of the Records of Scotland 1991-

Date of birth: 17 March 1941 *Education/professional qualifications:* Merchiston Castle School, Edinburgh; Trinity College, Cambridge, history (BA 1962); Toulouse University, France, French (diploma 1964) *Marital status:* married Sarah Margaret Florence King 1968; 1 daughter, 2 sons *Publications:* The County of West Lothian (Scottish Academic Press 1992); For the Encouragement of Learning: Scotland's National Library (HMSO 1989) *Recreations:* walking, French

Patrick M Cadell Esq, Keeper of the Records of Scotland, Scottish Record Office, HM General Register House, Edinburgh EH1 3YY
Telephone: 0131-535 1314 *Fax:* 0131-535 1360

CADOGAN, Professor Sir JOHN IVAN GEORGE Director-General of the Research Councils, Office of Science and Technology/Cabinet Office

Career: Purdie professor of chemistry St Andrews University 1963-69; Forbes professor of organic chemistry Edinburgh University 1969-79; BP 1979-92: director of research 1981-92; member Royal Commission on Criminal Justice 1991-93; director-general of research councils Office of Science and Technology/Cabinet Office 1993- *Current non-Whitehall posts:* visiting professor of chemistry Imperial College of Science, Technology and Medicine 1979-

Date of birth: 8 October 1930 *Education/professional qualifications:* Swansea Grammar School; Kings College, London, chemistry (BSc, PhD, DSc); CChem, FRSC; FRSE; FRS *Honours, decorations:* CBE *Marital status:* widowed; 1 son, 1 daughter *Publications:* about 250 scientific papers *Clubs:* Athenaeum

Professor Sir John Cadogan CBE, Director-General of Research Councils, Office of Science and Technology, Albany House, 84-86 Petty France, London SW1H 9ST *Telephone:* 0171-271 2000
Fax: 0171-271 2018

CAHN, ANDREW THOMAS Deputy Head of European Secretariat, Cabinet Office Grade: 3

Career: Ministry of Agriculture, Fisheries and Food (MAFF) 1973-75; 2nd secretary, Brussels 1976-77; MAFF 1977-82: private secretary to permanent secretary, external relations, fisheries; 1st secretary UK permanent representation to EC, Brussels 1982-85; cabinet of EC vice-president 1985-88; MAFF 1988-92: head of sheep division 1988-89, of research policy 1989-92; principal private secretary (PPS) to Chancellor of Duchy of Lancaster, Cabinet Office (CO) 1992-94; PPS to Minister of Agriculture MAFF 1994; deputy head of European secretariat CO 1995-

Date of birth: 1 April 1951 *Education/professional qualifications:* Bedales School; Trinity College, Cambridge, English (BA 1973) *Marital status:* married Virginia Beardshaw 1976; 1 daughter, 2 sons *Recreations:* family, mountains, squash

Andrew T Cahn Esq, Deputy Head of European Secretariat, Cabinet Office, 70 Whitehall, London SW1A 2AS *Telephone:* 0171-270 0177

CAINE, J Special Adviser to Secretary of State for Northern Ireland

J Caine Esq, Special Adviser, Northern Ireland Office, Stormont Castle, Belfast NT4 3ST
Telephone: 01232 520700

CAINES, Miss J Director of Information, Department of Trade and Industry Grade: 4

Miss J Caines, Director of Information, Department of Trade and Industry, Ashdown House, 123 Victoria Street, London SW1H 0ET *Telephone:* 0171-215 5951

CALCUTT, Sir DAVID CHARLES Chairman, Panel on Takeovers and Mergers; Chairman of the Council, Office of the Banking Ombudsman

Career: barrister 1955-, recorder 1972-89; chairman Bar Council 1984-85, Civil Service Arbitration Tribunal 1979-94; master Magdalene College, Cambridge 1986-94; chairman Panel on Takeovers and Mergers 1989-, council, Office of Banking Ombudsman 1994- *Current non-Whitehall posts:* president Lloyds of London Appeal Tribunal

Date of birth: 2 November 1930 *Education/professional qualifications:* King's College, Cambridge, law (MA 1951, LLB 1954, MusB 1954); Middle Temple (barrister 1955, bencher 1981) *Honours, decorations:* QC 1972; Kt 1991 *Marital status:* married Barbara Walker 1969

Sir David Calcutt QC, Chairman, Panel on Takeovers and Mergers, 226 Stock Exchange Building, London EC2P 2JX *Telephone:* 0171-382 9026 *Fax:* 0171-638 1554

CALDER, JULIAN RICHARD Head of Division, Government Statistical Service and General Division, Central Statistical Office Grade: 3

Career: Central Statistical Office 1973-81: statistician 1973-78, chief statistician (CS) 1978-81; Inland Revenue 1981-: CS 1981-85, director of statistics and economics office 1985-94; head of division, government statistical service and general division Central Statistical Office 1994-

Date of birth: 6 December 1941 *Education/professional qualifications:* Dulwich College, London; Brasenose College, Oxford, mathematics (BA 1962); Newcastle University, mathematics (MSc 1963); Birkbeck College, London University, statistics (MSc 1972) *Marital status:* married Avril Tucker 1965; 2 sons *Recreations:* cycling, listening to music

Julian R Calder Esq, Central Statistical Office, PO Box 1333, Millbank Tower, London SW1P 4QP
Telephone: 0171-217 4362 *Fax:* 0171-217 4338

CALDWELL, EDWARD GEORGE Parliamentary Counsel, Office of the Parliamentary Counsel Grade: 2

Career: solicitor; Law Commission (LC) 1967-69; Office of the Parliamentary Counsel 1969-: seconded to LC 1975-77, 1986-88; parliamentary counsel (drafting government bills) 1981-

Date of birth: 21 August 1941 *Education/professional qualifications:* St Andrews School, Singapore; Clifton College, Bristol; Worcester College, Oxford, law (BA 1963) *Honours, decorations:* CB 1990 *Marital status:* married Bronwen Crockett 1965, divorced 1992; married Dr Helen Beynon 1992; 2 daughters *Recreations:* motorcycling

Edward G Caldwell Esq CB, Parliamentary Counsel, Office of the Parliamentary Counsel, 36 Whitehall, London SW1A 2AY *Telephone:* 0171-210 6633 *Fax:* 0171-210 6632

CALDWELL, Dr HELEN JANET **Parliamentary Counsel, Parliamentary Counsel's Office** Grade: 4

Career: barrister 1975-; law lecturer Reading University 1979-87; Parliamentary Counsel's Office (drafting government bills): parliamentary counsel 1994-

Date of birth: 13 September 1952 *Education/professional qualifications:* Reigate County School; Girton College, Cambridge, law (BA 1974), Lincoln's Inn (barrister 1975), Wolfson College, Oxford (DPhil 1982) *Marital status:* married Edward George 1992; 2 daughters, 2 stepdaughters

Dr Helen J Caldwell, Parliamentary Counsel, Parliamentary Counsel Office, 36 Whitehall, London SW1A 2AY *Telephone:* 0171-210 3000 *Fax:* 0171-210 6632

CALMAN, Dr KENNETH CHARLES **Chief Medical Officer, Department of Health** Grade: 1A

Career: Glasgow University 1968-88: surgery lecturer 1968-74, oncology professor 1974-84, postgraduate dean 1984-88; chief medical officer (CMO) Scottish Office 1989-91; CMO Department of Health (advice to government on public health safeguards) 1991-

Date of birth: 25 December 1941 *Education/professional qualifications:* Allan Glen's School, Glasgow; Glasgow University, biochemistry (BSc 1964), medicine (MB ChB 1967, MD 1973, PhD 1971); FRCSGlas 1971; FRSE 1979; FRCP 1985; FRCPEd 1989; FRCGP 1989; FFCM 1989; FRCR 1990; FRCSE 1991; FRCPath 1992 *Marital status:* married Ann Wilkie 1967; 1 son, 2 daughters *Publications:* Healthy Respect (Faber & Faber 1987, 94) *Clubs:* New, Edinburgh; Reform *Recreations:* golf, gardening

Dr Kenneth C Calman, Chief Medical Officer, Department of Health, Richmond House, 79 Whitehall, London SW1A 2NS
Telephone: 0171-210 5150 *Fax:* 0171-210 5407

CAMERON, JAMES **Industrial Director, Welsh Office** Grade: 4

Career: private industry 1962-91: Rolls-Royce 1974-77; plant manager Zenith Carburettors 1977-80; manufacturing director Langley Insulation Ltd 1980-84; managing director Rexel Engineering Ltd 1984-91; industrial director Welsh Office (stimulating regional industrial growth) 1991-

Date of birth: 14 March 1949 *Education/professional qualifications:* Dumfries Academy; Dumfries Technical College, mechanical engineering (HNC 1972); Strathclyde University, mechanical engineering (BSc 1974); CEng 1976; FIMechE 1988 *Marital status:* married Susan Price 1994; 1 daughter, 1 son *Clubs:* Cardiff Golf, Austin Counties Car, Rover Sports Register *Recreations:* golf, classic cars

James Cameron Esq, Industrial Director, Welsh Office, Cathays Park, Cardiff CF1 3NQ *Telephone:* 01222 825685 *Fax:* 01222 823204

CAMERON, (THOMAS ANTHONY) TONY **Under Secretary, Agriculture, Scottish Office Agriculture and Fisheries Department** Grade: 3

Career: Scottish Office 1966-: private secretary to deputy under secretary 1972, to permanent under secretary 1973-74; principal 1977-82; assistant secretary 1982-92; under secretary agriculture 1992-

Date of birth: 3 February 1947 *Education/professional qualifications:* Stranraer High School *Marital status:* married Elizabeth Sutherland 1970; 2 sons *Recreations:* reading, mountaineering, cycling

Tony Cameron Esq, Under Secretary, Scottish Office Agriculture and Fisheries Department, Pentland House, 47 Robbs Loan, Edinburgh EH14 17W *Telephone:* 0131-244 6032 *Fax:* 0131-244 6116

CAMPBELL, NIALL GORDON Under Secretary, Social Work Services Group, Scottish Office Home and Health Department Grade: 3

Career: Scottish Office 1964-: assistant secretary 1978-89; under secretary social work services group Home and Health Department 1989-

Date of birth: 9 November 1941 *Education/professional qualifications:* The Edinburgh Academy; Merton College, Oxford, history (BA 1962) *Marital status:* married Alison Rigg 1975; 3 sons

Niall G Campbell Esq, Under Secretary, Scottish Office Home and Health Department, 43 Jeffrey Street, Edinburgh EH1 1DN *Telephone:* 0131-244 5530 *Fax:* 0131-244 5387

CARDEN, RICHARD JOHN DEREK Deputy Secretary, Food Safety, Ministry of Agriculture, Fisheries and Food Grade: 2

Career: Ministry of Agriculture, Fisheries and Food (MAFF) 1970-77; HM Treasury 1977-79; MAFF 1979-93: chief regional officer, midlands and western 1983-86; under secretary 1987-94: European Community and external trade policy 1987-91; fisheries secretary 1991-93; European secretariat Cabinet Office 1993-94; deputy secretary food safety directorate MAFF 1994-

Date of birth: 12 June 1943 *Education/professional qualifications:* Merchant Taylors' School, Northwood; St John's College, Oxford, literae humaniores (BA 1966, MA, DPhil 1970); Freie Universität, Berlin, Germany 1969-70 *Marital status:* married Pamela Haughton 1971; 1 daughter, 1 son *Publications:* The Papyrus Fragments of Sophocles (De Gruyter 1974) *Recreations:* cycling, reading to children

Richard J D Carden Esq, Deputy Secretary, Ministry of Agriculture, Fisheries and Food, Whitehall Place, London SW1A 2HH *Telephone:* 0171-270 8119

CARLETON, Air Vice-Marshal G W Director of Legal Services, RAF, Ministry of Defence

Air Vice-Marshal G W Carleton, Director of Legal Services, RAF, Innsworth, Gloucestershire GL3 1EZ *Telephone:* 01452 712612

CARLISLE, MARK (The Rt Hon Lord CARLISLE OF BUCKLOW) Chairman, Criminal Injuries Compensation Board and Authority; Chairman, Advisory Committee on Business Appointments of Crown Servants

Career: member Home Office advisory council on penal system 1966-70; Conservative MP for Runcorn 1964-83, for Warrington 1983-87: front bench spokesman on home affairs 1969-70, parliamentary under secretary Home Office (HO) 1970-72, minister of state HO 1972-74, Secretary of State for Education and Science 1979-81; chairman Conservative Home Affairs committee 1983-87; Crown Court recorder 1976-79; chairman Parole Review Committee 1987-88, Criminal Injuries Compensation Board/Authority 1989-; Chairman Advisory Committee on Business Appointments of Crown Servants 1988- *Current non-Whitehall posts:* Crown Court recorder 1981-; Courts of Appeal judge, Jersey and Guernsey 1990-

Date of birth: 7 July 1929 *Education/professional qualifications:* Radley College; Manchester University, law (LLB 1953); Gray's Inn (barrister 1953, bencher 1980) *Honours, decorations:* DL, QC 1971, PC 1979 *Marital status:* married Sandra Joyce Des Yoeux 1959; 1 daughter *Clubs:* Garrick, St James's, Mandrake *Recreations:* golf

The Rt Hon Lord Carlisle of Bucklow QC, DL, Chairman, Criminal Injuries Compensation Board and Authority, Morley House, 26-30 Holborn Viaduct, London EC1A 2JQ *Telephone:* 0171-842 6801 *Fax:* 0171-842 0804

CARMICHAEL, W G Regional Procurator Fiscal, South Strathclyde, Dumfries and Galloway Region, Crown Office Grade: 4

W G Carmichael Esq, Regional Procurator Fiscal, South Strathclyde, Dumfries and Galloway Region, Crown Office, Cameronian House, 3/5 Almada Street, Hamilton ML3 0HG *Telephone:* 01698 284000 *Fax:* 01698 422929

CARR, (EDWARD ARTHUR) JOHN Chief Executive, CADW: Welsh Historic Monuments (Executive Agency) Grade: 5

Career: journalist Thomson Regional Newspapers 1960-65, Financial Times 1965-67; production editor Sunday Times 1967-70; Times Newspapers Ltd 1970-81: project manager 1970-75, assistant general manager 1975-81; chief executive Waterlow and Sons printers 1981-82; director Neath Development Partnership 1982-85; CADW: Welsh Historic Monuments 1985-: chief executive 1991-

Date of birth: 31 August 1938 *Education/professional qualifications:* The Leys School, Cambridge; Christ's College, Cambridge, archaeology and anthropology part 1, English part 1 (BA 1960, MA) *Marital status:* married Verity Martin (divorced 1980); Patrice Metro 1980; 3 daughters (2 from previous marriage), 1 son *Recreations:* gardening, newspapers, historic structures

E A John Carr Esq, Chief Executive, CADW: Welsh Historic Monuments Executive Agency, 2 Fitzalan Road, Cardiff CF2 1UY *Telephone:* 01222 465511 *Fax:* 01222 450859

CARR, PETER DEREK Chairman, Occupational Pensions Board

Career: construction industry; special adviser National Board for Prices and Incomes 1967-69; director Commission on Industrial Relations 1969-74; divisional director Advisory, Conciliation and Arbitration Service 1974-78; counsellor Washington DC embassy 1978-83; regional director and city action team leader Department of Employment 1984-90; chairman Northern Regional Health Authority 1990-94, Occupational Pensions Board 1994- *Current non-Whitehall posts:* chairman County Durham Development Co 1989-, Northern Screen Commission 1990-; visiting fellow Durham University; fellow Nottingham University

Date of birth: 12 July 1930 *Education/professional qualifications:* Fircroft College, Birmingham, economic history, politics; Ruskin College, Oxford, economics, politics (dipPolEcon 1957); Garnett College, London, education *Honours, decorations:* CBE 1988 *Marital status:* married Geraldine Pamela Ward 1956; 1 son, 1 daughter *Clubs:* Royal Over-Seas League *Recreations:* cycling, photography, grandson

Peter D Carr Esq, CBE, Chairman, Occupational Pensions Board, PO Box 2EE, Newcastle-upon-Tyne NE99 2EE *Telephone:* 0191-225 6247 *Fax:* 0191-225 6422

CARTER, C P Deputy Director-General, Office of Electricity Regulation Grade: 3

C P Carter Esq, Deputy Director-General, Office of Electricity Regulation, Hagley House, Hagley Road, Birmingham B16 8QG *Telephone:* 0121-456 2100 *Fax:* 0121-456 4664

CARTER, Dr (JOHN) TIMOTHY Director of Field Operations, Health and Safety Executive Grade: 3

Career: medical officer British Petroleum 1974-78; senior medical officer BP Chemicals 1978-83; Health and Safety Executive 1983-: director of medical services 1983-89, of health policy 1989-92, of field operations 1992-

Date of birth: 12 February 1944 *Education/professional qualifications:* Dulwich College; Corpus Christi College, Cambridge (MB 1965, MA); University College Hospital London (FFOM 1984, FRCP 1987); London School of Hygiene (MSc 1974) *Marital status:* married Judith Ann Lintott 1967; 1 son, 2 daughters *Recreations:* history – natural, medical and local

Dr J Timothy Carter, Director of Field Operations, Health and Safety Executive, Daniel House, Trinity Road, Bootle, Merseyside L20 7HE *Telephone:* 0151-951 4702 *Fax:* 0151-922 7918

CARTWRIGHT, JOHN CAMERON Deputy Chairman, Police Complaints Authority

Career: War Office, Board of Trade 1952-55; Labour Party organiser/agent 1955-67; Royal Arsenal Co-operative Society 1967-74: director 1972-74; MP for Woolwich East 1974-92; Police Complaints Authority (independent investigation public complaints) 1992-: member 1992-93; deputy chairman (responsible for investigations) 1993-

Date of birth: 29 November 1933 *Education/professional qualifications:* Woking County Grammar School *Marital status:* married Iris June Tant 1959; 1 son, 1 daughter *Publications:* co-author Cruise, Pershing and SS 20 (Brasseys 1985) *Recreations:* DIY, football, jazz

John C Cartwright Esq, Deputy Chairman, Police Complaints Authority, 10 Great George Street, London SW1P 3AE *Telephone:* 0171-273 6468 *Fax:* 0171-273 6421

CASE, ANTHEA FIENDLEY Under Secretary, Budget and Public Finances Directorate, HM Treasury Grade: 3

Career: HM Treasury 1966-: assistant principal 1966-74; principal 1974-78; assistant secretary 1978-88: public enterprises division 1978-82, deputy establishment officer 1982-83, aid and export finance division 1983-88; under secretary 1988-: home, education and transport group 1988-90, pay group (civil service management and pay) 1990-93, fiscal policy 1993-95, deputy director budget and public finances directorate 1995-

Date of birth: 7 February 1945 *Education/professional qualifications:* Christ's Hospital, Hertford; St Anne's College, Oxford, history (BA 1966) *Marital status:* married David Charles 1967; 2 daughters *Recreations:* family, contemporary art, theatre, gardening

Mrs Anthea F Case, Under Secretary, HM Treasury, Parliament Street, London SW1P 2AG *Telephone:* 0171-270 4419 *Fax:* 0171-270 4827

CASTALDI, Dr PETER Chief Medical Adviser and Director of Medical Services, Social Security Benefits Agency (Executive Agency) Grade: 3

Career: hospital clinical and general practice posts 1966-79; Department of [Health and] Social Security 1979-: medical officer (MO) Wales and South West regional office 1979-82; MO North Fylde central office 1982-84; senior MO HQ 1984-85; North Fylde central office 1985-92: senior MO 1985-86, principal MO 1986-92; chief medical adviser and director of medical services (medical advice on social security benefits and war pensions) Social Security Benefits Agency 1992-

Date of birth: 13 January 1942 *Education/professional qualifications:* Neath Grammar School for Boys; Welsh National School of Medicine (MB BCh 1966) *Honours, decorations:* OStJ 1977, CStJ 1993 *Marital status:* married Florence Joan Sherratt 1967; 1 daughter, 1 son *Clubs:* Lytham St Anne's Lawn Tennis and Squash; Fylde Rugby Football *Recreations:* squash, swimming, birdwatching, watching rugby

Dr Peter Castaldi, Chief Medical Adviser and Director of Medical Services, Social Security Benefits Agency, Quarry House, Quarry Hill, Leeds LS2 7UA *Telephone:* 01132 324259 *Fax:* 01132 324407

CATLIN, JOHN ANTHONY Deputy Solicitor, Environment, Countryside and Planning, Department of the Environment Grade: 3

Career: solicitor 1970-75; Treasury Solicitor's Department 1975-84; Department of Environment 1984-: assistant solicitor 1984-89; deputy solicitor 1989-

Date of birth: 25 November 1947 *Education/professional qualifications:* Ampleforth College, York; Birmingham University, law (LLB 1969) *Marital status:* married Caroline Jane Goodman 1974; 1 son, 2 daughters *Recreations:* music, travel

John A Catlin Esq, Deputy Solicitor, Department of the Environment, 2 Marsham Street, London SW1P 3EB *Telephone:* 0171-276 4702 *Fax:* 0171-276 0505

CAYLEY, MICHAEL FORDE Director, Capital and Valuation Division and Financial Institutions Division, Inland Revenue Grade: 3

Career: administration trainee Inland Revenue (IR) 1971-73; private secretary to chairman Price Commission 1973-75; IR 1975-: principal 1975-82, assistant secretary 1982-91, under secretary and director capital and valuation division (advising ministers on capital gains and inheritance tax) 1991-, financial institutions division (advising on financial sector and financial transactions taxation) 1994-

Date of birth: 26 February 1950 *Education/professional qualifications:* Brighton College; St John's College, Oxford, English (BA 1971, MA) *Marital status:* married Jennifer Athalie 1987; 1 stepdaughter, 2 stepsons *Publications:* Moorings [poems] (Carcanet Press 1971); The Spider's Touch [poems] (Carcanet Press 1973) *Recreations:* classical music, piano-playing, choral singing, poetry, walking, old churches and prehistoric sites

Michael Cayley Esq, Under Secretary, Inland Revenue, Somerset House, Strand, London WC2R 1LB *Telephone:* 0171-438 7290 *Fax:* 0171-438 7488

CHANT, (ELIZABETH) ANN Chief Executive, Child Support Agency (Executive Agency) Grade: 3

Career: National Assistance Board 1963-70; Department of [Health and] Social Security 1970-94: principal 1982-87: principal private secretary to permanent secretary 1985-87; head of contributions branch 1987-89, of contributions unit implementation 1989-90, of contributions unit 1990-91; chief executive Social Security Contributions Agency 1991-94, Child Support Agency (assessment and enforcement child maintenance) 1994- *Current non-Whitehall posts:* member council and executive committee Industrial Society

Date of birth: 16 August 1945 *Education/professional qualifications:* Collegiate Grammar School for Girls, Blackpool *Marital status:* single *Recreations:* classical music and jazz, reading

Miss Ann Chant, Chief Executive, Child Support Agency, Millbank Tower, London SW1 4QU *Telephone:* 0171-217 4792 *Fax:* 0171-217 4824

CHAPMAN, (JAMES KEITH) BEN Director, Trade and Industry, Government Office for the North West Grade: 4

Career: Ministry of Pensions and National Insurance 1958-62; Ministry of Aviation/British Airports Authority 1962-67; Rochdale committee of inquiry into shipping 1967-70; Board of Trade 1970-74; 1st secretary, commercial, Dar es Salaam 1974-78, economic, Accra 1978-81; principal, assistant secretary Department of Trade and Industry (DTI) 1981-87; commercial counsellor Peking 1987-90; DTI 1991-: deputy regional director north west and director Merseyside 1991-93; regional director north west 1993-94; director trade and industry government office for north west 1994-

Date of birth: 8 July 1940 *Education/professional qualifications:* Appleby Grammar School; FIMgt *Marital status:* married Jane Deirdre Roffe 1967; 3 daughters *Recreations:* walking, music, opera

Ben Chapman Esq, Director Trade and Industry, Government Office for the North West, Sunley Tower, Piccadilly Plaza, Manchester M1 4BA *Telephone:* 0161-952 4102 *Fax:* 0161-952 4105

CHATAWAY, The Rt Hon CHRISTOPHER JOHN Chairman, Civil Aviation Authority

Career: Olympic Games athlete 1952, 1956, 5,000-metre world record holder; Arthur Guinness & Sons Ltd 1953-55; newscaster Independent Television News 1955; current affairs commentator BBC tv 1956-59; co-founder World Refugee Year 1959; MP 1959-74: joint parliamentary under secretary Department of Education and Science 1962-64, overseas development opposition spokesman 1964-66, Minister of Posts and Telecommunications 1970-72, for Industrial Development 1972-74; managing director and vice-chairman Orion Royal Bank Ltd 1974-88; non-executive chairman British Telecommunications Systems Ltd, United Medical Enterprises, Crown Communications Group 1988-93; several non-executive directorships; ActionAid 1975-: honorary treasurer 1975-86, chairman 1986-1992; chairman Groundwork Foundation 1985-90, Alcohol Education and Research Council 1991-94, Civil Aviation Authority 1991- *Current non-Whitehall posts:* non-executive director BET plc, Credito Italiano International Ltd; trustee ActionAid Foundation for Sports and the Arts

Date of birth: 31 January 1931 *Education/professional qualifications:* Sherborne School, Dorset; Magdalen College, Oxford, philosophy, politics and economics (BA 1953, MA) *Honours, decorations:* PC 1970 *Marital status:* married Carola Cecil Ashton 1976; 1 daughter, 4 sons, 1 stepson *Clubs:* Garrick *Recreations:* family, reading, running, skiing

The Rt Hon Christopher Chataway, Chairman, Civil Aviation Authority, CAA House, 45-49 Kingsway, London WC2B 6TE *Telephone:* 0171-379 7311 *Fax:* 0171-240 1153

CHESTERTON, DAVID Under Secretary, Heritage and Tourism Group, Department of National Heritage Grade: 3

Career: journalist 1961-74; Northern Ireland Office 1974-92: assistant secretary 1980-85, under secretary (US) 1985-92; US heritage and tourism group Department of National Heritage 1992-

Date of birth: 30 November 1939 *Education/professional qualifications:* St Catherine's College, Oxford, modern languages (BA 1961)

D Chesterton Esq, Under Secretary, Department of National Heritage, 2-4 Cockspur Street, London SW1Y 5DH *Telephone:* 0171-211 6000 *Fax:* 0171-211 6319

CHILTON, Dr BOB Director of Local Government Studies, Audit Commission *(see Addenda)*

Career: director of housing and property services Kensington and Chelsea council 1979-84; assistant director South Bank Polytechnic 1984-86; chief executive Gillingham council 1986-89; director of local community studies Audit Commission (external audit local government and NHS) 1989-

Date of birth: 20 April 1947 *Education/professional qualifications:* Acklam Hall Grammar School, Middlesbrough; Downing College, Cambridge, geography (BA 1969, MA), urban studies (PhD 1973) *Marital status:* married Neena Deborah 1976; 1 daughter, 1 son *Recreations:* sailing, walking

Dr Bob Chilton, Director of Local Government Studies, Audit Commission, 1 Vincent Square, London SW1P 2PN *Telephone:* 0171-828 1212 *Fax:* 0171-630 5667

CHISHOLM, JOHN ALEXANDER RAYMOND Chief Executive, Defence Evaluation and Research Agency (Executive Agency) Grade: 2

John A R Chisholm Esq, Chief Executive, Defence Evaluation and Research Agency, Farnborough, Hampshire GU14 6TD *Telephone:* 01252-394500

CHIVERS, KIT (CHRISTOPHER) JOHN ADRIAN Principal Establishment Officer, Department for National Savings Grade: 4

Career: HM Treasury 1968-94: junior private secretary to Chancellor of Exchequer 1971-73; 1st secretary, financial, Washington DC embassy 1976-78; head of industry division 1980-84; seconded to Prime Minister's efficiency unit 1984-86; head of pay division 1986-90, of specialist support group 1990-94; director of resources (principal establishment and finance officer, deputy to director) 1994-

Date of birth: 8 March 1945 *Education/professional qualifications:* Glasgow High School; Glasgow University, classics (MA 1966); Trinity College, Oxford, greats (MA 1968) *Marital status:* married Geertje Chivers-Bouwes 1969; 1 daughter, 1 son *Recreations:* charity work, writing on philosophy and theology

Kit Chivers Esq, Director of Resources, Department for National Savings, Charles House, 375 Kensington High Street, London W14 8SE *Telephone:* 0171-605 9462 *Fax:* 0171-605 9481

CHRISTOPHERSON, ROMOLA CAROL ANDREA Director of Information, Department of Health Grade: 4

Career: department of scientific and industrial research Ministry of Technology 1962-70; Department of Environment 1970-78; Ministry of Agriculture, Fisheries and Food 1978-81; chief press officer Northern Ireland Office 1981-83; deputy press secretary to prime minister 1983-84; head of information Department of Energy 1984-86; director of information Department of Health [and Social Security] 1986-

Date of birth: 10 January 1939 *Education/professional qualifications:* Collegiate School for Girls, Leicester; St Hugh's College, Oxford, English (BA 1961) *Marital status:* single *Recreations:* amateur dramatics, antiques

Miss Romola C A Christopherson, Director of Information, Department of Health, Richmond House, Whitehall, London SW1A 2NS
Telephone: 0171-210 5440 *Fax:* 0171-210 5433

CHRONNELL, R J Chief Crown Prosecutor, Anglia, Crown Prosecution Service Grade: 4

R J Chronnell Esq, Chief Crown Prosecutor, Anglia, Crown Prosecution Service, Queen's House, 58 Victoria Street, St Albans, Hertfordshire AL1 3HZ *Telephone:* 01727 818100 *Fax:* 01727 833144

CHURCH, IAN Editor, Hansard, House of Commons Grade: 4

Career: reporter Press Association 1964-66, Scotsman 1966-68, The Times 1968-72; House of Commons Official Report (Hansard) 1972-: reporter and sub-editor 1972-88, deputy editor 1988-89, editor and head of Department of the Official Report 1989- *Current non-Whitehall posts:* secretary Commonwealth Hansard Editors Association

Date of birth: 18 October 1941 *Education/professional qualifications:* Roan School, London *Marital status:* married Christine Stevenson 1964; 1 daughter *Recreations:* photography, writing fiction

Ian Church Esq, Editor, Official Report, House of Commons, London SW1A 0AA *Telephone:* 0171-219 3000 *Fax:* 0171-219 6323

CLAPHAM, Dr PETER Director and Chief Executive, National Physical Laboratory (Executive Agency) Grade: 3

Career: research National Physical Laboratory (NPL) 1960-81; assistant secretary research and technology policy division Department of Trade and Industry 1981-82; head of division mechanical and optical metrology NPL 1982-85; chief executive National Weights and Measures Laboratory 1985-90; chief executive NPL 1990-

Date of birth: 3 November 1940 *Education/professional qualifications:* Ashville College, Harrogate; University College, London, physics (BSc 1960); Imperial College, London, physics (PhD 1969) *Marital status:* married Jean Vigil 1965; 2 sons

Dr Peter Clapham, Director and Chief Executive, National Physical Laboratory, Teddington, Middlesex TW11 0LW
Telephone: 0181-943 6015 *Fax:* 0181-943 2155

CLARK, (CHARLES) ANTHONY Under Secretary, Higher Education, Department for Education Grade: 3

Career: Department of/for Education [and Science] 1965-: under secretary (US) teacher supply and international relations 1982-87; principal finance officer 1987-89; US higher education branch 1989-

Date of birth: 13 June 1940 *Education/professional qualifications:* King's College School, Wimbledon; Pembroke College, Oxford, physics (BA 1961, MA) *Honours, decorations:* CB *Marital status:* married Penelope Margaret Brett 1978; 2 daughters, 1 son *Recreations:* reading, gardening, golf

C Anthony Clark Esq CB, Under Secretary, Department for Education, Sanctuary Buildings, Great Smith Street, London SW1P 3PT *Telephone:* 0171-925 5192 *Fax:* 0171-925 6985

CLARK, DAVID JOHN Under Secretary, Principal Establishment Officer, Department of Health Grade: 3

Career: Department of Health (DoH) [and Social Security] (DSS) 1969-93: assistant secretary 1983-90; under secretary 1990-: head of pensions policy DSS 1990-93; head of recruitment studies Cabinet Office/Office of Public Service and Science 1994; head of departmental management division, principal establishment officer DoH 1994-

Date of birth: 20 September 1947 *Education/professional qualifications:* Kent University, history (MA 1972) *Marital status:* married Caroline Russell 1970; 2 sons, 3 daughters

David J Clark Esq, Under Secretary, Department of Health, Richmond House, 79 Whitehall, London SW1A 2NS *Telephone:* 0171-210 5833 *Fax:* 0171-210 5523

CLARK, GREGOR MUNRO Assistant Legal Secretary and Scottish Parliamentary Counsel, Lord Advocate's Department Grade: 3

Career: advocate 1972-; law practice 1972-74; Lord Advocate's Department 1974-: assistant, later deputy parliamentary draftsman 1974-79, assistant legal secretary and Scottish parliamentary counsel (assisting Scottish law officers on Scottish matters, drafting bills relating to Scotland and Scottish adaptations of bills) 1979-

Date of birth: 18 April 1946 *Education/professional qualifications:* Queen's Park Senior Secondary School, Glasgow; St Andrew's University, law (LLB 1970) *Marital status:* married Jane Maralyn Palmer 1974; 1 son, 2 daughters *Recreations:* music, Scandinavian languages and literature

Gregor M Clark Esq, Assistant Legal Secretary and Scottish Parliamentary Counsel, Lord Advocate's Department, 2 Carlton Gardens, London SW1Y 5AA *Telephone:* 0171-210 1046 *Fax:* 0171-210 1025

CLARK, ROBERT JOSEPH Administrator Western Circuit, Court Service (Executive Agency) Grade: 4

Career: Lord Chancellor's Department 1960-:/Court Service 1995-: Official Solicitor's office; industrial relations court; head of civil business 1988-91, of judicial appointments division 1991-93; administrator western circuit 1993-

Date of birth: 29 March 1942 *Education/professional qualifications:* various London schools *Marital status:* married Elke Agnes Schmidt 1970; 2 daughters *Recreations:* theatre, walking

Robert J Clark Esq, Circuit Administrator, Western Circuit Office, Bridge House, Clifton Down, Bristol BS8 4BN *Telephone:* 01179 743763 *Fax:* 01179 744133

CLARKE, A S R **Chief Crown Prosecutor, Severn/Thames, Crown Prosecution Service** Grade: 4

A S R Clarke, Chief Crown Prosecutor, Severn/Thames, Crown Prosecution Service, Artillery House, Victoria Square, Heritage Way, Worcester WR9 8QT *Telephone:* 01905 793763 *Fax:* 01905 796793

CLARKE, Rear-Admiral JOHN PATRICK **Flag Officer Training and Recruiting, Ministry of Defence; Chief Executive, Naval Recruiting and Training Agency (Executive Agency)**

Career: Royal Navy 1963-: commanding officer (CO) HMSs Finwhale 1975-76, Oberon 1976-77; staff operations officer first submarine squadron 1977-78; CO HMS Dreadnought 1979-80, submarine CO qualifying course 1980-82; submarine staff officer directorate of naval warfare 1983-85; executive officer HM Yacht Britannia 1985-86; captain submarine sea training 1986-88, 7th frigate squadron and HMS Argonaut 1988-90; Ministry of Defence 1990-: assistant director naval staff duties 1990-92; director of naval warfare 1992, of naval management, communication and information systems 1993-94; flag officer training and recruiting 1994-; chief executive Naval Recruiting and Training Agency 1995-

Date of birth: 12 December 1944 *Education/professional qualifications:* Epsom College, Surrey; Britannia Royal Naval College (commission 1966) *Honours, decorations:* LVO 1986, MBE 1978 *Recreations:* golf, bee keeping, reading history

Rear-Admiral John P Clarke LVO MBE, Flag Officer Training and Recruiting, Victory Building, HM Naval Base, Portsmouth PO1 3LS *Telephone:* 01705 727600 *Fax:* 01705 727613

CLARKE, OWEN J **Controller, Inland Revenue, Scotland** Grade: 4

Career: Inland Revenue 1955-: inspector of taxes 1961; district inspector 1970-73; Edinburgh 1973-80: enquiry branch 1973-76, in charge of special office 1976-80; group controller Merseyside 1980-81, Scotland 1981-88; controller north of England 1988-90, Scotland 1990-

Date of birth: 15 March 1937 *Education/professional qualifications:* Portobello Secondary School, Edinburgh *Marital status:* married Elizabeth More 1964; 2 sons, 1 daughter *Clubs:* Scottish Judo Federation; Tantallon Golf, North Berwick *Recreations:* sport, particularly judo, golf, jogging

Owen J Clarke Esq, Controller, Inland Revenue, Scotland, Lauriston House, 80 Lauriston Place, Edinburgh EH3 9SL *Telephone:* 0131-222 3780 *Fax:* 0131-229 0394

CLARKE, ROGER ERIC **Under Secretary, Shipping Policy Directorate, Department of Transport** Grade: 3

Career: principal, civil aviation posts Ministry of Aviation, Board of Trade, Department of Trade [and Industry] (DT[I]) 1964-72; seconded to Fiji government as air traffic rights adviser 1972-74; DT 1974-83: insurance division 1974-79: principal 1974-75, assistant secretary (AS) 1975-83: commercial relations and exports 1979-80, civil aviation policy 1980-83; Department of Transport 1983-: AS civil aviation policy 1983-85; under secretary 1985-: head of civil aviation policy 1985-89, of public transport 1989-91, of shipping policy 1991-, emergencies and security directorate 1991-94

Date of birth: 13 June 1939 *Education/professional qualifications:* University College School, London; Corpus Christi College, Cambridge, classics (BA 1960, MA) *Marital status:* married Elizabeth Pingstone 1983; 1 daughter *Clubs:* Reform *Recreations:* family, friends, church, garden, walking, theatre, music, languages, travel

Roger E Clarke Esq, Under Secretary, Department of Transport, 2 Marsham Street, London SW1P 3EB *Telephone:* 0171-276 5910 *Fax:* 0171-276 6309

CLARKE, Professor ROGER HOWARD Director, National Radiological Protection Board Grade: 3

Career: research officer Central Electricity Generating Board 1965-77; National Radiological Protection Board 1978-: head of nuclear power assessments 1978-82, board secretary 1983-87, director 1987- *Current non-Whitehall posts:* chairman International Commission on Radiological Protection 1993-; member Nuclear Safety Advisory Group, International Atomic Energy Agency 1992-; UK representative UN Scientific Committee on Effects of Atomic Radiation 1993-; member Group of Exports convened under Article 31 of the Euratom Treaty 1987-; visiting professor Imperial College of Science, Technology and Medicine 1993-, Surrey University 1994-

Date of birth: 22 August 1943 *Education/professional qualifications:* King Edward VI School, Stourbridge; Birmingham University, physics (BSc 1964), reactor physics and technology (MSc 1965); Central London Polytechnic, physical aspects of nuclear reactors in public and working environment (PhD 1973); honorary fellow Royal College of Radiologists 1994 *Marital status:* married Sandra Ann Buckley 1966; 1 son, 1 daughter *Publications:* co-author Carcinogenesis and Radiation Risk: A Biomathematical Reconnaissance (BIR 1977) *Recreations:* theatre, travel, gardening

Professor Roger H Clarke, Director, National Radiological Protection Board, Chilton, Didcot, Oxfordshire OX11 0RQ *Telephone:* 01235 822632 *Fax:* 01235 822630

CLEAVE, BRIAN E Solicitor of Inland Revenue Grade: 2

Career: Office of Solicitor of Inland Revenue 1967-: legal assistant (LA) 1967-72; senior LA 1972-78; assistant solicitor (AS) 1978-86; principal AS 1986-90; solicitor 1990-

Date of birth: 3 September 1939 *Education/professional qualifications:* Eastbourne College 1953-58; Exeter University, law (LLB 1961); Kansas University, USA, political science and law; Manchester University, law; solicitor 1966 *Honours, decorations:* CB *Marital status:* married Celia Williams 1979 *Recreations:* travel, theatre, walking on South Downs

Brian E Cleave Esq CB, Solicitor's Office, Inland Revenue, Somerset House, London WC2R 1LB *Telephone:* 0171-438 6645 *Fax:* 0171-438 6246

CLEAVER, Sir ANTHONY BRIAN Chairman, UK Atomic Energy Authority/AEA Technology

Career: IBM 1962-94: Europe general manager 1983-86, chief executive 1986-94, chairman 1990-94; UK: chairman IBM United Kingdom Holdings Ltd 1992-94; chairman UK Atomic Energy Authority/AEA Technology 1993- *Current non-Whitehall posts:* non-executive director General Accident Fire and Life Assurance Corp 1988-, Smith and Nephew plc 1993-; chairman Industrial Development Advisory Board 1993-, Independent Assessors (TECs) 1993-; non-executive director General Cable plc 1994-

Date of birth: 10 April 1938 *Education/professional qualifications:* Berkhamsted School; Trinity College, Oxford, literae humaniores (BA 1962, MA) *Honours, decorations:* FBCS 1976; Kt 1991 *Marital status:* married Mary Teresa Cotter 1962; 1 son, 1 daughter *Publications:* articles on information technology, management *Clubs:* MCC, Royal Automobile *Recreations:* opera, cricket, golf

Sir Anthony Cleaver, Chairman, UK Atomic Energy Authority/AEA Technology, 4-12 Regent Street, London SW1Y 4PE
Telephone: 0171-389 6553 *Fax:* 0171-389 6570

CLEVELAND, ALEXIS Territorial (Southern) and Development Director, Social Security Benefits Agency Grade: 4

Ms Alexis Cleveland, Territorial (Southern) and Development Director, Social Security Benefits Agency, Quarry House, Quarry Hill, Leeds LS2 7UA *Telephone:* 01132 327835

CLIVE, ERIC MCCREDIE Commissioner, Scottish Law Commission

Career: law faculty Edinburgh University 1962-80: lecturer, senior lecturer, reader, professor of Scots law; Scottish law commissioner 1981-

Date of birth: 24 July 1938 *Education/professional qualifications:* Stranraer High School; Edinburgh University, arts (MA 1958), law (LLB 1960); Michigan University, USA, law (LLM 1962); Virginia University, USA, law (SJD 1968) *Marital status:* married Kay McLeman 1962; 3 daughters, 1 son *Publications:* Scots Law for Journalists (W Green and Son 1988); Law of Husband and Wife in Scotland (W Green and Son 1982, 92) *Recreations:* hill walking, chess

Eric M Clive Esq, Commissioner, Scottish Law Commission, 140 Causewayside, Edinburgh EH9 1PR *Telephone:* 0131-668 2131
Fax: 0131-662 4900

CLOSE, ANTHONY Chairman, Health Education Authority

Anthony Close Esq, Chairman, Health Education Authority, Hamilton House, Mabledon Place, London WC1H 9TX *Telephone:* 0171-383 3833

COATES, DAVID R Chief Economic Adviser and Head of Economics and Statistics Division, Department of Trade and Industry Grade: 3

Career: research assistant Manchester University, Manchester Business School 1966-68; economic adviser (EA) Ministry of Technology and Department of Trade and Industry (DTI) 1968-74; DTI 1974-: senior EA 1974-82, assistant secretary 1982-89, under secretary, chief EA 1989-: economic management and education division 1990, economics, [market intelligence] and statistics division 1992-

Date of birth: 22 March 1942 *Education/professional qualifications:* Leeds Grammar School; Queen's College, Oxford (BA 1964); London School of Economics (MScEcon 1973) *Recreations:* family, gardening, travel, music

David R Coates Esq, Chief Economic Adviser, Department of Trade and Industry, Ashdown House, 123 Victoria Street, London SW1E 6RB *Telephone:* 0171-215 6059 *Fax:* 0171-215 6414

Government Departments

see page 372

COATES, DUDLEY JAMES Director of Regional Services, Ministry of Agriculture, Fisheries and Food Grade: 3

Career: assistant principal Ministry of Agriculture, Fisheries and Food (MAFF) 1968-70; second secretary UK delegation to EC, Brussels 1970-72; principal MAFF 1973-78; lecturer Civil Service College 1978-81; MAFF 1981-87: head of animal welfare division 1981-83, of financial management team 1983-87; director-general corporate services Intervention Board 1987-89; director regional services MAFF 1989-

Date of birth: 15 September 1946 *Education/professional qualifications:* Westcliff High School for Boys, Essex; Sussex University, politics (BA 1968) *Marital status:* married Dr Jean Margaret Walsingham 1969; 2 daughters *Publications:* contributor to Policies into Practice (Heinemann 1984) *Recreations:* Christian activities, singing, cycling

Dudley J Coates Esq, Director of Regional Services, Ministry of Agriculture, Fisheries and Food, Nobel House, 17 Smith Square, London SW1P 3JR *Telephone:* 0171-238 6717 *Fax:* 0171-238 6709

COCHLIN, M J A Head of Economic Development Welsh Office Grade: 3

M J A Cochlin Esq, Under Secretary, Welsh Office, Cathays Park, Cardiff CF1 3NQ *Telephone:* 01222 825111 *Fax:* 01222 823797

COE, J W Head of Information Branch, Department for Education Grade: 4

J W Coe Esq, Head of Information Branch, Department for Education, Sanctuary Buildings, Great Smith Street, London SW1P 3BT *Telephone:* 0171-925 5000 *Fax:* 0171-925 6000

COLES, Sir (ARTHUR) JOHN Permanent Under Secretary and Head of Diplomatic Service, Foreign and Commonwealth Office Senior grade

Career: HM Diplomatic Service 1960:- Middle East Centre for Arab Studies 1960-62; third secretary Khartoum 1962-64; Foreign and Commonwealth Office, London (FCO) UN Department 1964-68; assistant political agent Trucial States, Dubai 1968-71; Cabinet Office 1971-72; private secretary (PS) to ministers of state FCO 1972-75; head of chancery Cairo 1975-77; developing countries counsellor UK permanent representation to EC, Brussels 1977-80; head of S Asian department FCO 1980-81; PS foreign affairs and defence to Prime Minister 1981-84; ambassador to Jordan 1984-88; high commissioner to Australia 1988-91; FCO 1991-: deputy under secretary for Asia and the Americas 1991-93; permanent under secretary and head of diplomatic service 1994-

Date of birth: 13 November 1937 *Education/professional qualifications:* Magdalen College School, Brackley; Magdalen College, Oxford, history (BA 1960) *Honours, decorations:* CMG 1984, KCMG 1989 *Marital status:* married Anne Mary Sutherland Graham 1965; 2 sons, 1 daughter *Clubs:* United Oxford and Cambridge University *Recreations:* walking, birdwatching, reading, music, cricket

Sir John Coles KCMG, Permanent Under Secretary and Head of the Diplomatic Service, Foreign and Commonwealth Office, King Charles Street, London SW1A 2AH *Telephone:* 0171-270 3000 *Fax:* 0171-270 3776

COLEY, Dr G D Managing Director (Chemical and Biological Defence Establishment), Defence Evaluation and Research Agency (Executive Agency) Grade: 3

Dr G D Coley, Managing Director (CBDE), Defence Evaluation and Research Agency, Farnborough, Hampshire GU14 6TD *Telephone:* 01252 394500

COLLIER, MICHAEL Chief Executive, Funding Agency for Schools

Career: various posts in local government 1960-78: Macclesfield borough council 1960-67, Salop county council 1967-71, Birkenhead county borough council 1971-73, Stockport district council 1973-78; regional treasurer Mersey Regional Health Authority (HA) 1978-85; district general manager Liverpool HA 1985-90; director of finance NHS in Scotland, Scottish Office Home and Health Department 1990-94; chief executive Funding Agency for Schools 1994- *Current non-Whitehall posts:* Chartered Institute of Public Finance and Accountancy 1981: member council 1981- honorary treasurer 1994-

Date of birth: 30 March 1943 *Education/professional qualifications:* Kings School, Macclesfield; IPFA 1966 *Marital status:* married Cynthia Jean 1966; 1 daughter, 1 son *Recreations:* walking, theatre, bridge, badminton

Michael H Collier Esq, Chief Executive, Funding Agency for Schools, Albion Wharf, Skeldergate, York YO1 2XL *Telephone:* 01904 661604 *Fax:* 01904 661684

COLLINS, BRYAN HM Chief Inspector, Fire Service Inspectorate, Home Office

Career: HM chief inspector Fire Service Inspectorate Home Office 1993-

B Collins Esq, HM Chief Inspector, Fire Service Inspectorate, Home Office, 50 Queen Anne's Gate, London SW1H 9AT *Telephone:* 0171-217 8670

COLLON, MICHAEL HYDE Head of Legal Advice and Litigation Division, Lord Chancellor's Department Grade: 4

Career: barrister 1970-75; Lord Chancellor's Department 1975-: private secretary to Lord Chancellor 1980-82; head of European Community law division 1982-85, of property law and family law division 1985-87; secretary of Law Commission 1987-94; head of legal advice and litigation division 1994-

Date of birth: 11 May 1944 *Education/professional qualifications:* Eton College; Trinity College, Cambridge, natural sciences (BA 1965, MA); Middle Temple (barrister 1970) *Marital status:* married Josephine Ann Hearn 1971; 3 daughters, 1 son *Recreations:* music

Michael Collon Esq, Head of Legal Advice and Litigation Division, Lord Chancellor's Department, Southside, 105 Victoria Street, London SW1E 6QT *Telephone:* 0171-210 2110 *Fax:* 0171-210 2164

COLVILLE, Air Vice-Marshal CHRISTOPHER CHARLES COTTON Assistant Chief of Defence Staff, Operational Requirements (Air Systems), Ministry of Defence

Career: Royal Air Force (RAF) service 1964-: personal staff officer to UK military representative to NATO, Brussels; squadron command 1983-85; officer commanding RAF Coningsby; air commodore flying training HQ Support Command; air officer commanding training units 1992-94; head training group 1994; assistant chief of defence staff operational requirements (air systems) Ministry of Defence 1994-

Date of birth: 2 June 1945 *Education/professional qualifications:* RAF College, Cranwell (commission 1967); Open University, social science (BA 1975); Royal College of Defence Studies 1989; FRAeS; FIPD; QCVSA *Recreations:* microlight flying, shooting, mountaineering

Air Vice-Marshal C C C Colville, Assistant Chief of Defence Staff, Ministry of Defence, Whitehall, London SW1A 2HB *Telephone:* 0171-218 6596 *Fax:* 0171-218 7474

CONGDON, TIMOTHY GEORGE Member, Forecasting Panel, HM Treasury

Career: economic journalist The Times 1973-76; chief economist L Messel and Co 1976-86; chief London economist Shearson Lehman 1986-88; managing director Lombard Street Research Ltd economic forecasting consultancy 1989-; economic adviser Gerrard and National Holdings Ltd financial conglomerate 1989-; member forecasting panel HM Treasury 1992-

Date of birth: 28 April 1951 *Education/professional qualifications:* Colchester Royal Grammar School; St John's College, Oxford, modern history and economics (BA 1972); Nuffield College, Oxford, economics *Honours, decorations:* FRSA 1991 *Marital status:* married Dorianne Preston-Lowe 1988; 1 daughter *Publications:* Monetary Control in Britain (Macmillan 1982); The Debt Threat (Blackwell 1988); Reflections on Monetarism (Edward Elgar 1992) *Clubs:* Royal Automobile, Carlton *Recreations:* walking, reading, chess, opera

Timothy G Congdon Esq, Member, Forecasting Panel, HM Treasury, c/o Lombard Street Research Ltd, 33 Lombard Street, London EC3V 9BQ *Telephone:* 0171-623 9981 *Fax:* 0171-623 6173

COOKE, JOHN ARTHUR Under Secretary, International Trade Policy Division, Department of Trade and Industry Grade: 3

Career: assistant principal Board of Trade 1966-69; second/first secretary (FS) UK delegation to EC, Brussels 1969-73; principal Department of Trade and Industry (DTI) 1973-76; FS UK permanent representation to EC, Brussels 1976-77; DT[I] 1977-: principal 1977-80, assistant secretary (AS) 1980-84, seconded as assistant director to Morgan Grenfell and Co Ltd 1984-85; AS 1985-87, under secretary 1987-: head of overseas trade division 2 1987-89, of central unit 1989-92, director of deregulation unit 1990-92; head of international trade policy division 1992- *Current non-Whitehall posts:* member council Marie Curie Memorial Foundation 1992-

Date of birth: 13 April 1943 *Education/professional qualifications:* Dragon School and Magdalen College School, Oxford; Heidelberg University, Germany, German; King's College, Cambridge, history (BA 1964, MA); London School of Economics, history research *Marital status:* married Tania Frances Crichton 1970; 1 son, 2 daughters *Clubs:* United Oxford and Cambridge University; Cambridge Union *Recreations:* reading, travel, looking at buildings

John A Cooke Esq, Under Secretary, Department of Trade and Industry, Ashdown House, 123 Victoria Street, London SW1E 6RB *Telephone:* 0171-215 5000 *Fax:* 0171-215 6471

COOKSEY, Sir DAVID JAMES SCOTT Chairman, Audit Commission *(until August 1995)*; **Chairman, Local Government Commission for England**

Career: manufacturing industry -1981; director of various companies; chairman Audit Commission (external audit local government and NHS in England and Wales) 1986-95; chairman Local Government Commission for England 1995- *Current non-Whitehall posts:* chairman and chief executive Advent Ltd 1981-; director Bank of England 1993-

Date of birth: 14 May 1940 *Education/professional qualifications:* Westminster School; St Edmund Hall, Oxford, metallurgy (BA 1963, MA) *Honours, decorations:* Kt 1993 *Marital status:* married Janet Wardell-Yerburgh 1973; 1 daughter, 1 son, 1 stepdaughter *Clubs:* Royal Yacht Squadron, Royal Thames Yacht, Boodles *Recreations:* sailing, performing and visual arts

Sir David Cooksey, Chairman, Audit Commission, 1 Vincent Square, London SW1P 2PN; *Telephone:* 0171-828 1212 *Fax:* 0171-976 6187 *(until August 1995);* Chairman, Local Government Commission for England, Dolphyn Court, 10/11 Great Turnstile, London WC1V 7JU *Telephone:* 0171-430 8400 *Fax:* 0171-404 6142

CORLETT, CLIVE WILLIAM Deputy Chairman and Commissioner, Inland Revenue Grade: 2

Career: Inland Revenue (IR) 1960-: seconded to Civil Service Selection Board 1970, as private secretary to Chancellor of Exchequer 1972-74, as head of HM Treasury direct tax division 1979-81; director IR 1985-91, deputy secretary, commissioner 1992-; director-general 1992-94, deputy chairman 1994-

Date of birth: 14 June 1938 *Education/professional qualifications:* Birkenhead School; Brasenose College, Oxford, philosophy, politics and economics (BA 1960) *Marital status:* married Margaret Catherine Jones 1964; 1 son *Recreations:* walking

Clive W Corlett Esq, Deputy Chairman, Inland Revenue, Somerset House, Strand, London WC2R 1LB *Telephone:* 0171-438 6604 *Fax:* 0171-438 7002

CORP, Major General PHILIP JAMES GLADSTONE Director-General Equipment Support (Army), Ministry of Defence

Career: Royal Electrical and Mechanical Engineers (REME) 1962-: regimental duty, junior staff 1967-72; Ministry of Defence (MoD) 1975-76; REME posts 1977-80; deputy project manager MoD procurement executive 1981-83; commanding officer 7 Armoured Workshop 1984-86; quartermaster general's equipment support planning staff MoD 1987-89; commandant REME officers' school 1989-90; MoD equipment support 1990-: director 1990-93, director-general 1993- *Current non-Whitehall posts:* governor Welbeck College

Date of birth: 23 June 1942 *Education/professional qualifications:* Warwick School; Queen Elizabeth Grammar School, Crediton; Royal Military Academy Sandhurst; Pembroke College, Cambridge, mechanical sciences and law (BA 1966, MA); CEng 1971, FIMechE 1986; army staff college *Recreations:* music, furniture restoration, board sailing

Major General Philip J G Corp, Director-General Equipment Support (Army), Headquarters Quartermaster General, Portway, Monxton Road, Andover, Hampshire SP11 8HT *Telephone:* 01264 382571 *Fax:* 01264 382439

COTTRELL, Dr ELIZABETH Special Adviser to Secretary of State for Education

Career: consultant Charles Barker Lyons; special adviser to Richard Luce and David Mellor, Ministers for Arts and Libraries, to Gillian Shephard as Secretary of State for Employment 1992-93, as Minister of Agriculture, Fisheries and Food 1993-94, as Secretary of State for Education 1994- *Education/professional qualifications:* Cambridge University (MA, PhD) *Marital status:* widowed; 1 daughter *Publications:* A History of the British Steel Industry 1945-81; numerous on industrial policy, banking, finance, education

Dr Elizabeth Cottrell, Special Adviser to Secretary of State, Department for Education, Sanctuary Buildings, Great Smith Street, London SW1P 3BT *Telephone:* 0171-925 6251 *Fax:* 0171-925 6250

COURTNEY, ROGER GRAHAM Chief Executive, Building Research Establishment (Executive Agency) Grade: 3

Career: Building Research Station/Establishment (BRE) 1969-77; Department of Environment 1977-78; science and technology secretariat Cabinet Office 1978-84; technical director energy efficiency office Department of Energy 1984-86; BRE 1986-: deputy director 1986-88; director 1988-90, chief executive 1990-

Date of birth: 11 July 1946 *Education/professional qualifications:* Trinity College, Cambridge (BA, MA); Bristol University (MSc); Brunel University, operational research (MTech)

Roger G Courtney Esq, Chief Executive, Building Research Establishment, Garston, Watford, Hertfordshire WD2 7JR *Telephone:* 01923 894040 *Fax:* 01923 664089

COWAN, ALEC (ALEXANDER) FOSTER Chief Executive, NHS Pensions Agency (Executive Agency) Grade: 5

Career: Department of Environment 1965-68, of Education and Science 1968-92: information technology professional and manager 1973-82; senior administrator teachers' pension scheme 1982-86; deputy director information systems 1986-89: director and controller 1989-92; chief executive NHS Pensions Agency 1992-

Date of birth: 15 October 1946 *Education/professional qualifications:* Gateshead Grammar School; management (postgraduate diploma 1985) *Marital status:* married Pamela Webster 1978: divorced; 1 son, 1 daughter *Clubs:* Hesketh House *Recreations:* swimming, fishing, cooking, Newcastle United football team, reading

Alec F Cowan Esq, Chief Executive, NHS Pensions Agency, 200-220 Broadway, Fleetwood, Lancashire FY7 8LG *Telephone:* 01253 774401 *Fax:* 01253 774860

COWAN, Lieutenant-General S Inspector General Doctrine and Training, Ministry of Defence

Lieutenant-General S Cowan CBE, Inspector General Doctrine and Training, Ministry of Defence, Trenchard Lines, Upavon, Pewsey, Wiltshire SN9 6BE *Telephone:* 01980 615000

CRAIG, Surgeon Rear-Admiral ALEXANDER Medical Director-General (Naval), Ministry of Defence

Career: Royal Marine medical service 1969-: Ministry of Defence 1993-: surgeon rear-admiral support medical services 1993-94; medical director general (naval) 1994-

Date of birth: 22 November 1943 *Education/professional qualifications:* Edinburgh University, medicine (MB CLB 1967) and Royal Infirmary, Edinburgh

Surgeon Rear-Admiral A Craig QHP, Medical Director General (Naval), HM Naval Base, Portsmouth, Hampshire PO1 3LS *Telephone:* 01705 727802

"Next Steps" Executive Agencies
see page 875

CRAIG, GEORGE CHARLES GRAHAM Head of Transport, Planning and Environment Group, Welsh Office Grade: 3

Career: Ministry of Transport 1967-78; Welsh Office 1978-: private secretary to secretary of state 1978-80; assistant secretary 1980-86; under secretary, principal establishment officer 1986-95, head transport, planning and environment group 1995-

Date of birth: 8 May 1946 *Education/professional qualifications:* Brockley County Grammar School; Nottingham University, politics (BA 1967) *Marital status:* married Marian Gallagher 1968; 2 sons, 1 daughter

George C G Craig Esq, Under Secretary, Welsh Office, Cathays Park, Cardiff CF1 3NQ
Telephone: 01222 825111 *Fax:* 01222 823036

CRAIG, JOHN FRAZER Deputy Secretary, Agriculture, Economic Development, Industry and Training, Welsh Office Grade: 2

Career: HM Customs and Excise 1961-69; National Board for Prices and Incomes 1969-70; Welsh Office 1970-: private secretary to permanent secretary 1972-74, to secretary of state 1980-82; industry department 1982-87: assistant secretary 1982-85, under secretary 1985-87; principal finance officer 1987-90; deputy secretary 1990-, economic affairs 1990-95, agriculture, economic development, industry and training 1995

Date of birth: 8 November 1943 *Education/professional qualifications:* Robert Richardson Grammar School, Sunderland *Honours, decorations:* CB 1994 *Marital status:* married Janet Elizabeth Oswald 1973; 2 sons, 1 daughter

John F Craig Esq CB, Deputy Secretary, Welsh Office, Cathays Park, Cardiff CF1 3NQ
Telephone: 01222 823579 *Fax:* 01222 823199

CRAWFORD, IAIN Director, Veterinary Field Services, Ministry of Agriculture, Fisheries and Food Grade: 3

Career: veterinary practice 1961-68; Ministry of Agriculture, Fisheries and Food 1968-: various veterinary officer grades; assistant chief veterinary officer 1986-88, director veterinary field services 1988-

Date of birth: 8 April 1938 *Education/professional qualifications:* Glasgow University, veterinary medicine and surgery (BVMS 1961); MRCVS 1961 *Marital status:* married Janette Mary Allan 1962; 1 daughter, 2 sons *Recreations:* gardening, walking, sailing

Iain Crawford Esq, Director, Veterinary Field Services, Ministry of Agriculture, Fisheries and Food, Government Buildings, Hook Rise South, Tolworth, Surbiton, Surrey KT6 7NF
Telephone: 0181-330 8039 *Fax:* 0181-330 6872

CRAWFORD, Dr ROBERT MACKAY Managing Director, Operations, Scottish Enterprise Grade: 4

Career: Scottish National Party 1977-79; Strathclyde University 1981-83; Locate in Scotland (LIS) Scottish Office Industry Department 1983-: director North America LIS 1989-91, director 1991-

Date of birth: 14 June 1951 *Education/professional qualifications:* St Michael's Academy, Kilwinning, Ayrshire; Strathclyde University, politics (BA 1973); Harvard University, USA, politics and economics (JF Kennedy scholar 1976); Glasgow University, politics (PhD 1982) *Marital status:* married Linda Acheson 1975; 1 son, 1 daughter *Clubs:* Scottish RAC *Recreations:* jogging, reading, hill-walking, swimming

Dr Robert M Crawford, Managing Director, Operations, Scottish Enterprise, 120 Bothwell Street, Glasgow G2 7JP *Telephone:* 0141-248 2700 *Fax:* 0141-221 5129

CRICKHOWELL, (ROGER) NICHOLAS (The Rt Hon The Lord Crickhowell) Chairman, National Rivers Authority

Career: commercial insurance broking, latterly managing director and chairman William Brandt 1957-74; Conservative MP for Pembroke 1970-87: opposition spokesman (OS) on Welsh affairs 1974, chief OS on Welsh affairs Shadow Cabinet 1975-79, Secretary of State for Wales 1979-87; chairman National Rivers Authority 1989- *Current non-Whitehall posts:* director Automobile Association Ltd and Fanum Ltd 1988-, Associated British Ports Holdings plc, HTV Group plc 1987-, Cameron May Ltd; vice-chairman Anglesey Mining plc; president University of Wales College of Cardiff, South East Wales Arts Association, Contemporary Art Society for Wales

Date of birth: 25 February 1934 *Education/professional qualifications:* Westminster School, London; Trinity College, Cambridge, history (BA 1957, MA) *Honours, decorations:* PC 1979, baron 1987 *Marital status:* married Ankaret Healing 1963; 1 son, 2 daughters *Clubs:* Cardiff and County, Brookes's *Recreations:* fishing, gardening, collecting watercolours and drawings

The Rt Hon The Lord Crickhowell, Chairman, National Rivers Authority, 30-34 Albert Embankment, London SE1 7TL *Telephone:* 0171-820 0101 *Fax:* 0171-582 7840

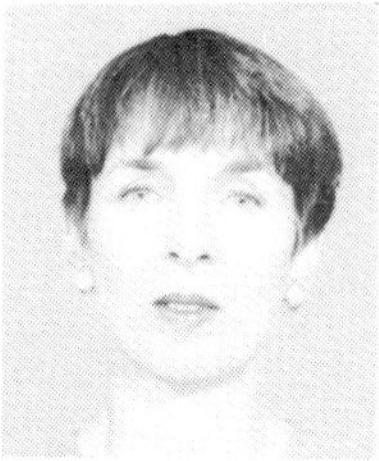

CRISHAM, CATHERINE ANN Head of Legal Group, Ministry of Agriculture, Fisheries and Food Grade: 4

Career: EC law lecturer Leiden University, Netherlands and London University 1977-82; lawyer Ministry of Agriculture, Fisheries and Food (MAFF) 1984-88; assistant to advocate general European Court of Justice, Luxembourg 1988-90; MAFF 1991-: lawyer 1991-94, head of legal group 1994-

Date of birth: 29 April 1950 *Education/professional qualifications:* Ursuline Convent School, Wimbledon, London; St Anne's College, Oxford, jurisprudence (BA 1972); Exeter University, European legal studies (LLM 1974); barrister 1982 *Marital status:* single *Recreations:* hill walking, theatre, cinema

Ms Catherine A Crisham, Head of Legal Group, Ministry of Agriculture, Fisheries and Food, 55 Whitehall, London SW1A 2EY
Telephone: 0171-270 8553 *Fax:* 0171-270 8166

CROFT, FRED(ERICK) LISTER Solicitor, Litigation Division, Treasury Solicitor's Department Grade: 4

Career: legal assistant 1977-80; senior legal assistant 1980-84; deputy head (policy) litigation division Treasury Solicitor's Department 1991-

Date of birth: 13 April 1951 *Education/professional qualifications:* Highgate School, London; Jesus College, Oxford, English (BA 1973, MA); Middle Temple (barrister 1975) *Marital status:* married Elizabeth May Cohen 1975; 2 sons, 1 daughter *Publications:* The Judge Over Your Shoulder (1994) *Clubs:* Thames, Hare and Hounds *Recreations:* running, film, theatre

Fred Croft Esq, Litigation Division, Treasury Solicitor's Department, Queen Anne's Chambers, 28 Broadway, London SW1H 9JS
Telephone: 0171-210 3091 *Fax:* 0171-210 3066

CRUICKSHANK, ALISTAIR RONALD Head of Agricultural Inputs, Ministry of Agriculture, Fisheries and Food Grade: 3

Career: Ministry of Agriculture, Fisheries and Food 1966-: assistant principal 1966-70, principal 1970-78, assistant secretary 1978-86; under secretary animal health 1986-89; principal finance officer 1989-94; head of agricultural inputs, plant protection and emergencies group 1994-

Date of birth: 2 October 1944 *Education/professional qualifications:* Aberdeen Grammar School; Aberdeen University, history (MA 1966) *Marital status:* married Alexandra Mary Noble 1967; 3 daughters *Recreations:* gardening, old buildings, church activities

Alistair R Cruickshank Esq, Under Secretary, Ministry of Agriculture, Fisheries and Food, Whitehall Place, London SW1A 2HH *Telephone:* 0171-270 8479 *Fax:* 0171-270 8289

CRUICKSHANK, DON Director-General, Office of Telecommunications (OFTEL)

Career: management consultant, McKinsey and Co Inc 1972-77; general manager Sunday Times 1977-80; finance director Pearson plc 1980-84; chairman Wandsworth health authority 1986-89; managing director Virgin Group plc 1984-89; chief executive NHS in Scotland, Scottish Office Home and Health Department 1989-93; director-general Office of Telecommunications 1993- *Current non-Whitehall posts:* non-executive director Christian Salvesen plc 1994-

Date of birth: 17 September 1942 *Education/professional qualifications:* Aberdeen University (MA 1962); Institute of Chartered Accountants Scotland (CA 1967); Manchester Business School (MBA 1972) *Marital status:* married Elizabeth Buchan Taylor 1964; 1 son, 1 daughter *Recreations:* sport, golf, opera

Don Cruickshank Esq, Director-General, Office of Telecommunications, 50 Ludgate Hill, London EC4M 7JJ *Telephone:* 0171-634 8801 *Fax:* 0171-634 8940

CUBIE, GEORGE Clerk of the Overseas Office, House of Commons Grade: 3

Career: House of Commons 1966-: clerk of financial committees 1987-89, of select committees 1989-91, of overseas office 1991-

Date of birth: 30 August 1943 *Education/professional qualifications:* Dollar Academy; Edinburgh University (MA)

George Cubie Esq, Clerk of the Overseas Office, House of Commons, London SW1A 0AA *Telephone:* 0171-219 3314

CULPIN, ROBERT Second Permanent Secretary, Spending Group, HM Treasury Grade: 1A

Career: HM Treasury 1965-: head of information and press secretary to Chancellor of Exchequer 1984-87; under secretary fiscal policy division 1987-93; deputy secretary public finance 1993-94; second permanent secretary public expenditure/spending group 1994-
Education/professional qualifications: Christ's College, Cambridge; Harvard and California Universities, USA

Robert Culpin Esq, Second Permanent Secretary, HM Treasury, Parliament Street, London SW1P 3AG *Telephone:* 0171-270 4370 *Fax:* 0171-270 5653

CURRIE, Professor DAVID ANTHONY Member, Forecasting Panel, HM Treasury

Career: economist Hoare Govett stockbrokers 1971-72; senior economist Economic Models consultants 1972; Queen Mary College, London 1972-88: economics lecturer 1972-79, reader 1979-81, professor 1981-88; deputy principal governor, professor and director Centre for Economic Forecasting London Business School 1988-; member forecasting panel HM Treasury 1992- *Current non-Whitehall posts:* trustee Joseph Rowntree Reform Trust 1991-; director International Schools of Business Management

Date of birth: 9 December 1946 *Education/professional qualifications:* Battersea Grammar School; Manchester University, mathematics (BSc 1968); Birmingham University, economics (MSocSc 1971); Queen Mary College, London, economics (PhD 1978) *Marital status:* married Saziye Gazioglu 1975, divorced 1992; 2 sons *Publications:* co-author Rules, Reputation and Macroeconomic Policy Coordination (Cambridge University Press 1993); co-editor Macroeconomic Policies in an Interdependent World (IMF 1989); co-author International Macroeconomic Policy Coordination (Group of Thirty 1988); co-editor Macroeconomic Interactions between North and South (Cambridge University Press 1988) *Clubs:* Reform *Recreations:* music, swimming, literature

Professor David A Currie, Member, Forecasting Panel, HM Treasury, c/o London Business School, Sussex Place, London NW1 4SA
Telephone: 0171-262 5050 *Fax:* 0171-724 6069

CUTLER, (TIMOTHY ROBERT) ROBIN Director-General and Deputy Chairman, Forestry Commission Grade: 2

Career: colonial forest service, Kenya 1958-64; New Zealand (NZ) forest service 1964-88: director of forest management 1978-86, deputy director-general 1986-88; chief executive NZ Ministry of Forestry 1988-90; director-general and deputy chairman UK Forestry Commission (policy advice, services and reporting to forestry ministers on relevant matters) 1990-

Date of birth: 24 July 1934 *Education/professional qualifications:* Banff Academy; Aberdeen University, forestry (BSc 1956) *Marital status:* married Ishbel Primrose 1958; 1 son, 1 daughter *Clubs:* New, Edinburgh; Commonwealth Trust, London *Recreations:* tennis, golf, gardening, stamps

Robin Cutler Esq, Director-General and Deputy Chairman, Forestry Commission, 231 Corstorphine Road, Edinburgh EH12 7AT
Telephone: 0131-334 0303 *Fax:* 0131-316 4891

D

DAIN, DAVID JOHN MICHAEL Assistant Under Secretary, South and South East Asia, Foreign and Commonwealth Office Senior grade

Career: HM Diplomatic Service 1963-: Teheran, Kabul 1964-68; seconded to Cabinet Office 1968-72; first secretary Bonn 1972-75; Foreign and Commonwealth Office, London (FCO) 1975-78; head of chancery Athens 1978-81; counsellor and deputy high commissioner Nicosia 1981-85; FCO 1985-90: head of western European department 1985-89; chairman Civil Service Selection Board 1989-90; high commissioner Nicosia 1990-94; assistant under secretary south and south east Asia FCO 1994-

Date of birth: 30 October 1940 *Education/professional qualifications:* St John's College, Oxford, literae humaniores (MA 1963) *Honours, decorations:* CMG 1991 *Marital status:* married Susan Kathleen Moss 1969; 1 son, 2 daughters *Clubs:* United Oxford and Cambridge University *Recreations:* tennis, sailing, flying, bridge, walking

David Dain Esq CMG, Assistant Under Secretary, Foreign and Commonwealth Office, Main Building, Downing Street, London SW1A 2AL *Telephone:* 0171-270 3000

DALES, R A Director, Marketing and Customer Services, Valuation Office Agency (Executive Agency) Grade: 4

Career: Valuation Office Agency: director of taxation and land services -1993, director customer services/marketing and customer services 1993-

R A Dales Esq, Director, Marketing and Customer Services, Valuation Office Agency, New Court, Carey Street, London WC2A 2JE *Telephone:* 0171-324 1183/1057 *Fax:* 0171-324 1073

DART, GEOFFREY STANLEY Head of Regional Development, Department of Trade and Industry Grade: 3

Career: Electricity Council 1974-77; Department of Energy (DEn) 1977-84; assistant private secretary (PS) to secretary of state (SoS) 1980-81; economic secretariat Cabinet Office 1984-85; DEn 1985-92: principal PS to SoS for Energy 1985-87, electricity division 1987-89, offshore safety division 1989-91, head of finance branch 1991-92; Department of Trade and Industry 1992-: competitiveness division 1992-94; under secretary 1994-: director deregulation unit 1994, head of regional development division 1995- *Current non-Whitehall posts:* non-executive director Laing Engineering Ltd 1991-; director European Investment Bank 1994-

Date of birth: 2 October 1952 *Education/professional qualifications:* Torquay Grammar School; St Peter's College, Oxford, modern history (BA 1974, MA) *Marital status:* married Rosemary Penelope 1974; 1 son, 1 daughter *Recreations:* books, films, music, sport

Geoffrey S Dart Esq, Under Secretary, Department of Trade and Industry, Kingsgate House, 66-74 Victoria Street, London SW1E 6SW *Telephone:* 0171-215 2510 *Fax:* 0171-215 8113

DAUNT, Sir TIMOTHY LEWIS ACHILLES Deputy Under Secretary, Foreign and Commonwealth Office Senior grade

Career: HM Diplomatic Service 1960-: second secretary Ankara embassy 1960-63; first secretary (FS) Foreign and Commonwealth Office London (FCO) 1964-67; FS Nicosia high commission 1967-70; private secretary to permanent under secretary FCO 1970-73; seconded to overseas department Bank of England 1973; FS UK mission to UN, New York 1974-75; counsellor UK delegation to OECD 1975-78; head of southern European department FCO 1978-81; associate Centre d'Etudes et Recherches Internationales, Paris 1981-82; deputy permanent representative UK delegation to NATO, Brussels 1982-85; assistant under secretary (defence) FCO 1985-86; ambassador to Turkey 1986-92; deputy under secretary FCO 1992-
Education/professional qualifications: Sherborne School, Dorset; St Catharine's College, Cambridge, history (BA 1959) *Honours, decorations:* CMG 1982, KCMG 1989 *Marital status:* married Patricia Susan Knight 1962; 1 son, 2 daughters *Clubs:* Cavalry and Guards

Sir Timothy Daunt KCMG, Deputy Under Secretary, Foreign and Commonwealth Office, King Charles Street, London SW1A 2AH *Telephone:* 0171-270 3000 *Fax:* 0171-839 2417

DAVIDSON, CHARLES KEMP (The Hon Lord Davidson) Chairman, Scottish Law Commission

Career: advocate 1956-83; dean Faculty of Advocates 1979-83; senator College of Justice in Scotland 1983-; chairman Scottish Law Commission 1988- *Current non-Whitehall posts:* deputy chairman Boundary Commission for Scotland 1985-

Date of birth: 13 April 1929 *Education/professional qualifications:* Fettes College, Edinburgh; Brasenose College, Oxford, literae humaniores (BA 1951, MA); Edinburgh University, law (LLB 1956) *Honours, decorations:* QC (Scotland 1969) *Marital status:* married Mary Mactaggart 1960; 2 daughters, 1 son

The Hon Lord Davidson, Chairman, Scottish Law Commission, 140 Causewayside, Edinburgh EH9 1PR *Telephone:* 0131-668 2131 *Fax:* 0131-662 4900

DAVIES, Professor Sir DAVID EVAN NAUNTON Chief Scientific Adviser, Ministry of Defence Grade: 1A

Career: electronic engineering lecturer Birmingham University 1961-67; assistant director of research British Railways Board 1967-71; University College, London 1971-88: professor of electrical engineering 1971-88, vice-provost 1986-88; vice-chancellor and chief executive Loughborough University of Technology 1988-93; chief scientific adviser Ministry of Defence 1993- *Current non-Whitehall posts:* president Institution of Electrical Engineers; member British Rail Research and Technology Committee

Date of birth: 28 October 1935 *Education/professional qualifications:* Birmingham University, electrical engineering (MSc 1958, PhD 1960, DSc 1968); FEng 1979; FRS 1984 *Honours, decorations:* CBE 1986, Kt 1994 *Publications:* various papers on antennas, signal processing, radar and fibre optics

Professor Sir David Davies, Chief Scientific Adviser, Ministry of Defence, Main Building, Whitehall, London SW1A 2HB *Telephone:* 0171-218 6588 *Fax:* 0171-218 6552

DAVIES, FRANK JOHN Chairman, Health and Safety Commission Grade: 1

Career: BPB Industries 1953-62, RTZ Pillar 1963-67; Alcan Aluminium (UK) Ltd 1967-83: director and divisional managing director 1977-83; group chief executive Rockware Group 1983-93; director BTR Nylex 1991-94; chairman Health and Safety Commission 1993- *Current non-Whitehall posts:* non-executive director Ardagh plc 1985-, Saltire plc 1993-; chairman Bardon Group plc 1994-

Date of birth: 24 September 1931 *Education/professional qualifications:* Monmouth School; University of Manchester Institute of Science and Technology, building construction *Honours, decorations:* OStJ 1977; CBE 1993 *Marital status:* married Sheila Margaret 1956; 3 sons *Clubs:* Carlton, Royal Automobile *Recreations:* gardening, theatre, walking

Frank J Davies Esq CBE, Chairman, Health and Safety Commission, Rose Court, Southwark Bridge Road, London SE1 9HS *Telephone:* 0171-717 6610 *Fax:* 0171-717 6644

DAVIES, GAVYN Member, Forecasting Panel, HM Treasury

Career: research Balliol College, Oxford 1972-74; economic adviser 10 Downing Street Policy Unit 1974-79; City economist 1979-; visiting economics professor London School of Economics 1988-; principal economics commentator The Independent 1991-; Goldman Sachs investment bank 1986-: chief UK economist 1986-, partner 1988-, head of European investment research (London) 1991-; member HM Treasury forecasting panel 1992- *Current non-Whitehall posts:* adviser to HoC Treasury Select Committee

Date of birth: 27 November 1950 *Education/professional qualifications:* St John's College, Cambridge, economics (BA 1972) *Honours, decorations:* OBE 1979 *Marital status:* married Susan Nye 1989; 1 daughter *Recreations:* sport

Gavyn Davies Esq OBE, Member, Forecasting Panel, HM Treasury, c/o Goldman Sachs, Peterborough Court, 133 Fleet Street, London EC4A 2BB *Telephone:* 0171-774 1161 *Fax:* 0171-774 1181

DAVIES, Professor GRAEME JOHN Chief Executive, Higher Education Funding Council for England *(until September 1995)* Grade: 1A

Career: lecturer metallurgy and materials science, Cambridge University 1962-77; professor of metallurgy Sheffield University 1978-86; vice-chancellor Liverpool University 1986-91; chief executive Universities Funding Council (UFC) 1991-93, Polytechnic and Colleges Funding Council (PCFC) 1992-93, Higher Education Funding Council for England (successor to UFC and PCFC) 1993-September 1995

Date of birth: 7 April 1937 *Education/professional qualifications:* Mount Albert Grammar School, Auckland, New Zealand; Auckland University, NZ, engineering metallurgy/materials science (BE, PhD 1962); Cambridge University, metallurgy and materials science (MA, ScD 1977) *Honours, decorations:* FEng 1988; CBIM 1990 *Marital status:* married Florence Isabelle Martin 1959; 1 son, 1 daughter *Publications:* Superplasticity (1981); Essential Metallurgy for Engineers (1985); Solidification and Casting (1973); Texture and the Properties of Materials (1976); Hot Working and Forming Processes (1980) *Clubs:* Athenaeum *Recreations:* cricket, birdwatching, golf

Professor Graeme Davies, Chief Executive, Higher Education Funding Council for England, Northavon House, Coldharbour Lane, Bristol BS16 1QD *Telephone:* 01179 317300 *Fax:* 01179 317150

Regulatory Organisations and Public Bodies

see page 1013

DAVIES, (JOHN) MICHAEL Clerk Assistant and Principal Finance Officer, House of Lords Grade: 2

Career: House of Lords 1964-: clerk 1964-71; private secretary (PS) to leader of House and government chief whip 1971-74; PS to chairman of committees, establishment officer, secretary of statute law committee 1974-83; principal clerk European and overseas office 1983-85, private bills 1985-88; reading clerk and clerk of public bills 1988-90; clerk assistant and clerk of public bills 1991-94, and principal finance officer 1994-

Date of birth: 2 August 1940 *Education/professional qualifications:* King's School, Canterbury; Peterhouse, Cambridge, history (BA 1963) *Marital status:* married Amanda Mary Atkinson JP 1971; 1 daughter, 2 sons *Recreations:* sport, travel

J Michael Davies, Clerk Assistant, House of Lords, London SW1A 0PW *Telephone:* 0171-219 3171 *Fax:* 0171-219 5933

DAVIES, PHILIP JOHN Parliamentary Counsel, Office of the Parliamentary Counsel Grade: 3

Career: law lecturer Manchester University 1977-82; Office of Parliamentary Counsel 1982-: assistant parliamentary counsel (PC) 1982-86, senior assistant PC 1986-90, deputy PC 1990-94, seconded to Law Commission 1992-94; PC (drafting government bills) 1994-

Date of birth: 19 September 1954 *Education/professional qualifications:* St Julian's High School, Newport, Gwent; Hertford College, Oxford, jurisprudence (BA 1976, BCL 1977); Middle Temple (barrister 1981) *Marital status:* married Jacqueline Sara Boutcher 1981; 1 daughter *Publications:* articles in legal periodicals *Recreations:* family, Welsh terrier

Philip J Davies Esq, Parliamentary Counsel, Office of the Parliamentary Counsel, 36 Whitehall, London SW1A 2AY *Telephone:* 0171-210 6630 *Fax:* 0171-210 6632

DAVIS, DEREK RICHARD Director-General, British National Space Centre, Department of Trade and Industry Grade: 3

Career: assistant principal Board of Trade 1967-70; principal Department of Trade and Industry (DTI) 1970-74; Department of Energy/DTI 1974-: principal 1974-77; assistant secretary 1977-85; under secretary and head of gas division 1985-87, and head of oil and gas division 1987-93; director-general British National Space Centre 1993-

Date of birth: 3 May 1945 *Education/professional qualifications:* Clifton College, Bristol; Balliol College, Oxford, literae humaniores (BA 1967) *Marital status:* married Diana Levinson 1987; 1 daughter, 1 son

Derek R Davis Esq, Director-General, British National Space Centre, Department of Trade and Industry, 88-89 Eccleston Square, London SW1V 1PT *Telephone:* 0171-215 0877 *Fax:* 0171-821 5387

DAVIS, PETER A Director-General, Office of the National Lottery Grade: 2

Career: general audit partner Price Waterhouse accountants 1974-80; various non-executive directorships 1984-89; Abbey National building society 1982-94: deputy chairman (DC) 1988-94; executive DC Harris Queensway plc 1980-87; Sturge Holdings plc 1988-93: DC 1991-93; director-general Office of the National Lottery 1993- *Current non-Whitehall posts:* chairman board for chartered accountants in business Institute of Chartered Accountants 1989-; non-executive director Provident Financial plc 1994-

Date of birth: 10 October 1941 *Education/professional qualifications:* Winchester College; Lincoln College, Oxford, law (BA 1963, MA); CA 1967 *Marital status:* married Vanessa Davis 1971; 2 sons *Clubs:* Hurlingham; Institute of Directors *Recreations:* tennis, fishing, football, theatre

Peter A Davis Esq, Director-General, Office of the National Lottery, 2 Monck Street, London SW1P 2BQ *Telephone:* 0171-227 2000 *Fax:* 0171-227 2005

DAWE, ROGER JAMES Head, Further Higher Education and International Command, Department for Education Grade: 2

Career: Ministry of Labour 1962-64: assistant principal safety, health and welfare and industrial relations divisions 1962-64; assistant principal Department of Economic Affairs 1964-65; private secretary (PS) to Prime Minister 1966-70; Department of Employment (DEmp) 1970-92: principal, pay policy 1970-72, PS to secretaries of state 1972-74, assistant secretary 1974-81: public service pay, manpower policy, head of group personnel unit, of unemployment benefit service; Manpower Services Commission 1981-85: under secretary, director of special programmes 1981-82, chief executive training division 1982-85; DEmp 1985-92: deputy secretary manpower policy 1985-88, director-general (DG) Training Commission 1988, DG Training Agency/Training, Enterprise and Education Directorate 1988-92; head further and higher education and international command Department for Education 1992-

Date of birth: 26 February 1941 *Education/professional qualifications:* Hardyes School, Dorchester; Fitzwilliam College, Cambridge, economics (BA 1962) *Honours, decorations:* OBE 1970, CB 1988 *Marital status:* married Ruth Day 1965; 1 son, 1 daughter *Recreations:* tennis, soccer, music, theatre

Roger J Dawe Esq CB OBE, Deputy Secretary, Department for Education, Sanctuary Buildings, Great Smith Street, London SW1P 3BT *Telephone:* 0171-925 6210 *Fax:* 0171-925 6966

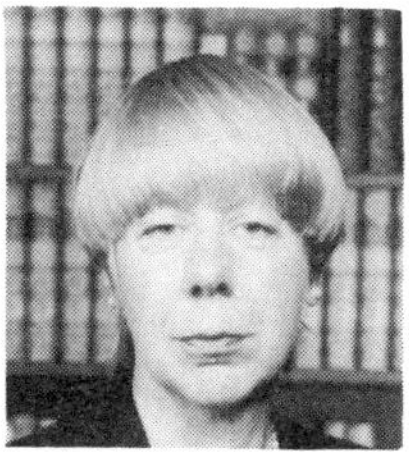

DAWES, (CAROLINE) HARRIET Deputy Chairman, Occupational Pensions Board

Career: Courtaulds Ltd 1965-77; solicitors Lovell White and King, 1977-80, Lovell White Durant 1980-: partner 1980-; deputy chairman Occupational Pensions Board 1992-

Date of birth: 22 August 1943 *Education/professional qualifications:* Oxford High School for Girls; Somerville College, Oxford, philosophy, politics and economics (BA 1965, MA) *Marital status:* married Michael Brooke Maunsell 1986 *Recreations:* opera, gardening, reading

Miss Harriet Dawes, Deputy Chairman, Occupational Pensions Board, c/o Lovell White Durrant, 65 Holborn Viaduct, London EC1A 2DY
Telephone: 0171-236 0066 *Fax:* 0171-248 7273

DAWSON, Dr PETER S Head of Veterinary Investigation Service, Ministry of Agriculture, Fisheries and Food Grade: 4

Date of birth: 3 March 1935 *Education/professional qualifications:* BSc, PhD; BVMS MRCVS *Marital status:* married; 2 daughters *Publications:* numerous scientific publications *Recreations:* gardening, bridge

Dr P S Dawson, Head of Veterinary Investigation Service, Ministry of Agriculture, Fisheries and Food, Government Buildings, Hook Rise South, Tolworth, Surbiton, Surrey KT6 7NF *Telephone:* 0181-330 8075
Fax: 0181-330 8623

DAYKIN, CHRISTOPHER DAVID Government Actuary, Government Actuary's Department

Career: actuarial officer (AO) Government Actuary's Department (GAD) 1970; VSO teacher 1971; GAD 1972-78: AO 1972-73, assistant actuary 1973-75, actuary 1976-78; principal HM Treasury 1978-80; GAD 1980-: actuary 1980-82, chief actuary 1982-84, directing actuary 1985-89; government actuary (head of actuarial profession in civil service; advice on social security, pensions, insurance, demography, consumer credit etc) 1989- *Current non-Whitehall posts:* chairman Civil Service Insurance Society 1990-; chairman education committee Groupe Consultatif 1992-; UK representative EC Observatory on Complementary Pension Schemes 1992-; chairman permanent committee on statistical, actuarial and financial studies, International Social Security Association 1992-; president Institute of Actuaries 1994-

Date of birth: 18 July 1948 *Education/professional qualifications:* Merchant Taylors' School, Northwood, Middlesex; Pembroke College, Cambridge, mathematics (BA 1970, MA); FIA 1973 *Honours, decorations:* CB 1993 *Marital status:* married Kathryn Ruth Tingey 1977; 1 daughter, 2 sons *Publications:* co-author Practical Risk Theory (Chapman and Hall 1993) *Clubs:* Actuaries, Gallio *Recreations:* travel, photography, music, languages

Christopher D Daykin Esq CB, Government Actuary, Government Actuary's Department, 22 Kingsway, London WC2B 6LE
Telephone: 0171-242 6828 *Fax:* 0171-831 6653

DEACON, KEITH VIVIAN Director of Quality Development Division, Inland Revenue Grade: 3

Career: Inland Revenue 1962-: principal inspector of taxes 1978; assistant secretary 1979-82; regional controller 1985-88; under secretary 1988-: director of technical division 1988, of insurance and specialist division 1988-91, of operations 1991-93, of quality development division 1993-

Date of birth: 19 November 1935 *Education/professional qualifications:* Sutton County Grammar School; Bristol University, English language and literature (BA) *Marital status:* married Brenda 1960; 1 son, 1 daughter *Recreations:* reading, photography, music

Keith V Deacon Esq, Under Secretary, Quality Development Division, Inland Revenue, Bush House, Strand, London WC2B 4RD *Telephone:* 0171-438 6622

DEAN, PETER HENRY Deputy Chairman, Monopolies and Mergers Commission

Career: RTZ Corporation plc 1966-85: solicitor 1966-72, secretary 1972-74, director 1974-85; Monopolies and Mergers Commission 1982-: member 1982-90, deputy chairman 1990- *Current non-Whitehall posts:* director Associated British Ports Holdings plc 1982-, Liberty Life Assurance Company Ltd 1986-, Seeboard plc 1993-

Date of birth: 24 July 1939 *Education/professional qualifications:* Rugby School; London University, law (LLB 1961); solicitor 1962 *Honours, decorations:* CBE 1993 *Marital status:* married Linda Louise Keating 1965; 1 daughter *Recreations:* choral singing, skiing

Peter H Dean Esq CBE, Deputy Chairman, Monopolies and Mergers Commission, New Court, 48 Carey Street, London WC2A 2JT
Telephone: 0171-324 1433 *Fax:* 0171-324 1400

DEARING, Sir RONALD ERNEST Chairman, School Curriculum and Assessment Authority

Career: Ministry of Labour and National Service 1946-49; Ministry of [Fuel and] Power (MoP) 1949-62: national service 1949-51; HM Treasury 1962-64; MoP/Technology/Department of [Trade and] Industry 1964-82: under secretary 1972-76: Newcastle regional director 1972-74; deputy secretary 1976-80; Post Office [Corporation] 1980-87: deputy chairman 1980-81, chairman 1981-87; chairman County Durham Development Corporation 1987-91, Accounting Standards Review Committee 1987-88, Polytechnics and Colleges Funding Council 1988-92, Financial Reporting Council 1990-93, Universities Funding Council 1991-92, Higher Education Funding Council for England 1992-93, School Curriculum and Assessment Authority 1993- *Current non-Whitehall posts:* member council Industrial Society 1985-; chairman Northern Development Company 1992-94, Camelot Group 1993-; chancellor Nottingham University 1993-

Date of birth: 27 July 1930 *Education/professional qualifications:* Malet Lambert High School, Hull; Doncaster Grammar School; Hull University, economics (BScEcon 1954); London Business School (Sloan Fellowship 1967, Fellowship of School 1987) *Honours, decorations:* CB 1979; Kt 1984 *Marital status:* married Margaret Patricia Riley 1954; 2 daughters *Clubs:* Royal Over-Seas League *Recreations:* gardening, stamps

Sir Ronald Dearing CB, Chairman, School Curriculum and Assessment Authority, Newcombe House, 45 Notting Hill Gate, London W11 3JB
Telephone: 0171-229 1234 *Fax:* 0171-243 1060

DE FONBLANQUE, JOHN ROBERT Assistant Under Secretary, International Organisations, Foreign and Commonwealth Office

Career: HM Diplomatic Service 1968-: south Asia department Foreign and Commonwealth Office, London (FCO) 1968-69; second secretary Jakarta 1970-71; first secretary UK permanent representation to EC, Brussels (UKREP) 1972-77; principal nationalised industries HM Treasury 1977-79; FCO 1980-83: Rhodesia department 1980, EC department 1980-83; assistant secretary Cabinet Office 1984-85; head of chancery New Delhi 1986-87; political and institutional counsellor UKREP 1988-93; assistant under secretary international organisations FCO 1994-

Date of birth: 20 December 1943 *Education/professional qualifications:* Ampleforth College; King's College, Cambridge, moral sciences (BA, MA 1966); London School of Economics, economics (MSc 1968) *Honours, decorations:* CMG 1993 *Marital status:* married Margaret Prest 1984; 1 son *Recreations:* mountain walking

John R de Fonblanque Esq CMG, Assistant Under Secretary, Foreign and Commonwealth Office, King Charles Street, London SW1A 2AH *Telephone:* 0171-270 2204 *Fax:* 0171-270 3902

DEMPSTER, JOHN WILLIAM SCOTT Deputy Secretary, Operations, Department of Transport Grade: 2

Career: tax inspector Inland Revenue 1961-64; various posts Departments of Transport (DTp) and Environment 1964-80; principal establishment and finance officer (PEFO) Lord Chancellor's Department 1980-84; DTp 1984-: head of marine directorate 1984-89, PEFO 1989-91, deputy secretary highways, safety and traffic/roads and local transport 1991-94, operations 1994-

Date of birth: 10 May 1938 *Education/professional qualifications:* Plymouth College; Oriel College, Oxford, politics, philosophy and economics (BA 1960, MA) *Marital status:* divorced *Clubs:* Alpine, Royal Southampton Yacht *Recreations:* mountaineering, sailing

John W S Dempster Esq, Deputy Secretary, Department of Transport, 2 Marsham Street, London SW1P 3EB *Telephone:* 0171-276 5240 *Fax:* 0171-276 6806

DENHAM, PAMELA ANNE Regional Director, Government Office for the North East, Departments of Environment, Transport, Trade and Industry and Employment Grade: 3

Career: Department of Trade and Industry 1967-: north east regional director 1990-94; regional director government office for the north east 1994-

Date of birth: 1 May 1943 *Education/professional qualifications:* King's College, London University (BSc 1964, PhD 1969) *Marital status:* divorced *Recreations:* walking, skiing, reading

Pamela Denham, Regional Director, Government Office for the North East, Stanegate House, 2 Groat Market, Newcastle-upon-Tyne NE1 1YN *Telephone and Fax:* 0191-235 7201

DENNER, Dr (WILLIAM) HOWARD BUTLER Chief Scientist (Food), Ministry of Agriculture, Fisheries and Food Grade: 3

Career: university posts 1968-72; Ministry of Agriculture, Fisheries and Food 1972-: senior scientific officer (SO) 1972-73; principal SO, head of food additives branch 1974-83; head of food composition and information unit 1984-88, of food science division II 1989-91; chief scientist (food) 1992-

Date of birth: 14 May 1944 *Education/professional qualifications:* Cyfarthfa Castle Grammar School, Merthyr Tydfil; University of Wales, Cardiff, biochemistry (BSc 1965, PhD 1969) *Marital status:* married Gwenda Williams 1966; 2 daughters *Recreations:* photography, golf, gardening

Dr Howard Denner, Chief Scientist (Food), Ministry of Agriculture, Fisheries and Food, Nobel House, 17 Smith Square, London SW1P 3JR *Telephone:* 0171-238 6192 *Fax:* 0171-238 6021

DENNING, Dr J H Head of Finance, Corporate Affairs and Safety Division, Railways Infrastructure, Department of Transport Grade: 4

Dr J H Denning, Railways Infrastructure, Department of Transport, 2 Marsham Street, London SW1P 3EB *Telephone:* 0171-276 6718 *Fax:* 0171-276 6160

DENZA, EILEEN Second Counsel to Chairman of Committees, House of Lords

Career: assistant law lecturer Bristol University 1961-63; Foreign and Commonwealth Office 1963-86: assistant legal adviser (LA) 1963-74, legal counsellor 1974-86: LA UK permanent representation to EC, Brussels 1980-83; barrister 1986-87; second counsel to chairman of committees (legal advice to EC committee) House of Lords 1987- *Current non-Whitehall posts:* part-time teacher University College, London 1989-

Date of birth: 23 July 1937 *Education/professional qualifications:* Aberdeen University, classics (MA 1958); Oxford University, jurisprudence (BA 1960, MA); Harvard University, USA, international law (LLM 1961); Lincoln's Inn (barrister 1963) *Honours, decorations:* CMG 1984 *Marital status:* married John 1966; 1 daughter, 2 sons *Publications:* Diplomatic Law (Oceana, New York 1976) *Recreations:* music

Mrs Eileen Denza CMG, Second Counsel to Chairman of Committees, Committee Office, House of Lords, London SW1A 0PW
Telephone: 0171-219 3043

DE RAMSEY, Lord (JOHN ALLWYN FELLOWES) Chairman, Environment Agency Advisory Committee, Department of the Environment

Career: chairman Cambridge Water Company 1985-89; president Country Landowners' Association 1991-93, Association of Drainage Authorities 1992-94; chair Environment Agency Advisory Committee, Department of Environment 1994- *Current non-Whitehall posts:* Crown Commissioner

Date of birth: 27 February 1942 *Education/professional qualifications:* Winchester College; Writtle Institute of Agriculture *Honours, decorations:* deputy lieutenant Cambridgeshire 1993; fellow Royal Agriculture Societies 1993 *Marital status:* married Alison Mary 1984; 2 sons, 2 daughters *Clubs:* Boodles *Recreations:* fishing, motor racing, golf, fine arts, wine and trees

Lord De Ramsey, Chairman, Environment Agency Advisory Committee, 2 Marsham Street, London SW1P 3EB *Telephone:* 0171-276 3728
Fax: 0171-276 4548

DERWENT, HENRY CLIFFORD SYDNEY Under Secretary, Road Infrastructure, Department of Transport Grade: 3

Career: Departments of Transport (DTp) and Environment 1974-87; DTp 1987-: head of vehicle licensing division Driver and Vehicle Licensing Agency 1987-90, of finance transport industries division 1990-92; under secretary highways/infrastructure 1992-

Date of birth: 19 November 1951 *Education/professional qualifications:* Berkhamsted School; Worcester College, Oxford, greats (BA 1973) *Marital status:* married Rosemary Meaker 1988; 3 daughters *Recreations:* riding, watercolours, languages, playing the flute

Henry C S Derwent Esq, Under Secretary, Department of Transport, 2 Marsham Street, London SW1P 3EB *Telephone:* 0171-276 5710
Fax: 0171-276 5967

DEVEREAU, (GEORGE) MICHAEL Chief Executive, Central Office of Information (Executive Agency)

Career: information officer (IO) Ministry of Public Building and Works, Building Research Establishment, Department of Environment (DoE) 1967-75; chief IO Price Commission 1975-78, DoE 1978-82, Department of Transport 1982-85; Central Office of Information 1985-: group director 1985-87, deputy director-general (DG) 1987-89, DG/chief executive 1989-

Date of birth: 10 November 1937 *Education/professional qualifications:* King William's College, Isle of Man; University College, London

G Michael Devereau Esq, Chief Executive, Central Office of Information, Hercules House, Hercules Road, London SE1 7DU *Telephone:* 0171-928 2345 *Fax:* 0171-261 0942

DEVERILL, NEIL Deputy Director Finance Regulation and Industry, HM Treasury Grade: 3

N Deverill Esq, Deputy Director, HM Treasury, Parliament Street, London SW1P 3AG *Telephone:* 0171-270 3000

DEVLIN, PATRICK Chief Executive, Northern Ireland Child Support Agency

Career: Northern Ireland (NI) Department of Health and Social Security 1957-92: social security offices regional manager 1984-88, head of information systems 1988-92; chief executive NI Child Support Agency (assessment and collection of child maintenance from absent parents) 1993-

Date of birth: 22 November 1938 *Education/professional qualifications:* Abbey Grammar School, Newry *Marital status:* married Sarah Ann Mackrell 1961; 1 daughter, 3 sons *Recreations:* walking, rambling, reading

Patrick Devlin Esq, Chief Executive, Northern Ireland Child Support Agency, Great Northern Tower, 21 Great Victoria Street, Belfast BT2 7AD *Telephone:* 01232 896800 *Fax:* 01232 896850

DIBBLE, ROY EDWIN Director, CCTA (Government Centre for Information Systems), Office of Public Service and Science/Cabinet Office Grade: 3

Career: GEC-Marconi-Elliott 1962-64; project leader Decca Navigator 1964-68; consultant Motorola Semiconductor 1968-71; Department of Trade and Industry 1971-72; Civil Service Department 1972-75; Government Centre for Information Systems (CCTA) HM Treasury 1975-93; director CCTA, Office of Public Service and Science, Cabinet Office 1993-

Date of birth: 16 December 1940 *Education/professional qualifications:* Maidstone Technical High School; electrical engineering diploma 1964; MIEE, CEng 1973; FBCS 1994 *Marital status:* married Valerie Jean Denham 1967 *Recreations:* sailing

Roy E Dibble Esq, Director, CCTA, Office of Public Service and Science, Rosebery Court, St Andrew's Business Court, Norwich, Norfolk NR7 0HS *Telephone:* 01603 704500 *Fax:* 01603 704860

DICKENSON, D V Chief Crown Prosecutor, North, Crown Prosecution Service Grade: 4

D V Dickenson Esq, Chief Crown Prosecutor, North, Crown Prosecution Service, Benton House, 136 Sandyford Road, Newcastle upon Tyne NE2 1QE *Telephone:* 0191-201 2390 *Fax:* 0191-230 0109

DICKINSON, BRIAN HENRY BARON Under Secretary, Food Safety, Ministry of Agriculture, Fisheries and Food Grade: 3

Career: Ministry of Agriculture, Fisheries and Food (MAFF) 1964-75: assistant principal 1964-68: assistant private secretary to minister 1967-68; principal general agricultural policy, milk 1968-75; assistant secretary (AS) food subsidies and prices Department of Prices and Consumer Protection 1975-78; MAFF 1978-: AS food policy and finance 1978-84; under secretary milk and finance 1984-89, food safety (general responsibility for protecting public) 1989-

Date of birth: 2 May 1940 *Education/professional qualifications:* Leighton Park School, Reading; Balliol College, Oxford, mathematics, literae humaniores (BA 1962) *Marital status:* married Sheila Lloyd 1971

Brian H B Dickinson Esq, Under Secretary, Ministry of Agriculture, Fisheries and Food, Ergon House, 17 Smith Square, London SW1P 3JR *Telephone:* 0171-238 6429 *Fax:* 0171-238 6430

DIGGLE, Dr GEOFF(REY) EDWARD Head of Toxicology, Food Safety and Nutrition Branch, Health Aspects of Environment and Food Division, Department of Health Grade: 4

Career: electronics industry -1962; Department of Health [and Social Security] 1973-: medical officer (MO) 1973-76, senior MO 1976-86; principal MO, head of toxicology, food safety and nutrition branch 1988- *Current non-Whitehall posts:* honorary senior lecturer in pharmaceutical medicine University of Wales 1986-, honorary lecturer Surrey University 1994-

Date of birth: 17 March 1936 *Education/professional qualifications:* Alsop High School, Liverpool; King's College, London, medicine (MB BS 1970); Royal Colleges of Medicine, pharmaceutical medicine (Dip Pharm Med 1988); MFPM 1988; FFPM 1993 *Marital status:* married Dr Sybil Elcoat 1959; 3 sons *Publications:* in medical textbooks and professional journals *Recreations:* study of human character

Dr Geoff E Diggle, Head of Toxicology, Food Safety and Nutrition Branch, Department of Health, Skipton House, Elephant and Castle, London SE1 6LW *Telephone:* 0171-972 5330 *Fax:* 0171-972 5156

DITMAS, H Transport Security, Department of Transport Grade: 4

H Ditmas Esq, Transport Security, Department of Transport, 2 Marsham Street, London SW1P 3EB *Telephone:* 0171-276 3000

DOBBIE, Dr BOB Under Secretary, Industrial Competitiveness Division, Department of Trade and Industry Grade: 3

Career: ICI fellow Bristol University 1967-68; chemistry lecturer Newcastle University 1968-76; chemistry tutor Open University 1975-85; Department of Trade and Industry 1976-: principal 1976-83, assistant secretary 1983-90; under secretary 1990-: director Merseyside Task Force Department of the Environment 1990-92; industrial competitiveness division, 1992- *Current non-Whitehall posts:* non-executive director Vickers Propulsion Technology Division 1988-

Date of birth: 16 January 1942 *Education/professional qualifications:* Dollar Academy; Edinburgh University, chemistry (BSc 1963); Fitzwilliam College, Cambridge, chemistry (PhD 1966) *Marital status:* married Elizabeth Charlotte Barbour 1964; 3 sons *Recreations:* theatre, hillwalking, malt whisky

Dr Bob Dobbie, Under Secretary, Industrial Competitiveness Division, Department of Trade and Industry, Ashdown House, 123 Victoria Street, London SW1E 6RB *Telephone:* 0171-215 6936 *Fax:* 0171-215 6984

DOBBIN, Revd Dr VICTOR **Chaplain General to the Forces, Ministry of Defence**

Career: army chaplain 1972-: service in Germany, Northern Ireland and UK 1972-73; assistant chaplain general (CG) Southern District 1993-95; CG to Forces 1995-

Date of birth: 12 March 1943 *Education/professional qualifications:* Bushmills Grammar School, Northern Ireland; Trinity College, Dublin, geography (MA 1970); Queen's University, Belfast, theology (MTh 1979, PhD 1984) *Honours, decorations:* MBE 1980, QHC 1993 *Recreations:* walking, reading, golf

Rev Dr Victor Dobbin MBE QHC, Chaplain General to the Forces, Ministry of Defence Chaplains, Bagshot Park, Bagshot, Surrey GU19 5PL *Telephone:* 01276 412831 *Fax:* 01276 412834

DOCHERTY, P **Senior Assistant Procurator Fiscal, Glasgow and Strathclyde Region, Crown Office** Grade: 4

P Docherty Esq, Senior Assistant Procurator Fiscal, Glasgow and Strathclyde Region, Crown Office, 10 Ballater Street, PO Box 185, Glasgow G5 9PZ *Telephone:* 0141-429 5566

DORKEN, (ANTHONY) JOHN **Head of Consumer Affairs Division, Department of Trade and Industry** Grade: 3

Career: Voluntary Service Overseas 1965-66; HM Diplomatic Service 1966-67; Board of Trade/Department of Trade and Industry (DTI) 1967-74: private secretary to parliamentary secretary for industry 1971-72; Department of Energy (DEn) 1974-77; Cabinet Office 1977-79; DEn 1980-92: assistant secretary 1980-89: seconded to Shell UK Exploration and Production 1986-89, director of resource management 1989-92; deputy director-general OFGAS 1992-93; under secretary, head of consumer affairs division DTI 1993-

Date of birth: 24 April 1944 *Education/professional qualifications:* Mill Hill School, London; King's College, Cambridge, classical tripos (BA 1965, MA) *Marital status:* married Satanay Mufti 1972; 1 daughter, 1 son *Recreations:* squash, tennis, music, walking

A John Dorken Esq, Under Secretary, Department of Trade and Industry, 10-18 Victoria Street, London SW1H 0NN *Telephone:* 0171-215 5000 *Fax:* 0171-222 9280

DOUGHTY, Dr PETER R **Contract Manager, Medical Services, Social Security Benefits Agency (Executive Agency)** Grade: 4

Career: medical practitioner; Department of Social Security 1985-: contracts manager, medical services Social Security Benefits Agency 1993-

Date of birth: 24 May 1947 *Education/professional qualifications:* St Bartholomew's Hospital medical college, medicine (BSc, MB BS, LRCP, MRCS, DObsRCOG) *Marital status:* married; 1 daughter *Recreations:* amateur radio

Dr Peter R Doughty, Contract Manager, Medical Services, Social Security Benefits Agency, Warbreck House, Warbreck Hill, Blackpool, Lancashire FY2 0YE *Telephone:* 01253 856123

DOUGLAS, HILARY KAY Director of Administration, Office for Standards in Education Grade: 4

Career: Department of Education and Science 1973-89; self-employed 1989-91; secretary Further Education Funding Council 1991-93; Department for Education 1992-94: school curriculum branch 1992-93; head of personnel 1993-94; administration director Office for Standards in Education (OFSTED) 1995-

Date of birth: 27 July 1950 *Education/professional qualifications:* Wimbledon High School for Girls, London; Cambridge University, history (BA 1971) *Marital status:* married Robert Harold 1972; 2 sons *Recreations:* family life; European languages and travel; music, theatre

Mrs Hilary K Douglas, Director of Administration, OFSTED, Alexandra House, 33 Kingsway, London WC2B 6SE *Telephone:* 0171-421 6764 *Fax:* 0171-421 6707

DOWDALL, JOHN MICHAEL Comptroller and Auditor General, Northern Ireland Audit Office Grade: 2

Career: economics lecturer Malta Royal University 1966-69; political economy lecturer Aberdeen University 1969-72; Northern Ireland (NI) civil service 1972-: economic adviser 1972-78; principal Department of Commerce 1978-81; assistant secretary Department of Finance and Personnel (DFP) 1981-85; deputy chief executive Industrial Development Board 1985-89; under secretary DFP 1989-94; comptroller and auditor general NI Audit Office

Date of birth: 6 September 1944 *Education/professional qualifications:* King Edward's School, Witley; Queen's University, Belfast, economics (BScEcon 1966) *Marital status:* married Aylerie 1964; 1 daughter, 3 sons

John M Dowdall Esq, Comptroller and Auditor General for Northern Ireland, The Audit Office, 106 University Street, Belfast BT7 1EU *Telephone:* 01232 251130 *Fax:* 01232 251051

DRACUP, D E J Chief Crown Prosecutor, South East, Crown Prosecution Service Grade: 4

D E J Dracup Esq, Chief Crown Prosecutor, South East, Crown Prosecution Service, Stoke Mill, Woking Road, Guildford, Surrey GU1 1AQ *Telephone:* 01483 573255 *Fax:* 01483 454271

DREW, Brigadier (JAMES) JIM ROBERT Chief Executive, Army Base Repair Organisation (Executive Agency)

Career: army service 1961-: force engineer UN peace-keeping force, Cyprus 1976-78; project officer electronic surveillance procurement 1978-80; chief of staff Royal Electrical and Mechanical Engineers (REME) training centre 1980-82; commanding officer army engineering facility 1982-84; general manager operations division AGB Research plc 1984-86; commandant REME officers' school 1986-89; colonel management of automatic test equipment, electronic diagnosis, reliability 1989-91; chief executive Army Base Repair Organisation (major overhaul army weapon systems; army units engineering support) 1993- *Current non-Whitehall posts:* Institution of Electrical Engineers: council member 1991-, member manufacturing division board 1991-; court member City University 1982-

Date of birth: 7 August 1941 *Education/professional qualifications:* Frimley and Camberley Grammar School; Welbeck College; Royal Military Academy,

Sandhurst (commission 1961); Royal Military College of Science, electronic engineering (BScEng 1965); staff college, Camberley (psc 1973); CEng MIEE 1976, FIEE 1983; FBIM 1983 *Honours, decorations:* CBE 1994 *Recreations:* sports, gardening, reading, chauffeuring children

Brigadier Jim R Drew CBE, Chief Executive, Army Base Repair Organisation, Portway, Monxton Road, Andover, Hampshire SP11 8HT *Telephone:* 01264 383148 *Fax:* 01264 383280

DREW, PHILIPPA C Assistant Under Secretary, Head of Personnel and Office Services, Home Office Grade: 3

Career: Home Office 1975-: seconded to Save the Children Fund, Nepal 1985-87; head of probation service division 1987-91; director of custody HM prison service 1992-95; head of personnel and office services 1995-

Date of birth: 11 May 1946 *Education/professional qualifications:* Oxford University; Pennsylvania University

Miss Philippa Drew, Assistant Under Secretary, Home Office, Grenadier House, Horseferry Road, London SW1P 2DD *Telephone:* 0171-217 0174 *Fax:* 0171-217 0002

DREWIENKIEWICZ, Major-General K J Engineer-in-Chief (Army), Ministry of Defence

Major-General K J Drewienkiewicz, Engineer-in-Chief (Army), Ministry of Defence, Northumberland House, Northumberland Avenue, London WC2N 5BP *Telephone:* 0171-218 0316

DREWRY, Dr DAVID JOHN Director of Science and Technology, Natural Environment Research Council Grade: 3

Career: director Scott Polar Research Institute, Cambridge University 1983-87, British Antarctic Survey 1987-94, of science and technology Natural Environment Research Council 1994- *Current non-Whitehall posts:* visiting fellow Green College, Oxford 1995-

Date of birth: 22 September 1947 *Education/professional qualifications:* Havelock School, Grimsby; Queen Mary College, London, geoscience (BSc 1969); Emmanuel College, Cambridge, geology/geophysics (PhD 1973) *Honours, decorations:* fellow Queen Mary and Westfield College, University of London 1979 *Marital status:* married Gillian Elizabeth Holbrook 1971 *Publications:* Glacial Geologic Processes (Edward Arnold 1986) *Clubs:* Geographical *Recreations:* classical music; skiing, tennis, cycling, hill walking; fine food and wines

Dr David J Drewry, Director of Science and Technology, Natural Environment Research Council, Polaris House, North Star Avenue, Swindon, Wiltshire SN2 1EU *Telephone:* 01793 411654 *Fax:* 01793 411780

DRURY, R M Executive Director, Pay, NHS Executive, Department of Health Grade: 3

R M Drury Esq, Executive Director, Pay, NHS Executive, Department of Health, Quarry House, Quarry Hill, Leeds LS2 7UE *Telephone:* 01132 545718

DUDDING, RICHARD SCARBROUGH Under Secretary, Pollution Control and Wastes, Department of the Environment Grade: 3

Career: Department of Environment (DoE) 1972-76; Privy Council Office 1976-78; Cabinet Office 1978; DoE 1978-: seconded to Overseas Containers Ltd 1983-85, secretary to committee of enquiry into local government 1985-86, under secretary 1990-: finance central 1990-93, pollution control and wastes 1993-

Date of birth: 29 November 1950 *Education/professional qualifications:* Cheltenham College; Jesus College, Cambridge, history (BA 1972, MA) *Marital status:* married Priscilla Diana Russell 1987; 2 sons *Recreations:* gardening, golf, walking

Richard S Dudding Esq, Under Secretary, Department of the Environment, 2 Marsham Street, London SW1P 3EB *Telephone:* 0171-276 3000 *Fax:* 0171-276 8847

DUFF, GRAHAM Director, Operations, Crown Prosecution Service Grade: 3

Career: Crown Prosecution Service 1986-: chief crown prosecutor Northumbria and Durham 1987-90, field director (operations) 1990-92, director operations 1992-

Date of birth: 7 January 1947 *Education/professional qualifications:* Durham University, law (BA 1969); Newcastle University (Cert Ed 1972); Lincoln's Inn (barrister 1976) *Marital status:* married; 1 son, 1 daughter *Recreations:* old Riley cars, breeding foreign birds, riding, target shooting, Northumbrian countryside

Graham Duff Esq, Director (Operations), Crown Prosecution Service, 50 Ludgate Hill, London EC4M 7JJ *Telephone:* 0171-273 8000

DUGDALE, SIMON Director of Communication, Department of the Environment Grade: 4

Simon Dugdale Esq, Director of Communication, Department of the Environment, 2 Marsham Street, London SW1P 3EB *Telephone:* 0171-276 3000

DUNCAN, Dr ALLAN GEORGE Director, Regulatory Systems Division, HM Inspectorate of Pollution, Department of the Environment Grade: 4

Career: research engineer California University, USA 1966-67, cryogenics division US National Bureau of Standards 1967-69; UK Atomic Energy Authority, Harwell 1969-79; Department of Environment 1979-: radiochemical inspectorate, latterly deputy chief inspector (DCI) 1979-90; DCI pollution inspectorate 1990-93; director of regulatory systems 1993- *Current non-Whitehall posts:* member Euratom Scientific and Technical Committee, IAEA International Nuclear Waste Advisory Committee, procedural and legal group EC Network of Environmental Regulators

Date of birth: 17 October 1940 *Education/professional qualifications:* Robert Gordon's College, Aberdeen; Aberdeen University, chemistry (BSc 1963); New College, Oxford, thermodynamics (DPhil 1966) *Marital status:* married Alison Patricia Reid 1972; 1 daughter, 2 sons *Publications:* contributions to learned journals *Recreations:* sailing, walking

Dr Allan G Duncan, Director, Regulatory Systems Division, HM Inspectorate of Pollution, Romney House, 43 Marsham Street, London SW1P 3PY *Telephone:* 0171-276 8129 *Fax:* 0171-276 8216

DUNNETT, ANTHONY GORDON Director, Industrial Development Unit, Department of Trade and Industry Grade: 3

Career: Royal Bank of Canada, Montreal 1977-80, 1982-86; corporate director Samuel Montagu bankers 1989-90; Midland Bank HQ 1986-88, 1990-: corporate director UK banking 1990-91, finance director corporate and industrial banking 1991-94; seconded as director of industrial development unit, regional development division Department of Trade and Industry 1994-

Date of birth: 17 June 1953 *Education/professional qualifications:* St Dunstan's College, Catford, London; McGill University, Canada, commerce and economics (BComm Econ 1974); Exeter University, economics (MA 1975); FCIB 1981 *Marital status:* married Ruth Elizabeth 1975; 1 son, 2 daughters *Recreations:* local church, youth leader; tennis, walking; opera, music

Anthony G Dunnett Esq, Director, Industrial Development Unit, Department of Trade and Industry, Kingsgate House, 66-74 Victoria Street, London SW1E 6SW *Telephone:* 0171-215 8199 *Fax:* 0171-215 2575

DUNSTAN, TESSA JANE Head of Legal Services, Investigations Division, Department of Trade and Industry Grade: 4

Career: Board of Trade/Department of Trade and Industry Solicitor's Office (DTI SO) 1968-84: legal assistant (LA) prosecutions 1968-73, senior LA 1973-84; legal adviser Office of Telecommunications 1984-87; DTI SO 1987-: adviser on insolvency and insider dealing 1987-89, head of investigations division legal services (companies, insider dealing, insolvency offences) 1989-

Date of birth: 18 July 1944 *Education/professional qualifications:* Convent of the Sacred Heart, Woldingham, Surrey; Lady Margaret Hall, Oxford, modern history (BA 1966, MA); Middle Temple (barrister 1967) *Marital status:* married Richard James Rowley 1973; 2 daughters, 2 sons *Recreations:* opera, gardening

Mrs Tessa J Dunstan, Head of Legal Services, Investigations Division, Department of Trade and Industry, Ashdown House, 123 Victoria Street, London SW1E 6RB *Telephone:* 0171-215 6406 *Fax:* 0171-215 6894

DUNT, Vice-Admiral JOHN HUGH Deputy Chief of Defence Staff (Systems), Ministry of Defence

Career: Royal Navy 1963-: captain HMS Defiance 1989-90; director defence systems Ministry of Defence 1991-93; director general fleet support (operations and plans) 1993-95, deputy chief of defence staff (systems) 1995-

Date of birth: 14 August 1944

Vice-Admiral John H Dunt, Deputy Chief of Defence Staff (Systems), Ministry of Defence, Whitehall, London SW1A 2HB *Telephone:* 0171-218 7165

DURHAM, DAVID EDWARD Chief Executive, Companies House (Executive Agency) and Registrar of Companies, England and Wales Grade: 4

Career: army 1956-82; director of housing, environmental health, public works Rochester city council 1982-86; unit general manager Parkside Health Authority, London 1986-90; chief executive and registrar of companies, England and Wales, Companies House (registers companies, collects statutory returns and provides information) 1990-

Date of birth: 8 August 1936 *Education/professional qualifications:* Magdalen College School, Oxford; Medway College, civil engineering (diploma 1959); RMCS and Staff College (graduate 1969); Open University, science and technology (BA 1971); South West London College, (ACIS 1982); MHSM 1988 *Marital status:* married Valerie Susan Wheeler 1960; 1 daughter, 1 son *Recreations:* squash, golf, DIY

David E Durham Esq, Chief Executive and Registrar of Companies, Companies House, Crown Way, Cardiff CF4 3UZ
Telephone: 01222 380400 *Fax:* 01222 380617

DURIE, D Deputy Secretary, Regional and Small Firms, Department of Trade and Industry Grade: 2

D Durie Esq, Deputy Secretary, Department of Trade and Industry, Kingsgate House, 66-74 Victoria Street, London SW1E 6SW *Telephone:* 0171-215 5000

E

EADIE, CHRISTOPHER JAMES Deputy Ombudsman, Office of the Banking Ombudsman

Career: RAF service 1958-89: RAF legal services 1964-89: director Cyprus 1976-78, Germany 1982-85; Office of the Banking Ombudsman (investigation public's complaints about banking services) 1989-: deputy obmudsman 1991-

Date of birth: 18 September 1934 *Education/professional qualifications:* Stranraer High School; Edinburgh University, law (BL 1957); solicitor (Scotland) 1957; London University (LLB 1981); FCIS *Marital status:* married Jane Elizabeth 1961; 1 son, 1 daughter *Clubs:* Royal Air Force

Christopher J Eadie Esq, Deputy Ombudsman, Office of the Banking Ombudsman, 70 Gray's Inn Road, London WC1X 8NB *Telephone:* 0171-404 9944 *Fax:* 0171-405 5052

EASTEAL, MARTIN Chief Executive, Local Government Commission for England Grade: 3 *(see Addenda)*

Career: HM Treasury 1970-74; deputy town clerk London borough Ealing 1974-78; general manager Harlow council, Essex 1978-83; director of public policy studies PA Consulting Group 1983-88; director National Audit Office 1988-92; chief executive Local Government Commission for England (review local authority structure, boundaries and electoral arrangements) 1992-

Date of birth: 4 November 1947 *Education/professional qualifications:* Buckhurst Hill High School, Essex; University College, Oxford, philosophy, politics and economics (BA 1970, MA); Knox Fellow, Harvard University, USA; FIPM 1981; FBIM 1978; MIMC 1984; FRGS 1992; FRSA 1993 *Marital status:* married Barbara Clark 1972; 2 daughters *Publications:* contributor The Labour Government 1964-70 (Penguin 1970); The Development of the General Manager (Nuffield Trust – NT 1986); Training for General Management (NT 1987); Management Information Systems in Whitehall (PA 1989) *Clubs:* Reform *Recreations:* vintage cars; trams

Martin Easteal Esq, Chief Executive, Local Government Commission for England, Dolphyn Court, 10-11 Great Turnstile, Lincoln's Inn Fields, London WC1V 7JU *Telephone:* 0171-430 8443 *Fax:* 0171-404 6143

ECCLESTONE, BARRY JAMES Solicitor, Health and Safety Commission and Executive Grade: 4

Career: solicitor 1968-71; assistant parliamentary counsel (APC) 1972-78, senior APC 1978-80; Treasury Solicitor's Department energy branch 1980-89: senior legal assistant 1980-83, assistant solicitor 1983-89; solicitor, Health and Safety Commission and Health and Safety Executive 1990-

Date of birth: 18 April 1944 *Education/professional qualifications:* King Edward's School, Birmingham; Bristol University, law (LLB 1965); Birmingham University, law (LLM 1972) *Marital status:* married Mary Penelope Susan Quicke 1973; 3 daughters *Recreations:* sailing, woodwork

Barry J Ecclestone Esq, Solicitor, Health and Safety Executive, Rose Court, 2 Southwark Bridge, London SE1 9HS *Telephone:* 0171-717 6650 *Fax:* 0171-717 6661

EDGAR, WILLIAM Chief Executive, National Engineering Laboratory (Executive Agency) Grade: 3

Career: principal engineer British Aircraft Corporation 1963-67; manufacturing general manager Weir Pumps 1967-73; director/chief executive Seaforth Maritime/Engineering 1973-86; director Vickers Marine 1986-88; executive chairman Cochrane Shipbuilders 1988-90; chief executive National Engineering Laboratory (preparing agency for privatisation) 1990-

Date of birth: 16 January 1938 *Education/professional qualifications:* St John's Grammar School, Hamilton; Strathclyde University, mechanical engineering (ARCST 1961); Birmingham University, mechanical engineering (MSc 1962) *Marital status:* married June Gilmour 1961; 2 sons *Clubs:* Sloane *Recreations:* reading, golf, music, soccer

William Edgar Esq, Chief Executive, National Engineering Laboratory, East Kilbride, Glasgow G75 0QU *Telephone:* 013552 72221 *Fax:* 013552 72132

EDWARDS, PATRICIA ANNE Deputy Parliamentary Commissioner, Office of the Parliamentary Commissioner for Administration (Ombudsman) Grade: 3

Career: Criminal Appeal Office 1965-74; Law Officers' Department 1974-77; Home Office 1977-: assistant legal adviser 1980-88; principal assistant legal adviser 1988-94; deputy parliamentary commissioner Office of the Parliamentary Commissioner for Administration 1994-

Date of birth: 29 May 1944 *Education/professional qualifications:* Barry and Purley County Grammar Schools; King's College, London, law (LLB 1965); Middle Temple (barrister 1967) *Marital status:* married Roger Cox 1970 *Recreations:* travel, reading, domestic pursuits

Miss Patricia A Edwards, Deputy Parliamentary Commissioner, Office of the Parliamentary Commissioner for Administration, Church House, Great Smith Street, London SW1P 3BW *Telephone:* 0171-276 2130 *Fax:* 0171-276 2099

EDWARDS, ROBERT NOEL Chief Executive, Chessington Computer Centre (Executive Agency) Grade: 5

Career: War Office 1962-63; Ministry of Pensions and National Insurance 1963-66; Civil Service Commission/Department 1966-82; HM Treasury 1982-92; chief executive Chessington Computer Centre 1992-

Date of birth: 25 December 1942 *Education/professional qualifications:* Chorlton Grammar School, Manchester *Marital status:* married Jean Margaret Ashton 1966; 2 sons, 1 daughter *Recreations:* music, choral singing

Robert Edwards Esq, Chief Executive, Chessington Computer Centre, Leatherhead Road, Chessington, Surrey KT9 2LT *Telephone:* 0181-391 3800 *Fax:* 0181-391 3986

ELAND, MICHAEL JOHN Commissioner, HM Customs and Excise Grade: 3

Career: HM Customs and Excise (C&E) 1975-82: private secretary (PS) to chairman of board 1979-81, principal 1981-88; Cabinet Office 1982-87: management and personnel office 1982-85, home affairs secretariat 1985-87; PS to Lord President of Council 1987-88; C&E 1988-: assistant secretary 1988-92; under secretary, commissioner central directorate 1992-94, customs policy 1994-

Date of birth: 26 September 1952 *Education/professional qualifications:* Worksop College, Nottinghamshire; Trinity College, Oxford, jurisprudence (BA 1974, MA); Middle Temple (barrister 1975) *Marital status:* married Rhiannon Wynn Jones 1981; 1 daughter, 1 son *Recreations:* walking, theatre

Michael J Eland Esq, Commissioner, HM Customs and Excise, New King's Beam House, 27 Upper Ground, London SE1 9JP
Telephone: 0171-865 5061 *Fax:* 0171-865 4051

ELLIS, Dr ADRIAN FOSS Head of Technology and Health Sciences Division, Health and Safety Executive Grade: 3

Career: research and development British Steel Corporation 1966-71; HM Alkali and Clean Air Inspectorate 1971-83; Health and Safety Executive 1983-: head of major hazards assessment unit 1985-86; deputy chief inspector (chemicals) 1986-90; field operations regional director 1990; director of hazardous installations policy and of technology 1990-91; under secretary, head of technology and health sciences division 1991- *Current non-Whitehall posts:* visiting professor Department of Applied Energy, Cranfield Institute of Technology/University 1992-

Date of birth: 15 February 1944 *Education/professional qualifications:* Dean Close School, Cheltenham; London University, chemical engineering (BSc 1966); Loughborough University, chemical engineering (PhD 1969), FIChemE 1977, FInstE 1977 *Marital status:* married Hilary Jean Miles 1973; 2 daughters, 1 son *Clubs:* Athenaeum *Recreations:* bridge, Swindon Town Football Club

Dr Adrian F Ellis, Under Secretary, Health and Safety Executive, St Anne's House, Stanley Precinct, Bootle, Merseyside L20 3MF
Telephone: 0151-951 4574 *Fax:* 0151-951 4232

ELLIS, (ARTHUR) JOHN Chairman, Intervention Board for Agricultural Produce (Executive Agency)

Career: Fyffes Group Ltd 1965-: financial director 1965-69, chief executive officer 1969-, managing director 1969-85, chairman 1985-; member economic development committee for agricultural industry 1978-85; part-time chairman national seed development organisation 1982-87; chairman Intervention Board for Agricultural Produce (implementation market support measures of EU common agricultural policy) 1989-

Date of birth: 22 August 1932 *Education/professional qualifications:* South West Essex Technical College and School of Art; City of London College, professional services; FCIS 1956; FCAA 1958; FICMA 1959; MBCS 1960 *Honours, decorations:* CBE 1986 *Marital status:* married Rita Patricia Blake 1956; 2 sons, 1 daughter *Clubs:* Reform, Farmers' *Recreations:* golf, fishing, reading

A John Ellis Esq CBE, Chairman, Intervention Board for Agricultural Produce, c/o 12 York Gate, Regent's Park, London NW1 4QJ
Telephone: 0171-487 4472 *Fax:* 0171-487 3645

ELTIS, Dr WALTER ALFRED Chief Economic Adviser to President of the Board of Trade

Career: fellow and economics tutor Exeter College, Oxford 1963-86; visiting economics professor Toronto University, Canada 1976-77, European University, Florence, Italy 1979; National Economic Development Office 1986-: economic director 1986-88, director-general 1988-92; chief economic adviser to president of the Board of Trade 1993- *Current non-Whitehall posts:* emeritus fellow Exeter College, Oxford 1988-; Gresham professor of commerce Gresham College, London 1993-; visiting professor of economics Reading University 1992-; council member European Policy Forum 1992-, Foundation for Manufacturing and Industry 1993-

Date of birth: 23 May 1933 *Education/professional qualifications:* Wycliffe College, Stonehouse, Gloucestershire; Emmanuel College, Cambridge, economics (BA 1956); Oxford University, economics (MA 1960, DLitt 1990) *Marital status:* married Shelagh Mary Owen 1959; 1 son, 2 daughters *Publications:* Growth and Distribution (Macmillan 1973); co-author Britain's Economic Problem: Too Few Producers (Macmillan 1976); The Classical Theory of Economic Growth (Macmillan 1984); Classical Economics, Public Expenditure and Growth (Edward Elgar 1993) *Clubs:* Reform, Royal Automobile *Recreations:* chess, music

Dr Walter A Eltis, Chief Economic Adviser to the President of the Board of Trade, Department of Trade and Industry, Ashdown House, 123 Victoria Street, London SW1E 6RB *Telephone:* 0171-215 6347 *Fax:* 0171-215 6471

ELVIDGE, JOHN WILLIAM Under Secretary, Scottish Office Industry Department Grade: 3

Career: Scottish Office 1973-: seconded as implementation director Scottish Homes 1988-89; Industry Department 1989-: assistant secretary 1989-93, under secretary (European funds and co-ordination, energy, transport and local roads, economics and statistics) 1993-

Date of birth: 9 February 1951 *Education/professional qualifications:* Sir George Monoux School, London; St Catherine's College, Oxford, English language and literature (BA 1972) *Marital status:* single *Recreations:* visual arts, music, theatre

John Elvidge Esq, Under Secretary, Scottish Office Industry Department, New St Andrew's House, Edinburgh EH1 3TG *Telephone:* 0131-244 4609 *Fax:* 0131-244 4599

EMMOTT, MICHAEL Deputy Director, Office of Manpower Economics Grade: 4

Career: Ministry of Labour/Department of Employment/Employment Department Group 1965-94: assistant principal 1965-68; private secretary (PS) to secretary of state (SoS) for employment and productivity 1968-70; principal incomes policy 1970-73; seconded to Australia Department of Labour 1973-75; PS to successive SoS for employment 1975-77; assistant secretary industrial relations 1977-81, employment policy 1981-84; seconded to enterprise and deregulation unit 1984-86; director of enterprise and special measures Manpower Services Commission 1986-87; director of programmes/business development Employment Service 1987-93; head of strategy unit 1993-94; deputy director Office of Manpower Economics (service of independent public sector salary review bodies) 1994-

Date of birth: 2 February 1943 *Education/professional qualifications:* Keighley Boys' Grammar School; Gonville and Caius College, Cambridge, law (BA 1965, MA) *Marital status:* married Janet Anita Gradecka 1964; 2 sons *Recreations:* running, reading

Michael Emmott Esq, Deputy Director, Office of Manpower Economics, Oxford House, 76 Oxford Street, London W1N 9FD
Telephone: 0171-467 7220 *Fax:* 0171-467 7248

ESSENHIGH, Rear-Admiral NIGEL R Hydrographer of the Navy and Chief Executive, Hydrographic Office (Executive Agency)

Career: Royal Navy 1963-: sea-going service; directorate of naval manpower and training Ministry of Defence (MoD) 1980-82; sea-going service in command; student Royal College of Defence Studies 1986; assistant director weapons and ships, naval plans MoD 1986-89; command HMS Exeter 1989-91; director naval plans and programmes MoD 1992-94; hydrographer of the navy and chief executive Hydrographic Office (supply charts and navigational publications for Royal Navy and others) 1994-

Date of birth: 1944 *Education/professional qualifications:* Royal College of Defence Studies; Army Staff College, Camberley

Rear-Admiral Nigel R Essenhigh, Hydrographer of the Navy, Hydrographic Office, Taunton, Somerset TA1 2DN *Telephone:* 01823 337900 *Fax:* 01823 284077

ESSERY, DAVID JAMES Under Secretary, Scottish Office Home and Health Department Grade: 3

Career: Scottish Office Departments 1956-: private secretary to minister of state 1968; principal Scottish Development Department (SDD) 1969; assistant secretary 1976-85: Scottish economic planning department 1976-81, SDD 1981-85; under secretary 1985-: Agriculture and Fisheries Department 1985-91, Home and Health Department (civil law, police, fire, home defence, emergency planning) 1991-

Date of birth: 10 May 1938 *Education/professional qualifications:* Royal High School, Edinburgh *Marital status:* married Nora Loughlin Sim 1963; 2 sons, 1 daughter *Recreations:* music, reading, cricket

David J Essery Esq, Under Secretary, Scottish Office, St Andrew's House, Edinburgh EH1 3DE
Telephone: 0131-244 2127 *Fax:* 0131-244 2683

ETHERINGTON, GORDON DAVID Chief Crown Prosecutor, London, Crown Prosecution Service Grade: 3

Career: solicitor 1968-; prosecuting solicitor (PS) Liverpool 1971; Cheshire prosecuting solicitors' department (PSD) 1972-85; PS, area PS; deputy PS Devon and Cornwall PSD 1985; Crown Prosecution Service 1986-: chief Crown prosecutor (CCP) Leicestershire/Northamptonshire 1986-89; CCP London north 1989-90; field director resources 1990-93; CCP London 1993-

Date of birth: 2 October 1944 *Education/professional qualifications:* Waterloo Grammar School, Lancashire *Marital status:* married Christine; 3 children *Recreations:* choral singing, sailing, walking

Gordon D Etherington Esq, Chief Crown Prosecutor, London, Crown Prosecution Service, 5th Floor, Portland House, Stag Place, London SW1E 5BH *Telephone:* 0171-915 5700 *Fax:* 0171-976 5418

EVANS, (CHRISTOPHER) PAUL Director of Housing and Urban Monitoring and Analysis; Housing Policy and Private Sector, Department of the Environment Grade: 3

Career: Department of Environment 1975-: private secretary to permanent secretary 1978-80; assistant secretary 1985-93: central policy planning 1985-87, inner cities 1987-90, personnel management 1990-92, central finance 1992-93; under secretary, director housing and urban monitoring and analysis 1993-, housing policy and private sector 1994-

Date of birth: 25 December 1948 *Education/professional qualifications:* St Julian's High School, Newport, Gwent; Trinity College, Cambridge, architecture (BA 1970, DipArch 1972, PhD 1975) *Marital status:* married Margaret Beckett 1971; 2 daughters

C Paul Evans Esq, Under Secretary, Department of the Environment, 2 Marsham Street, London SW1P 3EB *Telephone:* 0171-276 5594 *Fax:* 0171-276 3846

EVANS, D S International Aviation Directorate, Department of Transport Grade: 4

D S Evans Esq, International Aviation Directorate, Department of Transport, Suite 928, 1000 Sherbrooke Street West, Montreal, Quebec, HR3 3G4 Canada *Telephone:* 001-418 285 8302 *Fax:* 001-418 285 8001

EVANS, (JOHN) DEREK Chief Conciliation Officer, Advisory, Conciliation and Arbitration Service Grade: 4

Career: Department of Employment 1964-74: regional training service 1971-74; Advisory, Conciliation and Arbitration Service 1974-: director Wales 1982-88; director advisory services 1988-91, conciliation and arbitration 1991-92; chief conciliation officer 1992- *Current non-Whitehall posts:* industrial fellow Kingston University

Date of birth: 11 September 1942 *Education/professional qualifications:* Roundhay School, Leeds; FIPM 1986 *Marital status:* married Betty Wiseman 1964; 2 daughters *Clubs:* Sand Martins Golf *Recreations:* golf, sport, driving, music

J Derek Evans Esq, Chief Conciliation Officer, Advisory, Conciliation and Arbitration Service, 27 Wilton Street, London SW1X 7AZ *Telephone:* 0171-210 3669 *Fax:* 0171-210 3708

EVANS, RUTH Director, National Consumer Council Grade: 4

Career: co-ordinator Maternity Alliance 1981-86; MIND (National Association for Mental Health) 1986-90: deputy director 1986-89, acting director 1989-90; general secretary War on Want 1990; management consultant for National Rubella Council and Department of Health 1990-91; director National Consumer Council (independent body for domestic consumers of publicly and privately provided goods and services) 1992-

Date of birth: 12 October 1957 *Education/professional qualifications:* Camden School for Girls, London; Girton College, Cambridge, history (BA 1980, MA) *Honours, decorations:* FRSA 1992 *Marital status:* single *Recreations:* writing, music, swimming

Ms Ruth Evans, Director, National Consumer Council, 20 Grosvenor Gardens, London SW1W 0DH *Telephone:* 0171-730 3469 *Fax:* 0171-730 0191

EVANS, Dr (WILLIAM) DAVID Under Secretary, Technology and Innovation Policy, Industry Division, Department of Trade and Industry Grade: 3

Career: Department of Energy/Trade and Industry (DTI) 1974-80; first secretary science and technology Bonn embassy 1980-83; DTI 1984-: assistant secretary 1984-89; chief scientist 1989-92; under secretary environment division 1992-94, technology and innovation policy, industry division 1994-

Date of birth: 20 April 1949 *Education/professional qualifications:* St Catherine's College, Oxford, physics (BA 1971, DPhil 1974), FRAS 1975 *Marital status:* married Elizabeth Crowe 1980; 3 sons, 1 daughter *Recreations:* music, reading, history of technology

Dr David Evans, Under Secretary, Department of Trade and Industry, 151 Buckingham Palace Road, London SW1W 9SS *Telephone:* 0171-215 1659 *Fax:* 0171-215 4191

EVERED, Dr DAVID CHARLES Second Secretary, Medical Research Council

Career: junior hospital posts London and Leeds 1964-70; Newcastle University 1970-74: first assistant in medicine 1970-72, Wellcome senior research fellow 1972-74; consultant physician Newcastle Royal Victoria Infirmary 1974-78; director Ciba Foundation 1978-88; second secretary (deputy chief executive) Medical Research Council 1988- *Current non-Whitehall posts:* non-executive member Hammersmith and Queen Charlotte's Special Health Authority 1990-

Date of birth: 2 January 1940 *Education/professional qualifications:* Cranleigh School, Surrey; Middlesex Hospital medical school (BSc 1961, MB BS 1964, MD 1971); MRCP 1967; FRCP 1978; FIBiol 1978 *Marital status:* married Anne Elizabeth Massey Lings 1964; 2 daughters, 1 son *Publications:* Diseases of the Thyroid (Pitman 1976); Atlas of Endocrinology (Wolfe Medical 1979/90); Collaboration in Medical Research in Europe (Pitman 1981) *Recreations:* reading, history, antiques, gardening, tennis, sailing, walking

Dr David C Evered, Second Secretary, Medical Research Council, 20 Park Crescent, London W1N 4AL *Telephone:* 0171-636 5422 *Fax:* 0171-436 6179

EVERETT, CHARLES WILLIAM VOGT Director of Finance and Administration, Court Service (Executive Agency) Grade: 3

Career: Lord Chancellor's Department 1971-: assistant private secretary to Lord Chancellor 1974-76; seconded to Department of Transport 1982-84; head of legal aid bill division 1987-88; secretary to legal aid board 1988-89; head of court strategy division 1989-90, of central unit 1990-91, of policy and legal services group 1991-94; director of finance and administration Court Service 1994- *Current non-Whitehall posts:* member IBM (UK) strategy committee

Date of birth: 15 October 1949 *Education/professional qualifications:* Reading University (BA 1971) *Marital status:* married Elizabeth Vanessa Ellis 1978; 3 sons

Charles W V Everett, Director of Finance and Administration, Court Service, Southside, 105 Victoria Street, London SW1E 6QT *Telephone:* 0171-210 1696 *Fax:* 0171-210 1739

EVES, DAVID CHARLES THOMAS Deputy Director-General, Operations, and HM Chief Inspector of Factories, Health and Safety Executive Grade: 2

Career: schoolteacher 1963-64; factory inspector Ministry of Labour 1964-76; Health and Safety Executive 1977-: head of planning section 1977-78, director of corporate services 1978-80, head of planning 1981-83, deputy chief inspector of factories (CIF) 1983-85, CIF 1985-88, director of resources and planning 1988-89, deputy director-general (technology and health sciences, research, field operations, railways and mines) and CIF 1989-

Date of birth: 10 January 1942 *Education/professional qualifications:* King's School, Rochester; University College, Durham, English (BA 1963) *Honours, decorations:* CB *Marital status:* married Valerie Ann Carter 1964; 1 daughter *Clubs:* Athenaeum *Recreations:* sailing, fishing, painting, reading, music

David C T Eves Esq CB, Deputy Director-General, Health and Safety Executive, Rose Court, 2 Southwark Bridge, London SE1 9HS
Telephone: 0171-717 6450 *Fax:* 0171-717 6616

EWING, R S T Controller, Inland Revenue, Northern Ireland

R S T Ewing Esq, Controller, Inland Revenue, Northern Ireland, Level 9, Dorchester House, 52-55 Great Victoria Street, Belfast BT2 7QE *Telephone:* 01232 245123 *Fax:* 01232 328059

EWINS, PETER D Chief Scientist, Ministry of Defence Grade: 3

Career: Royal Aircraft Establishment (RAE) Farnborough 1966-78; staff of chief scientist RAF Ministry of Defence (MoD) 1978-81; head of helicopters research RAE 1981-84; seconded to civil service personnel policy Cabinet Office 1984-87; MoD 1987-91: director nuclear projects 1987, ARE procurement executive 1988-91; Defence Research Agency 1991-93: managing director maritime and electronics 1991, command and maritime systems 1992, operations 1993-94; Ministry of Defence 1994-: deputy chief scientific adviser 1994-95, chief scientist 1995-

Date of birth: 20 March 1943 *Education/professional qualifications:* BSc Eng, MSc; CEng *Publications:* technical papers on structural composite materials

P D Ewins Esq, Chief Scientist, Ministry of Defence, Main Building, Whitehall, London SW1A 2HB
Telephone: 0171-218 9000 *Fax:* 0171-218 6552

EYRE, Dr BRIAN LEONARD Deputy Chairman and Chief Executive, AEA Technology, UK Atomic Energy Authority

Career: training, research 1950-57; research Central Electricity Generating Board 1959-62; Harwell laboratory UK Atomic Energy Authority (UKAEA) 1962-79; visiting professor of materials science Liverpool University 1979-84; UKAEA 1984-: director fuel and engineering technology Risley 1984-87; London 1987-90: programmes board member 1987-89; deputy chairman (DC) and managing director businesses 1989-90; DC and chief executive AEA Technology (UKAEA trading name) 1990-

Date of birth: 29 November 1933 *Education/professional qualifications:* Greenford Grammar School; Surrey University, metallurgy (BSc 1959, DSc 1959) FEng 1992 *Honours, decorations:* CBE 1993 *Marital status:* married Caroline Elizabeth Rackham 1965; 2 sons *Clubs:* Athenaeum *Recreations:* walking, sailing

Dr Brian L Eyre CBE, Deputy Chairman and Chief Executive, AEA Technology, 329 Harwell, Didcot, Oxfordshire OX11 0RA
Telephone: 01235 433206 *Fax:* 01235 433823

F

FABER, DIANA **Commissioner, Law Commission**

Career: private practice barrister 1977-82; private practice solicitor 1982-93: partner 1988-93; commissioner (commercial and corporate law) Law Commission 1994-

Date of birth: 23 October 1955 *Education/professional qualifications:* Putney High School, London; University College, London, law (LLB 1976); Gray's Inn, College of Law (barrister 1977); solicitor 1983 *Marital status:* single *Recreations:* theatre, walking, books

Miss Diana Faber, Commissioner, Law Commission, Conquest House, 37-38 John Street, Theobald's Road, London WC1N 2BQ
Telephone: 0171-411 1204 *Fax:* 0171-411 1297

FAINT, (JOHN) ANTHONY LEONARD **Under Secretary, Eastern Europe and Western Hemisphere Division, Overseas Development Administration** Grade: 3

Career: Ministry of Overseas Development/Overseas Development Administration (ODA) 1965-86: assistant principal 1965-68; study leave 1968-69; principal, London 1969-70, 1974-80; first secretary (aid), Blantyre, Malawi 1971-73; head of SE Asia development division, Bangkok 1980-83; head of finance department, London 1983-86; alternate executive director World Bank, Washington DC 1986-89; ODA 1989-: head East Asia department 1989-90; under secretary international division 1990-; UK director European Bank for Reconstruction and Development 1991-92; eastern European division 1991-93, eastern Europe and western hemisphere division 1993-

Date of birth: 24 November 1942 *Education/professional qualifications:* Chigwell School; Magdalen College, Oxford, classics (BA 1965); Fletcher School, Massachusetts, USA, international economics (MA 1969) *Marital status:* married Elizabeth Theresa Winter 1979 *Recreations:* music, bridge, chess, squash

J Anthony L Faint Esq, Under Secretary, Overseas Development Administration, Old Admiralty Building, Whitehall, London SW1A 2AF *Telephone:* 0171-210 3809

FARMER, GEORGE WALLACE **President, Immigration Appeal Tribunal**

Career: private practice 1950-52, magistrate 1952-56, Barbados; (senior) resident magistrate 1956-64, director of public prosecutions 1964-65, Uganda; legal manager Road Transport Industry Training Board 1967-70; Immigration Appeals Tribunal 1970-: adjudicator 1970-82, vice-president 1982-91, president 1991-

Date of birth: 4 June 1929 *Education/professional qualifications:* Harrison College, Barbados; Middle Temple (barrister 1950)

George W Farmer Esq, President, Immigration Appeal Tribunal, Thanet House, 231 Strand, London WC2R 1DA *Telephone:* 0171-353 8060 *Fax:* 0171-583 1976

FARMER, PETER JOHN **Administrator, North-Eastern Circuit, Court Service (Executive Agency)** Grade: 4

Career: HM Customs and Excise 1975-79; HM Treasury 1979-81; Lord Chancellor's Department 1981-:/Court Service 1995-: principal, legal remuneration 1981-83; circuit principal, Leeds 1983-87; assistant secretary, management support 1987-88; assistant public trustee 1988-91, public trustee and accountant general of Supreme Court (executor, trustee and Mental Health Act receiver; protection of mentally incapable people's property and affairs) 1991-94, administrator north-eastern circuit (management area's high, crown and county courts' business) 1994-

Date of birth: 5 November 1952 *Education/professional qualifications:* King Edward VI School, Southampton; Gonville and Caius College, Cambridge, mathematics (BA 1975, MA); London University, psychology (certificate 1983); FIMgt *Marital status:* married Christine Ann Tetley 1986 *Clubs:* Royal Over-seas League; The Leeds *Recreations:* English folk dancing, hill walking

Peter J Farmer Esq, Circuit Administrator, North-Eastern Circuit Office, West Riding House, Albion Street, Leeds LS1 5AA
Telephone: 01132 441841 *Fax:* 01132 340948

FARQUHARSON, JONATHAN Commissioner, Charity Commission Grade: 4

Career: solicitor 1962-64; Charity Commission 1964-: legal assistant (LA) 1964-70, senior LA 1970-81, deputy commissioner 1981-85, commissioner 1985-

Date of birth: 27 December 1937 *Education/professional qualifications:* St Albans School; Manchester University, law (LLB 1959) *Marital status:* married Maureen Elsie Bright 1963; 2 daughters *Recreations:* geology, photography, painting, record collecting

Jonathan Farquharson Esq, Charity Commissioner, Charity Commission, 20 Kings Road, Queen's Dock, Liverpool L3 4DQ *Telephone:* 0151-703 1535 *Fax:* 0151-703 1556

FARRAND, Dr JULIAN THOMAS Pensions Ombudsman

Career: assistant law lecturer/lecturer King's College, London 1960-63; law lecturer Sheffield University 1963-65; reader in law Queen Mary College, London 1965-68; Manchester University 1968-88: professor of law 1968-88, dean law faculty 1970-72, 1976-78; chairman National Insurance Local Tribunal 1980-83, Supplementary Benefit Appeals Tribunal 1977-80, 1983-88; law commissioner 1984-88: chairman Government Conveyancing Committee 1984-85, London Rent Assessment Panel 1984-; insurance ombudsman 1989-94; pensions ombudsman 1994-

Date of birth: 13 August 1935 *Education/professional qualifications:* Portsmouth Grammar School; Haberdashers' Aske's Hampstead School; University College, London, law (LLB 1957, LLD 1966); solicitor 1960 *Marital status:* Brenda Marjorie Hale 1992; 2 daughters, 1 son *Publications:* Contract and Conveyance (1983); editor Emmet on Title (1986) *Recreations:* chess, bridge, wine

Dr Julian T Farrand, Pensions Ombudsman, 11 Belgrave Road, London SW1V 1RB *Telephone:* 0171-834 9144 *Fax:* 0171-821 0065

FAUSET, IAN DAVID Assistant Under Secretary, Civilian Management (Personnel), Ministry of Defence Grade: 3

Career: Ministry of Defence (MoD) 1968-: operational research department of chief scientist (CS), RAF 1968-72, 1973-78; technical staff officer to CS 1972-73; head of air studies at defence operational analysis organisation, Germany 1978-82; MoD 1982-: procurement executive (PE) 1982-91: project manager jet aircraft 1982-85, assistant project director helicopters 1985-87; assistant director civilian management 1987-88; head of civilian management policy division and director of personnel for PE 1988-89; project director Tornado aircraft 1989, EH101 helicopter 1989-91; assistant under secretary civilian management (personnel) 1991- *Current non-Whitehall posts:* non-executive director GEC Avery 1991-

Date of birth: 8 December 1943 *Education/professional qualifications:* Chester City Grammar School; King Edward VI Grammar School, Lichfield; London University (BSc); University College, Aberystwyth, statistics (diploma); CEng; FRAeS *Recreations:* bridge, cricket, tennis, squash

Ian D Fauset Esq, Assistant Under Secretary, Ministry of Defence, Lacon House, Theobald's Road, London WC1X 8RY *Telephone:* 0171-305 6148 *Fax:* 0171-305 6586

FELL, DAVID Second Permanent Secretary and Head of the Northern Ireland Civil Service, Northern Ireland Office Grade: 1A

Career: secondary school teacher 1966-67; research Queen's University, Belfast 1967-69; Northern Ireland civil service 1969-: Department of Agriculture 1969-72; Department of Commerce 1972-82: assistant secretary 1971-81, under secretary 1981-82; deputy chief executive Industrial Development Board 1982-84; permanent secretary Department of Economic Development 1984-91; second permanent under secretary and head of civil service 1991-

Date of birth: 20 January 1943 *Education/professional qualifications:* Royal Belfast Academical Institution; Queen's University, Belfast: pure mathematics (BSc 1963), applied mathematics (BSc 1964), physics (BSc 1965) *Honours, decorations:* CB 1990, CInstM 1991, FRSA 1992 *Marital status:* married Sandra Jesse 1967; 1 daughter, 1 son *Clubs:* Old Instonians *Recreations:* music, rugby, skiing, gastronomy

David Fell Esq CB, Second Permanent Secretary, Northern Ireland Office, Stormont Castle, Belfast BT4 3ST *Telephone:* 01232 528146 *Fax:* 01232 528495

FELLOWS, JOHN WALTER Director, Road Programme Directorate, Highways Agency (Executive Agency) Grade: 3

Career: private industry civil engineer 1954-59; civil engineer county boroughs of Dudley 1959-63, Coventry 1963-66, Wolverhampton 1966-69; Department of Transport (DTp) 1969-90: civil engineer 1969-84, assistant secretary highway maintenance division 1984-88, director south east region 1988-90; south east regional director Department of Environment/DTp (regional planning, house and trunk road network) 1990-94; Highways Agency 1994-: director network management and maintenance directorate 1994-45, road programme directorate 1995-

Date of birth: 27 July 1938 *Education/professional qualifications:* Dudley Technical High School; Wolverhampton Polytechnic/Birmingham University, civil engineering and transport planning (MSc 1974); FICE 1990 *Marital status:* married Maureen Lewis 1964; 2 sons *Recreations:* boating, sailing, golf, music, theatre

John W Fellows Esq, Director, Road Programme Directorate, Highways Agency, St Christopher House, Southwark Street, London SE1 0TE *Telephone:* 0171-921 4669 *Fax:* 0171-928 4664

FIGGIS, ANTHONY ST JOHN HOWARD Assistant Under Secretary, Vice-Marshal of the Diplomatic Corps, Foreign and Commonwealth Office Senior grade

Career: HM Diplomatic Service 1962-: Belgrade 1963-65, Bahrain 1968-70, Madrid 1971-74, Bonn 1988-89; assistant under secretary and vice-marshal diplomatic corps 1991-

Date of birth: 12 October 1940 *Education/professional qualifications:* Rugby School; King's College, Cambridge, modern languages (BA 1962) *Honours, decorations:* CMG 1993 *Marital status:* married (Miriam Ellen) Mayella Hardt 1964; 1 daughter, 2 sons *Recreations:* fly-fishing, tennis, piano playing, gardening

Anthony St J H Figgis Esq CMG, Assistant Under Secretary, Foreign and Commonwealth Office, Old Admiralty Building, Whitehall, London, SW1A 2AF *Telephone:* 0171-210 6360 *Fax:* 0171-210 6870

FILKIN, ELIZABETH JILL Adjudicator for the Inland Revenue, Customs and Excise and Contributions Agency

Career: local government and community work 1963-75; social administration lecturer Liverpool University 1975-83; chief executive National Association of Citizens' Advice Bureaux 1983-88; London Docklands Development Corporation 1988-92: assistant chief executive, director of community services; revenue adjudicator Revenue Adjudicator's Office Inland Revenue 1993-95, adjudicator for the Inland Revenue, Customs and Excise and Contributions Agency 1995- *Current non-Whitehall posts:* director Britannia Building Society 1992-, Hay Management Consultants 1992-

Date of birth: 24 November 1940 *Education/professional qualifications:* Clifton High School, Bristol; social administration, Birmingham University (BSocSci 1961) *Marital status:* divorced; 3 daughters *Publications:* The New Villagers (Cass 1968); Caring for Children (Owen Wells 1975) *Recreations:* walking, swimming

Ms Elizabeth J Filkin, Adjudicator's Office for the Inland Revenue, Customs and Excise and Contributions Agency, Haymarket House, 28 Haymarket, London SW1Y 4SP *Telephone:* 0171-930 3965 *Fax:* 0171-930 2298

FINER, Dr ELLIOT GEOFFREY Head of Chemicals and Biotechnology Division, Department of Trade and Industry Grade: 3

Career: research scientist Unilever Research 1968-75; Department of Energy 1975-90: principal, assistant secretary, director for industry and commerce 1983-86, Energy Efficiency Office 1986-90: director-general 1988-90; head of management development group Cabinet Office (Office of Minister for Civil Service) 1990-92; Department of Trade and Industry 1992-: head of enterprise initiative division 1992, of chemicals and biotechnology division 1992-

Date of birth: 30 March 1944 *Education/professional qualifications:* Royal Grammar School, High Wycombe; Cheadle Hulme School; East Barnet Grammar School; St Catharine's College, Cambridge, natural sciences (BA 1965); East Anglia University, nuclear magnetic resonance spectroscopy (MSc 1966, PhD 1968) *Marital status:* married Viviane Kibrit 1970; 2 sons *Publications:* papers in learned journals on nuclear magnetic resonance *Recreations:* home and family, reading, DIY, music

Dr Elliot G Finer, Under Secretary, Department of Trade and Industry, 151 Buckingham Palace Road, London SW1W 9SS *Telephone:* 0171-215 5000 *Fax:* 0171-215 4186

FINLAYSON, NIGEL KENNEDY Chief Executive, Fire Service College (Executive Agency) Grade: 5

Career: Home Office (HO) 1966-78; head of casino licensing Gaming Board for Great Britain 1978-83; HO 1983-: police department 1983-85; passport officer 1985-88; telecommunications directorate 1988-94: finance director 1988-91, chief executive (CE) 1991-94; CE Fire Service College 1994-

Date of birth: 23 June 1947 *Education/professional qualifications:* Acton County School, London *Marital status:* married Kathleen Celia 1978; 2 daughters, 1 son *Recreations:* gardening, sport, grandchildren

Nigel Finlayson Esq, Chief Executive, Fire Service College, Moreton-in-Marsh, Gloucestershire *Telephone:* 01608 652153 *Fax:* 01608 651788

FISHER, DAVID RICHARD Assistant Under Secretary (Systems), Ministry of Defence Grade: 3

Career: Ministry of Defence 1970-: defence secretariats for RN programmes and budget and for defence budget and PES negotiation 1976-83; research fellow Nuffield College, Oxford 1983-84; head of resources and programmes (air) 1984-88; defence counsellor UK delegation to NATO 1988-92; assistant under secretary, systems (establishing requirements for defence equipment projects) 1992-

Date of birth: 13 May 1947 *Education/professional qualifications:* Reading School; St John's College, Oxford, classics, philosophy and ancient history (BA 1969) *Publications:* Morality and the Bomb (Croom Helm 1985) *Recreations:* philosophy, music, theatre, gardening

David R Fisher Esq, Assistant Under Secretary, Ministry of Defence, Whitehall, London SW1A 2HB *Telephone:* 0171-218 2217 *Fax:* 0171-218 6134

FISK, Dr DAVID JOHN Chief Scientist, Air, Climate and Toxic Substances Directorate, Department of the Environment Grade: 3

Career: Department of Environment 1976-: Building Research Establishment 1976-84: head of systems dynamic branch 1976-79, of mechanical and electrical engineering division 1979-84; assistant secretary: environment policy planning and co-ordination 1985-87, air noise policy 1988; deputy chief scientist 1988-89; chief scientist (science of technology) and under secretary air, climate and toxic substances directorate 1988-

Date of birth: 9 January 1947 *Education/professional qualifications:* Stationers' Company's School, London; St John's College, Cambridge, natural sciences (BA 1968, MA); Manchester University, low temperature physics (PhD 1972); Cambridge University (ScD 1983); FCIBS 1983; CEng 1983 *Marital status:* married Anne Thoday 1972; 1 daughter, 1 son *Publications:* Thermal Control of Buildings (Applied Science 1981) *Recreations:* theatre, opera, concerts

Dr David J Fisk, Chief Scientist, Department of the Environment, 43 Marsham Street, London SW1P 3EB *Telephone:* 0171-276 3000

FITCHEW, GEOFFREY EDWARD Chairman and First Commissioner, Building Societies Commission; Chief Registrar of Friendly Societies Grade: 2

Career: HM Treasury (HMT) 1964-73: private secretary to minister of state 1968-69; research fellow Nuffield College, Oxford 1973-74; assistant secretary international finance HMT 1975-78; economics and finance counsellor UK permanent representation to EC, Brussels 1978-80; HMT 1981-86: under secretary EC group/external finance group 1983-86; director-general banking, financial services and company law (DG XV) EC Commission, Brussels 1986-93; head of European secretariat Cabinet Office 1993-94; chairman Building Societies Commission, Chief Registrar of Friendly Societies 1994-

Date of birth: 22 December 1939 *Education/professional qualifications:* Uppingham School; Magdalen College, Oxford, literae humaniores (BA 1962, MA); London School of Economics (MSc Econ 1964) *Honours, decorations:* CMG *Marital status:* married Mary Spillane 1966; 2 sons *Recreations:* tennis, golf

Geoffrey E Fitchew Esq CMG, Chairman, Building Societies Commission, 15 Great Marlborough Street, London W1V 2LL
Telephone: 0171-494 6688 *Fax:* 0171-437 1612

FLAXEN, DAVID WILLIAM Director of Statistics, Department of Transport Grade: 3

Career: Central Statistical Office (CSO), Department of Employment, Inland Revenue 1964-83; adviser UN Development Programme, Swaziland 1971-72; assistant director CSO 1983-89; director of statistics Department of Transport 1989-

Date of birth: 20 April 1941 *Education/professional qualifications:* Manchester Grammar School; Brasenose College, Oxford, physics (BA 1961, MA); University College, London, statistics (Dip Stat 1964) *Marital status:* married Eleanor Easton 1969; 2 daughters *Recreations:* bridge, music, wine, cooking

David W Flaxen Esq, Director of Statistics, Department of Transport, Romney House, 43 Marsham Street, London SW1P 3PY
Telephone: 0171-276 8030 *Fax:* 0171-276 8812

FLESHER, TIM(OTHY) JAMES Assistant Under Secretary, Chief Inspector of Immigration Service, Home Office Grade: 3

Career: Home Office (HO) 1974-82: private secretary (PS) to minister of state 1977-79, principal prisons department 1979-82; PS to prime minister 1982-86; HO 1986-92: head of immigration and refugees division 1986-87, of establishment division 1989-91; secretary to Sir Raymond Lygo's review of prison service management 1991; head of probation service division 1992; director of administration Office for Standards in Education 1992-94; assistant under secretary operations and resources and chief inspector immigration service HO 1994-

Date of birth: 25 July 1949 *Education/professional qualifications:* Haywards Heath Grammar School; Hertford College, Oxford, philosophy, politics and economics (BA 1970) *Marital status:* married Margaret McCormack 1986; 1 daughter *Recreations:* psephology, American football, squash

Tim J Flesher Esq, Assistant Under Secretary, Immigration and Nationality Department, Home Office, Lunar House, Wellesley Road, Croydon, Surrey
Telephone: 0181-760 2907

FLETCHER, PHILIP JOHN Deputy Secretary, Cities and Countryside Group, Department of the Environment Grade: 2

Career: Department of Environment 1973-: structure plans West Midlands 1973-76; central unit and private secretary posts 1976-79; private housebuilding and mortgage finance 1980-82; local government finance 1982-85; director central finance 1986-89; director planning and development control 1990-93; head of PSA Services and deputy secretary (DS) property holdings and central services 1993-94; DS cities and countryside group 1994-

Date of birth: 2 May 1946 *Education/professional qualifications:* Marlborough College; Trinity College, Oxford, history (BA 1967, MA) *Marital status:* married Margaret Anne Boys 1977; 2 daughters (1 deceased) *Recreations:* walking; reader, Church of England

Philip J Fletcher Esq, Deputy Secretary, Department of the Environment, 2 Marsham Street, London SW1P 3EB *Telephone:* 0171-276 3259
Fax: 0171-276 0625

FLYNN, DESMOND JAMES Deputy Inspector General, Insolvency Service (Executive Agency) Grade: 4

Career: Department of Economic Affairs 1968-69; Department of Trade and Industry (DTI) Insolvency Service (IS) companies winding up 1969-71; student 1971-74; IS 1974-: Official Receiver, Birmingham 1974-84: examiner 1974-80, assistant official receiver (AOR) 1980-84; AOR companies winding up, London 1984-86; seconded to DTI trade policy division 1986-88; principal inspector of official receivers 1988-89; deputy inspector general HQ operations (finance, personnel and training; disqualification and prosecution; procurement and common services) 1989-

Date of birth: 21 March 1949 *Education/professional qualifications:* Ealing Boys' Grammar School; University of East Anglia, philosophy, economic history (BA 1974) *Marital status:* married Kumari Ramdewar 1975; 1 daughter, 1 son *Publications:* contributor to Insolvency Law – Theory and Practice (1993) *Clubs:* Royston Golf *Recreations:* golf, reading

Desmond J Flynn Esq, Deputy Inspector General, Insolvency Service, 21 Bloomsbury Street, London WC1B 3QW *Telephone:* 0171-291 6720 *Fax:* 0171-291 6726

FOGDEN, MICHAEL ERNEST GEORGE Chief Executive, Employment Service (Executive Agency) Grade: 3

Career: Ministry of Pensions and National Insurance 1960-66; Ministry of Social Security 1966-68; Department of Health and Social Security 1968-83: private secretary to secretaries of state for social services Richard Crossman and Keith Joseph 1968-70, head of operational computer development 1981-83; Department of Employment 1983-: head of manpower policy division 1983-87, chief executive Employment Service (job centres and unemployment benefit services) 1987-

Date of birth: 30 May 1936 *Education/professional qualifications:* Worthing High School for Boys *Honours, decorations:* CB *Marital status:* married Ann Diamond 1957; 3 sons, 1 daughter *Clubs:* Institute of Directors *Recreations:* gardening, talking, music

Michael E G Fogden Esq CB, Chief Executive, Employment Service, St Vincent House, 30 Orange Street, London WC2H 7HT *Telephone:* 0171-389 1497 *Fax:* 0171-389 1457

FOLEY, Lieutenant General Sir JOHN PAUL Chief of Defence Intelligence, Ministry of Defence

Career: commanding officer 3rd battalion Royal Green Jackets 1978-81; junior division commandant Staff College 1981-82; arms director Ministry of Defence (MoD) 1983-85; student Royal College of Defence Studies 1986; chief of mission to Soviet forces in East Germany 1987-89; deputy chief of defence intelligence MoD 1989-92; commander British Forces Hong Kong 1992-94; chief of defence intelligence MoD 1994- *Current non-Whitehall posts:* colonel commandant The Light Division 1994-; trustee Gurkha Welfare Trust (UK)

Date of birth: 22 April 1939 *Education/professional qualifications:* Bradfield College *Honours, decorations:* MC 1973, OBE 1980, CB 1991, KCB 1994 *Recreations:* tennis, skiing, military history, photography, game shooting

Lieutenant General Sir John Foley KCB OBE MC, Chief of Defence Intelligence, Ministry of Defence, Old War Office Building, Whitehall, London SW1A 2EV *Telephone:* 0171-218 2407 *Fax:* 0171-218 3292

FORD, R I Regional Controller, Inland Revenue North

R I Ford Esq, Controller, Inland Revenue North, 100 Russell Street, Middlesbrough, Cleveland TS1 2RZ *Telephone:* 01642 213214 *Fax:* 01642 221991

FORD, (SYDNEY) JOHN Chief Executive, Driver and Vehicle Licensing Agency (Executive Agency) Grade: 3

Career: Hawker Siddeley 1960-61; Central Electricity Generating Board 1961-63; International Wool 1964-66; British Aluminium Company 1966-82: managing director (MD) 1982; deputy MD British Alcan 1982-85; William Holdings plc 1985-88: UK operations director 1985-87, director Europe 1987-88; director Christian Salvesen Continental Europe Distribution 1989-93; chief executive Driving Standards Agency 1993-94, Driver and Vehicle Licensing Agency 1995-

Date of birth: 23 August 1936 *Education/professional qualifications:* Swansea Grammar School; Bromsgrove High School; University College, Swansea, pure mathematics (BSc 1957, PhD 1960), mathematical statistics (diploma 1958) *Marital status:* married Morag Ann Munro 1990; 2 sons *Recreations:* rugby refereeing and coaching

Dr S John Ford, Chief Executive, Driver and Vehicle Licensing Agency, Longview Road, Morriston, Swansea SA6 7JL *Telephone:* 01792 782341 *Fax:* 01792 783331

FORRESTER, DAVID MICHAEL Under Secretary and Head of Further Education Branch, Department for Education Grade: 3

Career: Department of/for Education [and Science] (DES/DFE) 1967-76: assistant private secretary 1971-72, principal 1972-76; HM Treasury 1976-78; assistant secretary DES 1979-85; Department of Trade and Industry 1985-87; under secretary DES/DFE 1988-: head of schools' funding branch 1988-93, of further education branch 1994-

Date of birth: 22 June 1944 *Education/professional qualifications:* King's College, Cambridge, classics (BA 1966, MA); Kennedy School of Government, Harvard University, USA *Marital status:* married Helen Mary Hyatt; 1 son, 1 daughter *Clubs:* Pretenders *Recreations:* cricket, squash, mountain walking, skiing, opera

David M Forrester Esq, Under Secretary, Department for Education, Sanctuary Buildings, Great Smith Street, London SW1P 3BT *Telephone:* 0171-925 5800 *Fax:* 0171-925 6988

FOSTER, ANDREW WILLIAM Controller, Audit Commission

Career: social worker, London 1966-71; area social services officer 1971-75; assistant director of social services (DSS), Haringey 1975-79; DSS Greenwich 1979-82, North Yorkshire 1982-87; Department of Health 1987-92: general manager Yorkshire regional health authority 1987-91; deputy chief executive NHS management executive performance management directorate 1991-92; controller Audit Commission (external audit of local government and NHS in England and Wales) 1992-

Date of birth: 29 December 1944 *Education/professional qualifications:* Abingdon School; Newcastle Polytechnic, sociology (BSc 1966); London School of Economics, applied social studies (diploma 1968) *Marital status:* married Christine Marquiss 1967; 1 daughter, 1 son *Recreations:* golf, squash, walking, travel, theatre, food, wine

Andrew Foster Esq, Controller of Audit, Audit Commission, Vincent Square, London SW1P 2PN *Telephone:* 0171-828 1212 *Fax:* 0171-976 6187

FOSTER, ANN Director, Scottish Consumer Council

Career: lecturer College for Distributive Trades 1972-78; National Consumer Council 1978-91: consultant 1978-88, food policy adviser 1988-91; director Scottish Consumer Council 1991-

Date of birth: 28 September 1949 *Education/professional qualifications:* Hutchesons' Girls' Grammar School, Glasgow; St Andrew's University, French and medieval history (MA 1970); Reading University, education (MA Educ 1980) *Marital status:* single *Publications:* The Retail Handbook (McGraw Hill 1979); Food Policy and the Consumer (NCC 1989) *Clubs:* Westminster Dining; Western, Glasgow *Recreations:* theatre, skiing, opera, gardening

Mrs Ann Foster, Director, Scottish Consumer Council, Royal Exchange House, 100 Queen Street, Glasgow G1 3DN *Telephone:* 0141-226 5261 *Fax:* 0141-221 0731

FOSTER, RICHARD SCOTT Regional Director, London and South East, Employment Service (Executive Agency) Grade: 4

Career: Department of Employment (DEmp) 1973-79: private secretary to minister of state 1977-79; first secretary Stockholm embassy 1980-83; DEmp 1984-: head of personnel 1984-85; senior management support unit 1986-88; Employment Service (ES) (payment unemployment benefit, management job centres) 1988-: finance and planning director 1988-90; south west regional director Training Commission 1990-92; London and south east regional director 1992- *Current non-Whitehall posts:* director The London Brokerage

Date of birth: 26 March 1950 *Education/professional qualifications:* Devonport High School, Plymouth; Pembroke College, Cambridge, moral sciences (BA 1972, MA) *Marital status:* divorced *Clubs:* Ski Club of Great Britain *Recreations:* skiing, opera, tennis, theatre

Richard S Foster Esq, Regional Director, London and South East, Employment Service, 236 Gray's Inn Road, London WC1X 8HL *Telephone:* 0171-211 4175 *Fax:* 0171-278 3309

FOSTER, ROBERT Head of Aerospace Division, Department of Trade and Industry Grade: 3

Career: electronics and telecommunications industry 1964-77; Department of Trade and Industry (DTI) 1977-91: principal 1977-84, assistant secretary 1984-91; under secretary 1992-: Office of Science and Technology, Cabinet Office 1992-93; head of aerospace division DTI 1993-

Date of birth: 12 May 1943 *Education/professional qualifications:* Oundle School; Corpus Christi College, Cambridge, engineering (BA 1964, MA 1967); CEng; FIEE *Marital status:* married Judy Welsh 1967; 1 son, 1 daughter *Recreations:* squash, tennis, music, reading

Robert Foster Esq, Under Secretary, Department of Trade and Industry, 151 Buckingham Palace Road, London SW1W 9SS *Telephone:* 0171-215 1159 *Fax:* 0171-215 1319

FOTHERBY, GORDON Deputy Solicitor, HM Customs and Excise Grade: 3

Career: army legal corps 1973-77; HM Customs and Excise 1977-: senior principal legal assistant 1986; assistant secretary legal 1986-93: seconded to EC Commission as national expert 1989-91; deputy solicitor 1993-

Date of birth: 15 November 1950 *Education/professional qualifications:* Hull Grammar School; Sheffield University, law (LLB 1972); barrister 1973 *Marital status:* married Victoria Eloise 1974

Gordon Fotherby Esq, Deputy Solicitor, HM Customs and Excise, New King's Beam House, 22 Upper Ground, London SE1 9PJ
Telephone: 0171-865 5124 *Fax:* 0171-865 5022

FOX, Dr ALAN MARTIN Assistant Under Secretary (Quartermaster), Ministry of Defence Grade: 3

Career: Ministry of Aviation 1963-73; Foreign and Commonwealth Office aviation and defence first secretary Paris 1973-75; Ministry of Defence 1975-: head of defence intelligence service secretariat 1984-86; director intelligence resources 1987-88; assistant under secretary (AUS) (ordnance) 1988-92; visiting fellow Harvard University, USA 1992-93; (AUS) (quartermaster) 1994-

Date of birth: 5 July 1938 *Education/professional qualifications:* Bancroft's School, Woodford Green, Essex; Queen Mary College, London, physics (BSc 1959), mathematical physics (PhD 1963) *Recreations:* bridge, chess, computer games, sports spectator

Dr Alan M Fox, Assistant Under Secretary (Quartermaster), Ministry of Defence, Portway, Moxton Road, Andover, Hampshire SP11 8HT *Telephone:* 01264 382572 *Fax:* 01264 382090

FOX, DR (ANTHONY) JOHN Deputy Director and Chief Medical Statistician, Office of Population Censuses and Surveys Grade: 3

Career: Office of Population Censuses and Surveys (OPCS) 1975-79; professor of social statistics City University 1980-88; deputy director and chief medical statistician OPCS 1988-

Date of birth: 25 April 1946 *Education/professional qualifications:* University College, London (BSc); Imperial College, London (PhD, DIC)

Dr A John Fox, Deputy Director and Chief Medical Statistician, Office of Population Censuses and Surveys, St Catherine's House, 10 Kingsway, London WC2B 6JP *Telephone:* 0171-396 2160
Fax: 0171-396 2576

FOX, BRIAN MICHAEL Head of Senior Civil Service Group, Cabinet Office Grade: 3

Career: HM Treasury 1963-: private secretary to Financial Secretary 1967-69; seconded to 3is (Finance for Industry) 1981-82; deputy establishment officer 1983-87; head of defence policy and materiel division 1987-89; principal establishment and finance officer 1989-93; seconded as head of senior public appointments/civil service group Cabinet Office 1993-

Date of birth: 21 September 1944 *Education/professional qualifications:* East Ham Boys' Grammar School *Marital status:* married Maureen Shrimpton 1966; 1 daughter *Recreations:* table tennis, badminton, soccer

Brian M Fox Esq, Head of Senior Civil Service Group, Cabinet Office, 70 Whitehall, London SW1A 2AS *Telephone:* 0171-270 3000
Fax: 0171-270 6116

FRANCE, Sir CHRISTOPHER WALTER Staff Counsellor, Security and Intelligence Services Grade: 1

Career: HM Treasury 1959-84: various posts including private secretary to Chancellors of Exchequer 1959-80, seconded to Electricity Council 1980-81, to Ministry of Defence (MoD) 1981-84; Department of Health [and Social Security] 1984-92: deputy secretary 1984-86, second permanent secretary (PS) social security 1986-87, first PS 1987-88, PS 1988-92; PS MoD 1992-94; staff counsellor Security and Intelligence Services 1995-

Date of birth: 2 April 1934 *Education/professional qualifications:* East Ham Grammar School, London; New College, Oxford, philosophy, politics and economics (BA 1957) and education (Dip Ed 1958); CDipAF 1981 *Honours, decorations:* CB 1984, KCB 1989, GCB 1994 *Recreations:* keeping the house up and the garden down

Sir Christopher France GCB, c/o Cabinet Office, 70 Whitehall, London SW1A 2AS
Telephone: 0171-270 3000

FRANCE, ELIZABETH IRENE Data Protection Registrar Grade: 3

Career: Home Office 1971-94: principal 1977-86; assistant secretary 1986-94: head of crime prevention and police operations division 1986-88, of criminal justice conferences unit 1989, of information systems and pay services division 1990-94; registrar Office of Data Protection 1994-

Date of birth: 1 February 1950 *Education/professional qualifications:* Beauchamp School, Leicestershire; University College of Wales, Aberystwyth, political science (BScEcon 1971) *Marital status:* married Dr Michael William 1971; 2 sons, 1 daughter *Recreations:* family, cooking, skiing

Mrs Elizabeth I France, Registrar, Office of the Data Protection Registrar, Wycliffe House, Water Lane, Wilmslow, Cheshire SK9 5AF
Telephone: 01625 535711 *Fax:* 01625 524510

FRASER, ANDREW JOHN Chief Executive, Invest in Britain Bureau, Department of Trade and Industry Grade: 3

Career: advertising industry 1972-94: director of business development Saatchi and Saatchi 1980-92, managing director Europe Dentsu cdp europe 1992-94; chief executive Invest in Britain Bureau Department of Trade and Industry 1994-

Date of birth: 23 October 1950 *Education/professional qualifications:* Harvard School, California, USA; Sussex University, history (BA 1972) *Marital status:* divorced; 2 daughters *Clubs:* Marylebone Cricket, Royal Automobile *Recreations:* golf, tennis, wine, photography

Andrew Fraser Esq, Chief Executive, Invest in Britain Bureau, Department of Trade and Industry, Kingsgate House, 66-74 Victoria Street, London SW1E 6SW *Telephone:* 0171-215 8682 *Fax:* 0171-215 8451

FRASER, MAURICE Special Adviser to Foreign Secretary

Career: Conservative Research Department 1984-89: home affairs 1984-85, political desk 1985-86, head of political section 1986-87, assistant director 1987-89; special adviser to Foreign Secretaries Sir Geoffrey Howe March-July 1989, John Major July-October 1989, Douglas Hurd 1989-

Date of birth: 2 March 1960 *Education/professional qualifications:* French Lycée, London; London School of Economics, government and history (BSc Econ 1981) *Marital status:* married Louise Nicolette Le Pelley 1989; 1 son *Recreations:* history, philosophy, fine arts, tennis

Maurice Fraser Esq, Special Adviser, Foreign and Commonwealth Office, King Charles Street, London SW1A 2AL *Telephone:* 0171-270 2117 *Fax:* 0171-270 2111

FREEMAN, Dr PAUL ILLIFE Controller and Chief Executive, HM Stationery Office Grade: 2

Career: National Physical Laboratory 1964-74; Department of Industry 1974-77; director Computer Aided Design Centre 1977-83; director National Engineering Laboratory 1980-83; director Central Computer and Telecommunications Agency HM Treasury 1983-88; controller and chief executive HM Stationery Office 1989-

Date of birth: 11 July 1935 *Education/professional qualifications:* Manchester University, chemistry (BSc 1956, PhD 1959) *Honours, decorations:* CB 1992 *Marital status:* married Enid 1959; 1 son, 1 daughter *Publications:* scientific papers *Recreations:* reading, walking, gardening

Dr Paul I Freeman CB, Controller and Chief Executive, HMSO, St Crispins, Duke Street, Norwich NR3 1PD *Telephone:* 01603 695047 *Fax:* 01603 695045

FREEMAN, PETER DAVID MARK Principal Establishment Officer, Overseas Development Administration Grade: 3

Career: Overseas Development Administration (ODA) 1970-75: assistant private secretary to minister 1973-75; office of UK executive director World Bank 1975-78; ODA 1978-80; first secretary, aid, British high commission Harare 1980-83; ODA 1984-: head of EC department 1984-88, of central and southern Africa department 1988-90, of aid policy department 1990-91, of international division 1991-93, of personnel, organisation and services division 1993-

Date of birth: 8 December 1947 *Education/professional qualifications:* Oxford University, philosophy, politics and economics (BA 1969); Toronto University, Canada, political science (MA 1970) *Marital status:* married

Peter D M Freeman Esq, Principal Establishment Officer, Overseas Development Administration, 94 Victoria Street, London SW1E 5JL *Telephone:* 0171-917 7000 *Fax:* 0171-917 0769

FRERE, Vice-Admiral Sir TOBY Chief of Fleet Support, Ministry of Defence

Career: Royal Navy 1957-: director general fleet support 1988-91; flag officer submarines and commander submarines Eastern Atlantic 1991-94; chief of fleet support Ministry of Defence 1994-

Date of birth: 4 June 1938 *Education/professional qualifications:* Eton College; Britannia Royal Naval College; Royal College of Defence Studies *Honours, decorations:* KCB *Recreations:* sailing, walking

Vice-Admiral Sir Toby Frere KCB, Chief of Fleet Support, Ministry of Defence, Quay House, The Ambury, Bath BA1 5AB *Telephone:* 01225 472087

FRIEL, J D Regional Procurator Fiscal, North Strathclyde Region, Crown Office Grade: 4

Career: North Strathclyde regional procurator fiscal 1991-

J D Friel Esq, Regional Procurator Fiscal, North Strathclyde Region, Crown Office, 106 Renfrew Road, Paisley PA3 4DX *Telephone:* 0141-887 5225 *Fax:* 0141-887 6172

FRIES, RICHARD JAMES Chief Commissioner, Charity Commission Grade: 3

Career: Home Office 1965-92: head of equal opportunities and general department 1987-91; under secretary broadcasting and miscellaneous department 1991-92; Department of National Heritage 1992; chief commissioner Charity Commission 1992-

Date of birth: 7 July 1940 *Education/professional qualifications:* King's College, Cambridge, moral sciences (BA 1962) *Marital status:* married Carole Anne Buick 1970; 2 daughters, 1 son *Recreations:* music, chess

Richard J Fries Esq, Chief Commissioner, Charity Commission, 57 Haymarket, London SW1Y 4QX
Telephone: 0171-210 4465 *Fax:* 0171-210 4604

FRIZZELL, EDWARD WILLIAM Chief Executive, Scottish Prison Service (Executive Agency) Grade: 3

Career: Scottish Milk Marketing Board 1968-73; Scottish Council (development and industry) 1973-76; principal Scottish Office (SO) Department of Agriculture and Fisheries 1976-78; first secretary (fisheries) UK permanent representation to EC, Brussels 1978-82; SO 1982-: assistant secretary (AS) higher education Scottish Education Department 1982-86, AS finance division 1986-89; director Locate in Scotland, Industry Department 1989-91; chief executive Scottish Prison Service, Home and Health Department 1991- *Current non-Whitehall posts:* member board Quality Scotland Foundation

Date of birth: 4 May 1946 *Education/professional qualifications:* Paisley Grammar School; Glasgow University, history and political economy (MA 1968) *Marital status:* married Moira Calderwood 1969; 1 daughter, 2 sons *Clubs:* Mortonhall Golf, Edinburgh *Recreations:* mountain biking, running, painting, sculpture

Edward W Frizzell Esq, Chief Executive, Scottish Prison Service, Calton House, 5 Redheughs Rigg, Edinburgh EH12 9HW
Telephone: 0131-244 8522 *Fax:* 0131-244 8774

G

GADSBY, Brigadier ANDREW CHARLES IAN Director, Royal Armoured Corps, Ministry of Defence

Career: army service 1970-: 2 Royal Tank Regiment (2RTR) regimental posts 1970-79, 1982-85; student 1980-81, 1986; directing staff Royal Military College of Science 1987-88; commanding officer 2RTR 1988-91; student 1991; commander combat manoeuvre simulation centre, Germany 1991-94, Royal Armoured Corps (RAC) centre 1994-95; director RAC 1995-

Date of birth: 8 September 1950 *Education/professional qualifications:* Wellington School, Somerset; Royal Military Academy Sandhurst (commission 1970); Royal Military College of Science (psc(w) 1981); Army Staff College (psc 1982); Joint Service Defence College (jsdc 1987); higher command and staff course (HCSC 1991) *Recreations:* golf, aviation

Brigadier Andrew C I Gadsby, Director, Royal Armoured Corps, HQ RAC, Bovington Camp, Wareham, Dorset BH20 6JA *Telephone:* 01929 403301 *Fax:* 01929 403638

GAHAGAN, MICHAEL B Director, Cities and Countryside Policy Directorate, Department of the Environment Grade: 3

Career: civil service 1966-: north west and south east regional offices Department of Economic Affairs; Ministry of Housing and Local Government; Department of the Environment 1991-: director inner cities directorate 1991-94, cities and countryside directorate 1994-

Date of birth: 24 March 1943 *Education/professional qualifications:* St Mary's College, Southampton; Manchester University: ARICS *Marital status:* married; 2 sons *Recreations:* soccer, squash, bridge, sailing

Michael Gahagan Esq, Director, Cities and Countryside Policy Directorate, Department of the Environment, 2 Marsham Street, London SW1P 3EB *Telephone:* 0171-276 4473

GALLACHER, T N HM Senior Chief Inspector of Schools, Scottish Office Education Department Grade: 3

T N Gallacher Esq, HM Senior Chief Inspector of Schools, Scottish Office Education Department, New St Andrew's House, Edinburgh EH1 3S9 *Telephone:* 0131-244 4560

GALLAGHER, EDWARD PATRICK Chief Executive, National Rivers Authority

Career: Vauxhall Motors 1963-68; Sandoz Products Ltd 1968-70; Robinson Willey Ltd 1970-71; Black and Decker 1978-86: director of marketing services 1978-79, of service and distribution 1979-81, of business analysis 1981-83, of market and product development 1983-86; Amersham International 1986-92: director of corporate development 1986-88, divisional chief executive 1988-90, manufacturing director 1990-92; chief executive National Rivers Authority (water resources, quality, flood defence, fisheries, recreation, conservation, navigation) 1992-

Date of birth: 4 August 1944 *Education/professional qualifications:* Dunstable Grammar School; Sheffield University, engineering (BSc 1966); CEng 1976; FIWEM, FIEE *Marital status:* married Helen Wilkinson 1969; 2 sons *Recreations:* golf, tennis, theatre, rambling, guitar

Edward P Gallagher Esq, Chief Executive, National Rivers Authority, 30-34 Albert Embankment, London SE1 7TL *Telephone:* 0171-820 0101 *Fax:* 0171-820 1786

GALSWORTHY, ANTHONY CHARLES Chief of Assessments Staff, Joint Intelligence Organisation, Cabinet Office Grade: 3

Career: HM diplomatic service 1966-: third secretary Foreign and Commonwealth Office, London (FCO) 1966-67, Hong Kong 1967-70, Peking (later second secretary (SS) and consul) 1970-72; FCO 1972-77: SS, first secretary (FS); FS Rome 1977-81; FS, counsellor Peking 1981-84; FCO 1984-89: counsellor and head of Hong Kong department 1984-86, principal private secretary to secretary of state 1986-88, seconded to Royal Institute of International Affairs 1988-89; senior British representative Sino-British Joint Liaison Group, Hong Kong 1989-93; chief of assessments staff, Joint Intelligence Organisation, Cabinet Office 1993-

Date of birth: 20 December 1944 *Education/professional qualifications:* St Paul's School, London; Corpus Christi College, Cambridge, classics (BA 1966, MA 1973) *Honours, decorations:* CMG 1985 *Marital status:* married Jan Dawson-Grove 1970; 1 son, 1 daughter *Recreations:* wildlife, ornithology

Anthony C Galsworthy Esq CMG, Chief of Assessments Staff, Joint Intelligence Organisation, Cabinet Office, 70 Whitehall, London SW1A 2AS *Telephone:* 0171-270 3000 *Fax:* 0171-930 1419

GANT, JOHN Director of Personnel, Inland Revenue Grade: 3

Career: Inland Revenue 1966-: head officer adviser 1974-77; district inspector London 1977-81; group controller North London 1981-83; assistant director of operations (DO) 1983-88; regional controller eastern counties 1988-90; deputy DO 1990-92; director of personnel 1992-

Date of birth: 25 February 1944 *Education/professional qualifications:* King Edward VI Grammar School, Chelmsford; Newcastle University, French and German (BA 1966) *Marital status:* married Annette Cobb 1967; 2 sons *Recreations:* music, theatre, travel, fellwalking

John Gant Esq, Director of Personnel, Inland Revenue, Somerset House, Strand, London WC2 1LB *Telephone:* 0171-438 6780 *Fax:* 0171-438 7186

GARDEN, Air Marshal Sir TIMOTHY Commandant, Royal College of Defence Studies, Ministry of Defence

Career: Royal Air Force (RAF): flying appointments 1965-75; Ministry of Defence (MoD) staff officer 1976-78; squadron commander RAF 50 squadron 1979-81; director of defence studies RAF 1982-85; station commander RAF Odiham, Hampshire 1985-87; MoD 1987-: assistant director defence programmes 1987-88; director air force staff duties 1988-91, assistant chief of air staff 1991-2; assistant chief of defence staff (programmes) 1992-94; commandant Royal College of Defence Studies 1994-

Date of birth: 23 April 1944 *Education/professional qualifications:* King's School, Worcester; St Catherine's College, Oxford, physics (BA 1965, MA); Magdalene College, Cambridge, international relations (MPhil 1982) *Honours, decorations:* CB 1992; honorary fellow St Catherine's College, Oxford; KCB 1994 *Publications:* Can Deterrence Last? (Buchan and Enright 1984); The Technology Trap (Brasseys 1989) *Recreations:* bridge, computing, reading, windsurfing

Air Marshal Sir Timothy Garden KCB, Commandant, Royal College of Defence Studies, Seaford House, Belgrave Square, London SW1X 8NS *Telephone:* 0171-915 4830 *Fax:* 0171-915 4999

GARLAND, PETER Deputy Director of Finance, NHS Executive, Department of Health Grade: 3

Career: Department of Health: deputy director of performance management -1995, of finance NHS executive 1995-

Date of birth: 21 September 1946 *Education/professional qualifications:* Manchester University, history (BA) *Marital status:* married Janet Prescott 1979; 3 daughters

P Garland Esq, Director of Finance, NHS Management Executive, Department of Health, Quarry House, Quarry Hill, Leeds LS2 7US *Telephone:* 01132 545174

GATENBY, DAVID Chief Executive, UK Passport Agency (Executive Agency) Grade: 5

Career: Department of [Health and] Social Security 1962-94: group manager 1985-87; information technology project manager 1987-90; area manager Benefits Agency 1990-92; director information services and business planning Contributions Agency 1992-94; chief executive UK Passport Agency 1994-

Date of birth: 10 December 1942 *Education/professional qualifications:* Salt Grammar School, Shipley, Yorkshire *Marital status:* married Margaret 1965; 3 sons *Recreations:* jogging, travel, motor sports

David Gatenby Esq, Chief Executive, United Kingdom Passport Agency, Clive House, 70 Petty France, London SW1H 9HD
Telephone: 0171-271 8500 *Fax:* 0171-271 8824

GEORGE, Dr A M Deputy Chief Medical Officer, Health Professionals Group, Welsh Office Grade: 4

Dr A M George, Deputy Chief Medical Officer, Health Professionals Group, Welsh Office, Cathays Park, Cardiff CF1 3NQ *Telephone:* 01222 825396

GEORGE, (EDWARD) EDDIE ALAN JOHN Governor, Bank of England

Career: Bank of England 1962-: seconded to Moscow State University as student 1964-65; East European affairs 1965-66; seconded as economist to Bank of International Settlements, Basle, Switzerland 1966-69, as personal assistant to chairman of deputies International Monetary Fund committee on international monetary reform 1972-74; adviser overseas department 1974-77; deputy chief cashier banking department 1977-80; assistant director gilt-edged division 1980-82; executive director monetary policy, market operations and market supervision 1982-90; deputy governor 1990-93; governor 1993-

Date of birth: 11 September 1938 *Education/professional qualifications:* Dulwich College, London; Emmanuel College, Cambridge, economics (BA 1962, MA); Moscow State University, Russian *Marital status:* married (Clarice) Vanessa Williams 1962; 2 daughters, 1 son *Recreations:* family, sailing, bridge

Eddie A J George Esq, Governor, Bank of England, Threadneedle Street, London EC2R 8AH *Telephone:* 0171-601 4444 *Fax:* 0171-601 4771

GERRIE, IAN STEWART North West Regional Controller, Inland Revenue Grade: 4

Career: Inland Revenue: special office Edinburgh 1980-84, Solihull 1984-88; controller claims branch 1988-91; assistant controller Scotland 1991-92; performance management project manager 1992-93; controller north west 1993-

Date of birth: 1 December 1945 *Education/professional qualifications:* Ross High School, Tranent *Marital status:* married Dorothy Baillie 1968; 2 sons *Recreations:* sport, music, theatre

I S Gerrie Esq, Controller, Inland Revenue North West, The Triad, Stanley Road, Bootle, Merseyside L20 3PD *Telephone:* 0151-922 4055 *Fax:* 0151-944 2578

GIBBINGS, Sir PETER WALTER Chairman, Radio Authority

Career: army national service 1951-52; Associated Newspapers 1956-60; The Observer 1960-67: deputy manager and director 1965-67; Guardian Newspapers 1967-88: managing director 1967-73, chair 1973-88; director Press Association 1982-88: chair 1986-87, Reuters 1984-88, The Economist 1987-; Anglia Television 1988-94: chair 1988-94; chair Radio Authority 1995-

Date of birth: 25 March 1929 *Education/professional qualifications:* Rugby School; Wadham College, Oxford; Middle Temple (barrister 1953) *Honours, decorations:* Kt 1989 *Marital status:* married Elspeth Macintosh: 2 daughters; Louise Lambert: 1 son

Sir Peter Gibbings, Chairman, Radio Authority, Holbrook House, 14 Great Queen Street, London WC2B 5DG *Telephone:* 0171-430 2724

GIBBONS, Dr JOHN ERNEST Director of Building and Chief Architect, Scottish Office Environment Department Grade: 3

Career: private practice architect 1962-65; lecturer Birmingham School of Architecture and Aston University 1964-66; Edinburgh University 1967-72: research fellow 1967-69, lecturer 1967-72; Scottish Office Environment Department 1972-: assistant director building directorate 1978-82, deputy director and deputy chief architect (CA) 1982-84, director of building and CA 1984-

Date of birth: 20 April 1940 *Education/professional qualifications:* Oldbury Grammar School; Birmingham School of Architecture; Edinburgh University (PhD 1970); DipArch 1962; DipTP 1964; ARIBA 1964; ARIAS 1966; FSA 1970 *Marital status:* married Patricia Mitchell 1962; 1 son, 2 daughters *Clubs:* New, Edinburgh *Recreations:* photography, the arts

Dr John E Gibbons, Director of Building and Chief Architect, Scottish Office Environment Department, New St Andrew's House, Edinburgh EH1 3SY *Telephone:* 0131-244 4149 *Fax:* 0131-244 4785

GIEVE, (EDWARD) JOHN WATSON Under Secretary, Budget and Public Finances Directorate, HM Treasury Grade: 3

Career: Department of Employment 1974-78; HM Treasury 1978-: 3i (Finance for Industry) 1984-86; general expenditure policy 1987-88; press secretary 1988-89; principal private secretary to Chancellor of Exchequer 1989-91; under secretary banking group 1991-94, general expenditure policy 1994-95, deputy director budget and public finances directorate 1995-

Date of birth: 20 February 1950 *Education/professional qualifications:* Charterhouse; New College, Oxford, philosophy, politics and economics (BA 1971); philosophy (BPhil 1973) *Marital status:* married Katherine Vereker 1972; 2 sons

E John W Gieve, Under Secretary, HM Treasury, Parliament Street, London SW1P 3AG *Telephone:* 0171-270 4499 *Fax:* 0171-270 4980

GLASGOW, EDWIN JOHN Chairman, Financial Reporting Review Panel

Career: barrister 1969-; chairman Financial Reporting Review Panel (enforcement of proper accounting procedures by large companies) 1992-

Date of birth: 3 August 1945 *Education/professional qualifications:* St Joseph's College, Ipswich; University College, London, law (LLB 1966); Gray's Inn (barrister 1969) *Honours, decorations:* QC 1987 *Marital status:* married Janet Coleman 1967; 1 son, 1 daughter *Clubs:* Royal Automobile

Edwin J Glasgow Esq QC, Chairman, Financial Reporting Review Panel, Holborn Hall, 100 Gray's Inn Road, London WC1X 8AL *Telephone:* 0171-404 8818 *Fax:* 0171-404 1276

GLASS, NORMAN JEFFREY Deputy Director, Spending Directorate, HM Treasury Grade: 3

Career: economist Shell Mex and BP 1969-70, Economic Models Ltd 1970-72; economics lecturer Newcastle University 1972-74; economic adviser (EA) Department of Health and Social Security (DHSS) 1975-77, HM Treasury 1977-79, National Audit Office 1979-81; senior EA DHSS 1981-86; assistant secretary Department of Health 1986-89; director analytical services Department of Social Security 1989-92; chief economist, director of housing and urban monitoring and analysis/central management and analysis unit Department of Environment 1992-95; deputy director spending directorate HM Treasury 1995- *Current non-Whitehall posts:* member council Economic and Social Research Council 1992-; director CV Clothing plc

Date of birth: 31 May 1946 *Education/professional qualifications:* Stratford College, Dublin; Dublin University, economics and political science (BA 1968); Amsterdam University, Netherlands, economics (postgraduate diploma 1969) *Marital status:* married Marie-Anne Verger 1974; 1 daughter, 1 son *Recreations:* music, languages, gardening

Norman J Glass Esq, Deputy Director, Spending Directorate, HM Treasury, Parliament Street, London SW1P 3AG *Telephone:* 0171-270 3000

GLENCROSS, DAVID Chief Executive, Independent Television Commission

Career: producer BBC 1958-70; Independent Broadcasting Authority/Television Commission 1970-: senior television programme officer 1970-76; head of programme services 1976-77; deputy director of television 1977-83; director of television 1983-90; chief executive 1990-

Date of birth: 3 March 1936 *Education/professional qualifications:* Salford Grammar School; Trinity College, Cambridge, geography and history (BA 1958) *Honours, decorations:* CBE *Marital status:* married Elizabeth Louise Richardson 1965; 1 daughter *Recreations:* music, reading, radio, walking

David Glencross Esq CBE, Chief Executive, Independent Television Commission, 33 Foley Street, London W1P 7LB *Telephone:* 0171-255 3000 *Fax:* 0171-306 7800

GOBLE, JOHN F Deputy Chairman, Panel on Takeovers and Mergers

Career: solicitor Herbert Smith 1953-; director British Telecom 1983-91, Wren Underwriting Agencies 1988-91; deputy chairman Panel on Takeovers and Mergers 1989-

Date of birth: 1 April 1925 *Education/professional qualifications:* Brasenose College, Oxford

John F Goble Esq, Deputy Chairman, Panel on Takeovers and Mergers, 226 Stock Exchange Building, London EC2P 2JX *Telephone:* 0171-382 9026

GODFREY, Dr MALCOLM PAUL WESTON **Chairman, Public Health Laboratory Service Board**

Career: hospital posts 1950-60; Medical Research Council (MRC) 1960-74; dean Royal Postgraduate Medical School, London 1974-83; second secretary MRC 1983-88; chair Public Health Laboratory Service Board 1989-

Date of birth: 11 August 1926 *Education/professional qualifications:* Hertford Grammar School; King's College, London; King's College Hospital medical school (MB BS 1950); FRCP 1972 *Honours, decorations:* CBE 1986; QHP 1987-90 *Marital status:* married Barbara Goldstein 1955; 1 son, 2 daughters *Publications:* various in medical and scientific journals *Clubs:* Royal Society of Medicine *Recreations:* theatre, walking

Dr Malcolm P W Godfrey, Chairman, Public Health Laboratory Service Board, 61 Colindale Avenue, London NW9 5DF *Telephone:* 0181-200 1295 *Fax:* 0181-200 8130

GODLEY, Professor WYNNE **Member, Forecasting Panel, HM Treasury**

Career: HM Treasury (HMT) 1956-70; official adviser select committee on public expenditure 1971-73; department of applied economics Cambridge University 1970-: director 1970-85, acting director 1985-87, professor of applied economics 1980-; member HMT forecasting panel 1992-

Date of birth: 2 September 1926

Professor Wynne Godley, Member, Forecasting Panel, HM Treasury, c/o Department of Applied Economics, Cambridge University, Sidgwick Avenue, Cambridge CB3 9DD *Telephone:* 01223 337733

GOLDMAN, (AN)TONY JOHN **Under Secretary, International Aviation, Department of Transport** Grade: 3

Career: International Computers Ltd 1961-73; Department of the Environment 1973-76; Department of Transport 1976-: private secretary to secretary of state 1976-78; assistant secretary 1977-84; seconded to HM Treasury 1981-83; under secretary 1984-: public transport 1984-89, civil aviation policy 1989-93, international aviation 1993-

Date of birth: 28 February 1940 *Education/professional qualifications:* Marlborough College; Peterhouse, Cambridge, mathematics (BA 1961) and computer science (diploma 1961) *Marital status:* married Anne Rosemary Lane 1964; 3 sons *Recreations:* music, sailing

A J Goldman Esq, Under Secretary, Department of Transport, 2 Marsham Street, London SW1P 3EB *Telephone:* 0171-276 5399 *Fax:* 0171-276 5390

GOODENOUGH, ANTHONY MICHAEL **Assistant Under Secretary, Foreign and Commonwealth Office** Grade: DS3

Career: HM Diplomatic Service/Foreign [and Commonwealth] Office, London (FCO) 1964-: FCO 1964-67; Athens 1967-71; FCO 1971-74: private secretary to parliamentary under secretary 1971, to minister of state 1972-74; Paris 1974-77; FCO 1977-80; seconded to Cabinet Office 1980-82; head of chancery Islamabad 1982-86; counsellor FCO 1986-89; high commissioner to Ghana, accredited ambassador to Togo 1989-92; assistant under secretary Africa and Commonwealth FCO 1992-

Date of birth: 5 July 1941 *Education/professional qualifications:* Wellington College; New College, Oxford, modern history (BA 1963, MA) *Honours, decorations:* CMG 1990 *Marital status:* married Veronica Pender-Cudlip 1967; 1 daughter, 2 sons *Clubs:* United Oxford and Cambridge University

Anthony M Goodenough Esq CMG, Assistant Under Secretary, Foreign and Commonwealth Office, King Charles Street, London SW1A 2AH *Telephone:* 0171-270 2202 *Fax:* 0171-270 2946

GOODFELLOW, MIKE **Commercial Director, Defence Evaluation and Research Agency (Executive Agency)**

Mike Goodfellow Esq, Commercial Director, Defence Evaluation and Research Agency, Farnborough, Hampshire GU14 6TD *Telephone:* 01252 394500

GOODSON, Rear Admiral FREDERICK BRIAN **Assistant Chief of Defence Staff (Logistics), Ministry of Defence**

Career: Royal Navy 1958-: commander-in-chief, naval home command 1983-85; director, naval logistic planning 1985-87; commodore commanding HMS Centurion 1988-91, Royal College of Defence Studies 1992; rear admiral 1993-; assistant chief of defence staff (logistics) 1993-

Date of birth: 21 May 1938 *Education/professional qualifications:* Campbell College *Honours, decorations:* OBE 1982 *Recreations:* offshore sailing, squash, country pursuits

Rear Admiral F B Goodson OBE, Assistant Chief of Defence Staff (Logistics), Ministry of Defence, Main Building, Whitehall, London SW1A 2HB *Telephone:* 0171-218 3634

GORDON, J A **Director-General Air Systems 1, Ministry of Defence** Grade: 3

J A Gordon Esq, Director-General Air Systems 1, Ministry of Defence, Lacon House, Theobald's Road, London W1X 8RY *Telephone:* 0171-305 5555

GORDON, ROBERT **Director of Administrative Services, Central Services Division, Scottish Office** Grade: 3

Career: Scottish Office 1973-: principal town and country planning, transport Scottish Development Department 1979-85; principal private secretary to secretary of state 1985-87; assistant secretary 1987-91: department of agriculture and fisheries 1987-90; head of management and organisation 1990-91; director of administrative services 1991- *Current non-Whitehall posts:* warden Incorporation of Goldsmiths of the City of Edinburgh

Date of birth: 7 November 1950 *Education/professional qualifications:* The Gordon Schools, Huntly, Aberdeenshire; Aberdeen University, Italian studies (MA 1973) *Marital status:* married Joyce Cordiner 1976; 2 daughters, 2 sons *Recreations:* children, churches, chainsaws

Robert Gordon Esq, Director of Administrative Services, Central Services Division, Scottish Office, James Craig Walk, Edinburgh EH1 3BA *Telephone:* 0131-244 3768 *Fax:* 0131-244 3891

GOUGH, (CHARLES) BRANDON **Chairman, Higher Education Funding Council for England**

Career: chartered accountant 1964-: Coopers and Lybrand 1964-94: chairman 1983-94; chairman Higher Education Funding Council for England 1993- *Current non-Whitehall posts:* member Financial Reporting Council; chairman Doctors' and Dentists' Pay Review Body; director De La Rue plc 1994-, S G Warburg Group plc 1994-

Date of birth: 8 October 1937 *Education/professional qualifications:* Douai School, Berkshire; Jesus College, Cambridge, natural sciences, law (BA 1961,

MA); CA 1964, FCA *Honours, decorations:* Lloyd's Silver Medal 1986 *Marital status:* married Sarah Smith 1961; 2 daughters, 1 son *Recreations:* music, gardening

C Brandon Gough Esq, Chairman, Higher Education Funding Council for England, Northavon House, Coldharbour Lane, Bristol BS16 1QD *Telephone:* 01179 317317 *Fax:* 01179 317203

GOULD, DAVID JOHN Under Secretary, Defence and Overseas Secretariat, Cabinet Office Grade: 3

Career: Ministry of Defence 1973-: naval weapons department 1973-75; naval and NATO secretariat 1975-78; principal 1978-87: assistant head of branch managing finance for military aircraft 1978-80, NATO Defence College 1980-81, planning RAF forward programme 1981-83, seconded to UK delegation to NATO 1983-87; assistant secretary 1987-91; assistant under secretary 1991-: supply and organisation, air 1991-92, policy 1993; defence and overseas secretariat Cabinet Office 1993-

Date of birth: 9 April 1949 *Education/professional qualifications:* West Buckland School, Barnstaple; Sussex University, French and European Studies (BA 1971) *Marital status:* married Christiane Clara Krieger 1973; 1 daughter, 2 sons *Recreations:* music, especially opera and lieder; fitness; watching rugby

David J Gould Esq, Under Secretary, Cabinet Office, 70 Whitehall, London SW1A 2AS *Telephone:* 0171-270 0050 *Fax:* 0171-270 0416

GOYDER, DANIEL GEORGE Deputy Chairman, Monopolies and Mergers Commission

Career: private practice assistant solicitor/partner 1964-83; part-time law lecturer Essex University 1981-91; consultant private practice solicitor 1983-; Monopolies and Mergers Commission 1980-: member 1980-, deputy chairman 1991- *Current non-Whitehall posts:* consultant Birkett Westhorp and Long (solicitors) 1989-; visiting professor King's College, London 1991-, Essex University 1991-

Date of birth: 26 August 1938 *Education/professional qualifications:* Rugby School; Trinity College, Cambridge, law (BA 1959, LLB 1960); Harvard Law School, USA (LLM 1963) *Marital status:* married Jean Mary Dohoo 1962; 2 daughters, 2 sons *Publications:* co-author The Antitrust Laws of the USA (Cambridge University Press, 3rd ed 1981); EC Competition Law (Oxford University Press, 2nd ed 1992) *Clubs:* Law Society; Royal Society of Arts; Ipswich and Suffolk *Recreations:* choral singing, tennis

Daniel G Goyder Esq, Deputy Chairman, Monopolies and Mergers Commission, New Court, 48 Carey Street, London WC2A 2JT *Telephone:* 0171-324 1440 *Fax:* 0171-324 1400

GRAHAM, JOHN STRATHIE Under Secretary, Development Planning and Local Government, Scottish Office Environment Department Grade: 3

Career: Scottish Office 1972-: private secretary (PS) to minister of state 1975-76; Scottish economic planning department 1976-83; PS to secretary of state 1983-85; head of planning division 1985-90, of central finance division 1990-91; under secretary development planning and local government group Environment Department 1991-

Date of birth: 27 May 1950 *Education/professional qualifications:* Edinburgh Academy; Corpus Christi College, Oxford, literae humaniores (BA 1972)

Marital status: married Anne Stenhouse 1979; 1 daughter, 2 sons
Recreations: music, exploring Scotland

John S Graham Esq, Under Secretary, Scottish Office Environment Department, New St Andrew's House, Edinburgh EH1 3TG
Telephone: 0131-244 4722 *Fax:* 0131-244 4785

GRAHAM, Captain WADE STUART Chief Executive, Naval Aircraft Repair Organisation Defence Agency (Executive Agency)

Career: Royal Navy (RN) 1960-: Fleet Air Arm Squadrons, support appointments 1970-84; Ministry of Defence procurement executive 1984-87; director general aircraft (navy) 1987-91; production director RN aircraft yard Fleetlands 1991-94; chief executive Naval Air Repair Organisation 1994-

Date of birth: 17 June 1944 *Education/professional qualifications:* Chingford Secondary Modern School; RN College, Greenwich, electrical engineering; MIERE 1970; CEng 1983 *Marital status:* married Christine Mary 1965; 1 son, 2 daughters

Captain Wade Graham RN, Chief Executive, Naval Air Repair Organisation, RNAY Fleetlands, Gosport, Hampshire PO13 0AW
Telephone: 01329 826225 *Fax:* 01329 827193

GRANATT, (MICHAEL) MIKE STEPHEN DREESE Director of Information, Home Office Grade: 4

Career: journalist 1973-79; Employment Gazette Department of Employment 1979-81; press officer (PO) Home Office 1981-83; senior/chief PO/head of information Department of Energy 1983-89; director of public affairs and internal communication Metropolitan Police 1989-92; director of information ([DI])/of communication Department of Environment 1992-95; DI Home Office 1995-

Date of birth: 27 April 1950 *Education/professional qualifications:* Westminster City School; Queen Mary College, London *Marital status:* married Jane Veronica 1974; 1 son, 3 daughters *Clubs:* Royal Society of Arts *Recreations:* photography, short-wave radio, science fiction

Mike S D Granatt Esq, Director of Information, Home Office, Queen Anne's Gate, London SW1H 9AT *Telephone:* 0171-273 3757 *Fax:* 0171-273 4660

GRAY, PAUL RICHARD CHARLES Director of Personnel and Support Directorate, HM Treasury Grade: 3

Career: HM Treasury 1969-77, 1979-: Booker McConnell 1977-79; assistant secretary 1984-87, economic affairs private secretary to Prime Minister 1988-90; under secretary monetary group 1990-93; UK member EC monetary committee 1993; principal establishment and finance officer/director of personnel, finance and support 1994, of personnel and support directorate 1994- *Current non-Whitehall posts:* non-executive director Laing Management Ltd

Date of birth: 2 August 1948 *Education/professional qualifications:* London School of Economics, economics (BSc 1969) *Marital status:* married Lynda Braby 1972; 2 sons *Recreations:* family, walking, gardening, DIY

Paul R C Gray Esq, Director of Personnel and Support Directorate, HM Treasury, Allington Towers, Allington Street, London SW1E 5EB
Telephone: 0171-270 3000

GRAYDON, Air Chief Marshal Sir MICHAEL JAMES Chief of the Air Staff, Ministry of Defence

Career: Royal Air Force (RAF) 1960-: operations joint warfare Ministry of Defence (MoD) 1973-75; student National Defence College 1976; military assistant chief of defence staff MoD 1979-81; commander RAF stations Leuchars 1981-83, Stanley, Falkland Islands 1983; student Royal College of Defence Studies 1984; senior air staff officer HQ 11 Group 1985-86; assistant chief of staff (policy) Supreme Headquarters Allied Powers Europe 1986-89; air officer commanding-in-chief (AOCIC) RAF Support Command 1989-91; AOCIC/commander-in-chief Strike Command/UK air forces 1991-92; chief of air staff MoD 1992-

Date of birth: 24 October 1938 *Education/professional qualifications:* Wycliffe College, Gloucester; RAF College, Cranwell; National Defence College; Royal College of Defence Studies; FRAeS *Honours, decorations:* CBE 1984; KCB 1989, Air ADC to Queen 1992, GCB 1993 *Recreations:* golf, birdwatching, reading

Air Chief Marshal Sir Michael Graydon GCB CBE ADC, Chief of the Air Staff, Ministry of Defence, Whitehall, London SW1A 2HB *Telephone:* 0171-218 6314 *Fax:* 0171-218 3834

GREEN, ANDREW FLEMING Assistant Under Secretary, Foreign and Commonwealth Office

Career: diplomatic service 1965-: counsellor FCO 1988-90; ambassador to Syria 1991-94; assistant under secretary Middle East/Near East and North Africa FCO 1994-

Date of birth: 6 August 1941 *Education/professional qualifications:* Magdalene College, Cambridge (BA, MA)

Andrew F Green Esq CMG, Assistant Under Secretary, Foreign and Commonwealth Office, Downing Street, London SW1A 2AH *Telephone:* 0171-270 3000

GREENFIELD, JIM Deputy Chief Planning Inspector, Planning Inspectorate Agency (Executive Agency) Grade: 4

Jim Greenfield Esq, Deputy Chief Planning Inspector, Planning Inspectorate Agency, Room 1427, Tollgate House, Houlton Street, Bristol BS2 9DJ *Telephone:* 01179 878961

GREENSTOCK, JEREMY QUENTIN Deputy Under Secretary, Eastern Europe and Middle East and Commonwealth Office Senior grade

Career: teacher 1966-69; HM Diplomatic Service 1969-: second secretary (SS) Foreign and COmmonwealth Office (FCO) London 1969-70; language student Middle East Centre for Arab Studies 1970-72; SS and first secretary (FS) Dubai 1972-74; private secretary to ambassador Washington DC 1974-78; FS planning, personnel and Near East departments, FCO 1978-83; commercial counsellor Jedda, Riyadh 1983-86; head of chancery Paris 1987-90; assistant under secretary Eastern Adriatic, W and S Europe and Ireland, deputy political director FCO 1990-93; minister Washington DC 1994-95; deputy under secretary eastern Europe and Middle East FCO 1995-

Date of birth: 27 July 1943 *Education/professional qualifications:* Harrow School; Worcester College, Oxford, classics (BA 1966) *Honours, decorations:* CMG 1991 *Marital status:* married Anne Ashford Hodges 1969; 2 daughters, 1 son *Recreations:* travel, golf, skiing, music

Jeremy Q Greenstock Esq CMG, Deputy Under Secretary, Foreign and Commonwealth Office, Whitehall, London SW1A 2AH *Telephone:* 0171-270 3000

GREGORY, PETER ROLAND Director, NHS Directorate, Welsh Office Grade: 3

Career: Welsh Office 1971-: private secretary to permanent secretary 1974-75; principal 1976-82; assistant secretary health department 1982-90; under secretary transport, planning and environment group 1990-94; director health department/NHS directorate 1994-

Date of birth: 7 October 1946 *Education/professional qualifications:* Sexeys Grammar School, Blackford, Somerset; University College, Swansea, history (BA 1968); Manchester University (PhD 1972) *Marital status:* married Frances Margaret Hogan 1978 *Recreations:* music, walking

Peter R Gregory Esq, Director, NHS Directorate, Welsh Office, Cathays Park, Cardiff CF1 3NQ *Telephone:* 01222-823446 *Fax:* 01222 825021

GREGSON, Sir PETER LEWIS Permanent Secretary, Department of Trade and Industry Grade: 1

Career: various posts Board of Trade 1961-68; private secretary to prime minister 1968-72; assistant secretary, secretary Industrial Development Advisory Board, Department of Trade and Industry (DTI) 1972-74; secretary National Enterprise Board 1975-77; Department of Trade 1977-81: under secretary (US) 1977-80, deputy secretary (DS) 1980-81; DS Cabinet Office 1981-85; permanent US Department of Energy 1985-89; permanent secretary DTI 1989- *Current non-Whitehall posts:* council member Industrial Society 1990-

Date of birth: 28 June 1936 *Education/professional qualifications:* Nottingham High School; Balliol College, Oxford, classical moderations and greats (BA 1959, MA) *Honours, decorations:* CB 1983, KCB 1988 *Marital status:* single *Recreations:* gardening, listening to music

Sir Peter Gregson KCB, Permanent Secretary, Department of Trade and Industry, Ashdown House, 123 Victoria Street, London SW1E 6RB *Telephone:* 0171-215 4439

GREIG-SMITH, Dr PETER WILLIAM Director of Fisheries Research, Ministry of Agriculture, Fisheries and Food Grade: 4

Career: Ministry of Agriculture, Fisheries and Food 1980-: research scientist agricultural science service 1980-86; head of environmental research 1986-90, of conservation and environment protection Central Science Laboratory 1990-92; directorate of fisheries research 1992-: head of aquatic environment protection 1992-94, director 1994-

Date of birth: 17 May 1953 *Education/professional qualifications:* David Hughes School, Menai Bridge; Aberdeen University, zoology (BSc 1975); Sussex University, behavioural ecology (DPhil 1980) *Marital status:* married June Ann Fettes 1978: separated; 1 daughter, 1 son *Recreations:* mountains, golf DIY

Dr Peter W Greig-Smith, Director, Directorate of Fisheries Research, Ministry of Agriculture, Fisheries and Food, Pakefield Road, Lowestoft, Suffolk NR33 0HT *Telephone:* 01502 524217 *Fax:* 01502 524515

GRIBBON, (EDWARD) JOHN Director, Business Profits Division, Inland Revenue Grade: 3

Career: private practice accountant 1960-66; Inland Revenue 1966-: tax inspector (TI) 1966-81; principal TI 1981-89; deputy director of operations, compliance 1989-91; under secretary, director business profits division 1991-

Date of birth: 10 July 1943 *Education/professional qualifications:* Coleraine Academical Institution; Institute of Chartered Accountants in Ireland (ACA 1965, FCA 1976); London University, law (LLB 1980) *Marital status:* married Margaret Flanagan 1968; 2 daughters, 1 son *Clubs:* Civil Service *Recreations:* family, photography, local church

E John Gribbon Esq, Director, Business Profits Division, Inland Revenue, 22 Kingsway, London WC2R 6NR *Telephone:* 0171-438 6774 *Fax:* 0171-438 6073

GRIFFITHS, DAVID HUBERT Under Secretary, Arable Crops and Horticulture, Ministry of Agriculture, Fisheries and Food Grade: 3

Career: Ministry of Agriculture, Fisheries and Food 1963-: assistant secretary 1975, under secretary (US) 1982, fisheries secretary 1983-87, head of food, drink and marketing policy 1987-90, director of establishments 1990-95, US arable crops and horticulture 1995-

Date of birth: 24 December 1940 *Education/professional qualifications:* Kingswood School, Bath; St Catharine's College, Cambridge (BA, MA) *Marital status:* married Mary Abbott; 1 son, 1 daughter *Recreations:* golf, cooking, music

David H Griffiths Esq, Under Secretary, Ministry of Agriculture, Fisheries and Food, Whitehall Place, London SW1A 2HH *Telephone:* 0171-270 8659

GRIFFITHS, DOUGLAS ERIC GEORGE Deputy Chief Executive, The Crown Estate

Career: Ministry of Defence 1959-78; consultant Civil Service Department/HM Treasury (HMT) 1978-81; deputy director accountancy and audit Civil Service College 1981-86; finance officer HMT 1986-88; Crown Estate (administration of Crown landed property) 1988-: accountant and receiver general 1988-92, deputy chief executive finance and administration 1992-

Date of birth: 21 March 1940 *Education/professional qualifications:* FCMA 1972 *Marital status:* married Jascynthe Gwendoline Spenn 1970; 2 sons

Douglas E G Griffiths Esq, Deputy Chief Executive, The Crown Estate, 16 Carlton House Terrace, London SW1Y 5AH *Telephone:* 0171-210 4347 *Fax:* 0171-930 3752

GRIFFITHS, HOWARD Assistant Under Secretary/Command Secretary, Ministry of Defence Grade: 3

Career: Ministry of Defence (MoD) 1963-75; senior civilian director National Defence College 1976-78; assistant secretary (AS) MoD Procurement Executive 1978-80; counsellor and deputy head of delegation Mutual and Balanced Force Reduction negotiations, Vienna 1980-84; MoD 1984-91: AS general finance 1984-86; head of defence arms control unit 1986-88; assistant under secretary (AUS) policy 1988-91; fellow Centre for International Affairs Harvard University, USA 1991-92; AUS supply and organisation (air) MoD 1992-94; command secretary HQ logistics command 1994-

Date of birth: 20 September 1938 *Education/professional qualifications:* Gowerton Grammar School, Glamorgan; London School of Economics, international relations (BScEcon 1960, MScEcon 1962)

Howard Griffiths Esq, Assistant Under Secretary, HQ Logistics Command, RAF Brampton, Huntingdon, Cambridgeshire *Telephone:* 01480 52151 Ext 6900

GRIMSEY, COLIN ROBERT Under Secretary, Railways Infrastructure Directorate, Department of Transport Grade: 3

Career: assistant principal Department of Transport (DTp) 1968-72; principal Department of Environment 1972-79; DTp 1979-: assistant secretary 1979-89, under secretary 1989-: seconded to London Transport 1989-91, director of finance 1991-93, head of railways 1 directorate 1993-

Date of birth: 24 December 1943 *Education/professional qualifications:* Dartford Grammar School, Kent; King's College, London, physics (BSc 1964) *Marital status:* married Elizabeth Sermon 1976; 1 daughter, 1 son *Recreations:* family, opera, choral singing

Colin R Grimsey Esq, Under Secretary, Department of Transport, 2 Marsham Street, London SW1P 3EB *Telephone:* 0171-276 3000 *Fax:* 0171-276 0818

GROVE, VERNON CHARLES Circuit Administrator, Wales and Chester Circuit, Court Service Agency (Executive Agency)

Career: Lord Chancellor's Department 1956-: chief clerk Birmingham county court 1983-86; HQ operations and information technology 1986-90; courts administrator Birmingham 1990-94; circuit administrator Wales and Chester circuit Court Service Agency 1994-

Date of birth: 29 September 1940 *Education/professional qualifications:* Cathays High School, Cardiff *Marital status:* married Carol Ann Grove 1986; 1 daughter *Recreations:* sport, travel, reading

Vernon Grove Esq, Administrator, Wales and Chester Circuit, Churchill House, Churchill Way, Cardiff CF1 4HH *Telephone:* 01222 396925 *Fax:* 01222 373882

GROVER, DEREK JAMES LANGLANDS Deputy Chief Executive and Senior Director of Operations, Employment Service (Executive Agency) Grade: 3

Career: Department of Employment 1971-78; Cabinet Office 1978-80; Manpower Services Commission 1980-89: head of adult training policy 1984-86, of personnel 1986-89; Employment Department 1989-: director of youth training 1989, of training strategy and infrastructure 1989-94; deputy chief executive/senior director of operations Employment Service 1994-

Date of birth: 26 January 1949 *Education/professional qualifications:* Hove County Grammar School; Clare College, Cambridge, English literature (BA 1971, MA); MIPD 1993 *Marital status:* married Mary Katherine Morgan 1972; 1 son *Clubs:* Royal Society of Arts *Recreations:* music, reading, walking

Derek J L Grover Esq, Deputy Chief Executive, Employment Service, Rockingham House, 123 West Street, Sheffield S1 4ER *Telephone:* 01142 596246 *Fax:* 01142 795994

GRUNDY, DAVID STANLEY Policy and Resources Commissioner, Forestry Commission Grade: 3

Career: assistant principal Ministry of Power 1967-70; assistant private secretary to Minister of Technology 1970-71; principal Department of Trade and Industry 1971-76; economic adviser Foreign and Commonwealth Office 1976-78, Department of Environment 1978-79; chief economic adviser to Vanuatu government 1979-81; Forestry Commission 1982-: chief economist 1982-90, commissioner administration and finance 1990-92, of policy and resources 1992-

Date of birth: 10 April 1943 *Education/professional qualifications:* De la Salle College, Manchester; Jesus College, Cambridge, philosophy (BA, MA 1965); Jesus College, Oxford, economics (MPhil 1974) *Marital status:* married Elizabeth Jenny Schadla Hall 1965; 1 son *Clubs:* Dean Tennis, Edinburgh; Scottish Ornithological Club, Edinburgh *Recreations:* angling, bird-watching, gardening, tennis

David S Grundy Esq, Commissioner, Forestry Commission, 231 Corstorphine Road, Edinburgh EH12 7AT *Telephone:* 0131-334 0303 *Fax:* 0131-316 4891

GUNN, ROBERT NORMAN Chairman, Further Education Funding Council

Career: Boots Company 1951-90: vice-chairman and chief executive (CE) 1983-85, chairman and CE 1985-87, chairman 1987-90; Polytechnics and Colleges Funding Council 1988-93; Higher Education Funding Council for England 1992-94; chairman Further Education Funding Council 1992- *Current non-Whitehall posts:* director East Midland Electricity, Nottingham Building Society

Date of birth: 16 December 1925 *Education/professional qualifications:* Royal High School, Edinburgh; Worcester College, Oxford, history (BA, MA 1951); CBIM 1983, FInstD 1984 *Marital status:* married Joan Parry 1956; 1 daughter *Recreations:* gardening, theatre, travel

Robert N Gunn Esq, Chairman, Further Education Funding Council, Cheylesmore House, Quinton Road, Coventry CV1 2WT
Telephone: 01203 863000 *Fax:* 01203 863100

GUTHRIE, General Sir CHARLES Chief of the General Staff, Ministry of Defence

Career: army service 1959-: Ministry of Defence (MoD) 1973-74, 1980-82; command 1st battalion Welsh Guards 1977-80; commander British forces New Hebrides 1980, 4th Armoured Brigade 1982-84; chief of staff 1st British Corps (1BR) 1984-86; general officer commanding NE district and commander 2nd Infantry Division 1986-87; colonel commandant Intelligence Corps 1986-; assistant chief of general staff MoD 1987-89; commander 1BR Corps 1989-92; commander Northern Army Group 1992-93; commander-in-chief British Army of the Rhine 1992-94; chief of the general staff MoD 1994-

Date of birth: 17 November 1938 *Education/professional qualifications:* Harrow School; Royal Military Academy, Sandhurst (commission 1959); staff college 1972); *Honours, decorations:* LVO 1977; OBE 1980; KCB 1990; ADC Gen 1993; GCB 1994 *Recreations:* tennis, skiing, travel

General Sir Charles Guthrie GCB LVO OBE ADC Gen, Chief of the General Staff, Ministry of Defence, Main Building, Whitehall, London SW1A 2HB *Telephone:* 0171-218 7114
Fax: 0171-218 7840

H

HADDON, MARTIN THOMAS **Under Secretary, Animal Health and Veterinary Group, Ministry of Agriculture, Fisheries and Food** Grade: 3

Career: Ministry of Agriculture, Fisheries and Food (MAFF) 1966-74: assistant principal 1966-71, principal 1971-74; Cabinet Office 1974-76; MAFF 1976-: assistant secretary 1980-90; under secretary management services 1990-91, animal health and veterinary group 1991-

Date of birth: 8 December 1944 *Education/professional qualifications:* Beaumont College, Old Windsor; Worcester College, Oxford, literae humaniores (BA 1966) *Marital status:* married Helen Parry 1977; 2 daughters, 1 son

Martin T Haddon Esq, Under Secretary, Ministry of Agriculture, Fisheries and Food, Block B, Government Buildings, Hook Rise South, Tolworth, Surrey *Telephone:* 0181-330 8141 *Fax:* 0181-330 8140

HADLEY, DAVID ALLEN **Deputy Secretary, Agricultural Commodities, Trade and Food Production, Ministry of Agriculture, Fisheries and Food** Grade: 2

Career: Ministry of Agriculture, Fisheries and Food (MAFF) 1959-75: assistant principal 1959-64, principal 1964-71, assistant secretary (AS) 1971-75; AS HM Treasury 1975-78; MAFF 1979-89: AS 1979-81, under secretary 1981-87: cereals, sugar and external relations 1981-85, EC group 1985-87; deputy secretary (DS) agricultural commodities and trade 1987-89; DS EC affairs Cabinet Office 1989-93; DS agricultural commodities, trade and food production MAFF 1993-

Date of birth: 18 February 1936 *Education/professional qualifications:* Wyggeston Grammar School, Leicester; Merton College, Oxford, classics and philosophy (BA 1959) *Honours, decorations:* CB 1991 *Marital status:* married Veronica Ann Hopkins 1965; 1 son *Recreations:* gardening, music (especially opera)

David A Hadley Esq CB, Deputy Secretary, Ministry of Agriculture, Fisheries and Food, Whitehall Place, London SW1A 2HH *Telephone:* 0171-270 8109 *Fax:* 0171-270 8837

HALL, DAVID **Head of Projects and Export Promotion Division, Department of Trade and Industry** Grade: 3

Career: HM Diplomatic Service/Foreign [and Commonwealth] Office 1964-76; Department of Trade [and Industry] 1976-: assistant secretary 1982-91; under secretary, head of projects and export policy/promotion division 1991-

Date of birth: 15 July 1942 *Education/professional qualifications:* Pembroke College, Oxford, modern languages (BA)

David Hall Esq, Under Secretary, Department of Trade and Industry, Ashdown House, 1 Victoria Street, London SW1E 6RB *Telephone:* 0171-215 4933

HALLIDAY, JOHN FREDERICK **Deputy Under Secretary, Criminal Department, Home Office** Grade: 2

Career: volunteer teacher in Pakistan 1964-66; Home Office (HO) 1966-: seconded to Department of [Health and] Social Security 1987-90; deputy under secretary criminal department 1990-

Date of birth: 19 September 1942 *Education/professional qualifications:* Whitgift School, Croydon; St John's College, Cambridge, history (BA 1964, MA) *Honours, decorations:* CB *Marital status:* married; 4 sons *Recreations:* music, squash, theatre

John F Halliday Esq CB, Deputy Under Secretary, Home Office, 50 Queen Anne's Gate, London SW1H 9AT *Telephone:* 0171-273 3000 *Fax:* 0171-273 3420

HAMILL, J Secretary, Scottish Office Home and Health Department Grade: 2

J Hamill Esq, Secretary, Scottish Office Home and Health Department, St Andrew's House, Edinburgh EH1 3DG *Telephone:* 0131-244 2120 *Fax:* 0131-244 2683

HAMILTON, JOHN PATTERSON Director, Intelligence, National Criminal Intelligence Service

Career: police service 1963-: Royal Ulster Constabulary 1963-90; Greater Manchester police 1990-: seconded as director of intelligence and deputy director-general National Criminal Intelligence Service 1994-

Date of birth: 27 January 1944 *Education/professional qualifications:* Templemere Secondary School, Belfast; DipMan 1992; AdvDipCrim 1992; Open University (BA 1993) *Marital status:* married Patricia Johnston 1964; 1 daughter, 1 son *Recreations:* theatre, music

John Hamilton Esq, Director, Intelligence, National Criminal Intelligence Service, PO Box 8000, Spring Gardens, Tinworth Street, London SE11 5EN *Telephone:* 0171-238 8205 *Fax:* 0171-238 8446

HAMMOND, ANTHONY HILGROVE Deputy Secretary, Solicitor to the Department of Trade and Industry Grade: 2

Career: solicitor Greater London Council 1965-68; Home Office (HO) 1968-92: legal assistant (LA) 1968-70, senior LA 1970-74, assistant legal adviser (ALA) 1974-80; HO and Northern Ireland Office 1980-92: principal ALA 1980-88; deputy under secretary, legal adviser 1988-92; solicitor and deputy secretary Department of Trade and Industry 1992-

Date of birth: 27 July 1940 *Education/professional qualifications:* Malvern College; Emmanuel College, Cambridge, classics and law (BA 1962), public law (LLB 1963); solicitor 1965 *Honours, decorations:* CB 1992 *Marital status:* married Avril Collinson 1988 *Clubs:* Athenaeum *Recreations:* bridge, listening to music, birdwatching

Anthony H Hammond Esq CB, The Solicitor, Department of Trade and Industry, 10/18 Victoria Street, London SW1H 0NN *Telephone:* 0171-215 3039 *Fax:* 0171-215 3141

HAMPSON, STEPHEN F Under Secretary, Scottish Office Environment Department Grade: 3

Career: economics lecturer Aberdeen University 1969-71; economist National Economic Development Office 1971-75; economic adviser Scottish Office (SO) 1975-77, 1982-84; first secretary New Delhi 1978-81; SO 1984-: assistant secretary 1984-93; under secretary Environment Department (natural heritage, rural affairs, environmental protection, industrial pollution) 1993-

Date of birth: 27 October 1945 *Education/professional qualifications:* Leys School, Cambridge; University College, Cambridge, philosophy, politics and economics (BA 1967, MA), economics (BPhil 1969) *Marital status:* married Gunilla Brunk 1970; 1 daughter, 1 son *Recreations:* travel, hills

Stephen F Hampson Esq, Under Secretary, Scottish Office, New St Andrew's House, Edinburgh EH1 3TG *Telephone:* 0131-244 4851 *Fax:* 0131-244 4765

HANGARTNER, Dr (JOHN) ROBERT WILFRED Senior Principal Medical Officer, NHS Executive, Department of Health Grade: 3

Career: medical posts 1979-83; histopathology lecturer St George's Hospital medical school, London 1983-88; Department of Health 1988-: senior medical officer (MO) hospital policy and services 1988-91, principal MO health care medical 1 1991-93; senior principal MO medical education, training and staffing division 1993-

Date of birth: 5 February 1955 *Education/professional qualifications:* Merchant Taylors' School, Northwood; Guy's Hospital, medicine and surgery (BSc 1976, MB, BS, MRCS, LRCP 1979); MRCPath 1988; Open University, management (Dipl Mgmt 1991) *Marital status:* married Jillian Mary Ansell 1980; 1 daughter, 1 son *Clubs:* Royal Society of Medicine *Recreations:* photography, DIY

Dr J Robert W Hangartner, Senior Principal Medical Officer, Department of Health, Quarry House, Quarry Hill, Leeds LS2 7UE *Telephone:* 01132 545849 *Fax:* 01132 545959

HARBISON, Dr SAMUEL ALEXANDER HM Chief Inspector of Nuclear Installations and Director of Nuclear Safety, Health and Safety Executive Grade: 3

Career: reactor physicist United Kingdom Atomic Energy Authority, Windscale 1962-64; teaching, research assistant California University, USA 1964-66; research student Rutherford High Energy Laboratory 1966-68; research fellow London University 1969; senior lecturer Royal Naval College Greenwich nuclear science and technology department 1969-74; Health and Safety Executive HM Nuclear Inspectorate 1974-: head of hazardous substances policy branch 1988-91; chief inspector and director of nuclear safety 1991-

Date of birth: 9 May 1941 *Education/professional qualifications:* Ballymena Academy, Co Antrim; Queen's University, Belfast, physics (BSc 1962); California University, USA, nuclear physics (MS 1966); Westfield College, London University, nuclear physics (PhD 1969) *Marital status:* married Margaret Gail Healy 1991; 3 daughters from previous marriage *Publications:* An Introduction to Radiation Protection (Chapman and Hall 1986) *Recreations:* sport, gardening, travel and music

Dr Samuel A Harbison, HM Chief Inspector of Nuclear Installations, Health and Safety Executive, Rose Court, 2 Southwark Bridge, London SE1 9HS *Telephone:* 0171-717 6850 *Fax:* 0171-717 6095

HARDING, Air Vice-Marshal PETER JOHN Defence Services Secretary, Ministry of Defence

Career: RAF 1960-: deputy chief of staff, operations HQ Allied Air Forces Central Europe 1991-94; defence services secretary Ministry of Defence 1994-

Date of birth: 1 June 1940

Air Vice-Marshal P J Harding CB CBE AFC, Defence Services Secretary, Ministry of Defence, Main Building, Whitehall, London SW1A 2HB *Telephone:* 0171-218 9000

HARGREAVES, ROBERT Secretary, Broadcasting Complaints Commission

Career: home affairs, Washington correspondent, foreign editor Independent Television News 1962-80; deputy director programmes Independent Broadcasting Authority/Television Commission 1984-93; secretary Broadcasting Complaints Authority 1993-

Date of birth: 12 January 1933 *Publications:* several, including Superpower; America, Americans; Sadat: A biography

Robert Hargreaves Esq, Secretary, Broadcasting Complaints Commission, Grosvenor Gardens House, 35-37 Grosvenor Gardens, London SW1W 0BS *Telephone:* 0171-630 1966 *Fax:* 0171-828 7316

HARLEY, Lieutenant-General ALEXANDER GEORGE HAMILTON Deputy Chief of the Defence Staff, Ministry of Defence (Commitments)

Career: army service 1962-: assistant chief of defence staff MoD 1990-93; commander British forces Cyprus 1993-95; deputy chief of the defence staff MoD 1995-

Date of birth: 3 May 1941

Lieutenant-General Alexander G Harley CB OBE, Deputy Chief of the Defence Staff, Ministry of Defence, Whitehall, London SW1A 2HB *Telephone:* 0171-218 9000

HARP, GRAHAME JOHN ANTHONY Inspector of Companies; Head of Company Investigation Branches, Department of Trade and Industry Grade: 4

Career: Department of Trade [and Industry] (DT[I]) insolvency service (IS) 1963-78; assistant official receiver (OR) High Court 1978-80; DT[I] 1980-: principal internal audit 1980, international trade policy 1980-82; chief examiner IS policy 1982-85, principal examiner IS HQ 1985-89; OR High Court 1990; inspector of companies, head of company investigation branches 1990-

Date of birth: 1 May 1944 *Education/professional qualifications:* Southend Boys' School; ACCA 1973, FCCA 1980 *Marital status:* married Carole Madeleine Williams 1968 *Clubs:* Thames Estuary Yacht *Recreations:* sailing

Grahame J A Harp Esq, Inspector of Companies, Ashdown House, 123 Victoria Street, London SW1E 6RB *Telephone:* 0171-215 6798 *Fax:* 0171-215 5916

HARPUM, CHARLES Commissioner, Law Commission

Career: Cambridge University 1977-: fellow Downing College 1977-; assistant law lecturer 1979-84, law lecturer 1984-; visiting scholar Virginia University, USA 1991; commissioner Law Commision 1994-

Date of birth: 29 March 1953 *Education/professional qualifications:* Queen Elizabeth Grammar School, Penrith, Cumberland; Cheltenham Grammar School; Downing College, Cambridge, law (BA 1975, LLB 1977); Lincoln's Inn (barrister 1976) *Marital status:* single *Recreations:* travel, music, swimming, trees and gardens, the natural world

Charles Harpum Esq, Commissioner, Law Commission, Conquest House, 37-38 John Street, Theobald's Road, London WC1N 2BQ *Telephone:* 0171-411 1202 *Fax:* 0171-411 1297

HARRIS, CHRISTOPHER JOHN Chief Executive, Coastguard Agency (Executive Agency) Grade: 4

Career: marine engineer officer Royal Navy 1957-74; Department of Transport 1974-: head of aviation security 1986-91; director marine emergency operations (marine pollution control unit and HM Coastguard) 1992-94, chief executive Coastguard Agency 1994- *Current non-Whitehall posts:* non-executive director Oil Spill Response Ltd 1992-

Date of birth: 19 May 1937 *Education/professional qualifications:* Roundhay School, Leeds; Royal Naval College, Dartmouth; Royal Naval Engineering College, Manadon (BScEng 1962); Royal Naval College, Greenwich (advanced marine engineering qualification); CEng; MIMechE, MIMarE *Honours, decorations:* MBE 1974 *Marital status:* married *Recreations:* sailing

Christopher J Harris, MBE, Chief Executive, Coastguard Agency, Spring Place, 105 Commercial Road, Southampton, Hampshire SO15 1EG *Telephone:* 01703 329100 *Fax:* 01703 329440

HARRIS, LEONARD JOHN Director VAT Policy and Commissioner, HM Customs and Excise Grade: 3

Career: HM Customs and Excise (C&E) 1964-70; Civil Service Selection Board 1970-71; C&E 1971; Cabinet Office (CO) 1971-74; UK permanent representation to EC, Brussels 1974-77: first secretary 1974-76, counsellor 1976-77; assistant secretary C&E 1977-80, CO 1980-83; C&E 1983-87: commissioner 1983-87, under secretary management and personnel office 1987; head of personnel policy HM Treasury 1987-91; C&E 1991-: commissioner 1991-, director of internal taxes 1991-94, VAT policy 1994-

Date of birth: 4 July 1941 *Education/professional qualifications:* Westminster City School, London; St John's College, Cambridge, English (BA 1964, MA) *Marital status:* married Jennifer Dilys Biddiscombe née Barker 1986; 2 daughters, 1 son from previous marriage, 1 stepson, 1 stepdaughter

Leonard J Harris Esq, Commissioner, HM Customs and Excise, New King's Beam House, 22 Upper Ground, London SE1 9PJ *Telephone:* 0171-865 5015 *Fax:* 0171-865 5366

HARRIS, PETER MICHAEL Official Solicitor to the Supreme Court, Lord Chancellor's Department Grade: 3

Career: naval service 1953-72; barrister 1972-74; Lord Chancellor's Department 1974-: circuit administrator northern circuit 1986-93; Official Solicitor (representation of minors and mentally unsound) 1993-

Date of birth: 13 April 1937 *Education/professional qualifications:* Dursley Grammar School, Gloucestershire; Cirencester Grammar School; Royal Naval College, Dartmouth (commission 1958); Gray's Inn (barrister 1971) *Marital status:* married Bridget Burke 1963; 2 daughters, 1 son *Publications:* The Children Act 1989: A Procedural Handbook (Butterworths 1991) *Recreations:* walking, gardening, reading, theatre

Peter Michael Harris Esq, Official Solicitor, 81 Chancery Lane, London WC2A 1DD *Telephone:* 0171-911 7116 *Fax:* 0171-911 7105

HARRISON, Air Vice-Marshal A J Assistant Chief of Defence Staff (Operations and Security), Ministry of Defence

Air Vice-Marshal A J Harrison CBE, Assistant Chief of Defence Staff, Ministry of Defence, Main Building, Whitehall, London SW1A 2HB *Telephone:* 0171-218 9000

HART, GRAHAM ALLAN **Permanent Secretary, Department of Health** Grade: 1

Career: Ministry of Health [and Social Security] (DH[SS]) 1962-69: assistant principal 1962-67, principal 1967-69; assistant registrar General Medical Council 1969-71; DHSS 1972-82: principal private secretary to secretary of state for social services 1972-74; assistant secretary 1974; under secretary 1979; under secretary Central Policy Review Staff 1982-83; deputy secretary DH 1984-89; seconded as secretary Scottish Office Home and Health Department 1990-92; permanent secretary DH 1992-

Date of birth: 13 March 1940 *Education/professional qualifications:* Brentwood School; Pembroke College, Oxford, literae humaniores (BA 1962) *Honours, decorations:* CB 1987 *Marital status:* married Margaret Aline Powell 1964; 2 sons

Graham A Hart Esq CB, Permanent Secretary, Department of Health, Richmond House, 79 Whitehall, London SW1A 2NS *Telephone:* 0171-210 5310 *Fax:* 0171-210 5409

HARTLEY, BRYAN HOLROYD **Chief Pharmaceutical Officer, Department of Health; Business Head, Inspection and Enforcement, Medicines Control Agency (Executive Agency)** Grade: 4

Career: pharmaceutical development pharmacist Wellcome 1962-64; community pharmacy manager 1964-65; process development and quality assurance pharmacist Winthrop Laboratories 1965-68; process development manager Wyeth Laboratories 1968-71; Department of Health [and Social Security] 1971-: medicines division 1971-79: medicines inspectorate 1971-76, principal, Medicines Act advertising policy 1976-79, pharmaceutical division 1979-82; deputy chief pharmaceutical officer 1982-85; chief medicines inspector 1985-90; chief pharmaceutical officer 1990-, and business head, inspection and enforcement Medicines Control Agency 1990-

Date of birth: 27 April 1939 *Education/professional qualifications:* Municipal Grammar School, Wolverhampton; London University, pharmacy (BPharm 1962); FRPharmS 1986 *Marital status:* married Wendy Barbara Mills 1963; 2 daughters *Clubs:* Civil Service; Worshipful Society of Apothecaries of London *Recreations:* trekking; voluntary youth work

Bryan H Hartley Esq, Chief Pharmaceutical Officer, Department of Health, Richmond House, Whitehall, London SW1A 2NS
Telephone: 0171-273 0500 *Fax:* 0171-273 0676

HARTLEY, NICHOLAS JOHN **Head of Energy Policy Analysis Unit, Department of Trade and Industry** Grade: 4

Career: Department of Education and Science 1965-68; economic assistant, economic adviser (EA) HM Treasury 1968-84: seconded as assistant secretary to Royal Commission on Press 1974-77, as adviser Central Policy Review Staff, Cabinet Office 1978-80; EA, senior EA Office of Telecommunications 1984-89; senior EA Department of Environment 1989-92; head of energy policy analysis unit Department of Trade and Industry 1992-

Date of birth: 12 April 1944 *Education/professional qualifications:* St Clement Dane's Grammar School, Hammersmith, London; St Catharine's College, Cambridge, economics (BA 1965, MA); York University, economics (BPhil 1971) *Marital status:* married Jenny Stern 1974; 2 sons *Publications:* co-author The Ownership of the Provincial Press (HMSO 1977) *Recreations:* visual arts, theatre

Nicholas J Hartley Esq, Head of Energy Policy Analysis Unit, Department of Trade and Industry, 1 Palace Street, London SW1E 5HE *Telephone:* 0171-238 3409 *Fax:* 0171-238 3121

HARTNACK, PAUL RICHARD SAMUEL Comptroller General and Chief Executive, Patent Office (Executive Agency) Grade: 3

Career: Board of Trade 1961-67; assistant secretary (AS) committee of enquiry into civil air transport 1967-68; second secretary Paris embassy 1969-72; export promotion Department of Trade 1973-78; AS National Enterprise Board 1979-80; secretary British Technology Group 1980-85; AS finance and resource management division Department of Trade and Industry 1985-89; comptroller general and chief executive Patent Office 1989-

Date of birth: 17 November 1942 *Education/professional qualifications:* Hastings Grammar School *Marital status:* married Marion Quirk 1966; 2 sons *Recreations:* gardening, watching rugby

Paul R S Hartnack Esq, Comptroller General and Chief Executive, Patent Office, Concept House, Cardiff Road, Newport, Gwent NP9 1RH *Telephone:* 01633 814500 *Fax:* 01633 814504

HARTOP, BARRY Chief Executive, Welsh Development Agency

Career: Unilever 1965-83; chairman and managing director (MD) Lever Industrial 1983-89; MD Gestetner plc 1989-92; chief executive Welsh Development Agency 1994- *Current non-Whitehall posts:* non-executive chairman Hammicks Bookshops

Date of birth: 15 August 1942 *Education/professional qualifications:* Durham University, chemical engineering (BSc 1965) *Marital status:* married Sandra Swan 1967; 1 daughter, 1 son *Recreations:* tennis, squash, gardening, keep-fit, food

Barry Hartop Esq, Chief Executive, Welsh Development Agency, Pearl House, Greyfriars Road, Cardiff CF1 3XX *Telephone:* 01222 828669 *Fax:* 01222 345730

HARVEY, DEREK WILLIAM Chief Executive, Vehicle Certification Agency (Executive Agency) Grade: 5

Career: development engineer Leyland Vehicles 1968-73; project engineer Science and Research Council 1973-75, Forestry Commission 1975-78; Department of Transport 1978-: vehicle and component approvals (VCA) 1978-85, director operations vehicle inspectorate 1985-87, head of division VCA 1987-90; chief executive Vehicle Certification executive agency (testing and approval of new road vehicles and their components) 1990-

Date of birth: 2 January 1948 *Education/professional qualifications:* Royal Grammar School, Worcester; University College of Wales, Swansea, mechanical engineering (BSc 1968); CEng 1976; MIMechE 1976 *Marital status:* married Veronica Wallace 1973; 1 daughter *Clubs:* Rotary *Recreations:* motoring, camping, angling, DIY

Derek W Harvey Esq, Chief Executive, Vehicle Certification Agency, 1 Eastgate Office Centre, Eastgate Road, Bristol BS5 6XX *Telephone:* 01179-524100 *Fax:* 01179-524103

Parliamentary Offices

see page 347

HASTINGS, ALFRED JAMES Clerk of the Journals, House of Commons Grade: 3

Career: clerk's department House of Commons 1960-

Date of birth: 10 February 1938 *Education/professional qualifications:* New College, Oxford (MA)

A J Hastings Esq, Clerk of the Journals, House of Commons, Westminster, London SW1A 0AA
Telephone: 0171-219 3315

HATFIELD, RICHARD PAUL Director-General, Management Audit, Ministry of Defence Grade: 3

Career: Ministry of Defence 1974-: private secretary (PS) to under secretary for army 1978-79; seconded as PS to Cabinet secretary 1982-85; head of defence lands 1986-87, of overseas secretariat 1987-91, of programme and policy 1991-93; joint leader defence costs study 1993-94; director general management audit (central consultancy services, internal audit, agency development) 1993-

Date of birth: 8 February 1953 *Education/professional qualifications:* University College, Oxford, philosophy, politics and economics (BA 1974, MA) *Honours, decorations:* CBE 1991

Richard P Hatfield Esq, Director-General, Management and Audit, Ministry of Defence, Northumberland House, Northumberland Avenue, London WC2N 5BP *Telephone:* 0171-218 4096

HAWKINS, Professor ANTHONY DONALD Director of Fisheries Research for Scotland, Scottish Office Agriculture and Fisheries Department Grade: 4

Career: Department of Agriculture and Fisheries for Scotland (DAFS) 1965-72: scientific officer (SO) 1965-69, senior SO 1969-72; consultant UN Food and Agriculture Organisation 1972; DAFS 1972-: principal SO 1972-78, senior principal SO 1978-83, deputy chief SO 1983-87; chief SO, director of fisheries research for Scotland, Scottish Office Agriculture and Fisheries Department 1987- *Current non-Whitehall posts:* honorary research professor Aberdeen University 1987-; honorary lecturer St Andrew's University 1983-

Date of birth: 25 March 1942 *Education/professional qualifications:* Poole Grammar School, Dorset; Bristol University, zoology (BSc 1963) and physiology (PhD 1968) *Honours, decorations:* AB Wood Medal and Prize, Institute of Acoustics 1978; FRSE 1989 *Marital status:* married Susan Mary Fulker 1966; 1 son *Publications:* Sound Reception in Fish (Elsevier 1976); Aquarium Systems (Academic Press 1981) *Recreations:* whippet racing, salmon fishing, walking

Professor Anthony D Hawkins, Director of Fisheries Research for Scotland, Marine Laboratory, PO Box 101, Victoria Road, Torry, Aberdeen
Telephone: 01224 876544 *Fax:* 01224 259413

HAWKINS, Air Vice-Marshal DAVID RICHARD Yeoman Usher of the Black Rod, Deputy Serjeant-at-Arms, House of Lords

Career: Royal Air Force (RAF) Regiment 1959-: director RAF personal services 1 Ministry of Defence 1989-90; director 1990-91, commandant general 1991-; director-general RAF security 1991-94; Yeoman Usher of the Black Rod, Deputy Serjeant-at-Arms, House of Lords 1994-

Date of birth: 5 April 1937 *Education/professional qualifications:* Downside School; Royal Military Academy, Sandhurst *Honours, decorations:* MBE 1975; CB 1992

Air Vice-Marshal David R Hawkins CB MBE, Yeoman Usher of the Black Rod, Deputy Serjeant-at-Arms, House of Lords, London SW1A 0PW *Telephone:* 0171-219 3000

HAWTIN, BRIAN RICHARD Assistant Under Secretary (Commitments), Ministry of Defence Grade: 3

Career: Ministry of Defence 1967-: assistant secretary 1981-89; private secretary to Secretary of State for Defence 1987-89; assistant under secretary material/naval 1989-92, programmes 1992-94, commitments 1994-

Date of birth: 31 May 1946 *Education/professional qualifications:* Portsmouth Grammar School; Christ Church, Oxford, history (BA 1967, MA) *Recreations:* ceramics, walking

Brian R Hawtin Esq, Assistant Under Secretary, Ministry of Defence, Main Building, Whitehall, London SW1A 2HB *Telephone:* 0171-218 9000

HAWTIN, MICHAEL VICTOR Director, Underwriting Group, Export Credits Guarantee Department Grade: 3

Career: HM Treasury (HMT) 1964-83: assistant principal 1964-69, principal 1969-77: seconded to Barclays Bank 1969-71, assistant secretary 1977-83; under secretary 1983-: principal finance officer Property Services Agency, Department of Environment 1983-86; head of local government group HMT 1986-88; Export Credits Guarantee Department 1988-: director resource management group and principal establishment and finance officer 1988-92, underwriting group 1992-

Date of birth: 7 September 1942 *Education/professional qualifications:* Bournemouth School; St John's College, Cambridge, economics (BA 1963, MA); University of California, Berkeley, USA, economics (MA 1964) *Marital status:* married Judith Mary Eeley 1966; 1 son, 1 daughter *Recreations:* music, travel

Michael V Hawtin Esq, Director Underwriting Group, Export Credits Guarantee Department, 2 Exchange Tower, Harbour Exchange Square, London E14 9GS *Telephone:* 0171-512 7008 *Fax:* 0171-512 7400

HAY, Dr ROBERT KING MILLER Director and Chief Executive, Scottish Agricultural Science Agency (Executive Agency) Grade: 5

Career: agricultural science lecturer Edinburgh and Malawi Universities 1974-77; biology/ecology lecturer Lancaster University 1977-82; head of plant science Scottish Agricultural College, Auchincruive 1982-90; director and chief executive Scottish Agricultural Science Agency 1990-

Date of birth: 19 August 1946 *Education/professional qualifications:* Forres Academy, Moray; Aberdeen University, chemistry (BSc 1967); East Anglia University, biophysics (MSc 1968), plant physiology (PhD 1971) *Marital status:* married Dorothea Harden 1969; 2 sons, 1 daughter *Publications:* Chemistry for Agriculture and Ecology (Blackwell 1981); Environmental Physiology of Plants (Academic Press 1981, 87); An Introduction to the Physiology of Crop Yield (Longman 1989); Volatile Oil Crops: their Biology, Chemistry and Production (Longman 1993); Science Policies in Europe: Unity and Diversity (HMSO 1994)

Dr Robert Hay, Director and Chief Executive, Scottish Agricultural Science Agency, East Craigs, Edinburgh EH12 8NJ *Telephone:* 0131-244 8843 *Fax:* 0131-244 8947

Government Departments

see page 372

HAYMAN-JOYCE, Lieutenant General ROBERT JOHN Deputy Chief of Defence Procurement (London), Procurement Executive, Ministry of Defence

Career: army service 1963-: military assistant to chief of general staff Ministry of Defence (MoD) 1977-80; commanding officer Royal Hussars (Prince of Wales' Own) 1980-82; colonel operational requirements 1983; commander Royal Armoured Corps (RAC), BAOR 1984-85; National Defence College, India 1986; deputy commandant Royal Military College of Science 1987; MoD procurement executive 1988-92: director tanks 1988, director-general land fighting systems 1989-92; director RAC 1992-94; MoD 1994-: military secretary 1994-95; master general of ordnance 1995-

Date of birth: 16 October 1940 *Education/professional qualifications:* Radley College; Magdalene College, Cambridge, geography (BA 1963, MA); National Defence College, New Delhi *Honours, decorations:* OBE 1979, CBE 1989 *Recreations:* horses, skiing, listening to music, travel, reading

Lieutenant General R J Hayman-Joyce CBE, Deputy Chief of Defence Procurement (London), Procurement Executive, Ministry of Defence, Whitehall, London SW1A 2HB
Telephone: 0171-218 9000

HAYNES, LAWRIE JOHN Chief Executive, Highways Agency (Executive Agency) Grade: 2

Career: Royal Air Force 1969-78; British Aerospace 1983-94; chief executive Highways Agency 1994-

Date of birth: 6 December 1952 *Education/professional qualifications:* North Axholme School, Crowle, Humberside; Stevenson College, Edinburgh, business studies (SNC 1978); Heriot-Watt University, business law (BA 1983) *Marital status:* married Carol Anne 1978; 3 daughters *Clubs:* The Little Ship *Recreations:* sailing

L Haynes Esq, Chief Executive, Highways Agency, St Christopher House, Southwark Street, London SE1 0TE *Telephone:* 0171-928 3666
Fax: 0171-921 3920

HAYTER, PAUL DAVID GRENVILLE Reading Clerk and Principal Clerk of Public Bills, House of Lords Grade: 3

Career: House of Lords 1964-: clerk parliament office 1964-74; private secretary to leader of house and government chief whip 1974-77; clerk of committees 1977-85; principal clerk of committees 1985-90; reading clerk (ceremonial duties) 1991-; principal finance officer 1991-94; principal clerk of public bills 1994-

Date of birth: 4 November 1942 *Education/professional qualifications:* Eton College; Christ Church, Oxford, history (BA 1964, MA) *Honours, decorations:* LVO 1991 *Marital status:* married Hon Deborah Gervaise Maude 1973; 2 sons, 1 daughter *Recreations:* music, gardening, botanising, archery, painting

Paul D G Hayter Esq LVO, Public Bill Office, House of Lords, London SW1A 0PW *Telephone:* 0171-219 3151 *Fax:* 0171-219 5979

HEAD, MICHAEL EDWARD Under Secretary, Equal Opportunities and General Department, Home Office Grade: 3

Career: Home Office 1960-: assistant principal immigration and general departments, private secretary to parliamentary under secretary 1964-66; principal fire, general department 1966-72: secretary Erroll Committee on Liquor Licensing 1970-72; assistant secretary probation and aftercare, community programmes, equal opportunities and criminal departments 1972-84; assistant under secretary 1984-: general 1984-86, criminal justice and constitutional 1986-91, broadcasting and miscellaneous 1991, equal opportunities and general departments (race relations; voluntary sector policy, charity law; national, local and European elections; gambling; deregulation; cults) 1991-

Date of birth: 17 March 1936 *Education/professional qualifications:* Kingston Grammar School; Woking Grammar School; University College, London, history (BA 1957); Michigan University, USA, history (MA 1958) *Honours, decorations:* CVO 1991 *Marital status:* married Wendy Elizabeth Davies 1963; 2 sons, 2 daughters *Clubs:* Reform *Recreations:* reading, theatre, golf

Michael E Head Esq CVO, Under Secretary, Home Office, 50 Queen Anne's Gate, London SW1H 9AT *Telephone:* 0171-273 3383 *Fax:* 0171-273 2893

HEAP, DAVID Chief Dental Officer, Welsh Office Grade: 4

Career: chief dental officer Welsh Office health professional group 1986-

Date of birth: 5 July 1938 *Education/professional qualifications:* High School, Bury, Lancashire; Sheffield University, dentistry (BDS 1963) *Marital status:* married Margaret Leah 1970; 2 sons

David Heap Esq, Chief Dental Officer, Welsh Office, Cathays Park, Cardiff CF1 3NQ
Telephone: 01222 823470 *Fax:* 01222 823982

HEATH, (LETTYCE) ANGELA Under Secretary, Local Government Directorate, Department of the Environment Grade: 3

Career: Department of Environment 1971-: principal private secretary to minister of housing 1979-80; assistant secretary 1983-92: head of central policy planning unit 1983-85; local government reorganisation 1985-87; personnel management 1987-90; Housing Corporation sponsorship and finance 1990-91; under secretary 1992-: director London 1992-95, local government 1995-

Date of birth: 27 May 1944 *Education/professional qualifications:* Herbert Strutt Grammar School, Belper, Derbyshire; Birmingham University, English (BA 1966, MA 1968) *Marital status:* married Roger Gordon 1985; 2 stepdaughters *Recreations:* books, music, gardens

Mrs Angela Heath, Under Secretary, Local Government Directorate, Department of the Environment, 2 Marsham Street, London SW1P 3EB
Telephone: 0171-276 5258

HEATHCOTE, Dr (FREDERIC) ROGER Under Secretary, Services Management Division, Department of Trade and Industry Grade: 3

Career: research associate Birmingham University 1969-70; Ministry of Technology/Department of Trade and Industry (DTI) 1970-73: private secretary (PS) to secretary for industrial development 1973; Department of Energy 1974-92: PS to permanent under secretary 1974; Offshore Technology Unit 1975-81; petroleum engineering division 1981-82; gas division 1982-84; electricity division 1984-87; establishment and finance division 1987-89; head of finance branch 1987-88; director of resource management 1988-89; head of coal division 1989-91; principal establishment and finance officer 1991-92; under secretary services management divison DTI 1992-

Date of birth: 19 March 1944 *Education/professional qualifications:* Bromsgrove School, Worcestershire; Birmingham University, physics (BSc 1966) and high-energy nuclear physics (PhD 1969) *Marital status:* married Mary Campbell Syme Dickson 1986; 1 step-daughter, 1 son *Recreations:* reading, gardening, painting

Dr F Roger Heathcote, Under Secretary, Department of Trade and Industry, Kingsgate House, 66-74 Victoria Street, London SW1E 6SW
Telephone: 0171-215 3609 *Fax:* 0171-215 8449

HEATLEY, BRIAN ANTHONY Director of Adult Training, Employment Department Group Grade: 3

Career: Department of Trade and Industry 1974-89; Department of Employment/Employment Department Group 1989-: head of resource planning branch 1990-93, director adult learning 1993-94, adult training 1994-

Date of birth: 20 April 1947 *Education/professional qualifications:* St John's College, Cambridge, mathematics (BA 1968), Warwick University (MPhil 1974) *Marital status:* divorced; 1 daughter *Recreations:* history, running, walking, cooking, photography

Brian Heatley Esq, Director, Adult Training, Employment Department Group, Moorfoot, Sheffield S1 4PQ *Telephone:* 01142 593978 *Fax:* 01142 594821

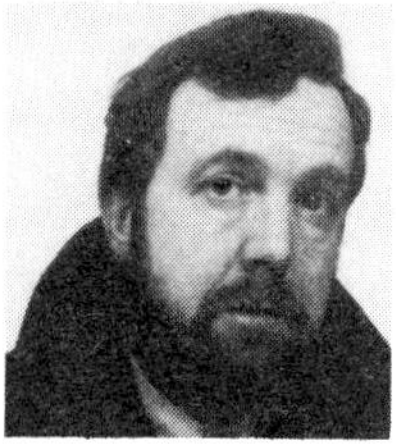

HEDGER, JOHN CLIVE Deputy Secretary, Schools' Command, Department for Education Grade: 2

Career: Department of/for Education [and Science] 1969-: assistant private secretary 1969-70; principal 1970-77: secretary to Committee of Enquiry into Education of Handicapped 1974-76; assistant secretary schools and further and higher education branches 1977-88; under secretary schools 1988-92; deputy secretary teachers' command 1992-94, schools' command 1994-

Date of birth: 17 December 1942 *Education/professional qualifications:* Quirister School, Winchester College; Victoria College, Jersey; Sussex University, English (BA 1965, MA 1966) *Marital status:* married Jean Felstead 1966; 2 sons, 1 daughter *Clubs:* Odney (Cookham) *Recreations:* coarse acting, coarse sailing, walking, growing things

Mr J C Hedger, Deputy Secretary, Department for Education, Sanctuary Buildings, Great Smith Street, London SW1P 3BT
Telephone: 0171-925 6211 *Fax:* 0171-925 6970

HENDERSON, CHARLES EDWARD Deputy Secretary, Energy Command, Department of Trade and Industry Grade: 2

Career: investment manager Equity and Law Life 1960-70; principal Export Credit Guarantee Department 1971-73, Departments of Trade and Industry (DTI) and of Energy (DEn) 1973-75; DEn 1975-88: assistant secretary 1975-82; under secretary1982-88: head of atomic energy division 1982-84, of oil division 1984-85, principal finance and establishment officer 1985-88; deputy secretary (DS) 1989-: head of Office of Arts and Libraries 1989-92; DTI 1992-: DS of corporate and consumer affairs command 1992, of energy command 1992-

Date of birth: 19 September 1939 *Education/professional qualifications:* Charterhouse; Pembroke College, Cambridge, mathematics (BA 1960, MA); FIA 1966 *Honours, decorations:* CB 1992 *Marital status:* married Rachel Hall 1966; 1 daughter, 1 son *Recreations:* music, golf, mountain walking, reading

Charles E Henderson Esq CB, Deputy Secretary, Department of Trade and Industry, 1 Palace Street, London SW1E 5HE *Telephone:* 0171-238 3139 *Fax:* 0171-238 3485

HENDERSON, Air Vice-Marshal D F A Assistant Chief of the Defence Staff (Policy and Nuclear)

Air Vice-Marshal D F A Henderson CBE, Assistant Chief of the Defence Staff, Ministry of Defence, Main Building, Whitehall, London SW1A 2HB *Telephone:* 0171-218 3150 *Fax:* 0171-218 7956

HENES, JOHN DEREK Director, Freight, Ports and International Division, Department of Transport Grade: 3

Career: Ministry of Aviation 1963-71; Department of Trade [and Industry] 1971-83: assistant secretary 1975-83; Department of Transport 1983-: director of international transport and freight division 1989-94, of freights, ports and international division 1994-

Date of birth: 8 June 1937 *Education/professional qualifications:* Christ's Hospital; Gonville and Caius College, Cambridge (BA, MA)

John D Henes Esq, Director of Freights, Ports and International Division, Department of Transport, 2 Marsham Street, London SW1P 3EB *Telephone:* 0171-276 5330

HENRY, JOHN Principal Finance Officer, Property Holdings Division, Department of the Environment Grade: 3

Career: psychologist Transport and Road Research Laboratory 1968-72; Department of Environment (DoE) 1972-: principal 1977-83, assistant secretary housing, radioactive waste and water divisions 1983-89; under secretary 1990-: regional director Yorkshire and Humberside DoE/Department of Transport 1990-94, principal finance officer property holdings division DoE 1994-

Date of birth: 8 October 1946 *Education/professional qualifications:* Cheltenham College; Queen's College, Oxford, philosophy and psychology (BA 1968, MA) *Marital status:* married Gillian Mary Richardson 1992; 1 daughter *Recreations:* walking, reading, art

John Henry Esq, Principal Finance Officer, Property Holdings Division, Department of the Environment, St Christopher House, Southwark Street, London SE1 0TE *Telephone:* 0171-921 4303 *Fax:* 0171-921 4926

HEPBURN, JOHN WILLIAM Under Secretary, Food, Drink and Marketing Policy, Ministry of Agriculture, Fisheries and Food Grade: 3

Career: Ministry of Agriculture, Fisheries and Food 1961-: assistant secretary 1973-81, under secretary (US) animal health 1982-86; director of establishments 1987-90; US food, milk/food and marketing 1990-

Date of birth: 8 September 1938 *Education/professional qualifications:* Hutchesons' Grammar School, Glasgow; Glasgow University, classics (MA 1959); Brasenose College, Oxford, classics *Marital status:* married Isla Marchbank 1972; 1 son *Recreations:* golf

John W Hepburn Esq, Under Secretary, Ministry of Agriculture, Fisheries and Food, Whitehall Place, London SW1A 2HH *Telephone:* 0171-270 8529 *Fax:* 0171-270 8838

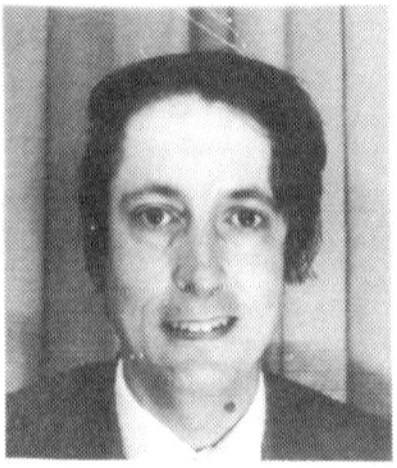

HEWITSON, (THOMAS) WILLIAM Chief Actuary, Life Insurance Division, Government Actuary's Department Grade: 4

Career: private practice actuarial training 1977-82; Government Actuary's Department 1982-: actuary, insurance division 1982-84; senior actuary, pensions division 1984-89; chief actuary, life insurance division 1989-

Date of birth: 31 December 1956 *Education/professional qualifications:* George Watson's College, Edinburgh; Edinburgh University, mathematics (BSc 1977); FFA 1981 *Marital status:* single *Recreations:* reading, music, travel

T William Hewitson Esq, Chief Actuary, Government Actuary's Department, 22 Kingsway, London WC2B 6LE *Telephone:* 0171-242 6828 *Fax:* 0171-831 6653

HEWITT, STEPHEN Under Secretary, Corporate Strategy and Personnel Division, Department of Social Security Grade: 3

Career: civil service 1975-: various positions 1975-90; Department of Social Security 1990-: under secretary corporate strategy and personnel division, resource management policy group 1992-

Date of birth: 9 March 1950 *Education/professional qualifications:* Dulwich College; Sussex University, chemistry (BSc 1971), history of science (MSc 1972) *Marital status:* married

Stephen Hewitt Esq, Under Secretary, Department of Social Security, Richmond House, 79 Whitehall, London SW1A 2NS *Telephone:* 0171-210 5831 *Fax:* 0171-930 3101

HEY, Miss C M Deputy Chief Inspector, Social Services Inspectorate, Department of Health Grade: 4

Miss C M Hey, Deputy Chief Inspector, Social Services Inspectorate, Department of Health, Richmond House, 79 Whitehall, London SW1A 2NS *Telephone:* 0171-210 5730

HEYWOOD, BARRY KEITH Regional Procurator Fiscal, Tayside Central and Fife, Crown Office Grade: 4

Career: Procurator Fiscal Service, Crown Office (public prosecution; sudden death and fire investigation) 1971-: depute procurator fiscal (PF) Ayr 1971-76, Glasgow 1976-77; PF Wick 1978-83; assistant PF Glasgow 1983-86; PF Inverness 1986-91; regional PF Tayside Central and Fife 1991- *Current non-Whitehall posts:* member council Law Society of Scotland

Date of birth: 24 July 1946 *Education/professional qualifications:* Kirkcaldy High School; Edinburgh University, law (MA 1967, LLB 1969) *Marital status:* married Mary Hutchison 1970; 1 daughter, 1 son *Recreations:* Roman and Byzantine history; walking

Barry K Heywood Esq, Regional Procurator Fiscal, 15 West Bell Street, Dundee *Telephone:* 01382 27535 *Fax:* 01382 202719

HICKEY, STEPHEN Chief Executive, Civil Service College (Executive Agency) Grade: 3

Career: Department of [Health and] Social Security (DSS) 1974-94: social security and health policy and legislation, assistant private secretary to Secretary of State 1978-79, 1984-85; social security operational strategy development 1979-84; family benefits policy and legislation 1985-88; DSS agency study 1988-89; seconded to Rank Xerox 1989-90; benefits agency strategic planning 1990-92; DSS finance 1992-94; chief executive Civil Service College 1994-

Date of birth: 10 July 1949 *Education/professional qualifications:* St Lawrence College, Ramsgate; Corpus Christi College, Oxford, history (BA 1970); St Antony's College, Oxford (DPhil 1978) *Marital status:* married Dr Janet Hunter 1976; 3 sons *Publications:* Workers in Imperial Germany: The Miners of the Ruhr (OUP 1985) *Recreations:* music, swimming, walking, history

Stephen Hickey Esq, Chief Executive, Civil Service College, Sunningdale Park, Ascot, Berks SL5 0QE *Telephone:* 01344 634000 *Fax:* 01344 842491

HICKS, Dr COLIN PETER Under Secretary, Environment and Energy Technologies Division, Department of Trade and Industry Grade: 3

Career: chemistry lecturer University of West Indies 1970-73; ICI research fellow Exeter University 1973-75; researcher National Physical Laboratory 1975-80; Department of Trade and Industry (DTI) 1980-84: research policy 1980-83, seconded as technical adviser to Barclays Bank 1983-84; deputy director Laboratory of Government Chemist 1984-87; DTI 1988-: secretary Industrial Development Advisory Board 1988-90, under secretary 1990-: innovation policy 1990-94, environment and energy technologies division 1994-

Date of birth: 1 May 1946 *Education/professional qualifications:* Rutlish Grammar School, Merton; Bristol University, chemistry (BSc 1967, PhD 1970) *Marital status:* married Elizabeth Joan Payne 1967; 2 daughters *Recreations:* computing

Dr Colin P Hicks, Under Secretary, Department of Trade and Industry, 1 Palace Street, London SW1E 5HE *Telephone:* 0171-215 4197 *Fax:* 0171-215 1062

HIGGINS, JOHN ANDREW Assistant Auditor General, National Audit Office Grade: 3 equivalent

Career: Exchequer and Audit Department 1958-84: audit manager 1977-81, deputy director 1981-84: seconded officer Office of Auditor General, Canada 1983-84; National Audit Office (examination of accounts of government departments, certain public bodies and international organisations) 1984-: director 1984-88, assistant auditor general 1988-

Date of birth: 19 February 1940 *Education/professional qualifications:* Hendon Grammar School; Hastings Grammar School; organ playing, Royal College of Organists (associateship 1988) *Marital status:* married Susan Jennifer Mathis 1965; 1 son *Clubs:* Ifield Golf and Country *Recreations:* classical organ, bridge, golf, supporting Crystal Palace

John A Higgins Esq, Assistant Auditor General, National Audit Office, 157-197 Buckingham Palace Road, London SW1W 9SP *Telephone:* 0171-798 7380 *Fax:* 0171-931 8614

"Next Steps" Executive Agencies

see page 875

HILL, (ROBERT) CHARLES Chairman, Standing Advisory Commission on Human Rights

Career: barrister; deputy county court judge 1979-80; Standing Advisory Commission on Human Rights 1991-: chairman 1992-

Date of birth: 22 March 1936 *Education/professional qualifications:* St Malachy's College, Belfast; Queen's University, Belfast, law (LLB 1957); Trinity College, Dublin, history/philosophy (BA 1959, MA 1962); Inn of Court, Northern Ireland (barrister 1959); Gray's Inn, London (barrister 1971); King's Inn, Dublin (barrister 1986); Queen's Counsel 1974; Senior Counsel (Ireland) 1987; Bencher Northern Ireland Inn of Court 1988 *Marital status:* married Kathleen Allen 1961; 1 daughter, 3 sons *Clubs:* Kildare Street and University, Dublin *Recreations:* art, forestry, shooting

R Charles Hill Esq QC, Chairman, Standing Advisory Commission on Human Rights, Temple Court, 39 North Street, Belfast BT1 1NA *Telephone:* 01232 243987 *Fax:* 01232 247844

HILLHOUSE, Sir (ROBERT) RUSSELL Permanent Under Secretary of State, Scottish Office Grade: 1

Career: Scottish Education Department (SED) 1962-71: assistant principal 1962-66, principal 1966-71; principal HM Treasury 1971-74; assistant secretary: Scottish Office (SO) 1974-77, Scottish Home and Health Department 1977-80; under secretary (US), principal finance officer SO 1980-85; SED 1985-88: US 1985-87, secretary 1987-88; permanent under secretary of state SO 1988- *Current non-Whitehall posts:* director Scottish Business in the Community 1990-

Date of birth: 23 April 1938 *Education/professional qualifications:* Hutchesons' Grammar School, Glasgow; Glasgow University, mathematics and physics (MA 1960) *Honours, decorations:* KCB 1991 *Marital status:* married Alison Janet Fraser 1966; 2 daughters *Clubs:* New (Edinburgh), Royal Society of Arts *Recreations:* making music; countryside

Sir Russell Hillhouse KCB, Permanent Under Secretary of State, Scottish Office, St Andrew's House, Regent Road, Edinburgh EH1 3DG *Telephone:* 0131-244 4026 *Fax:* 0131-244 2756

HILLIER, RICHARD Director, Resources and Planning Division, Health and Safety Executive Grade: 3

Career: director industrial relations division Employment Department Group -1994, of resources and planning division Health and Safety Executive 1994-

Richard Hillier Esq, Director, Resources and Planning Division, Health and Safety Executive, Rose Court, 2-10 Southwark Bridge Road, London SE1 9HF *Telephone:* 0171-717 6000 *Fax:* 0171-727 2254

HILTON, BRIAN JAMES GEORGE Deputy Secretary, Corporate and Consumer Affairs/Laboratories, Department of Trade and Industry Grade: 2

Career: Export Credits Guarantee Department 1958-69; Board of Trade 1968-71; first secretary UK delegation to OECD, Paris, Foreign and Commonwealth Office 1971-74; Department of [Trade and] Industry (DTI) 1974-89: textiles division 1974-76; assistant secretary 1976-82: Royal College of Defence Studies 1981; head financial services 1984-87, under secretary 1987-89; deputy secretary (DS) 1989-: countryside, marine, environment, fisheries Ministry of Agriculture, Fisheries and Food 1989-91; director Citizen's Charter Unit Cabinet Office 1991-94; DS corporate and consumer affairs/laboratories DTI 1994-

Date of birth: 21 April 1940 *Education/professional qualifications:* St Marylebone Grammar School, London *Honours, decorations:* CB 1992 *Marital status:* married Mary Margaret Kirkpatrick 1965; 2 daughters, 1 son *Recreations:* cricket, rugby, opera, music, gardening

Brian J G Hilton Esq CB, Deputy Secretary, Department of Trade and Industry, 151 Buckingham Palace Road, London SW1W 9SS
Telephone: 0171-215 1189 *Fax:* 0171-215 1400

HINE, Dr DEIRDRE JOAN Chief Medical Officer, Welsh Office Grade: 3

Career: hospital, general practice and public health posts 1961-74; community medicine specialist S Glamorgan Health Authority 1974-82; senior lecturer in geriatric medicine University of Wales College of Medicine (UWCM) 1982-84; deputy chief medical officer (CMO) Welsh Office (WO) 1984-88; senior lecturer, director breast screening service for Wales UWCM 1988-90; CMO (health policy and NHS management advice) WO 1990-

Date of birth: 16 September 1937 *Education/professional qualifications:* Charlton Park School, Cheltenham; Welsh National School of Medicine (MB BCh 1961); University of Wales, public health (DPH 1964); MFPHM 1974; FFPHM 1980 *Marital status:* married Raymond 1963; 2 sons *Recreations:* reading, music, walking, canal cruising, travel

Dr Deirdre J Hine, Chief Medical Officer, Welsh Office, Cathays Park, Cardiff CF1 3NQ
Telephone: 01222 823911 *Fax:* 01222 825242

HINSLEY, Dr RICHARD Deputy Chief Executive, Transport Research Laboratory (Executive Agency) Grade: 4

Career: Transport Research Laboratory: operations director -1994, deputy chief executive 1994-

Dr Richard Hinsley, Deputy Chief Executive, Transport Research Laboratory, Old Wokingham Road, Crowthorne, Berkshire RG11 6AU *Telephone:* 01344 773131

HOBSON, JOHN Director-General, Energy Efficiency Office, Department of the Environment Grade: 3

Career: assistant principal Ministry of Transport 1967-72; principal Department of the Environment (DoE) 1972-74, Civil Service Department 1974-78, DoE 1978-79; assistant secretary (AS) Department of Transport 1979-80; DoE 1980-: AS 1980-86, under secretary 1986-: director pollution control and wastes directorate 1988-93, energy efficiency office 1993-

Date of birth: 30 March 1946 *Education/professional qualifications:* Northampton Grammar School; Manchester Grammar School; King's College, Cambridge, mathematics (BA 1967, MA) *Marital status:* married Jeanne Gerrish 1970; 1 son, 1 daughter *Recreations:* gardening, reading, walking

John Hobson Esq, Under Secretary, Department of the Environment, 2 Marsham Street, London SW1P 3EB *Telephone:* 0171-276 3837
Fax: 0171-276 3714

HODGSON, MARTIN JOHN Controller, Inland Revenue East Grade: 4

Career: Inland Revenue 1967-: inspector of taxes 1967-73; training centre tutor 1973-76; district inspector (DI) Workington 1976-77; inspector (senior principal) head office 1977-81; DI Holborn 1981-82; principal inspector in charge of Centre 1 Scotland 1982-85; DI City 24 1985-87; assistant director head office 1987-90; controller east region 1990-

Date of birth: 1 May 1943 *Education/professional qualifications:* Bradford Grammar School; St Andrew's University, Latin and Greek (MA 1965) *Marital status:* married Doreen Burnie 1968; 1 son, 1 daughter *Recreations:* music, walking, gardening, swimming

Martin J Hodgson Esq, Controller, Inland Revenue East, Midgate House, Peterborough PE1 1TD *Telephone:* 01733 63241 *Fax:* 01733 313426

HOGARTH, ADRIAN JOHN Deputy Parliamentary Counsel, Office of the Parliamentary Counsel Grade: 3

Career: Office of Parliamentary Counsel (drafting government bills) 1985-: seconded as principal assistant parliamentary counsel (PC) to Law Commission 1992-94; deputy PC 1994-

Date of birth: 7 July 1960 *Education/professional qualifications:* St Paul's School, London; Magdalene College, Cambridge, archaeology, anthropology and law (BA 1981, MA, LLM 1982); Inner Temple (barrister 1983) *Marital status:* single *Recreations:* cricket, tennis

Adrian J Hogarth Esq, Deputy Parliamentary Counsel, Office of the Parliamentary Counsel, 36 Whitehall, London SW1A 2AY *Telephone:* 0171-210 6646 *Fax:* 0171-210 6632

HOGG, DAVID ALAN Deputy Treasury Solicitor, Treasury Solicitor's Department Grade: 2

Career: private practice solicitor 1969-78; Treasury Solicitor's Department (TSD) 1978-89: senior legal assistant 1978-85, assistant treasury solicitor (ATS) 1985-89; ATS Department of Energy 1989-90; principal assistant solicitor, head of litigation division (civil litigation in England and Wales for most government departments) 1990-92, deputy treasury solicitor 1993-

Date of birth: 8 October 1946 *Education/professional qualifications:* Brighton College; College of Law, Guildford (solicitor 1969) *Marital status:* married Pauline Pamela Papworth 1981; 3 sons, 1 daughter *Clubs:* National Liberal *Recreations:* theatre, inland waterways

David A Hogg Esq, Deputy Treasury Solicitor, Treasury Solicitor's Department, Queen Anne's Chambers, 28 Broadway, London SW1H 9JS *Telephone:* 0171-210 3129 *Fax:* 0171-210 3087

HOLLAND, (DAVID ANTHONY) TONY Technical Services Director, Highways Agency (Executive Agency) Grade: 4

Career: Department of Transport 1969-: deputy chief highway engineer 1987-90; director highway programme support services 1990-93, London regional office 1993-94, Highways Agency 1994-: London regional office 1994-95, technical services director 1995- *Current non-Whitehall posts:* council member Steel Construction Institute 1988-

Date of birth: 15 October 1939 *Education/professional qualifications:* Highgate School, London; Pembroke College, Cambridge, mechanical sciences (BA 1962); MICE 1966 *Marital status:* married Susan Elizabeth Riddy 1962; 1 daughter, 2 sons *Recreations:* gardening, walking, woodwork, bridge

Tony Holland Esq, Director, Technical Services, Highways Agency, St Christopher House, Southwark Street, London SE1 0TE
Telephone: 0171-928 5428 *Fax:* 0171-928 0373

HOLLIS, GEOFFREY ALAN Head of Livestock Group, Ministry of Agriculture, Fisheries and Food Grade: 3

Career: Gulf Oil 1967-74; Ministry of Agriculture, Fisheries and Food 1974-: seconded as first secretary to UK permanent representation to EC, Brussels 1977-80; under secretary and head of livestock group 1991- *Current non-Whitehall posts:* non-executive director Lucas Ingredients (Dalgety plc)

Date of birth: 25 November 1943 *Education/professional qualifications:* Hastings Grammar School; Hertford College, Oxford, mathematics (BA 1966, MA); Central London Polytechnic, management studies (diploma 1971) *Marital status:* married Ann Prentice 1967; 2 sons

Geoffrey A Hollis Esq, Under Secretary, Ministry of Agriculture, Fisheries and Food, Whitehall Place, London SW1A 2HH *Telephone:* 0171-270 8679 *Fax:* 0171-270 8837

HOLMES, ROBIN EDMOND KENDALL Head of Judicial Appointments Group, Lord Chancellor's Department Grade: 3

Career: Wolverhampton County Borough Council 1961-64; assistant principal/principal Ministry of Housing and Local Government 1965-73; assistant colonial secretary Hong Kong government 1973-75; assistant secretary 1976-83: Department of the Environment 1976-78, Property Services Agency 1978-82; Lord Chancellor's Department 1982-: under secretary 1983-: Midland and Oxford circuit administrator 1983-92, head of judicial appointments group 1992-

Date of birth: 14 July 1938 *Education/professional qualifications:* Wolverhampton Grammar School; Clare College, Cambridge, law (BA 1961); Birmingham University, law (LLM 1963); Law Society (solicitor 1964) *Marital status:* married Karin Kutter 1964; 2 sons *Recreations:* travel

Robin E K Holmes Esq, Head of Judicial Appointments Group, Lord Chancellor's Department, 105 Victoria Street, London SW1E 6QT *Telephone:* 0171-210 1602 *Fax:* 0171-210 1652

HOLMES, ROGER DE LACY Deputy Master/Chief Executive, Royal Mint (Executive Agency) Grade: 3

Career: Departments of Trade and Industry 1969-73, Prices and Consumer Protection 1974-77, Industry 1977-79; assistant to chairman British Leyland 1980-82; company secretary Mercury Communications 1982-83; director corporate affairs ICL 1984; executive director Dunlop Holdings 1984-85; executive director Chloride Group 1986-92; deputy master/chief executive Royal Mint 1993- *Current non-Whitehall posts:* non-executive director Cygnet Health Care plc

Date of birth: 15 January 1948 *Education/professional qualifications:* Huddersfield New College; Balliol College, Oxford, modern history (BA 1969); certified diploma in accounting and finance 1980 *Marital status:* married Jennifer Anne Heal 1970; 1 daughter, 1 son *Recreations:* chess, gol´ cricket

Roger de L Holmes Esq, Deputy Master, Royal Mint, 7 Grosvenor Garder London SW1W 0BH *Telephone:* 0171-828 8724 *Fax:* 0171-630 6592

Regulatory Organisations and Public Bodies

see page 1013

HOLROYD, JOHN HEPWORTH Prime Minister's Secretary for Appointments, and Ecclesiastical Secretary to the Lord Chancellor Grade: 2

Career: Ministry of Agriculture, Fisheries and Food 1959-85: assistant secretary 1969-78; under secretary 1978-89; Cabinet Office 1985-: deputy head of European secretariat 1985-89; deputy secretary 1989-: first civil service commissioner 1989-93; prime minister's secretary for appointments, and ecclesiastical secretary to Lord Chancellor 1993- *Current non-Whitehall posts:* treasurer to governors Kingswood School, Bath 1985-

Date of birth: 10 April 1935 *Education/professional qualifications:* Kingswood School, Bath; Worcester College, Oxford, history (BA 1959, MA) *Honours, decorations:* CB 1993 *Marital status:* married Judith Mary Hudson 1963; 1 son, 1 daughter *Clubs:* United Oxford and Cambridge University *Recreations:* choral singing, travel, joinery, bee-keeping

John H Holroyd Esq CB, Prime Minister's Secretary for Appointments, and Ecclesiastical Secretary to the Lord Chancellor, 10 Downing Street, London SW1A 2AA *Telephone:* 0171-930 4433

HOLT, Dr ANDREW ANTHONY Director, Information Systems, Department of Health Grade: 4

Career: operations research (OR) consultant HM Treasury 1974-78; head of OR Inland Revenue 1978-87; Department of Health [and Social Security] 1987-: director OR services 1987-90; director information services directorate 1990-

Date of birth: 4 January 1944 *Education/professional qualifications:* Latymer Upper School, Hammersmith; University College, London, mathematics (BSc 1965, PhD 1969) *Marital status:* married Janet Margery Crabtree 1969; 3 sons *Recreations:* soccer

Dr Andrew A Holt, Director Information Systems, Department of Health, Skipton House, 80 London Road, London SE1 6LW *Telephone:* 0171-972 6557 *Fax:* 0171-972 6534

HOPKINSON, (GEORGE) WILLIAM Assistant Under Secretary (Policy), Ministry of Defence Grade: 3

Career: Inland Revenue 1965-73; Civil Service Department 1973-81; HM Treasury 1981-86; Ministry of Defence 1986-: head defence arms control unit 1988-91; visiting fellow Cambridge University 1991-92; head defence lands service 1992-93; assistant under secretary (policy) 1993-

Date of birth: 13 September 1943 *Education/professional qualifications:* Tupton Hall Grammar School, Clay Cross; Pembroke College, Cambridge, history (BA 1965, MA) *Recreations:* reading, walking

G William Hopkinson Esq, Assistant Under Secretary (Policy), Ministry of Defence, Whitehall, London SW1A 2HB *Telephone:* 0171-218 2502 *Fax:* 0171-218 8292

HORNE, ROBERT DRAKE Under Secretary, Finance Branch, Department for Education Grade: 3

Career: Department of/for Education [and Science] 1968-: assistant secretary 1980-88: supply of teachers and finance under secretary teachers' pay and general branch 1988-92, finance 1993-

Date of birth: 23 April 1945 *Education/professional qualifications:* Mill Hill School, London; Oriel College, Oxford, classics (BA 1967) *Marital status:* married Jennifer Mary Gill 1972; 3 daughters *Recreations:* entertaining Australians, running

Robert D Horne Esq, Under Secretary, Department for Education, Sanctuary Buildings, Great Smith Street, London SW1P 3BT *Telephone:* 0171-925 6100 *Fax:* 0171-925 6998

HORNER, PHILIP Deputy Chief Executive, Government Property Lawyers (Executive Agency) Grade: 4

P Horner Esq, Deputy Chief Executive, Government Property Lawyers, Riverside Chambers, Castle Street, Taunton, Somerset TA1 4AP *Telephone:* 01823 345200 *Fax:* 01823 345330

HORSMAN, (MICHAEL) MIKE JOHN Director, Office of Manpower Economics Grade: 3

Career: Department of Employment/Employment Department Group 1974-: regional director London and south east, Employment Service 1989-92; director Office of Manpower Economics (service of independent public sector pay review bodies) 1992-

Date of birth: 3 March 1949 *Education/professional qualifications:* Dollar Academy, Glasgow; Glasgow University, history and politics (MA 1971); Balliol College, Oxford (scholar, exhibitioner) *Marital status:* married Dr Anne Margaret Marley 1977; 3 sons *Recreations:* cycling, history, literature

Mike Horsman Esq, Director, Office of Manpower Economics, Oxford House, 76 Oxford Street, London W1N 9FD *Telephone:* 0171-467 7200 *Fax:* 0171-467 7208

HOSKER, Sir GERALD ALBERY Queen's Proctor, Procurator General and Treasury Solicitor, Treasury Solicitor's Department *(until October 1995)* Grade: 1

Career: Treasury Solicitor's Department (TSD) (legal services for government departments; administration of estates of intestate) 1960-87: deputy treasury solicitor 1984-87; solicitor Department of Trade and Industry 1987-92; Queen's Proctor, Procurator General (matrimonial suits and legitimation cases) and Treasury Solicitor 1992-

Date of birth: 28 July 1933 *Education/professional qualifications:* Berkhamsted School, Hertfordshire; Law Society's School of Law (solicitor 1956); FRSA 1964; AFSA 1964 *Honours, decorations:* CB 1987, QC 1991, KCB 1994 *Marital status:* married Rachel Victoria Beatrice Middleton 1956; 1 daughter, 1 son *Clubs:* Royal Over-seas *Recreations:* study of biblical prophecy

Sir Gerald Hosker Esq KCB QC, Procurator General and Treasury Solicitor, Treasury Solicitor's Department, Queen Anne's Chambers, 28 Broadway, London SW1H 9JS *Telephone:* 0171-210 3050 *Fax:* 0171-210 3087

HOUGHAM, JOHN WILLIAM Chairman, Advisory, Conciliation and Arbitration Service

Career: army service 1955-57; Ford 1963-93: director industrial relations (DIR) Spain 1976-80; DIR manufacturing Europe 1982-86; executive director personnel 1986-93; chairman Advisory, Conciliation and Arbitration Service 1993- *Current non-Whitehall posts:* visiting professor East London University 1991-, visiting fellow City University 1991-

Date of birth: 18 January 1937 *Education/professional qualifications:* Sir Roger Manwood's Grammar School, Sandwich, Kent; Leeds University, English,

French, industrial relations (BA 1960); CIPM 1986; CBIM 1986 *Marital status:* married Peggy Grove 1961; 1 daughter, 1 son *Publications:* co-author Legal Intervention in Industrial Relations (Blackwell 1992) *Recreations:* family research, bird-watching, vintage cars, watching rugby

John W Hougham Esq, Chairman, Advisory, Conciliation and Arbitration Service, 27 Wilton Street, London SW1X 7AZ *Telephone:* 0171-210 3670 *Fax:* 0171-210 3708

HOULDSWORTH, W Deputy Director and Head of Support Services, CCTA (Government Centre for Information Systems) Grade: 4

W Houldsworth Esq, Deputy Director and Head of Support Services, CCTA, Gildengate House, Upper Green Lane, Norwich, Norfolk NR3 1DW *Telephone:* 01603 694700

HOWARD, DAVID JOHN Director, Excise and Central Policy, HM Customs and Excise Grade: 3

Career: Exchequer and Audit Department 1960-69; HM Customs and Excise (C&E) 1969-72: assistant principal 1969, principal 1969-72; private secretary to Chief Secretary to Treasury 1972-74; C&E 1974-91: assistant secretary 1976-84; director of VAT control 1985-87, of personnel 1987-90, of organisation 1990-91; deputy director of savings, principal establishment and finance officer Department for National Savings 1991-94; director excise and central policy C&E 1994- *Current non-Whitehall posts:* chairman governors Coulsdon High School, Old Coulsdon, Surrey 1993-

Date of birth: 1 June 1941 *Education/professional qualifications:* Whitgift School, Croydon *Marital status:* married Anne Westmore 1969; 2 sons, 2 daughters *Recreations:* vintage films, walking

David J Howard Esq, Director, Excise and Central Policy, HM Customs and Excise, 22 Upper Ground, London SE1 9PJ *Telephone:* 0171-865 5018 *Fax:* 0171-865 5120

HOWE, ELSPETH ROSALIND MORTON (Lady Howe of Aberavon) Chairman, Broadcasting Standards Council

Career: magistrate 1964-90: chairman Inner London Juvenile Court 1970-90; member Parole Board for England and Wales 1972-75; Inner London Education Authority 1967-79; member National Association for the Care and Resettlement of Offenders; deputy chairman Equal Opportunities Commission 1975-79; chairman Broadcasting Standards Council 1993- *Current non-Whitehall posts:* chairman BOC Foundation for the Environment 1990-; non-executive director Kingfisher plc 1986-, Legal and General Group 1989-

Date of birth: 8 February 1932 *Education/professional qualifications:* Wycombe Abbey School; London School of Economics, social science and administration (BSc 1985) *Marital status:* married Geoffrey 1953; 2 daughters, 1 son *Publications:* Women at the Top (1990); co-author Women on the Board (1991); Women and Credit (1978); numerous newspaper articles *Recreations:* bridge, walking, travel

Lady Howe, Chairman, Broadcasting Standards Council, 5-8 The Sanctuary, London SW1P 3JS *Telephone:* 0171-976 7670 *Fax:* 0171-976 7492

HOWE, JOHN FRANCIS Deputy Under Secretary, Civilian Management, Ministry of Defence Grade: 2

Career: Ministry of Defence 1967-: private secretary (PS) to permanent under secretary 1975-78; seconded as defence counsellor to UK delegation to NATO 1981-84; head of arms control unit 1984-86; PS to secretary of state 1986-87; assistant under secretary (personnel and logistics) 1988-91; deputy under secretary (civilian management) 1992-

Date of birth: 29 January 1944 *Education/professional qualifications:* Balliol College, Oxford, philosophy, politics and economics (BA 1964, MA) *Honours, decorations:* OBE 1974 *Recreations:* gardening, reading, travel

John F Howe Esq OBE, Deputy Under Secretary, Ministry of Defence, Main Building, Whitehall, London SW1A 2HB *Telephone:* 0171-218 9000

HOWE, MARTIN Director, Competition Policy Division, Office of Fair Trading Grade: 3

Career: economics lecturer Manchester, Illinois, USA and Sheffield Universities 1959-72; senior economic adviser Monopolies and Mergers Commission 1973-77; Office of Fair Trading 1977-: assistant secretary 1980-84; director, competition policy division 1984-

Date of birth: 9 December 1936 *Education/professional qualifications:* Leeds University, economics and accountancy (BCom 1957); Sheffield University, economics (PhD 1961) *Marital status:* married Anne Lawrenson 1959; 3 sons *Recreations:* theatre (including amateur dramatics), gardening, cricket

Martin Howe Esq, Director, Competition Policy Division, Office of Fair Trading, Field House, Breams Buildings, London EC4A 1PR *Telephone:* 0171-269 8843 *Fax:* 0171-269 8800

HOWES, CHRISTOPHER KINGSTON Second Commissioner and Chief Executive, Crown Estate Grade: 2

Career: planning and valuation assistant Greater London Council 1965-67; private practice 1967-79; Department of Environment 1979-89: deputy director land economy 1979-81, chief estates officer 1981-85, director land and property division 1985-89; second commissioner, chief executive and deputy chairman Crown Estate 1989- *Current non-Whitehall posts:* visiting professor Bartlett School of Architecture and Planning, University College, London 1984-; member Prince of Wales's Council 1990-, East Anglia University Court 1992-, Duchy of Lancaster 1993-

Date of birth: 30 January 1942 *Education/professional qualifications:* Gresham's School, Holt, Norfolk; London University College of Estate Management (BSc 1965); Reading University, land values research (MPhil 1976); ARICS 1967 *Marital status:* married Clare Cunliffe 1967; 2 daughters (1 deceased), 2 sons *Publications:* Value Maps: Aspects of Land and Property Values (Geoabstracts 1979) *Clubs:* Athenaeum, Aldeburgh Yacht, Royal Household Golf *Recreations:* music, sailing, painting

Christopher K Howes Esq, Chief Executive, Crown Estate, 16 Carlton House Terrace, London SW1Y 5AH *Telephone:* 0171-210 4231 *Fax:* 0171-930 1295

HUDSON, Dr CAROL Personnel and Professional Development Manager, Benefits Agency Medical Services Grade: 4

Dr Carol Hudson, Personnel and Professional Development Manager, Benefits Agency Medical Services, Warbreck House, Warbreck Hill, Blackpool, Lancashire FY2 0YE *Telephone:* 01253 337878

HUDSON, (NORMAN) BARRIE Under Secretary, International Division, Overseas Development Administration Grade: 3

Career: economist Tube Investments Ltd 1960-62, Economic Intelligence Unit 1962-63; statistics technical assistance adviser to Jordan government 1963-65; Overseas Development Ministry/Administration 1966-: statistician 1966-67, economic adviser British Middle East development division 1967-72, senior economic adviser 1973-74, head SE Asia development division 1974-76, assistant secretary 1977-80, under secretary 1981-: principal establishment officer 1981-85, Africa division (Africa and Middle East) 1986-93, international division 1993-

Date of birth: 21 June 1937 *Education/professional qualifications:* King Henry VIII School, Coventry; Sheffield University, economics and French (BA 1958); University College, London, economics (MSc Econ 1960) *Marital status:* married Hazel Cotterill 1963; 2 sons, 1 daughter *Recreations:* reading, theatre, football, cricket

N Barrie Hudson Esq, Under Secretary, Overseas Development Administration, 94 Victoria Street, London SW1E 5JL
Telephone: 0171-917 0156 *Fax:* 0171-917 0734

HUEBNER, MICHAEL DENIS Chief Executive, Court Service (Executive Agency); Deputy Clerk of the Crown in Chancery, Lord Chancellor's Department Grade: 2

Career: Lord Chancellor's Department 1966-: seconded to Law Officers' Department 1968-70; assistant solicitor 1978-85; under secretary 1985-89: NE circuit administrator 1985-88, principal establishment and finance officer 1988-89; deputy secretary 1989-: appointments and legislation 1989-91, head of law and policy groups 1991-93, of court service 1993-, chief executive 1995-; deputy clerk of the Crown in Chancery 1993-

Date of birth: 3 September 1941 *Education/professional qualifications:* Rugby School; St John's College, Oxford, modern history (BA 1963); Gray's Inn (barrister 1965, bencher 1994) *Honours, decorations:* CB 1994 *Marital status:* married Wendy Crosthwaite 1965; 1 son, 1 daughter

Michael D Huebner Esq CB, Chief Executive, Court Service, 105 Victoria Street, London SW1E 6QT
Telephone: 0171-210 1733 *Fax:* 0171-210 1739

HUGGINS, RODNEY PHILIP National Chairman, Independent Tribunal Service

Career: private practice lawyer, Kenya 1959-61; chair national insurance local tribunal 1975-84, industrial tribunals 1981-84; regional chair social security appeal tribunals 1984-92, chair VAT tribunals 1988-; member tribunals committee Judicial Studies Board 1991-; national chair Independent Tribunal Service (control social security and medical appeal tribunals) 1992-

Date of birth: 26 November 1935 *Education/professional qualifications:* Lycée Lakanal, Sceaux, Paris; solicitor 1958; advocate (Kenya) 1960; FCIArb 1981 *Marital status:* married José Rhoda 1959; 1 son *Publications:* Guide to Procedure in Social Security Appeal Tribunals (HMSO 1985) *Clubs:* Marylebone Cricket, Royal Automobile, Leander *Recreations:* golf, singing, scuba diving, bridge

Rodney P Huggins Esq, National Chairman, Independent Tribunal Service, City Gate House, 39-45 Finsbury Square, London EC2A 1PX
Telephone: 0171-814 6502 *Fax:* 0171-814 6542

HUGHES, Dr (ANTHONY) DAVID Research Director, ADAS (Executive Agency) Grade: 4

Career: Ministry of Agriculture, Fisheries and Food 1970-: soil scientist National Agricultural Advisory Service/Agricultural Development and Advisory Service (ADAS) 1970-84; administrative principal 1984-86; regional agricultural scientist ADAS/science adviser to Welsh Office 1986-88; ADAS 1988-: director field research and development 1988-91, research director 1991-

Date of birth: 22 September 1943 *Education/professional qualifications:* Dialstone Secondary Modern School, Stockport; Stockport School; Newcastle University, soil science (BSc 1967); Leeds University, soil science (PhD 1970) *Marital status:* married Janet Christine Whitehead 1970; 1 daughter, 1 son *Publications:* contributor The Agricultural Notebook *Clubs:* Civil Service *Recreations:* gardening, swimming

Dr A David Hughes, Research Director, ADAS, Oxford Spires Business Park, The Boulevard, Kidlington, Oxfordshire OX5 1NZ *Telephone:* 01865 845006 *Fax:* 01865 845091

HUGHES, (LEWIS) LEW HARRY Assistant Auditor General, National Audit Office

Career: Exchequer and Audit Department/National Audit Office (examination of accounts of government departments, certain public bodies and international organisations) 1979-: audit manager, deputy director 1979-85; director of health audit 1985-88, of defence audit 1988-90; assistant auditor general 1991- *Current non-Whitehall posts:* board member Auditing Practices Board 1991-

Date of birth: 6 March 1945 *Education/professional qualifications:* Devenport High School, Plymouth; City of London College, accountancy audit and law (internal public sector qualification 1966); CIPFA *Marital status:* married Irene Nash 1975; 1 son *Clubs:* Tavistock Golf *Recreations:* golf, violin and piano-playing, vintage cars

Lew H Hughes Esq, Assistant Auditor General, National Audit Office, Buckingham Palace Road, London SW1W 9SP *Telephone:* 0171-798 7678 *Fax:* 0171-931 8874

HULL, Dr ROB(ERT) DAVID Secretary, Higher Education Funding Council for England Grade: 3

Career: Civil Service Department 1974-81; Department of/for Education [and Science] 1982-94; secretary Higher Education Funding Council for England 1994-

Date of birth: 17 December 1950 *Education/professional qualifications:* Jesus College, Cambridge, mathematics (BA 1971, MA), linguistics (PhD 1975) *Marital status:* married Sally Ann 1973; 1 son, 1 daughter *Recreations:* chess

Dr Rob D Hull, Secretary, Higher Education Funding Council for England, Northavon House, Coldharbour Lane, Bristol BS16 2QD *Telephone:* 01179 317303 *Fax:* 01179 317150

HUM, CHRISTOPHER OWEN Assistant Under Secretary, Northern Asia and Pacific, Foreign and Commonwealth Office Grade: DS3

Career: HM Diplomatic Service 1967-: posts in Hong Kong, Peking, UK permanent representation to EC, Brussels, Paris, Foreign and Commonwealth Office, London (FCO) 1968-83; FCO 1983-89: assistant head Hong Kong department 1983-84, counsellor, deputy head Falkland Islands department 1985-86, head Hong Kong department 1986-89; political counsellor and head of chancery UK mission to UN, New York 1989-92; FCO 1992-: assistant under secretary northern Asia 1992-, and Pacific 1994-

Date of birth: 27 January 1946 *Education/professional qualifications:* Berkhamsted School, Hertfordshire; Pembroke College, Cambridge, modern and medieval languages (BA 1967, MA); Hong Kong University, Mandarin Chinese *Marital status:* married Julia Mary Park 1970; 1 daughter, 1 son *Recreations:* piano, viola, walking

Christopher O Hum Esq, Assistant Under Secretary, Foreign and Commonwealth Office, King Charles Street, London SW1A 2AH *Telephone:* 0171-270 2214 *Fax:* 0171-270 3387

HUMPHREYS, PETER JOHN Director of Personnel, National Rivers Authority Grade: 3

Career: personnel officer GEC Hotpoint 1970-72, William Press & Son 1972-75; pipework engineering group industrial relations manager British Steel 1975-83; personnel director Stanton plc 1983-89; director of personnel National Rivers Authority 1989-

Date of birth: 19 September 1947 *Education/professional qualifications:* St Ambrose College, Hale Barns, Cheshire; Newcastle Polytechnic, sociology (BSc 1969); Salford University, management (diploma 1970); FIPM 1994 *Marital status:* married Glynis Megan Roberts 1971; 1 daughter, 1 son *Recreations:* swimming, squash

Peter J Humphreys Esq, Director of Personnel, National Rivers Authority, Rivers House, Waterside Drive, Aztec West, Almondsbury, Bristol BS12 4UD *Telephone:* 01454 624400 *Fax:* 01454 624479

HUNT, Professor JULIAN CHARLES ROLAND Chief Executive, Meteorological Office (Executive Agency) Grade: 2

Career: Cambridge University 1970-: lecturer in applied mathematics and engineering 1970-78; reader in fluid mechanics 1978-90, professor 1990-; founder director Cambridge Environmental Research Consultants 1986-; chief executive Meteorological Office 1992-

Date of birth: 5 September 1941 *Education/professional qualifications:* Westminster School; Trinity College, Cambridge, mechanical sciences (BA 1963), aspects of magnetohydrodynamics (PhD 1967); Warwick University, engineering sciences *Honours, decorations:* FRS 1989; fellow Trinity College, Cambridge; honorary professor Cambridge University *Marital status:* married Marylla Shephard 1965; 2 daughters, 1 son *Publications:* numerous *Recreations:* family, art, theatre, running

Professor Julian C R Hunt FRS, Chief Executive, Meteorological Office, Bracknell, Berkshire RG12 2SZ *Telephone:* 01344 854600 *Fax:* 01344 856909

HUTCHISON, Sir PETER CRAFT **Chairman, Forestry Commission**

Career: army national service 1953-55; insurance industry 1959-; chairman Ailsa Shipbuilding; director Stakis plc 1979-91; chairman, trustee Edinburgh Royal Botanic Gardens 1985-94; chairman Loch Lomond and Trossachs working party 1991-94; board member Scottish Natural Heritage 1994; chairman Forestry Commission 1994- *Current non-Whitehall posts:* vice-chairman British Waterways 1988-; chairman Hutchison & Craft Ltd 1974-

Date of birth: 5 June 1935 *Honours, decorations:* CBE 1992; honorary fellow Royal Scottish Geographical Society 1994 *Marital status:* married Virginia 1966; 1 son *Clubs:* Western, Glasgow; Cavalry and Guards *Recreations:* gardening, plant collecting, calligraphy

Sir Peter Hutchison Bt CBE, Chairman, Forestry Commission, 231 Corstorphine Road, Edinburgh EH12 7AT *Telephone:* 0131-334 0303 *Fax:* 0131-334 4473

HUTTON, ANTHONY CHARLES **Principal Establishment and Finance Officer, Department of Trade and Industry** Grade: 2

Career: tax inspector Inland Revenue 1962-64; Board of Trade/Department of Trade [and Industry] 1964-: assistant principal 1964-68; principal 1968-77: principal private secretary to secretary of state for trade 1974-77; assistant secretary 1977-84; under secretary 1984-91; deputy secretary, principal establishment and finance officer 1991-

Date of birth: 4 April 1941 *Education/professional qualifications:* Brentwood School, Essex; Trinity College, Oxford, modern history (BA 1962, MA) *Marital status:* married Sara Flemming 1963; 2 sons, 1 daughter *Clubs:* Athenaeum *Recreations:* music, reading, odd-jobbing, walking

Anthony C Hutton Esq, Principal Establishment and Finance Officer, Department of Trade and Industry, Ashdown House, 123 Victoria Street, London, SW1E 6RB *Telephone:* 0171-215 6911 *Fax:* 0171-215 6917

HUTTON, DEIRDRE MARY **Chairman, Scottish Consumer Council**

Career: administrative housing associations 1970-74; general research Glasgow Chamber of Commerce 1975-83; freelance political research 1984-90; chairman Scottish Consumer Council 1990- *Current non-Whitehall posts:* member National Consumer Council 1991-; chairman Enterprise Music Scotland 1992-, Rural Forum 1992-; member Parole Board Scotland 1993-, consumer panel and ombudsman council Personal Investment Authority 1994-

Date of birth: 15 March 1949 *Education/professional qualifications:* Sherborne School for Girls *Marital status:* married Alasdair Henry 1975; 2 sons *Clubs:* Royal Society of Medicine *Recreations:* music, gardening, reading

Mrs Deirdre M Hutton, Chairman, Scottish Consumer Council, Royal Exchange House, 100 Queen Street, Glasgow G1 3DH *Telephone:* 0141-226 5261 *Fax:* 0141-221 0731

HYDES, OWEN DOUGLAS Deputy Chief Inspector, Drinking Water Inspectorate, Department of the Environment Grade: 6

Career: industrial water treatment 1965-73; Department of Environment water directorate 1973-: superintending chemist 1988-90; deputy chief inspector drinking water inspectorate 1990-

Date of birth: 3 May 1941 *Education/professional qualifications:* Millom Grammar School, Cumbria; Hull University, chemistry (BSc 1962); MRSC 1969; CChem 1977; FRSA *Marital status:* married Carol Ann 1966; 1 daughter *Publications:* The Treatment and Quality of Swimming Pool Water (HMSO 1984) *Recreations:* arts, natural history, environment, ornithology, sport

Mr Owen D Hydes Esq, Deputy Chief Inspector, Drinking Water Inspectorate, Romney House, 43 Marsham Street, London SW1P 3PY
Telephone: 0171-276 8213 *Fax:* 0171-276 8405

I

INGE, Field Marshal Sir PETER   Chief of the Defence Staff, Ministry of Defence

Career: army service 1956-: staff college student 1966; Ministry of Defence (MoD) 1967-69; joint services staff college student 1971; brigade major 11th Armoured Brigade (AB) 1972-73; staff college instructor 1973-74; commanding officer 1st battalion Green Howards 1974-76; commandant junior division staff college 1977-79; commander 4th AB 1979-82; chief of staff 1st British Corps (1BC) 1982-84; commander North East District and 2nd Infantry Division 1984-86; director-general logistic policy MoD (army) 1986-87; commander 1BC 1987-89, Northern Army Group and BAOR 1989-92; MoD 1992-: chief of the general staff, army, of the defence staff 1994- *Current non-Whitehall posts:* colonel commandant Army Physical Training Corps 1988-

Date of birth: 5 August 1935 *Education/professional qualifications:* Summer Fields School; Wrekin College; Royal Military Academy, Sandhurst *Honours, decorations:* KCB 1988, ADC Gen 1991, GCB 1992 *Recreations:* military history, tennis, cricket, walking

Field Marshal Sir Peter Inge GCB, Chief of the Defence Staff, Ministry of Defence, Main Building, Whitehall, London SW1A 2HB *Telephone:* 0171-218 3353 *Fax:* 0171-218 6799

INGLESE, ANTHONY MICHAEL CHRISTOPHER   Legal Director, Office of Fair Trading   Grade: 3

Career: Home Office legal adviser's branch 1975-91: seconded to legal secretariat to law officers 1986-88; legal director Office of Fair Trading (advising on consumer and competition law) 1991-

Date of birth: 19 December 1951 *Education/professional qualifications:* Salvatorian College, Harrow Weald; Fitzwilliam College, Cambridge, law (BA 1974, LLB 1975) *Marital status:* married Jane Elizabeth Kerry Bailes 1974; 1 son, 1 daughter *Clubs:* ICA *Recreations:* organising theatricals; watching football

Anthony M C Inglese Esq, Legal Director, Office of Fair Trading, Field House, 15-25 Bream's Buildings, London EC4A 1PR *Telephone:* 0171-269 8892 *Fax:* 0171-269 8830

INNES, JAMES   Director of Roads and Chief Road Engineer, Scottish Office Industry Department   Grade: 4

Career: engineer Lanark County Council (CC) 1966-67; civil engineer Inverness CC 1967-73; Scottish Office (SO) 1973-85; senior engineer 1973-82, principal engineer 1982-85; superintending engineer Department of Transport 1985; SO Industry Department roads directorate 1985-: assistant chief engineer (CE) 1985-88, deputy CE 1988-94, director of roads and chief road engineer 1995- *Current non-Whitehall posts:* visiting professor Strathclyde University 1992-

Date of birth: 7 August 1944 *Education/professional qualifications:* Woodside Secondary School, Glasgow; Strathclyde University, civil engineering (BSc 1966) *Marital status:* married June 1966; 1 daughter, 1 son *Recreations:* golf, hill walking; foreign travel

James Innes Esq, Director of Roads and Chief Road Engineer, Scottish Office Industry Department, New St Andrew's House, Regent Road, Edinburgh EH1 3DG *Telephone:* 0131-244 4283 *Fax:* 0131-244 4872

IRETON, BARRIE ROWLAND **Head of Africa Division, Overseas Development Administration** Grade: 3

Career: economist Zambia government 1965-69; development secretary Gambia government 1970-73; Overseas Development Administration 1973-: economic adviser (EA) 1973-76, senior EA 1976-84; assistant secretary 1984-88; under secretary 1988-: principal finance officer 1988-93; head of Africa division 1993-

Date of birth: 15 January 1944 *Education/professional qualifications:* Alleyne's Grammar School; Trinity College, Cambridge, economics (BA 1965, MA); London School of Economics (MSc 1970) *Marital status:* married June Collins 1985; 1 son, 1 daughter (1 son deceased) *Recreations:* tennis, gardening, walking

Barrie R Ireton Esq, Under Secretary, Overseas Development Administration, Eland House, Stag Place, London SW1E 5DH *Telephone:* 0171-917 0468 *Fax:* 0171-917 0652

IRWIN, HELEN ELIZABETH **Second Clerk of Select Committees, House of Commons** Grade: 4

Career: House of Commons Clerk's Office 1970-72, 1977-: clerk of public accounts committee 1977-81, Table Office clerk 1981-85, clerk of social services committee 1985-89, of health committee 1989-91, of foreign affairs committee 1991-94; second clerk of select committees 1994-

Date of birth: 21 April 1948 *Education/professional qualifications:* Whalley Range High School, Manchester; King's College, London, history (BA 1969); School of Slavonic and East European Studies, London University, social studies and administration (MA 1970) *Marital status:* married Robert 1972; 1 daughter *Recreations:* family and friends

Ms Helen E Irwin, Committee Office, House of Commons, London SW1A 0AA
Telephone: 0171-219 6257 *Fax:* 0171-219 2731

J

JACKLING, ROGER TUSTIN Deputy Under Secretary (Resources, Programmes and Finance) Ministry of Defence Grade: 2

Career: Ministry of Defence (MoD) 1969-84: fellow Center for International Affairs, Harvard University, USA 1985; principal Civil Service College 1986-89; MoD 1989-: assistant under secretary (programmes) 1989-91; deputy under secretary resources and programmes 1991-, and finance 1993-

Date of birth: 23 November 1943 *Education/professional qualifications:* Wellington College; New York University, USA, economics and politics (BA 1966); Jesus College, Oxford *Honours, decorations:* CBE *Recreations:* books, theatre, golf

Roger T Jackling Esq CBE, Deputy Under Secretary, Ministry of Defence, Main Building, Whitehall, London SW1A 2HB *Telephone:* 0171-218 9000 *Fax:* 0171-218 1885

JAFFRAY, TOM Director, Resource Management Group and Principal Establishment and Finance Officer, Export Credits Guarantee Department Grade: 3

Career: Department of Trade and Industry and Export Credits Guarantee Department (ECGD); director resource management and principal establishment and finance officer 1992-

Date of birth: 12 February 1952 *Education/professional qualifications:* Wallington High School; Imperial College, London, physics (BSc); Trinity College, Cambridge, mathematics; ARCS *Marital status:* married Nicolette Jane 1984

Tom Jaffray Esq, Director, Resource Management Group, Export Credits Guarantee Department, PO Box 2200, 2 Exchange Tower, Harbour Exchange, London E14 9GS *Telephone:* 0171-512 7731 *Fax:* 0171-512 7400

JAMES, HOWELL MALCOLM Political Secretary to the Prime Minister

Career: special adviser to Lord Young at Cabinet Office, Departments of Employment and of Trade and Industry 1985-87; corporate affairs director BBC 1987-92; corporate and government affairs director Cable and Wireless 1992-94; political secretary to the Prime Minister 1994-

Date of birth: 13 March 1954 *Education/professional qualifications:* Mill Hill School, London *Marital status:* single *Recreations:* theatre, food, films

Howell M James Esq, Political Secretary, Prime Minister's Office, 10 Downing Street, London SW1A 2AA *Telephone:* 0171-930 4433

JAMES, ROY LEWIS HM Chief Inspector of Schools (Wales) Grade: 4

Career: mathematics teacher/head of department, Surrey and Wales 1959-70; Welsh Office 1970-: schools inspector 1970-84: seconded as secretary to Schools Council committee for Wales 1975-77, staff inspector 1984-90, chief schools inspector 1990-92, HM chief inspector of schools (Wales) 1992-

Date of birth: 9 February 1937 *Education/professional qualifications:* Llandysul Grammar School; University College of Wales, Aberystwyth, mathematics (BSc 1958); education (postgraduate diploma 1959) *Marital status:* married Mary Williams 1962; 1 daughter *Recreations:* travel, walking, reading

Roy L James Esq, HM Chief Inspector of Schools, Office of HM Chief Inspector of Schools in Wales, Government Buildings, Tyglas Road, Llanishen, Cardiff CF4 5PL *Telephone:* 01222 761456 *Fax:* 01222 758182

JAMIESON, J L Divisional Solicitor, Solicitor's Office, Central Services, Scottish Office Grade: 4

J L Jamieson Esq, Divisional Solicitor, Solicitor's Office, Central Services, Scottish Office, New St Andrew's House, Edinburgh EH1 3SY *Telephone:* 0131-244 5251

JARROLD, KEN WESLEY Director of Human Resources, NHS Executive, Department of Health Grade: 2

Career: Department of Health (DoH) 1970-71; hospital administration Sheffield, Derby and Nottingham 1971-79; assistant district administrator (DA) South Tees health authority (HA) 1979-82; Gloucester HA 1982-89: DA 1982-84, district general manager 1984-89; chief executive Wessex regional HA 1990-94; human resources director NHS executive DoH 1994-

Date of birth: 19 May 1948 *Education/professional qualifications:* St Lawrence College, Ramsgate; Sidney Sussex College, Cambridge, history (BA 1969) *Marital status:* married Patricia Hadaway 1973; 2 sons *Publications:* Challenges for Health Services in the 1990s (Southampton University)

Ken W Jarrold Esq, Director of Human Resources, NHS Executive, Quarry House, Leeds LS2 7UE *Telephone:* 01132 545172 *Fax:* 01132 545173

JARVIE, Miss A Chief Nursing Officer, Scottish Office Home and Health Department Grade: 3

Miss A Jarvie, Chief Nursing Officer, Scottish Office Home and Health Department, St Andrew's House, Regent Road, Edinburgh EH1 3DG *Telephone:* 0131-244 2314

JAY, MICHAEL HASTINGS Deputy Under Secretary and Economic Director, Foreign and Commonwealth Office Senior Grade

Career: Ministry of Overseas Development (ODM) 1969-73; UK delegation to International Monetary Fund/World Bank, Washington DC 1973-75; ODM 1976-78; HM Diplomatic Service 1978-: first secretary New Delhi high commission 1978-81; Foreign and Commonwealth Office (FCO), London 1981-85; seconded as counsellor to Cabinet Office 1985-87; financial and commercial counsellor Paris embassy 1987-90; FCO 1990-: assistant under secretary for EC 1990-93, deputy under secretary and economic director 1993-

Date of birth: 19 June 1946 *Education/professional qualifications:* Winchester College; Magdalen College, Oxford, philosophy, politics and economics (BA, MA); School of Oriental and African Studies, London University (MSc 1969) *Honours, decorations:* CMG 1992 *Marital status:* married Sylvia Mylroie 1975

Michael H Jay Esq CMG, Deputy Under Secretary, Foreign and Commonwealth Office, Downing Street West, London SW1A 2AL *Telephone:* 0171-270 1500 *Fax:* 0171-270 2320

JEFFERSON, (JOHN) BRYAN Architectural Adviser to Secretary of State, Department of National Heritage

Career: director-general design services Property Services Agency (PSA) 1984-90; architectural adviser to secretary of state (SoS) Department of Environment 1984-93; chairman PSA Projects 1990-92; architectural adviser to SoS Department of National Heritage 1993- *Current non-Whitehall posts:* design adviser Tarmac Construction 1992-; visiting professor Sheffield University 1992-

Date of birth: 26 April 1928 *Education/professional qualifications:* Lady Manners School, Bakewell, Derbyshire; Sheffield University, architecture (diploma 1952) *Honours, decorations:* CBE 1983; CB 1990 *Marital status:* divorced; 3 sons *Clubs:* Royal Western Yacht *Recreations:* music, sea sailing

J Bryan Jefferson Esq CB CBE, Architectural Adviser, Department of National Heritage, 2-4 Cockspur Street, London SW1Y 5DH
Telephone: 0171-211 6000 *Fax:* 0171-211 6210

JEFFERYS, Dr DAVID BARRINGTON Head of Licensing Division, Medicines Control Agency (Executive Agency) Grade: 4

Career: medical posts Guy's and St Thomas's hospitals, London 1976-83; locum consultant physician Tunbridge Wells 1983-84; Medicines Control Agency 1984-: business manager of European and new drug licensing 1986-94; head of licensing division 1994- *Current non-Whitehall posts:* alternate delegate to Committee on Proprietary Medicinal Products (CPMP); chairman CPMP operations working party 1992-; member Pharmaceutical Report Scheme Committee; visiting professor of medicine Newcastle University

Date of birth: 1 August 1952 *Education/professional qualifications:* St Dunstan's College, London; London University (BSc 1973, MD 1983); Guy's Hospital (MB BS 1976); MRCP 1978; FFPM 1990; FRCP Edinburgh 1990, London 1992 *Marital status:* married Ann-Marie Smith 1985; 1 daughter, 1 son *Clubs:* Surrey County Cricket *Recreations:* sport, theatre, music, photography, art

Dr David B Jefferys, Head of Licensing Division, Medicines Control Agency, 1 Nine Elms Lane, London SW8 5NP *Telephone:* 0171-273 0200 *Fax:* 0171-273 0196

JEFFREY, BILL Deputy Head of Economic, Home, Social Affairs and Legislation Secretariat, Cabinet Office Grade: 3

Career: Home Office 1971-94: assistant secretary responsible for sentencing, criminal policy 1984-86, for criminal justice legislation 1986-88; head of prison service personnel management division 1988-91; under secretary (operations and resources) immigration and nationality department 1991-94; deputy head of economic, home, social affairs and legislation secretariat, Cabinet Office 1994-

Date of birth: 28 February 1948 *Education/professional qualifications:* Allen Glen's School, Glasgow; Glasgow University, mathematics (BSc 1970) *Marital status:* married Joan MacNaughton 1979 *Recreations:* reading, hill walking, watching football

W A Jeffrey Esq, Under Secretary, Cabinet Office, 70 Whitehall, London SW1A 2AS
Telephone: 0171-270 0189

JENKINS, (JAMES) CHRISTOPHER First Parliamentary Counsel, Parliamentary Counsel Office Grade: 1

Career: Parliamentary Counsel Office (drafting government bills) 1967-: seconded to Law Commission 1970-72, 1983-86; parliamentary counsel (PC) 1978-91; second PC 1991-; first PC 1994-

Date of birth: 20 May 1939 *Education/professional qualifications:* Magdalen College, Oxford, jurisprudence (BA 1961); solicitor 1965 *Honours, decorations:* CB 1987; QC 1994 *Marital status:* married Margaret Edwards 1962; 2 sons, 1 daughter

Christopher Jenkins Esq CB QC, First Parliamentary Counsel, Parliamentary Counsel Office, 36 Whitehall, London SW1A 2AY *Telephone:* 0171-210 6629 *Fax:* 0171-210 6632

JENKINS, Dr RACHEL Principal Medical Officer, Planning, Primary Care and NHS Community Care Directorate, Department of Health Grade: 4

Career: registrar Maudsley hospital 1975-77; Institute of Psychiatry 1977-85: researcher, honorary senior registrar, Wellcome fellow 1977-82, senior lecturer 1982-85; consultant and senior lecturer in psychological medicine St Bartholomew's hospital medical school 1985-87; Department of Health 1987-: principal medical officer mental health, elderly, disability unit 1988-95, planning, primary care and NHS community care directorate 1995-

Date of birth: 17 April 1949 *Education/professional qualifications:* St Paul's Girls' School, London; Girton College, Cambridge, medical sciences (BA 1971), clinical sciences (MB BChir 1974); MRCPsych 1978; MD (Cantab) 1984; FRCPsych 1992; FRIPHH 1992 *Marital status:* married David Keith 1974; 1 daughter, 1 son *Publications:* editor Post-Viral Fatigue Syndrome (Wiley 1991); co-author Promoting Mental Health at Work (HMSO 1992) and Creating a Common Profile (HMSO 1992); Promoting Mental Health Policies in the Workplace (HMSO 1993); Prevention of Suicide (HMSO 1994) *Recreations:* botany, ornithology, walking

Dr Rachel Jenkins, Principal Medical Officer, Department of Health, Wellington House, 133-155 Waterloo Road, London SE1 8UG
Telephone: 0171-972 4333 *Fax:* 0171-972 4340

JOHNS, MICHAEL ALAN Director, Business Operations Division, Inland Revenue Grade: 3

Career: Inland Revenue (IR) 1967-79: principal 1971-79; adviser to Cabinet Office Central Policy Review Staff 1979-80; IR 1980-: assistant secretary (AS) 1980-84; seconded to Orion Royal Bank 1985; AS 1986-87; under secretary 1987-; director policy division P7 1987-88, oil and financial division 1988-91, central division 1992-93, business operations division 1993-

Date of birth: 20 July 1946 *Education/professional qualifications:* Judd School, Tonbridge; Queen's College, Cambridge, history (BA 1967, MA) *Marital status:* single *Recreations:* skiing, teaching adults, moral philosophy

Michael A Johns Esq, Director, Business Operations Division, Inland Revenue, Somerset House, Strand, London WC2R 1LB
Telephone: 0171-438 6171 *Fax:* 0171-438 6440

JOHNSON, ALBERT GEORGE Director of Finance and Resources, Employment Service (Executive Agency) Grade: 4

Career: Department of Employment/Employment Department Group 1979-90; director of finance and resources Employment Service 1990-

Date of birth: 28 May 1937 *Education/professional qualifications:* Bancroft's School, Woodford; St Peter's College, Oxford, history (BA 1960, MA); Birkbeck College, London, psychology (BSc 1971); FCIS 1992 *Marital status:* married Laura Webster 1967; 2 sons, 1 daughter

Albert G Johnson Esq, Director of Finance and Resources, Employment Service, St Vincent House, 30 Orange Street, London WC2H 7HT
Telephone: 0171-389 1538 *Fax:* 0171-389 1457

JOHNSTON, ANDREW IAN Chief Actuary, Public Service Pensions, Government Actuary's Department Grade: 4

Career: Government Actuary's Department 1978-: trainee 1978-82; actuary social security income/expenditure forecasting 1982-90; chief actuary, public services pensions 1991-

Date of birth: 10 January 1956 *Education/professional qualifications:* Harrogate Grammar School; St Edmund Hall, Oxford, mathematics (BA 1978); FIA 1984 *Marital status:* married Sara Lesley Lewis 1988; 1 daughter *Clubs:* National Liberal

Andrew I Johnston Esq, Chief Actuary, Government Actuary's Department, 22 Kingsway, London WC2B 6LE *Telephone:* 0171-242 6828
Fax: 0171-831 6653

JOHNSTON, CATHERINE ELIZABETH Parliamentary Counsel, Office of the Parliamentary Counsel

Career: solicitor 1978-80; Office of the Parliamentary Counsel (OPC) 1980-: seconded to Law Commission 1983-85, 1990-92, to OPC Australia 1987-88; deputy PC 1989-94, PC 1994-

Date of birth: 4 January 1953 *Education/professional qualifications:* St Paul's Girls' School, London; St Hugh's College, Oxford, history (BA 1974); solicitor 1978 *Marital status:* married Brendan Keith 1989; 2 children

Miss Catherine E Johnston, Parliamentary Counsel, Office of the Parliamentary Counsel, 36 Whitehall, London SW1A 2AY *Telephone:* 0171-210 6612 *Fax:* 0171-210 6632

JOHNSTON, Dr IAN ALISTAIR Director-General, Training, Enterprise and Education Directorate, Employment Department Group Grade: 2

Career: Department of Employment (DEmp) 1969-75; labour attache Brussels embassy 1975-77; director Advisory Conciliation and Arbitration Service 1978-83; DEmp/Employment Department Group 1983-: head of financial management initiative 1983; under secretary 1984-92: director planning and resources Manpower Services Commission 1984, of education and training operations and policy 1985-92; deputy secretary 1992-: head resource and strategy directorate 1992; director-general training, enterprise and education directorate 1992- *Current non-Whitehall posts:* deputy chairman Sheffield Hallam University 1989-; honorary treasurer, council member Industry Society

Date of birth: 2 May 1944 *Education/professional qualifications:* High Wycombe Royal Grammar School; Birmingham University, metallurgy (BSc 1966, PhD 1969); CIMgt; FIPD *Marital status:* married Mary Bridget Lube 1973; 1 daughter, 1 son *Publications:* part-author Gower Handbook of Training and Development (Gower 1991) *Recreations:* birdwatching

Dr Ian A Johnston, Director-General, TEED, Employment Department Group, Moorfoot, Sheffield S1 4PQ *Telephone:* 01142 594108
Fax: 01142 751479

JOHNSTON, JOHN DOUGLAS HARTLEY Principal Assistant Solicitor, Solicitor's Office, Inland Revenue Grade: 3

Career: barrister; solicitor's office Inland Revenue 1968-: assistant solicitor 1976-86, under secretary 1986-

Date of birth: 19 March 1935 *Education/professional qualifications:* Jesus College, Cambridge (MA, LLB, PhD); Harvard Law School (LLM); Lincoln's Inn (barrister 1963)

John Johnston Esq, Solicitor's Office, Inland Revenue, Somerset House, Strand, London WC2R 1LB
Telephone: 0171-438 6228

JONES, COLIN LESLIE Director of Health Financial Management Division, Welsh Office Grade: 4

Career: Ministry of Health/Department of Health and Social Security 1961-76; Welsh Office 1976-: principal private secretary to secretary of state 1983-85; assistant secretary, head of local government finance policy and local government reorganisation 1985-91; director training, education and enterprise department 1992-94, health financial management division 1994-

Date of birth: 22 May 1941 *Education/professional qualifications:* Tonypandy Grammar School, Rhondda *Marital status:* married Angela Mary Lock 1962; 2 sons *Clubs:* Rotary *Recreations:* music, travel, keep fit

Colin Jones Esq, Director of Health Financial Management Division, Welsh Office, Companies House, Crown Way, Cardiff CF4 3UT
Telephone: 01222 823137 *Fax:* 01222 825021

JONES, DAVID GEORGE Director-General Supplies and Transport (Naval), Ministry of Defence Grade: 3

Career: War Office/Ministry of Defence 1960-: assistant private secretary (PS) to army minister 1970-71; PS to minister of state 1977-80; defence sales regional marketing director 1980-84; assistant secretary air systems controllerate (ASC) 1984-85; deputy director-general (DG) Al Yamamah project 1985-88; DG aircraft 2ASC 1988-89; civil secretary British forces Germany 1989-92; DG supplies and transport (navy) 1993-

Date of birth: 31 May 1941 *Education/professional qualifications:* High Storrs Grammar School, Sheffield *Recreations:* gardening, travel

David G Jones Esq, Director-General Supplies and Transport (Navy), Ministry of Defence, Ensleigh, Bath BA1 5AB *Telephone:* 01225 467707 *Fax:* 01225 468307

JONES, DEREK WILLIAM Director of Industry and Training, Welsh Office Grade: 3

Career: Department of Trade and Industry (DTI) 1977-83; HM Treasury 1983-87: public expenditure, industry 1983-84, financial institutions and markets 1984-87; Japan desk overseas trade division DTI 1987-89; Welsh Office 1989-: head of industrial policy division 1989-92, of finance programmes division 1992-94; director industry and training department 1994-

Date of birth: 8 December 1952 *Education/professional qualifications:* Cardiff High School; University College, Cardiff, philosophy (BA) *Marital status:* married; 2 sons

Derek W Jones Esq, Under Secretary, Welsh Office, Cathays Park, Cardiff CF1 3NQ
Telephone: 01222 823325 *Fax:* 01222 825478

JONES, IAN MICHAEL Head of Textiles and Retailing, Department of Trade and Industry Grade: 3

Career: Home Office 1972-81: police liaison division 1978-81; head of radio licensing Department of Trade and Industry (DTI) 1981-85; small firms division Department of Employment 1985-89; secretary British Overseas Trade Board 1989-90; DTI 1990-: south east regional director 1990-94; head of textiles and retailing division 1994- *Current non-Whitehall posts:* non-executive director Glynwed Consumer Products 1994-

Date of birth: 5 September 1945 *Education/professional qualifications:* St Bartholomew's Grammar School, Newbury; Fitzwilliam College, Cambridge, economics and politics (BA 1972) *Marital status:* married Vivien Mary Hepworth 1976; 2 sons *Recreations:* cricket, birds

Ian M Jones Esq, Under Secretary, Department of Trade and Industry, 151 Buckingham Palace Road, London SW1W 9SS *Telephone:* 0171-215 2969 *Fax:* 0171-215 1579

JONES, Dr KEITH HOWARD Chief Executive, Medicines Control Agency (Executive Agency) Grade: 3

Career: clinical and research posts Cardiff, Edinburgh and Cambridge teaching hospitals 1960-67; toxicologist; industry 1967-89: head of medical department Fisons Agrochemical Division, of safety assessment and clinical pharmacology Beecham Pharmaceuticals; medical affairs executive director Merck Sharp and Dohme Research Laboratories, USA; Medicine Control Agency 1989-: director 1989-, chief executive 1991- *Current non-Whitehall posts:* UK delegate to EC's Committee for Proprietary Medicines and Pharmaceutical Committee

Date of birth: 14 October 1937 *Education/professional qualifications:* medicine *Publications:* numerous publications on clinical and metabolic medicine, pesticide and drug toxicology, clinical pharmacology and drug development *Recreations:* sailing, tennis

Dr Keith H Jones, Chief Executive, Medicines Control Agency, Market Towers, 1 Nine Elms Lane, London SW8 5NQ *Telephone:* 0171-273 0100 *Fax:* 0171-273 0548

JONES, (RICHARD) DICK ADRIAN JEREMY Controller Large Groups Office, Inland Revenue Grade: 4

Career: Inland Revenue 1956-: West Country tax offices; head office technical establishments; district inspector Paignton, Woking and City of London; East London region controller 1988-94; large groups office controller 1994-

Date of birth: 9 October 1936 *Education/professional qualifications:* Bideford Grammar School *Marital status:* married Ida Elizabeth Crocker 1961; 1 son *Publications:* contributor to One Day for Life (Bantam 1987); The Tree (David and Charles 1990); The Sea (David and Charles 1993) *Clubs:* Royal Photographic Society *Recreations:* photography, tennis, walking, reading

Dick Jones Esq, Controller Large Groups Office, Inland Revenue, New Court, 48 Carey Street, London WC2A 2JE *Telephone:* 0171-324 1321 *Fax:* 0171-324 1353

JORDAN, GRAHAM HAROLD BEN Deputy Chief Scientist (Scrutiny and Analysis), Ministry of Defence Grade: 3

Career: Defence Operational Analysis Establishment 1967-82; Royal Aircraft Establishment, Farnborough 1982-87: head of defence weapons department 1985-87; head of civil service personnel management policy HM Treasury 1987-90; Ministry of Defence 1990-: scientific adviser command information systems 1990-91, assistant chief scientific adviser, capabilities 1991-94, deputy chief scientist (scrutiny and analysis) 1995-

Date of birth: 1 April 1945 *Education/professional qualifications:* Chislehurst and Sidcup Grammar School; Downing College, Cambridge, natural sciences and chemical engineering (BA 1966, MA); Brunel University, operational research (MTech 1974) *Publications:* Learning from Experience: A Report on the Arrangements for Managing Major Projects in the Procurement Executive (HMSO 1988) *Recreations:* riding, small-scale farming, music, DIY

Graham H B Jordan Esq, Deputy Chief Scientist, Ministry of Defence, Whitehall, London SW1A 2HB
Telephone: 0171-218 2034

JORDAN, KENNETH JOHN Director of Business Services, Employment Department Group Grade: 4

Career: Board of Trade (BoT) 1961-63; HM Treasury (HMT) 1963-64; BoT 1964-68: private secretary (PS) to minister of state 1964-66; Department of Economic Affairs 1968-69; Harkness fellow Harvard University, USA 1969-70; Department of Trade and Industry 1971-72; assistant secretary 1972-90: Northern Ireland Office 1972-75: principal PS to secretary of state 1974-75; HMT 1975-76; Department of Employment (DEmp) 1976-79; Manpower Services Commission 1979-81; Health and Safety Executive 1981-86; DEmp/Employment Department Group 1986-: director of financial services 1986-90, industrial relations division 1990-92, director of business services 1992-

Date of birth: 3 October 1938 *Education/professional qualifications:* Kingston Grammar School, Surrey; London School of Economics, economics (BScEcon 1961); Harvard University, USA, public administration (MPA 1970); FRSA; MBCS *Marital status:* married Beverly Anne Turner 1961 (divorced); Wendy Frances Thompson 1974; 1 son, 1 daughter *Recreations:* cooking, gardening, walking

Kenneth J Jordan Esq, Director of Business Services, Employment Department Group, Caxton House, Tothill Street, London SW1H 9NF
Telephone: 0171-273 5383 *Fax:* 0171-273 5384

JOYCE, PETER ROBERT Inspector General and Chief Executive, Insolvency Service (Executive Agency) Grade: 3

Career: Department of Trade [and Industry] 1960-: Insolvency Service (IS) (administration and investigation of bankruptcies and compulsory liquidations) 1960-79; consumer affairs division 1979-81; IS 1981-: chief examiner 1981-82, official receiver 1982-84, principal examiner 1984-85, deputy inspector general 1985-89, inspector general and chief executive 1989-

Date of birth: 14 January 1942 *Education/professional qualifications:* Westwood's Grammar School, Northleach, Gloucestershire; FCCA 1970 *Marital status:* married Marian Neal 1988

Peter R Joyce Esq, Inspector General and Chief Executive, Insolvency Service, PO Box 203, 21 Bloomsbury Street, London WC1B 3QW
Telephone: 0171-291 6717 *Fax:* 0171-291 6731

K

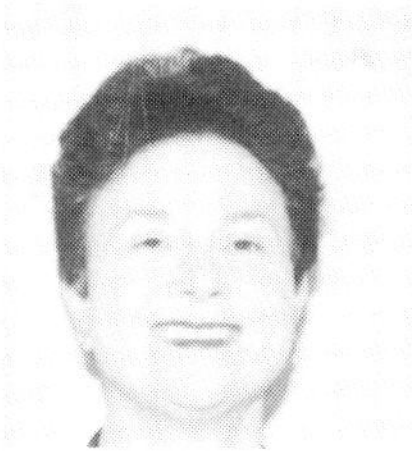

KAHN, DIANA SUSAN Deputy Director-General, Office of the National Lottery Grade: 5

Career: computer consultancy 1970-74; Department of Environment 1974-92: local government finance policy 1984-86; head of urban land policy 1986-88, of Crown Suppliers privatisation Property Services Agency 1988-91, of local authority competition policy 1991-92; deputy head Efficiency Unit, Cabinet Office 1992-94; deputy director general Office of the National Lottery 1994-

Date of birth: 6 November 1948 *Education/professional qualifications:* Benenden School, Kent; Lady Margaret Hall, Oxford, philosophy, politics and economics (BA 1970) *Marital status:* married Terence Anthony Mitchison 1982; 1 daughter, 1 son *Recreations:* hill walking

Ms Diana Kahn, Deputy Director-General, Office of the National Lottery, 2 Monck Street, London SW1P 2BQ *Telephone:* 0171-227 2000 *Fax:* 0171-227 2005

KAVANAGH, (THOMAS) TOM Secretary, Gaming Board for Great Britain Grade: 5

Career: statistician/reliability engineer Hawker Siddeley Aviation 1968-72; statistician Department of Employment 1972-82, Central Statistical Office 1982-84; Home Office 1984-91: chief statistician 1984-88, immigration and nationality department 1988-91; secretary Gaming Board for Great Britain (regulation of casinos, bingo clubs, gaming machines, lotteries) 1991-

Date of birth: 5 July 1947 *Education/professional qualifications:* Gunnersbury Roman Catholic Grammar School, London; Exeter University, economics and statistics (BAEcon 1968) *Marital status:* married Shirley Jane Harries 1977; 1 daughter, 3 sons *Recreations:* reading, sports

Tom Kavanagh Esq, Secretary, Gaming Board for Great Britain, Berkshire House, 168-173 High Holborn, London WC1V 7AA *Telephone:* 0171-306 6253 *Fax:* 0171-306 6267

KEITH, B P Secretary to Chairman of Committees; Principal Clerk, Private Bills Office, House of Lords Grade: 4

B P Keith Esq, Secretary to Chairman of Committees, House of Lords, Westminster, London SW1A 0PW *Telephone:* 0171-219 3231

KELLY, CHRISTOPHER WILLIAM Deputy Secretary, Director, Budget and Public Finances, Directorate, HM Treasury Grade: 2

Career: HM Treasury 1970-: private secretary to Financial Secretary 1971-73; principal 1973-80: secretary to Wilson Committee of Inquiry into Financial Institutions 1978-80; assistant secretary 1980-87; under secretary 1987-94: pay and industrial relations group 1987-91, social services group 1991-92, general expenditure policy group 1992-94; deputy secretary public finance/budget and public finances directorate 1994-

Date of birth: 18 August 1946 *Education/professional qualifications:* Beaumont College, Windsor; Trinity College, Cambridge, economics (BA 1968); Manchester University, sociology (MA Econ 1970) *Marital status:* married

Alison Durant 1970; 2 sons, 1 daughter *Recreations:* narrow boating, walking

Christopher W Kelly Esq, Deputy Secretary, HM Treasury, Parliament Street, London SW1P 3AG *Telephone:* 0171-270 5939 *Fax:* 0171-270 5287

KEMP, Dr ALAN Special Adviser to President of the Board of Trade

Dr Alan Kemp, Special Adviser, Department of Trade and Industry, Ashdown House, 123 Victoria Street, London SW1E 6RB *Telephone:* 0171-215 5000

KENDELL, Dr ROBERT EVAN Chief Medical Officer, Scottish Office Home and Health Department

Career: visiting professor University of Vermont College of Medicine, USA 1969-70; reader in psychiatry Institute of Psychiatry, London University 1970-74; psychiatry professor Edinburgh University 1974-91; member Medical Research Council 1984-88; dean of Edinburgh Medical School 1986-90; chief medical officer Scottish Office Home and Health Department 1991- *Current non-Whitehall posts:* member World Health Organisation expert advisory panel on mental health 1979-

Date of birth: 28 March 1935 *Education/professional qualifications:* Mill Hill School, London; Peterhouse, Cambridge, biochemistry and medicine (BA 1956, MB, BChir, MA 1959, MD 1967); King's College Medical School, London; Maudsley Hospital, London; Institute of Psychiatry, London *Honours, decorations:* Gaskell Gold Medal of Royal College of Psychiatrists 1967; Paul Hoch Medal of American Psychopathological Association 1988; FRSE 1993; Marcé Society Medal 1994 *Marital status:* married Dr Ann Whitfield 1961; 2 daughters, 2 sons *Publications:* The Classification of Depressive Illnesses (OUP 1968); Psychiatric Diagnosis in New York and London (OUP 1972); The Role of Diagnosis in Psychiatry (Blackwell Scientific 1975); Companion to Psychiatric Studies (Churchill Livingstone 1983, 1988, 1993) *Clubs:* Climbers' *Recreations:* overeating, hill walking

Dr Robert E Kendell, Chief Medical Officer, Scottish Office Home and Health Department, St Andrew's House, Edinburgh EH1 3DG *Telephone:* 0131-244 2264 *Fax:* 0131-244 2835

KENT, ALAN Chief Executive, Medical Devices Agency (Executive Agency) Grade: 4

Career: Vickers Medical -1986, 1991-93: managing director 1980-86, director regulatory affairs 1991-93; executive vice-president Air-Shields Inc, USA 1986-91; chief executive Medical Devices Agency 1993-

Date of birth: 20 January 1940 *Education/professional qualifications:* Wanstead County High School; Exeter University, physics (BSc 1961) *Marital status:* married Gillian Anne 1963; 2 daughters *Recreations:* golf, skiing, theatre

Alan Kent Esq, Chief Executive, Medical Devices Agency, 14 Russell Square, London WC1B 5EP *Telephone:* 0171-972 8140 *Fax:* 0171-972 8141

KERBY, JOHN VYVYAN Under Secretary, Asia and the Oceans, Overseas Development Administration Grade: 3

Career: assistant principal Colonial Office 1965-67; Ministry of Overseas Development 1967-70; private secretary to parliamentary under secretary Foreign and Commonwealth Office 1970-71; principal Overseas Development Administration (ODA) 1971-74, Civil Service Selection Board 1974-75; ODA 1975-: principal 1975-77, assistant secretary 1977-83, head of British development division in Southern Africa 1983-86, principal establishment officer and under secretary (US) overseas manpower division 1986-93, US Asia and the Oceans 1993- *Current non-Whitehall posts:* governor Centre for International Briefing 1986-

Date of birth: 14 December 1942 *Education/professional qualifications:* Eton College; Christ Church, Oxford, classics (BA 1965, MA) *Marital status:* married Shirley Elizabeth Pope 1977; 1 stepson, 1 stepdaughter *Recreations:* gardening, cricket, entomology

John V Kerby Esq, Under Secretary, Overseas Development Administration, 94 Victoria Street, London SW1E 5JL
Telephone: 0171-917 0352 *Fax:* 0171-917 0078

KERMAN, JOHN ALLISON Deputy Director, Civil Engineering and Environmental Policy, Highways Agency (Executive Agency) Grade: 4

Career: head of engineering policy and programme Department of Transport 1988-93; Highways Agency 1993-: director eastern region road programmes 1993-95; deputy director civil engineering and environmental policy directorate 1995-

Date of birth: 2 May 1946 *Education/professional qualifications:* University College School, Hampstead; Willesden and Westminster College of Technology *Marital status:* married Susan Humpherston 1967; 2 daughters, 1 son *Recreations:* music

J A Kerman Esq, Deputy Deputy, Civil Engineering and Environmental Policy, Highways Agency, St Christopher House, Southwark Street, London SE1 0TE *Telephone:* 0171-928 3666

KERR, The Rt Hon Sir MICHAEL ROBERT EMMANUEL Chairman, Appeal Committee, Panel on Takeovers and Mergers

Career: second world war air force service 1941-45; barrister 1948-: high court judge 1972-78; chairman Law Commission 1978-81; Lord Justice of Appeal 1981-89; president Chartered Institute of Arbitrators 1983-86, London Court of International Arbitration 1984-94; chairman Takeover Panel appeal committee 1992-

Date of birth: 1 March 1921 *Education/professional qualifications:* Aldenham School; Clare College, Cambridge, law (BA 1947, MA); Lincoln's Inn (barrister 1948, QC 1968, bencher 1968) *Honours, decorations:* KB 1972, PC 1983; Order of Merit (Germany 1990) *Marital status:* married Diana Patricia Sneezum 1983; 1 daughter, 2 sons, plus 1 daughter, 1 son from previous marriage *Publications:* McNair's Law of the Air (1953,65); articles on commercial law and arbitration *Clubs:* Garrick, Pilgrims *Recreations:* travel, music, family

The Rt Hon Sir Michael Kerr KB, Chairman, Appeal Committee, Panel on Takeovers and Mergers, c/o Essex Court Chambers, 24 Lincoln's Inn Fields, London WC2A 3ED *Telephone:* 0171-813 8000 *Fax:* 0171-813 8080

KERRIGAN, GREER SANDRA **Principal Assistant Solicitor, Division A, Department of Social Security** Grade: 3

Career: Department of Health [and Social Security] 1974-: legal assistant (LA) 1974-77, senior LA 1977-85, assistant solicitor 1985-91, under secretary, solicitor's office Department of Social Security 1991-

Date of birth: 7 August 1948 *Education/professional qualifications:* Bishop Anstey High School, Port of Spain, Trinidad; Council of Legal Education, law (barrister 1971) *Marital status:* married Donal Brian 1974; 1 son, 1 daughter *Recreations:* reading, bridge, squash

Mrs Greer S Kerrigan, Under Secretary, Department of Social Security, New Court, 48 Carey Street, London WC2A 2LS *Telephone:* 0171-412 1341 *Fax:* 0171-412 1583

KERSE, CHRISTOPHER STEPHEN **Head of Division B, Solicitor's Office, Department of Trade and Industry** Grade: 3

Career: law lecturer Bristol University 1968-72, Manchester University 1972-76; visiting assistant law professor British Columbia University, Canada 1974-75; Office of Fair Trading 1976-81; Department of Trade and Industry 1981-: senior legal assistant 1981-82; assistant solicitor 1982-88; under secretary 1988-: head of consumer affairs division 1991-93, solicitor division B 1993-

Date of birth: 12 December 1946 *Education/professional qualifications:* Hull University (LLB 1968); solicitor 1972

Christopher S Kerse Esq, Under Secretary, Department of Trade and Industry, 10-18 Victoria Street, London SW1H 0NN *Telephone:* 0171-215 5000 *Fax:* 0171-215 3141

KIDGELL, JOHN EARLE **Head of Economic Accounts Division, Central Statistical Office** Grade: 3

Career: Central Statistical Office (CSO) and HM Treasury 1970-79; Department of Environment and Property Services Agency 1979-88; CSO 1988-: head of division 3/sector accounts division 1991-94, of economic accounts division 1994-

Date of birth: 18 November 1943 *Education/professional qualifications:* St Andrew's University, economics (MA 1965); London School of Economics, statistics (MSc 1967) *Marital status:* married Penelope Jane Tarry 1968; 2 daughters, 1 son *Recreations:* tennis, hillwalking, music

John E Kidgell Esq, Head of Economic Accounts Division, Central Statistical Office, Great George St, London SW1P 3AQ *Telephone:* 0171-270 6040 *Fax:* 0171-270 6085

KING, JOHN CHARLES **Chief Executive, Security Facilities Executive (Executive Agency)** Grade: 5

Career: Ministry of Defence 1959-63; Ministry of Public Building and Works 1963-69; Property Services Agency 1969-91: head of strategy and planning unit 1983-85, of parliamentary works secretariat 1985, of design services secretariat 1986-89; assistant secretary 1989-: director of administration and personnel 1989-91; Department of Environment 1991-: head of transport and security services division 1991-93; chief executive Security Facilities Executive (provision public service security services) 1993-

Date of birth: 3 January 1940 *Education/professional qualifications:* Newquay Grammar School; Regent Street Polytechnic, management studies (diploma 1970) *Marital status:* married Jill Susan Youlton 1968; 2 sons *Recreations:* music, outdoor sports, especially rugby and swimming

John C King Esq, Chief Executive, Security Facilities Executive, St Christopher House, Southwark Street, London SE1 0TE
Telephone: 0171-921 4813 *Fax:* 0171-921 4012

KINGHAN, NEIL Director, Departmental Task Force, Department of the Environment Grade: 3

Career: Department of the Environment 1975-: private secretary (PS) to parliamentary under secretary 1978-80; principal 1980-87: PS to minister for housing 1984-87; assistant secretary 1987-92; director housing policy and private sector 1992-94, task force (reviewing DoE structures) 1994-

Date of birth: 20 August 1951 *Education/professional qualifications:* Brentwood School; Hertford College, Oxford, philosophy, politics and economics (BA 1973, MA), Latin American studies (MPhil 1975) *Marital status:* married *Clubs:* Surrey County Cricket *Recreations:* walking dog, watching cricket, skiing

Neil Kinghan Esq, Under Secretary, Department of the Environment, 2 Marsham Street, London SW1P 3EB *Telephone:* 0171-276 3120 *Fax:* 0171-276 4466

KIRBY, Brigadier RICHARD TAYLOR HARRISON Chief Executive, Defence Clothing and Textiles Agency (Executive Agency)

Career: army service 1967-: seconded to Royal Brunei Armed Forces 1981; commander supply and senior logistician Hong Kong 1985; director of supply management (army) 1990-92; student Royal College of Defence Studies 1992; director clothing and textiles 1993, chief executive Defence Clothing and Textiles Agency 1994-

Date of birth: 8 November 1945 *Education/professional qualifications:* Rhyl Grammar School; Royal Military College of Science; Army Staff College; Royal College of Defence Studies *Honours, decorations:* Pahlawan Negara Brunei for gallantry 1983; CBE 1990

Brigadier Richard Kirby CBE, Chief Executive, Defence Clothing and Textiles Agency, Portway, Monxton Road, Andover, Hampshire SP11 8HT *Telephone:* 01264 382791 *Fax:* 01264 382652

KIRK, MALCOLM WINDSOR Controller, Inland Revenue Wales and Midlands Grade: 4

Career: Inland Revenue 1972-: district inspector (DI) Newport, Gwent 1972-74; claims branch advisory division 1974-80; DI Soho, London 1980-81; management division personnel 1981-; group controller Wales 1981-83; head of Llanishen tax complex 1983-87; DI Bristol 1987-89; controller Wales 1989-, and Midlands 1994-

Date of birth: 9 July 1943 *Education/professional qualifications:* Canton High School for Boys, Cardiff; Leicester University, geography and industrial location (BA 1966) *Marital status:* married Glenys 1965; 1 daughter *Recreations:* bonsai trees, averting gaze from rugby field

Malcolm W Kirk Esq, Controller, Inland Revenue Wales and Midlands, First Floor, Phase II Building, Ty Glas, Llanishen, Cardiff CF4 5TS *Telephone:* 01222 755789 *Fax:* 01222 755730

KNAPP, TREVOR FREDERICK WILLIAM BERESFORD Assistant Under Secretary, Infrastructure and Logistics, Ministry of Defence Grade: 3

Career: Ministry of Aviation 1961; secretary Downey committee on development cost estimating 1965-66; secretary British Defence Research and Supply Staff, Canberra 1968-72; assistant secretary

Ministry of Defence (MoD) 1974; GEC Turbine Generators Ltd 1976; Central Policy Review Staff, Cabinet Office 1977-79; MoD 1979-: head of international collaboration 1979-83, director-general marketing 1983-88, assistant under secretary supply and organisation, air 1988-92, infrastructure and logistics 1992-

Date of birth: 26 May 1937 *Education/professional qualifications:* Christ's Hospital; King's College, London University, chemistry (BSc 1958); ARIC 1960

Trevor F W B Knapp Esq, Assistant Under Secretary, Ministry of Defence, Whitehall, London SW1A 2HB *Telephone:* 0171-218 9000 *Fax:* 0171-218 2432

KNOWLES, PETER FRANCIS ARNOLD Parliamentary Counsel, Draftsman in Charge, Law Commission Grade: 2

Career: barrister 1973-75; Parliamentary Counsel's Office (drafting government bills) 1975-: seconded to Law Commission (LC) 1979-81; parliamentary counsel 1991-: seconded to LC as draftsman in charge 1993-

Date of birth: 10 July 1949 *Education/professional qualifications:* University College, Oxford, law (BA 1970, MA); Gray's Inn (barrister 1971) *Marital status:* married Patricia Clifford 1972; 2 sons

Peter F A Knowles Esq, Parliamentary Counsel, Law Commission, Conquest House, 37-38 John Street, Theobald's Road, London WC1N 2BQ *Telephone:* 0171-453 1238 *Fax:* 0171-453 1297

KNOX, JOHN ANDREW Deputy Director, Serious Fraud Office Grade: 3

Career: chartered accountancy 1961-72; civil service 1972-: assistant secretary 1976: head of industrial financial appraisal Department of Trade and Industry 1985-87; Serious Fraud Office 1987-: chief accountant 1987-90; deputy director 1990-

Date of birth: 22 July 1937 *Education/professional qualifications:* Merton College, Oxford (MA); ACA 1964; FCA 1974

John A Knox Esq, Deputy Director, Serious Fraud Office, 10-16 Elm House, Elm Street, London WC1X 0BJ *Telephone:* 0171-239 7272

KOWALSKI, GREGOR Assistant Legal Secretary and Scottish Parliamentary Counsel, Lord Advocate's Department Grade: 3

Career: solicitor 1971-74; Procurator Fiscal Service 1974-78; Lord Advocate's Department 1978-: assistant legal secretary to Lord Advocate 1978-, Scottish parliamentary counsel (drafting legislation for Scotland) 1987-

Date of birth: 7 October 1949 *Education/professional qualifications:* Airdrie Academy; Strathclyde University, law (LLB 1971) *Marital status:* married Janet McFarlane Pillatt 1974; 2 sons *Recreations:* singing, music

Gregor Kowalski Esq, Assistant Legal Secretary and Scottish Parliamentary Counsel, Lord Advocate's Department, 2 Carlton Gardens, London SW1Y 5AA *Telephone:* 0171-210 1053 *Fax:* 0171-210 1025

KREBS, Professor JOHN RICHARD Chief Executive, Natural Environment Research Council

Career: ornithology demonstrator Oxford University (OU) 1969-70; assistant professor of ecology British Columbia University, Canada 1970-73; zoology lecturer University College of North Wales 1973-75; OU zoology department 1976-94: lecturer 1976-88, Royal Society research professor 1988-94; director Agricultural and Food Research Council ecology and behaviour unit 1989-94; Natural Environment Research Council 1989-: director behavioural ecology unit 1989-94, chief executive 1994- *Current non-Whitehall posts:* fellow Pembroke College, Oxford

Date of birth: 11 April 1945 *Education/professional qualifications:* City of Oxford High School for Boys; Pembroke College, Oxford, zoology (BA 1966, MA, DPhil 1970) *Honours, decorations:* scientific medal Zoological Society 1981; Linnean Society bicentenary medal 1983; FRS 1984; foreign member Max Planck Society 1985 *Marital status:* married Katherine Anne Fullerton 1968; 2 daughters *Publications:* Introduction to Behavioural Ecology (Blackwell Scientific 1st ed 1981, 2nd 1986, 3rd 1993); Behavioural Ecology: An Evolutionary Approach (Blackwell Scientific 1st ed 1978, 2nd 1984, 3rd 1991); Foraging Theory (Princeton University Press 1987); Behavioural and Neural Aspects of Learning and Memory (Clarendon Press 1991) *Recreations:* running, violin, gardening

Professor John R Krebs FRS, Chief Executive, Natural Environment Research Council, Polaris House, North Star Avenue, Swindon, Wiltshire SN2 1EU *Telephone:* 01793 411653 *Fax:* 01793 411780

KYLE, Air Vice-Marshal Richard Henry Air Officer Commanding Maintenance Units; Chief Executive, RAF Maintenance Group Defence Agency (Executive Agency)

Career: Royal Air Force (RAF) service 1965-: service in UK, Far East, Europe; Ministry of Defence 1976-78, 1982-85, director of ground training (RAF) 1989-90, director-general support services (RAF) 1992-93; chief executive RAF Maintenance Group Defence Agency and air officer commanding maintenance units HQ Logistics Command 1993-

Date of birth: 4 January 1943 *Education/professional qualifications:* Cranbrook School, Kent; RAF Technical College, Henlow; Southampton University (BScEng 1964); CEng 1971; RAF Staff College; Royal College of Defence Studies; FRAeS *Honours, decorations:* MBE 1977 *Recreations:* orienteering, squash, golf

Air Vice-Marshal Richard H Kyle MBE, Chief Executive, RAF Maintenance Group Defence Agency, RAF Brampton, Huntingdon, Cambridgeshire PE18 8QL *Telephone and Fax:* 01480 52151

L

LAING, I K Solicitor, Scotland, Inland Revenue

I K Laing Esq, Solicitor, Scotland, Inland Revenue, 80 Lauriston Place, Edinburgh EH3 9SL
Telephone: 0131-229 9344

LAMBERT, DAVID GEORGE Solicitor and Legal Adviser, Welsh Office Grade: 3

Career: solicitor 1964-; Welsh Office 1966-: lawyer 1966-74, assistant legal adviser 1974-91, solicitor and legal adviser 1991- *Current non-Whitehall posts:* diocesan registrar and deputy chapter clerk Llandaff diocese, Church in Wales 1986-; tutor University College of Wales, Cardiff 1972-

Date of birth: 7 August 1940 *Education/professional qualifications:* Boys' Grammar School, Barry; University of Wales, Aberystwyth, law (LLB 1961); Law Society (solicitor 1964); Notary Public 1986 *Marital status:* married Diana Mary Ware 1966; 1 son, 1 daughter *Recreations:* ecclesiastical law, classical music

David G Lambert Esq, Solicitor and Legal Adviser, Welsh Office, Cathays Park, Cardiff CF1 3NQ *Telephone:* 01222 823510 *Fax:* 01222 823204

LAMBERT, SOPHIA Under Secretary, Head of Road and Vehicle Safety and Traffic Area Offices Directorate, Department of Transport Grade: 3

Career: Foreign and Commonwealth Office 1966-82; assistant secretary Cabinet Office 1982-85; Department of Transport 1985-: head of international transport 1985-87, of public transport metropolitan division 1987-92, of international railways division 1992, of road and vehicle safety directorate 1992-, and Traffic Area Offices 1995-
Education/professional qualifications: London School of Economics

Miss S J Lambert, Head of Road and Vehicle Safety Directorate, Department of Transport, 2 Marsham Street, London SW1P 3EB *Telephone:* 0171-276 3000 *Fax:* 0171-276 6353

LAMING, (WILLIAM) HERBERT Chief Inspector, Social Services Inspectorate, Department of Health

Career: Nottinghamshire probation department/Nottingham city and county combined probation and aftercare department 1961-71; Hertfordshire County Council social services 1971-91: deputy director 1971-75, director 1975-91; chief social services inspector Department of Health 1991-

Date of birth: 19 July 1936 *Education/professional qualifications:* Durham University, social administration (diploma 1960); probation training 1961; London School of Economics, mental health course 1966 *Honours, decorations:* CBE 1985 *Marital status:* married Aileen Margaret Pollard 1962 *Clubs:* Reform

W Herbert Laming Esq CBE, Chief Inspector, Social Services Inspectorate, Department of Health, Richmond House, 79 Whitehall, London SW1A 2NS *Telephone:* 0171-210 5561 *Fax:* 0171-210 4982

LANDERS, BRIAN JAMES Director of Finance, HM Prison Service (Executive Agency) Grade: 3

Career: Commercial Union 1973-79; management auditor International Planned Parenthood Federation 1979-82; senior assistant auditor Tenneco Automotive Europe 1982-83; chief internal auditor, financial controller J Sainsbury plc 1985-88; management consultancy Price Waterhouse 1988-90; Habitat 1990-93: finance director Habitat UK, Habitat Group, managing director Habitat Spain; director of finance HM Prison Service 1993-

Date of birth: 21 April 1949 *Education/professional qualifications:* Exeter University, politics (BA 1970); London Business School, business administration (MSc 1985) *Marital status:* married Sarah Catherine Martin-Cuthbert 1993; 1 son, 1 daughter

B Landers Esq, Director of Finance, HM Prison Service, Cleland House, Page Street, London SW1P 4LN *Telephone:* 0171-217 6275 *Fax:* 0171-217 6746

LANE, ANTHONY JOHN Deputy Secretary, Property, Department of the Environment Grade: 2

Career: Department of [Trade and] Industry and predecessors 1965-94: under secretary 1980-90: deputy director-general Office of Fair Trading 1987-90; deputy secretary (DS) industrial policy 1991-94; DS property Department of Environment 1994-

Date of birth: 30 May 1939 *Education/professional qualifications:* Caterham School, Surrey; Balliol College, Oxford, philosophy, politics and economics (BA 1961, MA) *Honours, decorations:* CB 1990 *Marital status:* married Judith Sheila Dodson 1967; 2 sons, 1 daughter *Recreations:* travel, music, gardening

Anthony J Lane Esq CB, Deputy Secretary, Department of the Environment, 2 Marsham Street, London SW1P 3EB *Telephone:* 0171-276 0631 *Fax:* 0171-276 3483

LANGFORD, (ANTHONY) JOHN Chief Executive, Valuation Office (Executive Agency) Grade: 2

Career: Inland Revenue Valuation Office (valuation of land and buildings for taxation) 1957-: superintending valuer northern region 1981-83; chief valuer's office 1983-91: assistant chief valuer 1983-88, deputy chief valuer 1988-91; deputy chief executive (personnel, training, management planning, operational services) 1988-94, chief executive 1994-

Date of birth: 25 June 1936 *Education/professional qualifications:* Soham Grammar School; FRICS *Marital status:* married Joan Barber 1958; 1 son, 1 daughter *Recreations:* fell walking, bowls

A John Langford Esq, Chief Executive, Valuation Office, New Court, Carey Street, London WC2A 2JE *Telephone:* 0171-324 1155 *Fax:* 0171-324 1190

LANGHORNE, RICHARD TRISTAN BAILEY Director and Chief Executive Wilton Park Conference Centre (Executive Agency) Grade: 5

Career: Kent University 1966-75, 1994-: history lecturer 1966-75, master Rutherford College 1971-75, visiting professor in international relations 1994-; Cambridge University 1975-93: fellow St John's College 1975-93, director Centre of International Studies 1987-93; director and chief executive Wilton Park Conference Centre (conferences on international affairs, FCO sponsored) 1993- *Current non-Whitehall posts:* honorary professor of international relations, Kent University

Date of birth: 6 May 1940 *Education/professional qualifications:* St Edward's School, Oxford; St John's College, Cambridge, history (BA 1961, MA; Cert HS 1962) *Marital status:* married Helen Logue Donaldson 1971; 1 son, 1 daughter *Publications:* Collapse of the Concert of Europe (Macmillan 1982); Diplomacy and Intelligence during the Second World War (CUP 1985); The Practice of Diplomacy (Routledge 1994) *Clubs:* Athenaeum *Recreations:* cooking

Richard T B Langhorne Esq, Chief Executive, Wilton Park Conference Centre, Wiston House, Steyning, West Sussex BN44 3DZ *Telephone:* 01903 815020 *Fax:* 01903 815931

LANGLANDS, (ROBERT) ALAN Chief Executive, NHS Management Executive, Department of Health Grade: 2

Career: Argyll and Clyde health board 1976-78; South Lothian district maternity services 1978-81; unit administrator Middlesex Hospital (MH) and NE Westminster community services 1981-82, MH and University College Hospital and Soho Hospital for women 1982-85; district general manager (GM) Harrow health authority (HA) 1985-89; private practice healthcare management consultant 1989-90; regional GM NW Thames regional HA 1990-93; Department of Health NHS Management Executive 1993-: deputy chief executive 1993-94, chief executive 1994- *Current non-Whitehall posts:* member education committee Royal College of Nursing

Date of birth: 29 May 1952 *Education/professional qualifications:* Allan Glen's School, Glasgow; Glasgow University, pure science (BSc 1974); Institute of Health Service Management (AHSM 1979) *Marital status:* married Elizabeth McDonald 1977; 1 daughter, 1 son *Recreations:* family life, reading, gardening, tennis

R Alan Langlands Esq, Chief Executive, NHS Management Executive, Department of Health, Quarry House, Quarry Hill, Leeds LS2 7OE
Telephone: 01132 545671 *Fax:* 01132 545683

LANGRIDGE, CAROLINE MARY ELIZABETH Head of NHS Women's Unit, NHS Management Executive, Department of Health Grade: 5

Career: various local authorities 1962-68; Department of Trade and Industry 1968-75; Wandsworth community health council 1975-86; community unit general manager West Lambeth health authority 1986-89; NHS Management Executive, Department of Health (DH) 1989-: NHS trust unit 1989-92; head of NHS women's unit (policy and positive action for NHS women staff, DH shadow cabinet committee on women representatives) 1991-

Date of birth: 20 June 1946 *Education/professional qualifications:* Fulham County Grammar School, London; Bristol University, advanced urban studies (MPPS 1986) *Honours, decorations:* FRSA 1992 *Marital status:* married Martin Lipson 1993; 1 son *Clubs:* Royal Society of Arts, Forum UK, Parrot, Demos *Recreations:* theatre, cinema, good food

Ms Caroline Langridge, Head of NHS Women's Unit, Department of Health, Eileen House, 80-94 Newington Causeway, London SE1 6EF
Telephone: 0171-972 2877 *Fax:* 0171-972 2728

LANKESTER, Sir TIM(OTHY) PATRICK Permanent Secretary, Department for Education Grade: 1

Career: VSO, Belize 1960-61; Fereday Fellow St John's College, Oxford 1965-66; economist World Bank (IBRD) 1966-73: Washington DC 1966-69, New Delhi 1970-73; HM Treasury (HMT) 1973-78: principal 1973-77, assistant secretary 1977-78; private secretary to prime ministers James Callaghan 1978-79, Margaret Thatcher 1979-81; seconded to SG Warburg & Co Ltd 1981-83; under secretary HMT 1983-85; economic minister Washington DC and executive International Monetary Fund and IBRD 1985-88; deputy secretary HMT 1988-89; permanent secretary Overseas Development Administration 1989-94, Department for Education 1994-

Date of birth: 15 April 1942 *Education/professional qualifications:* Monkton Combe School, Somerset; St John's College, Cambridge, economics (BA 1964); Henry fellow Yale University, USA, economics (MA 1965) *Honours, decorations:* KCB 1994 *Marital status:* married Patricia Cockcroft 1968; 3 daughters

Sir Tim Lankester KCB, Permanent Secretary, Department for Education, Sanctuary Buildings, Great Smith Street, London SW1P 3BT
Telephone: 0171-925 6234 *Fax:* 0171-925 5841

LANYON, (HARRY) MARK Regional Director, Government Office for the East Midlands, Departments of Environment, Transport, Trade and Industry and Employment Grade: 3

Career: Concorde project Ministry of Aviation 1963-73; Department of Trade and Industry (DTI) 1973-90: deputy director south west 1977-82; regional director West Midlands 1982-85; advance manufacturing technology programme 1985-90; Office of Fair Trading 1990-93; regional director DTI Yorkshire and Humberside 1993-94, government office for the East Midlands 1994-

Date of birth: 15 July 1939 *Education/professional qualifications:* Ardingly College, Sussex; St Andrew's University (BSc 1962); CEng, MIMechE, DMS *Marital status:* married Elizabeth Morton 1970; 1 daughter, 1 son *Recreations:* caravanning, making things

Mark Lanyon Esq, Regional Director, Government Office for the East Midlands, Cranbrook House, Cranbrook Street, Nottingham NG1 1EY
Telephone: 01159 352420

LARGE, ANDREW McLEOD BROOKS Chairman, Securities and Investments Board

Career: British Petroleum 1964-71; managing director Orion Bank 1971-79; Swiss Bank Corporation 1980-89: member executive board 1987-89; chairman Securities Association 1986-87; member London stock exchange international council 1987-87; member Takeover and Mergers Panel 1987-88; chairman Large, Smith and Walter 1990-92; chairman Securities and Investments Board 1992- *Current non-Whitehall posts:* non-executive director English China Clays 1991-

Date of birth: 7 August 1942 *Education/professional qualifications:* Winchester College; Cambridge University, economics (MA 1964); INSEAD, France, business administration (MBA 1970) *Marital status:* married Susan Mary Melville 1967; 1 daughter, 2 sons *Clubs:* Brooks's *Recreations:* skiing, walking, gardening, photography, music

Andrew M Large Esq, Chairman, Securities and Investments Board, Gavrelle House, 2-14 Bunhill Row, London EC1Y 8RA *Telephone:* 0171-638 1240 *Fax:* 0171-638 5900

LAURANCE, (ANTHONY) TONY Scotland and Northern England, Territorial and Benefits Director, Social Security Benefits Agency (Executive Agency) Grade: 3

Career: journalist: Drum Publications, Zambia 1973-74, BBC 1974-75; Department of [Health and] Social Security 1975-: policy strategy unit 1980-82; finance policy division 1982-85; principal private secretary to Secretary of State for Social Services 1985-87; head of central management services 1987; establishment officer Newcastle central office 1987-89, controller 1989-90; Social Security Benefits Agency 1990-: director: territorial (Scotland and Northern England) 1990-, benefits 1993- *Current non-Whitehall posts:* board member The Newcastle Initiative

Date of birth: 11 November 1950 *Education/professional qualifications:* Bryanston School; Clare College, Cambridge, economics and philosophy (BA 1972) *Marital status:* married Judith Allen 1981; 2 daughters *Recreations:* walking, gardening, reading modern fiction

Tony Laurance Esq, Territorial and Benefits Director, Social Security Benefits Agency, Quarry House, Quarry Hill, Leeds LS2 7UE
Telephone: 01132 324222 *Fax:* 01132 324234

LAWS, STEPHEN CHARLES Parliamentary Counsel, Parliamentary Counsel Office

Career: assistant lecturer Bristol University 1972-73; private practice barrister 1973-75; legal assistant Home Office 1975-76; Parliamentary Counsel's Office (drafting government bills) 1976-: seconded to Law Commission 1980-82, 1989-91: assistant parliamentary counsel (PC) 1976-82, senior assistant PC 1982-85, deputy PC 1985-91, PC 1991-

Date of birth: 28 January 1950 *Education/professional qualifications:* St Dunstan's College, London; Bristol University, law (LLB 1972); Middle Temple (barrister 1973) *Marital status:* married Angela Mary Deardon 1972; 3 daughters, 2 sons *Publications:* co-author Statutes File, Halsbury's Laws *Recreations:* theatre, film, family life

Stephen Laws Esq, Parliamentary Counsel, Parliamentary Counsel Office, 36 Whitehall, London SW1A 2AY *Telephone:* 0171-210 6648 *Fax:* 0171-210 6632

LAWSON, Professor DAVID HAMILTON Chairman, Medicines Commission

Career: clinical posts Glasgow Western Infirmary 1966-72; visiting scientist Boston Collaborative Drug Surveillance Program, USA 1970-71; consultant physician Glasgow Royal Infirmary 1973-; visiting professor Strathclyde University 1976-; chairman Medicines Commission 1994- *Current non-Whitehall posts:* honorary professor of medicine Glasgow University 1993-

Date of birth: 27 May 1939 *Education/professional qualifications:* High School, Glasgow; Glasgow University, medicine (MB ChB 1962, MD 1973); FRCPEd 1976; FRCPGlas 1986; FFPM 1989 *Honours, decorations:* CBE 1993 *Marital status:* married Alison Diamond 1963; 3 sons *Publications:* Clinical Pharmacy and Hospital Drug Management (Chapman Hall 1982); Current Medicine 2, 3 and 4 (Churchill Livingstone 1990, 91, 93) *Clubs:* Royal Commonwealth Society *Recreations:* photography, hillwalking, birdwatching

Professor David H Lawson CBE, Chairman, Medicines Commission, c/o Department of Clinical Pharmacology, Royal Infirmary, Glasgow G4 0SF *Telephone:* 0141-552 3535 *Fax:* 0141-552 8933

LAYDEN, PATRICK JOHN Assistant Legal Secretary and Scottish Parliamentary Counsel, Lord Advocate's Department Grade: 3

Career: practising advocate 1973-77; Lord Advocate's Department 1977-: deputy Scottish parliamentary counsel and assistant legal secretary 1977-87, assistant legal secretary and Scottish parliamentary counsel (drafting legislation for Scotland, assisting Scottish law officers; legal advice to government departments) 1987- *Current non-Whitehall posts:* chairman London Scottish Benevolent Fund

Date of birth: 27 June 1949 *Education/professional qualifications:* Holy Cross Academy, Edinburgh; Edinburgh University, law (LLB 1971) *Honours, decorations:* TD 1981 *Marital status:* married Patricia Mary Bonnar 1984; 1 daughter, 3 sons *Recreations:* reading, walking

Patrick J Layden Esq TD, Assistant Legal Secretary and Scottish Parliamentary Counsel, Lord Advocate's Department, 2 Carlton Gardens, London SW1Y 5AA *Telephone:* 0171-210 1023 *Fax:* 0171-210 1025

LEADBEATER, Dr DAVID Deputy Director-General, British National Space Centre, Department of Trade and Industry

Career: civil service 1970-: principal scientific officer 1975-: sonar department 1975-83; head of sonar data processing division 1980-82, of submarine sonar systems division 1982-83; assistant director (underwater) naval analysis directorate 1983; head of sonar department Admiralty Research Establishment (ARE) Portland 1984-86; head of electronic warfare and weapons systems directorate ARE 1986-89; Defence Operational Analysis Establishment/Centre 1989-94: chief executive 1992-94, deputy director-general British National Space Centre 1994-

Date of birth: 7 November 1944 *Education/professional qualifications:* Tottenham Grammar School, London; Wanstead County High School; Bristol University, electrical engineering (BSc, PhD 1970) *Marital status:* married; 1 son, 1 daughter *Recreations:* music, science, armchair sport

Dr David Leadbeater, Deputy Director-General, British National Space Centre, 88 Eccleston Square, London SW1V 1PT *Telephone:* 0171-215 0705 *Fax:* 0171-821 5387

LEDLIE, JOHN Deputy Under Secretary (Personnel and Logistics), Ministry of Defence Grade: 2

Career: Ministry of Defence (MoD) 1967-73; UK delegate to NATO, Brussels 1973-76; MoD 1977-90: deputy chief of public relations 1977-79; seconded to Northern Ireland Office (NIO) and Cabinet Office 1979-81; procurement executive 1981-83; head of defence secretariat 19 1983; defence sales regional marketing director 1983-85; chief of public relations 1985-87; fellow Center for International Affairs, Harvard University, USA 1987-88; sea systems controllerate 1989-90; deputy under secretary NIO 1990-93; personnel and logistics MoD 1993-

Date of birth: 19 March 1942 *Education/professional qualifications:* Westminster School; Brasenose College, Oxford, philosophy, history, classical languages (BA 1963, MA) *Honours, decorations:* OBE 1977, CB 1994 *Recreations:* cricket, tennis, squash, hillwalking, theatre, opera

John Ledlie Esq CB OBE, Deputy Under Secretary, Ministry of Defence, Whitehall, London SW1A 2HB *Telephone:* 0171-218 7152 *Fax:* 0171-218 3660

Parliamentary Offices

see page 347

LEE, DEREK WILLIAM Chairman, Friendly Societies Commission, Registrar of Friendly Societies Grade: 4

Career: army service 1953-55; Lloyds Bank 1955-73; general manager/director Mercantile Credit 1973-87; chief executive H&H Factors 1988-89; Registrar of Friendly Societies 1989-: registrar 1989-, chairman 1992-

Date of birth: 11 April 1935 *Education/professional qualifications:* St Dunstan's College, London; London University, law (LLB 1973); FCIB 1973 *Marital status:* married Dorothy Joan 1960; 1 daughter *Recreations:* tennis, clarinet

Derek W Lee Esq, Chairman, Friendly Societies Commission, 15 Great Marlborough Street, London W1V 2AX *Telephone:* 0171-494 6540 *Fax:* 0171-494 7016

LEECH, Dr PHILIP ANDREW Principal Medical Officer, Planning, Primary Care and NHS Community Care Directorate, NHS Executive, Department of Health Grade: 4

Career: general practice 1973-89; Department of Health 1989-: senior medical officer 1989-92; principal medical officer, primary care division, later planning, primary care and NHS community care directorate NHS Management Executive 1992-

Date of birth: 20 February 1945 *Education/professional qualifications:* Manchester Grammar School; Sheffield University, medicine (MRCS LRCP 1969); diploma, medical jurisprudence (clinical) 1990; MRCGP 1993

Dr Philip A Leech, Principal Medical Officer, NHS Executive, Quarry House, Quarry Hill, Leeds LS2 7UE *Telephone:* 01132 545814 *Fax:* 01132 546347

LEES, Dr DEREK JOHN Head of Computing for Quality, Ministry of Defence Grade: 3

Career: Central Electricity Generating Board 1973-85; Rolls-Royce and Associates 1985-: chief metallurgist 1985-90, senior project manager 1990-94, executive manager 1994-; seconded as head of market testing and contractorisation/computing for quality Ministry of Defence 1994- *Current non-Whitehall posts:* executive manager Rolls-Royce & Associates Ltd 1994-

Date of birth: 2 December 1944 *Education/professional qualifications:* Erith Grammar School, Kent; Surrey University, metallurgy and materials science (BSc 1966), metallic corrosion and anodic passivation (PhD 1969); stress corrosion cracking research, Cambridge University 1969-72; CEng 1980; FIM 1987 *Recreations:* running, windsurfing, music

Dr Derek Lees, Head of Computing for Quality, Ministry of Defence, Northumberland House, Northumberland Avenue, London WC2N 5BP *Telephone:* 0171-218 8240 *Fax:* 0171-218 8250

LEES, Rear Admiral R B Director-General Naval Personnel, Strategy and Plans, Ministry of Defence

Rear Admiral R B Lees, Director-General Naval Personnel, Strategy and Plans, Ministry of Defence, Victory Building, HM Naval Base, Portsmouth PO1 3LS *Telephone:* 01705 727102

LEES, ROBERT FERGUSON Regional Procurator Fiscal, Lothian and Borders, Crown Office Grade: 3

Career: Crown Office Procurator Fiscal Service (public prosecution; sudden death and fire investigations) 1972-: procurator fiscal (PF) depute Paisley 1972-75, Glasgow 1975-78; senior depute PF Glasgow 1978-81; assistant PF Dundee 1982-88; regional PF North Strathclyde 1989-91, Lothian and Borders 1991-

Date of birth: 15 September 1938 *Education/professional qualifications:* Bellshill Academy; Strathclyde University, law (LLB 1970) *Marital status:* married Elsie Loughridge 1966 *Publications:* co-author Criminal Procedure (Butterworths 1990) *Recreations:* music, photography, travel, painting

Robert F Lees Esq, Regional Procurator Fiscal, Lothian and Borders, Procurator Fiscal's Office, 29 Chambers Street, Edinburgh EH1 1LD *Telephone:* 0131-226 4962 *Fax:* 0131-220 4669

LEGG, Sir THOMAS STUART Permanent Secretary, Lord Chancellor's Department and Clerk of the Crown in Chancery Grade: 1

Career: Lord Chancellor's Department 1962-: private secretary to Lord Chancellor 1965-68; assistant solicitor 1975; under secretary 1977-82: SE circuit administrator 1980-82; deputy secretary 1982-89: deputy clerk of Crown in Chancery 1986-89; secretary of commissions 1989; permanent secretary and clerk of the Crown in Chancery 1989- *Current non-Whitehall posts:* Master of the Bench, Inner Temple 1984-; member board Institute of Advanced Legal Studies 1989-; chairman Civil Service Benevolent Fund 1993-; member council Brunel University 1993-

Date of birth: 13 August 1935 *Education/professional qualifications:* Horace Mann-Lincoln School, New York, USA; Frensham Heights School, Surrey; St John's College, Cambridge, history and law (BA 1958, MA), law (LLM 1959); barrister 1960 *Honours, decorations:* CB 1985, QC 1990, KCB 1993 *Marital status:* married Marie-Louise Clarke 1983; 2 daughters by previous marriage *Clubs:* Garrick

Sir Thomas Legg KCB QC, Permanent Secretary, Lord Chancellor's Department, House of Lords, London SW1A 0PW
Telephone: 0171-219 3246 *Fax:* 0171-219 4711

LEISER, HELEN Head of Industrial Relations 1, Employment Department Group Grade: 3

Career: Trades Union Congress 1968-73; Department of Employment (DEmp) 1974-78; Manpower Services Commission 1978-81; DEmp 1981-83; Cabinet Office 1983-85; DEmp/Employment Department Group (EDG) 1985-86; Health and Safety Executive (HSE) 1986-91; offshore safety directorate Department of Energy/HSE 1991-93; business development director and executive board member Employment Service 1993-94; head of industrial relations division 1 EDG 1994-

Date of birth: 3 June 1947 *Education/professional qualifications:* Twickenham County Grammar School; London School of Economics, economics (BSc 1968) *Marital status:* single *Recreations:* reading, swimming, travel

Ms Helen Leiser, Head of Industrial Relations 1, Employment Department Group, Caxton House, Tothill Street, London SW1H 9NF
Telephone: 0171-273 5774 *Fax:* 0171-273 6060

Government Departments

see page 372

LE MARECHAL, ROBERT NORFORD Deputy Comptroller and Auditor General, National Audit Office Grade: 2

Career: army national service 1958-60; Exchequer and Audit Department/National Audit Office (auditing government department accounts) 1961-: housing, local government, finance, environment, trade and industry, energy, Foreign Office, Overseas Development Administration, UK Atomic Energy Authority, Civil Aviation Authority, nationalised industries; policy and planning director 1984-86; assistant auditor general 1986-89; deputy comptroller and auditor general 1989-

Date of birth: 29 May 1939 *Education/professional qualifications:* Taunton's School, Southampton *Honours, decorations:* CB *Marital status:* married Linda Mary Williams 1963; 2 daughters *Recreations:* reading, gardening

Robert N Le Marechal Esq CB, Deputy Comptroller and Auditor General, National Audit Office, 157-197 Buckingham Palace Road, London SW1W 9SP *Telephone:* 0171-798 7381 *Fax:* 0171-233 6163

LEONARD, BRIAN HENRY Regional Director, Government Office for the South West, Departments of Environment, Transport, Trade and Industry and Employment Grade: 3

Career: Heal and Son Ltd 1969-73; economic adviser Price Commission 1973-74; Departments of the Environment and Transport 1974-94; regional director government office for the south west 1994-

Date of birth: 6 January 1948 *Education/professional qualifications:* Dr Challoner's Grammar School, Amersham, Bucks; London School of Economics, economics, geography, politics (BScEcon 1969) *Marital status:* married Maggy Meade-King 1975; 2 sons *Clubs:* Marylebone Cricket *Recreations:* friends, games

B H Leonard Esq, Regional Director, Government Office for the South West, 4th Floor, The Pithay, Bristol BS1 2NQ; Phoenix House, Notte Street, Plymouth PL1 2HF
Telephone: 01179 456670 (Bristol); 01752 221891 (Plymouth)
Fax: 01179 226553 (Bristol); 01752 227647 (Plymouth)

LEONARD, JOHN PATRICK Deputy Director-General; Director of External Relations, Ordnance Survey (Executive Agency) Grade: 5

Career: Ordnance Survey: head of surveys 1978-85, of production 1985-87; director of marketing, planning and development 1987-93, of external relations, deputy director-general 1993- *Education/professional qualifications:* Glasgow Academy; Glenalmond School, Perth; Cambridge University: Selwyn College, English, geography (BA 1960), University College, development studies (diploma 1972) *Marital status:* married Christine Joan 1960; 1 daughter *Recreations:* mountaineering, photography, golf

John P Leonard Esq CBE, Deputy Director-General, Ordnance Survey, Romsey Road, Maybush, Southampton SO9 4DH *Telephone:* 01703 792558 *Fax:* 01703 792660

"Next Steps" Executive Agencies

see page 875

LEVENE, Sir PETER KEITH Prime Minister's Adviser on Efficiency and Effectiveness; Special Adviser to President of the Board of Trade

Career: United Scientific Holdings plc 1963-85: managing director 1968-85, chairman 1982-85; Ministry of Defence: personal adviser to secretary of state (PASS) 1984, to chief of defence procurement 1985-91; PASS Department of Environment 1991-92; prime minister's adviser on efficiency and effectiveness (in public service management) 1992-; special adviser to president of Board of Trade 1992- *Current non-Whitehall posts:* deputy chairman and managing director Wasserstein Perella & Co Ltd 1991-; chairman and chief executive Canary Wharf Ltd 1993-; City of London alderman 1984-; City of London magistrate 1984-

Date of birth: 8 December 1941 *Education/professional qualifications:* City of London School; Manchester University, economics and politics (BAEcon 1963) *Honours, decorations:* KBE 1989 *Marital status:* married Wendy Fraiman 1966; 2 sons, 1 daughter *Clubs:* City Livery, Guildhall, Royal Automobile *Recreations:* skiing, watching football

Sir Peter Levene KBE, Prime Minister's Adviser on Efficiency and Effectiveness, 70 Whitehall, London SW1A 2AS *Telephone:* 0171-270 0257 *Fax:* 0171-270 0099

LEVER, PAUL Deputy Secretary, Head of Defence and Overseas Secretariat and Chairman, Joint Intelligence Committee Grade: 2

Career: HM Diplomatic Service/Foreign and Commonwealth Office, London (FCO) 1966-81: third secretary FCO 1966-67; second secretary Helsinki embassy 1967-71; first secretary (FS) UK delegation to NATO 1971-73; FS FCO 1973-81: assistant private secretary to minister of state 1978-81; chef de cabinet to EC vice-president Christopher Tugendhat 1982-84; FCO 1985-90: head of UN department 1985-86, of defence department 1986-87, of security policy department 1987-90; assistant under secretary (AUS) 1990-94: ambassador and head of UK delegation to conventional arms control negotiations, Vienna 1990-92; AUS defence FCO 1992-94; seconded as deputy secretary, head of defence and overseas secretariat and chairman Joint Intelligence Committee Cabinet Office 1994-

Date of birth: 31 March 1944 *Education/professional qualifications:* St Paul's School, London; Queen's College, Oxford, philosophy and ancient history (BA 1966, MA) *Honours, decorations:* CMG 1991 *Marital status:* married Patricia Anne Ramsey 1990 *Recreations:* walking, art deco pottery

Paul Lever Esq, Deputy Secretary, Cabinet Office, 70 Whitehall, London SW1A 2AS *Telephone:* 0171-270 0360 *Fax:* 0171-930 1419

LEWIS, DEREK COMPTON Director-General and Chief Executive, HM Prison Service (Executive Agency)

Career: Ford Motor Company 1968-82; Imperial Group 1982-84; Granada Group 1984-91: group chief executive 1990-91; director Courtaulds Textiles 1990-93; chairman UK Gold Television Ltd 1992-; director-general and chief executive prison service 1993-

Date of birth: 9 July 1946 *Education/professional qualifications:* Queens' College, Cambridge (BA, MA); London Business School (MSc)

Derek C Lewis Esq, Director-General, HM Prison Service, Cleland House, Page Street, London SW1P 4LN *Telephone:* 0171-217 6703 *Fax:* 0171-217 6961

LEWIS, Dr GWYNETH HELEN Principal Medical Officer, AIDS and Communicable Disease Unit, Health Promition Division, Department of Health Grade: 4

Career: medical posts 1973-81; anatomy lecturer Cambridge University 1976-77; hospital medical director, Newfoundland, Canada 1978-79; general practitioner 1979-81; Department of Health 1981-: principal medical officer, medical head of AIDS and communicable disease unit 1989-

Date of birth: 4 October 1951 *Education/professional qualifications:* Oxford High School for Girls; University College Hospital, London (MB BS 1975); Royal College of General Practitioners (MRCGP 1980); London University, public health (MSc 1989) *Marital status:* married Dr Colin Sanderson 1990; 1 son *Recreations:* choral music

Dr Gwyneth H Lewis, Principal Medical Officer, Department of Health, 133-155 Waterloo Road, London SE1 8UG *Telephone:* 0171-972 4344 *Fax:* 0171-972 4348

LEWIS, LEIGH WARREN Director, Finance and Resource Management Division, Employment Department Group Grade: 3

Career: Department of Employment/Employment Department Group 1973-: private secretary (PS) to parliamentary under secretary 1975-76; manager department personnel unit 1976-78; principal, head of section, incomes division 1978-79; team manager departmental efficiency unit 1979-81; head of section, industrial relations policy division: member Employment Act 1982 and Trade Union Act 1984 legislation teams 1981-84; principal PS to Lord Young minister without portfolio, subsequently secretary of state 1984-86; assistant secretary, head of EC branch 1986-87; director of operations Unemployment Benefit Service 1987-88; seconded as group personnel director to Cable and Wireless plc 1988-91; under secretary, director international division 1991-93, finance and resource management division 1994-

Date of birth: 17 March 1951 *Education/professional qualifications:* Harrow County Grammar School for Boys; Liverpool University, Hispanic studies (BA 1973); MIPD *Marital status:* married Susan Evelyn Gold 1973; 2 sons *Recreations:* tennis, phone card collecting, Watford Football Club

Leigh W Lewis Esq, Under Secretary, Employment Department Group, Caxton House, Tothill Street, London SW1H 9NF
Telephone: 0171-273 5789 *Fax:* 0171-273 6059

LEWIS, PETER Director, Company Tax Division and Policy Co-ordination Unit, Inland Revenue Grade: 3

Career: naval national service 1955-57; Inland Revenue 1960-: tax inspector (TI) 1960-66; higher grade TI 1966-69; principal 1969-74; assistant secretary 1974-86; under secretary 1986-: director personal tax division 1986-91, company tax division (company and oil taxation) 1991-, policy co-ordination unit 1994-

Date of birth: 24 June 1937 *Education/professional qualifications:* Ealing Grammar School; St Peter's Hall, Oxford, modern history (BA 1960) *Marital status:* married Ursula Brigitte Kilian 1962; 1 son, 1 daughter *Recreations:* walking, gardening, canoeing

Peter Lewis Esq, Under Secretary, Inland Revenue, Somerset House, Strand, London WC2R 1LB
Telephone: 0171-438 6371 *Fax:* 0171-438 6148

LIDDELL, ALASDAIR Director of Planning, Primary Care and NHS Community Services, Department of Health Grade: 2

Career: NHS management posts, London 1973-82; district administrator Hammersmith and Fulham Health Authority (HA) 1982-84; district general manager (GM) Bloomsbury HA 1984-88; regional GM East Anglia Regional HA 1988-94; director of planning, primary care and NHS community services NHS Executive, Department of Health 1994-

Date of birth: 15 January 1949 *Education/professional qualifications:* Fettes College, Edinburgh; Balliol College, Oxford, jurisprudence (BA 1970); Thames Polytechnic (DipMan 1974) *Marital status:* married Jenny Abransky 1976; 1 son, 1 daughter

Alasdair Liddell Esq, Director of Planning, Primary Care and NHS Community Services, NHS Executive, Quarry House, Quarry Hill, Leeds LS2 7UE *Telephone:* 01132 545807 *Fax:* 01132 545809

LIESNER, HANS HUBERTUS Deputy Chairman, Monopolies and Mergers Commission

Career: teaching posts London School of Economics and Cambridge University 1955-70; HM Treasury 1970-76; Department of Trade and Industry and predecessors 1976-89: deputy secretary and chief economic adviser; deputy chairman Monopolies and Mergers Commission 1989-

Date of birth: 30 March 1929 *Education/professional qualifications:* Bristol University (BA); Nuffield College, Oxford *Honours, decorations:* CB *Marital status:* married *Publications:* monographs, contributions to books and journals *Clubs:* Reform *Recreations:* skiing, gardening, walking

Hans Liesner Esq CB, Deputy Chairman, Monopolies and Mergers Commission, New Court, Carey Street, London WC2A 2JT *Telephone:* 0171-324 1443 *Fax:* 0171-324 1400

LIKIERMAN, (JOHN) ANDREW Chief Accountancy Adviser, Director, Financial Management, Reporting and Audit Directorate, HM Treasury Grade: 1A

Career: management accountant Tootal Ltd 1965-68; lecturer Leeds University 1968-69, 1972-74; Qualitex Ltd 1969-72; lecturer London Business School (LBS) 1974-76; Central Policy Review Staff, Cabinet Office 1976-78; LBS 1979-: lecturer, senior lecturer, professor 1987, deputy principal 1990-1993; HM Treasury 1933-: seconded as head of government accountancy service, chief accountancy adviser 1993-, director of financial management, reporting and audit, principal finance officer 1995- *Current non-Whitehall posts:* observer Financial Reporting Council 1990-, Accounting Standards Board 1993-; member Cadbury Committee on financial aspects of corporate governance 1991-

Date of birth: 30 December 1943 *Education/professional qualifications:* Stowe School, Buckingham; Balliol College, Oxford, philosophy, politics, economics (BA 1965, MA); FCMA 1982; FCCA 1985 *Marital status:* married Meira 1987; 1 stepdaughter, 1 stepson *Publications:* Public Expenditure (Penguin 1988); co-author Public Sector Accounting and Financial Control (Van Nostrand 4th ed 1992) *Clubs:* Reform *Recreations:* cycling, tennis, choral singing, architecture, wine

J Andrew Likierman, Chief Accountancy Adviser, HM Treasury, Parliament Street, London SW1P 3AG *Telephone:* 0171-270 4530 *Fax:* 0171-270 5287

Regulatory Organisations and Public Bodies

see page 1013

LIMON, DONALD WILLIAM Clerk of the House of Commons Grade: 2

Career: clerk's department House of Commons (HoC) 1956-: assistant clerk 1956-60; senior clerk 1960-73; deputy principal clerk 1973-81; secretary HoC commission 1979-81; clerk of financial committees 1981-84; principal clerk Table Office 1985-89; clerk of committees 1989-90; clerk assistant 1990-94; clerk of the House 1994-

Date of birth: 29 October 1932 *Education/professional qualifications:* Durham Cathedral Chorister School; Durham School; Lincoln College, Oxford, philosophy, politics and economics (BA 1956, MA 1960) *Honours, decorations:* CB 1993 *Marital status:* married Joyce Beatrice Clifton 1987; 1 stepson, 1 stepdaughter *Publications:* contributor to Erskine May's Parliamentary Practice *Recreations:* cricket, golf, singing

Donald W Limon Esq CB, Clerk of the House, House of Commons, London SW1A 0AA *Telephone:* 0171-219 3311 *Fax:* 0171-219 5568

LINDSAY, (FRANCIS) FRANK DAVID HM Chief Agricultural Inspector and Midlands Regional Director, Health and Safety Executive Grade: 4

Career: occupational health and safety Factory Inspectorate/Health and Safety Executive: director accident prevention advisory unit 1987-92; HM chief agricultural inspector (agriculture, fisheries and forestry health and safety) and Midlands regional director of field operations 1993- *Education/professional qualifications:* BA, MSc; FIMgt; FIOSH *Marital status:* married Ann; 2 daughters *Publications:* Management Safety (HMSO 1981) *Recreations:* hill-walking, reading, swimming

F D Lindsay Esq, HM Chief Agricultural Inspector, Health and Safety Executive, Daniel House, Trinity Road, Bootle, Merseyside L20 7HE *Telephone:* 0151-951 4589 *Fax:* 0151-951 4889

LING, JEFFREY Assistant Under Secretary and Director of Information Systems Division, Foreign and Commonwealth Office

Career: HM Diplomatic Service 1966-: assistant under secretary and director of information systems 1989-

Date of birth: 9 September 1939 *Education/professional qualifications:* Bristol University (BSc) *Honours, decorations:* CMG *Marital status:* married

Jeffrey Ling Esq CMG, Director of Information Systems, Foreign and Commonwealth Office, 3 Matthew Parker Street, London SW1H 9NL *Telephone:* 0171-210 8200

LIPWORTH, Sir (MAURICE) SYDNEY Chairman, Financial Reporting Council

Career: practising barrister, South Africa 1956-64; various directorships, including non-executive, SA and UK 1957-; Allied Dunbar Assurance/Unit Trusts 1970-88: chairman 1982-88; chairman Monopolies and Mergers Commission 1988-93, Financial Reporting Council 1994- *Current non-Whitehall posts:* deputy chairman National Westminster Bank 1993-; non-executive director Carlton Communications 1993-; chairman Zeneca 1995-

Date of birth: 13 May 1931 *Education/professional qualifications:* King Edward VII School, Johannesburg, South Africa; Witwatersrand University, SA (BComm 1951, LLB 1954) *Honours, decorations:* Kt 1990, QC 1993 *Marital status:* married Rosa Liwarek 1957; 2 sons *Clubs:* Reform, Queen's *Recreations:* tennis, music, theatre

Sir Sydney Lipworth, Chairman, Financial Reporting Council, Holborn Hall, 100 Gray's Inn Road, London WC1X 8AL *Telephone:* 0171-404 8818 *Fax:* 0171-404 4497

LITCHFIELD, Dr PAUL Director of Medical Services, Occupational Health Service (Executive Agency) Grade: 4

Career: Royal Navy occupational medicine 1978-94: consultant 1986-94; director of medical services occupational Health Service 1994-

Date of birth: 26 October 1953 *Education/professional qualifications:* University College School, London; St Andrews University, medical science (BSc 1975); Manchester University, medicine (MB ChB 1977); London University, occupational medicine (MSc 1982); AFOM 1983, MFOM 1986, FFOM 1993 *Honours, decorations:* O St J 1993 *Marital status:* married Lindsay Helen 1979; 3 daughters

Dr Paul Litchfield, Director of Medical Services, Occupational Health Service, 18-20 Hill Street, Edinburgh EH2 3NB *Telephone:* 0131-220 4177 *Fax:* 0131-220 4183

LITTLE, Dr (THOMAS WILLIAM ANTHONY) TONY Director and Chief Executive, Central Veterinary Laboratory (Executive Agency) Grade: 3

Career: private practice veterinary surgeon 1963-66; Ministry of Agriculture, Fisheries and Food 1966-: Central Veterinary Laboratory (CVL) 1966-82: research officer (RO) 1966-72, senior RO 1972-82; animal health and veterinary group 1982-86: deputy regional veterinary officer 1982-85, veterinary head of section 1985-86; CVL 1986-: deputy director 1986-90, director and chief executive 1990- *Current non-Whitehall posts:* member court of governors London School of Hygiene and Tropical Medicine 1991-

Date of birth: 27 June 1940 *Education/professional qualifications:* Dame Allan's School, Newcastle-upon-Tyne; Santa Clara Union High School, California, USA; Edinburgh University, veterinary medicine (BVMS 1963); London University, veterinary micro-biology (DipBact 1968, PhD 1973); MRCVS 1963 *Marital status:* married Sally Anne Headlam 1985; 1 daughter, 3 sons (1 daughter and 1 son from previous marriage) *Publications:* contributions to veterinary journals and books *Clubs:* Littleton Sailing *Recreations:* sailing, walking, good food, theatre

Dr T W A Little, Director and Chief Executive, Central Veterinary Laboratory, New Haw, Weybridge, Surrey KT15 3NB *Telephone:* 01932 341111 *Fax:* 01932 347046

LITTLECHILD, Professor STEPHEN CHARLES Director-General, Office of Electricity Regulation Grade: 2

Career: professor of commerce and head of industrial economics and business studies department Birmingham University 1975-94; on leave of absence as director-general Office of Electricity Regulation 1989- *Current non-Whitehall posts:* honorary professor Birmingham University 1994-

Date of birth: 27 August 1943 *Education/professional qualifications:* Wisbech Grammar School; Birmingham University, commerce (BCom 1964); Texas University (PhD 1969) *Marital status:* married Kate Crombie 1974 (died 1982); 1 daughter, 2 sons *Publications:* Operational Research for Managers (1977); The Fallacy of the Mixed Economy (1978, 1986); Elements of Telecommunications Economics (1979); Energy Strategies for the UK (1982) *Recreations:* football, genealogy

Professor Stephen C Littlechild, Director-General, Office of Electricity Regulation, Hagley House, Hagley Road, Edgbaston, Birmingham B16 8QG *Telephone:* 0121-456 2100 *Fax:* 0121-456 6365

LITTLER, SHIRLEY (Lady Littler) Chairman, Gaming Board for Great Britain

Career: HM Treasury 1953-64, 1966-69; Department of Trade and Industry 1964-66; National Board for Prices and Incomes 1969-71; secretary Vehicle and General Tribunal 1971-72; Home Office 1972-83; Independent Broadcasting Authority 1983-90: director-general 1990; chairman Gaming Board for Great Britain (regulation of casinos, bingo clubs, gaming machines, lotteries) 1992- *Current non-Whitehall posts:* chairman National Advisory Board for Confidential Enquiries into Stillbirths and Deaths in Infancy 1992-; trustee Police Foundation

Date of birth: 8 June 1932 *Education/professional qualifications:* Headington School, Oxford; Girton College, Cambridge, history (BA 1953, MA) *Marital status:* married Sir Geoffrey 1958; 1 son *Recreations:* reading history

Lady Littler, Chairman, Gaming Board for Great Britain, Berkshire House, 168-73 High Holborn, London WC1V 7AA *Telephone:* 0171-306 6249 *Fax:* 0171-306 6267

LITTMODEN, CHRIS(TOPHER) Special Adviser, Ministry of Defence

Career: general manager BOC 1968-72; audit manager Ernst & Whinney 1972-74; Marks and Spencer plc 1974-: textiles financial controller, personal assistant to chairman, foods buying executive, company financial controller, finance divisional director, finance director 1991-94, executive director North America 1994-; Ministry of Defence 1992-: special adviser competition programme 1992-, defence cost study 1994- *Current non-Whitehall posts:* director British-America Chamber of Commerce 1994-, Samaritans (USA) 1995-

Date of birth: 28 September 1943 *Education/professional qualifications:* Brentwood School, Essex; FCA 1965 *Honours, decorations:* CBE 1995 *Recreations:* music, opera, history, reading, squash, theatre

Chris Littmoden Esq CBE, Marks and Spencer Services Inc, 10th Floor, 346 Madison Avenue and 44th Street, NY 10017, New York, USA *Telephone:* 0101 212 697 3886 *Fax:* 0101 212 697 3857

LLOYD, ANTHONY JOHN LESLIE (The Rt Hon Lord Lloyd of Berwick) Chairman, Security Commission

Career: barrister 1955-, high court judge 1978-84, Lord Justice of Appeal 1984-93, Lord of Appeal in Ordinary 1993-; vice-chairman Parole Board 1984-85; Security Commission (public service security breaches) 1985-: vice-chairman 1985-92, chairman 1992-

Date of birth: 9 May 1929 *Education/professional qualifications:* Eton College; Trinity College, Cambridge, classics, law; Inner Temple (barrister 1955, QC 1967, bencher 1976) *Honours, decorations:* Kt 1978, DL 1983, PC 1984 *Marital status:* married Jane Shelford 1960

The Rt Hon Lord Lloyd of Berwick, Chairman, Security Commission, c/o Cabinet Office, Whitehall, London SW1A 2AS *Telephone:* 0171-270 0170

LLOYD, JOHN WILSON Deputy Secretary, Welsh Office Grade: 2

Career: assistant principal HM Treasury (HMT) 1962-67: private secretary (PS) to financial secretary 1965-67; principal HMT, Civil Service Department 1967-74; Welsh Office (WO) 1974-: principal, PS to secretary of state 1974-75; assistant secretary 1975-82; under secretary 1982-88: principal establishment officer 1982-86, head of housing, health and social services policy group 1986-88; deputy secretary health and social services policy, education, transport planning, housing and environment 1988-

Date of birth: 24 December 1940 *Education/professional qualifications:* Swansea Grammar School; Clifton College, Bristol; Christ's College, Cambridge, biochemistry (BA 1962, MA) *Honours, decorations:* CB 1992 *Marital status:* married Buddug Roberts 1967; 1 daughter, 2 sons *Clubs:* United Oxford and Cambridge University *Recreations:* golf, swimming, hillwalking

John W Lloyd Esq, Deputy Secretary, Welsh Office, Cathays Park, Cardiff CF1 3NQ *Telephone:* 01222 825706 *Fax:* 01222 823234

LOADES, DAVID HENRY Directing Actuary, Social Security and Demography Division, Government Actuary's Department Grade: 3

Career: Government Actuary's Department 1956-: directing actuary and under secretary 1983-, social security and research/demography division 1991-

Date of birth: 16 October 1937 *Education/professional qualifications:* Beckenham and Penge County Grammar School for Boys; FIA 1961 *Marital status:* married; 3 *Recreations:* art galleries

David H Loades, Directing Actuary, Government Actuary's Department, 22 Kingsway, London WC2B 6LE *Telephone:* 0171-242 6828 *Fax:* 0171-831 6653

LOCK, Professor DAVID PETER Chief Planning Adviser, Department of the Environment Grade: 3

Career: area planning officer Leicester city council 1970-73; planning aid officer Town and Country Planning Association 1973-78; planning manager Milton Keynes development corporation 1978-82; associate director Conran Roche Ltd 1982-88; chairman City Discovery Centre Ltd 1987-, David Lock Associates 1990-; chief planning adviser Department of Environment 1994- *Current non-Whitehall posts:* visiting professor of town planning Central England University, Birmingham

Date of birth: 12 March 1948 *Education/professional qualifications:* Sir Roger Manwood's School, Sandwich, Kent; Trent Polytechnic, town planning (diploma 1970); MRTPI 1976; member Institute of Logistics 1992 *Honours, decorations:* FRSA 1993 *Marital status:* married Jeanette Anita Jones 1970; 3 daughters *Publications:* Riding the Tiger: Planning the South of England (Town and Country Planning Association 1991); Alternative Development Patterns: New Settlements (HMSO 1993) *Recreations:* loud music, clay shooting, town planning and architecture history

Professor David P Lock, Chief Planning Adviser, Department of the Environment, 2 Marsham Street, London SW1P 3EB
Telephone: 0171-276 3502 *Fax:* 0171-276 6344

LOCKE, JOHN CHRISTOPHER Chief Executive, NHS Estates (Executive Agency) Grade: 3

Career: Prudential Assurance Co Ltd 1964-91: surveyor 1964-86, estate management director 1987-88, estate management divisional director Prudential Portfolio Managers Ltd 1989-91; Southbank Technopark Ltd 1985-90: director 1985-91, chairman 1989-90; chairman Briggait Co Ltd 1987-90; surveyor to Watling Street Properties 1989-90; chief executive NHS Estates (property advice and consultancy) 1991-

Date of birth: 4 March 1947 *Education/professional qualifications:* Nautical College, Pangbourne; Regent Street Polytechnic, Brixton School of Building, Northern Polytechnic, surveying (ARICS 1971, FRICS 1984); honorary FIHospE 1992 *Marital status:* married Jacqueline Mercer Pamment 1969 (divorced); Maria Patricia Rogers 1990; 2 sons *Recreations:* opera, music, theatre, the arts, travel, family

John C Locke Esq, Chief Executive, NHS Estates, 1 Trevelyan Square, Boar Lane, Leeds LS1 6AE *Telephone:* 01132 547000 *Fax:* 01132 547299

LOMAS, JULIA CAROLE Chief Executive, Public Trust Office Grade: 4

Career: deputy borough solicitor Waltham Forest 1980-89; borough solicitor Haringey 1989-94; chief executive Public Trust Office (protection and management of affairs and property of the mentally incapacitated) 1994-

Date of birth: 9 December 1954 *Education/professional qualifications:* Pontefract and District Girls' High School; Coventry Polytechnic/University, business law (BA 1977) *Marital status:* divorced; 1 son *Recreations:* theatre, cricket, cookery

Ms Julia C Lomas, Chief Executive, Public Trust Office, Stewart House, 24 Kingsway, London WC2B 6JX *Telephone:* 0171-269 7022 *Fax:* 0171-831 0060

LORD, (JOHN) STUART Head of Planning and Finance Division, Department of Social Security Grade: 3

Career: Department of [Health and] Social Security 1972-: assistant secretary 1988-94: principal private secretary to secretary of state 1988-91, seconded to Department of Environment local government review team 1991, to Prudential Life and Pensions marketing department 1993; head of Benefits Agency security branch 1993-94; under secretary, head of planning and finance division 1994-

Date of birth: 10 February 1951 *Education/professional qualifications:* Manchester Grammar School; University College of Wales, Swansea, sociology and social statistics (BSc Econ 1972) *Marital status:* married Dwynwen Williams 1970; 1 sons, 1 daughter *Recreations:* holidays, photography

J S Lord Esq, Under Secretary, Department of Social Security, Richmond House, 79 Whitehall, London SW1A 2NS *Telephone:* 0171-210 5126 *Fax:* 0171-210 5219

LOUGHEAD, PETER Head of Coal Division, Department of Trade and Industry Grade: 3

Career: Department of Trade and Industry (DTI) 1975-: UK permanent representation to EC, Brussels 1982-85; assistant secretary DTI 1985-92: European policy division 1985-89, Radiocommunications Agency 1989-90, financial services division DTI 1990-92/HM Treasury 1992; DTI 1992-: under secretary coal review team 1992-93, coal privatisation unit 1993-94, coal division 1994-

Date of birth: 26 August 1950 *Education/professional qualifications:* Liverpool Institute High School; Lincoln College, Oxford, modern history (BA 1971, MA, DPhil 1981) *Marital status:* married Virginia 1993 *Recreations:* football

Peter Loughead Esq, Under Secretary, Department of Trade and Industry, 1 Palace Street, London SW1E 5HE *Telephone:* 0171-238 3489 *Fax:* 0171-238 3253

LOVE, GRAHAM CARVELL Finance Director, Defence Evaluation and Research Agency (Executive Agency) Grade: 3

Graham C Love Esq, Finance Director, Defence Evaluation and Research Agency, Farnborough, Hampshire GU14 6TD *Telephone:* 01252 394513 *Fax:* 01252 372042

LOVE, Professor PHILIP NOEL Commissioner, Scottish Law Commission Grade: 2

Career: partner in firm of solicitors 1963-74, consultant 1974-; Aberdeen University 1974-92: professor of conveyancing and professional practice of law 1974-92, dean of law faculty 1979-82, 1991-92, vice-principal 1986-90; chairman Scottish conveyancing and executry services board 1991-; commissioner Scottish Law Commission, Scottish Courts Administration (reviewing Scots law) 1986- *Current non-Whitehall posts:* vice-chancellor University of Liverpool 1992-

Date of birth: 25 December 1939 *Education/professional qualifications:* Aberdeen Grammar School; Aberdeen University, arts (MA 1961) and law (LLB 1963) *Honours, decorations:* CBE 1983 *Marital status:* married Isabel Leah Mearns 1963; widowed; 3 sons *Clubs:* New, Edinburgh; Liverpool Racquet; Athenaeum *Recreations:* sport, music

Professor Philip N Love CBE, c/o Senate House, University of Liverpool, Abercromby Square, PO Box 147, Liverpool L69 3BX *Telephone:* 0151-794 2003 *Fax:* 0151-708 7092

LOVEMAN, STEPHEN CHARLES GARDNER Under Secretary, Director of Operations, Training Enterprise and Education Directorate, Employment Department Group Grade: 3

Career: Department of Employment/Employment Department Group 1967-: Health and Safety Executive 1974-80; Manpower Services Commission skill centre policy 1981-86; under secretary 1986-: deputy chief executive Employment Service 1986-88; Cabinet Office inner cities coordination 1988-89; director of youth and adult training 1989-92, of operations, training, enterprise and education directorate 1992-

Date of birth: 26 December 1943 *Education/professional qualifications:* Arnold School, Blackpool; Emmanuel College, Cambridge, economics and history (BA 1965) *Marital status:* married Judith Roberts 1972; 1 daughter, 1 son *Recreations:* opera, walking, reading

S Loveman Esq, Under Secretary, Employment Department Group, Moorfoot, Sheffield S1 4PQ *Telephone:* 01142 594812 *Fax:* 01142 594676

LOWE, (JOHN) DUNCAN Crown Agent, Crown Office, Scotland Grade: 2

Career: solicitor in private practice 1971-73; Procurator Fiscal (PF) Service 1974-: regional PF Lothian and Borders 1988-91; crown agent (criminal prosecution in Scotland) 1991-

Date of birth: 18 May 1948 *Education/professional qualifications:* Hamilton Academy; Glasgow University, law (MA 1969, LLB 1971) *Marital status:* married Jacqueline McGregor Egan 1971; 2 sons *Recreations:* fishing, golf

J Duncan Lowe Esq, Crown Agent, Crown Office, 25 Chambers Street, Edinburgh EH1 1LA *Telephone:* 0131-226 2626 *Fax:* 0131-226 6910

LUCAS, Air Vice-Marshal The Venerable BRIAN HUMPHREY Chaplain-in-Chief, Royal Air Force, Ministry of Defence

Career: priest 1965-: air force service 1970-: Ministry of Defence 1987-: assistant chaplain-in-chief (CIC) 1987-91, CIC 1991- *Current non-Whitehall posts:* canon and prebendary Lincoln Cathedral; member council RAF Benevolent Fund

Date of birth: 20 January 1940 *Education/professional qualifications:* St David's College, Lampeter, humanities (BA 1962); St Stephen's House, Oxford, theology *Honours, decorations:* QHC 1989, CB 1993 *Recreations:* archaeology of Mediterranean and Near East, rugby, poetry

Air Vice-Marshal The Venerable Brian H Lucas CB, Chaplain-in-Chief, Royal Air Force, RAF Innsworth, Gloucestershire GL3 1EZ *Telephone:* 01452 712612 *Fax:* 01452 510828

LUCE, THOMAS RICHARD HARMAN Under Secretary, Social Care Policy, Department of Health Grade: 3

Career: tax inspector Inland Revenue 1965-67; Ministry of Aviation, of Technology 1967-69; Civil Service Department 1969-72; Department of Health [and Social Security] (DH[SS]) 1972-: under secretary (US) 1984; seconded to HM Treasury 1987-90; DH 1990-: US community services division 1990-95, social care policy 1995-

Date of birth: 11 July 1939 *Education/professional qualifications:* Christ's College, Cambridge (BA); Indiana University, USA

Thomas R H Luce Esq, Under Secretary, Social Care Group, Department of Health, Wellington House, 133-135 Waterloo Road, London SE1 8UG *Telephone:* 0171-972 4039

LYNN, (MICHAEL) MIKE DAVID Deputy Chief Executive, HMSO (Executive Agency)

Career: Her Majesty's Stationery Office 1960-: director of publications distribution 1980-83, of finance 1983-84, of print procurement 1984-86; director general of information technology and supply 1986-87, of corporate services 1987-89; deputy chief executive (trading operations) 1989-

Date of birth: 18 July 1942 *Education/professional qualifications:* Lincoln School *Marital status:* married Hilary Smyth 1965; 1 daughter, 1 son *Recreations:* swimming, chess, rough gardening

Mike Lynn Esq, Deputy Chief Executive, HMSO, St Crispins, Duke Street, Norwich NR3 1PD *Telephone:* 01603 694200 *Fax:* 01602 695045

LYON, JOHN Assistant Under Secretary, Criminal Policy, Home Office Grade: 3

John Lyon Esq, Assistant Under Secretary, Home Office, Queen Anne's Gate, London SW1H 9AT *Telephone:* 0171-273 2178 *Fax:* 0171-273 2967

LYTLE, Major-General SIMON WILLIAM ST JOHN   Director, Army Air Corps, Ministry of Defence

Career: Royal Irish Fusiliers 1960-69; Army Air Corps (AAC) 1969-: Staff College staff 1979-81; commanding officer 1 Regiment AAC 1981-84; Ministry of Defence 1984-86; command aviation BAOR 1986-88; student Royal College of Defence Studies 1989; director of army recruiting 1989-92, of Army Air Corps 1992- *Current non-Whitehall posts:* chairman Middle Wallop International Air Show 1992-; vice-chairman Museum of Army Flying 1992-; chairman trustees Army Historic Aircraft Flight

Date of birth: 1 October 1940 *Education/professional qualifications:* Sherborne School, Dorset; Royal Military Academy, Sandhurst (commission 1960; Staff College, Camberley 1973); Royal College of Defence Studies *Recreations:* offshore sailing, bridge, tennis, golf

Major-General Simon W St J Lytle, Director, Army Aviation, Ministry of Defence, Middle Wallop, Stockbridge, Hampshire SO20 8DY *Telephone:* 01980 384400 *Fax:* 01980 384481

M

MABBERLEY, JOHN C Managing Director, Defence Research Agency, Defence Evaluation and Research Agency (Executive Agency) Grade: 3

Career: director-general avionics, weapons and information systems, procurement executive, Ministry of Defence -1994; managing director operations Defence Research Agency 1994-

J C Mabberley Esq, Managing Director (DRA), Defence Evaluation and Research Agency, Farnborough, Hants GU14 6TD *Telephone:* 01252 392000

McAFEE, Major-General ROBERT WILLIAM MONTGOMERY Director-General, Army Training, Ministry of Defence

Career: chief of staff HQ 1 (BR) Corps 1991-92; colonel commandant RTR 1993-; director general army training Ministry of Defence 1993-

Date of birth: 8 November 1944

Major-General Robert W M McAfee, Director-General, Army Training, Ministry of Defence, Whitehall, London SW1A 2HB *Telephone:* 0171-218 9000

McCLOY, Dr ELIZABETH CAROL Chief Executive and Director, Civil Service Occupational Health Service (Executive Agency) Grade: 3

Career: clinical posts University College, London, West Middlesex University and Westminster hospitals 1969-83; occupational medicine Manchester Royal Infirmary 1984-88; director of health and safety Manchester Central Healthcare Trust 1989-93; chief executive and director Civil Service Occupational Health Service (medical adviser to civil service) 1993-

Date of birth: 25 April 1945 *Education/professional qualifications:* Guildford County Grammar School for Girls; University College, London (UCL), pharmacology (BSc 1966); UCL and UCL medical school (MB BS 1969); FFOM; FRSM; FRSA *Marital status:* divorced; 2 sons *Publications:* joint editor Practical Occupational Medicine (Edward Arnold) *Recreations:* gardening, theatre, reading, DIY

Dr Elizabeth C McCloy, Chief Executive, Civil Service Occupational Health Service, 18-20 Hill Street, Edinburgh EH2 3NB *Telephone:* 0131-220 4177 *Fax:* 0131-220 4183

McCLUSKIE, JOHN CAMERON Legal Secretary to Lord Advocate and First Scottish Parliamentary Counsel, Lord Advocate's Department Grade: 2

Career: apprentice solicitor in private practice 1967-69; assistant town clerk Cumbernauld Burgh Council 1969-70; private practice 1970; solicitor South of Scotland Electricity Board 1970-72; Lord Advocate's Department (LAD) 1972-: junior/senior assistant legal secretary and parliamentary draftsman 1972-89, legal secretary to Lord Advocate and first Scottish parliamentary counsel (head of LAD, responsible for assisting Scottish law officers; drafting bills relating to Scotland) 1989-

Date of birth: 1 February 1946 *Education/professional qualifications:* Hyndland School, Glasgow; Glasgow University (LLB 1967); Law Society of Scotland (solicitor 1970); Faculty of Advocates (advocate 1974) *Honours, decorations:* QC (Scotland) 1989 *Marital status:* married Janis Mary Helen McArthur 1970; 1 daughter, 1 son *Recreations:* vegetable growing

John C McCluskie Esq QC, Legal Secretary to Lord Advocate and First Scottish Parliamentary Counsel, Lord Advocate's Department, 2 Carlton Gardens, London SW1Y 5AA *Telephone:* 0171-210 1048
Fax: 0171-210 1025

McCREADIE, DOUGLAS OGILVIE Director, Land and Property/Building Regulations Directorate, Department of the Environment Grade: 4

Career: Ministry of Transport 1964-71; Department of Environment 1971-: director property and buildings division 1993-94, housing and construction division, property holdings and central services division 1994, property and buildings directorate/land and propert y and building regulations 1994-

Date of birth: 9 November 1941 *Education/professional qualifications:* George Watson's College; Edinburgh University, French with Russian (MA 1964) *Marital status:* married Claudine Spencer 1973; 2 sons, 3 daughters

D O McCreadie Esq, Director, Land and Property/Building Regulations Directorate, Department of the Environment, 2 Marsham Street, London SW1P 3EB *Telephone:* 0171-276 3553
Fax: 0171-276 0626

MACDONALD, ALASTAIR JOHN PETER Deputy Secretary, Industry Division, Department of Trade and Industry Grade: 2

Career: journalist 1962-68; Department of Economic Affairs 1968-71; Department of [Trade and] Industry (DTI) 1971-90: deputy secretary (DS) 1985-90; deputy under secretary procurement executive Ministry of Defence 1990-92; DS industry division DTI 1992-

Date of birth: 11 August 1940 *Education/professional qualifications:* Trinity College, Oxford *Honours, decorations:* CB 1989

Alastair Macdonald Esq CB, Deputy Secretary, Department of Trade and Industry, 151 Buckingham Palace Road, London SW1W 9SS *Telephone:* 0171-215 5000

MACDONALD, COLIN CAMERON Principal Establishment Officer, Central Services Division, Scottish Office Grade: 3

Career: Scottish Office 1967-: Scottish Development Department 1967-91; research officer (RO) 1970-71, senior RO 1971-75, senior principal RO 1975-81, chief RO 1981-88; assistant secretary 1988-92: housing 1988-91, central services 1991-: management organisation division 1991-92; under secretary and principal establishment officer 1992- *Current non-Whitehall posts:* non-executive director TSB Bank Scotland plc 1989-

Date of birth: 13 July 1943 *Education/professional qualifications:* Allan Glen's School, Glasgow; Strathclyde University, economics (BA 1967) *Marital status:* married Kathryn Mary Campbell 1969; 1 daughter, 1 son *Recreations:* tennis, fishing, music

Colin C MacDonald Esq, Under Secretary, Central Services Division, Scottish Office, 16 Waterloo Place, Edinburgh EH1 3DN
Telephone: 0131-244 3938 *Fax:* 0131-244 3896

McDONALD, MAVIS Principal Finance Officer, Establishments and Finance Division, Department of the Environment Grade: 3

Career: Ministry of Housing and Local Government/Department of Environment 1966-: under secretary 1988-: directorate of administrative resources 1990-91, of personnel management 1991-94, of housing resources and management 1994, of local government 1994-95, principal finance officer, establishments and finance division 1995-

Date of birth: 23 October 1944 *Education/professional qualifications:* London School of Economics, economics (BScEcon) *Marital status:* married David Arthur 1971; 1 son

Mrs Mavis McDonald, Director, Principal Finance Officer, Establishments and Finance Division, Department of the Environment, Lambeth Bridge House, Albert Embankment, London SE1 7SB *Telephone:* 0171-238 4090

MACE, BRIAN ANTHONY Director, Savings and Investment Division, Inland Revenue Grade: 3

Career: Inland Revenue (IR) 1971-73; secretariat Department of Trade and Industry inflation accounting committee 1974-75; IR 1975-: assistant secretary 1982-90; under secretary, director savings and investment division (tax on savings; stamp duty; charities' taxation) 1990-

Date of birth: 9 September 1948 *Education/professional qualifications:* Maidstone Boys' Grammar School; Gonville and Caius College, Cambridge, mathematics (BA 1971, MA) *Marital status:* married Anne Margaret Cornford 1973 *Recreations:* opera, cricket, recitals

Brian A Mace Esq, Under Secretary, Inland Revenue, Somerset House, Strand, London WC2R 1LB *Telephone:* 0171-438 6614 *Fax:* 0171-438 6766

MACFADYEN, Air Marshal IAN DAVID Director-General, Saudi Arabian Project, Ministry of Defence

Career: Royal Air Force (RAF) 1963-: squadron duties 1964-68; HQ Strike Command 1968-69; flying instructor RAF College, Cranwell 1970-73; student RAF Staff College 1973; squadron duties 1974-76; HQ2 Allied Tactical Air Force 1976-79; squadron duties 1980-84; Ministry of Defence (MoD) 1984-85; station commander RAF Leuchars 1985-87; student Royal College Defence Studies 1988; MoD 1989-90; chief of staff, later commander British Forces Middle East, Riyadh 1990-91; MoD 1991-: assistant chief of the defence staff operational requirements (air systems) 1991-94; director general Saudi Arabian Projects 1994-

Date of birth: 19 February 1942 *Education/professional qualifications:* Marlborough College; RAF College, Cranwell; RAF Staff College; Royal College of Defence Studies *Honours, decorations:* QCVSA 1973, OBE 1984, CB 1991 *Recreations:* shooting, golf, gliding, woodworking, philately

Air Marshal Ian D Macfadyen CB OBE, Director-General, Saudi Arabian Project, 77-91 New Oxford Street, London WC1A 1DS *Telephone:* 0171-829 8505 *Fax:* 0171-829 8469

McFADYEN, NORMAN Deputy Crown Agent, Crown Office Grade: 4

Career: procurator fiscal depute 1978-86; Crown Office (criminal prosecution in Scotland) 1986-: senior legal assistant 1986-88; head of fraud and specialist services 1988-94; deputy crown agent operations group 1994-

Date of birth: 24 June 1955 *Education/professional qualifications:* High School of Glasgow; Glasgow University, law (LLB 1976) *Marital status:* married Pauline Brown 1988; 1 son *Recreations:* walking

Norman McFadyen Esq, Deputy Crown Agent, Crown Office, 25 Chambers Street, Edinburgh EH1 1LA *Telephone:* 0131-226 2626 *Fax:* 0131-226 6564

McGOWRAN, TERRY (TERENCE) MARTIN Chief Crown Prosecutor, Crown Prosecution Service Midlands Grade: 4

Career: private practice solicitor 1967-70; assistant prosecuting solicitor (PS) Durham Constabulary 1970-73; PS Derbyshire 1973-75; area PS West Midlands 1975-86; Crown Prosecution Service (CPS) 1986-: West Midlands area 1986-93: branch crown prosecutor Dudley 1986-87, Birmingham 1987-90; chief crown prosecutor (CCP) 1990-93, CCP Midlands 1993-

Date of birth: 2 October 1941 *Education/professional qualifications:* Durham University, law (LLB 1963); solicitor 1967 *Marital status:* married Jennifer Sturgess 1969; 2 *Recreations:* fell walking, bridge, wine

T M McGowran, Chief Crown Prosecutor, CPS Midlands, Colmore Gate, Colmore Row, Birmingham B3 2QA *Telephone:* 0121-629 7202 *Fax:* 0121-629 7314

MACGREGOR, W A Chief Agricultural Officer, Scottish Office Grade: 4

W A MacGregor Esq, Chief Agricultural Officer, Scottish Office, St Andrew's House, Regent Road, Edinburgh EH1 3DG *Telephone:* 0131-656 8400

McINNES, Dr DIANA Principal Medical Officer, Health Promotion Division, Health and Social Services Group, Department of Health Grade: 4

Date of birth: 28 February 1952 *Education/professional qualifications:* London University (MSc 1991; MB, BS 1975), DCH 1979, DRCOG 1976, MRCGP 1979 *Marital status:* married Ian 1975; 2 sons

Dr D McInnes, Principal Medical Officer, Department of Health, Richmond House, 79 Whitehall, London SW1A 2NS *Telephone:* 0171-972 4226 *Fax:* 0171-972 4141

McINTOSH, Dr MALCOLM KENNETH Chief of Defence Procurement, Ministry of Defence Grade: 1

Career: Australia 1970-90: research scientist Weapons Research Establishment 1970-72; army service 1972-74; Economic Ministries 1974-82; Department of Defence 1982-90: chief of defence production 1987, deputy secretary acquisitions and logistics 1988; secretary Department of Industry, Technology and Commerce 1990; chief of defence procurement Procurement Executive Ministry of Defence 1991-

Date of birth: 14 December 1945 *Education/professional qualifications:* Telopea Park High School, Canberra, Australia; Australian National University, science (BSc 1967), physics (PhD 1972)

Dr Malcolm K McIntosh, Chief of Defence Procurement, Ministry of Defence, Whitehall, London SW1A 2HB *Telephone:* 0171-218 6304 *Fax:* 0171-218 2483

MACINTYRE, WILLIAM IAN Head of Telecommunications Division, Department of Trade and Industry Grade: 3

Career: BP Co Ltd 1965-72; principal: Export Credits Guarantee Department 1972-73, oil division Department of Trade and Industry (DTI)/Department of Energy (DEn) 1973-77; seconded as controller Industrial and Commercial Finance Corporation 1977-79; DEn 1979-92/DTI 1992-: assistant secretary gas division 1979-83, director-general energy efficiency office 1983-87, under secretary 1987-: electricity 1987-91, coal 1991-94; head of telecommunications division 1994-

Date of birth: 20 July 1943 *Education/professional qualifications:* Merchiston Castle School, Edinburgh; St Andrew's University, history and political economy (MA 1965) *Honours, decorations:* CB 1992 *Marital status:* married Jennifer Mary Pitblado 1967; 2 daughters, 1 son

William I Macintyre Esq CB, Under Secretary, Department of Trade and Industry, 151 Buckingham Palace Road, London SW1W 9SS *Telephone:* 0171-215 1839 *Fax:* 0171-931 7194

McIVOR, (FRANCES) JILL Northern Ireland Parliamentary Commissioner for Administration; Northern Ireland Commissioner for Complaints [Ombudsman] Grade: 3

Career: Queen's University, Belfast: librarian 1952-55, law tutor 1965-74; NI Legal Quarterly 1966-76; member lay panel Juvenile Court 1976-77, General Dental Council 1979-91; librarian director of public prosecutions department 1977-79; NI member Independent Broadcasting Authority 1980-86; member Fair Employment Agency/Commission 1984-91; deputy chairman Radio Authority 1990-94; Northern Ireland parliamentary commissioner for administration and commissioner for complaints [Ombudsman] 1991- *Current non-Whitehall posts:* chairman Ulster-New Zealand Trust 1987-; member Queen's University, Belfast Board of Visitors 1988-

Date of birth: 10 August 1930 *Education/professional qualifications:* Methodist College, Belfast; Lurgan College, County Armagh; Queen's University, Belfast, law (LLB 1951); barrister 1980 *Honours, decorations:* QSM 1993, CBE 1994 *Marital status:* married William Basil 1953; 2 sons, 1 daughter *Publications:* contributor and consultant Manual of Law Librarianship (1976); editor Elegentia Juris: selected writings of FH Newark (1973); Chart of the English Reports (1982) *Clubs:* Royal Over-Seas League *Recreations:* gardening, New Zealand

Mrs F Jill McIvor CBE, Ombudsman, Office of the Ombudsman, Progressive House, 33 Wellington Place, Belfast BT1 6HN
Telephone: 01232 233821 *Fax:* 01232 234912

MacKAY, Professor DONALD IAIN Chairman, Scottish Enterprise

Career: English Electric 1959-62; lecturer in political economy (PE) Aberdeen University 1962-65, in applied economics Glasgow University 1965-71; professor of PE Aberdeen University 1971-76, of economics 1976-82; professional fellow Heriot-Watt University 1982-; chairman Scottish Enterprise (development Scottish economy, skills and environment) 1993- *Current non-Whitehall posts:* chair Pieda Ltd 1976-; director Grampian Holdings 1987-; consultant to Secretary of State for Scotland 1971-; industrial arbitrator Advisory, Conciliation and Arbitration Service; member Scottish Economic Council 1985-; governor National Institute of Economic and Social Research 1981-

Date of birth: 27 February 1937 *Education/professional qualifications:* Dollar Academy; Aberdeen University, economics (MA 1959) *Honours, decorations:* FRSE 1988 *Marital status:* married Diana Raffan 1961; 1 son, 2 daughters *Publications:* Geographical Mobility and the Brain Drain (George Allen & Unwin 1969); Local Labour Markets and Wage Structures (1970); Labour Markets under Different Employment Conditions (George Allen & Unwin 1971); The Political Economy of North Sea Oil (Martin Robertson 1975); Scotland 1980: The Economics of Self-Government (Q Press 1977) *Recreations:* golf, tennis, bridge

Professor Donald I MacKay, Chairman, Scottish Enterprise, 120 Bothwell Street, Glasgow G2 7JP *Telephone:* 0141-248 2700 *Fax:* 0141-221 2250

MACKAY, EILEEN ALISON Principal Finance Officer, Central Services Division, Scottish Office Grade: 3

Career: research officer Department of Employment 1965-72; principal Scottish Office (SO) 1972-78, HM Treasury 1978-80; policy adviser Central Policy Review Staff, Cabinet Office 1980-83; SO 1983-: assistant secretary 1983-88, under secretary 1988-: housing group 1988-92, central services 1992, principal finance officer 1992- *Current non-Whitehall posts:* non-executive director Moray Firth Maltings plc 1988-

Date of birth: 7 July 1943 *Education/professional qualifications:* Dingwall Academy, Ross-shire; Edinburgh University, geography (MA 1965) *Marital status:* married (Alasdair) Muir Russell 1983 *Recreations:* gardening

Miss Eileen A Mackay, Principal Finance Officer, Central Services Division, Scottish Office, St Andrew's House, Edinburgh EH1 3DE *Telephone:* 0131-244 4714 *Fax:* 0131-244 5228

MacKAY, GREGOR Special Adviser to Secretary of State for Scotland

Career: special adviser to secretary of state for Scotland 1992-

Date of birth: 23 July 1969 *Education/professional qualifications:* St Andrew's University, economics (MA) *Marital status:* single

Gregor MacKay Esq, Special Adviser, Scottish Office, St Andrew's House, Edinburgh EH1 3DG *Telephone:* 0131-244 2757; 0171-270 6816 *Fax:* 0131-244 2756; 0171-270 6815

MACKAY, PETER Secretary, Scottish Office Industry Department *(until Autumn 1995)* Grade: 2

Career: Scottish Office (SO) 1963-78; Nuffield travelling fellowship 1978-79; director for Scotland, Manpower Services Commission 1982-85; under secretary Department of Employment 1985-87, Scottish Education Department 1987-89; principal establishment officer SO 1989-90; secretary SO Industry Department 1990-

Date of birth: 6 July 1940 *Education/professional qualifications:* Glasgow High School; St Andrew's University, political economy (MA 1962) *Marital status:* married Sarah Holdich 1964; 2 daughters, 1 son *Clubs:* Clyde Canoe, Scottish Arctic *Recreations:* dinghy sailing, sea canoeing, rock climbing, Alps, Arctic

Peter Mackay Esq, Secretary, Scottish Office Industry Department, New St Andrew's House, Edinburgh EH1 3TG *Telephone:* 0131-244 4602 *Fax:* 0131-244 4599

McKAY, WILLIAM ROBERT Clerk Assistant, House of Commons Grade: 3

Career: House of Commons 1961-: clerk of financial committees 1985-87; of the journals 1987-91, of public bills 1991-94; assistant 1994-

Date of birth: 18 April 1939 *Education/professional qualifications:* Trinity Academy, Leith; Edinburgh University (MA)

William R McKay Esq, Clerk Assistant, House of Commons, London SW1A 0AA *Telephone:* 0171-219 3311

MACKENZIE, A Chief Planner, Scottish Office Environment Department Grade: 4

A Mackenzie Esq, Chief Planner, Scottish Office Environment Department, New St Andrew's House, Edinburgh EH1 3SY *Telephone:* 0131-556 8400

MACKENZIE, KENNETH JOHN Head of Economic, Home, Social Affairs and Legislation Secretariat, Cabinet Office Grade: 2

Career: Scottish Home and Health Department (SHHD) 1965-70: assistant principal 1965-69, private secretary (PS) to joint parliamentary under secretary (US) 1969-70; principal General Register Office 1970, Scottish Office (SO) regional development division 1970-73; civil service fellow (CSF) Downing College, Cambridge 1972; principal Scottish Education Department 1973-77; CSF department of politics Glasgow University 1974-75; SO 1977-: principal PS to secretary of state 1977-79; assistant secretary economic planning department 1979-83, finance division 1983-85; US 1985-92: principal finance officer 1985-88, SHHD 1988-91; Agriculture and Fisheries Department 1991-: secretary, head of department and accounting officer 1992-95; head of economic, home, social affairs and legislation secretariat, Cabinet Office 1995- *Current non-Whitehall posts:* member Biotechnology and Biological Sciences Research Council 1994-

Date of birth: 1 May 1943 *Education/professional qualifications:* Birkenhead School, Cheshire; Pembroke College, Oxford, modern history (BA 1964, MA); Stanford University, USA: history (AM 1965) *Marital status:* married Irene Mary Hogarth 1975; 1 son, 1 daughter *Clubs:* Farmers *Recreations:* Congregational Board convener, amateur dramatics

Kenneth J MacKenzie Esq, Head of Economic, Home, Social and Legislation Secretariat, Cabinet Office, 70 Whitehall, London SW1A 2AS
Telephone: 0171-270 0240 *Fax:* 0171-270 0057

MACKEY, Air Vice-Marshal J Director, Defence Dental Services Directorate, Ministry of Defence

Air Vice-Marshal J Mackey QHDS, Defence Dental Services, Ministry of Defence, First Avenue House, High Holborn, London WC1V 6HE *Telephone:* 0171-305 5555

McLAUCHLAN, DEREK JOHN Chief Executive, National Air Traffic Services, Civil Aviation Authority

Career: engineer British Aircraft Corporation 1954-66; project manager European Space Technology Centre, Netherlands 1966-70; space general manager Marconi Space and Defence Systems 1970-76; engineering director ICL 1976-88; managing director Renishaw Research Ltd 1988-89; National Air Traffic Services, Civil Aviation Authority 1989-: director-general projects and engineering 1989-91, chief executive 1991-

Date of birth: 5 May 1933 *Education/professional qualifications:* Queen Elizabeth's Hospital School, Bristol; Bristol University, physics (BSc 1954); CEng 1988; FIEE 1988; FRAeS 1992 *Marital status:* married Sylvia June Smith 1963; 2 daughters *Recreations:* music, theatre, badminton

Derek J McLauchlan Esq, Chief Executive, National Air Traffic Services, 45-59 Kingsway, London WC2B 6TE *Telephone:* 0171-832 5772
Fax: 0171-832 6368

MACLAY, MICHAEL WILLIAM Special Adviser to Foreign Secretary

Career: Foreign and Commonwealth Office 1976-84; producer London Weekend Television (LWT) 1984-88; policy editor Sunday Correspondent 1988-90; senior producer LWT 1991; associate editor The European 1991-93; special adviser to Foreign Secretary 1993- *Current non-Whitehall posts:* trustee Citizenship Foundation

Date of birth: 14 July 1953 *Education/professional qualifications:* Churchers College, Petersfield; Trinity College, Cambridge, modern history (BA 1976) *Marital status:* married Elfi Lunkenheimer 1980; 1 daughter, 1 son *Publications:* Multi-speed Europe? The Community beyond Maastricht (RIAA 1982); Maastricht Made Simple (1983) *Clubs:* United Oxford and Cambridge University *Recreations:* sport, music, family

Michael W Maclay Esq, Special Adviser, Foreign and Commonwealth Office, King Charles Street, London SW1A 2AH
Telephone: 0171-270 2112 *Fax:* 0171-270 2111

McLEAN, MALCOLM Occupational Pensions Board Grade: 6

Career: National Assistance Board/Ministry of Social Security/Department of [Health and] Social Security 1961-: branch head Benefits Agency 1992-94; secretary, general manager Occupational Pensions Board 1994-

Date of birth: 28 January 1943 *Education/professional qualifications:* St Mary's College, Blackburn *Marital status:* married Dorothy 1966; 1 daughter *Recreations:* fell walking

Malcolm McLean Esq, Secretary, Occupational Pensions Board, Sandyford House, Archbold Terrace, Jesmond, Newcastle-upon-Tyne NE99 2EE
Telephone: 0191-225 6247 *Fax:* 0191-225 6422

MACLEOD, ANDREW KENNETH Chief Executive, Scottish Fisheries Protection Agency (Executive Agency) Grade: 5

Career: National Economic Development Office 1974-78; economic adviser (EA) Manpower Services Commission 1978-83; Industry Department for Scotland 1983-90: EA 1983-87, principal Highland and tourism division 1987-90; assistant secretary fisheries department Department of Agriculture and Fisheries for Scotland 1990-91; chief executive Scottish Fisheries Protection Agency 1991-

Date of birth: 28 March 1950 *Education/professional qualifications:* Larchfield School, Helensburgh; Fettes College, Edinburgh; St John's College, Oxford, philosophy, politics and economics (BA 1971); Nuffield College, Oxford, labour economics *Marital status:* married Sheila Janet McWilliam 1980; 2 daughters

Andrew K Macleod Esq, Chief Executive, Scottish Fisheries Protection Agency, Pentland House, 47 Robb's Loan, Edinburgh EH14 1TW
Telephone: 0131-244 6059 *Fax:* 0131-244 6001

MACLEOD, NORMAN Chief Executive, Scottish Office Pensions Agency (Executive Agency)

Career: Department of Health and Social Security -1968; Scottish Office 1968-: Home and Health Department 1968-73, 1979-82, 1990-92; central services 1973-79; Education Department 1982-87: Secretary to Scottish Tertiary Education Advisory Council; Industry Department 1987-90; chief executive Scottish Office Pensions Agency 1992-

Date of birth: 26 April 1938 *Education/professional qualifications:* Oban High School *Marital status:* married; 2 sons, 1 daughter *Recreations:* golf, Gaelic language and song, reading, walking

Norman MacLeod Esq, Chief Executive, Scottish Office Pensions Agency, St Margaret's House, 151 London Road, Edinburgh EH8 7TG
Telephone: 0131-244 3211 *Fax:* 0131-244 3334

MacMANUS, C F HM Chief Fire Inspector, Scottish Office

C F MacManus Esq, HM Chief Fire Inspector, Scottish Office, St Andrew's House, Regent Road, Edinburgh EH1 3DG *Telephone:* 0131 244 2314

McMANUS, Dr JAMES JOHN Commissioner, Scottish Prisons Complaints Commission Grade: 5

Career: law lecturer University College, Cardiff 1974-76; Dundee University 1976-: law lecturer 1976-78, senior lecturer 1978-; commissioner Scottish Prisons Complaints Commission 1994-

Date of birth: 23 June 1950 *Education/professional qualifications:* Our Lady's High School, Motherwell; law, Edinburgh University (LLB 1972), Dundee University (PhD 1985) *Marital status:* married Catherine MacKellaig 1974; 4 daughters, 1 son *Publications:* Lay Justice? (T&T Clark 1987) *Recreations:* cycling, skiing

Dr James J McManus, Commissioner, Scottish Prisons Complaints Commission, Saughton House, Broomhouse Drive, Edinburgh EH11 3XA
Telephone: 0131-244 8423 *Fax:* 0131-244 8430

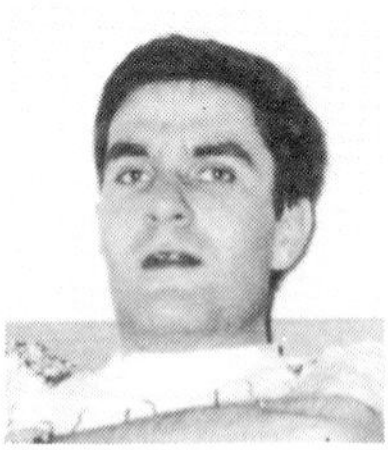

McMANUS, MICHAEL NOEL Special Adviser to Chancellor of the Duchy of Lancaster

Career: researcher Conservative Central Office 1990-92; special adviser to Secretary of State for Wales 1992-93, for Employment 1993-94, to Chancellor of Duchy of Lancaster 1994-

Date of birth: 25 December 1967 *Education/professional qualifications:* Tiffin School; Winchester College; Lincoln College, Oxford, philosophy, politics and economics (BA 1990) *Marital status:* single *Recreations:* watching and playing football, classical music, theatre

Michael N McManus Esq, Special Adviser to Chancellor of Duchy of Lancaster, 70 Whitehall, London SW1A 2AS *Telephone:* 0171-270 0429
Fax: 0171-270 0619

McNEE, IAN Chairman, Parole Board for Scotland

Career: Parole Board for Scotland: vice-chairman -1994, chairman 1994-

Ian McNee Esq, Chairman, Parole Board for Scotland, Calton 5, Redheughs Rigg, Edinburgh EH12 9HW *Telephone:* 0131-244 8528 *Fax:* 0131-244 8794

McQUAID, Dr JAMES Director, Strategy and General Division and Chief Scientist, Health and Safety Executive Grade: 3

Career: engineer British Nylon Spinners Ltd 1961-63; Safety in Mines Research Establishment 1966-74; Health and Safety Executive 1975-: research and laboratory service division 1975-85: seconded to ICI 1976-77; research director 1985-92; director strategy and general division and chief scientist 1992-

Date of birth: 5 November 1939 *Education/professional qualifications:* University College, Dublin, mechanical engineering (BEng 1961); Jesus College, Cambridge, aeronautical engineering (PhD 1966); National University of Ireland, engineering (DSc 1978) *Honours, decorations:* FEng *Marital status:* married Catherine Anne Hargan 1968; 1 daughter, 2 sons *Publications:* various in technical press *Clubs:* Athenaeum *Recreations:* ornamental turning, industrial archaeology

Dr James McQuaid, Director, Strategy and General Division, Health and Safety Executive, Rose Court, 2 Southwark Bridge, London SE1 9HS *Telephone:* 0171-717 6497 *Fax:* 0171-717 6996

MADDEN, MICHAEL Under Secretary, Environmental Policy, Ministry of Agriculture, Fisheries and Food Grade: 3

Career: Ministry of Transport and Civil Aviation 1955-63; Ministry of Agriculture, Fisheries and Food 1963-: principal 1967-73; assistant secretary 1973-85; under secretary, head management services group 1985-90, flood defence, plant protection and agricultural resources 1990-91, environment policy 1991-

Date of birth: 12 February 1936 *Education/professional qualifications:* King Edward VII School, Sheffield *Marital status:* married Angela Grace Abell; 2 sons, 1 daughter *Recreations:* hillwalking, tennis

Michael Madden Esq, Under Secretary, Ministry of Agriculture, Fisheries and Food, 3 Whitehall Place, London SW1A 2HH *Telephone:* 0171-270 8099

MAGEE, BRENDAN Chief Executive, Driver and Vehicle Licensing Agency Northern Ireland (Executive Agency) Grade: 6

Career: Home Office 1968-74; Price Commission 1974-76; Department of Employment/Employment Department Group 1976-93; chief executive Driver and Vehicle Licensing Agency Northern Ireland 1993-

Date of birth: 17 December 1949 *Education/professional qualifications:* St Michael's College, Enniskillen; Slough College of Further Education, business studies (HNC); Open University, politics, psychology (BA 1986) *Marital status:* married Margaret Henry 1976 *Recreations:* walking, theatre, real ale

Brendan Magee Esq, Chief Executive, Driver and Vehicle Licensing Agency Northern Ireland, County Hall, Castlerock Road, Coleraine BT51 3HS *Telephone:* 01265 44133 *Fax:* 01265 320447

MAGEE, IAN Chief Executive, Social Security Information Technology Services Agency (Executive Agency); Acting Chief Executive, Social Security Benefits Agency (Executive Agency) Grade: 3

Career: Department of [Health and] Social Security (D[H]SS) 1976-84: private secretary to minister for social security 1976-78, various policy and management posts 1978-84; member Enterprise Unit, Cabinet Office 1984-86; D[H]SS 1986-: deputy director of personnel 1986-89, DSS London south regional controller 1989-90, director southern territory Social Security Benefits Agency 1990-93; chief executive Social Services Information Technology Services Agency 1993-; acting chief executive Social Security Benefits Agency 1995-

Date of birth: 9 July 1946 *Education/professional qualifications:* St Michael's College, Leeds; Leeds University, history (BA 1968) *Marital status:* married; 2 sons, 1 daughter *Clubs:* MCC, Verulam Golf *Recreations:* cricket, golf, reading

Ian Magee Esq, Chief Executive, Social Security Information Technology Services Agency, Verulam Point, Station Way, St Albans, Hertfordshire *Telephone:* 01727 815839 *Fax:* 01727 833740

MAIN, Air Vice-Marshal JOHN BARTRAM Air Officer Communications and Information Systems, and Commanding Signals Units

Career: Royal Air Force (RAF) 1960-: director scientific and technical intelligence 1970-74; officer commanding 33 Signals Unit, Cyprus 1974-77, RAF Digby 1977-79; RAF Signals Engineering Establishment Henlow 1980-83; head technical intelligence (air) 1983-86; deputy command aerosystem eng 2 HQ Strike Command 1987-88; commandant RAFSEE and air commodore Signals RAF support command 1988-89; director command, control, communications and information systems (policy and operational requirements; director general support services (RAF) 1993-94; air officer communications and information systems and commanding signals units 1994-

Date of birth: 28 January 1941 *Education/professional qualifications:* Portsmouth Grammar School; Birmingham University, electrical engineering (BSc 1959); staff college 1979-80; Royal College of Defence Studies 1986; CEng 1968, FIEE 1968, FIEIE 1991, FRAeS 1984 *Honours, decorations:* MBE 1977, OBE 1979 *Recreations:* gardening, cycling, tennis, windsurfing, sailing, reading

Air Vice-Marshal John B Main OBE, Air Officer, HQ Logistics Command, RAF Brampton, Huntingdon, Cambridgeshire PE18 8QL *Telephone and Fax:* 01480 52151

MAINES, (JAMES) DENNIS Director-General, Command and Information Systems, Procurement Executive, Ministry of Defence Grade: 3

Career: various research posts Royal Radar and Signals Establishment with the Ministries of Aviation of Technology and of Defence 1981-: head of guided weapons optics and electronics group 1981-83, of microwave and electro-optics group 1983-84, of sensors, electronic warfare and guided weapons 1984-86; deputy director weapons Royal Aerospace Establishment, Farnborough 1986-88; director-general guided weapons and electronic systems procurement executive 1988-95, of Command and Information Systems 1995-

Date of birth: 26 July 1937 *Education/professional qualifications:* Leigh Grammar School; City University, London, applied physics (BSc 1960); CEng, FIEE 1985 *Publications:* numerous technical papers; contributor to Surface Wave Filters (1977) *Recreations:* sailing, painting, squash, gardening

J Dennis Maines Esq, Director-General, Command and Information Systems, Procurement Executive, Ministry of Defence, Lacon House, Theobald's Road, London WC1X 8RY *Telephone:* 0171-305 5555

MAKEHAM, PETER DEREK JAMES Director, Strategy and Employment Division, Employment Department Group Grade: 3

Career: Department of Employment 1971-: economist 1971-82, on secondment as economic adviser to Unilever 1982-83; speechwriter for Chancellor of Exchequer and Chief Secretary HM Treasury 1983-84; economist Cabinet Office Enterprise Unit 1984-85; Employment Department Group 1985-: enterprise and deregulation unit 1985-86, employment policy branch 1986-87; seconded to Department of Trade and Industry 1987-90, financial services branch 1990-91, director business services division 1991-92; under secretary, director strategy and employment policy division 1992-

Date of birth: 15 March 1948 *Education/professional qualifications:* Chichester High School for Boys; Nottingham University, economics and economic history (BA 1970); Leeds University, labour economics (MA 1971) *Marital status:* married Carolyne Rosemary Dawe 1972; 1 son, 3 daughters

Peter D J Makeham Esq, Under Secretary, Employment Department Group, Caxton House, Tothill Street, London SW1H 9NF
Telephone: 0171-273 5766 *Fax:* 0171-273 6088

MALONE-LEE, MICHAEL CHARLES Head of Policy Group, Lord Chancellor's Department *(until August 1995)* Grade: 2

Career: Department of Health and Social Security 1968-79, 1984-87; area administrator City and East London area health authority (HA) 1979-81; district administrator Bloomsbury HA 1981-84; principal finance officer Home Office 1987-90; deputy secretary 1990-: director of corporate affairs NHS Management Executive, Department of Health 1990-93; Lord Chancellor's Department 1993-: head of law and policy groups 1993-94, of policy group 1993-

Date of birth: 4 March 1941 *Education/professional qualifications:* Stonyhurst College; Campion Hall, Oxford, classics (BA 1968, MA) *Marital status:* married Claire Frances Cockin 1971; 2 sons *Recreations:* marathon running, cycling, natural history, France

Michael C Malone-Lee Esq, Deputy Secretary, Lord Chancellor's Department, Trevelyan House, Great Peter Street, London SW1P 2BY
Telephone: 0171-210 8719 *Fax:* 0171-210 8752

MALPAS, ROBERT Chairman, Natural Environment Research Council

Career: ICI 1948-78: director 1975-78; president Halcon International Corporation 1978-82; managing director BP 1983-89; chairman Powergen 1988-90, Natural Environment Research Council 1993- *Current non-Whitehall posts:* non-executive director BOC Group 1981-, Eurotunnel 1987-, Barings 1989-, Repsol (Spain) 1989-; chairman Cookson 1991-

Date of birth: 9 August 1927 *Education/professional qualifications:* Taunton School, Somerset; St George's College, Buenos Aires, Argentina; King's College, Durham University, engineering (BSc 1948) *Honours, decorations:* Order of Civil Merit (Spain) 1967; CBE 1976; FEng *Marital status:* married Josephine Dickenson 1956 *Clubs:* River, New York; Mill Reef, Antigua; Royal Automobile, London *Recreations:* tennis, swimming, golf, reading, music

Robert Malpas Esq CBE, Chairman, Natural Environment Research Council, Polaris House, North Star Avenue, Swindon, Wiltshire SN2 1EU
Telephone: 01793 411653 *Fax:* 01793 411780

MANN, Dr THOMAS JOSEPH Head of Public Health, NHS Executive, Department of Health Grade: 4

Career: hospital and general practice medical posts 1979-89; Department of Health NHS Executive 1989-: resident medical officer 1989-90; medical officer (MO) 1990-91; senior MO 1991-: performance management branch head north of England 1991-94; head of public health division 1994-

Date of birth: 4 December 1954 *Education/professional qualifications:* Finchley Catholic Grammar School, London; Royal Free Hospital, Hampstead, London; London University; Keele University; MBBS 1979, MRCGP 1984, MBA 1994 *Marital status:* married Eveleen; 3 sons, 1 daughter *Recreations:* reading, art

Dr Thomas J Mann, Head of Public Health Division, NHS Executive, Quarry House, Quarry Hill, Leeds LS2 7UE *Telephone and Fax:* 01132 545000

MANNING, DAVID GEOFFREY Head of Policy Planning, Foreign and Commonwealth Office

Career: HM Diplomatic Service 1972-: 3rd secretary Foreign and Commonwealth Office, London (FCO) 1972-74; 3rd/2nd secretary Warsaw embassy 1974-76; 2nd/1st secretary (FS) New Delhi high commission 1977-80; FCO 1980-84: east European and Soviet department 1980-82, policy planning staff (PPS) 1982-84; FS political internal Paris embassy 1984-88; counsellor 1988-: seconded to Cabinet Office 1988-90; head of political section Moscow embassy 1990-93; head of Eastern (formerly Soviet) department FCO 1993-94; UK representative International Conference on the Former Yugoslavia 1994; head of PPS FCO 1994-

Date of birth: 5 December 1949 *Education/professional qualifications:* Ardingley College, Sussex; Oriel College, Oxford, history (BA 1971); Johns Hopkins School of Advanced International Studies 1972 *Honours, decorations:* CMG 1992 *Marital status:* married Dr Catherine Parkinson 1973

David G Manning Esq CMG, Head of Policy Planning Staff, Foreign and Commonwealth Office, Whitehall, London SW1A 2AH *Telephone:* 0171-270 2910

MANNING, R G M Head of Aid Policy and Finance Division, Overseas Development Administration Grade: 3

R G M Manning Esq, Head of Aid Policy and Finance Division, Overseas Development Administration, 94 Victoria Street, London SW1E 5JL *Telephone:* 0171-917 7000

MANSFIELD, WILLIAM DAVID MUNGO JAMES MURRAY (The Earl of Mansfield) First Crown Estate Commissioner

Career: barrister 1958-71; House of Lords: opposition spokesman 1975-79, minister of state Scottish Office 1979-83, Northern Ireland Office 1983-84; first commissioner, chairman Crown Estate (administration of Crown landed property) 1985- *Current non-Whitehall posts:* director General Accident plc 1985-, American Trust plc 1985-

Date of birth: 7 July 1930 *Education/professional qualifications:* Eton College; Christ Church, Oxford; Inner Temple (barrister 1958) *Marital status:* married; 2 sons, 1 daughter *Clubs:* Turf, Pratts, Beefsteak, Whites

The Earl of Mansfield, First Commissioner, Crown Estate, 16 Carlton House Terrace, London SW1Y 5AH *Telephone:* 0171-210 4232
Fax: 0171-930 8259

MANTHORPE, JOHN Chief Land Registrar and Chief Executive, HM Land Registry (Executive Agency) Grade: 2

Career: HM Land Registry 1952-: head of plans and survey branch 1974-78; controller of registration 1978-85; principal finance officer 1985-90 and chief executive 1985-; chief land registrar 1991-

Date of birth: 16 June 1936 *Education/professional qualifications:* Beckenham and Penge Grammar School; honorary ARICS CIMgt *Honours, decorations:* CB *Marital status:* married Kathleen Mary Ryan 1967; 1 daughter, 3 sons *Recreations:* Sussex and Ashdown Forest

John Manthorpe Esq CB, Chief Land Registrar, HM Land Registry, Lincoln's Inn Fields, London WC2A 3PH *Telephone:* 0171-917 8888 *Fax:* 0171-955 0110

MARCHANT, RON Assistant Comptroller (Patents and Designs), Patent Office (Executive Agency) Grade: 4

Career: Patent Office 1969-: assistant comptroller (patents and designs) 1992-

Date of birth: 6 November 1945 *Education/professional qualifications:* Finchley Catholic Grammar School; London University, chemistry (BSc) *Marital status:* married Helen 1969; 3 daughters, 1 son *Recreations:* hillwalking, natural history

Ron Marchant Esq, Assistant Comptroller, Patent Office, Concept House, Cardiff Road, Newport, Gwent NP9 1RH *Telephone:* 01633 814555 *Fax:* 01633 814554

MARKEY, Air Vice-Marshal P D Director-General Support Management, RAF, Ministry of Defence

Air Vice-Marshal P D Markey, Director-General, Support Management, RAF, Ministry of Defence, RAF Brampton, Huntingdon, Cambridgeshire PE18 8QL *Telephone:* 01408 52151

MARKS, FREDERICK CHARLES Commissioner for Local Administration in Scotland [Ombudsman]

Career: legal posts Motherwell and Wishaw Burgh Council (BC) 1960-61, Kirkcaldy BC 1961-63; depute town clerk Dunfermline BC 1963-68; town clerk and manager Hamilton BC 1968-75; chief executive Motherwell District Council 1974-83; general manager Scottish Special Housing Association 1983-89; deputy chairman Local Government Boundary Commission for Scotland 1989-94; commissioner for Local Administration in Scotland (local government ombudsman) 1994- *Current non-Whitehall posts:* vice-chairman Queen Margaret Hospital Trust 1994-

Date of birth: 3 December 1934 *Education/professional qualifications:* Wishaw High School; Glasgow University, arts (MA 1957), law (LLB 1960); Law Society of Scotland (solicitor 1960) *Honours, decorations:* OBE *Marital status:* married Agnes Miller 1959; 1 daughter, 3 sons *Recreations:* hill walking

Frederick C Marks Esq OBE, Local Government Ombudsman, 23 Walker Street, Edinburgh EH3 7HX *Telephone:* 0131-225 5300 *Fax:* 0131-225 9495

MARSDEN, B Deputy Director of Finance, NHS Executive, Department of Health Grade: 3

B Marsden Esq, Deputy Director of Finance, Department of Health, Quarry House, Quarry Hill, Leeds LS2 7UE *Telephone:* 01132 545000

MARSDEN, WILLIAM Assistant Under Secretary, Americas, Foreign and Commonwealth Office Senior grade

Career: 3rd secretary (TS) Foreign Office, London 1962-64; TS UK delegation to NATO 1964-66; Rome 1966-70; assistant to general manager Joseph Lucas Ltd 1970-71; 1st secretary (FS) Foreign and Commonwealth Office, London (FCO) 1971-76; FS and cultural attache Moscow 1976-78; assistant head EC department FCO 1978-81; counsellor UK permanent representation to EC, Brussels 1981-85; head of East Africa department and commissioner British Indian Ocean Territory FCO 1985-89; ambassador to Costa Rica, accredited to Nicaragua 1989-92; minister Washington DC 1992-94; assistant under secretary Americas FCO 1994-

Date of birth: 15 September 1940 *Education/professional qualifications:* Winchester College; Laurenceville School, New Jersey, USA; Cambridge University (MA 1962); London University (BScEcon 1972) *Honours, decorations:* CMG 1991 *Marital status:* married Kaia Collingham 1964; 1 son, 1 daughter

William Marsden Esq CMG, Assistant Under Secretary, Foreign and Commonwealth Office, King Charles Street, London SW1A 2AH *Telephone:* 0171-270 2217 *Fax:* 0171-270 2476

MARSH, RICHARD Special Adviser to Secretary of State for Health

Career: Conservative Research Department 1987-90; special adviser Department of Environment 1990-91, to secretaries of state for health William Waldegrave 1991-92, Virginia Bottomley 1992-

Date of birth: 22 January 1963 *Education/professional qualifications:* Forest School, London; Christchurch, Oxford, chemistry (BA, MA) *Marital status:* single

Richard Marsh Esq, Special Adviser, Department of Health, Richmond House, 79 Whitehall, London SW1A 2NS *Telephone:* 0171-210 3000 *Fax:* 0171-210 5613

MARSHALL, JAMES Assistant Auditor General, National Audit Office Grade: 3

Career: Inland Revenue (IR) 1966-74; first secretary budget and fiscal UK permanent representation to EC, Brussels 1974-77; first assistant to UK member EC Court of Auditors, Luxembourg 1977-80; IR 1980-88; commercial recruitment consultant 1988-89; National Audit Office (examination of accounts and financial efficiency of government departments and some public bodies) 1989-: director of social security studies 1989-91, of privatisation and regulation studies 1991-93; assistant auditor general (accounts and studies of Departments of Employment, Health and Social Security; privatisation and regulation) 1993-

Date of birth: 16 March 1944 *Education/professional qualifications:* Sacred Heart College, Droitwich; King Charles I Grammar School, Kidderminster; Jesus College, Cambridge, history (BA 1966, MA) *Marital status:* married Patricia Anne Smallbone 1980; 1 son *Recreations:* reading, walking, opera

James Marshall Esq, Assistant Auditor General, National Audit Office, 157-197 Buckingham Palace Road, London SW1W 9SP *Telephone:* 0171-798 7390 *Fax:* 0171-931 9072

MARTIN, JOHN SHARP BUCHANAN Under Secretary, School Education and Sport, Scottish Office Education Department Grade: 3

Career: Scottish Office 1968-: assistant principal Education Department (ED) 1968-73: private secretary to junior minister 1971-73; principal education, personnel, health 1973-79, Rayner Scrutinies 1979-80; assistant secretary industry, housing, transport 1980-92; under secretary school education and sport, ED 1992-

Date of birth: 7 July 1946 *Education/professional qualifications:* Bell Baxter High School, Cupar, Fife; St Andrew's University, chemistry (BSc 1968) *Marital status:* married Catriona Meldrum 1971; 1 son, 1 daughter *Clubs:* Colinton Lawn Tennis, Woodcutters Cricket *Recreations:* tennis, cricket, philately

John S B Martin Esq, Under Secretary, Scottish Office Education Department, New St Andrew's House, Edinburgh EH1 3TG *Telephone:* 0131-244 4413 *Fax:* 0131-244 4785

MARTIN, R R Principal Finance Officer, Inland Revenue Grade: 3

Career: Inland Revenue: director management support group -1993, principal finance officer 1993-

R R Martin Esq, Principal Finance Officer, Inland Revenue, Somerset House, Strand, London WC2R 1LB *Telephone:* 0171-438 7270

MARTIN, (STEPHEN) STEVE HARCOURT Head of Education Department, Welsh Office Grade: 3

Career: Welsh Office 1974-: private secretary to permanent secretaries 1979-81; principal health policy and housing divisions 1981-87; assistant secretary health and social services division 1987-92; under secretary education group (education, Welsh language, sport, arts, museums and libraries) 1992-

Date of birth: 4 September 1952 *Education/professional qualifications:* Watford and Haywards Heath Grammar Schools; Hull University, politics *Marital status:* married Amanda Suna Hodges 1987; 1 son, 1 daughter *Recreations:* music, theatre, Welsh, literature, cricket

Steve H Martin Esq, Under Secretary, Welsh Office, Cathays Park, Cardiff CF1 3NQ *Telephone:* 01222 823207 *Fax:* 01222 825438

MASEFIELD, C Head of Defence Export Services Ministry of Defence Grade: 2

C Masefield Esq, Head of Defence Export Services, Ministry of Defence, Main Building, Whitehall, London SW1A 2HB *Telephone:* 0171-218 9000

MASON, (JAMES) STEPHEN Counsel to the Speaker, House of Commons

Career: barrister 1961-67; Parliamentary Counsel's Office 1967-94: assistant parliamentary counsel (PC) 1967-72, senior assistant PC 1972-75, deputy PC 1975-80, PC 1980-94; counsel to Speaker, House of Commons 1994-

Date of birth: 6 February 1935 *Education/professional qualifications:* Windsor County Grammar School; Brasenose College, Oxford, law (BA 1956, BCL 1957, MA); Middle Temple (barrister 1958) *Honours, decorations:* CB 1988 *Marital status:* married Tania Jane Moeran 1961; 2 daughters, 1 son *Clubs:* United Oxford and Cambridge University *Recreations:* reading, walking, playing piano

Stephen Mason Esq CB, Speaker's Office, House of Commons, London SW1A 0AA *Telephone:* 0171-219 3000

MASON, Dr PAUL JAMES Chief Scientist and Director of Research, Meteorological Office (Executive Agency) Grade: 4

Career: Meteorological Office 1967-: scientific officer (SO) 1967-71; senior SO 1971-74; principal SO 1974-82; assistant director boundary layer research 1982-89; deputy director physical processes 1989-91; chief scientist and director of research 1991- *Current non-Whitehall posts:* vice-president Royal Meteorological Society 1994-

Date of birth: 16 March 1946 *Education/professional qualifications:* Whitchurch Grammar School, Cardiff; Nottingham University, physics (BSc 1967), geophysics (PhD 1972) *Marital status:* married Elizabeth Mary Slaney 1968; 1 daughter, 1 son *Recreations:* walking

Dr Paul J Mason, Chief Scientist and Director of Research, Meteorological Office, London Road, Bracknell, Berkshire RG12 2SZ
Telephone: 01344 854604 *Fax:* 01344 856909

MATHESON, (STEPHEN) STEVE CHARLES TAYLOR Commissioner, Deputy Chairman, Inland Revenue Grade: 2

Career: Inland Revenue 1961-: tax inspector 1961-70; principal 1970-75; private secretary to Paymaster General 1975-76, to Chancellor of Exchequer 1976-77; assistant secretary, manager computerisation of PAYE project 1977-84; under secretary, director of information technology 1984-89; deputy secretary, commissioner 1989-: director-general, principal establishment officer 1989-94; deputy chairman (policy) 1993-

Date of birth: 27 June 1939 *Education/professional qualifications:* Aberdeen Grammar School; Aberdeen University, English language and literature (MA 1961); FBCS *Honours, decorations:* CB *Marital status:* married Marna Rutherford Burnett 1960; 2 sons *Publications:* Maurice Walsh, Storyteller (Brandon 1985); The North Kerry Phenomenon (contributor, 1992) *Recreations:* reading, cooking, cardplaying

Steve C T Matheson CB, Deputy Chairman, Inland Revenue, Somerset House, Strand, London WC2R 1LB *Telephone:* 0171-438 6789
Fax: 0171-438 7444

MATHEWS, (TERENCE) TERRY FRANCIS Commissioner, Building Societies Commission, Registry of Friendly Societies Grade: 4

Career: HM Treasury 1952-86; air force national service 1953-55; Building Societies Commission 1986-: assistant commissioner 1986-88, commissioner 1988-

Date of birth: 1 May 1935 *Education/professional qualifications:* Balham Central School *Marital status:* married Barbara Eleanor Scott 1977; 1 son, 1 daughter *Recreations:* amateur theatre, naval history

T F Mathews Esq, Commissioner, Building Societies Commission, Registry of Friendly Societies, 15 Great Marlborough Street, London W1V 2AX
Telephone: 0171-494 6627 *Fax:* 0171-287 6102

MATHISON, PETER YORKE Chief Executive, War Pensions Agency (Executive Agency) Grade: 5

Career: Leyland 1970-89: managing director (MD) engines 1987-89; MD Lucas Aerospace 1989-90, Royal Ordnance guns vehicle division 1990-92; chief executive War Pensions Agency 1993-

Date of birth: 29 March 1945 *Education/professional qualifications:* business studies (BA 1984); FCMA 1980 *Marital status:* married *Recreations:* swimming, walking

Peter Y Mathison Esq, Chief Executive, War Pensions Agency, Norcross, Blackpool, Lancashire FY5 3WP *Telephone:* 01253 333092 *Fax:* 01253 332391

MAY, Air Vice-Marshal JOHN A G Air Officer Training, and Commanding Training Group; Chief Executive RAF Training Group Defence Agency (Executive Agency)

Career: Royal Air Force (RAF) 1961-: flying service in Cyprus, UK and Germany; Ministry of Defence (MoD): staff officer to assistant chief of air staff (policy) 1978-79; chief flying instructor RAF College, Cranwell 1979-82; air plans MoD 1982-84; commander RAF Binbrook 1984-86; deputy director of air defence MoD 1986-88; air commodore policy and plans Support Command 1989; deputy chief of staff operations UK air forces, senior air staff officer Strike Command and air officer commanding (AOC) 38 Group 1993-94; AOC training group, air officer training, chief executive Training Group Defence Agency 1994-
Education/professional qualifications: City of London School; Staff College; RAF College, Cranwell *Honours, decorations:* CBE 1993; CB 1995
Recreations: classic cars, skiing

Air Vice-Marshal John May CB CBE, Chief Executive, RAF Training Group Defence Agency, RAF Innsworth, Gloucester GL3 1EZ
Telephone: 01452 712612 *Fax:* 01452 510833

MAYES, Major-General FREDERICK BRIAN Director General, Army Medical Services, Ministry of Defence

Career: Royal Army Medical Corps 1960-: BAOR 1988-93: consultant surgeon 1988-90, commander medical 1990-93; Director General army medical services 1993-

Date of birth: 24 August 1934

Major-General Frederick B Mayes, Director General, Army Medical Services, Keogh Barracks, Ash Vale, Aldershot, Hampshire GU12 5RR *Telephone:* 01252 340326

MAYHEW, Dr L D Principal Establishment and Finance Officer, Head of Central Services Division, Central Statistical Office Grade: 4

Dr L D Mayhew, Head of Central Services Division, Central Statistical Office, Great George Street, London SW1P 3AQ *Telephone:* 0171-270 6496

MEADWAY, (RICHARD) JOHN Under Secretary, Export Control and Non-Proliferation Division, Department of Trade and Industry Grade: 3

Career: Ministry of Technology 1970; Department of Trade [and Industry] (DT[I] 1973-: private secretary to Minister for Trade and Consumer Affairs 1973-74, to Secretary of State for Prices and Consumer Protection 1974, to Prime Minister 1976-78; assistant secretary international trade policy 1979-83, vehicles, management services 1983-89; under secretary overseas trade division 2 1989-94, export control and non-proliferation division 1994-

Date of birth: 30 December 1944 *Education/professional qualifications:* Collyer's School, Horsham; Peterhouse, Cambridge, natural sciences (BA 1965, MA); Edinburgh University, molecular biology (PhD 1969), Oxford University, molecular biology (MA 1969) *Marital status:* married Rev Dr Jeanette Partis 1968; 2 daughters *Clubs:* Reform *Recreations:* reading, travel

John Meadway Esq, Under Secretary, Department of Trade and Industry, Kingsgate House, 66-74 Victoria Street, London SW1E 6SW
Telephone: 0171-215 5230 *Fax:* 0171-931 0397

MEARS, Dr ADRIAN LEONARD Technical and Quality Director, Defence Evaluation and Research Agency (Executive Agency) Grade: 3

Dr A L Mears, Technical and Quality Director, Defence Evaluation and Research Agency, Meudon Avenue, Farnborough, Hampshire GU14 7TU *Telephone:* 01252-394555

MELDRUM, KEITH CAMERON Chief Veterinary Officer, Ministry of Agriculture, Fisheries and Food Grade: 3

Career: private veterinary practice 1961-63; Ministry of Agriculture, Fisheries and Food 1963-: veterinary officer (VO) 1963-72; divisional VO 1972-78; deputy regional VO 1978-80; regional VO 1980-83; assistant chief VO 1983-86; director veterinary field service 1986-88; chief VO animal health and veterinary group (for GB) 1988-

Date of birth: 19 April 1937 *Education/professional qualifications:* Uppingham School; Edinburgh University, veterinary studies (MRCVS 1961, BVM&S 1961, DVSM 1966) *Honours, decorations:* CB *Marital status:* married Vivien Mary Fisher 1982; 1 daughter, 2 sons *Clubs:* North London Rifle, Farmers' *Recreations:* competitive target rifle shooting, outdoor activities

Keith C Meldrum Esq CB, Chief Veterinary Officer, Government Buildings, Hook Rise South, Tolworth, Surbiton, Surrey KT6 7NF
Telephone: 0181-330 8050 *Fax:* 0181-330 6872

MELLING, ROSEMARY Chief Inspector, HM Magistrates' Court Service Inspectorate Grade: 5

Mrs Rosemary Melling, Chief Inspector, HM Magistrates' Courts Service Inspectorate, Southside, 105 Victoria Street, London SW1E 6QT *Telephone:* 0171-210 1661

MERIFIELD, ANTHONY JAMES Ceremonial Officer Cabinet Office; Secretary, Political Honours Scrutiny Committee Grade: 3

Career: district officer Overseas Civil Service, Kenya 1958-65; Ministry/Department of Health and Social Security (DH[SS]) 1965-82: principal 1965-71, assistant secretary 1971-78, under secretary industries and exports division 1978-79, director of establishments (HQ) 1979-82; assistant under secretary Northern Ireland Office 1982-85; DH[SS] 1986-91: regional liaison director NHS management board/executive 1986-91; Cabinet Office 1991: head of senior and public appointments group 1991-94; ceremonial officer and secretary Political Honours Scrutiny Committee 1994- *Current non-Whitehall posts:* trustee Whitehall and Industry Group

Date of birth: 5 March 1934 *Education/professional qualifications:* Chesterfield School; Shrewsbury School; Wadham College, Oxford, history (BA 1957, MA) *Honours, decorations:* CB 1994 *Marital status:* married Pamela Pratt 1980 *Clubs:* Commonwealth Trust, Achilles

Anthony J Merifield Esq CB, The Ceremonial Officer, 53 Parliament Street, London SW1A 2NG *Telephone:* 0171-210 5059 *Fax:* 0171-210 5046

METCALFE, DENYSE Chief Executive, Teachers' Pensions Agency (Executive Agency) Grade: 5

Career: accountant Bolton Metropolitan Borough Council (MBC) 1976-82; principal finance and administration officer Newcastle City Council housing department 1983-85; assistant director of finance (DOF) Middlesbrough BC 1985-89; deputy DOF Gateshead MBC 1989-91; chief executive Teachers' Pensions Agency 1991-

Date of birth: 15 October 1953 *Education/professional qualifications:* Convent of Assumption, Richmond; Manchester University, botany (BSc 1976); CIPFA 1980; MBA 1986 *Marital status:* married Derek 1976; 1 son, 1 daughter *Recreations:* riding, theatre, dogs

Mrs Denyse Metcalfe, Chief Executive, Teachers' Pensions Agency, Mowden Hall, Staindrop Road, Darlington DL3 9EE *Telephone:* 01325 392287 *Fax:* 01325 392571

METTERS, Dr JEREMY STANLEY Deputy Chief Medical Officer, Department of Health Grade: 2

Career: hospital posts 1963-66, 1970-72; Department of Health [and Social Security] 1972-: deputy chief scientist 1986-89; deputy chief medical officer health and social services group 1989-, group head Medical Devices Agency 1994

Date of birth: 6 June 1939 *Education/professional qualifications:* Eton College; Magdalene College, Cambridge; St Thomas's Hospital, London (MB BChir 1963, MA 1965); member 1970, fellow 1982 RCOG *Marital status:* married Margaret Howell 1962; 2 sons, 1 daughter

Dr Jeremy S Metters, Deputy Chief Medical Officer, Department of Health, Richmond House, 79 Whitehall, London SW1A 2NS *Telephone:* 0171-210 3000 *Fax:* 0171-930 4636

METZ, Dr DAVID HENRY Chief Scientist, Department of Transport Grade: 4

Career: Medical Research Council 1967-76; Department of Energy 1967-89: principal 1976-81, assistant secretary 1981-92: seconded as deputy director-general Office of Gas Supply 1986-89; chief scientist Department of Transport 1992-

Date of birth: 11 March 1941 *Education/professional qualifications:* City of London School; University College, London, chemistry (BSc 1962), biochemistry (MSc 1963); King's College, London, biophysics (PhD 1968) *Marital status:* married; 1 son *Recreations:* cooking, riding, sailing

Dr David H Metz, Chief Scientist, Department of Transport, 2 Marsham Street, London SW1P 3EB *Telephone:* 0171-276 5909 *Fax:* 0171-276 5875

MEYER, CHRISTOPHER JOHN ROME Chief Press Secretary to the Prime Minister Grade: 2

Career: HM Diplomatic Service 1966-: third secretary Moscow 1968-70; second secretary Madrid 1970-73; first secretary Foreign and Commonwealth Office (FCO), London 1973-78, UK representation to EC, Brussels 1978-82; counsellor and head of chancery Moscow 1982-84; chief Foreign Office spokesman and head of news department FCO 1984-88; visiting fellow Harvard University, USA 1988-89; Washington DC 1989-93: commercial minister 1989-92, minister and deputy head of mission 1992-93; seconded as chief press secretary to prime minister 1994-

Date of birth: 22 February 1944 *Education/professional qualifications:* Lancing College; Peterhouse, Cambridge, history (BA 1965, MA); Johns Hopkins School of Advanced International Studies, Bologna, Italy (diploma 1966) *Honours, decorations:* CMG 1988 *Marital status:* married Françoise Elizabeth Hedges 1976; 1 stepson, 2 sons *Recreations:* squash, jazz

Christopher J R Meyer Esq CMG, Chief Press Secretary to the Prime Minister, 10 Downing Street, London SW1A 2AA
Telephone: 0171-930 4433

MICHELL, M J Under Secretary, Oil and Gas, Energy Division, Department of Trade and Industry Grade: 3

M J Michell Esq, Under Secretary, Energy Division, Department of Trade and Industry, 1 Palace Street, London SW1E 5HE *Telephone:* 0171-215 5000

MILBANK, NEIL OSCAR Deputy Chief Executive and Director Materials Group, Building Research Establishment (Executive Agency) Grade: 4

Career: apprentice, design engineer de Havilland 1953-60; design engineer English Electric nuclear power division 1960-63; Building Research Establishment 1963-: deputy chief executive and director materials group (materials research; energy economy advice to EC) 1991- *Current non-Whitehall posts:* director TRADA Certification

Date of birth: 21 December 1935 *Education/professional qualifications:* Enfield Grammar School; City University, London, mechanical engineering (BScEng 1957); Birmingham University, thermo and gas dynamics (MSc 1958); MIMechE 1970; MCIBSE 1971; CEng 1976 *Honours, decorations:* bronze medal Chartered Institute of Building Services Engineers 1971 *Marital status:* married Sheila Evans 1960; 2 daughters *Publications:* The Energy Labelling of Buildings – The Principles (1991); Environmental Influence of Buildings (1992); Making Buildings Perform: The BRE Contribution (1993) *Clubs:* Rumford *Recreations:* bridge, golf

Neil O Milbank Esq, Deputy Chief Executive, Building Research Establishment, Garston, Watford, Hertfordshire WD2 7JR *Telephone:* 01923 664212 *Fax:* 01923 664089

MILLAR, DOUGLAS GEORGE Clerk of Select Committees, House of Commons Grade: 3

Career: joint secretary Association of Secretaries General of Parliaments 1971-77; House of Commons Department of the Clerk 1968-: clerk of defence committee 1979-83; clerk private members' bills, public bill office 1983-87; clerk of home affairs committee 1987-89, of financial and of treasury and civil service committees 1989-91; second clerk of select committees 1991-94; clerk of select committees and departmental finance officer 1994-

Date of birth: 15 February 1946 *Education/professional qualifications:* City of Norwich School; Bristol University, history (BA 1967); Reading University, politics (MA 1968) *Marital status:* married Victoria Smith 1987; 2 daughters, 2 sons *Clubs:* Roehampton, Parliamentary Golfing Society *Recreations:* golf, family

Douglas Millar Esq, Clerk of Select Committees, Committee Office, House of Commons, London SW1A 0AA *Telephone:* 0171-219 3286

MILLER, BARRY Assistant Under Secretary, Finance, Procurement Executive, Ministry of Defence Grade: 3

Career: Ministry of Aviation/Defence (MoD) 1961-: Royal Aircraft Establishment, Farnborough 1961-65; assistant principal 1965-69, principal 1969-75; seconded as principal Civil Service Department 1975-77; assistant secretary 1977-86, assistant under secretary and director-general (DG) defence quality assurance 1986-92; procurement executive 1992-: DG test and evaluation 1992-94; assistant under secretary finance 1994- *Current non-Whitehall posts:* chairman Civil Service Club 1990-

Date of birth: 11 May 1942 *Education/professional qualifications:* Royal Grammar School, Lancaster *Recreations:* military uniforms

Barry Miller Esq, Assistant Under Secretary, Procurement Executive, Ministry of Defence, Whitehall, London SW1A 2HB *Telephone:* 0171-218 6384

MILLETT, ANTHEA CHRISTINE Chief Executive, Teacher Training Agency Grade: 3

Career: teaching and school administrative posts 1963-78; Department of Education and Science schools inspector 1978-92; director of inspection Office of HM Chief Inspector of Schools (OFSTED) 1992-94; chief executive Teacher Training Agency 1995-

Date of birth: 2 November 1941 *Education/professional qualifications:* Erdington Grammar School, Birmingham; Bedford College, London, geography (BA 1963) *Marital status:* single *Recreations:* walking, reading, gardening, travel

Ms Anthea C Millett, Chief Executive, Teacher Training Agency, Portland House, Stag Place, London SW1E 5TT *Telephone:* 0171-925 3711 *Fax:* 0171-925 3792

MILLS, BARBARA JEAN LYON Director of Public Prosecutions, Crown Prosecution Service Grade: 1

Career: barrister 1967-90: prosecuting counsel to Inland Revenue 1977-81, junior Treasury Counsel 1981-86; director Serious Fraud Office 1990-92; director of public prosecutions Crown Prosecution Service (independent review and conduct of criminal proceedings) 1992-

Date of birth: 10 August 1940 *Education/professional qualifications:* St Helen's School, Northwood, Middlesex; Lady Margaret Hall, Oxford, jurisprudence (BA 1962, MA); Middle Temple (barrister 1963, Bencher 1990) *Honours, decorations:* QC 1986 *Marital status:* married John Angus Donald 1962; 3 daughters, 1 son

Mrs Barbara J L Mills QC, Director of Public Prosecutions, Crown Prosecution Service, 50 Ludgate Hill, London EC4M 7EX
Telephone: 0171-273 8098 *Fax:* 0171-329 8366

MILLS, HAROLD Secretary, Scottish Office Environment Department Grade: 2

Career: cancer research scientist Roswell Park Memorial Institute, USA 1962-64; chemistry lecturer Glasgow University 1964-69; principal Scottish Home and Health Department 1970-76; assistant secretary 1976-84: Scottish Office (SO) 1976-81, Privy Council Office 1981-83, Scottish Development Department (SDD) 1983-84; under secretary 1984-92: SDD 1984-88, SO, principal finance officer 1988-92; secretary environment department 1992-

Date of birth: 2 March 1938 *Education/professional qualifications:* Greenock High School; Glasgow University, chemistry (BSc 1959) and X-ray crystallography (PhD 1962) *Marital status:* married Marion Elizabeth Beattie 1973

Harold Mills Esq, Secretary, Scottish Office Environment Department, New St Andrew's House, Edinburgh EH1 3DE *Telephone:* 0131-244 4047
Fax: 0131-244 4822

MINFORD, Professor (ANTHONY) PATRICK LESLIE Member, Forecasting Panel, HM Treasury

Career: economic assistant Ministry of Overseas Development 1966; economist Ministry of Finance, Malawi 1967-69; economic adviser Courtaulds 1970-71; HM Treasury (HMT) 1971-74: HMT delegation in Washington DC, USA 1973-74; visiting fellow Manchester University 1974-75; professor of applied economics Liverpool University 1976-; director Merseyside Development Corporation 1988-89; member Monopolies and Mergers Commission 1990-; member forecasting panel HMT 1992- *Current non-Whitehall posts:* visiting professor Cardiff Business School 1993; director Welsh National Opera 1993-

Date of birth: 17 May 1943 *Education/professional qualifications:* Winchester College; Balliol College, Oxford (BA); London School of Economics (MScEcon, PhD) *Marital status:* married Rosemary Allcorn 1970; 1 daughter, 2 sons *Publications:* Substitution Effects, Speculation and Exchange Rate Stability (1978); The Supply Side Revolution in Britain (1991); Rational Expectations Macroeconomics (1992); plus several co-authorships

Professor Patrick Minford, Member, Forecasting Panel, HM Treasury, c/o

Department of Economics and Accounting, University of Liverpool, PO Box 147, Liverpool L69 2BX *Telephone:* 0151-794 3031
Fax: 0151-794 3028

MINGAY, (FREDERICK) RAY Director-General, Export Promotion, Department of Trade and Industry and Foreign and Commonwealth Office Grade: 3

Career: Ministry of Transport 1962-64; Board of Trade 1964-70: seconded to Rootes Motors 1969-70; commercial consul, Milan 1970-73; assistant secretary Department of Trade 1973-78; commercial counsellor Washington DC embassy 1978-83; under secretary 1988-: Department of Trade and Industry (DTI) 1983-88; consul general Chicago 1988-92; DTI/Foreign and Commonwealth Office 1992-: head of overseas trade export services 1992-93, director-general export promotion 1993-

Date of birth: 7 July 1938 *Education/professional qualifications:* Tottenham Grammar School, London; St Catharine's College, Cambridge, history (BA 1959); London University extramural, public administration (postgraduate diploma 1969) *Honours, decorations:* CMG 1992 *Marital status:* married Joan Heather Roberts 1963; 3 sons, 1 daughter *Recreations:* theatre, beekeeping, travel

F Ray Mingay Esq CMG, Under Secretary, Department of Trade and Industry, Kingsgate House, 66-74 Victoria Street, London SW1E 6SW
Telephone: 0171-215 5343 *Fax:* 0171-215 8237

MITCHELSON, IAN SYDNEY Chief Executive, HQ Service Children's Schools (North West Europe) (Executive Agency) Grade: 4

Career: teacher 1960-65; administrative assistant Worcestershire County Council (CC) local education authority 1966-69; assistant education officer (EO) North Riding CC 1969-74; North Yorkshire CC 1974-90: principal EO 1974-85, deputy county EO1985-90; chief executive HQ Service Children's Schools (North West Europe) 1991-

Date of birth: 10 December 1936 *Education/professional qualifications:* Morecambe Grammar School, Lancashire; Downing College, Cambridge, geography (BA 1959, MA); Cambridge University (Cert Ed 1960) *Marital status:* married Betty Hornby 1964; 2 daughters, 1 son *Recreations:* walking, gardening

Ian S Mitchelson, Chief Executive, HQ Service Children's Schools (North West Europe), HQ UKSC (G), BFPO 140 *Telephone:* (00) 49 2161 4723296
Fax: (00) 49 2161 4723487

MOIR, Dr (ALEXANDER THOMAS) BOYD Deputy Chief Scientist, Scottish Office Home and Health Department Grade: 4

Career: Medical Research Council brain metabolism unit 1968-72; Scottish [Office] Home and Health Department 1972-: senior medical officer (MO) 1972-77, principal MO 1977-86; deputy chief scientist and director chief scientist office (research and development) 1986-

Date of birth: 1 August 1939 *Education/professional qualifications:* George Heriot's School, Edinburgh; Edinburgh University, medicine (MB ChB 1963, PhD 1967), pharmacology (BSc 1964); MRCP 1972, FRCPEd 1979. FRCPSG 1985, MRCPath 1976, FRCPath 1988; FRInstB 1979, FIFST 1985, MFPHM 1986, FFPHM 1993, MFOM 1984, MIHSM 1993 *Marital status:* married Isabel May Sheeham 1962; 2

daughters, 1 son *Publications:* scientific, medical and professional papers *Recreations:* games, reading, music, gardening

Dr A T Boyd Moir, Deputy Chief Scientist, Chief Scientist's Office, Scottish Office Home and Health Department, St Andrew's House, Edinburgh EH1 3DE *Telephone:* 0131-244 2254 *Fax:* 0131-244 2368

MOMAN, PRAVEEN Special Adviser to Lord President of the Council/Leader of the House of Commons, Privy Council Office

Career: special adviser to arts minister Tim Renton -1992, to Antony Newton Lord President of the Council/Leader of the House of Commons 1994-

Praveen Moman Esq, Special Adviser, Privy Council Office, 68 Whitehall, London SW1A 2AT *Telephone:* 0171-270 0479

MONTAGU, NICHOLAS LIONEL JOHN Deputy Secretary, Infrastructure, Department of Transport Grade: 2

Career: philosophy assistant lecturer/lecturer Reading University 1966-74; Department of [Health and] Social Security 1974-92: principal 1974-81: seconded to Cabinet Office 1978-79, assistant secretary 1981-86, under secretary 1986-90, deputy secretary (DS) resource management and planning 1990-92; Department of Transport 1992-: DS public transport 1992-94, infrastructure 1994-

Date of birth: 12 March 1944 *Education/professional qualifications:* Rugby School; New College, Oxford, literae humaniores (BA 1966, MA) *Honours, decorations:* CB 1993 *Marital status:* married Dr Jennian Ford Geddes 1974; 2 daughters *Publications:* Brought to Account (HMSO 1981) *Recreations:* cooking, shopping, wild flowers

Nicholas L J Montagu Esq CB, Deputy Secretary, Department of Transport, 2 Marsham Street, London SW1P 3EB *Telephone:* 0171-276 5219 *Fax:* 0171-276 6806

MOORES, YVONNE Chief Nursing Officer and Director of Nursing, Department of Health

Career: hospital nursing 1964-70; principal nursing officer (NO) 1971-74; district NO 1974-76, area NO Manchester 1976-81; chief NO Welsh Office 1982-88, Scottish Office 1988-92, Department of Health 1992-; director of nursing 1992

Date of birth: 14 June 1941 *Education/professional qualifications:* Royal South Hampshire Hospital (RGN 1962); Southampton general hospital (RM 1963) *Marital status:* married *Clubs:* Sloane *Recreations:* golf

Mrs Yvonne Moores, Chief Nursing Officer and Director of Nursing, Department of Health, Richmond House, 79 Whitehall, London SW1A 2NS *Telephone:* 0171-210 3000 *Fax:* 0171-210 5296

Parliamentary Offices

see page 347

MOORHOUSE, PETER WILLIAM **Deputy Chairman, Police Complaints Authority**

Career: Cadbury Schweppes 1960-87: divisional managing director 1982-87; deputy chair Police Complaints Authority (independent investigation of public complaints) 1991-

Date of birth: 25 December 1938 *Education/professional qualifications:* Stonyhurst College *Marital status:* married Jane Catton 1962; 2 sons, 1 daughter *Recreations:* walking, gardening, opera, fine art

Peter W Moorhouse Esq, Deputy Chairman, Police Complaints Authority, 10 Great George Street, London SW1P 3AE *Telephone:* 0171-273 6414 *Fax:* 0171-273 6401

MORDUE, RICHARD ERIC **Under Secretary, Director of Economics and Statistics, Ministry of Agriculture, Fisheries and Food** Grade: 3

Career: Ministry of Agriculture, Fisheries and Food 1964-: various economics posts 1964-82; head of horticulture division 1982-89, director of economics and statistics 1989-

Date of birth: 14 June 1941 *Education/professional qualifications:* Royal Grammar School, Newcastle-upon-Tyne; King's College, Durham University (BScAgric 1964); Michigan State University, USA (MS Ag Econ 1968) *Marital status:* married Christine Phillips 1979; 1 son, 1 daughter *Clubs:* Civil Service *Recreations:* golf

Richard E Mordue Esq, Under Secretary, Ministry of Agriculture, Fisheries and Food, 3 Whitehall Place, London SW1A 2HH *Telephone:* 0171-270 8539 *Fax:* 0171-270 8558

MORGAN, (EVAN) ROGER **Under Secretary, International Relations and Youth, Department for Education** Grade: 3

Career: Department of Education and Science/for Education: under secretary 1991-: further education 1991-94, international relations and youth 1994-

Date of birth: 18 April 1945 *Education/professional qualifications:* Battersea College of Advanced Technology *Marital status:* married Libby Lewis 1967; 1 son, 1 daughter *Recreations:* music, cycling, gadgets

E Roger Morgan Esq, Under Secretary, Department for Education, Sanctuary Buildings, Great Smith Street, London SW1P 3BT *Telephone:* 0171-925 6050 *Fax:* 0171-925 6954

MORGAN, MARILYNNE ANN **Solicitor and Legal Adviser, Department of the Environment** Grade: 2

Career: Department of [Health and] Social Security 1973-91: under secretary, principal assistant solicitor 1985-91; Department of Environment 1991-: deputy solicitor 1991-92, solicitor and legal adviser 1992-

Date of birth: 22 June 1946 *Education/professional qualifications:* Gads Hill Place, Higham by Rochester; Bedford College, London, history (BA 1967); Middle Temple (barrister 1972) *Marital status:* married *Publications:* contributor, Halsbury's Laws of England (1982, 1986) *Clubs:* University Women's *Recreations:* homely pursuits

Mrs Marilynne A Morgan, Solicitor and Legal Adviser, Department of the Environment, 2 Marsham Street, London SW1P 3EB *Telephone:* 0171-276 3000

MORIARTY, MICHAEL JOHN **Deputy Chairman, Radio Authority**

Career: Home Office (HO), Cabinet Office, Civil Service Commission 1954-75; assistant under secretary 1975-84: criminal policy HO 1975-79; Northern Ireland Office 1979-81; HO 1981-90: broadcasting department 1981-84, deputy under secretary, principal establishment officer 1984-90; Radio Authority 1991-: deputy chairman 1994- *Current non-Whitehall posts:* sub-treasurer Chichester Cathedral; member Redundant Churches Committee 1992-; independent member Disasters Emergency Committee 1992-

Date of birth: 3 July 1930 *Education/professional qualifications:* Reading School; St John's College, Oxford, literae humaniores (BA 1954, MA) *Honours, decorations:* CB 1988 *Marital status:* married Rachel Milward 1960; 2 daughters, 1 son *Recreations:* music, walking

Michael J Moriarty Esq CB, Deputy Chairman, Radio Authority, Holbrook House, 14 Great Queen Street, London WC2B 5DG
Telephone: 0171-430 2724 *Fax:* 0171-405 7062

MORRIS, DOMINIC **Member of Prime Minister's Policy Unit**

Dominic Morris Esq, Prime Minister's Policy Unit, Prime Minister's Office, 10 Downing Street, London SW1A 2AA *Telephone:* 0171-930 4433

MORRIS, NORMA FRANCES **Administrative Secretary, Medical Research Council** Grade: 3

Career: assistant English lecturer Hull University 1959-60; Medical Research Council 1960-: posts in publications, accommodation, industrial liaison, finance; administrative secretary 1989- *Current non-Whitehall posts:* member National Biological Standards Board 1990-

Date of birth: 17 April 1935 *Education/professional qualifications:* Ilford County High School; University College, London, English (BA 1956, MA 1960) *Marital status:* married Samuel 1960; 2 daughters, 1 son *Recreations:* opera, edible fungi

Ms Norma Morris, Administrative Secretary, Medical Research Council, 20 Park Crescent, London W1N 4AL *Telephone:* 0171-637 6036
Fax: 0171-580 4369

MORRIS, ROBERT MATTHEW **Head of Criminal Justice and Constitutional Department, Home Office** Grade: 3

Career: Home Office (HO) 1961-66; Civil Service Department 1969-71; HO 1976-: principal private secretary to Home Secretary 1976-78; head of crime policy planning unit 1979-81; assistant under secretary and head of criminal justice and constitutional department 1983-

Date of birth: 11 October 1937 *Education/professional qualifications:* Christ's College, Cambridge

Robert M Morris Esq, Assistant Under Secretary, Home Office, 50 Queen Anne's Gate, London SW1H 9AP *Telephone:* 0171-273 3000

MORRIS, TREFOR ALFRED **HM Chief Inspector of Constabulary, Home Office**

Trefor A Morris Esq CBE, HM Chief Inspector of Constabulary, Home Office, 50 Queen Anne's Gate, London SW1H 9AT *Telephone:* 0171-273 3000 *Fax:* 0171-273 2190

MORRISON, (ALEXANDER) FRASER Chairman, Highlands and Islands Enterprise

Career: Morrison Construction Group 1970-: managing director 1976-84, chairman 1984-; chairman (non-executive supervision and spokesmanship) Highlands and Islands Enterprise (stimulation regional economic and social development) 1992- *Current non-Whitehall posts:* several company directorships

Date of birth: 20 March 1948 *Education/professional qualifications:* Tain Royal Academy; Edinburgh University, civil engineering (BSc 1970); CEng FICE 1993; EurIng 1993; MIHT *Honours, decorations:* FRSA 1990; CBE 1993 *Marital status:* married Patricia Janice Murphy 1972; 2 daughters, 1 son *Recreations:* sport, shooting, opera, art

Fraser Morrison Esq CBE, Chairman, Highlands and Islands Enterprise, Bridge House, 20 Bridge Street, Inverness IV1 1QR *Telephone:* 01463 234171 *Fax:* 01463 244469

MORRISON, DENNIS JOHN Director, Environment and Transport, Government Office for the East Midlands Grade: 4

Career: planning Lancashire county 1966-70, Cardiff Welsh Office 1970-75; Department of Environment (DoE) 1975-: NW region 1975-81, NW enterprise unit regional controller 1981-84, Merseyside Task Force urban and economic affairs regional controller 1984-89, East Midlands regional director DoE/Department of Transport (DTp) 1989-94, director environment and transport government office for the East Midlands 1994-

Date of birth: 20 May 1942 *Education/professional qualifications:* Lymm Grammar School, Cheshire; Manchester University, geography (BA 1964), town and country planning (DipTP 1969); FRGS; MRTPI *Marital status:* married Frances Pollard 1967; 1 daughter, 1 son *Clubs:* Altrincham 41 *Recreations:* antiquarian horology, antiquarian book collecting, gardening, hill walking

Dennis J Morrison Esq, Director, Environment and Transport, Government Office for the East Midlands, Cranbrook House, Cranbrook Street, Nottingham NG1 1EY *Telephone:* 01159 350602 *Fax:* 01159 242882

MORTIMER, (JAMES) JAMIE EDWARD Under Secretary, Financial Management, Reporting and Audit Directorate, HM Treasury Grade: 3

Career: HM Treasury 1971-: economic assistant 1971-74: private secretary to chief economic adviser 1973-74; economic adviser 1974-81; principal 1981-83; head of EC budget division 1983-89, of Home Office, legal departments and Department of Transport expenditure division 1989-91; under secretary aid and export finance group (overseas debt; export credit insurance; Foreign and Commonwealth Office and Overseas Development Administration expenditure) 1991-95, deputy director financial management, reporting and audit directorate 1995-

Date of birth: 9 November 1947 *Education/professional qualifications:* Latymer Upper School, Hammersmith; Wadham College, Oxford, philosophy, politics and economics (BA 1969, MA), economics (B Phil 1971) *Marital status:* married Lesley Patricia Young 1969 *Clubs:* Old Latymerians Association, Sunbury Golf, Royal Automobile *Recreations:* cinema, soccer, golf, cricket, birdwatching

Jamie Mortimer Esq, Under Secretary, HM Treasury, Parliament Street, London SW1P 3AG *Telephone:* 0171-270 4479 *Fax:* 0171-270 5804

MORTON, KATHRYN MARY STUART Head of Solicitors' E Division, Department of Trade and Industry Grade: 3

Career: economics research Lancaster University 1969-71; research officer Overseas Development Institute (ODI) 1971-74; research associate ODI and freelance 1974-80; solicitor 1978-82; Office of Fair Trading 1982-85: legal assistant (LA) 1982-83, senior LA 1983-85; Department of Trade and Industry 1985-: senior LA 1985-86, assistant solicitor 1986-92; under secretary, head of solicitors' E division (energy sector) 1992-

Date of birth: 2 June 1946 *Education/professional qualifications:* Ealing Grammar School for Girls, London; economics, school of Afro-Asian studies, Sussex University (BA 1967); solicitor 1980 *Marital status:* single *Publications:* Aid and Dependence (Croom Helm 1975); co-author Trade and Developing Countries (Croom Helm 1977)

Miss Kathryn M S Morton, Under Secretary, Department of Trade and Industry, 1 Palace Street, London SW1E 5HE *Telephone:* 0171-238 3470 *Fax:* 0171-238 3452

MOSELEY, ELWYN RHYS Local Commissioner, Commission for Local Administration in Wales (Local Government Ombudsman)

Career: assistant solicitor (AS) Newport County Borough Council (CBC) 1969-72; principal AS Cardiff CBC 1972-74; Cardiff City Council 1974-91: city solicitor 1974-91, deputy chief executive 1979-91, director administrative and legal services 1987-91; local commissioner for local administration [ombudsman] in Wales (investigation of local authority and other bodies' maladministration) 1991-

Date of birth: 6 August 1943 *Education/professional qualifications:* Caterham School, Surrey; Queens' College, Cambridge, law (BA 1965, MA); College of Law (solicitor 1969) *Marital status:* married Annick Andrée Guyomard 1968; 2 sons, 1 daughter *Recreations:* rugby, travel

Elwyn R Moseley Esq, Local Commissioner, Commission for Local Administration in Wales, Derwen House, Court Road, Bridgend CF31 1BN *Telephone:* 01656 661325 *Fax:* 01656 658317

MOTTON, ROGER Secretary, Medicines Commission

Roger Motton Esq, Secretary, Medicines Commission, Market Towers, 1 Nine Elms Lane, London SW8 5NQ *Telephone:* 0171-273 0393 *Fax:* 0171-273 0387

MOTTRAM, RICHARD CLIVE Permanent Secretary, Ministry of Defence Grade: 1A

Career: Ministry of Defence (MoD) 1968-92: seconded to Cabinet Office (CO) 1975-77; private secretary to permanent under secretary 1979-81, to secretary of state 1982-86; assistant under secretary defence programme 1986-89; deputy under secretary policy 1989-92; permanent secretary Office of Public Service and Science CO 1992-95, MoD 1995-

Date of birth: 23 April 1946 *Education/professional qualifications:* King Edward VI Camp Hill School, Birmingham; Keele University, international relations (BA 1968) *Recreations:* cinema, theatre, tennis

Richard C Mottram Esq, Permanent Secretary, Ministry of Defence, Whitehall, London SW1A 2HB *Telephone:* 0171-218 2839 *Fax:* 0171-218 3048

MOUATT, (RICHARD) BRIAN Chief Dental Officer, NHS Executive, Department of Health Grade: 3

Career: dental officer (DO) RAF 1960-65; public health DO Bournemouth 1965-68; chief DO, Zambia 1968-72; general practice 1972-74; Department of Health 1984-: DO/senior DO 1984-91, chief DO 1991- *Current non-Whitehall posts:* regional DO South East Thames Regional Health Authority

Date of birth: 4 September 1936 *Education/professional qualifications:* Blundell's School, Tiverton; Edinburgh University, dental surgery (BDS 1960); Royal College of Surgeons, dental surgery (MGDS RCS 1979) *Marital status:* married Ursula Wälti 1962; 1 son, 1 daughter *Recreations:* watercolour painting, travel

R Brian Mouatt Esq, Chief Dental Officer, NHS Executive, Department of Health, Richmond House, 79 Whitehall, London SW1A 2NS
Telephone: 0171-210 5247 *Fax:* 0171-210 5774

MOUNTFIELD, ROBIN Permanent Secretary, Office of Public Service and Science, Cabinet Office Grade: 1A

Career: Ministry of Power/of Technology/Department of [Trade and] Industry 1961-92: assistant principal 1961-65: private secretary (PS) to permanent secretary 1963-65; principal 1965-74: petroleum division 1965-68, iron and steel division 1968-72, PS to Minister for Industry 1972-74; assistant secretary 1974-80: air division 1974-77, seconded to Stock Exchange 1977-78, industrial and commercial policy division 1978-80; under secretary, head of vehicle division 1980-84; deputy secretary 1984-95: manufacturing industry 1984-87, financial services, company and competition affairs 1987-92, HM Treasury 1992-95: industry 1992-93, civil service management and pay 1993-95; permanent secretary Office of Public Service and Science, Cabinet Office 1995-

Date of birth: 16 October 1939 *Education/professional qualifications:* Merchant Taylors' School, Crosby, Liverpool; Magdalen College, Oxford, modern history (BA 1961) *Honours, decorations:* CB 1988 *Marital status:* married Anne Newsham 1963; 1 daughter, 2 sons

Robin Mountfield Esq CB, Permanent Secretary, Office of Public Service and Science, Cabinet Office, 70 Whitehall, London SW1A 2AS
Telephone: 0171-270 0002 *Fax:* 0171-270 0202

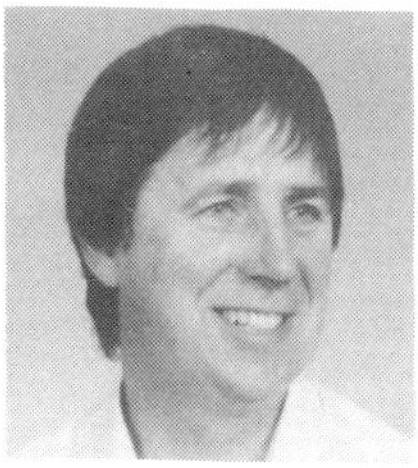

MOWL, COLIN JOHN Deputy Director, Macroeconomic Policy and Prospects Directorate, HM Treasury Grade: 3

Career: Ministry of Transport 1970-72; HM Treasury 1972-: senior economic adviser 1983-90; under secretary and head of economic analysis, forecasting and briefing, and public sector finances group 1990-95, deputy director macroeconomic policy and prospects directorate 1995-

Date of birth: 19 October 1947 *Education/professional qualifications:* London School of Economics, economics (BSc 1969, MSc 1970) *Marital status:* married Kathleen Patricia Gallagher 1980; 1 son, 1 daughter *Recreations:* family, home, sport

Colin J Mowl Esq, Under Secretary, HM Treasury, Parliament Street, London SW1P 3AG *Telephone:* 0171-270 4459 *Fax:* 0171-270 4992

MUNRO, GRAEME NEIL Chief Executive, Historic Scotland (Executive Agency) Grade: 3

Career: assistant principal Scottish Development Department (SDD) 1968-72; principal SDD, Scottish Home and Health Department (SHHD) 1972-79; assistant secretary Department of Agriculture and Fisheries for Scotland, SHHD, Scottish Office (SO) central services 1979-90; director Historic Buildings and Monuments SO Environment Department 1990-91; chief executive Historic Scotland (conservation and presentation of Scotland's built heritage) 1991-

Date of birth: 28 August 1944 *Education/professional qualifications:* Daniel Stewart's College, Edinburgh; St Andrew's University, French (MA 1967) *Marital status:* married Nicola Susan Wells 1972; 1 daughter, 1 son *Recreations:* local history, walking, swimming

Graeme N Munro Esq, Chief Executive, Historic Scotland, Longmore House, Salisbury Place, Edinburgh EH9 1SH *Telephone:* 0131-668 8696 *Fax:* 0131-668 8699

MUNRO, NEIL CHRISTOPHER Director of Management Services, Inland Revenue Grade: 4

Career: Inland Revenue (IR) 1970-78; resident observer Civil Service Selection Board 1978; IR 1978-: seconded to Confederation of British Industry as head of taxation department 1978-80; international division 1980-82; assistant secretary savings and investment division 1982-88; relocation project director 1988-; personnel division 1988-93: deputy director 1991-93; director management services division 1993-

Date of birth: 25 July 1947 *Education/professional qualifications:* Wallasey Grammar School; St John's College, Oxford, modern history (BA 1969); Cert Ed 1970; MIPM 1993 *Marital status:* married Caroline Anne Virginia 1987; 1 daughter *Clubs:* Marylebone Cricket *Recreations:* books, music, cricket, cooking

Neil C Munro Esq, Director of Management Services, Inland Revenue, Barkley House, PO Box 20, Castle Meadow Road, Nottingham NG2 1BA *Telephone:* 01159 740810 *Fax:* 01159 740812

MURPHY, (PATRICK) PAT WALLACE Under Secretary, Land Use, Conservation and Countryside Group, Ministry of Agriculture, Fisheries and Food Grade: 3

Career: Ministry of Agriculture, Fisheries and Food (MAFF) 1966-74: assistant principal 1966-71, principal 1971-74; first secretary Washington DC embassy 1974-78; MAFF 1978-: assistant secretary 1978-86; under secretary milk 1986-89, veterinary medicines, emergencies and biotechnology group 1989-93, European Community group 1993-94, land use, conservation and countryside group 1994-

Date of birth: 16 August 1944 *Education/professional qualifications:* St Chad's College, Wolverhampton; Trinity Hall, Cambridge, history (BA 1966) *Marital status:* married Denise Lillieth Fullarton-Fullarton 1972; 2 sons *Clubs:* Elstead Cricket, Elstead Tennis, Mandarins Cricket *Recreations:* cricket, tennis, gardening, travel

Pat W Murphy Esq, Under Secretary, Ministry of Agriculture, Fisheries and Food, Nobel House, 17 Smith Square, London SW1P 3JR *Telephone:* 0171-238 5684 *Fax:* 0171-238 5686

MURPHY, THOMAS Managing Director, Civil Aviation Authority

Career: British Petroleum 1955-86; Civil Aviation Authority 1986-: non-executive director 1986-87, managing director 1987-

Date of birth: 13 November 1928 *Education/professional qualifications:* Glasgow University (MA) *Honours, decorations:* CBE 1991 *Marital status:* married; 4 *Clubs:* Wentworth

Thomas Murphy Esq CBE, Managing Director, Civil Aviation Authority, CAA House, 45-59 Kingsway, London WC2B 6TE
Telephone: 0171-832 5766 *Fax:* 0171-379 3264

MURRAY, DAVID EDWARD Deputy Chief Executive (Property), The Crown Estate

Career: private sector quantity surveyor and project manager 1961-68; Greater London Council planning and transport department 1968-72; Berkshire county council 1972-93: county quantity surveyor 1977-88, director of property 1988-93; deputy chief executive (property) Crown Estate (administration of Crown landed property) 1993- *Current non-Whitehall posts:* external examiner Portsmouth University

Date of birth: 22 January 1944 *Education/professional qualifications:* Abbotsholme School, Hampshire; Hammersmith College of Art and Building; Brixton School of Building; AIQS 1971; Southampton College of Technology, construction economics (DipCE 1973); FRICS 1983 *Marital status:* married Barbara Joan Collins 1968; 2 sons *Clubs:* Parkstone Yacht *Recreations:* sailing, golf, family life

David E Murray Esq, Deputy Chief Executive (Property), The Crown Estate, 16 Carlton House Terrace, London SW1Y 5AH *Telephone:* 0171-210 4390 *Fax:* 0171-930 1295

NAISH, PETER Chief Executive, Equal Opportunities Commission

Career: various housing organisations 1970-89: chief executive (CE) English Churches Housing Group 1977-89; CE Research and Development for Psychiatry 1989-91, CLS Care Services 1991-94, Equal Opportunities Commission 1994-

Date of birth: 24 January 1945 *Education/professional qualifications:* Hampton Grammar School; King's College, London, theology; FCIH 1978; FIM 1979 *Marital status:* separated; 2 daughters, 1 son *Recreations:* walking, music, poetry

Peter Naish Esq, Chief Executive, Equal Opportunities Commission, Overseas House, Quay Street, Manchester M3 3HN
Telephone: 0161-838 8204 *Fax:* 0161-832 8816

NEEDHAM, PHILLIP Operations Director, ADAS (Executive Agency) Grade: 3

Career: National Agricultural Advisory Service/Agricultural Development and Advisory Service (ADAS), Ministry of Agriculture, Fisheries and Food 1961-: deputy director of research and development 1987-88; director of farm and countryside service and commercial director 1988-92, of operations 1992-

Date of birth: 21 April 1940 *Education/professional qualifications:* Birmingham University, chemistry (BSc 1961); Imperial College, London, plant physiology (MSc, DIC) *Marital status:* married Patricia Ann Farr 1962; 2 sons, 2 daughters

Phillip Needham Esq, Operations Director, ADAS, Oxford Spires Business Park, The Boulevard, Kidlington, Oxfordshire OX5 1NZ *Telephone:* 01865 845004 *Fax:* 01865 845091

NEVILLE-JONES, (LILIAN) PAULINE Political Director, Foreign and Commonwealth Office Grade: 2

Career: HM Diplomatic Service 1963-76: third, later second secretary Rhodesia 1965-66; second secretary, Singapore 1966-68, Foreign and Commonwealth Office London (FCO) 1968-71, Washington DC 1971-75, FCO 1975-77; member then chef de cabinet to Christopher Tugendhat, EC Commissioner for budget, financial institutions, personnel and administration 1977-82; head of policy planning staff, FCO 1983-87; minister Bonn embassy 1987-91; deputy secretary, head of overseas and defence secretariat Cabinet Office 1991-94: chairman Joint Intelligence Committee 1993-94; political director FCO 1994-

Date of birth: 2 November 1939 *Education/professional qualifications:* Leeds Girls' High School; Lady Margaret Hall, Oxford, modern history (BA 1961); Harkness Fellow, USA 1961-63 *Honours, decorations:* CMG 1987 *Marital status:* single

Miss L Pauline Neville-Jones CMG, Political Director, Foreign and Commonwealth Office, King Charles Street, London SW1A 2AH
Telephone: 0171-270 2167 *Fax:* 0171-270 3851

NEVILLE-ROLFE, LUCY JEANNE Director, Deregulation Unit, Department of Trade and Industry Grade: 3

Career: Ministry of Agriculture, Fisheries and Food 1973-92: private secretary 1977-79; sheep and livestock subsidies division 1979-81; milk and milk products division 1981-86; head of land use and tenure division 1986-89, of food legislation division (Food Safety Act 1990) 1989-90, of personnel 1990-92; member Prime Minister's Policy Unit 1992-94; director deregulation unit Department of Trade and Industry 1995-

Date of birth: 2 January 1953 *Education/professional qualifications:* St Mary's School, Shaftesbury; Cambridge; Somerville College, Oxford, philosophy, politics and economics (BA 1973, MA) *Marital status:* married Richard John Packer; 4 sons *Recreations:* cricket, racing, art and architecture, theatre, gardening

Miss Lucy J Neville-Rolfe, Director, Deregulation Unit, Department of Trade and Industry, Ashdown House, 123 Victoria Street, London SW1E 6RB *Telephone:* 0171-215 6637 *Fax:* 0171-215 6471

NEVILLE-ROLFE, MARIANNE TERESA Regional Director, Government Office for the North West, Departments of Environment, Transport, Trade and Industry and Employment Grade: 3

Career: Confederation of British Industry 1965-73; Department of Trade and Industry 1973-: principal 1973-82, assistant secretary 1982-87, under secretary 1987-90; seconded to Cabinet Office (Office of Public Service and Science) as chief executive Civil Service College and director top management programme 1990-94; regional director government office for north west 1994- *Current non-Whitehall posts:* member Higher Education Quality Council 1992-; member Council of Careers Research Advisory Council (CRAC) 1991-

Date of birth: 9 October 1944 *Education/professional qualifications:* St Mary's Convent, Shaftesbury; Lady Margaret Hall, Oxford, philosophy, politics and economics (BA 1965) *Honours, decorations:* FRSA *Marital status:* married David William John Blake 1972 (divorced 1992) *Clubs:* Royal Society of Arts *Recreations:* travel; opera; walking; reading, especially history

Miss Marianne T Neville-Rolfe, Regional Director, Government Office for the North West, Sunley Tower, Piccadilly Plaza, Manchester M1 4BA *Telephone:* 0161-838 5500 *Fax:* 0161-838 5503

NEWELL, CHRISTOPHER WILLIAM PAUL Director, Casework, Crown Prosecution Service Grade: 3

Career: Department of Director of Public Prosecutions (DPP) 1975-79; Law Officers' Department (LOD) 1979-83; DPP 1983-86; Crown Prosecution Service (CPS) 1986-87; assistant legal secretary LOD 1987-89; CPS 1989-: director of headquarters casework 1989-93, director, casework 1993-

Date of birth: 30 November 1950 *Education/professional qualifications:* Southampton University, law; Middle Temple (barrister 1973)

Christopher W P Newell Esq, Director, Casework, Crown Prosecution Service, 50 Ludgate Hill, London EC4M 7EX *Telephone:* 0171-273 8000

NEWEY, MAURICE R Director of Central Services, Department of Transport Grade: 4

Career: Departments of Transport (DTp), Environment and Property Services Agency: regional managing director PSA Southern 1976-82; director of central services DTp 1992-

Date of birth: 6 October 1944 *Education/professional qualifications:* Burton-on-Trent Grammar School *Marital status:* married; 1 son, 1 daughter *Recreations:* cricket, badminton, music

M R Newey Esq, Director of Central Services, Department of Transport, Lambeth Bridge House, London SE1 7SB *Telephone:* 0171-238 4509
Fax: 0171-238 4391

NICHOLLS, NIGEL HAMILTON Clerk of the Council, Privy Council Office Grade: 3

Career: assistant principal Admiralty 1962-64; Ministry of Defence (MoD) 1964-92: assistant private secretary (APS) to minister for Royal Navy 1965-66; principal 1966-74: directing staff Royal College of Defence Studies 1971-73, APS to secretary of state 1973-74; assistant secretary 1974-84: head of naval matters ashore secretariat 1974-77, defence counsellor UK delegation to Mutual and Balanced Force Reductions talks, Vienna 1977-80; head of naval operations secretariat 1980-84; assistant under secretary (AUS) 1984-: air staff 1984, defence staff 1984-86; seconded as under secretary Cabinet Office 1986-89; AUS systems Office of Management and Budget (defence equipment requirements) MoD 1989-92; Clerk of Privy Council 1992-

Date of birth: 19 February 1938 *Education/professional qualifications:* King's School, Canterbury; St John's College, Oxford, literae humaniores (BA 1962, MA) *Honours, decorations:* CBE 1982 *Marital status:* married Isobel Judith Dean 1967; 2 sons *Clubs:* United Oxford and Cambridge University *Recreations:* choral singing, genealogy, mountain walking

Nigel H Nicholls Esq CBE, Clerk of the Council, Privy Council Office, Whitehall, London SW1A 2AT *Telephone:* 0171-270 0510
Fax: 0171-270 0494

NICHOLS, DINAH ALISON Deputy Secretary, Housing and Construction, Department of the Environment Grade: 2

Career: Ministry of Transport 1965-74: assistant private secretary (PS) to minister 1969-70, principal 1970-74, seconded to Cabinet Office 1974-77; Department of the Environment (DoE) 1978-; assistant secretary radioactive waste policy 1977-80; inner city policy 1981-83; principal PS to Secretary of State for Transport 1983-85; director of administrative resources DoE/Department of Transport 1985-88; under secretary water directorate 1988-91; deputy secretary property holdings, construction and central support services 1991-94, housing and construction 1994- *Current non-Whitehall posts:* non-executive director Anglian Water plc 1992-

Date of birth: 28 September 1943 *Education/professional qualifications:* Wyggeston Girls' Grammar School, Leicester; Bedford College, London University, history (BA 1965) *Marital status:* single *Clubs:* Swiss Alpine, Hampstead Cricket, Royal Society of Arts *Recreations:* mountaineering and walking, choral singing, music, theatre, travel

Ms Dinah A Nichols, Deputy Secretary, Department of the Environment, 2 Marsham Street, London SW1P 3EB *Telephone:* 0171-276 3623
Fax: 0171-276 3638

NICKLEN, STEVE Director Audit Support, Audit Commission

Career: tutor, research scientist, molecular biology laboratory Pembroke College, Cambridge 1974-79; commercial management consultants 1984-93; director audit support directorate Audit Commission (independent audit local authorities and NHS) 1994-

Date of birth: 2 May 1953 *Education/professional qualifications:* King Edward VI School, Southampton; Leeds University, biochemistry (BSc 1974); Pembroke College, Cambridge, molecular biology research *Marital status:* married Mary Jane Madden Budd 1983; 1 daughter, 1 son *Recreations:* music, swimming, walking

Steve Nicklen Esq, Director, Audit Commission, 1 Vincent Square, London SW1P 2PN
Telephone: 0171-828 1212 *Fax:* 0171-396 1335

NIEDUSZYŃSKI, ANTHONY JOHN Secretary, Monopolies and Mergers Commission Grade: 3

Career: Board of Trade (BOT)/Department of [Trade and] Industry (D[T]I) 1964-74: assistant principal 1964-67, private secretary to President BOT 1967-68, principal 1968-72; principal private secretary to Minister for Trade and Consumer Affairs 1972-74, to Secretary of State for Trade 1974; assistant secretary Department of Prices and Consumer Protection 1974-77, DI 1977-82, Home Office 1982-83; DTI 1983-: assistant secretary 1983-85; under secretary 1985-: head of radiocommunications division, of air division, of business task forces division 2 (aerospace, shipbuilding and vehicles; defence industries) 1990-92, of aerospace division 1992-93; secretary to Monopolies and Mergers Commission 1993-

Date of birth: 7 January 1939 *Education/professional qualifications:* St Paul's School, London; Merton College, Oxford, literae humaniores (BA 1961, MA) *Marital status:* married Frances Oxford 1980; 1 daughter *Clubs:* Polish Hearth *Recreations:* gardening, fell walking, riding, opera, ballet

Anthony J Nieduszyński Esq, Secretary, Monopolies and Mergers Commission, New Court, 48 Carey Street, London WC2A 2JT
Telephone: 0171-324 1427 *Fax:* 0171-324 1400

NILSSON, PETER CARL Proceedings Operational Director, Solicitor's Office, Departments of Health and of Social Security Grade: 4

Career: captain Army Legal Services 1962-64; Ministry of Pensions and National Insurance 1964-69: legal assistant 1964-70, clerk to adjudicator 1967-69; Department of Health and Social Security 1970-83: senior legal assistant 1970-83 (principal administrator EC Commission, Brussels 1974-80), assistant solicitor 1983-90; proceedings operational director, Office of the Solicitor (provision of legal services and advice) Departments of Social Security 1990-, of Health 1990- and Office of Population Censuses and Surveys 1990-

Date of birth: 10 June 1938 *Education/professional qualifications:* East Barnet Grammar School, Hertfordshire; King's College, London, law (LLB, AKC 1961); Inner Temple (barrister 1962) *Marital status:* married Alish Veronica 1969; widower *Publications:* joint editor Law Relating to Supplementary Benefits and Family Income Supplements (HMSO 1972), editor Law Relating to National Insurance and Family Allowances (HMSO 1973) *Recreations:* theatre, music, walking

Peter C Nilsson Esq, Proceedings Operational Director, Solicitor's Office, Departments of Health and Social Security, New Court, 48 Carey Street, London WC2A 2LS *Telephone:* 0171-412 1369 *Fax:* 0171-412 1244

NIMMO SMITH, WILLIAM AUSTIN Commissioner, Scottish Law Commission

Career: advocate 1969-: statutory junior counsel to Department of Employment 1977-82; advocate depute 1983-86; chairman Medical Appeal Tribunals and Vaccine Damage Tribunals 1986-91; member Scottish Law Commission 1988- *Current non-Whitehall posts:* practising member Faculty of Advocates (Scottish Bar)

Date of birth: 6 November 1942 *Education/professional qualifications:* Dragon School, Oxford; Eton College; Balliol College, Oxford, literae humaniores (BA 1965); Edinburgh University, law (LLB 1967); member Faculty of Advocates 1969 *Honours, decorations:* QC 1982 *Marital status:* married Jennifer Main 1968; 1 daughter, 1 son *Publications:* contributions to legal publications *Clubs:* New, Edinburgh *Recreations:* hillwalking, music

William A Nimmo Smith Esq QC, Commissioner, Scottish Law Commission, 140 Causewayside, Edinburgh EH9 1PR
Telephone: 0131-668 2131 *Fax:* 0131-662 4900

NISBET, I Deputy Director, Corporate Affairs, NHS Executive, Department of Health Grade: 4

Miss I Nisbet, Deputy Director, Corporate Affairs, NHS Executive, Department of Health, Quarry House, Quarry Hill, Leeds LS2 7UE *Telephone:* 01132 545000

NISSEN, DAVID EDGAR JOSEPH The Solicitor, HM Customs and Excise Grade: 3

Career: prosecuting solicitor Sussex Police Authority 1970-73; HM Customs and Excise (C&E) 1973-90: senior legal assistant 1976-83; assistant solicitor (AS) 1983-87, principal AS 1987-90; principal AS Department of Energy (DEn) division Treasury Solicitor's Department (legal adviser to DEn) 1990-92; solicitor's division Department of Trade and Industry 1992-; the solicitor C&E 1992-

Date of birth: 27 November 1942 *Education/professional qualifications:* King's School, Chester; University College, London, law (LLB 1964) *Marital status:* married Pauline Jennifer Meaden 1969; 2 daughters *Recreations:* opera, gardening

David E J Nissen Esq, The Solicitor, HM Customs and Excise, New King's Beam House, 22 Upper Ground, London SE1 9PJ
Telephone: 0171-865 5121 *Fax:* 0171-865 5022

NIVEN, R A Under Secretary and Director, Industrial Relations II, Employment Department Group Grade: 3

R A Niven Esq, Under Secretary, Employment Department Group, Caxton House, Tothill Street, London SW1H 9NF *Telephone:* 0171-273 3000

NOBLE, GILLIAN M Under Secretary, Spending Directorate, HM Treasury Grade: 3

Career: economist Ministry of Transport/Department of Environment 1969-76; HM Treasury 1976-: public expenditure control 1976-87; head of banking division 1987-92, of education, science and heritage division 1992-93; under secretary, social services and territorial departments group 1993-95, deputy director spending directorate 1995-

Date of birth: 18 November 1947 *Education/professional qualifications:* Aberdeen University, economic science (MA 1969); University College, London, public sector economics (MSc 1974) *Marital status:* single *Recreations:* music, walking, historic houses

Miss Gillian Noble, Under Secretary, HM Treasury, Parliament Street, London SW1P 3AG
Telephone: 0171-270 4500 *Fax:* 0171-270 5356

NOLAN, MICHAEL PATRICK (The Rt Hon Lord Nolan) Chairman, Committee on Standards in Public Life

Career: barrister 1953-: crown court recorder 1975-82; high court judge 1982-91; western circuit presiding judge 1985-88; appeal judge 1991-; chairman Committee on Standards of Conduct in Public Life 1994-

Date of birth: 10 September 1928 *Education/professional qualifications:* Ampleforth College, York; Wadham College, Oxford, law (BA, MA 1952); Middle Temple (barrister 1953, bencher 1975); barrister Northern Ireland (NI) 1974, QC NI 1974 *Honours, decorations:* QC 1968, Kt Bachelor 1982, PC 1991, Baron 1994 *Marital status:* married Margaret Elizabeth Noyes 1953; 4 daughters, 1 son *Clubs:* Army and Navy, Boodles, Marylebone Cricket *Recreations:* walking, swimming, fishing, travel

The Rt Hon Lord Nolan, Chairman, Committee on Standards in Public Life, Horseguards Road, London SW1P 3AL *Telephone:* 0171-270 5875

NOONEY, DAVID MATTHEW Principal Establishment and Finance Officer, Crown Prosecution Service Grade: 3

Career: HM Treasury 1965-89: management accounting adviser (MAA) to home and education group division 1984-86; seconded to Lord Chancellor's Department (LCD) as MAA 1986-88, as head of resources 1988-89; LCD 1989-: head of resources division 1989-91, of civil business division 1991-93, of legal services and agencies division 1993; seconded to Crown Prosecution Service as principal establishment and finance officer 1993-

Date of birth: 2 August 1945 *Education/professional qualifications:* St Joseph's Academy, London; FICMA *Marital status:* married Maureen Georgina Revell 1973; 1 daughter *Recreations:* sport, theatre, crosswords

David M Nooney Esq, Principal Establishment and Finance Officer, Crown Prosecution Service, 50 Ludgate Hill, London EC4M 7EX
Telephone: 0171-273 8114 *Fax:* 0171-329 8168

NORMAND, A C Regional Procurator Fiscal (Glasgow and Strathclyde), Crown Office Grade: 3

A C Normand Esq, Regional Procurator Fiscal for Glasgow and Strathclyde, Procurator Fiscal's Office, 10 Ballater Street, Glasgow G5 9PS *Telephone:* 0141-429 5566 *Fax:* 0141-420 3575

Government Departments

see page 372

NORMINGTON, DAVID JOHN Director of Personnel and Development, Employment Department Group Grade: 3

Career: Department of Employment/Employment Department Group 1973-: East London area training manager Manpower Services Commission 1982-84; principal private secretary to secretary of state 1984-85; head of long-term unemployment policy branch 1985-87; London and SE regional director and leader London City Action Team 1987-89; head of strategy and employment policy division 1989-92; director of personnel and development 1992-

Date of birth: 18 October 1951 *Education/professional qualifications:* Bradford Grammar School; Corpus Christi College, Oxford, modern history (BA 1973, MA) *Marital status:* married Winifred Anne Charlotte Harris 1985 *Recreations:* gardening, walking, tennis, watching ballet

David J Normington Esq, Director of Personnel and Development, Employment Department Group, Caxton House, Tothill Street, London SE1H 9NF *Telephone:* 0171-273 5786 *Fax:* 0171-273 5787

NORRIS, SYDNEY GEORGE Assistant Under Secretary and Principal Finance Officer, Home Office Grade: 3

Career: army service 1956-58; Home Office (HO) 1963-79: private secretary (PS) to parliamentary secretary 1967; PS to Home Secretary 1973-74; assistant secretary 1974-81; HM Treasury 1979-81; HO 1981-82; establishment and finance officer Northern Ireland Office 1982-85; HO 1985-: director of operational policy prison service 1985-88; police department 1988-90; principal finance officer 1990-

Date of birth: 22 August 1937 *Education/professional qualifications:* Liverpool Institute High School for Boys; University College, Oxford, literae humaniores (BA 1962, MA); Trinity Hall, Cambridge, criminology (DipCrim 1963); University of California at Berkeley, USA, criminology (MCrim 1970) *Marital status:* married Brigid Fitzgibbon 1965; 1 daughter, 2 sons *Recreations:* running, fellwalking, piano, theatre, choral singing

Sydney G Norris Esq, Assistant Under Secretary, Home Office, 50 Queen Anne's Gate, London SW1H 9AT *Telephone:* 0171-273 3902 *Fax:* 0171-273 2190

NORRISS, Air Vice-Marshal PETER COULSON Director-General Air Systems 2, Procurement Executive, Ministry of Defence

Career: flying instructor RAF College Cranwell 1969-71; pilot 1972-76; personal air secretary to under secretary of state (RAF) Ministry of Defence (MoD) 1977-79; No 16 squadron commander 1980-83; MoD 1983-85: staff officer 1983-84, head of RAF presentation team 1984-85; station commander RAF Marham 1985-87; MoD 1988-: deputy director operational requirements (OR) (air) 1988-89, director OR (air) 1989-91, director-general aircraft 2/air systems 2 (all helicopters and aircraft except European fighter aircraft and Tornado for all armed forces) procurement executive 1991-

Date of birth: 22 April 1944 *Education/professional qualifications:* Beverley Grammar School, Yorkshire; Magdalene College, Cambridge, modern languages (BA 1966, MA 1970); FRAeS *Honours, decorations:* AFC 1977 *Recreations:* golf, squash

Air Vice-Marshal Peter C Norriss AFC, Director-General, Air Systems 2, Ministry of Defence Procurement Executive, St Giles Court, 1 St Giles High Street, London WC2H 8LD *Telephone:* 0171-305 1043 *Fax:* 0171-305 1045

NORTON, (MICHAEL JAMES) JIM Chief Executive, Radiocommunications Agency (Executive Agency) Grade: 3

Career: Post Office Telecommunications/British Telecom 1970-87; vendor consultancy director Butler Cox plc 1987-90; marketing director Cable and Wireless Europe 1990-93; chief executive Radiocommunications Agency (civil radio concerns, including use of radio spectrum) 1993-

Date of birth: 15 December 1952 *Education/professional qualifications:* Roan School for Boys, London; Sheffield University, electronic engineering (BEng 1974) *Honours, decorations:* FRSA 1993 *Marital status:* married Barbara Foster 1976; 1 son *Recreations:* music, theatre

M J Norton Esq, Chief Executive, Radiocommunications Agency, Waterloo Bridge House, Waterloo Road, London SE1 8UA
Telephone: 0171-215 2339 *Fax:* 0171-401 8673

NURSAW, Sir JAMES Counsel to the Chairman of Committees, House of Lords

Career: senior research officer in criminal science Cambridge University 1958-59; Home Office 1959-80; legal secretary Law Officers' Department 1980-83; legal adviser Home Office 1983-88; Treasury Solicitor's Department 1988-92; counsel to chairman of committees (legal advice) House of Lords 1993-

Date of birth: 18 October 1932 *Education/professional qualifications:* Bancroft's School, Woodford Wells, Essex; Christ's College, Cambridge, mathematics and law (MA 1953), law (LLB 1954); Middle Temple (barrister 1955) *Honours, decorations:* CB 1983, QC 1988, KCB 1991 *Marital status:* married Eira Caryl-Thomas 1959; 2 daughters *Clubs:* United Oxford and Cambridge University, Marylebone Cricket

Sir James Nursaw KCB QC, Counsel to the Chairman of Committees, House of Lords, London SW1A 0PW

NUTT, P E Deputy Director and Operations Director, Network Management and Maintenance Directorate, Highways Agency (Executive Agency) Grade: 4

P E Nutt Esq, Deputy Director, Network Management and Maintenance Directorate, Highways Agency, St Christopher House, Southwark Street, London SE1 0TE *Telephone:* 0171-928 3666

NUTTALL, CHRISTOPHER PETER Assistant Under Secretary, Director of Research and Statistics, Home Office Grade: 3

Career: Home Office (HO) 1963-82; assistant deputy solicitor general (SG), SG's Office, Ottawa, Canada 1982-89; assistant under secretary, director of research and statistics HO 1989-

Date of birth: 20 April 1939 *Education/professional qualifications:* Keele University (BA); University of California at Berkeley, USA (MA)

Christopher P Nuttall Esq, Assistant Under Secretary, Home Office, 50 Queen Anne's Gate, London SW1H 9AT *Telephone:* 0171-273 2616

O

OATES, LAURENCE Associate Head, Policy Group, Lord Chancellor's Department Grade: 3

Career: barrister 1970-77; legal assistant (LA)/senior LA Department of Employment 1977-81, Law Officers' Department 1981-84; assistant solicitor advising Department of Transport, Treasury Solicitor's Department 1984-89; Lord Chancellor's Department 1989-: under secretary 1989-: head of legal and law reform group 1989-92; administrator Midland and Oxford circuit 1992-94; associate head policy group 1995-

Date of birth: 14 May 1946 *Education/professional qualifications:* Beckenham and Penge Grammar School; Bristol University, law (LLB 1967); Middle Temple (barrister 1968) *Marital status:* married Brenda Lilian Hardwick 1968; 1 daughter, 1 son *Recreations:* flute, golf

Laurence Oates Esq, Under Secretary, Lord Chancellor's Department, Trevelyan House, Great Peter Street, London SW1Y 2BY
Telephone: 0171-210 8809 *Fax:* 0171-210 8549

O'BRIEN, Air Vice-Marshal ROBERT PETER Air Secretary, Ministry of Defence

Career: Royal Air Force (RAF) 1962-: pilot 1962-73; student Army Staff College 1974; staff/flying appointments HQ RAF Germany, Tri-national Tornado Training Establishment, Cottesmore 1979-82; station commander RAF Marham 1983-85; air offensive staff Ministry of Defence (MoD) 1985-87; deputy commander HQ British forces Cyprus 1988-91; infrastructure staff MoD 1991-92; commandant Joint Services Defence College 1992-94; Air Secretary MoD 1994-

Date of birth: 1 November 1941 *Education/professional qualifications:* Salesian College, Farnborough; RAF College, Cranwell (commission 1962); BA(gen) London external 1962 *Honours, decorations:* OBE *Clubs:* Royal Air Force *Recreations:* tennis, golf, walking

Air Vice-Marshal Robert O'Brien OBE, Air Secretary, HQ Personnel and Training Command, Innsworth, Gloucester GL3 1EZ *Telephone and Fax:* 01452 712612

O'CONNOR, LIAM Special Adviser to Secretary of State for the Environment

Liam O'Connor Esq, Special Adviser, Department of the Environment, 2 Marsham Street, London SW1P 3EB *Telephone:* 0171-276 3000

ODGERS, GRAEME DAVID WILLIAM Chairman, Monopolies and Mergers Commission

Career: International Finance Corporation 1959-62; consultancy, merchant banking and insurance 1962-73; director industrial development unit Department of Trade and Industry 1974-77; associate financial director GEC 1977-78; Tarmac 1979-86: group finance director 1979-86, group managing director (MD) 1983-86; MD British Telecom 1987-90; chief executive Alfred McAlpine 1990-93; chairman Monopolies and Mergers Commission 1993-

Date of birth: 10 March 1934 *Education/professional qualifications:* St John's College, Johannesburg, South Africa; Gonville and Caius College, Cambridge, engineering (BA 1955, MA); Harvard Business School, USA (MBA 1959) *Marital status:* married Diana Berge 1957; 2 daughters, 1 son *Clubs:* Wildernesse, City of London, Reform *Recreations:* golf

Graeme Odgers Esq, Chairman, Monopolies and Mergers Commission, New Court, 48 Carey Street, London WC2A 2JT
Telephone: 0171-324 1423 *Fax:* 0171-324 1400

O'DONNELL, (AUGUSTINE) GUS THOMAS Deputy Director, Macroeconomic Policy and Prospects Directorate, HM Treasury Grade: 3

Career: political economy lecturer Glasgow University 1975-79; economist HM Treasury (HMT) 1979-85; economic first secretary Washington DC embassy 1985-88; HMT 1988-: senior economic adviser 1988-89; chief press secretary to John Major as Chancellor of Exchequer 1989-90, as Prime Minister 1990-94; HMT 1994-: head of monetary group 1994-95, deputy director macroeconomic policy and prospects directorate 1995-

Date of birth: 1 October 1952 *Education/professional qualifications:* Salesian College, London; Warwick University, economics (BA 1973); Nuffield College, Oxford, economics (MPhil 1975) *Honours, decorations:* CB 1994 *Marital status:* married Melanie Timmis 1979; 1 daughter *Clubs:* Old Salesians Football *Recreations:* football, tennis

Gus T O'Donnell Esq CB, Under Secretary, HM Treasury, Parliament Street, London SW1P 3AG *Telephone:* 0171-270 3000 *Fax:* 0171-270 5557

OGLEY, (WILLIAM) BILL DAVID Director of Finances and Resources, Audit Commission

Career: accountant Derbyshire county council (CC) 1976-83, Oxfordshire CC 1983-85; Hertfordshire CC 1985-93: director of finance 1991-93; director of finance and resources, deputy controller Audit Commission (external audit local government and NHS) 1993-

Date of birth: 26 May 1955 *Education/professional qualifications:* Sir Roger Manwood's Grammar School, Sandwich, Kent; Manchester University, physics and psychology (BSc 1976); Sheffield University (CIPFA 1979) *Marital status:* married Ann Dolores 1978; 1 daughter, 1 son *Recreations:* sailing, golf, riding, tennis

W D Ogley Esq, Deputy Controller, Audit Commission, 1 Vincent Square, London SW1P 2PN *Telephone:* 0171-828 1212 *Fax:* 0171-976 6187

OLIVER, RON(ALD) JAMES Chief Executive, Vehicle Inspectorate (Executive Agency) Grade: 4

Career: engineering and automotive industry 1964-74; Department of Transport 1974-: vehicle engineering and safety divisions; vehicle inspection division 1978-: Vehicle Inspectorate 1985-: head 1985-, chief executive 1988-

Date of birth: 28 October 1945 *Education/professional qualifications:* Windsor Grammar School; Brunel University, engineering (BEng 1968); CEng 1973; MIMechE 1973 *Marital status:* married Fiona Hatton 1992; 1 daughter, 2 sons *Recreations:* cooking, swimming, walking, travel

Ron J Oliver Esq, Chief Executive, Vehicle Inspectorate, Berkeley House, Croydon Street, Bristol BS5 0DA *Telephone:* 01179 543210 *Fax:* 01179 543391

"Next Steps" Executive Agencies

see page 875

OMAND, DAVID BRUCE Deputy Under Secretary (Policy), Ministry of Defence Grade: 2

Career: Ministry of Defence 1970-: assistant principal 1970-75; assistant private secretary (PS) to secretary of state (SoS) 1974-75, 1979-81; PS to SoS 1981-82; head of management services and organisation 1982-84; defence reorganisation team 1984; on secondment as defence counsellor UK delegation to NATO, Brussels 1985-88; assistant under secretary management strategy 1988-91, programmes (annual defence long-term planning) 1991-92; deputy under secretary (policy) 1992-

Date of birth: 15 April 1947 *Education/professional qualifications:* Glasgow Academy; Corpus Christi College, Cambridge, economics (BA 1969) *Recreations:* opera, hill walking

David B Omand Esq, Deputy Under Secretary, Ministry of Defence, Whitehall, London SW1A 2HB *Telephone:* 0171-218 9000 *Fax:* 0171-218 1042

O'MARA, MARGARET Under Secretary, Libraries, Galleries and Museums Group, Department of National Heritage Grade: 3

Career: HM Treasury 1973-92: various positions 1973-85; head economic briefing division, monetary group division and expenditure group 1985-92; Department of National Heritage 1992-: under secretary arts group 1992-93, libraries, galleries and museums group 1993-

Date of birth: 10 May 1951 *Education/professional qualifications:* St Hilda's College, Oxford, literae humaniores (BA 1973); University College, London, public policy economics (MSc 1982) *Marital status:* single *Recreations:* walking, cooking

Miss Margaret O'Mara, Under Secretary, Department of National Heritage, 2-4 Cockspur Street, London SW1Y 5DH *Telephone:* 0171-211 6000 *Fax:* 0171-211 6230

OPPENHEIMER, NICOLA ANNE Principal Establishment and Finance Officer, Lord Chancellor's Department Grade: 3

Career: Lord Chancellor's Department 1973-: legal assistant 1973-78; senior legal assistant 1978-85; judicial appointments 1985-87; head of personnel management division 1987-91, of legal services and agencies division 1991-93; principal establishment and finance officer 1993-

Date of birth: 30 September 1950 *Education/professional qualifications:* St Margaret's School, Bushey; Queen's College, London; Queen Mary College, London University, law (LLB 1971); Middle Temple (barrister 1972) *Marital status:* married Michael 1973; 1 daughter, 1 son *Recreations:* early music, theatre, skiing, walking

Mrs Nicola A Oppenheimer, Principal Establishment and Finance Officer, Lord Chancellor's Department, 30 Great Peter Street, London SW1P 2BY *Telephone:* 0171-210 8519 *Fax:* 0171-210 8752

OSBORN, (FREDERIC ADRIAN) DEREK Director-General, Environmental Protection, Department of the Environment Grade: 2

Career: Ministry of Housing and Local Government 1965-74: private secretary to minister of state and permanent secretary 1967; Royal Commission on Standards of Conduct in Public Life 1974; assistant secretary (AS) Department of Transport 1975-77; Department of Environment 1977-: AS 1977-82, under secretary 1982-87: finance 1982-86, housing group 1986-87; deputy secretary 1987-: local government and finance 1987-89, director-general environmental protection 1990-

Date of birth: 14 January 1941 *Education/professional qualifications:* Leys School, Cambridge; Balliol College, Oxford, mathematics (BA 1963), philosophy (BPhil 1965) *Honours, decorations:* CB 1991 *Marital status:* married Caroline Niebuhr Tod 1971; 1 daughter, 1 son *Recreations:* music, reading, chess

Derek Osborn Esq CB, Deputy Secretary, Department of the Environment, 2 Marsham Street, London SW1P 3EB *Telephone:* 0171-276 3570 *Fax:* 0171-276 0590

OSBORNE, ANTHONY DAVID Chief Executive, Government Property Lawyers (Executive Agency) Grade: 3

Career: private practice solicitor 1958-65; Treasury Solicitor's Department (legal services to government departments) 1965-: solicitor to Health and Safety Executive 1985-90; under secretary (legal), head of property division 1990-93/chief executive Government Property Lawyers 1993-

Date of birth: 21 March 1935 *Education/professional qualifications:* solicitor 1958 *Marital status:* married Ethelwyn Grieve 1958; 2 sons, 1 daughter *Recreations:* music, theatre, travel, photography

Anthony D Osborne Esq, Chief Executive, Government Property Lawyers, Riverside Chambers, Castle Street, Taunton, Somerset TA1 4AP *Telephone:* 01823 345200 *Fax:* 01823 345202

OSBORNE, MICHAEL CHARLES ANTHONY Deputy Inspector General and Senior Official Receiver, Insolvency Service (Executive Agency) Grade: 4

Career: private industry 1956-62; Department of Trade and Industry Insolvency Service 1962-: companies winding up, London 1962-71; companies investigation branch (CIB) 1971-81; assistant official receiver High Court, London 1981-84, deputy inspector of companies CIB 1984-93; deputy inspector general and senior official receiver 1993-

Date of birth: 2 April 1938 *Education/professional qualifications:* St John's School, Leatherhead *Marital status:* married Jean Margaret Mazdon 1967; 3 sons *Recreations:* tennis, theatre, music

Michael C A Osborne Esq, Deputy Inspector General and Senior Official Receiver, Insolvency Service, 21 Bloomsbury Street, London WC1B 3SS *Telephone:* 0171-291 6724 *Fax:* 0171-291 6726

O'SHEA, MIKE KENT Under Secretary, Finance and Resource Management, Department of Trade and Industry Grade: 3

Career: Department of Trade and Industry 1973-: privatisation British Aerospace, British Telecom and Rolls Royce -1988; finance and resource management 1988-91; director Inner Cities Unit 1991-92, under secretary finance and resource management 1992- *Current non-Whitehall posts:* non-executive director Seven Seas Limited

Date of birth: 12 March 1951 *Education/professional qualifications:* Bristol Grammar School; Corpus Christi College, Cambridge, history (BA 1972) *Marital status:* married Linda Szpala 1988 *Clubs:* Gloucestershire County Cricket; Mandarins Cricket *Recreations:* cricket, walking, Wagner, beer and wine

M K O'Shea Esq, Under Secretary, Department of Trade and Industry, Ashdown House, 123 Victoria Street, London SW1E 6RB *Telephone:* 0171-215 6869

OSLER, DOUGLAS ALEXANDER HM Depute Senior Chief Inspector, HM Inspectors of Schools, Scottish Office Education Department Grade: 4

Date of birth: 11 October 1942 *Education/professional qualifications:* history (MA); teacher's certificate *Marital status:* married; 1 son, 1 daughter *Recreations:* golf, Rotary International

D A Osler Esq, HM Depute Senior Chief Inspector, HM Inspectors of Schools, Scottish Office Education Department, New St Andrew's House, Edinburgh EH1 3SY *Telephone:* 0131-244 4521 *Fax:* 0131-244 4785

OSMOTHERLY, EDWARD BENJAMIN CROFTON Chairman, Commission for Local Administration in England; Local Government Ombudsman Grade: 2

Career: Ministry of Housing and Local Government/Department of Environment 1963-78: assistant principal, principal; Harkness fellow (Brookings Institution, Washington DC and UCLA) 1972-73; assistant secretary 1976-82; seconded to British Rail (BR) 1979; head of machinery of government Civil Service Department 1980-82; Department of Transport 1982-93: under secretary 1982-89, deputy secretary public transport and research 1989-92, principal establishment and finance officer 1992-93; Commission for Local Administration (investigating complaints of maladministration by local authorities and certain other bodies) 1993-: commissioner (ombudsman) 1993-94; chairman 1994-

Date of birth: 1 August 1942 *Education/professional qualifications:* East Ham Grammar School, London; Fitzwilliam College, Cambridge, economics, anthropology, history (BA 1963, MA) *Honours, decorations:* CB 1992 *Marital status:* married Valerie Mustill 1970; 1 daughter, 1 son *Recreations:* squash, reading

Edward B C Osmotherly Esq CB, Chairman Commission for Local Administration, 21 Queen Anne's Gate, London SW1H 9BU *Telephone:* 0171-915 3210 *Fax:* 0171-233 0396

OSWALD, RICHARD ANTHONY Deputy Health Service Commissioner, Office of the Health Service Commissioners [Ombudsman] Grade: 3

Career: NHS administrative posts 1961-72; hospital secretary London Hospital 1972-74; support services manager South Camden Health District (HD) 1974-77; district administrator Leeds West HD 1977-84; district general manager Leeds Western Health Authority 1985-89; deputy health service commissioner Ombudsman's Office (complaints about NHS services in GB) 1989-

Date of birth: 12 January 1941 *Education/professional qualifications:* The Leys School, Cambridge; MHSM, DipHSM 1966 *Marital status:* married Janet Iris Penticost 1963; 3 sons, 1 daughter *Recreations:* classical music, acting, bird-watching

Richard A Oswald Esq, Deputy Health Service Commissioner, Office of the Health Service Commissioners, Millbank Tower, Millbank, London SW1P 4PU *Telephone:* 0171-217 4019 *Fax:* 0171-217 4000

OUGHTON, JOHN RAYMOND CHARLES Head of Efficiency and Effectiveness Group, Cabinet Office Grade: 3

Career: Ministry of Defence 1974-93: assistant private secretary (PS) to minister of state (MOS) 1979-80; seconded to Canadian government 1980-81; defence sales policy, East/West trade controls 1981-84; PS to personal adviser to secretary of state 1984, to MOS armed forces 1984-85; procurement policy directorate 1986-90: director 1987-90; head of navy resources and programmes 1990-93; head of Prime Minister's efficiency unit Cabinet Office 1993-

Date of birth: 21 September 1952 *Education/professional qualifications:* Reading School; University College, Oxford, modern history (BA 1974) *Marital status:* single *Clubs:* United Oxford and Cambridge University; Middlesex County Cricket; Tottenham Hotspur *Recreations:* squash, tennis, bridge, football

John R C Oughton Esq, Head of Efficiency and Effectiveness Group, Cabinet Office, 70 Whitehall, London SW1A 2AS *Telephone:* 0171-270 0257 *Fax:* 0171-270 0099

OUSELEY, HERMAN Chairman, Commission for Racial Equality

Career: principal race relations adviser Greater London Council 1981-84; assistant chief executive London Borough of Lambeth (LBL) 1984-86; director of education/chief executive Inner London Education Authority 1986-88; chief executive LBL 1988-93; chairman Commission for Racial Equality 1993-

Herman Ouseley Esq, Chairman, Commission for Racial Equality, Elliot House, 10-12 Allington Street, London SW1E 5EH *Telephone:* 0171-828 7022

OWEN, JOHN AUBREY Director, Regeneration Programmes, Government Office for London, Departments of the Environment, Employment, Trade and Industry and Transport Grade: 3

Career: assistant principal Ministry of Transport 1969-72; Department of Environment (DoE) 1972-75: assistant private secretary to minister for transport industries 1972-73, principal 1973-75; principal Department of Transport 1975-80: seconded to Cambridgeshire county council 1978-80; DoE 1980-: assistant secretary 1980-87, northern regional director 1987-91, director of personnel management 1991-95, director regeneration programmes, government office for London 1995- *Current non-Whitehall posts:* non-executive director Tarmac housing division 1992-

Date of birth: 1 August 1945 *Education/professional qualifications:* City of London School; St Catharine's College, Cambridge, classics (BA 1967, MA) *Marital status:* married Julia Margaret Jones 1971; 1 daughter, 1 son *Recreations:* opera, gardening

John A Owen Esq, Director, Regeneration Programmes, Government Office for London, Millbank Tower, 21-24 Millbank, London SW1P 4QU *Telephone:* 0171-217 4529

OWEN, PETER FRANCIS Deputy Secretary, Teachers and School Curriculum, Department for Education Grade: 2

Career: Department of the Environment (DoE) 1975-90: assistant secretary housing policy review 1975-77, local government finance (LGF) 1977-80; regional director DoE/Department of Transport 1980-82; director rural affairs 1982-83; under secretary LGF 1984-86; deputy secretary housing and construction 1986-90, economic secretariat Cabinet Office 1990-94, teachers and school curriculum Department for Education 1994-

Date of birth: 4 September 1940 *Education/professional qualifications:* Liverpool Institute; Liverpool University, French (BA 1963) *Honours, decorations:* CB 1990 *Marital status:* married Ann Preece 1963; 1 son, 1 daughter *Recreations:* reading, gardening, French language and literature

Peter F Owen Esq CB, Deputy Secretary, Department for Education, Sanctuary Buildings, Great Smith Street, Westminster, London SW1P 3BT *Telephone:* 0171-925 5000 *Fax:* 0171-925 6000

P

PACEY, ALBERT HOWARD Director-General, National Criminal Intelligence Service

Career: police service 1955-: cadet to chief superintendent Lincolnshire Constabulary 1955-76; staff officer to HM Inspector of Constabulary Home Office 1976; assistant chief constable Humberside Police 1977-83; deputy chief constable Lancashire Constabulary 1983-87; chief constable Gloucestershire Constabulary 1987-93; director-general National Criminal Intelligence Service 1993-

Date of birth: 18 December 1938 *Education/professional qualifications:* City School, Lincoln; National Defence College, Latimer; police staff college *Honours, decorations:* CBE 1994, QPM 1985 *Marital status:* married Ann Elizabeth 1960; 2 sons, 1 daughter *Clubs:* Cormorant *Recreations:* golf, gardening, reading

Albert H Pacey Esq CBE QPM, Director-General, National Criminal Intelligence Service, PO Box 8000, Spring Gardens, Tinworth Street, London SE11 5EN *Telephone:* 0171-238 8204 *Fax:* 0171-238 8208

PACKER, RICHARD JOHN Permanent Secretary, Ministry of Agriculture, Fisheries and Food Grade: 1

Career: Ministry of Agriculture, Fisheries and Food (MAFF) 1967-73: assistant principal 1967-71, principal 1971-73; first secretary UK permanent representation to EC, Brussels 1973-76; MAFF 1976-: principal private secretary to minister 1976-78, assistant secretary fisheries, EC divisions 1979-85, under secretary food, regions 1985-89, deputy secretary agricultural commodities, trade and production 1989-93, permanent secretary 1993-

Date of birth: 18 August 1944 *Education/professional qualifications:* City of London School; Manchester University, chemistry (BSc 1965) and organic chemistry (MSc 1966) *Marital status:* married Lucy Jeanne Neville-Rolfe; 6 sons (2 from previous marriage), 1 daughter (from previous marriage) *Recreations:* sports spectator, theatre, books

Richard J Packer Esq, Permanent Secretary, Ministry of Agriculture, Fisheries and Food, Whitehall Place, London SW1A 2HH *Telephone:* 0171-270 8701 *Fax:* 0171-270 8845

PAIN, (GILLIAN) JILL MARGARET Chief Reporter, Inquiry Reporters' Unit, Scottish Office Grade: 3

Career: teacher 1957-58; photogrammetrist Hunting Aerosurveys Ltd 1957-60; assistant map research officer War Office directorate of military survey 1960-62; planning assistant – chief assistant planning adviser Essex County Council 1962-73; planning inspectorate Department of Environment 1973-93: senior housing and planning inspector (HPI) 1973-77, principal HPI 1977-87, assistant chief PI 1987-93; chief reporter Inquiry Reporters' Unit (planning appeals) Scottish Office 1993-

Date of birth: 29 May 1936 *Education/professional qualifications:* Felixstowe College; St Andrew's University, geography/political economy (MA 1957); University College, London, town and country planning (Dip Tp 1965); Royal Town Planning Institute (MRTPI 1965) *Marital status:* single *Publications:* Planning and the Shopkeeper (Barrie and Rockcliffe 1967)

Clubs: Blackwater Sailing, Ski Club of Great Britain *Recreations:* sailing, skiing, ice dance, classical music, hillwalking

Miss Gillian M Pain, Chief Reporter, Inquiry Reporters' Unit, Scottish Office, 2 Greenside Lane, Edinburgh EH1 3AG *Telephone:* 0131-244 5644 *Fax:* 0131-244 5680

PARKER, (JAMES) GEOFFREY Chairman, Teacher Training Agency Grade: 2

Career: army national service 1954-56; teacher, head of department, headmaster various secondary state and private schools 1957-85; high [head] master Manchester Grammar School 1985-94; chairman Teacher Training Agency 1994-

Date of birth: 27 March 1933 *Education/professional qualifications:* Alderman Newton's School, Leicester; Christ's College, Cambridge, history (BA 1954); Wadham College, Oxford, teacher training (PGCE 1957) *Marital status:* married Ruth Major 1956; 2 daughters *Clubs:* East India *Recreations:* sailing, gardening, bees

J Geoffrey Parker Esq, Chairman, Teacher Training Agency, Portland House, Stag Place, London SW1E 5TT *Telephone:* 0171-925 3710

PARKER, ROBERT STEWART Parliamentary Counsel, Office of the Parliamentary Counsel Grade: 2

Career: classics teacher 1971-74; private practice barrister 1975-80; Parliamentary Counsel's Office (drafting government bills) 1980-: assistant parliamentary counsel (PC) 1980-84, senior assistant PC 1984-87: seconded to Law Commission 1985-87, deputy PC 1987-92, PC 1992-

Date of birth: 13 January 1949 *Education/professional qualifications:* Brentwood School, Essex; Trinity College, Oxford, classics (BA 1971, MA); Middle Temple (barrister 1975); British Institute of Management (MBIM 1984); MIMgt 1992 *Honours, decorations:* freeman City of London 1984 *Marital status:* single *Publications:* co-author Cases and Statutes on General Principles of Law (Sweet and Maxwell 1980) *Clubs:* Athenaeum, City Livery, Langbourn Ward *Recreations:* cricket, bridge, books, music, the livery

Robert S Parker Esq, Parliamentary Counsel, Office of the Parliamentary Counsel, 36 Whitehall, London SW1A 2AY *Telephone:* 0171-210 6611 *Fax:* 0171-210 6632

PARTRIDGE, Sir MICHAEL JOHN ANTHONY Permanent Secretary, Department of Social Security *(until August 1995)* Grade: 1

Career: assistant principal Ministry of Pensions and National Insurance (MPNI) 1960-64: private secretary to permanent secretary 1962-64; principal, pensions policy MPNI/Ministry of Social Security/Department of [Health and] Social Security (D[H]SS) 1964-71; D[H]SS 1971-83: assistant secretary NI contributions 1971-75, regional organisation 1975-76; under secretary supplementary benefit commission 1976-79, director social security regional organsiation 1979-81; deputy secretary, administration and principal establishment officer 1981-82, social security policy 1982-83; deputy under secretary police department Home Office 1983-87; D[H]SS 1987-: second permanent secretary (health policy and NHS) 1987-88, permanent secretary 1988- *Current non-Whitehall posts:* senior treasurer Methodist church 1980-; Liveryman Merchant Taylors; COmpany 1987-; trustee Harefield Hospital Trust 1991-; member of the court University of York 1991-, and of board of governors Middlesex University 1993-

Date of birth: 29 September 1935 *Education/professional qualifications:* Merchant Taylors' School, London; St John's College, Oxford, greats (BA 1960, MA) *Honours, decorations:* CB 1983, KCB 1990 *Marital status:* married Joan Elizabeth Hughes 1968; 2 sons, 1 daughter *Clubs:* United Oxford and Cambridge University *Recreations:* DIY, reading, skiing, sailing

Sir Michael Partridge KCB, Permanent Secretary, Department of Social Security, Richmond House, 79 Whitehall, London SW1A 2NS *Telephone:* 0171-210 5543 *Fax:* 0171-210 5838

PATON, ALASDAIR CHALMERS Director and Chief Engineer, Scottish Office Environment Department Grade: 3

Career: assistant engineer Clyde Port Authority 1967-71, Department of Agriculture and Fisheries for Scotland 1971-72; senior engineer Scottish Development Department (SDD) 1972-77; engineer Hong Kong Public Works Department 1977-80; SDD/Scottish Office Environment Department 1980-: senior engineer 1980-84, principal engineer 1984-87, deputy chief engineer 1987-91, chief engineer; under secretary civil engineering and water services; later director and chief engineer engineering, water and waste directorate 1991- *Current non-Whitehall posts:* council member Foundation for Water Research 1991-

Date of birth: 28 November 1944 *Education/professional qualifications:* John Neilson Institution, Paisley; Glasgow University, civil engineering (BScEng 1966) and management (DipMS); MIWEM 1984; FICE 1989; FIWEM 1991 *Marital status:* married Zona Gill 1969; 1 daughter, 1 son *Recreations:* rotary, golf, sailing

Alasdair C Paton Esq, Director and Chief Engineer, Scottish Office Environment Department, 27 Perth Street, Edinburgh EH3 5RB
Telephone: 0131-244 3035 *Fax:* 0131-244 6902

PATON, WILLIAM Operations Director, National Engineering Laboratory (Executive Agency) Grade: 4

Career: oil and steel industry 1963-64; National Engineering Laboratory (NEL) 1964-78; principal offshore supplies office Department of Energy 1978-80; NEL 1980-: division manager 1980-85, business controller 1985-88, deputy director 1988-90, operations director 1990-

Date of birth: 29 November 1941 *Education/professional qualifications:* Douglas Ewart School, Newton Stewart, Wigtown, Scotland; Glasgow University, physics (BSc 1963) *Marital status:* married Elizabeth Anne Marr 1964; 2 sons *Recreations:* golf

William Paton Esq, Operations Director, National Engineering Laboratory, East Kilbride, Glasgow G75 0QU *Telephone:* 013552 20222
Fax: 013552 72132

PATTEN, GARRY JOHN Deputy Chief Crown Prosecutor, London, Crown Prosecution Service Grade: 3

Career: private practice solicitor 1979-81; Director of Public Prosecutions department 1981-85; Crown Prosecution Service 1985-: deputy chief crown prosecutor London 1993-

Date of birth: 22 February 1950 *Education/professional qualifications:* BA, solicitor *Marital status:* married; 2 sons, 1 daughter *Recreations:* tennis

G J Patten Esq, Deputy Chief Crown Prosecutor, London, Crown Prosecution Service, Portland House, London SW1E 5BH
Telephone: 0171-915 5700 *Fax:* 0171-915 5872

PAWLEY, ROBERT JOHN Deputy Chief Executive, Valuation Office Agency (Executive Agency) Grade: 3

Career: Inland Revenue Valuation Office/Valuation Office Agency 1972-: superintending valuer Chief Valuer's Office, London 1981-84, Cambridge 1984-87; assistant chief valuer 1987-88; deputy chief executive (technical) 1989-

Date of birth: 10 September 1939 *Education/professional qualifications:* Plymouth College; Exeter University (BA); FRICS *Marital status:* married Simone Elizabeth Tayar 1965; 2 sons

Robert J Pawley Esq, Deputy Chief Executive, Valuation Office Agency, New Court, Carey Street, London WC2A 2JE *Telephone:* 0171-324 1183 *Fax:* 0171-324 1073

PAWSON, ANTHONY JOHN DALBY Assistant Under Secretary, Fleet Support, Ministry of Defence Grade: 3

Career: Ministry of Defence (MoD) 1967-: private secretary (PS) to chief of air staff 1978-80; first secretary nuclear affairs Foreign and Commonwealth Office delegation to NATO 1981-83; assistant secretary MoD 1983-90; non-executive director Cleanaway Ltd industrial waste management company 1988-90; seconded as principal PS to secretary of state for Northern Ireland 1990-92; student Royal College of Defence Studies 1992; assistant under secretary fleet support (policy and financial responsibility for Royal Navy support) MoD 1993-

Date of birth: 14 October 1946 *Education/professional qualifications:* Kent College, Canterbury; City University, London, computer science (BSc 1973) *Recreations:* cricket, rugby

Anthony J D Pawson Esq, Assistant Under Secretary, Ministry of Defence, Quay House, Bath, Avon BA1 5AB *Telephone:* 01225 472041 *Fax:* 01225 472199

PAYNTER, ALAN GUY HADLEY Director, Information Systems, HM Customs and Excise Grade: 4

Career: Ministry of [Public Building and] Works 1960-72: assistant private secretary to minister 1968-71; HM Customs and Excise 1972-: principal general customs directorate 1978-81, seconded to Overseas Containers Ltd 1981-83; senior principal, assistant secretary computer services division 1983-89; head of information technology divisions 1989-92, of information systems 1993-94; director of information systems 1994-

Date of birth: 5 November 1941 *Education/professional qualifications:* East Ham Grammar School; Central London Polytechnic, management studies (diploma 1972) *Marital status:* married Mary Houghton 1964; 2 daughters *Recreations:* theatre, books, running, swimming, golf

Alan G H Paynter Esq, Director Information Systems, HM Customs and Excise, Alexander House, Victoria Avenue, Southend, Essex SS99 1AA *Telephone:* 01702 367038 *Fax:* 01702 366089

PEACE, LIZ Company Secretary, Defence Research and Evaluation Agency (Executive Agency)

Ms Liz Peace, Company Secretary, Defence Research and Evaluation Agency, Farnborough, Hampshire GU14 6TD *Telephone:* 01252 394500

PEACH, Sir LEONARD HARRY Chairman, Police Complaints Authority

Career: IBM 1962-92: group director of personnel Europe, Africa and Middle East 1972-75; director of personnel and corporate affairs 1975-85, 1989-92; seconded to Department of Health and Social Security as chief executive NHS management board 1985-89; chairman Police Complaints Authority 1992- *Current non-Whitehall posts:* chairman Policy Studies Institute 1991-, IPM Personnel Services Ltd 1991-; non-executive director Coutts Consultants plc 1993-, Personal Investment Authority 1993-; chairman Westminster University 1993-

Date of birth: 17 December 1932 *Education/professional qualifications:* Queen Mary's Grammar School, Walsall, Staffordshire; Pembroke College, Oxford, history (BA 1956, MA); London School of Economics, personnel management (diploma 1958); CIPM 1985; CIMgt 1987 *Honours, decorations:* FRSA 1978; Kt 1989 *Marital status:* married Doreen Lilian Barker 1958; 2 sons *Recreations:* opera, theatre, cricket, gardening

Sir Leonard Peach Kt, Chairman, Police Complaints Authority, 10 Great George Street, London SW1P 3AE *Telephone:* 0171-273 6400 *Fax:* 0171-273 6401

PEARCE, Sir (DANIEL NORTON) IDRIS Deputy Chairman, English Partnerships

Career: Richard Ellis chartered surveyors 1959-92: partner 1959-61, shareholding partner 1961-92, consultant 1992-; chairman English Estates 1989-94; special adviser to John MacGregor, Secretary of State for Transport on BR privatisation 1992-94; deputy chairman English Partnerships 1994- *Current non-Whitehall posts:* non-executive director National Mortgage Bank 1992-, Higgs and Hill 1992-, Dusco (UK) 1993-; chairman Higher Education Council for Wales 1992-

Date of birth: 28 November 1933 *Education/professional qualifications:* West Buckland School, Barnstaple; College of Estate Management (FRICS) *Honours, decorations:* TD 1973, CBE 1984, DL 1986, Kt 1990 *Marital status:* married Ursula Helene Langley 1963; 2 daughters *Publications:* The Profession of the Land: A Call to Talent (College of Estate Management 1993) *Clubs:* Brooks's *Recreations:* opera, ballet, reading

Sir Idris Pearce DL CBE, Deputy Chairman, English Partnerships, 3 The Parks, Lodge Lane, Newton-le-Willows, Merseyside WA12 0JQ *Telephone:* 0194-229 6900 *Fax:* 0194-229 6927

PEARL, His Honour Judge DAVID STEPHEN Chief Adjudicator, Immigration Appeals Authority

Career: fellow and director of law studies Fitzwilliam College, Cambridge 1969-89; professor and dean, school of law East Anglia University 1989-94; chief adjudicator Immigration Appeals Authority 1994-

Date of birth: 11 August 1944 *Education/professional qualifications:* Westminster City School; Birmingham University, law (LLB 1965); Cambridge University: Queen's College (LLM 1967) and Fitzwilliam College (PhD 1970) *Marital status:* married Gillian Loraine 1985; 3 sons, 1 stepdaughter, 1 stepson *Publications:* co-author: A Textbook on Muslim Family Law (Croom Helm 1987); Family Law and Immigrant Communities (Jordans 1986)

His Honour Judge Pearl, Chief Adjudicator, Immigration Appeals Authority, Thanet House, 231 Strand, London WC2R 1DA *Telephone:* 0171-353 8060 *Fax:* 0171-353 3960

PEARSON, TONY (ANTHONY) Director of Operatons, North, HM Prison Service Grade: 3

Date of birth: 2 November 1939

A J Pearson Esq, Director of Operations, North, HM Prison Service, Cleland House, Page Street, London SW1P 4LN *Telephone:* 0171-217 6700

PEARSON, D J Principal Assistant Solicitor, Ministry of Agriculture, Fisheries and Food Grade: 3

D J Pearson Esq, Principal Assistant Solicitor, Ministry of Agriculture, Fisheries and Food, 55 Whitehall, London SW1A 2EY *Telephone:* 0171-270 3000

PECKHAM, Professor MICHAEL JOHN Director, Research and Development, Department of Health

Career: civilian medical consultant Royal Navy 1974-86; professor Institute of Cancer Research (ICR) and Royal Marsden Hospital radiotherapy department 1974-86; dean ICR 1984-86; director British Postgraduate Medical Research 1986-90; director of research and development Department of Health 1991- *Current non-Whitehall posts:* founder Bob Champion Cancer Trust 1986-; patron Jenny Wood Environmental Trust 1990-; chairman ECCO5 Cancer Trust 1991-

Date of birth: 2 August 1935 *Education/professional qualifications:* William Jones West Monmouthshire School; St Catharine's College, Cambridge, natural sciences (BA 1956); University College London Medical School (MB 1959); MD 1969; FRCR 1971; FRCPGlas 1979; FRCP 1986; FRCPath 1991; FRSA 1993; foreign associate member National Academy of Sciences, Institute of Medicine, Washington DC *Marital status:* married Catherine Stevenson King 1958; 3 sons *Publications:* The Management of Testicular Tumours (Edward Arnold 1981); The Biological Basis of Radiotherapy (Elsevier 1983); Conservative Management of Early Breast Cancer (Edward Arnold 1985); joint editor Oxford Textbook of Oncology (1995) *Clubs:* Reform *Recreations:* painting

Professor Michael J Peckham, Director Research and Development, Department of Health, Richmond House, 79 Whitehall, London SW1A 2NS *Telephone:* 0171-210 5556 *Fax:* 0171-210 5868

PEEL, DAVID ALEXANDER ROBERT Director of Administration Resources, Department of the Environment Grade: 3

Career: Ministry/Department of Transport (DTp) 1964-67; Department of Environment (DoE) 1968-71; first secretary UK permanent representation to EC, Brussels 1972-74; private secretary to Minister of Transport 1975; assistant secretary DTp, DoE and Property Services Agency 1976-89; under secretary, director of administration resources DoE 1990- *Current non-Whitehall posts:* member Business Advisory Group, Middlesex University Business School

Date of birth: 12 November 1940 *Education/professional qualifications:* St

Edmund's College, Ware, Hertfordshire; University College, Oxford, classics (BA 1963) *Marital status:* married Patricia Essery 1971; 2 sons *Recreations:* vegetable gardening, European architectural history, opera, classical music, ballet

David A R Peel Esq, Under Secretary, Department of the Environment, 2 Marsham Street, London SW1P 3EB *Telephone:* 0171-276 3544 *Fax:* 0171-276 4124

PEIRSON, MARGARET ELLEN Under Secretary, Occupational and Personal Pensions, Department of Social Security Grade: 3

Career: HM Treasury 1965-: seconded to Bank of England 1982-84; under secretary (US) 1986-: seconded to Department of Social Security 1990-: US B division 1990-94, C division (occupational and personal pensions) 1994-

Date of birth: 28 November 1942 *Education/professional qualifications:* North London Collegiate School; Somerville College, Oxford, mathematics (BA 1964); Yale University, USA, mathematics *Marital status:* single *Recreations:* choral singing, theatre

Miss Margaret E Peirson, Under Secretary, Department of Social Security, Adelphi, 1-11 John Adam Street, London WC2N 6HT *Telephone:* 0171-962 8451 *Fax:* 0171-962 8766

PENTREATH, Dr RICHARD JOHN Member, Environment Agency Advisory Committee Secretariat Grade: 3

Career: Ministry of Agriculture, Fisheries and Food 1969-89: fisheries radiobiological laboratory 1969-85, head of radioecology 1985-88, of aquatic environment protection division 1988-89; chief scientist National Rivers Authority 1989-; seconded as consultant to Department of the Environment/Environment Agency advisory committee secretariat 1994- *Current non-Whitehall posts:* council member Natural Environment Research Council 1992-

Date of birth: 28 December 1943 *Education/professional qualifications:* Humphry Davy Grammar School, Penzance; Queen Mary College, London University, zoology (BSc 1965); Auckland University, New Zealand, zoology (PhD 1968); London University, zoology (DSc 1980), FIBiol, FSRP *Marital status:* married Elizabeth Amanda Leach 1965; 2 daughters *Publications:* Nuclear Power, Man and the Environment (Taylor and Francis 1980) *Recreations:* visual arts, Cornish history, tall ship sailing

Dr Richard J Pentreath, Environment Agency Advisory Committee Secretariat, Government Buildings, Department of the Environment, Burghill Road, Westbury-on-Trym, Bristol BS10 6NH *Telephone:* 01179 873270 *Fax:* 01179 873272

PERETZ, DAVID LINDSAY CORBETT Under Secretary, International Finance Directorate, HM Treasury Grade: 3

Career: Ministry of Technology 1965-69; Inter-Bank Research Organisation 1969-76; HM Treasury (HMT) 1976-: assistant secretary 1980-84; principal private secretary to Chancellor of Exchequer 1984-85; under secretary 1985-: home finance/monetary group 1985-90; UK executive director International Monetary Fund and World Bank and economic minister Washington DC 1990-94; international finance directorate 1994-

Date of birth: 29 May 1943 *Education/professional qualifications:* Leys School, Cambridge; Exeter College, Oxford, chemistry (BA 1965) *Marital status:*

married Jane Wildman 1966; 1 son, 1 daughter *Clubs:* Reform *Recreations:* walking, sailing, skiing, opera

David L Peretz Esq, Under Secretary, HM Treasury, Parliament Street, London SW1P 3AG *Telephone:* 0171-270 3000

PERKINS, ALICE ELIZABETH Deputy Director, Spending Directorate, HM Treasury Grade: 3

Career: Department of [Health and] Social Security (D[H]SS) 1971-: private secretary to minister of state for social security 1974-75; assistant to Supplementary Benefits Commission chairman 1975-77; responsible for local implementation of social security legislation in GB 1984-88; implementation of split of DHSS into DH and DSS, central resource management and planning DSS 1988-90; under secretary, director of personnel DSS 1990-93; HM Treasury 1993-: head of defence policy, manpower and materiel policy group 1993-95, deputy director spending directorate 1995- *Current non-Whitehall posts:* trustee Whitehall and Industry Group

Date of birth: 24 May 1949 *Education/professional qualifications:* North London Collegiate School; St Anne's College, Oxford, modern history (BA 1971) *Marital status:* married J W Straw 1978; 1 son, 1 daughter

Ms Alice E Perkins, Under Secretary, HM Treasury, Parliament Street, London SW1P 3AG *Telephone:* 0171-270 4510 *Fax:* 0171-270 5587

PERRETT, ANTHONY JAMES Registrar, Registry of Friendly Societies Grade: 4

Career: industry 1963-73; legal assistant (LA) Department of Trade and Industry 1973-74, Department of Energy 1974-79; senior LA Treasury Solicitor's Department 1979-84, Ministry of Defence 1984-85; assistant director, legal Office of Fair Trading 1985-89; registrar and legal adviser Registry of Friendly Societies; legal adviser to Building Societies Commission, Friendly Societies Commission, Building Societies Investment Protection Board 1989-

Date of birth: 14 October 1939 *Education/professional qualifications:* Westminster College, Buenos Aires, Argentina; Monkton Combe School, Somerset; MIEE, CEng 1971; Lincoln's Inn (barrister 1972); Open University, arts, astronomy, relativity (BA 1986) *Marital status:* married Francisca Crommelin 1980; 2 sons, 2 daughters *Recreations:* reading, trains, gardening, travel

Anthony J Perrett Esq, Registrar, Registry of Friendly Societies, 15 Great Marlborough Street, London W1V 2LL *Telephone:* 0171-494 6629 *Fax:* 0171-494 6587

PETT, Major-General RAYMOND AUSTIN Director, Infantry, Ministry of Defence

Major-General R A Pett MBE, Director, Infantry, Ministry of Defence, Warminster, Wiltshire BA1 5AA *Telephone:* 01985 214000

PFLEGER, MARTIN CHARLES Assistant Auditor General, National Audit Office Grade: 3

Career: National Audit Office (examination of accounts of government departments and some public bodies) 1967-: private secretary to comptroller and auditor general 1978-79; audit manager/deputy director audit Department of Environment 1979-86; director of finance and information systems 1986-90, of corporate policy and finance 1990-93; assistant auditor general, principal finance officer and principal establishment officer 1993-

Date of birth: 5 May 1948 *Education/professional qualifications:* Park School, Swindon; rule 6 CIPFA 1982 *Marital status:* separated; 2 sons, 1 daughter *Clubs:* Institute of Directors *Recreations:* golf, bridge

Martin C Pfleger Esq, Assistant Auditor General, National Audit Office, 157-97 Buckingham Palace Road, London SW1W 9SP
Telephone: 0171-798 7314 *Fax:* 0171-931 8303

PHILLIPS, DIANE SUSAN Director, Housing Resources and Management, Department of the Environment Grade: 3

Career: National Economic Development Office 1964-72; Department of Environment 1972-: deputy director local government finance 1988-90; director government estates division 1990-91; principal finance officer and director transport and security services division 1991-94, director housing resources and management 1994-

Date of birth: 29 August 1942 *Education/professional qualifications:* Headlands Grammar School, Swindon; University College, Swansea, economics (BA 1964) *Marital status:* married John 1967; 2 daughters

Mrs Diane S Phillips, Director, Housing Resources and Management, Department of the Environment, 2 Marsham Street, London SW1P 3EB *Telephone:* 0171-276 3473

PHILLIPS, (GERALD) HAYDEN Permanent Secretary, Department of National Heritage Grade: 1A

Career: Home Office (HO) 1967-77: assistant principal, economic adviser, principal 1967-74, assistant secretary and principal private secretary to Home Secretary 1974-76; deputy chef de cabinet to EC Commission president Roy Jenkins 1977-79; HO 1979-86: assistant secretary 1979-81, assistant under secretary police department 1981-83, head of immigration and nationality department 1983-86; deputy secretary Cabinet Office 1986-88; HM Treasury 1988-92: deputy secretary public services 1988-90, civil service management and pay 1990-92; permanent secretary Department of National Heritage 1992- *Current non-Whitehall posts:* member council King's College, London; board of Henley Management Centre

Date of birth: 9 February 1943 *Education/professional qualifications:* Cambridgeshire High School; Clare College, Cambridge, history (BA 1965, MA); Yale University, USA, political science and economics (MA 1967) *Honours, decorations:* CB 1989 *Marital status:* married Hon Laura Grenfell 1980; 2 sons, 3 daughters (1s, 1d by previous marriage) *Clubs:* Brooks's *Recreations:* fishing, arts, sports, India

G Hayden Phillips Esq CB, Permanent Secretary, Department of National Heritage, 2-4 Cockspur Street, London SW1Y 5DH
Telephone: 0171-211 6000 *Fax:* 0171-211 6259

PHILLIPS, JONATHAN Under Secretary, Executive Agencies, Department of Transport Grade: 3

Career: Department of Trade [and Industry] 1977-93: seconded to CBI economics directorate 1982-83, as secretary to committee of inquiry into regulatory arrangements at Lloyd's 1986-87; assistant secretary 1987-93; under secretary, head of executive agencies' directorate Department of Transport 1993- *Current non-Whitehall posts:* non-executive director Forward Trust Group Ltd

Date of birth: 21 May 1952 *Education/professional qualifications:* Queen Mary's Grammar School, Walsall; St John's College, Cambridge, history (BA 1973, PhD 1978); London University Institute of Education (PGCE 1974) *Marital status:* married Amanda Rosemary Broomhead 1974; 2 sons *Recreations:* music, walking

Jonathan Phillips Esq, Under Secretary, Department of Transport, 2 Marsham Street, London SW1P 3EB *Telephone:* 0171-276 4750 *Fax:* 0171-276 0537

PICKFORD, MICHAEL A Directing Actuary, Supervision of Insurance Companies and Friendly Societies Division, Government Actuary's Department Grade: 3

Career: Government Actuary's Department 1957-: directing actuary, supervision of insurance companies and friendly societies 1989-

Date of birth: 22 August 1937 *Education/professional qualifications:* City of Oxford School; FIA *Honours, decorations:* CB 1994 *Marital status:* single *Clubs:* Actuaries *Recreations:* sport, travel, music

M A Pickford Esq CB, Directing Actuary, Government Actuary's Department, 22 Kingsway, London WC2B 6LE *Telephone:* 0171-242 6828 *Fax:* 0171-831 6653

PICKUP, DAVID FRANCIS WILLIAM Legal Adviser, Ministry of Defence/Treasury Solicitor's Department Grade: 3

Career: barrister 1976-; Treasury Solicitor's Department 1978-: legal assistant litigation division 1978-81; senior legal assistant Department of Energy advisory division 1981-87; litigation division 1987-88; principal establishment, finance and security officer 1988-90; litigation division 1990-91; legal adviser Ministry of Defence advisory division 1991-

Date of birth: 28 May 1953 *Education/professional qualifications:* Poole Grammar School; Central London Polytechnic, law (LLB 1975), Inns of Court School of Law (barrister 1976) *Marital status:* married Anne Elizabeth Round 1975 *Clubs:* Pyrford Cricket *Recreations:* cricket, skiing, music, food and wine, travel

David F W Pickup Esq, Legal Adviser, Ministry of Defence, Metropole Building, Northumberland Avenue, London WC2N 5BL *Telephone:* 0171-218 0723 *Fax:* 0171-218 0844

PILKINGTON, The Reverend Canon PETER Chairman, Broadcasting Complaints Commission

Career: curate, Bakewell, Derbyshire 1959-62; schoolmaster Eton College 1962-75; headmaster King's School, Canterbury 1975-86; high master, St Paul's School, London 1986-92; member Parole Board 1990-; chairman Broadcasting Complaints Commission 1992-

Date of birth: 5 September 1933 *Education/professional qualifications:* Dame Allan's Boys' School, Newcastle-upon-Tyne; Jesus College, Cambridge, history (BA 1955, MA) *Marital status:* married Helen Wilson 1966; 2 daughters *Clubs:* Beefsteak, Garrick

The Reverend Canon Peter Pilkington, Chairman, Broadcasting Complaints Commission, Grosvenor Gardens House, 35 Grosvenor Gardens, London SW1W 0BS *Telephone:* 0171-630 1966 *Fax:* 0171-828 7316

PILL, Sir MALCOLM THOMAS (The Hon Mr Justice Pill) Deputy Chairman, Boundary Commission for Wales

Career: army national service 1956-58; third secretary Foreign Office 1963-64; private practice barrister 1964-87, recorder 1976-87, judge Queen's Bench Division 1988-; deputy chairman Boundary Commission for Wales (review of parliamentary and European parliament constituencies) 1992-; chairman European Parliamentary Constituency Committee for Wales 1993- *Current non-Whitehall posts:* high court judge Queen's Bench Division 1988-; judicial member Employment Appeal Tribunal 1991-

Date of birth: 11 March 1938 *Education/professional qualifications:* Whitchurch Grammar School; Trinity College, Cambridge, law (MA, LLM); Hague Academy of International Law, Netherlands (diploma 1962); Gray's Inn (barrister 1962) *Honours, decorations:* QC 1978, Kt 1988 *Marital status:* married Roisin Mary Riordan 1966; 2 sons, 1 daughter *Clubs:* Army and Navy; Cardiff and County

Sir Malcolm Pill, Deputy Chairman, Boundary Commission for Wales, St Catherine's House, 10 Kingsway, London WC2B 6JP
Telephone: 0171-396 2105 *Fax:* 0171-396 2253

PILLING, JOSEPH GRANT Deputy Secretary, Departmental Resources and Services, Department of Health Grade: 2

Career: Home Office (HO) 1966-71; Northern Ireland Office (NIO) 1972; HO 1974-78; NIO 1978-79; HO 1979-84; Department of Health [and Social Security] (DH[SS]) 1984-87; director of personnel and finance HM Prison Service HO 1987-90; deputy under secretary NIO 1990-91; director-general HM Prison Service HO 1991-93; deputy secretary departmental resources and services DH 1993-

Date of birth: 8 July 1945 *Education/professional qualifications:* King's College, London; Harvard, USA

Joseph G Pilling Esq, Deputy Secretary, Department of Health, Richmond House, Whitehall, London SW1A 2NS *Telephone:* 0171-210 3000

PITTMAN, NIGEL Director of Resources and Services, Department of National Heritage Grade: 4

Career: Scottish Office 1971-85: various posts in Education, Agriculture and Housing departments; head of arts branch/secretary to Museums Advisory Board 1980-85; museum administrator and secretary to trustees National Museums of Scotland 1985-89; head of museums and galleries division, principal finance officer Office of Arts and Libraries 1989-92; director of resources and services Department of National Heritage 1992-

Date of birth: 3 September 1948 *Education/professional qualifications:* Epsom College; Royal Academy of Dramatic Art (diploma 1969) *Marital status:* married Dr Riitta Heino 1971; 1 daughter *Clubs:* National Liberal *Recreations:* walking, mountaineering, the arts, countryside, travel, family, friends

Nigel Pittman Esq, Director of Resources and Services, Department of National Heritage, 2-4 Cockspur Street, London SW1Y 5DH
Telephone: 0171-211 6189 *Fax:* 0171-211 6230

PLASTOW, Sir DAVID ARNOLD STUART Chairman, Medical Research Council

Career: managing director (MD) Rolls Royce Motors 1972-80; Vickers 1980-92: MD and chief executive (CE) 1980-87, chairman and CE 1987-92; chairman Medical Research Council 1990- *Current non-Whitehall posts:* chairman Inchcape 1992-

Date of birth: 9 May 1932 *Education/professional qualifications:* Culford School, Bury St Edmunds *Honours, decorations:* Kt 1986 *Marital status:* married Barbara Ann May 1954; 1 daughter, 1 son *Clubs:* Buck's *Recreations:* golf, music

Sir David Plastow, Chairman, Medical Research Council, 20 Park Crescent, London W1N 4AL *Telephone:* 0171-636 5422 *Fax:* 0171-436 6179

PLATT, (TERENCE) TERRY CHARLES Deputy Under Secretary, Principal Establishment Officer; Fire and Emergency Planning, Home Office Grade: 2

Career: Home Office (HO) 1957-69; Cabinet Office 1970-72, Northern Ireland Office 1972-73, 1981-82; HO 1982-: assistant under secretary Prison Department regimes and services director 1982-86, Immigration and Nationality Department operations and resources 1986-92; deputy under secretary, principal establishment officer 1992-, fire and emergency planning 1992-

Date of birth: 22 September 1936 *Education/professional qualifications:* St Olave's and St Saviour's Grammar School, London *Marital status:* married Margaret Anne Cotmore 1959; 2 sons *Recreations:* rose growing, photography, butterflies

Terry C Platt Esq, Deputy Under Secretary, Home Office, Queen Anne's Gate, London SW1H 9AT *Telephone:* 0171-273 2143 *Fax:* 0171-273 3420

PLOWMAN, JOHN PATRICK Director, Wildlife and Countryside, Department of the Environment Grade: 3

Career: principal Ministry of Defence 1967-82: seconded to Civil Service Selection Board 1975, to Cabinet Office 1976-78; assistant secretary 1982-93: Department of Environment (DoE) 1982-86: Property Services Agency (supplies) board 1982-84; counsellor UK permanent representation to EC, Brussels 1987-90; DoE 1990-: under secretary, north west regional director DoE and Department of Transport (DTp) 1993-94, director DoE/DTp government office for the north west 1994-; director wildlife and countryside 1994-

Date of birth: 20 March 1944 *Education/professional qualifications:* Lansdowne School; St Edward's School, Oxford; Grenoble University, France 1964; University College, Durham (BA 1967); FBIM 1984 *Marital status:* married Daphne Margaret Brock Kennett 1973; 1 daughter, 2 sons *Clubs:* Royal Over-Seas League *Recreations:* fishing, music, cricket, tennis

John Plowman Esq, Under Secretary, Department of the Environment, 2 Marsham Street, London SW1 *Telephone:* 0171-276 3682 *Fax:* 0171-276 3349

PODGER, G J F Under Secretary, Health Promotion Division, Department of Health Grade: 3

Career: Department of Health: head of international relations -1993; under secretary health promotion division 1993-

G J F Podger Esq, Under Secretary, Department of Health, Wellington House, 133-135 Waterloo Road, London SE1 8UG *Telephone:* 0171-972 2000 *Fax:* 0171-972 4725

POOLEY, Dr DEREK Chief Executive, Government Division, UK Atomic Energy Authority

Career: UK Atomic Energy Authority (UKAEA) Harwell 1963-83: director of energy research 1981-83; chief scientist Department of Energy 1983-86; UKAEA 1986-: deputy director, director Winfrith technology centre 1986-90; director thermal reactor services, then managing director nuclear business group AEA Technology (commercial division) 1990-94; chief executive government division (all decommissioning and waste management activities) 1994- *Current non-Whitehall posts:* chairman Euratom Scientific and Technical Committee 1994-

Date of birth: 28 October 1937 *Education/professional qualifications:* Sir James Smith's Grammar School, Camelford, Cornwall; Birmingham University, chemistry (BSc 1958), physics (PhD 1961); FIP 1979 *Honours, decorations:* honorary fellow Institute of Nuclear Engineers 1993; CBE 1995 *Marital status:* married Jennifer Mary Davey 1961; 2 sons, 1 daughter *Publications:* Real Solids and Radiation (Wykeham 1975); Shaping Tomorrow (Methodist Church 1981); Energy Technologies for the UK: Energy Paper 54 (HMSO 1987) *Recreations:* walking, gardening, photography, DIY

Dr Derek Pooley CBE, Chief Executive, Government Division, UK Atomic Energy Authority, Harwell, Didcot, Oxfordshire OX11 0RA
Telephone: 01235 433818 *Fax:* 01235 432232

POULTER, BRIAN HENRY Secretary, Northern Ireland Audit Office Grade: 3

Career: commercial chartered accountancy 1959-62; Department of Health and Social Services Northern Ireland (NI) 1962-71; Department of Commerce 1971-75; Exchequer and Audit Department/NI Audit Office 1975-: chief auditor 1975-81, deputy director 1981-82, director 1982-89, secretary 1989-

Date of birth: 1 September 1941 *Education/professional qualifications:* Regent House Grammar School, Newtownards, County Down *Marital status:* married (Margaret) Ann Dodds 1968; twin daughters, 1 son *Recreations:* reading, walking, cricket

Brian H Poulter Esq, Secretary, Northern Ireland Audit Office, 106 University Street, Belfast BT7 1EU
Telephone: 01232 251129 *Fax:* 01232 251051

POWNALL, MICHAEL GRAHAM Principal Clerk of Committees and of the Overseas Office, House of Lords Grade: 3

Career: House of Lords (HoL) Parliament Office 1971-: seconded as private secretary to leader of HoL and government chief whip 1980-83; establishment officer 1983-88; principal clerk (PC) and examiner of private bills 1988-90; PC of committees and of overseas office (also clerk of HoL EC committee) 1991-

Date of birth: 11 October 1949 *Education/professional qualifications:* Repton School; Exeter University, history (BA 1971) *Marital status:* married Deborah Ann McQueen 1974; 2 daughters *Clubs:* Riverside *Recreations:* birdwatching, music, squash

Michael G Pownall Esq, Principal Clerk of Committees, Committee Office, House of Lords, London SW1A 0PW *Telephone:* 0171-219 3218
Fax: 0171-219 6715

PRATT, TIMOTHY JEAN GEOFFREY Speaker's Counsel, House of Commons Grade: 2

Career: barrister 1959-; Treasury Solicitor's Department (TSD) 1961-72: legal assistant (LA) 1961-67, senior LA 1967-72; senior LA Law Officers' Department 1972-74; assistant solicitor Department of Trade and Industry 1974-79; legal adviser Office of Fair Trading 1979-85, Cabinet Office European Secretariat 1985-90; deputy treasury solicitor TSD 1990-93; speaker's counsel (European legislation etc) House of Commons 1993-

Date of birth: 25 November 1934 *Education/professional qualifications:* Brighton College; Trinity Hall, Cambridge, law (BA 1958, MA), Middle Temple (barrister 1959) *Honours, decorations:* CB *Marital status:* married Pamela Ann Blake 1963; 2 daughters *Clubs:* United Oxford and Cambridge University

Timothy J G Pratt Esq CB, Speaker's Counsel, House of Commons, London SW1A 0AA
Telephone: 0171-219 5561 *Fax:* 0171-219 2509

PRESTON, JEFFREY WILLIAM Deputy Director-General, Office of Fair Trading Grade: 2 *(see Addenda)*

Career: assistant principal Ministry of Aviation 1963-66; Board of Trade 1966-70: private secretary to permanent secretary 1966-67, principal 1967-70; principal HM Treasury 1970-73; Department of Trade and Industry 1973-85: principal 1973-75, assistant secretary 1975-82, under secretary and Yorkshire and Humberside regional director 1982-85; deputy secretary industrial and economic affairs Welsh Office 1985-90; deputy director-general Office of Fair Trading (administration of fair trading legislation) 1990-

Date of birth: 28 January 1940 *Education/professional qualifications:* Liverpool Collegiate School; Hertford College, Oxford, literae humaniores (BA 1963, MA) *Honours, decorations:* CB 1989 *Marital status:* single *Clubs:* United Oxford and Cambridge University *Recreations:* opera, swimming, motoring

Jeffrey Preston Esq CB, Deputy Director-General, Office of Fair Trading, Field House, Bream's Building, London EC4A 1PR
Telephone: 0171-242 2858 *Fax:* 0171-269 8800

PRICE, DAVID BROOKHOUSE Director of Human Resources, Employment Service (Executive Agency) Grade: 4

Career: army national service 1958-60; Ministry of Labour/Department of Employment 1960-74; Manpower Services Commission 1974-87: deputy chief executive employment services division 1977-84, director of personnel and central services 1984-87; Employment Service 1987-: director of personnel and business services 1987-92, of human resources 1992-

Date of birth: 9 September 1936 *Education/professional qualifications:* Boys' Grammar School, Woking; St John's College, Cambridge, history (BA 1958, MA); FIPM *Marital status:* married Judith Anne Ebben 1967; 2 daughters, 1 son *Clubs:* Commonwealth Trust *Recreations:* walking, reading, history, piano

David B Price Esq, Director of Human Resources, Employment Service, Porterbrook House, 7 Pear Street, Sheffield S11 8JF
Telephone: 01142 597977 *Fax:* 01142 597969

PRICKETT (ROBERT), ANDREW Chief Crown Prosecutor, Wales, Crown Prosecution Service Grade: 4

Career: Crown Prosecution Service: chief prosecuting solicitor Wiltshire 1985-86; chief crown prosecutor Gloucestershire and Wiltshire 1986-93, Wales 1993-

Date of birth: 2 August 1948 *Education/professional qualifications:* Sheffield University, law (LLB 1968); solicitor 1971 *Marital status:* married Margaret

R A Prickett Esq, Chief Crown Prosecutor, Wales, Crown Prosecution Service, Tudor House, 16 Cathedral Road, Cardiff CF1 9LJ
Telephone: 01222 783000 *Fax:* 01222 783098

PRINCE, DAVID Chief Executive, District Audit, Audit Commission

Career: director of finance and administration Cambridgeshire County Council (CC) 1986-91; chief executive Leicestershire CC 1991-94; chief executive district audit Audit Commission (external audit local government and NHS) 1994-

Date of birth: 31 May 1948 *Education/professional qualifications:* Buxton College, Derbyshire; Exeter University, English (BA 1969); IPFA 1972 *Marital status:* married Davina Ann 1976 *Recreations:* music, theatre, gardening

David Prince Esq, Chief Executive, District Audit, Audit Commission, 1 Vincent Square, London SW1P 2PN *Telephone:* 0171-828 1212
Fax: 0171-630 5668

PRINGLE, Sir JOHN KENNETH (The Hon Mr Justice Pringle) Deputy Chairman, Northern Ireland Boundary Commission

Career: barrister 1953-: Queen's Counsel 1970-84; recorder of Belfast 1984-93; Northern Ireland High Court judge 1993-; deputy chairman Boundary Commission for Northern Ireland (review of parliamentary and European parliament constituencies) 1993-

Date of birth: 23 June 1929 *Education/professional qualifications:* Campbell College, Belfast; Queen's University, Belfast, experimental physics (BSc 1950), law (LLB 1953) *Marital status:* married Ruth Henry 1960; 1 daughter, 2 sons *Recreations:* gardening, outdoor pursuits

The Hon Mr Justice Pringle, Deputy Chairman, Boundary Commission for Northern Ireland, Frances House, 9-11 Brunswick Street, Belfast BT2 7GE *Telephone:* 01232 311210 *Fax:* 01232 321294

PROCTOR, BILL Clerk of Financial Committees and of Treasury and Civil Service Select Committee Grade: 4

Career: research associate in comparative government Manchester University 1970-72; House of Commons (HoC) 1968-: public bill office 1968-70; European office 1972-74; clerk: select committee on science and technology 1974-77, on procedure 1977-79; transport 1979-82, foreign affairs 1982-87; secretary HoC Commission, clerk of domestic committees 1987-92, of financial committees and of treasury and civil service select committee 1992-

Date of birth: 1 May 1945 *Education/professional qualifications:* Bristol Cathedral School; Keele University, politics and English (BA 1968) *Marital status:* married Susan Mottram 1969; 2 sons, 1 daughter *Publications:* co-author The European Parliament: Structure, Procedure and Practice (HMSO 1973) and The Parliamentary Assembly: Procedure and Practice (Council of Europe 1990) *Recreations:* reading, music, amateur acting

Bill Proctor, Committee Office, House of Commons, London SW1A 0AA *Telephone:* 0171-219 3285
Fax: 0171-219 2782

PRYOR, ARTHUR JOHN Head of Competition Policy Division, Department of Trade and Industry Grade: 3

Career: Spanish and Portuguese lecturer University College, Cardiff 1963-66; Board of Trade and Export Credits Guarantee Department 1966-69; Department of Trade and Industry (DTI) 1970-73; first secretary Washington DC embassy 1973-75; D[T]I 1975-: assistant secretary shipping policy 1977-80, air division 1980-83, international trade policy 1984-85; under secretary 1985-: West Midlands regional director 1985-88; director-general British National Space Centre 1988-93; head of competition policy 1993-

Date of birth: 7 March 1939 *Education/professional qualifications:* Harrow County Grammar School; Downing College, Cambridge, modern languages (BA 1960, MA), history (PhD 1964) *Marital status:* married Marilyn Kay Petley 1964; 1 son, 1 daughter *Recreations:* tennis, golf, book collecting

Arthur J Pryor Esq, Under Secretary, Department of Trade and Industry, Ashdown House, 123 Victoria Street, London SW1E 6RB *Telephone:* 0171-215 5000 *Fax:* 0171-215 6726

PULVERTAFT, Rear-Admiral DAVID MARTIN Secretary, Defence, Press and Broadcasting Advisory Committee

Career: naval submarine engineering posts 1963-82; Royal College of Defence Studies 1983; Ministry of Defence 1984-92: chairman naval nuclear technical safety panel 1984-85, director surface ship refitting 1986-87, director-general (DG) aircraft (navy) 1988-90; DG procurement and support organisation (navy) 1990-92; secretary Defence, Press and Broadcasting Advisory Committee (management defence advisory notices voluntary system for media coverage of national security matters) 1992-

Date of birth: 26 March 1938 *Education/professional qualifications:* Canford School, Dorset; Britannia Royal Naval College, Dartmouth; Royal Naval Engineering College (BScEng 1962); Royal College of Defence Studies 1983; MIMechE 1974; FIMechE 1989; FBIM (now FIMgt) 1990 *Honours, decorations:* CB 1990 *Marital status:* married Mary Rose Jeacock 1961; 1 son, 2 daughters *Clubs:* Naval *Recreations:* genealogy, naval history, printing and bookbinding

Rear-Admiral David M Pulvertaft CB, Secretary, Defence, Press and Broadcasting Advisory Committee, Ministry of Defence, Whitehall, London SW1A 2HB *Telephone:* 0171-218 2206 *Fax:* 0171-218 5857

PURSE, HUGH ROBERT LESLIE Legal Adviser and Principal Assistant Treasury Solicitor, Employment Department Group/Treasury Solicitor's Department Grade: 3

Career: legal assistant Department of Employment/Employment Department Group (EDG) 1969-78; legal adviser (LA) Prices Commission 1978-79; government legal service 1979-: LA and principal assistant treasury solicitor, EDG division Treasury Solicitor's Department 1988-

Date of birth: 22 October 1940 *Education/professional qualifications:* King's College, London (LLB 1963); Gray's Inn (barrister 1964)

Hugh R L Purse Esq, Legal Adviser and Principal Assistant Treasury Solicitor, Employment Department Group, Caxton House, Tothill Street, London SW1H 9NF *Telephone:* 0171-273 5849

Regulatory Organisations and Public Bodies

see page 1013

PYM, FRANCIS LESLIE (The Rt Hon The Lord Pym) Chairman, Political Honours Scrutiny Committee

Career: Conservative MP for Cambridgeshire 1961-83, for Cambridgeshire SE 1983-87: parliamentary secretary to Treasury and government chief whip 1970-73; Secretary of State (SoS) for Northern Ireland (NI) 1973-74; opposition spokesman on NI and agriculture 1974, on agriculture, fisheries and food 1974-76, on House of Commons (HoC) and devolution 1976-78, on foreign and Commonwealth affairs 1978-79; SoS for Defence 1979-81; Chancellor of Duchy of Lancaster, Paymaster General, Leader HoC 1981; Lord President of Council, Leader HoC 1981-82; SoS for Foreign and Commonwealth Affairs 1982-83; Political Honours Scrutiny Committee 1987-: chairman 1992- *Current non-Whitehall posts:* chairman English Cable Enterprises 1990-, St Andrew's (Ecumenical) Trust 1990-; director Christie Brockbank Shipton Ltd 1990-; vice-president Register of Engineers for Disaster Relief 1987-; member council British Executive Service Overseas 1988-; member Landscape Foundation Board

Date of birth: 13 February 1922 *Education/professional qualifications:* Eton College; Magdalene College, Cambridge *Honours, decorations:* MC 1945, PC 1970, DL 1973, Baron 1987 *Marital status:* married Valerie Daglish 1949; 2 sons, 2 daughters *Publications:* The Politics of Consent (Hamish Hamilton 1984) *Clubs:* Buck's, Cavalry and Guards *Recreations:* gardens

The Rt Hon The Lord Pym, Chairman, Political Honours Scrutiny Committee, 55 Parliament Street, London SW1A 2NH
Telephone: 0171-210 5059 *Fax:* 0171-210 5046

Q

QUIGLEY, (ANTHONY) TONY LESLIE COUPLAND Head of Science and Engineering Base Group, Office of Science and Technology, Office of Public Service and Science/Cabinet Office Grade: 3

Career: Ministry of Defence 1967-: Admiralty Service Weapons Establishment 1967-81; Royal Armament Research and Development Establishment 1981-87; seconded to Cabinet Office on science and technology policy 1987-90; director strategic defence initiative participation office 1990-93; assistant chief scientific adviser, nuclear 1993-95; head of science and engineering base group, Office of Science and Technology, Office of Public Service and Science/Cabinet Office 1995-

Date of birth: 14 July 1946 *Education/professional qualifications:* Aspley Grammar School, Hemel Hempstead; Queen Mary College, London, electrical engineering (BSc Eng 1967); FIEE 1986 *Recreations:* playing and umpiring cricket, golf, flying model aircraft

Tony Quigley Esq, Under Secretary, Office of Science and Technology, Office of Public Service and Science, Albany House, 84-86 Petty France, London SW1H 9ST *Telephone:* 0171-271 2070 *Fax:* 0171-271 2018

R

RAMAGE, ALAN WILLIAM Chief Executive and Keeper of the Registers of Scotland Grade: 4

Career: Registers of Scotland 1991-: principal establishment and financial officer 1991-94, chief executive 1994-

Date of birth: 4 December 1943 *Education/professional qualifications:* Boroughmuir School, Edinburgh *Marital status:* married Fiona Alexandra 1983 *Recreations:* reading, running, swimming, eating out

Alan W Ramage Esq, Chief Executive, Registers of Scotland, Meadowbank House, 153 London Road, Edinburgh EH8 7AV *Telephone:* 0131-659 6111 *Fax:* 0131-459 1221

RAMSAY, ANDREW CHARLES BRUCE Head of Arts, Sports and Lottery Group, Department of National Heritage Grade: 3

Career: Department of Transport 1979-83; Department of Environment 1983-93: local government finance (LGF) 1983-88, urban development 1988-91, LGF 1991-93, international environment protection 1993; under secretary, head of arts and lottery group Department of National Heritage 1993-, and sports 1994-

Date of birth: 30 May 1951 *Education/professional qualifications:* Winchester College; Bedford College, London, history (BA 1973) *Marital status:* married Katharine Celia Marsh 1983; 2 daughters *Recreations:* gardening, opera, birdwatching

Andrew C B Ramsay Esq, Under Secretary, Department of National Heritage, 2-4 Cockspur Street, London SW1Y 5DH *Telephone:* 0171-211 6122 *Fax:* 0171-211 6170

RAMSAY, DOUGLAS JOHN Principal Assistant Parliamentary Counsel, Office of the Parliamentary Counsel Grade: 4

Career: private practice solicitor 1984-87; Parliamentary Counsel's Office (drafting government bills) 1987-: assistant parliamentary counsel (APC) 1987-91, senior APC 1991-94, principal APC 1994-

Date of birth: 29 November 1959 *Education/professional qualifications:* Northgate Grammar School, Ipswich; Leeds University, law (LLB 1981) *Marital status:* single *Recreations:* football, reading

Douglas J Ramsay Esq, Principal Assistant Parliamentary Counsel, Office of the Parliamentary Counsel, 36 Whitehall, London SW1A 2AY *Telephone:* 0171-210 6606 *Fax:* 0171-210 6632

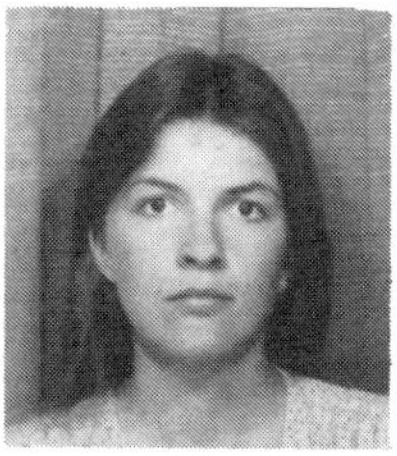

RAMSAY, KATHARINE CELIA Member, Prime Minister's Policy Unit

Career: Citibank NA 1977-79; desk officer, later head of economics section Conservative Research Department 1979-83; special adviser Departments of Transport, Environment, Trade and Industry 1983-90, of Health 1990-92; member Prime Minister's Policy Unit 1992-

Date of birth: 28 May 1955 *Education/professional qualifications:* St Paul's Girls' School, London; Girton College, Cambridge, history (BA, MA 1977) *Marital status:* married Andrew 1983; 2 daughters

Mrs Katharine C Ramsay, Prime Minister's Policy Unit, 10 Downing Street, London SW1A 2AA *Telephone:* 0171-270 3000

RATHBONE, J C A Chief Actuary, Insurance Companies and Friendly Societies Division, Government Actuary's Department Grade: 4

J C A Rathbone Esq, Chief Actuary, Insurance Companies and Friendly Societies Division, Government Actuary's Department, 22 Kingsway, London WC2B 6LE *Telephone:* 0171-242 6828

RAWLINS, Professor MICHAEL DAVID Chairman, Committee on Safety of Medicines, Medicines Commission

Career: medicine lecturer St Thomas's hospital medical school, London 1967-71; clinical pharmacology senior registrar Royal Postgraduate Medical School 1971-72; research fellow Karolinska Institute, Stockholm, Sweden 1972-73; professor of clinical pharmacology Newcastle University 1973-; vice-chairman northern regional health authority 1990-94; chairman committee on safety of medicines (advice to health ministers on the safety, efficacy and quality of medicinal products) 1993-

Date of birth: 28 March 1941 *Education/professional qualifications:* Uppingham School; St Thomas's medical school, London, medicine (BSc 1962, MB BS 1965, MD 1972); MRCP 1968, FRCP 1977; FRCPE 1987; FFPM 1989 *Marital status:* married Elizabeth Cadbury Hambly 1963; 3 daughters *Publications:* Variability in Human Drug Response (Butterworth 1973) *Clubs:* Royal Society of Medicine, Bamburgh Castle Golf *Recreations:* music, golf

Professor Michael D Rawlins, Chairman, Committee on Safety of Medicines, Market Towers, 1 Nine Elms Lane, London SW8 5NQ *Telephone:* 0171-273 0451 *Fax:* 0171-273 0387

RAWSTHORNE, ANTHONY ROBERT Assistant Under Secretary, Immigration and Nationality, Home Office Grade: 3

Career: Home Office (HO) 1966-82: posts dealing with prisons, race relations, magistrates courts, urban deprivation, head of crime policy planning unit 1977-79, of division establishment department 1979-82; secretary Falkland Islands Review Committee Cabinet Office 1982; HO 1983-: principal private secretary 1983, head of division, immigration and nationality department (IND) 1983-86, of establishment department 1986-91, of equal opportunities and general department 1991, assistant under secretary IND 1991-

Date of birth: 25 January 1943 *Education/professional qualifications:* Ampleforth College, York; Wadham College, Oxford, literae humaniores (BA 1965) *Marital status:* married Beverley Jean Osborne 1967; 1 son, 2 daughters *Recreations:* bridge, cycling, squash

Anthony R Rawsthorne, Assistant Under Secretary, Immigration and Nationality Department, Home Office, Lunar House, 40 Wellesley Road, Croydon CR9 2BY *Telephone:* 0181-760 2733 *Fax:* 0181-760 2435

READER, NIGEL F Finance Director, National Rivers Authority

Date of birth: 11 February 1948 *Education/professional qualifications:* Cambridge University, modern languages (BA, MA) *Honours, decorations:* CIMA *Marital status:* married; 3 daughters *Recreations:* running, skiing

N Reader Esq, Finance Director, National Rivers Authority, Rivers House, Waterside Drive, Aztec West, Almondsbury, Bristol BS12 4UD *Telephone:* 01454 624480 *Fax:* 01454 624031

REES, Sir DAI (DAVID ALLAN) Secretary, Medical Research Council

Career: chemistry lecturer Edinburgh University 1960-70; various posts, latterly principal scientist Unilever Research 1970-82; Medical Research Council 1982-: director National Institute of Medical Research 1982-87, secretary (chief executive) 1987- *Current non-Whitehall posts:* president European Science Foundation 1993-

Date of birth: 28 April 1936 *Education/professional qualifications:* Hawarden Grammar School, Clwyd; University College of North Wales, chemistry (BSc 1956, PhD 1959); Edinburgh University, chemistry (DSc 1970); FRS 1981; FRCPath 1992 *Honours, decorations:* Kt 1993 *Marital status:* married Myfanwy Owen 1959; 1 daughter, 2 sons *Publications:* Polysaccharide Shapes (Chapman & Hall 1977) *Clubs:* Royal Society of Medicine *Recreations:* reading, walking, river boats

Sir Dai Rees, Secretary, Medical Research Council, 20 Park Crescent, London W1N 4AL *Telephone:* 0171-636 5422 *Fax:* 0171-436 6179

REES, JONATHAN NIGEL Member Prime Minister's Policy Unit Grade: 5

Career: Department of Prices and Consumer Protection 1977-79; Department of Trade [and Industry] 1979-94: private secretary to secretary of state and minister for trade 1981-83; seconded to DG VII Transport EC Commission 1984-86; central unit European division 1986-89; seconded as industry counsellor UK permanent representation to EC, Brussels 1989-93; competitiveness division 1994; member Prime Minister's Policy Unit 1994-

Date of birth: 29 September 1955 *Education/professional qualifications:* Jesus College, Oxford, modern history (BA 1977, MA) *Marital status:* single *Clubs:* Marylebone Cricket *Recreations:* sport, travel

Jonathan N Rees Esq, Prime Minister's Policy Unit, 10 Downing Street, London SW1A 2AA *Telephone and Fax:* 0171-930 4433

REID, GRAHAM LIVINGSTONE Deputy Secretary, Industrial Relations and International Directorate, Employment Department Group Grade: 2

Career: Glasgow University 1960-73; Scottish Office 1973-75; Manpower Services Commission 1975-84; Department of Employment 1984-: deputy secretary manpower policy 1988-90, resources and strategy 1990, industrial relations and international directorate 1990-

Date of birth: 30 June 1937 *Education/professional qualifications:* St Andrew's University (MA); Queen's University, Kingston, Canada (MA) *Honours, decorations:* CB 1991

Graham L Reid Esq CB, Deputy Secretary, Employment Department Group, Caxton House, Tothill Street, London SW1H 9NF *Telephone:* 0171-273 3000

REID, WILLIAM KENNEDY Parliamentary Commissioner for Administration and Health Service Commissioner for England, for Scotland and for Wales [Ombudsman] Grade: 1 equivalent

Career: Ministry of Education 1956-64; Cabinet Office 1964-67; Department of Education and Science 1967-78; Scottish Office central services 1978-84; Scottish Home and Health Department 1984-89; parliamentary commissioner for administration and health service commissioner for England, for Scotland and for Wales (ombudsman: investigation of complaints of maladministration and failures in service) 1990- *Current non-Whitehall posts:* ex officio member Council on Tribunals 1990-,

Commission for Local Administration in England 1990-, Commission for Local Administration in Wales 1990-

Date of birth: 15 February 1931 *Education/professional qualifications:* George Watson's College, Edinburgh; Edinburgh University, classics (MA 1952); Trinity College, Cambridge (MA 1956) *Honours, decorations:* CB 1981 *Marital status:* married Ann Campbell 1959; 2 sons, 1 daughter *Publications:* Reports to Parliament 1990-94 (HMSO) *Clubs:* New, Edinburgh *Recreations:* verse and worse

William K Reid Esq CB, Parliamentary Commissioner for Administration, Church House, Great Smith Street, London SW1P 3BW
Telephone: 0171-276 3000 *Fax:* 0171-276 2104

RENSHALL, (JAMES) MICHAEL Deputy Chairman, Financial Reporting Review Panel

Career: Pilkington Brothers 1957-60; Institute of Chartered Accountants in England and Wales 1960-77: assistant secretary 1960-69, technical director 1969-70; partner/consultant private practice accountancy 1977-; deputy chairman Financial Reporting Review Panel (company accounts presentation standards) 1991-

Date of birth: 27 July 1930 *Education/professional qualifications:* Rydal School, Colwyn Bay; Clare College, Cambridge, English literature (BA 1953, MA); FCA, MSI *Honours, decorations:* CBE 1991 *Marital status:* married Kathleen Valerie Tyson 1960; 1 daughter *Publications:* co-author Added Value in External Financial Reporting (Institute of Chartered Accountants in England and Wales [ICA] 1979) and Purchase of Own Shares (ICA 1983); joint editor The Companies Act Handbook 1981 (ICA 1981); general editor Butterworth's Company Law Guide *Clubs:* United Oxford and Cambridge University *Recreations:* art, music, theatre, military history, gardens

J Michael Renshall Esq CBE, Deputy Chairman, Financial Reporting Review Panel, Holborn Hall, 100 Gray's Inn Road, London WC1X 8AZ
Telephone: 0171-404 8818 *Fax:* 0171-404 4497

RENTON, JANICE HELEN Deputy Commissioner and Secretary, Commissioner for Local Administration in Scotland [Ombudsman]

Career: private practice legal training 1967-69; legal assistant (LA) Clackmannan county council (CC) 1969-71; depute reporter to children's panel Glasgow Corporation 1971-72; senior LA Aberdeen CC 1972-74; depute director of law and administration Grampian Regional Council 1974-76; senior depute director of administration Edinburgh district council 1976-84; Commissioner for Local Administration in Scotland (ombudsman: investigation complaints of local government maladministration): deputy commissioner and secretary 1991- *Current non-Whitehall posts:* deputy adjudicator for Local Government Adjudicator for Scotland 1990-

Date of birth: 20 April 1947 *Education/professional qualifications:* The Academy, Bo'ness, West Lothian; Edinburgh University, law (LLB 1967) *Marital status:* single *Recreations:* eating, talking

Miss Janice H Renton, Deputy Commissioner and Secretary, Commissioner for Local Administration in Scotland, 23 Walker Street, Edinburgh EH3 7HX *Telephone:* 0131-225 5300 *Fax:* 0131-225 9495

REVELL, Surgeon Vice-Admiral ANTHONY LESLIE Surgeon General, Defence Medical Services, Ministry of Defence

Career: naval service 1960-: shipborne service 1960-63, 1965-67; naval, civilian and RAF hospital service UK, Cyprus, Singapore 1964-65, 1967-79, 1982-84; director studies Institute of Naval Medicine 1980-82, medical personnel 1984-86; medical officer in command RN hospital, Plymouth 1987-88; staff commander-in-chief (C-in-C) fleet 1988-90; Ministry of Defence (MoD) 1990-: director clinical services defence medical directorate 1990-91; operational medical services 1991-92; chief staff officer medical and dental to C-in-C fleet 1992-93; medical director-general (naval) and deputy surgeon-general 1993-94; surgeon general defence medical services 1994-

Date of birth: 26 April 1935 *Education/professional qualifications:* Birmingham University Medical School (MB, ChB 1959); DA 1968; FRCA 1969; Royal College of Defence Studies 1986; National Defence College 1979 *Honours, decorations:* OStJ 1984, QHS

Surgeon Vice-Admiral Anthony L Revell QHS, Surgeon General, Defence Medical Services, Ministry of Defence, Lacon House, Theobald's Road, London WC1X 8RY *Telephone:* 0171-305 5418 *Fax:* 0171-305 5468

RHIND, Professor DAVID WILLIAM Director-General and Chief Executive, Ordnance Survey (Executive Agency) Grade: 3

Career: geology research fellow Edinburgh University 1968-69, Royal College of Art 1969-73; reader in geography Durham University 1973-81; geography professor Birkbeck College, London 1982-91; director-general and chief executive Ordnance Survey 1992-

Date of birth: 29 November 1943 *Education/professional qualifications:* Berwick Grammar School, Berwick-upon-Tweed; Bristol University, geography (BSc 1965); Edinburgh University, geomorphology (PhD 1969); London University, geographical information systems (DSc 1991) *Marital status:* married Christine Young 1966; 2 daughters, 1 son *Publications:* eight books including co-editor Geographical Information Systems (Longman 1991); co-author Land Use (Methuen 1980); 200 papers and articles *Clubs:* Athenaeum *Recreations:* walking, house-painting, music

Professor David W Rhind, Director-General and Chief Executive, Ordnance Survey, Romsey Road, Maybush, Southampton SO16 4GU *Telephone:* 01703 792559 *Fax:* 01703 792660

RICHARDSON, JANE PHILLIPS Senior Legal Adviser, Monopolies and Mergers Commission Grade: 4

Career: private practice solicitors 1971-73; legal assistant (LA) Law Commission 1973-75; LA, senior LA Department of Trade and Industry (DTI) 1976-83; senior LA Foreign and Commonwealth Office 1983-84; DTI 1985-92; Department of Transport branch Treasury Solicitor's Department 1993-94; senior legal adviser Monopolies and Mergers Commission 1993-

Date of birth: 4 May 1949 *Education/professional qualifications:* Leeds Girls' High School; Bristol University, law (LLB 1970) *Marital status:* single *Recreations:* gardening, walking, music, reading

Ms Jane P Richardson, Senior Legal Adviser, Monopolies and Mergers Commission, New Court, 48 Carey Street, London WC2A 2JT *Telephone:* 0171-324 1426 *Fax:* 0171-324 1400

RICHARDSON, MICHAEL JOHN Under Secretary, Schools Organisation Branch, Department for Education Grade: 3

Career: HM Diplomatic Service 1968-87: East Africa department Foreign and Commonwealth Office, London (FCO) 1968-69; Chinese language student 1969-71; Peking embassy 1972-74; Near East and north Africa department FCO 1974-75; seconded to cabinet of EC commissioner Sir Christopher Soames 1976-77; western Europe department FCO 1977-78; private secretary to minister of state, later to Lord Privy Seal 1978-80; first secretary (economic) Rome embassy 1980-85; FCO 1985-87: assistant head of European co-ordination department 1985; head of EC presidency secretariat 1986-87; Department of/for Education [and Science] 1987-: head of teacher supply 1987-89; schools branch 1 (organisation and supply)/schools' organisation branch 1989-: head of division 1989-92; under secretary 1992-

Date of birth: 17 March 1946 *Education/professional qualifications:* Eton College; St Edmund Hall, Oxford, literae humaniores (BA 1968) *Marital status:* married Celia Bradshaw 1967; 1 son, 1 daughter *Recreations:* gardening, walking

Michael J Richardson Esq, Under Secretary, Department for Education, Sanctuary Buildings, Great Smith Street, London SW1P 3ET *Telephone:* 0171-925 5650 *Fax:* 0171-925 5629

RICHARDSON, THOMAS LEGH Deputy Political Director, Foreign and Commonwealth Office Senior Grade

Career: HM Diplomatic Service 1962-: head of economic relations department Foreign and Commonwealth Office, London (FCO) 1986-89; UK deputy permanent representative to UN 1989-94; assistant under secretary, deputy political director 1994-

Date of birth: 6 February 1941 *Education/professional qualifications:* Christ Church, Oxford, history (BA 1962, MA) *Honours, decorations:* CMG 1991 *Marital status:* married Alexandra Frazier Ratcliff 1979 *Recreations:* walking, reading, music, Italy

T L Richardson Esq CMG, Assistant Under Secretary, Foreign and Commonwealth Office, King Charles Street, London SW1A 2AL *Telephone:* 0171-270 3000

RICHMOND, Dr (JENNIFER) KAY Principal Medical Officer, Health Professional Group, Welsh Office Grade: 4

Career: general practitioner 1973-76, 1978-88; public health medicine registrar 1976-78; Welsh Office 1988-: medical officer (MO) 1988-89; senior MO 1989-92, principal MO 1992-: community and primary care, health professional group 1992-

Date of birth: 16 July 1945 *Education/professional qualifications:* Girls' Grammar School, Pontypool, Gwent; National Welsh School of Medicine, Cardiff, medicine (MB BCh 1968); Royal College of Physicians, child health (DCH 1970); Royal College of Obstetrics and Gynaecology, obstetrics (DObstRCOG 1972); MRCGP 1976, FRCGP 1987; MICGP 1987; MFPHM 1989 *Marital status:* married 1972; widowed 1975; 1 son, 1 daughter *Clubs:* Mensa, British Red Cross *Recreations:* choral singing, walking, skiing, reading

Dr Kay Richmond, Principal Medical Officer, Health Professional Group, Welsh Office, Cathays Park, Cardiff CF1 3NQ *Telephone:* 01222 823431 *Fax:* 01222 825438

RICKETT, WILLIAM FRANCIS SEBASTIAN Under Secretary, Finance Central Directorate, Department of the Environment Grade: 3

Career: Department of Energy (DEn) 1975-81: private secretary (PS) to permanent under secretary 1977-78, principal atomic energy division 1978-81; PS to prime minister 1981-83; seconded to corporate finance division Kleinwort Benson Ltd 1983-85; DEn/Department for Environment 1985-: assistant secretary oil division 1985-87, electricity division 1987-89, grade 4 electricity division 1989-90; under secretary (US) and director-general Energy Efficiency Office 1990-92; US finance central directorate 1993-

Date of birth: 23 February 1953 *Education/professional qualifications:* Eton College; Trinity College, Cambridge, natural sciences (BA 1974) *Marital status:* married Lucy Caroline Clark 1979; 1 son, 1 daughter *Clubs:* Royal Society of Arts *Recreations:* sport, painting, children

William F S Rickett Esq, Under Secretary, Department of the Environment, 2 Marsham Street, London SW1P 3EP *Telephone:* 0171-276 3000 *Fax:* 0171-276 4040

RICKS, ROBERT NEVILLE Legal Adviser to Department for Education, Treasury Solicitor's Department Grade: 3

Career: private practice 1965-69; Treasury Solicitor's Department 1969-: legal assistant (LA) 1969-73, senior LA 1973-81, assistant treasury solicitor (ATS) 1981-86, principal ATS 1986-: senior legal adviser and head of legal branch Department for Education 1990-

Date of birth: 29 June 1942 *Education/professional qualifications:* Highgate School, London; Worcester College, Oxford, jurisprudence (BA 1964, MA); solicitor 1967 *Marital status:* single *Clubs:* United Oxford and Cambridge University *Recreations:* collecting original cartoons, wine

Robert N Ricks Esq, Legal Adviser, Department for Education, Sanctuary Buildings, Great Smith Street, London SW1P 3BJ *Telephone:* 0171-925 6174

RIDD, PHILIP L Principal Assistant Solicitor, Litigation Division, Treasury Solicitor's Department Grade: 3

Career: principal assistant solicitor: Board of Inland Revenue -93; Treasury Solicitor's Department 1993-

P L Ridd Esq, Principal Assistant Solicitor, Treasury Solicitor's Department, Queen Anne's Chambers, 28 Broadway, London SW1H 9JS *Telephone:* 0171-210 3000 *Fax:* 0171-222 6006

RIDDELL, ALAN GORDON Secretary, Committee on Standards in Public Life (Nolan Committee) Grade: 5

Career: secondary school history teacher 1971-75; Department of Environment 1975-94: assistant private secretary (PS) to minister of housing and construction 1981-83; inner cities division 1983-86; private rented sector housing division (PRSH) 1986-87; PS to minister for local government, for water and planning 1987-90; head of PRSH 1990-92; principal PS to secretary of state 1992-94; secretary Committee on Standards of Conduct in Public Life 1994-

Date of birth: 8 September 1948 *Education/professional qualifications:* Greenock Academy; Glasgow University, modern history and political economy (MA 1970); teaching training (certificate 1971) *Marital status:* married Barbara Elizabeth Kelly 1976; 2 daughters *Recreations:* walking, boats

Alan G Riddell Esq, Secretary, Committee on Standards in Public Life, Horseguards Road, London SW1P 3AL *Telephone:* 0171-270 5879 *Fax:* 0171-270 5874

RIGGS, DAVID GEORGE Finance Director, Social Security Benefits Agency (Executive Agency) Grade: 3

Career: Bury County Borough Council 1958-68; Greater London Council 1968-82: finance officer 1968-74, head of public services finance 1974-76, assistant comptroller of finance 1976-82; director of finance Inner London Education Authority 1982-90; acting director of finance London borough of Hammersmith and Fulham 1990-91; finance director Social Security Benefits Agency 1991-

Date of birth: 6 May 1942 *Education/professional qualifications:* Bury Grammar School, Lancashire; Manchester University, economics (BA Econ 1968); IPFA 1963 *Marital status:* separated; 2 sons, 2 daughters *Recreations:* choral singing, running

David G Riggs Esq, Finance Director, Social Security Benefits Agency, Quarry House, Quarry Hill, Leeds LS2 7UA *Telephone:* 01132 324229 *Fax:* 01132 324235

RILEY, CHRIS(TOPHER) JOHN Chief Economist; Director Central Management and Analysis Unit, Department of the Environment Grade: 3

Career: HM Treasury (HMT) 1969-77: economic assistant 1969-72, senior economic assistant 1972-74, economic adviser 1974-77; research fellow Nuffield College, Oxford 1977-78; HMT 1978-: senior economic adviser 1978-88, under secretary medium-term and policy analysis group 1988-95; chief economist and director central management and analysis unit Department of the Environment 1995-

Date of birth: 20 January 1947 *Education/professional qualifications:* Ratcliffe College, Leicester; Wadham College, Oxford, mathematics (BA 1967, MA); East Anglia University, economics (MA 1969) *Marital status:* married Helen Marion Mynett 1982; 2 sons *Recreations:* music, especially choral singing

Chris Riley Esq, Chief Economist, Department of the Environment, 2 Marsham Street, London SW1P 3EB *Telephone:* 0171-276 4665 *Fax:* 0171-276 3846

RIMINGTON, STELLA Director-General, Security Service Grade: 2

Career: Security Service 1969-: director-general 1992-

Date of birth: 1935 *Education/professional qualifications:* Nottingham High School for Girls; Edinburgh University (MA 1958) *Marital status:* married John David 1963; 2 daughters

Mrs Stella Rimington, Director-General, Security Service, PO Box 3255, London SW1P 1AE

RIPPENGAL, DEREK Counsel to Chairman of Committees, House of Lords Grade: 3

Career: barrister 1953-55; academic posts Exeter and Cambridge Universities 1955-58; adviser Treasury Solicitor's Office 1958-72; solicitor and legal adviser Department of Trade and Industry 1972-73; parliamentary counsel Law Commission 1973-77; counsel to chairman of committees (advice on private bills, general legal advice) House of Lords 1977-

Date of birth: 8 September 1928 *Education/professional qualifications:* Hampton Grammar School, Middlesex; St Catharine's College, Cambridge, law (BA 1952, MA); Middle Temple (barrister 1953) *Honours, decorations:* QC 1980, CB 1982 *Marital status:* married Elizabeth Melrose 1963 (died 1973); 1 daughter, 1 son *Clubs:* Athenaeum *Recreations:* music, fishing

Derek Rippengal Esq CB QC, Counsel to Chairman of Committees, House of Lords, London SW1A 0PW *Telephone:* 0171-219 3211 *Fax:* 0171-219 2571

RITCHIE, DAVID ROBERT Regional Director, Government Office for the West Midlands, Departments of Environment, Transport, Trade and Industry and Employment Grade: 3

Career: Ministry of Transport 1970-; Department of the Environment (DoE) 1970-: principal, planning and inner cities NW regional office 1975-79, water legislation 1979-83; NW regional housing and environment controller 1983-86; head of water legislation division 1986-88, of housing association (capital) division 1988-89; W Midlands regional director DoE and Transport 1989-94; regional director government office for the West Midlands 1994-

Date of birth: 10 March 1948 *Education/professional qualifications:* Manchester Grammar School; St John's College, Cambridge, classics, theology (BA 1970), theology (MA 1976) *Marital status:* married Joan Gibbons 1989 *Recreations:* fell walking, gardening, cooking

David R Ritchie Esq, Regional Director, Government Office for the West Midlands, 77 Paradise Circus, Queensway, Birmingham B1 2DT *Telephone:* 0121-212 5055 *Fax:* 0121-212 5132

ROACHE, Colonel ANDREW HUGH Chief Executive, Defence Animal Centre (Executive Agency)

Career: private practice vet 1972-80; Royal Army Veterinary Corps (RAVC) 1980-: US Army health services command 1982-85; RAVC laboratory and stores 1985-87; Ministry of Defence 1987-89; Household Cavalry mounted regiment 1989-91; BAOR Defence Animal Support Unit 1991-94; chief executive Defence Animal Centre (supply dogs, handlers, horses, veterinary services to MoD) 1994-

Date of birth: 18 December 1949 *Education/professional qualifications:* Bablake School, Coventry; Bristol University, veterinary science (BVSc 1972) *Marital status:* married Glynis 1971; 2 sons *Recreations:* riding, swimming

Colonel Andrew Roache, Chief Executive, Defence Animal Centre, Welby Lane, Melton Mowbray, Leicestershire LE13 0SL *Telephone:* 01664 63281 *Fax:* 01664 410694

ROBERTS, Dr ALAN FREDERICK Chief Executive, Health and Safety Laboratory, Health and Safety Executive Grade: 4

Career: Health and Safety Executive: director explosion and flame laboratory 1981-89, nuclear safety management unit 1989-92; chief executive health and safety laboratory 1992-
Education/professional qualifications: DSc; FIChemE; FEng *Marital status:* married; two *Publications:* 60 technical papers; The Coal Mines of Buxton; Turnpike Roads around Buxton *Recreations:* local history, walking

Dr A F Roberts, Chief Executive, Health and Safety Laboratory, Health and Safety Executive, Broad Lane, Sheffield S3 7HQ *Telephone:* 01142 892301 *Fax:* 01142 892429

ROBERTS, ALLAN DEVERELL Head of Division, Solicitor's Office, Departments of Health and Social Security Grade: 3

Career: private practice solicitor 1974-76; Department(s) of Health [and Social Security] 1976-: head of division C, Solicitor's Office (legal services to Department of Health other than litigation and prosecution) 1989-

Date of birth: 14 July 1950 *Education/professional qualifications:* Eton College; Magdalen College, Oxford, jurisprudence (BA 1971, MA) *Marital status:* married Dr Irene Anne Graham Reilly 1991; 1 son *Recreations:* walking, music, football

Allan D Roberts Esq, Solicitor's Office, Departments of Health and Social Security, New Court, Carey Street, London WC2 2LS *Telephone:* 0171-412 1465 *Fax:* 0171-412 1211

ROBERTS, CHRISTOPHER WILLIAM Deputy Secretary, Trade Policy and Export Promotion, Department of Trade and Industry Grade: 2

Career: Cabinet Office 1966-68; private secretary to Prime Minister 1970-73; Department of Trade [and Industry] (DT[I]) 1973-77; under secretary Department of Prices and Consumer Protection 1977-79; DT[I] 1979-: deputy secretary 1983-: external trade policy, single European market and other EC matters 1991-92, trade policy and export promotion 1992-

Date of birth: 4 November 1937 *Education/professional qualifications:* Magdalen College, Oxford (MA) *Honours, decorations:* CB 1986

Christopher W Roberts CB Esq, Deputy Secretary, Department of Trade and Industry, 1 Victoria Street, London SW1E 6RB *Telephone:* 0171-215 5000 *Fax:* 0171-828 0931

ROBERTS, DENNIS LAURIE HAROLD Director of Statistics, Office of Population Censuses and Surveys Grade: 3

Career: Department of Environment: head of local government finance 1985-89, of water environment 1989-92, of finance 1992-94; director of statistics Office of Population Censuses and Surveys 1994-

Date of birth: 24 January 1949 *Education/professional qualifications:* Dartford Grammar School; Sheffield University, maths and statistics (BA 1970); Manchester University, statistics (MSc 1971) *Marital status:* married Anne Mary 1980; 1 son *Recreations:* walking, reading

Dennis L H Roberts Esq, Director of Statistics, Office of Population Censuses and Surveys, St Catherine's House, 10 Kingsway, London WC2B 6JP *Telephone:* 0171-396 2138 *Fax:* 0171-396 2576

ROBERTS, M G Head of Investigations, Solicitor's Office, Department of Trade and Industry Grade: 3

M G Roberts Esq, Head of Investigations, Solicitor's Office, Department of Trade and Industry, Ashdown House, 123 Victoria Street, London SW1E 6RB *Telephone:* 0171-215 5000

ROBERTSON, Air Vice-Marshal GRAEME ALAN Assistant Chief of the Defence Staff, Programmes, Ministry of Defence

Career: Royal Air Force (RAF) 1968-: officer commanding 92 squadron, RAF Wattisham; Ministry of Defence (MoD); deputy commander RAF Germany; air officer commanding No 2 group 1993-94; assistant chief of the defence staff, programmes MoD 1994-

Date of birth: 22 February 1945 *Education/professional qualifications:* Bancroft's School; RAF College, Cranwell; Open University (BA) *Honours, decorations:* CBE *Recreations:* shooting, golf, sailing, winter sports

Air Vice-Marshal G A Robertson CBE, Assistant Chief of the Defence Staff, Programmes, Ministry of Defence, Main Building, Whitehall, London SW1A 2HB *Telephone:* 0171-218 9000

ROBERTSON, IAIN ALASDAIR Chief Executive, Highlands and Islands Enterprise

Career: British Petroleum 1975-90: director of acquisitions and divestitures BP America 1987-90; chief executive Highlands and Islands Enterprise (economic, social, training and environmental development) 1990- *Current non-Whitehall posts:* member board Scottish Tourist Board 1993-

Date of birth: 30 October 1949 *Education/professional qualifications:* Perth Academy; Aberdeen University, law (LLB 1971); solicitor 1973 *Marital status:* married Judith Helen Stevenson 1977; 2 sons, 1 daughter *Recreations:* skiing, music, sailing

Iain A Robertson Esq, Chief Executive, Highlands and Islands Enterprise, Bridge House, 20 Bridge Street, Inverness 1VI 1QR
Telephone: 01463 234171 *Fax:* 01463 244469

ROBERTSON, Dr JAMES A S Chief Economic Adviser, Employment Department Group Grade: 3

Career: Department of Employment 1975-82, of Energy 1982-86, of Trade and Industry (DTI) 1986-90, of Transport 1990-91; head of industrial and regional economics, economics, market intelligence and statistics division DTI 1990-93; chief economic adviser Employment Department Group 1993-

Dr James A S Robertson, Chief Economic Adviser, Employment Department Group, Caxton House, Tothill Street, London SW1H 9NF *Telephone:* 0171-273 5772 *Fax:* 0171-273 5067

ROBERTSON, STANLEY STEWART JOHN Chief Inspecting Officer of Railways, Health and Safety Executive

Career: electrical engineer private industry 1961-74, Health and Safety Executive 1974-: senior electrical inspector of factories (FI) 1974-77, deputy superintending FI 1977-80, superintending FI 1980-91; deputy chief inspector and regional director 1991-93, chief inspecting officer of railways 1993- *Current non-Whitehall posts:* chairman National Inspection Council for Electrical Installation Contracting 1993-

Date of birth: 14 July 1938 *Education/professional qualifications:* Liverpool Polytechnic, electrical engineering (degree 1961); CEng 1973; FIEE 1987 *Marital status:* married Valerie Housley 1961; 2 sons, 2 daughters *Recreations:* listening to music, gardening

Stanley S J Robertson Esq, HM Chief Inspecting Officer of Railways, Health and Safety Executive, Rose Court, 2 Southwark Bridge, London SE1 9HS
Telephone: 0171-717 6501 *Fax:* 0171-717 6598

ROBINS, Major-General WILLIAM (BILL) J P Assistant Chief of Defence Staff and Director-General Communications and Information Systems, Ministry of Defence

Career: Royal Signals 1961-: Ministry of Defence (MoD) 1974-76, 1977-78; MoD 1982-: military assistant to Master of Ordnance 1982-84; army co-ordinator for general purpose information technology 1984-87; director command and information systems (CIS) 1987-89; director CIS (army) 1989-92; assistant chief of defence staff (command, control, communications and information systems) 1993-

Date of birth: 28 July 1941 *Education/professional qualifications:* Henry Mellish Grammar School, Nottingham; Welbeck College; Royal Military Academy, Sandhurst (commission 1961); Royal Military College of Science, electrical engineering (BSc 1966); Cranfield Institute of Technology, information systems design (MPhil); CEng, FIEE *Honours, decorations:* OBE *Recreations:* paintings, hill walking

Major-General W J P Robins OBE, Assistant Chief of Defence Staff, Ministry of Defence, Main Building, Whitehall, London SW1A 2HB *Telephone:* 0171-218 9000

ROBSON, GODFREY Under Secretary, Industrial Expansion and Inward Investment, Scottish Office Industry Department Grade: 3

Career: Scottish Office 1970-: private secretary (PS) to parliamentary under secretary 1973-74, PS to minister of state 1974, principal PS to secretary of state 1979-81, assistant secretary, roads and transport 1981-86, local government finance 1986-89; fisheries secretary, Agriculture and Fisheries Department 1989-93, under secretary, industrial expansion and inward investment Industry Department 1993-

Date of birth: 5 November 1946 *Education/professional qualifications:* Edinburgh University (MA)

Godfrey Robson Esq, Under Secretary, Scottish Office Industry Department, Meridian Court, Cadogan Street, Glasgow G2 6AT *Telephone:* 0141-248 2855 *Fax:* 0141-242 5404

ROBSON, STEPHEN ARTHUR Deputy Secretary, Finance Regulation and Industry, HM Treasury Grade: 2

Career: HM Treasury 1969-: private secretary to Chancellor of Exchequer 1974-76; under secretary defence policy and materiel group 1987-89, public enterprises and privatisation group 1990-93; deputy secretary [public expenditure], industry and financial institutions group 1993-95, director finance regulation and industry directorate 1995-

Date of birth: 30 September 1943 *Education/professional qualifications:* St John's College, Cambridge (MA, PhD); Stanford University, USA (MA) *Marital status:* married Meredith Hilary Lancashire 1974; 2 sons *Clubs:* Bosham Sailing *Recreations:* sailing

Stephen A Robson Esq, Deputy Secretary, HM Treasury, Parliament Street, London SW1P 3AG *Telephone:* 0171-270 3000

ROCHESTER, T A Director, Civil Engineering and Environmental Policy Directorate, Highways Agency (Executive Agency) Grade: 3

T A Rochester Esq, Director, Civil Engineering and Environmental Policy Directorate, Highways Agency, St Christopher House, Southwark Street, London SE1 0TE *Telephone:* 0171-928 3666

ROCK, PATRICK Special Adviser to Home Secretary

Career: Conservative Research Department; Tricentrol; special adviser to Secretaries of State for Environment Chris Patten 1989-91, Michael Heseltine 1991-92, Michael Howard 1992-93, and as Home Secretary 1993-

Patrick Rock Esq, Special Adviser, Home Office, 50 Queen Anne's Gate, London SW1H 9AT *Telephone:* 0171-273 3000 *Fax:* 0171-273 3965

RODDA, JIM Director of Finance and Administration, House of Commons Grade: 3

Career: finance posts in various companies 1967-91; director of finance and administration House of Commons 1991-

Date of birth: 16 August 1945 *Education/professional qualifications:* Maldon Grammar School; Reading University (BA); Leicester University; FCA 1971 *Marital status:* married Angela Hopkinson 1967; 1 son, 2 daughters *Recreations:* rambling, music

Jim Rodda Esq, Director of Finance and Administration, House of Commons, London SW1A 0AA *Telephone:* 0171-219 5460 *Fax:* 0171-219 2637

RODGERS, (WILLIAM) BILL THOMAS (The Rt Hon Lord Rodgers of Quarry Bank) Chairman, Advertising Standards Authority

Career: St Marylebone London borough councillor 1958-62; MP for Stockton-on-Tees 1962-74, for Teesside, Stockton 1974-83: minister of state Board of Trade 1968-69, HM Treasury 1969-70, Ministry of Defence 1974-76, Secretary of State for Transport 1976-79; founder member, vice-president Social Democratic Party 1982-87; director-general Royal Institute of British Architects 1987-94; chairman Advertising Standards Authority 1995-

Date of birth: 28 October 1928 *Education/professional qualifications:* Quarry Bank High School, Liverpool; Magdalen College, Oxford *Honours, decorations:* baron 1992 *Marital status:* married Silvia Szulman 1955; 3 daughters

The Rt Hon Lord Rodgers of Quarry Bank, Chairman, Advertising Standards Authority, 2 Torrington Place, London WC1E 7HW *Telephone:* 0171-580 5555 *Fax:* 0171-631 3051

ROE, GEOFFREY ERIC Director-General Commercial, Procurement Executive, Ministry of Defence Grade: 3

Career: Ministry of Aviation 1963-67; Ministry of Technology 1967-74: exports and international relations division 1969-74; procurement executive Ministry of Defence 1974-: guided weapons contracts branch 1974-76, seconded to British Aerospace 1976-78, secretary rocket motor executive 1978-81, assistant director contracts (air) 1981-86, director contracts (underwater weapons) 1986-89, head of materiel co-ordination (navy) 1989-90, principal director navy and nuclear contracts 1990-91, director-general defence contracts/commercial 1991-

Date of birth: 20 July 1944 *Education/professional qualifications:* Tottenham Grammar School *Recreations:* skiing, fell walking, sailing, flying

Geoffrey E Roe Esq, Director-General Commercial, Procurement Executive, Ministry of Defence, Foxhill, Bath BA1 5AB *Telephone:* 01225 884884

ROGERS, JOHN M Deputy Director Human Resources, NHS Executive, Department of Health Grade: 3

Career: Department of Health NHS management executive: head of Thames group, performance management directorate -1993; deputy director of personnel 1993-

Date of birth: 30 January 1947 *Education/professional qualifications:* King's School, Worcester; Marling School, Stroud; Bristol University, drama (BA) *Marital status:* divorced; 1 daughter

John M Rogers Esq, Head of Thames Group, Deputy Director Human Resources, NHS Executive, Department of Health, Quarry House, Quarry Hill, Leeds LS2 7UE *Telephone:* 01132 545225 *Fax:* 01132 545722

ROGERS, RAYMOND THOMAS Director, Information Management Group, NHS Executive, Department of Health Grade: 3

Career: hospital medical physicist 1962-70; Department of Health [and Social Security] 1970-: assistant secretary health information 1984-91; under secretary, director information management group NHS executive 1991-

Date of birth: 19 October 1940 *Education/professional qualifications:* Birmingham University, physics (BSc 1962); CPhys, FInstP *Marital status:* married Carmel Anne Saunders 1964; 3 children *Publications:* numerous *Recreations:* trekking, music, science

Raymond T Rogers Esq, Under Secretary, NHS Executive, Quarry House, Quarry Hill, Leeds LS2 7UE *Telephone:* 01132 546250 *Fax:* 01132 546278

ROLLINSON, TIMOTHY JOHN DENIS **Secretary to the Commissioners, Forestry Commission** Grade: 5

Career: Forestry Commission 1976-: district officer Kent 1976-78, New Forest 1978-81; research division 1981-88; head of land use planning 1988-90, of parliamentary and policy division 1990-93; secretary to Forestry Commissioners 1994-

Date of birth: 6 November 1953 *Education/professional qualifications:* Chigwell School, Essex; Edinburgh University, ecological science (BSc 1976) *Marital status:* married Dominique Christine Favardin 1975; 2 daughters, 1 son *Clubs:* Craigmillar Park Golf *Recreations:* golf, tennis, swimming, food, France

Timothy J D Rollinson Esq, Secretary, Forestry Commission, 231 Corstorphine Road, Edinburgh EH12 7AT *Telephone:* 0131-334 0303 *Fax:* 0131-316 4891

ROLLO, (JAMES) JIM MAXWELL CREE **Chief Economic Adviser, Foreign and Commonwealth Office** Grade: 3

Career: Ministry of Agriculture, Fisheries and Food 1968-79; economic adviser (EA) Foreign and Commonwealth Office (FCO) 1979-81; senior EA Overseas Development Administration 1981-84, FCO 1984-89; economics director Royal Institute of International Affairs 1989-93, chief EA FCO 1993-

Date of birth: 20 January 1946 *Education/professional qualifications:* Gourock High School; Greenock High School; Glasgow University, agricultural economics (BSc 1968); London School of Economics (MScEcon 1974) *Marital status:* married Sonia Ann Halliwell 1970; 1 daughter, 1 son *Publications:* The New Eastern Europe: Western Responses (Pinter 1990); co-author Trade Payments and Adjustment in Central and Eastern Europe (RIIA 1992) *Recreations:* books, performing arts, travel, food

J M C Rollo Esq, Chief Economic Adviser, Foreign and Commonwealth Office, London SW1A 2AH *Telephone:* 0171-270 2721 *Fax:* 0171-270 3369

ROSE, JAMES **Deputy Director of Inspection, Office for Standards in Education (OFSTED)** Grade: 4

Career: Department of/for Education [and Science]/Office for Standards in Education: chief inspector primary education; deputy director of inspection (national curriculum, primary education, special needs, international relations and research) 1991-

Date of birth: 15 June 1939 *Education/professional qualifications:* Leicester University; Kesteven College *Marital status:* married Pauline Alice Russell 1964; 1 daughter *Recreations:* gardening, walking

James Rose Esq, Deputy Director of Inspection, Office for Standards in Education, 29-33 Kingsway, London WC2B 6SE *Telephone:* 0171-421 6576 *Fax:* 0171-421 6707

ROSE, PETER GEORGE Press Secretary, Committee on Standards in Public Life (Nolan Committee) Grade: 5

Career: information officer Department of Trade and Industry 1971-75; press officer (PO) Department of Prices and Consumer Protection 1975-79; senior PO Department of Trade 1979-82; chief PO Health and Safety Executive 1982-85; head of news Home Office 1985-89; director of corporate communications Citygate Communications Ltd public relations company 1989-90; media director G7 economic summit Foreign and Commonwealth Office 1991; press secretary (PS) and head of information Cabinet Office 1992-94; PS Committee on Standards in Public Life 1994-

Date of birth: 12 July 1947 *Education/professional qualifications:* Southern Grammar School, Portsmouth *Marital status:* married Margaret Elizabeth 1973; 1 daughter, 1 son *Recreations:* reading, music, swimming

Peter G Rose Esq, Press Secretary, Committee on Standards in Public Life, Horse Guards Road, London SW1P 3AL *Telephone:* 0171-270 6345 *Fax:* 0171-270 5874

ROUS, Lieutenant General The Hon Sir (WILLIAM) WILLIE EDWARD Quartermaster General, Ministry of Defence

Career: military assistant to Field Marshal Lord Carver, Foreign and Commonwealth Office 1977-79; commanding officer 2nd battalion Coldstream Guards 1979-81; colonel staff duties HQ BAOR 1981-82; commander 1st Infantry Brigade 1983-84; director public relations (army) Ministry of Defence (MoD) 1985-87; general officer commanding 4th Armoured Division 1988-89; commandant staff college, Camberley 1990-91; military secretary MoD (army officers' careers; honours and awards administration) 1990-94; quartermaster general 1994-

Date of birth: 22 February 1939 *Education/professional qualifications:* Harrow School; Royal Military Academy, Sandhurst *Honours, decorations:* MBE 1974, OBE 1980, KCB 1992

Lieutenant General The Hon Sir William Rous KCB OBE, Quartermaster General, Portway, Andover, Hampshire SP11 8HT *Telephone:* 01264 382377

ROUSE, MICHAEL JOHN Chief Inspector, Drinking Water Inspectorate, Department of the Environment Grade: 5

Career: project engineer Massey Ferguson UK Ltd 1961-66; British Gas Engineering Research Station 1967-74: project leader, division manager; Water Research Centre 1974-93: division manager, director of engineering, managing director, chairman; chief inspector drinking water inspectorate water directorate Department of the Environment 1993-

Date of birth: 1 October 1939 *Education/professional qualifications:* Alcester Grammar School; Birmingham University, mechanical engineering (BSc 1961); MIGasE 1971, FIMechE 1973, FIWES 1985, FRSA 1989, EurIng 1989, FIWO 1992 *Marital status:* married Valerie Ann Penelope 1962; 1 daughter, 1 son *Recreations:* tennis, music

Michael J Rouse Esq, Chief Inspector, Drinking Water Inspectorate, Water Directorate, Department of the Environment, Romney House, 43 Marsham Street, London SW1P 3PY *Telephone:* 0171-276 8199 *Fax:* 0171-276 8405

ROWE-BEDDOE, DAVID SYDNEY Chairman, Welsh Development Agency

Career: Royal Navy reserve national service 1956-58; [Thomas] De La Rue Co 1961-76; Revlon Inc 1976-81; president GFTA Trandanalysen BGA and Herrdum and Co 1981-87; president, later board member Morgan Stanley GFTA Ltd 1982-92; chairman Welsh Development Agency 1993- *Current non-Whitehall posts:* chairman Cavendish Services Group 1987-, Development Board for Rural Wales 1994- non-executive director US Banknote Corporation 1990-, Development Securities plc 1994-

Date of birth: 19 December 1937 *Education/professional qualifications:* Stowe School, Buckingham; St John's College, Cambridge, economics and law (BA 1961, MA); Harvard University Graduate School of Business Administration, USA (PMD 1971); FInstD 1975 *Honours, decorations:* freeman City of London 1993 *Marital status:* married Malinda Collison (divorced 1982): Madeleine Harrison 1984; 3 daughters *Clubs:* Garrick, Turf, Cardiff and County, The Brook (New York) *Recreations:* music, theatre

David S Rowe-Beddoe Esq, Chairman, Welsh Development Agency, Pearl House, Greyfriars Road, Cardiff CF1 3XX *Telephone:* 01222 222667
Fax: 01222 237166

ROWLANDS, DAVID Deputy Secretary and Principal Establishment and Finance Officer, Department of Transport Grade: 2

Career: civil service 1974-: private secretary to minister of state Department of Industry 1978-80; Departments of Transport/Trade 1980-: assistant secretary 1984-90; under secretary head of railway 1 directorate 1991-93; deputy secretary, principal establishment and finance officer 1993-

Date of birth: 31 May 1947 *Education/professional qualifications:* St Mary's College, Crosby; St Edmund Hall, Oxford, philosophy, politics and economics (BA 1969) *Honours, decorations:* CB 1991 *Marital status:* married Louise Marjorie Brown 1975; 2 sons

David Rowlands Esq CB, Deputy Secretary, Department of Transport, 2 Marsham Street, London SW1P 3EB *Telephone:* 0171-276 5279
Fax: 0171-276 6806

RUBERY, Dr EILEEN DORIS Head of Health Aspects of Environment and Food Division, Department of Health Grade: 3

Career: biochemistry research Cambridge University 1967-73; Addenbrookes Hospital, Cambridge 1973-83: radiotherapy and oncology registrar 1973-78, honorary consultant and Wellcome research fellow 1978-83; Department of Health 1983-: senior medical officer toxicology, radiation and environmental protection 1983-87; principal medical officer (PMO) 1987-88; senior PMO 1988-: head of communicable diseases division 1988-90, head of health promotion (medical) division 1990-94; head of health aspects of environment and food division 1994-

Date of birth: 16 May 1943 *Education/professional qualifications:* Westcliff High School for Girls, Essex; Sheffield University Medical School (MB ChB 1966); Cambridge University, biochemistry (PhD 1973); DMRT 1974; FRCR 1976; MRCPath 1990; MFPHM 1993 *Honours, decorations:* QHP 1993 *Marital status:* married Philip 1970; 1 daughter *Publications:* Indications for Iodine Prophylaxis after a Nuclear Accident

(Pergamon/WHO 1990); Medicine – A Degree Course Guide (CRAC 1974-83); papers on radiation protection, communicable diseases, toxicology, public health medicine *Clubs:* Royal Society of Medicine *Recreations:* music, tapestry, theatre, reading

Dr Eileen D Rubery, Head of Health Aspects of Environment and Food Division, Department of Health, Skipton House, 80 London Road, London SE1 6LW *Telephone:* 0171-972 4420 *Fax:* 0171-972 4319

RUFFLEY, DAVID Special Adviser to Chancellor of the Exchequer

Career: private practice solicitor Coward Chance, later Clifford Chance 1985-91; special adviser to Secretary of State for Education and Science 1991-92, to Home Secretary 1992-93, to Chancellor of the Exchequer/HM Treasury 1993- *Current non-Whitehall posts:* governor Pimlico School

Date of birth: 18 April 1962 *Education/professional qualifications:* Queens' College, Cambridge, history, law (BA 1985, MA); solicitor 1989 *Marital status:* single *Clubs:* Athenaeum *Recreations:* golf, watching football

David Ruffley Esq, Special Adviser, HM Treasury, Parliament Street, London SW1P 3AG *Telephone:* 0171-270 5051 *Fax:* 0171-270 4836

RUMBELOW, MARTIN Under Secretary, Electronics and Engineering Division, Department of Trade and Industry Grade: 3

Career: air force national service 1955-57; British Aircraft Corporation 1958-74: technical sales 1958-65, personal assistant to managing director and corporate planning 1966-67, deputy production controller 1967-73, Concorde manufacturing project manager 1973-74; Department of [Trade and]Industry 1974-: principal 1974-78, assistant secretary 1979-86, under secretary services management division 1987-92, electronics and electrical engineering and mechanical engineering divisions 1992-94, electronics and engineering division 1994-

Date of birth: 3 June 1937 *Education/professional qualifications:* Cardiff High School; Bristol University, aeronautical engineering (BSc 1961); Cranfield Institute of Technology (MSc 1965); CEng *Marital status:* married Marjorie Elizabeth Glover 1965 *Clubs:* Royal Air Force *Recreations:* tennis, theatre, opera, singing, electronics, computing

Martin Rumbelow Esq, Under Secretary, Department of Trade and Industry, 151 Buckingham Palace Road, London SW1W 9SS *Telephone:* 0171-215 4188 *Fax:* 0171-215 4189

RUNCIMAN, (WALTER GARRISON) GARRY (Viscount Runciman of Doxford) Deputy Chairman, Securities and Investments Board

Career: army national service 1953-55; fellow Trinity College, Cambridge 1959-63, 1971-; part-time sociology lecturer Sussex University 1969-; visiting professor Harvard University, USA 1970; visiting fellow Nuffield College, Oxford 1979-87; chairman Walter Runciman 1976-90, Runciman Investments 1990-, Andrew Weir and Co 1991-; president General Council of British Shipping 1986-87; member Securities and Investments Board (regulation financial services industry) 1986-: deputy chairman 1990

Date of birth: 10 November 1934 *Education/professional qualifications:* Eton College; Trinity College, Cambridge *Honours, decorations:* FBA 1975; CBE 1987 *Marital status:* married Ruth Hellmann 1963; 1 son, 2 daughters *Publications:* A Treatise on Social Theory vol I 1983, vol II 1989 (Cambridge University Press) *Clubs:* Brooks's

Viscount Runciman of Doxford CBE, Deputy Chairman, Securities and Investments Board, Gavrelle House, 2-14 Bunhill Row, London EC1Y 8RA *Telephone:* 0171-638 1240 *Fax:* 0171-382 5900

RUSSELL, (ALASTAIR) MUIR Deputy Secretary, Scottish Office Agriculture and Fisheries Department Grade: 2

Career: Scottish Office (SO) 1970-83: assistant principal 1970-74, principal 1974-81: seconded as secretary to Scottish Development Agency 1975-76; assistant secretary 1981-90: principal private secretary to secretary of state 1981-83; under secretary Cabinet Office 1990-92; SO 1992-: head of housing group Environment Department 1992-95, deputy secretary Agriculture and Fisheries Department 1995- *Current non-Whitehall posts:* non-executive director Stagecoach Holdings plc 1992-

Date of birth: 9 January 1949 *Education/professional qualifications:* Glasgow High School; Glasgow University, natural philosophy (BSc 1970) *Marital status:* married Eileen Alison Mackay 1983 *Clubs:* Commonwealth Trust *Recreations:* music, food, wine

A Muir Russell Esq, Deputy Secretary, Scottish Office Agricultural and Fisheries Department, Pentland House, 47 Robb's Loan, Edinburgh EH14 1TW *Telephone:* 0131-244 6021 *Fax:* 0131-244 6001

RUSSELL, ALEXANDER WILLIAM Deputy Chairman, HM Customs and Excise Grade: 2

Career: Scottish Office 1961-76: water, housing and industrial development 1961-72, principal private secretary to secretary of state 1972-73, head of local transport division 1973-76; Civil Service Department 1976-82: head of machinery of government division 1976-79, of efficiency group 1979-82; head of financial management unit HM Treasury and Management and Personnel Office 1982-85; HM Customs and Excise 1985-: director organisation 1985-90, customs directorate 1990-92; director-general internal taxation and customs group 1992-94; deputy chairman 1994-

Date of birth: 16 October 1938 *Education/professional qualifications:* Royal High School, Edinburgh; Edinburgh University, history (MA 1960); Manitoba University, Canada, political science (MA 1961) *Marital status:* married Elspeth Rae Robertson 1962

Alexander W Russell Esq, Deputy Chairman, HM Customs and Excise, New Kings Beam House, 22 Upper Ground, London SE1 9PJ
Telephone: 0171-865 5011 *Fax:* 0171-865 5048

RUSSELL, Sir GEORGE Chairman, Independent Television Commission

Career: senior posts in industry, including ICI and Alcan 1958-; member Northern Development Board 1977-80; board member Washington Development Corporation 1978-80; Megaw inquiry into civil service pay 1981; council member Confederation of British Industry 1984-85; member Widdicombe inquiry into conduct of local authority business 1985; deputy chairman Channel 4 TV 1987-88; chairman Independent Television News 1988, Independent Broadcasting Authority 1989-90, Independent Television Commission 1990- *Current non-Whitehall posts:* director Northern Rock Building Society 1985-; group chief executive Marley plc 1986-; director Alcan Aluminium Ltd, Montreal 1987-; non-executive chairman 3is Group 1993-

Date of birth: 25 October 1935 *Education/professional qualifications:* Gateshead Grammar School; King's College, Durham University, politics and economics (BA 1958) *Honours, decorations:* CBE 1985, Kt 1992 *Marital status:* married Dorothy Brown 1959; 3 daughters *Recreations:* theatre, opera, tennis, badminton, bird watching

Sir George Russell CBE, Chairman Independent Television Commission, 33 Foley Street, London W1P 7LB *Telephone:* 0171-306 7850
Fax: 0171-306 7800

RUSSELL, TERRY **Secretary, Parole Board for England and Wales** Grade: 7

Career: HM Customs and Excise 1958-86; Home Office 1986-90; secretary Parole Board for England and Wales 1990-

T E Russell Esq, Secretary, Parole Board for England and Wales, Abell House, John Islip Street, London SW1P 4LH *Telephone:* 0171-217 5314 *Fax:* 0171-217 5677

RUTLEY, DAVID **Special Adviser to Minister of Agriculture, Fisheries and Food**

Career: associate consultant Bain and Company 1985-87; investment manager Advent Management Opportunities 1989-90; business development director Pepsico International 1991-93; special adviser to William Waldegrave as Chancellor of Duchy of Lancaster, Office of Public Service and Science 1993-94, as Minister for Agriculture, Fisheries and Food 1994-

Date of birth: 7 March 1961 *Education/professional qualifications:* Lewes Priory School, East Sussex; London School of Economics, international relations, (BScEcon 1985); Harvard Business School, USA, business administration (MBA 1989) *Marital status:* married *Recreations:* rockclimbing, mountaineering, skiing

David Rutley Esq, Special Adviser, Ministry of Agriculture, Fisheries and Food, 3 Whitehall Place West, London SW1A 2HH
Telephone: 0171-270 8482 *Fax:* 0171-270 8180

RUTTER, Dr (JAMES) MICHAEL **Chief Executive and Director of Veterinary Medicines, Veterinary Medicines Directorate (Executive Agency)** Grade: 4

Career: research assistant Edinburgh University 1964-69; Institute for Research on Animal Diseases/Institute for Animal Health 1969-89: seconded to Department of Education and Science 1975-78; head of microbiology department 1984-89, acting head of Compton laboratory 1986-89; director of veterinary medicines Ministry of Agriculture, Fisheries and Food 1989-; chief executive and director of veterinary medicines Veterinary Medicines Directorate 1990-

Date of birth: 20 August 1941 *Education/professional qualifications:* BVMandS 1964; BSc 1965; PhD 1968; MRCVS 1964 *Marital status:* married Jacqueline Patricia Watson 1967; 1 daughter *Publications:* numerous scientific papers, articles and book contributions; editor Perinatal Illhealth in Calves (1973); co-editor Pasteurella and Pasteurellosis (1989) *Recreations:* gardening, sport

Dr J M Rutter, Chief Executive, Veterinary Medicines Directorate, Woodham Lane, New Haw, Weybridge, Surrey KT15 3NB
Telephone: 01932 336911 *Fax:* 01932 336618

RYDER, (EDWARD) EDDY ALEXANDER **Head of Delegation, Channel Tunnel Safety Authority, Department of Transport** Grade: 3

Career: air force national service 1953-55; engineering posts GEC, Hawker Siddeley Nuclear Power Co, Central Electricity Generating Board 1955-71; Health and Safety Executive 1980-91: head of major hazards branch 1980-85; nuclear installations inspectorate 1985-91: deputy chief inspector (CI) 1985, CI and director of nuclear safety 1985-91; chair nuclear safety standards advisory group International Atomic Energy Authority 1985-91, Channel Tunnel Safety Authority 1992-

Date of birth: 9 November 1931 *Education/professional qualifications:* Cheltenham Grammar School; Bristol University, physics (BSc 1953); FInstP, CPhys 1971 *Honours, decorations:* CB 1992 *Marital status:* married Janet 1956; 1 son, 1 daughter *Recreations:* golf, gardening

E A Ryder Esq CB, Chairman, Channel Tunnel Safety Authority, Department of Transport, Church House, Great Smith Street House, London SW1P 3BL *Telephone:* 0171-276 2079 *Fax:* 0171-276 2078

RYDER, Dr PETER Director of Operations and Deputy Chief Executive, Meteorological Office (Executive Agency) Grade: 3

Career: research assistant Leeds University 1966-67; Meteorological Office 1967-: upper atmosphere research 1968-71; cloud physics research 1971-82: project manager 1971-76, assistant director 1976-82; assistant director of systems development 1982-84; deputy director of observational services 1984-88, of forecasting services 1988-89; director of operations and deputy chief executive 1989-

Date of birth: 10 March 1942 *Education/professional qualifications:* Yorebridge Grammar School, Askrigg, Yorkshire; Leeds University, physics (BSc 1963), cosmic ray research (PhD 1966) *Honours, decorations:* CB 1994 *Marital status:* married Jacqueline Doris Sylvia Rigby 1965; 2 sons, 1 daughter *Publications:* various on cloud physics research and meteorological service organisation *Recreations:* gardening, walking, fishing, photography, philately

Dr Peter Ryder CB, Director of Operations, Meteorological Office, London Road, Bracknell, Berkshire RG12 2SZ *Telephone:* 01344 854608 *Fax:* 01344 854948

S

SAGE, STEPHEN PAUL Chief Executive, The Buying Agency (Executive Agency) Grade: 5

Career: Crown Agents 1978-80; Departments of Environment (DoE) and Transport 1980-84; DoE 1984-93: assistant private secretary to minister for housing and construction 1984-85; controller Merseyside Task Force 1989-93; chief executive Buying Agency (public sector, including NHS, purchasing) 1993-

Date of birth: 3 June 1953 *Education/professional qualifications:* Bristol Grammar School; Peterhouse, Cambridge University, classics (BA 1974, MA); MCIPS 1993 *Marital status:* married Anne Jennifer Mickleburgh 1982; 2 sons, 1 daughter *Recreations:* reading, music, Alfa Romeos

Stephen P Sage Esq, Chief Executive, The Buying Agency, Royal Liver Building, Pier Head, Liverpool L3 1PE *Telephone:* 0151-224 2209 *Fax:* 0151-258 1249

SALISBURY, Dr D M Principal Medical Officer, Health Promotion Division, Department of Health Grade: 4

Career: senior lecturer King's College, London; fellow department of infectious disease epidemiology Oxford University; principal medical officer Department of Health

Date of birth: 10 August 1946 *Education/professional qualifications:* MB BS, FRCP, MFPHM *Marital status:* married; 2 children

Dr D M Salisbury, Principal Medical Officer, Department of Health, Wellington House, 133-135 Waterloo Road, London SE1 8UG *Telephone:* 0171-972 4488 *Fax:* 0171-972 4468

SALMON, ROGER BRUCE Director, Office of Passenger Rail Franchising

Career: N M Rothschild and Sons merchant bankers 1973-90: director 1981-90; self-employed 1990-93; special adviser on privatisation of passenger rail services Department of Transport 1993; director Office of Passenger Rail Franchising 1993- *Current non-Whitehall posts:* chairman Cuff and Co Ltd 1991-; King's College school of medicine and dentistry: member governing body 1986-, chairman planning and resources committee

Date of birth: 16 February 1946 *Education/professional qualifications:* Malvern College, Worcestershire; Jesus College, Cambridge, mathematics (BA 1966, MA); Stanford University, California, USA (MBA 1971) *Marital status:* married Erika Lueders 1970; 1 son, 1 daughter *Recreations:* hiking, bridge

Roger Salmon Esq, Director, Office of Passenger Rail Franchising, 26 Old Queen Street, London SW1H 9HP *Telephone:* 0171-799 8827 *Fax:* 0171-799 8830

SALVIDGE, PAUL Under Secretary, Posts Division, Department of Trade and Industry Grade: 3

Career: Ministry of Power 1967-72; Department of Trade and Industry 1972-: assistant secretary 1982-89; under secretary telecommunications and posts division 1989-94, posts division 1994-

Date of birth: 22 August 1946 *Education/professional qualifications:* Birmingham University, law (LLB 1967) *Marital status:* married Heather Johnson 1972; 1 daughter *Recreations:* reading, walking

Paul Salvidge Esq, Under Secretary, Department of Trade and Industry, 151 Buckingham Palace Road, London SW1W 9SS *Telephone:* 0171-215 5000 *Fax:* 0171-215 1971

SAMUEL, GILL(IAN) PATRICIA Press Secretary and Chief of Information, Ministry of Defence Grade: 4

Career: BBC Television current affairs group 1968-70; Plessey Co 1970-72; Department for National Savings 1972-75; chief press officer, head of news Department of [Trade and] Industry 1975-87; director of information Department of Transport 1987-92; press secretary and chief of information Ministry of Defence 1992-
Education/professional qualifications: Exeter University, history (BA 1967)

Miss Gill P Samuel, Press Secretary and Chief of Information, Ministry of Defence, Main Building, Whitehall, London SW1A 2HB *Telephone:* 0171-218 7900 *Fax:* 0171-218 7376

SANDARS, CHRISTOPHER THOMAS Assistant Under Secretary, Export Policy and Finance, Procurement Executive, Ministry of Defence Grade: 3

Career: Ministry of Defence (MoD) 1967-: assistant private secretary (PS) to minister of state; seconded to Central Policy Review Staff, Cabinet Office (CO) 1971-74; PS to minister of state 1975-77, head of general finance division 1 1977-80, of defence secretariat 13 1980-84; Royal College of Defence Studies 1985; head of secretariat 9 (air) 1986-90, assistant under secretary export policy and finance 1990-: defence and overseas secretariat CO 1993

Date of birth: 6 March 1942 *Education/professional qualifications:* Oundle; Corpus Christi College, Cambridge, history (BA 1964, MA) *Recreations:* tennis, badminton, painting, gardening

Christopher T Sandars Esq, Assistant Under Secretary, Export Policy and Finance, Procurement Executive, Ministry of Defence, Main Building, Whitehall, London SW19 2HB
Telephone: 0171-270 3000

SANDERS, NICHOLAS JOHN Head of Teachers' Branch, Department for Education Grade: 3

Career: Department of/for Education [and Science] 1971-: accountant general finance branch 1989-93, head of teachers' branch 1993-

Nicholas J Sanders Esq, Head of Teachers' Branch, Department for Education, Sanctuary Buildings, Great Smith Street, London SW1P 3ET *Telephone:* 0171-925 5000

SANDS, ROGER BLAKEMORE Clerk of Public Bills, House of Commons Grade: 3

Career: House of Commons (HoC) Department of the Clerk 1965-: clerk of European legislation committee 1977-81, of Scottish affairs committee 1981-85; secretary of HoC Commission 1985-87; principal clerk Overseas Office 1987-91, of select committees and registrar of members' interests 1991-94; clerk of public bills 1994- *Current non-Whitehall posts:* chairman Study of Parliament Group 1993-

Date of birth: 6 May 1942 *Education/professional qualifications:* University College School, London; Oriel College, Oxford, literae humaniores (BA 1965, MA) *Marital status:* married Jennifer Ann Cattell 1966; 2 daughters *Recreations:* gardening, occasional golf

Roger B Sands Esq, Public Bill Office, House of Commons, London SW1A 0AA *Telephone:* 0171-219 3000

SAUNDERS, BARBARA Chairman of the Council, Insurance Ombudsman Bureau

Career: deputy general secretary National Federation of Women's Institutes 1976-85; freelance consumer consultant 1985-: member Ministry of Agriculture, Fisheries and Food food advisory committee 1989-; member Department of Health advisory committee on microbiological safety of food 1991-, chairman council Insurance Ombudsman Bureau *Current non-Whitehall posts:* director Personal Investment Authority 1992-, member training standards panel Investment Management Regulatory Organisation; non-executive director St Albans and Hemel Hempstead NHS Trust 1994-; visiting fellow Institute of Food Research 1992-

Date of birth: 14 December 1950 *Education/professional qualifications:* York University, economics/economic history (BA 1972) *Honours, decorations:* honorary fellow College of Preceptors 1982 *Marital status:* married Derek John Palmer 1980; 1 daughter *Publications:* Understanding Additives (1988); Homeless Young People in Britain (1986) *Recreations:* tennis, badminton, theatre

Ms Barbara Saunders, Chairman of the Council, Insurance Ombudsman Bureau, City Gate One, 135 Park Street, London SE1 9EA
Telephone: 0171-928 4488 *Fax:* 0171-401 8700

SAUNDERS, Air Vice-Marshal DAVID JOHN Air Officer, Engineering and Supply, Ministry of Defence

Career: Royal Air Force (RAF) 1961-: head of RAF mobility study 1993; air officer engineering and supply 1993-

Date of birth: 12 June 1943

Air Vice-Marshal David J Saunders CBE, Air Officer Engineering and Supply, HQ Strike Command, RAF High Wycombe, Buckinghamshire HP14 4UE *Telephone:* 01494 461461

SAUNDERS, DAVID WILLIAM Second Parliamentary Counsel, Parliamentary Counsel Office Grade: 2

Career: solicitor 1964-70; Parliamentary Counsel Office (drafting government bills) 1970-: deputy parliamentary counsel (PC) 1978-80, PC 1980-94; seconded to Law Commission 1972-74, 1986-87; deputy secretary and second PC 1980-

Date of birth: 4 November 1936 *Education/professional qualifications:* Hornchurch Grammar School; Worcester College, Oxford, law (BA 1960, MA) *Honours, decorations:* CB 1989 *Marital status:* married Margaret Susan Rose Bartholomew 1963 *Clubs:* United Oxford and Cambridge University, Redhill Flying *Recreations:* bridge, golf, flying

David W Saunders Esq CB, Parliamentary Counsel, Office of the Parliamentary Counsel, 36 Whitehall, London SW1A 2AY
Telephone: 0171-210 6600 *Fax:* 0171-210 6632

SAUNDERS, JOHN DAVID Secretary, Council on Tribunals Grade: 5

Career: Lord Chancellor's Department 1980-: legal assistant (LA) 1980-83; legal group 1986-93; secretary Council on Tribunals (supervision of 60 appeals tribunals) 1993-

Date of birth: 15 March 1953 *Education/professional qualifications:* Brentwood School, Essex; Bristol University, law (LLB 1974); solicitor 1977 *Marital status:* single

John D Saunders Esq, Secretary, Council on Tribunals, 22 Kingsway, London WC2B 6LE
Telephone: 0171-936 7042

SAUNDERS, MICHAEL LAWRENCE Legal Adviser to the Home Office and Northern Ireland Office Grade: 2

Career: third secretary Hague Conference on Private International Law 1966-72; senior legal assistant Department of Trade and Industry 1972-73, of Energy 1973-76, Law Officers' Department (LOD) 1976-79; assistant legal adviser Cabinet Office European secretariat 1979-83; LOD 1983-89: assistant legal secretary 1983-86, legal secretary to Law Officers 1986-89; solicitor to HM Customs and Excise 1989-92; legal adviser Home Office and Northern Ireland Office 1992-

Date of birth: 13 April 1944 *Education/professional qualifications:* Clifton College, Bristol; Birmingham University, law (LLB 1965); Jesus College, Cambridge, international law (LLB 1966); Gray's Inn (barrister 1971) *Honours, decorations:* CB 1990 *Marital status:* married Anna Stobo 1970; 1 daughter, 1 son *Clubs:* United Oxford and Cambridge University *Recreations:* theatre, squash, cricket

Michael L Saunders Esq CB, Legal Adviser, Home Office, Queen Anne's Gate, London SW1H 9AT *Telephone:* 0171-273 2681 *Fax:* 0171-273 4075

SAVILLE, CLIVE HOWARD Head of Schools' Curriculum Branch, Department for Education Grade: 3

Career: Department of Education and Science (DES) 1965-: private secretary (PS) to minister for the arts 1968-70; University Grants Committee 1973-75, Cabinet Office 1975, principal PS to Lord President of the Council and Leader of House of Commons 1975-77; DES/Department for Education 1977-: assistant secretary 1977-87, under secretary supply and training of teachers, international relations 1987-92, head of school curriculum branch 1992-

Date of birth: 7 July 1943 *Education/professional qualifications:* Bishop Gore Grammar School, Swansea; University College, Swansea, English (BA 1965) *Marital status:* married Camille Kathleen Burke 1967

Clive Saville, Under Secretary, Department for Education, Sanctuary Buildings, Great Smith Street, London SW1P 3BT
Telephone: 0171-925 5700 *Fax:* 0171-925 6932

SAWYER, ANTHONY CHARLES Director, Operations (Prevention) and Commissioner, HM Customs and Excise Grade: 3

Career: HM Customs and Excise 1964-: deputy collector South Wales and Borders 1982-83; collector Edinburgh 1984-88; outfield directorate (regional operations and investigation division) 1988-: deputy director 1988-91, director 1991-94; commissioner 1991-: director operations (prevention) 1994- *Current non-Whitehall posts:* non-executive director branch banking division, Royal Bank of Scotland

Date of birth: 3 August 1939 *Education/professional qualifications:* Redhill and Croydon technical colleges *Marital status:* married Kathleen Josephine McGill 1962; 1 daughter, 2 sons *Clubs:* National Liberal, Royal Scots *Recreations:* sports, theatre, music

Anthony C Sawyer Esq, Commissioner, HM Customs and Excise, New King's Beam House, 22 Upper Ground, London SE1 9PJ
Telephone: 0171-865 5017 *Fax:* 0171-865 5354

SAYERS, MICHAEL WARWICK Secretary, Law Commission Grade: 5

Career: barrister Central Criminal Court 1966-72; advocate Criminal Injuries Compensation Board 1972-76; legal adviser Law Commission (LC) 1976-78, Council on Tribunals 1978-87: secretary 1978-87; Lord Chancellor's Department 1987-94: criminal policy, judicial appointments, family law; secretary (management, staffing and law reform) LC 1994-

Date of birth: 25 August 1943 *Education/professional qualifications:* Charterhouse; Oxford University, jurisprudence, (BA 1965); Middle Temple (barrister 1967) *Marital status:* married Elizabeth Ruth Wood 1969; 1 daughter, 1 son *Recreations:* church, sport, socialising

Michael W Sayers Esq, Secretary, Law Commission, Conquest House, 37-38 John Street, Theobalds Road, London WC1N 2BQ *Telephone:* 0171-453 1250 *Fax:* 0171-453 1297

SCAIFE, GEOFFREY RICHARD Chief Executive, National Health Service in Scotland Scottish Office Home and Health Department Grade: 3

Career: Department of Health and Social Security (DHSS) 1968-71; prime minister's office 1971-74; DHSS 1975-83; Merseyside regional health authority 1983-93: chief executive 1989-93; chief executive management executive NHS in Scotland Scottish Office Home and Health Department 1993-

Date of birth: 12 January 1949 *Education/professional qualifications:* Workington Grammar School *Marital status:* married Janet Elizabeth Woodward 1971; 2 daughters, 2 sons *Recreations:* outdoors, family, sport

Geoffrey R Scaife Esq, Chief Executive, NHS in Scotland, Scottish Office Home and Health Department, New St Andrew's House, Regent Road, Edinburgh EH1 3DS *Telephone:* 0131-244 2410 *Fax:* 0131-244 2162

SCHOFIELD, NEILL Director, Training, Infrastructure and Employers, Employment Department Group Grade: 3

Career: economist Departments of Environment 1970-78, of Energy 1978-82, of Employment/Employment Department Group 1982-: director business and enterprise 1990-92, of quality assurance, training, enterprise and education 1992-93, of training strategy and infrastructure 1994-, of training infrastructure and employers 1994- *Current non-Whitehall posts:* member of court Cranfield University; director Investors in People UK

Date of birth: 2 August 1946 *Education/professional qualifications:* Leeds University, economics (BA 1967); Queen Mary College, London University, economics (MSc 1975) *Marital status:* married Carol 1969; 2 daughters *Recreations:* walking, theatre, family

Neill Schofield Esq, Director, Training Infrastructure and Employers, Employment Department Group, Moorfoot, Sheffield S1 4PQ *Telephone:* 01142 593948 *Fax:* 01142 593677

SCHOLAR, MICHAEL CHARLES Permanent Secretary, Welsh Office Grade: 1

Career: HM Treasury 1969-93: assistant principal 1969-72; principal 1972-76: private secretary (PS) to chief secretary 1974-76; assistant secretary 1976-83: seconded to Barclays Bank International 1979-81; PS to prime minister 1981-83; under secretary 1983-87; deputy secretary public finance 1987-92, civil service management and pay 1992-93; permanent secretary Welsh Office 1993-

Date of birth: 3 January 1942 *Education/professional qualifications:* St Olave's and St Saviour's Grammar School, Bermondsey; St John's College, Cambridge, classics and moral sciences (BA 1963, PhD 1969); University of California at Berkeley and Harvard University, USA *Honours, decorations:* CB 1991 *Marital status:* married Angela Mary Sweet 1964; 3 sons (1 daughter deceased) *Recreations:* walking, playing the piano

Michael C Scholar Esq CB, Permanent Secretary, Welsh Office, Cathays Park, Cardiff CF1 3NQ *Telephone:* 01222 823289/0171-270 0539 *Fax:* 01222 825649/0171-270 0590

SCOBLE, CHRISTOPHER LAWRENCE Assistant Under Secretary, Police Department, Home Office Grade: 3

Career: Home Office 1965-: assistant principal 1965-70; seconded to Welsh Office 1969-70; principal 1970-78; assistant secretary 1978-88; assistant under secretary, broadcasting and miscellaneous 1988-91, establishment 1991-94, police 1994-

Date of birth: 21 November 1943 *Education/professional qualifications:* Kent College, Canterbury; Corpus Christi College, Oxford, modern history (BA 1966) *Marital status:* married Rosemary Hunter 1972; 1 son, 1 daughter

Christopher L Scoble Esq, Assistant Under Secretary, Home Office, 50 Queen's Anne Gate, London SW1H 9AT *Telephone:* 0171-273 2435 *Fax:* 0171-273 2703

SCOTT, Major General MICHAEL IAN ELDON Military Secretary, Ministry of Defence

Career: army service 1960-: second military assistant to chief of general staff Ministry of Defence (MoD); command 2nd battalion Scots Guards; staff Camberley staff college; commander 8th Infantry Brigade 1984-86; deputy military secretary MoD; general officer commanding Scotland, governor Edinburgh Castle 1993-95; military secretary (army officers' careers) MoD 1995- *Education/professional qualifications:* Sandhurst Royal Military Academy (commission 1960); staff college 1974; armed forces staff college, USA; Royal College of Defence Studies 1987 *Recreations:* art, travel, outdoor pursuits

Major General Michael I E Scott CBE DSO, Military Secretary, Ministry of Defence, Whitehall, London SW1A 2HB *Telephone:* 0171-218 9000

SCOURSE, Rear-Admiral F P Director-General Surface Ships, Procurement Executive, Ministry of Defence

Rear-Admiral F P Scourse, Director-General Surface Ships, Procurement Executive, Ministry of Defence, Foxhill, Bath BA1 5AB *Telephone:* 01225 884884

SCULLY, (MARIE ELIZABETH) ANN Vice-Chairman, National Consumer Council

Career: member European Coal and Steel Consultative Committee, Energy Advisory Panel, British Standards Institute consumer policy committee; National Consumer Council (representation of consumers' interests to government and manufacturers and suppliers): vice-chairman 1990- *Current non-Whitehall posts:* chairman Domestic Coal Consumers' Council; member board Investment Management Regulatory Organisation *Education/professional qualifications:* Notre Dame High School, Sheffield; Lanchester College, social studies; London University *Honours, decorations:* OBE 1995 *Children:* 1 daughter, 2 sons

Mrs M E Ann Scully OBE, Vice-Chairman, National Consumer Council, 20 Grosvenor Gardens, London SW1W 0DH *Telephone:* 071-730 3469 *Fax:* 071-730 0191

SEAMMEN, DIANA JILL Assistant Under Secretary (Programmes), Ministry of Defence Grade: 3

Career: HM Treasury 1969-89; commissioner and director VAT control, HM Customs and Excise 1989-92; seconded to Ministry of Defence as assistant under secretary 1992-: finance procurement executive 1992-94, programmes 1994-

Date of birth: 24 March 1948 *Education/professional qualifications:* Sussex University (BA 1969)

Ms Diana J Seammen, Assistant Under Secretary, Ministry of Defence, Main Building, Whitehall, London SW1A 2HB *Telephone:* 0171-218 9000

SEDDON, JON(ATHAN) MICHAEL Finance Director, Highway Agency (Executive Agency) Grade: 4

Career: accountant Metal Box and Dunlop Groups 1976-84; Dixons Group 1984-90: financial controller 1987-89, strategic planning accountant 1989-90; British Aerospace 1990-: finance director (FD) Communications Ltd 1992-, Enterprises Ltd 1993-; FD ABB Nera Ltd 1994, Highways Agency (responsible for national trunk roads) 1994-

Date of birth: 4 December 1956 *Education/professional qualifications:* Quarrybank Comprehensive School, Liverpool; Liverpool Polytechnic, accountancy; ACMA 1984 *Marital status:* married Maureen 1987; 1 son, 1 daughter *Recreations:* scuba diving, parachuting, riding, motorcycling

J M Seddon Esq, Finance Director, Highways Agency, St Christopher House, Southwark Street, London SE1 0TE *Telephone:* 0171-921 4185 *Fax:* 0171-921 4107

SEDGWICK, PETER NORMAN Under Secretary, Spending Directorate, HM Treasury Grade: 3

Career: HM Treasury 1969-: economic assistant 1969-71; economic adviser (EA) 1971-77; senior EA 1977-84; under secretary 1984-: head of finance economic unit 1984-86, of economic assessment group 1986-90, of international finance group 1990-94, of education, training and employment 1994-95, deputy directorate spending directorate 1995-

Date of birth: 4 December 1943 *Education/professional qualifications:* Westminster Cathedral Choir School; Downside School; Lincoln College, Oxford, philosophy, politics and economics (BA 1967), economics (BPhil

1969) *Marital status:* married Catherine Jane Saunders 1984; 2 daughters, 2 sons *Recreations:* choral singing

Peter N Sedgwick Esq, Under Secretary, HM Treasury, Parliament Street, London SW1P 3AG *Telephone:* 0171-270 4430 *Fax:* 0171-270 4380

SELBORNE, JOHN ROUNDELL (The Earl of Selborne) Chairman, Joint Nature Conservation Committee

Career: chairman Hops Marketing Board 1978-82, Agricultural and Food Research Council 1983-89; president Royal Agricultural Society of England 1988-89; chairman Joint Nature Conservation Committee 1991- *Current non-Whitehall posts:* director Blackmoor Estate Ltd 1958-, Agricultural Mortgage Corporation plc 1990-, Lloyds Bank plc 1994-; chairman House of Lords Select Committee on Science and Technology 1993-

Date of birth: 24 March 1940 *Education/professional qualifications:* Eton College; Christ Church, Oxford *Honours, decorations:* KBE 1987; FRS 1991 *Marital status:* married Joanna van Antwerp James 1969; 3 sons, 1 daughter *Clubs:* Brooks's, Farmers'

The Earl of Selborne KBE FRS, Chairman, Joint Nature Conservation Committee, Monkstone House, City Road, Peterborough PE1 1JY *Telephone:* 01733 62626 *Fax:* 01733 555948

SELLERS, GEOFFREY BERNARD Parliamentary Counsel, Office of the Parliamentary Counsel Grade: 2

Career: Office of Parliamentary Counsel (OPC) (drafting government bills) 1974-: parliamentary counsel 1987-, Law Commission 1982-85, 1991-93; OPC 1993-

Date of birth: 5 June 1947 *Education/professional qualifications:* Manchester Grammar School; Magdalen College, Oxford; Gray's Inn (barrister 1971) *Honours, decorations:* CB 1991

Geoffrey B Sellers Esq CB, Parliamentary Counsel, Office of the Parliamentary Counsel, 36 Whitehall, London SW1A 2AY *Telephone:* 0171-210 6633 *Fax:* 0171-210 6632

SELLERS, JOHN MARSLAND Deputy Parliamentary Counsel, Parliamentary Counsel Office Grade: 3

Career: law lecturer Lincoln College, Oxford 1973-75, London School of Economics 1975-77; private practice solicitor 1977-83; Parliamentary Counsel's Office (drafting government bills) 1983-: assistant parliamentary counsel (PC) 1983-88, senior assistant PC 1988-91, deputy PC 1991-

Date of birth: 15 July 1951 *Education/professional qualifications:* Manchester Grammar School; Magdalen College, Oxford, jurisprudence (BA 1972, BCL 1973); Law Society (solicitor 1980) *Marital status:* married Patricia Burns 1975; 2 sons *Recreations:* reading, fine wine

John M Sellers Esq, Deputy Parliamentary Counsel, Parliamentary Counsel Office, 36 Whitehall, London SW1A 2AY *Telephone:* 0171-210 6649 *Fax:* 0171-210 6632

SELWOOD, DEREK Director of Information Technology, Ministry of Agriculture, Fisheries and Food Grade: 4

Career: Inland Revenue 1960-88: tax officer 1960, surtax assessor 1960-69, systems analyst, senior programmer 1969-72, computer project manager 1972-75, manager computerised personnel system 1975-78, PAYE computerisation project team management 1978-80, procurement manager 1980-84, assistant director information technology 1984-88; government liaison manager Racal Data Networks 1988-89; director of information technology Ministry of Agriculture, Fisheries and Food 1989-

Date of birth: 19 December 1942 *Education/professional qualifications:* Boys' Grammar School, Woking *Marital status:* married Margaret Turner 1982; 1 daughter, 1 son *Recreations:* orienteering, running, skiing, golf

Derek Selwood, Director of Information Technology, Ministry of Agriculture, Fisheries and Food, Victory House, 30-34 Kingsway, London WC2B 6TV *Telephone:* 0171-413 2694 *Fax:* 0171-413 2692

SEYMOUR, DAVID Principal Assistant Legal Adviser, Home Office Grade: 3

Career: Home Office 1976-: assistant legal adviser (ALS) 1987-94, principal ALS 1994-

Date of birth: 24 January 1951 *Education/professional qualifications:* Trinity School, Croydon; The Queen's College, Oxford, law (BA 1972, MA 1977); Fitzwilliam College, Cambridge (LLB 1974); Gray's Inn (barrister 1975) *Marital status:* married Elisabeth Huitson 1972; 1 son, 2 daughters *Clubs:* United Oxford and Cambridge University; Marylebone Cricket *Recreations:* squash, hockey, walking

David Seymour Esq, Principal Assistant Legal Adviser, Home Office, 50 Queen Anne's Gate, London SW1H 9AT *Telephone:* 0171-273 3000 *Fax:* 0171-273 4075

SEYMOUR, SUSAN MARGARET Director, Trade, Industry and Europe, Government Office for Yorkshire and Humberside Grade: 4

Career: Department of Trade [and Industry] (DTI) 1974-: commercial consul British Trade Development Office, New York, USA 1982-85; Soviet Union market branch 1985-87; inner cities unit 1987-90; insurance division 1990-94; director trade, industry and Europe (DTI services to business; European Structural Funds; Energy Efficiency Office) Government Office for Yorkshire and Humberside 1994-

Date of birth: 13 July 1950 *Education/professional qualifications:* Barr's Hill Grammar School; Queen Mary College, London, history (BA 1971, MA 1972, PhD 1979) *Marital status:* married Theodore Conde Johnson 1985 *Publications:* Anglo-Danish Relations and Germany 1933-45 (Odense University Press 1982) *Recreations:* singing, hiking, classical music

Ms Susan M Seymour, Director Trade, Industry and Europe, Government Office for Yorkshire and Humberside, 25 Queen Street, Leeds LS1 2TW *Telephone:* 0113 233 8200 *Fax:* 0113 233 8306

SHANNON, Dr DAVID WILLIAM FRANCIS Chief Scientist, Agriculture, Ministry of Agriculture, Fisheries and Food Grade: 3

Career: Poultry Research Centre, Agriculture and Food Research Council 1967-86: research scientist 1967-78, director 1978-86; chief scientist agriculture, Ministry of Agriculture, Fisheries and Food 1986- *Current non-Whitehall posts:* member executive council CAB International 1988-; member Biotechnology and Biological Sciences Research Council agricultural systems directorate 1994-; member European Agricultural Research Initiative; UK representative on EU Standing Committee on Agricultural Research

Date of birth: 16 August 1941 *Education/professional qualifications:* Wallace High School, Lisburn, Northern Ireland; Queen's University, Belfast, agriculture (BAgr 1963, PhD 1966); Napier College, Edinburgh (DMS 1975) *Marital status:* married Rosamond Elizabeth Mary Bond 1967; 1 daughter, 1 son *Publications:* papers on poultry nutrition and hepato-toxicology *Recreations:* golf, bridge

Dr David W F Shannon, Chief Scientist, Agriculture, Ministry of Agriculture, Fisheries and Food, Nobel House, 17 Smith Square, London SW1P 3HX *Telephone:* 0171-238 5526 *Fax:* 0171-238 6129

SHARMA, SUKHDEV Executive Director, Commission for Racial Equality

S Sharma Esq, Executive Director, Commission For Racial Equality, Elliot House, 10-12 Allington Street, London SW1E 5EH *Telephone:* 0171-828 7022

SHARP, DUNCAN Chief Crown Prosecutor, Yorkshire, Crown Prosecution Service Grade: 4

Career: deputy town clerk Bridlington; county prosecuting solicitor Cumbria 1979-86; Crown Prosecution Service 1986-: chief crown prosecutor Cleveland/North Yorkshire 1986-93, Yorkshire 1993-

Date of birth: 29 April 1936 *Education/professional qualifications:* Leeds University, law (LLB 1957); solicitor 1959 *Marital status:* married Maureen 1959; 3 daughters, 2 sons *Recreations:* Victorian genealogy, gardening

D Sharp Esq, Chief Crown Prosecutor, CPS Yorkshire, 6th Floor, Ryedale Building, 60 Piccadilly, York, North Yorkshire YO1 1NS *Telephone:* 01904 610726 *Fax:* 01904 610394

SHARP, ROBIN JOHN ALFRED Under Secretary, Director, Global Environment, Department of the Environment Grade: 3

Career: Methodist minister 1960-66; Ministry of Housing and Local Government/Department of Environment 1968-: assistant secretary 1972-81: special assistant on European Communities Bill Cabinet Office 1972; road safety division 1972-75, housing 1975-81; under secretary 1981-: right to buy and public housing 1981-86, local government 1986-91, rural affairs 1991-94, global environment 1994- *Current non-Whitehall posts:* member council Flora and Fauna Preservation Society

Date of birth: 30 July 1935 *Education/professional qualifications:* Oxford University, classics (BA 1957, MA); Cambridge University, theology (BA 1959) *Honours, decorations:* CB 1993 *Marital status:* married 1963 *Recreations:* birdwatching, travel, music, theatre

Robin J A Sharp Esq CB, Under Secretary, Department of the Environment, 2 Marsham Street, London SW1P 3EB *Telephone:* 0171-276 8636 *Fax:* 0171-276 8626

SHAW, COLIN DON Director, Broadcasting Standards Council Grade: 3

Career: BBC 1953-77: secretary 1969-71, chief secretary 1971-77; director of television Independent Broadcasting Authority 1977-83; director of programme planning secretariat Independent Television Companies Association 1983-87; freelance writer and lecturer 1987-88; director Broadcasting Standards Council 1988-

Date of birth: 2 November 1928 *Education/professional qualifications:* Merton House School, Penmaenmawr; Liverpool College; St Peter's Hall, Oxford, English literature (BA 1952, MA); Inner Temple (barrister 1960) *Honours, decorations:* CBE 1993 *Marital status:* married Elizabeth Ann Bowker 1955; 2 daughters, 1 son *Publications:* children's and radio plays; articles on broadcasting *Clubs:* Reform *Recreations:* reading, theatre, travel

Colin D Shaw Esq CBE, Director, Broadcasting Standards Council, 5-8 The Sanctuary, London SW1P 3JS *Telephone:* 0171-233 0544 *Fax:* 0171-233 0397

SHAW, ELIZABETH ANGELA Executive Director, Charity Commission Grade: 4

Career: Home Office 1965-67; Foreign and Commonwealth Office 1967-70; Department of Health [and Social Security] (DH[SS]) 1970-87: principal 1977-84, assistant secretary 1984-87; Civil Service College 1987-90: director of finance and planning 1987-89, acting chief executive 1989-90; head of staff development DH 1990-91; executive director Charity Commission 1991-

Date of birth: 5 June 1946 *Education/professional qualifications:* Sydenham High School, London *Marital status:* married Adrian Carter 1993; 2 sons, 1 daughter *Recreations:* classical music, singing, English literature, theatre, cinema, walking, swimming

Mrs Elizabeth E Shaw, Executive Director, Charity Commission, St Alban's House, 57-60 Haymarket, London SW1Y 4QX *Telephone:* 0171-210 4420 *Fax:* 0171-210 4604

SHAW, JOHN FREDERICK Director Corporate Affairs, NHS Management Executive, Department of Health Grade: 2

Career: army national service 1955-57; Church Commissioners 1960-62; accountant Industrial Christian Fellowship 1962-63; head of recruitment Voluntary Service Overseas 1963-73; Department of Health [and Social Security] 1973-: principal 1973-78, assistant secretary 1978-87, under secretary NHS management executive: deputy director performance management 1987-93, director corporate affairs 1993-

Date of birth: 7 December 1936 *Education/professional qualifications:* Loretto School, Musselburgh; Worcester College, Oxford, law (BA 1960, MA) *Marital status:* married Ann Rodden 1964; 1 daughter, 2 sons *Recreations:* church activities, singing, gardening, pig keeping

John F Shaw Esq, Director of Corporate Affairs, NHS Management Executive, Department of Health, Quarry House, Quarry Hill, Leeds LS2 7UE *Telephone:* 01132 545673 *Fax:* 01132 545607

Parliamentary Offices

see page 347

SHAW, PETER ALAN Director of Services and Head of Personnel and Organisation Branch, Department for Education Grade: 3

Career: Department of Education and Science (DES) 1972-85: private secretary to secretary of state 1979-81, head of local government expenditure division 1982-85; head of employment division HM Treasury 1985-86; DES 1986-91: head of school teachers' pay division 1986-88, of information branch 1988-89, of grant-maintained schools division 1989-91; regional director northern regional office Departments of Environment and Transport 1991-93; principal establishments officer/director of services and head of personnel and organisation branch Department for Education 1993-

Date of birth: 31 May 1949 *Education/professional qualifications:* Bridlington School; Bede College, Durham University, geography (BSc 1970); Bradford University, traffic engineering and planning (MSc 1972); Regent College, British Columbia University, Canada, Christian studies (MCS 1974) *Marital status:* married Frances Willcox 1975; 1 daughter, 2 sons *Clubs:* Civil Service *Recreations:* walking, Anglican lay reader

Peter A Shaw Esq, Director of Services and Head of Personnel and Organisation Branch, Department for Education, Sanctuary Buildings, Great Smith Street, London SW1P 3BT *Telephone:* 0171-925 5486
Fax: 0171-925 6986

SHEPLEY, CHRIS(TOPHER) JOHN Chief Planning Inspector and Chief Executive, Planning Inspectorate (Executive Agency) Grade: 3

Career: [Greater] Manchester [city] council 1966-85: assistant/deputy county planning officer 1973-85; city planning officer/director of development Plymouth city council 1985-94; chief planning inspector and chief executive Planning Inspectorate (planning, housing, environmental highways appeals) 1994-

Date of birth: 27 December 1944 *Education/professional qualifications:* Stockport Grammar School; London School of Economics, geography (BA 1966); Manchester University, town planning (DipTP 1969) *Honours, decorations:* FRSA 1991; honorary visiting professor Manchester University 1990 *Marital status:* divorced; 1 son, 1 daughter *Publications:* The Grotton Papers (Royal Town Planning Institute 1979) *Recreations:* sport, music, opera, walking

C J Shepley, Chief Executive, Planning Inspectorate, Tollgate House, Houlton Street, Bristol BS2 9DJ *Telephone:* 0117-987 8963
Fax: 0117-987 8408

SHEPPARD, Major General PETER JOHN Chief of Staff, HQ Quartermaster General, Ministry of Defence

Career: staff officer military operations Ministry of Defence (MoD) 1980-82; commanding officer 35 Engineer Regiment 1982-84; HQ 1 (BR) Corps, Germany: deputy chief of staff (COS) 1984-86, commander Royal Engineers 1986-88; director army plans and programmes MoD 1989-91; COS HQ BAOR 1991-93, HQ Quartermaster General 1993-

Date of birth: 15 August 1942 *Education/professional qualifications:* Dover School; Welbeck College; Royal Military College Sandhurst; London University, civil engineering (BScEng 1965) *Honours, decorations:* mention in despatches 1978; OBE 1982, CBE 1992 *Recreations:* golf, reading, philately

Major General Peter J Sheppard CBE, Chief of Staff, HQ Quartermaster General, Portway, Monxton Road, Andover, Hampshire SP11 8HT *Telephone:* 01264 382976 *Fax:* 01264 382053

SHIFFNER, Rear-Admiral JOHN ROBIN Director-General, Fleet Support (Equipment and Systems), Ministry of Defence

Career: naval service 1967-: marine engineer officer HM ships and ship design offices Ministry of Defence (MoD) 1967-80; navy staff Washington DC embassy 1980-82; procurement executive MoD 1984-89: project manager T42 destroyers 1984-87, director mechanical engineering 1988-89; captain Britannia Royal Naval College, Dartmouth 1989-91; chief of staff to commander-in-chief naval home command 1991-93; director general fleet support (equipment and systems) naval support command MoD 1993-

Date of birth: 30 August 1941 *Education/professional qualifications:* Sedbergh School; Royal Naval Engineering College, mechanical engineering (BSc Eng 1966); Royal College of Defence Studies: CEng 1971; FIMarE 1984 *Honours, decorations:* CB *Recreations:* golf, gardening, winter sports

Rear-Admiral J R Shiffner CB, Director-General, Fleet Support, Ministry of Defence, Foxhill, Bath BA1 5AB *Telephone:* 01225 882348 *Fax:* 01225 884313

SHORT, BERNARD DAVID Head of Further Education Support Unit, Department for Education

Career: HM Inspectorate of Schools 1976-93: chief inspector further education 1986-93; head of further education support unit Department for Education 1993-

Date of birth: 9 June 1935 *Education/professional qualifications:* St Edmund Hall, Oxford (BA, MA)

Bernard D Short Esq, Head of Further Education Support Unit, Department for Education, Sanctuary Buildings, Great Smith Street, London SW1P 3BT *Telephone:* 0171-925 5000

SHORTRIDGE, JON DEACON Head of Local Government Reorganisation Group, Welsh Office Grade: 3

Career: Ministry of Housing/Countryside Commission 1969-71; Department of Environment 1973-75; planning posts Shropshire County Council 1975-84; Welsh Office 1984-: private secretary to secretary of state 1987-88; head of finance programmes division 1988-92; under secretary, head of local government reorganisation group 1992-

Date of birth: 10 April 1947 *Education/professional qualifications:* Chichester High School; St Edmund Hall, Oxford, philosophy, politics and economics (BA 1969, MA); Edinburgh University, urban design and regional planning (MSc 1973); MRTPI 1974 *Marital status:* married Diana Gordon 1972; 1 daughter, 1 son *Recreations:* family, sailing, tennis, reading

Jon D Shortridge, Under Secretary, Welsh Office, Crown Buildings, Cathays Park, Cardiff CF1 2NQ *Telephone:* 01222 823060 *Fax:* 01222 825096

SHOTTON, KEITH CRAWFORD Head of Management and Technology Services, Department of Trade and Industry Grade: 3

Career: Department of Trade and Industry 1987-: director radio technology, radio communications division 1987-90; head of information technology division 1990-92, of information and manufacturing technologies division 1992-94, of management and technology services 1994-

Date of birth: 11 September 1943 *Education/professional qualifications:* Trinity College, Cambridge (MA, PhD)

Dr Keith C Shotton, Head of Management and Technology Services, Department of Trade and Industry, 151 Buckingham Palace Road, London SW1W 9SS *Telephone:* 0171-215 1239
Fax: 0171-215 1967

SHURMAN, LAURENCE PAUL Banking Ombudsman, Office of the Banking Ombudsman

Career: private practice solicitor 1957-89: partner 1961-89; banking ombudsman (for complaints from individuals and small businesses) 1989-

Date of birth: 25 November 1930 *Education/professional qualifications:* Newcastle-upon-Tyne Royal Grammar School; Magdalen College, Oxford, law (BA 1954, MA) *Marital status:* married Mary Seamans 1963; 2 sons, 1 daughter *Publications:* The Practical Skills of the Solicitor (Longmans 1981, 85); contributor to 'Mental Health Tribunals', Atkin's Encyclopedia of Court Forms (Butterworth 1985) *Clubs:* Leander, Henley *Recreations:* fell walking, law reform

Laurence P Shurman Esq, Ombudsman, Office of the Banking Ombudsman, 70 Gray's Inn Row, London WC1X 8NB *Telephone:* 0171-404 9944 *Fax:* 0171-405 5052

SHUTLER, MAURICE FRANCIS Chief Industrial Adviser, Monopolies and Mergers Commission Grade: 4

Career: commercial operational research 1957-68; National Board for Prices and Incomes 1968-71; special adviser Civil Service Department 1971-77; Price Commission 1977-79: senior operational research adviser 1977-78, head of industrial advisers 1978-79; chief industrial adviser Monopolies and Mergers Commission 1979- *Current non-Whitehall posts:* visiting professor of operational research London School of Economics 1982-

Date of birth: 30 December 1931 *Education/professional qualifications:* Wolverhampton Grammar School; Hardye's School, Dorchester; Balliol College, Oxford, literae humaniores (BA 1954, MA); London School of Economics, operational research (diploma 1962) *Honours, decorations:* FOR 1973 *Marital status:* married Josephine Anne Boulding 1959; 2 daughters, 1 son *Publications:* co-author Operations Research in Management (Prentice Hall 1991) *Recreations:* railways, photography, singing Gregorian chant, trumpet playing

Maurice F Shutler Esq, Chief Industrial Adviser, Monopolies and Mergers Commission, New Court, 48 Carey Street, London WC2A 2JT *Telephone:* 0171-324 1315 *Fax:* 0171-324 1400

SILBER, STEPHEN ROBERT Law Commissioner

Career: barrister 1968-: recorder 1987-; law commissioner (review and revision of law) 1994-

Date of birth: 26 March 1944 *Education/professional qualifications:* University College, London; Trinity College, Cambridge

Stephen R Silber Esq, Law Commissioner, Law Commission, Conquest House, 37-38 John Street, London WC1N 2BQ *Telephone:* 0171-411 1219

SIMMONDS, MICHAEL Special Adviser to Secretary of State for Transport

Michael Simmonds Esq, Special Adviser, Department of Transport, 2 Marsham Street, London SW1P 3EB *Telephone:* 0171-276 3000

SIMS, GRAEME LINDSAY Deputy Director-General (Scotland), Office of Electricity Regulation Grade: 5

Career: associate consultant Boston Consulting Group 1985-87; business development officer Scottish Co-operative Development Committee 1988-91; Office of Electricity Regulation 1991-: economic adviser 1991-93, deputy director-general (Scotland) 1993-

Date of birth: 31 October 1963 *Education/professional qualifications:* Calday Grange Grammar School, Wirral; Magdalen College, Oxford, philosophy, politics and economics (BA 1985) *Marital status:* married June Kennedy Russell 1989; 1 daughter *Recreations:* cooking, reading, eating out, music, cinema, cycling

Graeme L Sims Esq, Deputy Director-General, Office of Electricity Regulation, 70 West Regent Street, Glasgow G2 2QZ
Telephone: 0141-331 1166 *Fax:* 0141-331 2777

SINCLAIR, C Assistant Under Secretary of State, Police Department, Home Office Grade: 3

Miss C Sinclair, Assistant Under Secretary of State, Police Department, Home Office, 50 Queen Anne's Gate, London SW1H 9AT *Telephone:* 0171-273 3000

SKINNER, ANGUS Chief Inspector of Social Work Services, Home and Health Department, Scottish Office Grade: 4

Career: social work Kent County Council 1973-75; social work manager Lothian region 1975-88; deputy director of social work Borders region 1988-91; Scottish Office Home and Health Department social work services group 1991-: chief social work adviser to secretary of state 1991-92, chief inspector 1992- *Current non-Whitehall posts:* governor National Institute of Social Work

Date of birth: 4 January 1950 *Education/professional qualifications:* Daniel Stewart's College, Edinburgh; Edinburgh University, social science (BSc 1971); London University, social work (CQSW 1973); Strathclyde University, management (MBA 1988) *Marital status:* married Kate Brewer 1971; 2 daughters, 1 son *Publications:* Another Kind of Home (HMSO 1992)

Angus Skinner Esq, Chief Adviser, Social Work Services Group, Scottish Office Home and Health Department, 43 Jeffrey Street, Edinburgh *Telephone:* 0131-244 5414 *Fax:* 0131-244 5496

SKINNER, Dr R Principal Medical Officer, Health Aspects of Environment and Food (Medical), Department of Health Grade: 4

Dr R Skinner, Principal Medical Officer, Department of Health, Skipton House, 80 London Road, Elephant and Castle, London SE1 6LW *Telephone:* 0171-972 2000

SLADE, LAURIE Insurance Ombudsman, Insurance Ombudsman Bureau

Career: legal adviser and registrar Chartered Institute of Arbitrators 1982-88; Insurance Ombudsman Bureau 1988-: deputy ombudsman 1988-94, ombudsman 1994-

Date of birth: 12 February 1944 *Education/professional qualifications:* Duke of York School, Nairobi, Kenya; Magdalen College, Oxford, law (BA, MA); FCIArb 1993 *Marital status:* single

Laurie Slade Esq, Insurance Ombudsman, Insurance Ombudsman Bureau, City Gate One, 135 Park Street, London SE1 9EA
Telephone: 0171-928 4488 *Fax:* 0171-401 8700

SLATER, Dr DAVID HOMFRAY Chief Inspector, HM Inspectorate of Pollution, Department of the Environment Grade: 3

Career: lecturer in combustion Imperial College, London 1970-75; Cremer and Warner (environmental and engineering risk projects) 1975-81: senior scientist 1975-79, partner 1979-81; founding director Technica Ltd 1981-91; chief inspector HM Inspectorate of Pollution Department of Environment 1991- *Current non-Whitehall posts:* professor of life sciences University College of Wales, Aberystwyth

Date of birth: 16 October 1940 *Education/professional qualifications:* University College of Wales, Aberystwyth, chemistry (BSc 1963, PhD 1966); FRSC, CChem, FIChemE, CEng, FInstE *Marital status:* married Edith Mildred Price 1964; 4 daughters *Publications:* numerous contributions to books, science journals and conference proceedings *Clubs:* Athenaeum *Recreations:* music, photography, fishing

Dr David H Slater, Chief Inspector, HM Inspectorate of Pollution, Romney House, 43 Marsham Street, London SW1P 3PY *Telephone:* 0171-276 8080 *Fax:* 0171-276 8800

SLATER, Admiral Sir JOCK First Sea Lord and Chief of the Naval Staff, Ministry of Defence

Career: Royal Navy 1956-: command HMSs Soberton 1965-72, Jupiter 1972-73; Kent 1976-77, Illustrious 1982-83; captain School of Maritime Operations 1983-85; assistant chief of defence staff Ministry of Defence (MoD) 1985-87; flag officer Scotland and Northern Ireland and commander Rosyth naval base 1987-89; chief of fleet support MoD 1989-91; commander-in-chief Fleet 1991-92; MoD 1993-; vice-chief of defence staff 1993-95; First Sea Lord and chief of naval staff 1995-

Date of birth: 27 March 1938 *Education/professional qualifications:* Edinburgh Academy, Sedburgh and Royal Naval College Dartmouth *Honours, decorations:* LVO 1971, KCB 1988, GCB 1992 *Recreations:* outdoor

Admiral Sir Jock Slater, GCB LVO, First Sea Lord and Chief of the Naval Staff, Ministry of Defence, Main Building, Whitehall, London SW1A 2HB *Telephone:* 0171-218 9000

SLEEMAN, TONY Controller, South Yorkshire, Inland Revenue Grade: 4

Career: Inland Revenue 1966-: local districts Wales/east region 1966-81; group controller Midlands 1981-91; controller South Yorkshire 1991-

Date of birth: 3 July 1945 *Education/professional qualifications:* Lockleaze Comprehensive School, Bristol; University College, Swansea, physics (BSc 1966) *Marital status:* married Pearl Edwards 1966; 3 daughters *Recreations:* golf, gardening

Tony Sleeman Esq, Controller, Inland Revenue, South Yorkshire, Sovereign House, 110 Queen Street, Sheffield S1 2EN *Telephone:* 01142 739099 *Fax:* 01142 750258

SLEIGH, ANDREW Managing Director, (Centre for Defence Analysis), Defence Evaluation and Research Agency Grade: 4

Andrew Sleigh Esq, Managing Director (CDA), Defence Evaluation and Research Agency, Farnborough, Hampshire GU4 6TD *Telephone:* 01252 24461

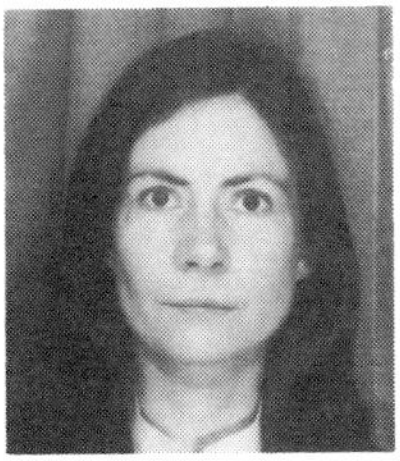

SMALES, Dr ELIZABETH Principal Medical Officer, Health Aspects of Environment and Food Division, Department of Health Grade: 4

Career: Royal Marsden hospital 1975-86: registrar in radiotherapy 1975-78, senior registrar 1978-86; Department of Health [and Social Security] 1986-: medical officer (MO) 1986-87, senior MO environmental radiation 1987-90, private secretary to chief MO 1990-91; principal MO head of environmental chemicals and radiation branch, health aspects of environment and food division, 1991-

Date of birth: 16 November 1948 *Education/professional qualifications:* University College, London, pharmacology (BSc 1969); Westminster hospital, medicine (MB BS 1972); Royal College of Radiologists (FRCR 1978) *Marital status:* married Frederick Charles 1974; 1 daughter, 1 son *Recreations:* family, reading, music, walking, gardening

Dr Elizabeth Smales, Principal Medical Officer, Department of Health, Skipton House, 80 London Road, London SE1 6LW
Telephone: 0171-972 5116 *Fax:* 0171-972 5167

SMART, KENNETH PETER ROSS Chief Inspector of Air Accidents, Department of Transport Grade: 4

Career: Ministry of Aviation 1967-75; Department of Transport Air Accidents Investigation Branch 1975-: inspector of accidents (IA) 1975-78, senior IA 1978-80, principal IA 1980-86, deputy chief IA 1986-90, chief IA 1990- *Current non-Whitehall posts:* president European Societies of Air Safety Investigations

Date of birth: 28 April 1946 *Education/professional qualifications:* Aylesford School; Ministry of Aviation College of Electronics, aeronautical engineering (certificate 1968); Worcester College of Technology, mechanical engineering (HNC 1970); Open University, technology (BA 1976) *Marital status:* married Chris 1993; 1 son, 1 daughter (from previous marriage) *Recreations:* hill walking, sailing, classic motor cycles

Kenneth P R Smart Esq, Chief Inspector, Air Accidents Investigation Branch, Defence Research Agency, Farnborough, Hampshire GU14 6TD
Telephone: 01252 510300 *Fax:* 01252 520050

SMEE, CLIVE HARROD Chief Economic Adviser, Department of Health Grade: 3

Career: economic adviser (EA) Ministry of Overseas Development 1969-75; senior EA Department of Health and Social Security (DHSS) 1975-82; adviser Central Policy Review Staff 1982-83; senior EA HM Treasury 1983-84; chief EA DHSS 1984-89; under secretary, chief EA economic and operational research directorate Department of Health 1989-

Date of birth: 29 April 1942 *Education/professional qualifications:* Royal Grammar School, Guildford; London School of Economics (BSc Econ 1963); Indiana University, USA, business administration (MBA 1965) *Marital status:* married Denise Eileen Sell 1976; 2 daughters, 1 son *Publications:* in academic journals *Recreations:* running, family, gardening

Clive H Smee Esq, Under Secretary, Department of Health, Skipton House, 80 London Road, London SE1 6LW *Telephone:* 0171-972 5220 *Fax:* 0171-972 5187

SMITH, Dr BRUCE GORDON **Chairman, Economic and Social Research Council**

Career: research associate Chicago University, USA 1964-65; technical staff Bellcomm Inc 1965-68; principal engineer Decca Radar Ltd 1968-71; Smith System Engineering 1971-: proprietor/managing director 1971-87, chair 1987-; chairman Economic and Social Research Council 1994-

Date of birth: 4 October 1939 *Education/professional qualifications:* Dulwich College, London; Christ Church, Oxford, physics (BA 1961), theoretical physics (DPhil 1964); FIEE 1978 *Honours, decorations:* OBE 1992 *Marital status:* married Rosemary Jane Martineau 1964; 2 daughters, 2 sons *Recreations:* sailing, cycling, walking

Dr Bruce G Smith OBE, Chairman, Economic and Social Research Council, Polaris House, North Star Avenue, Swindon, Wiltshire SN2 1UJ *Telephone:* 01793 413000 *Fax:* 01793 413001

SMITH, GRAHAM WILLIAM **Chief Inspector of Probation, Home Office**

Career: Home Office Probation Service 1965-: Durham combined probation area 1965-71: probation officer (PO) 1965-69, senior PO 1969-71; Inner London probation service 1971-92: senior PO 1971-73, assistant chief PO 1973-78, deputy chief PO 1978-80, chief PO 1981-92; HM chief inspector of probation 1992-

Date of birth: 15 August 1939 *Education/professional qualifications:* Bishop Wordsworth School, Salisbury; King's College, Durham University, social studies (DipSocSA 1964); Newcastle University, social studies (CQSW 1965) *Honours, decorations:* CBE 1990; Margaret Mead Award 1990 *Marital status:* married Jeanne Goodyear 1958; 1 daughter, 2 sons *Recreations:* theatre, gardening, sport

Graham W Smith Esq CBE, HM Chief Inspector of Probation, Home Office, 50 Queen Anne's Gate, London SW1H 9AT *Telephone:* 0171-273 3766 *Fax:* 0171-273 2131

SMITH, ROB(ERT) LEE **Head of Pupils and Parents Branch, Department for Education** Grade: 3

Career: Department of/for Education [and Science]: principal private secretary to secretary of state 1985-87; head of local authority financing and of grant-maintained schools divisions 1987-93; under secretary, head of pupils and parents branch (special needs, attendance, behaviour, independent schools) 1994-

Date of birth: 9 February 1952 *Education/professional qualifications:* St Dunstan's College, Catford, London; Magdalene College, Cambridge, English literature (BA, MA 1974) *Marital status:* married Susan Elizabeth Armfield 1986; 1 daughter, 1 son *Recreations:* folk dancing and music

R L Smith Esq, Under Secretary, Department for Education, Sanctuary Buildings, Great Smith Street, London SW1P 3BT *Telephone:* 0171-925 5510 *Fax:* 0171-925 6221

SNELL, DAVID CHARLES Director of Finance and Corporate Services and Deputy Chief Executive, Royal Mint (Executive Agency) Grade: 4

Career: Royal Mint 1971-: finance director 1976-83; marketing and finance director 1983-87; finance director 1987-88, deputy chief executive and director of finance and corporate services 1988- *Current non-Whitehall posts:* chairman Royal Mint Services Ltd 1989-; vice-chairman Enterprise Taff Ely Ogwr Partnership Ltd 1990-

Date of birth: 30 September 1940 *Education/professional qualifications:* Devonport High School, Plymouth; FCMA 1970; MBCS 1966 *Marital status:* divorced; 1 son, 1 daughter *Recreations:* travel, golf

David C Snell Esq, Deputy Chief Executive, Royal Mint, Llantrisant, Pontyclun, Mid-Glamorgan CF7 8YT *Telephone:* 01443 222111 *Fax:* 01443 237039

SPARROW, Sir JOHN Chairman, Horserace Betting Levy Board

Career: Morgan Grenfell Group 1963-88: director 1970-88; seconded as head of Central Policy Review Staff, Cabinet Office 1982-83; director and chairman various organisations, including chairman Process Plant EDC 1984-85, National Stud 1988-91; deputy chairman Short Brothers plc 1984-85; director Peterborough Development Corporation 1981-88; vice-chairman of Court London School of Economics 1984-93; chairman Horserace Betting Levy Board 1991- *Current non-Whitehall posts:* chairman Universities' Superannuation Scheme Ltd 1988-; National & Provincial Building Society 1989-: director 1989-, deputy chairman 1994-

Date of birth: 4 June 1933 *Education/professional qualifications:* Stationers' Company's School, London; London School of Economics, economics (BSc Econ 1954); FCA 1957 *Honours, decorations:* Kt 1984 *Marital status:* married Cynthia Naomi Whitehouse 1967 *Clubs:* Marylebone Cricket *Recreations:* cricket, crosswords, horseracing

Sir John Sparrow, Chairman, Horserace Betting Levy Board, 52 Grosvenor Gardens, London SW1W 0AU *Telephone:* 0171-333 0043 *Fax:* 0171-333 0041

SPEDDING, DAVID ROLLAND Chief, Secret Intelligence Service

Career: Secret Intelligence Service (MI6) 1967-: Chief 1994-

Date of birth: 7 March 1945 *Education/professional qualifications:* Sherborne School; Hertford College, Oxford, modern history (BA) *Honours, decorations:* OBE 1980, CVO 1984 *Marital status:* married; 2 sons

David R Spedding Esq, Chief, Secret Intelligence Service, PO Box 1300, London SE1 1BD

SPENCE, IAN RICHARD Director, International Division, Board of Inland Revenue Grade: 3

Career: Inland Revenue 1962-: assistant director finance division 1988-91, director international division 1991-

Date of birth: 15 October 1938 *Education/professional qualifications:* Jesus College, Cambridge, history (BA) *Marital status:* married; 2 daughters *Recreations:* opera, theatre, bridge, tennis

Ian R Spence Esq, Director, International Division, Board of Inland Revenue, Somerset House, London WC2R 1LB *Telephone:* 0171-438 6762 *Fax:* 0171-438 6396

SPENCER, Dr JONATHAN PAGE Under Secretary, Insurance Division, Department of Trade and Industry Grade: 3

Career: Department of [Trade and] Industry (D[T]I) 1974-: principal private secretary to secretaries of state 1982-83, policy planning unit 1983-85, minerals and metals (international steel negotiations) 1985-87; seconded to machinery of government division, Cabinet Office 1987-89; DTI 1989-: personnel management I 1989-91, under secretary insurance division 1991-

Date of birth: 24 April 1949 *Education/professional qualifications:* Bournemouth School; Downing College, Cambridge, natural sciences (BA 1970); Oxford University, metallurgy (D Phil 1974) *Marital status:* married Caroline Armitage 1976; 2 daughters, 1 son *Recreations:* making music, keeping house up and garden down

Dr Jonathan P Spencer, Under Secretary, Insurance Division, Department of Trade and Industry, 10-18 Victoria Street, London SW1H 0NN
Telephone: 0171-215 3120 *Fax:* 0171-215 3192

SPOTTISWOODE, CLARE MARY JOAN Director-General, Office of Gas Supply (OFGAS) Grade: 2

Career: HM Treasury 1977-80; Spottiswoode Trading/and Spottiswoode Ltd 1980-90: chairman and managing director 1984-90; freelance consultant 1990-93; director-general Office of Gas Supply 1993-

Date of birth: 20 March 1953 *Education/professional qualifications:* Cheltenham Ladies College; Clare College, Cambridge, mathematics, economics (BA 1975, MA); Yale University, USA, economics (MPhil 1977) *Marital status:* married Oliver William Richards 1977; 3 daughters, 1 son *Publications:* Quill (Century Hutchinson – CH 1985); Abacus (CH 1985) *Recreations:* theatre, opera, gardening, children

Ms Clare M J Spottiswoode, Director-General, Office of Gas Supply, Stockley House, 130 Wilton Road, London SW1V 1LQ
Telephone: 0171-828 9158 *Fax:* 0171-630 8164

SPURGEON, PETER GREGORY Director, Criminal Injuries Compensation Board/Authority Grade: 5

Career: Ministry of Defence 1958-62; Home Office 1962-: immigration officer 1962-67; parole unit 1967-73, probation department 1973-78, criminal policy department 1978-83, security branch 1983-86; chief inspector drugs branch 1986-90; head of fire services division 1990-92; director Criminal Injuries Compensation Board 1992-,/Authority 1994-

Date of birth: 23 March 1939 *Education/professional qualifications:* Sudbury Grammar School *Marital status:* married Jacqueline Holtam 1963; 1 daughter, 1 son *Recreations:* travel, guitar, swimming, reading

Peter G Spurgeon Esq, Director, Criminal Injuries Compensation Board/Authority, Morley House, 26-30 Holborn Viaduct, London EC1A 2JQ *Telephone:* 0171-842 6802 *Fax:* 0171-436 0804

SQUIRE, Air Vice-Marshal PETER TED Assistant Chief of the Air Staff, Ministry of Defence

Career: Royal Air Force (RAF) 1966-: training, flying, flying instruction and squadron posts 1966-80; student Royal Naval Staff College 1980; commanding officer (CO) 1 Squadron RAF Wittering 1981-83; briefing and presentation team, personal staff officer to air officer commanding (AOC)-in-chief HQ Strike

Command (STC) 1984-86; CO tri-national Tornado training establishment 1986-88; Ministry of Defence (MoD) 1988-91: air plans department 1988-89, director air offensive 1989-91; senior air staff officer HQ STC and deputy chief of staff operations UK air forces 1991-93; AOC No 1 Group 1993-94; assistant chief of air staff MoD 1994-
Education/professional qualifications: King's School, Bruton *Honours, decorations:* AFC 1979, DFC 1982
Recreations: cricket, golf

Air Vice-Marshal Peter Squire DFC AFC, Assistant Chief of the Air Staff, Ministry of Defence, Whitehall, London SW1A 2HB *Telephone:* 0171-218 6565 *Fax:* 0171-218 3834

STANLEY, JOHN MALLALIEU Under Secretary, Solicitors' Office, Department of Trade and Industry Grade: 3

Career: practising solicitor 1967-75; Department of [Trade and] Industry solicitors' office 1975-: assistant solicitor 1982-89, under secretary solicitors' office 1989-

Date of birth: 30 September 1941 *Education/professional qualifications:* Clare College, Cambridge, natural sciences; law (BA 1964, MA); solicitor 1967 *Marital status:* married Christine Mary Cunningham 1968; 2 sons, 1 daughter

John M Stanley Esq, Under Secretary, Solicitors' Office, Department of Trade and Industry, 10-18 Victoria St, London SW1H 0NN *Telephone:* 0171-215 3470 *Fax:* 0171-215 3141

STANLEY, MARTIN EDWARD Head of Vehicles, Metals and Minerals Division, Department of Trade and Industry Grade: 3

Career: Inland Revenue 1971-80; Department of Trade and Industry 1980-: principal private secretary to secretaries of state Nicholas Ridley 1990-91, Peter Lilley 1991-92; under secretary, head of vehicles divisions/vehicles, metals and minerals division 1992-

Date of birth: 1 November 1948 *Education/professional qualifications:* Royal Grammar School, Newcastle-upon-Tyne; Magdalen College, Oxford, chemistry and economics (BA 1970) *Marital status:* divorced; partner Janice Munday; 1 son from previous marriage *Clubs:* Hurlingham *Recreations:* travel, including walking and sailing

Martin Stanley Esq, Under Secretary, Department of Trade and Industry, 151 Buckingham Palace Road, London SW1W 9SS
Telephone: 0171-215 4193 *Fax:* 0171-215 4194

STANLEY, Dr PETER IAN Chief Executive, Central Science Laboratory Agency (Executive Agency) Grade: 3

Career: Ministry of Agriculture, Fisheries and Food 1970-: director Central Science Laboratory 1988-, chief executive 1992-

Date of birth: 25 June 1946 *Education/professional qualifications:* Dursley Grammar School, Gloucestershire; University College, London *Recreations:* ornithology, rugby, sailing

Dr Peter I Stanley, Chief Executive, Central Science Laboratory Agency, London Road, Slough, Berkshire SL3 7JH *Telephone:* 01753-534626 *Fax:* 01753 824058

STANTON, DAVID Director, Analytical Services Division, Department of Social Security Grade: 3

Career: HM Treasury 1974-75; seconded to Hong Kong Government 1975-77; Department of Employment/Employment Department Group 1977-92; director analytical services division Department of Social Security 1992-

Date of birth: 5 November 1942 *Education/professional qualifications:* Bishops Stortford College; Worcester College, Oxford, philosophy, politics and economics (BA 1965); London School of Economics, economics (MSc 1970) *Marital status:* married Isobel Joan Blair 1967; 1 son, 1 daughter *Recreations:* people, dogs and other animals, singing

David Stanton Esq, Director, Analytical Services Division, Department of Social Security, The Adelphi, 1-11 John Adam Street, London WC2N 6HT *Telephone:* 0171-962 8611 *Fax:* 0171-962 8795

STAPLE, GEORGE WARREN Director, Serious Fraud Office Grade: 2

Career: solicitor/partner Clifford Turner/Clifford Chance 1964-92; director Serious Fraud Office 1992- *Current non-Whitehall posts:* council member Law Society 1986-;

Date of birth: 13 September 1940 *Education/professional qualifications:* Haileybury College; solicitor *Marital status:* married Olivia Lowry 1968; 2 daughters, 2 sons *Clubs:* Brooks's; City of London; MCC *Recreations:* cricket, hill walking, gardening

George W Staple Esq, Director, Serious Fraud Office, Elm House, 10-16 Elm Street, London WC1X 0BJ *Telephone:* 0171-239 7272 *Fax:* 0171-837 1689

STAPLE, WILLIAM PHILIP Director-General, Panel on Takeovers and Mergers

Career: stockbroker Cazenove & Co 1973-81; NM Rothschild merchant bankers 1982-: director 1986-; director-general Panel on Takeovers and Mergers (protection of shareholders' interests) 1994-

Date of birth: 28 September 1947 *Education/professional qualifications:* Haileybury College, Hertford; College of Law (barrister 1970) *Marital status:* married Jennifer Frances Walker 1977: divorced; 1 son, 1 daughter *Clubs:* White's *Recreations:* skiing, tennis, theatre

William P Staple Esq, Director-General, Panel on Takeovers and Mergers, PO Box 226, Stock Exchange Building, London EC2P 2JX *Telephone:* 0171-382 9026 *Fax:* 0171-638 1554

STAPLETON, GUY Chief Executive, Intervention Board (Executive Agency) Grade: 3

Career: Ministry of Transport and Civil Aviation/of Aviation 1954-65: civil aviation assistant Rome embassy 1960-63, private secretary (PS) to national air traffic control services controller 1963-65; Ministry of Agriculture, Fisheries and Food (MAFF) 1965-74: assistant principal 1965-68: PS to joint parliamentary secretary 1967-68, principal 1968-73, assistant secretary 1973-81: Department of Prices and Consumer Protection 1974-76; under secretary 1981-: deputy head European Secretariat Cabinet Office 1982-85, director of establishments MAFF 1985-86; chief executive Intervention

Board (implementation market support measures of the EC common agricultural policy) 1986-

Date of birth: 10 November 1935 *Education/professional qualifications:* Hill Place School, Stow-on-the-Wold; Malvern College *Marital status:* single *Publications:* A Walk of Verse (Citizens Press 1961); 6 vols in Poets' England Series (Brentham Press 1977-93); Memories of Moreton (Drinkwater 1989); Four Shire Memories (1992) *Clubs:* Civil Service, Royal Over-seas League *Recreations:* local and family history, topographical verse

Guy Stapleton Esq, Chief Executive, Intervention Board, PO Box 69, Reading RG1 7QW *Telephone:* 01734 531700 *Fax:* 01734 393817

STEVENS, CLIFFORD DAVID Principal Establishment Officer, Welsh Office Grade: 3

Career: Foreign Office 1959-63; Board of Trade 1963-64; Department of Economic Affairs 1964-70; Civil Service Department (CSD) 1970-76; Cabinet Office 1976-78; CSD 1978-86; Welsh Office 1986-: director industry department 1987-94; principal establishment officer 1994-

Date of birth: 11 June 1941 *Education/professional qualifications:* Stationer's Company's School, London *Marital status:* married Mary Olive Bradford 1964; 1 son, 2 daughters *Recreations:* gardening, bowls

Clifford D Stevens Esq, Principal Establishment Officer, Welsh Office, Cathays Park, Cardiff CF1 3NQ *Telephone:* 01222-823307 *Fax:* 01222 825650

STEWART, G M Under Secretary, Criminal Justice, Licensing, Parole and Life Imprisonment, Scottish Office Home and Health Department Grade: 3

Mrs G M Stewart, Under Secretary, Scottish Office Home and Health Department, St Andrew's House, Edinburgh EH1 3DG *Telephone:* 0131-556 8400

STEWART, I Territorial (Wales and Central) and Support Services Director, Social Security Benefits Agency Grade: 4

I Stewart Esq, Territorial (Wales and Central) and Support Services Director, Social Security Benefits Agency, Quarry House, Quarry Hill, Leeds LS2 7UA *Telephone:* 01132 327836

STEWART, (JAMES) MORAY Second Permanent Under Secretary, Resources, Programmes and Finance, Ministry of Defence Grade: 1A

Career: Air Ministry/Ministry of Defence (MoD) 1962-: assistant secretary-general for defence planning and policy NATO 1984-86; deputy under secretary personnel and logistics 1986-88, defence procurement 1988-90, second permanent under secretary office of management and budget/resources and finance programmes 1990-

Date of birth: 21 June 1938 *Education/professional qualifications:* Marlborough College; Keele University, history and economics (BA) *Honours, decorations:* CB 1990 *Recreations:* reading, listening to music, walking

J M Stewart Esq CB, Second Permanent Under Secretary, Ministry of Defence, Whitehall, London SW1A 2HB *Telephone:* 0171-218 7115 *Fax:* 0171-218 2324

STIBBARD, PETER JACK Director of Statistics, Employment Department Group Grade: 3

Career: Kodak Ltd 1959-64; Thos Potterton Ltd 1964-66; Greater London Council 1966-68; Central Statistical Office 1968-82; HM Treasury 1982-84; under secretary statistics division 2, Department of Trade and Industry 1985-89; director of statistics Employment Department Group 1989-

Date of birth: 15 May 1936 *Education/professional qualifications:* Hull University (BSc Econ 1959); MIS 1963 *Marital status:* married Christine Fuller 1964; 2 daughters *Recreations:* family life, local environment

Peter J Stibbard Esq, Under Secretary, Employment Department Group, Caxton House, Tothill Street, London SW1H 9NF
Telephone: 0171-273 3000 *Fax:* 0171-273 5215

STOATE, RICHARD CHARLES Administrator, Midlands and Oxford Circuit, Court Service (Executive Agency) Grade: 4

Career: legal assistant Law Commission 1976-79; Lord Chancellor's Department (LCD) 1979-92: principal private secretary to LC 1983-87; head of criminal policy division Home Office 1992-95; administrator Midlands and Oxford circuit (management area's high, crown and county courts' business) LCD/Court Service 1995-

Date of birth: 5 November 1952 *Education/professional qualifications:* King's College School, Wimbledon, London; Christ's College, Cambridge, law (BA 1974, MA); barrister 1975 *Marital status:* separated; partner Samantha Jayne Maybury 1991-; 1 daughter; 1 daughter, 1 son from marriage *Recreations:* cricket, rugby, reading, theatre

Richard C Stoate Esq, Circuit Administrator, Midlands and Oxford Circuit,, Court Service, The Priory, 33 Bull Street, Birmingham B4 6DW *Telephone:* 0121-681 3200 *Fax:* 0121-681 3202

STOKER, JOHN FRANCIS Regional Director, Government Office for Merseyside, Departments of the Environment, Transport, Trade and Industry and Employment Grade: 3

Career: Department of Environment (DoE) 1973-83; Cabinet Office 1983-85; DoE 1985-: assistant secretary establishments, housing, environmental policy, finance 1985-92; under secretary, director Merseyside Task Force (economic, physical and environmental regeneration) 1992-94; regional director government office for Merseyside 1994- *Current non-Whitehall posts:* non-executive director Hanson Brick Division 1991-

Date of birth: 11 September 1950 *Education/professional qualifications:* King Edward's School, Birmingham; Brasenose College, Oxford, literae humaniores (BA 1972) *Marital status:* married Julie Puddicombe 1982 *Clubs:* Athenaeum, Liverpool; Middlesex County Cricket *Recreations:* music, travel, garden

John F Stoker Esq, Regional Director, Government Office for Merseyside, Graeme House, Derby Square, Liverpool L2 7SU
Telephone: 0151-227 4111 *Fax:* 0151-258 1154

STOW, (WILLIAM) BILL LLEWELLYN Head of European Community and Trade Relations Division, Department of Trade and Industry Grade: 3

Career: Department of Trade [and Industry] 1971-: 1st secretary (FS) UK delegation to Organisation for Economic Co-operation and Development, Paris 1980-83; international trade division 1983-85; FS UK permanent representation to EC, Brussels 1985-88; European policy division 1988-91; finance and resource management division 1991-94; under secretary, head of EC and trade relations division 1994-

Date of birth: 11 January 1948 *Education/professional qualifications:* Eastbourne Grammar School; Churchill College, Cambridge, history (BA 1970, MA) *Marital status:* married Rosemary Ellen 1976; 2 sons *Recreations:* cricket, hill and coast walking, birdwatching, reading history

W L Stow Esq, Under Secretary, Department of Trade and Industry, Ashdown House, 123 Victoria Street, London SW1E 6RB *Telephone:* 0171-215 6153 *Fax:* 0171-215 6131

STRACHAN, VALERIE PATRICIA MARIE Chairman, HM Customs and Excise Grade: 1

Career: assistant principal HM Customs and Excise (C&E) 1961-64, Department of Economic Affairs 1964-66, Home Office 1966; principal C&E 1966-72, HM Treasury (HMT) 1972-74; C&E 1974-85: assistant secretary 1974-80, commissioner, director VAT control 1980-83, director organisation 1983-85; head of joint management unit HMT/Cabinet Office 1985-87; C&E 1987-: deputy chairman, principal establishments and finance officer 1987-89, director-general 1989-93, chairman 1993- *Current non-Whitehall posts:* board of companions Institute of Management; management committee Royal National Lifeboat Institute

Date of birth: 10 January 1940 *Education/professional qualifications:* Newland High School, Hull; Manchester University, politics and modern history (BA 1961) *Honours, decorations:* CB 1991 *Marital status:* married John 1965; 1 son, 1 daughter *Clubs:* Reform *Recreations:* Scottish country dancing

Mrs Valerie Strachan CB, Chairman, HM Customs and Excise, New King's Beam House, 22 Upper Ground, London SE1 9PJ
Telephone: 0171-865 5001 *Fax:* 0171-865 5048

STRATHNAVER, EILEEN Special Adviser to President of Board of Trade

Career: personal assistant 1986-90, later special adviser to Michael Heseltine, as Secretary of State for Environment 1990-92, as President of Board of Trade, Department of Trade and Industry 1992-

Lady Strathnaver, Special Adviser, Department of Trade and Industry, Ashdown House, 123 Victoria Street, London SW1E 6RB *Telephone:* 0171-215 6620 *Fax:* 0171-215 6876

STUART, (NICHOLAS) NICK W Deputy Secretary, Director of Resources and Strategy, Employment Department Group Grade: 2

Career: Department of Education and Science (DES) 1964-73: assistant principal 1964-68, private secretary (PS) to Minister for Arts Jenny Lee 1968-69, principal 1969-73; PS to head of civil service, to prime ministers Edward Heath, Harold Wilson and James Callaghan 1973-76; assistant secretary DES 1976-78, member cabinet of European Commission president Roy Jenkins 1978-81; DES 1981-92: under secretary (schools) 1981-85, principal finance officer 1985-87, deputy secretary schools policy 1987-92; director of resources and strategy Employment Department Group 1992-

Date of birth: 2 October 1942 *Education/professional qualifications:* Harrow School; Christ Church, Oxford, modern history (BA 1963, MA) *Honours, decorations:* CB 1990 *Marital status:* married Susan J Fletcher 1974; 2 daughters, 1 son *Recreations:* allotment, collecting antiques

Nick W Stuart Esq CB, Deputy Secretary, Employment Department Group, Caxton House, Tothill Street, London SW1H 9NF
Telephone: 0171-273 5763 *Fax:* 0171-273 5030

STUART-SMITH, The Rt Hon Sir MURRAY (The Rt Hon Lord Justice Stuart-Smith) Commissioner, Security Service Tribunal and Intelligence Services Tribunal

Career: barrister 1952-; crown court recorder 1972-81; high court judge 1981-86; presiding judge western circuit 1983-87; lord justice of appeal 1988-; commissioner Security Service Tribunal (investigation of public complaints against the security service) 1989-, Intelligence Services Tribunal 1994- *Current non-Whitehall posts:* Lord Justice of Appeal 1988-

Date of birth: 18 November 1927 *Education/professional qualifications:* Radley College; Corpus Christi College, Cambridge, law (MA 1951, LLM 1950); Gray's Inn (barrister 1952) *Honours, decorations:* QC 1970; Bencher 1977; Kt 1981; PC 1988 *Marital status:* married Joan Elizabeth Mary Motion 1953; 3 daughters, 3 sons *Clubs:* Beefsteak *Recreations:* cello-playing, shooting, building, bridge

The Rt Hon Lord Justice Stuart-Smith, Commissioner, Security Service Tribunal, PO Box 18, London SE1 0TZ; Intelligence Services Tribunal, PO Box 4823, London SW1A 9XD
Telephone: 0171-273 4095 (SST); 0171-273 4383 (IST)

STUBBS, Sir WILLIAM HAMILTON Chief Executive, Further Education Funding Council for England Grade: 1A

Career: research Arizona University 1963-64, Shell Oil, San Francisco, USA 1964-67; teacher 1967-72; assistant director of education Carlisle 1972-74, Cumbria 1974-76; Inner London Education Authority 1977-88: education officer and chief executive 1982-88; chief executive Polytechnics and Colleges Funding Council 1988-92, Further Education Funding Council 1992- *Current non-Whitehall posts:* trustee Thames/LWT Telethon 1987-

Date of birth: 5 November 1937 *Education/professional qualifications:* Workington Grammar School; St Aloysius College, Glasgow; Glasgow University, chemistry (BSc 1959, PhD 1963) *Honours, decorations:* Kt 1994 *Marital status:* married Marie Margaret Pierce 1963; 3 daughters

Sir William Stubbs, Chief Executive, Further Education Funding Council, Cheylesmore House, Quinton Road, Coventry CV1 2WT
Telephone: 01203 863194 *Fax:* 01203 863199

SUGDEN, ALEC Assistant Comptroller, Intellectual Property Policy, Patent Office (Executive Agency)

Career: electronic engineer International Computers and Tabulators 1959-61; Patent Office 1961-: examiner 1961-69; senior examiner 1969-77; principal examiner 1977-84: head of international classification documentation 1977-79, in charge of policy 1980-84; superintending examiner, head of industrial property policy 1984-91; assistant comptroller, head of intellectual property policy directorate (international and EU harmonisation of intellectual property laws; UK policy) 1991-

Date of birth: 14 January 1936 *Education/professional qualifications:* Lowestoft Grammar School; Downing College, Cambridge, natural sciences (BA 1959, MA) *Marital status:* married Valerie Jones 1963; 2 sons

Alec Sugden Esq, Assistant Comptroller, Patent Office, Hazlitt House, 45 Southampton Buildings, London WC2A 1AR *Telephone:* 0171-438 4788 *Fax:* 0171-438 4713

SULIVAN, Major General TIM(OTHY) JOHN Director-General, Land Warfare, Ministry of Defence
Education/professional qualifications: civil engineering (BSc 1971) *Honours, decorations:* CBE 1991

Major General T J Sulivan CBE, Director-General Land Warfare, Ministry of Defence, Upavon Barracks, Pewsey, Wiltshire SN9 6BE *Telephone:* 01980 633371

SULLENS, KEITH Assistant Paymaster General and Chief Executive, Paymaster General's Office (Executive Agency) Grade: 5

Career: Ministry of Pensions and National Insurance 1962-64; Paymaster General's Office 1964-: head of pensions division 1980-82; pension services manager 1982-87; corporate planning manager 1987-89; director banking services and information technology 1989-90; establishment officer 1990-91; assistant paymaster general/chief executive 1991-

Date of birth: 9 May 1944 *Education/professional qualifications:* Hove Grammar School *Marital status:* married Penelope Judith Simmons 1968; 2 sons, 1 daughter *Recreations:* tennis, squash, badminton, soccer

Keith Sullens Esq, Assistant Paymaster General and Chief Executive, Paymaster General's Office, Sutherland House, Russell Way, Crawley, West Sussex RH10 1UH *Telephone:* 01293 560999 *Fax:* 01293 530942

SUMMERS, NICHOLAS Under Secretary, School Funding Branch, Department for Education Grade: 3

Career: Ministry of Education/Department of Education and Science (DES) 1961-74: private secretary to Minister for Arts 1965-66; Cabinet Office 1974-76; DES/Department for Education 1976-: teachers' branch 1976-80, school curriculum and examinations branch 1980-86, under secretary 1981-: further and higher education branch 3 1986-94, student affairs branch 1994; school funding 1994-

Date of birth: 11 July 1939 *Education/professional qualifications:* Tonbridge School; Corpus Christi College, Oxford, literae humaniores (BA 1961, MA); FRSA 1993 *Marital status:* married Marian Elizabeth Ottley 1965; 4 sons *Recreations:* family, music

Nicholas Summers Esq, Under Secretary, Department for Education, Sanctuary Buildings, Great Smith Street, London SW1P 3ET *Telephone:* 0171-925 5000 *Fax:* 0171-925 6965

SUMMERTON, Dr NEIL WILLIAM Under Secretary, Water Directorate, Department of the Environment Grade: 3

Career: Ministry of Transport 1966-69; King's College, London 1969-74: personal assistant to principal 1969-71, assistant secretary 1971-74; Department of Environment 1974-: assistant secretary 1978-85: housing policy and public expenditure 1978-81, right to buy implementation 1981-83, defective housing 1983-85; under secretary 1985-: planning and development control directorate 1985-88, local government finance policy directorate 1988-91, water directorate 1991- *Current non-Whitehall posts:* director London Christian Housing plc

Date of birth: 5 April 1942 *Education/professional qualifications:* Wellington Grammar School, Shropshire; King's College, London, history (BA 1963), war studies (PhD 1970) *Marital status:* married Pauline Webb 1965; 2 sons *Publications:* A Noble Task: Eldership and Ministry in the Local Church (Paternoster Press 1987, 94) *Recreations:* historical, ethical and theological writing

Dr Neil W Summerton, Under Secretary, Department of the Environment, 43 Marsham Street, London SW1P 3PY *Telephone:* 0171-276 8259 *Fax:* 0171-276 8639

SUTCLIFFE, P M Deputy Chief Scientist (Research and Technology), Ministry of Defence Grade: 3

P M Sutcliffe Esq, Deputy Chief Scientist (Research and Technology), Ministry of Defence, Main Building, Whitehall, London SW1A 2HB *Telephone:* 0171-218 6237

SUTHERLAND, E R **Parliamentary Counsel, Parliamentary Counsel Office** Grade: 3

E R Sutherland CB Esq, Parliamentary Counsel, Parliamentary Counsel Office, 36 Whitehall, London SW1A 2AY *Telephone:* 0171-210 6633

SUTTON, Dr (HOWARD) MICHAEL **Director, Trade and Industry, Government Office for the West Midlands** Grade: 4

Career: Department of Trade and Industry (DTI) 1970-: Warren Spring Laboratory 1970-88: head of planning and marketing 1978-85, deputy director 1985-88; head of shipbuilding and marine engineering 1988-91, of single market campaign 1991-93, of mechanical engineering 1993-94; trade and industry director Government Office for the West Midlands 1994-

Date of birth: 12 November 1942 *Education/professional qualifications:* Skegness Grammar School; Edinburgh University, chemistry (BSc 1965), physical chemistry (PhD 1968); CChem, FRSC 1977 *Marital status:* married Diane 1967; 1 daughter, 1 son *Recreations:* music, writing

Dr H M Sutton, Trade and Industry Director, Government Office for the West Midlands, 77 Paradise Circus, Queensway, Birmingham B1 2DY *Telephone:* 0121-212 5210 *Fax:* 0121-212 5063

SWEETMAN, JOHN FRANCIS **Clerk of Committees, House of Commons** Grade: 2

Career: army national service 1949-51; House of Commons Department of the Clerk 1954-: clerk of select committees on nationalised industries 1962-65, on science and technology 1970; second clerk of select committees 1979-83; clerk of the overseas office 1983-87; clerk assistant 1987-90; clerk of committees (overall direction of all staff of select committees, advice on working of committee system, oversight of all administrative matters affecting committees) 1990-

Date of birth: 31 October 1930 *Education/professional qualifications:* Cardinal Vaughan School, London; St Catharine's College, Cambridge, law (BA 1954, MA) *Honours, decorations:* TD 1964, CB 1990 *Marital status:* married Celia Elizabeth Nield 1983; 1 daughter, 3 sons (2 from previous marriage) *Clubs:* Marylebone Cricket

John F Sweetman Esq CB TD, Clerk of Committees, House of Commons, London SW1A 0AA *Telephone:* 0171-219 3313 *Fax:* 0171-219 6864

SWIFT, JOHN ANTHONY **Rail Regulator, Office of the Rail Regulator**

Career: barrister in competition law; special adviser on railway privatisation regulatory framework to Secretary of State for Transport 1993; rail regulator 1993-

Date of birth: 11 July 1940 *Education/professional qualifications:* Birkenhead School; University College, Oxford, jurisprudence (BA 1963, MA); Inner Temple (barrister 1965, bencher 1992) *Honours, decorations:* QC 1981 *Marital status:* married Jane Carol Sharples 1972; 1 son, 1 daughter *Clubs:* Reform *Recreations:* golf, walking, gardening

John Swift Esq QC, Rail Regulator, Office of the Rail Regulator, 1 Waterhouse Square, 138-142 Holborn, London EC1N 2SU *Telephone:* 0171-282 2000 *Fax:* 0171-282 2041

SWINNERTON, Dr CLIVE JERRY Director of Water Management, National Rivers Authority

Career: senior assistant hydrologist Great Ouse River Authority 1971-74; Wessex Water 1974-88: regional hydrologist, hydrologist 1974-78, resource planning manager 1978-84, Somerset divisional manager 1984-88; National Rivers Authority 1988-: regional general manager Wessex Rivers shadow unit 1988-89; technical director/director of water management 1989-

Date of birth: 27 February 1945 *Education/professional qualifications:* King Henry VIII Grammar School, Abergavenny; University College of Wales, Swansea, civil engineering (BSc 1967); Imperial College, London, engineering hydrology (MSc DIC 1968), water resources (PhD 1971); MICE; MIWEM; CEng *Marital status:* married Janet Mary Thomas 1968; 2 daughters *Recreations:* sport, running, cycling, skiing, gym, golf, fishing

Dr Clive J Swinnerton, Director of Water Management, National Rivers Authority, Rivers House, Waterside Drive, Aztec West, Almondsbury, Bristol BS12 4UD *Telephone:* 01179 624400 *Fax:* 01179 624409

SZÉLL, PATRICK JOHN Head of International Environmental Law Division, Department of the Environment Grade: 3

Career: Ministry of Housing and Local Government/Department of the Environment 1969-: legal assistant (LA) 1969-73; senior LA 1973-85; head of international environmental law division 1985-: assistant solicitor 1985-92, under secretary 1992-

Date of birth: 10 February 1942 *Education/professional qualifications:* Reading School; Trinity College, Dublin, law (BA LLB 1964, MA 1967); Inner Temple (barrister 1966) *Marital status:* married Olivia Brain 1967; 2 sons, 1 daughter *Recreations:* travel, butterflies, hockey

Patrick Széll Esq, Under Secretary, Legal Directorate, Department of the Environment, 2 Marsham Street, London SW1P 3EB *Telephone:* 0171-276 4230 *Fax:* 0171-276 6658

T

TAIT, JOHN Deputy Chief Nursing Officer, Nursing Division, Department of Health Grade: 4

Career: National Health Service -1973; Department of Health 1973-: nursing officer (NO) 1973-80; principal NO 1980-92; deputy chief NO Department of Health 1992-

Date of birth: 22 January 1935 *Education/professional qualifications:* RMN; RGN *Honours, decorations:* OBE *Marital status:* married; 4 *Recreations:* travel, walking, music, opera

John Tait OBE, Deputy Chief Nursing Officer, Department of Health, Richmond House, 79 Whitehall, London SW1A 2NS *Telephone:* 0171-210 5620 *Fax:* 0171-210 5570

TANFIELD, JENNIFER Librarian, House of Commons Grade: 3

Career: House of Commons Library 1963-: library clerk 1963-72; head of economic affairs section 1972-77, of statistical section 1977-87, of parliamentary division 1987-91; deputy librarian (establishment officer) 1991-93, librarian 1993-

Date of birth: 19 July 1941 *Education/professional qualifications:* School of SS Mary and Anne, Abbots Bromley; London School of Economics (BSc Econ 1962) *Marital status:* single *Publications:* In Parliament 1939-50 (HMSO 1991) *Recreations:* theatre, opera, travel, squash

Miss Jennifer Tanfield, Librarian, House of Commons Library, London SW1A 0AA *Telephone:* 0171-219 3635 *Fax:* 0171-219 2518

TATE, Dr (EDWARD) NICHOLAS Chief Executive, School Curriculum and Assessment Authority Grade: 3

Career: secondary school history teacher 1966-71; lecturer Birmingham College of Education (CE) 1972-74; lecturer, senior lecturer Moray House CE, Edinburgh 1974-88; National Curriculum Council 1989-91; School Examinations and Assessment Council 1991-93; School Curriculum and Assessment Authority 1993- chief executive 1994-

Date of birth: 18 December 1943 *Education/professional qualifications:* Huddersfield New College; Balliol College, Oxford, modern history (BA 1964); Liverpool University, history (MA 1976, PhD 1984) *Marital status:* married Nadya 1973; 2 daughters, 1 son *Publications:* Pizarro and the Incas (Longman 1982); Modern World History (Hodder and Stoughton [H&S] 1989); People and Events in the Modern World (H&S 1989); A History of the Modern World (Federal 1994)

Dr E N Tate, Chief Executive, School Curriculum and Assessment Authority, Newcombe House, 45 Notting Hill Gate, London W11 3JB *Telephone:* 0171-243 9376 *Fax:* 0171-243 1060

TAYLOR, A R Chief Crown Prosecutor, North West, Crown Prosecution Service Grade: 4

A R Taylor Esq, Chief Crown Prosecutor, North West, Crown Prosecution Service, PO Box 377, Sunlight House, Quay Street, Manchester M60 3LU *Telephone:* 0161-832 8628 *Fax:* 0161-834 0677

TAYLOR, BRIAN ARTHUR EDWARD Assistant Under Secretary, Civilian Management (Policy), Ministry of Defence Grade: 3

Career: Ministry of Defence (MoD) 1965-81: assistant private secretary (PS) to secretary of state 1969-70; PS to chief of air staff 1973-75; assistant secretary 1977-86: head of management services 1977-79, of naval personnel division 1979-81; student Royal College of Defence Studies 1982; central policy review staff Cabinet Office 1983; MoD 1984-91: head of civilian management 1984-86; assistant under secretary 1986-92: quartermaster 1986-88, air (procurement executive) 1988-91; under secretary personnel policy group HM Treasury 1992-94; assistant under secretary civilian management policy MoD 1994- *Current non-Whitehall posts:* non-executive director North British Newsprint Ltd 1988-

Date of birth: 10 January 1942 *Education/professional qualifications:* St Benedict's School, Ealing, London; Corpus Christi College, Oxford, literae humaniores (BA 1965, MA); Royal College of Defence Studies *Recreations:* sport, music, reading

Brian A E Taylor Esq, Assistant Under Secretary, Ministry of Defence, Northumberland House, Northumberland Avenue, London WC2N 5BP *Telephone:* 0171-218 4527 *Fax:* 0171-218 4020

TAYLOR, DAVID WILSON Chief Executive, English Partnerships

Career: managing director Lancashire Enterprises 1982-89, Amec Developments 1989-93; chief executive English Partnerships (Urban Regeneration Agency) 1993-

Date of birth: 9 May 1950 *Education/professional qualifications:* Galashiels Academy; Dundee University, architecture (I Dip 1973); Architectural Association, architecture (diploma 1976), urban and regional planning (postgraduate diploma 1977) *Marital status:* married Brenda Elizabeth; 2 sons *Recreations:* sport

David W Taylor Esq, Chief Executive, English Partnerships, 3 The Parks, Lodge Lane, Newton-le-Willows, Merseyside WA12 0JQ *Telephone:* 0194-229 6900 *Fax:* 0194-229 6927

TAYLOR, HUGH HENDERSON Head of Civil Service Employer Group, Cabinet Office Grade: 3

Career: Home Office 1972-93: principal private secretary to Home Secretary 1983-85; seconded to Cabinet Office (CO) 1987-91; head of prison service personnel division 1992-93; under secretary, head of management development/civil service employer group CO 1993-

Date of birth: 22 March 1950 *Education/professional qualifications:* Brentwood School; Emmanuel College, Cambridge, English (BA 1972) *Marital status:* married Diane Heather Baron 1988; 2 daughters *Recreations:* reading, opera

Hugh H Taylor Esq, Under Secretary, Cabinet Office, Horse Guards Road, London SW1P 3AL *Telephone:* 0171-270 6129

Government Departments

see page 372

TAYLOR, Dr JOHN FREDERICK Chief Medical Adviser, Department of Transport Grade: 4

Career: medical adviser British Rail 1960-64; medical officer HM Treasury medical service 1964-66; physician Moscow embassy 1966-68; medical adviser Civil Service Department 1968-72; Department of Transport 1972-: head of medical advisory branch Driver and Vehicle Licensing Centre 1972-86, chief medical adviser 1986-

Date of birth: 19 August 1930 *Education/professional qualifications:* Wimbledon College, London; King's College, London University and St George's Hospital (MB BS 1957); Royal Institute of Public Health and Hygiene, occupational medicine (DIH 1960); Royal College of Physicians, occupational medicine MFOM 1978, FFOM 1985; FRCP 1992 *Honours, decorations:* CBE 1991 *Marital status:* divorced; 1 son, 1 daughter *Publications:* contributor to Recent Advances in Occupational Medicine (Churchill Livingston 1987) *Clubs:* Royal Society of Medicine *Recreations:* history, historic buildings

Dr John F Taylor CBE, Chief Medical Adviser, Department of Transport, 2 Marsham Street, London SW1P 3EB *Telephone:* 0171-276 4039 *Fax:* 0171-276 0818

TAYLOR, KEVIN CHRISTOPHER Assistant Chief Veterinary Officer, Minister of Agriculture, Fisheries and Food Grade: 4

Career: private practice veterinary surgeon 1960-70; Ministry of Agriculture, Fisheries and Food veterinary service 1970-: veterinary head of notifiable diseases section 1986-91; assistant chief veterinary officer 1991-

Date of birth: 6 August 1937 *Education/professional qualifications:* Birkenhead School; Liverpool University, veterinary science (BVSc 1960); MRCVS 1960; Edinburgh University, veterinary state medicine (DVSM 1973) *Marital status:* married Jean Bradshaw 1961; 1 daughter, 1 son *Recreations:* photography, railway history and preservation, music, theatre, hillwalking

Kevin C Taylor Esq, Assistant Chief Veterinary Officer, Ministry of Agriculture, Fisheries and Food, Government Buildings, Hook Rise South, Tolworth, Surbiton, Surrey KT6 7NF *Telephone:* 0181-330 8056 *Fax:* 0181-337 3640

TEBBIT, KEVIN REGINALD Chief Inspector, Foreign and Commonwealth Office

Career: Foreign and Commonwealth Office 1982-: head of economic relations department 1992-94; assistant under secretary and chief inspector 1994-

Date of birth: 18 October 1946 *Education/professional qualifications:* St John's College, Cambridge (BA 1969)

Kevin R Tebbit Esq, Assistant Under Secretary, Foreign and Commonwealth Office, King Charles Street, London SW1A 2AH *Telephone:* 0171-270 3000

TEMPLE, S R Telecommunications Division, Department of Trade and Industry Grade: 4

Career: Ministry of Posts and Telecommunications; Home Office; Department of Trade and Industry: telecommunications division

Date of birth: 21 November 1944 *Education/professional qualifications:* MSc, CEng FIEE *Marital status:* married; 3 *Publications:* technical papers; ETSI a Revolution in European Telecommunications Standards Making

S R Temple Esq, Telecommunications, Department of Trade and Industry, 151 Buckingham Palace Road, London SW1 9SS *Telephone:* 0171-215 5000 *Fax:* 0171-215 1971

TERRY, Air Vice-Marshal COLIN GEORGE Chief of Staff, Headquarters Logistics Command, Ministry of Defence Grade: 3

Career: Royal Air Force (RAF) 1962-: station commander RAF Abingdon 1986-88; student Royal College of Defence Studies 1989; Ministry of Defence 1990-: director support management and senior director Harrogate 1990-92, director-general support management RAF 1993-95; chief of staff HQ Logistics Command 1995-

Date of birth: 8 August 1943 *Education/professional qualifications:* RAF College; Imperial College, engineering (BSc); CEng; FRAeS; ACGI *Honours, decorations:* OBE *Recreations:* sailing, fishing

Air Vice-Marshal C G Terry OBE, Chief of Staff, Headquarters Logistics Command, RAF Brampton, Huntingdon, Cambridgeshire PE18 8QL *Telephone and Fax:* 01480 52151

THEW, ROSEMARY CONSTANCE EVELYN West Midlands Regional Director, Employment Service Grade: 5

Career: Lord Chancellor's Department 1967-70; Inland Revenue 1970-79, Employment Department Group 1979-: West Midlands regional director 1995-

Date of birth: 3 November 1949 *Education/professional qualifications:* Preston Manor County Grammar School, Wembley *Marital status:* single *Recreations:* reading, golf

Miss Rosemary C E Thew, Regional Director, West Midlands Employment Service, 2 Duchess Place, Hagley Road, Edgbaston, Birmingham *Telephone:* 0121-456 1144 *Fax:* 0121-452 5412

THOMAS, KEITH JOHN Director of Highways, Welsh Office Grade: 4

Career: British Transport Docks Board 1956-69; Ministry of Public Buildings and Works/Property Services Agency, Department of Environment 1969-88: civil engineer (CE) 1969-77; principal CE 1977-80; area officer east Wales 1980-83, Colchester 1983-85; deputy director southern region 1985-88; director of highways Welsh Office 1988-

Date of birth: 26 December 1939 *Education/professional qualifications:* Cardiff High School; University College, Cardiff, civil engineering (BSc 1963); FICE 1985; FIHT 1988; FCS 1993 *Marital status:* married Vivienne Ann Weare 1962; 4 sons *Clubs:* Civil Service *Recreations:* squash, windsurfing

Keith J Thomas Esq, Director of Highways, Welsh Office, Government Buildings, Ty Glas Road, Llanishen, Cardiff CF4 5PL *Telephone:* 01222 761456 *Fax:* 01222 747558

"Next Steps" Executive Agencies

see page 875

THOMAS, MICHAEL CHRISTOPHER PRYCE Legal Adviser, Department of Transport/Treasury Solicitor's Department Grade: 3

Career: solicitor 1976-79; Ministry of Agriculture, Fisheries and Food (MAFF) 1980-86: legal assistant (LA) 1980-85, senior LA 1985-86; Law Officers' Department 1986-88; MAFF 1988-92; principal assistant solicitor Treasury Solicitor's Department/legal adviser Department of Transport 1993-

Date of birth: 31 October 1949 *Education/professional qualifications:* Barry Boys' Comprehensive School, Glamorgan; St John's College, Oxford, philosophy, politics and economics (BA 1971); Sussex University, international relations (MA 1972); Law Society (solicitor 1976) *Marital status:* married Pauline Marie Buckman 1978 *Clubs:* ICA *Recreations:* theatre, music

Michael C P Thomas Esq, Legal Adviser, Department of Transport, 2 Marsham Street, London SW1P 3EB *Telephone:* 0171-276 5700 *Fax:* 0171-276 3330

THOMAS, Rear Admiral MICHAEL RICHARD President of the Ordnance Board and Director-General Technical Services, Procurement Executive, Ministry of Defence

Career: naval assistant to chief of fleet support 1985-87; production director Portsmouth Dockyard 1987-88; superintendent ships Devonport, director-general ship refitting 1989-92; captain HMS Drake 1992-93; president of Ordnance Board, director-general technical services procurement executive Ministry of Defence 1993-

Date of birth: 11 February 1942 *Education/professional qualifications:* Latymer Upper School, London; Royal Naval Engineering College Manadon, electrical engineering (BScEng) FIEE 1982, CEng 1983; FIMgt 1986; MInst D 1992 *Recreations:* rugby management, classic cars, scouting management

Rear Admiral Michael R Thomas, President of the Ordnance Board, Procurement Executive, Ministry of Defence, Empress State Building, Lillie Road, London SW6 1TR *Telephone:* 0171-824 2800

THOMAS, PATRICIA ANNE Vice-Chairman and Commissioner for Local Administration in England (Local Government Ombudsman)

Career: law assistant lecturer, lecturer Leeds University 1962-68: teaching fellow Illinois University, USA 1963-64; Lancashire Polytechnic 1973-85: senior lecturer 1973-75, principal lecturer 1975-78, head of law school 1978-85, professor 1985; member Greater Manchester and Lancashire rent assessment panel 1977-85: vice-chairman 1984, chairman 1985; chairman Blackpool Supplementary Benefit Appeal Tribunal 1980-85; Commission for Local Administration in England 1985-: commissioner 1985-, vice-chairman for north and north midlands 1993-

Date of birth: 3 April 1940 *Education/professional qualifications:* Mitcham County Grammar School for Girls; King's College, London, law (LLB 1961, LLM 1962) *Marital status:* married Joseph Glyn 1968; 2 daughters, 1 son *Publications:* Law of Evidence (Cracknell's Companion) 1972 *Recreations:* walking, family, friends

Mrs Patricia Thomas, Vice-Chairman, Commission for Local Administration in England, Beverley House, 17 Shipton Road, York YO3 6FZ *Telephone:* 01904 630151 *Fax:* 01904 624058

THOMPSON, Dr JANET Director-General, Forensic Science Service (Executive Agency) Grade: 3

Career: Home Office 1971-: head of emergency planning division 1982-87, of prison service management services 1987-88; director-general Forensic Science Service 1988-

Date of birth: 23 October 1941 *Education/professional qualifications:* North London Collegiate School; Brighton College of Technology, applied physics (BSc 1963); Somerville College, Oxford, physics (DPhil 1968) *Marital status:* divorced; 1 daughter, 2 sons *Recreations:* family life, gardening, riding

Dr Janet Thompson, Director-General, Forensic Science Service, Home Office, 50 Queen Anne's Gate, London SW1H 9AT
Telephone: 0171-273 2167 *Fax:* 0171-273 2256

THOMPSON, PETER KENNETH JAMES Solicitor to Departments of Health and Social Security Grade: 2

Career: private practice barrister 1961-73; Law Commission; Lord Chancellor's Department 1974-83; Department of [Health and] Social Security (DH/SS) 1983-: under secretary 1983-; solicitor DH and DSS 1989-

Date of birth: 30 July 1937 *Education/professional qualifications:* Christ's College, Cambridge, law (MA, LLB); Lincoln's Inn (barrister) 1961

Peter K J Thompson Esq, Solicitor, Departments of Health and Social Security, New Court, 48 Carey Street, London WC2A 2LS *Telephone:* 0171-412 1404 *Fax:* 0171-412 1501

THORNTON, NEIL ROSS Under Secretary, Exports to Europe and the Americas, Department of Trade and Industry Grade: 3

Career: Ministry of Posts and Telecommunications 1971-75; private secretary (PS) to permanent secretary Department of Industry 1975-79; principal HM Treasury 1979-81; Department of [Trade and] Industry 1981-: assistant secretary 1984-90: principal PS to secretaries of state 1988-90; under secretary Europe division 1990-93, exports to Europe and the Americas 1993-

Date of birth: 11 February 1950 *Education/professional qualifications:* Sedbergh School, Cumbria; Pembroke College, Cambridge, engineering (BA 1971, MA) *Marital status:* married Christine Boyes 1977; 2 daughters *Recreations:* literature, choral singing, golf

Neil R Thornton Esq, Under Secretary, Department of Trade and Industry, Kingsgate House, 66-74 Victoria Street, London SW1E 6SW
Telephone: 0171-215 8120 *Fax:* 0171-215 4743

TILT, RICHARD Director of Security and Programmes, HM Prison Service (Executive Agency) Grade: 3

Career: HM Prison Service (HMPS): assistant governor Wellingborough borstal 1967-71; tutor Wakefield officers' training school and staff college 1971-74; governor Pollington borstal 1974-75; deputy governor Ranby 1975-78, Gartree 1978-80 prisons 1978-80; governor Bedford prison 1980-82; head of manpower 1982-84; governor Gartree prison 1984-88; deputy regional director Midlands 1988-89; head of industrial relations 1989-92; head of finance police department Home Office 1992-94; under secretary director of security and services HMPS 1994-95, of security and programmes 1995-

Date of birth: 11 March 1944 *Education/professional qualifications:* King's School, Worcester; Nottingham University, social administration (BA 1965); Open University, industrial relations (diploma 1978) *Honours, decorations:* Churchill Fellow 1991 *Marital status:* married Kate 1966; 2 sons, 1 daughter *Recreations:* walking, reading, theatre

Richard Tilt Esq, Director of Security and Programmes, HM Prison Service, Cleland House, Page Street, London SW1P 4LN *Telephone:* 0171-217 6393 *Fax:* 0171-217 6403

TIMMS, KATE **Principal Finance Officer, Ministry of Agriculture, Fisheries and Food** Grade: 3

Career: agricultural counsellor Paris embassy 1984-88; under secretary Ministry of Agriculture, Fisheries and Food (MAFF) 1988-89; agriculture minister UK permanent representation to EC 1990-95; principal finance officer MAFF 1995-

Date of birth: 8 October 1944

Ms Kate Timms, Principal Finance Officer, Ministry of Agriculture, Fisheries and Food, 19-29 Woburn Place, London WC1H 0LU *Telephone:* 0171-917 3600

TOMLINSON, MICHAEL JOHN **Director of Inspection, Office for Standards in Education (OFSTED)** Grade: 4

Career: chemistry teacher, head of department 1965-77; seconded as ICI schools/industry liaison officer 1977; Department of/for Education [and Science], HM Schools Inspectorate/Office for Standards in Education 1978-: staff inspector, chief inspector; deputy director of inspection 1992-94, director of inspection 1995-

Date of birth: 17 October 1942 *Education/professional qualifications:* Bournemouth School for Boys; King's College, Durham, chemistry (BSc 1964); Nottingham University, education (PGCE 1965) *Marital status:* married Maureen Janet Tupling 1965; 1 son, 1 daughter *Publications:* New Movements in the Study and Teaching of Chemistry (Temple-Smith 1975); Organic Chemistry: A Problem-Solving Approach (Bell and Hyman – B&H 1977); Mechanisms in Organic Chemistry (B&H 1978) *Recreations:* gardening, food and wine

Michael J Tomlinson Esq, Director of Inspection, Office for Standards in Education, Elizabeth House, York Road, London SE1 7PH *Telephone:* 0171-421 6786 *Fax:* 0171-421 6707

TREADGOLD, SYDNEY WILLIAM **Secretary, Financial Reporting Council**

Career: RAF 1951-53; chartered accountant 1954-62; assistant finance officer Liverpool University 1963-65; principal Ministry of Aviation 1965-67, Ministry of Technology 1967-71; assistant secretary Department of Trade and Industry (DTI) 1972-78; under secretary Price Commission 1978-79, DTI 1979-89; member Accounting Standards Task Group 1989-90; secretary Financial Reporting Council 1990-

Date of birth: 10 May 1933 *Education/professional qualifications:* Larkmead School, Abingdon; ACA 1960; FCA 1970; IPFA 1987 *Marital status:* married Elizabeth White 1961; 2 sons

Sydney Treadgold Esq, Secretary, Financial Reporting Council, Holborn Hall, 100 Gray's Inn Road, London WC1X 8AL *Telephone:* 0171-404 8818 *Fax:* 0171-404 4497

TREWBY, Rear-Admiral JOHN ALLAN Assistant Chief of the Defence Staff Operational Requirements (Sea Systems), Ministry of Defence

Career: naval service 1963-: specialist weapons officer 1968-: dockyard and sea-going posts 1980-84; Ministry of Defence (MoD) 1984-88: directorate naval operational requirements 1984-85; assistant director (AD) procurement executive 1985-88; Royal College of Defence Studies 1989; AD navy plans (manpower and support) MoD 1989-92; commodore Clyde, commander Clyde naval base 1992-94; assistant chief of defence staff operational requirements (sea systems) MoD 1994-

Date of birth: 12 September 1945 *Education/professional qualifications:* Marlborough College; Trinity College, Cambridge, mechanical sciences (BA 1968, MA); RN staff course 1977; Royal College of Defence Studies 1989; FIEE 1988, CEng 1975, FIMarE 1993 *Recreations:* walking, golf, squash, tennis

Rear-Admiral John A Trewby, Assistant Chief of the Defence Staff, Ministry of Defence, Whitehall, London SW1A 2HB *Telephone:* 0171-218 6070 *Fax:* 0171-218 3606

TROSS, JONATHAN Director of Resource Management and Planning, Department of Social Security Grade: 2

Career: teacher Nairobi, Kenya 1971; Department of [Health and] Social Security D[H]SS 1972-: principal 1977-84; assistant secretary (AS) 1984-87; seconded to Barclays Bank as assistant director 1987-90; AS DH 1990-91; DSS 1991-: under secretary planning and finance division 1991-94; deputy secretary, director resource management and planning group 1994-

Date of birth: 21 January 1949 *Education/professional qualifications:* Chislehurst and Sidcup Grammar School, Kent; University College, Oxford, modern history (BA 1970) *Marital status:* married Ann Humphries 1972; 1 son, 1 daughter *Clubs:* Fulham Football *Recreations:* theatre, reading, football

Jonathan Tross Esq, Deputy Secretary, Department of Social Security, Richmond House, 79 Whitehall, London SW1A 2NS
Telephone: 0171-210 5470 *Fax:* 0171-210 5480

TRUE, NICHOLAS EDWARD Deputy Head, Prime Minister's Policy Unit *(see Addenda)*

Career: member Conservative Research Department 1975-82; special adviser to secretary of state for health and social security 1982-86; director Public Policy Unit plc 1986-90; borough councillor Richmond-upon-Thames 1986-90; deputy head Prime Minister's Policy Unit 1991- *Current non-Whitehall posts:* director Orange Tree Theatre 1990-

Date of birth: 31 July 1951 *Education/professional qualifications:* Nottingham High School; Peterhouse, Cambridge, classics and history (BA 1973) *Honours, decorations:* CBE 1993 *Marital status:* married Anne-Marie Hood 1979; 2 sons, 1 daughter *Clubs:* Traveller's, Beefsteak *Recreations:* Byzantine history, music, gardening, Italy

Nicholas E True Esq CBE, Deputy Head, Prime Minister's Policy Unit, 10 Downing Street, London SW1A 2AA *Telephone:* 0171-270 3000

TUCKER, CLIVE FENEMORE Under Secretary, Director of International Division, Employment Department Group Grade: 3

Career: Department of Employment/Employment Department Group 1970-: assistant secretary 1978-87, under secretary 1987-, director of industrial relations division 1 1989-93, of international division 1993-

Date of birth: 13 July 1944 *Education/professional qualifications:* Balliol College, Oxford (BA) *Marital status:* married Caroline Macready 1978; 2 daughters

Clive F Tucker Esq, Under Secretary, Employment Department Group, Caxton House, Tothill Street, London SW1H 9NF *Telephone:* 0171-273 5775 *Fax:* 0171-273 6060

TUMIM, His Honour Judge STEPHEN HM Chief Inspector of Prisons, England and Wales, HM Inspectorate of Prisons

Career: county court judge 1978-; president Mental Health Tribunal 1983-87; chief inspector of prisons in England and Wales, 1987- *Current non-Whitehall posts:* president Royal Literary Fund; chairman Koestler Award Trust; chairman British Art Market Standing Committee

Date of birth: 15 August 1930 *Education/professional qualifications:* St Edward's School, Oxford; Worcester College, Oxford, law (degree 1953); Middle Temple (barrister 1955, bencher 1990) *Marital status:* married Winifred Borthwick 1962; 3 daughters *Publications:* Great Legal Disasters (Weidenfeld and Nicolson 1983); Great Legal Fiascos (Weidenfeld and Nicolson 1985) *Clubs:* Garrick, Beefsteak *Recreations:* books and pictures

His Honour Judge Stephen Tumim, HM Chief Inspector of Prisons in England and Wales, HM Inspectorate of Prisons, Home Office, 50 Queen Anne's Gate, London SW1H 9AT *Telephone:* 0171-273 3000 *Fax:* 0171-273 4087

TURNBULL, ANDREW Permanent Secretary, Department of the Environment Grade: 1

Career: economist Zambia government 1968-70; HM Treasury (HMT) 1970-94: assistant principal 1970-72, principal 1972-76; seconded to International Monetary Fund 1976-78; assistant secretary 1978-85: economic affairs private secretary (PS) to prime minister (PM) 1983-85; head of general expenditure policy division 1985-88; principal PS to PM 1988-92; deputy secretary public finance 1992-93, second permanent secretary public expenditure group 1993-94, permanent secretary Department of the Environment 1994-

Date of birth: 21 January 1945 *Education/professional qualifications:* Enfield Grammar School; Christ's College, Cambridge, economics (BA 1967) *Honours, decorations:* CB 1990, CVO 1992 *Marital status:* married Diane Clarke 1967; 2 sons *Recreations:* running, opera, fell walking

Andrew Turnbull Esq CB CVO, Permanent Secretary, Department of the Environment, 2 Marsham Street, London SW1P 3EB *Telephone:* 0171-276 3600 *Fax:* 0171-276 5995

Regulatory Organisations and Public Bodies

see page 1013

TURNER, JOHN Regional Director, Government Office for the Eastern Region, Departments of the Environment, Transport, Trade and Industry and Employment Grade: 3

Career: industrial policy and sponsorship Department of Trade and Industry 1967-81; Department of Employment (DEmp) 1981-87: seconded to Manpower Services Commission 1981-84, assistant secretary 1985, principal private secretary to secretaries of state Lord Young and Norman Fowler 1986-87; Central Policy Review Staff 1987-88; head of small firms and tourism division DEmp 1988-89; deputy chief executive Employment Service 1989-94; regional director government office for the eastern region 1994-

Date of birth: 22 April 1946 *Education/professional qualifications:* Ramsey Abbey Grammar School, Huntingdonshire; Northwood Hills Grammar School, Middlesex *Marital status:* married Susan Georgina Cameron 1971; 1 daughter, 2 sons *Recreations:* music, motoring, outdoors

John Turner Esq, Regional Director, Government Office for the Eastern Region, Enterprise House, Chivers Way, Vision Park, Histon, Cambridge CB4 4ZR *Telephone:* 01223 202064 *Fax:* 01223 202066

TURTON, (EU)GENIE CHRISTINE Director, Citizen's Charter Unit, Cabinet Office Grade: 2

Career: Department/Ministry of Transport 1970-85: assistant principal 1970-74, principal 1974-80: principal private secretary to secretary of state 1978-80, assistant secretary 1980-81, seconded to Midland Bank channel link financing group 1981-82, to Cabinet Office (CO) machinery of government 1982-85; Department of Environment 1986-94: under secretary 1986-91, deputy secretary housing and urban group 1991-93, cities and countryside group 1993-94; director Citizen's Charter unit CO 1994- *Current non-Whitehall posts:* trustee Pilgrim Trust 1991-

Date of birth: 19 February 1946 *Education/professional qualifications:* Nottingham Girls' High School; Girton College, Cambridge, classics (BA 1967, MA) *Marital status:* divorced *Recreations:* books, music, shopping

Miss E C Turton, Director, Citizen's Charter Unit, Cabinet Office, Horseguards Road, London SW1P 3AL *Telephone:* 0171-270 5786 *Fax:* 0171-270 5824

TWEEDIE, Professor Sir DAVID PHILIP Chairman, Accounting Standards Board

Career: private practice chartered accountancy, Glasgow 1969-72; Edinburgh University 1973-78: accounting and business methods lecturer 1973-78, director of studies 1973-75, associate dean social sciences faculty 1975-78; technical director Institute of Chartered Accountants of Scotland 1978-81; national research partner KMG Thomson McLintock 1982-87; national technical partner Peat Marwick McLintock 1987-90; chairman Accounting Standards Board 1990-

Date of birth: 7 July 1944 *Education/professional qualifications:* Grangemouth High School; Edinburgh University, business administration (BCom 1966), incomes policy (PhD 1969); CA 1972 *Honours, decorations:* KC 1994 *Marital status:* married Jan Brown 1970; 2 sons *Publications:* co-author The Private Shareholder and the Corporate Report (ICAEW 1977); Financial Reporting Inflation – the Capital Maintenance Concept (ICRA 1979); co-author The Institutional Investor and Financial Information (ICAEW

1981) and The Debate on Inflation Accounting (CUP 1984) *Recreations:* golf, watching rugby and athletics, gardening

Professor Sir David P Tweedie KC, Chairman, Accounting Standards Board, 100 Gray's Inn Road, London WC1X 8AL *Telephone:* 0171-404 8818 *Fax:* 0171-404 4497

TWIST, KENNETH LYNDON Chief Inspector, HM Inspectorate of Mines, Health and Safety Executive Grade: 3

Date of birth: 13 January 1938 *Education/professional qualifications:* CEng. FI(Min)E *Marital status:* married; 3 sons *Recreations:* IT

K L Twist Esq, HM Chief Inspector, HM Inspectorate of Mines, Health and Safety Executive, St Anne's House, University Road, Bootle L20 3RA *Telephone:* 0151-951 4190 *Fax:* 0151-951 4230

TYACKE, SARAH JACQUELINE Chief Executive and Keeper of Public Records, Public Record Office (Executive Agency) Grade: 3

Career: British Museum 1968-73; British Library 1973-92: director of special collections 1986-91; chief executive and keeper of Public Records 1992- *Current non-Whitehall posts:* trustee *Mappa Mundi,* Hereford Cathedral 1989-; chairman European board International Council on Archives 1992-

Date of birth: 29 September 1945 *Education/professional qualifications:* Chelmsford County High School; Bedford College, London, history (BA 1968); FSA *Marital status:* married Nicholas 1971; 1 daughter *Publications:* London Map Sellers (1978); English Mapmaking 1500-1650 (1983); Catalogue of Samuel Pepys's Map Collection (1990) *Recreations:* hillwalking, swimming, painting

Mrs Sarah J Tyacke, Chief Executive and Keeper of Public Records, Public Record Office, Ruskin Avenue, Kew, Richmond, Surrey TW9 4DU *Telephone:* 0181-878 1250 *Fax:* 0181-878 8905

TYRRELL, ALAN Legal Visitor, Office of the Lord Chancellor's Visitors, Lord Chancellor's Department

Career: private practise barrister 1956-72; recorder 1972-; member European parliament 1979-84; legal visitor Lord Chancellor's Department *Current non-Whitehall posts:* director Medical Protection Society, Papworth Hospital NHS Trust

Date of birth: 23 June 1933 *Education/professional qualifications:* LLB; FCIArb *Honours, decorations:* QC 1976 *Marital status:* married; 2 *Publications:* The Legal Professions in the New Europe (Basil Blackwell 1993) *Clubs:* Athenaeum *Recreations:* bridge; budgerigars

A Tyrrell Esq, Legal Visitor, Office of the Lord Chancellor's Visitors, Lord Chancellor's Department, Rochester House, 33 Greycoat Street, London SW1 2QF *Telephone:* 0171-757 7250 *Fax:* 0171-727 7299

TYTE, Dr DAVID CHRISTOPHER Rationalisation Director, Defence Evaluation and Research Agency (Executive Agency) Grade: 3

Dr David C Tyte, Rationalisation Director, Defence Evaluation and Research Agency, Farnborough, Hampshire GU14 6TD *Telephone:* 01252 394532

U

UNERMAN, SANDRA DIANE Deputy Solicitor, Department of the Environment Grade: 3

Career: Department of Environment 1974-: legal assistant (LA)/senior LA 1974-83; assistant solicitor 1983-92: civil service fellow Minnesota University, USA 1989-90; deputy solicitor 1992-

Date of birth: 23 August 1950 *Education/professional qualifications:* Bristol University, history (BA 1971); barrister 1973 *Marital status:* single *Publications:* Trial of Three (Dobsons 1979) *Clubs:* Folklore Society *Recreations:* reading, writing, theatregoing, listening to music

Ms Sandra D Unerman, Deputy Solicitor, Department of the Environment, 2 Marsham Street, London SW1P 3EB *Telephone:* 0171-276 3000

UPTON, PETER Director of Operations, Valuation Office Agency (Executive Agency) Grade: 4

Career: Valuation Office Agency (valuation of land and buildings for taxation) 1984-: superintending valuer south-eastern region 1984-89; director of operations and information technology 1989-

Date of birth: 22 July 1937 *Education/professional qualifications:* ARICS 1962 *Marital status:* married; 3 children

Peter Upton Esq, Director of Operations, Valuation Office Agency, New Court, Carey Street, London WC2A 2JE *Telephone:* 0171-324 1021 *Fax:* 0171-324 1073

V

VALLANCE WHITE, JAMES ASHTON Principal Clerk and Judicial Taxing Officer, Judicial Office, House of Lords

Career: Department of the Clerk of the Parliaments, House of Lords 1961-: principal clerk judicial office and fourth clerk at the table (judicial) 1983-

Date of birth: 25 February 1938 *Education/professional qualifications:* Allhallows School; St Peter's College, Oxford, philosophy, politics and economics (BA 1961, MA) *Marital status:* married Anne Margaret O'Donnell 1987 *Clubs:* Brooks's

James A Vallance White Esq, Principal Clerk and Judicial Taxing Officer, Judicial Office, House of Lords, London SW1A 0PW *Telephone:* 0171-219 3111

VANNET, ALFRED DOUGLAS Regional Procurator Fiscal, Grampian, Highland and Islands Grade: 4

Career: private practice solicitor 1973-76; Crown Office (CO) and Procurator Fiscal Service (public prosecution in Scotland) 1976-: procurator fiscal (PF) depute, Dundee 1976-77, PF depute/senior PF depute, Glasgow 1977-84; CO headquarters 1984-94: assistant solicitor 1984-90; deputy Crown Agent 1990-94; regional PF Grampian, Highland and Islands 1994-

Date of birth: 31 July 1949 *Education/professional qualifications:* High School of Dundee; Dundee University, law (LLB 1973) *Marital status:* married Pauline Margaret Renfrew 1979; 1 daughter, 1 son *Recreations:* music

Alfred D Vannet Esq, Regional Procurator Fiscal, Grampian, Highland and Islands, Inverlair House, West North Street, Aberdeen AB9 1AL *Telephone:* 01224 645132 *Fax:* 01224 647005

VAUX, JOHN ESMOND GEORGE Principal Assistant Solicitor, European Division, Treasury Solicitor's Department Grade: 3

Career: solicitor; Ministry of Agriculture, Fisheries and Food (MAFF) 1979-83; EC Commission 1983-85; MAFF 1985-90; Treasury Solicitors' Department 1990-: legal adviser Cabinet Office and head of European division 1990-94, principal assistant solicitor European division 1994-

Date of birth: 3 September 1948 *Education/professional qualifications:* Gosport County Grammar School; Selwyn College, Cambridge, history (BA 1971) *Marital status:* married; 1 daughter, 1 son *Clubs:* Institute of Contemporary Arts

J Vaux Esq, Principal Assistant Solicitor, Treasury Solicitor's Department, Queen Anne's Chambers, 28 Broadway, London SW1H 9JS *Telephone:* 0171-210 3021

VENABLES, ROBERT MICHAEL COCHRANE Commissioner, Head of Legal Division, Charity Commission Grade: 3

Career: solicitor 1962-70; Treasury Solicitor's Department 1970-89: legal assistant (LA) conveyancing 1970-73, senior LA conveyancing 1973-76; Department of Energy (DEn) 1976-80; assistant treasury solicitor: DEn 1980-83, establishments finance 1983-85, DEn 1985-87, conveyancing 1987-89; commissioner, head of legal division Charity Commissioners for England and Wales 1989- *Current non-Whitehall posts:* member Law Society council 1993-

Date of birth: 8 February 1939 *Education/professional qualifications:* Portsmouth Grammar School; solicitor (1962) *Marital status:* married Hazel Lesley Gowing 1972; 2 sons, 2 daughters *Clubs:* Civil Service, Law Society *Recreations:* opera, theatre, collecting domestic anachronisms

Robert M C Venables Esq, Head of Legal Division, Charity Commission for England and Wales, St Alban's House, 57-60 Haymarket, London SW1Y 4QX *Telephone:* 0171-210 4419 *Fax:* 0171-210 4604

VENNING, (ROBERT) BOB WILLIAM DAWE Principal Establishment and Finance Officer, Cabinet Office Grade: 3

Career: philosophy tutor Birmingham University 1968-69; logic and scientific method lecturer Lanchester Polytechnic 1969-70; Department of Health [and Social Security] 1971-93: private secretary (PS) to Minister for Disabled 1974-75, principal 1975-81, PS to Minister for Health 1981-83, assistant secretary 1983-90, under secretary NHS Management Executive health authority personnel division 1990-93; principal establishment and finance officer Cabinet Office 1993-

Date of birth: 25 July 1946 *Education/professional qualifications:* Midhurst School, Sussex; Birmingham University, mental and moral philosophy (BA 1968) *Marital status:* married Jennifer Mei-ling Jackson 1969; 1 son, 1 daughter *Recreations:* playing classical and flamenco guitar, electronics and computing

Bob Venning Esq, Principal Establishment and Finance Officer, Cabinet Office, Government Offices, Great George Street, London SW1P 3AL *Telephone:* 0171-270 6030

VEREKER, JOHN MICHAEL MEDLICOTT Permanent Secretary, Overseas Development Administration Grade: 1A

Career: assistant principal Overseas Development Ministry (ODM) 1967-69; World Bank, Washington 1970-72; ODM 1972-78: principal 1972-77, private secretary to ministers 1977-78, assistant secretary 1978; Prime Minister's Office 1980-83; Overseas Development Administration (ODA)/Foreign and Commonwealth Office 1983-88: under secretary 1983, principal finance officer 1986-88; Department of Education and Science/for Education 1988-94: deputy secretary further and higher education 1988-92, schools 1993-94; permanent secretary ODA 1994- *Current non-Whitehall posts:* member board British Council, Voluntary Service Overseas, British Executive Service Overseas

Date of birth: 9 August 1944 *Education/professional qualifications:* Marlborough College; Keele University (BA 1967) *Honours, decorations:* CB 1992 *Marital status:* married Judith Diane Rowen 1971; 1 daughter, 1 son

John M M Vereker Esq CB, Permanent Secretary, Overseas Development Administration, 94 Victoria Street, London SW1E 5JL *Telephone:* 0171-917 0500 *Fax:* 0171-917 0732

VINCENT, ROBIN ANTHONY Administrator, Northern Circuit, Court Service (Executive Agency) Grade: 4

Career: Worcestershire quarter sessions and magistrate's courts posts 1962-72; Lord Chancellor's Department 1972-:/Court Service 1995-: deputy chief clerk Worcester crown and county courts 1972-77; Birmingham circuit administrator's office 1977-81; chief clerk Worcester Crown Court 1981-85; headquarters 1986-93: head of court service development division 1986-91, of personnel 1991-93, of judicial appointments 1993; northern circuit administrator 1993-

Date of birth: 27 February 1944 *Education/professional qualifications:* King's School, Worcester *Marital status:* married Hazel Ruth Perkins 1971; 2 sons *Recreations:* soccer, cricket, music

Robin A Vincent Esq, Administrator, Northern Circuit, 15 Quay Street, Manchester M60 9FD *Telephone:* 0161-833 1005 *Fax:* 0161-832 8596

W

WAKEHAM, JOHN (The Rt Hon Lord Wakeham of Maldon) Chairman, Press Complaints Commission

Career: magistrate Inner London 1972-; Conservative MP for Maldon 1974-83, for Colchester South and Maldon 1983-92: minister of state 1982-83, parliamentary secretary 1983-87, parliamentary under secretary Department of Industry 1981-82, Lord Privy Seal 1987-88, Leader of House of Commons 1987-89; Secretary of State for Energy 1989-92, Lord Privy Seal and Leader House of Lords 1992-94; Chairman Press Complaints Commission 1995-

Date of birth: 22 June 1932 *Education/professional qualifications:* Charterhouse School; FCA *Honours, decorations:* PC 1983; baron 1992 *Marital status:* married Anne Roberta Bailey (died 1984): 2 sons; Alison Bridget Ward 1985: 1 son

The Rt Hon Lord Wakeham, Chairman, Press Complaints Commission, 1 Salisbury Square, London EC4Y 8AE *Telephone:* 0171-353 1248 *Fax:* 0171-353 8355

WALFORD, Dr DIANA MARION Director, Public Health Laboratory Service Board

Career: hospital medical posts 1968-75; research (training) fellow Medical Research Council 1975-76; Department of Health 1976-92: senior principal medical officer (MO) and under secretary 1983-89; deputy chief MO and director of health care NHS Management Executive 1989-92; director Public Health Laboratory Service 1992- *Current non-Whitehall posts:* member board of management London School of Hygiene and Tropical Medicine; member British Society for Haematology 1978-; founder member British Blood Transfusion Society 1983-

Date of birth: 26 February 1944 *Education/professional qualifications:* Calder High School for Girls, Liverpool; Liverpool University (BSc 1965); MB ChB 1968; MD 1976; London University, epidemiology (MSc 1987); FRCP 1990; FRCPath 1986; MFPHM 1989, FFPHM 1994 *Marital status:* married Arthur David; 1 daughter, 1 son *Publications:* contributor to Meyler's Side Effects of Drugs (9th edn 1980), Side Effects of Drugs Annual (1980) and Drug-Induced Emergencies (1980) *Clubs:* Royal Society of Medicine *Recreations:* theatre, painting, travel

Dr Diana Walford, Public Health Laboratory Service Board, 61 Colindale Avenue, London NW9 5DF *Telephone:* 0181-200 1295 *Fax:* 0181-905 9742

WALKER, ALAN ROBERT Director of Operations, South, HM Prison Service Grade: 3

Career: local government audit Hull Corporation 1956-58; air force national service 1958-60; Colonial Police Northern Rhodesia 1960-63, Papua New Guinea 1964-67; Scottish Prison Service 1968-: various prisons 1968-73, 1976-78, 1979-82, 1983-87, 1990-91; prison service college tutor 1973-76; seconded to Whitehall Efficiency Services, Cabinet Office 1982-83; prison service headquarters 1978-79, 1986-87, 1990-: deputy director 1990-92, deputy chief executive 1992-95; director of operations, south, HM Prison Service 1995-

Date of birth: 23 January 1939 *Education/professional qualifications:* Marist Brothers College; FBIM 1981 *Marital status:* married Judith Anne McNaught 1969; 1 son, 1 daughter *Recreations:* orchid growing, reading, music

Alan R Walker Esq, Director of Operations, South, HM Prison Service, Cleland House, Page Street, London SW1P 4LN *Telephone:* 0171-217 6700 *Fax:* 0171-217 6694

WALKER, ANNA Deputy Director-General, Office of Telecommunications (OFTEL) Grade: 3

Career: administrator British Council 1972-73, Confederation of British Industry 1973-74, Department of [Trade and] Industry 1975-: private secretary to Secretary of State for Industry 1977-78; shipping policy with USA, USSR and Europe 1978-82; finance and resources management 1982-83; inter-departmental review of budgetary control 1984; seconded to Cabinet Office machinery of government 1986; personnel 1987-88; competition policy 1988-91; OFTEL 1991-: director of competition 1991-94, deputy director-general 1994-

Date of birth: 5 May 1951 *Education/professional qualifications:* Benenden School; Lady Margaret Hall, Oxford, history (BA 1972) *Marital status:* married Thomas Edward Hanson 1983; 3 daughters

Mrs Anna Walker, Deputy Director-General, Office of Telecommunications, 50 Ludgate Hill, London EC4M 7JJ *Telephone:* 0171-634 8804 *Fax:* 0171-634 8940

WALKER, (CHRISTOPHER) ROY Chief Officer, Joint Nature Conservation Committee Grade: 5

Career: Board of Trade 1958-68; Civil Service Department 1968-73; HM Treasury 1973; Department of Trade and Industry/Energy (DEn) 1973-74; Cabinet Office (CO) 1974-75; DEn 1975-77; under secretary 1977-93: Department of Education and Science 1977-86; Department of Employment 1986-89: seconded to Business the Cities 1989; CO 1989-92: deputy head science and technology secretariat 1989-92, seconded to Royal Institute of Public Administration 1992; Department for Education 1992-93; chief officer Joint Nature Conservation Committee 1993-

Date of birth: 5 December 1934 *Education/professional qualifications:* Sir George Monoux Grammar School, London; Sidney Sussex College, Cambridge, geography (BA 1957) *Honours, decorations:* CB 1992 *Marital status:* married Hilary Mary Biddiscombe 1961; 2 sons *Clubs:* Chipstead Sailing *Recreations:* dinghy sailing, hill walking, photography

Roy Walker Esq, Chief Officer, Joint Nature Conservation Committee, Monkstone House, City Road, Peterborough PE1 1JY *Telephone:* 01733 866900 *Fax:* 01733 555948

WALKER, JEREMY Regional Director, Government Office for Yorkshire and Humberside, Departments of the Environment, Transport, Trade and Industry and Employment Grade: 3

Career: Department of Employment (DEmp) 1971-73; Manpower Services Commission (MSC) 1974-75; Health and Safety Executive 1975-76; MSC 1976-82; exchange officer Australian Department of Employment and Industrial Relations 1982-84; MSC 1984-88: regional employment manager 1984-86, head of community programme and new job training scheme 1986-88; Yorkshire and Humberside (Y&H) regional director Training Agency and DEmp 1988-94: leader Leeds/Bradford city action team

1990-94; regional director government office for Y&H 1994- *Current non-Whitehall posts:* member council Leeds University; member board Yorkshire and Humberside Arts

Date of birth: 12 July 1949 *Education/professional qualifications:* Brentwood School, Essex; Birmingham University, history (BA 1971) *Marital status:* married Patricia June Lockhart 1968; 2 sons, 1 daughter *Recreations:* smallholding

Jeremy Walker, Regional Director, Government Office for Yorkshire and Humberside, City House, New Station Street, Leeds LS1 4JD
Telephone: 01532 835200 *Fax:* 01532 449313

WALKER, PETER EDWARD (The Rt Hon Lord Walker of Worcester) Chairman, English Partnerships

Career: MP for Worcester 1961-92: Secretary of State (SoS) for Environment 1970-72, Trade and Industry 1972-74; Minister for Agriculture 1979-83; SoS for Energy 1983-87, for Wales 1987-90; chairman English Partnerships (Urban Regeneration Agency) 1994- *Current non-Whitehall posts:* Chairman Thornton and Co 1991-, Cornhill Insurance 1992-; director Smith New Court, British Gas, Tate & Lyle

Date of birth: 25 March 1932 *Education/professional qualifications:* Latymer Upper School *Honours, decorations:* MBE 1960; PC *Marital status:* married Tessa Pout 1969; 3 sons, 2 daughters *Publications:* Ascent of Britain; Trust the People; Staying Power *Clubs:* Carlton, Bucks *Recreations:* tennis

The Rt Hon Lord Walker of Worcester MBE, Chairman, English Partnerships, 3 The Parks, Lodge Lane, Newton-le-Willows, Merseyside WA12 0JQ *Telephone:* 0194-229 6900 *Fax:* 0194-229 6927

WALKER, TIMOTHY EDWARD HANSON Deputy Under Secretary, Equal Opportunities and General; Immigration and Nationality Department, Home Office Grade: 2

Career: Weir junior research fellow in theoretical chemistry University College, Oxford 1969-71; exhibitioner of Royal Commission of 1851, Paris 1969-71; Harkness fellow Commonwealth Fund of New York 1971-73; strategic planner Greater London Council 1974-77; principal Department of Trade 1977-83; Sloan Fellow London Business School 1983; Department of Trade and Industry (DTI) 1983-89: assistant secretary 1983, administration director Alvey programme 1983-85, head of policy planning unit 1985-86, principal private secretary to secretaries of state 1986-87, under secretary 1987, director of information engineering directorate 1987-89; non-executive director ICI Chemicals and Polymers Ltd 1988-89; UK governor International Atomic Energy Agency 1989-94; head of atomic energy division Department of Energy/DTI 1989-95; deputy under secretary equal opportunities and general, immigration and nationality department Home Office 1995- *Current non-Whitehall posts:* non-executive director UKAEA government division 1994-; chairman assembly of donors/nuclear safety account European Bank for Reconstruction and Development 1993-

Date of birth: 27 July 1945 *Education/professional qualifications:* Tonbridge School; Brasenose College, Oxford, chemistry (BA 1967, MA, DPhil 1969) *Marital status:* married Judith Mann 1969 (died 1976); Anna Butterworth 1983; 3 daughters (1d from previous marriage) *Publications:* contributions to scientific journals *Recreations:* cooking, gardening, collecting modern prints

Timothy E H Walker Esq, Deputy Under Secretary, Home Office, 50 Queen Anne's Gate, London SW1H 9AT *Telephone:* 0171-273 3000

WALLACE, RICHARD ALEXANDER Principal Finance Officer, Welsh Office Grade: 3

Career: Ministry of Social Security/Department of Health and Social Security 1968-1986: principal 1972-81, assistant secretary 1981-86; Welsh Office 1986-: under secretary, head of transport, planning and environment group 1988-90; principal finance officer 1990-

Date of birth: 24 November 1946 *Education/professional qualifications:* Clifton College, Bristol; King's College, Cambridge, English (BA 1967, MA) *Marital status:* married Teresa Caroline Harington Smith 1970; 3 children (and 1 deceased)

R A Wallace Esq, Principal Finance Officer, Welsh Office, Cathays Park, Cardiff CF1 3NQ *Telephone:* 01222 825111 *Fax:* 01222 823199

WALLARD, Dr ANDREW JOHN Deputy Director and Controller of Scientific Services, National Physical Laboratory (Executive Agency) Grade: 4

Career: researcher National Physical Laboratory (NPL) 1968-81; Department of Trade and Industry 1981-: head of technical information section 1981-82, deputy head policy planning unit 1982-83, branch head: research and technology policy division 1983-86, electronics applications division 1986-88; international affairs director information engineering directorate 1988-90; deputy director and controller of scientific services NPL (national measurement standards) 1990- *Current non-Whitehall posts:* non-executive director Rank CINTEL 1987-

Date of birth: 11 October 1945 *Education/professional qualifications:* Liverpool Institute; St Andrew's University, physics (BSc 1968, PhD 1971) *Marital status:* married Barbara Jean Pritchard 1969; 2 sons *Clubs:* Papercourt Sailing *Recreations:* music, gardening, sailing, wine

Dr Andrew J Wallard, Deputy Director, National Physical Laboratory, Teddington, Middlesex TW11 0LW *Telephone:* 0181-943 6013 *Fax:* 0181-943 1350

WALMSLEY, Vice Admiral ROBERT Deputy Chief of Defence Procurement (South of England), Procurement Executive, Ministry of Defence

Vice Admiral Robert Walmsley, Deputy Chief of Defence Procurement, Procurement Executive, Ministry of Defence, Main Building, Whitehall, London SW1A 2HB *Telephone:* 0171-218 9000

WALSH, HENRY GEORGE Deputy Chairman, Building Societies Commission Grade: 3

Career: HM Treasury (HMT) 1966-74; Cabinet Office 1974-80: private secretary to chancellor of Duchy of Lancaster 1974-76, European secretariat 1976-80; economic counsellor Washington DC embassy 1980-85; HMT 1985-91: head of monetary policy division 1985-86, of International Monetary Fund and debt division 1986-89, under secretary financial institutions and markets 1989-91; deputy chairman Building Societies Commission 1991-

Date of birth: 28 September 1939 *Education/professional qualifications:* West Hill School; McGill University, Canada; Cambridge University *Marital status:* separated; 3 daughters *Clubs:* Dulwich and Sydenham Golf *Recreations:* golf

H G Walsh Esq, Deputy Chairman, Building Societies Commission, 15 Great Marlborough Street, London W1V 2LL *Telephone:* 0171-494 6642 *Fax:* 0171-437 1612

WALSH, Dr JULIA **Chief Executive, ADAS (Executive Agency)** Grade: 2

Career: chief executive ADAS (research and consultancy to food and farming industries)

Dr Julia Walsh, Chief Executive, ADAS, Oxford Spires Business Park, The Boulevard, Kidlington, Oxfordshire OX5 1NZ *Telephone:* 01865 845002 *Fax:* 01865 845090

WALTERS, RHODRI HAVARD **Establishment Officer, House of Lords** Grade: 4

Career: House of Lords Clerks Office 1975-: clerk to select committee on overseas trade 1984-85; seconded to Cabinet Office as private secretary to Leader of House and government chief whip 1986-89; clerk to select committee on science and technology 1990-93; establishment officer 1993-

Date of birth: 28 February 1950 *Education/professional qualifications:* Cyfarthfa Castle Grammar School, Merthyr Tydfil; Jesus College, Oxford, modern history (BA 1971, MA, DPhil 1975) *Marital status:* single *Publications:* co-author How Parliament Works (Longman 1987) *Recreations:* rowing, gardening, music

Rhodri H Walters Esq, Establishment Officer, House of Lords, London SW1A 0PW *Telephone:* 0171-219 3186 *Fax:* 0171-219 4868

WARD, (ANTHONY) TONY JOHN **Deputy Chief Executive, Child Support Agency (Executive Agency)** Grade: 5

Career: Department of Health and Social Security and predecessors 1959-84: manager national insurance office 1980-81, social security offices 1981-84; consultant Cabinet Office 1984-89; chief executive Resettlement Agency (for the single homeless) 1989-94; deputy chief executive Child Support Agency 1994-

Date of birth: 3 November 1940 *Education/professional qualifications:* Devonport High School, Plymouth *Marital status:* divorced; 1 son, 1 daughter *Recreations:* cricket, travel

Tony J Ward Esq, Deputy Chief Executive, Child Support Agency, Millbank Tower, 21-24 Millbank, London SW1 4QU *Telephone:* 0171-217 4154 *Fax:* 0171-217 4683

WARD, PHILLIP DAVID **Director, Construction Sponsorship, Department of the Environment** Grade: 3

Career: Department of Environment 1973-: head of local government finance policy 1985-88, of global atmosphere division 1989-90; principal private secretary to secretary of state 1990-92; director construction sponsorship (sponsorship of the construction and building products industries; EC construction issues; building material standards) 1992- *Current non-Whitehall posts:* governor Handsworth Primary School 1988-

Date of birth: 1 September 1950 *Education/professional qualifications:* Sir John Talbot's Grammar School, Whitchurch, Shropshire; Sheffield University, law (BJur 1973) *Marital status:* married Barbara Patricia Taylor 1974; 2 daughters *Recreations:* cinema, travel, sailing

Phillip D Ward Esq, Director Construction Sponsorship, Department of the Environment, 2 Marsham Street, London SW1P 3EB *Telephone:* 0171-276 4139 *Fax:* 0171-276 3369

WARD, REGINALD GEORGE Director of Statistics and Economics Office, Inland Revenue Grade: 3

Career: HM Treasury 1978-82; Cabinet Office 1982-86; Department of Trade and Industry 1986-89; head of division 1/government statistical service and general division Central Statistical Office 1989-94; director of statistics and economics office Inland Revenue 1994-

Date of birth: 6 July 1942 *Education/professional qualifications:* Leicester University (BSc 1963); Aberdeen University (MSc 1964); Oxford University (DipStat 1965); London Business School (MBA 1987) *Marital status:* married 1964; 2 sons, 1 daughter *Publications:* Keeping Score: History of the CSO (HMSO 1991) *Recreations:* sailing

Reginald G Ward Esq, Director of Statistics and Economics Office, Inland Revenue, Somerset House, London WC2R 1LB *Telephone:* 0171-438 6609 *Fax:* 0171-438 7582

WARNE, (FREDERICK) JOHN Under Secretary, Police Department, Home Office Grade: 3

Career: Home Office 1975-: assistant secretary 1984-93; under secretary police department 1993-

Date of birth: 7 March 1944 *Education/professional qualifications:* Liskeard Grammar School, Cornwall *Marital status:* divorced; 2 sons

F John Warne Esq, Under Secretary, Home Office, 50 Queen Anne's Gate, London SW1H 9AT *Telephone:* 0171-273 2830

WARNER, GERRY CHIERICI Intelligence Co-ordinator, Cabinet Office Grade: 2

Career: Foreign [and Commonwealth] Office 1954-89; Police Complaints Authority 1989-90; intelligence co-ordinator Cabinet Office 1990-

Date of birth: 27 September 1931 *Education/professional qualifications:* Lindisfarne School, Yorkshire; St Peter's College, Oxford, history (BA 1954) *Honours, decorations:* CMG 1986 *Marital status:* married Mary Wynne Davis 1956; 2 daughters, 1 son *Clubs:* Royal Air Force *Recreations:* walking

Gerry C Warner Esq CMG, Intelligence Co-ordinator, Cabinet Office, 70 Whitehall, London SW1A 2AS *Telephone:* 0171-270 0368 *Fax:* 0171-930 1419

WATSON, (ANGUS) GAVIN Under Secretary, Cities, Countryside and Private Finance, Department of the Environment Grade: 3

Career: Department of Environment 1971-: head of construction manpower division 1980-81, of building regulations division 1981-84, of finance (housing and general) division 1984-86; under secretary 1986-: director of public housing management and resources 1986-90, of water resources 1990; environmental policy analysis directorate 1990-94; cities, countryside and private finance 1994- *Current non-Whitehall posts:* non-executive director DENCO 1988-

Date of birth: 14 April 1944 *Education/professional qualifications:* Carlisle Grammar School; Merton College, Oxford, history (BA 1965, MA) *Marital status:* divorced; 2 sons *Recreations:* industrial archaeology, fell walking, looking at buildings

Gavin Watson Esq, Under Secretary, Department of the Environment, Romney House, 43 Marsham Street, London SW1P 3PY
Telephone: 0171-276 8636 *Fax:* 0171-276 8626

WATSON, DAVID Chief Executive, Oil and Gas Projects and Supplies Office, Department of Trade and Industry Grade: 3

Career: private practice chartered accountant 1973-76; BP 1977-94: BP Exploration 1985-91: manager acquisitions and disposals 1985-89, manager business support 1989-91, vice-president corporate development BP Canada 1991-92, manager UK Land 1992-94; seconded from BP as chief executive oil and gas projects and supplies office Department of Trade and Industry 1994-

Date of birth: 9 April 1952 *Education/professional qualifications:* Oundle School; Kentucky University, USA 1970; Worcester College, Oxford, engineering (BA 1973); FCA 1973 *Marital status:* mrried Elizabeth Anne 1978; 1 daughter, 1 son *Recreations:* cricket, gardening, music

D Watson Esq, Chief Executive, Oil and Gas Projects and Supplies Office, Department of Trade and Industry, Alhambra House, 45 Waterloo Street, Glasgow G2 6AS; 1 Palace Street, London SW1E 5HE
Telephone: 0141-228 3601; 0171-238 3611
Fax: 0141-204 4998; 0171-233 8794

WATSON, GARRY SANDERSON Scottish Legal Services Ombudsman

Career: finance manager Upper Clyde Shipbuilders 1968-69; Hill Samuel Bank 1969-91: director 1976-90, managing director 1990-91; Scottish legal services ombudsman 1994-

Date of birth: 31 July 1940 *Education/professional qualifications:* Glasgow Academy; Institute of Chartered Accountants of Scotland (CA 1964) *Marital status:* married Elizabeth Ann 1967; 4 daughters *Recreations:* hillwalking, shooting, family pursuits

Garry S Watson Esq, Scottish Legal Service Ombudsman, 2 Greenside Lane, Edinburgh EH1 3AH
Telephone: 0131-556 5574 *Fax:* 0131-556 1519

WATSON, PETER Chief Executive, Commercial Division, AEA Technology, UK Atomic Energy Authority

Career: British Rail 1971-76, 1991-94; GKN 1976-91; chief executive AEA Technology (commercial division of UK Atomic Authority) 1994-

Date of birth: 9 January 1944 *Education/professional qualifications:* Waterloo University, Canada (MSc 1968, PhD 1971)

Peter Watson Esq, Chief Executive, Commercial Division, AEA Technology, UK Atomic Energy Authority, Harwell, Oxfordshire OX11 0RA *Telephone:* 01235 821111

WATT, Dr ROBERT MACKAY Chief Inspector, Animals (Scientific Procedures) Inspectorate, Home Office Grade: 4

Career: physiology lecturer Edinburgh University medical school 1970-75; community medicine fellow Scottish Health Service 1975-77; Home Office 1977-: inspector (Cruelty to Animals Act 1876) 1977-84, superintending inspector 1984-87, chief inspector animals (scientific procedures) inspectorate (implementing legal controls on animal use in research) 1987-

Date of birth: 5 February 1941 *Education/professional qualifications:* Aberdeen Grammar School; Manchester Grammar School; Edinburgh University, physiology (BSc 1963), medicine (MB ChB 1966), micro-chemistry (PhD 1972), community medicine (diploma 1976) *Marital status:* married Christine Wendy Gregory 1969; 2 sons *Recreations:* painting, model-making, wood carving, armchair aviation

Dr Robert M Watt, Chief Inspector, Animals (Scientific Procedures) Inspectorate, Home Office, Queen Anne's Gate, London SW1H 9AT *Telephone:* 0171-273 2347 *Fax:* 0171-273 2423

WEATHERSTON, (WILLIAM) ALASTAIR (PATERSON) Under Secretary, Scottish Office Education Department (*until November 1995*) Grade: 3

Career: Scottish Office 1959-: seconded to Cabinet Office 1972-74; assistant secretary 1974-82; director Scottish Courts Administration 1982-86; fisheries secretary Agriculture and Fisheries Department 1986-89; under secretary further and higher education and arts Education Department 1989-

Date of birth: 20 November 1935 *Education/professional qualifications:* Edinburgh University, history (MA 1957) *Honours, decorations:* CB 1993 *Marital status:* married Margaret Jardine 1961; 1 daughter, 2 sons *Recreations:* reading, music

Alastair Weatherston Esq CB, Under Secretary, Scottish Office Education Department, 43 Jeffrey Street, Edinburgh EH1 1DN *Telephone:* 0131-244 5322 *Fax:* 0131-244 5387

WEBBER, HENRY Director of Parliamentary Works, House of Commons and House of Lords Grade: 4

Career: civil engineering industry 1964-71; Department of Environment 1971-91: area officer Portsmouth 1982-85; assistant director London region 1985-87; director, civil engineering services 1987-91; director of parliamentary works Houses of Parliament 1991- *Current non-Whitehall posts:* member board Quality Scheme for Ready Mixed Concrete; UK member board International Association for Bridge and Structural Engineering

Date of birth: 12 April 1943 *Education/professional qualifications:* Reading School; Loughborough University, engineering (BSc 1964); CEng 1968; MICE 1968; FICE 1988; FBIM 1988 *Marital status:* married Gwalia Elizabeth Owen 1968; 2 sons *Publications:* co-author Design Life of Structures (Blackie 1991); various papers in professional journals *Recreations:* keep fit, tennis, theatre

Henry Webber Esq, Director of Parliamentary Works, House of Commons, London SW1A 0AA *Telephone:* 0171-219 3920 *Fax:* 0171-219 6409

WEBBER, MICHAEL Charity Commissioner Grade: 4

Career: charity commissioner 1989- *Current non-Whitehall posts:* chairman and chief executive Pifco Holdings plc 1983-

Date of birth: 7 February 1946 *Education/professional qualifications:* Carmel College, Berkshire; FCA 1968 *Marital status:* single

Michael Webber Esq, Charity Commissioner, Charity Commission, St Alban's House, 57-60 Haymarket, London SW1Y 4QX *Telephone:* 0171-210 4540 *Fax:* 0171-930 9174

WEEPLE, ED(WARD) JOHN Under Secretary, Scottish Office Industry Department Grade: 3

Career: assistant principal Ministry of Health/Department of Health and Social Security 1971-78: private secretary to Minister of Health 1971-73, principal 1973-78; Scottish Office 1978-: principal Industry Department (ID) 1978-80; assistant secretary Home and Health Department 1980-85, Agriculture and Fisheries Department 1985-90; under secretary (enterprise networks; employment and training; tourism; new towns; urban regeneration) ID 1990- *Current non-Whitehall posts:* chairman Wester Hailes Partnership Board 1990-; chairman Ferguslie Park Partnership Board 1990-;

member Scottish Business in the Community executive council 1990-; member Edinburgh Common Purpose

Date of birth: 15 May 1945 *Education/professional qualifications:* St Aloysius College, Glasgow; Glasgow University, history (MA 1967) *Marital status:* married Joan Shaw 1970; 3 sons, 1 daughter

Ed J Weeple Esq, Under Secretary, Scottish Office Industry Department, New St Andrew's House, Edinburgh EH1 3TD *Telephone:* 0131-244 4605 *Fax:* 0131-244 5157

WEISS, JOHN ROGER Director, Asset Management Group, Export Credits Guarantee Department Grade: 3

Career: Inland Revenue 1961-64; Export Credits Guarantee Department 1964-: principal 1978-82; head of finance division 1982-87, of chief executive's division 1987-90; director asset management group 1990-

Date of birth: 27 December 1944 *Education/professional qualifications:* St Helen's College, Thames Ditton *Marital status:* married Hazel Kay Lang 1967 *Recreations:* music, walking

John R Weiss Esq, Under Secretary, Export Credits Guarantee Department, 2 Exchange Tower, Harbour Exchange Square, London E14 9GS *Telephone:* 0171-512 7376 *Fax:* 0171-512 7400

WELCH, DAVID Chief Executive, Royal Parks (Executive Agency) Grade: 5

Career: local government; chief executive Royal Parks 1992-

David Welch Esq, Chief Executive, Royal Parks, Old Police House, Hyde Park, London W2 2UH *Telephone:* 0171-298 2125 *Fax:* 0171-298 2005

WENBAN-SMITH, HUGH BOYD Under Secretary, Head of Civil Aviation Directorate, Department of Transport Grade: 3

Career: economist, Zambia government and central bank 1964-67; economic adviser (EA) Ministry of Overseas Development 1968-71; economic first secretary New Delhi high commission 1971-74; EA Department of Trade and Industry 1975-77; senior EA Prices Commission 1977-79; senior consultant commercial accountancy practice 1979-81; head of water finance and economics division Department of Environment 1981-85; Department of Transport 1985-: director financial management 1985-89, under secretary 1989-: head of marine directorate 1989-93, of civil aviation directorate 1993-

Date of birth: 6 November 1941 *Education/professional qualifications:* Bradfield College, Berkshire; King's College, Cambridge, economics (MA 1964); University College, London, public policy economics (MSc 1975)

Hugh B Wenban-Smith Esq, Under Secretary, Department of Transport, 2 Marsham Street, London SW1P 3EB *Telephone:* 0171-276 5379 *Fax:* 0171-276 5562

WENTWORTH, STEPHEN **Fisheries Secretary, Ministry of Agriculture, Fisheries and Food** Grade: 3

Career: Ministry of Agriculture, Fisheries and Food 1967-: seconded to civil service selection board 1974, to UK permanent representation to EC, Brussels as first secretary 1976-78; head of beef division 1978-80; seconded to Cabinet Office 1980-82; head of milk division 1982-85, of EC division 1985-86; under secretary, head of meat group 1986-89, of livestock products group 1989-91, of EC group 1991-93; fisheries secretary 1993-

Date of birth: 23 August 1943 *Education/professional qualifications:* Wimbledon College, London; Merton College, Oxford (MA, MSc)

Stephen Wentworth Esq, Fisheries Secretary, Ministry of Agriculture, Fisheries and Food, Nobel House, London SW1P 3HX *Telephone:* 0171-238 5796

WEST, Rear-Admiral ALAN WILLIAM JOHN **Naval Secretary; Director-General, Naval Manning, Ministry of Defence**

Career: naval service 1965-: sea-going posts 1966-73; command HMS Yarnton 1973-76; principal warfare office 1977; specialist sea-going posts 1977-82: command HMS Ardent 1980-82; Ministry of Defence (MoD) 1982-87: naval plans division, naval staff duties division, interim working group; command HMS Bristol 1987-88; MoD 1989-: head of maritime intelligence 1989-92; 1993-: director naval staff duties 1993-94; naval secretary (responsible for naval service staff) 1994-, director-general naval manning 1994-

Date of birth: 21 April 1948 *Education/professional qualifications:* Windsor Grammar School; Clydebank High School; Royal Naval College, Dartmouth (commission 1966); Royal College of Defence Studies 1992; higher command and staff course 1993 *Honours, decorations:* DSC 1982 *Clubs:* Royal Yacht Squadron *Recreations:* keel boat racing, swimming, cricket, tennis

Rear-Admiral Alan W J West DSC, Naval Secretary, Victory Building, HM Naval Base, Portsmouth PO1 3LS *Telephone:* 01705 727400 *Fax:* 01705 727413

WEST, CHRISTOPHER JOHN **Solicitor, HM Land Registry (Executive Agency)** Grade: 3

Date of birth: 4 May 1941 *Education/professional qualifications:* Lincoln's Inn (barrister 1966) *Marital status:* married; 1 daughter *Publications:* Registered Conveyancing (Ruoff and Roper 1991) *Recreations:* theatre, jazz, cricket

C J West Esq, Solicitor HM Land Registry, 32 Lincoln's Inn Fields, London WC2A 3PH *Telephone:* 0171-917 8888 *Fax:* 0171-955 0110

WHEELER, (RICHARD) DICK JOHN **Director of Information Technology, Department of Trade and Industry** Grade: 4

Career: Inland Revenue 1961-83; Ministry of Agriculture, Fisheries and Food 1983-89: deputy head computer services 1983-85, assistant director information technology (IT) planning 1985-89; director IT Department of Trade and Industry services management division 1990-

Date of birth: 5 January 1943 *Education/professional qualifications:* Glyn Grammar School, Epsom *Marital status:* married Carol Pople 1979; 1 daughter, 2 sons *Recreations:* bridge, golf, gardening

Dick Wheeler Esq, Director of Information Technology, Department of Trade and Industry, Kingsgate House, 66-74 Victoria Street, London SW1E 6SW *Telephone:* 0171-215 3630 *Fax:* 0171-215 8160

WHEELER-BOOTH, Sir MICHAEL ADDISON JOHN Clerk of the Parliaments, House of Lords Grade: 1

Career: Parliament Office, House of Lords (HoL) 1960-: seconded as private secretary to leader of house and government chief whip 1965-67, as joint secretary inter-party conference on HoL reform 1967-69; clerk of the journals 1970-72, of select committee on procedures for scrutiny of European legislation 1972-73; chief clerk Overseas and European Office 1972-78; principal clerk 1978-83; reading clerk and clerk of the journals 1983-88; clerk assistant of the parliaments and clerk of the journals 1988-91; Clerk of the Parliaments (appointment of Parliament Office staff; HoL accounting officer; procedural advice; records custodian for both houses; authentication of Acts) 1991-

Date of birth: 25 February 1934 *Education/professional qualifications:* Leighton Park School, Reading; Magdalen College, Oxford, modern history (BA 1957, MA) *Honours, decorations:* KCB 1995 *Marital status:* married Emily Frances Smith 1982; 2 daughters, 1 son *Publications:* contributor, Griffith and Ryle, Parliament (1989); contributions to other parliamentary journals *Clubs:* Brooks's, Garrick

Sir Michael Wheeler-Booth KCB, Clerk of the Parliaments, Parliament Office, House of Lords, London SW1A 0PW *Telephone:* 0171-219 3181 *Fax:* 0171-219 2571

WHELDON, JULIET LOUISE Legal Secretary, Legal Secretariat to the Law Officers Grade: 2

Career: legal assistant Treasury Solicitor's Department (TSD) 1976-83; senior legal assistant Law Officers' Department (LOD) 1983-84; assistant solicitor TSD 1984-86, LOD 1986-87; principal assistant solicitor in charge of Treasury advisory work TSD 1987-89; legal secretary Legal Secretariat to Law Officers (senior official in Attorney General and Solicitor General's Office; briefing law officers) 1989-

Date of birth: 26 March 1950 *Education/professional qualifications:* Sherborne School for Girls; Lady Margaret Hall, Oxford, history (BA 1971); College of Law (bar finals 1975); Gray's Inn (barrister 1975) *Honours, decorations:* CB 1994 *Marital status:* single

Miss Juliet L Wheldon CB, Legal Secretary, Legal Secretariat to the Law Officers, 9 Buckingham Gate, London SW1E 6JP *Telephone:* 0171-828 1968 *Fax:* 0171-828 0593

WHETNALL, ANDREW DONARD Under Secretary, Machinery of Government and Standards Group, Cabinet Office Grade: 3

Career: Department of Transport 1980-83, Department of the Environment 1983-89: assistant secretary (AS) 1987-93, inner cities 1987-88, water legislation 1988-89; AS then under secretary machinery of government division Cabinet Office 1989-

Date of birth: 18 May 1948 *Education/professional qualifications:* King's Norton Grammar School, Birmingham; Sussex University, English (BA 1969, MA 1970); University College, Cambridge, education (CertEd 1971) *Marital status:* married Jane Lepel 1972; 2 daughters, 2 sons *Recreations:* music, reading

Andrew D Whetnall Esq, Under Secretary, Cabinet Office, 70 Whitehall, London SW1A 2AS *Telephone:* 0171-270 0067 *Fax:* 0171-270 0345

WHIPPMAN, MICHAEL Under Secretary, Social Security Policy Group, Department of Social Security Grade: 3

Career: University of Pennsylvania, USA 1963-71: post-doctoral fellow 1963-65, assistant professor of physics 1965-71; senior research fellow, theoretical physics Helsinki University, Finland 1971-73; Department of [Health and] Social Security (D[H]SS) 1973-90: principal 1973-80, assistant secretary 1980-88, under secretary (US) 1988-90; US home and education group HM Treasury 1990-93, division B social security policy group DSS 1993-

Date of birth: 20 September 1938 *Education/professional qualifications:* King Edward VII School, Johannesburg, South Africa; University of Witwatersrand, SA, theoretical physics (BSc 1960); Clare College, Cambridge, theoretical physics (PhD 1963); FAPS 1972 *Marital status:* married Constance Baskett 1967; 2 daughters *Recreations:* opera, walking

Michael Whippman, Under Secretary, Department of Social Security, The Adelphi, 1-11 John Adam Street, London WC2N 6HT
Telephone: 0171-962 8361 *Fax:* 0171-962 8439

WHITBREAD, LESLIE RUSSELL Secretary, Committee on Safety of Medicines

Leslie Whitbread Esq, Secretary, Committee on Safety of Medicines, Market Towers, 1 Nine Elms Lane, London SW8 5NQ *Telephone:* 0171-273 0451 *Fax:* 0171-273 0453

WHITE, KEVIN CHARLES GORDON Director of Business Development Directorate, Employment Service Grade: 4

Career: Department of Employment 1976-: director training systems division, training enterprise and education directorate 1990-92, of renamed planning division 1992-94, of business development Employment Service 1994-

Date of birth: 20 July 1950 *Education/professional qualifications:* Haberdashers' Aske's School, Elstree; East Anglia University, English and history (BA 1972); Warwick University, English (MA 1974) *Marital status:* married Louise Sarah Watt 1977; 3 sons *Recreations:* sport, theatre, cooking

Kevin C G White Esq, Director of Business Development, Employment Service, Rockingham House, 123 West Street, Sheffield S1 4ER
Telephone: 01142 596250 *Fax:* 01142 595700

WHITE, RICHARD HAMILTON HAYDEN Head of Legal Group, Lord Chancellor's Department Grade: 3

Career: private practice solicitor 1963-67; lecturer/senior lecturer in law Birmingham University 1967-74; Lord Chancellor's Department 1974-: under secretary, head of legal group 1992-

Date of birth: 9 August 1939 *Education/professional qualifications:* Sutton Valence School; Trinity College, Oxford (BA, MA); solicitor 1963 *Recreations:* country pursuits, Sicily

Richard H H White Esq, Under Secretary, Lord Chancellor's Department, Southside, 105 Victoria Street, London SW1A 6QT *Telephone:* 0171-210 3530 *Fax:* 0171-210 8549

WHITING, ALAN Under Secretary, Finance Regulation and Industry Directorate, HM Treasury Grade: 3

Career: HM Treasury (HMT) 1968-69; economic assistant Department of Economic Affairs/Ministry of Technology 1969-70; economist European Free Trade Association, Geneva 1970-72, Confederation of British Industry 1972-74; Department of Trade and Industry 1974-92: economic adviser (EA) 1974-79, senior EA 1979-83, assistant secretary 1983-85, under secretary 1985-: economics division 1985-89, economic management and education 1989, finance and resource management 1989-92, financial services 1992 (responsibility transferred to HMT); HMT 1992-: US securities and investment services group/financial services regulation 1992-95, deputy director finance regulation and industry directorate 1995-

Date of birth: 14 January 1946 *Education/professional qualifications:* Acklam Hall Grammar School, Middlesbrough; East Anglia University, social studies (BA 1967); University College, London, economics (MScEcon 1969) *Marital status:* married Annette Frances Pocknee 1968; 2 daughters, 2 sons *Publications:* co-author The Trade Effects of EFTA and the EEC 1959-1967 (EFTA 1972); editor The Economics of Industrial Subsidies (HMSO 1976) *Clubs:* Littleton Sailing *Recreations:* building, sailing, sport, gardening, photography

Alan Whiting Esq, Under Secretary, HM Treasury, Parliament Street, London SW1P 3AG *Telephone:* 0171-270 4448 *Fax:* 0171-270 5563

WHITTY, NIALL RICHARD Commissioner, Scottish Law Commission

Career: private practice solicitor 1965-66; solicitor Office of Solicitor to Secretary of State for Scotland 1967-71; Scottish Law Commission 1971-: solicitor 1971-94, commissioner 1994-

Date of birth: 28 October 1937 *Education/professional qualifications:* John Watson's School, Edinburgh; Morrison's Academy, Crieff; St Andrew's University, history (MA 1960); Edinburgh University, law (LLB 1963); solicitor 1965 *Marital status:* married Elke Mechthild Maria Gillis 1977; 3 sons, 1 daughter *Publications:* articles on Scottish law

Niall R Whitty Esq, Commissioner, Scottish Law Commission, 140 Causewayside, Edinburgh EH9 1PR *Telephone:* 0131-668 2131 *Fax:* 0131-662 4900

WICKS, Sir NIGEL LEONARD Second Permanent Secretary, Director, International Finance, HM Treasury Grade: 1A

Career: British Petroleum 1958-68; HM Treasury (HMT) 1968- private secretary to prime minister (PS to PM) 1975-78; HMT 1978-83; economic minister Washington DC embassy and UK executive director IMF and World Bank 1983-85; principal PS to PM 1985-88; HMT 1989-: second permanent secretary finance 1989-94, overseas/international finance 1994-

Date of birth: 16 June 1940 *Education/professional qualifications:* Cambridge University (MA); London University (MA) *Honours, decorations:* CBE 1979; CVO 1989; KCB 1992

Sir Nigel L Wicks KCB CVO CBE, Second Permanent Secretary, HM Treasury, Parliament Street, London SW1P 3AG *Telephone:* 0171-270 3000

WILCOCK, CHRISTOPHER CAMPLIN Head of Electricity and Nuclear Fuels Division, Department of Trade and Industry Grade: 3

Career: HM Diplomatic Service 1962-72: Foreign and Commonwealth Office, London (FCO) 1962-63; Middle East Centre for Arab Studies 1963-64; 3rd secretary Khartoum 1964-66, FCO 1966-68, 2nd secretary UK delegation to NATO 1968-70; hospital building division Department of Health and Social Security 1972-74; Department of Energy/Trade and Industry 1974-: continental shelf policy division 1974-78, electricity division 1978-81, seconded to Shell UK 1982-83, head of finance branch 1983-86, director of resource management 1986-88, head of electricity division A 1988-91, of electricity division 1991-, and of nuclear fuels division 1994-

Date of birth: 13 September 1939 *Education/professional qualifications:* Berkhamsted School; Ipswich School; Trinity Hall, Cambridge, modern languages (BA Tripos parts I & II 1960), oriental languages (Tripos part I 1962) *Honours, decorations:* Order of the Two Niles, Fifth Class (Sudan) 1965 *Marital status:* married Evelyn Clare Gollin 1965; 2 daughters *Recreations:* reading, cinema, travel

Christopher C Wilcock, Under Secretary, Department of Trade and Industry, 1 Palace Street, London SW1E 5HE *Telephone:* 0171-238 3734 *Fax:* 0171-630 9570

WILCOX, JUDITH (Lady Wilcox) Chairman, National Consumer Council

Career: financial director Capstan Foods 1970-78, chairman Channel Foods Ltd 1980-88; president directeur général Pecheries de la Morinie, France 1988-90; chair National Consumer Council (independent body for domestic consumers of publicly and privately provided goods and services) 1990- *Current non-Whitehall posts:* director Automobile Association Ltd 1991-, Fanum Ltd 1991-, Morinie et Cie, France 1990-

Date of birth: 31 October 1940 *Education/professional qualifications:* St Mary's Convent, Wantage; Plymouth Polytechnic *Marital status:* widowed; 1 son *Clubs:* Reform *Recreations:* sailing, horseracing, 14th-century calligraphy

Lady Wilcox, Chairman, National Consumer Council, 20 Grosvenor Gardens, London SW1W 0DH *Telephone:* 0171-730 3469 *Fax:* 0171-730 0191

WILD, (JOHN) ROBIN Chief Dental Officer, Scottish Office Home and Health Department Grade: 4

Career: general dental practice 1965-71; dental officer (DO) East Lothian county council 1971-74; chief administrative DO Borders health board 1974-87: regional dental postgraduate adviser Edinburgh postgraduate board for medicine 1982-87; Scottish Office Home and Health Department 1987-: deputy chief DO 1987-93, chief DO 1993-

Date of birth: 12 September 1941 *Education/professional qualifications:* Sedbergh School, Yorkshire; Edinburgh University, dentistry (BDS 1965); Dundee University, public dentistry (DPD 1973) *Honours, decorations:* JP 1982 *Marital status:* married Daphne 1965; 2 daughters, 1 son *Clubs:* Royal Scottish Automobile; Royal Commonwealth Society; Bentley Drivers *Recreations:* vintage cars, music, gardening

J Robin Wild Esq, Chief Dental Officer, Scottish Office Home and Health Department, St Andrew's House, Edinburgh EH1 3DG *Telephone:* 0131-244 2302 *Fax:* 0131-244 2683

WILKINSON, Rear-Admiral NICHOLAS JOHN Commandant, Joint Service Defence College

Career: HM Ships Venus, Vidal, Hermes, Neptune, Hardy, Fife, Endurance, London 1960-78; Ministry of Defence (MoD) 1968-80: offices of vice chief naval staff and assistant chief naval staff (policy) 1968-77; assistant director naval officer appointments 1978-80; training commander, Chatham 1980-82; military assistant to director international military staff NATO HQ 1983-85; MoD 1986-90: director defence logistics co-ordination 1986-89; secretary to First Sea Lord 1989-90; military member Prospect Defence Organisation Project 1991-92; director-general naval manpower and training MoD 1992-94; commandant Joint Service Defence College 1994-

Date of birth: 14 April 1941 *Education/professional qualifications:* Cheltenham College; Britannia Royal Naval College, Dartmouth (commission 1961); Lieutenants' Greenwich course; army staff course; NATO defense course; Royal College of Defence Studies 1986; FIM 1991 *Honours, decorations:* CB 1993 *Recreations:* cricket, opera, swimming, cuisine périgourdine

Rear-Admiral Nicholas J Wilkinson CB, Commandant, Joint Service Defence College, Greenwich, London SE10 9NN *Telephone:* 0181-858 2154 *Fax:* 0181-853 5739

WILLCOCKS, VALERIE MICHELLE Chief Executive, Independent Tribunal Service Grade: 6

Career: nurse, sister 1963-66; community midwife 1967-70; health visitor 1970-76; South Lincolnshire Health Authority 1976-88: nursing officer 1976-80, senior community services nursing officer 1980-82, manpower/capital planning officer 1982-85, research/quality assurance/planning officer 1985-88; Department of Health 1988-93: health promotion/services for ethnic minority groups 1988-89, senior principal research officer medical division 1990-91, editor Health Trends 1991-93; chief executive Independent Tribunal Service 1993-

Date of birth: 10 June 1941 *Education/professional qualifications:* Prince Rupert School, Germany; RGN 1961, RM 1962, RHV 1972, NCDN 1974; Open University, social sciences (BA 1979); Nottingham University, social administration (MPhil 1986) *Marital status:* Arthur John (partner); 1 son *Recreations:* herb gardening, charity fundraising, theatre, music, crafts

Mrs Valerie M Willcocks, Chief Executive, Independent Tribunal Service, City Gate House, 39-45 Finsbury Square, London EC2A 1PX *Telephone:* 0171-814 6505 *Fax:* 0171-814 6540

WILLIAMS, HELEN MARY Head of Transdepartmental Group, Office of Science and Technology, Office of Public Service and Science Grade: 3

Career: Department of Education and Science (DES) 1972-78; resident observer Civil Service Selection Board 1978-79; DES 1979-93: assistant secretary 1984-93: advisory board for research councils 1984-87, national curriculum policy 1987-91, local education authority spending policy 1991-93; head of transdepartmental group Office of Science and Technology, Office of Public Service and Science/Cabinet Office 1993-

Date of birth: 30 June 1950 *Education/professional qualifications:* Allerton High School; St Hilda's College, Oxford, modern history (BA 1972) *Marital status:* married David Michael Forrester 1983; 1 son, 1 daughter *Recreations:* family life, walking

Mrs Helen M Williams, Office of Science and Technology, Office of Public Service and Science, Albany House, 84-86 Petty France, London SW1H 9ST *Telephone:* 0171-271 2020 *Fax:* 0171-271 2018

WILLIAMS, HYWELL **Special Adviser, Welsh Office**

Career: schoolmaster Rugby School 1982-91; journalist and writer 1991-93; special adviser to John Redwood, Secretary of State for Wales 1993-

Date of birth: 1956 *Education/professional qualifications:* St John's College, Cambridge (MA)

Hywell Williams Esq, Special Adviser, Welsh Office, Gwydyr House, Whitehall, London SW1A 2ER *Telephone:* 0171-210 0549

WILLIAMS, JENNY MARY **Under Secretary and Head of Railways Privatisation Directorate, Department of Transport** Grade: 3

Career: Department of Transport: under secretary, head of railways directorate (privatisation) 1993- *Current non-Whitehall posts:* director Morley College 1993-

Date of birth: 26 September 1948 *Marital status:* married 1970; 3 sons

Ms Jenny M Williams, Under Secretary, Department of Transport, 2 Marsham Street, London SW1P 3EB *Telephone:* 0171-276 5849 *Fax:* 0171-276 0307

WILLIAMS, MARJORIE EILEEN **South West Regional Controller, Inland Revenue** Grade: 4

Career: Inland Revenue 1972-: south west regional controller 1994-

Date of birth: 18 December 1946 *Education/professional qualifications:* Stretford Girls' Grammar School, Lancashire; Reading University, geography with geology (BSc 1968) *Marital status:* married Graham Terence 1970 *Recreations:* birdwatching, flying, gardening

Mrs Marjorie Williams, Regional Controller, Inland Revenue, Longbrook House, New North Road, Exeter EX4 4UA *Telephone:* 01392 453210 *Fax:* 01392 216803

WILLIAMS, MIKE **Under Secretary, Finance Regulation and Industry Directorate, HM Treasury** Grade: 3

Career: HM Treasury 1973-: seconded to Cabinet Office 1976-77, to Price Waterhouse 1980-81; head of industry group 1992-95, deputy director finance regulation and industry directorate 1995-

Date of birth: 22 January 1948 *Education/professional qualifications:* Wycliffe College, Stonehouse, Gloucestershire; Trinity Hall, Cambridge, economics (BA 1969, MA); Nuffield College, Oxford, development economics research *Marital status:* married Jennifer Mary Donaldson 1970; 3 sons

Michael L Williams Esq, Under Secretary, HM Treasury, Parliament Street, London SW1P 3AG *Telephone:* 0171-270 4449 *Fax:* 0171-270 4332

WILLIAMSON, (GEORGE) EDWARD **HM Chief Inspector of Explosives, Health and Safety Executive**

Career: fluoro-chemical research University of Manchester Institute of Science and Technology (UMIST) 1959-64; production management ICI 1964-73; explosives inspectorate Home Office 1973-74, Health and Safety Executive 1974-: head of policy section 1976-85; deputy chief inspector of explosives (CIE) 1985-86, CIE 1986-

Date of birth: 8 February 1938 *Education/professional qualifications:* King's School, Macclesfield; UMIST, chemistry (BSc Tech 1959) *Marital status:* married Beryl Ann Rowley 1960; 2 sons, 1 daughter *Clubs:* West Kirby Sailing *Recreations:* sailing, walking, family

Edward Williamson Esq, HM Chief Inspector of Explosives, Health and Safety Executive, Magdalen House, Stanley Precinct, Bootle, Merseyside L20 3QZ *Telephone:* 0151-951 4018 *Fax:* 0151-951 3891

WILLIS, Air Chief Marshal Sir JOHN FREDERICK Vice Chief of the Defence Staff, Ministry of Defence

Career: Royal Air Force (RAF) 1955-: squadron flying and flying instructor posts 1958-77: officer commanding (OC) No 27 squadron; Ministry of Defence (MoD) 1977-82; OC RAF Akrotiri, Cyprus 1982-84; director of air staff briefing MoD 1984-85; chief of special weapons branch Supreme Headquarters Allied Powers Europe 1985-89; assistant chief of defence staff (policy and nuclear) MoD 1989-91; director general training RAF 1991-92; air officer commanding in chief Support Command 1992-94; chief of staff Logistics Command 1994-95; vice chief of the defence staff MoD 1995-

Date of birth: 27 October 1937 *Education/professional qualifications:* Dulwich College, London; RAF College, Cranwell (commission 1958) *Honours, decorations:* CBE 1988, CB 1991, KCB 1993 *Recreations:* model aircraft

Air Chief Marshal Sir John Willis KCB CBE, Vice Chief of the Defence Staff, Ministry of Defence, Whitehall, London SW1A 2HB *Telephone:* 0171-218 7657 *Fax:* 0171-218 6799

WILLOTT, (WILLIAM) BRIAN Chief Executive, Export Credits Guarantee Department Grade: 2

Career: low-temperature physics research Maryland University, USA 1965-67; Board of Trade 1967-73: assistant principal 1967-69, principal, shipping policy division 1969-73; HM Treasury 1973-75; Department of [Trade and] Industry 1975-80: assistant secretary 1975-80: industrial and commercial policy 1975-78, industrial development unit 1978-80; under secretary 1980-92: seconded to National Enterprise Board/British Technology Board 1980-84: secretary 1980, chief executive 1981-84, head of information technology 1984-87, of financial services 1987-92; chief executive Export Credits Guarantee Department 1992-

Date of birth: 14 May 1940 *Education/professional qualifications:* Solihull School; Queen Elizabeth Grammar School, Wakefield; Trinity College, Cambridge, natural sciences (BA 1961, MA), physics (PhD 1965) *Marital status:* married Alison Leyland Pyke-Lees 1970; 2 daughters, 2 sons *Recreations:* reading, music, walking, cycling, gardening

W Brian Willott Esq, Chief Executive, Export Credits Guarantee Department, 2 Exchange Tower, Harbour Exchange Square, London E14 9GS *Telephone:* 0171-512 7004 *Fax:* 0171-512 7146

WILLOUGHBY, ROGER JAMES Clerk of Private Bills and Registrar of Members' Interests, House of Commons Grade: 3

Career: House of Commons Department of the Clerk 1962-: deputy principal clerk 1975; secretary to UK delegation to European Parliament 1976-79; clerk of Home Affairs Committee 1979-84, of supply, Public Bill Office 1984-88, of private bills (conduct of private business in committee and the chamber; examiner of petitions for private bills) 1988-, registrar of members' interests 1994-

Date of birth: 30 September 1939 *Education/professional qualifications:* Shrewsbury School; Balliol College, Oxford, literae humaniores; English language and literature (BA 1962) *Marital status:* married Veronica Lepper 1970 *Recreations:* literature, cricket, walking

Roger J Willoughby Esq, Clerk of Private Bills, House of Commons, London SW1A 0AA *Telephone:* 0171-219 3269

WILMSHURST, JON BARRY Under Secretary, Economic and Social, Overseas Development Administration Grade: 3

Career: statistician Rhodesia and Nyasaland 1960-63; economist National Institute of Economic and Social Research 1964; Overseas Development Ministry/Administration (ODA) 1964-78: economist 1964-71, senior economist (SE) 1971-78; SE Department of Transport 1979-83, Monopolies and Mergers Commission 1983-85; ODA 1985-: under secretary economic and social department (chief economist, head of statistics, social, financial and public administration advisory services) 1990-

Date of birth: 25 October 1936 *Education/professional qualifications:* Beckenham Grammar School; Manchester University, economics (BA 1960) *Marital status:* married June Taylor 1960; 4 daughters *Clubs:* Langley Park Golf *Recreations:* golf, gardening

Jon B Wilmshurst Esq, Under Secretary, Overseas Development Administration, 94 Victoria Street, London SW1E 5JL *Telephone:* 0171-917 0522 *Fax:* 0171-917 0797

WILSON, AUSTIN PETER Head of Fire and Emergency Planning, Home Office Grade: 3

Career: Home Office (HO) 1961-88: seconded to Northern Ireland Office (NIO) 1977-80; assistant under secretary 1981-; NIO 1988-92; head of criminal policy department (HO) 1992-94, of fire and emergency planning department 1994-

Date of birth: 31 March 1938 *Education/professional qualifications:* St Edmund Hall, Oxford, modern history (BA 1961) *Marital status:* married Norma Louise Mill 1962; 1 son, 2 daughters *Recreations:* theatre, rough walking

Austin P Wilson Esq, Assistant Under Secretary, Home Office, Horseferry Road, Dean Ryle Street, London SW1P 2AW *Telephone:* 0171-217 8209 *Fax:* 0171-217 8731

WILSON, COLIN ALEXANDER MEGAW Assistant Legal Secretary and Scottish Parliamentary Counsel, Lord Advocate's Department Grade: 3

Career: private practice solicitor 1975-79; Lord Advocate's Department (Scottish legal system) 1979-: assistant legal secretary 1979-: assistant Scottish parliamentary counsel (SPC) 1979-83, depute SPC 1983-93, SPC (drafting bills relating to Scotland) 1993-

Date of birth: 4 January 1952 *Education/professional qualifications:* High School of Glasgow; Edinburgh University, law (LLB 1973) *Marital status:* married Mandy Esca Clay 1987; 1 son, 1 daughter *Recreations:* choral singing, walking, reading

Colin A M Wilson Esq, Scottish Parliamentary Counsel, Lord Advocate's Department, 2 Carlton Gardens, London SW1Y 5AA *Telephone:* 0171-210 1022 *Fax:* 0171-210 1025

WILSON, GERALD ROBERTSON Secretary, Scottish Office Education Department; Deputy Secretary, Central Services, Scottish Office Grade: 2

Career: Scottish Office (SO) 1961-72: assistant principal 1961-66; principal Home and Health Department 1966-72; private secretary to Lord Privy Seal 1972-74; assistant secretary (AS) SO 1974-77; counsellor UK Permanent Representation to the EC, Brussels 1977-82; SO 1982-: AS 1982-84, under secretary Industry Department 1984-88, deputy secretary (DS) and secretary of Education Department 1988-, DS Central Services 1991-

Date of birth: 7 September 1939 *Education/professional qualifications:* Holy Cross Academy, Edinburgh; Edinburgh University, history (MA 1961) *Honours, decorations:* CB 1991 *Marital status:* married Margaret Wight 1963; 1 daughter, 1 son *Clubs:* New, Edinburgh *Recreations:* music

Gerald R Wilson Esq CB, Secretary, Scottish Office Education Department, New St Andrew's House, Edinburgh EH1 3TG *Telephone:* 0131-244 4409 *Fax:* 0131-244 5210

WILSON, Colonel GORDON HANCE Headmaster and Chief Executive, Duke of York's Royal Military School (Executive Agency)

Career: teacher 1974-78; administrator educational services, Cyprus 1978-80; personnel manager army education recruiting and assessment 1980-81; BAOR 1983-86: building construction manager 1983-85, education centre manager 1985-86; budget and plans administrator army education Ministry of Defence 1986-88; BAOR 1989-92: senior careers adviser education service 1989-90, station commander Verden 1990-91; chief education officer first armoured division 1991-92; headmaster and chief executive Duke of York's Royal Military School (secondary co-educational boarding for armed forces' children) 1992-

Date of birth: 29 March 1950 *Education/professional qualifications:* Queen's University, Belfast, modern history (BA 1972), education (Dip Ed 1973); Royal Military Academy, Sandhurst (commission 1974); University College, Cardiff, education (MEd 1990); Army Staff College (psc 1981) *Marital status:* married Margaret Elizabeth Smyth 1971; 1 son, 1 daughter *Recreations:* music, swimming, running, skiing

Colonel Gordon H Wilson, Headmaster, Duke of York's Royal Military School, Dover, Kent CT15 5EQ *Telephone:* 01304 245024 *Fax:* 01304 245019

WILSON, (JAMES) BRIAN Director, Planning, Government Office for the South East Grade: 4

Career: architect/planner various private practices 1966-70, Edinburgh town planning department 1970-71, Richmond London borough 1971-73; private practice project director 1973-75; Department of Environment 1975-: principal planning officer (PO) historic areas and conservation 1975-78; superintending PO south-east region 1978-82; Yorkshire and Humberside regional controller 1982-88; chief planning adviser 1988-93; regional controller, planning/director planning, government office for the south east 1993-

Date of birth: 19 May 1940 *Education/professional qualifications:* Daniel Stewart's College, Edinburgh; Heriot Watt University, architecture (DA 1965), town planning (Dip TP 1967) *Marital status:* married Irenee Elizabeth 1972; 2 sons *Recreations:* history, francophilia, old buildings

J Brian Wilson Esq, Director, Planning, Government Office for the South East, 375 Kensington High Street, London W14 8QH *Telephone:* 0171-605 9000 *Fax:* 0171-605 9249

WILSON, Major General MICHAEL PETER BRUCE GRANT Director-General and Chief Executive, Military Survey (Executive Agency)

Career: director-general and chief executive Military Survey (provision of geographic support to defence) 1993-

Date of birth: 19 August 1943 *Education/professional qualifications:* Duke of York's School, Nairobi, Kenya; University College, London, photogrammetry (diploma 1976); ARICS 1988; FRGS 1990; FIMgt 1991 *Marital status:* married Margaret Ritchie 1968; 2 sons, 1 daughter *Recreations:* climbing, mountaineering, shooting, stalking, fishing, cricket, golf

Major General M P B G Wilson, Military Survey, Elmwood Avenue, Feltham, Middlesex TW13 7AH *Telephone:* 0181-818 2130 *Fax:* 0181-818 2148

WILSON, RICHARD THOMAS JAMES Permanent Secretary, Home Office Grade: 1

Career: Board of Trade 1966-71; Cabinet Office (CO) 1971-73; Department of Energy 1974-86: assistant secretary 1977-82, under secretary 1982-87, principal establishment and finance officer 1982-86; CO 1986-90: deputy secretary 1987-92: industry HM Treasury 1990-92; permanent secretary Department of the Environment 1992-94, Home Office 1994-

Date of birth: 11 October 1942 *Education/professional qualifications:* Radley College; Clare College, Cambridge (BA 1964); Middle Temple (barrister 1965) *Honours, decorations:* CB 1991 *Marital status:* married Caroline Margaret Lee 1972; 1 son, 1 daughter *Recreations:* gardening, water colours

Richard T J Wilson CB, Permanent Secretary, Home Office, 50 Queen Anne's Gate, London SW1H 9AT *Telephone:* 0171-273 2199 *Fax:* 0171-273 2972

WILSON, ROBERT WILLIAM GORDON Principal Clerk of Domestic Committees, House of Commons Grade: 4

Career: House of Commons Department of the Clerk 1967-: senior clerk 1972-81: secretary to UK delegation to parliamentary assemblies of Council of Europe, Western European Union and North Atlantic Assembly 1974-77, deputy principal clerk 1981-91: clerk of European legislation 1981-86, environment 1986-87 and foreign affairs 1987-91 committees; principal clerk of financial committees 1991-92, of domestic committees, secretary of the House of Commons Commission and clerk of the finance and services committee 1992-

Date of birth: 8 July 1946 *Education/professional qualifications:* Lancing College; Christ Church, Oxford, modern history (BA 1967, MA) *Marital status:* single *Publications:* Guide to the Houses of Parliament (1988, 1993) *Clubs:* Traveller's *Recreations:* theatre, opera, travel, architectural conservation

Robert Wilson Esq, Principal Clerk, Domestic Committees, Committee Office, House of Commons, London SW1A 0AA *Telephone:* 0171-219 3270

WINCKLER, ANDREW STUART Head of Supervision, Securities and Investments Board

Career: HM Treasury 1970-82; Lloyds Bank 1982-87: syndications manager international bank 1982-85, director merchant bank 1985-87; director Security Pacific Hoare Govett Ltd 1987-90; deputy chair European Capital Co Ltd 1990-94; executive director, head of Supervision Securities and Investments Board (financial services regulation) 1994-

Date of birth: 8 January 1949 *Education/professional qualifications:* Bedford Modern School; Christ's College, Cambridge, history (BA 1970), economics (DipEcon 1975); MSI 1993 *Marital status:* married Marie Estelle Sigwart 1971; 3 sons *Clubs:* United Oxford and Cambridge University

Mr Andrew Winckler, Executive Director, Securities and Investments Board, Gavrelle House, 2-14 Bunhill Row, London EC1Y 8RA
Telephone: 0171-638 1240 *Fax:* 0171-382 5904

WINNIFRITH, CHARLES BONIFACE Principal Clerk, Table Office, House of Commons Grade: 3

Career: army national service 1958-60; House of Commons Department of the Clerk 1960-: assistant clerk 1960-64; senior clerk 1964-72; deputy principal clerk 1972-83; select committees 1983-89: second clerk 1983-87, clerk 1987-89; principal clerk Table Office (advice to speaker and MPs on parliamentary questions and early day motions; preparation of order paper, notice paper and order book) 1989-

Date of birth: 12 May 1936 *Education/professional qualifications:* Tonbridge School, Kent; Christ Church, Oxford, literae humaniores (BA, 1958, MA 1961) *Marital status:* married Josephine Poile MBE 1962 (died 1991); Sandra Stewart 1993; 1 son, 2 daughters *Clubs:* MCC *Recreations:* cricket, American soap opera

Charles B Winnifrith Esq, Principal Clerk, Table Office, House of Commons, London SW1A 0AA *Telephone:* 0171-219 3312

WINSTANLEY, PAUL Chief Executive, Social Security Resettlement Agency (Executive Agency) Grade: 6

Career: civil service 1969-: chief executive Social Security Resettlement Agency (for single homeless) 1994-

Date of birth: 29 September 1945 *Education/professional qualifications:* St Margaret's Grammar School, Liverpool *Marital status:* married 1987; 2 daughters

Paul Winstanley Esq, Chief Executive Social Security Resettlement Agency, Euston Tower, 286 Euston Road, London NW1 3DN
Telephone: 0171-388 1188 *Fax:* 0171-383 6069

WINYARD, Dr GRAHAM P A Medical Director, NHS Executive, Department of Health Grade: 2

Career: principal health officer Papua New Guinea 1977-79; senior registrar Oxford Regional Health Authority (RHA), lecturer London School of Hygiene 1979-82; district medical officer Lewisham and of Southwark HA 1982-87; Department of Health (DoH) 1987-90; regional medical director and director of public health Wessex 1990-93; medical director NHS Executive DoH 1993-

Date of birth: 19 January 1947 *Education/professional qualifications:* Southend High School; Hertford

College, Oxford (MA); BM, BCh; FRCP; FF PHM *Marital status:* married Sandra Catherine Bent 1979; 1 son, 2 daughters

Dr Graham Winyard, Medical Director, NHS Executive, Department of Health, Quarry House, Quarry Hill, Leeds LS2 7UE *Telephone:* 01132 545823

WISEMAN, Dr M J Health Aspects of Environment and Food (Medical), Department of Health Grade: 4

Dr M J Wiseman, Health Aspects of Environment and Food (Medical), Department of Health, Skipton House, 80 London Road, Elephant and Castle, London SE1 6LW *Telephone:* 0171-972 2000

WOOD, PHILIP Under Secretary and Head of Railway Privatisation Directorate, Department of Transport Grade: 3

Career: Department of Transport 1979-: under secretary and head of railways 2/privatisation directorate 1986-

Date of birth: 30 June 1946 *Education/professional qualifications:* Queen's College, Oxford *Honours, decorations:* OBE 1979

Philip Wood Esq OBE, Under Secretary, Department of Transport, 2 Marsham Street, London SW1P 3EB *Telephone:* 0171-276 3000

WOOD, Dr SUSAN MARION Director of Post Licensing Division, Medicines Control Agency Grade: 4

Career: medical posts St Bartholomew's Hospital, London 1979-80; research and clinical posts Hammersmith Hospital and Royal Postgraduate Medical School, London 1980-83; medicines division Department of Health 1983-90: senior medical officer 1983-84, head of review of medicines, principal medical officer 1988; head of adverse drug reactions unit 1988-90; Medicines Control Agency (post-marketing surveillance of medicines) 1990-: head of pharmacovigilance unit 1990-94, director post licensing division 1994-

Date of birth: 20 July 1952 *Education/professional qualifications:* Tormead School; County School for Girls; King's College, London, pharmacology (BSc 1973); St Bartholomew's Hospital Medical School (MB, BS 1977); Royal Postgraduate Medical School, London (MD 1985) *Marital status:* married John 1978 *Recreations:* walking, gardening, oriental cuisine, travel, primitive tribal cultures

Dr Susan M Wood, Director of Post Licensing Division, Medicines Control Agency, Market Towers, 1 Nine Elms Lane, London SW8 5NQ *Telephone:* 0171-273 0400 *Fax:* 0171-273 0675

WOODCOCK, E C Chief Crown Prosecutor, Mersey/Lancashire, Crown Prosecution Service Grade: 4

E C Woodcock Esq, Chief Crown Prosecutor, Mersey/Lancashire, Crown Prosecution Service, Royal Liver Building, Pier Head, Liverpool L3 1HN *Telephone:* 0151-236 7575 *Fax:* 0151-255 0642

WOODHEAD, CHRIS HM Chief Inspector of Schools, OFSTED Grade: 2

Career: English teacher 1969-76; English education tutor Oxford University 1976-82; Shropshire local education authority (LEA) 1982-88: English adviser 1982-84, chief adviser 1984-88; deputy chief education officer Devon LEA 1988-90, Cornwall LEA 1990; National Curriculum Council 1990-93: deputy chief executive 1990-91, chief executive (CE) 1991-93; CE School Curriculum and Assessment Authority 1993-94; chief inspector of schools Office for Standards in Education 1994-

Date of birth: 20 October 1946 *Education/professional qualifications:* Wallington Grammar School, Surrey; Bristol University: English (BA 1968), PGCE 1969; Keele University (MA) *Marital status:* divorced; 1 daughter *Publications:* Writing and Responding (Oxford University Press – OUP 1982); 19th and 20th Century English Poetry (OUP 1984) *Recreations:* climbing

Chris Woodhead Esq, HM Chief Inspector, OFSTED, Alexandra House, 29-33 Kingsway, London WC2B 6SE *Telephone:* 0171-421 6800 *Fax:* 0171-421 6546

WOODHEAD, Sir PETER Prisons Ombudsman, Prisons Ombudsman Office Grade: 5

Career: Royal Navy 1962-94: director naval operations Ministry of Defence 1985; command HMS Illustrious 1986-88; flag officer 1st and 2nd flotillas 1988-91; deputy supreme commander Atlantic NATO 1991-94; prisons ombudsman (investigating complaints and grievances in prisons) 1994-

Date of birth: 30 July 1939 *Education/professional qualifications:* Leeds Grammar School; Conway MN training ship; Britannia Royal Naval College, Dartmouth; national defence college, Royal College Defence Studies *Honours, decorations:* KCB 1992; Legion of Honour, USA 1994 *Marital status:* married Carol 1964; 1 son, 1 daughter *Clubs:* Royal Navy *Recreations:* travel, Christian activities, sport

Sir Peter Woodhead KCB, Prisons Ombudsman, Prisons Ombudsman Office, St Vincent House, 30 Orange Street, London WC2 7HH *Telephone:* 0171-389 1527 *Fax:* 0171-389 1492

WOODS, (ELISABETH) LIS ANN Director Operations (Compliance) HM Customs and Excise Grade: 3

Career: assistant principal Ministry of Pensions and National Insurance and successors 1963-69; Department of [Health and] Social Security (D[H]SS) 1970-80: principal 1970-76, assistant secretary (AS) 1976-80; AS HM Treasury 1980-82; AS DHSS 1976-88; under secretary 1988-; head of finance DSS 1988-91; HM Customs and Excise 1991-: director VAT control 1991-94, operations (compliance) 1994-

Date of birth: 27 October 1940 *Education/professional qualifications:* South Hampstead High School for Girls, London; Girton College, Cambridge, modern languages (BA 1963) *Marital status:* married James Maurice 1976 *Recreations:* cycling, cooking, reading

Mrs Lis Woods, Under Secretary, HM Customs and Excise, New King's Beam House, 22 Upper Ground, London SE1 9PJ *Telephone:* 0171-865 5020 *Fax:* 0171-865 5354

WOOL, Dr ROSEMARY JANE Director of Health Care, HM Prison Service (Executive Agency) Grade: 3

Career: general practice 1963-74; Home Office Prison Service 1974-: medical officer (MO), senior MO, principal MO prison medicine service 1974-89; director prison medical services/health care 1989-

Date of birth: 19 July 1935 *Education/professional qualifications:* High School, March, Cambridgeshire; Charing Cross Hospital, London (MB BS 1960, D Obst RCOG 1965, DPM 1972, MRC Psych 1974, FRC Psych 1988) *Marital status:* single *Recreations:* walking, piano playing, music

Dr Rosemary J Wool, Director of Health Care, HM Prison Service, Cleland House, Page Street, London SW1P 4LN *Telephone:* 0171-217 6419 *Fax:* 0171-217 6224

WOOLER, STEPHEN JOHN Deputy Legal Secretary and Deputy Head of Department, Legal Secretariat to the Law Officers Grade: 4

Career: private practice barrister 1969-73; Director of Public Prosecutions (DPP) Office 1973-87: legal assistant (LA) 1973-76, senior LA 1976-82, assistant DPP 1982-83, seconded as legal adviser to law officers 1983-87; chief crown prosecutor London north 1987-89; assistant/deputy legal secretary and deputy head of department to law officers/legal secretariat to the law officers 1989-

Date of birth: 16 March 1948 *Education/professional qualifications:* Bedford Modern School; University College, London, law (LLB 1969); Gray's Inn (barrister 1969) *Marital status:* married Jonquil Elizabeth Wilmshurst-Smith 1974; 1 son, 1 daughter *Recreations:* rugby, walking, gardening, reading

Stephen J Wooler Esq, Deputy Legal Secretary, Legal Secretariat to the Law Officers, Attorney General's Chambers, 9 Buckingham Gate, London SW1E 6JP *Telephone:* 0171-828 7155 *Fax:* 0171-828 0593

WOOLLEY, Dr DAVID Director, Fire Research Station, Building Research Establishment (Executive Agency) Grade: 4

Career: postdoctoral fellow National Research Council, Canada 1964-66; Fire Research Station, Building Research Establishment 1966-: head of combustion products section 1973-83, of buildings and structures division 1983-88; director 1988- *Current non-Whitehall posts:* visiting professor in chemistry Salford University

Date of birth: 8 April 1939 *Education/professional qualifications:* St Andrew's University, chemistry (BSc 1961, PhD 1964); FIFireE; CChem; FRSC; FPRI, MIFS *Marital status:* married Maureen; 2 sons *Publications:* numerous on fire safety *Recreations:* woodwork, metalwork, car mechanics, classic cars

Dr David Woolley, Director, Fire Research Station, Building Research Establishment, Garston, Watford WD2 7JR *Telephone:* 01923 894040 *Fax:* 01923 664910

Parliamentary Offices

see page 347

WOOLMAN, ROGER Solicitor to Ministry of Agriculture, Fisheries and Food, Intervention Board and Forestry Commission Grade: 2

Career: legal assistant (LA) Office of Fair Trading (OFT) 1976-78; Department of Trade and Industry (DTI) 1978-88, 1991-92: senior LA 1978-81, assistant solicitor 1981-84, under secretary (US) 1985-88, 1991-92; legal director OFT 1988-91; DTI Solicitor's Office division B (legal advice on company law, insurance, insolvency) 1991-92; solicitor to Ministry of Agriculture, Fisheries and Food, Intervention Board and Forestry Commission 1993-

Date of birth: 13 February 1937 *Education/professional qualifications:* Perse School, Cambridge; Trinity Hall, Cambridge, law (BA 1960, MA) *Marital status:* married Elizabeth Ingham 1973; 1 daughter, 1 son *Clubs:* Reform, Hampstead Golf

Roger Woolman Esq, The Solicitor, Ministry of Agriculture, Fisheries and Food, 55 Whitehall, London SW1A 2EY *Telephone:* 0171-270 8379 *Fax:* 0171-270 8096

WOOTTON, (HAROLD) JOHN Chief Executive, Transport Research Laboratory (Executive Agency) Grade: 3

Career: civil engineering lecturer Leeds University 1959-62; technical director Freeman, Fox, Wilbur Smith and Associates transport consultants 1963-67; director SIA Ltd computer service bureau 1967-71; chairman Wootton Jeffreys Consultants Ltd transport and planning consultants 1971-91; chief executive Transport [and Road] Research Laboratory 1991-

Date of birth: 17 November 1936 *Education/professional qualifications:* Queen Mary's Grammar School, Walsall; Queen Mary College, London, civil engineering (BScEng 1958); University of California, Berkeley, USA, transport engineering (MEng 1963) *Marital status:* married Patricia Ann Riley 1960; 2 sons *Clubs:* Royal Automobile *Recreations:* cricket, golf, rotary, photography

John Wootton Esq, Chief Executive, Transport Research Laboratory, Crowthorne, Berkshire RG11 6AU *Telephone:* 01344 770001 *Fax:* 01344 770761

WORMALD, PETER JOHN Director and Registrar General for England and Wales, Office of Population Censuses and Surveys Grade: 2

Career: Ministry of Health (MoH) 1958-65: assistant principal 1958-63, principal 1963-65; principal HM Treasury 1965-67, MoH 1967-70; Department of Health and Social Security 1970-87: assistant secretary 1970-78, under secretary 1978-87; director of personnel NHS management board/executive 1987-90; director and registrar general for England and Wales Office of Population Censuses and Surveys 1990-

Date of birth: 10 March 1936 *Education/professional qualifications:* Doncaster Grammar School; Queen's College, Oxford, jurisprudence (BA 1958, MA) *Honours, decorations:* CB 1990 *Marital status:* married Elizabeth North 1962; 3 sons *Clubs:* United Oxford and Cambridge University, Home Park Golf, St Enodoc Golf *Recreations:* music, golf, bridge

Peter J Wormald Esq CB, Director and Registrar General for England and Wales, Office of Population Censuses and Surveys, St Catherine's House, 10 Kingsway, London WC2B 6JP *Telephone:* 0171-396 2139 *Fax:* 0171-396 2576

WORSWICK, Dr RICHARD DAVID Chief Executive and Government Chemist, Laboratory of the Government Chemist (Executive Agency) Grade: 3

Career: Science Research Council research assistant department of inorganic chemistry, Oxford 1972-73; research product manager Boots Company plc 1973-76; Harwell Laboratory, United Kingdom Atomic Energy Authority 1976-90: marketing and planning 1976-85, head of research planning 1985-88, of environmental and medical sciences division 1988-90; director process technology and instrumentation division Atomic Energy Authority industrial technology 1990-91; chief executive and Government Chemist Laboratory of Government Chemist 1991-

Date of birth: 22 July 1946 *Education/professional qualifications:* Magdalen College School, Oxford; New College, Oxford, chemistry (BA 1969); Department of Inorganic Chemistry, Oxford (DPhil 1972); FRIC 1991 *Marital status:* married Jacqueline Adcock 1970; 3 daughters *Recreations:* violin playing

Dr Richard D Worswick, Chief Executive and Government Chemist, Laboratory of the Government Chemist, Queen's Road, Teddington, Middlesex TW11 0LY *Telephone:* 0181-943 7300 *Fax:* 0181-943 2767

WRIGHT, DAVID JOHN Deputy Under Secretary, Foreign and Commonwealth Office Grade: DS2

Career: Foreign Office 1966; third/second secretary Tokyo 1966-72; Foreign and Commonwealth Office, London (FCO) 1972-75; Ecole Nationale d'Administration, Paris 1975-76; first secretary Paris 1976-80; private secretary (PS) to secretary of Cabinet 1980-82; economic counsellor Tokyo 1982-85; head of FCO personnel services 1985-88; seconded as deputy PS to Prince of Wales 1988-90; ambassador to South Korea 1990-94; deputy under secretary Asia, Americas, Africa and joint export promotion directorate FCO 1994- *Current non-Whitehall posts:* non-executive director AEA Technology 1994-

Date of birth: 16 June 1944 *Education/professional qualifications:* Wolverhampton Grammar School; Peterhouse, Cambridge, history (BA 1966, MA) *Honours, decorations:* LVO 1990, CMG 1992 *Marital status:* married Sally Ann Dodkin 1968; 1 son, 1 daughter *Clubs:* United Oxford and Cambridge University *Recreations:* running, cooking, military history, golf

David J Wright Esq CMG LVO, Deputy Under Secretary, Foreign and Commonwealth Office, King Charles Street, London SW1A 2AH *Telephone:* 0171-270 2156 *Fax:* 0171-270 2780

WRIGHT, (LESTER) PAUL Under Secretary, Broadcasting and Media Group, Department of National Heritage Grade: 3

Career: Home Office 1971-92: asssistant private secretary (PS) to Home Secretary 1972-73; Harkness fellowship 1976-78; PS to permanent under secretary 1980-82; head of prison building 1983-87, of broadcasting 1987-91, of drugs divisions 1991-92; Department of National Heritage 1992-: under secretary broadcasting, film and sport group 1992-94, broadcasting and media group 1994-

Date of birth: 2 July 1946 *Education/professional qualifications:* Bedford School; Gonville and Caius College, Cambridge, history (BA 1967, MA, PhD 1970) *Marital status:* married Jill Wildman 1969; 1 son *Recreations:* music, theatre, walking

Paul Wright Esq, Under Secretary, Department of National Heritage, 2-4 Cockspur Street, London SW1Y 5DH *Telephone:* 0171-211 6410 *Fax:* 0171-211 6460

WRIGHT, STEPHEN JOHN LEADBETTER Assistant Under Secretary, EU Affairs, Foreign and Commonwealth Office Grade: 3

Career: HM Diplomatic Service 1968-: third secretary Havana 1969-71; Civil Service College 1971-72; second/first secretary (FS) Foreign and Commonwealth Office, London (FCO) 1972-75; FS British Information Services, New York 1975-80; FS UK permanent representation to EC, Brussels (UKPR) 1980-84; deputy head of energy, science and space department FCO 1984-85; seconded as counsellor to Cabinet Office 1985-87; counsellor and head of chancery New Delhi 1988-91; external relations counsellor UKPR 1991-94; assistant under secretary EC/EU affairs FCO 1994-

Date of birth: 7 December 1946 *Education/professional qualifications:* Shrewsbury School; Queen's College, Oxford, modern history (BA 1968) *Marital status:* married Georgina Susan Butler 1970 *Recreations:* photography, reading, music, rowing, riding, walking

Stephen J L Wright Esq, Assistant Under Secretary, Foreign and Commonwealth Office, London SW1A 2AH *Telephone:* 0171-270 2277 *Fax:* 0171-270 2320

WROE, DAVID CHARLES LYNN Deputy Director, Central Statistical Office Grade: 2

Career: Ministry of Pensions and National Insurance 1965-68; Central Statistical Office (CSO) 1968-70, 1973-75; 1976-82; Department of Environment 1982-91: under secretary (US) regional policy 1982-86, director of statistics 1982-91, US housing monitoring and analysis 1986-91; CSO 1991-: director of national accounts 1991-94, deputy director 1991- *Current non-Whitehall posts:* non-executive director John Laing Construction Ltd; member Royal Statistical Society council

Date of birth: 20 February 1942 *Education/professional qualifications:* Trinity College, Cambridge (BA 1967, MA); Trinity College, Oxford, statistics; Birkbeck College, London (MSc 1967) *Marital status:* married; 3 daughters *Publications:* articles on economic statistics *Clubs:* Reform *Recreations:* sailing

David C L Wroe Esq, Deputy Director, Central Statistical Office, Great George Street, London SW1P 3AQ *Telephone:* 0171-270 3000 *Fax:* 0171-270 5866

WYLIE, ROBERT D S Deputy Solicitor, HM Customs and Excise Grade: 3

Career: HM Customs and Excise: principal assistant solicitor -1994, deputy solicitor 1994-

Robert D S Wylie Esq, Deputy Solicitor, HM Customs and Excise, New King's Beam House, 22 Upper Ground, London SE1 9PJ *Telephone:* 0171-620 1313 *Fax:* 0171-865 5022

Y

YARD, JOHN Director, Business Services Office, Inland Revenue Grade: 3

Career: Inland Revenue 1963-: tax inspector 1971-84; deputy director systems and policy 1984-91; head of change management group 1992; under secretary 1993-: director information technology office 1993-94, business services offices 1994-

Date of birth: 29 July 1944 *Education/professional qualifications:* St Marylebone Grammar School, London *Marital status:* married Jean Murray 1992; 2 sons, 1 daughter *Recreations:* holidays, property renovation

John Yard Esq, Under Secretary, Inland Revenue, 10 Maltravers Street, c/o Somerset House, Strand, London WC2R 1LB *Telephone:* 0171-438 6562 *Fax:* 0171-438 7239

YASS, IRVING Director, Planning and Transport, Government Office for London, Departments of the Environment, Transport, Trade and Industry, and Employment Grade: 3

Career: Ministries of Transport (MoT) and Civil Aviation 1958-67; HM Treasury 1967-70; MoT 1970-71; Department of Environment 1971-76: assistant secretary (AS) urban planning 1971-73, central policy planning 1973-74, secretary Layfield committee on local government finance 1974-76; Department of Transport 1976-: AS finance, roads and local transport 1976-78, general policy highways 1978-81, public transport policy 1981-82; under secretary 1982-: director of finance 1982-86, London regional director 1987-94, director of London transport policy/planning and transport Government Office for London 1992-

Date of birth: 20 December 1935 *Education/professional qualifications:* Harrow County Boys' Grammar School; Balliol College, Oxford, modern history (BA 1956) *Honours, decorations:* CB 1993 *Marital status:* married Marion Ruth Leighton 1962; 1 daughter, 2 sons

Irving Yass Esq CB, Under Secretary, Government Office for London, 2 Marsham Street, London SW1P 3EB *Telephone:* 0171-276 6089 *Fax:* 0171-276 0727

YEO, DIANE HELEN Commissioner, Charity Commission Grade: 4

Career: production BBC radio 1968-74; clearing house director Africa Educational Trust 1974-79; head of fundraising Girl Guides Association 1979-82; director of fundraising and public relations Young Women's Christian Association 1982-85; director Institute of Charity Fundraising Managers 1985-88; charity commissioner 1989- *Current non-Whitehall posts:* consultant London School of Economics Centre for Voluntary Organisation 1988-; director Charity Appointments 1985-

Date of birth: 22 July 1945 *Education/professional qualifications:* Blackheath High School, London; Birkbeck College, London University, psychology (BSc 1970); FICFM; FRSA 1990 *Marital status:* married Timothy Stephen Kenneth 1970; 1 daughter, 1 son *Recreations:* photography, tennis, swimming

Mrs Diane H Yeo, Commissioner, Charity Commission, St Albans House, 57-60 Haymarket, London SW1Y 4QX *Telephone:* 0171-210 3000 *Fax:* 0171-210 4604

YORK, D Operations Director and Deputy Road Programme Director, Highways Agency (Executive Agency) Grade: 4

D York Esq, Operations Director, Highways Agency, 5 Broadway, Broad Street, Birmingham B15 1BL *Telephone:* 0121-631 8000 *Fax:* 0121-631 8186

YOUNG, Dr ANDREW BUCHANAN Deputy Chief Medical Officer, Scottish Office Home and Health Department Grade: 3

Career: hospital medical superintendent, Kenya 1965-72; fellow in community health medicine Scottish Health Service 1972-75; Home and Health Department Scottish Office 1975-: principal medical officer 1985-89; deputy chief medical officer 1989-

Date of birth: 11 August 1937 *Education/professional qualifications:* Edinburgh University (MB, ChB 1961); FRCPEd 1983, MRCPEd 1970; FFPHM 1984, MFPHM 1974; DTM&H 1964 *Honours, decorations:* QHP 1993 *Marital status:* married Lois; 1 son, 1 daughter

Dr Andrew B Young Esq, Deputy Chief Medical Officer, Scottish Office Home and Health Department, St Andrew's House, Edinburgh EH1 3DG *Telephone:* 0131-244 2270 *Fax:* 0131-244 2835

YOUNG, ANDREW GEORGE Chief Actuary, Social Security Division, Government Actuary's Department Grade: 4

Date of birth: 15 June 1949 *Education/professional qualifications:* Glasgow University (BSc); FIA *Marital status:* married; 4 *Recreations:* rock and pop music; theatre, football

A G Young Esq, Chief Actuary, Social Security Division, Government Actuary's Department, 22 Kingsway, London WC2B 6LE *Telephone:* 0171-242 6828

YOUNG, JOHN ROBERT CHESTER Chief Executive and Executive Director, Securities and Investments Board

Career: Simon and Coates stockbrokers 1961-82: investment analyst 1961-65, partner 1965-82: deputy senior partner, head of institutional sales 1976-82; Stock Exchange 1978-87: member council 1978-82, executive director (ED) policy planning and markets 1982-87; chief executive Securities Association/Securities and Futures Authority 1987-93; chief executive and ED Securities and Investments Board 1993- *Current non-Whitehall posts:* non-executive director East Surrey Hospital and Community Healthcare NHS Trust 1992-

Date of birth: 6 September 1937 *Education/professional qualifications:* Bishop Vesey's Grammar School, Sutton Coldfield; St Edmund Hall, Oxford, jurisprudence (BA, MA) *Honours, decorations:* CBE *Marital status:* married Pauline Joyce Yates 1963; 1 daughter, 2 sons (1 son deceased) *Clubs:* City, Vincents, Harlequins, Dorking RFC *Recreations:* rugby, cooking

John R C Young Esq, Chief Executive, Securities and Investments Board, Gavrelle House, 2-4 Bunhill Row, London EC1Y 8RA *Telephone:* 0171-638 1240 *Fax:* 0171-382 5927

Government Departments

see page 372

YOUNG, (JOHN ROBERTSON) ROB Deputy Under Secretary of State, Chief Clerk, Foreign and Commonwealth Office Grade: DS2

Career: third secretary Foreign and Commonwealth Office, London (FCO) 1967-68; Middle East Centre for Arab Studies 1968-70; third/second secretary Cairo 1970-72; FCO 1972-76: first secretary (FS) 1972-75; private secretary to minister of state 1975-76; Ecole Nationale d'Administration, Paris 1976-77; FS Paris 1977-81, FCO 1981-83; counsellor Damascus 1984-86; head of Middle East department FCO 1987-91; minister Paris 1991-94; deputy under secretary former Soviet Union, eastern Europe, Middle East FCO 1994-95, chief clerk 1995-

Date of birth: 21 February 1945 *Education/professional qualifications:* King Edward VI School, Norwich; Leicester University, French and Latin (BA 1967) *Honours, decorations:* CMG 1991 *Marital status:* married Catherine Suzanne Françoise 1967; 2 daughters, 1 son *Clubs:* Cruising Association *Recreations:* music, theatre, sailing

J R Young Esq CMG, Chief Clerk, Foreign and Commonwealth Office, King Charles Street, London SW1A 2AH *Telephone:* 0171-210 8239
Fax: 0171-210 8022

YOUNG, ROBIN URQUHART Regional Director, Government Office for London Grade: 2

Career: Department of the Environment (DoE) 1973-: private secretary to secretaries of state 1985-88; under secretary housing 1988-89, environment policy 1989-91, local government review 1991-92, local government 1992-94; regional director government office for London 1994-

Date of birth: 7 September 1948 *Education/professional qualifications:* Fettes College, Edinburgh; University College, Oxford (BA 1971) *Marital status:* single *Recreations:* squash, tennis, cinema

Robin Young Esq, Regional Director, Government Office for London, 2 Marsham Street, London SW1P 3EB *Telephone:* 0171-276 0410
Fax: 0171-276 5827

Institutions

Parliamentary Offices

Government Departments

House of Commons

Organisation

The House of Commons Service is the permanent service of the House although its staff are not civil servants of the Crown. The work of this permanent staff, which is divided between six departments, revolves around the activity of the House of Commons and its committees.

Responsibilities

administration and finance
catering
chamber
committees
Hansard
library
private bills
public bills (Government and private members)
public information
research

Number of staff 927

House of Commons

Westminster, London SW1A 0AA
Tel 0171-219 3000

All staff are based at the House of Commons unless otherwise indicated.
For other addresses and telephone numbers see the end of this section.

Principal Officers and Officials

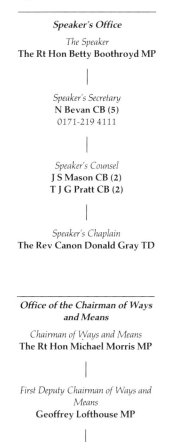

Speaker's Office

The Speaker
The Rt Hon Betty Boothroyd MP

Speaker's Secretary
N Bevan CB (5)
0171-219 4111

Speaker's Counsel
J S Mason CB (2)
T J G Pratt CB (2)

Speaker's Chaplain
The Rev Canon Donald Gray TD

Office of the Chairman of Ways and Means

Chairman of Ways and Means
The Rt Hon Michael Morris MP

First Deputy Chairman of Ways and Means
Geoffrey Lofthouse MP

Second Deputy Chairman of Ways and Means
Dame Janet Fookes MP

Chairman's Secretary
Ms P A Helme (7)
0171-219 3771

House of Commons Commission

Members of the Commission
The Rt Hon Betty Boothroyd MP (Chairman)
The Rt Hon Alan Beith MP
The Rt Hon Paul Channon MP
John Garrett MP
The Rt Hon Antony Newton MP
Miss Ann Taylor MP

Secretary
R W G Wilson (4)
0171-219 3270

Overview

Grade 1	Grade 2	Grade 3	Grade 4	Department/Office
	Principal Officers and Officials			
	Clerk of the House			
D W Limon	W R McKay	R B Sands M R Jack		Public Bill Office
		A J Hastings		Journal Office
		C B Winnifrith		Table Office
		G Cubie		Overseas Office
		R J Willoughby		Private Bill Office
	J F Sweetman	D G Millar	Ms H E Irwin R W G Wilson W A Proctor	Committee Office
			H C Foster (5)	Vote Office
	Serjeant at Arms			
		P N W Jennings		Serjeant at Arms
	Library			
		Miss J B Tanfield	Miss P J Baines	Library
	Official Report			
			I D Church (4)	Official Report
	Refreshment			
			Mrs S Harrison (5)	Refreshment
	Finance and Administration			
		J Rodda		Finance and Administration

Principal Officers and Officials

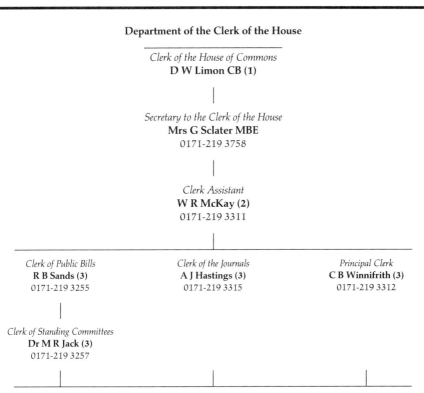

Department of the Clerk of the House

Clerk of the House of Commons
D W Limon CB (1)

Secretary to the Clerk of the House
Mrs G Sclater MBE
0171-219 3758

Clerk Assistant
W R McKay (2)
0171-219 3311

Clerk of Public Bills
R B Sands (3)
0171-219 3255

Clerk of Standing Committees
Dr M R Jack (3)
0171-219 3257

Clerk of the Journals
A J Hastings (3)
0171-219 3315

Principal Clerk
C B Winnifrith (3)
0171-219 3312

Public Bill Office

Government and private members' bills
Public legislation
Standing committees on: bills, statutory instruments, European Community documents, Scottish and Welsh Grand Committees

Journal Office

Minutes of the House
Procedural records and indices
Procedure and privilege

Table Office

Preparation of Order and Notice Papers (including Questions and Motions)

Clerk of the Overseas Office
G Cubie (3)
0171-219 3314

Clerk of Private Bills
Taxing Officer and Examiner of Petitions for Private Bills, Registrar of Members' Interests
R J Willoughby (3)
0171-219 3277

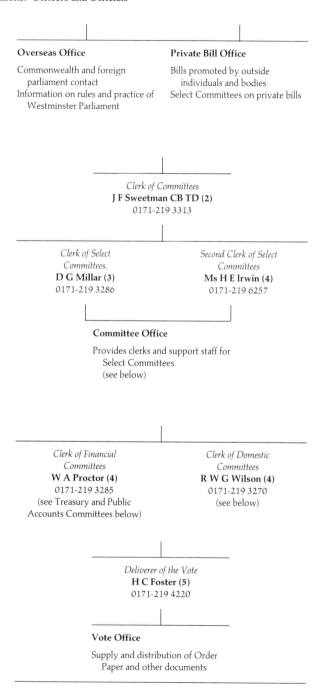

Overseas Office

Commonwealth and foreign parliament contact
Information on rules and practice of Westminster Parliament

Private Bill Office

Bills promoted by outside individuals and bodies
Select Committees on private bills

Clerk of Committees
J F Sweetman CB TD (2)
0171-219 3313

Clerk of Select Committees,
D G Millar (3)
0171-219 3286

Second Clerk of Select Committees
Ms H E Irwin (4)
0171-219 6257

Committee Office

Provides clerks and support staff for Select Committees
(see below)

Clerk of Financial Committees
W A Proctor (4)
0171-219 3285
(see Treasury and Public Accounts Committees below)

Clerk of Domestic Committees
R W G Wilson (4)
0171-219 3270
(see below)

Deliverer of the Vote
H C Foster (5)
0171-219 4220

Vote Office

Supply and distribution of Order Paper and other documents

Clerks of Select Committees (Departmentally-related)

Agriculture
N P Walker
0171-219 3263

Defence
D L Natzler
0171-219 3280

Education
M D Hamlyn
0171-219 6243

Employment
P C Seaward
0171-219 3268

Environment
S J Priestley
0171-219 3289

Foreign Affairs
Dr C R M Ward
0171-219 3278

Health
R G James
0171-219 6244

Home Affairs
C Poyser
0171-219 3260

National Heritage
Mrs J Sharpe
0171-219 6120

Northern Ireland
R I S Phillips
0171-219 2171

Science and Technology
Ms E Samson
0171-219 2792

Scottish Affairs
A H Doherty
0171-219 6125

Social Security
L C Smyth
0171-219 5831

Trade and Industry
D J Gerhold
0171-219 5469

Transport
C D Stanton
0171-219 6242

Treasury and Civil Service
W A Proctor (4)
0171-219 3285

Welsh Affairs
B M Hutton
0171-219 3261

Sub-Committee
P M Hensher
0171-219 5766

Clerks of Select Committees (Scrutiny Committees, etc)

Consolidation etc, Bills (Joint Committee)
M Hennessy
0171-219 3256

Deregulation
D R Lloyd
0171-219 2830

European Legislation
R J Rogers
0171-219 5467

Parliamentary Commissioner for Administration
A Y A Azad
0171-219 3259

Public Accounts
K Brown
0171-219 3273

Statutory Instruments
Ms P A Helme
0171-219 3281

Clerks of Select Committees (Domestic)

Accommodation and Works
P G Moon
0171-219 2420

Administration
M Clark
0171-219 3275

Broadcasting
D W N Doig
0171-219 3253

Catering
M Clark
0171-219 3275

Finance and Services
R W G Wilson (4)
0171-219 3270

Information
P G Moon
0171-219 2420

Liaison
J F Sweetman CB (2)
0171-219 3313

Members' Interests
R J Willoughby (3)
0171-219 3277

Privileges
A J Hastings (3)
0171-219 3315

Procedure
A R Kennon
0171-219 3316

Selection
G R Devine
0171-219 3250

Department of the Serjeant at Arms

Serjeant at Arms
P N W Jennings (3)
0171-219 3030

Deputy Serjeant at Arms
M Cummins (5)
0171-219 3040

Director of Works
H P Webber (4)
0171-219 3920
(1 Cannon Row)

Serjeant at Arms

Order, security and ceremonial
Housekeeping
Works and accommodation

Department of the Library

Librarian
Miss J B Tanfield (3)
0171-219 3635

Deputy Librarian
Miss P J Baines (4)
0171-219 6179
(Derby Gate)

Head of Division
K G Cuninghame (5)
0171-219 5781
(Derby Gate)

Head of Division
S Z Young (5)
0171-219 3622
(Derby Gate)

Parliamentary Division

Computer etc services
International affairs and defence
Reference services
Public Information Office

Research Division

Business and transport
Economic policy and statistics
Education and social services
Home affairs
Science and environment
Social and general statistics

Department of the Official Report

Editor
I D Church (4)
0171-219 3388

Official Report

Produces verbatim report (Hansard) of sittings of House and its Standing Committees

Refreshment Department

Director of Catering Services
Mrs S Harrison (5)
0171-219 3686

Refreshment

Catering and refreshment service for Members, staff and guests

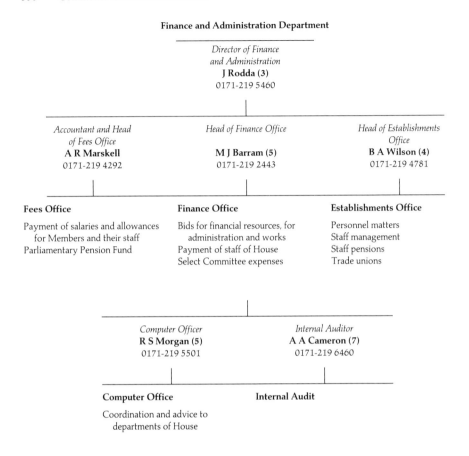

Finance and Administration Department

Director of Finance and Administration
J Rodda (3)
0171-219 5460

Accountant and Head of Fees Office
A R Marskell
0171-219 4292

Head of Finance Office
M J Barram (5)
0171-219 2443

Head of Establishments Office
B A Wilson (4)
0171-219 4781

Fees Office

Payment of salaries and allowances for Members and their staff
Parliamentary Pension Fund

Finance Office

Bids for financial resources, for administration and works
Payment of staff of House
Select Committee expenses

Establishments Office

Personnel matters
Staff management
Staff pensions
Trade unions

Computer Officer
R S Morgan (5)
0171-219 5501

Internal Auditor
A A Cameron (7)
0171-219 6460

Computer Office

Coordination and advice to departments of House

Internal Audit

House of Commons Addresses

1 Canon Row
London SW1A 2JN
Tel 0171-219 3920

1 Derby Gate
Westminster
London SW1A 2DG
Tel 0171-219 3000

House of Lords

Organisation	The departments of the Clerk of the Parliaments and the Gentleman Usher of the Black Rod together make up the staff of the House of Lords. Staff are not civil servants of the Crown. The work of this permanent staff revolves round the activity of Peers, House committees and the parliamentary process generally.
Responsibilities	committees Hansard judicial business of the House library private bills public bills sittings of the House
Number of staff	310

House of Lords

Westminster, London SW1A 0PW
Tel 0171-219 3000

Principal Officers and Officials

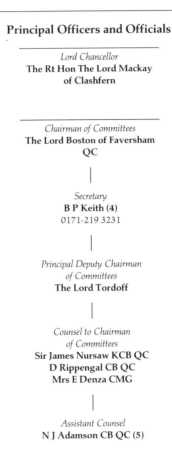

Lord Chancellor
The Rt Hon The Lord Mackay of Clashfern

Chairman of Committees
The Lord Boston of Faversham QC

Secretary
B P Keith (4)
0171-219 3231

Principal Deputy Chairman of Committees
The Lord Tordoff

Counsel to Chairman of Committees
Sir James Nursaw KCB QC
D Rippengal CB QC
Mrs E Denza CMG

Assistant Counsel
N J Adamson CB QC (5)

Overview

Grade 1	Grade 2	Grade 3	Grade 4	Department/Office
Clerk of the Parliaments				
Sir Michael Wheeler-Booth		P D G Hayter	E C Ollard (5)	Public Bill Office
			Mrs M E E C Villiers (5)	Official Report
			Mrs M B Bloor (HEOD)	Printed Paper Office
			B P Keith	Private Bill and Chairman of Committees Office
Sir Michael Wheeler-Booth			A D O Bibbiani	Refreshment
Sir Michael Wheeler-Booth	J M Davies		C Preece (6/7)	Accountant's Office
			R H Walters	Establishment Office
			D L Jones (5)	Library
			D L Johnson (5)	Record Office
Sir Michael Wheeler-Booth		J A Vallance White		Judicial Office
Sir Michael Wheeler-Booth		M G Pownall	Dr F P Tudor (5)	Committee Office
			T V Mohan (5)	Overseas Office
Sir Michael Wheeler-Booth			D R Beamish	Journal and Information Office
Gentleman Usher of the Black Rod and Serjeant-at-Arms				
		General Sir Edward Jones	A V M David Hawkins (7)	Gentleman Usher of the Black Rod

Principal Officers and Officials: Grades 1–4.

Principal Officers and Officials

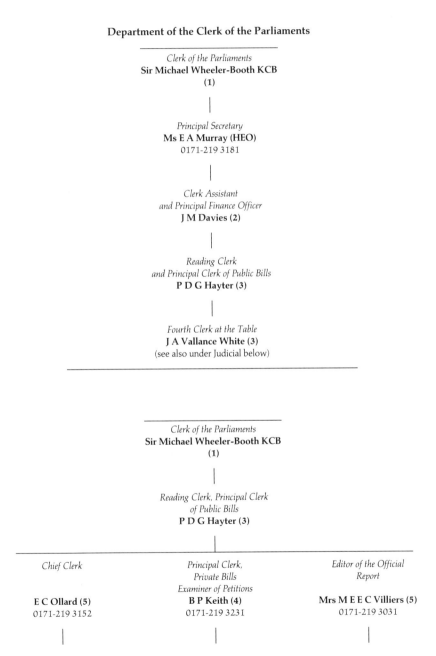

Department of the Clerk of the Parliaments

Clerk of the Parliaments
Sir Michael Wheeler-Booth KCB
(1)

Principal Secretary
Ms E A Murray (HEO)
0171-219 3181

Clerk Assistant
and Principal Finance Officer
J M Davies (2)

Reading Clerk
and Principal Clerk of Public Bills
P D G Hayter (3)

Fourth Clerk at the Table
J A Vallance White (3)
(see also under Judicial below)

Clerk of the Parliaments
Sir Michael Wheeler-Booth KCB
(1)

Reading Clerk, Principal Clerk
of Public Bills
P D G Hayter (3)

Chief Clerk	*Principal Clerk, Private Bills Examiner of Petitions*	*Editor of the Official Report*
E C Ollard (5)	**B P Keith (4)**	**Mrs M E E C Villiers (5)**
0171-219 3152	0171-219 3231	0171-219 3031

'ublic Bill Office

;overnment and private members' bills
rocedural advice
ıssistance in drafting bills and amendments
reparation of acts, bills and amendments for publishing

Private Bill Office

Bills promoted by outside organisations
Opposed local legislation
Procedural and administrative support to Chairman of Committees

Official Report of Debates

Produces verbatim report of sittings of the House (Hansard)

Clerk
Mrs M B Bloor (HEO D)
0171-219 3037

Printed Paper Office

Ordering, storage and supply of working papers and official publications

---

Clerk of the Parliaments
Sir Michael Wheeler-Booth KCB (1)

Superintendent
A D O Bibbiani (SCO)

Refreshment Department

Catering facilities for Lords, guests and staff

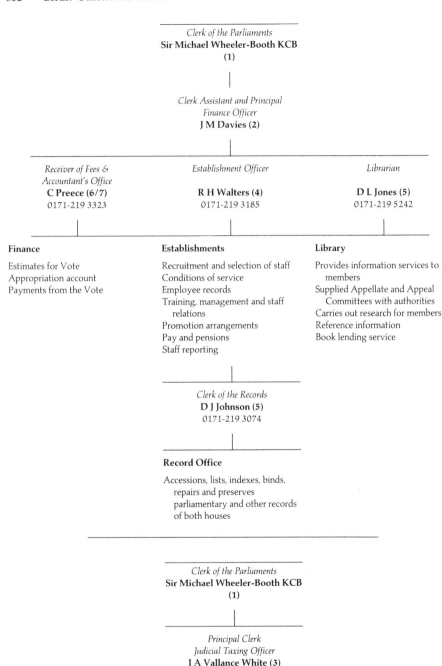

Clerk of the Parliaments
Sir Michael Wheeler-Booth KCB (1)

Clerk Assistant and Principal Finance Officer
J M Davies (2)

Receiver of Fees & Accountant's Office
C Preece (6/7)
0171-219 3323

Establishment Officer
R H Walters (4)
0171-219 3185

Librarian
D L Jones (5)
0171-219 5242

Finance

Estimates for Vote
Appropriation account
Payments from the Vote

Establishments

Recruitment and selection of staff
Conditions of service
Employee records
Training, management and staff relations
Promotion arrangements
Pay and pensions
Staff reporting

Library

Provides information services to members
Supplied Appellate and Appeal Committees with authorities
Carries out research for members
Reference information
Book lending service

Clerk of the Records
D J Johnson (5)
0171-219 3074

Record Office

Accessions, lists, indexes, binds, repairs and preserves parliamentary and other records of both houses

---

Clerk of the Parliaments
Sir Michael Wheeler-Booth KCB (1)

Principal Clerk
Judicial Taxing Officer
J A Vallance White (3)
0171-219 3111

Judicial Office

Judicial business of the House
Preparation and arrangements for hearing of appeals
Taxation of judicial costs
Channels peerage claims

Clerk of the Parliaments
Sir Michael Wheeler-Booth KCB (1)

Principal Clerk
M G Pownall (3)
0171-219 3218

Chief Clerks
Dr F P Tudor (5)
T V Mohan (5)

Committee and Overseas Offices

Administers select committees on public business

Clerk of the Parliaments
Sir Michael Wheeler-Booth KCB (1)

Principal Clerk
D R Beamish (4)
0171-219 3187

Journal and Information Office

Compilation and issue of records of the House
Statistics on business of the House
Bulletins on membership
Computers

Department of Gentleman Usher of the Black Rod and Serjeant-at-Arms

Gentleman Usher of the Black Rod and Serjeant-at-Arms, Secretary to the Lord Great Chamberlain
General Sir Edward Jones KCB CBE

Yeoman Usher of the Black Rod
Deputy Serjeant-at-Arms
Air Vice-Marshal David Hawkins CB MBE (7)

Black Rod

Security of Palace as a whole
Maintenance of order
Accommodation and services for Lords
Administration of Royal Apartments on behalf of the Lord Great Chamberlain

National Audit Office

Founded	1866 as the Exchequer and Audit Department and reconstituted as the NAO in 1984
Status	An independent body. The head of the National Audit Office, the Comptroller and Auditor General, is an officer of the House of Commons
Responsible to	Public Accounts Committee/Commission and thence to Parliament
Responsibilities	Auditing the accounts of government departments, certain public bodies and international organisations Value for money audits which investigate the economy, efficiency and effectiveness with which any department, authority or other body under its jurisdiction has used its resources in discharging its functions
Number of Staff	737

National Audit Office

157–197 Buckingham Palace Road, London SW1W 9SP
Tel 0171-798 7000   Fax 0171-828 3774

22 Melville Street, Edinburgh EH3 7NS
Tel 0131-244 2736   Fax 0131-244 2721

Officials

Comptroller and Auditor General
Sir John Bourn KCB (1)

Private Secretary
F Grogan
0171-798 7383

Deputy Comptroller and Auditor General
R N Le Marechal CB (2)

Assistant Auditors General
M C Pfleger (3)
T J Burr (3)
J Marshall (3)
J A Higgins (3)
L H Hughes (3)

Overview

Grade 1	Officials Grade 2	Department Grade 3	
Sir John Bourn	R N Le Marechal	M C Pfleger	***Unit A*** Corporate Policy and Finance Human resources Office Services Policy Management and Provision Value for Money Audit and Financial Audit Policy and Management
		T J Burr	***Unit B*** Customs and Excise Environment Home Affairs and Courts Inland Revenue Parliamentary and Government Finance Transport
		J Marshall	***Unit C*** Employment Health Privatisation/Regulation Social Security
		J A Higgins	***Unit D*** Agriculture Estate Management International Audit including the UN Scotland Overseas Service
		L H Hughes	***Unit E*** Defence Education National Heritage Trade and Industry Welsh Affairs

Officials and Departments

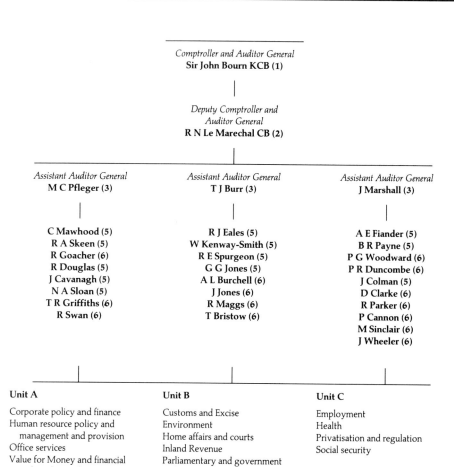

Comptroller and Auditor General
Sir John Bourn KCB (1)

Deputy Comptroller and Auditor General
R N Le Marechal CB (2)

Assistant Auditor General
M C Pfleger (3)

C Mawhood (5)
R A Skeen (5)
R Goacher (6)
R Douglas (5)
J Cavanagh (5)
N A Sloan (5)
T R Griffiths (6)
R Swan (6)

Assistant Auditor General
T J Burr (3)

R J Eales (5)
W Kenway-Smith (5)
R E Spurgeon (5)
G G Jones (5)
A L Burchell (6)
J Jones (6)
R Maggs (6)
T Bristow (6)

Assistant Auditor General
J Marshall (3)

A E Fiander (5)
B R Payne (5)
P G Woodward (6)
P R Duncombe (6)
J Colman (5)
D Clarke (6)
R Parker (6)
P Cannon (6)
M Sinclair (6)
J Wheeler (6)

Unit A

Corporate policy and finance
Human resource policy and management and provision
Office services
Value for Money and financial audit policy and management

Unit B

Customs and Excise
Environment
Home affairs and courts
Inland Revenue
Parliamentary and government finance
Transport

Unit C

Employment
Health
Privatisation and regulation
Social security

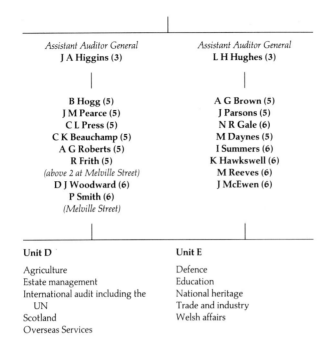

Assistant Auditor General
J A Higgins (3)

B Hogg (5)
J M Pearce (5)
C L Press (5)
C K Beauchamp (5)
A G Roberts (5)
R Frith (5)
(above 2 at Melville Street)
D J Woodward (6)
P Smith (6)
(Melville Street)

Unit D

Agriculture
Estate management
International audit including the UN
Scotland
Overseas Services

Assistant Auditor General
L H Hughes (3)

A G Brown (5)
J Parsons (5)
N R Gale (6)
M Daynes (5)
I Summers (6)
K Hawkswell (6)
M Reeves (6)
J McEwen (6)

Unit E

Defence
Education
National heritage
Trade and industry
Welsh affairs

Northern Ireland Audit Office

Founded	1987 under the provisions of the Audit (Northern Ireland) Order 1987, and replaced the former Exchequer and Audit Department
Status	independent body: the head of the Office, the Comptroller and Auditor General for Northern Ireland, is an officer of the House of Commons
Responsible to	in the absence of an elected Northern Ireland Assembly, the Comptroller and Auditor General for Northern Ireland is responsible to the Public Accounts Commission and the Committee of Public Accounts of the House of Commons at Westminster
Responsibilities	Controlling receipts into and issues from the Northern Ireland Consolidated Fund Examining the accounts of government departments and certain public bodies in Northern Ireland Examinations of the economy, efficiency and effectiveness of the use of resources by government bodies and various other bodies in receipt of public funds
Number of staff	102

Northern Ireland Audit Office

106 University Street, Belfast BT7 1EU
Tel 01232 251000 Fax 01232 251051

Officials

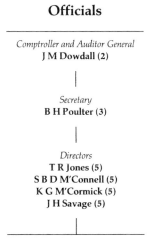

Comptroller and Auditor General
J M Dowdall (2)

Secretary
B H Poulter (3)

Directors
T R Jones (5)
S B D M'Connell (5)
K G M'Cormick (5)
J H Savage (5)

Audit Office

Audit of all departments and certain public bodies
Control of receipts into and issues from the Northern Ireland Consolidated Fund

Ministry of Agriculture, Fisheries and Food

Founded	1889 as Board of Agriculture
Ministers	Minister of Agriculture, Fisheries and Food, one minister of state and two parliamentary secretaries
Responsibilities	agricultural land use animal health and welfare arable crops biotechnology dairy produce quotas disease control (animals, plants and fish) diversification EC common agricultural policy and common fisheries policy environmental protection (countryside and marine) farm woodlands flood and coastal defence food regulation, safety and quality food industry fisheries forestry horse industry land tenure organic farming pesticides plant health set aside veterinary medicine scientific, technical and professional services and advice to farmers, growers and ancillary industries
Number of staff	7740
Executive Agencies	ADAS* Central Science Laboratory Central Veterinary Laboratory Intervention Board Meat Hygiene Service Pesticides Safety Directorate Veterinary Medicines Directorate

**Joint MAFF/Welsh Office Agricultural Department agency*

Ministry of Agriculture, Fisheries and Food

Whitehall Place, London SW1A 2HH
Tel 0171-270 3000   Fax 0171-270 8125

All personnel are based at Whitehall Place unless otherwise indicated.
For other addresses and telephone numbers see end of this section.

Ministers

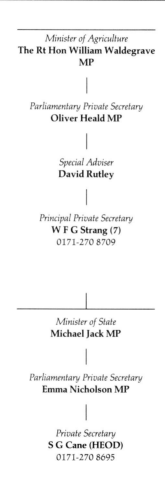

Minister of Agriculture
The Rt Hon William Waldegrave MP

Parliamentary Private Secretary
Oliver Heald MP

Special Adviser
David Rutley

Principal Private Secretary
W F G Strang (7)
0171-270 8709

Minister of State
Michael Jack MP

Parliamentary Private Secretary
Emma Nicholson MP

Private Secretary
S G Cane (HEOD)
0171-270 8695

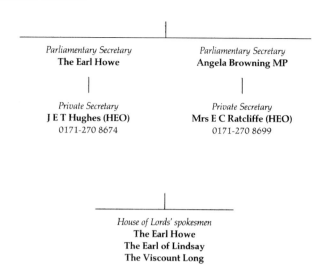

Parliamentary Secretary
The Earl Howe

Private Secretary
J E T Hughes (HEO)
0171-270 8674

Parliamentary Secretary
Angela Browning MP

Private Secretary
Mrs E C Ratcliffe (HEO)
0171-270 8699

House of Lords' spokesmen
The Earl Howe
The Earl of Lindsay
The Viscount Long

Ministerial Responsibilities

William Waldegrave	overall responsibility for all food, farming, fisheries and countryside R&D Citizen's Charter
Michael Jack	agricultural commodities European Community (Common Agricultural Policy; Common Fisheries Policy; and matters falling within the areas of responsibility of the Parliamentary Secretary, Lord Howe) export promotion external trade policy fisheries and marine environmental protection food and drink industry including marketing and promotion Intervention Board relations with overseas countries and international organisations set-aside R&D on all the above
The Earl Howe	ADAS agricultural grants agricultural land use agricultural resources policy departmental central services deregulation diversification economics and statistics environment and conservation farm woodlands flood and coastal defence forestry land tenure organic farming plant health plant varieties and seeds regional administration research and development rural affairs structures R&D on all the above

Angela Browning	animal health and medicines animal welfare biotechnology issues emergency services food safety and regulation food science horse industry meat hygiene pesticide safety R&D on all the above

Departmental Overview

Grade 1	Civil Servants Grade 2	Grade 3	Group	Minister
R J Packer	These Groups report directly to the Permanent Secretary	C J A Barnes	Establishments	Earl Howe
		Ms K Timms	Finance	Earl Howe
		J Haslam (5)	Information	Earl Howe
	Agricultural Commodities, Trade and Food Production			
R J Packer	D A Hadley	A J Lebrecht (5)	European Union Group	M Jack
		D H Griffiths	Arable Crops and Horticulture Group	M Jack
		J W Hepburn	Food, Drink and Marketing Policy	M Jack
		G A Hollis	Livestock Group	M Jack
	Food Safety			
R J Packer	R J Carden	B H B Dickinson	Food Safety	A Browning
		A R Cruickshank	Agricultural Inputs, Plant Protection and Emergencies Group	A Browning
		K C Meldrum M T Haddon	Animal Health and Veterinary Group	A Browning
		I Crawford	State Veterinary Service	A Browning
		Dr W H B Denner	Chief Scientist (Food)	A Browning
	Countryside, Marine Environment and Fisheries			
R J Packer	C R Cann	P W Murphy	Land Use, Conservation and Countryside	Earl Howe
		M Madden	Environment Policy Group	Earl Howe
		R E Mordue	Economics and Statistics	Earl Howe
		S Wentworth	Fisheries	M Jack
	Chief Scientific Adviser and Regional Organisation			
R J Packer	Dr P J Bunyan	Dr D W F Shannon	Chief Scientist (Agriculture)	Earl Howe
		D J Coates	Regional Services	Earl Howe
	Legal			
R J Packer	R Woolman	B T Atwood	Legal	Earl Howe
		D J Pearson	Legal	Earl Howe

Civil Servants and Groups

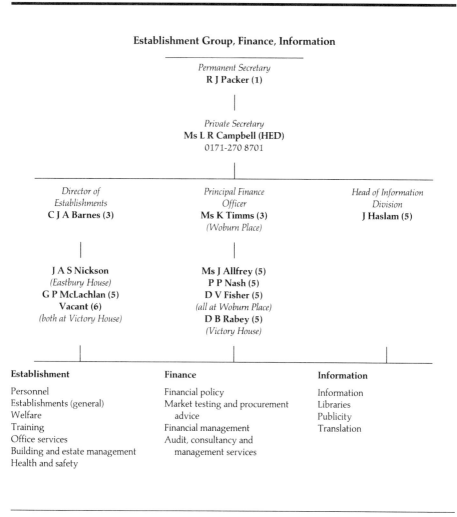

Establishment Group, Finance, Information

Permanent Secretary
R J Packer (1)

Private Secretary
Ms L R Campbell (HED)
0171-270 8701

Director of Establishments
C J A Barnes (3)

J A S Nickson
(Eastbury House)
G P McLachlan (5)
Vacant (6)
(both at Victory House)

Principal Finance Officer
Ms K Timms (3)
(Woburn Place)

Ms J Allfrey (5)
P P Nash (5)
D V Fisher (5)
(all at Woburn Place)
D B Rabey (5)
(Victory House)

Head of Information Division
J Haslam (5)

Establishment

Personnel
Establishments (general)
Welfare
Training
Office services
Building and estate management
Health and safety

Finance

Financial policy
Market testing and procurement advice
Financial management
Audit, consultancy and management services

Information

Information
Libraries
Publicity
Translation

Agricultural Commodities, Trade and Food Production

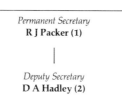

Permanent Secretary
R J Packer (1)

Deputy Secretary
D A Hadley (2)

A J Lebrecht (5)

L G Mitchell (6)

Under Secretary
D H Griffiths (3)

Mrs A M Blackburn (5)
R A Saunderson (5)
(Ergon House)

Under Secretary
J W Hepburn (3)

R W Melville (5)
D V Orchard (5)
Miss S E Brown* (5)
G M Trevelyan (4)
P M Boyling (5)
H B Brown (5)
(both above at Nobel House)

European Union Group

Common Agricultural Policy
Channel Islands and IoM
HM Customs & Excise liaison
Surplus food

Arable Crops and Horticulture

Cereals
Set aside
Sugar, tobacco, oilseeds and proteins
Horticulture and potatoes

Food, Drink and Marketing Policy

Food industry, marketing and competition
Tropical foods
External relations
Trade promotion
Trade policy
Alcoholic drinks

Under Secretary
G A Hollis (3)

J R Cowan (5)
T D Rossington (5)
G W Noble (5)
B J Harding (5)

Livestock Group

Beef
Sheep and livestock
Pigs, eggs and poultry
Milk and milk products

**Miss Brown also reports to P W Murphy (EC Group) on GATT Uruguay Round issues*

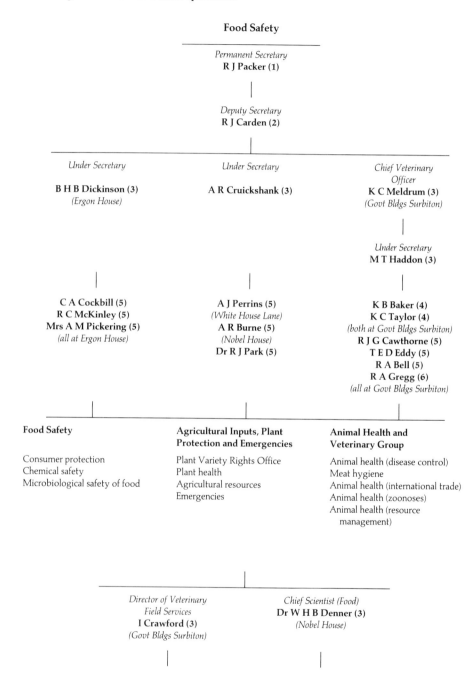

Food Safety

Permanent Secretary
R J Packer (1)

Deputy Secretary
R J Carden (2)

Under Secretary
B H B Dickinson (3)
(Ergon House)

Under Secretary
A R Cruickshank (3)

Chief Veterinary Officer
K C Meldrum (3)
(Govt Bldgs Surbiton)

Under Secretary
M T Haddon (3)

C A Cockbill (5)
R C McKinley (5)
Mrs A M Pickering (5)
(all at Ergon House)

A J Perrins (5)
(White House Lane)
A R Burne (5)
(Nobel House)
Dr R J Park (5)

K B Baker (4)
K C Taylor (4)
(both at Govt Bldgs Surbiton)
R J G Cawthorne (5)
T E D Eddy (5)
R A Bell (5)
R A Gregg (6)
(all at Govt Bldgs Surbiton)

Food Safety

Consumer protection
Chemical safety
Microbiological safety of food

Agricultural Inputs, Plant Protection and Emergencies

Plant Variety Rights Office
Plant health
Agricultural resources
Emergencies

Animal Health and Veterinary Group

Animal health (disease control)
Meat hygiene
Animal health (international trade)
Animal health (zoonoses)
Animal health (resource management)

Director of Veterinary Field Services
I Crawford (3)
(Govt Bldgs Surbiton)

Chief Scientist (Food)
Dr W H B Denner (3)
(Nobel House)

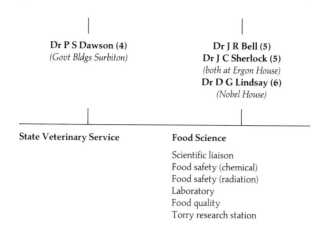

Dr P S Dawson (4)
(Govt Bldgs Surbiton)

State Veterinary Service

Dr J R Bell (5)
Dr J C Sherlock (5)
(both at Ergon House)
Dr D G Lindsay (6)
(Nobel House)

Food Science

Scientific liaison
Food safety (chemical)
Food safety (radiation)
Laboratory
Food quality
Torry research station

Countryside, Marine Environment and Fisheries

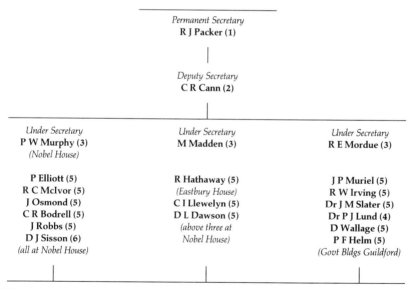

Permanent Secretary
R J Packer (1)

Deputy Secretary
C R Cann (2)

Under Secretary
P W Murphy (3)
(Nobel House)

P Elliott (5)
R C McIvor (5)
J Osmond (5)
C R Bodrell (5)
J Robbs (5)
D J Sisson (6)
(all at Nobel House)

Land Use, Conservation and Countryside

Countryside
Land use and tenure
Conservation policy
Environment taskforce
Land use planning unit

Under Secretary
M Madden (3)

R Hathaway (5)
(Eastbury House)
C I Llewelyn (5)
D L Dawson (5)
(above three at Nobel House)

Environment

Environmental protection
Salmon and inland fisheries
Whaling
Flood and coastal defence
Marine environment protection

Under Secretary
R E Mordue (3)

J P Muriel (5)
R W Irving (5)
Dr J M Slater (5)
Dr P J Lund (4)
D Wallage (5)
P F Helm (5)
(Govt Bldgs Guildford)

Economics and Statistics

Farm business
International
Resource use
Economics and statistics (food)
Agricultural commodities
Census and prices

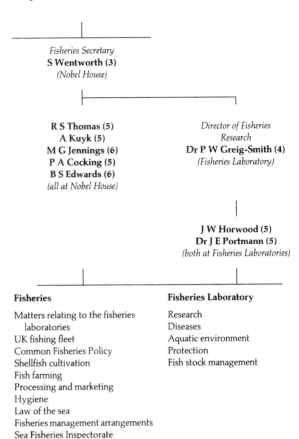

Fisheries Secretary
S Wentworth (3)
(Nobel House)

R S Thomas (5)
A Kuyk (5)
M G Jennings (6)
P A Cocking (5)
B S Edwards (6)
(all at Nobel House)

Director of Fisheries Research
Dr P W Greig-Smith (4)
(Fisheries Laboratory)

J W Horwood (5)
Dr J E Portmann (5)
(both at Fisheries Laboratories)

Fisheries

Matters relating to the fisheries laboratories
UK fishing fleet
Common Fisheries Policy
Shellfish cultivation
Fish farming
Processing and marketing
Hygiene
Law of the sea
Fisheries management arrangements
Sea Fisheries Inspectorate

Fisheries Laboratory

Research
Diseases
Aquatic environment
Protection
Fish stock management

Chief Scientific Adviser and Regional Organisation

Permanent Secretary
R J Packer (1)

Chief Scientific Adviser
Dr P J Bunyan (2)
(Nobel House)

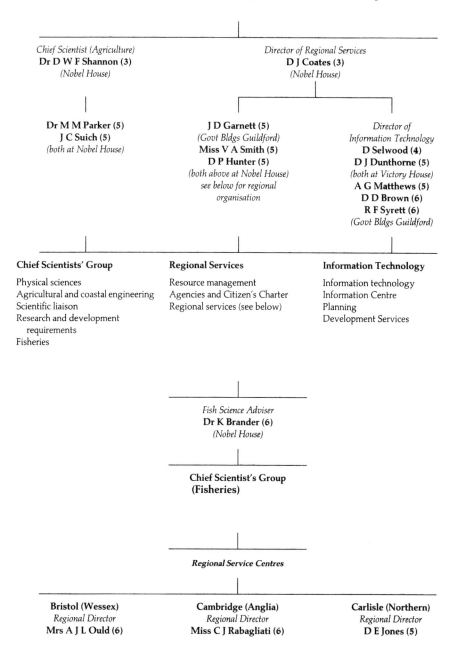

Chief Scientist (Agriculture)
Dr D W F Shannon (3)
(Nobel House)

Dr M M Parker (5)
J C Suich (5)
(both at Nobel House)

Director of Regional Services
D J Coates (3)
(Nobel House)

J D Garnett (5)
(Govt Bldgs Guildford)
Miss V A Smith (5)
D P Hunter (5)
(both above at Nobel House)
see below for regional organisation

Director of Information Technology
D Selwood (4)
D J Dunthorne (5)
(both at Victory House)
A G Matthews (5)
D D Brown (6)
R F Syrett (6)
(Govt Bldgs Guildford)

Chief Scientists' Group

Physical sciences
Agricultural and coastal engineering
Scientific liaison
Research and development requirements
Fisheries

Regional Services

Resource management
Agencies and Citizen's Charter
Regional services (see below)

Information Technology

Information technology
Information Centre
Planning
Development Services

Fish Science Adviser
Dr K Brander (6)
(Nobel House)

Chief Scientist's Group (Fisheries)

Regional Service Centres

Bristol (Wessex)
Regional Director
Mrs A J L Ould (6)

Cambridge (Anglia)
Regional Director
Miss C J Rabagliati (6)

Carlisle (Northern)
Regional Director
D E Jones (5)

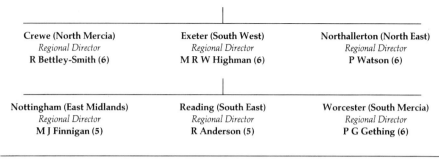

Crewe (North Mercia)
Regional Director
R Bettley-Smith (6)

Exeter (South West)
Regional Director
M R W Highman (6)

Northallerton (North East)
Regional Director
P Watson (6)

Nottingham (East Midlands)
Regional Director
M J Finnigan (5)

Reading (South East)
Regional Director
R Anderson (5)

Worcester (South Mercia)
Regional Director
P G Gething (6)

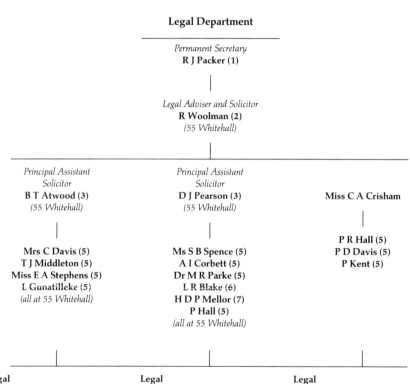

Legal Department

Permanent Secretary
R J Packer (1)

Legal Adviser and Solicitor
R Woolman (2)
(55 Whitehall)

Principal Assistant Solicitor
B T Atwood (3)
(55 Whitehall)

Mrs C Davis (5)
T J Middleton (5)
Miss E A Stephens (5)
L Gunatilleke (5)
(all at 55 Whitehall)

Legal

Agricultural commodities
Animal health and welfare
Plant health
Set aside
Fisheries
Pesticides
Food safety
Meat Hygiene Service
Marine environmental protection

Principal Assistant Solicitor
D J Pearson (3)
(55 Whitehall)

Ms S B Spence (5)
A I Corbett (5)
Dr M R Parke (5)
L R Blake (6)
H D P Mellor (7)
P Hall (5)
(all at 55 Whitehall)

Legal

Civil litigation
Commercial matters
Employment
Investigation unit
Central resources
Prosecutions
Agricultural Wages Board
Defence matters

Miss C A Crisham

P R Hall (5)
P D Davis (5)
P Kent (5)

Legal

ECJ litigation
EC matters, Channel Islands and Isle of Man
Common Agricultural Policy
Land use, land drainage (other than plant health and litigation)
Environmental matters
Dairy produce quotas
Fertilisers and feeding stuffs

Ministry of Agriculture Addresses

National addresses

Colney Lane
Norwich NR4 7UQ
Tel 01603 259350
Fax 01603 501123

Eastbury House
30–34 Albert Embankment
London SE1 7TL
Tel 0171-238 3000
Fax 0171-238 6616

Ergon House
17 Smith Square
London SW1P 3JR
Tel 0171-238 3000
Fax 0171-238 6591

Fisheries Laboratory
Pakefield Road
Lowestoft
Suffolk NR33 0HT
Tel 01502 562244
Fax 01502 513865

Government Buildings
Epsom Road
Guildford
Surrey GU1 2LD
Tel 01483 68121
Fax 01483 37396

Government Buildings
Hook Rise South
Tolworth
Surbiton
Surrey KT6 7NF
Tel 0181-330 4411
Fax 0181-337 3640

Nobel House
17 Smith Square
London SW1P 3JR
Tel 0171-238 3000
Fax 0171-238 6591

Tolworth Tower
Surbiton
Surrey KT6 7DX
Tel 0181-330 4411
Fax 0181-390 4425

Torry Research Station
PO Box 31
135 Abbey Road
Aberdeen AB9 8DG
Tel 01224 877071
Fax 01224 874246

Victory House
30–34 Kingsway
London WC2B 6TU
Tel 0171-405 4310

White House Lane
Huntingdon Road
Cambridge CB3 0LF
Tel 01223 277151
Fax 01223 342386

55 Whitehall
London SW1A 2EY
Tel 0171-270 3000
Fax 0171-270 8125

19–29 Woburn Place
London WC1H 0LU
Tel 0171-270 8080
Fax 0171-917 3602

Regional Service Centres

Anglia
Block B
Government Buildings
Brooklands Avenue
Cambridge CB2 2DR
Tel 01223 462727
Fax 01223 455652

Wessex
Block C
Government Buildings
Burghill Road
Westbury-on-Trym
Bristol BS10 6NJ
Tel 01179 591000
Fax 01179 505392

East Midlands
Block 7
Government Buildings
Chalfont Drive
Nottingham NG8 3SN
Tel 01159 291191
Fax 01159 425846

North East
Government Buildings
Crosby Road
Northallerton
North Yorks DL6 1AD
Tel 01609 773751
Fax 01609 780179

North Mercia
Berkeley Towers
Nantwich Road
Crewe
Cheshire CW2 6PT
Tel 01270 69211
Fax 01270 669494

Northern
Eden Bridge House
Lowther Street
Carlisle
Cumbria
CA3 8DX
Tel 01228 23400
Fax 01228 23400 (Ext 468)

South East
Block A
Government Buildings
Coley Park
Reading RG1 6DT
Tel 01734 581222
Fax 01734 392399

South Mercia
Block C
Government Buildings
Whittington Road
Worcester WR5 2LQ
Tel 01905 763355
Fax 01905 763180

South West
Government Buildings
Alphington Road
Exeter
Devon EX2 8NQ
Tel 01392 77951
Fax 01392 410936

Founded In 1916 the War Cabinet and War Cabinet Secretariat were constituted from the Secretariat of the Committee for Imperial Defence (CID) which had been set up in 1904. After the war in 1920 a Cabinet Secretariat was set up on an established basis. The CID had a separate secretariat but both secretariats remained in the combined Offices of the Cabinet and CID. In 1939 a War Cabinet was again formed and the CID suspended and in 1940 the title of the Office became the Offices of the War Cabinet and the Minister of Defence. An economic section was formed and the Central Statistical Office established in 1941.

In 1947 many staff transferred to the new Ministry of Defence. In 1953 the Economic Section transferred to the Treasury. The CSO, which had become a department of the Chancellor of the Exchequer in 1989, was established as an executive agency in 1991.

Over the years the functions of the Cabinet Office (CO) have changed frequently. From 1970–83 the Central Policy Review Staff (CPRS) provided policy analysis and advice to ministers. When the CPRS disbanded, its Chief Scientist remained in the CO as Chief Scientific Adviser.

In 1983 the Management and Personnel Office (MPO) became an integral part of the CO and the Secretary of the Cabinet became Head of the Home Civil Service. In 1987 some MPO functions were transferred to the Treasury and the MPO was reconstituted as the Office of the Minister for the Civil Service (OMCS).

After the 1992 election the new Chancellor of the Duchy of Lancaster assumed responsibility for the OMCS but, because of a significant increase in the scope of the department's work, which now includes the Citizen's Charter, the Efficiency Unit, the Market Testing Initiative, the Office of Science and Technology, and the

Open Government initiative (see below for full list of responsibilities) the name has been changed to the Office of Public Service and Science (OPSS).

It also took over from the Treasury responsibility for the Central Office of Information, HMSO, the Chessington Computer Centre and CCTA, the Government Centre for Information Systems, in 1992.

Ministers The Prime Minister, the Chancellor of the Duchy of Lancaster (Minister of Public Service and Science) and one parliamentary under secretary

Responsibilities
Support of ministers collectively in the conduct of Cabinet business
CCTA, the Government Centre for Information Systems
Citizen's Charter
Civil service personnel management issues
Efficiency and effectiveness of the civil service
Machinery of government including open government
Market testing programme
Next Steps programme
Office of the Civil Service Commissioners
Office of Science and Technology

Number of staff 1440

Executive agencies
Central Office of Information
Chessington Computer Centre
Civil Service College
HMSO
Occupational Health Service
Recruitment and Assessment Services

Cabinet Office/
Office of Public Service and Science

70 Whitehall, London SW1A 2AS
Tel 0171-270 3000
Fax *Telephone the above number and when through to the Cabinet Office ask for appropriate fax number*
All personnel are based at 70 Whitehall unless otherwise indicated.
For other addresses and telephone numbers see end of this section.

Ministers

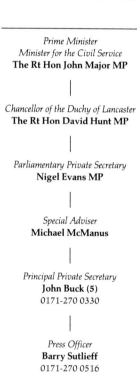

Prime Minister
Minister for the Civil Service
The Rt Hon John Major MP

Chancellor of the Duchy of Lancaster
The Rt Hon David Hunt MP

Parliamentary Private Secretary
Nigel Evans MP

Special Adviser
Michael McManus

Principal Private Secretary
John Buck (5)
0171-270 0330

Press Officer
Barry Sutlieff
0171-270 0516

Parliamentary Secretary for Public Service and Science
John Horam MP

Private Secretary
Ms D Williams
0171-270 0411

House of Lords Spokesmen
The Rt Hon The Viscount Cranborne
The Earl Howe
The Baroness Miller of Hendon

Ministerial Responsibilities

David Hunt/ John Horan	Citizen's Charter Civil service personnel management issues CCTA, the government Centre for Information Systems Efficiency and effectiveness of the civil service. Machinery of government including open government Market testing initiative Next Steps programme Office of the Civil Service Commissioners Office of Science and Technology Open government

Departmental Overview

Civil Servants			Division	Minister
Grade 1	*Grade 2*	*Grade 3*		
Sir Robin Butler (0)		A J Merifield (5)	Ceremonial	J Major
Sir Robin Butler (0)/ R Mountfield (1A)		A D Whetnall	Machinery of Government and Standards Group	J Major D Hunt
	Cabinet Secretariat			
Sir Robin Butler (0)	P Lever	D J Gould	Defence and Overseas	J Major
	P Lever G C Warner	A C Galsworthy	Joint Intelligence Organisation	J Major
	K J MacKenzie	W A Jeffrey	Economic, Home, Social Affairs and Legislation	J Major
	B G Bender	A T Cahn	European Affairs	J Major
		R Hope (6)	Telecoms	J Major
	Office of Public Service and Science			
R Mountfield (1A)	Miss E C Turton		Citizen's Charter Unit (Sir James Blyth, Chairman of the Advisory Panel)	J Major D Hunt
		J Oughton	Efficiency and Effectiveness Group (Sir Peter Levene, Prime Minister's Adviser)	J Major D Hunt
		C Brendish	AUMA (Advice to ministers on OPSS agencies)	J Major D Hunt
	M Bett		Office of the Civil Service Commissioner	J Major D Hunt
R Mountfield (1A)/Vacant		Sir John Cadogan A L C Quigley Mrs H Williams	Office of Science and Technology	J Major D Hunt

Departmental Overview

Civil Servants			Division	Minister
Grade 1	*Grade 2*	*Grade 3*		
R Mountfield (1A)		H H Taylor	Civil Service Employer Group	J Major D Hunt
		T Perks (5)	Information Officer Management Unit*	J Major D Hunt
		R E Dibble	CCTA	J Major D Hunt
Sir Robin Butler (0)/ R Mountfield (1A)		R W D Venning	Establishment Officers Group	J Major D Hunt
		B Fox	Senior Civil Service Group	J Major D Hunt

* Reports to Robin Mountfield on administrative matters. On professional matters reports to the Head of the Government Information Service

Civil Servants and Divisions

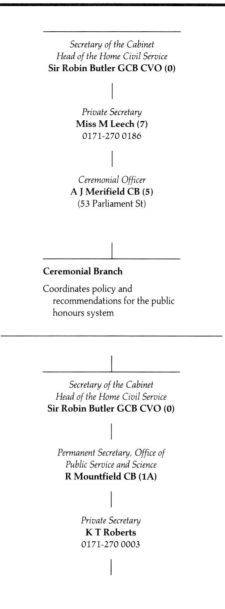

Secretary of the Cabinet
Head of the Home Civil Service
Sir Robin Butler GCB CVO (0)

Private Secretary
Miss M Leech (7)
0171-270 0186

Ceremonial Officer
A J Merifield CB (5)
(53 Parliament St)

Ceremonial Branch

Coordinates policy and recommendations for the public honours system

Secretary of the Cabinet
Head of the Home Civil Service
Sir Robin Butler GCB CVO (0)

Permanent Secretary, Office of Public Service and Science
R Mountfield CB (1A)

Private Secretary
K T Roberts
0171-270 0003

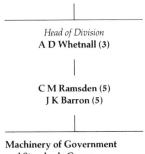

Head of Division
A D Whetnall (3)

C M Ramsden (5)
J K Barron (5)

Machinery of Government and Standards Group

Machinery of government
Parliamentary issues
Open government
Public bodies
Public appointments
Security
Conduct
Discipline
Business appointments

Cabinet Secretariat

Secretary of the Cabinet
Head of the Home Civil Service
Sir Robin Butler GCB CVO (0)

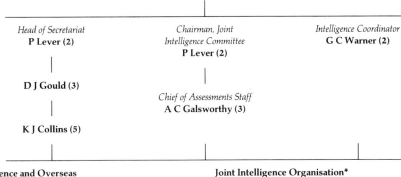

Head of Secretariat
P Lever (2)

D J Gould (3)

K J Collins (5)

Chairman, Joint Intelligence Committee
P Lever (2)

Chief of Assessments Staff
A C Galsworthy (3)

Intelligence Coordinator
G C Warner (2)

Defence and Overseas Secretariat

Foreign and defence policy-making
Intelligence agencies
Northern Ireland and Anglo-Irish relations
Civil Contingencies Unit

Joint Intelligence Organisation*

Monitoring of foreign threats to British interests and security
Assessments of foreign events and situations

Intelligence requirements and priorities
Intelligence resources and programmes

* *For details of structure and functions of the Security and Intelligence Services see under that title in this section of the book*

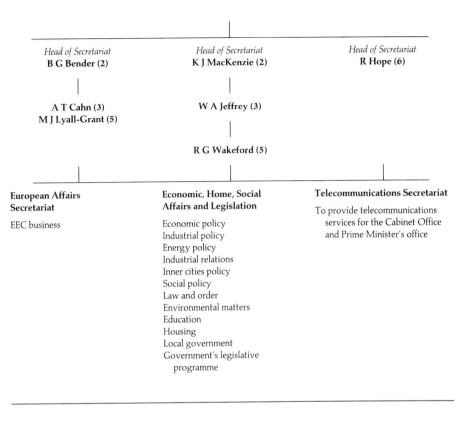

Head of Secretariat
B G Bender (2)

A T Cahn (3)
M J Lyall-Grant (5)

European Affairs Secretariat

EEC business

Head of Secretariat
K J MacKenzie (2)

W A Jeffrey (3)

R G Wakeford (5)

Economic, Home, Social Affairs and Legislation

Economic policy
Industrial policy
Energy policy
Industrial relations
Inner cities policy
Social policy
Law and order
Environmental matters
Education
Housing
Local government
Government's legislative programme

Head of Secretariat
R Hope (6)

Telecommunications Secretariat

To provide telecommunications services for the Cabinet Office and Prime Minister's office

---

Office of Public Service and Science

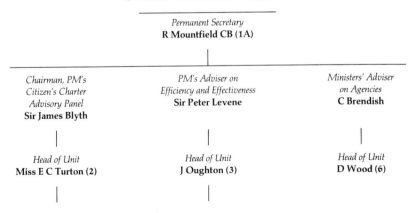

Permanent Secretary
R Mountfield CB (1A)

Chairman, PM's Citizen's Charter Advisory Panel
Sir James Blyth

Head of Unit
Miss E C Turton (2)

PM's Adviser on Efficiency and Effectiveness
Sir Peter Levene

Head of Unit
J Oughton (3)

Ministers' Adviser on Agencies
C Brendish

Head of Unit
D Wood (6)

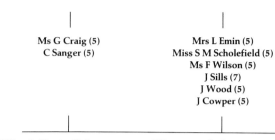

Ms G Craig (5)
C Sanger (5)

Mrs L Emin (5)
Miss S M Scholefield (5)
Ms F Wilson (5)
J Sills (7)
J Wood (5)
J Cowper (5)

Citizen's Charter Unit

Implement, develop and coordinate the Citizen's Charter initiative

Efficiency and Effectiveness Group

Improving efficiency and effectiveness in the civil service
Market testing initiative
Next Steps project team

Advisory Unit on Ministers' Agencies

Advice to OPSS ministers on the performance and strategic management of the department's executive agencies

First Civil Service Commissioner
M Bett CBE (2)

Head of the Office of the Civil Service Commissioners
Miss E M Goodison
(24 Whitehall)

Office of the Civil Service Commissioner

Responsible for senior appointments and recruitment to the fast stream
Advising the Chancellor of the Duchy of Lancaster and the Secretary of State for Foreign Affairs on the rules for recruitment to the civil service
Monitoring the application of those rules by departments and agencies
Liaison with careers services of academic institutions
Advising on nationality and character standards for entry to the Home Civil Service

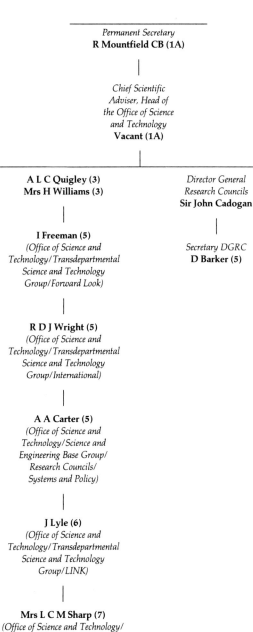

Permanent Secretary
R Mountfield CB (1A)

Chief Scientific Adviser, Head of the Office of Science and Technology
Vacant (1A)

A L C Quigley (3)
Mrs H Williams (3)

I Freeman (5)
(Office of Science and Technology/Transdepartmental Science and Technology Group/Forward Look)

R D J Wright (5)
(Office of Science and Technology/Transdepartmental Science and Technology Group/International)

A A Carter (5)
(Office of Science and Technology/Science and Engineering Base Group/Research Councils/Systems and Policy)

J Lyle (6)
(Office of Science and Technology/Transdepartmental Science and Technology Group/LINK)

Mrs L C M Sharp (7)
(Office of Science and Technology/Transdepartmental Science and Technology Group/Women in Science, Engineering and Technology)

Director General Research Councils
Sir John Cadogan

Secretary DGRC
D Barker (5)

Dr K Root (6)
(Office of Science and Technology/Science and Engineering Base Group/Finance and Statistics)

Office of Science and Technology

Provides the central focus for consideration for science and technology issues across government
Responsibility for the science budget and the work of the five research councils
Responsible for the Advisory Council for Science and Technology and the Research Councils (DGRC)

Permanent Secretary
R Mountfield CB (1A)

Head of Group
H H Taylor (3)

Mrs J I Britton (5)
C J Parry (5)
Dr S Mitha (5)
Mrs N M Tompkinson (5)
Dr J G Fuller (5)
Miss E M Goodison (5)
I Strachan (5)
D G Pain (5)
G Davies

*Head of Information Officer Management Unit**
T Perks (5)

Civil Service Employer Group

Equal opportunities
Development division
Top management programme
European and fast stream division
Office of the Civil Service Commissioners
Personnel management and civil service statistics
Civil service pensions
OPSS secretariat

Information Officer Management Unit

Central management for members of GIS
Career advice and development
Central promotion boards
Transfer of staff
Secondments
Marketing of GIS recruitment and training

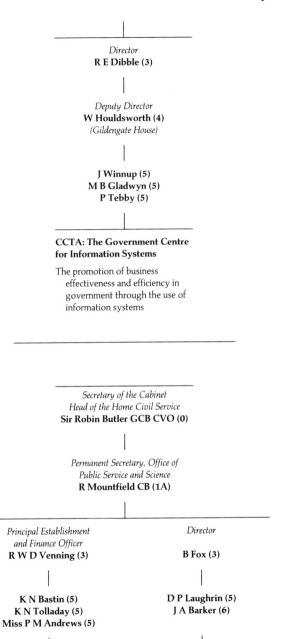

Director
R E Dibble (3)

Deputy Director
W Houldsworth (4)
(Gildengate House)

J Winnup (5)
M B Gladwyn (5)
P Tebby (5)

CCTA: The Government Centre for Information Systems

The promotion of business effectiveness and efficiency in government through the use of information systems

---

Secretary of the Cabinet
Head of the Home Civil Service
Sir Robin Butler GCB CVO (0)

Permanent Secretary, Office of Public Service and Science
R Mountfield CB (1A)

Principal Establishment and Finance Officer
R W D Venning (3)

K N Bastin (5)
K N Tolladay (5)
Miss P M Andrews (5)

Director
B Fox (3)

D P Laughrin (5)
J A Barker (6)

Establishment and Finance

Personnel management
Training
IT
Internal consultancy
Office services
Finance
Internal audit
Official histories and public records

Senior Civil Service Group

Senior staff and interchange
Senior pay and contracts

* IOMU reports to Robin Mountfield on administrative matters. On professional matters it reports to the Head of the Government Information Service.

Cabinet Committees

Although much unofficial material has been written about cabinet committees, very little official information was published before the list of committees was made public on 19 May 1992. Nor has an official history of cabinet committees and the way in which they have evolved been written.

However, the Cabinet Office has provided the following commentary on their functions: the main role of cabinet committees is to facilitate the work of the government by ensuring that issues requiring collective discussion are properly considered. There are two types of committee – standing committees, which have titles and ad hoc groups, which are numbered. The standing committees are commonly known by their initials – for ease of reference, eg the Economic and Domestic Policy Committee is known as EDP and so on. Standing committees consider issues of long-term or continuing interest; ad hoc groups, called GEN or MISC groups deal with particular issues and are more ephemeral.

The committees are served by Cabinet Office staff with assistance from departments where appropriate. In general, the committees do not have a set programme of meetings. Some meet more often than others. In some cases issues are dealt with by correspondence between committee members without a meeting.

The Cabinet Office advises the prime minister on what committees need to be established. Cabinet members and their ministers are invited by the prime minister to join cabinet committees. Ministers do not usually see papers for committees of which they are not members.

There are also a series of sub-committees which deal with different aspects of policy within a particular subject area. For example, Health Strategy, Drug Misuse and Women's Issues are sub-committees of the main standing committee, Home and Social Affairs (EDH).

In February 1994 a revised list of committees was published and the main changes included the following: the replacement of the sub-committee on Coordination of Urban Policy (EDH[U]) by a full committee, Regeneration (EDR); the responsibilities of the full committee on Civil Service Pay (EDC) transferred to the sub-committee on Public Sector Pay (EDI[P]); and the responsibilities of the sub-committee on Alcohol Misuse (EDH[A]) transferred to the sub-committee on Health Strategy (EDH[H]).

The February 1994 update also revealed that the Chancellor of the Exchequer had become a full member of the Intelligence Services committee (IS).

A further updated list of cabinet committees and sub-commitees was published in *Hansard* on 22 November (*col 89w ff*). The main changes included the following:

Wound up: **Gulf (OPDG)**, **European Security (OPDSE)**, and the sub-committee **Eastern Europe (OPD[AE])**. Future questions on these issues will be dealt with either by Defence and Overseas Policy (OPD) or European Questions (OPD[E]). The ad hoc **Refugees from former Yugoslavia (Gen 24)** has also been wound up. There are two ad hoc additions: **Smart Card Technology (Gen 34)** and **Competitiveness (Gen 29)**.

The former Chancellor of the Duchy of Lancester, William Waldegrave, was a member of Intelligence Services (IS) but this invitation is no longer extended to his successor **David Hunt**. Mr Hunt now chairs a number of committees previously headed by Lord Wakeham, former leader of the House of Lords including Industrial, Commercial and Consumer Affairs (EDI), Environment (EDE), Local Government (EDL), Regeneration (EDR) and Public Sector Pay (EDI[P]). Mr Hunt also chairs Women's Issues (EDH[W]) and Smart Card Technology (Gen 34).

A new committee, **Coordination and Presentation of Government Policy (EDCP)**, was established on 20 March 1995.

In addition to cabinet committees there are many committees of officials throughout Whitehall.

Main Committees

Economic and Domestic Policy (EDP)
Prime Minister *(Chairman)*
Chancellor of the Exchequer
Home Secretary
President of the Board of Trade
Leader of the House of Commons
Secretary of State for the Environment
Chancellor of the Duchy of Lancaster
Secretary of State for Scotland
Secretary of State for Northern Ireland
Secretary of State for Employment
Secretary of State for Wales
Chief Secretary, Treasury
Minister without Portfolio

Other Ministers will be invited to attend for items in which they have a departmental interest.

Terms of Reference: To consider strategic issues relating to the government's economic and domestic policies.

Defence and Overseas Policy (OPD)
Prime Minister *(Chairman)*
Foreign Secretary
Chancellor of the Exchequer
President of the Board of Trade
Secretary of State for Defence
Attorney General

The Chancellor of the Duchy of Lancaster and the Leader of the House of Lords also receive papers and may be invited to attend as necessary.

The Chief of Defence Staff will attend as required, as will the Chiefs of Staff when necessary.

Terms of Reference: To keep under review the government's defence and overseas policy.

Nuclear Defence Policy (OPDN)
Prime Minister *(Chairman)*
Foreign Secretary
Chancellor of the Exchequer
Secretary of State for Defence

Terms of Reference: To keep under review the government's policy on nuclear defence.

Hong Kong and Other Dependent Territories (OPDK)
Prime Minister *(Chairman)*
Foreign Secretary
Chancellor of the Exchequer
Home Secretary
President of the Board of Trade
Secretary of State for Defence
Leader of the House of Commons
Chancellor of the Duchy of Lancaster
Minister of State, Foreign and Commonwealth Office

Others, including the Attorney General, the Governor of Hong Kong and the British Ambassador in Peking, may be invited to attend as appropriate. The Minister without Portfolio (Jeremy Hanley) also receives papers.

Terms of Reference: To keep under review the implementation of the agreement with the Chinese on the future of Hong Kong and the implications of that agreement for the government of Hong Kong and the wellbeing of its people; and to keep under review as necessary the government's policy towards other Dependent Territories.

Northern Ireland (NI)
Prime Minister *(Chairman)*
Foreign Secretary
Home Secretary
Secretary of State for Defence
Secretary of State for Northern Ireland
Leader of the House of Lords
Chief Secretary, Treasury
Attorney General

Other ministers are invited to attend as the business requires.

Terms of Reference: To oversee the government's policy on Northern Ireland issues and relations with the Republic of Ireland on these matters.

Science and Technology (EDS)
Prime Minister *(Chairman)*
Foreign Secretary
President of the Board of Trade
Secretary of State for Defence
Secretary of State for the Environment
Chancellor of the Duchy of Lancaster
Minister of Agriculture, Fisheries and Food
Secretary of State for Scotland
Secretary of State for Health
Secretary of State for Education
Secretary of State for Transport
Leader of the House of Lords
Chief Secretary, Treasury

The Chief Scientific Adviser is in attendance. The Minister without Portfolio also receives papers.

Terms of Reference: To review science and technology policy.

Intelligence Services (IS)*
Prime Minister *(Chairman)*
Foreign Secretary
Chancellor of the Exchequer
Home Secretary
Secretary of State for Defence

The Leader of the House of Commons and the Attorney General may be invited to attend as appropriate.

Terms of Reference: To keep under review policy on the security and intelligence services.

* *For details of the structure and functions of the Security and Intelligence Services see under that title in this section of the book*

Coordination and Presentation of Government Policy (EDCP)
Chancellor of the Duchy of Lancaster *(Chairman)*
Leader of the House of Commons
Leader of the House of Lords
Minister without Portfolio

Other members will be invited to attend as necessary

Terms of Reference: To consider the coordination and presentation of government policy

Industrial, Commercial and Consumer Affairs (EDI)
Chancellor of the Duchy of Lancaster *(Chairman)*
Chancellor of the Exchequer
Home Secretary
President of the Board of Trade
Leader of the House of Commons
Secretary of State for the Environment
Minister of Agriculture, Fisheries and Food
Secretary of State for Scotland
Secretary of State for Northern Ireland
Secretary of State for Employment
Secretary of State for Wales
Secretary of State for Transport
Leader of the House of Lords
Chief Secretary, Treasury
Minister without Portfolio

The Attorney General also receives papers and may be invited to attend as necessary.

Terms of Reference: To consider industrial, commercial and consumer issues including questions of competition and deregulation.

Environment (EDE)
Chancellor of the Duchy of Lancaster *(Chairman)*
Foreign Secretary
Chancellor of the Exchequer
President of the Board of Trade
Leader of the House of Commons
Secretary of State for the Environment
Minister of Agriculture, Fisheries and Food
Secretary of State for Scotland
Secretary of State for Northern Ireland
Secretary of State for Wales
Secretary of State for Transport
Secretary of State for National Heritage
Leader of the House of Lords
Chief Secretary, Treasury

The Minister without Portfolio also receives papers.

Terms of Reference: To consider questions of environmental policy.

Home and Social Affairs (EDH)
Leader of the House of Commons *(Chairman)*
Lord Chancellor
Home Secretary
President of the Board of Trade
Secretary of State for the Environment
Chancellor of the Duchy of Lancaster
Secretary of State for Social Security

Minister of Agriculture, Fisheries and Food
Secretary of State for Scotland
Secretary of State for Northern Ireland
Secretary of State for Health
Secretary of State for Education
Secretary of State for Employment
Secretary of State for Transport
Secretary of State for Wales
Secretary of State for National Heritage
Leader of the House of Lords
Minister without Portfolio
Chief Whip in the House of Commons

The Attorney General, the Lord Advocate and the Chief Whip in the House of Lords also receive papers and are invited to attend as necessary.

Terms of Reference: To consider home and social policy issues.

Local Government (EDL)

Chancellor of the Duchy of Lancaster *(Chairman)*
Chancellor of the Exchequer
Home Secretary
Leader of the House of Commons
Secretary of State for the Environment
Secretary of State for Social Security
Secretary of State for Scotland
Secretary of State for Health
Secretary of State for Education
Secretary of State for Wales
Secretary of State for Transport
Secretary of State for National Heritage
Leader of the House of Lords
Chief Secretary, Treasury
Minister without Portfolio
Minister of State, Department of the Environment (Minister for Local Government, Housing and Urban Regeneration)

Terms of Reference: To consider issues affecting local government, including the annual allocation of resources.

Regeneration (EDR)
Chancellor of the Duchy of Lancaster *(Chairman)*
Home Secretary
President of the Board of Trade
Leader of the House of Commons
Secretary of State for the Environment
Secretary of State for Education
Secretary of State for Employment
Secretary of State for Transport
Minister without Portfolio
Chief Secretary, Treasury
Minister of State, Department of the Environment (Minister for Local Government, Housing and Urban Regeneration)

The Secretaries of State for Scotland, Northern Ireland and Wales are invited to attend as appropriate.

Terms of Reference: To consider regeneration policies and their coordination.

Public Expenditure (EDX)
Chancellor of the Exchequer *(Chairman)*
Home Secretary
President of the Board of Trade
Leader of the House of Commons
Chancellor of the Duchy of Lancaster
Minister of Agriculture, Fisheries and Food
Chief Secretary to the Treasury

The Minister without Portfolio also receives papers.

Terms of Reference: To consider the allocation of the public expenditure control totals and make recommendations to the cabinet.

Queen's Speeches and Future Legislation (FLG)
Leader of the House of Commons *(Chairman)*
Lord Chancellor
Chancellor of the Duchy of Lancaster
Leader of the House of Lords
Minister without Portfolio
Attorney General
Lord Advocate
Chief Whip in the House of Commons
Financial Secretary, Treasury
Chief Whip in the House of Lords

The Foreign Secretary may be invited to attend or be represented for discussion of the Queen's speeches.

Terms of Reference: To prepare and submit to the Cabinet drafts of the Queen's speeches to Parliament, and proposals for the government's legislative programme for each session of Parliament.

Legislation (LG)

Leader of the House of Commons *(Chairman)*
Lord Chancellor
Secretary of State for Scotland
Secretary of State for Wales
Leader of the House of Lords
Attorney General
Lord Advocate
Chief Whip in the House of Commons
Minister of State, Foreign and Commonwealth Office
Minister of State, Home Office
Financial Secretary, Treasury
Chief Whip in the House of Lords

The Secretary of State for Northern Ireland also receives papers and is invited to attend as necessary.

Terms of Reference: To examine all draft bills, to consider the parliamentary handling of government bills, European Community documents and private members' business, and such other related matters as may be necessary; and to keep under review the government's policy in relation to issues of parliamentary procedures.

Sub-Committees

Health Strategy (EDH[H])

Leader of the House of Commons *(Chairman)*
President of the Board of Trade
Secretary of State for the Environment
Chancellor of the Duchy of Lancaster
Secretary of State for Social Security
Minister of Agriculture, Fisheries and Food
Secretary of State for Scotland
Secretary of State for Northern Ireland
Secretary of State for Health
Secretary of State for Education
Secretary of State for Wales
Secretary of State for Transport
Minister of State, Home Office
Paymaster General, Treasury
Parliamentary Under Secretary, Department of Employment
Parliamentary Under Secretary, Department of Health
Parliamentary Under Secretary, Department of National Heritage

The Chief Medical Officer is in attendance. The Minister without Portfolio also receives papers.

Terms of Reference: To oversee the development, implementation and monitoring of the government's health strategy, to coordinate the government's policies on UK-wide issues affecting health, and report as necessary to the Cabinet Committee on Home and Social Affairs.

Public Sector Pay (EDI[P])

Chancellor of the Duchy of Lancaster *(Chairman)*
Chancellor of the Exchequer
Home Secretary
President of the Board of Trade
Secretary of State for Defence
Secretary of State for the Environment
Secretary of State for Social Security
Secretary of State for Scotland
Secretary of State for Health
Secretary of State for Education
Secretary of State for Employment
Secretary of State for Transport
Chief Secretary, Treasury
Parliamentary Secretary, Office of Public Service and Science

The Lord Chancellor also receives papers and may be invited to attend as necessary. The Minister without Portfolio also receives papers.

Terms of Reference: To coordinate the handling of pay issues in the public sector, and report as necessary to the Cabinet Committee on Industrial, Commercial and Consumer Affairs.

European Questions (OPD[E])

Foreign Secretary *(Chairman)*
Chancellor of the Exchequer
Home Secretary
President of the Board of Trade
Secretary of State for Defence
Leader of the House of Commons
Secretary of State for the Environment
Chancellor of the Duchy of Lancaster
Minister for Agriculture, Fisheries and Food
Secretary of State for Scotland
Secretary of State for Northern Ireland
Secretary of State for Employment
Secretary of State for Wales
Secretary of State for Transport
Minister without Portfolio
Attorney General
Chief Whip in the House of Commons
Minister of State, Foreign and Commonwealth Office

The Lord Advocate also receives papers. He and other ministers will be invited to attend as the nature of the business requires. The UK Permanent representative to the European Union is also in attendance.

Terms of Reference: To consider questions relating to the UK's membership of the European Union and to report as necessary to the Cabinet Committee on Defence and Overseas Policy.

Terrorism (OPD[T])

Home Secretary *(Chairman)*
Foreign Secretary
President of the Board of Trade
Secretary of State for Defence
Secretary of State for Scotland
Secretary of State for Northern Ireland
Secretary of State for Transport
Attorney General

Terms of Reference: To keep under review the arrangements for countering terrorism and for dealing with terrorist incidents and their consequences, and to report as necessary to the Cabinet Committee on Defence and Overseas Policy.

Drug Misuse (EDH[D])

Leader of the House of Commons *(Chairman)*
Solicitor General
Minister of State, Home Office
Paymaster General, Treasury
Minister of State, Ministry of Defence (Minister for the Armed Forces)
Minister of State, Scottish Office
Minister of State, Department for Education
Parliamentary Under Secretary, Foreign and Commonwealth Office
Parliamentary Under Secretary, Department of Health
Parliamentary Under Secretary, Welsh Office

Others, including the Minister for Overseas Development and Parliamentary Under Secretaries from the Departments of the Environment and Employment may be invited to attend as appropriate and receive all papers.

Terms of Reference: To coordinate the government's national and international policies for tackling drugs misuse, and report as necessary to the Cabinet Committee on Home and Social Affairs.

Women's Issues (EDH[W])

Chancellor of the Duchy of Lancaster *(Chairman)*
Secretary of State for Education
Minister of State, Home Office
Paymaster General, Treasury
Minister of State, Department of the Environment (Minister for Construction and Planning)
Minister of State, Scottish Office
Minister of State, Department of Employment
Parliamentary Secretary, Ministry of Agriculture, Fisheries and Food
Parliamentary Under Secretary of State, Department of Health
Parliamentary Under Secretary of State, Northern Ireland Office
Parliamentary Secretary, Office of Public Service and Science
Parliamentary Under Secretary, Department of Social Security
Parliamentary Under Secretary of State for Trade and Technology, Department of Trade and Industry
Parliamentary Under Secretary of State, Department of Transport
Parliamentary Under Secretary of State, Welsh Office

The Minister of State, Ministry of Defence (Minister for the Armed Forces) and the Parliamentary Secretary, Lord Chancellor's Department also receive papers and may be invited to attend as necessary. The Minister without Portfolio also receives papers.

Terms of Reference: To review and develop the government's policy and strategy on issues of special concern to women; to oversee their implementation; and to report as necessary to the Cabinet Committee on Home and Social Affairs.

London (EDL[L])

Secretary of State for the Environment *(Chairman)*
Minister without Portfolio
Minister of State, Home Office
Financial Secretary, Treasury
Minister of State, Department of Trade and Industry (Minister for Industry and Energy)
Minister of State, Department of the Environment (Minister for Local Government, Housing and Urban Regeneration)
Minister of State, Department of Health (Minister for Health)
Parliamentary Under Secretary, Department of Education
Parliamentary Under Secretary, Department of Employment
Parliamentary Under Secretary, Department of Environment
Parliamentary Under Secretary, Department of National Heritage
Parliamentary Secretary, Office of Public Service and Science
Parliamentary Under Secretary, Department of Social Security
Parliamentary Under Secretary, Department of Transport (Minister for Transport in London)

Terms of Reference: To coordinate the government's policies on London.

Sanctions against the Federal Republic of Yugoslavia (GEN 27)

Minister of State, Foreign and Commonwealth Office *(Chairman)*
Paymaster-General, Treasury
Minister of State, Treasury
Minister of State, Department of Trade and Industry (Minister for Trade)
Minister of State, Ministry of Defence (Minister for Defence Procurement)
Minister of State, Department of Transport

Terms of Reference: To keep under review the implementation of the sanctions against the Federal Republic of Yugoslavia imposed under United Nations Security Council Resolutions 757, 787 and 820, and to report to the Cabinet Committee on Overseas and Defence Policy as necessary.

Ministerial Group on Competitiveness (GEN 29)

President of the Board of Trade *(Chairman)*
Chancellor of the Exchequer
Secretary of State for the Environment
Chancellor of the Duchy of Lancaster
Minister of Agriculture, Fisheries and Food
Secretary of State for Scotland
Secretary of State for Education
Secretary of State for Employment
Secretary of State for Wales
Secretary of State for Transport

Representatives of other Departments may be invited to attend as necessary. The Minister without Portfolio also receives papers.

Terms of Reference: To keep issues affecting the United Kingdom's competitiveness under review; and to update, in whole or part, as appropriate, from time to time the White Paper on Competitiveness for consideration by the Cabinet Committee on Economic and Domestic Policy.

Ministerial Group on Card Technology (GEN 34)

Chancellor of the Duchy of Lancaster *(Chairman)*
Secretary of State for Foreign and Commonwealth Affairs
Secretary of State for the Home Department
President of the Board of Trade
Leader of the House of Commons
Secretary of State for Social Security
Secretary of State for Scotland
Secretary of State for Northern Ireland
Secretary of State for Health
Secretary of State for Employment
Secretary of State for Wales
Secretary of State for Transport
Chief Secretary, Treasury
Parliamentary Secretary, Office of Public Service and Science

The Minister without Portfolio also receives papers.

Terms of Reference: To consider the developing technology of card systems, and the potential demand for such systems from Government Departments, to ensure a co-ordinated approach across the Government taking account of the impact on the individual citizen.

Cabinet Office Addresses

For fax numbers telephone the number below and ask for the appropriate fax number

Gildengate House
Upper Green Lane
Norwich NR3 1DW
Tel 01603 660181

Horse Guards Road
London SW1P 3AL
Tel 0171-270 3000

53 Parliament Street
London SW1A 2NH
Tel 0171-270 3000

Riverwalk House
157/61 Millbank
London SW1P 4RT
Tel 0171-217 3800

24 Whitehall
London SW1A 2ED
Tel 0171-210 6681

The Crown Estate

Founded	1760
Status	Statutory body
Responsibilities	Administration of the hereditary land revenues of the Crown under the provisions of the Crown Estate Act 1961. The estate includes properties in England, Wales, Scotland, Windsor Great Park, and foreshore and seabed around the coast of the United Kingdom
Number of staff	557

The Crown Estate

16 Carlton House Terrace, London SW1Y 5AH

Tel 0171-210 4377 Fax 0171-930 8259/3752

All staff are based at Carlton House Terrace unless otherwise indicated.
For other addresses and telephone numbers see the end of this section.

Commissioners

First Commissioner
Chairman
The Rt Hon The Earl of Mansfield

Second Commissioner
Deputy Chairman
C K Howes CB

Commissioners
R B Caws CBE
J N C James CBE
A Macdonald CBE
J H M Norris CBE
The Lord De Ramsey

Overview

Chairman	Staff: Deputy Chairman Chief Executive	Deputy Chief Executive	Senior Management Team	Department
Earl of Mansfield	C K Howes		M L Davies	Legal
			J R Mulholland	Agricultural Estates
			M J Gravestock	Scottish Estates
			M J O'Lone	Windsor Estate
	Property			
Earl of Mansfield	C K Howes	D E Murray	C F Hynes	Urban Estates
			F G Parrish	Marine Estates
			R Wyatt	Housing Estates
	Finance and Administration			
Earl of Mansfield	C K Howes	D E G Griffiths	M E Beckwith	Corporate Services
			R Blake	Personnel
			J Ford	Internal Audit
			D Kingston-Smith	Information Systems
			J Lelliott	Finance
			P Shearmur	Valuation and Investment Analysis

Staff and Departments

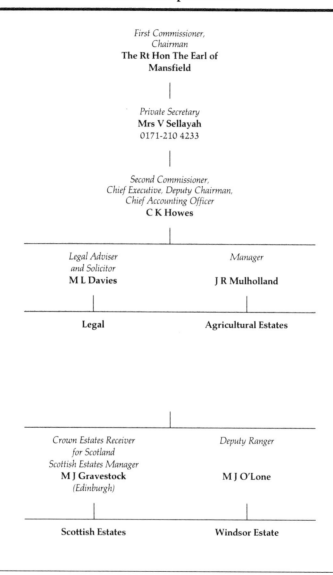

First Commissioner, Chairman
The Rt Hon The Earl of Mansfield

Private Secretary
Mrs V Sellayah
0171-210 4233

Second Commissioner, Chief Executive, Deputy Chairman, Chief Accounting Officer
C K Howes

Legal Adviser and Solicitor
M L Davies

Legal

Manager
J R Mulholland

Agricultural Estates

Crown Estates Receiver for Scotland
Scottish Estates Manager
M J Gravestock
(Edinburgh)

Scottish Estates

Deputy Ranger
M J O'Lone

Windsor Estate

Property

First Commissioner, Chairman
The Rt Hon The Earl of Mansfield

Second Commissioner, Chief Executive, Deputy Chairman, Chief Accounting Officer
C K Howes

Deputy Chief Executive
D E Murray

Crown Estate Surveyor and Urban Estates Manager
C F Hynes
Urban Estates

Marine Estates Manager
F G Parrish
Marine Estates

Chief Housing Manager
R Wyatt
Housing Estates

Finance and Administration

First Commissioner, Chairman
The Rt Hon The Earl of Mansfield

Second Commissioner, Chief Executive, Deputy Chairman, Chief Accounting Officer
C K Howes

Deputy Chief Executive
D E G Griffiths

Manager
M E Beckwith
Corporate Services

Manager
R Blake
Personnel

Manager
J Ford
Internal Audit

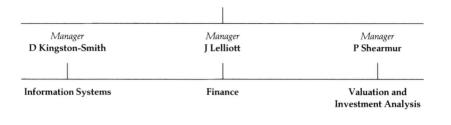

Manager **D Kingston-Smith**	*Manager* **J Lelliott**	*Manager* **P Shearmur**
Information Systems	**Finance**	**Valuation and Investment Analysis**

The Crown Estate Addresses

Crown Estate Office
10 Charlotte Square
Edinburgh EH2 4DR
Tel 0131-226 7241
Fax 0131-220 1366

Crown Estate Office
The Great Park
Windsor
Berks SL4 2HT
Tel 017538 60222
Fax 017538 59617

Crown Office (Scotland)

Founded	1765
Minister	Lord Advocate
Responsibilities	The public prosecution of crime in Scotland. All prosecutions in the High Court of Justiciary are conducted by Crown Counsel instructed by the Crown Office. In the Sheriff and District Courts prosecutions are conducted by the Procurator Fiscal Service which is administered by the Crown Office
Number of staff	Fiscal Service: 928 Crown Office: 132

Crown Office

25 Chambers Street, Edinburgh EH1 1LA
Tel 0131-226 2626   Fax 0131-2266910

All staff are located at Chambers Street unless otherwise indicated.
For other addresses and telephone numbers see end of this section.

Officials

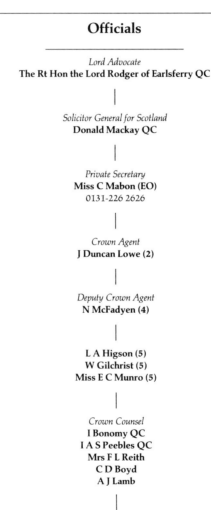

Lord Advocate
The Rt Hon the Lord Rodger of Earlsferry QC

Solicitor General for Scotland
Donald Mackay QC

Private Secretary
Miss C Mabon (EO)
0131-226 2626

Crown Agent
J Duncan Lowe (2)

Deputy Crown Agent
N McFadyen (4)

L A Higson (5)
W Gilchrist (5)
Miss E C Munro (5)

Crown Counsel
I Bonomy QC
I A S Peebles QC
Mrs F L Reith
C D Boyd
A J Lamb

Mrs V E Stacey
S MacGibbon
W Totten
S Brady
M O'Grady
D A Turnbull
C A L Scott
P B Cullen

Departmental Overview

Civil Servants			Department	Minister/ Solicitor General
Grade 2	*Grade 3*	*Grade 4*		
J D Lowe		N McFadyen	Crown Office	Lord Rodger D Mackay
	Procurator Fiscal Service			
J D Lowe	A C Normand	P Docherty	Glasgow and Strathkelvin	Lord Rodger D Mackay
	R F Lees		Lothian and Borders	Lord Rodger D Mackay
		A D Vannet	Grampian, Highlands and Islands	Lord Rodger D Mackay
		B K Heywood	Tayside Central and Fife	Lord Rodger D Mackay
		J D Friel	North Strathclyde	Lord Rodger D Mackay
		W G Carmichael	South Strathclyde, Dumfries and Galloway	Lord Rodger D Mackay

Civil Servants and Departments

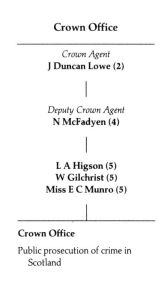

Crown Office

Crown Agent
J Duncan Lowe (2)

Deputy Crown Agent
N McFadyen (4)

L A Higson (5)
W Gilchrist (5)
Miss E C Munro (5)

Crown Office

Public prosecution of crime in Scotland

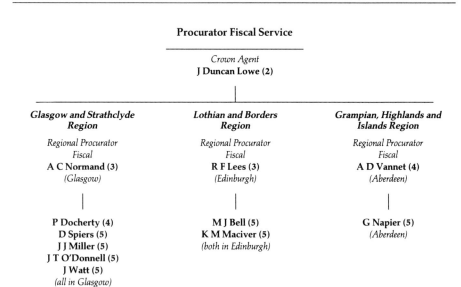

Procurator Fiscal Service

Crown Agent
J Duncan Lowe (2)

Glasgow and Strathclyde Region

Regional Procurator Fiscal
A C Normand (3)
(Glasgow)

P Docherty (4)
D Spiers (5)
J J Miller (5)
J T O'Donnell (5)
J Watt (5)
(all in Glasgow)

Lothian and Borders Region

Regional Procurator Fiscal
R F Lees (3)
(Edinburgh)

M J Bell (5)
K M Maciver (5)
(both in Edinburgh)

Grampian, Highlands and Islands Region

Regional Procurator Fiscal
A D Vannet (4)
(Aberdeen)

G Napier (5)
(Aberdeen)

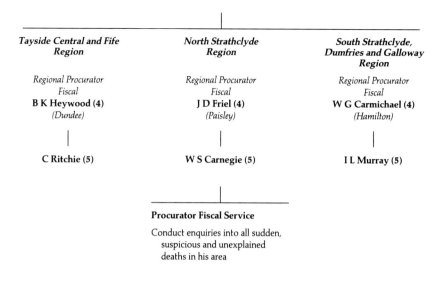

Tayside Central and Fife Region	North Strathclyde Region	South Strathclyde, Dumfries and Galloway Region
Regional Procurator Fiscal	*Regional Procurator Fiscal*	*Regional Procurator Fiscal*
B K Heywood (4) *(Dundee)*	**J D Friel (4)** *(Paisley)*	**W G Carmichael (4)** *(Hamilton)*
C Ritchie (5)	**W S Carnegie (5)**	**I L Murray (5)**

Procurator Fiscal Service

Conduct enquiries into all sudden, suspicious and unexplained deaths in his area

Crown Office Addresses

Regional Offices

Aberdeen Regional Office
Inverlair House
West North Street
Aberdeen AB9 1AL
Tel 01224 645132
Fax 01224 647005

Dundee Regional Office
15 West Bell Street
Dundee DD1 1HB
Tel 01382 27535
Fax 01382 202719

Edinburgh Regional Office
Sheriff Court House
29 Chambers Street
Edinburgh EH1 1LD
Tel 0131-226 4962
Fax 0131-220 4669

Glasgow Regional Office
10 Ballater Street
Glasgow G5 9PZ
Tel 0141-429 5566
Fax 0141-429 2066

Hamilton Regional Office
Cameronian House
3/5 Almada Street
Hamilton ML3 0HG
Tel 01698 284000
Fax 01698 422929

Paisley Regional Office
106 Renfrew Road
Paisley PA3 4DX
Tel 0141-887 5225
Fax 0141-887 6172

Crown Prosecution Service

Founded	1986
Responsibilities	The independent review and conduct of criminal proceedings instituted by police forces in England and Wales (with the exception of cases conducted by the Serious Fraud Office and certain minor offences) The Director of Public Prosecutions is the Head of the Service and discharges her statutory functions under the superintendence of the Attorney General The service comprises a headquarters office and 13 areas covering England and Wales each of which is supervised by a Chief Crown Prosecutor
Number of staff	6400

Crown Prosecution Service

50 Ludgate Hill, London EC4M 7EX

Tel 0171-273 8000   Public Enquiry Point 0171-273 8152   Fax 0171-329 8002

All staff are based at Ludgate Hill unless otherwise indicated.
For other addresses and telephone numbers see the end of this section.

Superintending Minister

Attorney General
The Rt Hon Sir Nicholas Lyell QC MP
(for details of his office
see Legal Secretariat to the Law Officers)

Officials

Director of Public Prosecutions
Mrs B J L Mills QC (1)

Private Secretary to the Director
Mrs T Newlyn (7)
0171-273 8100

Departmental Overview

	Civil Servants	Department
Grade 1	*Grade 3*	
	Headquarters	
Mrs B J L Mills QC	D M Nooney	Establishment and Finance Group
	K R Ashken	Policy Group
	G Duff	Operations Group
	C Newell	Casework Group
	C P S Areas	
Mrs B J L Mills QC	for names and districts see body of entry below	

Civil Servants and Departments

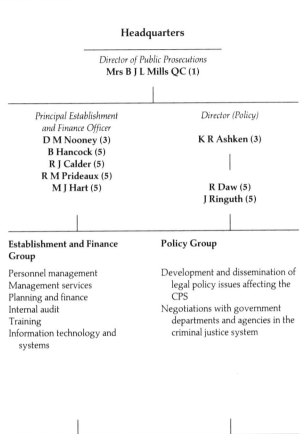

Headquarters

Director of Public Prosecutions
Mrs B J L Mills QC (1)

Principal Establishment and Finance Officer
D M Nooney (3)
B Hancock (5)
R J Calder (5)
R M Prideaux (5)
M J Hart (5)

Director (Policy)
K R Ashken (3)

R Daw (5)
J Ringuth (5)

Establishment and Finance Group

Personnel management
Management services
Planning and finance
Internal audit
Training
Information technology and systems

Policy Group

Development and dissemination of legal policy issues affecting the CPS
Negotiations with government departments and agencies in the criminal justice system

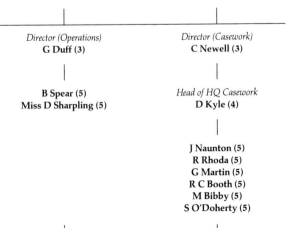

Director (Operations)
G Duff (3)

B Spear (5)
Miss D Sharpling (5)

Director (Casework)
C Newell (3)

Head of HQ Casework
D Kyle (4)

J Naunton (5)
R Rhoda (5)
G Martin (5)
R C Booth (5)
M Bibby (5)
S O'Doherty (5)

Operations Group

National operational practice
Area plans and resource allocations
Performance measures
Counsel fees
Operational systems

Casework Group

Fraud
International provision
Special casework
Police complaints
Casework standards

CPS Areas

Chief Crown Prosecutors	*Area*
D V Dickenson (4)	**CPS North:** Northumbria, Durham, Cumbria and Cleveland police forces
D Sharp (4)	**CPS Yorkshire:** North Yorkshire and West Yorkshire police forces
C Woodcock (4)	**CPS Mersey/Lancashire:** Merseyside and Lancashire police forces
D Adams (4)	**CPS Humber:** South Yorkshire, Humberside and Lincolnshire police forces
A R Taylor (4)	**CPS North West:** Greater Manchester and Cheshire police forces
B T McArdle (4)	**CPS East Midlands:** Derbyshire, Nottinghamshire, Leicestershire and Northamptonshire police forces
R A Prickett (4)	**CPS Wales:** North Wales, Dyfed, Powys, South Wales and Gwent police forces
T M McGowran (4)	**CPS Midlands:** West Midlands, Staffordshire and Warwickshire police forces
R J Chronnell (4)	**CPS Anglia:** Essex, Norfolk, Suffolk, Hertfordshire, Bedfordshire and Cambridgeshire police forces
A S R Clarke (4)	**CPS Severn/Thames:** West Mercia, Gloucestershire, Wiltshire and Thames Valley police forces
P Boeuf (4)	**CPS South West:** Avon, Somerset, Devon and Cornwall and Dorset police forces
G D Etherington (3) *Deputy Chief Crown Prosecutor* G Patten (4)	**CPS London:** Metropolitan and City of London police forces
D E J Dracup (4)	**CPS South East:** Kent, Sussex, Surrey and Hampshire police forces

Crown Prosecution Service Addresses

CPS Anglia
Queen's House
58 Victoria Street
St Albans AL1 3HZ
Tel 01727 818100
Fax 01727 833144

CPS East Midlands
2 King Edward Court
King Edward Street
Nottingham NG1 1EL
Tel 01159 480480
Fax 01159 418397

CPS Humber
Belgrave House
47 Bank Street
Sheffield S1 2EH
Tel 01142 731261
Fax 01142 762468

CPS London
Portland House
Stag Place
London SW1E 5BH
Tel 0171-915 5700
Fax 0171-828 8766

CPS Mersey/Lancashire
7th Floor (South)
Royal Liver Building
Pier Head
Liverpool L3 1HN
Tel 0151-236 7575
Fax 0151-255 0642

CPS Midlands
14th Floor
Colmore Gate
2 Colmore Row
Birmingham B3 2QA
Tel 0121-629 7202
Fax 0121-629 7314

CPS North
Benton House
136 Sandyford Road
Newcastle upon Tyne NE2 1QE
Tel 0191-201 2390
Fax 0191-230 0109

CPS North West
PO Box 377
8th Floor
Sunlight House
Quay Street
Manchester M60 3LU
Tel 0161-837 7402
Fax 0161-832 3628

CPS Severn/Thames
Artillery House
Heritage Way
Worcester WR9 8YB
Tel 01905 793763
Fax 01905 796793

CPS South East
Stoke Mill
Woking Road
Guildford
Surrey GU1 1AQ
Tel 01483 573255
Fax 01483 454271

CPS South West
8 Kew Court
Pynes Hill
Rydon Lane
Exeter
Devon EX2 5SS
Tel 01392 445422
Fax 01392 445353

CPS Yorkshire
6th Floor
Ryedale Building
60 Piccadilly
York
North Yorkshire YO1 1NS
Tel 01904 610726
Fax 01904 610394

CPS Wales
Tudor House
16 Cathedral Road
Cardiff
CF1 9LJ
Tel 01222 783000
Fax 01222 783098

Crown Solicitor's Office (Northern Ireland)

Founded 1 January 1974 replacing Chief Crown Solicitor's Office

Status Non-ministerial department

Responsible to Attorney General

Responsibilities Legal services for United Kingdom and Northern Ireland government departments

Administration of estates of people dying intestate and without known kin; dissolved companies; and failure of trustees

The Crown Solicitor also acts as Queen's Proctor in Northern Ireland (interventions and advisory functions in matrimonial suits and cases dealing with the legitimation of children)

Number of staff 110

Crown Solicitor's Office for Northern Ireland

Royal Courts of Justice, Chichester Street, Belfast PO Box 410
Tel 01232 235111 Fax 01232 248741

Minister

Attorney General
The Rt Hon Nicholas Lyell QC MP
(for details of his office see Law Officers' Department)

Officials

Crown Solicitor (2)

|

Private Secretary
01232 235111

|

Deputy Crown Solicitor (4)

|

4 Assistant Solicitors (5)

Her Majesty's Customs and Excise

Founded	1909 (by merger of the Boards of Customs and Excise, founded 1671 and 1683 respectively)
Minister	Chancellor of the Exchequer
Responsibilities	Collection and management of Value Added Tax, insurance premium tax and the excise duties including air passenger duty Fighting drug trafficking and enforcement of import and export prohibitions and restrictions such as those imposed to prevent the spread of weapons of mass destruction or as sanctions in support of international peacekeeping Collection of customs duties and agricultural levies on behalf of the European Union Compilation of trade statistics Providing advice to Ministers on these subjects
Executive units	HM Customs and Excise is a government department operating fully on Next Steps lines. It has 22 executive units, including 14 Collections
Number of staff	24,000

Her Majesty's Customs and Excise

New King's Beam House, 22 Upper Ground, London SE1 9PJ
Tel 0171-620 1313   Fax 0171-620 1313 x5005

All staff are based at New King's Beam House unless otherwise indicated.
For other addresses and telephone numbers see the end of this section.

Minister

The Chancellor of the Exchequer
The Rt Hon Kenneth Clarke MP
(for details of his office see HM Treasury)

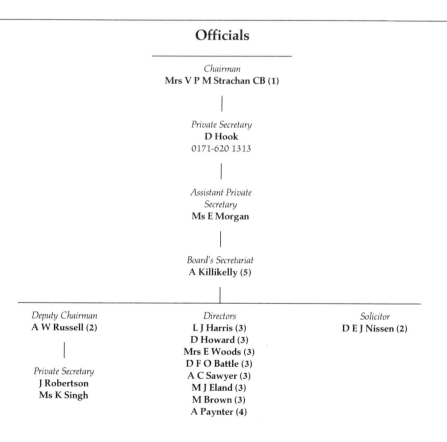

Officials

Chairman
Mrs V P M Strachan CB (1)

Private Secretary
D Hook
0171-620 1313

Assistant Private Secretary
Ms E Morgan

Board's Secretariat
A Killikelly (5)

Deputy Chairman
A W Russell (2)

Private Secretary
J Robertson
Ms K Singh

Directors
L J Harris (3)
D Howard (3)
Mrs E Woods (3)
D F O Battle (3)
A C Sawyer (3)
M J Eland (3)
M Brown (3)
A Paynter (4)

Solicitor
D E J Nissen (2)

Departmental Overview

Civil Servants			Department
Grade 1	*Grade 2*	*Grade 3*	
Mrs V P M Strachan	A W Russell		Deputy Chairman's Group: Information Systems; Quality, Communications and Business Service; Change Management Unit
Mrs V P M Strachan		Mrs E Woods	Operations (Compliance) Directorate
		A C Sawyer	Operations (Prevention) Directorate
		M Brown	Operations (Central) Directorate
		L J Harris	VAT Policy Directorate
		D Howard	Excise and Central Policy Directorate
		M J Eland	Customs Policy Directorate
		D F O Battle	Personnel and Finance Directorate
Mrs V P M Strachan	D E J Nissen	R D S Wylie	Solicitor's Office
		G Fotherby	Solicitor's Office
Mrs V P M Strachan			Collections For names and districts see body of entry below

Civil Servants and Departments

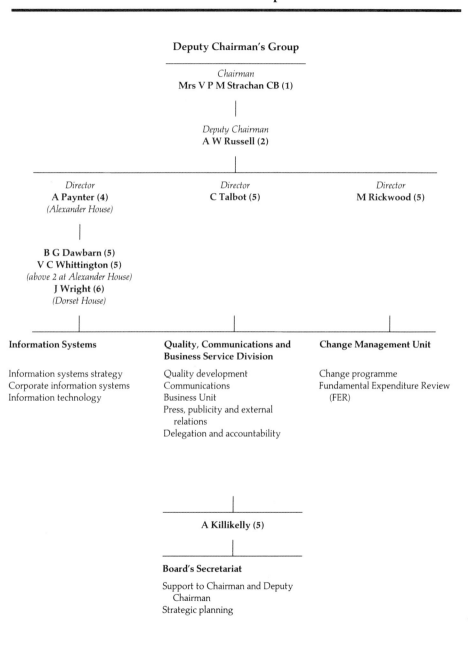

Deputy Chairman's Group

Chairman
Mrs V P M Strachan CB (1)

Deputy Chairman
A W Russell (2)

Director
A Paynter (4)
(Alexander House)

B G Dawbarn (5)
V C Whittington (5)
(above 2 at Alexander House)
J Wright (6)
(Dorset House)

Information Systems

Information systems strategy
Corporate information systems
Information technology

Director
C Talbot (5)

Quality, Communications and Business Service Division

Quality development
Communications
Business Unit
Press, publicity and external relations
Delegation and accountability

A Killikelly (5)

Board's Secretariat

Support to Chairman and Deputy Chairman
Strategic planning

Director
M Rickwood (5)

Change Management Unit

Change programme
Fundamental Expenditure Review (FER)

Operations (Compliance, Prevention and Central); VAT Policy; Excise and Central Policy; Customs Policy; Personnel and Financial

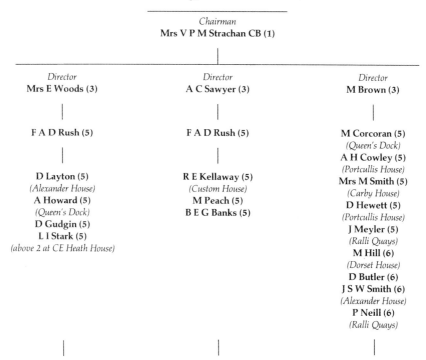

Chairman
Mrs V P M Strachan CB (1)

Director
Mrs E Woods (3)

F A D Rush (5)

D Layton (5)
(Alexander House)
A Howard (5)
(Queen's Dock)
D Gudgin (5)
L I Stark (5)
(above 2 at CE Heath House)

Director
A C Sawyer (3)

F A D Rush (5)

R E Kellaway (5)
(Custom House)
M Peach (5)
B E G Banks (5)

Director
M Brown (3)

M Corcoran (5)
(Queen's Dock)
A H Cowley (5)
(Portcullis House)
Mrs M Smith (5)
(Carby House)
D Hewett (5)
(Portcullis House)
J Meyler (5)
(Ralli Quays)
M Hill (6)
(Dorset House)
D Butler (6)
J S W Smith (6)
(Alexander House)
P Neill (6)
(Ralli Quays)

Operations (Compliance) Directorate

Operational policy and management relating to: control of imported freight, EC CAP imports and exports, End-use control, Free zones, Warehousing, Preferences, Quotas, Anti-dumping duty, Community transit, Customs freight systems, Duty-free shops, Valuation
Debt Management Policy (VAT) including: Civil recovery, Distress/diligence procedures, Missing traders, Insolvency, Working with the Inland Revenue, Insurance Premium Tax
Customs business information systems
Customs freight 2000 implementation team

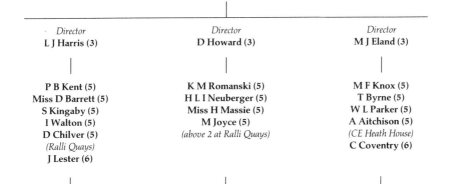

Director
L J Harris (3)

P B Kent (5)
Miss D Barrett (5)
S Kingaby (5)
I Walton (5)
D Chilver (5)
(Ralli Quays)
J Lester (6)

Operations (Prevention) Directorate

Operational policy and management relating to:Outfield organisation, Allocation and oversight of use of resources, Monitoring performance against plans, Administration and personnel
Information and risk analysis systems
Traveller's Charter
Aviation, maritime and rail traffic control
Operational anti-smuggling matters
Excise anti-smuggling risk analysis
Drug dogs
Liaison with other enforcement agencies at home and abroad
Intelligence gathering
Investigations relating to prohibitions and restrictions, revenue fraud, EC fraud and smuggling
Tracing proceeds of drug smuggling and other investigations under the Drugs Trafficking Offences Act
Standards of investigation
Revenue cutters

Director
D Howard (3)

K M Romanski (5)
H L I Neuberger (5)
Miss H Massie (5)
M Joyce (5)
(above 2 at Ralli Quays)

Operations (Central) Directorate

VAT Central Unit: accounting and adjustment, European sales listings, credibility and repayment supplements
VAT Central Unit: returns, payments, repayments
HQ personnel and financial management units
HQ accommodation and office service units
Pensions services
Libary and information
Museum
Tariff and Statistical Office
Vocational and developmental training
HQ Training Units
Accounting services
Management consultancy services
Purchasing Unit

Director
M J Eland (3)

M F Knox (5)
T Byrne (5)
W L Parker (5)
A Aitchison (5)
(CE Heath House)
C Coventry (6)

VAT Policy Directorate

VAT strategy and planning
VAT liability, supply, machinery and collection policy
Single market VAT
Insurance premium tax (IPT)
Tax avoidance
VAT tribunals policy

Excise and Central Policy Directorate

Budget and central unit
Economics and statistics division
Revenue duties

Customs Policy Directorate

European Union
Customs Union
International relations
International assistance
Anti-smuggling legislation
Memoranda of understanding and anti-drug alliance
International liaison
Traveller's Charter principles
Duty-free shopping
EU third pillar
Import and export prohibitions and restrictions
UN sanctions
Money laundering
Controlled drugs
Precursor chemicals, weapons and explosives
Obscene material
Scott Inquiry
Policy on valuation, preference, quotas, anti-dumping, exports, transit, warehousing, inwards processing relief, outwards processing relief
Tariff

Director
D F O Battle (3)

J Bone (5)
R N McAfee (5)
Ms A French (5)
M Norgrove (5)
C Outhwaite (5)
(Baryta House)
P Freeborn (6)
R McMurray (6)

Personnel and Finance Directorate

Human resource development

Recruitment, (alternative working patterns), transfers, manpower planning

Staff appraisal, promotion, succession planning, staff development, trawls, honours

Pay and allowances, overtime, travelling and removal expenses, staff records

Superannuation, discipline and inefficiency, data protection, absence, welfare, occupational health, health and safety

Accommodation policy and office services, and security

Communications, industrial relations, civil emergencies, equal opportunities

Solicitor's Office

Chairman
Mrs V P M Strachan CB (1)

Solicitor
D E J Nissen (2)

Principal Assistant Solicitors
R D S Wylie (3)
G Fotherby (3)

H J Flood (5)
D N Pratt (5)
(Ralli Quays)
P Dangerfield (5)
J A Quin (5)
C Allen (5)
Miss S G Linton (5)
M C K Gasper (5)
M Michael (5)
D M North (5)
J W N Tester (5)
Mrs S Edwards (5)
Miss A E Bolt (5)
I D Napper (5)

Solicitor's Office

Preparation and conduct of penalty proceedings in England and Wales
Forfeitures and seizures, prosecutions
VAT tribunals
Excise tribunals
International matters
Mutual assistance, VAT questions relating to importation, exportation and valuation
General customs matters
General, civil litigation, debt recovery and enforcement in the High Court and County Court (and Civil Courts in N Ireland and Scotland)
Insolvency and bankruptcy
Employment, Industrial Tribunal matters and hearings
VAT and IPT liability
Zero-rating and exemptions, input tax, partial exemption
EU questions
VAT machinery, control and enforcement
Car tax
Prosecutions

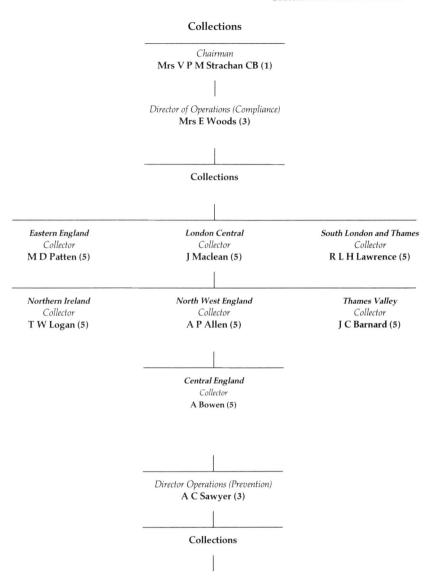

Collections

Chairman
Mrs V P M Strachan CB (1)

Director of Operations (Compliance)
Mrs E Woods (3)

Collections

Eastern England
Collector
M D Patten (5)

London Central
Collector
J Maclean (5)

South London and Thames
Collector
R L H Lawrence (5)

Northern Ireland
Collector
T W Logan (5)

North West England
Collector
A P Allen (5)

Thames Valley
Collector
J C Barnard (5)

Central England
Collector
A Bowen (5)

Director Operations (Prevention)
A C Sawyer (3)

Collections

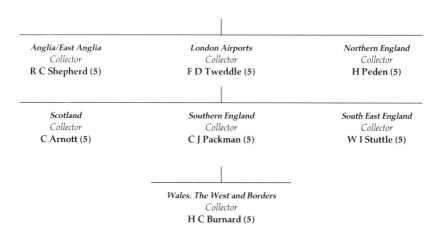

Anglia/East Anglia
Collector
R C Shepherd (5)

London Airports
Collector
F D Tweddle (5)

Northern England
Collector
H Peden (5)

Scotland
Collector
C Arnott (5)

Southern England
Collector
C J Packman (5)

South East England
Collector
W I Stuttle (5)

Wales, The West and Borders
Collector
H C Burnard (5)

HM Customs and Excise Addresses

National addresses

Alexander House
21 Victoria Avenue
Southend-on-Sea SS99 1AA
Tel 01702 348944

Baryta House
29 Victoria Avenue
Southend-on-Sea SS2 6AP
Tel 01702 348944

Carby House
73 Victoria Avenue
Southend-on-Sea SS2 6EB
Tel 01702 348944

CE Heath House
61 Victoria Avenue
Southend-on-Sea SS2 6EY
Tel 01702 348944

Customs House
Lower Thames Street
London EC3R 6EE
Tel 0171-283 5353
Fax 0171-696 7799

Dorset House
Stamford Street
London SE1 9PS
Tel 0171-928 3344

Portcullis House
27 Victoria Avenue
Southend-on-Sea SS2 6AL
Tel 01702 348944

Queens Dock
Liverpool
L74 4AA
Tel 0151-703 8000

Ralli Quays
3 Stanley Street
Salford M60 9LA
Tel 0161-839 7839

Collections addresses

Anglia/East Anglia
17 Lower Brook Street
Ipswich
Suffolk IP4 1DN
Tel 01473 235700

Central England
Alpha Tower
Suffolk Street
Queensway
Birmingham B1 1TX
Tel 0121-643 2777
Fax 0121-643 9657

Eastern England
Bowman House
100–102 Talbot Street
Nottingham NG1 5NF
Tel 01159 470451
Fax 01159 483487

London Airports
Custom House
Nettleton Road
North Side
Heathrow Airport
Hounslow
Middlesex TW6 2LA
Tel 0181-910 3615

London Central
Thomas Paine House
3rd Floor
Angel Square
Torrens Street
London EC1V 1TA
Tel 0171-865 3000
Fax 0171-865 3105

Northern England
Peter Bennett House
Redvers Close
West Park Ring Road
Leeds LS16 6RQ
Tel 01132 304444
Fax 01132 883322

Northern Ireland
Design Centre
39 Corporation Street
Belfast BT1 3AB
Tel 01232 234466
Fax 01232 232903

North West England
First Floor
Queens Dock
Liverpool L4 4AA
Tel 0151-703 1200
Fax 0151-236 3350

Scotland
44 York Place
Edinburgh EH1 3JW
Tel 0131-469 2000

South East England
Priory Court
St Johns Road
Dover
Kent CT17 9SH
Tel 01304 206789
Fax 01304 224420

Southern England
Custom House
Orchard Place
Southampton SO9 1ZD
Tel 01703 330330
Fax 01703 827088

South London and Thames
Dorset House
Stamford Street
London SE1 9PS
Tel 0171-928 3344

Thames Valley
Eaton Court
104-112 Oxford Road
Reading RG1 7FU
Tel 01734 583921
Fax 01734 505618

Wales, The West and Borders
Portcullis House
21 Cowbridge Road East
Cardiff CF1 9SS
Tel 01222 238531
Fax 01222 387302

Where there is no fax number shown, please phone the switchboard and ask for the fax number of the department you wish to contact

Ministry of Defence

Founded 1946 as a small coordinating department; became a ministry in 1964 with the amalgamation of the Admiralty, War Office and Air Ministry

Ministers one secretary of state, two ministers of state and one parliamentary under secretary of state

Responsibilities
Command and administration of the armed forces
Formulation and implementation of defence policy
Research, development, production and purchase of weapons systems and equipment

Number of Staff

	Service	*Civilian*	*Total*
Centre staff: (ie staff directly employed by MoD)	14,200	15,700	30,000
Procurement executive and research:	1,200	12,200	13,300
Services:	219,300	80,800	300,100
Totals	234,800	108,700	343,400

Figures may not add to totals because of rounding. Does not include staff employed in MoD executive agencies.

Executive and Support Agencies
Army Base Repair Organisation
Army Base Storage and Distribution Agency
Defence Accounts Agency
Defence Analytical Services Agency
Defence Animal Centre
Defence Clothing and Textiles Agency
Defence Postal and Courier Services
Defence Evaluation and Research Agency
Defence Transport and Movements Executive (DTMX)
Disposal Agency
Duke of York's Military School
HQ Service Children's Schools (NW Europe)
Hydrographic Office
Logistics and Information Systems Agency
Meteorological Office

Military Survey
Naval Aircraft Repair Organisation
Naval Recruiting and Training Agency
Queen Victoria School
RAF Maintenance Group Defence Agency
RAF Signals Engineering Establishment
RAF Training Group Defence Agency
Service Children's Schools (NW Europe)

Because of security considerations the Whitehall Companion has agreed to an MoD request that it should publish only the names of civil servants and members of the armed forces at grade 3/equivalent and above. Most grade 5s/equivalents and below are signified as Director (*).

The MoD is currently undergoing changes. Although the Whitehall Companion has provided as much up-to-date information as is available, a number of jobs within the ministry will probably change over the next 12 months. If readers have difficulty contacting anyone listed in this section they should telephone MoD general enquiries on 0171-218 9000 or the public enquiry office 0171-218 6645.

Ministry of Defence

Main Building, Whitehall, London SW1A 2HB
Tel 0171-218 9000 Public Enquiry Office 0171-218 6645
Fax *Telephone above number and ask for appropriate fax number*
All staff are based at Main Building unless otherwise indicated.
For other addresses and telephone numbers see the end of this section.

Ministers

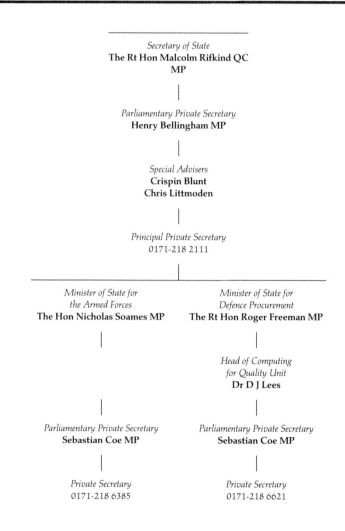

Secretary of State
The Rt Hon Malcolm Rifkind QC MP

Parliamentary Private Secretary
Henry Bellingham MP

Special Advisers
Crispin Blunt
Chris Littmoden

Principal Private Secretary
0171-218 2111

Minister of State for the Armed Forces
The Hon Nicholas Soames MP

Parliamentary Private Secretary
Sebastian Coe MP

Private Secretary
0171-218 6385

Minister of State for Defence Procurement
The Rt Hon Roger Freeman MP

Head of Computing for Quality Unit
Dr D J Lees

Parliamentary Private Secretary
Sebastian Coe MP

Private Secretary
0171-218 6621

Parliamentary Under Secretary of State for Defence
The Lord Henley

Private Secretary
0171-218 2452

House of Lords' Spokesmen
The Lord Henley
The Earl Howe
The Viscount Long
The Viscount Ullswater

Ministerial Responsibilities

Malcolm Rifkind	Overall responsibility for the ministry
Nicholas Soames	all operational matters and overseas commitments arms control operational logistics reserve forces policy size and shape of the 3 services strategy and general financial issues women in the armed forces
Roger Freeman	defence equipment programme defence exports defence procurement and contracts equipment projects nuclear issues quality assurance policy for market testing and contracting out research and development Royal dockyards Trident programme
The Lord Henley	Citizen's Charter defence estate and service housing environmental matters heritage low flying medicine and hospitals (military) NAAFI "Next steps" works services service and civilian personnel matters including equal opportunities House of Lords spokesman

List of MOD Departments in order shown

List of MOD Departments in order shown

Higher Organisation of Defence

Secretary of State
Rt Hon Malcolm Rifkind QC MP

Defence Council*

Admiralty Board	**Army Board**	**Air Force Board**
Chief of the Naval Staff **Admiral Sir Jock Slater GCB LVO (4*)**	*Chief of the General Staff* **General Sir Charles Guthrie KCB LVO OBE (4*)**	*Chief of the Air Staff* **Air Chief Marshal Sir Michael Graydon GCB CBE ADC (4*)**
Executive Committee of the Admirality Board	**Executive Committee of the Army Board**	**Executive Committee of the Air Force Board**

*see next page for membership

Defence Council

Secretary of State *Chairman of Defence Council*	**The Rt Hon Malcolm Rifkind QC MP**
Ministers:	
Armed Forces	**The Hon Nicholas Soames MP**
Defence Procurement	**The Rt Hon Roger Freeman MP**
Parliamentary Under Secretary for the Armed Forces	**The Lord Henley**
Chief of the Defence Staff	**Field Marshal Sir Peter Inge GCB ADCGen (5*)**
Permanent Under Secretary of State	**R C Mottram**
Chief of the Naval Staff	**Adm Sir Jock Slater GCB LVO (4*)**
Chief of the General Staff	**Gen Sir Charles Guthrie KCB LVO OBE (4*)**
Chief of the Air Staff	**Air Chief Mshl Sir Michael Graydon GCB CBE ADC (4*)**
Vice-Chief of the Defence Staff	**Air Chief Mshl Sir John Willis KCB CBE (4*)**
Chief of Defence Procurement	**Dr M K McIntosh**
Chief Scientific Adviser	**Prof Sir David Davies**
Second Permament Under Secretary of State	**J M Stewart CB**

Higher Organisation of Defence

Secretary of State
The Rt Hon Malcolm Rifkind QC MP

Ministers
The Hon Nicholas Soames MP
The Rt Hon Roger Freeman MP
The Lord Henley

Chief of the Defence Staff (CDS)
Field Marshal Sir Peter Inge GCB ADCGen (5*)

Permanent Under Secretary of State
R C Mottram (1)

Chief of the Naval Staff (CNS)
Admiral Sir Jock Slater GCB LVO (4*)

Chief of the General Staff (CGS)
General Sir Charles Guthrie KCB LVO OBE (4*)

Chief of the Air Staff (CAS)
Air Chief Marshal Sir Michael Graydon GCB CBE ADC (4*)

Vice Chief of the Defence Staff (VCDS)
Air Marshal Sir John Willis KCB CBE (4*)

Single Service Executive Staffs

Defence Staff

Higher Organisation of Defence

Secretary of State
The Rt Hon Malcolm Rifkind QC MP

Ministers
The Hon Nicholas Soames MP
The Rt Hon Roger Freeman MP
The Lord Henley

Permanent Under Secretary of State
R C Mottram (1)

Second Permanent Under Secretary of State (2nd PUS)
J M Stewart CB (1A)

Office of Management and Budget (OMB)

Chief Scientific Adviser (CSA)
Prof Sir David Davies (1A)

Defence Scientific Staff

Chief of Defence Procurement (CDP)
Dr M K McIntosh (1)

Procurement Executive

Departmental Overview

Civil Servants and Defence Staff				Department	Minister
*Grade 1/5**	*Grade 1A/4**	*Grade 2/3**	*Grade 3/2**		
Defence Council					
		Admirality Board			
	Adm Sir Jock Slater			Executive Committee	M Rifkind
		Army Board			
	Gen Sir Charles Guthrie			Executive Committee	M Rifkind
		Air Force Board			
	Air Chief Mshl Sir Michael Graydon			Executive Committee	M Rifkind

KEY

Grade 1/5*
1 = civil service grade 1
5* = 5 star general

Grade 1A/4*
1A = Civil Service Grade 1A
4* = 4 star general

Grade 2/3*
2 = civil service grade 2
3* = 3 star general

Grade 3/2*
3 = civil service grade 2
2* = 2 star general

Miscellaneous
(*) 1 star brigadier etc
† rank lower than (*)

Departmental Overview

Civil Servants and Defence Staff Grade 1/5*	Grade 1A/4*	Grade 2/3*	Grade 3/2*	Department	Minister
Central Staffs					
		Defence Services Secretary			
Field Marshal Sir Peter Inge			Air Vice-Mshl Peter Harding	Defence Services Secretariat	M Rifkind
		Chiefs of Staff Secretariat			
Field Marshal Sir Peter Inge	Air Chief Mshl Sir John Willis		Director (*)	Chiefs of Staff Secretariat	M Rifkind
		Defence Staff Budget Manager Unit			
Field Marshal Sir Peter Inge and R C Mottram	Air Chief Mshl Sir John Willis		D C R Heyhoe	General Finance Unit	M Rifkind
		Defence Information Division			
Field Marshal Sir Peter Inge and R C Mottram			Miss G Samuel (4)	Information Services	M Rifkind

Departmental Overview

Civil Servants and Defence Staff Grade 1/5*	Grade 1A/4*	Grade 2/3*	Grade 3/2*	Department	Minister
		Commitments			
Field Marshal Sir Peter Inge and R C Mottram	Air Chief Mshl Sir John Willis	Lt Gen A G H Harley	Air Vice-Mshal A J Harrison	Operations and Security	N Soames
			Air Vice Mshl N B Baldwin	Overseas	N Soames
			Rear Admiral F B Goodson	Logistics	N Soames
			B R Hawtin	Commitments	N Soames
		Systems			
Field Marshal Sir Peter Inge and R C Mottram	Air Chief Mshl Sir John Willis	Vice Adm J H Dunt	R Adm J A Trewby	Sea Systems	N Soames
			Maj Gen E F G Burton	Land Systems	N Soames
			Air Vice Mshl C C C Colville	Air Systems	N Soames
			Maj Gen W J P Robins	Communications and Information Systems	N Soames
		Programmes and Personnel			
Field Marshal Sir Peter Inge and R C Mottram	Air Chief Mshl Sir John Willis	Lt Gen The Hon Sir Thomas Boyd-Carpenter	Air Vice Marshal G A Robertson	Programmes	N Soames
			Miss A Walker	Personnel and Reserves	N Soames

Departmental Overview

Civil Servants and Defence Staff: Grade 1/5*	Grade 1A/4*	Grade 2/3*	Grade 3/2*	Department	Minister
Defence Medical Services Directorate					
		Lt Gen The Hon Sir Thomas Boyd-Carpenter and Surgeon Rear Adm A L Revell	Air Vice-Mshl J Mackey	Directorate of Defence Dental Services	Ld Henley
			Director (*)	Directorate of Defence Nursing Services	Ld Henley
Policy					
Field Marshal Sir Peter Inge and R C Mottram		D B Omand	Air Vice Marshal D F A Henderson	Policy and Nuclear	N Soames
			G W Hopkinson	Policy	N Soames R C Mottram

Departmental Overview

Civil Servants and Defence Staff *Grade 1/5**	*Grade 1A/4**	*Grade 2/3**	*Grade 3/2**	Department	Minister
		Resources, Programmes and Finance			
R C Mottram	J M Stewart	R T Jackling	D Fisher	Systems	N Soames
			Ms D J Seammen	Programmes	N Soames
			C V Balmer	Management Strategy	N Soames
			P J Trevelyan	Defence Accounts	N Soames
			T J Brack	General Finance	N Soames
			P P Altobell	Defence Analytical Services	N Soames
			Director (5)	Resources and Programmes	N Soames
			Director (5)	Economic Advice	N Soames

Departmental Overview

Civil Servants and Defence Staff

Grade 1/5*	Grade 1A/4*	Grade 2/3*	Grade 3/2*	Department	Minister
		Personnel and Logistics			
R C Mottram	J M Stewart	J Ledlie	Miss A Walker	Service Personnel	Ld Henley
			T F W B Knapp	Infrastructure and Logistics	Ld Henley
				Defence Works Services	Ld Henley
		Civilian Management			
R C Mottram	J M Stewart	J F Howe	B A E Taylor	Policy	Ld Henley
			I D Fauset	Personnel	Ld Henley
			J Reddington	MOD Police	Ld Henley
			R P Hatfield	Management and Organisation	Ld Henley

Chiefs of Staff

		Naval Staff			
Field Marshal Sir Peter Inge	Adm Sir Jock Slater		R Adm J J Blackham	Naval Staff	All

Departmental Overview

Grade 1/5*	Grade 1A/4*	Grade 2/3*	Grade 3/2*	Department	Minister
		General Staff			
Field Marshal Sir Peter Inge	Gen Sir Charles Guthrie		Maj Gen T Granville-Chapman	General Staff	All
		Air Staff			
Field Marshal Sir Peter Inge	Air Chief Mshl Sir Michael Graydon		Air Vice Mshl P T Squire	Air Staff	All

Defence Intelligence

Grade 1/5*	Grade 1A/4*	Grade 2/3*	Grade 3/2*	Department	Minister
Field Marshal Sir Peter Inge and R C Mottram		Lt Gen Sir John Foley	Director (2*)	Intelligence Assessments	M Rifkind
			Assistant Under Secretary	Scientific and Technical Intelligence	M Rifkind
			Director (2*)	Management and Support of Intelligence	M Rifkind
			Director (2*)	Military Survey	M Rifkind

Departmental Overview

Civil Servants and Defence Staff				Department	Minister
*Grade 1/5**	*Grade 1A/4**	*Grade 2/3**	*Grade 3/2**		
Scientific Staff					
R C Mottram	Prof Sir David Davies	Dr A Ferguson		Nuclear Weapons Safety Adviser	R Freeman
		P D Ewins	G H B Jordan	Scrutiny and Analysis	R Freeman
			Director (5)	Budget and Finance	R Freeman
			P M Sutcliffe	Research and Technology	R Freeman
			P W Roper (4)	Nuclear Policy	R Freeman
Navy Department					
		Second Sea Lord; Commander-in-Chief Naval Home Command			
Field Marshal Sir Peter Inge	Adm Sir Jock Slater	Adm Sir Michael Boyce	R Adm J P Clarke	Flag Officer, Training and Recruiting	Ld Henley
			Rear Adm A W J West	Naval Secretary's Office; Naval Manning	Ld Henley
			R Adm R B Lees	Naval Personnel Strategy and Plans	Ld Henley
			Surgeon Rear Adm A Craig	Naval Medical and Dental Services	Ld Henley
			The Ven Archdeacon M W Bucks	Naval Chaplaincy Services	Ld Henley

Departmental Overview

Grade 1/5*	Grade 1A/4*	Grade 2/3*	Grade 3/2*	Department	Minister
		Naval Support Command			
Field Marshal Sir Peter Inge	Adm Sir Jock Slater	Vice Adm Sir Toby Frere	A J D Pawson	Fleet Support	N Soames R Freeman
			D G Jones	Supplies and Transport (Naval)	N Soames R Freeman
			R Adm P Spencer	Fleet Support (Operations and Plans)	N Soames R Freeman
			Rear Adm D J Wood	Aircraft (Navy)	N Soames R Freeman
			R Adm N R Essenhigh	Hydrographic Services	N Soames R Freeman
			B V Babbington	Fleet Support (Ships)	N Soames R Freeman
			R Adm J R Shiffner	Fleet Support (Equipment and Systems)	N Soames R Freeman

Civil Servants and Defence Staff (Grade columns); Department; Minister

Departmental Overview

Grade 1/5*	Grade 1A/4*	Grade 2/3*	Grade 3/2*	Department	Minister
Army Department					
		Quartermaster General			
Field Marshal Sir Peter Inge	Gen Sir Charles Guthrie	Lt Gen The Hon Sir William Rous	Dr A Fox	Quartermaster	R Freeman N Soames
			Maj Gen P J Sheppard	Chief of Staff (HQ/QMG)	R Freeman N Soames
			Maj Gen P J G Corp	Directorate General of Equipment (Army)	R Freeman N Soames
			Maj Gen M S White	Logistic Support (Army)	R Freeman N Soames
			Maj Gen A H Boyle	Communications and Information Systems (Army)	R Freeman N Soames
		Adjutant General			
Field Marshal Sir Peter Inge	Gen Sir Charles Guthrie		Maj Gen M I E Scott	Military Secretary	Ld Henley
			W A Perry (4)	Civil Secretary	Ld Henley
	Gen Sir Michael Rose		Maj Gen D L Burden	Army Manning and Recruiting	Ld Henley
			Dr J R Allan	Army Personnel Research Establishment	Ld Henley

Departmental Overview

Civil Servants and Defence Staff				Department	Minister
*Grade 1/5**	*Grade 1A/4**	*Grade 2/3**	*Grade 3/2**		
			Maj Gen M D Reagan	Personnel and Training	Ld Henley
			Maj Gen F B Mayes	Army Medical Services	Ld Henley
			Rev D V Dobbin	Chaplain's Services	Ld Henley
		Inspector General Doctrine and Training			
Field Marshal Sir Peter Inge	Gen Sir Charles Guthrie	Lt Gen S Cowan	Maj Gen R W M McAfee Maj Gen T J Sulivan Brig A C I Gadsby (1*) Maj Gen I G C Durie Maj Gen K J Drewienkiewicz Maj Gen R A Pett Maj Gen S W St J Lytle	Doctrine, Training and Land Warfare (including Directors of Royal Armoured Corps, Royal Artillery, Engineer-in-Chief, Infantry, Army Aviation	N Soames

Departmental Overview

Civil Servants and Defence Staff Grade 1/5*	Grade 1A/4*	Grade 2/3*	Grade 3/2*	Department	Minister
Air Force Department					
		Headquarters Strike Command			
Field Marshal Sir Peter Inge	Air Chief Mshl Sir Michael Graydon and Air Chief Mshl Sir William Wratten	Air Mshl J S Allison	Air Vice Mshl D J Saunders	Engineering and Supply	N Soames
			Air Vice Mshl T B Sherrington	Administration	N Soames
			Director (*)	Plans	N Soames
			A J Ward (4)	Command Secretariat	N Soames
		Headquarters Logistic Command			
Field Marshal Sir Peter Inge	Air Chief Mshl Sir Michael Graydon and Air Chief Mshl Sir Michael Alcock		H Griffiths	Command Secretary	N Soames
			Air Vice Mshl C G Terry	Chief of Staff; Deputy Air Officer Commanding in Chief	N Soames
			Air Vice Mshl R H Kyle	Air Officer Maintenance	N Soames
			Air Vice Mshl P D Markey	Support Management	N Soames
			Air Vice Mshl J B Main	Communications Information Systems	N Soames

Departmental Overview

Grade 1/5*	Grade 1A/4*	Grade 2/3*	Grade 3/2*	Department	Minister
		Personnel and Training Command			
Field Marshal Sir Peter Inge	Air Chief Mshl Sir Michael Graydon and Air Mshl D Cousins		Air Vice Mshl R P O'Brien	Air Secretary	Ld Henley
			Air Vice Mshl G W Carleton	Legal Services (RAF)	Ld Henley
			The Ven B H Lucas	Chaplaincy Services (RAF)	Ld Henley
			Air Vice Mshl J A Baird	Medical Services (RAF)	Ld Henley
			Air Vice Mshl P G Beer	Strategic Policy and Plans	N Soames
			Air Vice Mshl J A G May	Training Group	N Soames
Procurement Executive					
		Deputy Chief of Defence Procurement (Support)			
R C Mottram and Dr M K McIntosh		M J V Bell	G E Roe	Commercial	R Freeman
			B Miller	Finance	R Freeman
			R Adm M R Thomas	Technical Services; Ordnance Board	R Freeman
			J A Gulvin	Business Strategy	R Freeman

Departmental Overview

Civil Servants and Defence Staff				Department	Minister
*Grade 1/5**	*Grade 1A/4**	*Grade 2/3**	*Grade 3/2**		
		Deputy Chief of Defence Procurement (South of England)			
R C Mottram and Dr M K McIntosh		Vice Adm R Walmsley	R Adm R O Irwin	Strategic Systems Executive	R Freeman
			C V Betts	Submarines	R Freeman
			R Adm F P Scourse	Surface Ships	R Freeman
		Deputy Chief of Defence Procurement (London)			
R C Mottram and Dr M K McIntosh		Lt Gen R J Hayman-Joyce	Maj Gen A G Sharman	Land Systems	R Freeman
			J D Maines	Command and Information Systems	R Freeman
		Deputy Chief of Defence Procurement (Operations)			
R C Mottram and Dr M K McIntosh		Air Mshl Sir Roger Austin	J A Gordon	Air Systems 1	R Freeman
			Air Vice Mshl P C Norris	Air Systems 2	R Freeman
			G N Beaven	Weapons and Electronic Systems	R Freeman

Departmental Overview

Civil Servants and Defence Staff: Grade 1/5*	Grade 1A/4*	Grade 2/3*	Grade 3/2*	Department	Minister
		Defence Export Services			
R C Mottram and Dr M K McIntosh		C B G Masefield	I M S Faulkner	International Finance Advice	R Freeman
			Rear Adm J F T G Salt	Defence Export Services	R Freeman
			D J Bowen	Marketing	R Freeman
			C T Sandars (4)	Export Policy and Finance	R Freeman
			Air Mshl I D MacFadyen	Saudi Armed Forces Projects	R Freeman

Inter-Service Organisations

Grade 1/5*	Grade 1A/4*	Grade 2/3*	Grade 3/2*	Department	Minister
Field Marshal Sir Peter Inge		Air Mshl Sir Timothy Garden	R Adm J F Perowne	Royal College of Defence Studies	Ld Henley
			Maj Gen A I G Kennedy		
			Air Vice Mshl P Dodworth		
			Rear Adm N J Wilkinson	Joint Service Defence College	Ld Henley

KEY

Grade 1/5*
1 = civil service grade 1
5* = 5 star general

Grade 1A/4*
1A = civil service grade 1A
4* = 4 star general

Grade 2/3*
2 = civil service grade 2
3* = 3 star general

Grade 3/2*
3 = civil service grade 2
2* = 2 star general

Miscellaneous
(*) 1 star brigadier etc
† rank lower than (*)

Civil Servants and Armed Services

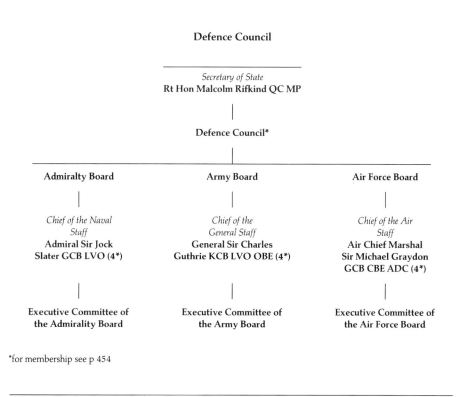

Defence Council

Secretary of State
Rt Hon Malcolm Rifkind QC MP

Defence Council*

Admiralty Board	Army Board	Air Force Board
Chief of the Naval Staff **Admiral Sir Jock Slater GCB LVO (4*)**	*Chief of the General Staff* **General Sir Charles Guthrie KCB LVO OBE (4*)**	*Chief of the Air Staff* **Air Chief Marshal Sir Michael Graydon GCB CBE ADC (4*)**
Executive Committee of the Admirality Board	**Executive Committee of the Army Board**	**Executive Committee of the Air Force Board**

*for membership see p 454

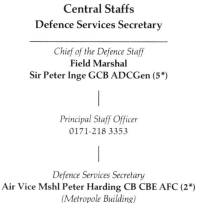

Central Staffs

Defence Services Secretary

Chief of the Defence Staff
Field Marshal
Sir Peter Inge GCB ADCGen (5*)

Principal Staff Officer
0171-218 3353

Defence Services Secretary
Air Vice Mshl Peter Harding CB CBE AFC (2*)
(Metropole Building)

Defence Services Secretariat

Service interface with Royal business
Senior appointments
Honours and awards

Chiefs of Staff Secretariat

Chief of the Defence Staff
Field Marshal
Sir Peter Inge GCB ADCGen (5*)

Permanent Under Secretary of State
R C Mottram (1)

Private Secretary
0171-218 2839

Vice Chief of the Defence Staff
Air Chief Marshal Sir John Willis KCB CBE (4*)

Secretary of Chiefs of Staff Committee
Director (*)

Chiefs of Staff Secretariat

Chiefs of Staff
Corporate Business

Budget Manager Unit

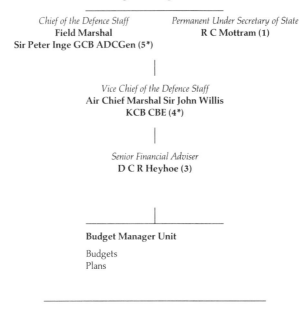

Chief of the Defence Staff
Field Marshal
Sir Peter Inge GCB ADCGen (5*)

Permanent Under Secretary of State
R C Mottram (1)

Vice Chief of the Defence Staff
Air Chief Marshal Sir John Willis
KCB CBE (4*)

Senior Financial Adviser
D C R Heyhoe (3)

Budget Manager Unit

Budgets
Plans

Defence Information Staff

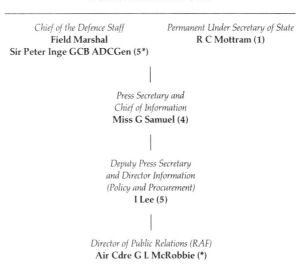

Chief of the Defence Staff
Field Marshal
Sir Peter Inge GCB ADCGen (5*)

Permanent Under Secretary of State
R C Mottram (1)

Press Secretary and
Chief of Information
Miss G Samuel (4)

Deputy Press Secretary
and Director Information
(Policy and Procurement)
I Lee (5)

Director of Public Relations (RAF)
Air Cdre G L McRobbie (*)

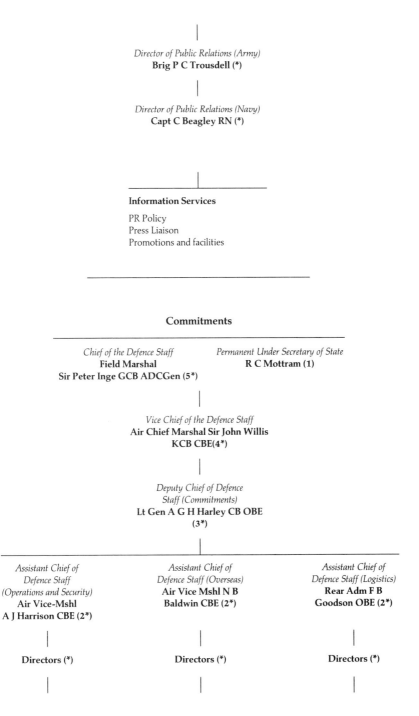

Director of Public Relations (Army)
Brig P C Trousdell (*)

Director of Public Relations (Navy)
Capt C Beagley RN (*)

Information Services

PR Policy
Press Liaison
Promotions and facilities

Commitments

Chief of the Defence Staff
Field Marshal Sir Peter Inge GCB ADCGen (5*)

Permanent Under Secretary of State
R C Mottram (1)

Vice Chief of the Defence Staff
Air Chief Marshal Sir John Willis KCB CBE(4*)

Deputy Chief of Defence Staff (Commitments)
Lt Gen A G H Harley CB OBE (3*)

Assistant Chief of Defence Staff (Operations and Security)
Air Vice-Mshl A J Harrison CBE (2*)

Directors (*)

Assistant Chief of Defence Staff (Overseas)
Air Vice Mshl N B Baldwin CBE (2*)

Directors (*)

Assistant Chief of Defence Staff (Logistics)
Rear Adm F B Goodson OBE (2*)

Directors (*)

Operations and Security

Military operations
Naval operations
Air offensive and defence directorates
Joint warfare directorate
Security

Overseas

Preparation of military advice for the Chief of the Defence Staff on policy and operational matters worldwide and on military assistance overseas

Logistics

Policy and plans for deployments, exercises (movements, stores, material)

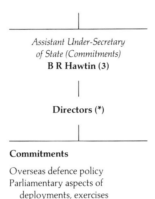

Assistant Under-Secretary of State (Commitments)
B R Hawtin (3)

Directors (*)

Commitments

Overseas defence policy
Parliamentary aspects of deployments, exercises

Systems

Chief of the Defence Staff
Field Marshal Sir Peter Inge GCB ADCGen (5*)

Permanent Under Secretary of State
R C Mottram (1)

Vice Chief of the Defence Staff
Air Chief Marshal Sir John Willis KCB CBE (4*)

Deputy Chief of Defence Staff (Systems)
Vice Admiral J H Dunt (3*)

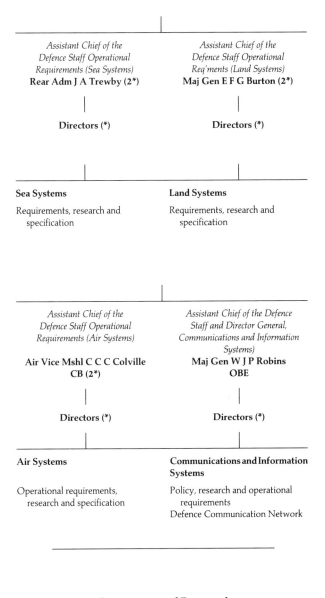

Assistant Chief of the Defence Staff Operational Requirements (Sea Systems)
Rear Adm J A Trewby (2*)

Directors (*)

Assistant Chief of the Defence Staff Operational Req'ments (Land Systems)
Maj Gen E F G Burton (2*)

Directors (*)

Sea Systems

Requirements, research and specification

Land Systems

Requirements, research and specification

Assistant Chief of the Defence Staff Operational Requirements (Air Systems)

Air Vice Mshl C C C Colville CB (2*)

Directors (*)

Assistant Chief of the Defence Staff and Director General, Communications and Information Systems)
Maj Gen W J P Robins OBE

Directors (*)

Air Systems

Operational requirements, research and specification

Communications and Information Systems

Policy, research and operational requirements
Defence Communication Network

Programmes and Personnel

Chief of the Defence Staff
Field Marshal Sir Peter Inge GCB ADCGen (5*)

Permanent Under Secretary of State
R C Mottram (1)

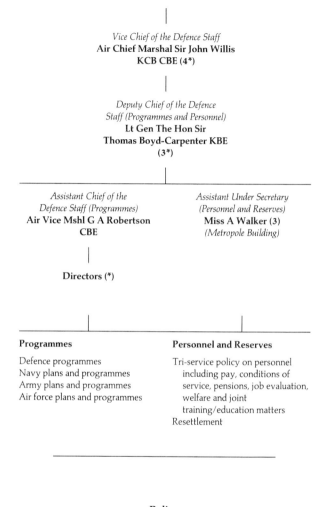

Vice Chief of the Defence Staff
Air Chief Marshal Sir John Willis KCB CBE (4*)

Deputy Chief of the Defence Staff (Programmes and Personnel)
Lt Gen The Hon Sir Thomas Boyd-Carpenter KBE (3*)

Assistant Chief of the Defence Staff (Programmes)
Air Vice Mshl G A Robertson CBE

Directors (*)

Assistant Under Secretary (Personnel and Reserves)
Miss A Walker (3)
(Metropole Building)

Programmes

Defence programmes
Navy plans and programmes
Army plans and programmes
Air force plans and programmes

Personnel and Reserves

Tri-service policy on personnel including pay, conditions of service, pensions, job evaluation, welfare and joint training/education matters
Resettlement

Policy

Chief of the Defence Staff
Field Marshal Sir Peter Inge GCB ADCGen (5*)

Permanent Under Secretary of State
R C Mottram (1)

Deputy Under-Secretary of State (Policy)
D B Omand (2)

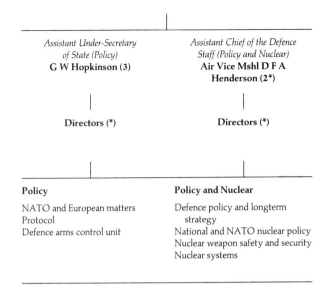

Assistant Under-Secretary of State (Policy)	*Assistant Chief of the Defence Staff (Policy and Nuclear)*
G W Hopkinson (3)	**Air Vice Mshl D F A Henderson (2*)**
Directors (*)	**Directors (*)**

Policy

NATO and European matters
Protocol
Defence arms control unit

Policy and Nuclear

Defence policy and longterm strategy
National and NATO nuclear policy
Nuclear weapon safety and security
Nuclear systems

Defence Medical Services Directorate

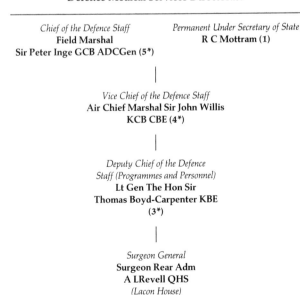

Chief of the Defence Staff
Field Marshal Sir Peter Inge GCB ADCGen (5*)

Permanent Under Secretary of State
R C Mottram (1)

Vice Chief of the Defence Staff
Air Chief Marshal Sir John Willis KCB CBE (4*)

Deputy Chief of the Defence Staff (Programmes and Personnel)
Lt Gen The Hon Sir Thomas Boyd-Carpenter KBE (3*)

Surgeon General
Surgeon Rear Adm A LRevell QHS
(Lacon House)

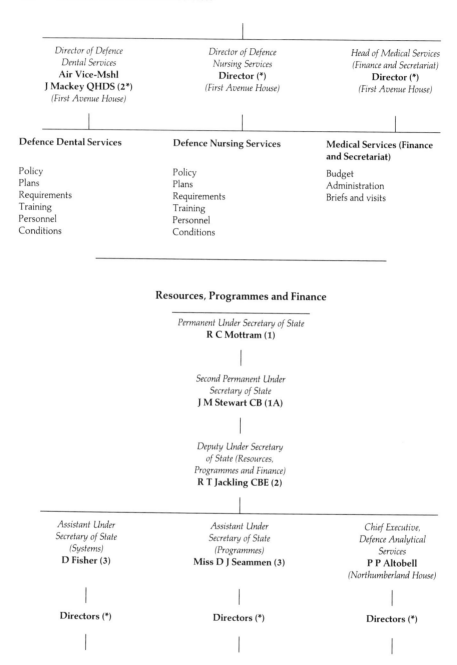

Director of Defence Dental Services
Air Vice-Mshl J Mackey QHDS (2*)
(First Avenue House)

Director of Defence Nursing Services
Director (*)
(First Avenue House)

Head of Medical Services (Finance and Secretariat)
Director (*)
(First Avenue House)

Defence Dental Services

Policy
Plans
Requirements
Training
Personnel
Conditions

Defence Nursing Services

Policy
Plans
Requirements
Training
Personnel
Conditions

Medical Services (Finance and Secretariat)

Budget
Administration
Briefs and visits

Resources, Programmes and Finance

Permanent Under Secretary of State
R C Mottram (1)

Second Permanent Under Secretary of State
J M Stewart CB (1A)

Deputy Under Secretary of State (Resources, Programmes and Finance)
R T Jackling CBE (2)

Assistant Under Secretary of State (Systems)
D Fisher (3)

Directors (*)

Assistant Under Secretary of State (Programmes)
Miss D J Seammen (3)

Directors (*)

Chief Executive, Defence Analytical Services
P P Altobell
(Northumberland House)

Directors (*)

Systems

Screening of Procurement Executive and MoD Centre
Long term costings
Secretariat

Programmes

Long term financial planning and resource allocation in relation to the defence programme
Associated parliamentary and NATO aspects

Defence Analytical Services

Statistical information

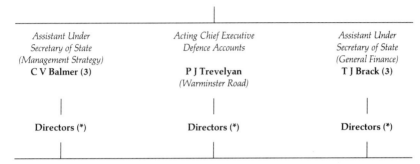

Assistant Under Secretary of State (Management Strategy)
C V Balmer (3)

Directors (*)

Management Strategy

Development unit
  Defence finance
  Training centre
Market testing service
Framework team

Acting Chief Executive Defence Accounts
P J Trevelyan
(Warminster Road)

Directors (*)

Defence Accounts

Bills and contract payments and receipts
Civilian pay
Financial and management accounting

Assistant Under Secretary of State (General Finance)
T J Brack (3)

Directors (*)

General Finance

Service and central finance
Estimates and votes
Expenditure control
Service works and accommodation policy
Charging policy
International cost sharing
Procurement executive
PAC & NAO liaison
Propriety, value for money, financial delegation issues
NATO funding
Economic and financial statistics
R&D expenditure
Risk assessment
Statistical surveys
Secretariat
Defence Support agencies (framework team)
Next Steps
Management strategy
Development team

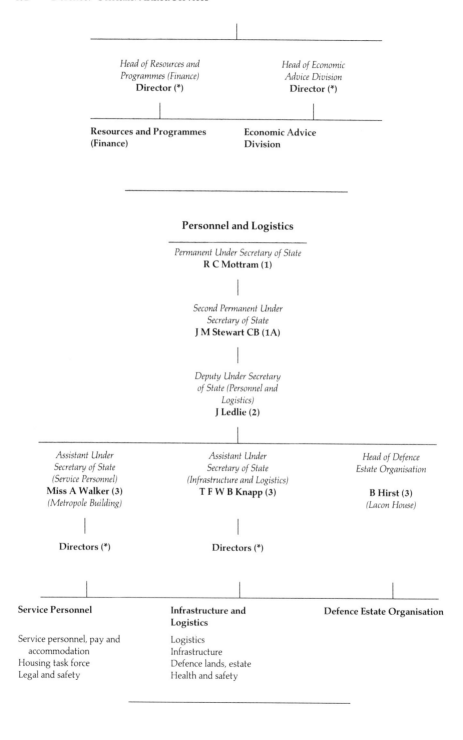

Head of Resources and Programmes (Finance)
Director (*)

Head of Economic Advice Division
Director (*)

Resources and Programmes (Finance)

Economic Advice Division

Personnel and Logistics

Permanent Under Secretary of State
R C Mottram (1)

Second Permanent Under Secretary of State
J M Stewart CB (1A)

Deputy Under Secretary of State (Personnel and Logistics)
J Ledlie (2)

Assistant Under Secretary of State (Service Personnel)
Miss A Walker (3)
(Metropole Building)

Directors (*)

Assistant Under Secretary of State (Infrastructure and Logistics)
T F W B Knapp (3)

Directors (*)

Head of Defence Estate Organisation
B Hirst (3)
(Lacon House)

Service Personnel

Service personnel, pay and accommodation
Housing task force
Legal and safety

Infrastructure and Logistics

Logistics
Infrastructure
Defence lands, estate
Health and safety

Defence Estate Organisation

Civilian Management

Permanent Under Secretary of State
R C Mottram (1)

Second Permanent Under Secretary of State
J M Stewart CB (1A)

Deputy Under-Secretary of State (Civilian Management)
J F Howe OBE (2)

Assistant Under-Secretary of State (Policy)
B A E Taylor (3)
(Northumberland House)

Directors (*)

Assistant Under-Secretary of State (Personnel)
I D Fauset (3)
(Lacon House)

Directors (*)

Policy

Industrial relations
Training
Pay and superannuation
Employment policy
Deployment and co-location

Personnel

Personnel management for all non-delegated civilian staff
Recruitment and career development

Ministry of Defence Police Chief Constable
J Reddington
(Empress State Bldg)

Deputy Chief Constable
N L Chapple
(Empress State Bldg)

Dir Gen Management Audit
R P Hatfield (3)
(Northumberland House)

Directors (*)

MOD Police

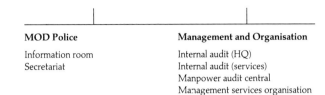

Information room
Secretariat

Management and Organisation

Internal audit (HQ)
Internal audit (services)
Manpower audit central
Management services organisation

Chiefs of Staff
Naval Staff

Chief of the Defence Staff
Field Marshal
Sir Peter Inge GCB ADCGen (5*)

Chief of Naval Staff
First Sea Lord
Admiral Sir Jock Slater
GCB LVO (4*)

Assistant Chief of Naval Staff
Rear Admiral J J Blackham
CB (2*)

Directors (*)

Naval Staff

Naval warfare
Operations and trade
Staff duties
Communications
Secretariat
Coordination and briefing
Presentation team
Strategic systems assessment

General Staff

Chief of the Defence Staff
Field Marshal
Sir Peter Inge GCB ADCGen (5*)

Chief of the General Staff
General Sir Charles Guthrie KCB LVO OBE (4*)

Assistant Chief of General Staff
Maj Gen T Granville-Chapman (2*)

Directors (*)

General Staff

Military operations
Army management services
Management accountancy services
Staff duties
Historical branch
Command and information systems
Engineer-in-chief
Signal officer-in-chief
General staff secretariat

Air Staff

Chief of the Defence Staff
Field Marshal
Sir Peter Inge GCB ADCGen (5*)

Chief of the Air Staff
Air Chief Marshal Sir Michael Graydon GCB CBE ADC (4*)

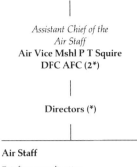

Assistant Chief of the Air Staff
Air Vice Mshl P T Squire DFC AFC (2*)

Directors (*)

Air Staff

Briefing coordination
Staff duties, personnel
Air offensive
Air defence
Secretariat (air staff)
Flight safety
Air historical branch
Publications clearance branch (air)
Anglo-American community relations

Defence Intelligence*

Chief of the Defence Staff
Field Marshal Sir Peter Inge GCB ADCGen (5*)

Permanent Under Secretary of State
R C Mottram (1)

Chief of Defence Intelligence
Lt Gen Sir John Foley KCB OBE MC (3*)
(Old War Office Building)

Director General Intelligence (Assessments) (2*)
(Old War Office Building)

Assistant Under Secretary (3) (Scientific and Technical Intelligence)
(Old War Office Building)

Director General Management and Support of Intelligence (2*)
(Old War Office Building)

Directorate General Intelligence (Assessments)

Directorate General of Scientific and Technical Intelligence

Directorate General Management and Support of Intelligence

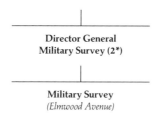

Director General
Military Survey (2*)

Military Survey
(Elmwood Avenue)

* *For a description of the structure and functions of this and other aspects of the Security and Intelligence Services see under that title in this section of the book*

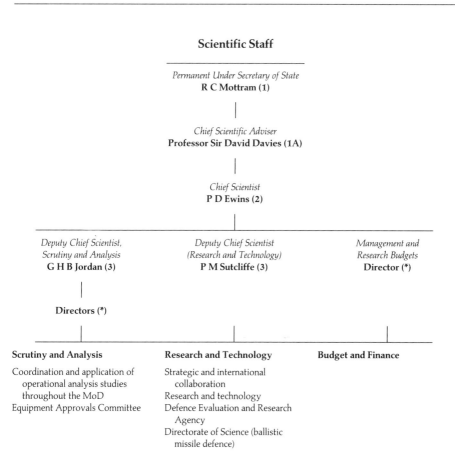

Scientific Staff

Permanent Under Secretary of State
R C Mottram (1)

Chief Scientific Adviser
Professor Sir David Davies (1A)

Chief Scientist
P D Ewins (2)

Deputy Chief Scientist, Scrutiny and Analysis
G H B Jordan (3)

Directors (*)

Deputy Chief Scientist (Research and Technology)
P M Sutcliffe (3)

Management and Research Budgets
Director (*)

Scrutiny and Analysis

Coordination and application of operational analysis studies throughout the MoD
Equipment Approvals Committee

Research and Technology

Strategic and international collaboration
Research and technology
Defence Evaluation and Research Agency
Directorate of Science (ballistic missile defence)

Budget and Finance

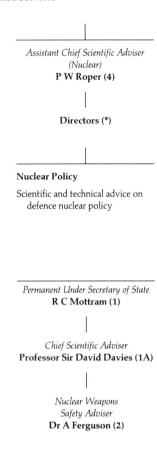

Assistant Chief Scientific Adviser (Nuclear)
P W Roper (4)

Directors (*)

Nuclear Policy

Scientific and technical advice on defence nuclear policy

Permanent Under Secretary of State
R C Mottram (1)

Chief Scientific Adviser
Professor Sir David Davies (1A)

Nuclear Weapons Safety Adviser
Dr A Ferguson (2)

Navy Department

Second Sea Lord; Commander-in-Chief Naval Home Command

Chief of the Defence Staff
Field Marshal Sir Peter Inge GCB ADCGen (5*)

Chief of Naval Staff First Sea Lord
Admiral Sir Jock Slater GCB LVO (4*)

Commander-in-Chief Naval Home Command
Second Sea Lord
Admiral Sir Michael Boyce KCB OBE (3*)
(Victory Building)

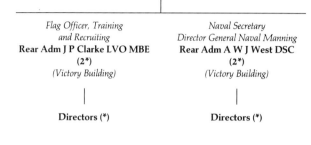

Flag Officer, Training and Recruiting
Rear Adm J P Clarke LVO MBE (2*)
(Victory Building)

Directors (*)

Naval Secretary
Director General Naval Manning
Rear Adm A W J West DSC (2*)
(Victory Building)

Directors (*)

Training and Recruiting

Manpower planning
Manning and training for seamen, engineering, supply and secretariat, instructors
Education and training support
Foreign and commonwealth training
Naval psychologist
Recruiting
Service conditions
Physical training and sport
Judge advocate
RN film corporation
Charities
Pay and manning

Naval Secretary's Office; Naval Manning

Officer appointments for seamen, engineers, supply, secretariat, instructors
Future structure and employment

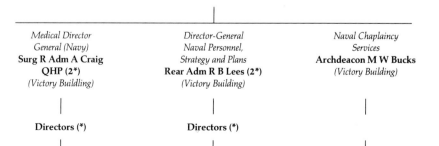

Medical Director General (Navy)
Surg R Adm A Craig QHP (2*)
(Victory Buildling)

Directors (*)

Director-General Naval Personnel, Strategy and Plans
Rear Adm R B Lees (2*)
(Victory Building)

Directors (*)

Naval Chaplaincy Services
Archdeacon M W Bucks
(Victory Building)

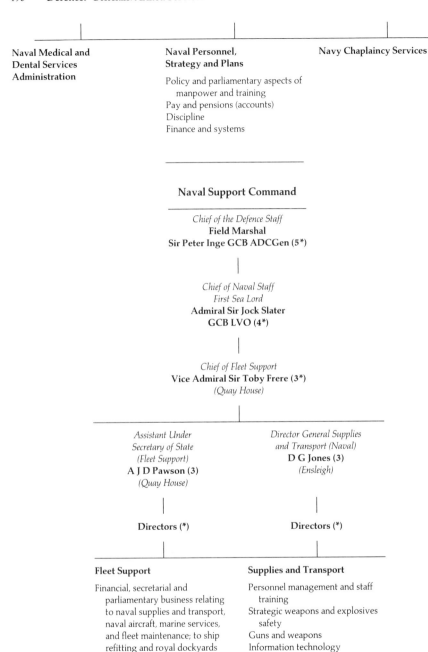

Naval Medical and Dental Services Administration

Naval Personnel, Strategy and Plans

Policy and parliamentary aspects of manpower and training
Pay and pensions (accounts)
Discipline
Finance and systems

Navy Chaplaincy Services

Naval Support Command

Chief of the Defence Staff
Field Marshal Sir Peter Inge GCB ADCGen (5*)

Chief of Naval Staff
First Sea Lord
Admiral Sir Jock Slater GCB LVO (4*)

Chief of Fleet Support
Vice Admiral Sir Toby Frere (3*)
(Quay House)

Assistant Under Secretary of State (Fleet Support)
A J D Pawson (3)
(Quay House)

Directors (*)

Fleet Support

Financial, secretarial and parliamentary business relating to naval supplies and transport, naval aircraft, marine services, and fleet maintenance; to ship refitting and royal dockyards

Director General Supplies and Transport (Naval)
D G Jones (3)
(Ensleigh)

Directors (*)

Supplies and Transport

Personnel management and staff training
Strategic weapons and explosives safety
Guns and weapons
Information technology
Engineering and weapon support
Finance and budgets

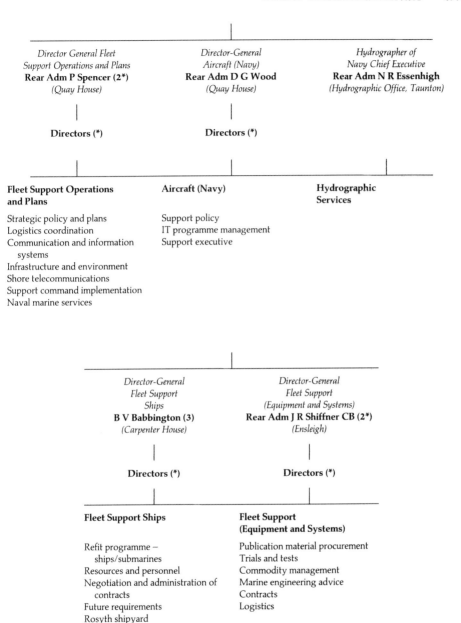

Director General Fleet Support Operations and Plans
Rear Adm P Spencer (2*)
(Quay House)

Directors (*)

Director-General Aircraft (Navy)
Rear Adm D G Wood
(Quay House)

Directors (*)

Hydrographer of Navy Chief Executive
Rear Adm N R Essenhigh
(Hydrographic Office, Taunton)

Fleet Support Operations and Plans

Strategic policy and plans
Logistics coordination
Communication and information systems
Infrastructure and environment
Shore telecommunications
Support command implementation
Naval marine services

Aircraft (Navy)

Support policy
IT programme management
Support executive

Hydrographic Services

Director-General Fleet Support Ships
B V Babbington (3)
(Carpenter House)

Directors (*)

Director-General Fleet Support (Equipment and Systems)
Rear Adm J R Shiffner CB (2*)
(Ensleigh)

Directors (*)

Fleet Support Ships

Refit programme – ships/submarines
Resources and personnel
Negotiation and administration of contracts
Future requirements
Rosyth shipyard

Fleet Support (Equipment and Systems)

Publication material procurement
Trials and tests
Commodity management
Marine engineering advice
Contracts
Logistics

Army Department

Quartermaster General

Chief of the Defence Staff
Field Marshal
Sir Peter Inge GCB ADCGen (5*)

Chief of the General Staff
Gen Sir Charles Guthrie KCB
LVO OBE (4*)

Quartermaster-General
The Hon Sir William Rous KCB
OBE
(Portway)

Assistant Under-
Secretary of State
(Quartermaster)
Dr A Fox (3)
(Portway)

Directors (*)

Chief of Staff
(HQ/QMG)
Maj Gen P J Sheppard
CBE (2*)
(Portway)

Directors (*)

Quartermaster

Financial and secretariat responsibilities

Logistic Policy

Logistic operations
Support planning
Army quartering
Information systems
Engineer support
Supply and pioneers
Postal and courier services
Transport and movements

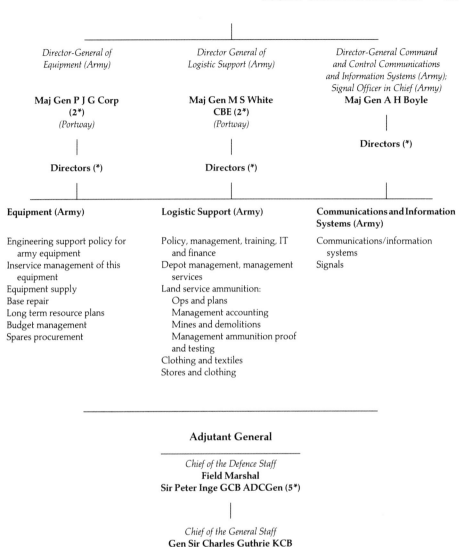

Director-General of Equipment (Army)

Maj Gen P J G Corp (2*)
(Portway)

Directors (*)

Director General of Logistic Support (Army)

Maj Gen M S White CBE (2*)
(Portway)

Directors (*)

Director-General Command and Control Communications and Information Systems (Army); Signal Officer in Chief (Army)
Maj Gen A H Boyle

Directors (*)

Equipment (Army)

Engineering support policy for army equipment
Inservice management of this equipment
Equipment supply
Base repair
Long term resource plans
Budget management
Spares procurement

Logistic Support (Army)

Policy, management, training, IT and finance
Depot management, management services
Land service ammunition:
- Ops and plans
- Management accounting
- Mines and demolitions
- Management ammunition proof and testing

Clothing and textiles
Stores and clothing

Communications and Information Systems (Army)

Communications/information systems
Signals

Adjutant General

Chief of the Defence Staff
Field Marshal Sir Peter Inge GCB ADCGen (5*)

Chief of the General Staff
Gen Sir Charles Guthrie KCB LVO OBE (4*)

Adjutant-General
Gen Sir Michael Rose KCB CBE (4*)
(Upavon)

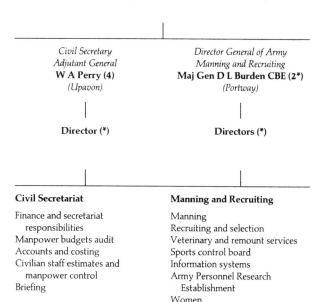

Civil Secretary
Adjutant General
W A Perry (4)
(Upavon)

Director (*)

Director General of Army
Manning and Recruiting
Maj Gen D L Burden CBE (2*)
(Portway)

Directors (*)

Civil Secretariat

Finance and secretariat responsibilities
Manpower budgets audit
Accounts and costing
Civilian staff estimates and manpower control
Briefing

Manning and Recruiting

Manning
Recruiting and selection
Veterinary and remount services
Sports control board
Information systems
Army Personnel Research Establishment
Women

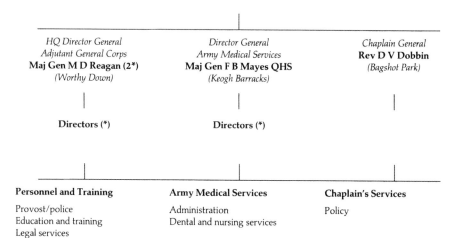

HQ Director General
Adjutant General Corps
Maj Gen M D Reagan (2*)
(Worthy Down)

Directors (*)

Director General
Army Medical Services
Maj Gen F B Mayes QHS
(Keogh Barracks)

Directors (*)

Chaplain General
Rev D V Dobbin
(Bagshot Park)

Personnel and Training

Provost/police
Education and training
Legal services

Army Medical Services

Administration
Dental and nursing services

Chaplain's Services

Policy

Chief of the Defence Staff
Field Marshal
Sir Peter Inge GCB ADCGen (5*)

Chief of the General Staff
Gen Sir Charles Guthrie KCB LVO OBE (4*)

Military Secretary
Maj Gen M I E Scott CBE DSO (2*)

Military Secretary

Career matters for officers

Doctrine and Training

Chief of the Defence Staff
Field Marshal
Sir Peter Inge GCB ADCGen (5*)

Chief of the General Staff
General Sir Charles Guthrie KCB LVO OBE (4*)

Inspector General Doctrine and Training
Lt Gen S Cowan CBE (3*)
(Upavon)

Dir Gen Army Training
Maj Gen R W M McAfee (2*)

Dir Gen Land Warfare
Maj Gen T J Sulivan (2*)
(Upavon)

Arms Directors

Dir Royal Artillery
Maj Gen I G C Durie (2*)
(Larkhill)

Dir Royal Armoured Corps
Brig A C I Gadsby (1*)
(Bovington Camp)

Dir Infantry
Maj Gen R A Pett MBE (2*)
(Warminster)

Dir Army Aviation
Maj Gen S W St J Lytle CB (2*)
(Middle Wallop)

Engineer-in-Chief (Army)
Maj Gen K J Drewienkiewicz (2)
(Northumberland House)

Doctrine and Training

Policy for doctrine training, exams and courses
CD, BD, TD, and NBC policy
ABCA national office
Training policy for regular and reserve armies
Coordination of collective training resources
Training assistance to other countries
Adventurous training
Royal Artillery
Royal Armoured Corps
Infantry
Army aviation
Engineer-in-Chief
Land warfare

Air Force Department

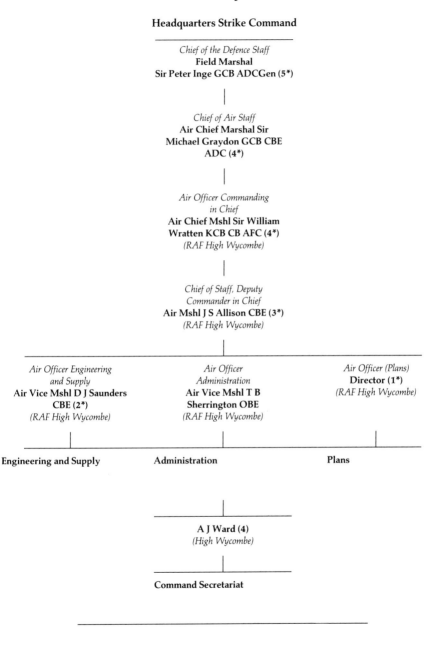

Headquarters Strike Command

Chief of the Defence Staff
Field Marshal
Sir Peter Inge GCB ADCGen (5*)

Chief of Air Staff
Air Chief Marshal Sir
Michael Graydon GCB CBE
ADC (4*)

Air Officer Commanding
in Chief
Air Chief Mshl Sir William
Wratten KCB CB AFC (4*)
(RAF High Wycombe)

Chief of Staff, Deputy
Commander in Chief
Air Mshl J S Allison CBE (3*)
(RAF High Wycombe)

Air Officer Engineering
and Supply
Air Vice Mshl D J Saunders
CBE (2*)
(RAF High Wycombe)

Engineering and Supply

Air Officer
Administration
Air Vice Mshl T B
Sherrington OBE
(RAF High Wycombe)

Administration

Air Officer (Plans)
Director (1*)
(RAF High Wycombe)

Plans

A J Ward (4)
(High Wycombe)

Command Secretariat

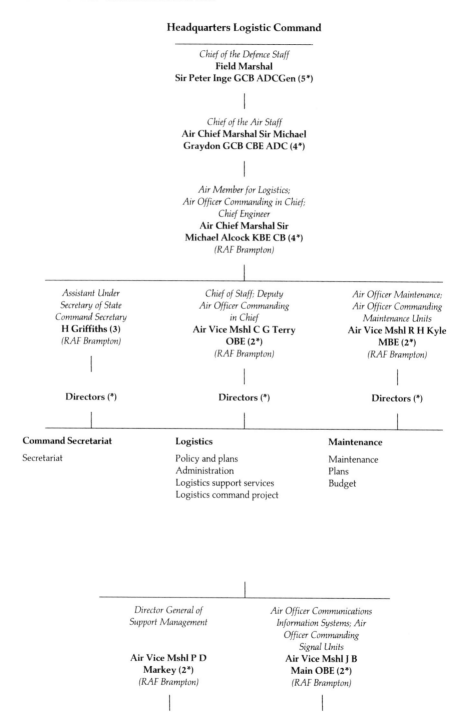

Headquarters Logistic Command

Chief of the Defence Staff
Field Marshal
Sir Peter Inge GCB ADCGen (5*)

Chief of the Air Staff
Air Chief Marshal Sir Michael
Graydon GCB CBE ADC (4*)

Air Member for Logistics;
Air Officer Commanding in Chief;
Chief Engineer
Air Chief Marshal Sir
Michael Alcock KBE CB (4*)
(RAF Brampton)

Assistant Under Secretary of State Command Secretary
H Griffiths (3)
(RAF Brampton)

Directors (*)

Chief of Staff; Deputy Air Officer Commanding in Chief
Air Vice Mshl C G Terry OBE (2*)
(RAF Brampton)

Directors (*)

Air Officer Maintenance; Air Officer Commanding Maintenance Units
Air Vice Mshl R H Kyle MBE (2*)
(RAF Brampton)

Directors (*)

Command Secretariat

Secretariat

Logistics

Policy and plans
Administration
Logistics support services
Logistics command project

Maintenance

Maintenance
Plans
Budget

Director General of Support Management
Air Vice Mshl P D Markey (2*)
(RAF Brampton)

Air Officer Communications Information Systems; Air Officer Commanding Signal Units
Air Vice Mshl J B Main OBE (2*)
(RAF Brampton)

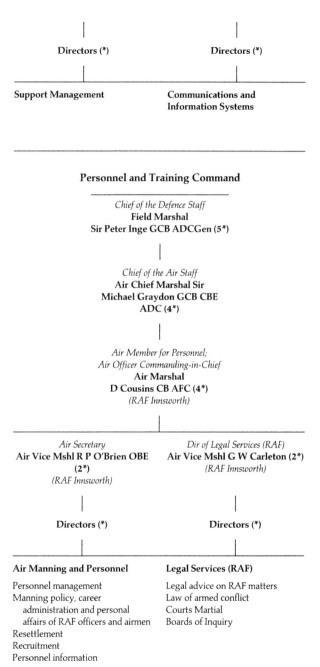

Directors (*)	Directors (*)
Support Management	**Communications and Information Systems**

Personnel and Training Command

Chief of the Defence Staff
Field Marshal
Sir Peter Inge GCB ADCGen (5*)

Chief of the Air Staff
Air Chief Marshal Sir
Michael Graydon GCB CBE
ADC (4*)

Air Member for Personnel;
Air Officer Commanding-in-Chief
Air Marshal
D Cousins CB AFC (4*)
(RAF Innsworth)

Air Secretary
Air Vice Mshl R P O'Brien OBE (2*)
(RAF Innsworth)

Directors (*)

Air Manning and Personnel

Personnel management
Manning policy, career administration and personal affairs of RAF officers and airmen
Resettlement
Recruitment
Personnel information

Dir of Legal Services (RAF)
Air Vice Mshl G W Carleton (2*)
(RAF Innsworth)

Directors (*)

Legal Services (RAF)

Legal advice on RAF matters
Law of armed conflict
Courts Martial
Boards of Inquiry

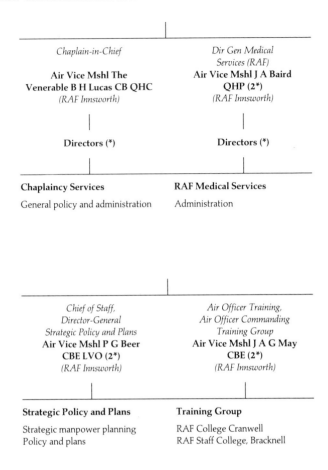

Chaplain-in-Chief
Air Vice Mshl The Venerable B H Lucas CB QHC
(RAF Innsworth)

Directors (*)

Chaplaincy Services

General policy and administration

Dir Gen Medical Services (RAF)
Air Vice Mshl J A Baird QHP (2*)
(RAF Innsworth)

Directors (*)

RAF Medical Services

Administration

Chief of Staff, Director-General Strategic Policy and Plans
Air Vice Mshl P G Beer CBE LVO (2*)
(RAF Innsworth)

Strategic Policy and Plans

Strategic manpower planning
Policy and plans

Air Officer Training, Air Officer Commanding Training Group
Air Vice Mshl J A G May CBE (2*)
(RAF Innsworth)

Training Group

RAF College Cranwell
RAF Staff College, Bracknell

Procurement Executive

Deputy Chief of Defence Procurement (Support)

Permanent Under Secretary of State
R C Mottram (1)

Chief of Defence Procurement
Dr M K McIntosh (1)

Deputy Chief of Defence Procurement (Support)
M J V Bell CB (2)

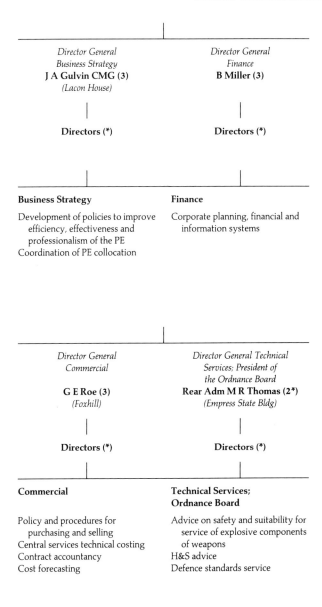

Director General
Business Strategy
J A Gulvin CMG (3)
(Lacon House)

Directors (*)

Director General
Finance
B Miller (3)

Directors (*)

Business Strategy

Development of policies to improve efficiency, effectiveness and professionalism of the PE
Coordination of PE collocation

Finance

Corporate planning, financial and information systems

Director General
Commercial

G E Roe (3)
(Foxhill)

Directors (*)

Director General Technical
Services; President of
the Ordnance Board
Rear Adm M R Thomas (2*)
(Empress State Bldg)

Directors (*)

Commercial

Policy and procedures for purchasing and selling
Central services technical costing
Contract accountancy
Cost forecasting

Technical Services;
Ordnance Board

Advice on safety and suitability for service of explosive components of weapons
H&S advice
Defence standards service

Deputy Chief of Defence Procurement (South of England)

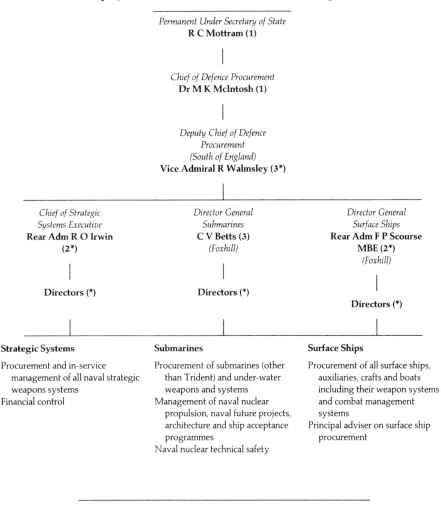

Permanent Under Secretary of State
R C Mottram (1)

Chief of Defence Procurement
Dr M K McIntosh (1)

Deputy Chief of Defence Procurement (South of England)
Vice Admiral R Walmsley (3*)

Chief of Strategic Systems Executive
Rear Adm R O Irwin (2*)

Directors (*)

Director General Submarines
C V Betts (3)
(Foxhill)

Directors (*)

Director General Surface Ships
Rear Adm F P Scourse MBE (2*)
(Foxhill)

Directors (*)

Strategic Systems

Procurement and in-service management of all naval strategic weapons systems
Financial control

Submarines

Procurement of submarines (other than Trident) and under-water weapons and systems
Management of naval nuclear propulsion, naval future projects, architecture and ship acceptance programmes
Naval nuclear technical safety

Surface Ships

Procurement of all surface ships, auxiliaries, crafts and boats including their weapon systems and combat management systems
Principal adviser on surface ship procurement

Deputy Chief of Defence Procurement (London)

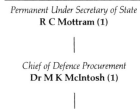

Permanent Under Secretary of State
R C Mottram (1)

Chief of Defence Procurement
Dr M K McIntosh (1)

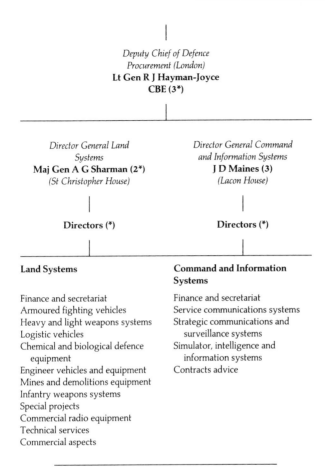

Deputy Chief of Defence Procurement (London)
Lt Gen R J Hayman-Joyce CBE (3*)

Director General Land Systems
Maj Gen A G Sharman (2*)
(St Christopher House)

Directors (*)

Director General Command and Information Systems
J D Maines (3)
(Lacon House)

Directors (*)

Land Systems

Finance and secretariat
Armoured fighting vehicles
Heavy and light weapons systems
Logistic vehicles
Chemical and biological defence equipment
Engineer vehicles and equipment
Mines and demolitions equipment
Infantry weapons systems
Special projects
Commercial radio equipment
Technical services
Commercial aspects

Command and Information Systems

Finance and secretariat
Service communications systems
Strategic communications and surveillance systems
Simulator, intelligence and information systems
Contracts advice

Deputy Chief of Defence Procurement (Operations)

Permanent Under Secretary of State
R C Mottram (1)

Chief of Defence Procurement
Dr M K McIntosh (1)

Deputy Chief of Defence Procurement (Operations)
Air Marshal Sir Roger Austin KCB AFC (3*)

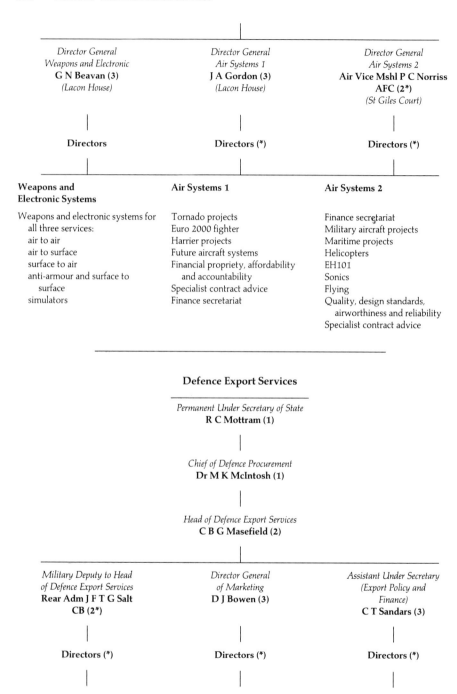

Director General
Weapons and Electronic
G N Beavan (3)
(Lacon House)

Directors

Weapons and Electronic Systems

Weapons and electronic systems for all three services:
- air to air
- air to surface
- surface to air
- anti-armour and surface to surface
- simulators

Director General
Air Systems 1
J A Gordon (3)
(Lacon House)

Directors (*)

Air Systems 1

- Tornado projects
- Euro 2000 fighter
- Harrier projects
- Future aircraft systems
- Financial propriety, affordability and accountability
- Specialist contract advice
- Finance secretariat

Director General
Air Systems 2
Air Vice Mshl P C Norriss AFC (2*)
(St Giles Court)

Directors (*)

Air Systems 2

- Finance secretariat
- Military aircraft projects
- Maritime projects
- Helicopters
- EH101
- Sonics
- Flying
- Quality, design standards, airworthiness and reliability
- Specialist contract advice

Defence Export Services

Permanent Under Secretary of State
R C Mottram (1)

Chief of Defence Procurement
Dr M K McIntosh (1)

Head of Defence Export Services
C B G Masefield (2)

Military Deputy to Head of Defence Export Services
Rear Adm J F T G Salt CB (2*)

Directors (*)

Director General of Marketing
D J Bowen (3)

Directors (*)

Assistant Under Secretary (Export Policy and Finance)
C T Sandars (3)

Directors (*)

Defence Export Services

Military advice, support and training
Exhibitions and inward visitors

Marketing

Overseas sales
Assistance to manufacturers in obtaining export orders

Export Policy and Finance

Sales support and disposals
Political and security aspects of defence sales
Financial services
Iranian contracts

Director General
Saudi Airforce Project
Air Mshl I D MacFadyen CB OBE (3*)
(Castlewood House)

Inter-Service Organisations

Chief of the Defence Staff
Field Marshal
Sir Peter Inge GCB ADCGen (5*)

Commandant Royal College of Defence Studies
Air Mshl Sir Timothy Garden CBE (2*)
(RCDS)

Rear Adm J F Perowne OBE (2*)
Maj Gen A I G Kennedy CBE (2*)
Air Vice Mshl P Dodworth CB OBE AFC (2*)
Vacant (5)
(all at RCDS)

Commandant Joint Service Defence College
Rear Adm N J Wilkinson CBE (2*)
(JSDC)

Ministry of Defence Addresses

For fax numbers telephone the number listed and ask for the appropriate fax number

Adastral House
Theobalds Road
London WC1X 8RU
Tel 0171-305 5555

AWE Aldermaston
Reading
Berks RG7 4PR
Tel 01734 814111

Bagshot Park
Surrey GU19 5PL
Tel 01276 471717

Bovington Camp
Wareham
Dorset BH20 6JA
Tel 01929 462721

Broadoaks
Parvis Road
West Byfleet
Surrey KT14 6LY
Tel 019323 41199

CAA House
45–59 Kingsway
London WC2B 6TE
Tel 0171-379 7311

Carpenter House
Broad Quay
Bath BA1 5AB
Tel 01225 884884

Castlewood House
77–91 New Oxford Street
London WC1A 1DS
Tel 0171-829 8500

Chemical and Biological Defence Establishment
(now part of DERA)
Porton Down
Salisbury
Wiltshire SP4 0JG
Tel 01980 613000

DERA Portsdown
Cosham
Hampshire PO6 4AA
Tel 01705 332000

DERA Southwell
Portland
Dorset DT5 2JS
Tel 01305 820381

Elmwood Avenue
Feltham
Middx TW13 7AE
Tel 0181-890 3622

Empress State Building
Lillie Road
London SW6 1TR
Tel 0171-824 4444

Ensleigh
Bath BA1 5AB
Tel 01225 884884

First Avenue House
High Holborn
London WC1V 6HE
Tel 0171-305 5555

Fleetbank House
2–6 Salisbury Square
London EC4Y 8AT
Tel 0171-305 5555

Foxhill
Bath BA1 5AB
Tel 01225 884884

Hydrographic Office
Taunton
Somerset TA1 2DN
Tel 01823 337900

Joint Service Defence College
Greenwich
London SE10 9NN
Tel 0181-858 2154 ext 4017

Keogh Barracks
Ash Vale
Aldershot
Hants GU12 5RR
Tel 01252 340340

Lacon House
Theobalds Road
London WC1X 8RY
Tel 0171-305 5555

Larkhill
Salisbury
Wiltshire SP4 8QB
Tel 01980 620922

Metropole Building
Northumberland Avenue
London WC2N 5BL
Tel 0171-218 9000

Middle Wallop
Stockbridge
Hampshire SO20 8YD
Tel 01264 62121

Northumberland House
Northumberland Avenue
London WC2N 5BP
Tel 0171-218 9000

Old War Office Building
Whitehall
London SW1A 2EU
Tel 0171-218 9000

Pinegates
Lower Bristol Road
Bath BA1 5AB
Tel 01225 884884

PO Box 1734
Rectory Road
Sutton Coldfield
West Midlands B75 7QB
Tel 0121-378 1281

Portway
Moxton Road
Andover
Hampshire SP11 8HT
Tel 01264 382111

Prospect House
100 New Oxford Street
London WC1A 1HE
Tel 0171-305 5555

Quay House
The Ambury
Bath BA1 5AB
Tel 01225 884884

RAF Brampton
Huntingdon
Cambs PE18 8QL
Tel 01480 52151

RAF High Wycombe
Bucks HP14 4UE
Tel 01494 461461

RAF PMC Innsworth
Gloucestershire
GL3 1EZ
Tel 01452 712612

Royal College of Defence Studies
Seaford House
37 Belgrave Square
London SW1X 8NS
Tel 0171-915 4800
Fax 0171-915 4999

St Christopher House
Southwark Street
London SE1 0TD
Tel 0171-921 plus ext

St George's Court
14 New Oxford Street
London WC1A 1EJ
Tel 0171-305 5555

St Giles Court
1–13 St Giles High Street
London WC2H 8LD
Tel 0171-305 5555

Stuart House
Soho Square
London W1V 5FJ
Tel 0171-305 5555

Turnstile House
98 High Holborn
London WC1V 6LL
Tel 0171-305 5555

Upavon Barracks
Pewsey
Wilts SN9 6BE
Tel 01980 615000

Victory Building
HM Naval Base
Portsmouth PO1 3LS
Tel 01705 822351

Warminster
Wiltshire BA12 0DJ
Tel 01985 214000

Warminster Road
Bath BA1 5AA
Tel 01225 884884

Worthy Down
Hampshire SO21 2RG
Tel 01962 880880

Department of the Director of Public Prosecutions for Northern Ireland

Founded	1972
Status	The Director of Public Prosecutions for Northern Ireland is a statutory office holder under the Crown
Responsible to	Attorney General
Responsibilities	The Director initiates and conducts on behalf of the Crown proceedings for indictable offences and for such summary offences or classes of summary offences as the Director considers should be dealt with by him
Number of staff	Unavailable

Department of the Director of Public Prosecutions for Northern Ireland

Royal Courts of Justice, Chichester Street, Belfast BT1 3NX
Tel 01232 235111 Fax 01232 240730

Statutory office holders

Director

Deputy Director

Officials

2 Senior Assistant Directors (3)

Department for Education

Founded 1899 as Board for Education. The Board became the Ministry of Education in 1945, the Department of Education and Science in 1964 and the Department for Education in 1992

Ministers secretary of state, one minister of state and two parliamentary under secretaries

Responsibilities
admissions
adult/continuing education
Assisted Places Scheme
collective worship
CTCs and grant-maintained schools
curriculum
discipline
further education
governors
health education
higher education
independent schools
local management
meals and milk
parents' charter
play
polytechnics
primary schools
school/industry links
special education
students (including overseas) and student support
teachers and teacher appraisal
tests, exams and assessment
transport
under-fives
universities
urban programme
youth service

Number of staff 1770

Executive agencies Teachers' Pension Agency

See also OFSTED, Office for Standards in Education, below

Department for Education

Sanctuary Buildings, Great Smith Street, London SW1P 3BT
Tel 0171-925 5000   Fax 0171-925 6000
Public Enquiries: Tel 0171-925 5555   Fax 0171-925 6971

All staff are based at Sanctuary House unless otherwise indicated.
For other addresses and telephone numbers see end of this section.

Ministers

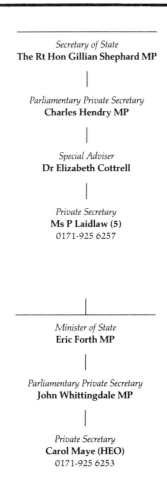

Secretary of State
The Rt Hon Gillian Shephard MP

Parliamentary Private Secretary
Charles Hendry MP

Special Adviser
Dr Elizabeth Cottrell

Private Secretary
Ms P Laidlaw (5)
0171-925 6257

Minister of State
Eric Forth MP

Parliamentary Private Secretary
John Whittingdale MP

Private Secretary
Carol Maye (HEO)
0171-925 6253

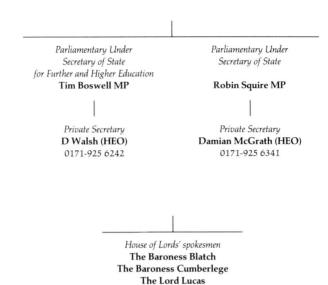

Parliamentary Under Secretary of State for Further and Higher Education	*Parliamentary Under Secretary of State*
Tim Boswell MP	**Robin Squire MP**
Private Secretary	*Private Secretary*
D Walsh (HEO)	**Damian McGrath (HEO)**
0171-925 6242	0171-925 6341

House of Lords' spokesmen
The Baroness Blatch
The Baroness Cumberlege
The Lord Lucas

Ministerial Responsibilities

Gillian Shephard
- Overall responsibility for the department
- Funding of education
- Implementation of education reforms including the Citizen's Charter
- Interface between education and training
- Pay
- Policy on women
- Public expenditure survey

Eric Forth
- Careers education and guidance
- Departmental purchasing
- Education/industry links
- Education exports
- IT in schools
- "Next Steps" agencies
- OFSTED
- Performance tables
- Research
- School curriculum
- School effectiveness and action on failing schools
- School transport
- Special education in schools
- Teachers' misconduct
- Testing and examinations 5-16
- Truancy, discipline and attendance
- Under-fives

Tim Boswell
- Adult/continuing education
- A/AS levels
- Departmental correspondence and manpower
- FE and HE Funding Councils
- Further education (FE) (content, quality, structure, funding, building)
- Higher education (HE) (content, quality, structure, funding, building)
- International including EU
- Links with Employment Department Group
- Overseas students
- Student issues and support
- Youth Service

Robin Squire

- Assisted Places Scheme
- Choice and diversity in schools
- Common Funding Formula
- City technology colleges
- Development and implementation of policy for schools
- Energy and environment
- Grant-maintained school issues
- Independent schools
- Local management of schools
- Pensions
- School governors
- School meals
- School reorganisation and admissions policies
- Schools' capital
- Schools' policies at inner city, regional and local level
- Section 11 matters
- Specialist schools
- Teacher matters including training, supply and appraisal
- Teacher Training Agency
- Teachers' Pension Agency
- Technology colleges

Departmental Overview

Civil Servants			Department	Minister
Grade 1	*Grade 2*	*Grade 3*		
	Schools Branches			
Sir Tim Lankester	J Hedger	M J Richardson	Schools' Organisation Branch	E Forth R Squire
		R L Smith	Schools' Pupils' Branch	E Forth R Squire
		N Summers	Schools' Funding Branch	R Squire
	Further and Higher Education and International			
Sir Tim Lankester	R Dawe	C A Clark	Higher Education Branch	T Boswell
		D M Forrester	Further Education Branch	T Boswell
		E R Morgan	Internation Relations and Youth Branch	T Boswell
	Teachers and Schools' Curriculum			
Sir Tim Lankester	P Owen	N J Sanders	Teachers	R Squire
		C H Saville	Schools' Curriculum Branch	E Forth
	Services Directorate			
Sir Tim Lankester		P A Shaw	Personnel and Organisation	G Shephard E Forth
		D E L Allnutt (4)	Analytical Services	
		A K Gibson (5)	Information Services	
	Other branches			
Sir Tim Lankester		R N Ricks	Legal Adviser	
		R D Horne	Finance Branch	G Shephard
Sir Tim Lankester		J Coe (4)	Information Branch	

Civil Servants and Departments

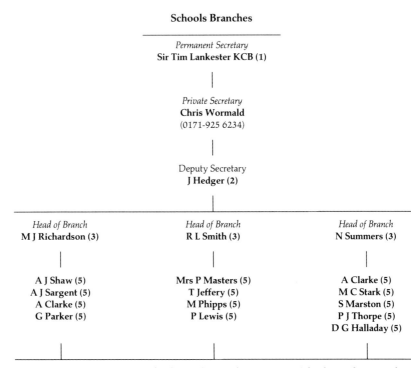

Schools Branches

Permanent Secretary
Sir Tim Lankester KCB (1)

Private Secretary
Chris Wormald
(0171-925 6234)

Deputy Secretary
J Hedger (2)

Head of Branch
M J Richardson (3)

A J Shaw (5)
A J Sargent (5)
A Clarke (5)
G Parker (5)

Head of Branch
R L Smith (3)

Mrs P Masters (5)
T Jeffery (5)
M Phipps (5)
P Lewis (5)

Head of Branch
N Summers (3)

A Clarke (5)
M C Stark (5)
S Marston (5)
P J Thorpe (5)
D G Halladay (5)

Schools' Organisation

Organisation of schools
Admissions and attendance
16-19s in schools
Capital expenditure
HMI reports
Leaving age
School government
Meals, milk, transport
Charging for school activities
Reorganisation of education in Inner London
Local management of schools
Parents' Charter
School building standards and controls
Guidance on design and property management

Schools' Pupils' Branch

Urban programme and policy for inner cities
Ethnic minorities
Travellers and refugees
Discipline
Attendance
Special educational needs
School health service
School–industry liaison
Careers
Health education
Under-fives
Educational technology
Broadcasting policy
Copyright
Personal and social education

Schools' Funding Branch

CTC unit
Independent schools team
Assisted places
Music and ballet schools
Grant-maintained schools
Local management of schools

Further and Higher Education and International

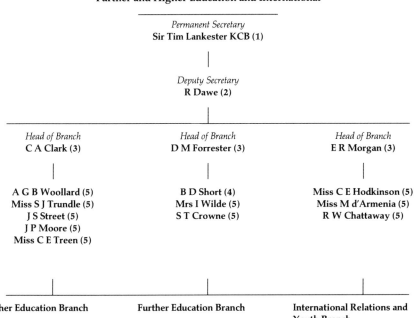

Permanent Secretary
Sir Tim Lankester KCB (1)

Deputy Secretary
R Dawe (2)

Head of Branch
C A Clark (3)

A G B Woollard (5)
Miss S J Trundle (5)
J S Street (5)
J P Moore (5)
Miss C E Treen (5)

Head of Branch
D M Forrester (3)

B D Short (4)
Mrs I Wilde (5)
S T Crowne (5)

Head of Branch
E R Morgan (3)

Miss C E Hodkinson (5)
Miss M d'Armenia (5)
R W Chattaway (5)

Higher Education Branch

General HE policy
Higher Education Funding Council for England: general policy and funding
Quality assurance in HE
HE links with industry and the professions
HE Charter
Performance indicators for HE
Research policy
Medical education
Engineering education
Access funds
Student support division

Further Education Branch

FE policy and funding
Post-16 curriculum and qualifications in schools and FE
Publication of information about post-16 achievements in schools and colleges
FE staff development
FE Charter
Further Education Funding Council
FE college governance and management
FE for adults

International Relations and Youth Branch

International Relations

Teachers and Schools' Curriculum

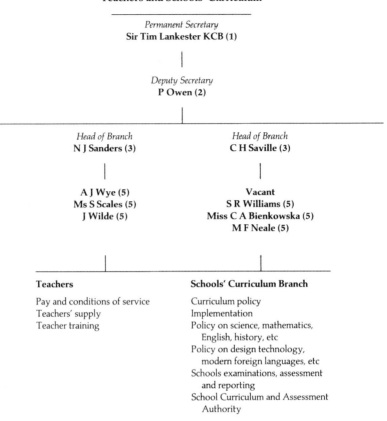

Permanent Secretary
Sir Tim Lankester KCB (1)

Deputy Secretary
P Owen (2)

Head of Branch
N J Sanders (3)

A J Wye (5)
Ms S Scales (5)
J Wilde (5)

Head of Branch
C H Saville (3)

Vacant
S R Williams (5)
Miss C A Bienkowska (5)
M F Neale (5)

Teachers

Pay and conditions of service
Teachers' supply
Teacher training

Schools' Curriculum Branch

Curriculum policy
Implementation
Policy on science, mathematics, English, history, etc
Policy on design technology, modern foreign languages, etc
Schools examinations, assessment and reporting
School Curriculum and Assessment Authority

Services Directorate

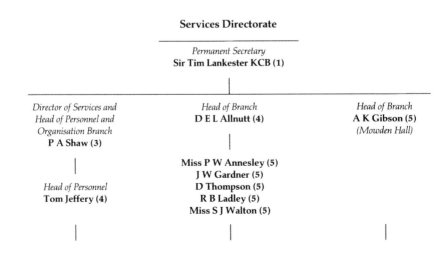

Permanent Secretary
Sir Tim Lankester KCB (1)

Director of Services and Head of Personnel and Organisation Branch
P A Shaw (3)

Head of Personnel
Tom Jeffery (4)

Head of Branch
D E L Allnutt (4)

Miss P W Annesley (5)
J W Gardner (5)
D Thompson (5)
R B Ladley (5)
Miss S J Walton (5)

Head of Branch
A K Gibson (5)
(Mowden Hall)

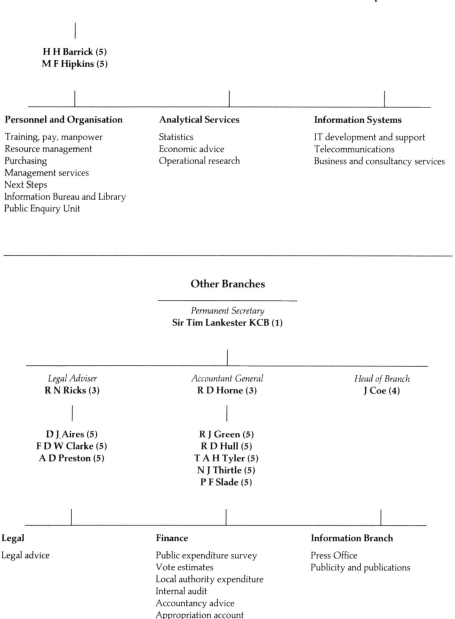

H H Barrick (5)
M F Hipkins (5)

Personnel and Organisation

Training, pay, manpower
Resource management
Purchasing
Management services
Next Steps
Information Bureau and Library
Public Enquiry Unit

Analytical Services

Statistics
Economic advice
Operational research

Information Systems

IT development and support
Telecommunications
Business and consultancy services

Other Branches

Permanent Secretary
Sir Tim Lankester KCB (1)

Legal Adviser
R N Ricks (3)

D J Aires (5)
F D W Clarke (5)
A D Preston (5)

Accountant General
R D Horne (3)

R J Green (5)
R D Hull (5)
T A H Tyler (5)
N J Thirtle (5)
P F Slade (5)

Head of Branch
J Coe (4)

Legal

Legal advice

Finance

Public expenditure survey
Vote estimates
Local authority expenditure
Internal audit
Accountancy advice
Appropriation account

Information Branch

Press Office
Publicity and publications

Department for Education Addresses

Mowden Hall
Staindrop Road
Darlington DL3 9BG
Tel 01325 460155
Fax 01325 392695

Employment Department Group (EDG)

The EDG comprises the department headquarters, the Employment Service, Health and Safety Commission and the Advisory Conciliation and Arbitration Service.

Founded	1916
Ministers	one secretary of state, one minister of state, two parliamentary under secretaries
Responsibilities	employee rights and involvement European and international employment matters Health and Safety Commission/Executive (liaison with) industrial relations pay and equal opportunities statistics Training and Enterprise Councils (vocational education, training and enterprise) women's issues
Number of staff	EDG: 62,244 Department of Employment: 5200
Executive agencies	Employment Service

Employment Department Group

Caxton House, Tothill Street, London SW1H 9NF
Tel 0171-273 3000 Fax 0171-273 5124

All personnel are based at Caxton House unless otherwise indicated.
Other addresses and telephone numbers are listed at the end of this section.

Ministers

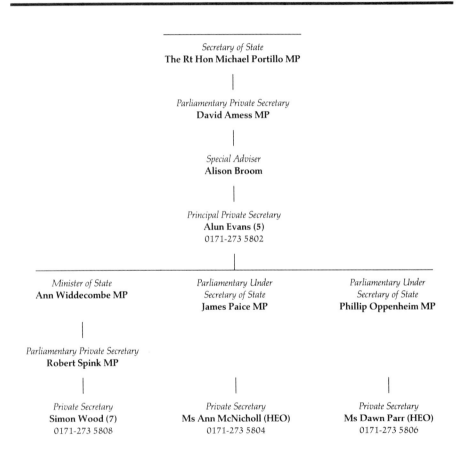

Secretary of State
The Rt Hon Michael Portillo MP

Parliamentary Private Secretary
David Amess MP

Special Adviser
Alison Broom

Principal Private Secretary
Alun Evans (5)
0171-273 5802

Minister of State
Ann Widdecombe MP

Parliamentary Private Secretary
Robert Spink MP

Private Secretary
Simon Wood (7)
0171-273 5808

Parliamentary Under Secretary of State
James Paice MP

Private Secretary
Ms Ann McNicholl (HEO)
0171-273 5804

Parliamentary Under Secretary of State
Phillip Oppenheim MP

Private Secretary
Ms Dawn Parr (HEO)
0171-273 5806

House of Lords' spokesmen
The Lord Henley
The Viscount Goschen
The Lord Inglewood

Ministerial Responsibilities

Michael Portillo	overall responsibility for the department
Ann Widdecombe	Citizen's Charter Employment agency licensing Employment policy and benefit issues Employment service European Union and international issues Jobseekers' allowance Older workers People with disabilities Women's employment issues and Equal Opportunities Commission
James Paice	Adult training Careers service Inner cities Quality assurance Regional and urban policy Special needs training Training and Enterprise Councils (TECs) and TEC performance Training strategy and infrastructure Youth and education policy and programmes
Phillip Oppenheim	ACAS Deregulation Environmental issues Health and Safety Industrial relations Industrial tribunals Market testing Pay issues Race equality issues Redundancy payments Statistics and research Work permits

Departmental Overview

Grade 1	Civil Servants *Grade 2*	*Grade 3*	Division	Minister
	Industrial Relations and International			
M Bichard	G L Reid	H Leiser	Industrial Relations 1	P Oppenheim
		R A Niven	Industrial Relations 2	P Oppenheim
		C F Tucker	International	A Widdecombe
		P J Stibbard	Statistical Services	P Oppenheim
	Resources and Strategy			
M Bichard	N Stuart	K Jordan (4)	Business Services	
		J Robertson	Economics, Research and Evaluation	P Oppenheim
		L Lewis	Finance and Resource Management	P Oppenheim
		D Normington	Personnel and Development	
		P Makeham	Strategy and Employment Policy	A Widdecombe
	Training, Enterprise and Education			
M Bichard	I A Johnston	S Loveman	Financial Control Unit; Employment Department, Regions*; Planning	J Paice
		B Heatley	Adult Learning	J Paice
		P Thomas (4)	Quality Assurance	J Paice
		N Schofield	Training, Infrastructure and Employers	J Paice
		Mrs V Bayliss	Youth and Education	J Paice

*For the government regional offices which bring together the existing regional offices of the Departments of Transport, Trade and Industry, Employment (Training, Enterprise and Education Directorate) and Environment, see separate entry in this section under **Government Offices for the Regions**.

Civil Servants and Departments

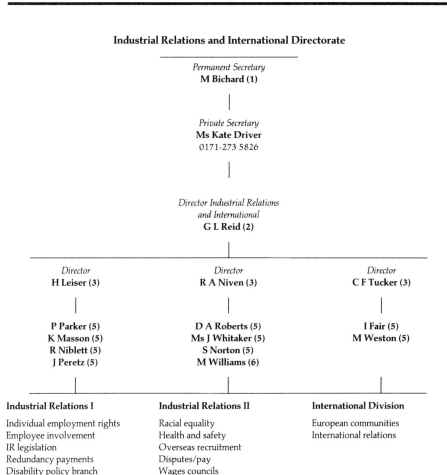

Industrial Relations and International Directorate

Permanent Secretary
M Bichard (1)

Private Secretary
Ms Kate Driver
0171-273 5826

Director Industrial Relations and International
G L Reid (2)

Director
H Leiser (3)

P Parker (5)
K Masson (5)
R Niblett (5)
J Peretz (5)

Director
R A Niven (3)

D A Roberts (5)
Ms J Whitaker (5)
S Norton (5)
M Williams (6)

Director
C F Tucker (3)

I Fair (5)
M Weston (5)

Industrial Relations I

Individual employment rights
Employee involvement
IR legislation
Redundancy payments
Disability policy branch

Industrial Relations II

Racial equality
Health and safety
Overseas recruitment
Disputes/pay
Wages councils
Employment agency licensing
Sex equality

International Division

European communities
International relations

Director
P J Stibbard (3)

T Orchard (5)
D Fenwick (5)
B Werner (5)
K R Perry (5)
(Runcorn office)
Ms M Rout (5)
(Sheffield office)

Statistical Services

Earnings and vocational training
Unemployment and LMS coordination
Labour force: surveys, projections and international
Employment and business registers
Statistical services to TEED

Resources and Strategy Directorate

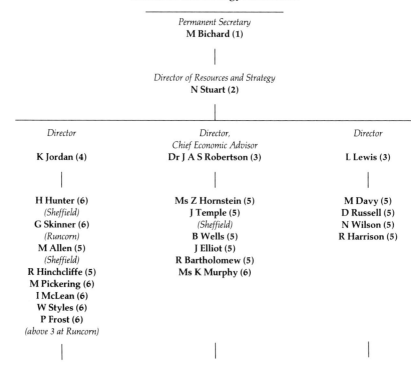

Permanent Secretary
M Bichard (1)

Director of Resources and Strategy
N Stuart (2)

Director
K Jordan (4)

H Hunter (6)
(Sheffield)
G Skinner (6)
(Runcorn)
M Allen (5)
(Sheffield)
R Hinchcliffe (5)
M Pickering (6)
I McLean (6)
W Styles (6)
P Frost (6)
(above 3 at Runcorn)

Director,
Chief Economic Advisor
Dr J A S Robertson (3)

Ms Z Hornstein (5)
J Temple (5)
(Sheffield)
B Wells (5)
J Elliot (5)
R Bartholomew (5)
Ms K Murphy (6)

Director
L Lewis (3)

M Davy (5)
D Russell (5)
N Wilson (5)
R Harrison (5)

Business Services

Corporate services
Estates
Information systems
Management services

Economics, Research and Evaluation

Employment market research unit
Economic briefing
Labour market analysis
Social science research
Economics research evaluation
TEC research and evaluation
Research management

Finance and Resource Management

Financial
Financial services
Market testing unit

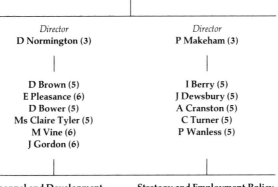

Director
D Normington (3)

D Brown (5)
E Pleasance (6)
D Bower (5)
Ms Claire Tyler (5)
M Vine (6)
J Gordon (6)

Personnel and Development

Group personnel unit
Group relocation project
Personnel branch
Personnel plus
Staff development
Group management development unit

Director
P Makeham (3)

I Berry (5)
J Dewsbury (5)
A Cranston (5)
C Turner (5)
P Wanless (5)

Strategy and Employment Policy

Information
Employment policy briefing
Strategy unit
Senior management support unit
Employment operation branch
Labour market briefing branch

P Robson (5)

Internal Audit: Group and non-Training, Enterprise and Education Directorate, (Employment Department HQ)

Training, Enterprise and Education Directorate

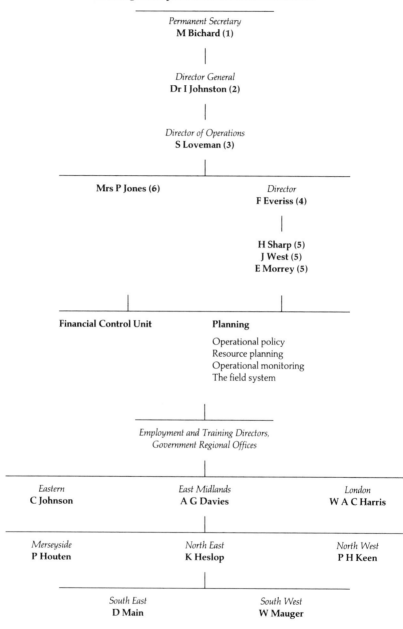

Permanent Secretary
M Bichard (1)

Director General
Dr I Johnston (2)

Director of Operations
S Loveman (3)

Mrs P Jones (6)

Director
F Everiss (4)

H Sharp (5)
J West (5)
E Morrey (5)

Financial Control Unit

Planning

Operational policy
Resource planning
Operational monitoring
The field system

Employment and Training Directors, Government Regional Offices

Eastern
C Johnson

East Midlands
A G Davies

London
W A C Harris

Merseyside
P Houten

North East
K Heslop

North West
P H Keen

South East
D Main

South West
W Mauger

West Midlands	*Yorkshire and Humberside*
H Tollyfield	**G Dyche**

* *For the full listing of government regional offices which bring together the existing offices of the Departments of Transport, Trade and Industry, Employment (Training, Enterprise and Education Directorate) and Environment, see separate entry in this section under* **Government Offices for the Regions**.

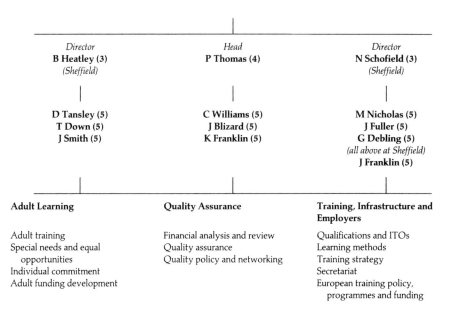

Director **B Heatley (3)** *(Sheffield)*	*Head* **P Thomas (4)**	*Director* **N Schofield (3)** *(Sheffield)*
D Tansley (5) **T Down (5)** **J Smith (5)**	**C Williams (5)** **J Blizard (5)** **K Franklin (5)**	**M Nicholas (5)** **J Fuller (5)** **G Debling (5)** *(all above at Sheffield)* **J Franklin (5)**
Adult Learning	**Quality Assurance**	**Training, Infrastructure and Employers**
Adult training Special needs and equal opportunities Individual commitment Adult funding development	Financial analysis and review Quality assurance Quality policy and networking	Qualifications and ITOs Learning methods Training strategy Secretariat European training policy, programmes and funding

Director
Mrs V Bayliss (3)
(Sheffield)

J Robertson (5)
Ms L Ammon (5)
R Wye (5)
T Fellowes (5)
M Brimmer (5)
(all above at Sheffield)

Youth and Education

Schools and partnership policy
Careers service
Young people at work
Further education and higher education

Employment Department Group Addresses

East Lane
Runcorn WA7 2DN
Tel 01928 715151

Moorfoot
Sheffield S1 4PQ
Tel 01142 753275

Department of the Environment

Founded	1970 with the merger of the Ministry of Housing and Local Government, Ministry of Transport and the Ministry of Public Building and Works
Ministers	secretary of state, three ministers of state and two parliamentary under secretaries
Responsibilities	conservation construction countryside energy efficiency environmental protection government civil estate management housing local government New Towns Commission PSA Services (see separate entry below) town and country planning urban regeneration water
Number of staff	4900
Executive agencies	Building Research Establishment The Buying Agency Ordnance Survey Planning Inspectorate Agency The Queen Elizabeth II Conference Centre Security Facilities Executive

Department of the Environment

2 Marsham Street, London SW1P 3EB
Tel 0171-276 3000
Fax *Telephone Department and ask for appropriate fax number*
All personnel are based at 2 Marsham Street unless otherwise indicated.
For other addresses and telephone numbers see end of this section.

Ministers

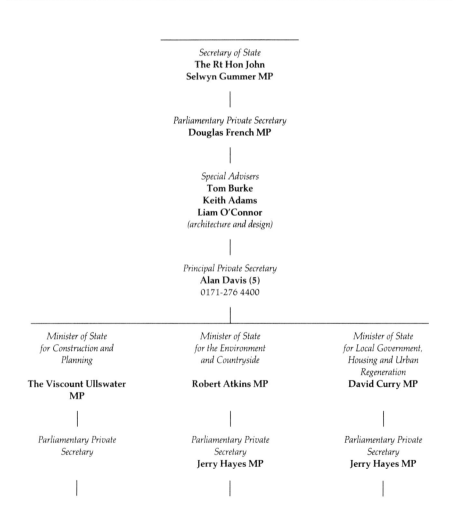

Secretary of State
The Rt Hon John Selwyn Gummer MP

Parliamentary Private Secretary
Douglas French MP

Special Advisers
Tom Burke
Keith Adams
Liam O'Connor
(architecture and design)

Principal Private Secretary
Alan Davis (5)
0171-276 4400

Minister of State for Construction and Planning
The Viscount Ullswater MP

Parliamentary Private Secretary

Minister of State for the Environment and Countryside
Robert Atkins MP

Parliamentary Private Secretary
Jerry Hayes MP

Minister of State for Local Government, Housing and Urban Regeneration
David Curry MP

Parliamentary Private Secretary
Jerry Hayes MP

Special Adviser
Gavin Barwell
(who advises the other Ministers of State)

Private Secretary
C Wood (7)
0171-276 0933

Special Adviser
Gavin Barwell

Private Secretary
Mrs T Vokes (7)
0171-276 0934

Special Adviser
Gavin Barwell

Private Secretary
B Hackland (7)
0171-276 3190

Parliamentary Under Secretary of State, Minister for Energy Efficiency
Robert Jones MP

Private Secretary
Miss D Butler (SEO)
0171-276 3229

Parliamentary Under Secretary of State
Sir Paul Beresford MP

Private Secretary
Miss M Cameron (HEO)
0171-276 0939

House of Lords' Spokesmen
The Viscount Ullswater
The Earl Howe
The Earl of Lindsay

Sponsor Ministers: Urban Regeneration

Minister for London	**John Gummer (DOE)**
Lambeth, Lewisham, Newham, Hackney, Southwark	**Robert Jones (DOE)**
Haringey, Tower Hamlets, Kensington and Chelsea, Brent	**Sir Paul Beresford**
Minister of Transport for London	**Steven Norris (DOT)**
Bristol	**The Viscount Astor (DNH)**
Plymouth	**The Baroness Cumberlege (DH)**
Birmingham, Sandwell, Walsall	**Richard Page (DTI)**
Wolverhampton	**John Watts (DOT)**
Nottingham, Derby, Leicester	**John Bowis (DH)**
Merseyside	**Robin Squire (DFE)**
Manchester, Salford, Blackburn, Bolton, Wigan	**Alistair Burt (DSS)**
Leeds, Bradford, Batley	**David Curry (DOE)**
Dearne Valley, Barnsley	**James Arbuthnot (DSS)**
Sheffield, Hull	**Ann Widdecombe (ED)**
Tyne and Wear	**Ian Taylor (DTI)**
Cleveland	**The Baroness Blatch (HO)**

Ministerial Responsibilities

John Gummer	Overall responsibility for the department and minister for London
The Viscount Ullswater	Building Research Establishment Buying agency Construction industry Queen Elizabeth II Conference Centre Security Facilities Executive Town and country planning Departmental spokesman in the House of Lords
David Curry	Housing PSA Services Local government Thames Gateway Urban regeneration
Robert Atkins	British Waterways Board Countryside Environmental protection Ordnance Survey Water
Sir Paul Beresford	Property Holdings PSA Services Supports Robert Atkins on environment, water and countryside; Viscount Ullswater on planning; David Curry on urban regeneration; and John Gummer on London
Robert Jones	Energy efficiency Supports David Curry on housing and local government; and Viscount Ullswater on construction

Departmental Overview

Civil Servants			Department	Minister
Grade 1	*Grade 2*	*Grade 3*		
A Turnbull		S Dugdale (4)	Communication	Sir P Beresford
		C Riley	Central Management and Analysis Unit	J S Gummer
	Environment Protection			
A Turnbull	F A Osborn	R S Dudding	Pollution Control and Waste	R Atkins/ Sir P Beresford
		Dr D J Fisk	Air, Climate, and Toxic Substances Chief Scientist	R Atkins/ Sir P Beresford
		R J A Sharp	Global Environment	R Atkins/ Sir P Beresford
		Dr D H Slater	HM Inspectorate of Pollution	R Atkins/ Sir P Beresford
		J Hobson	Energy Efficiency Office	R Atkins/ Sir P Beresford
		Dr N W Summerton	Water	R Atkins/ Sir P Beresford
		J Stevens (5)	Environment Protection Central	R Atkins/ Sir P Beresford
		Dr R J Pentreath	Environment Agency Advisory Committee Secretariat	R Atkins/ Sir P Beresford
	Establishments and Finance			
A Turnbull		Mrs M McDonald	Personnel	Vis Ullswater
		D A R Peel	Administration Resources	Vis Ullswater
		W F S Rickett	Finance Central	Vis Ullswater
	Local Government and Planning			
A Turnbull	C J S Brearley	Mrs A Heath	Local Government	D Curry/ R Jones
		P J J Britton	Local Government Finance Policy	D Curry/ R Jones
		J F Ballard D Lock	Town and Country Planning	Vis Ullswater/ Sir P Beresford

Departmental Overview

	Civil Servants		Department	Minister
Grade 1	*Grade 2*	*Grade 3*		
	Cities and Countryside			
A Turnbull	P J Fletcher	M B Gahagan	Cities and Countryside Policy	D Curry/ Sir P Beresford
		A G Watson	Cities and Countryside and Private Finance	D Curry/ Sir P Beresford
		J Plowman	Wildlife and Countryside	R Atkins/ Sir P Beresford
		Government Regional Offices*		
		J Turner	Eastern	As required
		M Lanyon	East Midlands	As required
	R U Young	J A Owen	London	As required
		J Stoker	Merseyside	As required
		Ms P Denham	North East	As required
		Ms M Neville-Rolfe	North West	As required
		Ms G Ashmore	South East	As required
		B Leonard S McQuillin	South West Devon and Cornwall	As required
		D Ritchie	West Midlands	As required
		J Walker	Yorkshire and Humberside	As required
	Housing and Construction			
A Turnbull	Ms D Nichols	Dr C P Evans	Housing Policy and Private Sector	D Curry/ R Jones
		Dr C P Evans	Housing and Urban Monitoring and Analysis	D Curry/ R Jones
		Mrs D Phillips	Housing Resources and Management	D Curry/ R Jones
		P Ward	Construction Sponsorship	Vis Ullswater/ R Jones
		D O McCreadie (4)	Land and Property; Building Regulations; Procurement and Prequalification Systems	Vis Ullswater/ Sir P Beresford

Departmental Overview

	Civil Servants		Department	Minister
Grade 1	*Grade 2*	*Grade 3*		
	Property			
A Turnbull	A J Lane	N E Borrett	Property Holdings	Sir P Beresford
		J Henry	Principal Finance Officer and Agency Sponsorship	Sir P Beresford
	Solicitor			
A Turnbull	Mrs M Morgan	Ms S Unerman	Legal Command	
		J A Catlin	Legal Command	
		P Szell	Legal Command	
		N Kingham	Departmental Task Force: Structure and Senior Management Review	

*The Department's regional offices are now integrated with those of Trade and Industry, Transport and Employment (Training, Enterprise and Education Directorate). Each regional director (see above) administers the new single budget and is equally responsible to whichever secretaries of state have operational programmes under the direction of their particular office at any one time. Regional directors do not always report to the secretary of state but will go through the relevant departmental permanent secretary as appropriate. Regional directors are accountable to the Secretary of State for the Environment on matters concerning the administration of the single budget.

For separate **Government Offices for the Regions** entry see under that name in this section.

The government offices in the regions operate in cooperation with English Partnerships; see the latter in the Regulatory Organisations' section of the *Whitehall Companion*.

Civil Servants and Departments

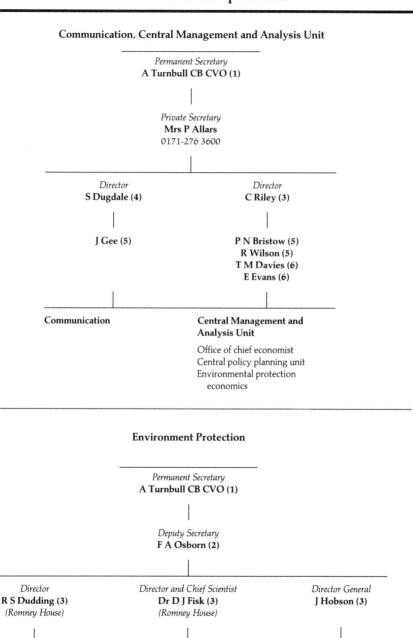

Communication, Central Management and Analysis Unit

Permanent Secretary
A Turnbull CB CVO (1)

Private Secretary
Mrs P Allars
0171-276 3600

Director
S Dugdale (4)

J Gee (5)

Director
C Riley (3)

P N Bristow (5)
R Wilson (5)
T M Davies (6)
E Evans (6)

Communication

Central Management and Analysis Unit

Office of chief economist
Central policy planning unit
Environmental protection economics

Environment Protection

Permanent Secretary
A Turnbull CB CVO (1)

Deputy Secretary
F A Osborn (2)

Director
R S Dudding (3)
(Romney House)

Director and Chief Scientist
Dr D J Fisk (3)
(Romney House)

Director General
J Hobson (3)

H Cleary (5)
N Williams (5)
Mrs L A C Simcock (5)
Dr P Hinchcliffe (5)
Dr S Brown (5)
J McBrayne (5)

Pollution Control and Waste

Local environmental quality
Environment Agency project team
Environment Agency Advisory Committee secretariat
Waste management
Contaminated land and liabilities
Policy and legislation
Waste technical
Radioactive substances

Dr N J King (5)
R Mills (5)
A Apling (5)
P Dykins (5)
Mrs H Hillier (5)

Air, Climate and Toxic Substances

Air quality
Global atmosphere
Toxic substances
Statistics

A K Galloway (5)
R Dinwiddy (5)
Dr P Clarke (5)
Dr D Vincent (5)
N Sanders (5)

Energy Efficiency Office

Energy efficiency in industry, commerce and domestic sector
Low income households
Energy Saving Trust
Appliance/home energy labelling
Environmental management in business and best practice
Regional energy efficiency offices
Environmental protection and industry
Eco-labelling
Advisory Committee on Business and the Environment

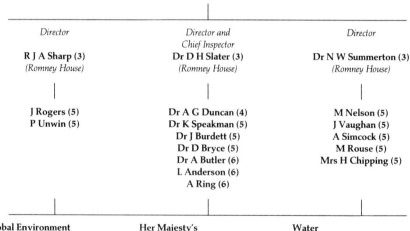

Director
R J A Sharp (3)
(Romney House)

J Rogers (5)
P Unwin (5)

Global Environment

Environmental protection international
Environmental protection Europe

Director and Chief Inspector
Dr D H Slater (3)
(Romney House)

Dr A G Duncan (4)
Dr K Speakman (5)
Dr J Burdett (5)
Dr D Bryce (5)
Dr A Butler (6)
L Anderson (6)
A Ring (6)

Her Majesty's Inspectorate of Pollution

Regulatory systems
Operations
Business strategy
Pollution policy
Corporate development and secretariat
Finance
Personnel

Director
Dr N W Summerton (3)
(Romney House)

M Nelson (5)
J Vaughan (5)
A Simcock (5)
M Rouse (5)
Mrs H Chipping (5)

Water

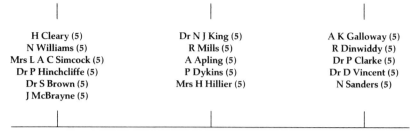

Water services
Water sponsorship and navigation
Water quality
Waterways, resources and marine
Drinking Water Inspectorate*

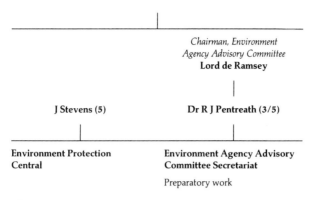

Chairman, Environment Agency Advisory Committee
Lord de Ramsey

J Stevens (5)

Dr R J Pentreath (3/5)

Environment Protection Central

Environment Agency Advisory Committee Secretariat

Preparatory work

**See under Regulatory Organisations' section*

Establishments and Finance

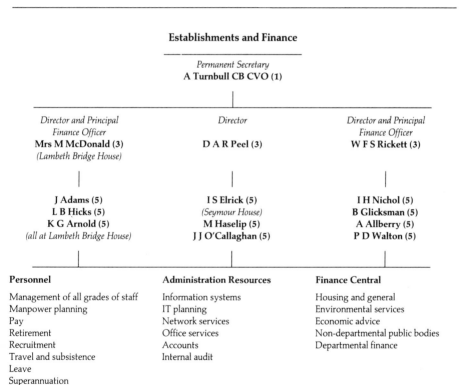

Permanent Secretary
A Turnbull CB CVO (1)

Director and Principal Finance Officer
Mrs M McDonald (3)
(Lambeth Bridge House)

J Adams (5)
L B Hicks (5)
K G Arnold (5)
(all at Lambeth Bridge House)

Personnel

- Management of all grades of staff
- Manpower planning
- Pay
- Retirement
- Recruitment
- Travel and subsistence
- Leave
- Superannuation

Director
D A R Peel (3)

I S Elrick (5)
(Seymour House)
M Haselip (5)
J J O'Callaghan (5)

Administration Resources

- Information systems
- IT planning
- Network services
- Office services
- Accounts
- Internal audit

Director and Principal Finance Officer
W F S Rickett (3)

I H Nichol (5)
B Glicksman (5)
A Allberry (5)
P D Walton (5)

Finance Central

- Housing and general
- Environmental services
- Economic advice
- Non-departmental public bodies
- Departmental finance

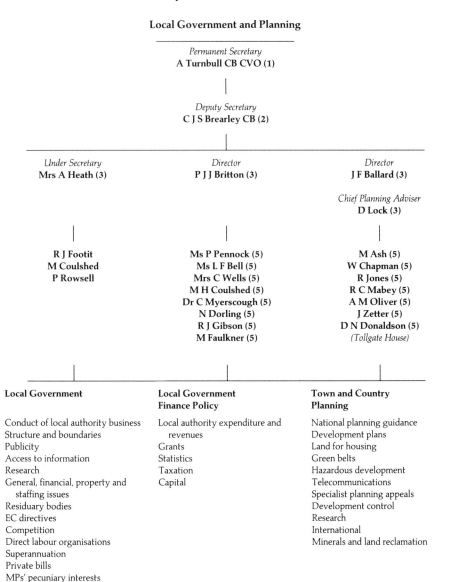

Local Government and Planning

Permanent Secretary
A Turnbull CB CVO (1)

Deputy Secretary
C J S Brearley CB (2)

Under Secretary
Mrs A Heath (3)

R J Footit
M Coulshed
P Rowsell

Director
P J J Britton (3)

Ms P Pennock (5)
Ms L F Bell (5)
Mrs C Wells (5)
M H Coulshed (5)
Dr C Myerscough (5)
N Dorling (5)
R J Gibson (5)
M Faulkner (5)

Director
J F Ballard (3)

Chief Planning Adviser
D Lock (3)

M Ash (5)
W Chapman (5)
R Jones (5)
R C Mabey (5)
A M Oliver (5)
J Zetter (5)
D N Donaldson (5)
(Tollgate House)

Local Government

Conduct of local authority business
Structure and boundaries
Publicity
Access to information
Research
General, financial, property and staffing issues
Residuary bodies
EC directives
Competition
Direct labour organisations
Superannuation
Private bills
MPs' pecuniary interests

Local Government Finance Policy

Local authority expenditure and revenues
Grants
Statistics
Taxation
Capital

Town and Country Planning

National planning guidance
Development plans
Land for housing
Green belts
Hazardous development
Telecommunications
Specialist planning appeals
Development control
Research
International
Minerals and land reclamation

Cities and Countryside

Permanent Secretary
A Turnbull CB CVO (1)

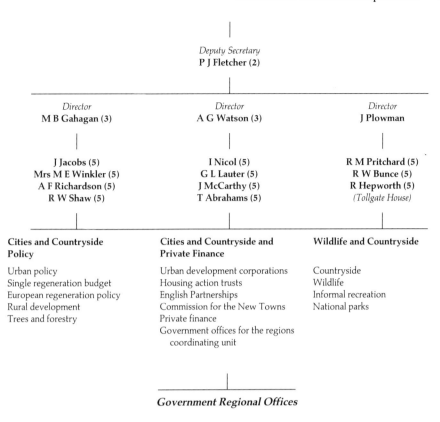

Deputy Secretary
P J Fletcher (2)

Director
M B Gahagan (3)

J Jacobs (5)
Mrs M E Winkler (5)
A F Richardson (5)
R W Shaw (5)

Cities and Countryside Policy

Urban policy
Single regeneration budget
European regeneration policy
Rural development
Trees and forestry

Director
A G Watson (3)

I Nicol (5)
G L Lauter (5)
J McCarthy (5)
T Abrahams (5)

Cities and Countryside and Private Finance

Urban development corporations
Housing action trusts
English Partnerships
Commission for the New Towns
Private finance
Government offices for the regions coordinating unit

Director
J Plowman

R M Pritchard (5)
R W Bunce (5)
R Hepworth (5)
(Tollgate House)

Wildlife and Countryside

Countryside
Wildlife
Informal recreation
National parks

Government Regional Offices

The Department's regional offices are now integrated with those of Trade and Industry, Transport and Employment (Training, Enterprise and Education Directorate). Brief details of senior staff are given below but a fuller entry can be found under **Government Offices for the Regions** in this section of the *Whitehall Companion.*

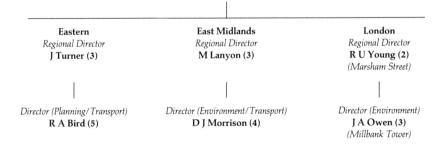

Eastern
Regional Director
J Turner (3)

Director (Planning/Transport)
R A Bird (5)

East Midlands
Regional Director
M Lanyon (3)

Director (Environment/Transport)
D J Morrison (4)

London
Regional Director
R U Young (2)
(Marsham Street)

Director (Environment)
J A Owen (3)
(Millbank Tower)

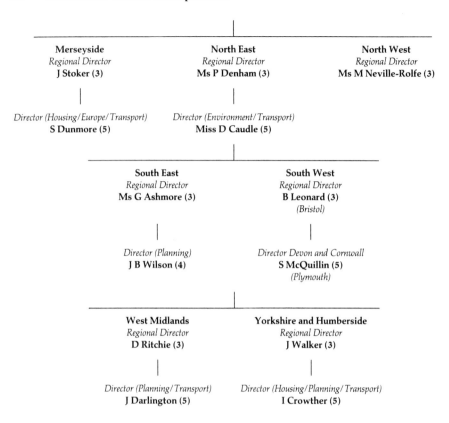

Merseyside
Regional Director
J Stoker (3)

Director (Housing/Europe/Transport)
S Dunmore (5)

North East
Regional Director
Ms P Denham (3)

Director (Environment/Transport)
Miss D Caudle (5)

North West
Regional Director
Ms M Neville-Rolfe (3)

South East
Regional Director
Ms G Ashmore (3)

Director (Planning)
J B Wilson (4)

South West
Regional Director
B Leonard (3)
(Bristol)

Director Devon and Cornwall
S McQuillin (5)
(Plymouth)

West Midlands
Regional Director
D Ritchie (3)

Director (Planning/Transport)
J Darlington (5)

Yorkshire and Humberside
Regional Director
J Walker (3)

Director (Housing/Planning/Transport)
I Crowther (5)

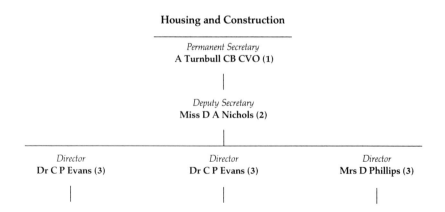

Housing and Construction

Permanent Secretary
A Turnbull CB CVO (1)

Deputy Secretary
Miss D A Nichols (2)

Director
Dr C P Evans (3)

Director
Dr C P Evans (3)

Director
Mrs D Phillips (3)

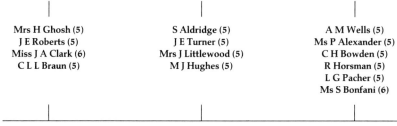

Mrs H Ghosh (5)
J E Roberts (5)
Miss J A Clark (6)
C L L Braun (5)

Housing Policy and Private Sector

Housing policy
Home ownership
Private renting and leasehold reform
Right to buy
Renovation grants
Housing and the environment

S Aldridge (5)
J E Turner (5)
Mrs J Littlewood (5)
M J Hughes (5)

Housing and Urban Monitoring and Analysis

Economic advice
Statistics
Building stock research
IT applications
Social research

A M Wells (5)
Ms P Alexander (5)
C H Bowden (5)
R Horsman (5)
L G Pacher (5)
Ms S Bonfani (6)

Housing Resources and Management

Housing transfer and private finance
Local authority housing financing
Homelessness
Gipsy sites
Special needs housing
Tenant participation
Housing investment programmes
Housing revenue accounts and subsidy
Council house rents
Local authority housing
Housing associations

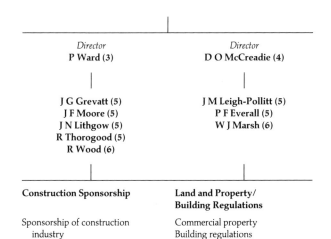

Director
P Ward (3)

J G Grevatt (5)
J F Moore (5)
J N Lithgow (5)
R Thorogood (5)
R Wood (6)

Construction Sponsorship

Sponsorship of construction industry
Competitiveness
Export promotion
EC
Innovation
Quality assurance
Statistics and research management

Director
D O McCreadie (4)

J M Leigh-Pollitt (5)
P F Everall (5)
W J Marsh (6)

Land and Property/ Building Regulations

Commercial property
Building regulations
Prequalification
Government works contracts

Property

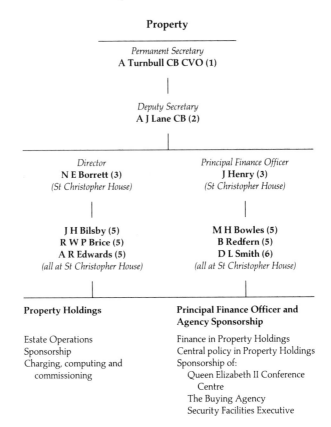

Permanent Secretary
A Turnbull CB CVO (1)

Deputy Secretary
A J Lane CB (2)

Director
N E Borrett (3)
(St Christopher House)

J H Bilsby (5)
R W P Brice (5)
A R Edwards (5)
(all at St Christopher House)

Property Holdings

Estate Operations
Sponsorship
Charging, computing and commissioning

Principal Finance Officer
J Henry (3)
(St Christopher House)

M H Bowles (5)
B Redfern (5)
D L Smith (6)
(all at St Christopher House)

Principal Finance Officer and Agency Sponsorship

Finance in Property Holdings
Central policy in Property Holdings
Sponsorship of:
- Queen Elizabeth II Conference Centre
- The Buying Agency
- Security Facilities Executive

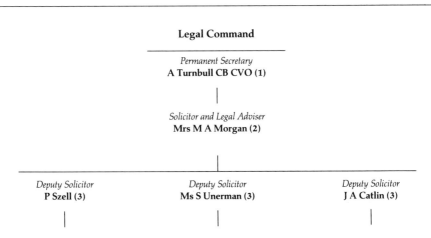

Legal Command

Permanent Secretary
A Turnbull CB CVO (1)

Solicitor and Legal Adviser
Mrs M A Morgan (2)

Deputy Solicitor
P Szell (3)

Deputy Solicitor
Ms S Unerman (3)

Deputy Solicitor
J A Catlin (3)

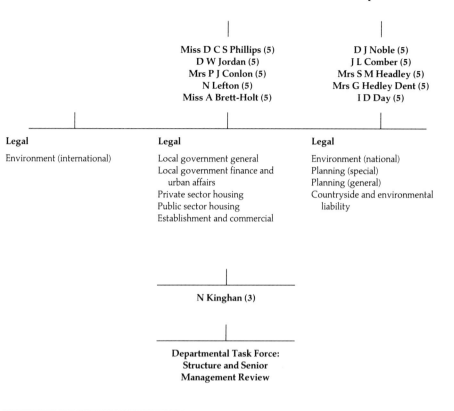

Miss D C S Phillips (5)
D W Jordan (5)
Mrs P J Conlon (5)
N Lefton (5)
Miss A Brett-Holt (5)

D J Noble (5)
J L Comber (5)
Mrs S M Headley (5)
Mrs G Hedley Dent (5)
I D Day (5)

Legal

Environment (international)

Legal

Local government general
Local government finance and urban affairs
Private sector housing
Public sector housing
Establishment and commercial

Legal

Environment (national)
Planning (special)
Planning (general)
Countryside and environmental liability

N Kinghan (3)

Departmental Task Force: Structure and Senior Management Review

Department of the Environment Addresses

Main addresses

Graeme House
Derby Square
Liverpool L2 7SU
Tel 0151-227 4111
Fax 0151-236 1199

Highwood Pavillions
Jupiter Road
Patchway
Bristol BS12 5SL
Tel 01179 319400
Fax 01179 319505

Lambeth Bridge House
London SE1 7SB
Tel 0171-238 3000
Fax 0171-238 4330

1 Palace Street
London SW1E 5HE
Tel 0171-238 3000
Fax 0171-828 6983

Romney House
43 Marsham Street
London SW1 3PY
Tel 0171-276 3000
Fax 0171-276 0818

St Christopher House
Southwark Street
London SE1 0TE
Tel 0171-928 3666
Fax 0171-921 2294

Seymour House
Whiteleaf Road
Hemel Hempstead
Herts HP3 9DE
Tel 01442 210400
Fax 01442 252048

Tollgate House
Houlton Street
Bristol BS2 9DJ
Tel 01179 218811
Fax 01179 218269

Regional addresses

Eastern
Enterprise House
Chivers Way
Vision Park
Histon
Cambridge CB4 4ZR
Tel 01223 202064
Fax 01223 202066

East Midlands
Cranbrook House
Cranbrook Street
Nottingham NG1 1EY
Tel 01159 350602
Fax 01159 799743

London
Millbank Tower
Millbank
London SW1P 4QU
Tel 0171-217 3000
Fax Telephone above number and ask for appropriate fax number

2 Marsham Street
London SW1P 3EB
Tel 0171-276 5825
Fax 0171-276 5827

Mersey
Graeme House
Derby Square
Liverpool L2 7SU
Tel 0151 227 4111
Fax 0151 236 1199

North Eastern
Stanegate House
2 Groat Market
Newcastle upon Tyne NE1 1YN
Tel 0191-201 3300
Fax 0191-201 3480

North West
Sunley Tower
Piccadilly Plaza
Manchester M1 4BE
Tel 0161-838 5555/0161-236 2171
Fax 0161-228 3740

South East
Charles House
375 Kensington High Street
London W14 8QH
Tel 0171-605 9000
Fax 0171-605 9253

South West
The Pithay
Bristol BS1 2PB
Tel 01179 878000
Fax 01179 878318

Plymouth Office
Phoenix House
Notte Street
Plymouth PL1 2HF
Tel 01752 221891
Fax 01752 227647

West Midlands
77 Paradise Circus
Queensway
Birmingham B1 2DT
Tel 0121-212 5000/0121-626 2000
Fax 0121-212 1010

Yorkshire and Humberside
City House
New Station Street
Leeds LS1 4JD
Tel 01132 800600
Fax 01132 338301

Export Credits Guarantee Department

Founded	1919
Responsible to	President of the Board of Trade/Secretary of State for Trade and Industry and Minister for Trade
Responsibilities	Facilitates UK exports by making available export credit insurance to British firms selling overseas Guarantees repayment to British banks providing finance for exports
Number of staff	489

Export Credits Guarantee Department

PO Box 2200, 2 Exchange Tower, Harbour Exchange, London E14 9GS
Tel 0171-512 7000 Fax 0171-512 7649

Ministers

President of the Board of Trade/ Secretary of State for Trade and Industry
The Rt Hon Michael Heseltine MP

Minister for Trade
Richard Needham MP

Officials

Chief Executive
W B Willott (2)

Management Board
M V Hawtin (3)
T M Jaffray (3)
J R Weiss (3)

General Counsel
R G Elden (5)

Departmental Overview

Civil Servants			Department	Minister
Grade 1	*Grade 2*	*Grade 3*		
	W B Willott	T M Jaffray	Resource Management Group	M Heseltine R Needham
		M V Hawtin	Underwriting Group	M Heseltine R Needham
		J R Weiss	Asset Management Group	M Heseltine
		R G Elden (5)	General Counsel's Office	M Heseltine R Needham

Civil Servants and Departments

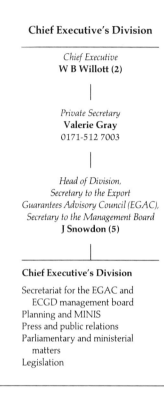

Chief Executive's Division

Chief Executive
W B Willott (2)

Private Secretary
Valerie Gray
0171-512 7003

Head of Division, Secretary to the Export Guarantees Advisory Council (EGAC), Secretary to the Management Board
J Snowdon (5)

Chief Executive's Division

Secretariat for the EGAC and ECGD management board
Planning and MINIS
Press and public relations
Parliamentary and ministerial matters
Legislation

Resource Management, Underwriting and Asset Management Groups

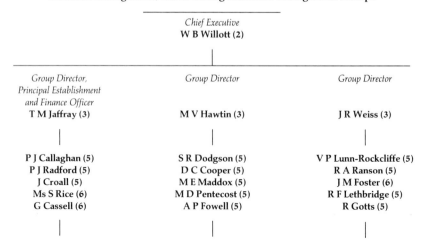

Chief Executive
W B Willott (2)

Group Director, Principal Establishment and Finance Officer
T M Jaffray (3)

P J Callaghan (5)
P J Radford (5)
J Croall (5)
Ms S Rice (6)
G Cassell (6)

Group Director
M V Hawtin (3)

S R Dodgson (5)
D C Cooper (5)
M E Maddox (5)
M D Pentecost (5)
A P Fowell (5)

Group Director
J R Weiss (3)

V P Lunn-Rockcliffe (5)
R A Ranson (5)
J M Foster (6)
R F Lethbridge (5)
R Gotts (5)

Resource Management Group

Finance
Personnel
IT services
Risk management
Management information
Audit, investigation and review
Operational research

Underwriting Group

Underwriting of capital goods and project business worldwide
Supporting policy and documentation
Financial analysis
Bank guarantees and bond facilities
Marketing and product development

Asset Management Group

Claims and recoveries
Treasury management
International debt
International relations
Reinsurance

General Counsel
R G Elden (5)

General Counsel's Office

Legal advice
Legal risk management
Legal advice procurement

Foreign and Commonwealth Office

Founded The Diplomatic Service was established in 1965 by the merger of the former Foreign, Commonwealth and Trade Commissioner services. Subsequently it incorporated the staffs of the Colonial Office in London, which merged with the Commonwealth Relations Office in 1966 to form the Commonwealth Office. The Foreign and Commonwealth offices continued as separate departments responsible to separate secretaries of state until 1968, when they combined as the Foreign and Commonwealth Office, responsible to one secretary of state.

Ministers Foreign Secretary, four ministers of state and one parliamentary under secretary

Responsibilities Provides, mainly through diplomatic missions, the means of communication between the British government and other governments and international governmental organisations for the discussion and negotiation of all questions of international relations.

It is responsible for alerting the government to the implications of developments overseas; for protecting British interests overseas; for protecting British citizens abroad; for explaining British policies to, and cultivating friendly relations with, governments overseas; and for the discharge of British responsibilities to the dependent territories.

Number of staff (London) 3266

Executive Agencies Wiston House Conference Centre (Wilton Park)
Natural Resources Institute

Foreign and Commonwealth Office

Downing Street, London SW1A 2AL
Tel 0171-270 3000
Fax *Telephone the above number and when through to the FCO ask for appropriate fax number*

All staff are based at Downing Street unless otherwise indicated.
For other addresses and telephone numbers see the end of this section.

Ministers

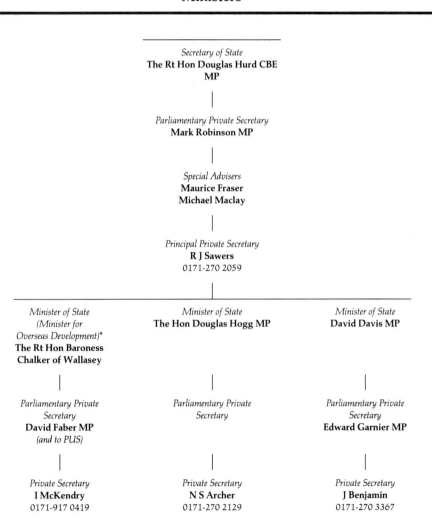

Secretary of State
The Rt Hon Douglas Hurd CBE MP

Parliamentary Private Secretary
Mark Robinson MP

Special Advisers
Maurice Fraser
Michael Maclay

Principal Private Secretary
R J Sawers
0171-270 2059

*Minister of State (Minister for Overseas Development)**
The Rt Hon Baroness Chalker of Wallasey

Parliamentary Private Secretary
David Faber MP
(and to PUS)

Private Secretary
I McKendry
0171-917 0419

Minister of State
The Hon Douglas Hogg MP

Parliamentary Private Secretary

Private Secretary
N S Archer
0171-270 2129

Minister of State
David Davis MP

Parliamentary Private Secretary
Edward Garnier MP

Private Secretary
J Benjamin
0171-270 3367

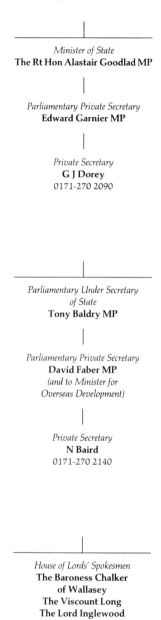

Minister of State
The Rt Hon Alastair Goodlad MP

Parliamentary Private Secretary
Edward Garnier MP

Private Secretary
G J Dorey
0171-270 2090

Parliamentary Under Secretary of State
Tony Baldry MP

Parliamentary Private Secretary
David Faber MP
(and to Minister for Overseas Development)

Private Secretary
N Baird
0171-270 2140

House of Lords' Spokesmen
The Baroness Chalker of Wallasey
The Viscount Long
The Lord Inglewood

**See Overseas Development Administration*

Ministerial Responsibilities

Douglas Hurd	Overall responsibility for the department
Baroness Chalker	Africa including South Africa FCO issues in the House of Lords Overseas Development Administration
Alastair Goodlad	commercial/trade promotion South East Asia, the Far East and Australasia FCO administration
Douglas Hogg	arms control east/west relations including former Soviet Union economic policy Middle East United Nations
David Davis	defence policy European Communities Latin and South America South Atlantic and Antarctica Western and Southern Europe
Tony Baldry	aviation and maritime consular questions energy environment immigration and nationality Indian sub-continent and Afghanistan information and cultural affairs narcotics control and AIDS nationality treaty and claims North America ODA issues in the House of Commons parliamentary liaison protocol science and technology West Indies

Departmental Overview

	Civil Servants		Department	Minister
Perm Under Secretary	**Deputy Under Secretary**	**Assistant Under Secretary**		
	Aid Policy; Legal Advisers; Policy Planning			
Sir John Coles		R G M Manning (ODA)	Aid Policy*	Ly Chalker
			Policy Planning Staff (Planning only)	As required
	Sir Franklin Berman	D H Anderson	Legal Advisers	As required
	Permanent Under-Secretary's Department; Security Coordination; Service Advisers and Attachés; CSCE Unit; Non-Proliferation and Defence; Security Policy; Ireland			
Sir John Coles	Sir Timothy Daunt	D G Martin (Head of Dept)	Permanent Under Secretary's Department	D Hurd
		J R de Fonblanque	Security Coordination	A Goodlad
		R B Smith	Service Advisers and Attachés CSCE Unit Non-Proliferation and Defence Security Policy	D Hogg D Hogg D Hogg D Hogg
		T L Richardson	Republic of Ireland	D Hurd
	Central European; Eastern; Joint Assistance Units; Middle and Near East			
Sir John Coles	J Q Greenstock	F N Richards	Central European Eastern Joint Assistance Unit (Central & Eastern)	D Hogg D Hogg D Hogg
		A F Green	Middle East Near East and North Africa	D Hogg D Hogg

Departmental Overview

Perm Under Secretary	Civil Servants: Deputy Under Secretary	Civil Servants: Assistant Under Secretary	Department	Minister
	The Americas and Antarctic; Atlantic and Southern Oceans; Far Eastern and Pacific; Asia; Africa; Commonwealth; Joint Directorate			
Sir John Coles	D J Wright	W Marsden	South Atlantic and Antarctic	D Davis
			Latin America	D Davis
			West Indian and Atlantic	D Davis
			North America	T Baldry
		C O Hum	Far Eastern and Pacific	A Goodlad
			Hong Kong	A Goodlad
		D J M Dain	South Asian	A Goodlad
			South East Asian	A Goodlad
		A M Goodenough	African (Equitorial)	Ly Chalker
			African (Southern)	Ly Chalker
			Commonwealth Coordination	Ly Chalker
		F R Mingay	FCO/DTI Joint Export Promotion Directorate	A Goodlad
	Aviation and Maritime; Environment, Science and Energy; Drugs, International Crime and Terrorism; Economic Relations; European Community			
Sir John Coles	M H Jay	J R de Fonblanque	Aviation and Maritime	T Baldry
			Environment, Science and Energy	T Baldry
			Drugs, International Crime and Terrorism	T Baldry
			Economic Relations*	D Davis
		S J L Wright	European Community (Internal and External)	D Davis
		J Rollo	Economic Advisers	As required

Departmental Overview

Perm Under Secretary	Civil Servants: Deputy Under Secretary	Civil Servants: Assistant Under Secretary	Department	Minister
	Consular; Information and News; Migration and Nationality; IT; Personnel, Establishment and Security; Finance and Management; Protocol; Overseas Estate; Library and Records			
Sir John Coles	J R Young	C C R Battiscombe	Consular	T Baldry
			Cultural Relations	T Baldry
			Information	T Baldry
			Migration and Visa	T Baldry
			Nationality, Treaty and Claims	T Baldry
			News	As required
			Parliamentary Relations	T Baldry
		J Ling	Information Systems (Operations and Projects)	T Baldry
			Services, Planning and Resources	T Baldry
			Support Services	A Goodlad
			Engineering Services	
			Library and Records	
		P J Torry	Personnel Management, Policy and Services	A Goodlad
			Security*	A Goodlad
			Training	A Goodlad
			Medical and Welfare*	A Goodlad
			PROSPER	A Goodlad
		K R Tebbit	Overseas Inspectorate*	A Goodlad
			Resources and Finance	A Goodlad
			Internal Audit*	A Goodlad
			Management Review*	A Goodlad
		A St J Figgis	Protocol, Royal Matters, Honours	T Baldry
			Overseas Estate	A Goodlad
		T L Richardson	Research and Analysis	As required
	Policy Planning; Europe; Joint Assistance Unit; United Nations; Human Rights; Common Foreign and Security Policy			
Sir John Coles	L P Neville-Jones	D G Manning (Head of Dept)	Policy Planning	As required
		F N Richards	Eastern Adriatic	D Davis
		T L Richardson	Southern Europe	D Davis
			Western Europe	
		J R de Fonblanque	United Nations	D Hogg
			Human Rights	A Goodlad
		S J L Wright	Common Foreign and Security Policy	D Davis

Departmental Overview

Civil Servants			Department	Minister
Perm Under Secretary	**Deputy Under Secretary**	**Assistant Under Secretary**		
	Government Hospitality Fund			
Sir John Coles		Col T Earl	Government Hospitality Fund	A Goodlad

* joint FCO/ODA departments

** joint FCO/DTI directorate

Civil Servants and Departments

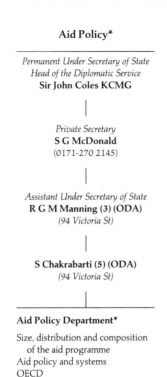

Aid Policy*

Permanent Under Secretary of State
Head of the Diplomatic Service
Sir John Coles KCMG

Private Secretary
S G McDonald
(0171-270 2145)

Assistant Under Secretary of State
R G M Manning (3) (ODA)
(94 Victoria St)

S Chakrabarti (5) (ODA)
(94 Victoria St)

Aid Policy Department*

Size, distribution and composition of the aid programme
Aid policy and systems
OECD
Other donors

* joint FCO/ODA department

Policy Planning Staff (Planning only)

Permanent Under Secretary of State
Head of the Diplomatic Service
Sir John Coles KCMG

Policy Planning Staff
(Planning only)

Legal Advisers

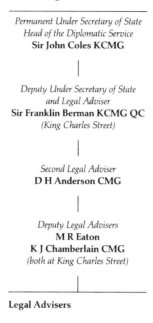

Permanent Under Secretary of State
Head of the Diplomatic Service
Sir John Coles KCMG

Deputy Under Secretary of State
and Legal Adviser
Sir Franklin Berman KCMG QC
(King Charles Street)

Second Legal Adviser
D H Anderson CMG

Deputy Legal Advisers
M R Eaton
K J Chamberlain CMG
(both at King Charles Street)

Legal Advisers

Overseas Police Advisers

Permanent Under Secretary of State
Head of the Diplomatic Service
Sir John Coles KCMG

Senior Police Adviser
L Grundy

Political Adviser
R Nicklin
(both at 94 Victoria Street)

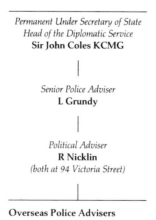

Overseas Police Advisers

Permanent Under Secretary's Department; Security Coordination; Service Advisers and Attachés; CSCE Unit; Non-proliferation and Defence; Security; Ireland

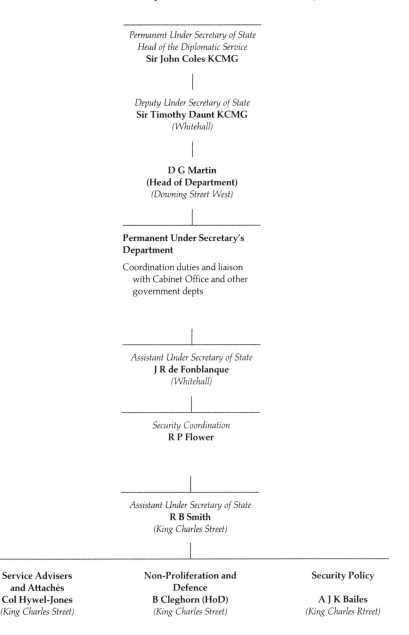

Permanent Under Secretary of State
Head of the Diplomatic Service
Sir John Coles KCMG

Deputy Under Secretary of State
Sir Timothy Daunt KCMG
(Whitehall)

D G Martin
(Head of Department)
(Downing Street West)

Permanent Under Secretary's Department

Coordination duties and liaison with Cabinet Office and other government depts

Assistant Under Secretary of State
J R de Fonblanque
(Whitehall)

Security Coordination
R P Flower

Assistant Under Secretary of State
R B Smith
(King Charles Street)

Service Advisers and Attachés
Col Hywel-Jones
(King Charles Street)

Non-Proliferation and Defence
B Cleghorn (HoD)
(King Charles Street)

Security Policy
A J K Bailes
(King Charles Rtreet)

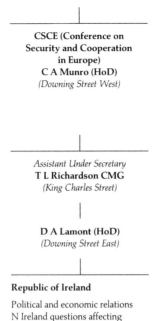

CSCE (Conference on Security and Cooperation in Europe)
C A Munro (HoD)
(Downing Street West)

Assistant Under Secretary
T L Richardson CMG
(King Charles Street)

D A Lamont (HoD)
(Downing Street East)

Republic of Ireland

Political and economic relations
N Ireland questions affecting Republic and other foreign countries

---

Central European; Eastern; Joint Assistance Units; Middle and Near East

Permanent Under Secretary of State
Head of the Diplomatic Service
Sir John Coles KCMG

Deputy Under Secretary of State
J Q Greenstock CMG
(Whitehall)

Assistant Under Secretary of State
F N Richards

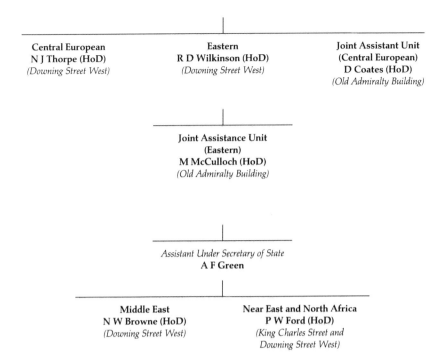

Central European
N J Thorpe (HoD)
(Downing Street West)

Eastern
R D Wilkinson (HoD)
(Downing Street West)

Joint Assistant Unit (Central European)
D Coates (HoD)
(Old Admiralty Building)

Joint Assistance Unit (Eastern)
M McCulloch (HoD)
(Old Admiralty Building)

Assistant Under Secretary of State
A F Green

Middle East
N W Browne (HoD)
(Downing Street West)

Near East and North Africa
P W Ford (HoD)
(King Charles Street and Downing Street West)

The Americas and Antarctic; Atlantic and Southern Oceans; Far Eastern, Pacific and Asia; Africa; Commonwealth; Joint Directorate

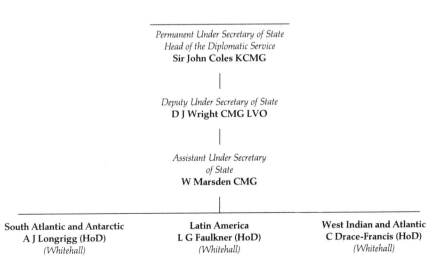

Permanent Under Secretary of State
Head of the Diplomatic Service
Sir John Coles KCMG

Deputy Under Secretary of State
D J Wright CMG LVO

Assistant Under Secretary of State
W Marsden CMG

South Atlantic and Antarctic
A J Longrigg (HoD)
(Whitehall)

Latin America
L G Faulkner (HoD)
(Whitehall)

West Indian and Atlantic
C Drace-Francis (HoD)
(Whitehall)

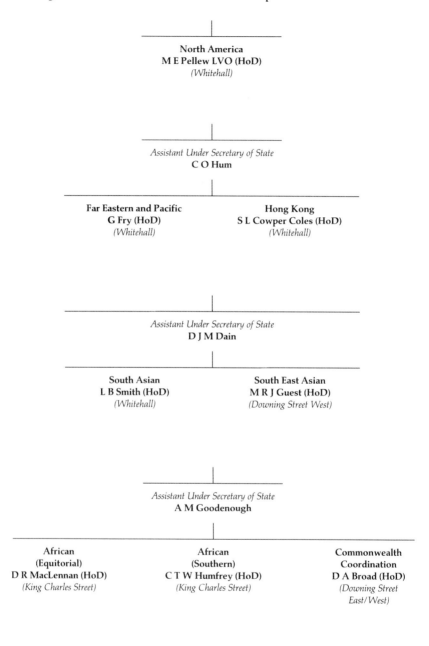

North America
M E Pellew LVO (HoD)
(Whitehall)

Assistant Under Secretary of State
C O Hum

Far Eastern and Pacific
G Fry (HoD)
(Whitehall)

Hong Kong
S L Cowper Coles (HoD)
(Whitehall)

Assistant Under Secretary of State
D J M Dain

South Asian
L B Smith (HoD)
(Whitehall)

South East Asian
M R J Guest (HoD)
(Downing Street West)

Assistant Under Secretary of State
A M Goodenough

African (Equitorial)
D R MacLennan (HoD)
(King Charles Street)

African (Southern)
C T W Humfrey (HoD)
(King Charles Street)

Commonwealth Coordination
D A Broad (HoD)
(Downing Street East/West)

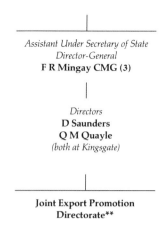

Assistant Under Secretary of State
Director-General
F R Mingay CMG (3)

Directors
D Saunders
Q M Quayle
(both at Kingsgate)

Joint Export Promotion Directorate**

***Joint FCO/DTI Directorate*

Aviation and Maritime; Environment, Science and Energy; Drugs, International Crime and Terrorism; Economic Advisers/Relations; European Community

Permanent Under Secretary of State
Head of the Diplomatic Service
Sir John Coles KCMG

Deputy Under Secretary of State
and Economic Director
M H Jay CMG

Assistant Under Secretary of State
J R de Fonblanque

Aviation and Maritime
A M Collins (HoD)
(Whitehall)

Economic Relations*
D F Richmond (HoD)
(Whitehall)

Environment, Science and Energy
G H Boyce (HoD)
(Whitehall)

Drugs, International Crime and Terrorism
R P Flower (HoD)
(Downing Street East)

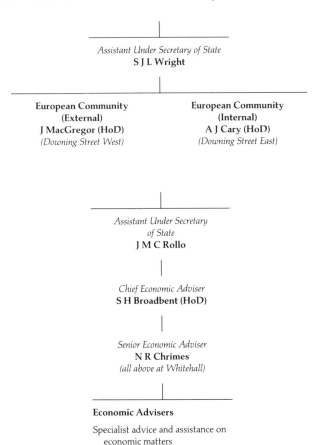

Assistant Under Secretary of State
S J L Wright

European Community (External)
J MacGregor (HoD)
(Downing Street West)

European Community (Internal)
A J Cary (HoD)
(Downing Street East)

Assistant Under Secretary of State
J M C Rollo

Chief Economic Adviser
S H Broadbent (HoD)

Senior Economic Adviser
N R Chrimes
(all above at Whitehall)

Economic Advisers

Specialist advice and assistance on economic matters

**Joint FCO/ODA department*

Consular; Information and News; Migration and Nationality; IT; Personnel; Establishment and Security; Finance and Management; Protocol; Overseas Estate; Library and Records

Permanent Under Secretary of State
Head of the Diplomatic Service
Sir John Coles KCMG

Deputy Under Secretary of State and Chief Clerk
J R Young CMG

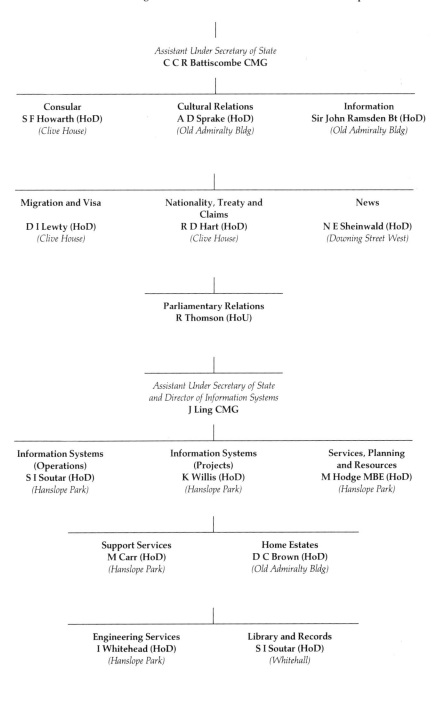

Assistant Under Secretary of State
C C R Battiscombe CMG

Consular
S F Howarth (HoD)
(Clive House)

Cultural Relations
A D Sprake (HoD)
(Old Admiralty Bldg)

Information
Sir John Ramsden Bt (HoD)
(Old Admiralty Bldg)

Migration and Visa
D I Lewty (HoD)
(Clive House)

Nationality, Treaty and Claims
R D Hart (HoD)
(Clive House)

News
N E Sheinwald (HoD)
(Downing Street West)

Parliamentary Relations
R Thomson (HoU)

Assistant Under Secretary of State and Director of Information Systems
J Ling CMG

Information Systems (Operations)
S I Soutar (HoD)
(Hanslope Park)

Information Systems (Projects)
K Willis (HoD)
(Hanslope Park)

Services, Planning and Resources
M Hodge MBE (HoD)
(Hanslope Park)

Support Services
M Carr (HoD)
(Hanslope Park)

Home Estates
D C Brown (HoD)
(Old Admiralty Bldg)

Engineering Services
I Whitehead (HoD)
(Hanslope Park)

Library and Records
S I Soutar (HoD)
(Whitehall)

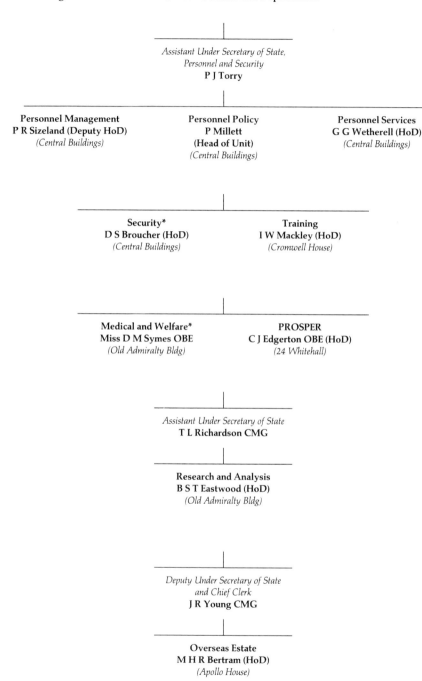

Assistant Under Secretary of State,
Personnel and Security
P J Torry

Personnel Management
P R Sizeland (Deputy HoD)
(Central Buildings)

Personnel Policy
P Millett
(Head of Unit)
(Central Buildings)

Personnel Services
G G Wetherell (HoD)
(Central Buildings)

Security*
D S Broucher (HoD)
(Central Buildings)

Training
I W Mackley (HoD)
(Cromwell House)

Medical and Welfare*
Miss D M Symes OBE
(Old Admiralty Bldg)

PROSPER
C J Edgerton OBE (HoD)
(24 Whitehall)

Assistant Under Secretary of State
T L Richardson CMG

Research and Analysis
B S T Eastwood (HoD)
(Old Admiralty Bldg)

Deputy Under Secretary of State
and Chief Clerk
J R Young CMG

Overseas Estate
M H R Bertram (HoD)
(Apollo House)

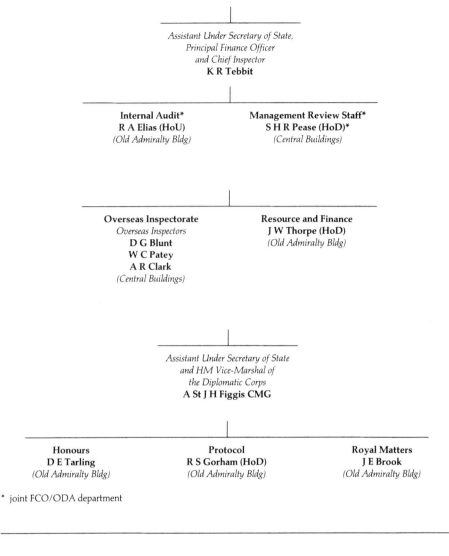

Assistant Under Secretary of State,
Principal Finance Officer
and Chief Inspector
K R Tebbit

Internal Audit*
R A Elias (HoU)
(Old Admiralty Bldg)

Management Review Staff*
S H R Pease (HoD)*
(Central Buildings)

Overseas Inspectorate
Overseas Inspectors
D G Blunt
W C Patey
A R Clark
(Central Buildings)

Resource and Finance
J W Thorpe (HoD)
(Old Admiralty Bldg)

Assistant Under Secretary of State
and HM Vice-Marshal of
the Diplomatic Corps
A St J H Figgis CMG

Honours
D E Tarling
(Old Admiralty Bldg)

Protocol
R S Gorham (HoD)
(Old Admiralty Bldg)

Royal Matters
J E Brook
(Old Admiralty Bldg)

* joint FCO/ODA department

Policy Planning; Europe; Eastern Adriatic; United Nations; Human Rights; Common Foreign and Security Policy

Permanent Under Secretary of State
Head of the Diplomatic Service
Sir John Coles KCMG

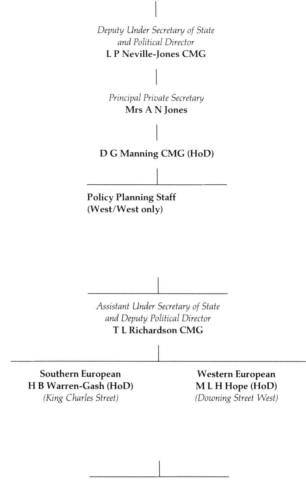

Deputy Under Secretary of State
and Political Director
L P Neville-Jones CMG

Principal Private Secretary
Mrs A N Jones

D G Manning CMG (HoD)

Policy Planning Staff
(West/West only)

Assistant Under Secretary of State
and Deputy Political Director
T L Richardson CMG

Southern European
H B Warren-Gash (HoD)
(King Charles Street)

Western European
M L H Hope (HoD)
(Downing Street West)

Assistant Under Secretary of State
S J L Wright

Common Foreign and
Security Policy
H J R Mortimer (HoD)
(Downing Street West)

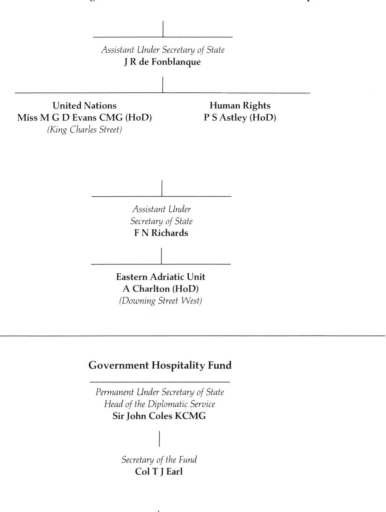

Assistant Under Secretary of State
J R de Fonblanque

United Nations
Miss M G D Evans CMG (HoD)
(King Charles Street)

Human Rights
P S Astley (HoD)

Assistant Under
Secretary of State
F N Richards

Eastern Adriatic Unit
A Charlton (HoD)
(Downing Street West)

Government Hospitality Fund

Permanent Under Secretary of State
Head of the Diplomatic Service
Sir John Coles KCMG

Secretary of the Fund
Col T J Earl

Government Hospitality Fund

Official hospitality for overseas ministerial visitors

Foreign and Commonwealth Office Addresses

For all fax numbers telephone the office concerned and ask for appropriate fax number

Apollo House
36 Wellesley Road
Croydon CR9 3RR
Tel 0181-686 5622

2/3/4 Central Buildings
Matthew Parker Street
London SW1H 9NL
Tel 0171-210 3000

Century House
Westminster Bridge Road
London SE1 7XF
Tel 0171-928 5600

Clive House
Petty France
London SW1H 9HD
Tel 0171-270 3000

Cornwall House
Stamford Street
London SE1 9NS
Tel 0171-211 3000

Cromwell House
Dean Stanley Street
London SW1P 3JG
Tel 0171-276 7676

Downing Street East
London SW1A 2AL
Tel 0171-270 3000

Downing Street West
London SW1A 2AL
Tel 0171-270 3000

Hanslope Park
Hanslope
Milton Keynes MK19 7BH
Tel 01908 510444

King Charles Street
London SW1A 2AL
Tel 0171-270 3000

Kingsgate House
66–74 Victoria Street
London SW1E 6SW
Tel 0171-215 5000

Old Admiralty Building
Whitehall
London SW1A 2AF
Tel 0171-210 3000

94 Victoria Street
London SW1E 5JL
Tel 0171-917 7000

Whitehall
London SW1A 2AP
Tel 0171-270 3000

24 Whitehall
London SW1A 2AF
Tel 0171-210 6058

Forestry Commission

Founded	1919
Ministers	Secretary of State for Scotland Minister of Agriculture, Fisheries and Food Secretary of State for Wales
Responsibilities	Administration of the woodland grant system Forestry research Management of the Commission's forest estate Regulation and monitoring standards in all forestry including the Forestry Enterprise
Number of staff	6650

Forestry Commission

231 Corstorphine Road, Edinburgh EH12 7AT
Tel 0131-334 0303 Fax 0131-334 3047, 0131-316 4891

All staff are based at Corstorphine Road unless otherwise indicated.
For other addresses and telephone numbers see the end of this section.

Ministers

Secretary of State for Scotland
The Rt Hon
Ian Lang MP
(for details of his office see Scottish Office)

Minister of Agriculture, Fisheries and Food
The Rt Hon
William Waldegrave MP
(for details of his office see MAFF)

Secretary of State for Wales
The Rt Hon
John Redwood MP
(for details of his office see Welsh Office)

Officials

Chairman, Executive Commissioner
Sir Peter Hutchison Bt CBE

Director General, Executive Commissioner
T R Cutler (2)

Secretary to the Commissioners
T J D Rollinson (5)

Executive Commissioners
D L Foot (3)
N A H McKerrow (3)
D S Grundy (3)

Non-Executive Commissioners
Robin Grove-White
John Edmonds
Harry Fetherstonhaugh
Bridget Bloom OBE
Terence Mallinson
Sir Michael Strang Steel Bt

Departmental Overview

Civil Servants			Department	Minister
Grade 1	*Grade 2*	*Grade 3*		
Chairman: Sir Peter Hutchison Bt CBE	T R Cutler	D L Foot	The Forestry Authority	All
		N A H McKerrow	Forest Enterprise*	All
		D S Grundy	Policy and Resources	All

*Forest Enterprise will become an Executive Agency late in 1995

Civil Servants and Departments

The Forestry Authority

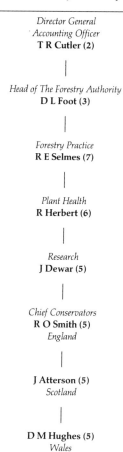

Director General
Accounting Officer
T R Cutler (2)

Head of The Forestry Authority
D L Foot (3)

Forestry Practice
R E Selmes (7)

Plant Health
R Herbert (6)

Research
J Dewar (5)

Chief Conservators
R O Smith (5)
England

J Atterson (5)
Scotland

D M Hughes (5)
Wales

Forest Enterprise

Director General and
Accounting Officer
T R Cutler (2)

Chief Executive
N A H McKerrow (3)

Enterprise Corporate Services
S E Quigley (5)

Estate Management
P C Ranken (5)

Business Enterprise
Dr R MacIntosh (5)

Regional Directors

G J Hamilton (5)
North Scotland

G M Cowie (5)
South Scotland

G R Hatfield (5)
North and East England

R J N Busby (5)
South and West England

J F Morgan (5)
Wales

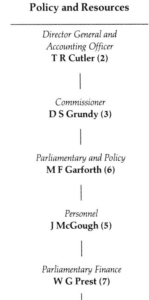

Policy and Resources

Director General and Accounting Officer
T R Cutler (2)

Commissioner
D S Grundy (3)

Parliamentary and Policy
M F Garforth (6)

Personnel
J McGough (5)

Parliamentary Finance
W G Prest (7)

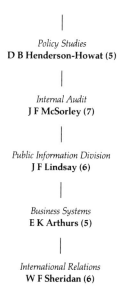

Policy Studies
D B Henderson-Howat (5)

Internal Audit
J F McSorley (7)

Public Information Division
J F Lindsay (6)

Business Systems
E K Arthurs (5)

International Relations
W F Sheridan (6)

Forestry Commission Addresses

Research

Alice Holt Lodge
Wrecclesham
Farnham
Surrey GU10 4LH
Tel 01420 22255
Fax 01420 23653

Northern Research Station
Roslin
Midlothian EH25 9SY
Tel 0131-445 2176
Fax 0131-445 5124

Forest Enterprise Regional Offices

North and East England Office
1a Grosvenor Terrace
York YO3 7BD
Tel 01904 620221
Fax 01904 610664

North Scotland Office
21 Church Street
Inverness IV1 1EL
Tel 01463 232811
Fax 01463 243846

South Scotland Office
55/57 Moffat Road
Dumfries DG1 1NP
Tel 01387 269171
Fax 01387 251491

South and West England Office
Avon Fields House
Somerdale
Keynsham
Bristol BS18 2BD
Tel 01179 869481
Fax 01179 861981

Wales Office
Victoria House
Victoria Terrace
Aberystwyth
Dyfed SY23 2DQ
Tel 01970 612367
Fax 01970 625282

The Forestry Authority National Offices

England Office
Great Eastern House
Tenison Road
Cambridge CB1 2DU
Tel 01223 314546
Fax 01223 460699

Scotland Office
Portcullis House
21 India Street
Glasgow G2 4PL
Tel 0141-248 3931
Fax 0141-226 5007

Wales Office
North Road
Aberystwyth
Dyfed SY23 2EF
Tel 01970 625866
Fax 01970 626177

Government Actuary's Department

Founded 1919

Status Established by Treasury Minute; for management purposes GAD is one of the departments for which the Chancellor of the Exchequer is responsible to Parliament. Ministerial responsibility currently rests with the Economic Secretary to the Treasury.

Responsibilities Consultancy service to government departments, the public sector and overseas governments

Advice on social security and occupational pension schemes, population and other studies

Advice on supervision of insurance companies and friendly societies and any actuarial matter

Number of staff 85

Government Actuary's Department

22 Kingsway, London WC2B 6LE
Tel 0171-242 6828   Fax 0171-831 6653

Minister

Minister of State,
Economic Secretary
Anthony Nelson MP
(for details of his office
see HM Treasury)

Officials

Government Actuary
C D Daykin CB (2)

Private Secretary
Mrs M Eskrick
0171-242 6828

Departmental Overview

Civil Servants		Directorate	Minister
Grade 2	*Grade 3*		
C D Daykin	D G Ballantine	Public Service Pensions	A Nelson*
	M A Pickford	Insurance Companies & Friendly Societies	A Nelson
	D H Loades	Social Security and Demography	A Nelson
	A C Beer (6)	Establishment and Accounts	A Nelson

* Currently the minister responsible to Parliament but the Department gives advice to any minister of home or overseas department

Civil Servants and Departments

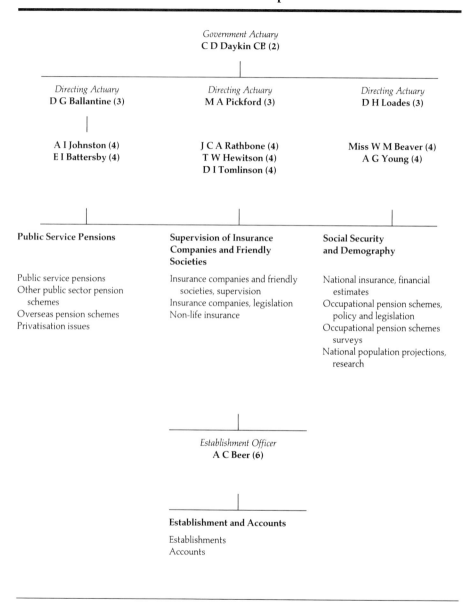

Government Actuary
C D Daykin CB (2)

Directing Actuary
D G Ballantine (3)

A I Johnston (4)
E I Battersby (4)

Directing Actuary
M A Pickford (3)

J C A Rathbone (4)
T W Hewitson (4)
D I Tomlinson (4)

Directing Actuary
D H Loades (3)

Miss W M Beaver (4)
A G Young (4)

Public Service Pensions

Public service pensions
Other public sector pension schemes
Overseas pension schemes
Privatisation issues

Supervision of Insurance Companies and Friendly Societies

Insurance companies and friendly societies, supervision
Insurance companies, legislation
Non-life insurance

Social Security and Demography

National insurance, financial estimates
Occupational pension schemes, policy and legislation
Occupational pension schemes surveys
National population projections, research

Establishment Officer
A C Beer (6)

Establishment and Accounts

Establishments
Accounts

Government Offices for the Regions

Established

The ten Government Offices for the Regions were established in April 1994, by combining the regional offices of the Departments of the Environment, Trade and Industry, Employment (Training) and Transport

Responsibilities

The Offices are responsible for administering the main regional programmes of the four departments, as well as programmes from the Home Office and the Department for Education in the regions. The Government Offices also administer the Single Regeneration Budget

Each regional director reports to the relevant secretary of state for each department's main programmes, and to the secretary of state for the environment for the single regeneration budget. Government Office staff remain members of their parent departments

The Government Offices Central Unit acts as a central coordinating point and secretariat for the Interdepartmental Management Board, which oversees the work of the Government Offices

Number of staff

Eastern	191
East Midlands	272
London	323
Merseyside	155
North East	303
North West	389
South East	236
South West	232
West Midlands	360
Yorkshire and Humberside	331
Total	2792

Government Offices for the Regions

Central Unit, Room N12/13, 2 Marsham Street, London SW1P 3EB
Tel 0171-276 4629 Fax 0171-276 3354
Addresses of all the regional offices can be found at the end of the section.

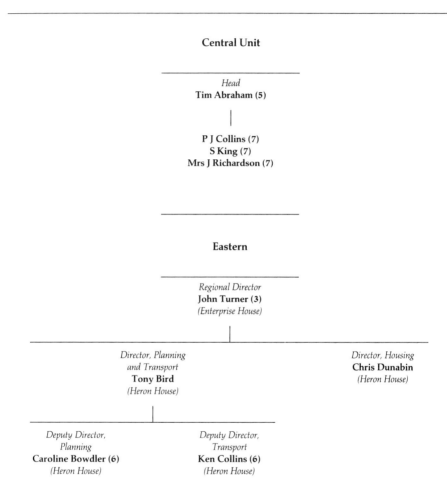

Central Unit

Head
Tim Abraham (5)

P J Collins (7)
S King (7)
Mrs J Richardson (7)

Eastern

Regional Director
John Turner (3)
(Enterprise House)

Director, Planning and Transport
Tony Bird
(Heron House)

Deputy Director, Planning
Caroline Bowdler (6)
(Heron House)

Deputy Director, Transport
Ken Collins (6)
(Heron House)

Director, Housing
Chris Dunabin
(Heron House)

Director, Employment and Training
Ms Celia Johnson (5)
(Victory House)

Director, Trade and Industry
Martin Oldham (5)

Deputy Director, Employment and Training
Mrs Carol Hunter (6)
(Victory House)

Deputy Director, Employment and Training
Peter Moss (6)
(Victory House)

Deputy Director, Trade and Industry
Rob Dennis (6)
(above 2 at Westbrook Centre)

East Midlands

Regional Director
Mark Lanyon (3)
(Cranbrook House)

Director, Environment and Transport
Dennis Morrison (4)
(Cranbrook House)

Assistant Director, Transport and Planning
Martin Gorman (6)
(Cranbrook House)

Assistant Director, Housing and Regeneration
Robert Smith (6)
(Cranbrook House)

Director, Trade and Industry
Martin Briggs (5)
(Severns House)

Director, Employment and Training
Alan Davies (5)

Assistant Director, Investment and Development
Graham Nevitte (6)
(Severns House)

Assistant Director, Exports and Enterprise
Roger Newell (6)
(Severns House)

Assistant Director, Training, Quality and Finance
Mrs Liz Lewis (6)
(above 2 at Castle Gate)

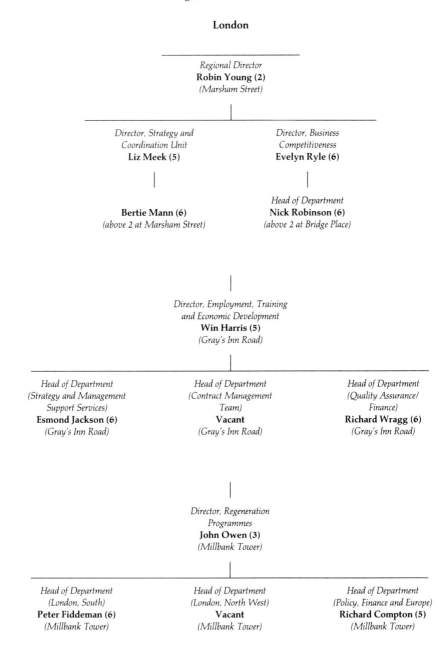

London

Regional Director
Robin Young (2)
(Marsham Street)

Director, Strategy and Coordination Unit
Liz Meek (5)

Bertie Mann (6)
(above 2 at Marsham Street)

Director, Business Competitiveness
Evelyn Ryle (6)

Head of Department
Nick Robinson (6)
(above 2 at Bridge Place)

Director, Employment, Training and Economic Development
Win Harris (5)
(Gray's Inn Road)

Head of Department (Strategy and Management Support Services)
Esmond Jackson (6)
(Gray's Inn Road)

Head of Department (Contract Management Team)
Vacant
(Gray's Inn Road)

Head of Department (Quality Assurance/ Finance)
Richard Wragg (6)
(Gray's Inn Road)

Director, Regeneration Programmes
John Owen (3)
(Millbank Tower)

Head of Department (London, South)
Peter Fiddeman (6)
(Millbank Tower)

Head of Department (London, North West)
Vacant
(Millbank Tower)

Head of Department (Policy, Finance and Europe)
Richard Compton (5)
(Millbank Tower)

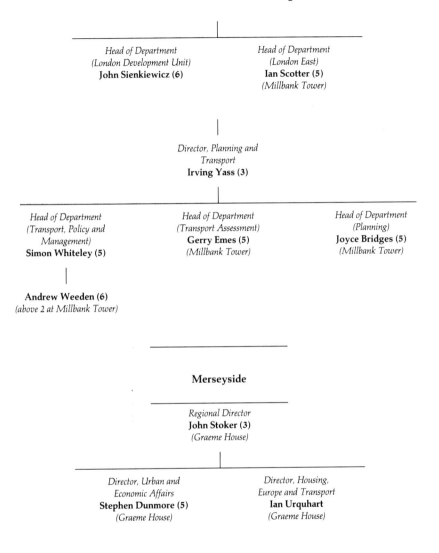

Head of Department
(London Development Unit)
John Sienkiewicz (6)

Head of Department
(London East)
Ian Scotter (5)
(Millbank Tower)

Director, Planning and Transport
Irving Yass (3)

Head of Department
(Transport, Policy and Management)
Simon Whiteley (5)

Andrew Weeden (6)
(above 2 at Millbank Tower)

Head of Department
(Transport Assessment)
Gerry Emes (5)
(Millbank Tower)

Head of Department
(Planning)
Joyce Bridges (5)
(Millbank Tower)

Merseyside

Regional Director
John Stoker (3)
(Graeme House)

Director, Urban and Economic Affairs
Stephen Dunmore (5)
(Graeme House)

Director, Housing, Europe and Transport
Ian Urquhart
(Graeme House)

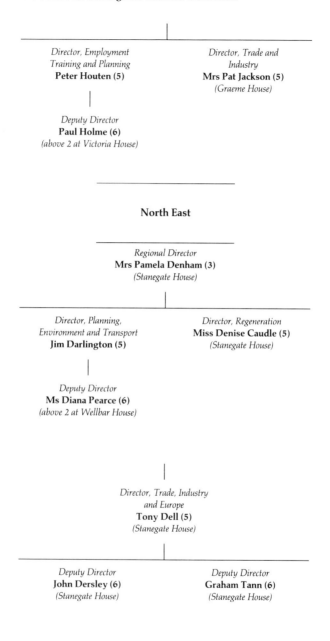

Director, Employment Training and Planning
Peter Houten (5)

Deputy Director
Paul Holme (6)
(above 2 at Victoria House)

Director, Trade and Industry
Mrs Pat Jackson (5)
(Graeme House)

North East

Regional Director
Mrs Pamela Denham (3)
(Stanegate House)

Director, Planning, Environment and Transport
Jim Darlington (5)

Deputy Director
Ms Diana Pearce (6)
(above 2 at Wellbar House)

Director, Regeneration
Miss Denise Caudle (5)
(Stanegate House)

Director, Trade, Industry and Europe
Tony Dell (5)
(Stanegate House)

Deputy Director
John Dersley (6)
(Stanegate House)

Deputy Director
Graham Tann (6)
(Stanegate House)

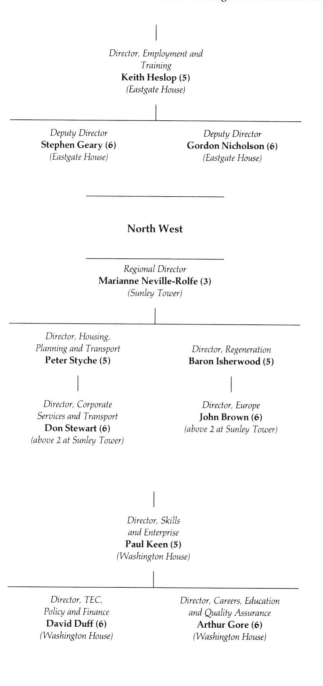

Director, Employment and Training
Keith Heslop (5)
(Eastgate House)

Deputy Director
Stephen Geary (6)
(Eastgate House)

Deputy Director
Gordon Nicholson (6)
(Eastgate House)

North West

Regional Director
Marianne Neville-Rolfe (3)
(Sunley Tower)

Director, Housing, Planning and Transport
Peter Styche (5)

Director, Corporate Services and Transport
Don Stewart (6)
(above 2 at Sunley Tower)

Director, Regeneration
Baron Isherwood (5)

Director, Europe
John Brown (6)
(above 2 at Sunley Tower)

Director, Skills and Enterprise
Paul Keen (5)
(Washington House)

Director, TEC, Policy and Finance
David Duff (6)
(Washington House)

Director, Careers, Education and Quality Assurance
Arthur Gore (6)
(Washington House)

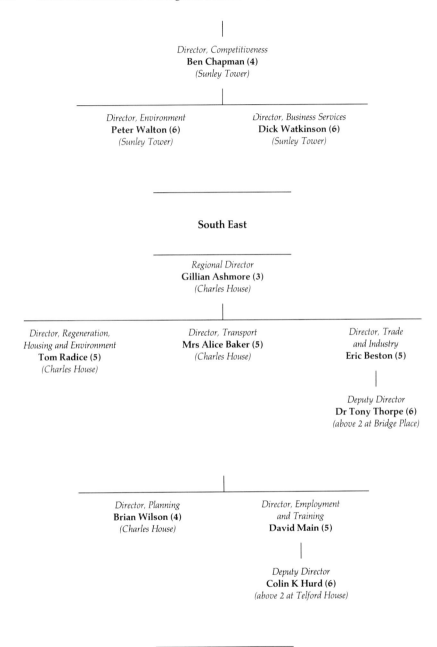

Director, Competitiveness
Ben Chapman (4)
(Sunley Tower)

Director, Environment
Peter Walton (6)
(Sunley Tower)

Director, Business Services
Dick Watkinson (6)
(Sunley Tower)

South East

Regional Director
Gillian Ashmore (3)
(Charles House)

Director, Regeneration, Housing and Environment
Tom Radice (5)
(Charles House)

Director, Transport
Mrs Alice Baker (5)
(Charles House)

Director, Trade and Industry
Eric Beston (5)

Deputy Director
Dr Tony Thorpe (6)
(above 2 at Bridge Place)

Director, Planning
Brian Wilson (4)
(Charles House)

Director, Employment and Training
David Main (5)

Deputy Director
Colin K Hurd (6)
(above 2 at Telford House)

South West

Regional Director
Brian Leonard (3)
(The Pithay)

Director, Employment and Training
Wendy Mauger (5)

Assistant Director
David Way (6)
(above 2 at The Pithay)

Director, Environment and Transport
Matthew Quinn (5)
(Tollgate House)

Deputy Director, Regeneration and Housing
Peter Botham (6)

Deputy Director, Planning
Peter Girling (6)

Deputy Director, Transport
David Woods (6)

Deputy Director, Regional Energy Efficiency Office
Robert Anthony (6)
(above 4 at Tollgate House)

Director, Trade and Industry
John Bowder (5)

Deputy Director
Wilfred Smith (6)
(above 2 at The Pithay)

Director, Devon and Cornwall
Steve McQuillin (5)

Deputy Director,
Steve Brooking (6)
(above 2 at Phoenix House)

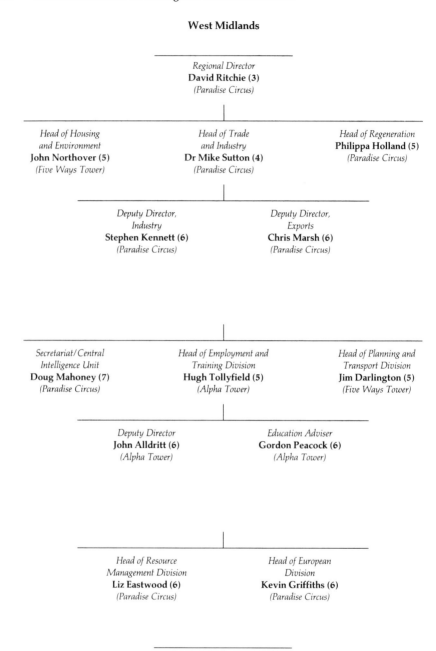

West Midlands

Regional Director
David Ritchie (3)
(Paradise Circus)

Head of Housing and Environment
John Northover (5)
(Five Ways Tower)

Head of Trade and Industry
Dr Mike Sutton (4)
(Paradise Circus)

Head of Regeneration
Philippa Holland (5)
(Paradise Circus)

Deputy Director, Industry
Stephen Kennett (6)
(Paradise Circus)

Deputy Director, Exports
Chris Marsh (6)
(Paradise Circus)

Secretariat/Central Intelligence Unit
Doug Mahoney (7)
(Paradise Circus)

Head of Employment and Training Division
Hugh Tollyfield (5)
(Alpha Tower)

Head of Planning and Transport Division
Jim Darlington (5)
(Five Ways Tower)

Deputy Director
John Alldritt (6)
(Alpha Tower)

Education Adviser
Gordon Peacock (6)
(Alpha Tower)

Head of Resource Management Division
Liz Eastwood (6)
(Paradise Circus)

Head of European Division
Kevin Griffiths (6)
(Paradise Circus)

Yorkshire and Humberside

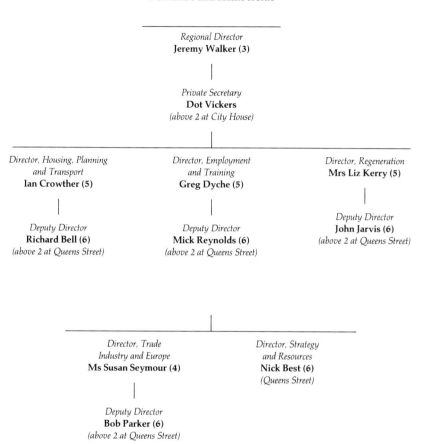

Regional Director
Jeremy Walker (3)

Private Secretary
Dot Vickers
(above 2 at City House)

Director, Housing, Planning and Transport
Ian Crowther (5)

Deputy Director
Richard Bell (6)
(above 2 at Queens Street)

Director, Employment and Training
Greg Dyche (5)

Deputy Director
Mick Reynolds (6)
(above 2 at Queens Street)

Director, Regeneration
Mrs Liz Kerry (5)

Deputy Director
John Jarvis (6)
(above 2 at Queens Street)

Director, Trade Industry and Europe
Ms Susan Seymour (4)

Deputy Director
Bob Parker (6)
(above 2 at Queens Street)

Director, Strategy and Resources
Nick Best (6)
(Queens Street)

Government Offices for the Regions Addresses

Eastern

Unit 7
Enterprise House
Vision Park
Histon
Cambridge CB4 4ZR
Tel 01223 202069
Fax 01223 202066

Heron House
49-53 Goldington Road
Bedford MK40 3LL
Tel 01234 363161
Fax, Tel the above number and ask for fax number

Victory House
Vision Park
Cambridge CB4 4DZ
Tel 01234 202000
Fax, Tel the above number and ask for fax number

Building A
Westbrook Centre
Milton Road
Cambridge CB4 1YG
Tel 01223 461939
Fax, Tel the above number and ask for fax number

East Midlands
21-23 Castle Gate
Nottingham NG1 7AQ
Tel 01159 410360
Fax 01159 581378

Cranbrook House
Cranbrook Street
Nottingham NG1 1EY
Tel 01159 935 2355
Fax, Tel the above number and ask for fax number

Severns House
Middle Pavement
Nottingham NG1 7DW
Tel 01159 506181
Fax 01159 587074

London
Bridge Place
88-89 Eccleston Square
London SW1V 1PT
Tel 0171-215 0585
Fax, Tel the above number and ask for fax number

236 Gray's Inn Road
London WC1X 8HL
Tel 0171-211 4221
Fax, Tel the above number and ask for fax number

2 Marsham Street
London SW1P 3EB
Tel 0171-276 5825
Fax 0171-276 5827

Millbank Tower
21-24 Millbank
London SW1P 4QU
Tel 0171-217 4529
Fax, Tel the above number and ask for fax number

Merseyside
Graeme House
Derby Square
Liverpool L2 7SU
Tel 0151-227 4111 (ext 6302)
Fax 0151-236 1199

Victoria House
James Street
Liverpool L2 7NX
Tel 0151-227 4111 (ext 2509)
Fax 0151-236 3391

North East
Eastgate House
Kings Manor
Newcastle upon Tyne NE1 6PA
Tel 0191-235 7000
Fax 0191-235 7002

Stanegate House
2 Groat Market
Newcastle upon Tyne NE1 1YN
Tel 0191-235 4722
Fax 0191-235 7798

Wellbar House
Gallowgate
Newcastle upon Tyne NE1 4TD
Tel 0191-201 3955
Fax 0191-201 3480

North West
Sunley Tower
Piccadilly Plaza
Manchester M1 4BA
Tel 0161-952 4000
Fax, Tel the above number and ask for fax number

Washington House
New Bailey Street
Manchester M3 5ER
Tel 0161-837 7038
Fax 0161-834 4374

South East
Bridge Place
88-89 Eccleston Square
London SW1V 1PT
Tel 0171-215 5000
Fax, Tel the above number and ask for fax number

Charles House
375 Kensington High Street
London W14 8QH
Tel 01345 125431
Fax, Tel the above number and ask for fax number

Telford House
Hamilton Close
Basingstoke
Hampshire RG21 2UZ
Tel 01256 799274
Fax, Tel the above number and ask for fax number

South West
Phoenix House
Notte Street
Plymouth PL1 2HF
Tel 01752 221891
Fax 01752 226658

4th/5th Floor
The Pithay
Bristol BS1 2NQ
Tel 01179 272666
Fax, Tel the above number and ask for fax number

Tollgate House
Houlton Street
Bristol BS2 9DJ
Tel 01179 878000
Fax, Tel the above number and ask for fax number

West Midlands
Alpha Tower
Suffolk Street
Queensway
Birmingham B1 1UR
Tel 0121-631 3555
Fax, Tel the above number and ask for fax number

Five Ways Tower
Frederick Road
Birmingham B15 1SJ
Tel 0121-626 2000
Fax, Tel the above number and ask for fax number

77 Paradise Circus
Queensway
Birmingham B1 2DT
Tel 0121-212 5050
Fax 0121-212 1010

Yorkshire and Humberside
City House
New Station Street
Leeds LS1 4JD
Tel 01132 800600
Fax, Tel the above number and ask for fax number

25 Queen Street
Leeds LS1 2TW
Tel 01132 443171
Fax, Tel the above number and ask for fax number

Department of Health

Founded	1948 as the Ministry of Health. In 1968 it became the Department of Health and Social Security and split to form separate departments in 1989
Ministers	one secretary of state, one minister of state, three parliamentary under secretaries
Responsibilities	National Health Service public health reciprocal health arrangements with other countries social services provided by local authorities for elderly and handicapped people, socially deprived families and children in care
Number of staff	5101
Executive agencies	Medical Devices Agency Medicines Control Agency NHS Estates NHS Pensions Agency

Department of Health

Richmond House, 79 Whitehall, London SW1A 2NS
Tel 0171-210 3000 Fax 0171-210 5523

All staff are based at Richmond House unless otherwise indicated.
For other addresses and telephone numbers see the end of this section.

Ministers

Secretary of State
The Rt Hon Virgina Bottomley JP MP

Parliamentary Private Secretary
Keith Mans MP

Special Adviser
R J Marsh

Principal Private Secretary
Clare Moriarty (5)
0171-210 5157

Minister of State
Gerald Malone MP

Special Adviser
Tony Hockley*

Parliamentary Private Secretary
Peter Butler MP

Private Secretary
Andy Taylor (7)
0171-210 5105

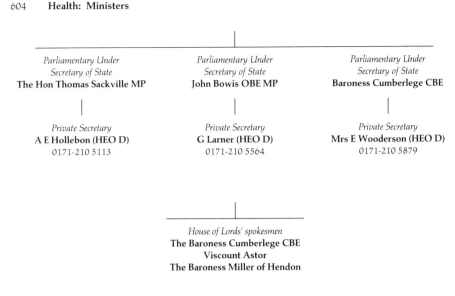

Parliamentary Under Secretary of State
The Hon Thomas Sackville MP

Private Secretary
A E Hollebon (HEO D)
0171-210 5113

Parliamentary Under Secretary of State
John Bowis OBE MP

Private Secretary
G Larner (HEO D)
0171-210 5564

Parliamentary Under Secretary of State
Baroness Cumberlege CBE

Private Secretary
Mrs E Wooderson (HEO D)
0171-210 5879

House of Lords' spokesmen
The Baroness Cumberlege CBE
Viscount Astor
The Baroness Miller of Hendon

*Tony Hockley also supports all the PUSs

Ministers' Responsibilities

Virginia Bottomley

Overall responsibility for the department
NHS Review
Office of Population Censuses and Surveys

Gerald Malone

Community health councils
Complaints and disciplinary issues
European Union and international affairs
General dental services
General medical services
General ophthalmic services
GP fundholding
Health Education Authority
Health exports
Junior doctors' hours
London
Medical and dental manpower and education
NHS appointments (overview; N and S Thames, Trent and W Midlands)
NHS general
  management
  pay and personnel
Patients' Charter
Pharmaceutical services and NHS drugs bill
Primary care services
Purchasing
Research
Tobacco advertising controls
Waiting lists

John Bowis

Alcohol abuse
Children's services/YTS
Community care
Drug abuse
All services for elderly, mentally ill, people with learning difficulties, disabled (including sensorily disabled)
Homeless people
NHS appointments (Anglia and Oxford, South West)
Personal social services
Special hospitals
Voluntary sector (including section 64 grants)

Tom Sackville

Abortion
Acute services (including cancer)
Ambulances
Blood
Capital investment
Civil defence
Confidentiality
Crown immunity
Clinical Standards Advisory Group
Deregulation
DoH management (including Next Steps)
Family planning
Human Fertilisation and Embryology Authority
Hospital security
Income generation
Information: systems and IT
Laboratories
Medicines Control Agency
NHS appointments (N West, Northern and Yorkshire)
- casework
- closures
- mergers
- "approvals in principle" of capital projects
- trusts

NHS Estates
OPCS
Pharmaceutical industry
Private finance initiative
Private sector
Statistics
Supplies
Transplantation
Value for money/competitive tendering

Baroness Cumberlege

AIDS/HIV
Alternative therapies
Environmental health
Ethnic issues
Food hygiene
Green issues
Health of the Nation
Health education and promotion
Health strategy
Hospices
Hospital chaplaincy
Infectious diseases
Inner cities

Nursing
Nutrition
Opportunity 2000
Professions allied to medicine
Public health
Smoking
Vaccine damage
Women's health (including maternity services, breast and cervical cancer services including screening)

Departmental Overview

Grade 1	Civil Servants: Grade 2	Grade 3	Department	Minister
	Departmental Resources and Services			
G Hart	J Pilling	A B Barton	Finance Division	T Sackville/ G Malone
		D Clark	Departmental Management Division	G Malone
		C Smee	Economics and Operational Research Division	T Sackville
		Mrs R J Butler	Statistics Division	T Sackville
		Dr A Holt (4)	Information Services Directorate	T Sackville
	Reports directly to Mr Hart	Ms R Christopherson (4)	Information Division	T Sackville
		J Barnes	Industry and International Division	G Malone
		N Boyd	Policy Management Unit	T Sackville
	Public Health Group			
G Hart and Dr K Calman	Dr J Metters	G Podger	Health Promotion	Baroness Cumberlege
		Dr E Rubery	Health Aspects of Environment and Food	Baroness Cumberlege
	Social Care Group			
G Hart		T R H Luce	Social Care Policy	J Bowis
		W H Laming	Social Services Inspectorate	J Bowis

Departmental Overview

Grade 1	Civil Servants Grade 2	Grade 3	Department	Minister
	NHS Executive			
A Langlands* and G Hart	Dr G Winyard**	Dr P Bourdillon	Specialist Clinical Services	G Malone
		Dr R Hangartner	Medical Education, Training and Staffing	G Malone
		Dr T Mann (4)	Public Health	Baroness Cumberlege
		Prof M Peckham	Research and Development	G Malone
		Mrs Y Moores**	Nursing	Baroness Cumberlege
	K W Jarrold	R M Drury	NHS Personnel	G Malone
		J M Rogers	NHS Personnel NHS Women's Unit NHS Training Directorate	G Malone
	J F Shaw	R T Rogers	Corporate Affairs Directorate/ Information Management Group	G Malone/ T. Sackville
	C Reeves*	P Garland B Marsden	Finance and Corporate Information	T Sackville/ G Malone
	A Liddell	R B Mouatt Dr S Adam A McKeon Dr R J Williams	Planning, Primary Care, Coummunity Care Directorate	T Sackville
	Solicitor's Office (part of Department of Social Security)			
G Hart	P K J Thompson	A D Roberts	Solicitor's Office	

* *On secondment from outside the Civil Service so do not have grades.*

** *Also responsible to Chief Medical Officer.*

Civil Servants and Departments

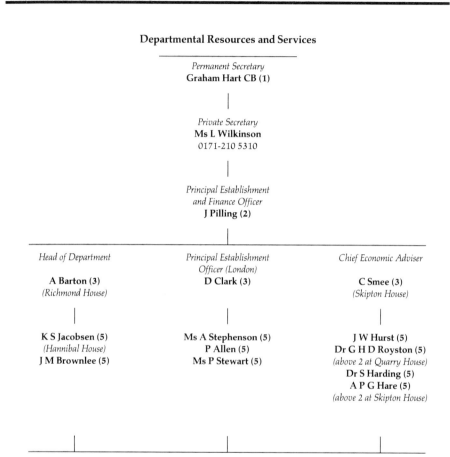

Departmental Resources and Services

Permanent Secretary
Graham Hart CB (1)

Private Secretary
Ms L Wilkinson
0171-210 5310

Principal Establishment and Finance Officer
J Pilling (2)

Head of Department
A Barton (3)
(Richmond House)

K S Jacobsen (5)
(Hannibal House)
J M Brownlee (5)

Principal Establishment Officer (London)
D Clark (3)

Ms A Stephenson (5)
P Allen (5)
Ms P Stewart (5)

Chief Economic Adviser
C Smee (3)
(Skipton House)

J W Hurst (5)
Dr G H D Royston (5)
(above 2 at Quarry House)
Dr S Harding (5)
A P G Hare (5)
(above 2 at Skipton House)

Finance Division

Supply estimates and appropriation accounts (HPSS)
Family health services
Centrally financed services
Departmental administrations' expenditure, investment, appraisals, personal social services
Local authority expenditure
Internal audit and accountancy services
Finance liaison for agencies

Departmental Management Division (London)

Personnel management
Corporate and manpower planning
Staff development
Facilities management
Next Steps and Citizen's Charter
Office services

Economics and Operational Research Division

Economic support and operational research studies

Director
Mrs R J Butler (3)
(Skipton House)
(also reports to J Shaw)

Mrs J Nash (5)
R K Willmer (5)
G J O Phillpotts (5)
Ms G Eastabrook (5)
(all above at Skipton House)

Statistics Division

Provision of statistics, management information and statistical analysis
Remuneration manpower statistics of general dental, pharmaceutical and ophthalmic services, prescription analysis, health service activities, preventative and environmental health, demographic, population, personal social services
Key indicators of local authority social services
Statistical publications
Social surveys

Director
Dr A Holt (4)
(Skipton House)

J Bilsby (5)
(Skipton House)
M O'Rourke (5)
(Hannibal House)
Miss S Blackburn (6)
C Horsey (6)
Mrs L Wishart (ISO) (6)
(above 3 at Skipton House)
A N Beer
(Hannibal House)

Information Services

Information systems
Library services
Information development centre
Telecommunications and office systems services

Director
Ms R Christopherson (4)
(reports directly to G Hart)

C P Wilson (6)
(Richmond House)
Mrs A Rea (6)
(Skipton House and Richmond House)

Information Division

Liaison with press, radio and television
Production and distribution of publicity material, promotion of publicity campaigns

Head of Division
J H Barnes (3)
(Richmond House)

Head of Unit
Dr W J Burroughs (4)
(Richmond House)

Head of Policy Management Unit
N Boyd (5)
(Richmond House)

S J Furniss (5)
M Brown (5)
Dr W Thorne (5)
D Bellamy (5)
(Above 4 at Richmond House)

Industry and International Division

International relations (health)
Relations with European Community, World Health Organisation and other international agencies
Bilateral health agreements
Pharmaceutical price regulation scheme
Sponshorship of the pharmaceutical industry
EC pharmaceutical pricing

Policy Management Unit

Public Health Group

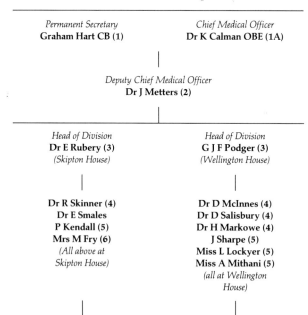

Permanent Secretary
Graham Hart CB (1)

Chief Medical Officer
Dr K Calman OBE (1A)

Deputy Chief Medical Officer
Dr J Metters (2)

Head of Division
Dr E Rubery (3)
(Skipton House)

Dr R Skinner (4)
Dr E Smales
P Kendall (5)
Mrs M Fry (6)
(All above at Skipton House)

Head of Division
G J F Podger (3)
(Wellington House)

Dr D McInnes (4)
Dr D Salisbury (4)
Dr H Markowe (4)
J Sharpe (5)
Miss L Lockyer (5)
Miss A Mithani (5)
(all at Wellington House)

Health Aspects of Environment and Food

Microbiology of the environment and food
Biotechnology
Nutrition
Welfare foods
Management of NDPBs
Aspects of public health
Environmental pollution (excluding radiation)
Information unit
Radiation
Food and chemical safety
Consumer products

Health Promotion

Health of the nation
Ethnic health
Substance misuse
Communicable diseases (excluding food and waterborne)
Immunisation
Abortion
Embryology
Sexual health
Child health
Ethics

Social Care Group

Permanent Secretary
Graham Hart CB (1)

Chief Inspector
W H Laming CBE (3)
(Richmond House)

D C Brand (4)
(also reports to Head of Social Care Policy)
Miss C M Hey (4)
(above 2 at Richmond House)
Mrs W Rose (5)
J G Smith (5)
F Tolan (5)
J Kennedy (5)
(all at Wellington House)

Under Secretary
T R H Luce (3)
(Wellington House)

R M Orton (5)
R Tyrell (5)
N Duncan (5)
E Hunter Johnston (5)
D P Walden (5)
(all at Wellington House)

Social Services Inspectorate

Inspection division
Regional social services inspectorates
Information and research
Assistant chief inspector-led regional business units
Analytical and information unit
Social services training
Joint reviews

Social Care Policy

General social services policy
Children's residential care
Secure accommodation
Juvenile justice
General community care
Elderly social care
Disabilities
Mental illness
Deprivation issues

NHS Executive

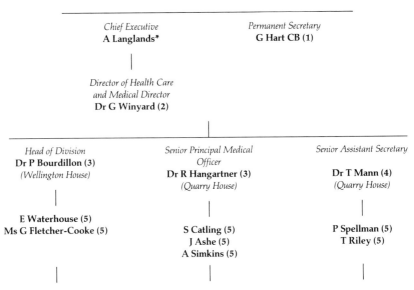

Chief Executive
A Langlands*

Permanent Secretary
G Hart CB (1)

Director of Health Care and Medical Director
Dr G Winyard (2)

Head of Division
Dr P Bourdillon (3)
(Wellington House)

E Waterhouse (5)
Ms G Fletcher-Cooke (5)

Senior Principal Medical Officer
Dr R Hangartner (3)
(Quarry House)

S Catling (5)
J Ashe (5)
A Simkins (5)

Senior Assistant Secretary
Dr T Mann (4)
(Quarry House)

P Spellman (5)
T Riley (5)

Specialist Clinical Services

Clinical Services A:
- Supra regional services
- cancer
- transplants
- surgery
- emergencies

Clinical Services B:
- maternity and services for women
- children's services
- medicine
- pathology
- imaging
- pharmacy
- head and neck services

Medical Education, Training and Staffing

Medical workforce planning
EC medical directives
Medical education regulation

Public Health

Clinical effectiveness and audit
"Health of the Nation"
Public health in the NHS
Guidelines and health outcomes
Public health aspects of primary care-led purchasing
Ethnic health
Occupational health

Director

Prof M Peckham
(Richmond House)

Deputy Director
Professor G Smith
(Skipton House/Quarry House)
Mrs B Soper (5)
Mrs J Griffin (5)
(above 2 at Skipton House)
Dr C Henshall (5)
(Quarry House)
Dr P Greenaway (5)
(Skipton House/Quarry House)

Chief Nursing Officer and Director of Nursing NHSME
Mrs Y Moores (3)
(Richmond House)

Dr G Chapman (5)
(above 3 at Quarry House)
J Tait (4)
M Hill (5)
(above 2 at Richmond House)

Research and Development

Development of departmental research and development strategy
Responsibility for research and development in health and personal social services
Content of NHS programme and framework

Nursing Directorate

Nursing
Midwifery
Health visiting services
Monitor scale and provision of nursing services
Nurse training and education
Clinical effectiveness/practise/audit
Professional and corporate management
Nursing services in NHS Executive

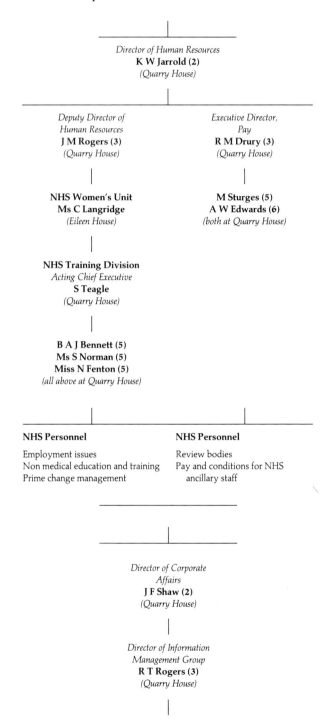

Director of Human Resources
K W Jarrold (2)
(Quarry House)

Deputy Director of Human Resources
J M Rogers (3)
(Quarry House)

NHS Women's Unit
Ms C Langridge
(Eileen House)

NHS Training Division
Acting Chief Executive
S Teagle
(Quarry House)

B A J Bennett (5)
Ms S Norman (5)
Miss N Fenton (5)
(all above at Quarry House)

Executive Director, Pay
R M Drury (3)
(Quarry House)

M Sturges (5)
A W Edwards (6)
(both at Quarry House)

NHS Personnel

Employment issues
Non medical education and training
Prime change management

NHS Personnel

Review bodies
Pay and conditions for NHS ancillary staff

Director of Corporate Affairs
J F Shaw (2)
(Quarry House)

Director of Information Management Group
R T Rogers (3)
(Quarry House)

Deputy Director of Corporate Affairs
Miss I Nisbet (4)

C Kenny (5)
Dr R Moore (5)
I Smith (5)
M A O'Flynn (5)
I G Nicholls (5)
Dr G Royston (5)
R Schofield (5)
(all above at Quarry House)

Corporate Affairs Directorate/Information Management Group

NHS Executive secretariat
Quality and consumers
Information management group of the NHS Executive
Intelligence unit
Operational policy
Business planning and budgets

Director of Finance and Corporate Information and NHS Performance
C Reeves*

Deputy Director Finance
P Garland (3)

Deputy Director Finance
B Marsden (3)

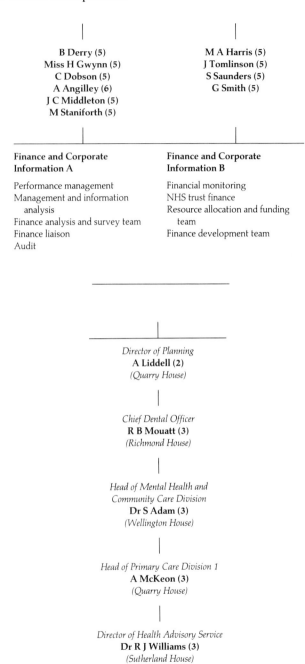

B Derry (5)
Miss H Gwynn (5)
C Dobson (5)
A Angilley (6)
J C Middleton (5)
M Staniforth (5)

M A Harris (5)
J Tomlinson (5)
S Saunders (5)
G Smith (5)

Finance and Corporate Information A

Performance management
Management and information analysis
Finance analysis and survey team
Finance liaison
Audit

Finance and Corporate Information B

Financial monitoring
NHS trust finance
Resource allocation and funding team
Finance development team

Director of Planning
A Liddell (2)
(Quarry House)

Chief Dental Officer
R B Mouatt (3)
(Richmond House)

Head of Mental Health and Community Care Division
Dr S Adam (3)
(Wellington House)

Head of Primary Care Division 1
A McKeon (3)
(Quarry House)

Director of Health Advisory Service
Dr R J Williams (3)
(Sutherland House)

B H Hartley (4)
(Richmond House)
Dr R Jenkins (4)
(Wellington House)
Dr P A Leech (4)
(Quarry House)
J A Thompson (4)
(Richmond House)
D Franklin (4)

Professor I Williams (5)
Mrs H McCallum (5)
W J A McCarthy (5)
D Hewlett (5)
B Slater (5)
Mrs L Wolstenholme (5)
(above 7 at Quarry House)
C Audrey (5)
I Copper (5)
K Eaton (5)
S Alcock (5)
(above 4 at Richmond House)
I Jewesbury (5)
A M McCulloch (5)
(above 2 at Wellington House)

Planning, Primary Care and NHS Community Care Directorate

Communications
Oversight of the NHS internal market
NHS policy and executive boards secretariat
General medical services including GP fundholding
NHS purchasing
Prescribing
Dental services
Pharmaceutical and opthalmic services
Prescription charges and fraud
Mental health policy and services
NHS community care
Health advisory service
Mental health review tribunals
Economic regulation

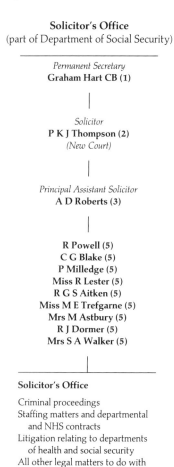

Solicitor's Office

(part of Department of Social Security)

Permanent Secretary
Graham Hart CB (1)

Solicitor
P K J Thompson (2)
(New Court)

Principal Assistant Solicitor
A D Roberts (3)

R Powell (5)
C G Blake (5)
P Milledge (5)
Miss R Lester (5)
R G S Aitken (5)
Miss M E Trefgarne (5)
Mrs M Astbury (5)
R J Dormer (5)
Mrs S A Walker (5)

Solicitor's Office

Criminal proceedings
Staffing matters and departmental and NHS contracts
Litigation relating to departments of health and social security
All other legal matters to do with health and personal social services

* on secondment from outside the Civil Service

Department of Health Addresses

For fax numbers, please phone the switchboard and ask for the relevant fax number

Adelphi
1-11 John Street
London WC2N 6HT
Tel 0171-962 8000

Eileen House
80–94 Newington Causeway
London SE1 6EF
Tel 0171-972 2000

Hannibal House
Elephant and Castle
London SE1 6TE
Tel 0171-972 2000

Market Towers
1 Nine Elms Lane
London SW8 5NQ
Tel 0171-720 2188

Millbank Tower
21–24 Millbank
London SW1P 4QU
Tel 0171-972 8505

New Court
48 Carey Street
London WC2A 2LS
Tel 0171-831 6111

Quarry House
Quarry Hill
Leeds LS2 7UE
Tel 01132 545000

Russell Square House
14 Russell Square
London WC1B 5EP
Tel 0171-636 6811

Skipton House
80 London Road
Elephant and Castle
London SE1 6LW
Tel 0171 972 2000

Wellington House
133–135 Waterloo Road
London SE1 8UG
Tel 0171-972 2000

Home Office

Founded	1782
Ministers	Home Secretary, three ministers of state and one parliamentary under secretary of state
Responsibilities	animal welfare Channel Islands/Isle of Man charities law civil defence community relations and inner cities coroners cremations and burials criminal injuries compensation scheme criminal law criminal policy data protection drugs electoral matters exhumations extradition fire safety in theatres and cinemas fire services firearms gaming and lotteries immigration liquor licensing local legislation/bye-laws marriage nationality passports police prisons probation and aftercare race relations refugees resettlement Royal matters shops summer time voluntary organisations

Number of staff	9627
Executive agencies	Forensic Science Service UK Passport Agency Fire Service College HM Prison Service

Home Office

50 Queen Anne's Gate, London SW1H 9AT
Tel 0171-273 3000 Fax 0171-273 2190

All personnel are based at 50 Queen Anne's Gate unless otherwise indicated.
For other addresses and telephone numbers see end of Home Office section.

Ministers

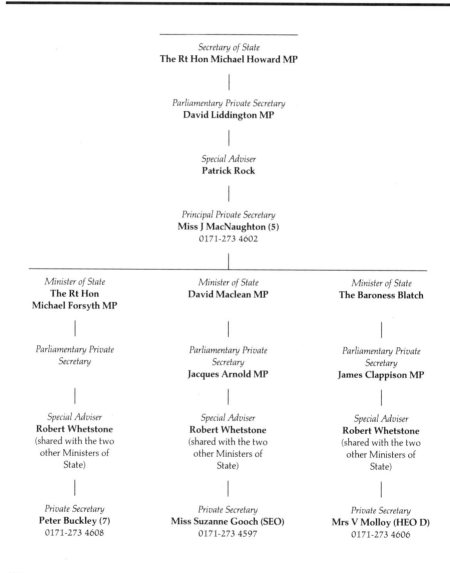

Secretary of State
The Rt Hon Michael Howard MP

Parliamentary Private Secretary
David Liddington MP

Special Adviser
Patrick Rock

Principal Private Secretary
Miss J MacNaughton (5)
0171-273 4602

Minister of State
The Rt Hon Michael Forsyth MP

Parliamentary Private Secretary

Special Adviser
Robert Whetstone
(shared with the two other Ministers of State)

Private Secretary
Peter Buckley (7)
0171-273 4608

Minister of State
David Maclean MP

Parliamentary Private Secretary
Jacques Arnold MP

Special Adviser
Robert Whetstone
(shared with the two other Ministers of State)

Private Secretary
Miss Suzanne Gooch (SEO)
0171-273 4597

Minister of State
The Baroness Blatch

Parliamentary Private Secretary
James Clappison MP

Special Adviser
Robert Whetstone
(shared with the two other Ministers of State)

Private Secretary
Mrs V Molloy (HEO D)
0171-273 4606

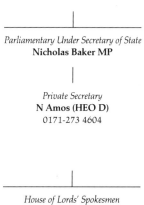

Parliamentary Under Secretary of State
Nicholas Baker MP

Private Secretary
N Amos (HEO D)
0171-273 4604

House of Lords' Spokesmen
The Baroness Blatch
The Lord Rodger of Earlsferry
The Baroness Trumpington

Ministerial Responsibilities

Michael Howard	Overall responsibility for department Deals personally with: Emergencies Establishment Finance and manpower Legal adviser's branch Royal matters Security
Michael Forsyth	Deregulation Drugs European matters Gambling Life sentences Liquor licensing Mentally disordered offenders Prisons Shops and Sunday trading
David Mclean	Criminal policy Crime prevention Police
The Baroness Blatch	Animals Bye-laws Channel Islands/Isle of Man Charities Coroners Cults Data protection and privacy Electoral law Emergency Planning Fire service Green issues Obscenity Probation and aftercare Race and community relations Summertime Voluntary sector Women's issues Departmental spokesman in the House of Lords

Nicholas Baker	Extradition Immigration and nationality Miscarriages of justice Passports Refugee resettlement UK Central Authority (clearing house for enquiries from judicial authorities in other countries) Departmental spokesman in the House of Commons on matters for which Lady Blatch is responsible

Departmental Overview

	Civil Servants		Department	Minister
Grade 1	*Grade 2*	*Grade 3*		
	Criminal, Research and Statistics Department and Constitutional Division			
Richard Wilson	J F Halliday	J M Lyon	Criminal Policy	D Maclean N Baker
		R M Morris	Criminal Justice and Constitutional	M Forsyth Ly Blatch N Baker
		C P Nuttall	Research and Statistics	
	Prisons†			
Richard Wilson		His Honour Judge Stephen Tumim	HM Chief Inspector of Prisons	M Forsyth
	Fire and Emergency Planning			
Richard Wilson	T C Platt	A P Wilson	Fire and Emergency Planning	Ly Blatch N Baker
		B Collins	HM Fire Service Inspectorate	Ly Blatch N Baker
	Personnel, Office Services and Finance			
Richard Wilson	T C Platt	Miss P Drew	Personnel and Office Services	M Howard
		S G Norris	Finance Information Technology	M Howard
		M Granatt (4)	Public Relations	
	Police			
Richard Wilson	S W Boys-Smith	Miss C Sinclair	Police	D Maclean
		C L Scoble	Police	D Maclean
		C Walters	Police: Science and Technology	D Maclean
		F J A Warne	Police	D Maclean
		T Morris	HM Inspectorate of Constabulary	D Maclean
	Legal Adviser's Branch			
Richard Wilson	Michael Saunders CB	D Seymour	Principal Assistant Legal Adviser	M Howard
		D J Bentley	Principal Assistant Legal Adviser	M Howard

Departmental Overview

	Civil Servants		Department	Minister
Grade 1	*Grade 2*	*Grade 3*		
	Equal Opportunities and General, Immigration and Nationality			
Richard Wilson	T E H Walker	M E Head	Equal Opportunities and General	M Forsyth
		A R Rawsthorne	Immigration: Policy and Nationality	Ly Blatch N Baker
		T J Flesher	Immigration: Operations and Resources	N Baker

†see HM Prison Service in the Next Steps Executive Agencies Section

Civil Servants and Departments

Criminal and Research and Statistics Departments and Constitutional Division

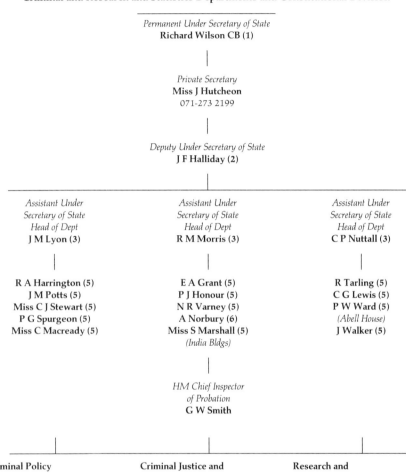

Permanent Under Secretary of State
Richard Wilson CB (1)

Private Secretary
Miss J Hutcheon
071-273 2199

Deputy Under Secretary of State
J F Halliday (2)

Assistant Under Secretary of State Head of Dept
J M Lyon (3)

R A Harrington (5)
J M Potts (5)
Miss C J Stewart (5)
P G Spurgeon (5)
Miss C Macready (5)

Assistant Under Secretary of State Head of Dept
R M Morris (3)

E A Grant (5)
P J Honour (5)
N R Varney (5)
A Norbury (6)
Miss S Marshall (5)
(India Bldgs)

HM Chief Inspector of Probation
G W Smith

Assistant Under Secretary of State Head of Dept
C P Nuttall (3)

R Tarling (5)
C G Lewis (5)
P W Ward (5)
(Abell House)
J Walker (5)

Criminal Policy Department

Criminal policy
Criminal law
Miscarriages of justice
Victims
Criminal injuries compensation scheme
International cooperation

Criminal Justice and Constitutional Department

Probation service
HM Inspectorate of Probation
Constitutional issues
Drugs
Central drug prevention
Criminal justice conferences

Research and Statistics Department

Research
Statistics

Prisons*

Permanent Under Secretary of State
Richard Wilson CB (1)

|

HM Chief Inspector of Prisons
His Hon Judge Stephen Tumim

|

HM Deputy Chief Inspector of Prisons
B V Smith (5)

*for details see HM Prison Service in Next Steps Executive Agencies section

---

Fire and Emergency Planning

Permanent Under Secretary of State
Richard Wilson CB (1)

|

Deputy Under Secretary of State
T C Platt (2)

|

HM Chief Inspector, Fire Service Inspectorate
B Collins
Lay Inspector
P Cummings

|

Assistant Under Secretary of State
A P Wilson (3)

|

M J Addison (5)
Dr D M Peace (5)
Mrs V V R Harris (5)
R J Miles (5)

|

Fire and Emergency Planning Department

Fire service
Fire prevention
Fire service inspectorate
Fire service college
Civil defence
Emergency planning

Personnel, Office Services and Finance

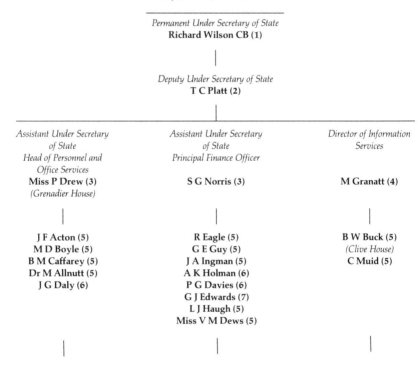

Permanent Under Secretary of State
Richard Wilson CB (1)

Deputy Under Secretary of State
T C Platt (2)

Assistant Under Secretary of State
Head of Personnel and Office Services
Miss P Drew (3)
(Grenadier House)

J F Acton (5)
M D Boyle (5)
B M Caffarey (5)
Dr M Allnutt (5)
J G Daly (6)

Assistant Under Secretary of State
Principal Finance Officer
S G Norris (3)

R Eagle (5)
G E Guy (5)
J A Ingman (5)
A K Holman (6)
P G Davies (6)
G J Edwards (7)
L J Haugh (5)
Miss V M Dews (5)

Director of Information Services
M Granatt (4)

B W Buck (5)
(Clive House)
C Muid (5)

Personnel and Office Services

Accommodation and common services
Staff development
Personnel management
Assessment consultancy
Security

Finance

Planning and control of expenditure
Local government
Central secretariat
Internal audit
Procurement
Accounts
Accountancy
Efficiency
Market testing

Public Relations, Information Technology

Public relations
Information technology

Police

Permanent Under Secretary of State
Richard Wilson CB (1)

Deputy Under Secretary of State
S W Boys-Smith (2)

Assistant Under Secretary of State
Miss C Sinclair (3)

Mrs C L Crawford (5)
Mrs F Clarkson (5)

Police Department

Metropolitan police
Value for money

Assistant Under Secretary of State
C L Scoble (3)

N C Sanderson (5)
P N Wrench (5)
Mrs P G W Catto (5)
Dr G K Laycock (6)

Police Department

Police powers
Complaints
Crime prevention
Training
Recruitment

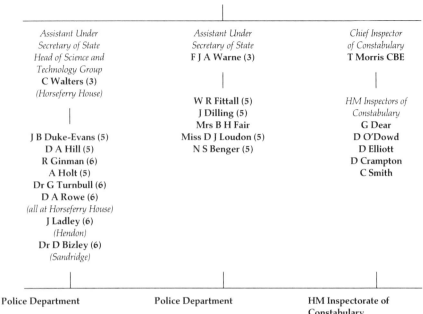

Assistant Under Secretary of State
Head of Science and Technology Group
C Walters (3)
(Horseferry House)

J B Duke-Evans (5)
D A Hill (5)
R Ginman (6)
A Holt (5)
Dr G Turnbull (6)
D A Rowe (6)
(all at Horseferry House)
J Ladley (6)
(Hendon)
Dr D Bizley (6)
(Sandridge)

Police Department

Scientific and technical support to police forces
Police national computer
Police requirements support unit
Police scientific development

Assistant Under Secretary of State
F J A Warne (3)

W R Fittall (5)
J Dilling (5)
Mrs B H Fair
Miss D J Loudon (5)
N S Benger (5)

Police Department

Public order

Chief Inspector of Constabulary
T Morris CBE

HM Inspectors of Constabulary
G Dear
D O'Dowd
D Elliott
D Crampton
C Smith

HM Inspectorate of Constabulary

Inspections
Professional policing matters
Promoting policy efficiency and effectiveness

Legal Adviser's Branch

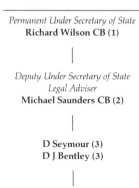

Permanent Under Secretary of State
Richard Wilson CB (1)

Deputy Under Secretary of State
Legal Adviser
Michael Saunders CB (2)

D Seymour (3)
D J Bentley (3)

Legal Adviser's Branch

Advice on legal matters
Preparation of bills
Drafting of statutory instruments
etc

Equal Opportunities and General; Immigration and Nationality

Permanent Under Secretary of State
Richard Wilson CB (1)

Deputy Under Secretary of State
T E H Walker (2)

Assistant Under Secretary of State Head of Department
M E Head CVO (3)

E Soden CBE (5)
R Kornicki (5)
H S Webber (5)
A Harding (5)
Dr R M Watt (4)

Equal Opportunities and General

Race relations
Sex discrimination
Electoral matters
Gambling
Voluntary sector
Charities
Refugee resettlement
Data protection and privacy
Coroners
Local legislation
Animals

Assistant Under Secretary of State
A R Rawsthorne (3)
(Lunar House)

R M Whalley (5)
Mrs E C L Pallett (5)
D A L Cooke (5)
M J Gillespie (5)
A Walmsley (6)
(Liverpool)

Immigration: Policy and Nationality

Immigration policy
Refugees and asylum
European business
Nationality

Assistant Under Secretary of State
T J Flesher (3)
(Lunar House)

R G Yates (5)
Miss A Smith (5)
K D Sutton (5)
E B Nicholls (5)
T Farrage *(Ports)*
C Manchip *(Enforcement)*

Immigration: Operations and Resources

Immigration service
After entry casework
Appeals and enforcement
Finance and management services
Information technology

Home Office Addresses

Abell House
John Islip Street
London SW1P 4LH
Tel 0171-217 3000
Fax 0171-828 7643

Calthorpe House
P O Box 2078
Edgbaston
Birmingham B16 8QZ
Tel 0121-455 9855
Fax 0121-454 6738

Cleland House
Page Street
London SW1P 4LN
Tel 0171-217 3000
Fax 0171-217 6635

Clive House
Petty France
London SW1H 9HD
Tel 0171-217 3000
Fax 0171-217 8553

Crown House
52 Elizabeth House
Corby
Northants NN17 1PJ
Tel 01536 202101
Fax 01536 68557

Grenadier House
99/105 Horseferry Road
London SW1P 2DD
Tel 0171-217 3000
Fax 0171-217 0002

Hendon Data Centre
Aerodrome Road
Colindale
London NW9 5LN
Tel 0181-205 1855
Fax 0181 200 3279

Horseferry House
Dean Ryle Street
London SW1P 2AW
Tel 0171-217 3000
Fax 0171-217 8619

Liverpool Nationality Office
India Buildings
Water Street
Liverpool LZ 0QN
Tel 0151-227 3939
Fax 0151-255 1160

Lunar House
40 Wellesley Road
Croydon CR9 2BY
Tel 0181-686 0688
Fax 0181-760 1181

Sandridge Laboratories
Woodcock Hill
Sandridge
St Albans
Herts AL4 9HQ
Tel 01727 865051
Fax 01727 850642

St John's House
Merton Road
Bootle
Merseyside L20 3QE
Tel 0151-934 7209
Fax 0151-933 6340

Whittington House
19/30 Alfred Place
London WC1E 7LU
Tel 0171-636 9501
Fax 0171-436 0804

Board of Inland Revenue

Founded 1849

Ministers Chancellor of the Exchequer, Financial Secretary to the Treasury and Economic Secretary to the Treasury

Responsibilities Administers and collects direct taxes, mainly income tax, corporation tax, capital gains tax, stamp duty – and advises the Chancellor of the Exchequer on policy questions

Number of staff 61,443

Executive agencies Valuation Office Agency

Executive offices The department is organised into a series of accountable management units under the Next Steps programme. The day-to-day operations in assessing and collecting tax and in providing internal support services are carried out by 27 executive offices. These are listed below and, where relevant, their directorates/divisions in brackets:

Regional Executive Offices (10)
(Business Operations Division)

Capital Taxes Office
(Business Operations Division)

Claims Branch and Inspector of Foreign Dividends
(Business Operations Division)

Information Technology Office

Corporate Communications Office

Internal Audit Office
(Finance Division)

Enforcement Office
(Business Operations Division)

Oil Taxation Office
(Business Operations Division)

Accounts Office (Cumbernauld)
(Business Operations Division)

Financial Accounting Office
(Finance Division)

Pensions Schemes Office
(Business Operations Division)

Accounts Office (Shipley)
(Business Operations Division)

Solicitor's Office (Scotland)

Special Compliance Office
(Business Operations Division)

Stamp Office
(Business Operations Division)

Statistics and Economics Office

Training Office

Solicitor's Office

Board of Inland Revenue

Somerset House, Strand, London WC2R 1LB
Tel 0171-438 6622
Fax *Telephone the above number and ask for the appropriate fax number*
All staff are based at Somerset House unless otherwise indicated.
For other addresses and telephone numbers see the end of this section.

Ministers

Chancellor of the Exchequer
The Rt Hon Kenneth Clarke MP

Financial Secretary to the Treasury
The Rt Hon Jonathan Aitken MP

Economic Secretary to the Treasury
Anthony Nelson MP

(for details of their offices see
HM Treasury section)

The Board

Chairman and Commissioner
Sir Anthony Battishill KCB (1)

|

Private Secretary
F Khan
0171-438 6615

|

Deputy Chairmen and Commissioners
S C T Matheson (2)
C W Corlett (2)

|

Director General and Commissioner
G H Bush (2)

Departmental Overview

	Civil Servants		**Department**
Grade 1	*Grade 2*	*Grade 3*	
Sir Anthony Battishill	These divisions report directly to the Chairman	R R Martin	Finance
		K V Deacon	Quality Development Division
		M A Johns	Business Operations Division
	Personal Tax; Capital and Valuation; Savings and Investment; Statistics and Economics Office; International; Business Profits; Company Tax; Financial Institutions		
Sir Anthony Battishill	S C T Matheson	E McGivern	Personal Tax
		M F Cayley	Capital and Valuation Financial Institutions
		B A Mace	Savings and Investment
		R G Ward	Statistics and Economics Office
		I R Spence	International
		E J Gribbon	Business profits
		P Lewis	Company Tax
	Personnel Division; Management Services Division; Information Technology Office; Training Office		
Sir Anthony Battishill	G H Bush	J Gant	Personnel Division
		N C Munro	Management Services Division
		J E Yard	Business Services Office
		D J Timmons	Training Office
	Planning		
Sir Anthony Battishill	C W Corlett	D A Smith	Change Management Division
		R Hooper	Corporate Communications Office

Departmental Overview

Civil Servants			Department
Grade 1	*Grade 2*	*Grade 3*	
	Solicitor's Office		
Sir Anthony Battishill	B E Cleave	J G H Bates	Taxation of Profits, Capital Gains Tax, Avoidance Schemes, Criminal Prosecutions
		J D H Johnston	Legislation, Inheritance Tax, Stamp Duties, Charities
		G F Butt	Personal Taxation, Rating, Recovery and Enforcement, International, Double Taxation, Oil
		I K Laing	Law on Tax in Scotland
	Regional Executive Offices		
Sir Anthony Battishill	M A Johns (3)	M J Hodgson	East Midlands
		R A J Jones	Large Groups Office
		J F Carling	London
		R I Ford	North
		I S Gerrie	North West
		D L S Bean	South East
		Mrs M E Williams	South West
		A C Sleeman	South Yorkshire
		R S T Ewing	Northern Ireland
		O J D Clarke	Scotland
		M W Kirk	Wales and Midlands

Civil Servants and Departments

Quality Development Division; Business Operations Division; Finance Division

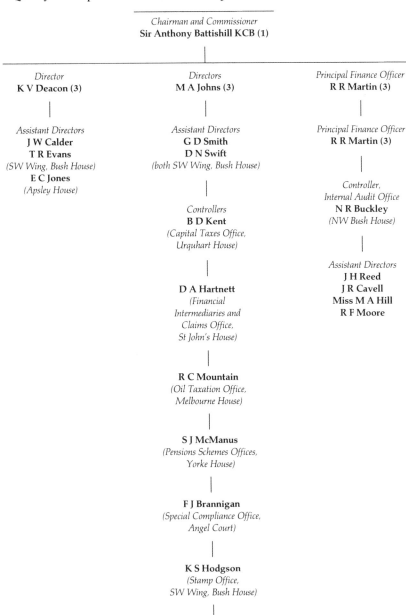

Chairman and Commissioner
Sir Anthony Battishill KCB (1)

Quality Development Division

Director
K V Deacon (3)

Assistant Directors
J W Calder
T R Evans
(SW Wing, Bush House)
E C Jones
(Apsley House)

Business Operations Division

Directors
M A Johns (3)

Assistant Directors
G D Smith
D N Swift
(both SW Wing, Bush House)

Controllers
B D Kent
(Capital Taxes Office, Urquhart House)

D A Hartnett
(Financial Intermediaries and Claims Office, St John's House)

R C Mountain
(Oil Taxation Office, Melbourne House)

S J McManus
(Pensions Schemes Offices, Yorke House)

F J Brannigan
(Special Compliance Office, Angel Court)

K S Hodgson
(Stamp Office, SW Wing, Bush House)

Finance Division

Principal Finance Officer
R R Martin (3)

Principal Finance Officer
R R Martin (3)

Controller, Internal Audit Office
N R Buckley
(NW Bush House)

Assistant Directors
J H Reed
J R Cavell
Miss M A Hill
R F Moore

Deputy Controller
A G Nield
(Fitzroy House)
H V Capon
(Urquhart House)
R J Draper
(Barkergate)
T R Diggins
(City House, Nottingham)
D Newlyn
I M Griffin
K C Cartwright
M P Wright
(above 4 at Melbourne House)
J T Cawdron
(New Court)
J E Whittles
D F Parrett
G W Lunn
(Angel Court)
I Fraser
(Capital Taxes Office, Mulberry House)
E C Jones
(Apsley House)
E A Harrison
M R Williams
R J Warner
(above 3 at SW Wing, Bush House)

Quality Development Division

Compliance and technical standards
Penalties
Subcontractors

Business Operations Division

Capital taxes offices
The Stamp Office
Oil Taxation Office
Claims branch and inspector foreign dividends
Pension Schemes Office
Special investigations
Criminal proceedings
Collection and audit procedures
Organisation and performance
Operational policy
Operational systems and support
Resources planning
Special compliance

Finance Division

Financial planning
Internal audit
Management planning
Financial Accounting Office
Central purchasing
Pay policy

Personal Tax; Capital and Valuation; Savings and Investment; Statistics; International; Business Profits; Company Tax; Financial Institutions

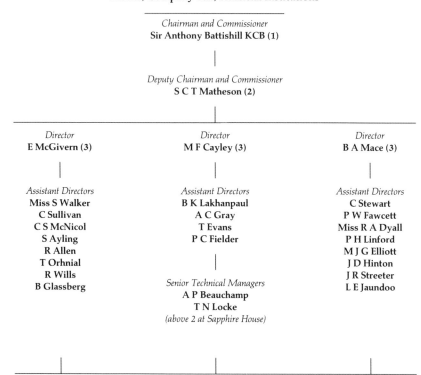

Chairman and Commissioner
Sir Anthony Battishill KCB (1)

Deputy Chairman and Commissioner
S C T Matheson (2)

Director
E McGivern (3)

Assistant Directors
Miss S Walker
C Sullivan
C S McNicol
S Ayling
R Allen
T Orhnial
R Wills
B Glassberg

Director
M F Cayley (3)

Assistant Directors
B K Lakhanpaul
A C Gray
T Evans
P C Fielder

Senior Technical Managers
A P Beauchamp
T N Locke
(above 2 at Sapphire House)

Director
B A Mace (3)

Assistant Directors
C Stewart
P W Fawcett
Miss R A Dyall
P H Linford
M J G Elliott
J D Hinton
J R Streeter
L E Jaundoo

Personal Tax

Income tax rates and allowances
Independent taxation
Schedule E
Benefits in kind and expenses
Foreign earnings
Lump sums
Employment/self-employment
Social security benefits
PAYE
Personal taxation
Company cars
Tax relief for vocational training
Simplified assessing

Capital and Valuation

Inheritance tax
Capital transfer tax
Capital gains tax
Development land tax

Savings and Investment

Charities
Stamp duty
Provision for retirement and pensions
Taxation on savings including PEPs and TESSAs
Trusts, settlements and administration of estates
Covenants, maintenance and alimony
TOBBI
MIRAs
Employee share schemes and financial participation schemes, profit-related pay

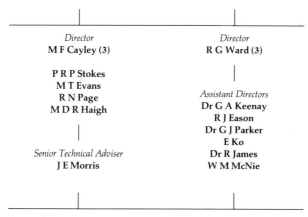

Director
M F Cayley (3)

P R P Stokes
M T Evans
R N Page
M D R Haigh

Senior Technical Adviser
J E Morris

Financial Institutions

Banks
Financial concerns
Lloyds
Stock Exchange
Building societies
Unit and investment trusts
New financial instruments
Taxation of interest received, relief for interest paid
Life assurance, general assurance

Director
R G Ward (3)

Assistant Directors
Dr G A Keenay
R J Eason
Dr G J Parker
E Ko
Dr R James
W M McNie

Statistics and Economics

Budgetary support and forecasting
Personal incomes
Company sector
Capital and wealth
Information technology
Economic advice

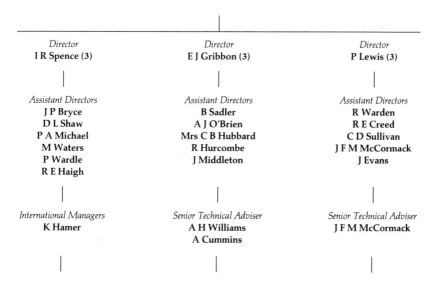

Director
I R Spence (3)

Assistant Directors
J P Bryce
D L Shaw
P A Michael
M Waters
P Wardle
R E Haigh

International Managers
K Hamer

Director
E J Gribbon (3)

Assistant Directors
B Sadler
A J O'Brien
Mrs C B Hubbard
R Hurcombe
J Middleton

Senior Technical Adviser
A H Williams
A Cummins

Director
P Lewis (3)

Assistant Directors
R Warden
R E Creed
C D Sullivan
J F M McCormack
J Evans

Senior Technical Adviser
J F M McCormack

International

OECD
Individual residence and domicile
Non-resident trusts
Double taxation agreements
Paying agents
Diplomatic privilege
International organisations
Company residence and migration
Offshore funds
Foreign partnerships
Thin capitalisation
Foreign companies and traders
International avoidance problems
Liaison with EC
Transfer pricing
Unitary tax
Non-residents' trading in UK
Schedule D, Cases IV and V

Business Profits

Cessations
New businesses
Company amalgamations
Partnerships
Capital allowance (except mines, oil wells)
Shipping and leasing
Land, farming, forestry
Stock relief
Schedule D
Privatisation
EC business tax proposals
Self-employed persons
Property income
Trading profits
Trade Protection Associations
Literary and artistic profits
Copyright royalties
Building and contracting
Particular trades

Company Tax

Corporation tax
Business expansion scheme
Purchase of own shares
Close companies
Demergers
Industrial and provident societies
Cooperatives
Capital allowances (mines and oil wells)
Group relief and losses
Housing Associations
North Sea fiscal regimes
Petroleum Revenue Tax
Policy coordination

Personnel Division; Management Services Division; Information Technology Office; Training Office

Chairman and Commissioner
Sir Anthony Battishill KCB (1)

Commissioner and Director General
G H Bush (2)

Director
J Gant (3)

Director
N C Munro

Director
J E Yard (3)

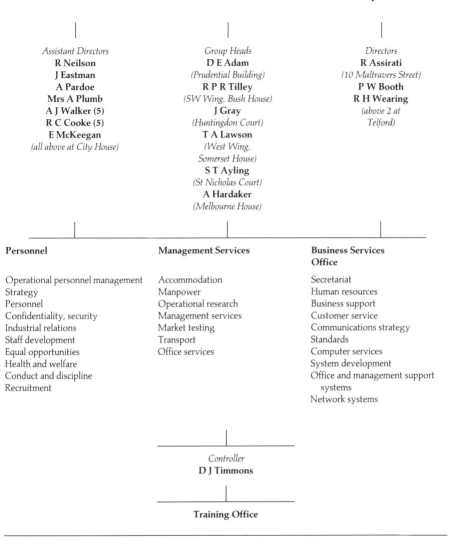

Assistant Directors
R Neilson
J Eastman
A Pardoe
Mrs A Plumb
A J Walker (5)
R C Cooke (5)
E McKeegan
(all above at City House)

Group Heads
D E Adam
(Prudential Building)
R P R Tilley
(SW Wing, Bush House)
J Gray
(Huntingdon Court)
T A Lawson
(West Wing, Somerset House)
S T Ayling
(St Nicholas Court)
A Hardaker
(Melbourne House)

Directors
R Assirati
(10 Maltravers Street)
P W Booth
R H Wearing
(above 2 at Telford)

Personnel

Operational personnel management
Strategy
Personnel
Confidentiality, security
Industrial relations
Staff development
Equal opportunities
Health and welfare
Conduct and discipline
Recruitment

Management Services

Accommodation
Manpower
Operational research
Management services
Market testing
Transport
Office services

Business Services Office

Secretariat
Human resources
Business support
Customer service
Communications strategy
Standards
Computer services
System development
Office and management support systems
Network systems

Controller
D J Timmons

Training Office

Planning

Chairman and Commissioner
Sir Anthony Battishill KCB (1)

Deputy Chairman and Commissioner
C W Corlett (2)

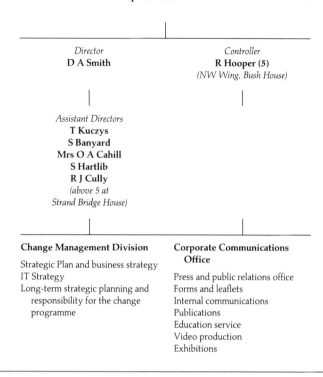

Director
D A Smith

Assistant Directors
T Kuczys
S Banyard
Mrs O A Cahill
S Hartlib
R J Cully
(above 5 at Strand Bridge House)

Controller
R Hooper (5)
(NW Wing, Bush House)

Change Management Division

Strategic Plan and business strategy
IT Strategy
Long-term strategic planning and responsibility for the change programme

Corporate Communications Office

Press and public relations office
Forms and leaflets
Internal communications
Publications
Education service
Video production
Exhibitions

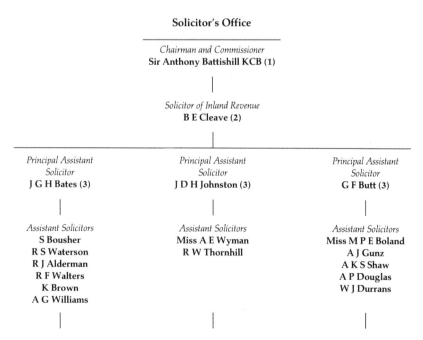

Solicitor's Office

Chairman and Commissioner
Sir Anthony Battishill KCB (1)

Solicitor of Inland Revenue
B E Cleave (2)

Principal Assistant Solicitor
J G H Bates (3)

Assistant Solicitors
S Bousher
R S Waterson
R J Alderman
R F Walters
K Brown
A G Williams

Principal Assistant Solicitor
J D H Johnston (3)

Assistant Solicitors
Miss A E Wyman
R W Thornhill

Principal Assistant Solicitor
G F Butt (3)

Assistant Solicitors
Miss M P E Boland
A J Gunz
A K S Shaw
A P Douglas
W J Durrans

Taxation of profits
Capital Gains Tax
Avoidance schemes
Criminal prosecutions

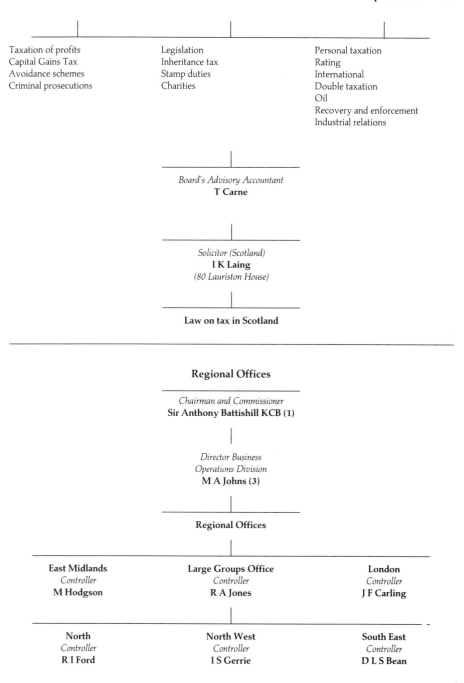

Legislation
Inheritance tax
Stamp duties
Charities

Personal taxation
Rating
International
Double taxation
Oil
Recovery and enforcement
Industrial relations

Board's Advisory Accountant
T Carne

Solicitor (Scotland)
I K Laing
(80 Lauriston House)

Law on tax in Scotland

Regional Offices

Chairman and Commissioner
Sir Anthony Battishill KCB (1)

Director Business Operations Division
M A Johns (3)

Regional Offices

East Midlands
Controller
M Hodgson

Large Groups Office
Controller
R A Jones

London
Controller
J F Carling

North
Controller
R I Ford

North West
Controller
I S Gerrie

South East
Controller
D L S Bean

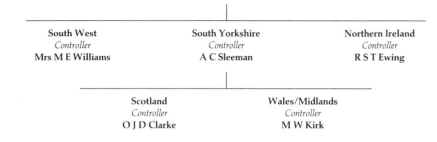

South West
Controller
Mrs M E Williams

South Yorkshire
Controller
A C Sleeman

Northern Ireland
Controller
R S T Ewing

Scotland
Controller
O J D Clarke

Wales/Midlands
Controller
M W Kirk

Board of Inland Revenue Addresses

For fax numbers telephone the office concerned and ask for the appropriate fax number

Angel Court
199 Borough High Street
London SE1 1HZ
Tel 0171-234 3716

Apsley House
Wellington Road North
Stockport SK4 1EY
Tel 0161-480 6009

21 Barkergate
Nottingham NG1 1JU
Tel 01159 522008

City House
Maid Marion Way
Nottingham NG1 6BH
Tel 01159 243111

Commerce Square
High Pavement
The Lace Market
Nottingham NG1 1HS
Tel 01159 243939

Fitzroy House
PO Box 46
Nottingham NG2 1BD
Tel 01159 740000

Huntingdon Court Annexe
90-94 Mansfield Road
Nottingham NG1 3HH
Tel 01159 414214

Lauriston House
80 Lauriston Place
Edinburgh EH3 9SL
Tel 0131-229 9344

10 Maltravers Street
London WC2R 1LB
Tel 0171-438 7483

Melbourne House
Aldwych
London WC2B 4LL
Tel 0171-438 6622

Mulberry House
16 Picardy Place
Edinburgh EH1 3NB
Tel 0131-556 8511

North West Wing
Bush House
Aldwych
London WC2B 4PP
Tel 0171-438 6622

New Court
Carey Street
London WC2A 2JE
Tel 0171-324 0000

Prudential Building
72 Maid Marion Way
Nottingham NG1 6AR
Tel 01159 242299

St John's House
Merton Road
Bootle
Merseyside L69 4EJ
Tel 0151-922 6363

St Nicholas Court
25/27 Castle Gate
Nottingham NG1 7AR
Tel 01159 243855

Sapphire House
550 Streetsbrooke Road
Solihull
West Midlands B91 1QU
Tel 0121-711 3232

South West Wing
Bush House
Strand
London WC2B 4QN
Tel 0171-438 6622

Strand Bridge House
138-142 Strand
London WC2R 1HH
Tel 0171-438 6662

Telford Development Centre
Matheson House
Telford
Shropshire
TF3 4ER
Tel 01952 290044

Urquhart House
3/5 High Pavement
Nottingham NG1 1HS
Tel 01159 243844

Yorke House
PO Box 62
Nottingham NG2 1BG
Tel 01159 740000

Regional Offices

East
Midgate House
Peterborough PE1 1TD
Tel 01733 63241

Large Groups Office
New Court
Carey Street
London WC2A 2JE
Tel 0171-324 1334

London
New Court
Carey Street
London WC2A 2JE
Tel 0171-324 1251

North
100 Russell Street
Middlesborough
Cleveland TS1 2RZ
Tel 01642 213214

North West
The Triad
Stanley Road
Bootle
Merseyside L20 3PD
Tel 0151-922 4055

South East
Albion House
Chertsey Road
Woking GU21 1BT
Tel 01483 723322

South West
3rd Floor
Longbrook House
New North Road
Exeter EX4 4UA
Tel 01392 453210

South Yorkshire
Sovereign House
10 Queen Street
Sheffield S1 2EN
Tel 01142 739099

Northern Ireland
Level 9
Dorchester House
52-58 Great Victoria Street
Belfast BT2 7QE
Tel 01232 245123

Scotland
80 Lauriston Place
Edinburgh EH3 9SL
Tel 0131-229 9344

Wales/Midlands
1st Floor
Phase II Building
Ty Glas
Llanishen
Cardiff CF4 5TS
Tel 01222 755789

Legal Secretariat to the Law Officers

(formerly Law Officers' Department)

Founded	1893
Ministers	Attorney General Solicitor General
Responsibilities	All major international and domestic legislation involving the government Enforcement of the criminal law Principal legal adviser to the government Questions referred to the Law Officers by MPs Work of the: Treasury Solicitor's Department Crown Prosecution Service Serious Fraud Office Legal Secretariat to the Law Officers The Director of Public Prosecutions for Northern Ireland is also responsible to the Attorney General
Number of staff	26
Executive agencies	Government Property Lawyers

Legal Secretariat to the Law Officers

Attorney General's Chambers, 9 Buckingham Gate, London SW1E 6JP
Tel 0171-828 7155 Fax 0171-828 0593

Ministers

Attorney General
The Rt Hon Sir Nicholas Lyell QC MP

Private Secretary
Stuart Moore
0171-828 1884

Parliamentary Private Secretary
Vacant

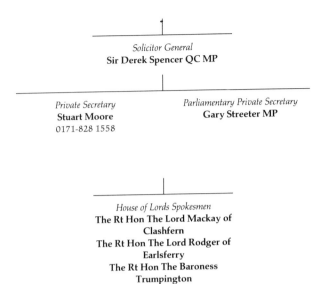

Solicitor General
Sir Derek Spencer QC MP

Private Secretary
Stuart Moore
0171-828 1558

Parliamentary Private Secretary
Gary Streeter MP

House of Lords Spokesmen
The Rt Hon The Lord Mackay of Clashfern
The Rt Hon The Lord Rodger of Earlsferry
The Rt Hon The Baroness Trumpington

Officials

Legal Secretary to the Law Officers
Miss J L Wheldon CB (2)

Deputy Legal Secretary
S J Wooler (4)

Ministerial Responsibilities

Sir Nicholas Lyell	Overall responsibility for the work of the Crown Prosecution Service Legal Secretariat to the Law Officers Serious Fraud Office Treasury Solicitor's Department All major international and domestic litigation involving the government Enforcement of criminal law Government's principal legal adviser The Director of Public Prosecutions for Northern Ireland is also superintended by the Attorney General Ex-officio head of the Bar
Sir Derek Spencer	Responsible for such matters as the Attorney General delegates to him Shares with Attorney General the handling of matters referred to the Law Officers by MPs

Departmental Overview

	Civil Servants		**Department**	**Minister**
Grade 2	*Grade 4*	*Grade 5*		
	Legal Secretariat			
Miss J L Wheldon	S J Wooler	R Jackson	Legal Secretariat	Attorney General Solicitor General

Civil Servants and Departments

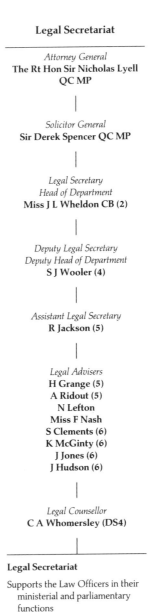

Legal Secretariat

Attorney General
The Rt Hon Sir Nicholas Lyell QC MP

Solicitor General
Sir Derek Spencer QC MP

Legal Secretary
Head of Department
Miss J L Wheldon CB (2)

Deputy Legal Secretary
Deputy Head of Department
S J Wooler (4)

Assistant Legal Secretary
R Jackson (5)

Legal Advisers
H Grange (5)
A Ridout (5)
N Lefton
Miss F Nash
S Clements (6)
K McGinty (6)
J Jones (6)
J Hudson (6)

Legal Counsellor
C A Whomersley (DS4)

Legal Secretariat

Supports the Law Officers in their ministerial and parliamentary functions

Lord Advocate's Department

Founded The Office of the Lord Advocate was founded in the 15th century. The department in its present form was created in 1925

Ministers The Lord Advocate
Solicitor General for Scotland
(who are the Law Officers of the Crown for Scotland and chief legal advisers to the government on Scottish questions)

Responsibilities The department assists the Law Officers on Scottish questions and acts as the legal adviser on Scottish matters to certain government departments

As Scottish parliamentary counsel, staff draft government legislation relating exclusively to Scotland and are responsible for the adaptation to Scotland of other legislation

All judicial work for the Lord Advocate's Department is carried out by the Crown Office, Scotland

Number of staff 20

Lord Advocate's Department

2 Carlton Gardens, London SW1Y 5AA
Tel 0171-210 1010 Fax 0171-210 1025

Ministers and Officials

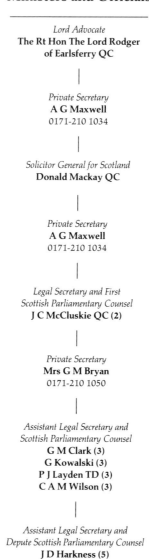

Lord Advocate
The Rt Hon The Lord Rodger of Earlsferry QC

Private Secretary
A G Maxwell
0171-210 1034

Solicitor General for Scotland
Donald Mackay QC

Private Secretary
A G Maxwell
0171-210 1034

Legal Secretary and First Scottish Parliamentary Counsel
J C McCluskie QC (2)

Private Secretary
Mrs G M Bryan
0171-210 1050

Assistant Legal Secretary and Scottish Parliamentary Counsel
G M Clark (3)
G Kowalski (3)
P J Layden TD (3)
C A M Wilson (3)

Assistant Legal Secretary and Depute Scottish Parliamentary Counsel
J D Harkness (5)

Lord Chancellor's Department

Founded	1885 (and assumed its present form and responsibilities in 1972 following the Courts Act 1971)
Ministers	The Lord Chancellor, one parliamentary secretary
Responsibilities	courts: procedure of the civil courts and administration of the appeal, high, crown and county courts and responsibility for the locally-administered magistrates' courts Great Seal of the Realm (custodian of) immigration appellate authorities judges (advice on the appointment of) Lands Tribunal land reform legal aid magistrates, masters and district judges of the High Court and county court district judges (appointment of) Magistrates' Courts Services Inspectorate Pensions Appeal Tribunal Social Security Commissioners Special Commissioners of Income Tax VAT Tribunals
Number of staff	1,200
Executive Agencies	Court Service HM Land Registry Public Record Office Public Trust Office

Lord Chancellor's Department

House of Lords, London SW1A 0PW
Trevelyan House, Great Peter Street, London SW1P 2BY
Tel 0171-210 8500   Fax 0171-210 8549

All staff are based at House of Lords or Trevelyan House unless otherwise indicated.
For other addresses and telephone numbers see the end of this section.

Officers and Officials

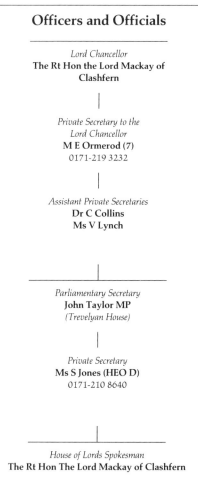

Lord Chancellor
The Rt Hon the Lord Mackay of Clashfern

Private Secretary to the Lord Chancellor
M E Ormerod (7)
0171-219 3232

Assistant Private Secretaries
Dr C Collins
Ms V Lynch

Parliamentary Secretary
John Taylor MP
(Trevelyan House)

Private Secretary
Ms S Jones (HEO D)
0171-210 8640

House of Lords Spokesman
The Rt Hon The Lord Mackay of Clashfern

Ministerial Responsibilities

Lord Mackay of Clashfern

Administration of the appeal, high, crown and county courts in England and Wales, and for the locally administered magistrates courts
Appointment of masters and district judges of the high court, county court district judges and magistrates
Advice to Crown and the prime minister on appointment of judges and other officers
Great Seal of the Realm (custodian thereof)
Immigration Appellate authorities
Lands Tribunal
Northern Ireland Court Service (separate department; see under that name)
Pensions Appeal Tribunal
Procedure of the civil courts
Promotion of general reforms in civil law
Social Security Commissioners
Special Commissioners of Income Tax
VAT tribunals

John Taylor

Assists on legal aid and the development of legal services and is responsible for:
- Budget and resource issues
- Energy efficiency
- Equal opportunities and women's issues
- HM Land Registry
- Public Record Office
- Spokesman in the House of Commons

Departmental Overview

Grade 1	Civil Servants: Grade 2	Grade 3	Department	Minister
	Crown Office			
Sir Thomas Legg	M Huebner		Letters patent and various ceremonial activity	Lord Chancellor
	Judicial Appointments Group, Establishment and Finance Group			
Sir Thomas Legg	These report directly to Sir Thomas Legg	R E K Holmes	Judicial Appointments	Lord Chancellor
		Mrs N A Oppenheimer	Establishment and Finance Group	J Taylor
	Policy Group			
Sir Thomas Legg	M Malone-Lee *(until August 1995)* then I M Burns	R H H White	Legal Group	Lord Chancellor
		L C Oates	Legal Advice and Litigation	J Taylor
		P G Harris (5)	Central Unit	J Taylor
	Official Solicitor's Department			
		P M Harris	Official Solicitor's Department	

Below are offices associated with the Lord Chancellor's Department

Grade 3	Department	Minister
A Tyrrell	Office of the Lord Chancellor's Visitors	Lord Chancellor
Mrs A B Macfar-lane	Court of Protection	Lord Chancellor
Judge Waley	Judge Advocate of the Fleet	
C Rant	Judge Advocate General of the Forces	Lord Chancellor
J H Holroyd (2)	Ecclesiastical Patronage	Prime Minister/ Lord Chancellor

Civil Servants and Departments

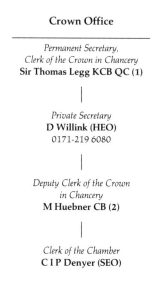

Crown Office

Permanent Secretary,
Clerk of the Crown in Chancery
Sir Thomas Legg KCB QC (1)

Private Secretary
D Willink (HEO)
0171-219 6080

Deputy Clerk of the Crown
in Chancery
M Huebner CB (2)

Clerk of the Chamber
C I P Denyer (SEO)

Judicial Appointments Group, Establishment and Finance Group

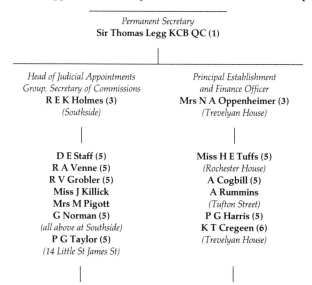

Permanent Secretary
Sir Thomas Legg KCB QC (1)

Head of Judicial Appointments
Group, Secretary of Commissions
R E K Holmes (3)
(Southside)

D E Staff (5)
R A Venne (5)
R V Grobler (5)
Miss J Killick
Mrs M Pigott
G Norman (5)
(all above at Southside)
P G Taylor (5)
(14 Little St James St)

Principal Establishment
and Finance Officer
Mrs N A Oppenheimer (3)
(Trevelyan House)

Miss H E Tuffs (5)
(Rochester House)
A Cogbill (5)
A Rummins
(Tufton Street)
P G Harris (5)
K T Cregeen (6)
(Trevelyan House)

Judicial Appointments Group

Circuit bench
District bench and tribunals
Magistrates (appointments)
Magistrates (training)
Judicial Studies Board
Policy and conditions of service

Establishment and Finance

Accommodation and magistrates courts building
Personnel management
Finance
Training
Internal finance
Procurement services
Planning and communications

Policy Group

Permanent Secretary
Sir Thomas Legg KCB QC (1)

Deputy Secretary
M Malone-Lee (2)
(until August 1995)
I M Burns (2)
(from August 1995)
(Trevelyan House)

Head of Legal Group
R H H White (3)
(Southside)

M Collon (4)
J A C Watherston (5)
M Kron (5)
(all at Southside)
J M Gibson (5)
(America House)

Associate Head of Policy Group
L C Oates (3)
(Trevelyan House)

W Arnold (5)
S Smith (5)
(both at Trevelyan House)

Legal

Legal advice and litigation
Rules and regulations
International
Statutory publication office

Policy and Legal Services

Legal services and agencies
Legal aid
Family law

Official Solicitor's Department

Official Solicitor
P M Harris (3)
(81 Chancery Lane)

Official Solicitor's Department

Confidential adviser to the Court
Representation of minors, persons of unsound mind, and persons committed for contempt of court
Judicial and other trusteeships
Administration of deceased estates

The following groups are independent offices associated with the Lord Chancellor's Department

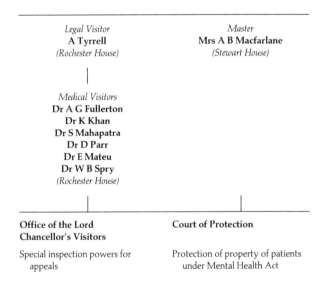

Legal Visitor
A Tyrrell
(Rochester House)

Medical Visitors
Dr A G Fullerton
Dr K Khan
Dr S Mahapatra
Dr D Parr
Dr E Mateu
Dr W B Spry
(Rochester House)

Office of the Lord Chancellor's Visitors

Special inspection powers for appeals

Master
Mrs A B Macfarlane
(Stewart House)

Court of Protection

Protection of property of patients under Mental Health Act

Judge Advocate of the Fleet
Vacant
(Law Courts, Maidstone)

Judge Advocate General of the Forces
C Rant
(22 Kingsway)

Secretary for Ecclesiastical Patronage
J H Holroyd CB (2)
(10 Downing St)

Judge Advocate of the Fleet

Naval courts martial and disciplinary courts
Naval Discipline Act
Assist Admiralty Board

Judge Advocate General of the Forces

Provision of Judge Advocates at courts martial and military courts in the UK and abroad
Post-trial legal advice to the army, RAF and MOD

Ecclesiastical Patronage

Lord Chancellor's Department Addresses

America House
Spring Gardens
London SW1A 2BP
Tel 0171-389 3253
Fax 0171-389 7490

81 Chancery Lane
London WC2A 1DD
Tel 0171-911 7131
Fax 0171-911 7105

10 Downing Street
London SW1
Tel 0171-930 4433
Fax: telephone the above number and ask for appropriate fax number

22 Kingsway
London WC2B 6LE
Tel 0171-305 7905
Fax: telephone the above number and ask for appropriate fax number

Law Courts
Barker Road
Maidstone
Kent ME16 8EQ
Tel 01622 754966
Fax 01622 687349

14 Little St James' Street
London SW1A 1DP
Tel 0171-925 0185
Fax 0171-321 0142

Rochester House
33 Greycoat Street
London SW1P 2QF
Tel 0171-210 3000
Fax 0171-210 1309

Royal Courts of Justice
Strand
London WC2A
Tel 0171-936 6000
Fax: telephone the above number and ask for appropriate fax number

Southside
105 Victoria Street
London SW1
Tel 0171-210 2182
Fax 0171-210 2059

Stewart House
24 Kingsway
London WC2B 6JX
Tel 0171-269 7000
Fax 0171-831 0060

Trevelyan House
30 Great Peter Street
London SW1P 2BY
Tel 0171-210 8500
Fax 0171-210 8549

67 Tufton Street
London SW1P 3QS
Tel 0171-210 0606
Fax 0171-976 0384

Department of National Heritage

Founded	1992, when it took over the functions of the old Office of Arts and Libraries and a number of other responsibilities (broadcasting, films, heritage, royal parks, sport and tourism) from other departments
Ministers	one secretary of state and two parliamentary under secretaries of state
Responsibilities	arts policy broadcasting films historic buildings and ancient monuments libraries national lottery national museums and galleries sport tourism
Number of staff	337
Executive agencies	Historic Royal Palaces Royal Parks

Department of National Heritage

2-4 Cockspur Street, London SW1Y 5DH
Tel 0171-211 6000   Fax 0171-211 6210

Ministers

Secretary of State
The Rt Hon Stephen Dorrell MP

Parliamentary Private Secretary
Gyles Brandreth MP

Special Adviser
Bryan Jefferson
(Architecture)

Private Secretary
J O F Kingman (7)
0171-211 6239

Parliamentary Under Secretary of State
The Viscount Astor

Private Secretary
Ms J Buggins
0171-211 6421

Parliamentary Under Secretary of State, Minister for Sport
Iain Sproat MP

Private Secretary
Niall MacKenzie
0171-211 6303

House of Lords' Spokesmen
The Viscount Astor
The Rt Hon The Baroness Trumpington
The Lord Annaly

Ministerial Responsibilities

Stephen Dorrell
- Major policies in each policy area
- Broadcasting
- European Union and international matters
- Film
- Media
- Performing arts
- Public appointments
- Public expenditure

Iain Sproat
- Deregulation
- Historic Royal Palaces Agency
- Libraries
- National Lottery
- Royal Estates
- Royal Parks Agency
- Sport
- Supports Stephen Dorrell on performing arts

Viscount Astor
- Access Initiative (increasing access to, and encouraging participation in, all the arts)
- Architecture and conservation
- Built heritage
- Citizen's Charter
- Cultural property
- Government Art Collection
- Green issues
- Museums and galleries
- Regional and local government issues
- Tourism
- Supports Stephen Dorrell on media, broadcasting and film

Departmental Overview

Civil Servants			Divisions	Minister
Grade 1	*Grade 3*	*Grade 5*		
	Information			
Hayden Phillips (1A)	Reports directly	Andrea MacLean P Bolt	Information Fundamental Expenditure Review	
	Arts, Sports and Lottery Group			
Hayden Phillips (1A)	A C B Ramsay	N Kroll (4) S MacDonald	Arts Policy National Lottery	S Dorrell/ I Sproat
		Dr W Baron (6)	Government Art Collection	Vis Astor
		Miss H Wilkin-son (7)	Millennium Commission Unit	S Dorrell/ I Sproat
		Miss A Stewart	Sport and Recreation	I Sproat
	Museums, Galleries and Libraries Group			
Hayden Phillips (1A)	Miss M O'Mara	P Gregory N Kroll (Acting)	Museums and Galleries Libraries	Vis Astor I Sproat
		E D'Silva (Acting)	British Library Project	I Sproat
		M Helston (7)	Cultural Property	Vis Astor
	Broadcasting and Media Group			
Hayden Phillips (1A)	P Wright	Miss S Booth	Broadcasting Policy	S Dorrell/ Vis Astor
		P C Edwards	Media	S Dorrell/ Vis Astor
	Heritage and Tourism Group			
Hayden Phillips (1A)	D Chesterton	A H Corner	Heritage	S Dorrell/ Vis Astor
		Dr K Gray	Royal Estates	S Dorrell/ I Sproat
		Ms J Evans	Tourism	S Dorrell/ Vis Astor
	Resources and Services Group			
Hayden Phillips (1A)	N Pittman (4)	R Maclachlan S Broadley	Finance and Corporate Planning Implementation and Review	S Dorrell S Dorrell
		G Jones	Personnel Management and Policy	S Dorrell

Civil Servants and Groups

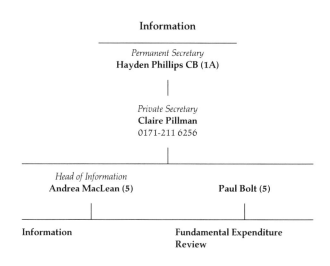

Information

Permanent Secretary
Hayden Phillips CB (1A)

Private Secretary
Claire Pillman
0171-211 6256

Head of Information
Andrea MacLean (5)

Information

Paul Bolt (5)

Fundamental Expenditure Review

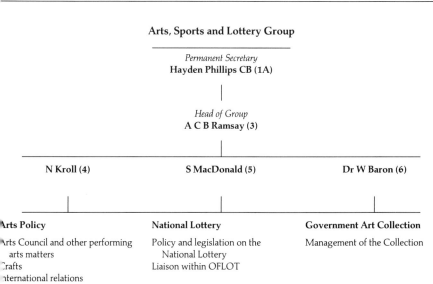

Arts, Sports and Lottery Group

Permanent Secretary
Hayden Phillips CB (1A)

Head of Group
A C B Ramsay (3)

N Kroll (4)

Arts Policy

Arts Council and other performing arts matters
Crafts
International relations
Arts taxation matters
Business sponsorship of the arts

S MacDonald (5)

National Lottery

Policy and legislation on the National Lottery
Liaison within OFLOT

Dr W Baron (6)

Government Art Collection

Management of the Collection

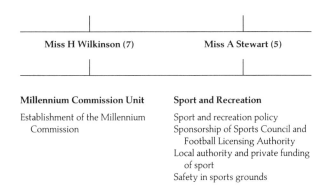

Miss H Wilkinson (7)

Millennium Commission Unit

Establishment of the Millennium Commission

Miss A Stewart (5)

Sport and Recreation

Sport and recreation policy
Sponsorship of Sports Council and Football Licensing Authority
Local authority and private funding of sport
Safety in sports grounds

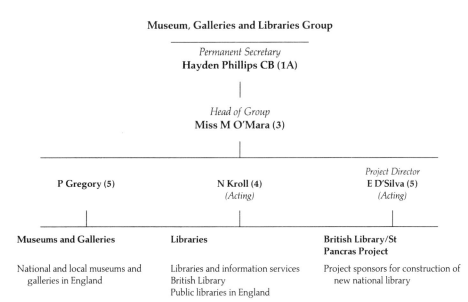

Museum, Galleries and Libraries Group

Permanent Secretary
Hayden Phillips CB (1A)

Head of Group
Miss M O'Mara (3)

P Gregory (5)

Museums and Galleries

National and local museums and galleries in England

N Kroll (4) *(Acting)*

Libraries

Libraries and information services
British Library
Public libraries in England

Project Director
E D'Silva (5) *(Acting)*

British Library/St Pancras Project

Project sponsors for construction of new national library

M Helston (7)

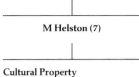

Cultural Property

Reviewing committee on export of works of art
Acceptance-in-Lieu Scheme
Government Indemnity Scheme

Broadcasting and Media Group

Permanent Secretary
Hayden Phillips CB (1A)

Head of Group
P Wright (3)

Miss S Booth CBE (5)

P C Edwards (5)

Broadcasting Policy

Broadcasting constitutional matters
Review of the BBC Charter
Broadcasting Act 1990
Radio, satellite and cable policy

Media

International and financial aspects of broadcasting policy
Press regulation
Films policy

Heritage and Tourism Group

Permanent Secretary
Hayden Phillips CB (1A)

Head of Group
D Chesterton (3)

A H Corner (5)

Dr K Gray (5)

Ms J Evans (5)

Heritage

Policy on the conservation and use of historic buildings and monuments
Sponsorship of English Heritage and the Royal Commission on the Historical Monuments of England

Royal Estates

Sponsorship of the Royal Armouries and Historic Royal Palaces Agency

Tourism

Sponsorship of BTA and ETB
Development of tourism's contribution to economic growth
Ensure tourist boards fulfil their objectives cost-effectively.

Resources and Services

Permanent Secretary
Hayden Phillips CB (1A)

Head of Group
N Pittman (4)

Director of Finance
R Maclachlan (5)

Director of Implementation and Review
S Broadley (5)

G Jones (5)

Finance and Corporate Planning

Financial management
Accounting systems
Estimates
Public Expenditure Survey forecasts

Implementation and Review

Establishment of accommodation and services for the department
Management of change and project management

Personnel Management and Policy

Personnel management
Equal opportunities
Welfare
Pay
Superannuation
Conditions of service

Department for National Savings

Founded 1861

Responsible to Economic Secretary, HM Treasury

Responsibilities The Department is the government's savings organisation and its products include:

- savings certificates
- income bonds
- pensioners' guaranteed income bond
- premium bonds
- savings bank ordinary and investment accounts
- capital bonds
- children's bonus bonds

Number of Staff 165

Department for National Savings

Charles House, 375 Kensington High Street, London W14 8SD
Tel 0171-605 9300 Fax 0171-605 9438

All staff are based at Charles House unless otherwise indicated.
For other addresses and telephone numbers see the end of this section.

Minister

Economic Secretary
Anthony Nelson MP
(for details of his office
see HM Treasury section)

Officials

Director
C D Butler (2)
(until the end of 1995)

Senior Personal Secretary
Mrs E Gould
0171-605 9463

Principal Establishment
and Finance Officer
C J A Chivers (4)

Departmental Overview

	Civil Servants		Department
Grade 2	*Grade 4*	*Grade 5*	
C D Butler *(until the end of 1995)*	C J A Chivers	P N S Hickman Robertson	Planning and Product Policy Division
		D S Speedie	Establishment
		M Nicholls	Finance
		Miss A Nash	Marketing and Information
		B G Rosser	Information Systems Division
C D Butler	These divisions report directly to the Director	D Monaghan	National Savings, Glasgow
		E B Senior	National Savings, Durham
		A S McGill	National Savings, Blackpool

Civil Servants and Departments

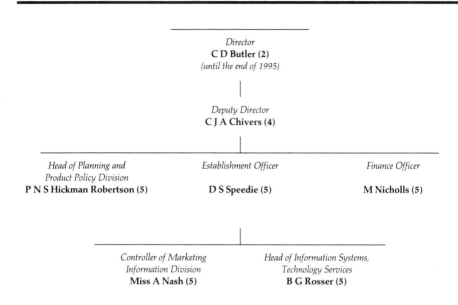

Director
C D Butler (2)
(until the end of 1995)

Deputy Director
C J A Chivers (4)

Head of Planning and Product Policy Division
P N S Hickman Robertson (5)

Establishment Officer
D S Speedie (5)

Finance Officer
M Nicholls (5)

Controller of Marketing Information Division
Miss A Nash (5)

Head of Information Systems, Technology Services
B G Rosser (5)

National Savings, Glasgow

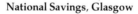

Director
C D Butler (2)
(until the end of 1995)

Controller
D H Monaghan (5)
(Boydstone Road)

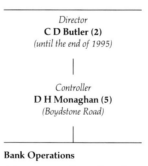

Bank Operations

Administration of Capital Bonds, National Savings Bank Investment, Ordinary Accounts, Children's Bonus Bonds

National Savings, Durham

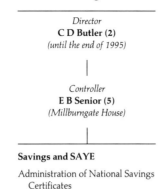

Director
C D Butler (2)
(until the end of 1995)

Controller
E B Senior (5)
(Millburngate House)

Savings and SAYE

Administration of National Savings Certificates

National Savings, Blackpool

Director
C D Butler (2)
(until the end of 1995)

Controller
A S McGill (5)
(Mythop Road)

Premium Bonds

Department for National Savings Addresses

Boydstone Road
Cowglen
Glasgow G58 1SB
Tel 0141-649 4555
Fax 0141-649 3998

Government Buildings
Heyhouses Lane
Lytham St Annes
Lancs FY0 1YN
Tel 01253 66151
Fax 01253 715667

Millburngate House
Durham DH99 1NS
Tel 0191-386 4900
Fax 0191-374 5495

Mythop Road
Marton
Blackpool
FY3 9YP
Tel 01253 766151
Fax 01253 793113

Northern Ireland Court Service

Founded	1979
Status	A unified and distinct civil service of the Crown
Minister	The Lord Chancellor
Responsibilities	To facilitate the conduct of the business of the Supreme Court, county courts, magistrates' courts, coroners' courts, office of the Social Security Commissioner for Northern Ireland and the Enforcement of Judgments Office Administrative responsibility for the Office of the Social Security Commissioner transferred during the 1980s to the Court Service The officers and other staff are appointed by the Lord Chancellor
Number of staff	670

Northern Ireland Court Service

Windsor House, Bedford Street, Belfast BT2 7LT
Tel 01232 328594 Fax 01232 439110

Ministers

Lord Chancellor
The Rt Hon The Lord Mackay of Clashfern
(for details of his office see Lord Chancellor's Department)

Officials

Director (3)

Personal Secretary
01232 328594 x244

Civil Servants and Departments

Northern Ireland Court Service

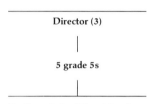

Director (3)

5 grade 5s

Northern Ireland Court Service

Court business
Press liaison
Legal aid
Policy evaluation
Judicial appointments
Judicial studies
Personnel
Finance
Training
Customer service
Communication
Enforcement of judgments
Management information systems
Accommodation and office services
Information technology
Internal audit
Legal advisers
Circuit administrators
Courts administrators, Supreme Court
Court Funds Office
Library service
Administration branch
Capital projects branch

Northern Ireland

The administration of the Province is carried out by the Northern Ireland Office (NIO) and the Northern Ireland departments. The NIO is staffed in part by Great Britain civil servants and in part by members of the Northern Ireland Civil Service.

The **Northern Ireland Office** deals mainly with security, law and order issues and political and constitutional developments. Social, economic and industrial policies are administered by the **Northern Ireland departments**.

For security reasons the names of most civil servants have been omitted.

Northern Ireland Office

Founded	1972 as a separate UK government department under the provisions of the Northern Ireland (Temporary Provisions) Act 1972, when the executive and legislative powers of the Northern Ireland Government and Parliament were transferred to the Secretary of State for Northern Ireland and the Parliament of the United Kingdom respectively
Ministers	secretary of state, two ministers of state and two parliamentary under secretaries of state
Responsibilities	To combat terrorism and to seek to establish stable political institutions in Northern Ireland The NIO is staffed by about 200 civil servants from the Home Civil Service and 1350 from the Northern Ireland Civil Service in London and Belfast, and is organised into the following divisions: Constitutional and Political Criminal Justice Economic and Social Finance and Personnel Forensic Science Police Political Affairs Prisons Probation and Training Schools Security and International Security Policy and Operations (I & II)
Executive Agencies	Compensation Agency (NI) Northern Ireland Prison Service

Northern Ireland Office

Stormont Castle, Belfast BT4 3ST
Tel 01232 520700 Fax 01232 768938
Whitehall, London SW1A 2AZ
Tel 0171-210 3000 Fax 0171-210 6549

For other addresses and telephone numbers see the end of this section.

Ministers

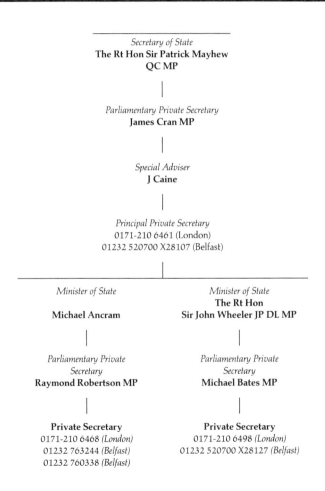

Secretary of State
The Rt Hon Sir Patrick Mayhew QC MP

Parliamentary Private Secretary
James Cran MP

Special Adviser
J Caine

Principal Private Secretary
0171-210 6461 (London)
01232 520700 X28107 (Belfast)

Minister of State
Michael Ancram

Parliamentary Private Secretary
Raymond Robertson MP

Private Secretary
0171-210 6468 *(London)*
01232 763244 *(Belfast)*
01232 760338 *(Belfast)*

Minister of State
The Rt Hon Sir John Wheeler JP DL MP

Parliamentary Private Secretary
Michael Bates MP

Private Secretary
0171-210 6498 *(London)*
01232 520700 X28127 *(Belfast)*

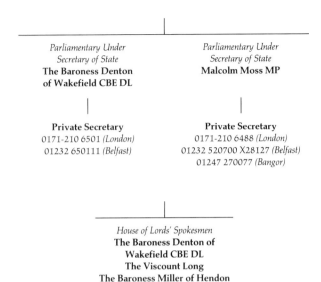

Parliamentary Under Secretary of State
The Baroness Denton of Wakefield CBE DL

Private Secretary
0171-210 6501 *(London)*
01232 650111 *(Belfast)*

Parliamentary Under Secretary of State
Malcolm Moss MP

Private Secretary
0171-210 6488 *(London)*
01232 520700 X28127 *(Belfast)*
01247 270077 *(Bangor)*

House of Lords' Spokesmen
The Baroness Denton of Wakefield CBE DL
The Viscount Long
The Baroness Miller of Hendon

Ministerial Responsibilities

Sir Patrick Mayhew	Economic questions Overall responsibility for the NIO and NI departments Constitutional and political Security policy and operations	
Sir John Wheeler	Information services Finance and personnel Law and order Security policy	see NICS departments below
Michael Ancram	Community relations Education Political development	see NICS departments below
Malcolm Moss	Environment Health and Social Services Roads Training and employment Transport Urban renewal Water	see NICS departments below
Baroness Denton	Agriculture Economic development Industrial development House of Lords spokesman on all NI matters	see NICS departments below

Departmental Overview

	Civil Servants		Department	Ministers
Sir John Chilcot	Reports directly to the PUS	Grade 3	Establishment and Finance	Sir J Wheeler
			Security	Sir J Wheeler
	Control and Coordination (London)			
Sir John Chilcot	Grade 2	Grade 3	Security and International	Sir J Wheeler
			Constitutional and Political	Sir J Wheeler/ M Ancram
			Economic and Social	Sir J Wheeler
		Grade 3	Political Affairs	Sir J Wheeler/ M Ancram
			Inter-Governmental Secretariat	Sir J Wheeler
		Grade 4	Information Services	Sir J Wheeler
	Control and Coordination (Belfast)			
Sir John Chilcot	Grade 2	Grade 3	Security Policy and Operations	Sir J Wheeler
			Forensic Science	Sir J Wheeler
		Grade 3	Criminal Justice	Sir J Wheeler
			Police	Sir J Wheeler
			Probation and Training Schools	Sir J Wheeler
			Compensation Agency	Sir J Wheeler
		Grade 3	Prisons	Sir J Wheeler

Civil Servants and Departments

Establishment and Finance

Permanent Under Secretary of State
Sir John Chilcot KCB (1)

Private Secretary
0171-210 6456 *(London)*
01232 520700 X28121 *(Belfast)*

Second Permanent Under Secretary of State and Head of Northern Ireland Civil Service
David Fell CB (1A)

Private Secretary
01232 520700 X28416 *(Belfast)*

Under Secretary (3)
(Belfast)

Grade 5
(London)
Grade 5
Grade 5
(both in Belfast)

Establishment

Personnel, accounts and general administration
Resources control
Services

Control and Coordination (London)

Permanent Under Secretary of State
Sir John Chilcot KCB (1)

Deputy Secretary (2)
(Control and Coordination London)

Under Secretary (3) *(London)*	**Under Secretary (3)** *(Belfast)*	**Grade 4** *(London and Belfast)*
Grade 5 **Grade 5** **Grade 5** *(all in London)*	**Grade 5** **Grade 5** *(both in Belfast)*	**Grade 5** *(Belfast)* **Grade 6** *(London)*
Security and International	**Political Affairs**	**Information Services**
Liaison on law and order matters Constitutional and Political Economic and Social	Inter-governmental secretariat	

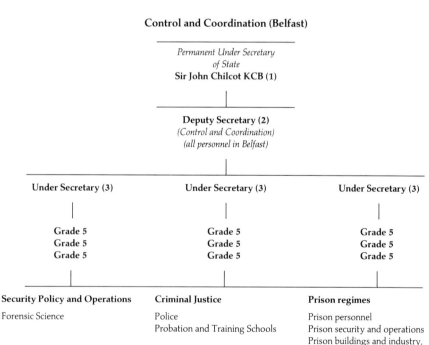

Control and Coordination (Belfast)

Permanent Under Secretary of State
Sir John Chilcot KCB (1)

Deputy Secretary (2)
(Control and Coordination)
(all personnel in Belfast)

Under Secretary (3)	**Under Secretary (3)**	**Under Secretary (3)**
Grade 5 **Grade 5** **Grade 5**	**Grade 5** **Grade 5** **Grade 5**	**Grade 5** **Grade 5** **Grade 5**
Security Policy and Operations	**Criminal Justice**	**Prison regimes**
Forensic Science	Police Probation and Training Schools	Prison personnel Prison security and operations Prison buildings and industry, education and service Prison secretariat Management systems, inspection and review, budgetary control

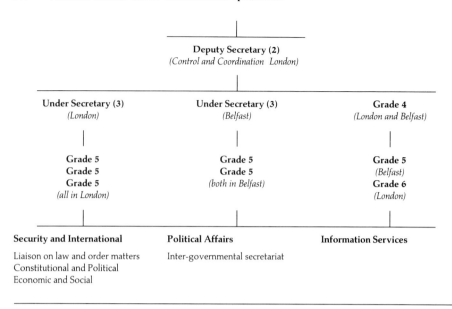

Northern Ireland Civil Service Departments

Department of Agriculture for Northern Ireland
Department of Economic Development Northern Ireland
Department of Education for Northern Ireland
Department of the Environment for Northern Ireland
Department of Finance and Personnel (including NI Civil Service Commission)
Department of Health and Social Services, Northern Ireland

Department of Agriculture for Northern Ireland

Founded	1974
Minister	parliamentary under secretary of state, Northern Ireland Office
Responsibilities	Development of the agricultural, forestry and fishing industries in Northern Ireland
	Provision of an advisory service for farmers, agricultural research and education
	Agent of the Ministry of Agriculture, Fisheries and Food in the administration of Northern Ireland of schemes affecting the whole of the United Kingdom
	Involvement with the application to Northern Ireland of the agricultural policy of the EC
	Promotion of community-led regeneration in areas of rural deprivation
Executive Agencies	None

Department of Agriculture for Northern Ireland

Dundonald House, Upper Newtownards Road, Belfast BT4 3SB
Tel 01232 520100   Fax 01232 525015

Minister

Parliamentary Under Secretary of State
Baroness Denton of Wakefield CBE DL

Private Secretary
0171-210 6500 (London)
01232 524611 (Belfast)

Departmental Overview

	Civil Servants	Division	Minister
Grade 2	Grade 3	Personnel and Finance	Ly Denton
	Grade 3	Food and Farm Policy	Ly Denton
	Grade 3	Agri-Environment Policy: Forestry and Fisheries	Ly Denton
	Grade 3	Agri-Food Development Service	Ly Denton
	Grade 3	Science Service	Ly Denton
	Grade 3	Veterinary Service	Ly Denton

Civil Servants and Divisions

Department of Agriculture for Northern Ireland

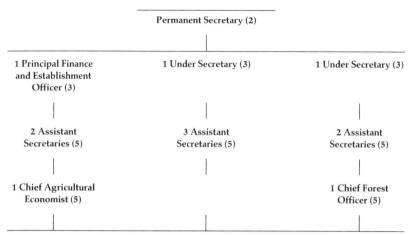

Permanent Secretary (2)

1 Principal Finance and Establishment Officer (3)	**1 Under Secretary (3)**	**1 Under Secretary (3)**
2 Assistant Secretaries (5)	**3 Assistant Secretaries (5)**	**2 Assistant Secretaries (5)**
1 Chief Agricultural Economist (5)		**1 Chief Forest Officer (5)**

Personnel and Finance

- Personnel
- Industrial personnel
- Information technology
- Efficiency and management services
- Finance, internal audit, resource control
- Economics and statistics
- Coordination
- Rural development

Food and Farm Policy Group

- Animal health and milk
- Cereals, horticulture, farm safety, intensive livestock
- Potatoes, plant health marketing, food policy, commodity group coordination
- Livestock production, subsidies and general livestock
- Meat marketing
- Integrated administration control system

Agri-Environment Policy; Forestry and Fisheries

- Forestry and fisheries policy and development
- Watercourse management
- Capital grants
- Agri-environment and countryside management policy

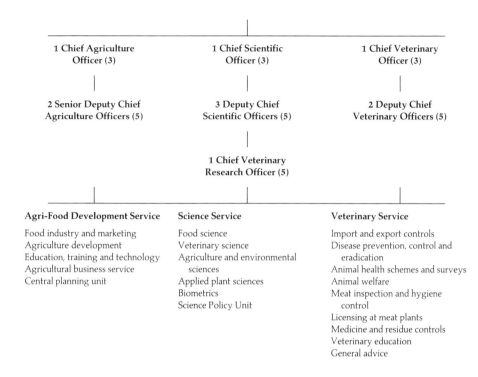

1 Chief Agriculture Officer (3)

2 Senior Deputy Chief Agriculture Officers (5)

1 Chief Scientific Officer (3)

3 Deputy Chief Scientific Officers (5)

1 Chief Veterinary Research Officer (5)

1 Chief Veterinary Officer (3)

2 Deputy Chief Veterinary Officers (5)

Agri-Food Development Service

Food industry and marketing
Agriculture development
Education, training and technology
Agricultural business service
Central planning unit

Science Service

Food science
Veterinary science
Agriculture and environmental sciences
Applied plant sciences
Biometrics
Science Policy Unit

Veterinary Service

Import and export controls
Disease prevention, control and eradication
Animal health schemes and surveys
Animal welfare
Meat inspection and hygiene control
Licensing at meat plants
Medicine and residue controls
Veterinary education
General advice

Department of Economic Development for Northern Ireland

Founded	1982
Minister	parliamentary under secretary of state, Northern Ireland Office
Responsibilities	company affairs consumer protection energy equality of opportunity in employment health and safety at work industrial development policy industrial relations mineral development promotion of small businesses through the Local Enterprise Development Unit (LEDU) promotion of industrially orientated research and development through the Industrial Research and Technology Unit (IRTU) promotion of tourism through the Northern Ireland Tourist Board (NITB) promotion of inward investment to Northern Ireland and the development and maintenance of existing industry through the Industrial Development Board (IDB)
Executive Agencies	Training and Employment Agency (NI) Industrial Research and Technology Unit (NI)

Department of Economic Development for Northern Ireland

Netherleigh, Massey Avenue, Belfast BT4 2JP
Tel 01232 529900 Fax 01232 529550/529551

Minister

Parliamentary Under Secretary of State
The Baroness Denton of Wakefield CBE DL

Private Secretary
0171-210 6501 (London)
01232 529209 (Belfast)

Departmental Overview

	Civil Servants		Divisions	Minister
	Grade 2	Grade 3	Resources Group	Ly Denton
		Grade 3	Regulatory Services Group	Ly Denton
		Grade 3	Science and Technology Group	Ly Denton
	Industrial Development Board			
Chairman	Grade 2	Grade 3	Inward Investment Group	Ly Denton
		Grade 3	Home Industry Group	Ly Denton
		Grade 3	Corporate Services Group	Ly Denton

Civil Servants and Divisions

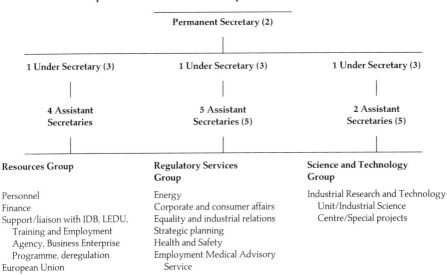

Department of Economic Development for Northern Ireland

Permanent Secretary (2)

1 Under Secretary (3)	1 Under Secretary (3)	1 Under Secretary (3)
4 Assistant Secretaries	5 Assistant Secretaries (5)	2 Assistant Secretaries (5)
Resources Group	**Regulatory Services Group**	**Science and Technology Group**
Personnel Finance Support/liaison with IDB, LEDU, Training and Employment Agency, Business Enterprise Programme, deregulation European Union	Energy Corporate and consumer affairs Equality and industrial relations Strategic planning Health and Safety Employment Medical Advisory Service	Industrial Research and Technology Unit/Industrial Science Centre/Special projects

Industrial Development Board for Northern Ireland (IDB)
(Department of Economic Development)

IDB House, 64 Chichester Street, Belfast BT1 4JX
Tel 01232 233233 Fax 01232 231328

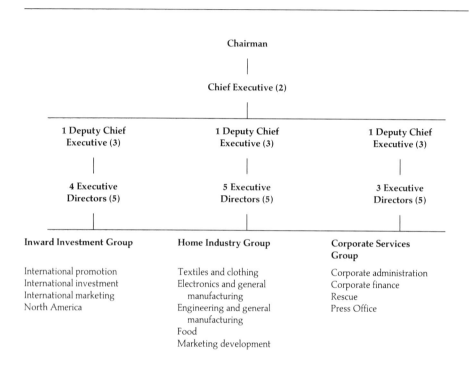

Chairman

Chief Executive (2)

1 Deputy Chief Executive (3)	1 Deputy Chief Executive (3)	1 Deputy Chief Executive (3)
4 Executive Directors (5)	5 Executive Directors (5)	3 Executive Directors (5)
Inward Investment Group	**Home Industry Group**	**Corporate Services Group**
International promotion International investment International marketing North America	Textiles and clothing Electronics and general manufacturing Engineering and general manufacturing Food Marketing development	Corporate administration Corporate finance Rescue Press Office

Department of Education for Northern Ireland

Founded 1973

Minister minister of state, Northern Ireland Office

Responsibilities The development of primary, secondary and further education, including:

- arts, libraries and museums
- community and adult education
- curriculum, examinations and assessment
- higher education
- improvement of community relations
- integrated education
- nursery education
- oversight of the five area Education and Library Boards
- special education
- sport and recreation
- teacher training
- teachers' salaries and superannuation
- youth services

Executive Agencies None

Department of Education for Northern Ireland

Rathgael House, Balloo Road, Bangor, Co Down BT19 7PR
Tel 01247 279279   Fax 01247 456451

Minister

Minister of State
Michael Ancram MP

Private Secretary
0171-210 6488 (London)
01232 528127 (Belfast)
01247 279303 (Bangor)

Departmental Overview

	Civil Servants	Divisions	Minister
Grade 2	Grade 3	Educational Services	M Ancram
	Grade 3	Establishment and Finance	M Ancram
	Grade 3	Education and and Training Inspectorate	M Ancram

Civil Servants and Divisions

Department of Education for Northern Ireland

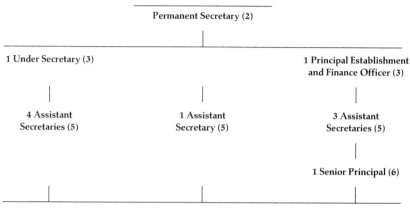

Permanent Secretary (2)

1 Under Secretary (3)

1 Principal Establishment and Finance Officer (3)

4 Assistant Secretaries (5)

1 Assistant Secretary (5)

3 Assistant Secretaries (5)

1 Senior Principal (6)

Educational Services

Area boards coordination and common services
Nursery and primary schools administration
Independent schools
Integrated schools administration
Teachers, administration, salaries and superannuation
Education reform finance
Area boards curriculum support service
Secondary schools administration
Voluntary grammar schools
Local management of schools
Curriculum and assessment
Special education

Policy

Policy evaluation
Policy development
Review of educational administration
Citizen's Charter issues
Liaison with SACHR
Policy appraisal and fair treatment
Women's issues
Open government
Legislation
Information services
Economic advisory service

Establishment and Finance

Finance and strategic planning
Planning
Higher education
Community relations
Recreation and youth
Education/industry links
Vocational qualifications
Further and continuing education
Initial teacher training
Student support
Arts, libraries and museums
European issues

1 Chief Inspector (3)

1 Deputy Chief Inspector (4)

5 Staff Inspectors (5)

53 Inspectors

Education and Training Inspectorate

Secondary education
Primary and nursery education
Special education needs/educational research
Teacher training and education for mutual understanding
Further and continuing education and youth service
Education and training

Department of the Environment for Northern Ireland

Founded 1976

Minister parliamentary under secretary of state, Northern Ireland Office

Responsibilities

- creation and management of country parks and the designation of areas of special scientific interest and of outstanding natural beauty
- disposal and management of department's land and property holdings
- environmental protection
- fire services
- housing policies
- listing and preservation of historic buildings and monuments
- overseeing and auditing the accounts of district councils
- planning
- registration of title of land and registration of deeds
- roads
- transport policies
- urban regeneration
- water and sewerage
- works services

Executive Agencies

- Driver and Vehicle Licensing Agency (NI)
- Driver and Vehicle Testing Agency (NI)
- Ordnance Survey (NI)
- The Public Record Office of Northern Ireland
- Rate Collection Agency (NI)

A new agency, the **Water Executive Agency** is likely to be launched later in 1995. Five more agencies dealing with **planning**, the **environment**, **roads and works services**, and the **Lands Registry/Registry of Deeds**, will be launched in April 1996.

Department of the Environment for Northern Ireland

Clarence Court, 10-18 Adelaide Street, Belfast BT2 8GB
Tel 01232 540540 Fax 01232 540028

Minister

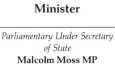

Parliamentary Under Secretary of State
Malcolm Moss MP

Private Secretary
0171-210 6468(London)
01232 541183 (Belfast)

Departmental Overview

	Civil Servants	Division	Minister
Grade 2	Grade 3	Personnel, Finance, Central Claims, Housing, Local Government and Land Registry	M Moss
	Grade 3	Planning and Urban Affairs	M Moss
	Grade 3	Central Policy and Management	M Moss
	Grade 3	Environment, Planning and Works	M Moss
	Grade 3	Transport, Fire Service, Road Service, Water Policy	M Moss
	Grade 3	Water Executive	M Moss

Civil Servants and Divisions

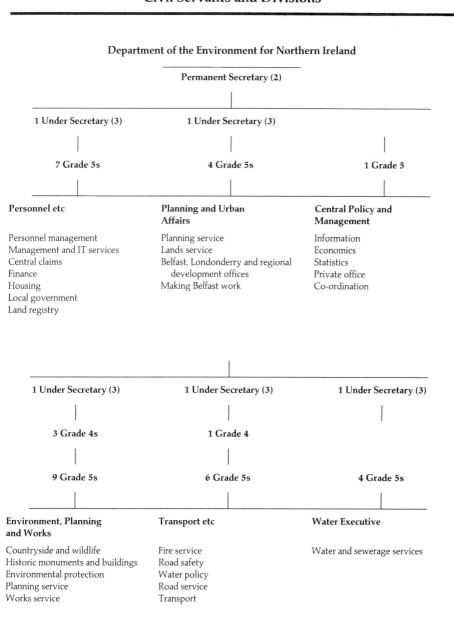

Department of the Environment for Northern Ireland

Permanent Secretary (2)

1 Under Secretary (3)

7 Grade 5s

Personnel etc

Personnel management
Management and IT services
Central claims
Finance
Housing
Local government
Land registry

1 Under Secretary (3)

4 Grade 5s

Planning and Urban Affairs

Planning service
Lands service
Belfast, Londonderry and regional development offices
Making Belfast work

1 Grade 5

Central Policy and Management

Information
Economics
Statistics
Private office
Co-ordination

1 Under Secretary (3)

3 Grade 4s

9 Grade 5s

Environment, Planning and Works

Countryside and wildlife
Historic monuments and buildings
Environmental protection
Planning service
Works service

1 Under Secretary (3)

1 Grade 4

6 Grade 5s

Transport etc

Fire service
Road safety
Water policy
Road service
Transport

1 Under Secretary (3)

4 Grade 5s

Water Executive

Water and sewerage services

Department of Finance and Personnel, Northern Ireland

Founded	1982
Minister	minister of state, Northern Ireland Office
Responsibilities	Northern Ireland Civil Service (equal opportunities policy, management and training consultancy and information technology service) census economic and social planning and research expenditure of NI departments General Register Office Government Purchasing Service (NI) law reform liaison with HM Treasury and NIO on financial matters personnel management provision of staff for the Civil Service Commission Ulster Savings
Executive Agencies	Valuation and Lands Agency

Department of Finance and Personnel, Northern Ireland

Rosepark House, Upper Newtownards Road, Belfast BT4 3NR
Tel 01232 520400 Fax 01232 485711

Minister

Minister of State
Sir John Wheeler MP

Private Secretary
0171-210 6498/9 (London)
01232 526545 (Belfast)
Fax: 01232 526440

Departmental Overview

	Civil Servants	Divisions	Minister
	Northern Ireland Civil Service		
D Fell CB (1A) Head of the Civil Service	Grade 3	Central Secretariat	Sir J Wheeler
	Grade 3	Legal Services	Sir J Wheeler
	First Legislative Counsel	Office of the Legislative Counsel	Sir J Wheeler
Grade 2	Grade 3	Supply Group	Sir J Wheeler
	Grade 3	Resources Control and Professional Services	Sir J Wheeler
	Grade 4	Establishment, Finance and Consultancy	Sir J Wheeler
	Grade 3	Central Personnel Group	Sir J Wheeler
	Grade 3	Valuation and Lands Agency	Sir J Wheeler
	Grade 3	Government Purchasing Service	Sir J Wheeler
	Grade 6	International Fund	Sir J Wheeler
	Grade 5	Law Reform	Sir J Wheeler

Civil Servants and Divisions

Northern Ireland Civil Service

Head of Northern Ireland Civil Service
David Fell CB (1A)

Under Secretary (3)

3 Assistant Secretaries (5)

Central secretariat

Protocol issues
Central appointments unit
Cross-border economic co-operation
NI legislative programme
Public Records scrutiny
Central Community Relations Unit
Central Planning Unit

1 Head of Legal Services (3)

1 Deputy Head of Legal Services (4)

8 Assistant Solicitors (5)

Legal Services

Provides legal advice and services to NI government departments

1 1st Legislative Counsel

1 2nd Legislative Counsel

2 Assistant Solicitors (5)

Office of the Legislative Counsel

Drafting of primary legislation (Orders in Council) for NI

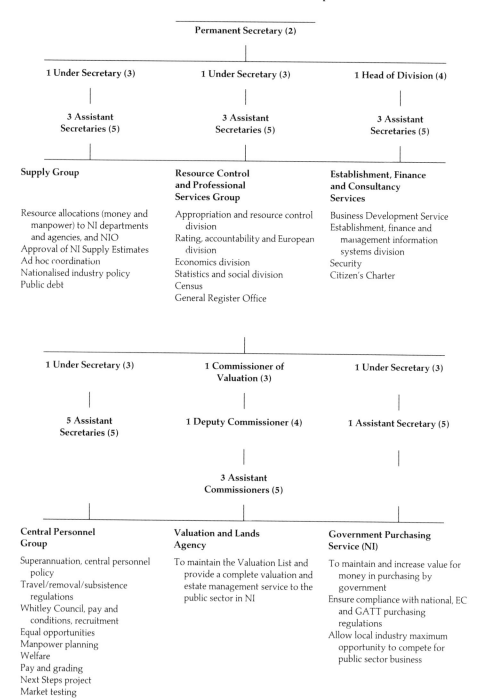

Permanent Secretary (2)

1 Under Secretary (3)

3 Assistant Secretaries (5)

Supply Group

- Resource allocations (money and manpower) to NI departments and agencies, and NIO
- Approval of NI Supply Estimates
- Ad hoc coordination
- Nationalised industry policy
- Public debt

1 Under Secretary (3)

3 Assistant Secretaries (5)

Resource Control and Professional Services Group

- Appropriation and resource control division
- Rating, accountability and European division
- Economics division
- Statistics and social division
- Census
- General Register Office

1 Head of Division (4)

3 Assistant Secretaries (5)

Establishment, Finance and Consultancy Services

- Business Development Service
- Establishment, finance and management information systems division
- Security
- Citizen's Charter

1 Under Secretary (3)

5 Assistant Secretaries (5)

Central Personnel Group

- Superannuation, central personnel policy
- Travel/removal/subsistence regulations
- Whitley Council, pay and conditions, recruitment
- Equal opportunities
- Manpower planning
- Welfare
- Pay and grading
- Next Steps project
- Market testing

1 Commissioner of Valuation (3)

1 Deputy Commissioner (4)

3 Assistant Commissioners (5)

Valuation and Lands Agency

- To maintain the Valuation List and provide a complete valuation and estate management service to the public sector in NI

1 Under Secretary (3)

1 Assistant Secretary (5)

Government Purchasing Service (NI)

- To maintain and increase value for money in purchasing by government
- Ensure compliance with national, EC and GATT purchasing regulations
- Allow local industry maximum opportunity to compete for public sector business

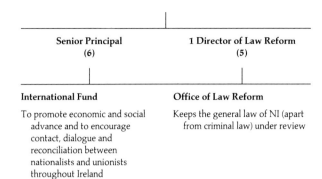

Senior Principal
(6)

1 Director of Law Reform
(5)

International Fund

To promote economic and social advance and to encourage contact, dialogue and reconciliation between nationalists and unionists throughout Ireland

Office of Law Reform

Keeps the general law of NI (apart from criminal law) under review

Department of Health and Social Services, Northern Ireland

Founded	1965
Minister	parliamentary under secretary of state, Northern Ireland Office
Responsibilities	health personal social services social legislation and administration social security and child support
Executive Agencies	Social Security Agency (NI) Child Support Agency (NI)

Department of Health and Social Services, Northern Ireland

Dundonald House, Upper Newtownards Road, Belfast BT4 3SF
Tel 01232 520100 Fax 01232 524972

Minister

Parliamentary Under Secretary of State
Malcolm Moss MP

Private Secretary
0171-210 6465 (London)
01232 524794 (Belfast)

Departmental Overview

	Civil Servants	Divisions	Minister
Grade 2	Grade 3	Health and Personal Social Services Management Executive	M Moss
	Grade 3	Health and Personal Social Services Policy and Strategy Group	M Moss
	Grade 4	Social Services Inspectorate	M Moss
	Grade 4	Nursing and Midwifery Advisory Group	M Moss
Chief Medical Officer (3)	Grade 3	Medical and Allied Services	M Moss
	Grade 4	Dental Services	M Moss
	Grade 5	Pharmaceutical Advice and Services	M Moss
	Grade 3	Central Group	M Moss

Civil Servants and Divisions

Department of Health and Social Services, Northern Ireland

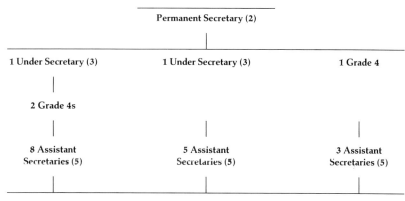

Permanent Secretary (2)

1 Under Secretary (3)

2 Grade 4s

8 Assistant Secretaries (5)

Health and Personal Social Services Management

- Purchasing and performance review directorate
- Office of the Chief Executive
- Financial management directorate
- Human resources directorate
- Provider development directorate
- Directorate of information systems
- Estates and property division
- Design and consultancy services division
- Project planning and procurement division
- Family health services directorate

1 Under Secretary (3)

5 Assistant Secretaries (5)

Health and Personal Social Services Policy and Strategy Group

- Health policy division
- Family policy unit
- Client groups division
- Social legislation division
- Strategy and intelligence group
- Social and community division (including voluntary activity unit)

1 Grade 4

3 Assistant Secretaries (5)

Social Services Inspectorate

- Family and child care programmes
- Belfast Action Team overview
- Physical handicap programme
- Mental health and substance abuse programme
- Elderly care programme
- Training schools and probation service
- Mental handicap programme

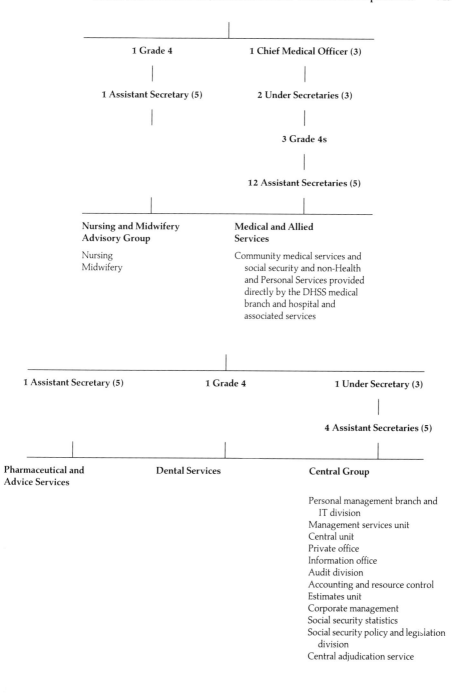

1 Grade 4

1 Assistant Secretary (5)

1 Chief Medical Officer (3)

2 Under Secretaries (3)

3 Grade 4s

12 Assistant Secretaries (5)

Nursing and Midwifery Advisory Group

Nursing
Midwifery

Medical and Allied Services

Community medical services and social security and non-Health and Personal Services provided directly by the DHSS medical branch and hospital and associated services

1 Assistant Secretary (5)

1 Grade 4

1 Under Secretary (3)

4 Assistant Secretaries (5)

Pharmaceutical and Advice Services

Dental Services

Central Group

Personal management branch and IT division
Management services unit
Central unit
Private office
Information office
Audit division
Accounting and resource control
Estimates unit
Corporate management
Social security statistics
Social security policy and legislation division
Central adjudication service

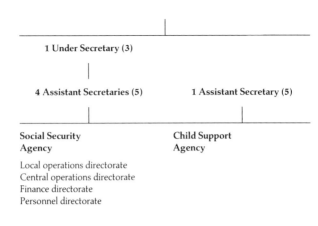

1 Under Secretary (3)

4 Assistant Secretaries (5)

1 Assistant Secretary (5)

Social Security Agency

Local operations directorate
Central operations directorate
Finance directorate
Personnel directorate

Child Support Agency

Office of Population, Censuses and Surveys

Founded	1970 when the General Register Office, established in 1837, merged with the Government Social Survey which started in 1941
Responsibilities	Analysis of vital, medical and demographic statistics and publication of reports Census of the population Registration of births, marriages and deaths in England and Wales Regulation of civil marriages Research
Number of staff	1700

OPCS is likely to merge with the Central Statistical Office (*see* Next Steps executive agencies section) and become an executive agency in April 1996

Office of Population, Censuses and Surveys

Head Office, St Catherine's House, 10 Kingsway, London WC2B 6JP
Tel 0171-396 2200 Fax 0171-396 2576

Minister

Parliamentary Under Secretary of State for Health
The Hon Tom Sackville MP
(for details of his office see Department of Health)

Officials

Director and Registrar General
P J Wormald CB

Private Secretary
Mrs J Morgan
0171-396 2161

Civil Servants and Departments

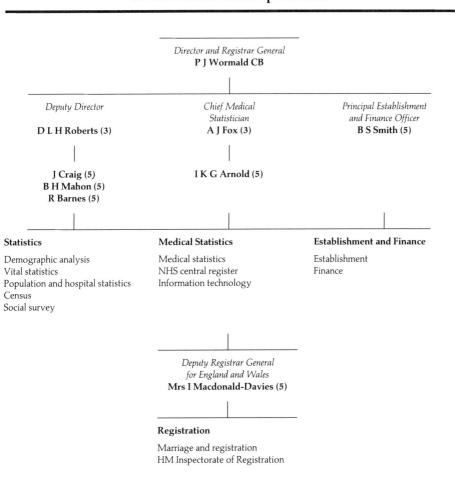

Director and Registrar General
P J Wormald CB

Deputy Director
D L H Roberts (3)

J Craig (5)
B H Mahon (5)
R Barnes (5)

Chief Medical Statistician
A J Fox (3)

I K G Arnold (5)

Principal Establishment and Finance Officer
B S Smith (5)

Statistics

Demographic analysis
Vital statistics
Population and hospital statistics
Census
Social survey

Medical Statistics

Medical statistics
NHS central register
Information technology

Establishment and Finance

Establishment
Finance

Deputy Registrar General for England and Wales
Mrs I Macdonald-Davies (5)

Registration

Marriage and registration
HM Inspectorate of Registration

Office for Standards in Education (OFSTED)

Founded	1992
Ministers	Non-ministerial department responsible to HM Chief Inspector of Schools
Responsibilities	Establishment and regulation of the system of school inspection set up by the Education (Schools) Act 1992
	Provision of advice to the Secretary of State for Education and aims on educational issues
	Specific inspection responsibilities including teacher education, independent schools and adult and continuing education
Number of staff	490

Office for Standards in Education (OFSTED)

Alexandra House, 29-33 Kingsway, London WC2B 6SE
Tel 0171-421 6800   Fax 0171-421 6707

Her Majesty's Chief Inspector
Chris Woodhead (2)

Personal Assistant
Ms Christine Kensett
0171-421 6768

Departmental Overview

Civil Servants *Grade 2*	*Grade 4*	Division
Chris Woodhead	Mrs H Douglas	Administration
	M J Tomlinson A J Rose	Inspection

Civil Servants and Divisions

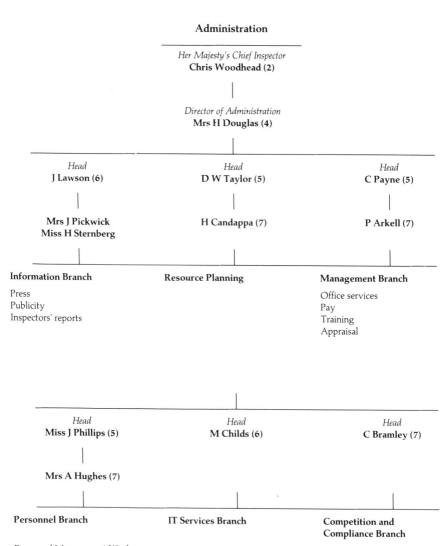

Administration

Her Majesty's Chief Inspector
Chris Woodhead (2)

Director of Administration
Mrs H Douglas (4)

Head
J Lawson (6)

Mrs J Pickwick
Miss H Sternberg

Information Branch

Press
Publicity
Inspectors' reports

Head
D W Taylor (5)

H Candappa (7)

Resource Planning

Head
C Payne (5)

P Arkell (7)

Management Branch

Office services
Pay
Training
Appraisal

Head
Miss J Phillips (5)

Mrs A Hughes (7)

Personnel Branch

Personnel Management Work Programme Team

Head
M Childs (6)

IT Services Branch

Head
C Bramley (7)

Competition and Compliance Branch

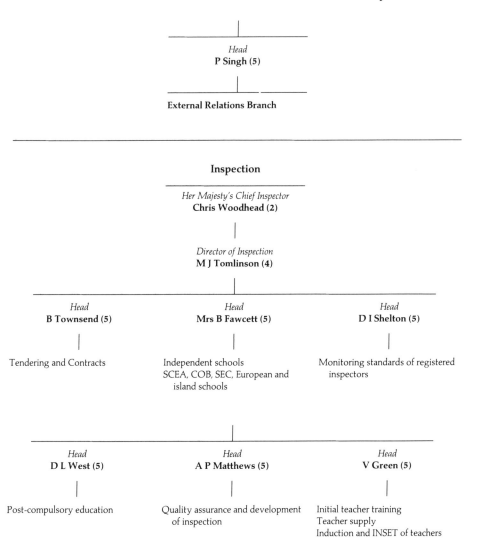

Head
P Singh (5)

External Relations Branch

Inspection

Her Majesty's Chief Inspector
Chris Woodhead (2)

Director of Inspection
M J Tomlinson (4)

Head
B Townsend (5)

Tendering and Contracts

Head
Mrs B Fawcett (5)

Independent schools
SCEA, COB, SEC, European and island schools

Head
D I Shelton (5)

Monitoring standards of registered inspectors

Head
D L West (5)

Post-compulsory education

Head
A P Matthews (5)

Quality assurance and development of inspection

Head
V Green (5)

Initial teacher training
Teacher supply
Induction and INSET of teachers

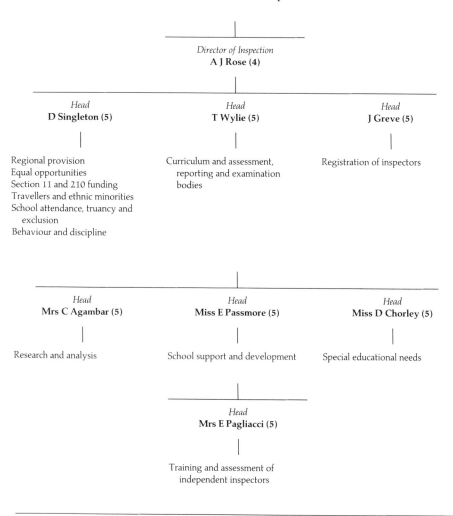

Director of Inspection
A J Rose (4)

Head
D Singleton (5)

Regional provision
Equal opportunities
Section 11 and 210 funding
Travellers and ethnic minorities
School attendance, truancy and exclusion
Behaviour and discipline

Head
T Wylie (5)

Curriculum and assessment, reporting and examination bodies

Head
J Greve (5)

Registration of inspectors

Head
Mrs C Agambar (5)

Research and analysis

Head
Miss E Passmore (5)

School support and development

Head
Miss D Chorley (5)

Special educational needs

Head
Mrs E Pagliacci (5)

Training and assessment of independent inspectors

Overseas Development Administration

Founded	1964
Ministers	Secretary of State for Foreign and Commonwealth Affairs and Minister for Overseas Development
Responsibilities	British aid to overseas countries. This includes capital aid on concessionary terms and technical cooperation provided directly to developing countries or through multilateral aid organisations, including the United Nations and its specialised agencies
Number of staff	1100
Executive agencies	Natural Resources Institute

Overseas Development Administration

94 Victoria Street, London SW1E 5JL
Tel 0171-917 7000 Fax 0171-917 0016/0019

All personnel are based at 94 Victoria Street unless otherwise indicated.
For other addresses and telephone numbers see the end of this section.

Ministers

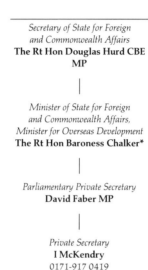

Secretary of State for Foreign and Commonwealth Affairs
The Rt Hon Douglas Hurd CBE MP

Minister of State for Foreign and Commonwealth Affairs, Minister for Overseas Development
The Rt Hon Baroness Chalker*

Parliamentary Private Secretary
David Faber MP

Private Secretary
I McKendry
0171-917 0419

*For details of Lady Chalker's responsibilities see under Foreign and Commonwealth Office

Departmental Overview

Civil Servants			Department	Minister
Grade 1A	*Grade 2*	*Grade 3*		
J M Vereker	These divisions report directly to the Permanent Secretary	R G M Manning	Aid Policy and Finance	Ly Chalker
		P M D Freeman	Establishment, Information Systems, Management Review Staff, Medical and Staff Welfare	Ly Chalker
		J B Wilmshurst	Economic and Social Development	Ly Chalker
		P A Bearpark (5)	Information, Emergency Aid	Ly Chalker
J M Vereker	R M Ainscow	P D M Freeman	Overseas Manpower and Pensions	Ly Chalker
		J A L Faint	Eastern Europe and Western Hemisphere	Ly Chalker
		B R Ireton	Africa	Ly Chalker
		J V Kerby	Asia and the Oceans	Ly Chalker
		N B Hudson	International	Ly Chalker
		Ms M A Harrison (5)	Education	Ly Chalker
		J W Hodges (5)	Engineering	Ly Chalker
		Dr D Nabarro (5)	Health and Population	Ly Chalker
		A J Bennett	Natural Resources and Environment	Ly Chalker

Civil Servants and Departments

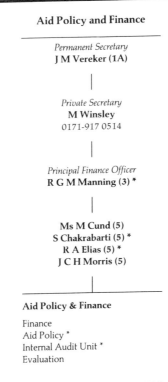

Aid Policy and Finance

Permanent Secretary
J M Vereker (1A)

Private Secretary
M Winsley
0171-917 0514

Principal Finance Officer
R G M Manning (3) *

Ms M Cund (5)
S Chakrabarti (5) *
R A Elias (5) *
J C H Morris (5)

Aid Policy & Finance

Finance
Aid Policy *
Internal Audit Unit *
Evaluation

* *Staff and divisions are part of a joint ODA/FCO department*

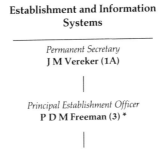

Establishment and Information Systems

Permanent Secretary
J M Vereker (1A)

Principal Establishment Officer
P D M Freeman (3) *

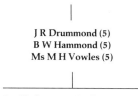

J R Drummond (5)
B W Hammond (5)
Ms M H Vowles (5)

Establishment and Information Systems

Establishment and organisation
Information systems department
Library *
Medical and staff welfare *
Management review staff *
Sponsored organisations and scholarships department

* *Staff and divisions are part of a joint ODA/FCO department*

Economic and Social Development

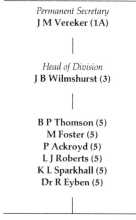

Permanent Secretary
J M Vereker (1A)

Head of Division
J B Wilmshurst (3)

B P Thomson (5)
M Foster (5)
P Ackroyd (5)
L J Roberts (5)
K L Sparkhall (5)
Dr R Eyben (5)

Economic and Social

Asia, Latin America and Oceans
Africa and Middle East group
Multilateral and research economics
Aid economics and small enterprises
Government and institutions
Social development

Information

Permanent Secretary
J M Vereker (1A)

P A Bearpark (5)

Information; Emergency Aid

Information
Publicity
Press office

Overseas Manpower and Pensions

Permanent Secretary
J M Vereker (1A)

Deputy Secretary
R M Ainscow (2)

Under Secretary
P M D Freeman (3)

D S Fish (5)
(Abercrombie House)

Overseas Manpower

Overseas appointments and contracts
Personnel services
Recruitment and consultancies

D Trotter (5)
(Abercrombie House)

Overseas Pensions

Eastern Europe and Western Hemisphere

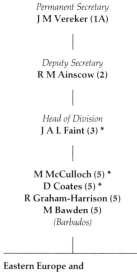

Permanent Secretary
J M Vereker (1A)

Deputy Secretary
R M Ainscow (2)

Head of Division
J A L Faint (3) *

M McCulloch (5) *
D Coates (5) *
R Graham-Harrison (5)
M Bawden (5)
(Barbados)

Eastern Europe and Western Hemisphere

Central Europe
Eastern Europe and former Soviet Union *
European Bank for Reconstruction and Development
British development division in the Caribbean (Barbados), Latin America and the Caribbean Atlantic

* *Staff and divisions are part of a joint ODA/FCO department*

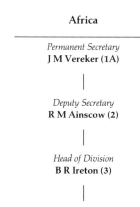

Africa

Permanent Secretary
J M Vereker (1A)

Deputy Secretary
R M Ainscow (2)

Head of Division
B R Ireton (3)

Ms B M Kelly (5)
G Leader (6)
S Ray (5)
M Wickstead (5)
(Kenya)
A G Coverdale (5)
(Zimbabwe)
G M Stegmann
(South Africa)

Africa

Eastern Africa
Central and Southern Africa
West and North Africa
British development division in East Africa
British development division in Central Africa
British development division in Southern Africa

Asia and the Oceans

Permanent Secretary
J M Vereker (1A)

Deputy Secretary
R M Ainscow (2)

Head of Division
J V Kerby (3)

A Davis (5)
Mrs P M Wilkinson (5)
Ms S E Unsworth (5)
Ms A M Archbold (5)
C P Raleigh (5)
(Thailand)

Asia and the Oceans

East Asia
Pacific department
South Asia
West Asia
South East Asia development division

International

Permanent Secretary
J M Vereker (1A)

Deputy Secretary
R M Ainscow (2)

Head of Division
N B Hudson (3)

Ms P Hilton (5)
J Machin (5)
M A Power (5)

International

European Community and Food Aid
United Nations and Commonwealth
International financial institutions

Education

Permanent Secretary
J M Vereker (1A)

Deputy Secretary
R M Ainscow (2)

Ms M Harrison (5)

Education

Education aid policy
Functional programmes of assistance
Technical cooperation programmes
British Council
Commonwealth education matters

Engineering

Permanent Secretary
J M Vereker (1A)

Deputy Secretary
R M Ainscow (2)

J Hodges (5)

Engineering

Research on new and renewable sources of energy
Engineering, geological and building research projects
Relations with Building Research Establishment, Hydraulics Research Station, Institute of Hydrology, Transport and Road Research Laboratory

Health and Population

Permanent Secretary
J M Vereker (1A)

Deputy Secretary
R M Ainscow (2)

Dr D Nabarro (5)

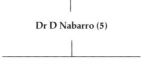

Health and Population

World Health Organisation
Medical and nutrition research projects
Population policy and family planning

Natural Resources and Environment

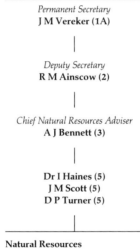

Permanent Secretary
J M Vereker (1A)

Deputy Secretary
R M Ainscow (2)

Chief Natural Resources Adviser
A J Bennett (3)

Dr I Haines (5)
J M Scott (5)
D P Turner (5)

Natural Resources

Policy on agricultural and rural development, cooperatives and institutions
Support for international research
Renewable natural resources research
Contract research
Relations with ODA scientific units, Overseas Surveys Directorate of Ordnance Survey
Relations with ODA core-funded associated bodies
Science and technology for development
Environment policy

Overseas Development Administration Addresses

Abercrombie House
Eaglesham Road
East Kilbride
Glasgow G75 8EA
Tel 0135584 4000
Fax 0135584 4097

Barbados
PO Box 167
Bridgetown
Barbados
Tel Barbados 436 9873
Fax Barbados 426 2194

Kenya
PO Box 30465
Bruce House
Standard Street
Nairobi
Kenya
Tel Nairobi 335944
Fax Nairobi 340260

South Africa
Suite 303
Infotech Building
1090 Arcadia Street
Hatfield 0083
Pretoria
South Africa
Tel Pretoria 3423360
Fax Pretoria 3423429

Thailand
c/o British Embassy
Bangkok
Thailand
Tel Bangkok 662 253-0191
Fax Bangkok 662 253-712

Zimbabwe
c/o British High Commission
Stanley House
Jason Moyo Avenue
PO Box 4490
Harare
Zimbabwe
Tel Harare 793781
Fax Harare 728380

Parliamentary Counsel Office

Founded	1868
Status	Part of the Cabinet Office
Responsible to	The Lord Privy Seal and the Lord President of the Council in respect of professional matters; and the Chancellor of the Duchy of Lancaster in respect of administrative matters
Responsibilities	Drafting of government bills (except for those relating exclusively to Scotland); drafting of amendments to, and motions etc. relating to, bills; advice on parliamentary procedure
Number of staff	60

Parliamentary Counsel Office

36 Whitehall, London SW1A 2AY
Tel 0171-210 6633   Fax 0171-210 6632

Ministers

The Lord Privy Seal
The Rt Hon The Viscount Cranborne

The Lord President of the Council
The Rt Hon Antony Newton MP
in respect of professional matters

The Chancellor of the Duchy of Lancaster
The Rt Hon David Hunt MP
in respect of administrative matters

Counsel

First Parliamentary Counsel
J C Jenkins CB QC

Private Secretary
P J Moore MBE (7)
0171-210 6629

Second Parliamentary Counsel
D W Saunders CB

Parliamentary Counsel
E G Caldwell CB
E G Bowman CB
G B Sellers CB
E R Sutherland CB
S C Laws
R S Parker
Miss C E Johnston
P J Davies

Deputy Parliamentary Counsel
J M Sellers
A Hogarth

Principal Assistant Parliamentary Counsel
Miss H J Caldwell
D J Ramsay

Assistant Parliamentary Counsel
R N Cory
D J Cook
Ms K A Cooper
D I Greenberg
Miss B A Waplington
Miss J M Piesse
Mrs A M Bertlin
Ms C Croft
E J Stell
Mrs H Rogers

Prime Minister's Office

10 Downing Street, London SW1A 2AA
Tel 0171-270 3000
Fax *Telephone the above number and ask for appropriate fax number*

70 Whitehall, London SW1A 2AS
Tel 0171-270 0260/0435 Fax 0171-930 1419

Prime Minister and
First Lord of the Treasury and
Minister for the Civil Service
The Rt Hon John Major MP

Principal Private Secretary
to the Prime Minister
Alex Allan (3)
0171-930 4433

Number of staff 105 (November 1994)

Overview

Civil Servants and Other Staff

Private Office

The Rt Hon John Major	Alex Allan (3)	*Private Secretaries*	
		R Lyne (3)	Overseas Affairs
		Mrs M Francis (5)	Economic Affairs
		M Adams (5)	Parliamentary Affairs
		Miss R Reynolds (7)	Home Affairs and Diary
		J H Holroyd (2)	Secretary for Appointments
		Miss L Wilkinson (SEO)	Personnel and Finance

Political Office

The Rt Hon John Major		Howell James	Political Secretary
		John Ward MP	Parliamentary Private Secretary (Commons)
		Lord McColl of Dulwich	Parliamentary Private Secretary (Lords)

No 10 Policy Unit

The Rt Hon John Major	Norman Blackwell (1A)	*Special Advisers* Dominic Morris Jonathan Rees Katharine Ramsay Sean Williams Carolyn Fairbairn David Soskin Tim Collins

Press Office

The Rt Hon John Major	C J R Meyer CMG (2)	Chief Press Secretary

Efficiency Unit*

The Rt Hon John Major	Sir Peter Levene	Prime Minister's Adviser on Efficiency
	J Oughton (3)	Head of Unit

* Under the general jurisdiction of the Chancellor of the Duchy of Lancaster

Civil Servants, Other Staff and Departments

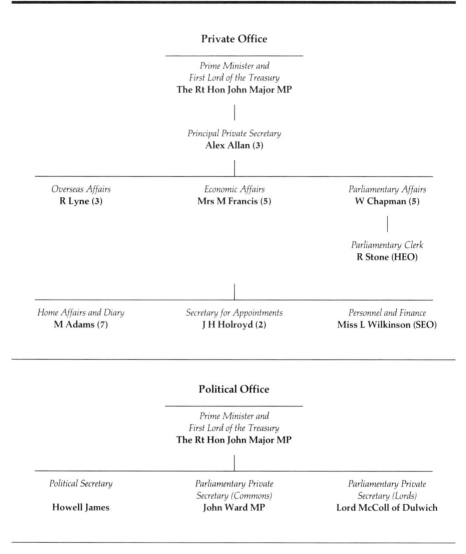

Private Office

Prime Minister and First Lord of the Treasury
The Rt Hon John Major MP

Principal Private Secretary
Alex Allan (3)

- *Overseas Affairs* — **R Lyne (3)**
- *Economic Affairs* — **Mrs M Francis (5)**
- *Parliamentary Affairs* — **W Chapman (5)**
  - *Parliamentary Clerk* — **R Stone (HEO)**
- *Home Affairs and Diary* — **M Adams (7)**
- *Secretary for Appointments* — **J H Holroyd (2)**
- *Personnel and Finance* — **Miss L Wilkinson (SEO)**

Political Office

Prime Minister and First Lord of the Treasury
The Rt Hon John Major MP

- *Political Secretary* — **Howell James**
- *Parliamentary Private Secretary (Commons)* — **John Ward MP**
- *Parliamentary Private Secretary (Lords)* — **Lord McColl of Dulwich**

No 10 Policy Unit

Prime Minister and
First Lord of the Treasury
The Rt Hon John Major MP

No 10 Policy Unit

Head of Unit **Norman Blackwell**	Economic and European issues
Dominic Morris	Industry, Education, Science
Jonathan Rees	Transport, Housing, Environment
Katharine Ramsay	Local government, Rural affairs
Sean Williams	Enterprise, Employment, Agriculture
Carolyn Fairbairn	Health, Family policy
David Soskin	Social Security
Tim Collins	Home affairs, Defence, Heritage

Press Office

Prime Minister and
First Lord of the Treasury
The Rt Hon John Major MP

Chief Press Secretary
C J R Meyer CMG (2)

Deputy Chief Press Secretary
A Marre (5)

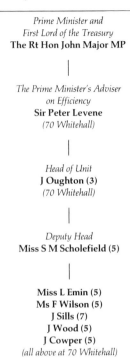

Efficiency and Effectiveness Group*

Prime Minister and
First Lord of the Treasury
The Rt Hon John Major MP

|

The Prime Minister's Adviser
on Efficiency
Sir Peter Levene
(70 Whitehall)

|

Head of Unit
J Oughton (3)
(70 Whitehall)

|

Deputy Head
Miss S M Scholefield (5)

|

Miss L Emin (5)
Ms F Wilson (5)
J Sills (7)
J Wood (5)
J Cowper (5)
(all above at 70 Whitehall)

* *see also Cabinet Office*

Privy Council Office

Founded	During the 13th and 14th centuries
Responsible to	Lord President of the Council (since 1940 most often the Leader of the House of Commons or the House of Lords and usually a senior member of the Cabinet) and thence the sovereign
Responsibilities:	*Lord President of the Council* Administering the appointments of Privy Counsellors (of whom there are about 400) Royal proclamations and Orders in Council Granting of royal charters Approval of bye-laws and statutes of chartered bodies Approval of regulations and rules made by the governing bodies of the medical and certain allied professions Appointment of high sheriffs and many Crown and Privy Council appointments to government bodies Administration of the judicial committee of the Privy Council (the final court of appeal for Commonwealth citizens), which is composed of all Privy Counsellors who hold or have held high judicial office *Leader of the Commons* Arranging government business Procedural matters Supervision of the government's legislative programme Upholding the rights and privileges of the House as a whole
Number of staff	38

There are no longer any responsibilities or functions of any kind attaching to the office of Lord Privy Seal (currently The Rt Hon The Viscount Cranborne, Leader of the House of Lords) as such. This office is currently based in the Privy Council Office as a matter of convenience.

Privy Council Office

68 Whitehall, London SW1A 2AT
Tel 0171-270 3000

Ministers

Lord President of the Council and Leader of the House of Commons
The Rt Hon Antony Newton OBE MP

Parliamentary Private Secretary

Special Adviser
Praveen Moman

Principal Private Secretary
P Cohen

Private Secretary
Mrs H Paxman
0171-270 0480

The Lord Privy Seal and Leader of the House of Lords
The Rt Hon The Viscount Cranborne

Parliamentary Private Secretary
Cheryl Gillan MP

Private Secretary
Mrs J M Bailey
0171-270 0501

Ministerial Responsibilities

Antony Newton *as Lord President*	Responsible for the work of the Privy Council Office: royal proclamations and Orders in Council granting of royal charters administers appointments of Privy Counsellors approval of statutes and byelaws of chartered bodies; rules and regulations of certain professions various Crown and Privy Council appointments administration of judicial committee
as Leader of the Commons	Advice on procedural matters and upholding the rights and privileges of the House Arrangement of government business in the House including legislation

Officials

Clerk of the Council
N H Nicholls CBE (3)

Deputy Clerk of the Council and Establishment Officer
R P Bulling (5)

Assistance to the Clerk in all his functions

Registrar of the Judicial Committee of the Privy Council
D H O Owen (5)

Organisation of the work of the Judicial Committee

Registry of Friendly Societies

Founded	RFS: 1875 Building Societies Commission: 1986 Friendly Societies Commission: 1992
Status	non-ministerial department serving three statutory bodies: the Building Societies Commission, the Friendly Societies Commission and the Central Office of the Registry of Friendly Societies
Responsible to	Minister of State, HM Treasury
Responsibilities	Advice to ministers on friendly societies, building societies and industrial and provident societies *The Building Societies Commission:* exercises prudential supervision over building societies in the interests of investors. It administers the system of regulation and promotes the financial stability of the building society industry generally *The Friendly Societies Commission:* established under the Friendly Societies Act 1992 with statutory responsibility for the regulation and supervision of friendly societies *The Central Office of the Registry of Friendly Societies:* exercises prudential supervision over friendly societies and credit unions Provides a public registry of mutual organisations registered under the Building Societies Act 1986, Friendly Societies Act 1974, and the Industrial and Provident Societies Act 1965.
Number of staff	176

Registry of Friendly Societies

15 Great Marlborough Street, London W1V 2AX
Tel 0171-437 9992 Fax 0171-437 1612

58 Frederick Street, Edinburgh EH2 1AB
Tel 0131-225 3224 Fax 0131-225 5687

Minister

Minister of State, HM Treasury
Anthony Nelson MP

Officials

Chief Registrar of Friendly Societies
Chairman and First Commissioner,
Building Societies Commission
G E Fitchew (2)

Private Secretary
Susan Jefferies
0171-494 6641

Deputy Chairman
H G Walsh (3)

Departmental Overview

Civil Servants			Department	Minister
Grade 2	*Grade 3*	*Grade 4*		
G E Fitchew	H G Walsh	T F Mathews	Building Societies Commission	A Nelson
		D W Lee	Friendly Societies Commission	A Nelson
G E Fitchew		D W Lee A J Perrett J L J Craig (5)	Central Office	A Nelson

Civil Servants and Departments

Chairman of the Building Societies Commission
G E Fitchew (2)

Deputy Chairman
H G Walsh (3)

Commissioner
T F Mathews (4)
J Palmer (5)

Assistant Commissioners
R Gabbertas (5)
D A W Stevens (5)
W J Champion (5)

Commissioners (part-time)
N Fox Bassett
F E Worsley
F G Sunderland
Sir James Birrell

Secretary
Ms J Dennis

Chief Registrar of Friendly Societies, Industrial Assurance Commissioner
G E Fitchew (2)

Assistant Registrars
D W Lee (4)
A J Perrett (4)

Registry of Friendly Society (Scotland) Assistant Registrar
J L J Craig (5)
(58 Frederick Street)

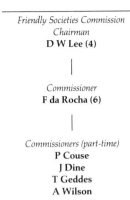

Friendly Societies Commission
Chairman
D W Lee (4)

Commissioner
F da Rocha (6)

Commissioners (part-time)
P Couse
J Dine
T Geddes
A Wilson

Scottish Courts Administration

Founded	1971
Ministers	The Lord Advocate Secretary of State for Scotland
Responsibilities	*Secretary of State* Performance of the Scottish Court Service. Central administration pertaining to the Judiciary in the Supreme and Sheriff Courts Accountant in Bankruptcy Central administration of associated departments Central authority under the Child Abduction and Custody Act 1986 and for reciprocal enforcement of international maintenance obligations *Lord Advocate* The jurisdiction and procedure of Scottish courts in civil proceedings The law of evidence in Scotland in civil and criminal matters The law and procedures relating to the enforcement of the judgements of Scottish courts in civil matters and the recognition and enforcement of judgements of foreign courts, other than orders for the payment of maintenance Private international law The law relating to arbitration in Scotland The law relating to fatal accident inquiries and to tribunals and in some cases responsibility for their conduct and administration Relations with the Scottish Law Commission and its functions and law reform in Scotland in those areas for which the Lord Advocate has ministerial responsibility
Number of staff	200
Executive Agency	Scottish Court Service

Scottish Courts Administration

Hayweight House, 23 Lauriston Street, Edinburgh EH3 9DQ
Tel 0131-229 9200   Fax 0131-221 6890

Ministers

Secretary of State for Scotland
The Rt Hon Ian Lang MP

The Lord Advocate
The Rt Hon The Lord Rodger of Earlsferry QC

Civil Servants

Director
J Hamill (2)*

Deputy Director
Court Procedures, Evidence and Legislation; Law Reform
P M Beaton (5)
Assistant Solicitor

Deputy Director
Resources, Policy (Non-Legal) and Liaison
D Stewart (6)

*Mr Hamill is also Secretary of the Scottish Office Home and Health Department which, like the rest of the Scottish Office, is undergoing a senior management review the results of which are likely to be known later this year, with a new structure in place by April 1996

Scottish Office

Founded 1885

Ministers secretary of state, one minister of state, three parliamentary under secretaries of state

Responsibilities a number of statutory functions administered by five main departments:

- Scottish Office Agriculture and Fisheries Department
- Scottish Office Education Department
- Scottish Office Environment Department
- Scottish Office Home and Health Department
- Scottish Office Industry Department;

and a group of central services divisions (excluding Forestry Commission, General Register Office and Scottish Courts Administration)

Other departments for which the Secretary of State has some degree of responsibility are:

- Forestry Commission
- General Register Office for Scotland
- Scottish Courts Administration

Number of staff 4835

Executive agencies

- Historic Scotland
- Registers of Scotland
- Scottish Agricultural Science Agency
- Scottish Courts Service
- Scottish Fisheries Protection Agency
- Scottish Office Pensions Agency
- Scottish Prison Service
- Scottish Record Office
- Student Awards Agency for Scotland

At the time of going to press a senior management review of the Scottish Office is underway. A new structure is expected to be in place from April 1996

Scottish Office

St Andrew's House, Regent Road, Edinburgh EH1 3DG
Tel 0131-556 8400 Fax 0131-244 2683
Dover House, Whitehall, London SW1A 2AU
Tel 0171-270 3000 Fax 0171-270 6719

All staff are based at St Andrew's House unless otherwise indicated.
For other addresses and telephone numbers see the end of this section.

Ministers

Secretary of State
The Rt Hon Ian Lang MP

Parliamentary Private Secretary
Simon Coombs MP

Special Advisers
Gregor MacKay
Mark Izatt

Principal Private Secretary
M B Foulis (5)
0131-244 4011

Minister of State
The Rt Hon Lord Fraser of Carmyllie QC

Private Secretary
Ms S J Morrell (HEO)
0131-244 4017

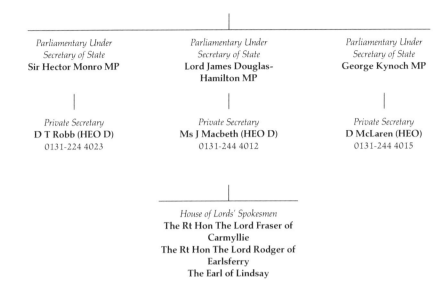

Parliamentary Under Secretary of State
Sir Hector Monro MP

Private Secretary
D T Robb (HEO D)
0131-224 4023

Parliamentary Under Secretary of State
Lord James Douglas-Hamilton MP

Private Secretary
Ms J Macbeth (HEO D)
0131-244 4012

Parliamentary Under Secretary of State
George Kynoch MP

Private Secretary
D McLaren (HEO)
0131-244 4015

House of Lords' Spokesmen
The Rt Hon The Lord Fraser of Carmyllie
The Rt Hon The Lord Rodger of Earlsferry
The Earl of Lindsay

Ministerial Responsibilities

Ian Lang	overall responsibility for the Scottish Office Forestry Commission General Register Office (Scotland) life prisoners Registers of Scotland royal prerogative of mercy Scottish Courts Administration Scottish Record Office
Lord Fraser of Carmyllie	European issues health and social work home affairs including women's issues and constitutional matters Scottish business in the House of Lords
Sir Hector Monro	agriculture arts co-ordination of rural affairs environment fisheries forestry heritage sport and recreation
George Kynoch	energy industry local government including finance and planning new towns
Lord James Douglas-Hamilton	building control education Highlands and Islands housing roads and transport tourism urban policy Commons spokesman on health and social work and home affairs

Departmental Overview

Grade 1	Civil Servants: Grade 2	Grade 3	Department	Minister
	Agriculture and Fisheries			
Sir Russell Hillhouse	A M Russell	A J Matheson (5)	Division A	Sir H Monro
		K W Moore (5)	Division C	Sir H Monro
		Dr T W Hegerty (5)	Scientific Adviser's Unit	Sir H Monro
		T A Cameron	Commodities and Land Groups	Sir H Monro
		A D Findlay	Fisheries	Sir H Monro
		W A Macgregor (4)	Agricultural staff	Sir H Monro
	Education			
Sir Russell Hillhouse	G R Wilson	J S B Martin	Schools	Ld J D Hamilton
		W A P Weather-ston	Formal Post-Schools Education; Arts and Sport	Ld J D Hamilton
		T N Gallacher	HM Inspectorate of Schools	Ld J D Hamilton
	Environment			
Sir Russell Hillhouse	H H Mills	S F Hampson	Rural Affairs and Environmental Protection	Sir H Monro
		D F Middleton	Housing	Ld J D Hamilton
		J S Graham	Development Planning and Local Government	G Kynoch
		J E Gibbons	Building Directorate	Ld J D Hamilton
		A C Paton	Engineering, Water and Waste Directorate	Sir H Monro
		Miss G M Pain	Inquiry Reporters	G Kynoch
		A Mackenzie (4)	Planning Services	G Kynoch
		Dr J R Cuthbert (5)	Statistical Services	

Departmental Overview

Grade 1	Civil Servants Grade 2	Grade 3	Department	Minister
	Home and Health			
Sir Russell Hillhouse	J Hamill	D J Essery	Police, Fire, Emergency, Law and General	Ld Fraser
		Mrs G M Stewart	Criminal Justice, Licensing, Parole and Life Imprisonment	Ld Fraser
		G Scaife	NHS in Scotland	Ld Fraser
		N G Campbell	Social Work Services	Ld Fraser
		D J Belfall	Health Policy and Public Health	Ld Fraser
		R J Wild (4)	Dental Services	Ld Fraser
		Miss A Jarvie	Nursing Services	Ld Fraser
		C F McManus	Fire Services	Ld Fraser
		C B Fairweather (5)	HM Inspectorate of Prisons	Ld Fraser
		Mrs J Richardson	Commissions	Ld Fraser
		Dr C P Levein (5)	Research	Ld Fraser
	Dr R E Kendell	Dr A B Young	Medical Services	Ld Fraser
	Prof I A D Bouchier	Dr A T R Moir	Chief Scientist's Office	Ld Fraser
	J M Boyd		HM Constabulary	Ld Fraser
	Industry Department			
Sir Russell Hillhouse	P Mackay *(until Autumn 1995)*	E J Weeple	Enterprise, Training and Employment, Urban Policy, New Towns, Highlands and Tourism	Ld J D Hamilton G Kynoch
		J W Elvidge	Coordination of European Matters, Energy, Economics and Statistics, Transport and Local Roads	Ld Fraser G Kynoch Ld J D Hamilton
		G Robson	Industrial Expansion, Inward Investment	G Kynoch
		J Innes	Roads Directorate	Ld J D Hamilton
	Central Services Divisions (providing common services to the five departments)			
Sir Russell Hillhouse	G R Wilson	C C MacDonald	Personnel Management and Organisation	
		Miss E A Mackay	Finance	
		E W Ferguson (5)	Liaison Division (London)	
		R S B Gordon (3)	Administrative Services	
		Ms E S D Drummond (5)	Scottish Office Information Directorate	
		M Grant	Management Group Support	
	R Brodie	N W Boe	Solicitor's Office	

Civil Servants and Departments

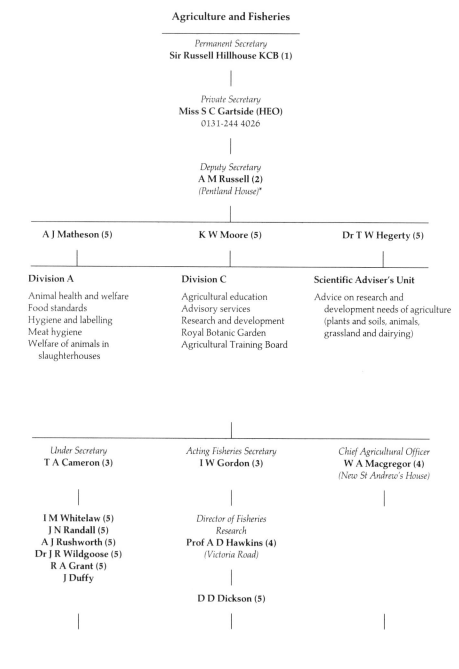

Agriculture and Fisheries

Permanent Secretary
Sir Russell Hillhouse KCB (1)

Private Secretary
Miss S C Gartside (HEO)
0131-244 4026

Deputy Secretary
A M Russell (2)
*(Pentland House)**

A J Matheson (5)

Division A

Animal health and welfare
Food standards
Hygiene and labelling
Meat hygiene
Welfare of animals in slaughterhouses

K W Moore (5)

Division C

Agricultural education
Advisory services
Research and development
Royal Botanic Garden
Agricultural Training Board

Dr T W Hegerty (5)

Scientific Adviser's Unit

Advice on research and development needs of agriculture (plants and soils, animals, grassland and dairying)

Under Secretary
T A Cameron (3)

I M Whitelaw (5)
J N Randall (5)
A J Rushworth (5)
Dr J R Wildgoose (5)
R A Grant (5)
J Duffy

Acting Fisheries Secretary
I W Gordon (3)

Director of Fisheries Research
Prof A D Hawkins (4)
(Victoria Road)

D D Dickson (5)

Chief Agricultural Officer
W A Macgregor (4)
(New St Andrew's House)

Commodities and Land

Land tenure, land use, crofting
Red deer
Extensification
Classification of agricultural land
Rural policy affecting agriculture
Cereals, horticulture, seed and plant varieties
Potatoes and plant health
Environmental pollution
Pesticides and pest control
Set aside
General agricultural policy
EC coordination
Cooperation and marketing
Structural support for both agriculture and fisheries
Fish and shellfish farming policy
Emergencies planning
Livestock products
Hillfarming and other subsidies
Economic advice and statistical services
Information services/information technology planning

Fisheries

EC common fisheries policy
Fishing industry structure and financial arrangements
Law of the Sea
Pelagic and whitefish quota management
Marketing policy
International trade
Statistics
Diseases and cultivation
Salmon and freshwater fisheries
Marine environment
Research and development
Seals
Liaison with offshore oil industry
Fleet structure policy
Marine laboratory
Freshwater fisheries laboratory

Agricultural Staff

Professional/technical services
Estate management
Surveying services

*all Agriculture and Fisheries staff at Pentland House unless otherwise indicated

---

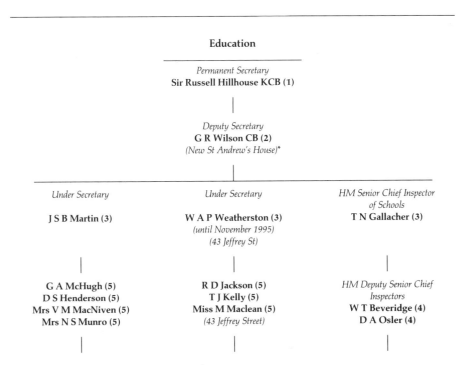

Education

Permanent Secretary
Sir Russell Hillhouse KCB (1)

Deputy Secretary
G R Wilson CB (2)
*(New St Andrew's House)**

Under Secretary
J S B Martin (3)

G A McHugh (5)
D S Henderson (5)
Mrs V M MacNiven (5)
Mrs N S Munro (5)

Under Secretary
W A P Weatherston (3)
(until November 1995)
(43 Jeffrey St)

R D Jackson (5)
T J Kelly (5)
Miss M Maclean (5)
(43 Jeffrey Street)

HM Senior Chief Inspector of Schools
T N Gallacher (3)

HM Deputy Senior Chief Inspectors
W T Beveridge (4)
D A Osler (4)

HM Chief Inspectors
H M Stalker (5)
(231 Corstophine Road)
G P D Gordon (5)
(Corunna House)
G H C Donaldson (5)
(Greyfriars House)
Miss K M Fairweather (5)
R Tuck (5)
J J McDonald (5)
J I Boyes (5)
A S McGlynn (5)
M Roebuck (5)

Chief Statistician
G Jones (5)
(43 Jeffrey Street)

Schools

Schools
Schools curriculum and examinations
Teachers
Sport, leisure and recreation

Formal Post-Schools Education, Arts and Sport

Vocational education
Higher education
Further education
Science and technology unit
Scottish Higher Education Funding Council
Scottish Arts Council
Broadcasting
Gaelic
National Lottery
National institutions

HM Inspectorate of Schools

Inspection of schools, colleges and other educational institutions
Educational needs
National development
Education research and technology
Educational statistics
Management of education and resources
Education statistics audit unit

*all Education staff at New St Andrew's House unless otherwise indicated

Environment

Permanent Secretary
Sir Russell Hillhouse KCB (1)

Deputy Secretary
H H Mills (2)
*(New St Andrew's House)**

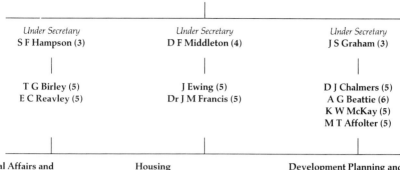

Under Secretary
S F Hampson (3)

T G Birley (5)
E C Reavley (5)

Rural Affairs and Environmental Protection

Rural affairs
Environmental protection
Radioactive waste management
Climatic change
Air and noise pollution
Oil pollution emergencies
Nuclear accidents overseas
Industrial pollution inspectorate
Scottish natural heritage

Under Secretary
D F Middleton (4)

J Ewing (5)
Dr J M Francis (5)

Housing

Local authority housing
Private sector housing
Housing associations
Castlemilk Partnership
Housing improvement policy and grants
Special needs
Special cases
Rent registration and assessment
Tenant's charter

Under Secretary
J S Graham (3)

D J Chalmers (5)
A G Beattie (6)
K W McKay (5)
M T Affolter (5)

Development Planning and Local Government, Local Government Finance

Territorial planning
Development planning and control
Land compensation
Local government
Direct labour organisations and competition
Local legislation and bye-laws
Dogs and feral cats
Local government finance reform
Community charge
Rating and valuation
Expenditure

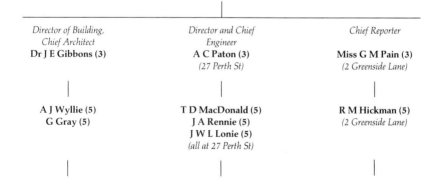

Director of Building, Chief Architect
Dr J E Gibbons (3)

A J Wyllie (5)
G Gray (5)

Director and Chief Engineer
A C Paton (3)
(27 Perth St)

T D MacDonald (5)
J A Rennie (5)
J W L Lonie (5)
(all at 27 Perth St)

Chief Reporter
Miss G M Pain (3)
(2 Greenside Lane)

R M Hickman (5)
(2 Greenside Lane)

Building Directorate

Education and social work building
Building control
Construction industry and procurement policy
Housing
Police and fire building

Engineering, Water and Waste Directorate

Water supply and sewerage
Water pollution control
Solid waste, litter and post-consumer recycling
Hazardous waste inspectorate
Engineering advice
Flood prevention and coast protection
Environmental protection appeals

Inquiry Reporters

Conduct of all land-use related public local inquiries in Scotland
Operation of planning appeals system

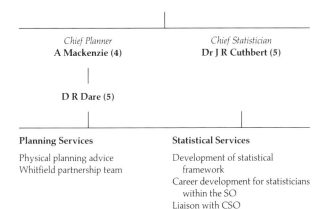

Chief Planner
A Mackenzie (4)

D R Dare (5)

Chief Statistician
Dr J R Cuthbert (5)

Planning Services

Physical planning advice
Whitfield partnership team

Statistical Services

Development of statistical framework
Career development for statisticians within the SO
Liaison with CSO

*all Environment staff at New St Andrew's House unless otherwise indicated

---

Home and Health

Permanent Secretary
Sir Russell Hillhouse KCB (1)

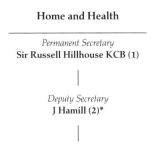

Deputy Secretary
J Hamill (2)*

*see also p 753

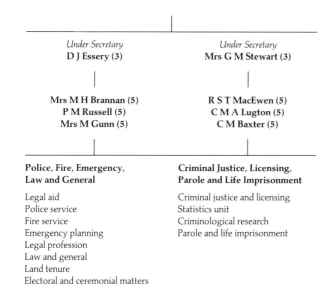

Under Secretary
D J Essery (3)

Mrs M H Brannan (5)
P M Russell (5)
Mrs M Gunn (5)

Police, Fire, Emergency, Law and General

Legal aid
Police service
Fire service
Emergency planning
Legal profession
Law and general
Land tenure
Electoral and ceremonial matters

Under Secretary
Mrs G M Stewart (3)

R S T MacEwen (5)
C M A Lugton (5)
C M Baxter (5)

Criminal Justice, Licensing, Parole and Life Imprisonment

Criminal justice and licensing
Statistics unit
Criminological research
Parole and life imprisonment

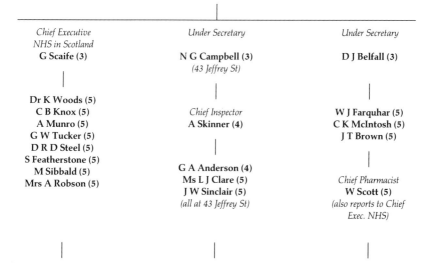

Chief Executive
NHS in Scotland
G Scaife (3)

Dr K Woods (5)
C B Knox (5)
A Munro (5)
G W Tucker (5)
D R D Steel (5)
S Featherstone (5)
M Sibbald (5)
Mrs A Robson (5)

Under Secretary
N G Campbell (3)
(43 Jeffrey St)

Chief Inspector
A Skinner (4)

G A Anderson (4)
Ms L J Clare (5)
J W Sinclair (5)
(all at 43 Jeffrey St)

Under Secretary
D J Belfall (3)

W J Farquhar (5)
C K McIntosh (5)
J T Brown (5)

Chief Pharmacist
W Scott (5)
(also reports to Chief Exec. NHS)

NHS in Scotland

Health boards, capital buildings, service provision
Development of purchasing
State hospitals
Health building
Estate surveys
Disposal of NHS land
Supplies and common services
Competitive tendering
Primary health care
Quality of service, service committee appeals
Emergency planning
Appointments
NHS trusts
Financial management
Manpower and cost monitoring
Economic advice
Information technology services
Personnel
NHS review implementation
Clinical resources and audit

Social Work Services

Manpower and education
Planning service and practice development
Capital programme for local authorities
Analysis research and statistics
Oversight recruitment
Deployment of professional staff
Offenders and addictions
Community care
Child care

Health Policy and Public Health Directorate

Specific diseases, acute services, maternity and family planning services
Child health
Private health care
Mental health services
Services for disabled
AIDS – education and prevention
Drug and alcohol misuse
Scottish Health Service Advisory Council
Pharmaceutical services

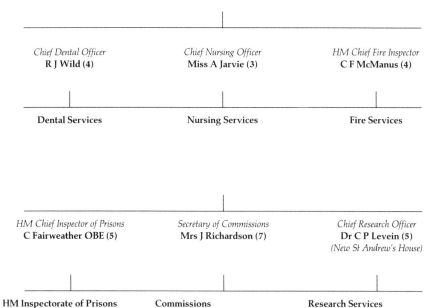

Chief Dental Officer
R J Wild (4)

Dental Services

Chief Nursing Officer
Miss A Jarvie (3)

Nursing Services

HM Chief Fire Inspector
C F McManus (4)

Fire Services

HM Chief Inspector of Prisons
C Fairweather OBE (5)

HM Inspectorate of Prisons

Secretary of Commissions
Mrs J Richardson (7)

Commissions

Appointment of JPs and general commissioners of income tax
Lieutenancy matters

Chief Research Officer
Dr C P Levein (5)
(New St Andrew's House)

Research Services

Central research unit
Research services for the SO depts

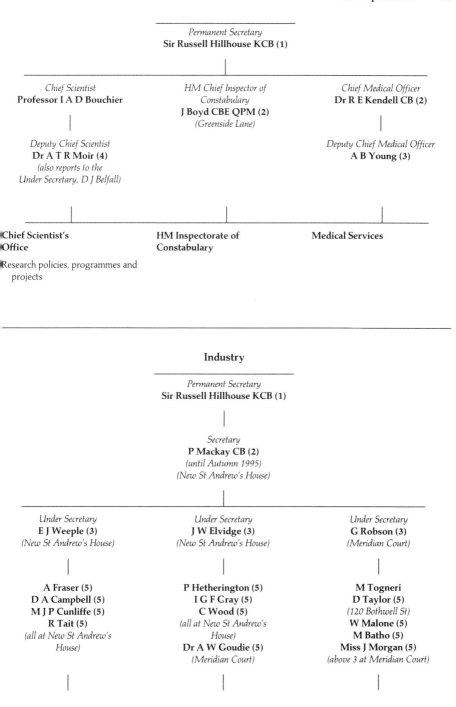

Permanent Secretary
Sir Russell Hillhouse KCB (1)

Chief Scientist
Professor I A D Bouchier

Deputy Chief Scientist
Dr A T R Moir (4)
(also reports to the Under Secretary, D J Belfall)

HM Chief Inspector of Constabulary
J Boyd CBE QPM (2)
(Greenside Lane)

Chief Medical Officer
Dr R E Kendell CB (2)

Deputy Chief Medical Officer
A B Young (3)

Chief Scientist's Office

Research policies, programmes and projects

HM Inspectorate of Constabulary

Medical Services

Industry

Permanent Secretary
Sir Russell Hillhouse KCB (1)

Secretary
P Mackay CB (2)
(until Autumn 1995)
(New St Andrew's House)

Under Secretary
E J Weeple (3)
(New St Andrew's House)

A Fraser (5)
D A Campbell (5)
M J P Cunliffe (5)
R Tait (5)
(all at New St Andrew's House)

Under Secretary
J W Elvidge (3)
(New St Andrew's House)

P Hetherington (5)
I G F Gray (5)
C Wood (5)
(all at New St Andrew's House)
Dr A W Goudie (5)
(Meridian Court)

Under Secretary
G Robson (3)
(Meridian Court)

M Togneri
D Taylor (5)
(120 Bothwell St)
W Malone (5)
M Batho (5)
Miss J Morgan (5)
(above 3 at Meridian Court)

Enterprise, Training and Employment, Urban Policy, European Funds, New Towns

Scottish enterprise, training and employment
New towns
Urban policy and programme
Highlands and Islands Enterprise
Tourism

Coordination of European Matters, Energy, Economics and Statistics, Transport and Local Roads

Electricity, energy, North Sea oil, and gas, coal, nuclear energy, energy efficiency
Transport: bus, ferry, ports and waterways, airports, rail, roads, freight
Coordination of European matters
Economics and statistics

Director of Roads, Chief Road Engineer
J Innes (3)

J Howison (5)
N Mackenzie (5)
R Irvine (5)
(all at New St Andrew's House)

Roads Directorate

Trunk roads policy and programme, legislation, traffic regulations, local roads, road safety
Schemes and territorial
Motorway and trunk road design and construction
Maintenance, minor works and speed limits
Planning application
Engineering and procurement
Technical standards, contracts, planning applications, bridges, traffic signs, lighting, landscaping
Private finance initiative

Industrial Expansion, Inward Investment

Regional policy, enterprise, development grants
Industrial policy and technology
Steel and shipbuilding
Export promotion, monitoring and common services
Locate in Scotland
Regional enterprise grants for innovation
Scottish Trade International

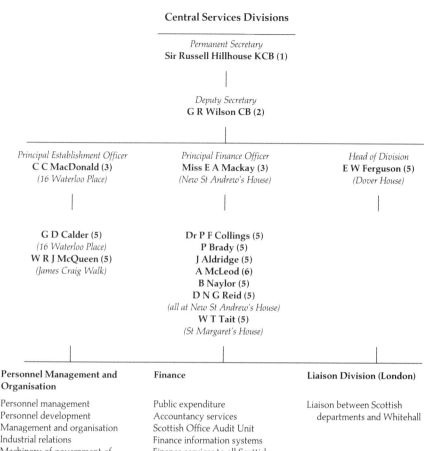

Central Services Divisions

Permanent Secretary
Sir Russell Hillhouse KCB (1)

Deputy Secretary
G R Wilson CB (2)

Principal Establishment Officer
C C MacDonald (3)
(16 Waterloo Place)

G D Calder (5)
(16 Waterloo Place)
W R J McQueen (5)
(James Craig Walk)

Personnel Management and Organisation

Personnel management
Personnel development
Management and organisation
Industrial relations
Machinery of government of Scotland
Market testing
Next Steps initiative
Industrial relations
Pay, leave and superannuation

Principal Finance Officer
Miss E A Mackay (3)
(New St Andrew's House)

Dr P F Collings (5)
P Brady (5)
J Aldridge (5)
A McLeod (6)
B Naylor (5)
D N G Reid (5)
(all at New St Andrew's House)
W T Tait (5)
(St Margaret's House)

Finance

Public expenditure
Accountancy services
Scottish Office Audit Unit
Finance information systems
Finance services to all Scottish departments

Head of Division
E W Ferguson (5)
(Dover House)

Liaison Division (London)

Liaison between Scottish departments and Whitehall

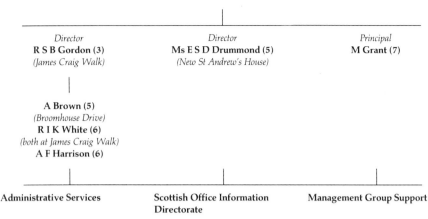

Director
R S B Gordon (3)
(James Craig Walk)

A Brown (5)
(Broomhouse Drive)
R I K White (6)
(both at James Craig Walk)
A F Harrison (6)

Director
Ms E S D Drummond (5)
(New St Andrew's House)

Principal
M Grant (7)

Administrative Services

Scottish Office Computer Services
Telecommunications
Purchase and supply unit
Efficiency unit
Office management
Library services
Travel and subsistence
Management of Scottish Office Estate
Development of accommodation strategy
Physical security matters
Property investment management and disposal
Graphics

Scottish Office Information Directorate

Information to the media
Publicity campaigns
Press arrangements for Royal and state visits
Agent for COI in Scotland

Management Group Support

Honours, public appointments
Royal and state visits
Government hospitality
Parliamentary Commissioner for Administration
Women's issues

Solicitor
R Brodie CB (2)
(New St Andrew's House)

Deputy Solicitor
N W Boe (3)
(New St Andrew's House)

J L Jamieson (4)
J B Allan (5)
I H Harvie (5)
R M Henderson (5)
H F MacDiarmid (5)
G C Duke (5)
Mrs L A Wallace (5)

Solicitor's Office

Legal services to all Scottish departments and to certain other Government departments

Scottish Office Addresses

120 Bothwell Street
Glasgow G2 7SP
Tel 0141-248 2700
Fax 0141-221 3217

Saughton House
Broomhouse Drive
Edinburgh EH11 3XD
Tel 0131-244 8119
Fax 0131-244 8176

Calton House
5 Redheughs Rigg
Edinburgh EH12 9HW
Tel 0131-244 8745
Fax 0131-244 8774

231 Corstophine Road
Edinburgh EH12 0PQ
Tel 0131-316 4639
Fax 0131-334 3047

Corunna House
29 Cadogan Street
Glasgow G2 7LP
Tel 0141-204 1220
Fax 0141-248 5736

Dover House
Whitehall
London SW1A 2AU
Tel 0171-270 3000
Fax 0171-270 6719

East Craigs
Edinburgh EH12 8NJ
Tel 0131-244 8843
Fax 0131-244 8940

2 Greenside Lane
Edinburgh EH1 3AH
Tel 0131-244 4510
Fax 0131-244 5616

Greyfriars House
Gallowgate
Aberdeen AB9 1UE
Tel 01224 642544
Fax 01224 625370

Gyleview House
3 Redheughs Rigg
South Gyle
Edinburgh EH12 9HH
Tel 0131-244 5819
Fax 0131-244 5887

James Craig Walk
Edinburgh EH1 3BA
Tel 0131-556 8400
Fax 0131-244 3891

43 Jeffrey Street
Edinburgh EH1 1DN
Tel 0131-556 8400
Fax 0131-244 5387

Meridian Court
Cadogan Street
Glasgow G2 6AT
Tel 0141-248 2855
Fax 0141-242 5404

New St Andrew's House
Edinburgh EH1 3SY
Tel 0131-556 8400
Fax 0131-244 4785

Pentland House
47 Robb's Loan
Edinburgh EH14 1TW
Tel 0131-556 8400
Fax 0131-244 6001/2/3

27 Perth Street
Edinburgh EH3 5RB
Tel 0131-556 8400
Fax 0131-244 2903

Robert Stevenson House
2 Greenside Place
Edinburgh EH1 3AH
Tel 0131-556 8400
Fax 0131-244 5680

St Margaret's House
Edinburgh EH8 7TG
Tel 0131-556 8400
Fax 0131-244 3334

Thainston Court
By Inverurie
AB51 57A
Tel 01467 626222
Fax 01467 626217

PO Box 101
Victoria Road
Aberdeen AB9 8DB
Tel 01224 876544
Fax 01224 879156

16 Waterloo Place
Edinburgh
EH1 3DN
Tel 0131 556 8400
Fax 0131 244 3972

The Security and Intelligence Services

The UK has three security and intelligence services, collectively known as the agencies: the Security Service (MI5), Secret Intelligence Service, SIS (MI6) and GCHQ. It also has a Defence Intelligence Staff which is an integral part of the Ministry of Defence.

Scrutiny of MI5, MI6 and GCHQ is provided by the Intelligence and Security Committee set up under the Intelligence and Security Act 1994. For details see the Committee below.

Security Service (MI5)

Director-General: **Mrs Stella Rimington**
Thames House, PO Box 3225, London SW1P 1AE

The Security Service is responsible for protecting national security as well as safeguarding the economic well-being of the UK against threats from overseas. The functions of the Service are set out in the Security Service Act 1989 – which for the first time put MI5 on a statutory basis – and its work was further explained in a booklet, published in July 1993, entitled *The Security Service* (ISBN 0 11 3410875).

The Security Tribunal was set up in 1989 to investigate complaints about the Service from the public (*see in the Regulatory Organisations' section*).

Secret Intelligence Service (SIS) (MI6)

Chief: **David Spedding CVO OBE**
Vauxhall Cross, PO Box 1300, London SE1 1BD

The principal function of SIS is the production of secret intelligence in support of the government's security, defence, foreign and economic policies as laid down by the Joint Intelligence Committee (*see Central Intelligence Machinery below*).

The Intelligence Services Act 1994 put SIS and GCHQ on a statutory footing – as has already happened with MI5.

The Intelligence Services Tribunal – provided for under the Act – was set up at the end of 1994 to investigate complaints from the public against the Service (*see under* the Regulatory Organisations' section). Both tribunals have the same commissioner, president and vice-president.

Government Communications Headquarters (GCHQ)

Director: **Sir John Adye KCMG**
Priors Road, Cheltenham, Gloucestershire GL52 5AJ
Tel: 01242 221491

GCHQ provides government departments and military commands with signal intelligence in support of the government's security, defence, foreign and economic policies, in accordance with requirements laid down by the Joint Intelligence Committee (*see Central Intelligence Machinery below*).

In addition GCHQ also produces advice and assistance to government departments and the armed forces on the security of their communications and information technology systems. This task is undertaken by the Communication Electronics Security Group.

Along with SIS (see above) GCHQ was put on a statutory footing in 1994.

The Intelligence Services Tribunal – provided for under the Act – was set up at the end of 1994 to investigate complaints from the public against the Service (*see under* the Regulatory Organisations' section). Both tribunals have the same commissioner, president and vice-president.

Defence Intelligence Staff (DIS)

Chief of Defence Intelligence: **Lieutenant General Sir John Foley KCB OBE MC**
Ministry of Defence, Whitehall, London SW1A 2HB
Tel: 0171-218 9000

The Ministry's defence intelligence capability encompasses the Defence Intelligence Staff (DIS) and intelligence elements throughout the armed forces and within the single service commands. The DIS, which was established in 1964, is run by the Chief of Defence Intelligence (CDI) under whom are three director-generals: DG intelligence (assessments); scientific and technical intelligence; and management and support of intelligence.

DIS assessments draw on all possible sources of information and much of its work is devoted exclusively to military subjects, although it also looks at weapons proliferation, arms sales and control, the defence industries, and scientific and technological developments.

There are many users including ministers, the chiefs of staff, the various armed forces and other government departments. More information about the work of defence intelligence can be found in *Statement on the Defence Estimates 1994*, Cm 2550.

Central Intelligence Machinery

In October 1993 the goverment published for the first time details of how the Cabinet Office-based central intelligence machinery works.

In their day-to-day activities the agencies operate under the immediate control of their respective heads who are personally responsible to ministers. The Prime Minister is responsible for intelligence and security matters overall and is supported in that capacity by the Cabinet Secretary. The lines of ministerial responsibility are set out in Annex A.

The functions and membership of the various committees which task, finance, oversee and coordinate the intelligence services are set out in Annex B.

These two annexes are based on material contained in the booklet mentioned above, *Central Intelligence Machinery* (ISBN 0 11 430091 7).

Intelligence and Security Committee

The committee, made up of MPs and one peer, and set up under the Intelligence and Security Act 1994, scrutinises the expenditure, administration and policy of MI5, MI6 (SIS) and GCHQ. The Committee, which is serviced by Cabinet Office officials and reports to the Prime Minister, held its first meeting in December 1994.

The members are:
The Rt Hon Tom King CH MP (Con) *(Chairman)*
The Rt Hon Alan Beith MP (Lib Dem)
The Rt Hon Dr John Gilbert MP (Lab)
The Rt Hon Sir Archie Hamilton MP (Con)
The Rt Hon The Lord Howe QC (Con)
Barry Jones MP (Lab)
Michael Mates MP (Con)
Allan Rogers MP (Lab)
Sir Giles Shaw MP (Con)

Intelligence Services Tribunal

PO Box 4823, London SE1 0TZ
Tel: 0171-273 4383

The Tribunal was set up under the Intelligence Services Act 1994 and investigates complaints from the public about the services. For more details *see under* the Regulatory Organisations' section.

Security Service Tribunal

PO Box 18, London SW1A 9XD
Tel: 0171-273 4095

Set up under the Security Service Act 1989 the Tribunal investigates complaints from the public about the services. For more details *see under* the Regulatory Organisations' section.

Staff Counsellor for the Security and Intelligence Services

Staff Counsellor: **Sir Christopher France GCB**
c/o Cabinet Office, 70 Whitehall, London SW1A 2AS
Tel: 0171-270 3000

The post of staff counsellor was established in 1987. He is not a member of the security and intelligence services but an independent adviser available to be consulted by any member of the services who has anxieties relating to the work of his or her service which it has not been possible to allay through ordinary processes of management/staff relations.

The staff counsellor has access to all relevant documents and to any level of management in each service. He is able to make recommendations to the head of the service concerned and also has access to the Cabinet Secretary if he wishes and has the right to make recommendations to him. He reports as appropriate to the heads of the services and once a year to the Prime Minister, the Foreign Secretary and the Home Secretary on his activities and on the working of the system.

Annex A UK Intelligence:

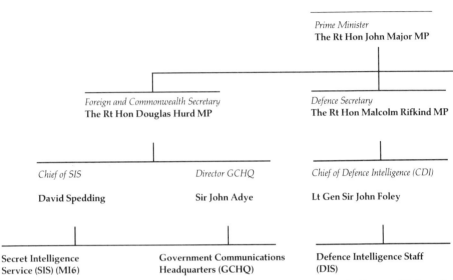

Prime Minister
The Rt Hon John Major MP

Foreign and Commonwealth Secretary
The Rt Hon Douglas Hurd MP

Defence Secretary
The Rt Hon Malcolm Rifkind MP

Chief of SIS

David Spedding

Director GCHQ

Sir John Adye

Chief of Defence Intelligence (CDI)

Lt Gen Sir John Foley

Secret Intelligence Service (SIS) (MI6)

Production of secret intelligence in support of HMG's security, defence, foreign and economic policies in response to requirements from JIC and approved by Ministers

It meets these requirements through a variety of sources and by liaison with a wide range of foreign intelligence and security services

Government Communications Headquarters (GCHQ)

Provides government departments and military commands with signal intelligence in support of HMG's security, defence, foreign and economic policies

Provides advice and assistance to government departments and the armed forces on the security of their communications and IT systems

Defence Intelligence Staff (DIS)

Serves the Ministry of Defence, the armed forces and other government departments

Analyses information from a wide variety of sources, both overt and covert

The CDI is responsible for the work of the DIS and coordinates intelligence for British defence

Ministerial Responsibility

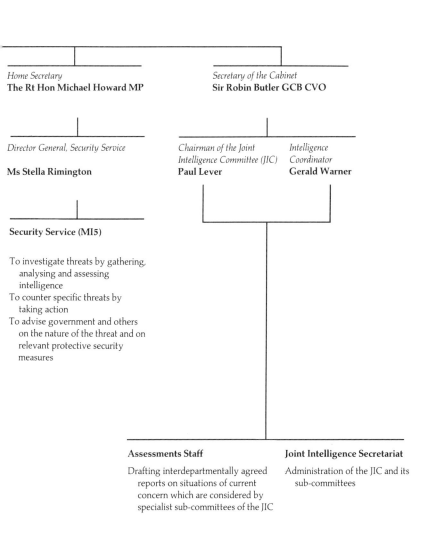

Home Secretary
The Rt Hon Michael Howard MP

Secretary of the Cabinet
Sir Robin Butler GCB CVO

Director General, Security Service
Ms Stella Rimington

Chairman of the Joint Intelligence Committee (JIC)
Paul Lever

Intelligence Coordinator
Gerald Warner

Security Service (MI5)

To investigate threats by gathering, analysing and assessing intelligence
To counter specific threats by taking action
To advise government and others on the nature of the threat and on relevant protective security measures

Assessments Staff

Drafting interdepartmentally agreed reports on situations of current concern which are considered by specialist sub-committees of the JIC

Joint Intelligence Secretariat

Administration of the JIC and its sub-committees

Annex B UK Intelligence

Prime Minister
The Rt Hon John Major MP

Secretary of the Cabinet
Sir Robin Butler GCB CVO

Permanent Secretaries Committee on the Intelligence Services (PSIS)

Members:
Secretary of the Cabinet *(Chairman)*
Permanent Secretaries at the:
- Foreign and Commonwealth Office
- Ministry of Defence
- Home Office
- HM Treasury

Intelligence Coordinator

Gerald Warner

PSIS

Scrutinises agencies' annual expenditure forecasts and management plans

Intelligence Coordinator

Advises PSIS
Chairs Advisory Committee which conducts first scrutiny of agencies expenditure forecasts
Advises Cabinet Secretary on coordination of intelligence machinery
Chairs formal and informal groups charged with intelligence management
Has particular responsibility for reviewing UK's intelligence requirements

Joint Intelligence Secretariat

Middle-ranking officers from various departments and disciplines and permanent Cabinet Office staff

JIS

Administration of the JIC and its sub-committees

:entral Organisation

Ministerial Committee on the Intelligence Services (IS)

Members:
Prime Minister *(Chairman)*
Foreign and Commonwealth Secretary
Chancellor of the Exchequer
Home Secretary
Secretary of State for Defence

The Attorney General attends as appropriate

IS

To keep under review policy on the security and intelligence services

Intelligence and Security Committee

Members:
The Rt Hon Tom King CH MP (Con) *(Chairman)*
The Rt Hon Alan Beith MP (Lib Dem)
The Rt Hon Dr John Gilbert MP (Lab)
The Rt Hon Sir Archie Hamilton MP (Con)
The Rt Hon The Lord Howe QC (Con)
Barry Jones MP (Lab)
Michael Mates MP (Con)
Allan Rogers MP (Lab)
Sir Giles Shaw MP (Con)

ISC

Scrutiny of the expenditure, administration and policy of MI5, MI6 (SIS) and GCHQ

nt Intelligence Committee (JIC)

embers:
ul Lever *(Chairman)*
nior officials in Foreign and Commonwealth Office, Ministry of Defence and Treasury
ads of SIS, GCHQ, MI5
elligence Coordinator
ief of the Assessment Staff

her departments (eg Home Office) attend as appropriate

:

give direction and to keep under review the organisation and working of British intelligence activity at home and overseas
submit requirements and priorities for intelligence gathering
coordinate interdepartmental plans for intelligence activity
monitor and give early warning of threats to British interests
assess events relating to external affairs, defence, nternational criminal activity, scientific, technical and nternational economic matters
maintain and supervise liaison with Commonwealth and foreign intelligence organisations

essments Staff

ef of Assessments Staff:
thony Galsworthy
ior and middle-ranking officers from various departments, services and disciplines

JIC Sub-Committees and Current Intelligence Groups (CIGs)

Experts from a range of government departments

sessments Staff

fting interdepartmentally agreed reports on ituations of current concern which are considered by pecialist sub-committees of the JIC

JIC Sub-Committees and CIGs

Consider reports from the Assessments Staff which are passed to JIC for consideration and submission to Ministers

Serious Fraud Office

Founded	1987
Status	Non-ministerial department
Responsible to	Attorney General
Responsibilities	Investigation and prosecution of cases involving serious and complex fraud in England, Wales and Northern Ireland
Number of staff	135 civil servants 38 police officers A varying number of people are employed on a case by case basis

Serious Fraud Office

Elm House, 10–16 Elm Street, London WC1X 0BJ
Tel 0171-239 7272   Fax 0171-837 1689

Minister

Attorney General
The Rt Hon Sir Nicholas Lyell QC MP
(for details of his office see Law Officers' Department)

Officials

Director of the Serious Fraud Office
G W Staple (2)

Personal Secretary
Mrs A Wright
0171-239 7272

Deputy Director of the Serious Fraud Office
J A Knox (3)

Departmental Overview

Grade 2	Civil Servants *Grade 3*	Department	Minister
G W Staple	J A Knox	Lawyers and Accountants	Attorney General
	P Rayner (5)	Establishment and Finance	Attorney General

Civil Servants and Departments

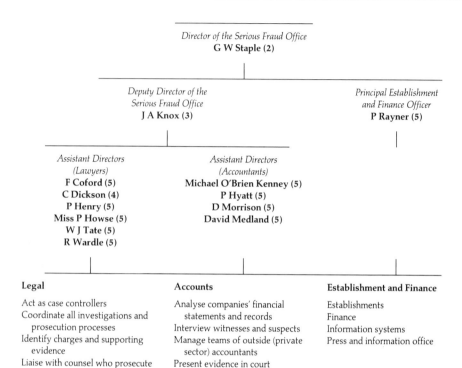

Director of the Serious Fraud Office
G W Staple (2)

Deputy Director of the Serious Fraud Office
J A Knox (3)

Assistant Directors (Lawyers)
F Coford (5)
C Dickson (4)
P Henry (5)
Miss P Howse (5)
W J Tate (5)
R Wardle (5)

Assistant Directors (Accountants)
Michael O'Brien Kenney (5)
P Hyatt (5)
D Morrison (5)
David Medland (5)

Principal Establishment and Finance Officer
P Rayner (5)

Legal

Act as case controllers
Coordinate all investigations and prosecution processes
Identify charges and supporting evidence
Liaise with counsel who prosecute SFO cases
Advise Director of the SFO

Accounts

Analyse companies' financial statements and records
Interview witnesses and suspects
Manage teams of outside (private sector) accountants
Present evidence in court

Establishment and Finance

Establishments
Finance
Information systems
Press and information office

Department of Social Security

Founded	The DSS became a separate department in 1988. Between 1968 and 1988 it had been part of the Department of Health and Social Security
Ministers	secretary of state, two ministers of state and three parliamentary under secretaries of state
Responsibilities	child benefit family credit income support industrial injuries scheme (payment of benefits, collection of contributions) legal aid (assessment of means) lone parents and maintenance National Insurance (payment of benefits, collection of contributions) non-contributory benefits one parent benefit social fund
Number of staff	1500
Executive agencies	Social Security Benefits Agency SS Child Support Agency SS Contributions Agency SS Information Technology Services Agency SS Resettlement Agency SS War Pensions Agency

Department of Social Security

Richmond House, 79 Whitehall, London SW1A 2NS
Tel 0171-210 5983   Fax 0171-210 5523

All staff are based at Richmond House unless otherwise indicated.
For other addresses and telephone numbers see the end of this section.

Ministers

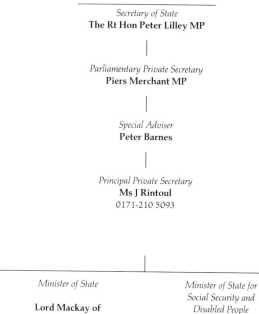

Secretary of State
The Rt Hon Peter Lilley MP

Parliamentary Private Secretary
Piers Merchant MP

Special Adviser
Peter Barnes

Principal Private Secretary
Ms J Rintoul
0171-210 5093

Minister of State
Lord Mackay of Ardbrecknish

Private Secretary
Miss C Payne (HEO)
0171-210 5135

Minister of State for Social Security and Disabled People
William Hague MP

Parliamentary Private Secretary
Jacqui Lait MP*

Private Secretary
Ms S Linaker (HEO)
0171-210 5121

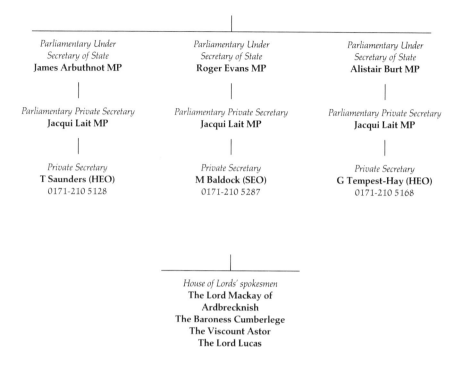

Parliamentary Under Secretary of State
James Arbuthnot MP

Parliamentary Private Secretary
Jacqui Lait MP

Private Secretary
T Saunders (HEO)
0171-210 5128

Parliamentary Under Secretary of State
Roger Evans MP

Parliamentary Private Secretary
Jacqui Lait MP

Private Secretary
M Baldock (SEO)
0171-210 5287

Parliamentary Under Secretary of State
Alistair Burt MP

Parliamentary Private Secretary
Jacqui Lait MP

Private Secretary
G Tempest-Hay (HEO)
0171-210 5168

House of Lords' spokesmen
The Lord Mackay of Ardbrecknish
The Baroness Cumberlege
The Viscount Astor
The Lord Lucas

*Ms Lait, principally, will be Mr Hague's PPS but she will provide support to all the PUSs

Ministerial Responsibilities

Peter Lilley	Overall responsibility for the department
William Hague	Disability Disability-related benefits Incapacity benefit Independent Living Fund Overview of occupational, personal and state pensions Social security policy Statutory maternity pay Statutory sick pay Vaccine damage
Lord Mackay of Ardbrecknish	Citizen's Charter Market testing IT Services Agency Resettlement Agency War Pensions Agency Departmental spokesman in the House of Lords
James Arbuthnot	Contributions Agency Deregulation Equal treatment Fraud and overpayment Methods of payment National insurance Pensions Widows' benefits
Alistair Burt	Child benefit Child support Child Support Agency Family issues Green issues Lone parents Low incomes One parent benefit

Roger Evans
Benefit adjudication
Benefits Agency
Council tax benefit
Family credit
Housing benefit
Income support
Jobseekers' allowance
Social Fund
Unemployment benefit
Work incentive issues

Departmental Overview

Civil Servants			Division	Minister
Grade 1	*Grade 2*	*Grade 3*		
Sir Michael Partridge *(until September 1995 and then Mrs A Bowtell)*		S Reardon (5)	Information Division	
	Social Security Policy Group			
Sir Michael Partridge	Mrs A Bowtell *(until September 1995)*	P R H Allen	Division A (Sick/Disabled/ Maternity Benefits/War Pensions/ Disability Unit	W Hague Ld Mackay of Ardbrecknish
		M Whippman	Division B (Unemployment Benefit/ Lone Parents and Maintenance)	A Burt R Evans
		Miss M Peirson	Division C (Occupational and Personal Pensions)	J Arbuthnot
		R B Brown	Division D (Income Support, Housing Benefit) (Social Fund)	R Evans
		D Brereton	Division E (State Pensions and National Insurance)	J Arbuthnot
	Resource Management Policy			
Sir Michael Partridge	J Tross	S Lord	Planning and Finance Division	
		S Hewitt	Corporate Strategy and Personnel Division	
		D Stanton	Analytical Services Division	
	Solicitor's Office			
Sir Michael Partridge	P K J Thompson	Mrs G S Kerrigan	Division A	
		P C Nilsson	Division B	
		A D Roberts	Division C	

Civil Servants and Divisions

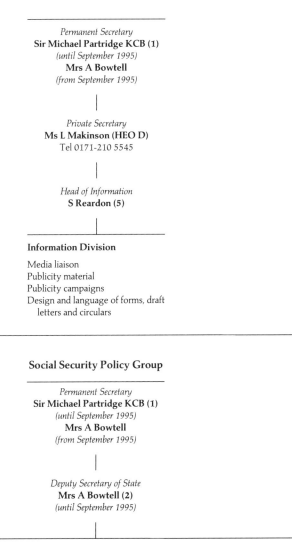

Permanent Secretary
Sir Michael Partridge KCB (1)
(until September 1995)
Mrs A Bowtell
(from September 1995)

Private Secretary
Ms L Makinson (HEO D)
Tel 0171-210 5545

Head of Information
S Reardon (5)

Information Division

Media liaison
Publicity material
Publicity campaigns
Design and language of forms, draft letters and circulars

Social Security Policy Group

Permanent Secretary
Sir Michael Partridge KCB (1)
(until September 1995)
Mrs A Bowtell
(from September 1995)

Deputy Secretary of State
Mrs A Bowtell (2)
(until September 1995)

Under Secretary
P R H Allen (3)
(Adelphi)

Under Secretary
M Whippman (3)
(Adelphi)

Under Secretary
Miss M Peirson (3)
(Adelphi)

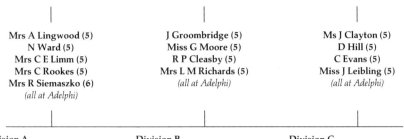

Mrs A Lingwood (5)
N Ward (5)
Mrs C E Limm (5)
Mrs C Rookes (5)
Mrs R Siemaszko (6)
(all at Adelphi)

Division A
Sick/Disabled/Maternity Benefits/Disability Unit

Cash benefits for sick and disabled people includes:
- war pensions
- industrial injuries
- sickness benefit
- invalidity benefit
- maternity allowance
- vaccine damage
- invalid care allowance
- severe disablement allowance
- statutory sick pay
- statutory maternity pay
- disability living allowance
- disability working allowance

SS policy on claims, payments and adjudication, overlapping benefits and common provisions including dependency increases
Liaison with Independent Tribunal Service, central adjudication services and Motability and Independent Living Fund
Inter-departmental Disability Unit
Disability and career benefits analysis and review

J Groombridge (5)
Miss G Moore (5)
R P Cleasby (5)
Mrs L M Richards (5)
(all at Adelphi)

Division B
Child, Family and Unemployment Benefits, Jobseeker's Allowance, Child Support Maintenance, International Aspects of Social Security, General Poverty and Low Income Issues

Policy on:
Cash benefits for the unemployed
Jobseeker's allowance
Child benefit, one-parent benefit, guardian's allowance
Family credit
General family issues
Work incentive issues
Poverty and low income issues, including tax/benefit interaction
Child support maintenance
Lone parent issues
Residual welfare foods, passported benefit and legal aid issues
International aspects of social security
Women's issues
EC poverty programme

Ms J Clayton (5)
D Hill (5)
C Evans (5)
Miss J Leibling (5)
(all at Adelphi)

Division C
Occupational and Personal Pensions

Policy on occupational and personal pensions
EC issues
Legislation

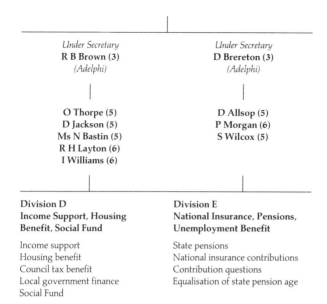

Under Secretary
R B Brown (3)
(Adelphi)

O Thorpe (5)
D Jackson (5)
Ms N Bastin (5)
R H Layton (6)
I Williams (6)

Under Secretary
D Brereton (3)
(Adelphi)

D Allsop (5)
P Morgan (6)
S Wilcox (5)

Division D
Income Support, Housing Benefit, Social Fund

Income support
Housing benefit
Council tax benefit
Local government finance
Social Fund

Division E
National Insurance, Pensions, Unemployment Benefit

State pensions
National insurance contributions
Contribution questions
Equalisation of state pension age

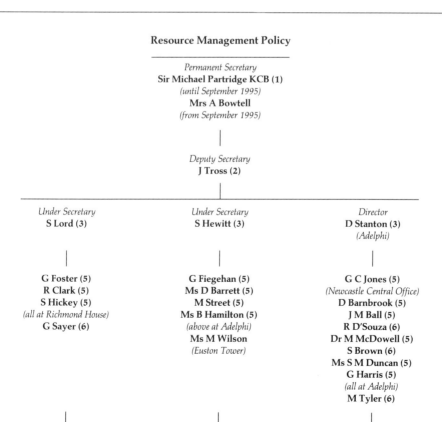

Resource Management Policy

Permanent Secretary
Sir Michael Partridge KCB (1)
(until September 1995)
Mrs A Bowtell
(from September 1995)

Deputy Secretary
J Tross (2)

Under Secretary
S Lord (3)

G Foster (5)
R Clark (5)
S Hickey (5)
(all at Richmond House)
G Sayer (6)

Under Secretary
S Hewitt (3)

G Fiegehan (5)
Ms D Barrett (5)
M Street (5)
Ms B Hamilton (5)
(above at Adelphi)
Ms M Wilson
(Euston Tower)

Director
D Stanton (3)
(Adelphi)

G C Jones (5)
(Newcastle Central Office)
D Barnbrook (5)
J M Ball (5)
R D'Souza (6)
Dr M McDowell (5)
S Brown (6)
Ms S M Duncan (5)
G Harris (5)
(all at Adelphi)
M Tyler (6)

Planning and Finance Division

Benefit expenditure
Administrative expenditure
Public expenditure survey
Liaison with agencies
Accountancy
Benefit accounting
Audit and liaison with NAO
Departmental IS/IT financial regime
Management of efficiency scrutinies

Corporate Strategy and Personnel Division

Departmental information systems strategy
Long-term IT supply issues
Support to departmental board
Strategic planning
Cross-departmental issues (eg Citizen's Charter, Next Steps)

Analytical Services Division

Collection of statistics
Operational issues
Economic advice
Forecasting and statistical advice
Research services
Incapacity, incomes and income-related benefits take-up

Solicitor's Office

Permanent Secretary
Sir Michael Partridge KCB (1)
(until September 1995)
Mrs A Bowtell
(from September 1995)

Solicitor
P K J Thompson (2)
(New Court)

Principal Assistant Solicitor
Mrs G S Kerrigan (3)
(New Court)
Mrs G Massiah (5)
Mrs M Astbury (5)
J H Swainson (5)
D P Dunleavy (5)
Miss A V Windsor (5)
K K Baublys (5)
(all at New Court)

Proceedings Operational Director
P C Nilsson (4)
(New Court)
Miss M Trefgarne (5)
R Aitken (5)
R S Powell (5)
G G Blake (5)
(all at New Court)

Principal Assistant Solicitor
A D Roberts (3)
(New Court)
Miss R Lester (5)
P Milledge (5)
R J Dormer (5)
J F McCleary (5)
J P Canlin (5)
(all at New Court)

Division A

Advice and services on SS policy
War pensions
Occupational and personal pensions

Division B

Civil and criminal proceedings
Industrial relations
Establishment matters
Legal services to Chief Adjudication Officer

Division C

Health and personal social services
EC and international matters

Department of Social Security Addresses

For fax numbers, contact the switchboard at the relevant location

Adelphi
1–11 John Adam Street
London WC2N 6HT
Tel 0171-962 8000

Millbank Tower
21–24 Millbank
London SW1P 4QU
Tel 0171-217 3000

New Court
48 Carey Street
London WC2A 2LS
Tel 0171-962 8000

Euston Tower
286 Euston Road
London NW1 3DN
Tel 0171-388 1188

Newcastle upon Tyne NE98 1YX
Tel 0191-213 5000

Department of Trade and Industry

Founded As the Board of Trade in 1786, as Department of Trade and Industry in 1970, split in 1974 and reconstituted in 1983

Ministers President of the Board of Trade/secretary of state; three ministers of state and three parliamentary under secretaries

Responsibilities
- company legislation
- competition policy
- consumer protection (including relations with the Office of Fair Trading, the Monopolies and Mergers Commission and OFTEL)
- deregulation policy
- energy
- industrial competitiveness
- industry and commerce policy
- information and manufacturing technology
- international trade policy
- promotion of UK exports
- regional development and inward investment
- regulation of insurance industry
- science and technology research and development policy
- small firms and Business Link
- sponsorship role for sectors where DTI has governmental responsibility

Number of staff 5125

Executive agencies
- Companies House
- Insolvency Service
- Laboratory of the Government Chemist
- National Engineering Laboratory
- National Physical Laboratory
- National Weights and Measures Laboratory
- Patent Office
- Radiocommunications Agency

Department of Trade and Industry

Ashdown House, 123 Victoria Street, London SW1E 6RB
Tel 0171-215 5000 Fax 0171-828 3258

The HQ address for the DTI will change to 1 Victoria Street, London SW1H 0ET from early August 1995. It is likely that telephone and fax numbers will remain as above

Business in Europe Tel 01179 444 888 Innovation Inquiry Line Tel 0800 44 2001

All personnel are based at Ashdown House/1 Victoria Street unless otherwise indicated.
For other addresses and telephone numbers see the end of this section.

Ministers

President of the Board of Trade and Secretary of State
The Rt Hon Michael Heseltine MP

Parliamentary Private Secretary
Richard Ottaway MP

Special Advisers
Lady Strathnaver
Dr Alan Kemp
Sir Peter Levene
Dr Walter Eltis
(chief economic adviser)

Principal Private Secretary
Mark Gibson
0171-215 5621

Minister for Consumer Affairs
The Rt Hon
Lord Ferrers

Minister for Energy
The Rt Hon
Tim Eggar MP

Parliamentary Private Secretary
Peter Luff MP

Minister for Trade
The Rt Hon
Richard Needham MP

Parliamentary Private Secretary
Andrew Rowe MP

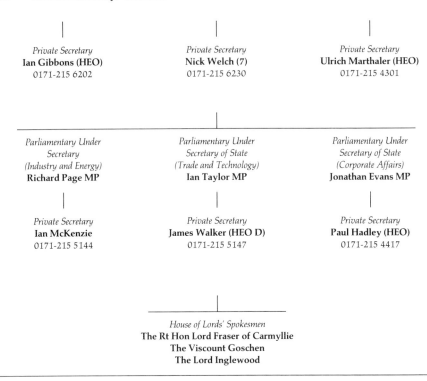

Private Secretary
Ian Gibbons (HEO)
0171-215 6202

Private Secretary
Nick Welch (7)
0171-215 6230

Private Secretary
Ulrich Marthaler (HEO)
0171-215 4301

Parliamentary Under Secretary (Industry and Energy)
Richard Page MP

Private Secretary
Ian McKenzie
0171-215 5144

Parliamentary Under Secretary of State (Trade and Technology)
Ian Taylor MP

Private Secretary
James Walker (HEO D)
0171-215 5147

Parliamentary Under Secretary of State (Corporate Affairs)
Jonathan Evans MP

Private Secretary
Paul Hadley (HEO)
0171-215 4417

House of Lords' Spokesmen
The Rt Hon Lord Fraser of Carmyllie
The Viscount Goschen
The Lord Inglewood

Ministerial Responsibilities

Michael Heseltine
- Overall responsibility for the Department
- Export Credits Guarantee Department
- Industry issues
- Post Office

Tim Eggar
- Atomic energy
- Competitiveness
- Coal
- Electricity and nuclear fuels
- Energy policy
- Invest in Britain Bureau
- Inward investment and regional selective assistance cases referred to the Industrial Development Advisory Board
- Oil and gas
- Oil and Gas Projects and Supplies Office (UK)
- Regional development
- Regional offices
- Sectors:
  - Aerospace
  - Chemicals and biotechnology
  - Information technology and electronics
  - Metals and minerals
  - Textiles and retailing
  - Vehicles and shipbuilding
- Regional industrial issues: South East, South West and London

Richard Needham
- Overall responsibility for exports and trade policy
- European Union trade relations
- Export Credits Guarantee Department
- Exports to Europe and the Americas
- Exports to Asia, Africa and Australasia
- Joint Export Promotion Directorate
- Oil and Gas Projects and Supplies Office (outside UK)
- Projects export promotion
- Regional industrial issues: West Midlands
- Responsible for DTI interests at the Foreign Affairs Council

The Earl Ferrers	Business links Consultancy Scheme Consumer affairs Design Public appointments Small firms Regional industrial issues: Eastern England and East Midlands Departmental spokesman in the House of Lords
Jonathan Evans	Companies Company law Companies House Agency Competition policy Consumer affairs (reporting to Earl Ferrers) Deregulation unit Insolvency Service Agency Insurance Investigations National Weights and Measures Laboratory Regional industrial issues: North West and Merseyside
Ian Taylor	British National Space Centre Common services Industrial research establishments including Laboratory of the Government Chemist and the National Physical Laboratory Management technology and technology services Market testing Patent Office Radiocommunications Agency Technology and innovation policy Telecommunications Responsible through Richard Needham for: European Union and trade relations Export control and non-proliferation International trade policy Regional industrial issues: North East Single Market Compliance Unit Represents HMG at the Internal Market Council Responsible for DTI interests at the Foreign Affairs Council

Richard Page

Small firms and Business Links (reporting through Earl Ferrers)

Supports President on the Post Office and industry issues as follows:

- biotechnology
- mechanical and electrical engineering
- non-ferrous metals
- furniture, paper and board
- ceramics and glass
- retailing
- advertising and other business support measures and trade association initiative

Supports Mr Eggar on all inward investment, energy and regional issues

Regional industrial issues: Yorkshire and Humberside

Departmental Overview

Grade 1	Grade 2	Grade 3	Department	Minister
Trade Policy and Export Promotion				
Sir Peter Gregson	C W Roberts	F R Mingay	Joint Export Promotion Directorate*	R Needham/ I Taylor
		D T Hall	Projects Export Promotion	R Needham/ I Taylor
		D Watson	Oil and Gas Projects and Supplies Office†	R Needham/ I Taylor
		M M Baker	Exports to Asia, Africa and Australasia	R Needham/ I Taylor
		N R Thornton	Exports to Europe and the Americas	R Needham/ I Taylor
		J Cooke	International Trade Policy	R Needham/ I Taylor
		W L Stow	European Community and Trade Relations	R Needham/ I Taylor
		R J Meadway	Export Control and Non-proliferation	R Needham/ I Taylor
Industry				
Sir Peter Gregson	A Macdonald	I M Jones	Textiles and Retailing	T Eggar/ R Page
		P S Salvidge	Posts	M Heseltine/ R Page
		W I Macintyre	Telecommunications	I Taylor
		Dr E G Finer	Chemicals and Biotechnology	T Eggar/ I Taylor
		M Stanley	Vehicles, Metals and Minerals	T Eggar/ I Taylor
		R Foster	Aerospace	T Eggar/ I Taylor
		R M Rumbelow	Electronics and Engineering Division	T Eggar/ I Taylor
		Dr W D Evans	Technology and Innovation Policy	I Taylor
		D R Davis	British National Space Centre	I Taylor

**a joint DTI/FCO department*

†Also works closely with Energy Division. Reports to C E Henderson on UK matters.

Departmental Overview

Civil Servants Grade 1	Grade 2	Grade 3	Department	Minister
Energy				
Sir Peter Gregson	C E Henderson	N Hirst	Atomic Energy	T Eggar/ R Page
		P Loughead	Coal	T Eggar/ R Page
		C C Wilcock	Electricity and Nuclear Fuels	T Eggar/ R Page
		M J Michell	Oil and Gas*	T Eggar/ R Page
		N Hartley	Energy Policy and Analysis Unit	T Eggar/ R Page
		Dr C Hicks	Environment and Energy Technologies	I Taylor
Laboratories				
Sir Peter Gregson	B J G Hilton	W Edgar	National Engineering Laboratory	J Evans
		Dr R D Worswick	Laboratory of the Government Chemist	I Taylor
		Dr P Clapham	National Physical Laboratory	I Taylor
		Dr S Bennett	National Weights and Measures Laboratory	J Evans
Regional and Small Firms				
Sir Peter Gregson	D Durie	G Dart	Regional Development	T Eggar/ R Page
		A Fraser	Invest in Britain Bureau	T Eggar/ R Page
		H V B Brown	Small Firms and Business Link	Earl Ferrers/ R Page
		Dr K C Shotton	Management and Technology Services	I Taylor

Departmental Overview

Civil Servants			Department	Minister
Grade 1	*Grade 2*	*Grade 3*		
		Government Regional Offices*		
		J Turner	Eastern	T Eggar/ R Page
		M Lanyon	East Midlands	T Eggar/ R Page
	R U Young		London	T Eggar/ R Page
		J Stoker	Merseyside	T Eggar/ R Page
		Ms P Denham	North East	T Eggar/ R Page
		Ms M Neville-Rolfe	North West	T Eggar/ R Page
		Ms G Ashmore	South East	T Eggar/ R Page
		B Leonard S McQuillin (5)	South West Devon and Cornwall	T Eggar/ R Page
		D Ritchie	West Midlands	T Eggar/ R Page
		J Walker	Yorkshire and Humberside	T Eggar/ R Page
	Corporate and Consumer Affairs			
Sir Peter Gregson	B J G Hilton	Dr J P Spencer	Insurance	J Evans
		Mrs S E Brown	Companies	J Evans
		A Pryor	Competition Policy	J Evans
		Ms L Neville-Rolfe	Deregulation Unit	J Evans
		A J Dorken	Consumer Affairs	Earl Ferrers/ J Evans

*The Department's regional offices are now integrated with those of Environment, Transport and Employment (Training, Enterprise and Education Directorate). Each regional director (see above) administers the new single budget and is directly responsible to whichever secretaries of state have operational programmes under their particular office at any one time. Regional directors do not always report to the secretary of state but go through the relevant departmental permanent secretary as appropriate. Regional directors are accountable to the Secretary of State for the Environment on matters concerning the administration of the single budget.

For more details of these offices see separate entry in this section under **Government Offices for the Regions**.

The integrated regional offices operate in cooperation with English Partnerships; see the latter in the Regulatory Organisations section of the *Whitehall Companion*).

Departmental Overview

Grade 1	Civil Servants: Grade 2	Grade 3	Department	Minister
	Solicitors' Office			
Sir Peter Gregson	A H Hammond	M G Roberts	Investigations Division	J Evans
		C Kerse	Solicitors Division B	J Evans
		J M Stanley	Solicitors Division C	J Evans
		P H Bovey	Solicitors Division D	J Evans
		Miss K M S Morton	Solicitors Division E	J Evans
	Establishment and Finance			
Sir Peter Gregson	A C Hutton	M K O'Shea	Finance and Resource Management	T Eggar/ R Page
		Miss J M Caines (4)	Information Division	T Eggar/ R Page
		A Elkington (5)	Internal Audit	T Eggar/ R Page
		Miss P Boys	Personnel	T Eggar/ R Page
		Dr F R Heath-cote	Services Management	T Eggar/ R Page
		D Coates	Economics and Statistics	T Eggar/ R Page
	Competitiveness			
Sir Peter Gregson		Dr R Dobbie	Competitiveness	T Eggar

Civil Servants and Departments

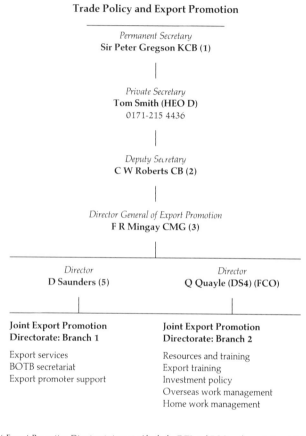

Trade Policy and Export Promotion

Permanent Secretary
Sir Peter Gregson KCB (1)

Private Secretary
Tom Smith (HEO D)
0171-215 4436

Deputy Secretary
C W Roberts CB (2)

Director General of Export Promotion
F R Mingay CMG (3)

Director
D Saunders (5)

Joint Export Promotion Directorate: Branch 1

Export services
BOTB secretariat
Export promoter support

Director
Q Quayle (DS4) (FCO)

Joint Export Promotion Directorate: Branch 2

Resources and training
Export training
Investment policy
Overseas work management
Home work management

The Joint Export Promotion Directorate is part of both the DTI and FCO and reports to ministers in both

---

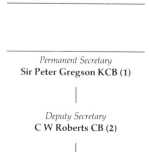

Permanent Secretary
Sir Peter Gregson KCB (1)

Deputy Secretary
C W Roberts CB (2)

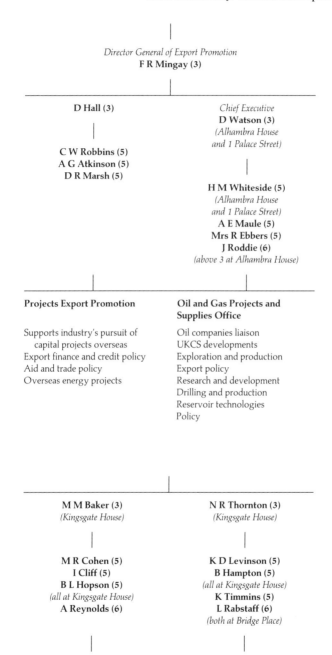

Director General of Export Promotion
F R Mingay (3)

D Hall (3)

C W Robbins (5)
A G Atkinson (5)
D R Marsh (5)

Chief Executive
D Watson (3)
(Alhambra House and 1 Palace Street)

H M Whiteside (5)
(Alhambra House and 1 Palace Street)
A E Maule (5)
Mrs R Ebbers (5)
J Roddie (6)
(above 3 at Alhambra House)

Projects Export Promotion

Supports industry's pursuit of capital projects overseas
Export finance and credit policy
Aid and trade policy
Overseas energy projects

Oil and Gas Projects and Supplies Office

Oil companies liaison
UKCS developments
Exploration and production
Export policy
Research and development
Drilling and production
Reservoir technologies
Policy

M M Baker (3)
(Kingsgate House)

M R Cohen (5)
I Cliff (5)
B L Hopson (5)
(all at Kingsgate House)
A Reynolds (6)

N R Thornton (3)
(Kingsgate House)

K D Levinson (5)
B Hampton (5)
(all at Kingsgate House)
K Timmins (5)
L Rabstaff (6)
(both at Bridge Place)

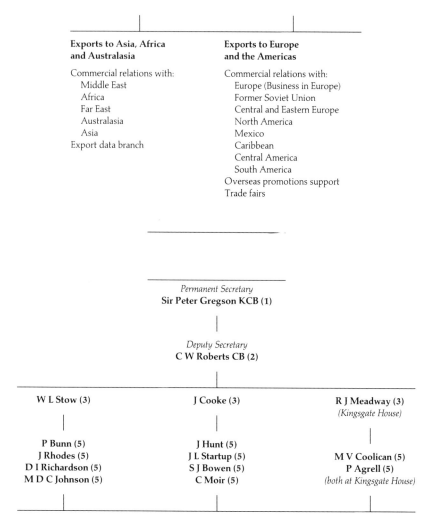

Exports to Asia, Africa and Australasia

Commercial relations with:
- Middle East
- Africa
- Far East
- Australasia
- Asia

Export data branch

Exports to Europe and the Americas

Commercial relations with:
- Europe (Business in Europe)
- Former Soviet Union
- Central and Eastern Europe
- North America
- Mexico
- Caribbean
- Central America
- South America

Overseas promotions support
Trade fairs

Permanent Secretary
Sir Peter Gregson KCB (1)

Deputy Secretary
C W Roberts CB (2)

W L Stow (3)

P Bunn (5)
J Rhodes (5)
D I Richardson (5)
M D C Johnson (5)

European Community and Trade Relations

EC policy issues
EC aid and industrial policy
Energy charter treaty unit
International energy unit
Trade policy:
- Former Soviet Union
- Central and Eastern Europe
- North America
- Asia/Pacific Rim and developing countries

J Cooke (3)

J Hunt (5)
J L Startup (5)
S J Bowen (5)
C Moir (5)

International Trade Policy

International and EC trade policy
Tariffs
Multilateral trade negotiations
International investment
General import policy
Unfair trade
Multifibre agreement
Economic advice on aid, trade investment, transitional economies

R J Meadway (3)
(Kingsgate House)

M V Coolican (5)
P Agrell (5)
(both at Kingsgate House)

Export Control and Non-Proliferation

Export control organisation including policy, sensitive technologies, export licensing, compliance units and sanctions unit
Nuclear non-proliferation policy
Safeguards Office
Chemical and biological weapons conventions

Industry

Permanent Secretary
Sir Peter Gregson KCB (1)

Deputy Secretary
A Macdonald CB (2)
(151 Buckingham Palace Road)

I M Jones (3)
(151 Buckingham Palace Road)

C L Jackson (5)
T L Roberts (5)
(both at 151 Buckingham Palace Road)

Textiles and Retailing

Textiles and consumer goods
Retailing, services and printing

W MacIntyre (3)
(151 Buckingham Palace Road)

S R Temple (4)
Mrs L Brown (5)
J Neilson (5)
N Worman (5)
D Hendon (5)
N M McMillan (5)
(all at 151 Buckingham Palace Road)

Telecommunications

National policy includes licensing and broadcasting
International telecommunications policy
Technical affairs and administration
Telecommunications, radiocommunications and broadcast sponsorship

P Salvidge (3)
(151 Buckingham Palace Road)

D Sibbick (5)
P Waller (5)
(both at 151 Buckingham Palace Road)

Posts

Post office and postal services

Dr E G Finer (3)

Mrs G Alliston (5)
Dr E A M Baker (5)
(all above at 151 Buckingham Palace Road)

M E Stanley (3)

B F Harding (5)
H P Brown (5)
T M H Shearer (5)
R Poole (6)
(all above at 151 Buckingham Palace Road)

Chemicals and Biotechnology

Chemical industry briefing
Bulk and speciality chemicals
Biotechnology
Technology transfer
Industrial competitiveness

Vehicles, Metals and Minerals

International and domestic steel issues
ISERBS
Mineral reconnaissance
Non-ferrous metals and minerals
Vehicle components and commercial vehicles
Vehicles: international and manufacturing strategy
Shipbuilding

R Foster (3)

Ms R J R Anderson (5)
S I Charik (5)
M Ralph (5)
Miss V Evans (5)
(all above at 151 Buckingham Palace Road)

Aerospace

Aero engines, helicopters and aviation equipment
Airframes and aerospace policy
Air market assessment and technical advice
Research and technology for civil aircraft

R M Rumbelow (3)

T J Soane (5)
Dr I Eddison (5)
C Bradley (5)
S C Pride (5)
(all above at 151 Buckingham Palace Road)

Electronics and Engineering

Industry sponsorship of IT and IT related industries, consumer electronics and components
Heavy electrical equipment
Power generation
Industry sponsorship:
- Process plant industries
- Production machinery industries
- Capital equipment industries
- Computing and optoelectronics
- Micro electronics
- Esprit

Mechanical engineering technologies

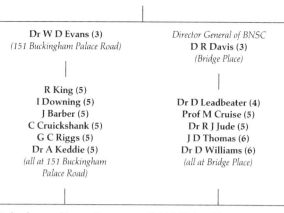

Dr W D Evans (3)
(151 Buckingham Palace Road)

R King (5)
I Downing (5)
J Barber (5)
C Cruickshank (5)
G C Riggs (5)
Dr A Keddie (5)
(all at 151 Buckingham Palace Road)

Technology and Innovation Policy

Science and technology policy
Technology transfer
Innovation and R&D policy
National Measurement System policy unit
Link
Science parks
International research and technology relations
EUREKA
Research and technology policy assessment unit
Standards policy
Innovation Unit

Director General of BNSC
D R Davis (3)
(Bridge Place)

Dr D Leadbeater (4)
Prof M Cruise (5)
Dr R J Jude (5)
J D Thomas (6)
Dr D Williams (6)
(all at Bridge Place)

British National Space Centre

Space technology
Industrial policy
Space applications
Space station issues
Space transportation
Satellite telecommunications
Space science
Microgravity

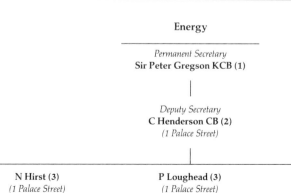

Energy

Permanent Secretary
Sir Peter Gregson KCB (1)

Deputy Secretary
C Henderson CB (2)
(1 Palace Street)

N Hirst (3)
(1 Palace Street)

P Loughead (3)
(1 Palace Street)

C C Wilcock (3)
(1 Palace Street)

Mrs H Haddon (5)
S D Spivey (5)
Dr D Lumley (5)
(all at 1 Palace Street)

J A V Collett (5)
A Berry (5)
Ms F S Price (5)
(all above at 1 Palace Street)

J H T Green (5)
S F D Powell (5)
Miss S Haird (5)
Dr P Fenwick (5)
(all at 1 Palace Street)

Atomic Energy Division

UKAEA
Management of nuclear liabilities
DRAWMOPS
Nuclear R&D programmes
Safety

Coal Division

British Coal privatisation
Safety and subsidence
Coal industry employment and operations

Electricity and Nuclear Fuels Division

Regulatory policy
Planning questions
Non-fossil fuel generation
Post flotation
Engineering Inspectorate
Nuclear Electric
BNFL issues
Uranium enrichment and procurement
Plutonium reprocessing and Thorp
Decommissioning and waste management
Health and safety issues

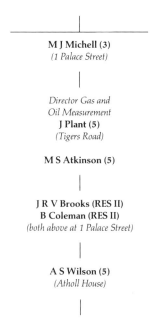

M J Michell (3)
(1 Palace Street)

Director Gas and Oil Measurement
J Plant (5)
(Tigers Road)

M S Atkinson (5)

J R V Brooks (RES II)
B Coleman (RES II)
(both above at 1 Palace Street)

A S Wilson (5)
(Atholl House)

Director of Oil and Gas Royalties Office
J Craven (6)
(1 Palace Street)

Oil and Gas

Downstream oil and gas markets
Policy coordination
Licensing and pipeline consents
Abandonment: UKCS boundaries
Royalties
Exploration and licensing
Reservoir development
Production engineering
Oil and gas: Field development
Gas and oil measurement

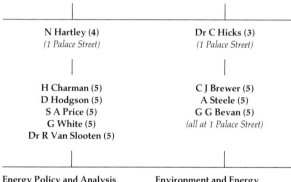

N Hartley (4)
(1 Palace Street)

H Charman (5)
D Hodgson (5)
S A Price (5)
G White (5)
Dr R Van Slooten (5)

Energy Policy and Analysis

Energy statistics
Energy projections
Energy economics
Energy policy issues; R&D
Oil and gas industry economics
North Sea statistics
Industry and environmental economics

Dr C Hicks (3)
(1 Palace Street)

C J Brewer (5)
A Steele (5)
G G Bevan (5)
(all at 1 Palace Street)

Environment and Energy Technologies

General environmental policy issues
Ozone depletion
EC legislation
Technology programmes
Waste issues
Vehicle emissions
Recycling policies
Energy and the environment
Global warming

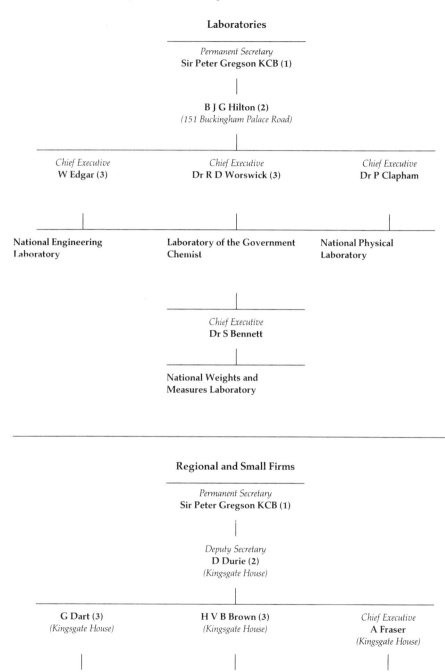

Laboratories

Permanent Secretary
Sir Peter Gregson KCB (1)

B J G Hilton (2)
(151 Buckingham Palace Road)

Chief Executive
W Edgar (3)

National Engineering Laboratory

Chief Executive
Dr R D Worswick (3)

Laboratory of the Government Chemist

Chief Executive
Dr P Clapham

National Physical Laboratory

Chief Executive
Dr S Bennett

National Weights and Measures Laboratory

Regional and Small Firms

Permanent Secretary
Sir Peter Gregson KCB (1)

Deputy Secretary
D Durie (2)
(Kingsgate House)

G Dart (3)
(Kingsgate House)

H V B Brown (3)
(Kingsgate House)

Chief Executive
A Fraser
(Kingsgate House)

Miss D Gane (5)
R H S Wells (5)
Mrs M A Wilks (5)
K Holt (5)
(all above at Kingsgate House)

Director IDU
A G Dunnett (3)
(Kingsgate House)

R Anderson (5)
J R Reid (5)
(St Mary's House c/o Moorfoot)
M Garrod (5)
(Kingsgate House)

Regional Development

Regional policy and activities of integrated regional offices
EC regional policy and funds
Regional Selective Assistance
Regional Development Grants
Industrial development unit
Accountancy services

Small Firms and Business Link

Small firms policy and finance
Loan guarantee scheme
Local delivery of support for small firms
TECs
Business links development
Consultancy scheme and successors

Invest in Britain Bureau

Inward investment promotion policy and activities
Promotion of England as a location for internationally mobile inward investment projects

Dr K C Shotton (3)
(151 Buckingham Palace Road)

Dr P Curtis (5)
D K Poulter (5)
Dr R Hinder (5)
Dr M S Draper (5)
(all at 151 Buckingham Palace Road)

Management and Technology Services

Technology access and adaption
Local innovation services
Technology – international projects
Best management practice in manufacturing and business process

Government Regional Offices

The Department's regional offices are now integrated with those of Environment, Transport and Employment (Training, Enterprise and Education Directorate). Each regional director (see below) administers the new single budget and is directly responsible to whichever secretaries of state have operational programmes under their particular office at any one time. Regional directors do not always report to the secretary of state but go through the relevant departmental permanent secretary as appropriate. Regional directors are accountable to the Secretary of State for the Environment on matters concerning the administration of the single budget.

For more details of these offices see separate entry in this section under **Government Offices for the Regions**.

The integrated regional offices operate in cooperation with English Partnerships; see the latter in the Regulatory Organisations section of the *Whitehall Companion*).

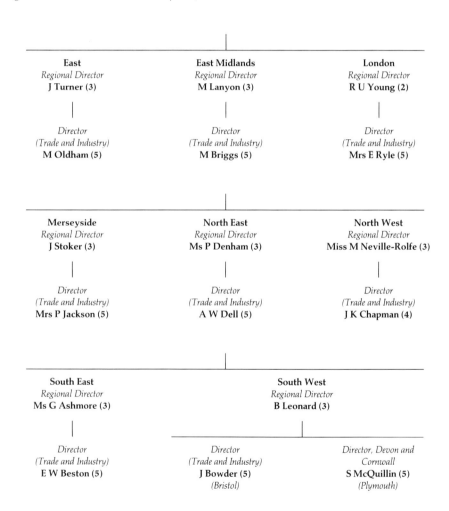

East
Regional Director
J Turner (3)

Director (Trade and Industry)
M Oldham (5)

East Midlands
Regional Director
M Lanyon (3)

Director (Trade and Industry)
M Briggs (5)

London
Regional Director
R U Young (2)

Director (Trade and Industry)
Mrs E Ryle (5)

Merseyside
Regional Director
J Stoker (3)

Director (Trade and Industry)
Mrs P Jackson (5)

North East
Regional Director
Ms P Denham (3)

Director (Trade and Industry)
A W Dell (5)

North West
Regional Director
Miss M Neville-Rolfe (3)

Director (Trade and Industry)
J K Chapman (4)

South East
Regional Director
Ms G Ashmore (3)

Director (Trade and Industry)
E W Beston (5)

South West
Regional Director
B Leonard (3)

Director (Trade and Industry)
J Bowder (5)
(Bristol)

Director, Devon and Cornwall
S McQuillin (5)
(Plymouth)

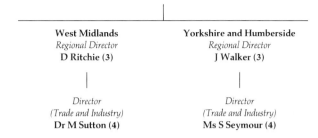

West Midlands	Yorkshire and Humberside
Regional Director	*Regional Director*
D Ritchie (3)	**J Walker (3)**
Director (Trade and Industry)	*Director (Trade and Industry)*
Dr M Sutton (4)	**Ms S Seymour (4)**

Corporate and Consumer Affairs

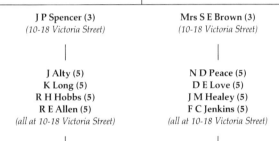

Permanent Secretary
Sir Peter Gregson KCB (1)

Deputy Secretary
B J G Hilton (2)

J P Spencer (3)	**Mrs S E Brown (3)**
(10-18 Victoria Street)	*(10-18 Victoria Street)*
J Alty (5)	**N D Peace (5)**
K Long (5)	**D E Love (5)**
R H Hobbs (5)	**J M Healey (5)**
R E Allen (5)	**F C Jenkins (5)**
(all at 10-18 Victoria Street)	*(all at 10-18 Victoria Street)*

Insurance

Insurance companies: authorisation and supervision (life and non-life)
Lloyds
Specialist re-insurance
Annual returns regulations
EC directive and single market
Insurance intermediaries
General policy
Public complaints and enquiries
Insurance against terrorist attacks

Companies

Directors and shareholders
Company legislation
European laws
Takeovers and shares
Accounting and audit policy
Company accounting
Disclosure of interests in shares
Registration of company charges
Accountancy advice
Company law and conduct

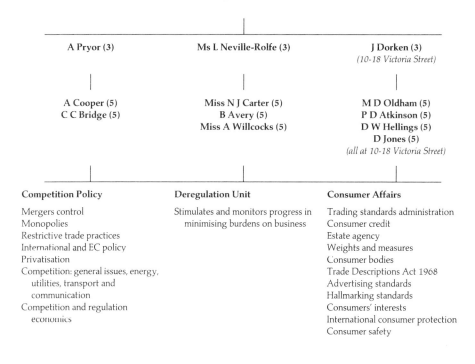

A Pryor (3)

A Cooper (5)
C C Bridge (5)

Ms L Neville-Rolfe (3)

Miss N J Carter (5)
B Avery (5)
Miss A Willcocks (5)

J Dorken (3)
(10-18 Victoria Street)

M D Oldham (5)
P D Atkinson (5)
D W Hellings (5)
D Jones (5)
(all at 10-18 Victoria Street)

Competition Policy

Mergers control
Monopolies
Restrictive trade practices
International and EC policy
Privatisation
Competition: general issues, energy, utilities, transport and communication
Competition and regulation economics

Deregulation Unit

Stimulates and monitors progress in minimising burdens on business

Consumer Affairs

Trading standards administration
Consumer credit
Estate agency
Weights and measures
Consumer bodies
Trade Descriptions Act 1968
Advertising standards
Hallmarking standards
Consumers' interests
International consumer protection
Consumer safety

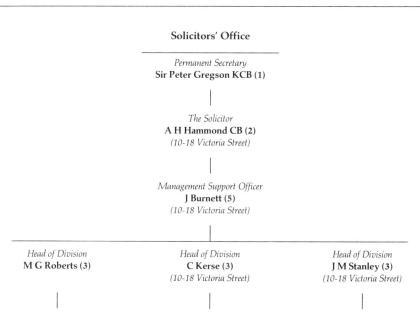

Solicitors' Office

Permanent Secretary
Sir Peter Gregson KCB (1)

The Solicitor
A H Hammond CB (2)
(10-18 Victoria Street)

Management Support Officer
J Burnett (5)
(10-18 Victoria Street)

Head of Division
M G Roberts (3)

Head of Division
C Kerse (3)
(10-18 Victoria Street)

Head of Division
J M Stanley (3)
(10-18 Victoria Street)

Inspector of Companies
G Harp (4)

Mrs T J Dunstan (4)
A Mier (5)
S L Parkinson (5)
Mrs B A Chase (5)
A H S Robertshaw (5)
H Bradshaw (5)

Investigations

Companies investigation
Case clerks
Investigation officers
Investigations policy
Companies inspections
Official Receivers' reports: prosecutions

I K Mathers (5)
J Roberts (5)
A S Hyett (5)
Miss N O'Flynn (5)
(all at 10-18 Victoria Street)

Solicitors' B

Insurance
Company law
Insolvency and EC company law

Mrs J Darvell (5)
Miss P A Granados (5)
C Raikes (5)
(all at 10-18 Victoria Street)

Solicitors' C

Industry and environment
Telecomms, radiocomms, PO, IT
Intellectual property
EC structural fund issues
Financial assistance for industry

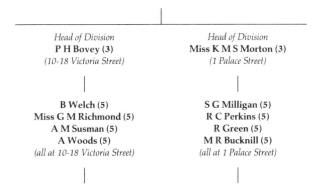

Head of Division
P H Bovey (3)
(10-18 Victoria Street)

B Welch (5)
Miss G M Richmond (5)
A M Susman (5)
A Woods (5)
(all at 10-18 Victoria Street)

Head of Division
Miss K M S Morton (3)
(1 Palace Street)

S G Milligan (5)
R C Perkins (5)
R Green (5)
M R Bucknill (5)
(all at 1 Palace Street)

Solicitors' D

Consumer issues
Overseas trade
Deregulation
Business law policy unit
Competition
Weights and measures etc
Exports, imports, trade sanctions
Export Credits Guarantee Branch

Solicitors' E

Atomic energy
Electricity
Energy: research and development
Gas, oil and petroleum licensing
Coal industry matters

Establishment and Finance

Permanent Secretary
Sir Peter Gregson KCB (1)

Principal Establishment and Finance Officer
A C Hutton (2)

M K O'Shea (3)*

J Clayton (5)
Dr S Sklaroff (5)
Keith Hills (5)
Mrs M Bloom (5)
J Hobday (5)

Director of Information
Miss J Caines (4)
A Marre (6)
(Bridge Place)

Head of Internal Audit
A C Elkington (5)
(Bridge Place)

Finance and Resource Management

Programme finance and coordination of Public Expenditure Survey
Value for money
MINIS
Vote management of running costs
Resource management
Organisational policy
Manpower audit
Citizen's Charter
Market testing

Information

Press
Promotions
Publicity
Publications

Internal Audit

Independent appraisal function which provides a service to management by reviewing and reporting on the adequacy, reliability and effectiveness of internal control systems

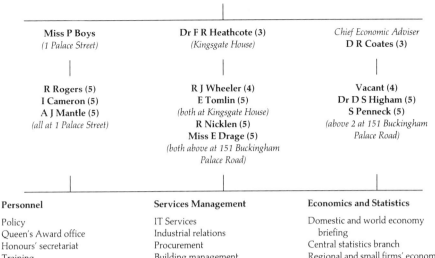

Miss P Boys
(1 Palace Street)

R Rogers (5)
I Cameron (5)
A J Mantle (5)
(all at 1 Palace Street)

Dr F R Heathcote (3)
(Kingsgate House)

R J Wheeler (4)
E Tomlin (5)
(both at Kingsgate House)
R Nicklen (5)
Miss E Drage (5)
(both above at 151 Buckingham Palace Road)

Chief Economic Adviser
D R Coates (3)

Vacant (4)
Dr D S Higham (5)
S Penneck (5)
(above 2 at 151 Buckingham Palace Road)

Personnel

Policy
Queen's Award office
Honours' secretariat
Training
Promotion, recruitment
Trawling units
Conditions of Service

Services Management

IT Services
Industrial relations
Procurement
Building management
Information management services
Office services
Competitive Service Unit

Economics and Statistics

Domestic and world economy briefing
Central statistics branch
Regional and small firms' economics and statistics
Trade statistics
Operational research unit
Small firms statistics
Economics and statistics of industry and innovation
Industrial economics and statistics

Competitiveness

Permanent Secretary
Sir Peter Gregson KCB (1)

Dr R Dobbie (3)

S Haddrill (5)
E Hosker (5)
Dr A Eggington (5)
(Kingsgate House)

Competitiveness

Responsible for ensuring that government policies, both of the DTI and other departments, are designed and implemented with full regard to the importance of making UK industry more competitive at home and abroad
Briefs ministers on general industrial competitiveness questions and on the policies of other government departments
Maintains a dialogue with national organisations on these issues

Department of Trade and Industry Addresses

Alhambra House
45 Waterloo Street
Glasgow G2 6AS
Tel 0141-248 2855
Fax 0141 221 1718

Atholl House
86-88 Guild Street
Aberdeen AB9 1DR
Tel 01224 254043
Fax (tel the no above and ask for relevant fax no)

Bridge Place
88-89 Eccleston Square
London SW1V 1PT
Tel 0171-215 5000
Fax (tel the no above and ask for relevant fax no)

151 Buckingham Palace Road
London SW1W 9SS
Tel 0171-215 5000
Fax 0171-215 2909

Export Credits Guarantee Dept
PO Box 2200
2 Exchange Tower
Harbour Exchange Square
London E14 9GS
Tel 0171-512 7000
Fax 0171-512 7649

Kingsgate House
66-74 Victoria Street
London SW1E 6SW
Tel 0171-215 5000
Fax 0171-931 0397

1 Palace Street
London SW1E 5HE
Tel 0171-215 5000
Fax 0171-834 3771

3 Tigers Road
(off Saffron Road)
Wigston
Leicestershire LE18 4UX
Tel 01162 785354
Fax 01162 780027

10-18 Victoria Street
London SW1H 0NN
Tel 0171-215 5000
Fax 0171-222 9280

Government Offices: Regions

East
Heron House
49-53 Goldington Road
Bedford MK40 3LL
Tel 01234 276161
Fax 01234 276272

Building A
Westbrook Centre
Milton Road
Cambridge CB4 1YG
Tel 01223 461939
Fax (tel above number and ask for fax number)

East Midlands
Cranbrook House
Cranbrook Street
Nottingham NG1 1EY
Tel 01159 350602
Fax 01159 352414

Severns House
Middle Pavement
Nottingham NG1 7DW
Tel 01159 506181
Fax 01159 587074

London
Bridge Place
88-89 Eccleston Square
London SW1V 1PT
Tel 0171-215 5000
Fax 0171-215 0875

Merseyside
Graeme House
Derby Square
Liverpool L2 7UP
Tel 0151 227 4111
Fax 0151 236 1140

North East
Stanegate House
2 Groat Market
Newcastle upon Tyne NE1 1YN
Tel 0191-232 4722
Fax 0191-235 7798

North West
Sunley Tower
Piccadilly Plaza
Manchester M1 4BA
Tel 0161-838 5555/236 2171
Fax 0161-228 3740

South East
Charles House
375 Kensington High Street
London W14 8QH
Tel 0171-605 9000
Fax 0171-605 9249

Bridge Place
88-89 Eccleston Square
London SW1V 1PT
Tel 0171-215 5000
Fax (tel above number and ask for fax number)

South West
The Pithay
Bristol BS1 2PB
Tel 01179 456661
Fax 01179 221799

Plymouth Office
Phoenix House
Notte Street
Plymouth PL1 2HF
Tel 01752 221891
Fax 01752 227647

West Midlands
77 Paradise Circus
Queensway
Birmingham B1 2DT
Tel 0121-212 5000
Fax 0121-212 1010

Yorkshire and Humberside
7th Floor
City House
New Station Street
Leeds LS1 4 JD
Tel 01132 835201
Fax 01132 449313

25 Queen Street
Leeds LS1 2TW
Tel 01132 443171
Fax (tel above number and ask for fax number)

Department of Transport

Founded 1919

Ministers secretary of state, two ministers of state and one parliamentary under secretary

Responsibilities
airports
bus and road freight licensing
bus industry, sponsorship of
civil aviation, domestic and international
driver testing and licensing
HM Coastguard
local authorities, oversight of transport planning
marine pollution
shipping and ports
motorways and trunk roads
rail industry, sponsorship of
road safety
taxis and private hire cars, regulation of
vehicle standards, registration and licensing

Number of Staff 2000

Executive agencies
Coastguard Agency
Driver and Vehicle Licensing Agency
Driving Standards Agency
Highways Agency
Marine Safety Agency
Transport Research Laboratory
Vehicle Certification Agency
Vehicle Inspectorate

Department of Transport

2 Marsham Street, London SW1P 3EB

Tel 0171-276 3000 Fax 0171-276 0818

All personnel are based at 2 Marsham Street unless otherwise indicated.
For other addresses and telephone numbers see end of section.

Ministers

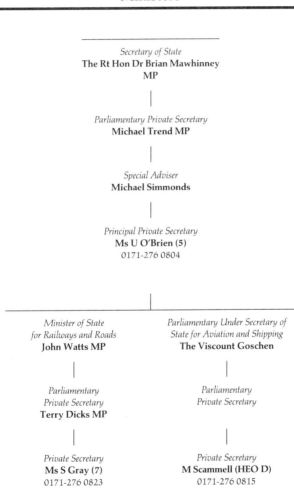

Secretary of State
The Rt Hon Dr Brian Mawhinney MP

Parliamentary Private Secretary
Michael Trend MP

Special Adviser
Michael Simmonds

Principal Private Secretary
Ms U O'Brien (5)
0171-276 0804

Minister of State for Railways and Roads
John Watts MP

Parliamentary Private Secretary
Terry Dicks MP

Private Secretary
Ms S Gray (7)
0171-276 0823

Parliamentary Under Secretary of State for Aviation and Shipping
The Viscount Goschen

Parliamentary Private Secretary

Private Secretary
M Scammell (HEO D)
0171-276 0815

Parliamentary Under Secretary of State for Transport in London and Minister for Local Transport and Road Safety
Steven Norris MP

Private Secretary
S E Heard
0171-276 0827

House of Lords' Spokesman
The Baroness Miller of Hendon

Ministerial Responsibilities

Brian Mawhinney	Overall responsibility for the work of the department Environmental aspects and financial planning of transport
John Watts	Channel Tunnel including Safety Unit Highways Agency Railways Roads infrastructure policy (including national roads)
Steve Norris	Disabled people Driver and vehicle licensing Driver testing and training Inner cities policy outside London Local and urban transport issues nationwide London transport issues including roads and traffic and London Underground Research Road and vehicle safety Road taxation Departmental spokesman in the House of Commons on matters for which Viscount Goschen is responsible
The Viscount Goschen	Airports Aviation Marine and shipping matters including the Coastguard and ports Departmental spokesman in the House of Lords

Departmental Overview

Civil Servants			Group	Minister
Grade 1	*Grade 2*	*Grade 3*		
Sir Patrick Brown		M J Helm (5)	Information	B Mawhinney
		M Thomas	Legal	B Mawhinney
	Infrastructure			
Sir Patrick Brown	N L J Montagu	C R Grimsey	Railways Infrastructure	J Watts
		P Wood	Railway Privatisation	J Watts
		Mrs J M Williams	Railway Privatisation	J Watts
		H Derwent	Road Infrastructure	J Watts
		J Henes	Freight, Ports and International	Vis Goschen
		E A Ryder	UK Delegation to Channel Tunnel Safety Authority	J Watts
		Government Regional Offices*		
		J Turner	Eastern	B Mawhinney
		M Lanyon	East Midlands	B Mawhinney
	R U Young	I Yass	London	B Mawhinney
		J Stoker	Merseyside	B Mawhinney
		Ms P Denham	North East	B Mawhinney
		Ms M Neville-Rolfe	North West	B Mawhinney
		Ms G Ashmore	South East	B Mawhinney
		B Leonard S McQuillin	South West Devon and Cornwall	B Mawhinney
		D Ritchie	West Midlands	B Mawhinney
		J Walker	Yorkshire and Humberside	B Mawhinney
	Operations			
Sir Patrick Brown	J W S Dempster	H B Wenban-Smith	Civil Aviation	Vis Goschen
		A J Goldman	International Aviation	Vis Goschen
		K P R Smart (4)	Air Accidents	B Mawhinney
		R E Clarke	Shipping Policy	Vis Goschen
		Capt P B Marriott (5)	Marine Accident Investigation Branch	B Mawhinney
		R A Allan	Urban and Local Transport	S Norris
		Miss S Lambert	Road and Vehicle Safety; Traffic Area Offices	S Norris

Departmental Overview

Grade 1	Civil Servants Grade 2	Grade 3	Department	Minister
	Finance and Central Services			
Sir Patrick Brown	D J Rowlands	B Wadsworth	Finance	B Mawhinney
		R Bird	Personnel	B Mawhinney
		D W Flaxen	Statistical Service	B Mawhinney
		Dr D Metz (4)	Chief Scientist's Unit	B Mawhinney
		M R Newey (4)	Central Services	B Mawhinney
		H Ditmas (4)	Transport Security	B Mawhinney
		J Phillips	Executive Agencies	B Mawhinney
		Miss A Frye (6)	Mobility Unit	B Mawhinney
		D R Instone (5)	Transport Policy Unit	B Mawhinney

*The Department's regional offices are now integrated with those of Environment, Trade and Industry, and Employment (Training, Enterprise and Education Directorate). Each regional director (see above) administers the new single budget and is equally responsible to whichever secretaries of state have operational programmes under the direction of their particular office at any one time. Regional directors do not always report to the secretary of state but go through the relevant departmental permanent secretary as appropriate. Regional directors are accountable to the Secretary of State for the Environment on matters concerning the administration of the single budget.

For separate **Government Offices for the Regions** entry see under that title in this section.

The government regional offices operate in cooperation with English Partnerships; see the latter in the Regulatory Organisations section of the *Whitehall Companion*).

Civil Servants and Departments

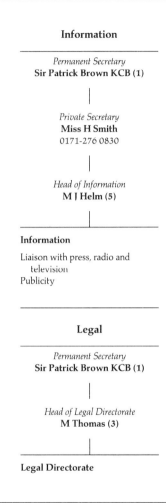

Information

Permanent Secretary
Sir Patrick Brown KCB (1)

Private Secretary
Miss H Smith
0171-276 0830

Head of Information
M J Helm (5)

Information

Liaison with press, radio and television
Publicity

Legal

Permanent Secretary
Sir Patrick Brown KCB (1)

Head of Legal Directorate
M Thomas (3)

Legal Directorate

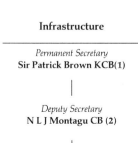

Infrastructure

Permanent Secretary
Sir Patrick Brown KCB(1)

Deputy Secretary
N L J Montagu CB (2)

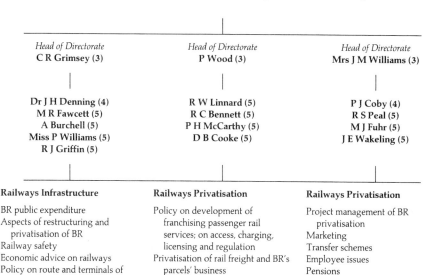

Head of Directorate
C R Grimsey (3)

Dr J H Denning (4)
M R Fawcett (5)
A Burchell (5)
Miss P Williams (5)
R J Griffin (5)

Railways Infrastructure

BR public expenditure
Aspects of restructuring and privatisation of BR
Railway safety
Economic advice on railways
Policy on route and terminals of channel tunnel rail link; privatisation of European passenger services and Channel Tunnel rail link/EPS competition
International railways

Head of Directorate
P Wood (3)

R W Linnard (5)
R C Bennett (5)
P H McCarthy (5)
D B Cooke (5)

Railways Privatisation

Policy on development of franchising passenger rail services; on access, charging, licensing and regulation
Privatisation of rail freight and BR's parcels' business
Freight grants unit

Head of Directorate
Mrs J M Williams (3)

P J Coby (4)
R S Peal (5)
M J Fuhr (5)
J E Wakeling (5)

Railways Privatisation

Project management of BR privatisation
Marketing
Transfer schemes
Employee issues
Pensions
Staff travel concessions
Systems
Coordination of secondary legislation under the Railways Act 1993

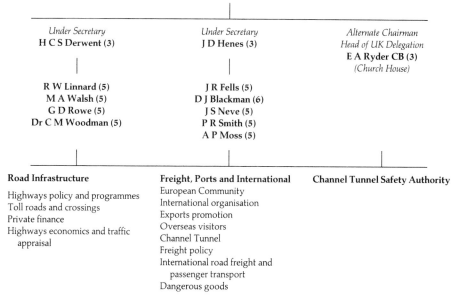

Under Secretary
H C S Derwent (3)

R W Linnard (5)
M A Walsh (5)
G D Rowe (5)
Dr C M Woodman (5)

Road Infrastructure

Highways policy and programmes
Toll roads and crossings
Private finance
Highways economics and traffic appraisal

Under Secretary
J D Henes (3)

J R Fells (5)
D J Blackman (6)
J S Neve (5)
P R Smith (5)
A P Moss (5)

Freight, Ports and International

European Community
International organisation
Exports promotion
Overseas visitors
Channel Tunnel
Freight policy
International road freight and passenger transport
Dangerous goods

Alternate Chairman
Head of UK Delegation
E A Ryder CB (3)
(Church House)

Channel Tunnel Safety Authority

Government Regional Offices

The Department's regional offices are now integrated with those of Environment, Trade and Industry, and Employment (Training, Enterprise and Education Directorate). Each regional director (see below) administers the new single budget and is equally responsible to whichever secretaries of state have operational programmes under the direction of their particular office at any one time. Regional directors do not always report to the secretary of state but will go through the relevant departmental permanent secretary as appropriate. Regional directors are accountable to the Secretary of State for the Environment on matters concerning the administration of the single budget.

For separate **Government Offices for the Regions** entry see under that title in this section.

The government regional offices operate in cooperation with English Partnerships; see the latter in the Regulatory Organisations section of the *Whitehall Companion*).

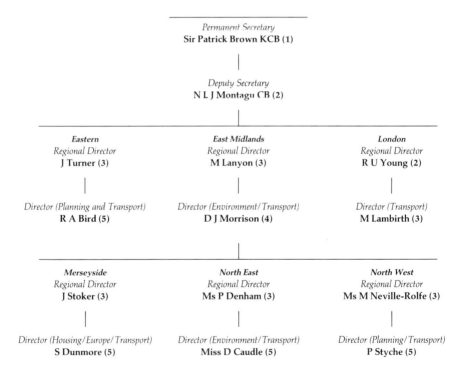

Permanent Secretary
Sir Patrick Brown KCB (1)

Deputy Secretary
N L J Montagu CB (2)

Eastern
Regional Director
J Turner (3)

Director (Planning and Transport)
R A Bird (5)

East Midlands
Regional Director
M Lanyon (3)

Director (Environment/Transport)
D J Morrison (4)

London
Regional Director
R U Young (2)

Director (Transport)
M Lambirth (3)

Merseyside
Regional Director
J Stoker (3)

Director (Housing/Europe/Transport)
S Dunmore (5)

North East
Regional Director
Ms P Denham (3)

Director (Environment/Transport)
Miss D Caudle (5)

North West
Regional Director
Ms M Neville-Rolfe (3)

Director (Planning/Transport)
P Styche (5)

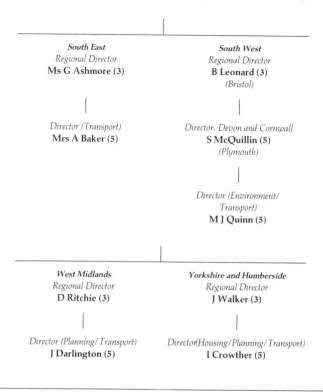

South East
Regional Director
Ms G Ashmore (3)

Director (Transport)
Mrs A Baker (5)

South West
Regional Director
B Leonard (3)
(Bristol)

Director, Devon and Cornwall
S McQuillin (5)
(Plymouth)

Director (Environment/ Transport)
M J Quinn (5)

West Midlands
Regional Director
D Ritchie (3)

Director (Planning/Transport)
J Darlington (5)

Yorkshire and Humberside
Regional Director
J Walker (3)

Director (Housing/Planning/Transport)
I Crowther (5)

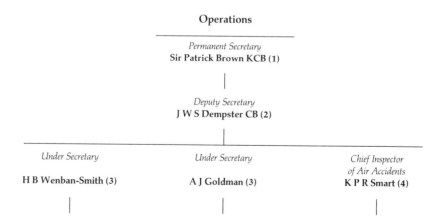

Operations

Permanent Secretary
Sir Patrick Brown KCB (1)

Deputy Secretary
J W S Dempster CB (2)

Under Secretary
H B Wenban-Smith (3)

Under Secretary
A J Goldman (3)

Chief Inspector of Air Accidents
K P R Smart (4)

Ms A Munro (5)
Ms M J Clare (5)
Ms E J Duthie (5)
M C Mann (5)

N S Starling (5)
A T Baker (5)
Dr P H Martin (5)
D S Evans (4)
(Montreal)

R C McKinlay (5)
(both at Farnborough)

Civil Aviation Directorate

- Airport policy
- Civil Aviation Authority
- Airline competition
- Airspace capacity
- Safety
- Search and rescue
- Environment and noise
- Economics
- Aviation
- Maritime International

International Aviation Directorate

- Relations with all countries
- Defence planning
- International Civil Aviation Organisation
- European Civil Aviation Conference
- EC
- International competition
- Tariffs
- Concorde routes

Air Accidents Investigation

- Civil air accidents in UK
- British registered or manufactured aircraft
- Investigations for MOD (Air)

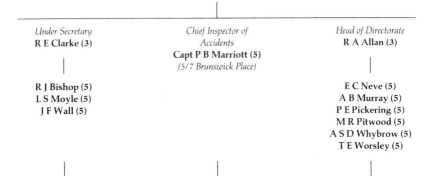

Under Secretary
R E Clarke (3)

R J Bishop (5)
L S Moyle (5)
J F Wall (5)

Chief Inspector of Accidents
Capt P B Marriott (5)
(5/7 Brunswick Place)

Head of Directorate
R A Allan (3)

E C Neve (5)
A B Murray (5)
P E Pickering (5)
M R Pitwood (5)
A S D Whybrow (5)
T E Worsley (5)

Shipping Policy

- Shipping policy
- Foreign relations
- EC
- Defence planning
- Shipping register
- Seamen's records
- Planning Board for Ocean Shipping
- Coordination of transport civil emergency planning
- Marine Safety Agency
- Coastguard Agency

Marine Accident Investigation

- UK registered ships anywhere in the world
- Non-UK registered ships in UK territorial waters
- Others at discretion of SoS

Urban and Local Transport

- Urban transport policy
- Traffic policy
- Buses and taxis
- Driver information systems
- Economics
- Local transport

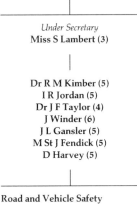

Under Secretary
Miss S Lambert (3)

Dr R M Kimber (5)
I R Jordan (5)
Dr J F Taylor (4)
J Winder (6)
J L Gansler (5)
M St J Fendick (5)
D Harvey (5)

Road and Vehicle Safety and Traffic Area Offices

Legislation and enforcement
Education and publicity
Vehicle safety
Environmental standards
Vehicle testing
Mechanical engineering
Medical adviser
Traffic area coordination
Traffic area offices
Vehicle Certification Agency

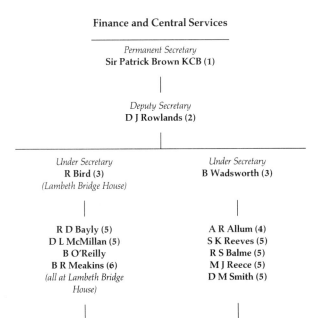

Finance and Central Services

Permanent Secretary
Sir Patrick Brown KCB (1)

Deputy Secretary
D J Rowlands (2)

Under Secretary
R Bird (3)
(Lambeth Bridge House)

R D Bayly (5)
D L McMillan (5)
B O'Reilly
B R Meakins (6)
(all at Lambeth Bridge House)

Under Secretary
B Wadsworth (3)

A R Allum (4)
S K Reeves (5)
R S Balme (5)
M J Reece (5)
D M Smith (5)

Personnel

Personnel management
Personnel policy
Secondments
Training
Pay and superannuation
Welfare service

Finance

Accounts
Public expenditure
Public appointments
Grants
Internal audit
Citizen's Charter

Director of Statistics
D W Flaxen (3)
(Romney House)
Miss B J Wood (5)
Dr R L Butchart (5)
P J Capell (5)
R P Donachie (5)
(all at Romney House)

Chief Scientist
Dr D Metz (4)

M R Newey (4)
(Lambeth Bridge House)

D E Bridge (5)
G L Jones (5)
(both above at Ashdown House)
I R Heawood (5)
(Lambeth Bridge House)

Statistics

National and London traffic
Roads and road vehicles
Buses and coaches
Domestic and international road haulage
London and urban transport
Road accidents
Ports
Shipping and sea passengers
Aviation
National Travel Survey

Chief Scientist's Unit

Research and development
Science and technology issues

Central Services Unit

Accommodation
Office services
Management support services
Contracts and procurement

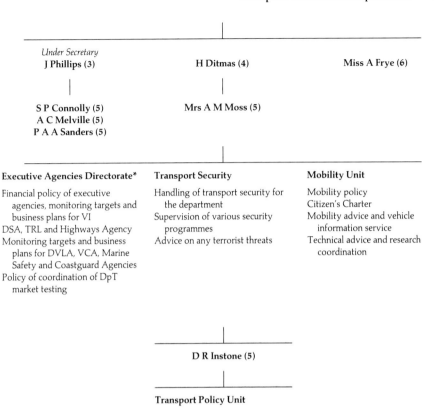

Under Secretary
J Phillips (3)

S P Connolly (5)
A C Melville (5)
P A A Sanders (5)

H Ditmas (4)

Mrs A M Moss (5)

Miss A Frye (6)

Executive Agencies Directorate*

Financial policy of executive agencies, monitoring targets and business plans for VI
DSA, TRL and Highways Agency
Monitoring targets and business plans for DVLA, VCA, Marine Safety and Coastguard Agencies
Policy of coordination of DpT market testing

Transport Security

Handling of transport security for the department
Supervision of various security programmes
Advice on any terrorist threats

Mobility Unit

Mobility policy
Citizen's Charter
Mobility advice and vehicle information service
Technical advice and research coordination

D R Instone (5)

Transport Policy Unit

*The Driver and Vehicle Licensing Agency, the Transport Research Laboratory and the Highways Agency report direct to D J Rowlands

Department of Transport Addresses

National addresses

Ashdown House
Sedlescombe Road North
St Leonards on Sea
East Sussex
Tel 01424 431344
Fax 01424 458550

5/7 Brunswick Place
Southampton
Hants SO1 2AN
Tel 01703 232424
Fax 01703 232459

Church House
Great Smith Street
London SW1P 3BL
Tel 0171-276 2014
Fax 0171-276 2078

Crowthorne
Berkshire RG11 6AU
Tel 01344 773131
Fax 01344 770356

Friars House
Warwick Road
Coventry CV1 2TN
Tel 01203 535101
Fax 01203 535330

Lambeth Bridge House
London SE1 7SB
Tel 0171-238 4449
Fax 0171-238 5215

Millbank Tower
London SW1P 4QU
Tel 0171-217 4479
Fax 0171-217 4399

2 Monck Street
London SW1 2BQ
Tel 0171-276 2820
Fax 0171-276 2770

83 Princes Street
Edinburgh EH2 2HH
Tel 0131-225 5567
Fax 0131-220 4066

Suite 928
1000 Sherbrook Street West
Montreal
Quebec
Canada H3A 3G4
Tel 001 418 285 8302
Fax 001 418 285 8001

Romney House
43 Marsham Street
London SW1P 3EB
Tel 0171-276 3000
Fax 0171-276 8355

Royal Aerospace Establishment
Farnborough
Hants GU14 6TD
Tel 01252 510300
Fax 01252 540535

Spring Place
105 Commercial Road
Southampton SO1 0ZD
Tel 01703 329 100
Fax 01703 329 351

St Christopher House
Southwark Street
London SE1 0TE
Tel 0171-928 3666
Fax 0171-928 4664

Sunley House
90–93 High Holborn
London WC1V 6LP
Tel 0171-405 6911
Fax 0171-831 2508

Tollgate House
Houlton Street
Bristol BS2 9DJ
Tel 01179 218283
Fax 01179 218264

Regional Offices

Eastern

Bedford
Heron House
49-53 Goldington Road
Bedford MK40 3LL
Tel 01234 363161
Fax 01234 276081

Cambridge
Enterprise House
Chivers Way
Vision Park
Histon
Cambridge CB4 4ZR
Tel 01223 202069
Fax 01223 202066

East Midlands

Cranbrook House
Cranbrook Street
Nottingham NG1 1EY
Tel 01159 350602
Fax 01159 799743

London

2 Marsham Street
London SW1P 3EB
Tel 0171-276 5825
Fax 0171-276 5827

Mersey

Graeme House
Derby Square
Liverpool L2 7SU
Tel 0151 227 4111
Fax 0151 236 1199

North Eastern

Stanegate House
2 Groat Market
Newcastle upon Tyne NE1 1YN
Tel 0191-201 3300
Fax 0191-261 6081

North West

Sunley Tower
Piccadilly Plaza
Manchester M1 4BE
Tel 0161-838 5555/0161 236 2171
Fax 0161-228 3740

South East

Charles House
375 Kensington High Street
London W14 4QH
Tel 0171-605 9003
Fax 0171-605 9253

South West

Bristol
4th Floor The Pithay
Bristol BS1 2NQ
Tel 01179 87800
Fax 01179 878318

Plymouth
Phoenix House
Notte Street
Plymouth P1 2HS
Tel 01752 221891

West Midlands

77 Paradise Circus
Queensway
Birmingham B1 2DT
Tel 0121-212 5000/0121-626 2000
Fax 0121-212 1010

Yorkshire and Humberside

City House
New Station Street
Leeds LS1 4JD
Tel 01132 800600
Fax 01132 338301

HM Treasury

The Prime Minister (who is also First Lord of Treasury), the government whips in both Houses and the Leader of the House of Lords are all officially part of HM Treasury. They do not, however, play a part in the day-to-day life of the departmental Treasury which is headed by the Chancellor of the Exchequer

Departmental Treasury

Founded	Eleventh century
Ministers	Chancellor of the Exchequer, Chief Secretary, Financial Secretary, Paymaster General and Minister of State/Economic Secretary
Responsibilities	To formulate and put into effect the government's financial and economic policy To plan public expenditure and see that it conforms to the approved plans Central oversight of civil service pay and personnel management Financial services and institutions Overseas financial relations, including international monetary affairs Privatisation and wider share ownership Procurement policy Taxation
Number of staff	1334
Executive agencies	Central Statistical Office Office of HM Paymaster General Royal Mint Valuation Office *Inland Revenue *HM Customs and Excise

*Government departments on "Next Steps" agency lines. See this section

HM Treasury

Parliament Street, London SW1P 3AG
Tel 0171-270 3000   Fax 0171-270 5653/0171-839 2082

All personnel are based at Parliament Street unless otherwise indicated.
For other addresses and telephone numbers see end of Treasury section.

Ministers

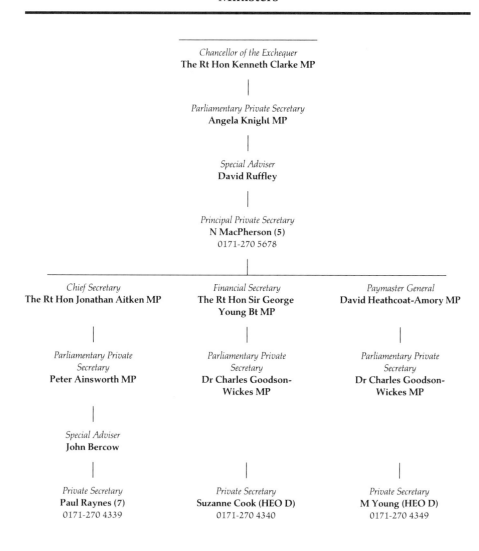

Chancellor of the Exchequer
The Rt Hon Kenneth Clarke MP

Parliamentary Private Secretary
Angela Knight MP

Special Adviser
David Ruffley

Principal Private Secretary
N MacPherson (5)
0171-270 5678

Chief Secretary
The Rt Hon Jonathan Aitken MP

Parliamentary Private Secretary
Peter Ainsworth MP

Special Adviser
John Bercow

Private Secretary
Paul Raynes (7)
0171-270 4339

Financial Secretary
The Rt Hon Sir George Young Bt MP

Parliamentary Private Secretary
Dr Charles Goodson-Wickes MP

Private Secretary
Suzanne Cook (HEO D)
0171-270 4340

Paymaster General
David Heathcoat-Amory MP

Parliamentary Private Secretary
Dr Charles Goodson-Wickes MP

Private Secretary
M Young (HEO D)
0171-270 4349

Minister of State,
Economic Secretary
Anthony Nelson MP

Private Secretary
S G Meek (HEO)
0171-270 4350

House of Lords' Spokesmen
The Lord Henley
The Lord Mackay of Ardbrecknish
The Lord Inglewood

Forecasting Panel
Andrew Britton
Tim Congdon
Professor David Currie
Gavyn Davies
Professor Wynne Godley
Professor Patrick Minford

Ministerial Responsibilities

Kenneth Clarke	ministerial head of the Treasury overall responsibility for – the economy – fiscal policy – finance and monetary policy – civil service management
Jonathan Aitken	competitive tendering and market testing export credit public expenditure planning control (including local authority and nationalised industry finance) public sector pay including nationalised industry pay, parliamentary pay, allowances and superannuation (but excluding civil service pay) value for money in the public services including Next Steps agencies
Sir George Young	Civil Service personnel management, industrial relations and relocation competition and deregulation policy Inland Revenue taxes legislative programme oversight of Inland Revenue, excluding Valuation Office parliamentary financial business privatisation and private finance
David Heathcoat-Amory	charities Customs and Excise duties and taxes environment, including energy efficiency EC budget and future financing ministerial correspondence oversight of Customs and Excise Paymaster General's office Treasury interest in general accounting issues Treasury interest in women's issues

Anthony Nelson

Central Statistical Office
Department for National Savings
economic and monetary union
export promotion
financial system, including banks, building societies and friendly societies and other financial institutions; and financial services
FORWARD (CISCO)
Government Actuary's Department
international finance issues and institutions
monetary policy
National Investment and Loans Office
procurement policy
public expenditure casework
Royal Mint
stamp duties
Treasury Bulletin and Economic Briefing
Valuation Office
wider share ownership

Departmental Overview

Civil Servants: Grade 1	Grade 1A	Grade 2	Grade 3	Directorates	Minister
Sir Terence Burns				Ministerial support	
				Communications	K Clarke
				Strategy	K Clarke
Macroeconomic Policy and Prospects Directorate					
Sir Terence Burns	A Budd		C J Mowl	Economic prcspects	J Aitken
			A O'Donnell	Fiscal and macroeconomic policy	J Aitken D Heathcoat Amory
				Economic briefing and analysis	A Nelson
				Inflation and economic policy	J Aitken A Nelson
				Debt and reserves management	A Nelson
				Economist group management unit	A Nelson

Departmental Overview

Civil Servants				Directorates	Minister
Grade 1	*Grade 1A*	*Grade 2*	*Grade 3*		
International Finance Directorate					
Sir Terence Burns	Sir Nigel Wicks		D L C Peretz P McIntyre	EU finances, future strategy, coordination	D Heathcoat Amory A Nelson
				Developing countries, debt and export finance	J Aitken A Nelson
				International financial institutions and former Soviet Union	A Nelson
				Trade policy and developments	A Nelson
				World economic issues	A Nelson
				Regional/country analysis	A Nelson
Budget and Public Finances Directorate					
Sir Terence Burns		C W Kelly	Mrs A F Case E J W Gieve	General expenditure policy and statistics	J Aitken
				Exchequer funds and accounts	D Heathcoat Amory
				Public sector finances	J Aitken
				Tax and Budget, tax economics and administration	Sir G Young D Heathcoat Amory
				Strategic management	J Aitken

Departmental Overview

Grade 1	Civil Servants Grade 1A	Grade 2	Grade 3	Directorates	Minister
				Public sector pay policy	J Aitken
				Departmental pay systems	J Aitken
				Public service pensions	J Aitken
	Spending Directorate				
Sir Terence Burns	R Culpin		N J Glass	Aid, diplomacy and intelligence	J Aitken
			Ms A Perkins	Defence	J Aitken
			Miss G M Noble	Agriculture	J Aitken
			P Sedgwick	Social security and pensions	J Aitken
				Health	J Aitken
				Heritage and central departments	J Aitken
				Education	J Aitken
				Employment and training	J Aitken
				Home Office and legal departments	J Aitken
				Local government	J Aitken
				Housing, urban and government property	J Aitken
				Scotland, Wales, Northern Ireland, environment, other DoE issues	J Aitken D Heathcoat Amory
				Central operational research and economics	J Aitken

Departmental Overview

Grade 1	Civil Servants: Grade 1A	Grade 2	Grade 3	Directorates	Minister
	Financial Management, Reporting and Audit Directorate				
Sir Terence Burns	J A Likierman		J E Mortimer	Treasury Officer of Accounts	D Heathcoat Amory
				Central accountancy	D Heathcoat Amory
				Government accountancy services management unit	D Heathcoat Amory
				Audit policy and advice	D Heathcoat Amory
				Resource accounting and budgeting	D Heathcoat Amory
				Finance and purchasing	D Heathcoat Amory
				Treasury internal audit	D Heathcoat Amory

Departmental Overview

Grade 1	Grade 1A	Grade 2	Grade 3	Directorates	Minister
	Finance, Regulation and Industry				
Sir Terence Burns		S A Robson	N Deverill	Credit institutions	A Nelson
			A Whiting	Financial services	A Nelson
			M L Williams	Securities and markets policy	A Nelson
				General financial issues	J Aitken
				Securities and investment services	A Nelson
				Industry issues	J Aitken
				Private finance	Sir G Young
				Transport issues	J Aitken
				Privatisation	Sir G Young
				Competition, regulation	Sir G Young
				Procurement policy and practice	A Nelson
	Personnel and Support Directorate				
			P R C Gray	Personnel policy project	Sir G Young
				Personnel management	Sir G Young
				Information systems	Sir G Young
				Accommodation and security	Sir G Young
				Outplacement services	Sir G Young

Standing Cross Directorate Teams

Sir Terence Burns (1)	Treasury Management Board
Mrs A F Case (3)	Deputy Directors' Group
C J Mowl (3)	Treasury Economic Forecasts
A O'Donnell (3)	EU Monetary Development Team
P McIntyre (3)	EU Budgetary Issues
Mrs A F Case (3)	Tax Issues
R Culpin (1A)	Survey Management Committee
J A Likierman (1A)	Steering Committee on Rsource Accounts Budgeting

Civil Servants and Directorates

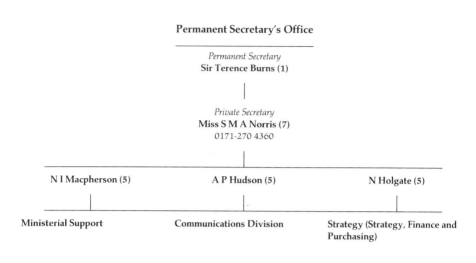

Permanent Secretary's Office

Permanent Secretary
Sir Terence Burns (1)

Private Secretary
Miss S M A Norris (7)
0171-270 4360

N I Macpherson (5)	**A P Hudson (5)**	**N Holgate (5)**
Ministerial Support	**Communications Division**	**Strategy (Strategy, Finance and Purchasing)**

Macroeconomic Policy and Prospects Directorate

Permanent Secretary
Sir Terence Burns (1)

Director
A Budd (1A)

Deputy Directors
C J Mowl (3)
A O'Donnell (3)

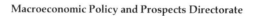

Macroeconomic Policy and Prospects Directorate

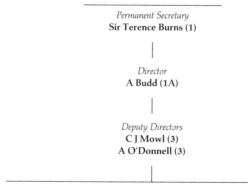

D Savage (5)	Economic prospects
S W Matthews (5)	Fiscal and macroeconomic policy
C M Kelly (5)	Economic briefing and analysis
S J Pickford (5)	Inflation and monetary policy
J S Cunliffe (5)	Debt and reserves management
Vacant	Economist group management unit

International Finance Directorate

Permanent Secretary
Sir Terence Burns (1)

Director
Sir Nigel Wicks (1A)

Deputy Directors
D L C Peretz (3)
P McIntyre (3)

International Finance Directorate

N J Ilett (5)	EU finances
Ms S Owen (5)	EU future strategy EU coordination
Ms J Rutter (5)	Developing countries, debt and export finance
D J Roe (5)	International financial institutions and former Soviet Union
S J Brooks (5)	Trade policy and developments World economic issues Regional/country analysis

Budget and Public Finances Directorate

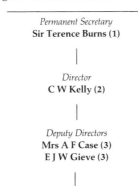

Permanent Secretary
Sir Terence Burns (1)

Director
C W Kelly (2)

Deputy Directors
Mrs A F Case (3)
E J W Gieve (3)

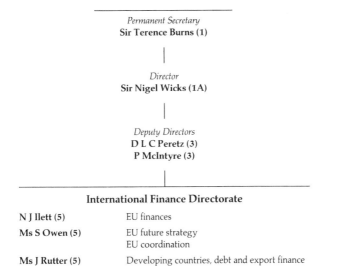

Budget and Public Finances Directorate

E J W Gieve (3)	General expenditure policy
D R Deaton (5)	General expenditure statistics
N M Hansford (5)	Exchequer funds and accounts
A W Ritchie (5)	Public sector finances
A J Sharples (5)	Tax and Budget
R P Short (5)	Tax economics
M N Parkinson (5)	Tax administration
S N Wood (5)	Strategic management
Dr R Kosmin (5)	Public sector pay policy
Mrs S D Brown (5)	Departmental pay systems
D W Rayson (5)	Public service pensions

Spending Directorate

Permanent Secretary
Sir Terence Burns (1)

Director
R Culpin (1A)

Deputy Directors
N J Glass (3)
Ms A Perkins (3)
Miss G M Noble (3)
P Sedgwick (3)

Spending Directorate

I Rogers (5)	Aid, diplomacy and intelligence
M E Donnelly (5)	Defence
T J Sutton (5)	Agriculture
J Halligan (5)	Social security and pensions
J W Grice (5)	Health
M Neale (5)	Heritage and central departments
Miss R Thompson (5)	Education
M C Mercer (5)	Employment and training
P H Brook (5)	Home Office and legal departments
I M V Taylor (5)	Local government
R M Bent (5)	Housing, urban and government property
Ms M Wallace (5)	Scotland, Wales, N Ireland, environment, other DoE issues
N J Glass (3)	Central operational research and economics

Financial Management, Reporting and Audit Directorate

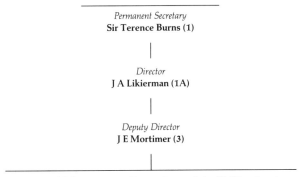

Permanent Secretary
Sir Terence Burns (1)

Director
J A Likierman (1A)

Deputy Director
J E Mortimer (3)

Financial Management, Reporting and Audit Directorate

J E Mortimer (3)	Treasury Officer of Accounts
K Bradley (5)	Central accountancy
P J C Holden (5)	Government accountancy service management unit
C Butler (5)	Audit policy and advice
Mrs R Dunn (5)	Resource accounting and budgeting
N Holgate (5)	Finance and purchasing (Strategy, finance and purchasing)
W P Tickner (5)	Treasury internal audit

Finance Regulation and Industry

Permanent Secretary
Sir Terence Burns (1)

Director
S A Robson (2)

Deputy Directors
N Deverill (3)
A Whiting (3)
M L Williams (3)

Finance Regulation and Industry Directorate

C Farthing (5)	Credit institutions
Mrs P Diggle (5)	Financial services
J Heywood (5)	Securities and markets policies
Mrs E I Young (5)	General financial issues
Miss J C Simpson (5)	Securities and investment services
C R Pickering (5)	Industry issues
R B Saunders (5)	Private finance
P Wynn Owen (5)	Transport issues
H T Bush (5)	Privatisation
Vacant	Competition, regulation and energy markets
J R Colling (5)	Procurement policy
A R Williams (5)	Procurement practice

Personnel and Support Directorate

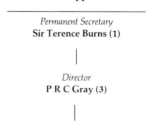

Permanent Secretary
Sir Terence Burns (1)

Director
P R C Gray (3)

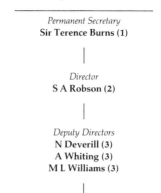

Personnel and Support Directorate

Ms C A Slocock (5)	Personnel policy project
D Hall (5)	Personnel management
S P Judge (5)	Information systems
E I Cooper (5)	Accommodation and security
D Truman (5)	Outplacement services

Standing Cross Directorate Teams

Sir Terence Burns (1)	Treasury Management Team
Mrs A F Case (3)	Deputy Directors' Group
C J Mowl (3)	Treasury Economic Forecasts
A O'Donnell (3)	EU Monetary Development Teams
P McIntyre (3)	EU Budgetary Issues
Mrs A F Case (3)	Tax Issues
R Culpin (1A)	Survey Management Committee
J A Likierman (1A)	Steering Committee on Resource Accounts Budgeting

HM Treasury Addresses

Allington Towers
19 Allington Street
London SW1E 5EB
Tel 0171-215 0434
Fax 0171-215 0482

Alencon Link
Basingstoke
Hants RG21 1JB
Tel 01256 29222

Treasury Solicitor's Department

Founded	17th century
Status	Non-ministerial department
Responsible to	Attorney General
Responsibilities	Litigation and conveyancing services for most government departments and some other public bodies and legal advice for those which do not have their own lawyers Administration of estates of people dying intestate and without known kin; dissolved companies; and failure of trustees Provision of legal advice on European Community law; conduct of litigation before the European Court of Justice The Treasury Solicitor is also the HM Procurator General and Queen's Proctor (interventions and advisory functions in matrimonial suits and legitimation cases)
Number of staff	550
Executive agencies	Government Property Lawyers

Treasury Solicitor's Department

Queen Anne's Chambers, 28 Broadway, London SW1H 9JS
Tel 0171-210 3000 Fax 0171-222 6006

Minister

Attorney General
The Rt Hon Sir Nicholas Lyell QC MP
(for details of his office see Legal Secretariat to the Law Officers)

Officials

HM Procurator General and Treasury Solicitor
Sir Gerald Hosker KCB QC (1)
(until October 1995)

Deputy Treasury Solicitor
D A Hogg (2)

Private Office
Mrs M S Powell
Tel 0171-210 3012

Mrs J Minall
Tel 0171-210 3031

Departmental Overview

Grade 1	Civil Servants Grade 2	Grade 3	Division
Sir Gerald Hosker *(until October 1995)*	D A Hogg	J E G Vaux	European Division
		P Ridd	Litigation Division
		H R L Purse	Department of Employment Division
		D F W Pickup	Ministry of Defence Division
		R N Ricks	Department for Education Division
		M C P Thomas	Department of Transport Division
	M A Blythe		Treasury Advisory Division
		Mrs M Harrop (5)	Lawyers' Management Unit
		A J E Hollis (5)	Resources and Services Division
		M C L Carpenter (5)	Office of Public Service and Science Division
		P C Jenkins (5)	National Heritage Division
		Mrs I G Letwin (5)	Central Advisory Division
		Miss S L Sargant (5)	Bona Vacantia Division
Reports directly to Sir Gerald Hosker		Mrs D Babar	Queen's Proctor

Civil Servants and Departments

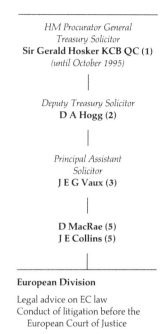

HM Procurator General
Treasury Solicitor
Sir Gerald Hosker KCB QC (1)
(until October 1995)

Deputy Treasury Solicitor
D A Hogg (2)

Principal Assistant Solicitor
J E G Vaux (3)

D MacRae (5)
J E Collins (5)

European Division

Legal advice on EC law
Conduct of litigation before the European Court of Justice

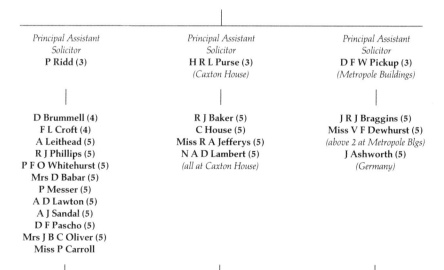

Principal Assistant Solicitor
P Ridd (3)

D Brummell (4)
F L Croft (4)
A Leithead (5)
R J Phillips (5)
P F O Whitehurst (5)
Mrs D Babar (5)
P Messer (5)
A D Lawton (5)
A J Sandal (5)
D F Pascho (5)
Mrs J B C Oliver (5)
Miss P Carroll

Principal Assistant Solicitor
H R L Purse (3)
(Caxton House)

R J Baker (5)
C House (5)
Miss R A Jefferys (5)
N A D Lambert (5)
(all at Caxton House)

Principal Assistant Solicitor
D F W Pickup (3)
(Metropole Buildings)

J R J Braggins (5)
Miss V F Dewhurst (5)
(above 2 at Metropole Blgs)
J Ashworth (5)
(Germany)

Litigation Division

Advice in and conduct of litigious matters

Department of Employment Division

Legal advice

Ministry of Defence Division

Legal advice

Principal Assistant Solicitor
R N Ricks (3)
(Sanctuary Buildings)

F D W Clarke (5)
S T Harker (5)
A D Preston (5)
(all at Sanctuary Buildings)

Principal Assistant Solicitor
M C P Thomas (3)
(2 Marsham Street)

D J Aries (5)
R G Bellis (5)
P D Coopman (5)
C W M Ingram (5)
R Lines (5)
A G Jones (5)
(all at 2 Marsham Street)

Department for Education Division

Legal advice

Department of Transport Division

Legal advice

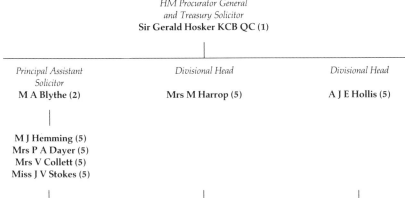

HM Procurator General and Treasury Solicitor
Sir Gerald Hosker KCB QC (1)

Principal Assistant Solicitor
M A Blythe (2)

M J Hemming (5)
Mrs P A Dayer (5)
Mrs V Collett (5)
Miss J V Stokes (5)

Divisional Head
Mrs M Harrop (5)

Divisional Head
A J E Hollis (5)

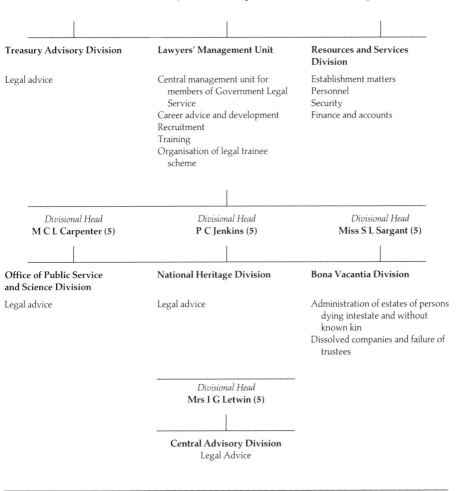

Treasury Advisory Division

Legal advice

Lawyers' Management Unit

Central management unit for members of Government Legal Service
Career advice and development
Recruitment
Training
Organisation of legal trainee scheme

Resources and Services Division

Establishment matters
Personnel
Security
Finance and accounts

Divisional Head
M C L Carpenter (5)

Office of Public Service and Science Division

Legal advice

Divisional Head
P C Jenkins (5)

National Heritage Division

Legal advice

Divisional Head
Miss S L Sargant (5)

Bona Vacantia Division

Administration of estates of persons dying intestate and without known kin
Dissolved companies and failure of trustees

Divisional Head
Mrs I G Letwin (5)

Central Advisory Division
Legal Advice

Queen's Proctor

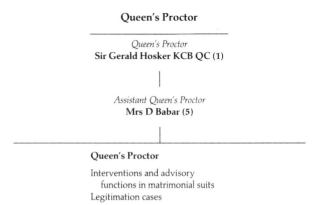

Queen's Proctor
Sir Gerald Hosker KCB QC (1)

Assistant Queen's Proctor
Mrs D Babar (5)

Queen's Proctor

Interventions and advisory functions in matrimonial suits
Legitimation cases

Treasury Solicitor's Department Addresses

Caxton House
Tothill Street
London SW1H 9NF
Tel 0171-273 3000
Fax 0171-273 5605

Metropole Buildings
Northumberland Avenue
London WC2N 5BL
Tel 0171-218 4691
Fax 0171-218 0844

Sanctuary Buildings
Great Smith Street
London SW1P 3BT
Tel 0171-925 5000
Fax 0171-925 6992

2 Marsham Street
London SW1P 3EB
Tel 0171-276 3000
Fax 0171-276 3330

Welsh Office

Founded	1964
Ministers	secretary of state and two parliamentary under secretaries of state
Responsibilities	agriculture and fisheries ancient monuments and historic buildings civil emergencies countryside and nature conservation economic affairs and regional planning (oversight) education environmental protection European Regional Development Fund forestry health housing industry (financial assistance) land use including planning local government personal social services roads sport tourism training and the careers service urban policy in Wales water and sewerage Welsh language, arts and culture non-departmental public bodies
Number of staff	2066
Executive agencies	ADAS (jointly with MAFF) CADW (Welsh Historic Monuments) Planning Inspectorate (jointly with DoE)

Welsh Office

New Crown Building, Cathays Park, Cardiff CF1 3NQ
Tel 01222 825111 Fax 01222 823036
Gwydyr House, Whitehall, London SW1A 2ER
Tel 0171-270 3000 Fax 0171-270 0561

All staff are based at Cathays Park unless otherwise indicated.
For other addresses and telephone numbers see the end of this section.

Ministers

Secretary of State
The Rt Hon John Redwood MP

Parliamentary Private Secretary
David Evennett MP

Special Adviser
Hywel Williams
(also advises Parliamentary Under Secretaries)

Principal Private Secretary
Ms K Jennings
0171-270 0549 (London)
01222 823200 (Cardiff)

Parliamentary Under Secretary of State
Gwilym Jones MP

Special Adviser
Hywel Williams
(also advises Secretary of State and other Parliamentary Under Secretary)

Private Secretary
V R Watkin
0171-270 0569 (London)
01222 823300 (Cardiff)

Parliamentary Under Secretary of State
Rod Richards MP

Special Adviser
Hywel Williams
(also advises Secretary of State and other Parliamentary Secretary)

Private Secretary
M D Parkinson
0171-270 0559 (London)
01222 825448 (Cardiff)

House of Lords' Spokesmen

The Rt Hon The Lord Rodger of Earlsferry

The Lord Lucas

Ministerial Responsibilities

John Redwood
Overall responsibility for the strategic direction of the department including:
Citizen's Charter
Development agencies
Funding councils
Housing for Wales
Welsh Health Common Services Authority

Gwilym Jones
Agriculture
CADW
Conservation
Countryside Council for Wales
Energy
Environmental protection
European Union issues
Exports
Forestry
"Four Motors" initiative (motor manufacturing areas in Europe with which Wales has trade links)
Historic buildings and ancient monuments
Housing
Industry
Inward investment
Land use planning
Local government
National parks
Programme for the Valleys
Public appointments
Regional selective assistance
Sport
Transport and roads
Urban affairs
Wales Youth Agency
Water
Youth issues

Rod Richards	Arts and culture Broadcasting Community care Education, training and enterprise Fisheries Health Holyhead Personal social services Rural affairs Small businesses Tourism Women's issues Welsh language

Departmental Overview

	Civil Servants		**Department**	**Minister**
Grade 1	***Grade 2***	***Grade 3***		
	Legal, Information, Establishment, Finance, NHS Directorate			
M C Scholar		D G Lambert	Legal Group	J Redwood
		H G Roberts (5)	Information	J Redwood
		C D Stevens	Establishment Group	J Redwood
		R A Wallace	Finance Group	J Redwood
		P R Gregory	NHS Directorate in Wales	J Redwood/ R Richards
	Agriculture, Economic Development, Industry and Training			
M C Scholar	J F Craig	L K Walford	Agriculture	J Redwood/ G Jones
		M J A Cochlin	Economic Development	J Redwood/ R Richards
		D W Jones	Industry and Training	G Jones/ R Richards
	Education; Health Professionals Group; Local Government Finance, Housing and Social Services Group; Nursing Division; Transport, Planning and Environment Group; Local Government Reorganisation Group; HM Chief Inspector of Schools			
M C Scholar	J W Lloyd	S H Martin	Education	J Redwood/ R Richards
		Dr D J Hine	Health Professionals Group	J Redwood/ R Richards
		R W Jarman	Local Government Finance, Housing and Social Services	J Redwood/ R Richards
		Miss M P Bull	Nursing	J Redwood/ R Richards
		G C G Craig	Transport, Planning and Environment	J Redwood/ G Jones
		J D Shortridge	Local Government Reorganisation	J Redwood/ G Jones
		R L James (4)	HM Chief Inspector of Schools	J Redwood/ R Richards

Civil Servants and Departments

Legal, Information, Establishment, Finance, NHS Directorate

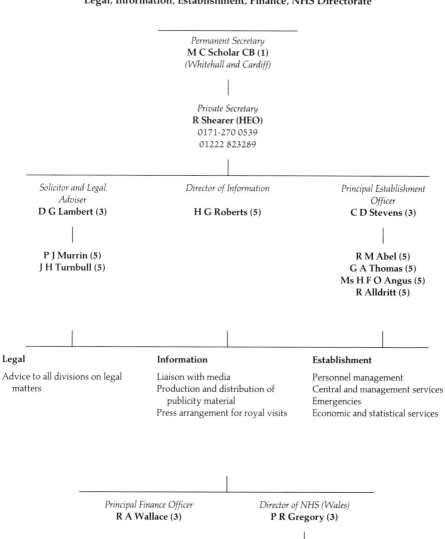

Permanent Secretary
M C Scholar CB (1)
(Whitehall and Cardiff)

Private Secretary
R Shearer (HEO)
0171-270 0539
01222 823289

Solicitor and Legal Adviser
D G Lambert (3)

P J Murrin (5)
J H Turnbull (5)

Director of Information
H G Roberts (5)

Principal Establishment Officer
C D Stevens (3)

R M Abel (5)
G A Thomas (5)
Ms H F O Angus (5)
R Alldritt (5)

Legal

Advice to all divisions on legal matters

Information

Liaison with media
Production and distribution of publicity material
Press arrangement for royal visits

Establishment

Personnel management
Central and management services
Emergencies
Economic and statistical services

Principal Finance Officer
R A Wallace (3)

Director of NHS (Wales)
P R Gregory (3)

C L Jones (4)

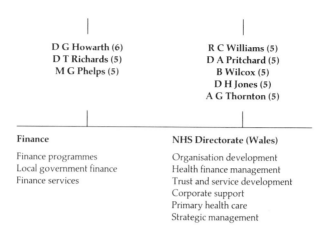

D G Howarth (6)
D T Richards (5)
M G Phelps (5)

R C Williams (5)
D A Pritchard (5)
B Wilcox (5)
D H Jones (5)
A G Thornton (5)

Finance

Finance programmes
Local government finance
Finance services

NHS Directorate (Wales)

Organisation development
Health finance management
Trust and service development
Corporate support
Primary health care
Strategic management

Agriculture, Economic Development, Industry and Training

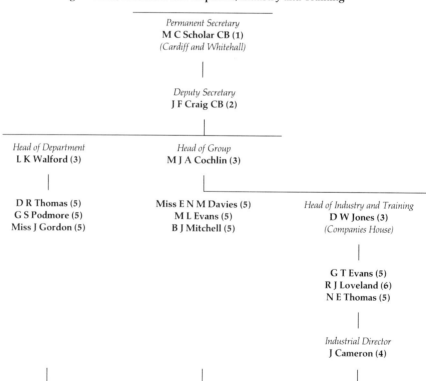

Permanent Secretary
M C Scholar CB (1)
(Cardiff and Whitehall)

Deputy Secretary
J F Craig CB (2)

Head of Department
L K Walford (3)

D R Thomas (5)
G S Podmore (5)
Miss J Gordon (5)

Head of Group
M J A Cochlin (3)

Miss E N M Davies (5)
M L Evans (5)
B J Mitchell (5)

Head of Industry and Training
D W Jones (3)
(Companies House)

G T Evans (5)
R J Loveland (6)
N E Thomas (5)

Industrial Director
J Cameron (4)

H D Brodie (5)
N E Thomas (5)

Agriculture

Commodities, structure, environmental and general policy
Animal health welfare, fisheries, R&D and emergencies
Land, agricultural subsidies and grants, training and plants

Economic Development

European affairs
Countryside and nature conservation
National parks
Development Board for Rural Wales
Tourism
Urban affairs

Industry and Training

Training
TECs
Further and higher education
Employment policy
Enterprise and small firms
Adult and youth guidance
Industrial policy
Exports
R&D
Energy efficiency
Industrial development

Education; Health Professionals Group; Local Government Finance, Housing and Social Services Group; Nursing Division; Transport, Planning and Environment Group; Local Government Reorganisation Group; HM Chief Inspector of Schools

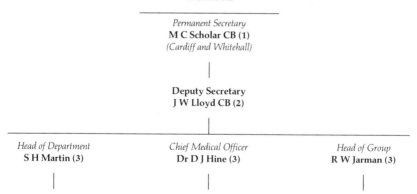

Permanent Secretary
M C Scholar CB (1)
(Cardiff and Whitehall)

Deputy Secretary
J W Lloyd CB (2)

Head of Department
S H Martin (3)

Chief Medical Officer
Dr D J Hine (3)

Head of Group
R W Jarman (3)

H Evans (5)
(Companies House)
R J Davies (5)
W G Davies (5)
Dr H F Rawlings (5)
(Tyglas Road)

Dr A M George (4)
Dr J K Richmond (4)
D M Heap (4)
Dr G B A Veitch (5)
Dr J A V Pritchard (5)
Dr J Ludlow (5)
Dr A K Thomas (5)
Dr B Fuge (5)
Dr D E Davies (5)
Dr D W Owen (5)
Dr D Salter (5)
Dr J G Avery (5)
Dr R Owen (5)
Dr P Lyne (5)
Dr H N Williams (5)
R Alexander (5)
Dr P Tromans (5)

R J Davies (5)
Mrs B J M Wilson (5)
A G Thornton (5)
Dr D Adams (5)
D G Evans (5)

Education

Schools curriculum
Schools administration
Further and higher education
Education services

Health Professionals Group

Advice to all divisions on health

Local Government Finance, Housing and Social Services Group

Public health and family
Community care
Health policy and resources
Social services inspectorate
Housing
Architects and surveyors
Nursing

Chief Nursing Officer
Miss M P Bull OBE

Head of Group
G C G Craig (3)

D I Westlake (5)
A H H Jones (5)
G K Hoad (6)
W P Roderick (5)
E A J Carr (5)
K J Thomas (4)

Head of Group
J D S Shortridge (3)

Nursing Division

Nursing advice

Transport, Planning and Environment Group

Environment
Planning
Estates
Transport policy
Roads administration
Roads construction
Roads (North Wales network management)
Highways

Local Government Reorganisation Group

Local government reorganisation
Local government administration, provision of services and commercial activities
Local Government Boundary Commission

HM Chief Inspector of Schools
R L James (4)
(Tyglas Road)

Staff Inspectors
S J Adams (5)
J R N Evans (5)
T E Parry (5)
G Thomas (5)
P Thomas (5)
(all at Tyglas Road)

Welsh Office Addresses

Companies House
Crown Way
Cardiff CF4 3UT
Tel 01222 388588
Fax 01222 222885

Brunel House
2 Fitzalan House
Cardiff CF2 1UY
Tel 01222 465511
Fax 01222 465511 X218

Government Buildings
Dinerth Road
Colwyn Bay
Clwyd LL28 4UL
Tel 01492 44261
Fax 01492 44261 X6581

Government Buildings
Tyglas Road
Llanishen
Cardiff CF4 5PL
Tel 01222 761456
Fax 01222 747901
Fax: HM Chief Inspector of Schools
01222 758182

'Next Steps' Executive Agencies

Next Steps is the name given to the civil service reforms under which agencies are being set up to deliver government services. The main aim is – within available resources – to improve the quality and efficiency of management in government for the benefit of taxpayers, the public and staff. Next Steps was launched in February 1988 following the recommendations of the Efficiency Unit report "Improving Management in Government: the Next Steps". The report recommended that, to the greatest extent practical, the executive functions of government should be carried out by units designated as agencies headed by chief executives.

Since then, 108 agencies have been established and over 369,000 civil servants, 66% of the total, are now working in agencies and other organisations operating on Next Steps lines.

Another 65 candidates have been announced covering over 84,000 more civil servants, and many more areas are under consideration. The candidates for agency status include Army Recruiting, the Youth Treatment Service, and the Welsh Office's Highways Directorate, as well as independent government departments such as the Crown Prosecution Service, Department for National Savings, Office of Population Censuses and Surveys, Serious Fraud Office and the Treasury Solicitor's Department. Details of these candidates will be found below, after the list of those agencies already established.

The role of the chief executive

Next Steps agencies are headed by a chief executive to whom day-to-day management of the agency has been delegated by the responsible minister within the terms of the agency's published framework document.

The minister sets the policy framework for the agency, delegates authority to carry out the specified task and allocates the agency's budget. He sets key performance targets for the agency and approves its corporate plan and annual business plan. He then monitors the agency's performance, measures its success against its targets and is accountable to Parliament for its activities. These arrangements are set out in each agency's framework document.

The chief executive manages the day-to-day operation and is accountable to the minister for the use of the resources provided, the performance of the agency and for ensuring that the agreed targets are met. Often, an element of the chief executive's salary is linked to the achievement of these targets. The chief executive will also be the accounting officer accountable to Parliament for the proper handling of the resources for which he or she is responsible.

Chief executives are civil servants, although many of them may be directly recruited from outside the civil service for a contract period. Their 'grading' in civil service terms is that appropriate to the job to be done.

New agencies and other changes

Thirteen new agencies have been established since the last edition of *The Whitehall Companion*. They are:

Army Base Storage and Distribution Agency
Court Service
Defence Clothing and Textiles Agency
Defence Transport and Movements Executive
Disposal Sales Agency
Industrial Research and Technology Unit (NI)

Logistic Information Systems Agency
Meat Hygiene Service
Naval Recruiting and Training Agency
Northern Ireland Prison Service
Public Record Office of Northern Ireland
RAF Signals Engineering Establishment
Scottish Court Service

Some changes have taken place over the past year:
The **Accounts Services Agency** has now been privatised.

The Defence Research Agency has been reorganised and is now called the **Defence Evaluation and Research Agency**. It now incorporates the work of two agencies listed separately last year in the Whitehall Companion: the **Chemical and Biological Defence Establishment** and the **Defence Operational Analysis Centre**.

The HQ Logistics Command Maintenance Group has been renamed the **RAF Maintenance Group Defence Agency**.

The Service Children's Schools (NW Europe) has been renamed the **HQ Service Children's Schools (NW Europe)**.

The following agencies will change their status over the next year:
ADAS: part of the organisation will probably be privatised and the likelihood is that the privatised body will include the whole of the commercial consultancy and commercial research and development arms and some other work.

The **Central Statistical Office** and the **Office of Population, Censuses and Surveys** (*see* Government Departments section) are likely to merge and become an executive agency in April 1996.

Insolvency Service: probable involvement of the private sector in the case administration work of the Official Receivers.

Laboratory of the Government Chemist: to be established as an independent non-profit distributing company in the private sector during 1995/96.

National Engineering Laboratory: a trade purchaser will be sought during 1995.

National Physical Laboratory: bids from potential management contractors are now being considered which may lead to the Laboratory moving out of government ownership in the long-term.

Transport Research Laboratory: to be privatised during 1995/96.

Next Steps Executive Agencies (108)

(July 1995)

*See under Government Departments Section

Candidates for Agency Status (65)

Agricultural Colleges	NI Civil Service (NICS)
Agricultural Development Service	NICS
Air Secretary's Command	Defence
Army Engineer Services	Defence
Army Personnel Agency	Defence
Army Procurement and Provisioning Branches	Defence
Army Recruiting	Defence
Army Technical Support Authority	Defence
Army Training	Defence
Business Development Services	NICS
Civil Service, Health and Social Services and Teachers' Superannuation	NICS
Crown Prosecution Service*	
Defence Central Services	Defence
Defence Codification Authority	Defence
Defence Communication Service	Defence
Defence Estates Organisation	Defence
Dental Care Agency	Defence
Department for National Savings*	
Departmental Information Systems Units	NICS
Environment Services	NICS
Estate Services Directorate	NICS
Fisheries Research Services	Scottish Office
Fleet Maintenance and Repair Organisation	Defence
Forensic Science Laboratory	Northern Ireland Office
Forest Enterprise	Forestry Commission
Forestry Service	NICS
Fuel Procurement Branch	Environment
Government Purchasing Service	NICS
Health and Safety	NICS
Health Service Information Systems	NICS
Highways Directorate	Welsh Office
Insolvency Service	NICS
Lands/Deeds Registration	NICS
Marine Services (Naval)	Defence
Medical Training Agency	Defence
MoD Police	Defence
Naval Bases Personnel Services	Defence
Naval Support Command	Defence
Office of Population, Censuses and Surveys*	
Other Defence Training	Defence
Personnel Vetting Agency	Defence
Planning Service	NICS
Pricing and Quality Service	Defence
Property Holdings	Environment
RAF Logistic Support Services	Defence
RAF Pay and Personnel Management	Defence
RAF Recruiting and Selection	Defence
RAF Support Management Group	Defence

Recruitment	NICS
RN Platform and Equipment Support	Defence
Roads Directorate	Scottish Office
Roads Services	NICS
Science Service	NICS
Secondary Care Agency	Defence
Serious Fraud Office*	
Service Children's Schools Overseas (Tri-Service)	Defence
Statistics, Census Office, General Register Office	NICS
Telecommunications	NICS
Trading Standards	NICS
Treasury Solicitor's Department*	
Veterinary Service	NICS
Watercourse Management	NICS
Water Executive	NICS
Works Service	NICS
Youth Treatment Service	Health

*independent government departments

ADAS

ADAS Headquarters, Oxford Spires Business Park, The Boulevard, Kidlington, Oxon OX5 1NZ
Tel 01865 842742 Fax 01865 845055

Staff

Chief Executive
Dr Julia M Walsh (2)

Director of Operations
Phillip Needham (3)

Director of Research
Dr David Hughes (4)

Director of Marketing
David Hall (5)

Director of Finance
Dr Chris Herring (5)

Director, Wales
Cyril Davies (5)

Non Executive Director
Charles Bystram (Chairman)

Consultancy Centres
(see next page)

Responsibilities

ADAS provides a comprehensive range of consultancy services to the food, farming, land and leisure industries. In addition, ADAS carries out research in these same areas; performs certain statutory functions; and provides advice on policy for MAFF and the Welsh Office.

Number of staff 2059

Department Agriculture, Fisheries and Food and the Welsh Office

Launched 1 April 1992

ADAS Consultancy Centre Addresses

Cardiff
St Agnes Road
Gabalfa
Cardiff CF4 4YH
Tel 01222 586000
Fax 01222 586228

Guildford
98 Epsom Road
Guildford GU1 2LD
Tel 01483 62881
Fax 01483 65356

Huntingdon
Chequers Court
Huntingdon
Cambs PE18 6LT
Tel 01480 52161
Fax 01480 412049

Leeds
Lawnswood
Otley Road
Leeds LS16 5PY
Tel 01132 611222
Fax 01132 300174

Taunton
Quantock House
Paul Street
Taunton TA1 3NX
Tel 01823 337922
Fax 01823 253284

Wolverhampton
Woodthorne
Wergs Road
Wolverhampton WV6 8TQ
Tel 01902 754190
Fax 01902 743602

ADAS Research Centres Addresses

Arthur Rickwood
Mepal
Ely
Cambs CB6 2BA
Tel 01354 692531
Fax 01354 694488

Boxworth
Boxworth
Cambridge CB3 8NN
Tel 01954 267666
Fax 01954 267659

Bridgets
Martyr Worthy
Winchester
Hants SO21 1AP
Tel 01962 779765
Fax 01962 779739

Drayton
Alcester Road
Stratford-upon-Avon
Warwick CV37 9RQ
Tel 01789 293057
Fax 01789 414393

Gleathorpe
The Grange
Meden Vale
Mansfield
Notts NG20 9PF
Tel 01623 844331
Fax 01623 844472

High Mowthorpe
Duggleby
Malton
N Yorks YO17 8BP
Tel 01944 738646
Fax 01944 738434

Pwllpeiran
Cwymystwyth
Aberystwyth
Dyfed SY23 4AB
Tel 0197422 229
Fax 0197422 302

Redesdale
Rochester
Otterburn
Northumberland NE19 1SB
Tel 01830 520608
Fax 01830 520451

Rosemaund
Preston Wynne
Hereford HR1 3PG
Tel 01432 820444
Fax 01432 820121

Soil and Water Research Centre
Anstey Hall
Maris Lane
Trumpington
Cambridge CB2 2LF
Tel 01223 840011
Fax 01223 841618

Terrington
Terrington St Clement
King's Lynn
Norfolk PE34 4PW
Tel 01553 828621
Fax 01553 827229

Army Base Repair Organisation

Monxton Road, Andover, Hants SP11 8HT
Tel 01264 383295 Fax 01264 383144

Staff	*Chief Executive* **Brigadier Jim Drew CBE**
Responsibilities	To provide in-depth overhaul of all army weapon systems. Immediate engineering support to army units in Great Britain
Number of staff	3500
Department	Defence
Launched	1 April 1993

Army Base Storage and Distribution Agency

Building 211, HQ QMG, Portway, Monxton Road, Andover, Hampshire SP11 8HT
Tel 01263 382424 Fax 01264 382574

Staff	*Chief Executive* **Brig Kevin Goad**
Responsibilities	The storage and distribution of all material needed to sustain the Field Army
Number of Staff	6400
Department	Defence
Launched	4 April 1995

Building Research Establishment

Garston, Watford WD2 7JR
Tel 01923 894040 Fax 01923 664010

Staff

Chief Executive
Roger Courtney (3)

Deputy Chief Executive
Director (Materials)
Neil Milbank (4)

Director (Fire Research Station)
Dr David Woolley (4)

Director (Finance)
Jim Horan (5)

Head of Personnel
Mrs Arran Elkeles (6)

Director (Construction and Application)
Brian Hall (5)

Director (Geotechnics and Structures)
Dr Nick Cook (5)

Director (Environmental Engineering)
Dr Tony Birtles (5)

Director (Building Energy and Efficiency)
Dr Vic Crisp (5)

Responsibilities

To support the Secretary of State for the Environment and other departments in their policy and executive responsibilities relating to construction and the health and safety of people in and around buildings

To carry out research and provide guidance on the design, construction and performance of built works, the prevention and control of fire and the protection of the environment

To provide research and consultancy services to non-government customers

To make available its research findings and knowledge through seminars and publications

Number of staff	705
Department	Environment
Launched	2 April 1990

The Buying Agency

Royal Liver Building, Pier Head, Liverpool L3 1PE
Tel 0151-227 4262 Fax 0151-227 3315

Staff

Chief Executive
S P Sage (5)

Finance Director
R S Munslow (6)

Marketing and Sales Director
C Hancock (6)

Procurement Director
C Poulter (6)

Secretariat
K Pope (7)

Responsibilities

To provide a professional purchasing service to central government departments, the NHS and other public sector bodies. TBA's core business encompasses mechanical, electrical, engineering, building and domestic products and accommodation services

Number of staff 110

Department Environment

Launched 31 October 1991

CADW (Welsh Historic Monuments)

Brunel House, 2 Fitzalan Road, Cardiff CF2 1UY
Tel 01222 465511 Fax 01222 450859

Staff

Chief Executive
John Carr (5)

Directors
J R Avent (6)
J D Hogg (6)
R W Hughes (6)

Responsibilities

To support directly and indirectly the preservation, conservation, appreciation and enjoyment of the built heritage in Wales through advice, education, example, persuasion and, where appropriate, intervention and financial support

Number of staff 262

Department Welsh Office

Launched 2 April 1991

Central Office of Information

Hercules Road, London SE1 7DU
Tel 0171-928 2345 Fax 0171-261 5037

Staff

Chief Executive
Mike Devereau (3)

Senior Personal Secretary
Mrs J Rodrigues
0171-261 8209

Management Board
K E Williamson (5)
R Smith (5)
R Windsor (5)
D A Low (5)

Secretary to the Board
Miss K Gilding (7)

Client Services and Marketing
Mike Richardson (6)

Press Officer
Miss M Thomas (10)

Directors

Advertising
Peter Buchanan (6)

Direct Marketing and Promotion
Colin Noble (6)

Research
Malcolm Rigg (6)

Films, Television and Radio
Ian Hamilton *(Acting)*

Publications
Jack Murray (6)

Events
Alan Chard (6)

References and Translations
David Beynon (6)

Network Services
Rob Haslam (6)

Emergency Planning and Head of Personnel Services
Mike Langhorne (6)

Press and Pictures

Head of News and Features
Huw Williams (7)

Head of Commercial Publicity
Malcolm Fare (7)

Head of Pictures
David Scrivener (7)

Library and Information Centre
0171-261 8241

Responsibilities To supply information and publicity services and give advice in all media for government departments, agencies and other public sector clients, on a repayment basis

Number of staff 500

Department The COI is a department in its own right. The Chief Executive was accountable to Treasury ministers until June 1992. He is now accountable to the Cabinet Office (Office of Public Service and Science)

Launched 5 April 1990

Central Science Laboratory

London Road, Slough, Berks SL3 7HJ
Tel 01753 534626 Fax 01753 824058

Staff

Chief Executive
Dr Peter Stanley (3)

Research Director (Agriculture/Environment)
Dr Tony Hardy (5)

Research Director (Food)
Dr John Gilbert (5)

Resource Director
Brian Simmons (5)

Head of Marketing and Communications Group
Dr Mike Tas (6)

Head Plant Health Group
Dr Stephen Hill (6)

Head Infestation Risk Evaluation Group
Dr Ken Wildey (6)

Head Pest Management Strategies Group
Dr Nick Price (6)

Head Pesticide Surveillance Group
Dr Michael Wilson (6)

Head Conservation and Environment Protection Group
Dr Stephen Hunter (6)

Head Chemical Safety of Food Group
Dr Rob Massey (6)

Head Food Quality Group
Dr Kevin Whittle (6)

Head Microbiology
Dr Rohan Kroll (6)

Responsibilities

To provide a wide range of research and development, and scientific support and advice to meet both the statutory and policy objectives of MAFF. In addition CSL may, on a commercial basis, provide R&D and advice to other government departments and to public and private sector organisations both overseas and UK-based.

The main areas are:
Consumer safety with the emphasis on the microbiological, radiological and chemical safety and the quality and nutritional value of food.
Safeguarding food supplies through the identification and control of invertebrate pests, and plant pests and diseases and the management of vertebrate wildlife.
Environmental protection through the investigation of the impact of agriculture on the environment and the promotion of biodiversity in agricultural habitats.

Number of staff 657

Department Agriculture, Fisheries and Food

Launched 1 April 1992. The CSL merged with the Food Science Laboratories in April 1994.

Central Statistical Office

Government Offices, Great George Street, London SW1P 3AQ
Tel 0171-270 3000 Fax 0171-270 5866

Millbank Tower, Millbank, London SW1P 4QU
Tel 0171-217 3000 Fax 0171-217 4338

Government Buildings, Cardiff Road, Newport NP9 1XG
Tel 01633 815696 Fax 01633 812863

Staff

Director and Head of the Government Statistical Service
Professor Tim Holt (1A)

Deputy Director
Director of National Accounts
D Wroe (2)

Board Members
Professor Tim Holt
David Wroe (2)
J C Calder (3)
Mike Pepper (3)
John Kidgell (3)
Les Mayhew (4)
Mrs Mary Berg
Paul Thornton

GSS and General Division
Head of Division
J C Calder (3)

D C K Stirling (5)
Miss J Church (5)
Mrs M Haworth (5)
(all at Millbank)
R J Scott (5)
(Newport)
T Jones (5)

Business Statistics Division
Head of Division
Dr M Pepper (3)

K Francombe (5)
C J Spiller (5)
J Kinder (5)
M Brand (5)
G Walker (5)
(all at Newport)

Economic Accounts Division
Head of Division
J E Kidgell (3)

G Jenkinson (5)
B J Buckingham (5)
Mrs P G Walker (5)
(above 2 at Millbank)
P Turnbull (5)
K Mansell (5)
R Lynch (5)

Central Services Division
Head of Division
Dr L Mayhew (4)

R Pape (5)
D R Lewis (5)
W H Joiner (5)
(above 2 at Newport)

Head of Policy Secretariat
J Pullinger (5)

Head of Information
I Scott (6)

Head of Marketing
P Powell (6)

Responsibilities
The CSO is responsible for compiling and publishing the key statistics needed for central economic management. CSO liaises with the EC and other international statistical institutions on domestic and international statistics. The CSO is also responsible for central management of the government statistical service

It also publishes press notices on macro-economic statistics and a range of publications on specific industries and activities

Number of staff
1280

Department
The CSO is a department in its own right. The Director is accountable to the Chancellor of the Exchequer

Launched
19 November 1991

The Central Statistical Office is likely to merge with the Office of Population, Censuses and Surveys (see government departments section) and become an executive agency in April 1996.

Central Veterinary Laboratory

New Haw, Addlestone, Surrey KT15 3NB
Tel 01932 341111 Fax 01932 347046

Staff

Chief Executive
Dr T W A Little (3)

Director of Research
Dr J A Morris (5)

Director of Operations
R W Saunders (5)

Responsibilities To provide specialist scientific and technical support and consultancy in the fields of animal health and welfare, food safety and the environment

Number of staff 651

Department Agriculture, Fisheries and Food

Launched 2 April 1990

Chessington Computer Centre

Leatherhead Road, Chessington, Surrey KT9 2LT
Tel 0181-397 5266 Fax 0181-391 3986

Staff

Chief Executive
R N Edwards (5)

Director, Product Development
J R Hebron (7)

Director, Customer Services
D J Trevliving (7)

Director, Human Resources
Mrs P A Wills (7)

Company Secretary
I D Kirkpatrick (7)

Director, Finance
M C Felstead (7)

Director, Marketing
H Manders (7)

Marketing Manager
B G Draper (SEO)

Responsibilities Chessington provides administrative and associated services to the public sector, including payroll, personnel, superannuation, financial management, training, pay assessment and superannuation assessment

Number of staff 390

Department Cabinet Office (Office of Public Service and Science)

Launched 1 April 1993

Civil Service College

Sunningdale Park, Ascot, Berks SL5 0QE
Tel 01344 634000 Fax 01344 842491

11 Belgrave Road, London SW1V 1RB
Tel 0171-834 6644 Fax 0171-630 6888

Staff

Chief Executive
Dr Stephen Hickey

Director of Studies
Dr R J Smith (5)

Secretary
Miss M A Wood (6)

Business Group Directors
Mrs M Chapman (5)
Miss E Chennels (6)
G Llewellyn (6)
Ms S McCarthy (6)
C Aitken (6)
M Barnes (6)
Ms J A Topham (6)

Responsibilities To help develop the managerial and professional skills of civil servants especially those at or aspiring to relatively senior levels, and to promote good practice in government in management and key professional areas

Number of staff 273

Department Cabinet Office (Office of Public Service and Science)

Launched 6 June 1989

The Coastguard Agency

105 Commercial Road, Southampton SO15 1EG
Tel 01703-329100 Fax 01703-329400

Staff

Chief Executive
Chris Harris (4)

Chief Coastguard
Cdr Derek Ancona (5)

Director Marine Pollution Control Unit
Cdr John Bywater (6)

Director of Administration
David Cockram (6)

Responsibilities

Initiation and coordination of civil maritime search and rescue within the United Kingdom Search and Rescue Region and discharge of HM Government's responsibility for dealing with major spillages of oil and other hazardous substances from ships at sea which threaten UK interests

Number of staff 570

Department Transport

Launched April 1994

Companies House

Crown Way, Maindy, Cardiff CF4 3UZ
Tel 01222 388588 Fax 01222 380900

Staff

Chief Executive
Registrar of Companies
for England and Wales
David Durham (4)

Operations and Marketing
Director
Wendy Alexander (5)

Finance and Planning
Director
Peter Lawrence (5)

Contracting Director
Katharine Elliott (5)

Information Systems
Director
David Garnett (6)

Responsibilities

To incorporate companies, register documents which companies are obliged to file, and provide company information

It also exercises certain statutory powers on behalf of the Secretary of State for Trade and Industry, eg the Registrar can authorise a change of company name

Number of staff 1054

Department Trade and Industry

Launched 3 October 1988. It became a trading fund on 1 October 1991

Compensation Agency (NI)

Royston House, 34 Upper Queen Street, Belfast BT1 6FD
Tel 01232 249944 Fax 01232 246956

Staff	*Chief Executive* **D A Stanley (5)**
Responsibilities	To administer statutory criminal injuries and criminal damage compensation schemes in Northern Ireland
Number of staff	150
Department	Northern Ireland Office
Launched	1 April 1992

Court Service

South Side, 105 Victoria Street, London SW1E 6QT
Tel 0171-210 2182 Fax 0171-210 2059

Staff

Chief Executive
Michael Hubener (2)

Director of Finance and Administration
C W V Everett (3)

Resources
K Pogson (5)

Personnel and Training
Miss B Kenny (5)

Major Reviews
J Jacob (5)

Accommodation and Court Building
A Shaw (5)

Information Technology
P White (5)

Operational Support
P Handcock (5)

Circuit Administrators

Midland and Oxford
R Stoate (4)

North-Eastern
P J Farmer (3)

Northern
R A Vincent

South-Eastern
J F Brindley (3)

Wales and Chester
V C Grove (4)

Western
R J Clark (4)

Responsibilities The Court Service provides administrative support to the Supreme Court of England and Wales (comprising the Court of Appeal, the High Court of Justice – including the probate service – and the Crown Court), county courts and a number of tribunals. While the outcome of cases coming before these courts and tribunals is determined by a judge or judicial officer, much of the work necessary to enable those decisions to be made and given effect is carried out by the staff of the Court Service. The Service does not provide support for the magistrates' courts, which are supported by a separate locally administered service

Number of Staff 10,500

Department Lord Chancellor's

Launched 1 April 1995

Court Service Addresses

Midland and Oxford
2 Newton Street
Birmingham B4 7LU
Tel 0121 200 1234
Fax 0121 212 1359

Northern
15 Quay Street
Manchester M60 9FD
Tel 0161 833 1005
Fax 0161 832 8596

North-Eastern
17th Floor
West Riding House
Albion Street
Leeds LS1 5AA
Tel 01132 441841
Fax 01132 438737

South-Eastern
New Cavendish House
18 Maltravers Street
London WC2R 3EU
Tel 0171-936 6000
Fax 0171-936 7230

Wales and Chester
3rd Floor
Churchill House
Churchill Way
Cardiff CF1 4HH
Tel 01222 396625
Fax 01222 373882

Western
Bridge House
Clifton Down
Bristol BS8 4BN
Tel 01179 743763
Fax 01179 744133

Defence Accounts Agency

Ministry of Defence, Warminster Road, Bath BA1 5AA
Tel 01225 884884 Fax 01225 828176

Staff

Acting Chief Executive and Director of Pay Services
Peter Trevelyan

Director of Financial and Management Accounting Services
Colin Spillane

Director of Bill Payments and Receipts
Mike Rowe

Director, Staff
Danny Thomas

Director of Finance and Corporate Affairs
Peter Chafer

Director of Information Technology
Gerry Pearce

Responsibilities

To provide the central accounting function for the MOD, comprising:
- production of the Appropriation Accounts
- management of banking and cash
- payment of bills and claims
- recovery of monies due
- payment of civilian salaries and wages
- awarding of civilian superannuation benefits

To provide accounting and other information for the management of the MOD

To define and promulgate MOD accounting policies and regulations

To provide civilian pay and pensions services to other government departments on a repayment basis

Number of staff 1808

Department Defence

Launched 1 April 1991

The Agency is in the process of being reorganised, and changes are likely to be announced in the late summer

Defence Analytical Services Agency

MoD, Northumberland House, Northumberland Avenue, London WC2N 5BP
Tel 0171-218 0872 Fax 0171-218 5203

Staff	*Chief Executive* **Paul Altobell**
Responsibilities	Compiles manpower, medical, financial and logistical management information. It also provides management systems, analyses and advice to the Ministry of Defence and armed services
Number of staff	121
Department	Defence
Launched	1 July 1992

Defence Animal Centre

Welby Lane Camp, Melton Mowbray, Leicestershire, LE13 0SL
Tel 01664 63281 Fax 01664 410694

Staff

Chief Executive
Colonel Andrew Roache

Responsibilities

To acquire all service animals and to train dogs and handlers, horses and equine managers for ceremonial and operational use throughout MoD-sponsored establishments. Specialist dog handler training for Home Office agencies and Foreign and Commonwealth governments is carried out on a repayment basis.

Number of staff

217

Department

Defence

Launched

June 1993

Defence Clothing and Textiles Agency

HQ QMG, Portway, Monxton Road, Andover, Hants SP11 8HT
Tel 01264 382791 Fax 01264 382652

Staff

Chief Executive
Brig R H T Kirby CBE

Head of Business Management
R J Mealing

Head of Product Management, Clothing and Textiles
Col J G H Robertson

Head of Product Management, General Stores
J Deas

Head of Quality and Product Support Division
J R Denyer

Head of Science and Technology Division
Professor C Lewis OBE

Head of Contracting Division
M Campbell

Responsibilities To provide uniforms, clothing and textile products to meet the operational needs of the MOD and other defined customers with agreed standards and in the most cost effective manner

Number of staff 520

Department Defence

Launched November 1994

Defence Evaluation and Research Agency

Farnborough, Hants GU14 6TD*
Tel 01252 392000 Fax 01252 392173

Staff

Chief Executive
John Chisholm

Finance Director
Graham Love

Commercial Director
Dr Mike Goodfellow

Technical and Quality Director
Dr Adrian Mears

Rationalisation Director
Dr David Tyte

Company Secretary
Mrs Liz Peace (5)

Defence Research Agency

Managing Director
John Mabberley

Sectors
Land systems
Air systems
Sea systems
Command and Information systems
Weapons systems
Electronics
Human Sciences
Structural materials

Defence Test and Evaluation Organisation

(formerly Director General, Test and Evaluation, MOD)

Managing Director
David Kimberley

Sectors
Air operations
Land capabilities
Sea capabilities
Air capabilities
Assessment and evaluation

Chemical, Biological and Defence Establishment

Managing Director
Dr Graham Coley

Sectors
Chemical and biological defence
Chemical and electrical systems

Centre for Defence Analysis
(formerly Defence Operational Analysis Centre, Executive Agency)

Managing Director
Andrew Sleigh

Sectors
High level studies
Land studies
Air studies
Naval studies

Responsibilities Provides non-nuclear research for the MoD, other government departments and the private sector

Number of staff 12,000

Department Defence

Launched Defence Research Agency: 1 April 1991. On 1 April 1995 it became the Defence Evaluation and Research Agency having taken over the running of two other executive agencies: the Defence Operational Analysis Centre and the Chemical and Biological Defence Establishment; and a division from within the MoD: Director General, Test and Evaluation

*Following reorganisation the final location of many staff has not yet been finalised. In the first instance contact the Farnborough address

Defence Postal and Courier Services

MoD, Inglis Barracks, Mill Hill, London NW7 1PX
Tel 0181-818 6300 Fax 0181-818 6309

Staff
Chief Executive
Brig T McG Brown OBE

Responsibilities
Provides a world-wide mail and secure courier service for service personnel and the MoD. It also supports forces post offices and provides a transit system for the MoD in the UK

Number of staff
503

Department
Defence

Launched
1 July 1992

Defence Transport and Movements Executive

HQ QMG, , Monxton Road, Andover, Hampshire SP11 8HT
Tel 01264 382410 Fax 01264 382881

Staff	*Chief Executive* **Brig Michael Hodson CBE**
Responsibilities	Provides military transport and movement expertise in support of exercises and operations
Number of Staff	250
Department	Defence
Launched	4 April 1995

Disposal Sales Agency

St Christopher House, Sourthwark Street, London SE1 0TD
Tel 0171-921 1143 Fax 0171-921 1443/1697

Staff

Chief Executive
Keith Ellender

Assistant Director,
Plans and Budget
Garry Thomas

Assistant Director,
Ships and Armaments
Mick Robinson

Assistant Director,
Contracts and Technical
Colin McPhee

Responsibilities

To dispose of surplus Ministry of Defence equipment, stores and spares. The Agency has two main tasks: to negotiate the sale of major capital assets on a government-to-government basis; to identify and make contractual arrangements for the most appropriate method of disposal by sale of all other items

Number of staff

65

Department

Defence

Launched

3 October 1994

Driver and Vehicle Licensing Agency

Longview Road, Morriston, Swansea SA6 7JL
Tel 01792 782341 Fax 01792 782793

Staff

Chief Executive
Dr John Ford

Head of Central Operations
Richard Verge

Head of Development
Trevor Horton

Head of Personnel and Services
Robin Hancock

Head of Local Operations
John Betts

Responsibilities

The registration and licensing of drivers and vehicles in Great Britain and collection of excise duty. It also runs the scheme to sell attractive registration marks.

It provides a wide range of services for the Department of Transport and other government departments, the police and the general public including answering queries; supplying information to the police, the courts, insurance companies and the public; and helping road safety

Number of staff 3100

Department Transport

Launched 1 April 1990

Driver and Vehicle Licensing Agency (Northern Ireland)

County Hall, Castlerock Road, Coleraine BT51 3HS
Tel 01265 44133 Fax 01265 320927

Staff

Chief Executive
Brendan Magee

Responsibilities

Issues driving licences to appropriately qualified drivers and, as an agent of the Secretary of State for Transport, registers and licenses vehicles in Northern Ireland and collects and enforces excise duty

Number of staff

239

Department

Department of the Environment for Northern Ireland

Launched

2 August 1993

Driver and Vehicle Testing Agency (NI)

Balmoral Road, Belfast BT12 6QL
Tel 01232 681831 Fax 01232 665520

Staff	*Chief Executive* **J B Watson (6)**
Responsibilities	To promote and improve road safety in Northern Ireland through the advancement of driving standards and implementation of the government's policies for improving the mechanical standards of vehicles
Number of staff	250
Department	Department of the Environment for Northern Ireland
Launched	1 April 1992

Driving Standards Agency

Stanley House, 56 Talbot Street, Nottingham NG1 5GU
Tel 0115 9667600 Fax 0115 9557734

Staff

Chief Executive
Bernard Herdan

Finance Director
Ms Laraine Manley (5)

Operations Director
A E Evans (6)

Registrar of Approved Driving Instructors
B G Austin (7)

Personnel Manager
J T Berwick (7)

Policy and External Relations Manager
P Butler (7)

Regional Operations Manager
G E Court (7)

Planning Manager
G C Morgan (7)

Chief Driving Examiner
D Norris

Responsibilities To test drivers of cars, motorcycles, large goods and passenger carrying vehicles, to maintain the Register of Approved Driving Instructors and to oversee compulsory basic training for motorcyclists

Number of staff 1760

Department Transport

Launched 2 April 1990

Duke of York's Royal Military School

Dover, Kent CT15 5EQ
Tel 01304 245024 Fax 01304 245019

Staff *Chief Executive*
Col Gordon H Wilson

Responsibilities To provide boarding school education for the dependents, aged between 11 and 18 years, of service personnel

Number of staff 100

Department Defence

Launched 1 April 1992

Employment Service

St Vincent House, 30 Orange Street, London WC2H 7HT
Tel 0171-839 5600   Fax 0171-389 1373

Staff

Chief Executive
M E G Fogden CB (3)

Corporate Development and Secretariat
C Wright (6)

Senior Director of Operations and Deputy Chief Executive
D Grover (3)
(Sheffield)

Network Development Branch
C Mackinnon (5)

Business Consultancy Service
D Benham (6)

Pay Strategy Project
C Wells (6)
(Above 3 in Sheffield)

Directorate of Human Resources
Director
D B Price (4)

Personnel
R Lasko (5)

Deputy Head of Personnel
M Pender (6)

Training and Development
P Benzies (6)

Occupational Psychology
Dr M Killcross (5)

Estates
J Davies (6)
(all in Sheffield)

Business Development Directorate
Director
K White (4)

Business Strategy
Ms K Walker (6)

Research and Evaluation
J S Child (5)

Job Placing and Programmes
Miss S Newton (5)

Claimant Advice
S Holt (5)

Disability Services
G Macnair (5)
(all in Sheffield)

Finance and Resources Directorate
Director
A G Johnson (4)

Internal Audit
Ms S Orr (6)
(Sheffield)

Finance, Resource and Planning
S Norton (6)

Financial Management Services
J B Stewart (5)

Information Technology
D Wood (5)
G Dodsworth (6)
R Harris (6)

Regional Organisation
Regional Directors
London and South East
Richard Foster (4)

Office for Scotland
A R Brown (5)

Northern
P Robson (5)

North West
J Roberts (5)

Yorkshire & Humberside
G Humphreys (5)

West Midlands
Miss R Thew (5)

East Midlands and Eastern
Mrs A Le Sage (5)

Office for Wales
E B Pearce (5)

South West
K Pascoe (5)

Responsibilities To help unemployed people get back into work and to pay benefits to those entitled to them. In addition it runs a number of special programmes for the unemployed and for people with disabilities

Number of staff 44,000

Department Employment

Launched 2 April 1990

Employment Service Addresses

Rockingham House
123 West Street
Sheffield S1 4ER
Tel 01142 59739190
Fax 01142 739190

Regional addresses

East Midlands and Eastern
Newton House
Maid Marion Way
Nottingham NG1 6GG
Tel 01159 483308

London and South East
236 Gray's Inn Road
London WC1X 8HL
Tel 0171-211 4175

Northern
Broadacre House
Market Street
Newcastle upon Tyne
NE1 6HH
Tel 0191-232 6181

North West
Ontario House
2 Furnace Quay
Salford M5 2XZ
Tel 0161-873 1000

South West
The Pithay
Bristol BS1 2NQ
Tel 01179 273710

West Midlands
2 Duchess Place
Hagley Road
Birmingham B16 8NS
Tel 0121-456 1144

Yorkshire and Humberside
Jubilee House
33–41 Park Place
Leeds LS1 2RE
Tel 01132 446299

Scotland
Argyle House
2 Lady Lawson Street
Edinburgh EH3 9SD
Tel 0131-229 9191

Wales
Companies House
Crown Way
Maindy
Cardiff CF4 3UW
Tel 01222 388588

Fire Service College

Moreton-in-Marsh, Gloucestershire GL56 0RH
Tel 01608 650831 Fax 01608 651788

Staff

Chief Executive
Nigel Finlayson

Commandant
Frank David

Responsibilities

To provide command, leadership and management training for the UK Fire Service through a progressive system of training, and also to provide training in finance and specialist fire-related subjects

To provide training for commerce and industry, and for students from overseas fire brigades

Number of staff 260

Department Home Office

Launched 1 April 1992 with Trading Fund status

Forensic Science Service

Room 736, Home Office, 50 Queen Anne's Gate, London SW1H 9AT
Tel 0171-273 2167 Fax 0171-273 2256
Priory House, Gooch Street North, Birmingham B5 6QQ
Tel 0121-666 6606 Fax 0121-622 3536

Staff

Chief Executive and Director-General
Dr Janet Thompson (3)

Director, Operations
Dr P D B Clarke (5)

Director, Finance and Administration
K C Cloran (5)

Chief Scientist
Dr A W Scaplehorn (5)

Director, Service Development
Dr D J Werrett (5)

Director, Business Development
T Howitt (5)

Responsibilities

To provide scientific support in the investigation of crime and expert evidence to the courts. Its customers include the police, the Crown Prosecution Service and the defence.

Number of staff

690

Department

Home Office

Launched

1 April 1991

Government Property Lawyers

Riverside Chambers, Castle Street, Taunton, Somerset TA1 4AP
Tel 01823 345200 Fax 01823 345202

Staff

Chief Executive
A D Osborne (3)

Deputy Chief Executive
P Horner (4)

Group Directors
P L Noble (5)
M Benmayor (5)
M Rawlins (5)
A M Scarfe (5)
I P Parker (5)

Director of Lands Advisory
R C Paddock (5)

Finance and Personnel Director
M J Robbins (7)

Responsibilities To provide conveyancing and lands advisory services to government departments and other public bodies in England and Wales

Number of staff 132

Department Treasury Solicitor's Department

Launched 1 April 1993

The Highways Agency

St Christopher House, Southwark Street, London SE1 0TE
Tel 0171-921 4999 Fax *Telephone the above number and ask for appropriate fax number*

All personnel based at St Christopher House unless otherwise indicated.
For other addresses and telephone numbers see end of this section.

Staff

Chief Executive
L J Haynes (2)

Human Resources Director
K A Wyatt (5)

Strategy Director
P G Collis (5)
(St Christopher House and Jefferson House)

Head of Public Relations
Miss L Austin (7)

Restructuring and Property Team Directorate
Director
N E Firkins (5)

Deputy Director
G Robertson (5)

Road Programme Directorate
Director
J W Fellows (3)
(St Christopher House and 5 Broadway)

Administrative Services Director
K McKenzie (5)

Technical Services Director
D A Holland (4)

Operations Director and Deputy Road Programme Director
D York (4)

Northern Operations Director
R R Bineham (5)

Construction Operations Director
J Boud (5)

Southern Operations Director
D W Ward (5)

Administrative Operations Director
J M Bradley (5)

Motorway Operations Director
D E Oddy (5)

Network Management and Maintenance Directorate
Director
B J Billington (3)

Deputy Director and Operations Director
P E Nutt (4)

Director, London
R T Thorndike (5)

Network Control Division Director
M G Quinn (5)
(St Christopher House and Tollgate House)

Operations Support Division
J Oliver (6)

Network Policy Director
R Eastman (5)

Director, Northern
K Lasbury (5)
(City House)

Director, Southern
A D Rowland (5)
(Federated House)

Director, Midland
W S C Wadrup (5)
(Heron House)

Finance Directorate
Director
J Seddon (4)

Finance Procurement Division
P A Houston (5)

Highways Computing Division
D J Kershaw (4)
(Jefferson House)

Lands and Compensation Division
Mrs B Bostock (5)

Lands North Office
P Davies (7)
(Sunley Tower)

Lands South Office
K Davies (7)
(Federated House)

Lands Midland Office
M Smith (7)
(Heron House)

Lands
P Wilson (7)

Civil Engineering and Environmental Policy Directorate
Director
T A Rochester (3)

Deputy Director
and Engineering Policy Division
J A Kerman (4)

Bridges Engineering Division
A Pickett (5)

Environmental Policy Division
Miss V Bodnar (5)

Roads, Engineering and Environment Division
N S Organ (5)

Responsibilities Managing, maintaining and improving the national trunk road network within England to secure the delivery of an efficient, reliable, safe and environmentally acceptable trunk road network. The Agency makes the best use of the existing network through efficient traffic management and maintenance policies and project manages the design and construction of further public investment as approved by the Secretary of State for Transport

Number of Staff 1900

Department Transport

Launched 1 April 1994

Highways Agency Addresses

5 Broadway
Broad Street
Birmingham B15 1BL
Tel 0121-631 8000
Fax 0121-631 8184

City House
New Station Street
Leeds LS1 4JD
Tel 01132 836300
Fax 01132 836625

Federated House
London Road
Dorking
Surrey RH4 1SZ
Tel 01306 870100
Fax 01306 870222

Heron House
Goldington Road
Bedford Road
Bedford MK40 3LL
Tel 01234 363161
Fax 01234 276081

Jefferson House
27 Park Place
Leeds LS1 2SZ
Tel 01132 541000
Fax 01132 541001

Sunley Tower
Piccadilly Plaza
Manchester M1 4BE
Tel 0161-832 9111
Fax 0161-952 4098

Tollgate House
Houlton Street
Bristol BS2 9DJ
Tel 01179 878087
Fax 01179 878264

Historic Royal Palaces

Hampton Court Palace, East Molesey, Surrey KT8 9AU
Tel 0181-781 9750 Fax 0181-781 9754

Staff

Chief Executive
David C Beeton

Director of Finance and Resources
Ms R Darbyshire

Public Affairs Director
P D Hammond

Curator
Dr S J Thurley

Surveyor of the Fabric
S Bond

Director (Hampton Court and Kew)
D McGuinnes *(Acting)*

Resident Governor (Tower of London)
Maj Gen G W Field CB OBE
0171-488 5630

Director (Kensington Palace)
N J Arch
0171-937 9561

Commercial Director
D J C MacDonald

Responsibilities To manage the five Historic Royal Palaces (Tower of London, Hampton Court Palace, The Banqueting House, Kensington and Kew Palaces)

Number of staff 500

Department National Heritage

Launched 1 October 1989

Historic Scotland

Longmore House, Salisbury Place, Edinburgh EH9 1SH
Tel 0131-668 8600 Fax 0131-668 8699

Staff

The Director and Chief Executive
Graeme N Munro (3)

Directors

Heritage Policy
F J Lawrie (5)

Corporate Planning and Resources
S Rosie (6)

Properties in Care
D Macniven (5)

Technical Conservation, Research and Evaluation
I Maxwell (5)

Responsibilities

To protect and promote public understanding and enjoyment of Scotland's ancient monuments and archaeological sites and landscapes, historic buildings, parks, gardens and designed landscapes

Number of staff

690

Department

Scottish Office Environment Department

Launched

2 April 1991

HM Land Registry

Lincoln's Inn Fields, London WC2A 3PH
Tel 0171-917 8888 Fax 0171-955 0110

Staff

Chief Land Registrar, Chief Executive
J J Manthorpe CB (2)

Solicitor
C J West (3)

Director (Corporate Services)
E G Beardsall (4)

Senior Land Registrar
Mrs J G Totty (5)

Director (Operations)
G N French (5)

Director (Information Technology)
P J Smith (5)

Director (Finance)
Miss H M Jackson (5)

Controller (Management Services)
P R Laker (6)

Land Registrar
M L Wood (5)

District Land Registrars

Birkenhead
M G Garwood (5)

Coventry
S P Kelway (5)

Croydon
D M J Moss (5)

Durham
C W Martin (5)

Gloucester
W W Budden (5)

Harrow
J V Timothy (5)

Kingston upon Hull
S R G Coveney (5)

Leicester
Mrs J A Goodfellow (6)

Lytham
J G Cooper (5)

Nottingham
P J Timothy (5)

Peterborough
L M Pope (5)

Plymouth
A J Pain (5)

Portsmouth
S R Sehrawat (6)

Stevenage
C Tate (5)

Swansea
G A Hughes (5)

Telford
M A Roche (5)

Tunbridge
G R Tooke (5)

Weymouth
Mrs P M Reeson (5)

York
Mrs R S Lovel (6)

Responsibilities

To maintain and develop a stable and effective land registration system throughout England and Wales as the cornerstone for the creation and free movement of interests in land

To grant legal title on behalf of the Crown to interests in land for the whole of England and Wales

To provide ready access to up-to-date and guaranteed land information so enabling confident dealings in property and security of title

Number of staff

8500

Department

HM Land Registry is a department in its own right. The Chief Executive is directly accountable to the Lord Chancellor

Launched

2 July 1990

District Land Registrars Addresses

Birkenhead
Old Market House
Hamilton Street
Birkenhead L41 5FL
Tel 0151-473 1110
Fax 0151-473 0251

Coventry
Leigh Court
Torrington Avenue
Tile Hill
Coventry CV4 9XZ
Tel 01203 860860
Fax 01203 860021

Croydon
Sunley House
Bedford Park
Croydon CR9 3LE
Tel 0181-781 9100
Fax 0181-781 9110

Durham
Southfield House
Southfield Way
Durham DH1 5TR
Tel 0191-301 3500
Fax 0191-301 0020

Gloucester
Twyver House
Bruton Way
Gloucester GL1 1DQ
Tel 01452 511111
Fax 01452 510050

Harrow
Lyon House
Lyon Road
Harrow HA1 2EU
Tel 0181-235 1181
Fax 0181-862 0176

Kingston upon Hull
Earle House
Portland Street
Hull HU2 8JN
Tel 01482 223244
Fax 01482 224278

Leicester
Thames Tower
99 Burleys Way
Leicester LE1 3UB
Tel 01162 654000
Fax 01162 654008

Lytham
Birkenhead House
East Beach
Lytham St Annes
Lancashire FY8 5AB
Tel 01253 849849
Fax 01253 840013

Nottingham
Chalfont Drive
Nottingham NG8 3RN
Tel 01159 351166
Fax 01159 350038

Peterborough
Touthill Close
City Road
Peterborough
Northants PE1 1XN
Tel 01733 288288
Fax 01733 280022

Plymouth
Plumer House
Tailyour Road
Crownhill
Plymouth PL6 5HY
Tel 01752 701234
Fax 01752 769051

Portsmouth
St Andrew's Court
St Michael's Road
Portsmouth
Hants PO1 2JH
Tel 01705 865022
Fax 01705 871075

Stevenage
Brickdale House
Swingate
Stevenage
Herts SG1 1XG
Tel 01438 788888
Fax 01438 780107

Swansea
Ty Bryn Glas
High Street
Swansea SA1 1PW
Tel 01792 458877
Fax 01792 473236

Telford
Parkside Court
Hall Park Way
Telford TF3 4LR
Tel 01952 290355
Fax 01952 290356

Tunbridge
Curtis House
Tunbridge Wells
Kent TN2 5AQ
Tel 01892 510015
Fax 01892 510032

Weymouth
1 Cumberland Drive
Weymouth
Dorset DT4 9TT
Tel 01305 776161
Fax 01305 774436

York
James House
James Street
York YO1 3YZ
Tel 01904 450000
Fax 01904 450086

HM Prison Service

Cleland House, Page Street, London SW1P 4LN
Tel 0171-217 3000 Fax 0171-217 6635

Staff

Director-General
Derek Lewis (2)

Executive Directors
Director of Personnel
Vacant (3)

Director of Operations North
A J Pearson (3)

Director of Operations South
A Walker (3)

Director of Health Care
Dr R Wool (3)

Director of Finance
B Landers (3)

Director of Security and Programmes
R R Tilt (3)

Director of Services
A J Butler (3)

Non-Executive Directors

Mrs U Banerjee
Mr F W Bentley
Mr G Keeys
Sir Duncan Nichol

Secretary
J Sarjantson

Directorate of Custody
P Wheatley (5)

Area Managers
T Murtagh
J Hunter
P Kitteridge
A Rayfield
J Wilkinson
J May
A de Frisching

Directorate of Programmes
K Heal (5)

Area Managers
J Mullens
A Papps
I Lockwood
T Bone
M Codd
J Blakey
D Curtis

Directorate of Health Care
Miss S Paul (5)
Dr L Joyce (5)
Dr D Howells (4)
R W Lockett (6)

Directorate of Personnel
Mrs E Grimsey
I Boon (5)

Directorate of Finance
S Hickson (5)
J Le Vay (5)
P Atherton (5)
S Moore
S Jenner (7)

Directorate of Security
Bill Abbott (5)

Directorate of Services
Miss L Gill (5)
R Haines (4)
R Fulton (5)
D Kent (5)

Contract and Competitions Group
D Ackland (5)

Press Office
Ms A Nelson (7)

Responsibilities The management of HM Prison Service in England and Wales.

Number of staff	39,012
Department	Home Office
Launched	1 April 1993

HMSO

St Crispins, Duke Street, Norwich NR3 1PD
Tel 01603 622211 Fax 01603 695582

Staff

Controller and Chief Executive
Dr Paul I Freeman CB

Deputy Chief Executive
M D Lynn

Director General, Corporate Services
P J Macdonald

HMSO Publications Director
C N Southgate

HMSO Print Director
E Hendry

HMSO Office Supplies Director
A Cole

HMSO Copiers Director
V G Bell

HMSO Business Systems Director
D C Kerry

HMSO Furniture Director
Gavin Turner
(HMSO Furniture)

HMSO Scotland Director
G W Bedford
(Edinburgh)

HMSO Northern Ireland Director
M McNeill
(Belfast)

Responsibilities The provision of publishing and printing services, office supplies, office machinery and furniture to Parliament, government departments and other publicly funded bodies

Number of staff 2900

Department HMSO is a department in its own right and a Trading Fund. The Chief Executive is accountable to the Chancellor of the Duchy of Lancaster (Office of Public Service and Science)

Launched 14 December 1988

HMSO Addresses

HMSO St Crispins
Duke Street
Norwich NR3 1PD
Tel 01603 622211
Fax 01603 695582

HMSO Furniture
City Reach One
5 Greenwich View Place
Mill Harbour
London E14 9NN
Tel 0171-512 3322
Fax 0171-512 0312

HMSO Scotland
Bankhead Avenue
Edinburgh EH11 4AB
Tel 0131-479 9000
Fax 0131-479 3336

HMSO Northern Ireland
IDB House
64 Chichester Street
Belfast BT1 4PS
Tel 01232 238451
Fax 01232 895151

HQ Service Children's Schools (North West Europe)

HQ UKSC(G) BFPO 140
Tel 00 49 2161 472-3296 Fax 010 49 2161 472-3487

Staff	*Chief Executive* **Ian S Mitchelson (4)** *Assistant Chief Executive* *(Strategic Direction of Service)* **Paul Niedzwiedzki (7 equivalent)** *Assistant Chief Executive* *(Quality Assurance)* **Ian Forrest (7 equivalent)** *Assistant Chief Executive* *(Strategic Plans and Budgets)* **Mervyn J Harvey (7)**
Responsibilities	To provide an education service for the dependant children living with MoD personnel in North West Europe
Number of staff	1450
Department	Defence
Launched	1 April 1991

Hydrographic Office

Taunton, Somerset TA1 2DN
Tel 01823 337900 Fax 01823 284077

Lacon House, Theobalds Road, London WC1X 8RY
Tel 0171-305 6632 Fax 0171-305 6919

Staff

Hydrographer of the Navy and Chief Executive
Rear Admiral N R Essenhigh

Deputy Chief Executive
Mrs B A Bond (5)

Director, Defence Requirements
Capt R A Cotton RN

Director, Finance and Administration
M R Pack (6)

Director, Production and Marketing
D H McPherson (6)

Director, Nautical Charts and Publications
W A A Huddy (6)

Director, Planning
S Parnell (6)

Director, Information Systems
Dr C R Drinkwater (6)

Responsibilities To produce charts and navigational publications for the Royal Navy and other customers at home and abroad

Number of staff 798

Department Defence

Launched 1 April 1990

Industrial Research and Technology Unit

Netherleigh House, Massey Avenue, Belfast BT4 2JP
Tel 01232 529900 Fax 01232 529548

Staff
Chief Executive
Greg McConnell

Responsibilities
Promotes industrially relevant research, development and technology transfer in Northern Ireland

Number of Staff
150

Department
Department of Economic Development for Northern Ireland

Launched
3 April 1995

Insolvency Service

PO Box 203, 21 Bloomsbury Street, London WC1B 3QW
Tel 0171-291 6724 Fax 0171-291 6726

Staff

Inspector General and Chief Executive
Peter Joyce (3)

Deputy Inspector General HQ Operations
D J Flynn (4)

Deputy Inspector General, Official Receiver Operations
M C A Osborne (4)

Head of Policy
Mrs J K Scoones (5)

Responsibilities

To administer and investigate the affairs of individuals in bankruptcy and companies wound up by the courts

To report criminal offences in those failures and take proceedings for the disqualification of directors in all corporate failures

To regulate, directly or through professional bodies, private sector insolvency practitioners

To provide banking and investment services for bankruptcy and liquidation funds (funds from the realisation of assets are required to be paid by trustees and liquidators into the Insolvency Services Account and may be invested in government securities)

To provide advice to ministers on insolvency policy issues

Number of staff 1685

Department Trade and Industry

Launched 21 March 1990

Intervention Board

Fountain House, Queen's Walk, Reading RG1 7QW
Tel 01734 583626 Fax 01734 583626 ext 2370

Staff

Chief Executive
Guy Stapleton (3)

Chairman
A J Ellis CBE

Secretary
S P Briggs (SEO)

Director (Finance)
G R R Jenkins (5)

Director (External Trade)
G N Dixon (5)

Director (Livestock Products)
M J Griffiths (5)

Director (Crops)
H MacKinnon (5)

Director (Corporate Services)
J W M Peffers (5)

Director (Legal)
J McCleary (5)

Responsibilities To implement the UK's obligations under the EC's Common Agricultural Policy by operating some 70 separate schemes to support the market in farm and food products

Number of staff 978

Department The Intervention Board is a department in its own right. The Chief Executive is accountable to the Secretaries of State for Scotland, Wales and Northern Ireland and the Minister of Agriculture, Fisheries and Food

Launched 1 April 1990

Laboratory of the Government Chemist

Queens Road, Teddington, Middlesex TW11 0LY
Tel 0181-943 7000 Fax 0181-943 2767

Staff

Chief Executive and Government Chemist
Dr R D Worswick (3)

Directors:
Business Operations
Dr B King (5)

Business Development
Dr R Dietz (5)

Heads of Division
Consultancy
Dr P B Baker (6)

Analytical Support
J Day (6)

Business Development
Dr R Ah-Sun (6)

Accounting and Finance
A Wilson (6)

Human Resources
J Rowe (7)

Responsibilities

To provide customers in both the public and private sectors with authoritative, independent and impartial consultancy and support on analytical chemistry, biomaterials and related sciences

It plays an important role in the enforcement of law, the maintenance of public health, the protection of government duty revenue, the consumer and the environment

Its customers include government departments, the European Community, local authorities, law enforcement agencies, and private industry

Number of staff 315

Department Trade and Industry

Launched 30 October 1989

Logistic Information Systems Agency

Monxton Road, Andover, Hants SP11 8HT
Tel 01264 382280 Fax 01264 38282

Staff

Chief Executive
Brig A W Pollard

Director, Strategy and Plans
Col J W Chuter

Director, Customer Support (Logistic Support)
Col T Byrd

Director, Customer Support (Equipment Support)
Col C W Paskell

Director, Project Support
T Wild

Director, Information Technology Services
J R Cooper

Director, Implementation
A C Targett

Responsibilities

To provide information systems, services and support to Army logistics. Systems provide the information which is needed for the supply, management, distribution and where appropriate, the repair of stores, equipment and combat supplies used by the Army

Number of staff 395

Department Defence

Launched November 1994

Marine Safety Agency

Spring Place, 105 Commercial Road, Southampton SO15 1EG
Tel 01703-329100 Fax 01703-329298

Staff	*Chief Executive* **Robin Bradley (4)** *Director Marine Safety (Ship Construction and Navigation)* **Bill Graham (5)** *Director Marine Safety (Marine Engineering and Equipment)* **Peter Hambling (5)** *Director Marine Safety (Operations and Seafarers' Standards)* **Captain Doug Bell (5)** *Director Marine Safety (Finance, Personnel and Corporate Services)* **Roy Padgett (6)**
Responsibilities	To develop, promote and enforce high standards of marine safety and to minimise the risk of pollution of the marine environment from ships
Number of staff	400
Department	Transport
Launched	1 April 1994

Meat Hygiene Service

Foss House, Kingspool, 1-2 Peasholme Green, York YO1 2PX
Tel 01904 455501 Fax 01904 455502

Staff

Chief Executive
Johnston McNeill

Head of Operations
Philip Corrigan

Head of Finance
Allan Ellison

Head of Information Technology
Graham Perry

Head of Human Resources
Monica Redmond

Responsibilities To safeguard public health and animal welfare through fair, consistent and effective enforcement of hygiene, inspection and welfare regulations

Number of staff 1100

Department Ministry of Agriculture, Fisheries and Food

Launched April 1995

Medical Devices Agency

14 Russell Square, London WC1B 5EP
Tel 0171-972 2000 Fax 0171-972 8104

Officials

Chief Executive
A Kent

Director of Finance
K Cornelius

Head of European Business
Dr D C Potter

Head of Device Evaluation and Publication
B Wignall

Head of Manufacturer Registration Scheme
R W B Allen

Head of Corporate Management
T F Crawley

Head of Device Technology and Safety
Dr E Hoxey

Medical and Nursing Business
Senior Medical Officers
Dr S M Ludgate
Dr S P Vahl
Senior Nursing Officer
Mrs P A Collinson

Responsibilities To protect the public health and safeguard the interests of patients and users by ensuring that medical devices for sale or use in the United Kingdom meet appropriate standards of safety, quality and performance and comply with relevant European directives

Number of staff 175

Department Health

Launched 27 September 1994

Medicines Control Agency

Market Towers, 1 Nine Elms Lane, London SW8 5NQ
Tel 0171-273 3000 Fax 0171-273 0334

Staff

Chief Executive
Dr Keith Jones (3)

Board Members

Licensing
Dr D Jeffreys (4)

Post-Licensing
Dr Susan Wood (4)

Inspection and Enforcement
B H Hartley (4)

Executive Support
R K Alder (4)

Information Technology
P Coulling (4)

Finance
M R Read (5)

Responsibilities

To safeguard public health by controlling medicines, through a system of licensing, monitoring, inspection and enforcement which ensures that medicines marketed in the UK are safe, efficacious and of good quality. It works closely with its statutory advisory committees: the Medicines Commission and the British Pharmacopoeia, and also with the Committee on the Safety of Medicines and the Committee on Dental and Surgical Materials *(see entry for Medicines Commission in the Regulatory Organisations and Public Bodies section).*

Number of staff 347

Department Health

Launched 11 July 1991

Meteorological Office

London Road, Bracknell, Berks RG42 1SZ
Tel 01344 420242 Fax 01344 854412

Staff

Chief Executive
Professor Julian C R Hunt FRS (2)

Deputy Chief Executive and Director of Operations
Dr P Ryder CB (3)

Director of Central Forecasting
C R Flood (5)

Director of Observations
J M Nicholls (5)

Director of Information Technology
Dr R L Wiley (5)

Director of Defence Services
Dr S J Caughey (5)

Chief Scientist and Director of Research
Dr P Mason (4)

Director of Atmospheric Process Research
Dr P W White (5)

Director of Forecasting Research
Dr M J P Cullen (5)

Director of Climate Research
Dr D J Carson (5)

Director of Commercial Services
Vacant (5)

Director of Finance and Administration
M A Bittleston (5)

Responsibilities

To provide an effective, modern and efficient national meteorological service for the United Kingdom

Number of staff 2300

Department Defence

Launched 2 April 1990

Military Survey

Elmwood Avenue, Feltham, Middlesex TW13 7AE
Tel 0181-890 3622 Fax 0181-818 2148

Staff	*Director General* **Major General M P B G Wilson (2*)†** *Directors* **Brigadier P R Wildman (*)** **Brigadier A J Hoon (*)** **P James**
Responsibilities	To ensure geographic support to the Ministry of Defence for planning, training and operations
Number of staff	807
Department	Defence
Launched	1 April 1991

† 2*, * = armed forces equivalent of Civil Service grades 3 and 5 respectively

National Engineering Laboratory

East Kilbride, Glasgow G75 0QU
Tel 013552 20222 Fax 013552 36930

Staff

Chief Executive
William Edgar (3)

Operations Director
W Paton (4)

Sales and Marketing Director
D W Lee (5)

Finance and Administration Director
G M MacDonald (5)

Divisional Managers
Dr F C Kinghorn (5)
Dr S M Langdon (6)

Responsibilities To provide comprehensive engineering technology services and consultancy to the government and the private sector in the fields of energy, process engineering, defence and transport

Number of staff 331

Department Trade and Industry

Launched 5 October 1990

National Physical Laboratory

Queens Road, Teddington, Middlesex TW11 0LW
Tel 0181-977 3222 Fax 0181-943 2155

Staff

Chief Executive and Director
Dr Peter Clapham (3)

Deputy Director
Dr A J Wallard (4)

Secretary
J M Whitlock (5)

Heads of Division
Electrical Science
Dr T G Blaney (5)

IT and Computing
A J Marks (5)

Materials Metrology
Dr M K Hossain (5)

Mechanical and Optical Metrology
Dr A R Colclough (5)

Quantum Metrology
Dr J R Gott (5)

Radiation Science and Acoustics
Dr P Christmas (5)

National Measurement Accreditation Service
W T K Henderson (5)

Responsibilities

To develop and maintain national standards for measuring physical quantities

To provide calibration services essential to UK industry

To undertake research on standards for engineering materials and for information technology

To ensure that accurate measurement standards, compatible with those of Britain's major trading partners, are available to UK organisations

To provide the base for the National Measurement Accreditation Service (NAMAS) which accredits public and private sector calibration and testing laboratories

Number of staff 720

Department Trade and Industry

Launched 3 July 1990

National Weights and Measures Laboratory

Stanton Avenue, Teddington, Middlesex TW11 0JZ
Tel 0181-943 7272 Fax 0181-943 7270

Staff	*Chief Executive and Director* **Dr Seton Bennett (5)**
Responsibilities	To administer weights and measures legislation, especially regulation and certification of equipment for use in shops etc
Number of staff	46
Department	Trade and Industry
Launched	18 April 1989

Natural Resources Institute

Central Avenue, Chatham Maritime, Chatham, Kent ME4 4TB
Tel 01634 880088 Fax 01634 880066/77

Staff

Chief Executive
Anthony Beattie (3)

Deputy Directors
T J Perfect (5)
Professor R D Cooke (5)
C I Myhill (5)
Dr R G Poulter (6)
Professor M Gill (6)

Responsibilities

To collaborate with developing countries to increase the sustainable productivity of their natural resources – farming, forestry and fisheries – through the application of science and technology

Number of staff

456

Department

Overseas Development Administration

Launched

2 April 1990

Naval Aircraft Repair Organisation

RN Aircraft Yard, Fleetlands, Gosport PO13 0AW
Tel 01705 822351 Xt 44910/01329 826225 Fax 01329 823043/2

Staff

Chief Executive
Captain Wade Graham

Responsibilities

To provide repair, modification, overhaul and storage services for the tri-service helicopter fleet, their engines and selected components and for marine gas turbine engines and their components

Number of staff

1549

Department

Defence

Launched

1 April 1992

Naval Recruiting and Training Agency

Victory Building, HM Naval Base, Portsmouth, Hampshire PO1 3LS
Tel 01705 727600 Fax 01705 727613

Staff	*Chief Executive* **Rear Admiral Johnny Clarke LVO MBE**
Responsibilities	Primarily improving and maintaining a pool of suitably trained manpower for deployment in the Naval Service
Number of Staff	5400
Department	Defence
Launched	1 April 1995

NHS Estates

1 Trevelyan Square, Boar Lane, Leeds LS1 6A1
Tel 01132 547000 Fax 01132 547299

Staff

Chief Executive
John Locke (3)

Director (Estate Policy)
Geof Mayers (5)

Director (Business Development)
Roger Tanner (5)

Director (Resources)
John Wardle (5)

Chief Engineer
Mike Arrowsmith (5)

Responsibilities

To act as property advisers and consultants to the NHS and the healthcare industry at home and abroad

To provide advice and support over the complete range of health care estate functions including monitoring services for the NHS

To provide cost effective services to help customers deliver health care in a well managed environment

To ensure optimum use of the estate for better health care

Its customers include the NHS Management Executive, health authorities, NHS trusts, government departments and others including substantial overseas interests

Number of staff 161

Department Health

Launched 1 April 1991

NHS Pensions Agency

Hesketh House, 200-220 Broadway, Fleetwood, Lancs FY7 8LG
Tel 01253 774774 Fax 01253 774860

Staff

Chief Executive
Alec Cowan (5)

Director of Systems and Business Processes
Bill McCallum

Director of Customer Services (Employers)
Michael Stewart (6)

Director of Operations
Martin Shearman (7)

Director of Finance
Nigel Holden (7)

Responsibilities To administer the NHS Occupational Pension Scheme on behalf of all NHS staff in England and Wales.

Number of staff 524

Department Health

Launched 20 November 1992

Northern Ireland Child Support Agency

Great Northern Tower, 17 Great Victoria Street, Belfast BT2 7AD
Tel 01232 896896 Fax 01232 896693

Staff	*Chief Executive* **Pat Devlin** *Director of Resources* **David Elwood** *Director of Business Development* **Sheila Barfoot** *Director of Northern Ireland Operations* **John Canavan** *Centre Manager* **John Johnston** *Personnel Officer* **Maureen Cullen**
Responsibilities	To operate the system created by the Child Support (Northern Ireland) Order 1991 in Northern Ireland
Number of staff	1005
Department	Department of Health and Social Services for Northern Ireland
Launched	5 April 1993

Northern Ireland Prison Service

Dundonald House, Upper Newtownards Road, Belfast BT4 3SB
Tel 01232 520700* Fax 01232 525160

Staff

Chief Executive
Alan Shannon

Divisions

Personnel Services

Finance and Estate Management

Operational Management

Policy and Planning

Press Office

Responsibilities

The Northern Ireland Prison Service aims to hold in secure and humane confinement persons who have been given into custody by the courts, and to reduce the risk of re-offending by encouraging them to take full advantage of the opportunities offered during their confinement within the financial resources allocated to it

Number of staff 3590

Department Northern Ireland Office

Launched April 1995

*The Northern Ireland Office number. Ask for the relevant Prison Service department when the operator answers

Occupational Health Service

18–20 Hill Street, Edinburgh EH2 3NB
Tel 0131-220 4177 Fax 0131-220 4183

Dacre House, 17-19 Dacre Street, London SW1H 0DH
Tel 0171-222 1202 Fax 0171-222 0373

Staff

Chief Executive and Director; Medical Adviser to the Civil Service
Dr Elizabeth McCloy

Deputy Medical Adviser
Dr P Litchfield (4)

Responsibilities

To improve health and safety at work in government departments, agencies and public bodies

To provide statutory and non-statutory health surveillance, health and safety audits, advice and rehabilitation of the disabled, clinical services for the staff and their families working overseas and a full range of health care services

Number of staff 125

Department Cabinet Office (Office of Public Service and Science)

Launched 2 April 1990

Office of HM Paymaster General

Sutherland House, Russell Way, Crawley, West Sussex RH10 1UH
Tel 01293 560999 Fax 01293 538979

Staff	*Assistant Paymaster General, Chief Executive* **Keith Sullens** *Banking Director* **Ron Hollands** *Pensions Director* **Mike West** *Finance Director* **David Nunn**
Responsibilities	To provide banking, pensions and financial information services for the government and public sector bodies
Number of staff	772
Department	H M Treasury
Launched	1 April 1993

Ordnance Survey

Romsey Road, Maybush, Southampton SO9 4DH
Tel 01703 792000 Fax 01703 792404

Staff

Director General
Professor D W Rhind

Deputy Director General and Director of External Relations
J P Leonard

Director of Business Services
I G Lock

Director of Business and Professional Markets
P Wesley

Director of Consumer and Education Markets
D Davies

Director of Information Management
B Nanson

Director of Data Collection
I Logan

Director of OS International
E Gilbert

Corporate Secretary
R Budden

Press Officer
Steve Yeates

Responsibilities The official topographic surveying and mapping organisation of Great Britain

Number of staff 2027

Department Ordnance Survey is a department in its own right. The Director General is accountable to the Secretary of State for the Environment

Launched 1 May 1990

Ordnance Survey of Northern Ireland

Colby House, Stanmillis Court, Belfast BT9 5BJ
Tel 01232 661244 Fax 01232 683211

Staff	*Chief Executive* **Michael Brand (5)**
Responsibilities	To maintain a topographical information archive for Northern Ireland To provide information from the archive to customers in forms most appropratе to their needs To undertake special surveys, aerial photography, cartographic and reprographic services and technical assistance to government departments and others at home and abroad
Number of staff	195
Department	Department of the Environment, Northern Ireland
Launched	1 April 1992

UK Passport Agency

Clive House, 70-78 Petty France, London SW1H 9HD
Tel 0171-271 3000 Fax 0171-271 8645

Staff

Chief Executive
David Gatenby

Deputy Chief Executive
Director (Operations)
T L Lonsdale

Director (Planning and Resources)
K J Sheehan

Director (Systems)
R G Le Marechal

Responsibilities To issue passports to British nationals in the United Kingdom

Number of staff 1300

Department Home Office

Launched 2 April 1991

Patent Office

Concept House, Cardiff Road, Newport, Gwent NP9 1RH
Tel 01633 814000 Fax 01633 814563

Staff	*Comptroller General* **Paul R S Hartnack (3)** *Assistant Comptrollers* *Intellectual Property and Copyright* **A Sugden (4)** *Patents and Designs* **R Marchant (4)** *Assistant Registrar* **Miss A Brimelow (5)** *Secretary* **T Cassidy (5)**
Responsibilities	To grant patents and trade marks, register designs, and formulate policy on intellectual property
Number of staff	957
Department	Trade and Industry
Launched	1 March 1990

Pesticides Safety Directorate

Mallard House, King's Pool, Peasholme Green, York YO1 2PX
Tel 01904 640500 Fax 01904 455711/455733

Staff

Chief Executive
G K Bruce (4)

Director (Policy)
J A Bainton (5)

Director (Finance)
A M Kerr (7)

Approvals Group

Director (Approvals)
Dr A D Martin (5)

Deputy Director (Approvals)
T E Tooby (6)

Responsibilities To protect consumers, users and the environment through the evaluation and approval of pesticides and the development of policies relating to them.

Number of staff 210

Department Ministry of Agriculture, Fisheries and Food

Launched 1 April 1993

Planning Inspectorate Agency

Tollgate House, Houlton Street, Bristol BS2 3NQ
Tel 01179 878927 Fax 01179 878769
Cathays Park, Cardiff CF1 3NQ
Tel 01222 823892 Fax 01222 825622

Staff

Chief Planning Inspector, Chief Executive
Chris Shepley (3)

Deputy Chief Planning Inspector
J Greenfield (4)

Assistant Chief Planning Inspectors
J T Graham (5)
R F Wilson (5)
Mrs S Bruton (5)
C A Jenkins (5)
J Acton (5)
D John (5)

Head of Planning Appeals Administration
Miss S Carter (5)

Director of Finance and Management Services
M Brasher (5)

Deputy Director of Finance and Management Services
M T Davey (6)

Information Systems
K Hoddee (7)

Responsibilities To carry out appeals and other casework involving planning, housing, environmental, highways and allied legislation

Number of staff 634

Department Environment and Wales

Launched 1 April 1992

Public Record Office

Ruskin Avenue, Kew, Richmond, Surrey TW9 4DU
Tel 0181-876 3444 Fax 0181-876 8905

Chancery Lane, London WC2A 1LR
Tel 0181-876 3444 Fax 0181-878 7231

Staff

Keeper of Public Records
Mrs S J Tyacke (3)

Director of Public Services
Dr E Hallam Smith (5)

Director of Government Services
N G Cox (5)

Director of Corporate Services
Dr D Simpson (5)

Responsibilities

Under the general direction of the Lord Chancellor the Public Record Office is responsible for the records of central government and the courts dating from the 14th century onwards.

It coordinates arrangements for the selection and disposal of public records, their safekeeping and their use by the public.

Records selected for preservation are normally transferred to the Public Record Office and made available for public inspection when they are thirty years old.

Number of staff 500

Department Lord Chancellor's Department

Launched 1 April 1992

Public Record Office of Northern Ireland

66 Balmoral Avenue, Belfast BT9 6NY
Tel 01232 661621 Fax 01232 665718

Staff	*Chief Executive* **Dr Anthony P Malcomson**
Responsibilities	Identifies and preserves Northern Ireland's archival heritage and ensures public access to that heritage which fully meets Open Government standards
Number of Staff	95
Department	Department of Environment for Northern Ireland
Launched	3 April 1995

Public Trust Office

Stewart House, 24 Kingsway, London WC2B 6JX
Tel 0171-269 7000 Fax 0171-831 0060

Staff

Chief Executive, Public Trustee and Accountant General of the Supreme Court
Ms Julia C Lomas

Assistant Public Trustee
Mrs S Hutcheson

Deputy Accountant General and Head of Trust and Funds Sector
F Eddy (6)

Head of Mental Health Sector
Mrs H Bratton (6)

Head of Establishments and Finance Sector
E A Bloomfield (6)

Chief Investment Manager
H Stevenson (6)

Responsibilities

To protect and manage the affairs of people with mental disability and provide a trustee and executorship service for the general public. The Office also provides a secure place of deposit for funds paid into court such as payments in satisfaction of debts.

Number of staff 586

Department Lord Chancellor's Department

Launched 1 July 1994

Queen Elizabeth II Conference Centre

Broad Sanctuary, London SW1P 3EE
Tel 0171-798 4000 Fax 0171-798 4200

Staff

Chief Executive
M C Buck

Commercial Director
Ms G Price

Finance and Personnel Director
D G Remington

Security Director
Group Captain D Reilly

Estates Director
G Booth

Responsibilities To provide and manage secure conference and banqueting facilities for national and international government meetings and to market the centre commercially for both private sector and government use

Number of staff 64

Department Environment

Launched 6 July 1989

Queen Victoria School

Dunblane, Perthshire FK15 0JY
Tel 01786 822288 Fax 0131-310 2519

Staff

Chief Executive and Head Master
Brian Raine

Bursar
Col (Retd) A Tapp

Responsibilities

To provide continuity of Scottish education in a stable boarding environment for the 10–18-year-old sons of Scottish servicemen and women, or those who have served in Scotland

To prepare them for entry to university, other higher or further education institutions, the armed services, professions, business or industry

Number of staff 74

Department Defence

Launched 1 April 1992

Radiocommunications Agency

Waterloo Bridge House, Waterloo Road, London SE1 8UA
Tel 0171-215 2150 Fax 0171-928 4309

Staff	*Chief Executive* **J Norton** *Heads of Branches* **M Goddard (5)** **R Louth (5)** **A Grilli (5)** **A D I Reed (5)** **B A Maxwell (5)** **R M Skiffins (5)**
Responsibilities	Most civil radio matters other than those concerned with telecommunications broadcasting policy and the radio equipment market To facilitate access to the radio spectrum for the widest range of services to promote competition, quality and choice. To ensure compliance by radio users with the Wireless Telegraphy Acts and other relevant legislation
Number of staff	541
Department	Trade and Industry
Launched	2 April 1990

RAF Maintenance Group Defence Agency

HQ Logistics Command, RAF Brampton, Huntingdon, Cambs PE18 8QL
Tel 01480 52151 Ext 6300 Fax 01480 451511 Ext 6309

Staff	*Chief Executive* **Air Vice-Marshal Richard H Kyle MBE (2*)†** *Air Commodore Defence Agency (Maintenance)* **Air Cdre J S Jones CBE (*)** *Head of Plans and Budgets (Maintenance Group)* **M Heritage-Owen (6)**
Responsibilities	To provide maintenance support to RAF fixed wing aircraft and the other Services To provide a comprehensive spares and materials storage and distribution system To provide specialist logistic services for all three services
Number of staff	9332
Department	Defence
Launched	1 April 1991

† 2*, * = armed forces ranking equivalent to Civil Service grades 3 and 5 respectively

RAF Signals Engineering Establishment

RAF Henlow, Bedfordshire SG16 6DN
Tel 01462 851515 Fax 01462 851515 ext 7687

Staff	*Chief Executive* **Air Commodore P C Ayee** *Directors* **Group Captain D R G Rennison** **M A Tyler** **A Palmer** **Wing Commander D E Eighteen**
Responsibilities	To provide a quick reaction signals engineering capability for military operations worldwide. This includes design, manufacture, installation and recovery over the full range of ground-based communications, radar and information and electronic systems and special avionic equipment for aircraft of the three services
Number of staff	1570
Department	Defence
Launched	22 November 1994

RAF Training Group Defence Agency

HQ Personnel and Training Command, RAF Innsworth, Gloucester GL3 1EZ
Tel 01452 712612 x5346 Fax 01452 510825 x5976

Staff	*Chief Executive* **Air Vice-Marshal J A G May CB CBE**
Responsibilities	Provides flying and ground training to meet the operational requirements of the RAF
Number of staff	8500
Department	Defence
Launched	1 April 1994

Rate Collection Agency (Northern Ireland)

Oxford House, 49/55 Chichester Street, Belfast BT1 4HH
Tel 01232 252252 Fax 01232 252113

Staff

Chief Executive
David Gallagher (6)

Responsibilities

To collect district rates on behalf of Northern Ireland's 26 district councils and the regional rate for the NI Department of Finance and Personnel

To administer the housing benefit scheme for those ratepayers who are owner-occupiers

Number of staff

270

Department

Department of the Environment for Northern Ireland

Launched

1 April 1991

Recruitment and Assessment Services Agency

Alencon Link, Basingstoke RG21 1JB
Tel 01256 29222 Fax 01256 846315

24 Whitehall, London SW1A 2ED
Tel 0171-210 6666 Fax 0171-210 6793

Staff

Chief Executive
Vacant

Director of Civil Service Selection Board Schemes
Acting Chief Executive
C A Muir (5)

Director of Selection Services Directorate
Vacant

Director of Research and Business Development
F D Bedford (6)

Director of Finance and Administration
Mrs J Lovegrove (6)

Responsibilities To provide a full range of professional recruitment and related services for government departments and agencies and the wider public sector

Number of staff 135

Department Cabinet Office (Office of Public Service and Science)

Launched 2 April 1991

Registers of Scotland

Meadowbank House, 153 London Road, Edinburgh EH8 7AU
Tel 0131-659 6111 Fax 0131-459 1221

Staff	*Chief Executive and Keeper* **Alan W Ramage (4)** *Deputy Keeper* **Alastair G Rennie (5)** *Deputy Chief Executive* **John K Mason**
Responsibilities	To maintain the public registers provided for the registration in Scotland of legal documents, in particular those deeds relating to rights in land, but also covering a wide range of deeds relating to succession, trusts, family agreements, state appointments and others
Number of staff	1100
Department	Scottish Office
Launched	6 April 1990

Royal Mint

Llantrisant, Pontyclun, Mid Glam CF7 8YT
Tel 01443 222111 Fax 01443 228799

7 Grosvenor Gardens, London SW1W 0BH
Tel 0171-828 8724 Fax 0171-630 6592

Staff

Master of the Mint
The Chancellor of the Exchequer

Deputy Master and Chief Executive
Roger de L Holmes

Director of Finance and Corporate Services and Deputy Chief Executive
D C Snell

Sales Director
A R Lotherington

Marketing Director
B D Williams

Director of Operations
R D Burchill (5)

Director of Personnel and Establishment Officer
C J J Boyle

Responsibilities The manufacture and distribution of UK and overseas circulating and commemorative coinage, medals and seals

Number of staff 991

Department The Royal Mint is a department in its own right. The Chief Executive is accountable to the Chancellor of the Exchequer

Launched 2 April 1990

Royal Parks

The Old Police House, Hyde Park, London W2 2UH
Tel 0171-298 2000 Fax 0171-298 2005

Staff	*Chief Executive* **David Welch** ***Park Managers*** *Central Parks* **Jennifer Adams** *Regent's Park* **David Caselton** *Richmond Park and Bushey Park* **Michael Fitt** *Greenwich Park* **Jim Buttress** *Estates Surveyor* **Alun Jones** *Head of Finance* **Alistair Bond** *Policy and Review* **Viviane Robertson** *Head of Procurement* **Joan Botfield** *Head of Royal Parks Constabulary* **Chief Officer W Ross** *Head of Personnel* **Mrs Ros Saper**
Responsibilities	To maintain and develop the Parks for public enjoyment
Number of staff	288
Department	National Heritage
Launched	1 April 1993

Scottish Agricultural Science Agency

East Craigs, Edinburgh EH12 8NJ
Tel 0131-244 8843 Fax 0131-244 8940

Staff

Director
Dr R K M Hay (5)

Heads of Divisions

Plant varieties and seeds
S R Cooper (Deputy Director) **(6)**

Pesticides and zoology
A D Ruthven (6)

Potato and plant health
W J Rennie (6)

Head of Administration
Ms V Glynn (7)

Responsibilities

To provide scientific information and advice on agricultural and horticultural crops and the environment. It also has statutory and regulatory functions in relation to plant health, bee health, plant variety registration and crop improvement, genetically manipulated organisms, and the protection of crops, food and the environment.

Number of staff

151

Department

Scottish Office Agriculture and Fisheries Department

Launched

1 April 1992

Scottish Court Service

Hayweight House, 23 Lauriston Street, Edinburgh EH3 9DQ
Tel 0131-229 9200 Fax 0131-221 6890

Staff

Chief Executive
M Ewart (4)

Deputy Chief Executive
I E Scott (5)

Responsibilities

Provision of staff, court houses and associated services for the Court of Session, the High Court of Justiciary and the 49 Sheriff Courts in Scotland

Number of staff

900

Department

Scottish Courts Administration

Launched

3 April 1995

Scottish Fisheries Protection Agency

Pentland House, 47 Robb's Loan, Edinburgh EH14 1TW
Tel 0131-556 8400 Fax 0131-244 6001

Staff	*Chief Executive* **A K MacLeod (5)** *Director, Corporate Strategy and Resources* **J B Roddin (6)** *Director of Operations* **R J Walker (6)** *Marine Superintendent* **Captain R Mill Irving (6)**
Responsibilities	Enforces UK, EC and international fisheries law and regulations in Scottish waters and ports to secure the conservation of fish stocks
Number of staff	263
Department	Scottish Office
Launched	12 April 1991

Scottish Office Pensions Agency

St Margaret's House, 151 London Road, Edinburgh EH8 7TG
Tel 0131-244 3585 Fax 0131-244 3334

Staff	*Chief Executive* **Norman MacLeod** *Director of Policy* **Gavin Mowat** *Director of Operations* **Alistair Small** *Director of Resources and Customer Service* **Jim Edgar**
Responsibilities	To regulate and administer public service pensions schemes for which the Secretary of State for Scotland is responsible
Number of staff	192
Department	The Scottish Office
Launched	1 April 1993

Scottish Prison Service

Calton House, 5 Redheughs Rigg, Edinburgh EH12 9HW
Tel 0131-556 8400 Fax 0131-244 8563

Staff

Chief Executive
E W Frizzell

Area Director, North and East
P Russell

Area Director, South and West
J Pearce

Director of Custody
P Withers

Strategy and Corporate Affairs Director
D A Stewart

Human Resources Director
J D Gallagher

Finance and Information Systems Director
W Pretswell

Responsibilities

To keep in custody those committed by the courts, maintain good order in each prison, care for prisoners with humanity and provide prisoners with a range of opportunities to exercise personal responsibility and prepare for release.

Number of staff

4451

Department

Scottish Office

Launched

1 April 1993

Scottish Record Office

HM General Register House, Edinburgh EH1 3YY
Tel 0131-535 1314 Fax 0131-535 1360

Officials

Keeper of the Records of Scotland
P M Cadell (5)

Deputy Keeper
Dr P D Anderson

Secretary, National Register of Archives (Scotland)
Dr I Barnes

Responsibilities

The Scottish Record Office is responsible for preserving the public records of Scotland and other records (including Church records and private archives) which have been transmitted to the Keeper of the Records of Scotland and for making them available for public inspection

The Office assists government departments and other public bodies and courts of law in Scotland with review of non-current records and advises local authorities over their records

The National Register of Archives (Scotland) surveys archives in private hands

Number of staff 137

Department Scottish Office

Founded Before 1286, but launched as an agency on 1 April 1993

Security Facilities Executive

St Christopher House, Southwark Street, London SE1 0TE
Tel 0171-921 4813 Fax 0171-921 4012

Staff

Chief Executive
John King (5)

Director, Finance and IT
Peter Jolly (7)

Director of Personnel
Barry Forrester (7)

Business Director, Government Car Service/ Inter-Despatch Service
Lavinia Allison (6)

Group Director, Special Services Group and Security Furniture Services
Martyn Sodergren (6)

Business Director, Custody Services
Mike Storey (7)

Head of Agency Planning
Nick Montague (7)

Responsibilities

Offers a comprehensive range of security related services covering: advice on electronic and physical security and explosive protection measures; the design, supply, installation, maintenance and repair of electronic security systems and equipment; the supply of new and renovated approved security furniture; a 24 hour guarding service; reception services; a full range of chauffeur and car hire services; and mail collection and delivery services including van service mainly in London, 1 hour motorbike courier service in Central London and a new nationwide service to be introduced in 1995/96

Number of staff 1225

Department Environment

Launched 15 October 1993

Social Security Agency (Northern Ireland)

Castle Buildings, Stormont, Belfast BT4 3SJ
Tel 01232 520520 Fax 01232 523337

Staff	**Chief Executive (3)**
	Finance Director (5)
	Personnel, Planning and Information Director (5)
	Central Operations Director (5)
	Local Operations Director (5)
Responsibilities	To administer the payment of social security benefits, and ensure compliance with the law relating to National Insurance and collecting contributions To provide benefits' processing services and to audit and store encashed social security payment orders for the Benefits Agency in Great Britain
Number of staff	5207
Department	Department of Health and Social Services for Northern Ireland
Launched	1 July 1991

Social Security Benefits Agency

Quarry House, Quarry Hill, Leeds LS2 7UA
Tel 01132 324000 Fax: telephone the SSBA for fax number

All personnel based at Quarry House unless otherwise indicated. For other addresses and telephone numbers see end of Benefits Agency section.

Staff

Acting Chief Executive
Ian Magee (2)*

Personal Assistant
Terry Moran (7)

Territorial and Personnel Director
Paul Murphy (4)

Managers
J Lutton (5)
J Parker (6)
M Pepper (6)
J Mason (5)

Finance Director
David Riggs (3)

Managers
P Brooke (5)
D Brown (5)
J Stuart (6)
D H Evans (6)
R Langford (6)
I Armstrong (6)

Territorial Directors:

Wales and Central England, Support Services Director
I Stewart (4)

I Watson (6)
B Butler (6)
P Chandler (6)

Southern Territory, Development Director
Ms A Cleveland (4)

A Stott (5)
J Sumner (6)

Scotland and Northern England, Benefits Director
Tony Laurance (3)

M Fisher (5)

Area Directors:

Benefits Agency Newcastle Benefits Directorates
S Godfrey (6)
G Goulding (6)
(all at Longbenton)

Fylde Benefits and War Pensions Directorate
M Coyne (5)
Mrs C Peters (6)
(all at Norcross)

Chief Medical Adviser, Director of Medical Services
Dr Peter Castaldi (3)

Principal Medical Officer
Dr David Findlay (4)

Contract Manager
Dr P Doughty (4)
(Warbreck House)

Business Development Manager
Dr M Aylward (4)
(Adelphi)

Personnel and Professional Development Manager
Dr C Hudson (4)
(Warbreck House)

Responsibilities To administer claims for and payments of social security benefits and war pensions

Number of staff 65,700

Department Social Security

Launched 2 April 1991

*Mr Magee is currently acting Chief Executive at the Social Security Benefits Agency until a new appointment is made, probably in early autumn 1995. He retains his job as Chief Executive of the Social Security Information Technology Services Agency

Social Security Benefits Agency Addresses

Adelphi
1-11 John Adam Street
London WC2N 6HT
Tel 0171-962 8000

DSS Longbenton
Newcastle upon Tyne NE98 1YX
Tel 0191-213 5000
Fax call above tel no and ask for relevant fax no

DSS Norcross
Blackpool
Lancashire FY5 3TA
Tel 01253 856123
Fax call above tel no and ask for relevant fax no

Warbreck House
Warbreck Hill
Blackpool
Lancs FY2 0YE
Tel 01253 856123

Social Security Child Support Agency

Millbank Tower, 21-24 Millbank, London SW1 4QU
Tel 0171-217 4486 Fax 0171-217 4766

Staff	*Chief Executive* **Miss Ann Chant** *Operations Director and Deputy Chief Executive* **Tony Ward** *Finance Director* **Derek Rutherford CBE** *Business Development and Support Director* **Peter Sharkey** *Policy Liaison Director* **John Hughes** *Personnel Director* **Ms Claudette Francis**
Responsibilities	The Agency operates the system created by the Child Support Act 1993 for the assessment, collection and enforcement of child maintenance
Number of staff	5500
Department	Social Security
Launched	April 1993

Social Security Contributions Agency

Longbenton, Newcastle upon Tyne NE98 1YX
Tel 0191-213 5000 Fax 0191-225 7380

Staff

Chief Executive
Faith Boardman (3)

Acting Chief Executive
George Bertram (5)

Acting Deputy Chief Executive
Director Information Services
and Business Planning
Steve Heminsley (5)

Acting Director
(Compliance and Education)
Charles Thomas (6)

Director (Finance and
Facilities Management)
Vacant (5)

Director of Facilities
Management
Keith Elliott (6)

Director (Personnel)
Ken Wilson (6)

Director (Central
Operations)
Robin J K Roberts OBE (6)

Non-Executive Director
John Wilson

Responsibilities

To collect and record National Insurance contributions

To maintain individual NI records

To provide an advisory service to the DSS, other government departments, the business community, members of the public and employers and contributors

Number of staff 10,527

Department Social Security

Launched 2 April 1991

Social Security Information Technology Services Agency

4th Floor, Verulam Point, Station Way, St Albans, Herts AL1 5HE
Tel 01727 815838 Fax 01727 833740

Staff

Chief Executive
Ian Magee (3)*

Departmental Information Technology Authority (DITA) Director
Kevin Caldwell (5)*

Planning and Headquarters Customer Director
Ursula Brennan (5)

BA Customer Director
Gordon Hextall (5)

Project Focus 1995 Director
George McCorkell (5)

Contributions Agency and Child Support Agency Customer Director
Norman Haighton (5)

Service Delivery Director
Peter Crahan (5)

Finance Director
John L Thomas (5)

Personnel Director
Steve Williams (5)

Non-Executive Director
Tom Drury

Responsibilities To develop, maintain and support computer systems which are used to administer the business of the DSS and its agencies and other customers within government

Number of staff 3800

Department Social Security

Launched 2 April 1990

*As well as being Chief Executive of SSITSA, Mr Magee is also acting Chief Executive of the Social Security Benefits Agency until a new appointment is made, probably in early autumn 1995. Kevin Caldwell will act as Chief Executive of SSITSA in Mr Magee's absence

Social Security Resettlement Agency

Euston Tower, 286 Euston Road, London NW1 3DN
Tel 0171-388 1188 Fax 0171-383 7199

Staff

Chief Executive
Paul Winstanley (6)

Responsibilities

To operate hostels for single homeless people with an unsettled way of life and at the same time to disengage the Government from the direct management of the hostels either by replacing them with more appropriate facilities or by making capital and revenue grants available to voluntary organisations and local authorities who may wish to purchase them and provide similar resettlement services.

The Agency will close on 31 March 1996 and its residual function of grant-aiding and monitoring organisations will revert to the Department of Social Security

Number of staff 170

Department Social Security

Launched 24 May 1989

Social Security War Pensions Agency

Norcross, Blackpool, Lancs FY5 3WP
Tel 01253 858858 Fax 01253 330561

Staff

Chief Executive
Peter Mathison

Director of Finance and Planning
Ian Little (6)

Personnel Manager
John W Ashton (7)

Operations Manager
Derek Clarke (7)

Business Implementation Manager
John R Sheppard (7)

Welfare Services Manager
Keith Briars (7)

Customer Services/General Sections Manager
Peter Hulme (7)

Information Technology Manager
Mrs Lesley Plank (7)

Responsibilities The assessment of war pensions, the welfare service for war pensioners and the Ilford Park Polish Home in Devon

Number of staff 1646

Department Social Security

Launched April 1994

Student Awards Agency for Scotland

Gyleview House, 3 Redheughs Rigg, Edinburgh EH12 9HH
Tel 0131-244 5823 Fax 0131-244 5887

Staff *Chief Executive*
Ken MacRae

Responsibilities Administers the Students' Allowances Scheme, the Post-Graduate Students' Allowances Scheme, the Scottish Studentships Scheme and the Nursing and Midwifery Bursary Scheme in Scotland

Number of staff 145

Department Scottish Office

Launched 5 April 1994

Teachers' Pensions Agency (TPA)

Mowden Hall, Staindrop Road, Darlington DL3 9EE
Tel 01325 392929 Fax 01325 392216

Staff	*Chief Executive* **Mrs D Metcalfe (5)**
Responsibilities	To administer the teachers' superannuation scheme (a contributory pension scheme for full and part-time teachers employed in England and Wales)
Number of staff	385
Department	Education
Launched	1 April 1992

Training and Employment Agency (Northern Ireland)

Clarendon House, 9–21 Adelaide Street, Belfast BT2 8DJ
Tel 01232 541541 Fax 01232 541543

Staff

Chairman
S J Spence

Chief Executive
J S Crozier (3)

Deputy Chief Executive
I Walters (4)

Director Corporate Services Division
C Thompson (5)

Director, Preparation for Work, Regional Operations Division
D Noble (5)

Director, Preparation for Work, Programme Development and Support Division
N Carson (5)

Director, Business Support Division
I Walters (5)

Director of Training Centres Division
T Scott (5)

Responsibilities To provide employment and training services in Northern Ireland

Number of staff 1305

Department Department of Economic Development for Northern Ireland

Launched 1 April 1990

Transport Research Laboratory

Old Wokingham Road, Crowthorne, Berkshire RG11 6AU
Tel 01344 773131 Fax 01344 770356

Staff

Chief Executive
Professor John Wootton (3)

Deputy Chief Executive
Dr Richard Hinsley (4)

Research Director
Dr Phil Bly (5)

Business Director
Garth Clarke (5)

Finance Director
David Goody (5)

Resource Director
Eric Gould (5)

Responsibilities To conduct and manage the Department of Transport's transport research and provide advice on scientific, technical and other matters in the transport field

Number of staff 416

Department Transport

Launched 1 April 1992

The Secretary of State has announced that he expects to privatise the TRL during 1995-96

Valuation and Lands Agency (NI)

Queen's Court, 56-66 Upper Queen Street, Belfast BT1 6FD
Tel 01232 439303 Fax 01232 235897

Staff

Chief Executive and Commissioner of Valuation
D J Bell (3)

Assistant Commissioners:

Client Services Division
G L Hughes (5)

Rating Valuation Division
N D Woods (5)

Finance and Personnel Division
J J Herron (5)

Responsibilities

To provide and maintain the Valuation List for rating purposes in Northern Ireland

To provide a comprehensive advisory service to government departments and statutory bodies on all aspects of the valuation of land and buildings, including negotiation of compensation, fixing rents, disposal of surplus land and property management

To provide Northern Ireland ministers with advice on matters relating to land management and valuation

Number of staff 312

Department Department of Finance and Personnel for Northern Ireland

Launched 1 April 1993

Valuation Office Agency

New Court, Carey Street, London WC2A 2JE
Tel 0171-324 1183/1057 Fax 0171-324 1073

Staff

Chief Executive
A J Langford (2)

Deputy Chief Executive
R J Pawley (3)

Chief Valuer, Scotland
A MacLaren (5)

Management Divisions

Director, Operations
P Upton (4)

Director, Marketing and Customer Services
R A Dales (4)

Director, Finance and Planning
D K Park (5)

Director, Personnel and IT
J H Ebdon (5)

Technical Divisions

Land Services and Taxation
W J Reed (5)

Revaluation and Council Tax
B J Jones (5)

Rating
P Sanderson (5)

Crown Property Unit,
Valuer-in-Charge
C J Brooks (6)

Responsibilities

To provide land and buildings valuation services to government departments, other public bodies and a number of local authorities

Number of staff	5900
Department	Inland Revenue
Launched	30 September 1991

Vehicle Certification Agency

1 Eastgate Office Centre, Eastgate Road, Bristol BS5 6XX
Tel 01179 515151 Fax 01179 524103

Staff

Chief Executive
Derek W Harvey (5)

Deputy Chief Executive
P F Nicholl (6)

Head of Compliance Systems
D Porritt (7)

Head of Finance and Business Support
L W Andrews (7)

Head of Test Operations
A W Stenning (7)

Responsibilities To test and certificate vehicles (and vehicle parts) to UK and international standards

Number of staff 75

Department Transport

Launched 2 April 1990

Vehicle Inspectorate

Berkeley House, Croydon Street, Bristol BS5 0DA
Tel 01179 543200 Fax 01179 543212

Staff

Chief Executive
Ron Oliver (4)

Deputy Chief Executive and
Head of Road Transport Enforcement Division
J A T David (5)

Head of Vehicle Testing Division
and Operations Director
R D Tatchell (6)

Head of Customer and Technical Services,
Road Transport Enforcement Division
H G Edwards (6)

Head of Corporate Affairs Division
and Finance Director
J A Belt (6)

Responsibilities

To carry out annual testing and inspection of heavy goods vehicles, public service vehicles and light goods vehicles

To administer and supervise the MOT testing scheme for motorcycles, cars and light goods vehicles

To carry out operator licensing and enforcement including checks on vehicle weights and drivers' hours

To investigate serious accidents and vehicle defects and oversee vehicle recall campaigns

Number of staff 1800

Department Transport

Launched 1 August 1988

Veterinary Medicines Directorate

Woodham Lane, New Haw, Addlestone, Surrey KT15 3NB
Tel 01932 336911 Fax 01932 336618

Staff	*Chief Executive and Director of Veterinary Medicines* **Dr J Michael Rutter (4)** *Director (Policy and Finance)* **C J Lawson (5)** *Director (Licensing)* **D K N Woodward (5)**
Responsibilities	To license and control the manufacture and marketing of animal medicines To provide post licensing surveillance of suspected adverse reactions and veterinary residues in meat To provide policy advice on these matters to the Agriculture and Health ministers in the UK
Number of staff	100
Department	Agriculture, Fisheries and Food
Launched	2 April 1990

Wilton Park Conference Centre

Wiston House, Steyning, Sussex BN44 3DZ
Tel 01903 815020 Fax 01903 815931

Staff

Chief Executive
Richard T B Langhorne

Manager
John Melser

Responsibilities

To organise conferences on international affairs for politicians, officials, academics and others from around the world

It is also hired out on commercial terms to government departments, business and other users

Number of staff

32

Department

Foreign and Commonwealth Office

Launched

1 September 1991

Regulatory Organisations and Public Bodies

This section includes 103 regulatory organisations and other public bodies ranging from OFTEL and the Civil Aviation Authority to the Boundary Commissions and parliamentary and other ombudsmen. New organisations in this edition are as follows:

Advisory Committee on Business Appointments of Crown Servants
Committee on Standards in Public Life
Funding Agency for Schools
Intelligence Services Tribunal
Prisons' Ombudsman
Scottish Prisons' Complaints Commission
Teacher Training Agency

The Revenue Adjudicator's Office now has the additional responsibility for investigating complaints against HM Customs and Excise and the Contributions Agency. It has been renamed the **Office of the Adjudicator for the Inland Revenue, Customs and Excise and the Contributions Agency**.

Advertising Standards Authority

Brook House, 2 Torrington Place, London WC1E 7HW
Tel 0171-580 5555 Fax 0171-631 3051

Officials

Chairman
The Rt Hon Lord Rodgers of Quarry Bank

Director General
Matti Alderson

Press Officer
Caroline Crawford

Responsibilities

To regulate the content of advertising in non-broadcast media in the United Kingdom

To supervise the British codes of advertising and sales promotion

Founded

1962

Advisory Committee on Business Appointments of Crown Servants

c/o Cabinet Office, 70 Whitehall, London SW1A 2AS
Tel 0171-270 0466 Fax 0171-270 0623

Members

Chairman
The Rt Hon The Lord Carlisle of Bucklow QC

Deputy Chairman
The Lord Bridges GCMG

Members
Sir John Blelloch KCB
Sir Denys Henderson
Sir Charles Huxtable KCB CBE
Sir Robin Ibbs KBE
The Rt Hon Peter Shore MP
The Rt Hon The Lord Thomson of Monifieth KT

Secretary
J K Barron

Responsibilities

The Committee considers applications from the two most senior grades of the civil service, and from the equivalent ranks and grades in the armed forces and the diplomatic service, under the rules governing the acceptance of outside appointments by former Crown servants. The Advisory Committee makes recommendations to the Prime Minister (to the Foreign Secretary in respect of the diplomatic service) who decides the outcome of each application

Founded

July 1975

Advisory, Conciliation and Arbitration Service

27 Wilton Street, London SW1X 7AZ
Tel 0171-210 3000 Fax 0171-210 3708

Officials

Chairman of Council
John Hougham

Personal Secretary
Miss J Simmons
071-210 3670

Chief Conciliation Officer
J D Evans (4)

Directors
H Canter (5)
P Syson (5)
F Noonan (5)

Responsibilities

A general duty to promote the improvement of industrial relations

To prevent and resolve disputes by fostering constructive relationships between employers, employees and trade unions; and by providing conciliation, arbitration and mediation

To help ensure that statutory protections, rights and obligations of individual employees are assured fairly and effectively; and to promote the settlement of complaints by conciliation

To provide information and advice on industrial relations and employment policies

Founded

1974 and then under the provisions of the Employment Protection Act 1975

Audit Commission for Local Authorities and the NHS in England and Wales

1 Vincent Square, London SW1P 2PN
Tel 0171-828 1212 Fax 0171-976 6187
Nicholson House, Lime Kiln Close, Stoke Gifford, Bristol BS12 6SU
Tel 01179 236757 Fax 01179 794100

Officials

Chairman
Sir David Cooksey
(until 31 August 1995)

Deputy Chairman
Clive Thompson

Commissioners
Sir Terence English
John Foster
Cllr David Heath CBE
Sir Donald Irvine
Kate Jenkins
Sir Peter Kemp
Jeremy Orme
Helena Shovelton
Peter Soulsby
Iris Tarry
Tony Travers
Ron Watson
Clive Wilkinson
Peter Wood

Controller
Andrew Foster (2)

Director, Health Studies
Dr Jonathan Boyce

Chief Executive
District Audit
David Prince

Director, Audit Support
S Nicklen

Director, Local Government Studies
Vacant

Director, Resources
W D Ogley

Director, Purchasing
M Bickerstaff

Responsibilities	To appoint auditors to local authorities and health authorities and to help authorities to bring about improvements in efficiency, directly through the auditing process and through the 'value for money' studies which the Commission carries out. The auditors appointed may be the District Audit Service or private firms of accountants The Commission members include senior people from industry, local government, the accounting profession and the trade unions
Founded	1983 under the provisions of the Local Government Finance Act 1982 and amended by the NHS and Community Care Act 1990

Bank of England

Threadneedle Street, London EC2R 8AH
Tel 0171-601 4444 Fax 0171-601 4471

Officials

Governor
E A J George

Deputy Governor
Howard Davies
(from September 1995)

Directors
Sir David Cooksey
Frances Heaton
Sir Christopher Hogg
Pen Kent
Sir Chips Keswick
Mervyn King
Sir David Lees
Sheila Masters
Sir Jeremy Morse KCMG
Ian Plenderleith
Brian Quinn
Sir David Scholey CBE
Neville Simms
David Simon CBE
Professor Sir Roland Smith
Sir Colin Southgate

Secretary
J R E Footman

Responsibilities

As the central bank of the UK, the Bank of England has three main objectives:

To maintain the value of the nation's money, mainly through policies and market operations agreed with the government

To ensure the soundness of the financial system, including direct supervision of banks and participants in some city financial markets

To promote the efficiency and competitiveness of the financial system, notably in the field of domestic and international payment and settlement systems

The Bank offers a range of services to its customers (the government, the clearing banks, other central banks and members of the staff) such as cheques, accounts, foreign exchange transactions, gold bullion deposits, and in the case of staff members, normal banking services

It is also responsible for:
The design, production and issue of banknotes in England and Wales

Government borrowing (in the form of Treasury bills, gilts and foreign currency borrowing)

Advising on the terms of new debt, and managing the stock of existing debt

Founded

1694 by Act of Parliament and Royal Charter. It was nationalised in 1946 and a new Royal Charter granted.

It is governed by a Court of Directors, all of whom are appointed by the Crown

Boundary Commission for England

St Catherine's House, 10 Kingsway, London WC2B 6JP
Tel 0171-396 2105 Fax 0171-396 2253

Officials

Chairman
The Speaker of the House of Commons

Deputy Chairman
The Hon Mr Justice Knox

Commission Members
Miss S C Cameron
D D Macklin

Joint Secretaries
R McLeod (6)
G Utteridge (7)

Responsibilities

To review parliamentary constituencies and European parliamentary constituencies in England

Founded

1944 under the provisions of the House of Commons (Redistribution of Seats) Act 1944. Currently constituted under the Parliamentary Constituencies Act 1986

Boundary Commission for Northern Ireland

Frances House, 9/11 Brunswick Street, Belfast BT2 7GE
Tel 01232 321292 Fax 01232 321294

Officials

Chairman
The Speaker of the House of Commons

Deputy Chairman
The Hon Mr Justice Pringle

Secretary
J R Fisher (7)

Commission Members
D J Clement
P G Duffy

Responsibilities

To review parliamentary constituencies in Northern Ireland and report on the number of members to be returned by each constituency to any future Northern Ireland Assembly

Founded

1944 under the provisions of the House of Commons (Redistribution of Seats) Act 1944. Currently constituted under the Parliamentary Constituencies Act 1986 and the Boundary Commissions Act 1992

Boundary Commission for Scotland

St Andrew's House, Edinburgh EH1 3DE
Tel 0131-244 2196/2027 Fax 0131-244 2683

Officials

Chairman
The Speaker of the House of Commons

Deputy Chairman
The Hon Lord Davidson

Secretary
D K C Jeffrey (7)

Commission Members
Dr C M Glennie
Professor U A Wannop

Responsibilities

To review parliamentary constituencies and European parliamentary constituencies in Scotland

Founded

1944 under the provisions of the House of Commons (Redistribution of Seats) Act 1944. Currently constituted under the Parliamentary Constituencies Act 1986 and the Boundary Commissions Act 1992

Boundary Commission for Wales

St Catherine's House, 10 Kingsway, London WC2B 6JP
Tel 0171-396 2105 Fax 0171-396 2253

Officials

Chairman
The Speaker of the House of Commons

Deputy Chairman
The Rt Hon Lord Justice Pill

Commission Members
W P Davey
M A McLaggan

Joint Secretaries
R McLeod (6)
G Utteridge (7)

Responsibilities

To review parliamentary constituencies and European parliamentary constituencies in Wales

Founded

1944 under the provisions of the House of Commons (Redistribution of Seats) Act 1944. Currently constituted under the Parliamentary Constituencies Act 1986

Broadcasting Complaints Commission

Grosvenor Gardens House, 35-37 Grosvenor Gardens, London SW1W 0BS
Tel 0171-630 1966 Fax 0171-828 7316

Members

Chairman of Commission
The Reverend Canon Peter Pilkington

Members
Donald Allen CMG
Tony Christopher CBE
Ms Danielle Barr
Ms Jane Leighton

Officials

Secretary
Robert Hargreaves

Responsibilities

To consider and adjudicate upon complaints of
- unjust or unfair treatment in sound or television programmes
- unwarranted infringement of privacy in, or in connection with the obtaining of material included in, such programmes

Founded

1981 under the provisions of the Broadcasting Act 1980. Now operates under the provisions of the Broadcasting Act of 1990

Broadcasting Standards Council

7 The Sanctuary, London SW1P 3JS
Tel 0171-233 0544 Fax 0171-233 0397

Council Members

Chairman
Lady Howe

Deputy Chairman
Lord Dubs

Members
Dr Jean Curtis-Raleigh
Robert Kernohan OBE
The Rev John Lang
Ms Sally O'Sullivan
Matthew Parris
Rhiannon Bevan

Officials

Director
Colin Shaw CBE (3)

Deputy Director
Norman McLean

Research Director
Andrea Millwood Hargrave

Press and Programmes Officer
Clare Reynolds

Responsibilities

To consider the portrayal of violence, sexual conduct and matters of taste and decency in television and radio programmes and broadcast advertisements

To consider and make findings on complaints, to monitor programmes, to undertake relevant research, to draw up a Code of Practice, and consult on developments in Europe concerning the future regulation of transfrontier broadcasting

Founded

Established as a non-statutory body in 1988; became a statutory body in 1991 under the provisions of the Broadcasting Act 1990

Building Societies Ombudsman

Grosvenor Gardens House, 35-37 Grosvenor Gardens, London SW1X 7AW
Tel 0171-931 0044 Fax 0171-931 8485

Officials

Chairman of the Council
Lord Barnett

Registrar to the Council
Kevin Shears

Ombudsman
Brian Murphy

Office Manager
Mrs Barbara Cheney

Responsibilities To settle complaints by customers against building societies

Founded 1987 under the provisions of the Building Societies Act 1986

Charity Commission

St Alban's House, 57-60 Haymarket, London SW1Y 4QX
Tel 0171-210 4477 Fax 0171-930 9173

Officials

Chief Commissioner
R J Fries (3)

Commissioner, Head of Legal Staff
R M C Venables (3)

Commissioners
J Farquharson (4)
Mrs D H Yeo (4)
M Webber (4)

Commissioners (part-time)
Tessa Baring
John Bonds

Secretary, Executive Director
Mrs E Shaw (4)
0171-210 4414

Controller of Operations
V F Mitchell (5)

Official Custodian
M Fry (7)

Senior Legal Staff
K M Dibble (5)
G S Goodchild (5)
J Dutton (5)
S Slack (5)

Head of External Relations
Andrew Crook (6)

Responsibilities

To maintain a register of charities in England and Wales

To encourage the development of better administration

To investigate and check abuses

Founded

1853 under the provisions of the Charitable Trusts Act 1853

Citizen's Charter Advisory Panel

Horse Guards Road, London SW1T 3AL
Tel 0171-270 6425 Fax 0171-270 6362

Members

Chairman
Sir James Blyth

Members
Anne Galbraith
Angela Heylin
Neil Johnson
The Baroness Perry of Southwark
Dr Madsen Pirie
Nick Rawlings
Lady Wilcox

Officials

Director of the Citizen's Charter Unit
Miss E C Turton

Secretary
Pauline Garnett

Responsibilities

To raise the standards of public service by developing the Citizen's Charter initiative

Founded

1991 as part of the Citizen's Charter initiative

Civil Aviation Authority

CAA House, 45/59 Kingsway, London WC2B 6TE
Tel 0171-379 7311 Fax 0171-240 1153

Officials

Chairman
The Rt Hon Christopher Chataway

Managing Director
Tom Murphy CBE

Secretary and Legal Adviser
R J Britton

Members
C Paice
D J McLauchlan
M J Willett
R Birdseye
R Sturt
Captain G Gray
L W Priestley
Ms A Burdus
A Blackman
R Lynch
Air Vice-Marshal J Brownlow CB OBE AFC

Responsibilities

The safety and economic regulation of British civil aviation and provision of air traffic services in UK airspace jointly with the Ministry of Defence

Founded

1972 under the provisions of the Civil Aviation Act 1971

Commission for Local Administration in England (Local Government Ombudsman)

21 Queen Anne's Gate, London SW1H 9BU
Tel 0171-915 3210 Fax 0171-233 0396

Officials

Chairman
E B C Osmotherly CB
(Local Government Ombudsman for London, Kent, Surrey, East Sussex and West Sussex)

Vice-Chairman
Mrs P A Thomas
(Local Government Ombudsman for East Midlands and North of England)

Members
J White
(Local Government Ombudsman for South West, South, West and most of Central England)

Parliamentary Commissioner
W K Reid CB *(ex officio)*

Secretary
G D Adams

Responsibilities

To investigate complaints of injustice arising from maladministration by local authorities and certain other bodies

Founded

1974 under the provisions of the Local Government Act 1974

Commissioner for Local Administration in Scotland (Local Government Ombudsman)

23 Walker Street, Edinburgh EH3 7HX
Tel 0131-225 5300 Fax 0131-225 9495

Officials

Commissioner
Frederick C Marks OBE

Deputy Commissioner, Secretary
Janice H Renton

Responsibilities

To investigate complaints from members of the public of injustice attributed to maladministration in local government

Founded

1975 under the provisions of the Local Government Scotland Act 1975

Commission for Local Administration in Wales (Local Government Ombudsman)

Derwen House, Court Road, Bridgend, Mid Glamorgan CF31 1BN
Tel 01656 661325 Fax 01656 658317

Officials

Local Commissioner
E R Moseley

Parliamentary Commissioner
W K Reid CB *(ex officio)*

Secretary to the Commission
D Bowen

Responsibilities

To consider complaints of maladministration made against local authorities in Wales

Founded

1974 under the provisions of the Local Government Act 1974

Commission for Racial Equality

Elliot House, 10-12 Allington Street, London SW1E 5EH
Tel 0171-828 7022 Fax 0171-630 7605

Officials

Executive Chairman
Herman Ouseley

Deputy Chairmen
Ranjit Sondhi
Tony Ward

Commissioners
Dr M C K Chan MBE
Dr Raj Chandran
Ms M Cunningham
M Hastings
H Harris
M Jogee
Dr Z Khan
Mrs Z Manzoor
Dr D Neil
B Purkiss
A Rose OBE
Dr J Singh

Executive Director
Sukhdev Sharma

Responsibilities

To promote equality of opportunity and good relations between different racial groups

To work towards elimination of discrimination

Founded

1977 under the provisions of the Race Relations Act 1976

Committee on Standards in Public Life

Horse Guards Road, London SW1P 3AL
Tel 0171-270 5875 Fax 0171-270 5874

Officials and Members

Chairman
The Rt Hon The Lord Nolan

Members
Sir Clifford Boulton GCB
Sir Martin Jacomb
Professor Anthony King
The Rt Hon Tom King CH MP
The Rt Hon Peter Shore MP
The Rt Hon the Lord Thompson of Monifieth KT DL
Sir William Utting CB
Dame Anne Warburton DCVO CMG
Diana Warwick

Secretary
Alan Riddell

Press Secretary
Peter Rose

Responsibilities

To examine current concerns about standards of conduct of all holders of public office, including arrangements relating to financial and commercial activities, and make recommendations as to any changes in present arrangements which might be required to ensure the highest standards of propriety in public life

For these purposes public office should include:

- ministers, civil servants and advisers;
- Members of Parliament and UK Members of the European Parliament;
- members and senior officers of all non-departmental public bodies and NHS bodies;
- non-Ministerial office holders;
- members and other senior officers of other bodies discharging publicly-funded functions; and
- elected members and senior officers of local authorities.

The committee does not investigate individual allegations of misconduct

Founded

October 1994

Council for Science and Technology

Albany House, 84/86 Petty France, London SW1H 9ST
Tel 0171-271 2105 Fax 0171-271 2028

Officials and Members

Chairman
The Rt Hon David Hunt MBE MP

Deputy Chairman
Vacant

Members
Professor S Kumar Bhattacharyya
Professor Sir Aaron Klug
Sir Robin Nicholson
Dr Bridget Ogilvie
Sir Ralph Robins
Dr Alan Rudge OBE
Professor Sir Stewart Sutherland
Sir Richard Sykes
John Towers
Dr Peter Williams CBE

Office of Science and Technology Secretariat
Mrs Helen Williams
Chris de Grouchy
Philip Dale

Responsibilities

To advise the government on science, engineering and technology issues central to the success of the United Kingdom, drawing as appropriate on the findings of the technology foresight programme

To advise the government on the balance and direction of government funded science, engineering and technology, taking account of international developments; and to advise the forward look of government funded science, engineering and technology

Founded

The formation of the Council was announced in the Government White Paper on Science, Engineering and Technology *Realising our Potential*, published in May 1993. The Council first met in November 1993

Council on Tribunals

22 Kingsway, London WC2B 6LE
Tel 0171-936 7045 Fax 0171-936 7044

Council Members

Chairman
The Rt Hon The Lord Archer of Sandwell QC
T N Biggart CBE WS *(Chairman, Scottish Committee)*
Mrs A Anderson
G A Anderson
M B Dempsey
Mrs S Friend MBE
C Heaps
B Hill CBE
Professor M J Hill
W N Hyde
R H Jones CVO
Professor T M Partington
I D Penman CB
Dr C A Kaplan
L F Read QC
W K Reid CB *(Parliamentary Commissioner for Administration)*

Officials

Secretary
J D Saunders (5)

Secretary (Scottish Committee)
Mrs A Scotland

Responsibilities

Tribunals cover a variety of subjects, including agriculture, immigration, employment, pensions, road traffic, social security, taxation and the allocation of school places. Examples include industrial tribunals which deal with alleged unfair dismissals and social security appeal tribunals which deal with disputes regarding benefits

The Council's main functions are:

To keep under review the constitution and working of some 70 tribunals which have been placed under its general supervision

To consider and report on administrative procedures relating to statutory inquiries, ie those set up as a result of situations specified in acts of parliament as needing such inquiries

To advise government departments on proposals for legislation affecting tribunals and inquiries, and on proposals where the need for an appeal procedure may arise

Members of the Council are appointed by the Lord Chancellor and the Lord Advocate

Founded

1958 and now operates under the provisions of the Tribunals and Inquiries Act 1992

Criminal Injuries Compensation Board and Authority

Morley House, 26-30 Holborn Viaduct, London EC1A 2JQ
Tel 0171-842 6800 Fax 0171-436 0804

Tay House, 300 Bath Street, Glasgow G2 4JR
Tel 0141-331 2726 Fax 0141-353 3148/331 2287

Officials

Chairman
Lord Carlisle of Bucklow QC

Director
P G Spurgeon (5)

Senior Solicitor
Mrs A M Johnstone (6)

Operations Manager
J S Lawson (7)

Responsibilities

The Criminal Injuries Compensation Board administers a scheme for financially compensating victims of crimes of violence and people injured while arresting an offender or preventing an offence.

A new body was set up in April 1994, the Criminal Injuries Compensation Authority, which now deals with all applications for compensation and operates the new Tariff Scheme. Most staff are common to both the Board and Authority and will operate from the same premises.

The Tariff Scheme provides for an independent appeals process which is to be run by the Criminal Injuries Compensation Appeals Panel whose chairman is Michael Lewer QC.

The CICB and CICA will coexist until such time as the Secretary of State may direct that the Board will cease to exist and transfer any remaining records.

Founded

1964 by the Home Secretary and Secretary of State for Scotland under the prerogative powers of the crown

Defence, Press and Broadcasting Advisory (DA Notices) Committee

Room 2235, Ministry of Defence, Main Building
London SW1A 2HB
Tel 0171-218 2206 Fax 0171-218 5857

Members

Chairman
R C Mottram

Vice-Chairman and Chairman
Press and Broadcasting Side
A C D Stuart (nominated by the Newspaper Society)

Government Members
Richard Wilson CB
Moray Stewart CB
Sir Timothy Daunt KCMG

Press and Broadcasting Members
R Ayre (British Broadcasting Corporation)
J D Bishop (Periodical Publishers Association)
T H S Cole (Sky Television)
G Elliott (Newspaper Society)
B Hitchen CBE (Newspaper Publishers Association)
A S M Hutchinson (Newspaper Publishers Association)
R Hutchinson (Periodical Publishers Association)
S Kuttner (Newspaper Publishers Association)
A J Macdonald (Nominated by Independent Television)
S Purvis (Independent Television News)
C T Webb (Press Association)
R J Williamson (Scottish Daily Newspaper Society)

Secretary
Rear Admiral D M Pulvertaft CB

Deputy Secretary
Commander F N Ponsonby LVO OBE Royal Navy

Responsibilities

The Defence, Press and Broadcasting Advisory Committee oversees the voluntary code which operates between those government departments which have responsibilities for national security and the media; using as its vehicle the DA Notice system.

DA Notices provide general guidance to national and provincial newspaper editors, to periodical editors, to radio and television organisations and to some book publishers. They describe those areas which the Government considers it has a duty to protect and invite editors, directors and publishers to consult the DA Notice Secretary whenever there may be doubt.

Founded 1912. The D notice system was restructured in 1982 following a House of Commons Defence Committee review. A further review in 1992-3 resulted in the change from Defence Notices to Defence Advisory Notices and the present committee title.

Drinking Water Inspectorate

Room B155, Romney House, 43 Marsham Street, London SW1P 3PY
Tel 0171-276 8808 Fax 0171-276 8405

Officials

Chief Inspector
Michael Rouse

Deputy Chief Inspector
Owen Hydes

Superintending Inspector
Tony Lloyd

Principal Inspectors
David Drury
Dr John Gray
Tony Hallas
Milo Purcell
Richard Vincent
Mike Waite
Dr David Westwood
Peter White

Responsibilities

The main task of the Inspectorate is to check that water companies supply wholesome water and meet the requirements of the water quality regulations. If standards are breached it initiates action to ensure that remedial measures are taken.

Founded

2 January 1990 under powers in the Water Act 1989, since consolidated into the Water Industry Act 1991

Economic and Social Research Council

Polaris House, North Star Avenue, Swindon SN2 1UJ
Tel 01793 413000 Fax 01793 413001

Officials

Chairman
Dr Bruce Smith OBE

Chief Executive
Professor Ronald Amann

Responsibilities

To support and encourage research in the social sciences

To make grants to students for postgraduate study and training in economic and social research

To provide advice and information about the social sciences

Founded

1965 by Royal Charter

English Partnerships

(Set up under statute as the Urban Regeneration Agency)

3 The Parks, Lodge Lane, Newton-le-Willows, Merseyside WA12 0JQ
Tel 0194-229 6900 Fax 0194-229 6927

Officials and Staff

Chairman
Lord Walker of Worcester PC MBE

Deputy Chairman
Sir Idris Pearce CBE TD DL

Chief Executive
David Taylor

Board Members
Michael Carr
Bill Jordan CBE
Stephen Massey
Dennis Stevenson CBE
Paula Hay-Plumb
David Taylor

Finance and Administration Director
Paula Hay-Plumb

Development Director
Mike Appleton

Head of Personnel and Agency Secretary
Stan Kirton

Head of Corporate Relations
Barbara Riddell

Responsibilities

To help create new and lasting employment opportunities, improve the environment, attract inward investment, stimulate local enterprise, and bring vacant, derelict and contaminated land throughout England, back into productive use

Founded

1993 through part III of the Leasehold Reform, Housing and Urban Development Act

Equal Opportunities Commission

Overseas House, Quay Street, Manchester M3 3HN
Tel 0161-833 9244 Fax 0161-835 1657

Officials

Chairwoman
Kamlesh Bahl

Deputy Chairwoman
Diana Brittan

Commissioners
Mary Berg
Noreen Bray
Robert Fleeman
Anne Gibson
Richard Grayson
Barbara Kelly
Clive Mather
Peter Smith
Dr Joan Stringer
Anne Watts
Cecilia Wells

Chief Executive
Peter Naish

Deputy Chief Executive
Susan Atkins

Head of Operations
Frank Spencer

Legal Adviser
Alan Lakin

Responsibilities

To keep under review the working of the Sex Discrimination Act and the Equal Pay Act

To promote the equality of opportunity between men and women

To work towards the elimination of unlawful sex and marriage discrimination

Founded

1976 under the provisions of the Sex Discrimination Act 1975

Financial Reporting Council

Holborn Hall, 100 Gray's Inn Road, London WC1X 8AL
Tel 0171-404 8818 Fax 0171-404 4497

Members

Chairman
Sir Sydney Lipworth QC

Deputy Chairmen
John Kemp-Welch
Roger Lawson
Sir Bryan Nicholson

There are 26 other members and observers

Officials

Secretary
Sydney Treadgold

Responsibilities

To promote good financial reporting

The FRC is the overarching and facilitating body for making appointments to, and providing guidance and support for, its operational bodies: the **Accounting Standards Board** (see below) and the **Financial Reporting Review Panel** (see below)

These three bodies are not government controlled but have its strong support. The Chairman and the three deputy chairmen of the FRC are appointed by the Secretary of State for Trade and Industry and the Governor of the Bank of England

Founded

1990 following the report of the Review Committee on the Making of Accounting Standards. Related provisions were introduced into company law by the Companies Act 1989

Financial Reporting Council: Accounting Standards Board

Holborn Hall, 100 Gray's Inn Road, London WC1X 8AL
Tel 0171-404 8818 Fax 0171-404 4497

Board Members

Chairman
Sir David Tweedie

Technical Director
Allan Cook

Members
David Allvey
Ian Brindle
Michael Garner
Raymond Hinton
Huw Jones
Professor Geoffrey Whittington
Ken Wild

Observers

Professor Andrew Likierman
Sarah Brown
Professor Robert Jack CBE

Secretary
Michael Butcher

Responsibilities

To make, amend and withdraw accounting standards

Prescribed by Statutory Instrument 1990 No 1667 for this purpose

Founded

1990, taking over from the Accounting Standards Committee. One of the Financial Reporting Council's operational bodies. See FRC above

Financial Reporting Council: Financial Reporting Review Panel

Holborn Hall, 100 Gray's Inn Road, London WC1X 8AL
Tel 0171-404 8818 Fax 0171-404 1276

Panel Members

Chairman
Edwin Glasgow QC

Deputy Chairman
Michael Renshall CBE

There are 18 other panel members

Officials

Secretary
Sydney Treadgold

Responsibilities

Authorised by the Secretary of State for Trade and Industry to examine departures from the accounting requirements of the Companies Act by large companies and where appropriate to invite the company to take corrective action. Failing that it will seek a remedy from the court

Founded

1991. One of the Financial Reporting Council's operational bodies. See FRC above

Funding Agency for Schools

Albion Wharf, 25 Skeldergate, York YO1 2XL
Tel 01904 661661 Fax 01904 661686

Officials

Chairman
Sir Christopher Benson

Chief Executive
Michael Collier

Shailendra Adwalpalkar
Sir Robert Balchin
The Rev Canon Gerald Greenwood
Dr Arthur Hearnden OBE
Stanley Kalms
Lee Karu
Mrs Lesley King
Mrs Pauline Latham OBE
Cllr Edward Lister
Brother Francis Patterson OBE
Mrs M G Ryding
Peter Turner OBE

Planning Director
Sandy Adamson

Finance Director
John Codling

Grants Director
David Halladay

Personnel and Services Director
Jim Walker

Communications Director
Roger Witts

Board Secretary
Miss Jane Thornhill

Responsibilities

The primary function of the Agency is to support GM (grant maintained) schools. This involves:

Calculation and repayment of recurrent, special purpose and capital grants and loans to GM schools in accordance with chapter V of Part II of the 1993 Act, regulations made under that chapter and any supplementary guidance provided by the Department for Education

Financial monitoring of GM schools

Value-for-money studies as determined by the Agency, or as directed by the Secretary of State for Education

Ensuring the provision of sufficient school places in specified local education authority areas in accordance with any order made under Section 12 of the 1993 Act

Provision of such information and advice to the Secretary of State as she may require in connection with any education function and any other information and advice the Agency thinks fit

Carrying out other activities in connection with the discharge of key functions, including the undertaking of research studies

The Secretary of State has the power to delegate further functions to the Agency under Section 17 of the 1993 Act

Founded On 1 April 1994 as a result of the Education Act 1993

Further Education Funding Council

Cheylesmore House, Quinton Road, Coventry CV1 2WT
Tel 01203 863000 Fax 01203 863100

Officials

Chairman
Robert Gunn

Chief Executive
Sir William Stubbs

Director of Finance
Roger McClure

Chief Inspector
Dr Terry Melia

Director of Education Programmes
Geoff Hall

Council

Robert Gunn
Nicholas Bennett
Tony Cann
John Capey
Anthony Close
Margaret Davey
Patricia Haikin
Margaret Hobrough
Christopher Jonas
Les Lawrence
Sir Michael Lickiss
Michael Rowarth
Sir William Stubbs
Anne Wright

Roger Dawe *(Secretary of State's representative)*
David Forrester
(alternative representative)

Secretary
Mike Wardle

Responsibilities

Responsible for allocating funds put at its disposal by Parliament to those colleges in England which comprise the FEFC sector, and to local education authorities and others for those further education courses prescribed in Schedule 2 of the Further and Higher Education Act 1992

Founded

July 1992 as a result of the Further and Higher Education Act 1992

Gaming Board for Great Britain

Berkshire House, 168-173 High Holborn, London WC1V 7AA
Tel 0171-306 6200 Fax 0171-306 6267

Officials

Chairman
Lady Littler

Secretary
T Kavanagh

Members
B P Austin
Sir Richard Barratt CBE QPM
Lady Trethowan JP
W B Kirkpatrick

Responsibilities

To ensure that those involved in organising gaming and lotteries are fit and proper to do so and to keep gaming free of criminal infiltration

To ensure that gaming and lotteries are run fairly and in accordance with the law

To advise the Home Secretary on developments in gaming and lotteries so that the law can respond to change

Founded

1968 under the provisions of the Gaming Act 1968. The Board also has responsibilities in relation to lotteries under the Lotteries and Amusements Act 1976

General Register Office for Scotland

New Register House, Edinburgh EH1 3YT
Tel 0131-334 0380 Fax 0131-314 4400

Ministers and Officials	**Minister of State, Scottish Office** (for details of his office see Scottish Office) *Registrar General* **James Meldrum (4)** *Deputy Registrar General* **B V Philp (5)**
Responsibilities	To administer the law on marriage To maintain the NHS Central Register To produce and supply a wide range of population and vital statistics To oversee registration of births, marriages and deaths To take censuses of population
Founded	1855

Health Education Authority

Hamilton House, Mabledon Place, London WC1H 9TX
Tel 0171-383 3833 Fax 0171-387 0550

Officials

Chairman
Anthony Close

Chief Executive
Vacant

Human Resources Director,
Deputy Chief Executive
Ms Jane Greenoak

Operations Manager
Donald Reid

Finance Director
Peter Trowell

Non-Executive Directors
Kriss Akabusi
The Baroness Brigstocke
Mrs Gillian Butler
Professor Alasdair Geddes
Dr Alan Gilmour CVO CBE
Ms Esther Rantzen OBE
The Rt Rev William J Westwood

Responsibilities

To advise the Secretary of State on matters relating to health education

To undertake health education activity

To plan and carry out programmes of other activities in cooperation with health authorities, Family Health Services Authorities, local authorities, local education authorities, voluntary organisations and other persons or bodies concerned with health education

To sponsor research and evaluation

To assist the provision of appropriate training

To prepare, publish or distribute material

To provide a national centre of health promotion information and advice

Founded

1987 after taking over the responsibilities in England of the Health Education Council. The HEA is a special health authority of the National Health Service

Health and Safety Commission

Rose Court, 2-10 Southwark Bridge, London SE1 9HF
Tel 0171-717 6000 Fax 0171-717 6644
All staff are based at Rose Court unless otherwise indicated
For other addresses and telephone numbers see the end of this section

Officials

Chairman
Frank Davies CBE OstJ

Members
Rex Symons
Peter Jacques
Alan Tuffin
Dame Rachel Waterhouse
Paul Gallagher
Edward Carrick
Nigel Pitcher
Christopher Chope
Dr Geraldine Schofield

Secretary
T A Gates (7)

Responsibilities

To reform health and safety law

To propose new regulations

To promote the protection of people at work and the public from hazards arising from industrial (including commercial) activity including major industrial accidents and the transportation of hazardous materials

The Commission guides and is advised by the Health and Safety Executive (see below for details)

Liaison with the Employment Department Group

Founded

1974 under the provisions of the Health and Safety at Work Act

---

See Health and Safety Executive over page

Health and Safety Executive

Rose Court, 2-10 Southwark Bridge, London SE1 9HF
Tel 0171-717 6000 Fax 0171-717 6644

Officials

Director General
Ms J H Bacon

Deputy Directors General
D C T Eves (2)
Vacant

Responsibilities

The HSE is a statutory body consisting of the Director General and two other people appointed by the Health and Safety Commission to which the HSE gives advice. HSE staff are the primary instrument for carrying out the Commission's policies which they do as necessary in liaison with other regulatory bodies.

The HSE has a special responsibility to ensure that the Health and Safety at Work Act and other law on health and safety is observed. This is achieved through HSE's field force who operate through a network of 21 area offices throughout the UK and HSE inspectors systematically visit and review a wide range of work activities.

Founded

1974 under the provisions of the Health and Safety at Work Act

Organisational Overview

	Civil Servants		Division
Grade 1	*Grade 2*	*Grade 3*	
	Health and Safety Executive		
Miss J H Bacon	These divisions report directly to the Director General	R Hillier	Resources and Planning Directorate of Information and Advisory Services
		B J Ecclestone (4)	Solicitor's Office
		Dr J T McQuaid	Strategy and General
	Operations		
Miss J H Bacon	D C T Eves	Dr A F Roberts (4)	Health and Safety Laboratory
		Dr A F Ellis	Technology and Health Sciences
		K L Twist	Mines Inspectorate
		S S J Robertson	Railways Inspectorate
		Dr J T Carter	Field Operations and Medical Services
	Policy		
Miss J H Bacon	Vacant	M Addison	Safety Policy
		Dr S Harbison	Nuclear Safety
		Dr P J Graham	Health Policy
		R S Allison	Offshore Safety

Civil Servants and Departments

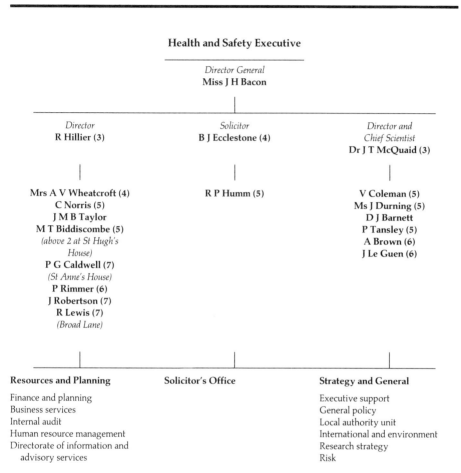

Health and Safety Executive

Director General
Miss J H Bacon

Director
R Hillier (3)

Mrs A V Wheatcroft (4)
C Norris (5)
J M B Taylor
M T Biddiscombe (5)
(above 2 at St Hugh's House)
P G Caldwell (7)
(St Anne's House)
P Rimmer (6)
J Robertson (7)
R Lewis (7)
(Broad Lane)

Solicitor
B J Ecclestone (4)

R P Humm (5)

Director and Chief Scientist
Dr J T McQuaid (3)

V Coleman (5)
Ms J Durning (5)
D J Barnett
P Tansley (5)
A Brown (6)
J Le Guen (6)

Resources and Planning

Finance and planning
Business services
Internal audit
Human resource management
Directorate of information and advisory services

Solicitor's Office

Strategy and General

Executive support
General policy
Local authority unit
International and environment
Research strategy
Risk

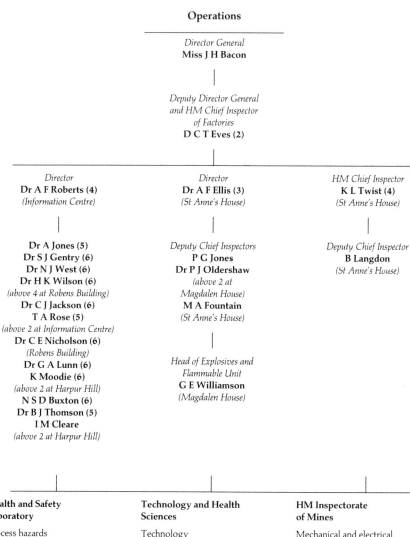

Operations

Director General
Miss J H Bacon

Deputy Director General and HM Chief Inspector of Factories
D C T Eves (2)

Director
Dr A F Roberts (4)
(Information Centre)

Dr A Jones (5)
Dr S J Gentry (6)
Dr N J West (6)
Dr H K Wilson (6)
(above 4 at Robens Building)
Dr C J Jackson (6)
T A Rose (5)
(above 2 at Information Centre)
Dr C E Nicholson (6)
(Robens Building)
Dr G A Lunn (6)
K Moodie (6)
(above 2 at Harpur Hill)
N S D Buxton (6)
Dr B J Thomson (5)
I M Cleare
(above 2 at Harpur Hill)

Director
Dr A F Ellis (3)
(St Anne's House)

Deputy Chief Inspectors
P G Jones
Dr P J Oldershaw
(above 2 at Magdalen House)
M A Fountain
(St Anne's House)

Head of Explosives and Flammable Unit
G E Williamson
(Magdalen House)

HM Chief Inspector
K L Twist (4)
(St Anne's House)

Deputy Chief Inspector
B Langdon
(St Anne's House)

Health and Safety Laboratory

Process hazards
Explosion control
Engineering control
Biomedical services
Workplace control
Electrical equipment certification

Technology and Health Sciences

Technology
Health sciences
Strategy and central services

HM Inspectorate of Mines

Mechanical and electrical
Field inspections

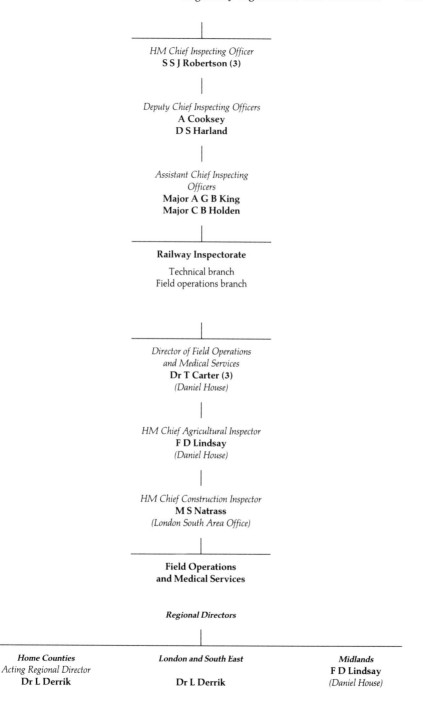

HM Chief Inspecting Officer
S S J Robertson (3)

Deputy Chief Inspecting Officers
A Cooksey
D S Harland

Assistant Chief Inspecting Officers
Major A G B King
Major C B Holden

Railway Inspectorate

Technical branch
Field operations branch

Director of Field Operations and Medical Services
Dr T Carter (3)
(Daniel House)

HM Chief Agricultural Inspector
F D Lindsay
(Daniel House)

HM Chief Construction Inspector
M S Natrass
(London South Area Office)

Field Operations and Medical Services

Regional Directors

Home Counties
Acting Regional Director
Dr L Derrik

London and South East
Dr L Derrik

Midlands
F D Lindsay
(Daniel House)

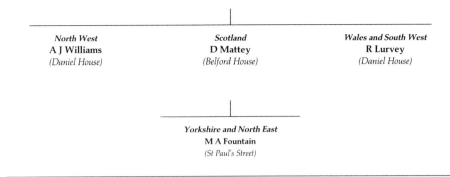

North West
A J Williams
(Daniel House)

Scotland
D Mattey
(Belford House)

Wales and South West
R Lurvey
(Daniel House)

Yorkshire and North East
M A Fountain
(St Paul's Street)

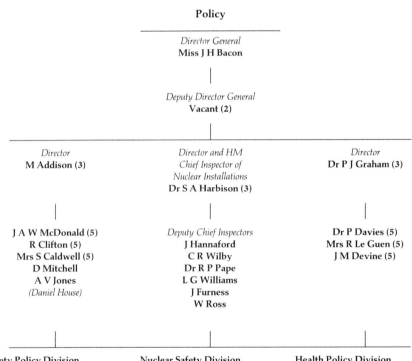

Policy

Director General
Miss J H Bacon

Deputy Director General
Vacant (2)

Director
M Addison (3)

J A W McDonald (5)
R Clifton (5)
Mrs S Caldwell (5)
D Mitchell
A V Jones
(Daniel House)

Director and HM Chief Inspector of Nuclear Installations
Dr S A Harbison (3)

Deputy Chief Inspectors
J Hannaford
C R Wilby
Dr R P Pape
L G Williams
J Furness
W Ross

Director
Dr P J Graham (3)

Dr P Davies (5)
Mrs R Le Guen (5)
J M Devine (5)

Safety Policy Division

Mechanical, electrical and work equipment
General and technical, radiation and noise
Mining and special industries
Transportation/explosives
Hazardous installations
Railways

Nuclear Safety Division

Strategy and international policy
Physics assessments
Engineering assessments
Inspection of chemical plant, small installations and non-licensed sites
Inspections of power stations
Radiation and technical policy
Radiation protection

Health Policy Division

Toxic substances: usage and chemicals supply
Pathology and research
Policy

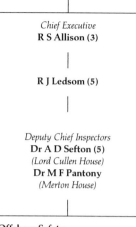

Chief Executive
R S Allison (3)

R J Ledsom (5)

Deputy Chief Inspectors
Dr A D Sefton (5)
(Lord Cullen House)
Dr M F Pantony
(Merton House)

Offshore Safety

Policy
Resources and systems
Operations
Technology

Health and Safety Executive Addresses

Belford House
59 Belford Road
Edinburgh EH4 3UE
Tel 0131-247 2000
Fax 0131-247 2121

14 Cardiff Road
Luton
Beds LU1 1PP
Tel 01582 34121
Fax 01582 459775

Daniel House
Trinity Road
Bootle
Merseyside L20 3QZ
Tel 0151-951 4000
Fax 0151-951 3827

Harpur Hill
Buxton
Derbyshire SK17 9JN
Tel 01298 26211
Fax 01298 79514

Information Centre
Broad Lane
Sheffield S3 7HQ
Tel 01142 892345
Fax 01142 892333

London South Area Office
1 Long Lane
London SE1 4PG
Tel 0171-407 8911
Fax 0171-403 7058

Lord Cullen House
Fraser Place
Aberdeen AB9 1UB
Tel 01224 252500
Fax 01224 252555

Magdalen House
Stanley Precinct
Bootle L20 3QZ
Tel 0151-951 4000
Fax 0151-922 7918

Merton House
Stanley Road
Bootle
Merseyside L20 3DL
Tel 0151-951 4000
Fax 0151-951 3131

Robens Building
Broad Lane
Sheffield S3 7HQ
Tel 01142 892000
Fax 01142 892500

Rose Court
2 Southwark Bridge
London SE1 9HS
Tel 0171-717 6000
Fax 0171-717 6644

St Anne's House
Stanley Precinct
Bootle L20 3RA
Tel 0151-951 4000
Fax 0151-951 4232

St Hugh's House
Stanley Precinct
Bootle L20 3QY
Tel 0151-951 4000
Fax 0151-922 5394

8 St Paul's Street
Leeds LS1 2LE
Tel 01132 446191
Fax 01132 450626

St Peter's House
Balliol Road
Bootle L20 3LZ
Tel 0151-951 4000
Fax 0151-922 5980/1158

Higher Education Funding Council for England

Northavon House, Coldharbour Lane, Bristol BS16 1QD
Tel 01179 317317 Fax 01179 317173

Officials

Chairman
Brandon Gough

Chief Executive
Professor Graeme Davies *(to 30 September 1995)*
Professor Brian Fender *(from 1 October 1995)*

Council

Brandon Gough
Professor Graeme Davies
Mrs Joan Bingley
Professor Sir John Cadogan
Professor Sir Colin Campbell
Michael Fallon
Professor Sir Brian Follett
Professor Kay-Tee Khaw
Sir Idris Pearce
Sir Robert Scholey
Miss Barbara Stephens
Dr J A Strickson
Dr R J G Telfer
Miss Janet Trotter
Professor David Watson

Secretary
Rob Hull

Responsibilities

The Higher Education Funding Council for England (HEFCE) is responsible under the Further and Higher Education Act 1992 for the distribution of funds made available by the Secretary of State for Education for the provision of education and the undertaking of research by institutions of higher education in England.

Founded

6 May 1992 and assumed its full responsibilities, in succession to the Universities' Funding Council and Polytechnics' and Colleges' Funding Council, on 1 April 1993.

Highlands and Islands Enterprise

Bridge House, 20 Bridge Street, Inverness IV1 1QR
Tel 01463 234171 Fax 01463 244469

Officials

Chairman
Fraser Morrison CBE

Chief Executive
Iain Robertson

Board

Mrs Valerie MacIver
Dr James Hunter
Angus Macdonald
John D M Robertson
Peter Timms
John Harrison
John Angus Mackay
John Goodlad
Jack Shaw Stewart
Nicolas McAndrew

Responsibilities

HIE has the statutory functions of stimulating economic and social development; enhancing skills and capacities relevant to employment and promoting self-employment; and improving the environment of the Highlands and Islands

There are ten Local Enterprise Companies (LECs) which are companies carrying out programmes of activities contracted by HIE. These activities differ according to the needs of their area.

In support of its functions HIE's principal activities are:

To encourage startup and growth of companies in their area

To ensure that such companies are provided with appropriate assistance, advice and information

To promote the Highlands and Islands as a location for investment

To reduce the amount of derelict land and return it to use

To help young people and the longterm unemployed to gain the skills required for employment

To exercise its social remit in a way which helps sustain population and thus creates and maintains viable and self-sustaining local economies

Founded

1991 under the provisions of the Enterprise and New Towns (Scotland) Act 1990. It took over the functions of the Highlands and Islands Development Board and those of the former Training Agency in the northern half of Scotland

Horserace Betting Levy Board

52 Grosvenor Gardens, London SW1V 0AU
Tel 0171-333 0043 Fax 0171-333 0041

Board Members

Chairman
Sir John Sparrow

Deputy Chairman
John Robb

Members
Mrs A A McCurley
Sir Paul Fox
P Jones
T Ricketts
P Smith
The Lord Wyatt of Weeford

Officials

Chief Executive
R L Brack

Head of Legal Affairs
Ms L Evers

Projects Development Executive
D M Stewart

Scientific Liaison Executive
Ms E K Archer

Chief Accountant
G Rogers

Responsibilities

To collect a levy on the turnover of bookmakers and the Horserace Totalisator Board, and apply it for the improvement of breeds, veterinary science and education, and the improvement of horseracing

To provide through the Horseracing Forensic Laboratory a research-backed drugscreening service for both the Jockey Club and commercial clients

To supervise the National Stud at Newmarket

Founded

1961 under the provisions of the Betting Levy Act 1961

Immigration Appeals, the Appellate Authorities

Thanet House, 231 Strand, London WC2R 1DA
Tel 0171-353 8060 Fax 0171-583 1976

Immigration Appeal Tribunal

President
G W Farmer

Vice-Presidents
Professor D C Jackson
Mrs J Chatwani

Adjudicators

Chief Adjudicator
Judge Pearl

Deputy Chief Adjudicator
R G Care

Chief Clerk
Mrs L Hedden (7)

Responsibilities To hear and determine appeals in the UK against immigration decisions

Founded 1971 under the provisions of the Immigration Act 1971

Independent Television Commission

33 Foley Street, London W1P 7LB
Tel 0171-255 3000 Fax 0171-306 7800

Officials	*Chairman* **Sir George Russell CBE** *Deputy Chairman* **Jocelyn Stevens CVO** *Chief Executive* **David Glencross**
Members	**Dr John Beynon** **The Earl of Dalkeith** **Roy Goddard** **Miss Jude Goffe** **Mrs Eleri Wynne Jones** **Mrs Pauline Mathias** **Dr Maria Maloney** **John Ranelagh** *Secretary* **Michael Redley**
Responsibilities	To license and regulate all commercially funded UK television services including cable and satellite services as well as terrestrial UHF services
Founded	1991 under the provisions of the Broadcasting Act 1990 The Independent Television Commission and the Radio Authority (see this section) replaced the Independent Broadcasting Authority

Independent Tribunal Service

(formerly Office of the President of Social Security Appeal Tribunals, Medical Appeal Tribunals and Vaccine Damage Tribunals)

City Gate House, 39-45 Finsbury Square, London EC2A 1PX
Tel 0171-814 6500 Fax 0171-814 6540

Officials

President
His Hon Judge Keith Bassingthwaighte

National Chairman
Mr Rodney P Huggins

Chief Executive
Mrs Valerie M Willcocks (6)

Responsibilities

To exercise judicial and administrative control over social security appeal tribunals, medical appeal tribunals, vaccine damage tribunals, disability appeal tribunals and child support appeal tribunals

Founded

1983 under the provisions of the Health and Social Services and Social Security Adjudications Act 1983

Insurance Ombudsman Bureau

City Gate One, 135 Park Street, London SE1 9EA
Tel 0171-928 4488 Fax 0171-401 8700

Officials

Chairman of the Council
Ms Barbara Saunders

Insurance Ombudsman
Laurie Slade

Deputy Ombudsman
Peter Hart

Bureau Manager and Clerk to the Council
Christopher Hamer

Responsibilities

To provide a dispute resolution service for personal insurance policy holders where the company involved is a member of the IOB scheme

Founded

1981

Intelligence Services Tribunal

PO Box 4823, London SW1A 9XD
Tel 0171-273 4383

Officials

Commissioner
The Rt Hon Lord Justice Stuart Smith

Tribunal President
The Rt Hon Lord Justice (Simon) Brown

Tribunal Vice-President
Sheriff John McInnes QC

Sir Richard Gaskell

Responsibilities To investigate public complaints against the intelligence services

Founded As a result of the Intelligence Services Act 1994

Joint Nature Conservation Committee

Monkstone House, City Road, Peterborough PE1 1JY
Tel 01733 62626 Fax 01733 555948

Officials

Chairman
The Earl of Selborne KBE FRS

Chief Officer
C R Walker CB

Director, Life Science Division
Dr M W Pienkowski (6)

Director, Earth and Aquatic Sciences Division
Dr M A Vincent (6)

Members

Professor D Q Bowen
The Earl of Cranbrook
Professor G M Dunnet OBE
Dr J S Faulkner
Mr E M W Griffith CBE
Sir John Knill
M Magnusson KBE
Professor R M May
Professor P J Newbould OBE
Dr D F Shaw
Professor J I Sprent

Responsibilities

Advising ministers on the development and implementation of policies for, or affecting, nature conservation in Great Britain as a whole, or nature conservation outside Great Britain

Establishment of common scientific standards for monitoring and research into nature conservation, and the analysis of resulting information

Provision of advice and the dissemination of knowledge about nature conservation

Provision of advice to the country agencies (see below) for nature conservation

Undertaking and commissioning of research

Founded

1990 under the provisions of the Environmental Protection Act 1990. JNCC and the three country agencies (English Nature, Scottish Natural Heritage and the Countryside Council for Wales) carry forward duties previously undertaken by the Nature Conservancy Council (NCC)

Law Commission

Conquest House, 37-38 John Street, Theobald's Road, London WC1N 2BQ
Tel 0171-453 1220 Fax 0171-453 1297

Commissioners

Chairman
The Hon Mr Justice Brooke

Professor Andrew Burrows (common and public law)
Miss Diana Faber (commercial and company law)
Charles Harpum (property and trust law)
Stephen Silber QC (criminal law)

Officials

Secretary
Michael Sayers (5)

Head of Statute Law Revision
C W Dyment (5)

Parliamentary Draftsmen
P F A Knowles
Sir Henry de Waal
Miss L A Nodder
P R de Val
Mrs E A F Gardiner

Responsibilities

Reform of the law with a view to its systematic development and its simplification and modernisation

To revise and consolidate statute law and repeal obsolete and unnecessary laws

Founded

1965 under the provisions of the Law Commissions Act 1965

Local Government Commission for England

Dolphyn Court, 10/11 Great Turnstile, London WC1V 7JU
Tel 0171-430 8400 Fax 0171-404 6142

Officials

Chairman
Sir David Cooksey

*Commissioners**

Chief Executive
Robert Chilton

Responsibilities

To review the structure, boundaries and electoral arrangements for local government in England.

Founded

1992 under the provisions of the Local Government Act 1992. It took over many of the responsibilities of the former Local Government Boundary Commission in that year.

Most of the commissioners are changing and at the time of going to press no appointments had been made. The new commissioners will take up their posts during July 1995. Telephone the press office for details.

Magistrates' Courts Service Inspectorate

Southside, 105 Victoria Street, London SW1E 6QT
Tel 0171-210 1661 Fax 0171-210 1663

Block 2, Government Buildings, Burghill Road, Westbury-on-Trym, Bristol BS10 6NH
Tel 01179 507960 Fax 01179 500408

City House, New Station Street, Leeds LS1 4JR
Tel 01132 836635 Fax 01132 836636

Officials

HM Chief Inspector
Rosemary Melling (5)

HM Senior Inspector, Central and Southern Team
Duncan Gear (6)

HM Senior Inspector, Eastern Team
Sue Steel (6)

HM Senior Inspector, Western Team
Julia Eeles (6)
(Bristol)

HM Senior Inspector, Northern Team
Colin Monson (6)
(Leeds)

Responsibilities

To inspect and report to the Lord Chancellor on the administration and management of the Magistrates' Courts Service in order to improve performance and disseminate good practice. The Inspectorate is not empowered to comment on the judicial decisions of magistrates or their clerks

Founded

The Magistrates' Courts Service Inspectorate (MCSI) was established in January 1993 with the appointment of the Chief Inspector and one Inspector. The Police and Magistrates' Courts Bill made provision for it to be placed on a statutory footing. Since 1 September 1994 MCSI has been designated HM Magistrates' Courts Service Inspectorate

Medical Research Council

20 Park Crescent, London W1N 4AL
Tel 0171-636 5422 Fax 0171-436 6179

Chairman
Sir David Plastow

Chief Executive,
Secretary of the Council
Sir Dai Rees

Second Secretary
Dr D C Evered

Administrative Secretary
Mrs Norma Morris (3)

Officials

Senior Staff
Dr M B Davies (5)
Dr D R Dunstan (5)
Dr M B Kemp (6)
Mrs J M Lee (5)
Dr D J McLaren (6)
Dr D A A Owen (5)
Dr D L Smith (5)
N H Winterton (5)

Responsibilities

To promote and support high-quality basic, strategic and applied research and related postgraduate training in all branches of biomedical science with the aim of maintaining and improving health, placing special emphasis on meeting the needs of users of its research and training output, thereby enhancing health, the quality of life and the United Kingdom's industrial competitiveness

Founded

1920 when it succeeded the Medical Research Committee established in 1913. Under the Science and Technology Act 1965 it was responsible to the Secretary of State for Education and Science and from 1992 to the Office of Public Service and Science, Cabinet Office

Medicines Commission

Market Towers, 1 Nine Elms Lane, London SW8 5NQ
Tel 0171-273 0393 Fax 0171-273 0387

Officials

Chairman
Professor David Lawson

Secretary
Roger Motton

Principal Assessor
Dr June Raine

Pharmaceutical Assessor
Miss Doreen Hepburn

Responsibilities

To advise the UK Health and Agriculture Ministers on matters relating to the Medicines Act 1968; and on the safety, quality and efficacy of medicinal products. The secretariat is provided by a statutory advisory committee of the Medicines Control Agency *(see entry for Medicines Control Agency in the Next Steps Executive Agencies section).*

Founded

1969 under the provisions of the Medicines Act 1968

Committees set up under Section 4 of the Medicines Act 1968

Committee on Safety of Medicines

Market Towers, 1 Nine Elms Lane, London SW8 5NQ
Tel 071-273 0451 Fax 071-273 0453

Officials

Chairman
Professor Michael Rawlins

Secretary
Leslie Whitbread

Assessor (New Drugs)
Dr Alex Nicholson

Assessor (Pharmacovigilance)
Dr Susan Wood

Assessor (Abridged Licensing)
Miss Doreen Hepburn

Responsibilities	To advise UK Health ministers on the safety, efficacy and quality of medicinal products To collect and investigate reports of adverse reactions to medicinal products
Founded	1970

Other: Veterinary Products Committee and the Advisory Board on the Registration of Homeopathic Products

Monopolies and Mergers Commission

New Court, 48 Carey Street, London WC2A 2JT
Tel 0171-324 1467 Fax 0171-324 1400

Commission Members

Chairman
G D W Odgers

Deputy Chairmen
P H Dean CBE
D G Goyder
H H Liesner CB

Members
A G Armstrong
I S Barter
Mrs C M Blight
P Brenan
J S Bridgeman
R O Davies
Professor S Eilon
J Evans
N H Finney OBE
Sir Archibald Forster
Sir Ronald Halstead CBE
Ms P A Hodgson
D J Jenkins MBE
A L Kingshott
R Lyons
N F Matthews
Professor J S Metcalfe CBE
Professor A P L Minford
J D Montgomery
Dr D J Morris
Professor J F Pickering
L Priestley
M R Prosser
Dr A Robinson
J K Roe
Dr L M Rouse
Mrs C Tritton QC
Professor G Whittington

Staff

Secretary
A J Nieduszynski

Team Managers
J A Banfield (5)
A O H Blair (5)
G M Field (5)
G Knight (5)
Mrs G D J Steel (5)

Senior Legal Adviser
Miss Jane Richardson

Chief Industrial Adviser
M F Shutler (4)

Accountant Adviser
Peter Le Mesurier

Senior Economic Adviser
G P Sumner (5)

Press and Information Adviser
G Edward
0171-324 1407

Responsibilities

To investigate and report on monopoly and merger situations, newspaper mergers, certain general questions, anti-competitive practices and questions of efficiency, costs and possible abuse of monopoly positions in the public sector

To conduct inquiries under the provisions of certain acts designed to effect the privatisation of undertakings formerly in the private sector

The Commission has no power to initiate its own investigations. References are made to it either by the Secretary of State for Trade and Industry, the Director General of Fair Trading or, in the case of the privatised industries, by the appropriate regulator. Completed reports are submitted to the Secretary of State for Trade and Industry or, in the case of the privatised industries, to the appropriate regulator

Founded

1948 as the Monopolies and Restrictive Practices Commission. Became the Monopolies and Mergers Commission under the provisions of the Fair Trading Act 1973. It also operates under the provisions of the Competition Act 1980

National Consumer Council

20 Grosvenor Gardens, London SW1W 0DH
Tel 0171-730 3469 Fax 0171-730 0191

Members

Chairman
Lady Wilcox

Vice-Chairman
Ann Scully

Members
Sir Geoffrey Allen
David Arculus
Mrs Anne Daltrop
Professor Paul Fairest
Jennifer Francis
David Gilchrist
John Hughes
Noel Hunter
George Jones
Ms Ruth Lea
Mary McAnally
Lady McCollum
Eric Smellie
Jean Varnam

Chairman, Scottish Consumer Council
Deirdre Hutton

Chairman, Welsh Consumer Council
Beata Brookes

Officials

Director (Chief Executive)
Ruth Evans

Head of Communications and Campaigns
Diana Whitworth

Senior Parliamentary Officer
Hazel Phillips

Responsibilities

To ensure that the consumer viewpoint is fully taken into account in the formation of economic, social and public service policies, and to persuade the suppliers of goods and services – both public and private – to be more responsive to consumers' needs and more caring in dealing with the problems of individual consumers

Founded

1975 as a result of a government White Paper

National Criminal Intelligence Service

PO Box 8000, Spring Gardens, Tinworth Street, London SE11 5EN
Tel 0171-238 8000 Fax 0171-238 8446

Officials

Director General
A H Pacey CBE QPM

Deputy Director General and Director (Intelligence)
J P Hamilton

Director International Division
P J Byrne MBE

Director UK Division
Vacant

National Coordinator, Regional Crime Squads, England and Wales
R A Penrose QPM

Responsibilities

To provide leadership and excellence in criminal intelligence, and to assist law enforcement and other relevant agencies by processing intelligence, giving direction and providing services and strategic analysis to combat serious criminal activity. The National Criminal Intelligence Service concentrates on major criminals of regional, national and international interest.

NCIS provides the National Central Bureau for Interpol, is the conduit for the newly-formed Europol and is the organisation to which reports of suspicious transactions must be made under the laws dealing with asset search and seizure, money laundering and the associated regulations. The following intelligence functions are also undertaken:

- Kidnap and extortion
- Paedophiles
- Organised crime
- National Drugs Intelligence Unit
- National Football Intelligence Unit
- Counterfeiting of valuable securities and currency

There are three main headquarters divisions and five regional offices in London, Bristol, Birmingham, Manchester and Wakefield. The office of the national co-ordinator of regional crime squads is also incorporated within headquarters complex.

Founded

1992, as a result of the work of a tripartite steering group set up by the Home Office, in consultation with the public service, local authority associations and HM Customs and Excise.

National Radiological Protection Board

Chilton, Didcot, Oxon OX11 0RQ
Tel 01235 831600 Fax 01235 833891

Officials

Chairman
Sir Keith Peters

Director
Professor R H Clarke

Board

Professor Sir Keith Peters
Professor M Bobrow
Professor E H Grant
Professor J M Harrington CBE
Professor T R Lee
Professor R M MacKie
Professor R M May FRS
The Hon Mrs Sara Morrison
Professor J Peto
Professor G M Roberts
Dr M F Spittle
Sir Martin Wood OBE FRS

Secretary
M C O'Riordan

Assistant Directors
Dr J W Stather
Miss F A Fry
Dr J R Harrison
Dr A D Wrixon

Responsibilities

To advance by research the acquisition of knowledge about the protection of mankind from radiation hazards

To provide advice to the government on the acceptability to the UK of standards recommended or proposed by international bodies, and on their application

To provide information and advice to those with responsibilities in the UK in relation to the protection from radiation hazards, either of the community as a whole, or particular sections of it

Founded

1970 under the provisions of the Radiological Protection Act 1970

National Rivers Authority*

30-34 Albert Embankment, London SE1 7TL
Tel 0171-820 0101 Fax 0171-820 1603

Rivers House, Waterside, Aztec West, Almondsbury, Bristol BS12 4UD
Tel 01454 624400 Fax 01454 624409

Officials

Chairman
The Rt Hon The Lord Crickhowell

Chief Executive
Ed Gallagher
(Bristol/London)

Director of Public Affairs
Miles Wilson
(Bristol)

Director of Operations
Dr Kevin Bond
(Bristol)

Chief Scientist and Director of Water Quality
Dr Richard Pentreath†

Director of Water Management
Dr Clive Swinnerton
(Bristol)

Personnel Director
Peter Humphreys††
(Bristol)

Finance Director
Nigel Reader
(Bristol)

Director of Market Testing
Dr Geoff Mance
(Bristol)

Secretary and Director of Legal Services
Chris Martin
(Bristol)

Responsibilities

An independent body with statutory responsibilities for water resources, pollution control, flood defence, fisheries, recreation, conservation and navigation in England and Wales

It also has substantial responsibilities for the marine environment around the coast of England and Wales:

- for pollution control and salmonid fisheries purposes it has duties and powers to distances of three nautical miles out respectively
- for flood defence it is responsible for a large number of sea defences (but not coastal protection which falls within the remit of local authorities)

Founded 1989 under the provisions of the Water Act 1989, now consolidated under the Water Resources Act 1991

**From April 1996 the NRA will have become part of the government's new environmental protection agency*

†Seconded to the Secretariat for the Environment Agency Advisory Committee (Room 102, Block 2, Government Buildings, Department of the Environment, Burghill Road, Westbury-on-Trym, Bristol BS10 6NH, Tel 01179 764608)

††Seconded part-time to the Secretariat for the Environment Agency Advisory Committee (see address and telephone number in paragraph above)

Natural Environment Research Council

Polaris House, North Star Avenue, Swindon SN2 1EU
Tel 01793 411500 Fax 01793 411501

Officials

Chairman of Council
Robert Malpas CBE

Chief Executive and Deputy Chairman
Professor John R Krebs FRS (2)

Director of Science and Technology
Dr David J Drewry (3)

Director Awards and Training
Professor J Bryan Ellis (5)

Establishment Officer
David G Griffiths (5)

Director, NERC Scientific Services
Brian J Hinde OBE (5)

Director Policy and Communications
Dr Richard K G Paul (5)

Director of Finance
Colin M Read (5)

Director of Technology Interaction
Dr Michael J Tricker (5)

Responsibilities

To encourage, plan and execute research in the physical and biological sciences which relate to man's natural environment and its resources

Founded

1965 by Royal Charter under the provisions of the Science and Technology Act 1965, and granted a Supplemental Charter in December 1993

Occupational Pensions Board

PO Box 2EE, Newcastle on Tyne NE99 2EE
Tel 0191-225 6414 Fax 0191-225 6283
Office of the Registrar, PO Box 1NN, Newcastle on Tyne NE99 1NN
Tel 0191-225 66237 Fax 0191-225 6390

Officials

Chairman
Peter Carr CBE

Deputy Chairman
Miss Harriet Dawes OBE

Secretary to the Board and General Manager of the Executive Office
Malcolm McLean

Members
R J Amy
J R Bowman
Mrs R Brown
R Ellison
H Harris Hughes
A Herbert
A V Lyburn
A Pickering
W M R Ramsay
M R Slack
K R Thomas OBE
P Triggs

Responsibilities

To report to the Secretary of State for Social Services on regulations relating to occupational pension schemes and to advise as required on particular matters relating to such schemes

To ensure compliance with the requirements for preservation of scheme benefits and for equal access to membership by men and women

To supervise arrangements for contracting-out of the state scheme to final salary schemes, money purchase and appropriate personnel pension schemes

To order the modification or winding up of an occupational pension scheme

To ensure that occupational pension schemes comply with the requirements for disclosure of information by giving advice to scheme administrators and, where appropriate, determining whether scheme rules conform with the requirements

To act as Registrar of Occupational and Personal Pension Schemes and to operate a tracing service to enable individuals to trace past preserved pension rights

To make grants to appropriate bodies providing advice or assistance in connection with occupational or personal pensions

Founded 1973 under the Social Security Act 1973

The Office of the Adjudicator for the Inland Revenue, Customs and Excise and the Contributions Agency

Haymarket House, 28 Haymarket, London SW1Y 4SP
Tel 0171-930 2292 Fax 0171-930 2298

Officials

The Adjudicator
Elizabeth Filkin

Head of Office
David Richardson

Adjudication Managers
Tim East
Ian Monk
Manju Sharma
Mike Sisk

Responsibilities

To consider impartially complaints about the way in which the Inland Revenue, Customs and Excise or the Contributions Agency have acted. The Adjudicator decides whether the complaints are justified and, if so, recommends what should be done. On this basis the Adjudicator publishes an annual report to the two departments and the agency

Founded

5 May 1993

Office of the Banking Ombudsman

70 Gray's Inn Road, London WC1X 8NB
Tel 0171-404 9944 Fax 0171-405 5052

Officials

Ombudsman
Laurence Shurman

Deputy Ombudsman
Chris Eadie

Assistant Ombudsman
Catherine Clarke

Administration Manager
Ian Pattison

Chairman of the Council
Sir David Calcutt QC

Clerk to the Council
Brendon Sewill CBE

Responsibilities

To settle complaints by individuals and small companies against member banks about banking services

Founded

1986

Office of the Data Protection Registrar

Wycliffe House, Water Lane, Wilmslow, Cheshire SK9 5AF
Tel 01625 535711 Fax 01625 524510

Officials

Data Protection Registrar
Mrs Elizabeth France (3)

Deputy Registrar
F G B Aldhouse (5)

Legal Adviser to the Registrar
Mrs R P Jay (5)

Responsibilities

To give information and advice on the operation of the Data Protection Act 1984

To promote the observance of the Data Protection Principles

To consider complaints that the Data Protection Principles or the Act have been contravened and take appropriate action

To encourage the preparation and dissemination of codes of practice for guidance in complying with the Data Protection Principles

To underpin compliance with the Act through prosecution for offences or via enforcement action for contraventions of the Data Protection Principles

To compile, maintain and publish a register of data users and computer bureaux

To give advice and support to other countries which have ratified the Council of Europe Convention and act as the United Kingdom authority

Founded

1984 under the provisions of the Data Protection Act 1984

Office of Electricity Regulation (OFFER)

Hagley House, Hagley Road, Birmingham B16 8QG
Tel 0121-456 2100 Fax 0121-456 4664

Regent Court, 70 West Regent Street, Glasgow G2 2QZ
Tel 0131-331 2678 Fax 0131-331 2777

Officials

Director General of Electricity Supply
Professor S C Littlechild

Deputy Director General
C P Carter (5)

Deputy Director General (Scotland)
G L Sims (5)

Legal Adviser
D Bevan (5)

Director Consumer Affairs
Dr D Hauser (5)

Directors Regulation and Business Affairs
A J Boorman (5)
Vacant (5)

Technical Director
Dr B Wharmby (5)

Chief Meter Examiner
J Cooper (6)

Director Public Affairs
Miss J D Luke (6)

Director Administration
H P Jones (6)

Responsibilities

To ensure that all reasonable demands for electricity are satisfied

To promote competition in the generation and supply of electricity

To protect consumers' interests on prices, security of supply and quality of services as well as to promote energy efficiency

Founded

1989 under the provisions of the Electricity Act 1989

Office of Fair Trading

Field House, Bream's Buildings, London EC4A 1PR
Tel 0171-242 2858 Fax 0171-269 8800

Chancery House, Chancery Lane, London WC2A 1SP
Tel 0171-242 2858 Fax 0171-269 8773

Officials

Acting Director-General of Fair Trading
J W Preston CB (2)*

Deputy Director-General
J W Preston CB (2)*

Director, Consumer Affairs
G H Horton (3)

Director, Competition Policy
Dr M Howe (3)

Director, Legal Department
A Inglese (3)

Senior Economics Adviser
D Elliott (5)
(Chancery House)

Establishments and Finance Officer
Miss C Banks (5)
(Chancery House)

Responsibilities

To keep watch on commercial activities and trading practices in the United Kingdom

To assess monopolies, mergers and trade practices that may be restrictive or anti-competitive and, where necessary, refer cases to the Monopolies and Mergers Commission or the Restrictive Practices Court, or offer advice to the Secretary of State for Trade and Industry

As a United Kingdom 'competent authority', to assist the European Commission enforce Community competition law

To propose and promote changes in law and practice if the interests of consumers are being harmed

To take legal action against businesses that persistently cause problems for consumers

To equip customers with the information and advice they need

To license traders offering credit or hire facilities

Founded

1973 under the provisions of the Fair Trading Act 1973, with additional responsibilities under the Consumer Credit Act 1974, the Restrictive Trade Practices Act 1976, the Estate Agents Act 1979 and the Competition Act 1980

*who will revert to being Deputy Director-General when a new Director-General is appointed

Office of Gas Supply (OFGAS)

Stockley House, 130 Wilton Road, London SW1V 1LQ
Tel 0171-828 0898 Fax 0171-630 8164

Officials

Director-General of Gas Supply
Clare Spottiswoode

Director, Regulation and Business Affairs
Dr Eileen Marshall (4)

Legal Adviser
Denys Long (5)

Director, Network Operations
Mark Higson (5)

Director, Consumer Affairs
Willie Macleod (5)

Director, Administration
Roy Field (7)

Director, Public Affairs
Chris Webb (7)

Responsibilities

To grant authorisations to other suppliers of gas through pipes

To fix and publish maximum charges for reselling gas

To investigate complaints where enforcement powers may be exercisable

To publish information and advice for the benefit of tariff customers

To settle the terms on which other suppliers have access to British Gas pipelines in the event of disagreement

To facilitate the development of competition in gas supply

Founded

1986 under the provisions of the Gas Act 1986

Office of the Health Service Commissioners (Ombudsman)

Millbank Tower, Millbank, London, SW1P 4PU
Tel 0171-276 2035 Fax 0171-217 3000

Commissioner

Health Service Commissioner (Ombudsman)
W K Reid CB (1)

Officials

Deputy Health Service Commissioner
R A Oswald (3)

Directors
Miss D C Fordham (5)
D Pinchin (5)
R Keynes (5)
N Jordan (5)
Ms H Bainbridge (5)

Responsibilities

To investigate complaints from members of the public about maladministration by, or failures in service by, or on behalf of National Health Service authorities, including trusts

Founded

Established by statute in 1973, the Commissioners' powers are now set out in the Health Service Commissioners Act 1993

Office of the Legal Services Ombudsman

22 Oxford Court, Oxford Street, Manchester M2 3WQ
Tel 0161-236 9532 Fax 0161-236 2651

Officials	*Ombudsman* **Michael Barnes** *Secretary* **Stephen Murray**
Responsibilities	To oversee the handling of complaints against solicitors, barristers and licensed conveyancers. In particular, to investigate allegations about the manner in which complaints have been dealt with by the relevant professional body. The Ombudsman may also investigate the matter to which a complaint relates
Founded	1991 under the provisions of the Courts and Legal Services Act 1990

Office of Manpower Economics

Oxford House, 76 Oxford Street, London W1N 9FD
Tel 0171-636 1742 Fax 0171-467 7248

Officials

Director
M J Horsman (3)

Deputy Director
Michael Emmott (4)

Chief Statistician
G S Charles (5)

Assistant Secretaries
P J H Edwards (5)
Mrs S Webber (5)
A Hughes (6)

Responsibilities

To service independent review bodies which advise on the pay of various public sector groups: School Teachers' Review Body, the Top Salaries Review Body, the Armed Forces Review Body, the Doctors' and Dentists' Review Body and the Review Body for Nurses and other NHS professions. The Office also provides services for the Pharmacists Review Panel, the Police Negotiating Board and the Civil Service Arbitration Tribunal.

To undertake research into pay and associated matters as requested by Government

Founded

1971

The Office of the National Lottery (OFLOT)

2 Monck Street, London SW1P 2BQ
Tel 0171-227 2000 Fax 0171-227 2005

Officials

Director-General
Peter Davis (2)

Deputy Director-General
Diana Kahn (5)

Head of Information
Colin Seabrook (7)

Lottery Marketing Adviser
Alan Chant (7)

Head of Compliance Regulation
Ken Dunn (5)

Lottery IT Adviser
Derek Woolley (7)

Head of Consumer Protection
Michael Richardson (7)

Head of Administration
Adrian Reed (7)

Responsibilities

To regulate the National Lottery operations during the seven year term of the Licence granted by the director-general under Section 5 of the National Lottery Act etc 1993

To license the individual games promoted as part of the National Lottery

The Director-General's duties include ensuring the propriety of the Lottery operation, including establishing that those involved in the running of the Lottery are fit and proper persons to do so; protection of the interests of participants and subject to those, to maximise revenues to the National Lottery Distribution Fund.

Launched

Established as a non-ministerial department in October 1993 under the National Lottery Act etc 1993

Office of the Northern Ireland Commissioner for Complaints (Ombudsman)*

33 Wellington Place, Belfast BT1 6HN
Tel 01232 233821 Fax 01232 234912

Officials

Commissioner for Complaints
Mrs J McIvor CBE QSM

Senior Director
G R Dawson (5)

Responsibilities

To investigate complaints by people claiming to have sustained injustice in consequence of maladministration in connection with the administrative actions of local authorities and certain public bodies

Founded

1969 under the provisions of the Commissioner for Complaints Act (NI) 1969

See also Office of the NI Parliamentary Commissioner for Administration

Office of the Northern Ireland Parliamentary Commissioner for Administration (Ombudsman)*

33 Wellington Place, Belfast BT1 6HN
Tel 01232 233821 Fax 01232 234912

Officials

Parliamentary Commissioner for Administration
Mrs J McIvor CBE QSM

Senior Director
G R Dawson (5)

Responsibilities

To investigate complaints by people claiming to have sustained injustice in consequence of maladministration arising from action taken by one of the various Northern Ireland government departments or agencies

Founded

1969 under the provisions of the Parliamentary Commissioner Act (NI) 1969

**See also Office of the NI Commissioner for Complaints*

Office of the Parliamentary Commissioner for Administration (Ombudsman)

Church House, Great Smith Street, London SW1P 3BW
Tel 0171-276 2130 Fax 0171-276 2104

Commissioner

Parliamentary Commissioner (Ombudsman)
W K Reid CB (1)

Officials

Deputy Parliamentary Commissioners
J E Avery (3)
Miss P Edwards (3)

Directors
Mrs S Maunsell (5)
A Watson (5)
Mrs H Bates (5)
L Railton (5)

Responsibilities

To investigate complaints about maladministration referred to him by MPs from members of the public against government departments and certain non-departmental bodies, including complaints that access to information has been wrongfully refused under the 1994 Code of Practice on Access to Government Information

Founded

1967 under the provisions of the Parliamentary Commissioner Act 1967

Office of Passenger Rail Franchising

26 Old Queen Street, London SW1H 9HP
Tel 0171-799 8800 Fax 0171-799 8810

Officials

Franchising Director
Roger Salmon

Assistant Directors
Chris Stokes
Nick Newton
Gary Backler
Adrian Clough
Neil McDonald

Principal Finance Officer
David Revotta

Principal Establishment Officer
Jane Marsh

Head of Public Affairs
Peter McDermott

Responsibilities

To secure the provision of improved railway passenger services through franchise agreements. The Franchise Director is responsible for franchising services, and channelling public subsidy into them (and into the remainder of the railway while it is unfranchised) where necessary. He will also monitor performance standards of operators. His principal considerations are: service and value for passengers, success and profit for franchisees; value for money for the taxpayer; and the long-term development of the railway

Founded

1993 under the provisions of the Railways Act, 1993

Office of the Rail Regulator

1 Waterhouse Square, 138-142 Holborn, London EC1N 2SU
Tel 0171-282 2000 Fax 0171-282 2040

Officials

Rail Regulator
John Swift QC

Director, Personnel, Finance and Administration
Peter Murphy (5)

Director, Passenger Services Regulation
John Rhodes (5)

Director, Network Regulation
Charles Brown (5)

Chief Legal Adviser
Michael Brocklehurst

Chief Information Officer
Ian Cooke (7)

Responsibilities

To protect the interests of rail customers

To promote the efficient use and development of the railway network for the carriage of both passengers and goods

To promote competition in the provision of railways services

To issue licences to new railway operators and impose the minimum restrictions on such operators consistent with the discharge of the Rail Regulator's other duties

To decide whether closures should occur

To ensure regular reviews of rail provision

To publish advice for rail users and annual reports on the service

Founded

1993 under the provisions of the Railway Act 1993

Office of Telecommunications (OFTEL)

50 Ludgate Hill, London EC4M 7JJ
Tel 0171-634 8700 Fax 0171-634 8943

Officials

Director-General
Don Cruickshank

Deputy Director General
Mrs A Walker

Director, Competition
Ann Taylor (5)

Director, Consumer Affairs
Mrs C Farnish

Director, Licensing
Mrs S Chambers

Director, Licence Enforcement and Fair Trading
Martin Owen (5)

Technical Director
P Walker

Legal Director
D H M Ingham (5)

Economic Director
A R Bell (5)

Director, Administration
D Smith

Director, Information
D Redding

Responsibilities

To advise the Secretary of State for Trade and Industry on licensing and other telecommunications issues

To approve apparatus

To enforce telecommunications licences

To initiate licence amendments

To investigate complaints

To maintain and promote effective competition in telecommunications and the international effectiveness of the UK telecommunications industry

	To maintain public registers of various documents including copies of licences
	To promote the interests of consumers, purchasers and other users in respect of prices, quality and variety
Founded	1984 under the provisions of the Telecommunications Act 1984

Office of Water Services (OFWAT)

Centre City Tower, 7 Hill Street, Birmingham B5 4UA
Tel 0121-625 1300 Fax 0121-625 1400

Officials

Director General of Water Services
I C R Byatt

Deputy Director General
G A Booker (3)

Head of Administration
M Toulmin (5)

Head of Costs and Performance Division
Dr W Emery (5)

Head of Legal Division
A Merry (5)

Head of Consumer Affairs
M Saunders (5)

Head of Information
Ms D Plant (6)

Responsibilities

To monitor the water and sewerage industry in England and Wales

To regulate charges

To promote economy and efficiency

To protect customers with regard to pricing and standards of service

To facilitate competition

To compare the performance of water companies

To determine certain disputes with companies

Ten regional Customer Services Committees represent consumer views and investigate complaints about companies. The chairman and members are appointed by the Director General

Founded

1989 under the provisions of the Water Act 1989

Panel on Takeovers and Mergers

226 Stock Exchange Building, London EC2P 2JX
Tel 0171-382 9026 Fax 0171-638 1554

Officials

Chairman
Sir David Calcutt QC

Deputy Chairmen
John F C Hull
John F Goble

Members
Dennis Stevenson
Sir Christopher Benson
Robert B Jack
Allan Bridgewater
Paul Myners
Julian G Tregoning
Sir Nicholas Goodison
John L Walker-Haworth
Antony R Beevor
Martin G Taylor
Roger H Lawson
Charles K R Nunneley
Geoffrey M Lindey
The Hon Christopher J Sharples
John Kemp-Welch

Director-General
William P Staple

Chairman of the Appeal Committee
The Rt Hon Sir Michael Kerr

Deputy Chairman of the Appeal Committee
The Rt Hon Sir Christopher Slade

Responsibilities

The Panel was set up as a non-statutory body following a proposal by the Governor of the Bank of England and the Chairman of the Stock Exchange, in response to concerns about practices unfair to shareholders at the time of take-overs.

The Panel, which continues to have the support of the Bank of England, draws its members from major UK financial and business institutions. The day-to-day work is carried out through its Executive, headed by the Director-General.

The principal objective of the Panel is to ensure fair conduct of a takeover bid from the point of view of shareholders.

The Panel requires those whom it regulates to adhere to the principles and rules set out in the City Code on Takeovers and Mergers and the rules governing substantial acquisitions of shares.

Founded 1968

Parole Board for England and Wales

Abell House, John Islip Street, London SW1P 4LH
Tel 0171-217 5314 Fax 0171-217 5677

Officials

Chairman
The Rt Hon Lord Belstead DL JP

Vice-Chairman
The Hon Mr Justice Potts

Secretary
T E Russell

Responsibilities

To advise the Home Secretary on the release of prisoners under licence, on the conditions of such licences, the revocation of licences, and allied matters in England and Wales, and to give directions for the release on licence of prisoners serving discretionary life sentences

Founded

1967 under the provisions of the Criminal Justice Act 1967, and continued under the Criminal Justice Act 1991

Parole Board for Scotland

Room 126, Calton House, 5 Redheughs Rigg, Edinburgh EH12 9HW
Tel 0131-244 8755 Fax 0131-244 8794

Officials

Chairman
Ian McNee

Vice-Chairman
Sheriff Gordon Shiach

Secretary
Hugh Boyle (7)

Responsibilities

To advise the Secretary of State for Scotland on the release of prisoners under licence, on the conditions of such licences, the revocation of such licences and allied matters in Scotland

Founded

1968 under the provisions of the Criminal Justice Act 1967

Pensions Ombudsman

11 Belgrave Road, London SW1V 1RB
Tel 0171-834 9144 Fax 0171-821 0065

Officials

Ombudsman
Dr Julian Farrand

Legal Advisers
Marjorie Wallach
Sarah Jacobs

Office Manager
Roy Roberts

Responsibilities

To investigate complaints or resolve disputes about occupational pensions. They also deal with complaints and disputes about some personal pension schemes.

Founded

1991 under the provisions of the Social Security Act 1990

Police Authority for Northern Ireland

River House, 48 High Street, Belfast BT1 2DR
Tel 01232 230111 Fax 01232 245098

Officials

Chairman
David S Cook

Secretary and Chief Executive
R T Armstrong (3)

Assistant Secretary, Establishment
H M Sloan (5)

Assistant Secretary, Support Services
D R McMillan (5)

Responsibilities

To secure the maintenance of an adequate and efficient police service in Northern Ireland, appoint the chief officers of the RUC and provide administrative support to the force. The Authority is responsible for financial and budgetary control and the provision of a wide range of support services including buildings, transport and supplies.

The Authority also promotes community and police liaison committees which, in most cases, are run by the local district council. A lay visitors scheme was established in 1991

Founded

1970 under the provisions of the Police Act (NI) 1970

Police Complaints Authority

10 Great George Street, London SW1P 3AE
Tel 0171-273 6450 Fax 0171-273 6401

Officials

Chairman
Sir Leonard Peach

Deputy Chairmen
J Cartwright (Investigations)
P W Moorhouse (Discipline)

Members
Mrs L Cawsey
M Chapman
N Dholakia
Miss L Haye
Miss A Kelly
Mrs M Meacher
L Spencer
Brigadier A Vivian
Miss B Wallis
E Wignall
A Williams MBE

Responsibilities

The independent body to oversee public complaints against police officers in England and Wales

Founded

1985 under the provisions of the Police and Criminal Evidence Act 1984

Political Honours Scrutiny Committee

53 Parliament Street, London SW1A 2NH
Tel 0171-210 5058

Officials

Chairman
The Rt Hon Lord Pym MC DL

Members
The Rt Hon The Lord Cledwyn of Penrhos CH
The Rt Hon The Lord Thomson of Monifieth KT DL

Secretary
A J Merifield CB

Responsibilities

To report to the Prime Minister on the suitability of those he proposes to recommend for an honour for political services

Founded

1923

Press Complaints Commission

1 Salisbury Square, London EC4Y 8AE
Tel 0171-353 1248/3732 (help-line) Fax 0171-353 8355

Officials

Chairman
The Rt Hon The Lord Wakeham

Members
Lady Browne-Wilkinson
Sir Brian Cubbon
Sir Denys Henderson
Sir Geoffrey Holland
Lord Irvine of Lairg
Harry Roche
Baroness Smith of Gilmorehill
Lord Tordoff

Complaints Commissioner
Professor Robert Pinker

Director
Mark Bolland

Responsibilities

To deal with complaints from the public about the contents and conduct of newspapers and magazines, enforcing a Code of Practice agreed by the press

Founded

1991 replacing the Press Council, following the recommendations of the Calcutt Committee on Privacy and Related Matters

Prisons Ombudsman

St Vincent House, 30 Orange Street, London WC2 7HH
Tel 0171-389 1527 Fax 0171-389 1492

Officials

Ombudsman
Sir Peter Woodhead

Assistant Ombudsmen
Adam Sampson
Michael Loughlin
Sara Down

Responsibilities

Investigating complaints and grievances in prisons in England and Wales

Founded

1994 as a result of Government commitment to implement a recommendation in the Woolf report

Public Health Laboratory Service Board

61 Colindale Avenue, London NW9 5DF
Tel 0181-200 1295 Fax 0181-200 8130

Board

Chairman
Dr Malcolm Godfrey CBE

Deputy Chairman
Mr A Graham-Dixon QC

Professor J P Arbuthnott
Dr W Bogie
Professor G Crompton
Professor C S F Easmon
Professor P E M Fine
Professor M J Forsythe
Dr D G Garvie
Mr J Godfrey
Dr D R L Hankinson
Sir Gordon Higginson
D Noble CBE
Professor F W O'Grady CBE
Dr M J Painter
Professor J R Pattison
Professor I Philips
Dr J J Skehel
Dr Geogina H Stewart
Mr J W Tiffney

Director
Dr Diana M Walford

Secretary
K M Saunders

Responsibilities

To provide a microbiological service for the diagnosis, prevention and control of infections and communicable diseases in England and Wales. A principal function of the Service is the monitoring and surveillance of the microbial diseases prevalent in the population.

It carries out its function by providing specialist diagnostic and public health microbiological services from its 53 regional and area laboratories for hospitals, general practitioners, consultants in communicable disease control and local authority environmental health departments. Following a Strategic Review of the PHLS in 1994 this network of laboratories is to be reorganised into groups during 1995 and 1996. Most of its specialised microbiological reference services are provided by the Central Public Health Laboratory and the national surveillance function by the Communicable Disease Surveillance Centre which also publishes the weekly Communicable Disease Report.

The Service also carries out research related to its areas of responsibility.

Founded

1961 under the provisions of the Public Health Laboratory Service Act 1960 (amended in the National Health Service Act 1977).

The Public Health Laboratory Service Act 1979 extended the powers of the Board to enable it to assume management responsibility for the Centre for Applied Microbiology and Research (CAMR), Porton Down. In 1993, the Government announced the transfer of responsibility for CAMR from April 1994 from the Board to a special Health Authority in recognition of developments in CAMR's role since 1979.

Radio Authority

Holbrook House, 14 Great Queen Street, London WC2B 5DG
Tel 0171-430 2724 Fax 0171-405 7062

Officials

Chairman
Sir Peter Gibbings

Deputy Chairman
Michael Moriarty CB

Members
Jennifer Francis
Andrew Reid
Michael Reupke
Lady Sheil

Chief Executive
Anthony Stoller

Deputy Chief Executive
Paul Brown

Secretary
John Norrington

Responsibilities

To plan frequencies, award licences, regulate programming and radio advertising (where necessary)

To play an active role in the discussion and formulation of policies which affect the independent radio industry and its listeners

Founded

1991 under the provisions of the Broadcasting Act 1990

The Radio Authority and the Independent Television Commission (see this section) replaced the Independent Broadcasting Authority

School Curriculum and Assessment Authority

Newcombe House, 45 Notting Hill Gate, London W11 3JB
Tel 0171-229 1234 Fax 0171-229 8526

Officials

Chairman
Sir Ron Dearing CB

Deputy Chairman
Graham Mackenzie

Chief Executive
Dr Nicholas Tate

(The chairman and other fourteen members of SCAA are appointed by the Secretary of State for Education and include teachers, educationalists and industrialists)

Responsibilities

To develop the National Curriculum and its assessment at ages 7, 11 and 14

To keep under review all aspects of the curriculum, school examinations and assessment for state schools in England and to advise the Secretary of State for Education on these matters, including appropriate research and development

To advise the Secretary of State on the approval of external qualifications

To publish and disseminate information relating to the curriculum, examinations and assessment

To make the necessary arrangements for school-based assessments

Founded

Established under the Education Act, 1993, SCAA assumed its responsibilities on 1 October 1993. It replaces the National Curriculum Council (NCC) and the School Examinations and Assessment Council (SEAC)

Scottish Consumer Council

Royal Exchange House, 100 Queen Street, Glasgow G1 3DN
Tel 0141-226 5261   Fax 0141-221 0731

Members

Chairman
Deirdre Hutton

Members
Mrs Margaret Agbemetsi-Sika
Mrs Margaret Burns
Mrs Elspeth Campbell
Mrs Gillian Campbell
H Bruce Collier
Peter Edmondson OBE
Bernard Forteath
Mrs May Kidd
Professor Gerry Maher
Jeremy Mitchell
Thomas O'Malley
Ms Yvonne Osman
Mrs Winifred Sherry JP *(Vice-Chairman)*

Officials

Director
Ann Foster

Information Officer
Katie Carr

Responsibilities

To represent the interests of Scottish consumers and to ensure that a consumer viewpoint is expressed wherever possible, when public and private services are under consideration

Founded

1975 as a result of a government White Paper

Scottish Enterprise

120 Bothwell Street, Glasgow G2 7JP
Tel 0141-248 2700 Fax 0141-221 3217

Officials

Chairman
Professor Donald MacKay

Deputy Chairman
Sir Ronald Garrick CBE

Chief Executive
Crawford W Beveridge CBE

Managing Director, Operations
Dr Robert M Crawford (4)

Board

Professor Donald Mackay
Dr Jim Adamson OBE
Professor Andrew Bain
Crawford Beveridge CBE
Tom Farmer CBE
Sir Ronald Garrick
Michael Gray OBE
Cllr Rosemary McKenna
Professor Jack Shaw CBE
Yvonne Strachan
Mrs Celia Urquhart
Sir Ian Wood

Responsibilities

To help develop a high output, high income and low unemployment economy in Scotland which provides a high quality of life and is sustainable both in economic and environmental terms

Through "Locate in Scotland", to diversify and develop the economy by attracting and assisting inward investors

Scottish Enterprise's 13 Local Enterprise Companies work in partnership with all sections of the community to develop the local economy, improve the environment and provide training at all levels

Founded

1991 when it took over the economic development and environmental improvement functions of the Scottish Development Agency and the training functions of the Training Agency in lowland Scotland

Scottish Law Commission

140 Causewayside, Edinburgh EH9 1PR
Tel 0131-668 2131 Fax 0131-662 4900

Members

Chairman
The Hon Lord Davidson

Commissioners
Dr E M Clive
Niall R Whitty
Professor P N Love CBE
W A Nimmo Smith QC

Officials

Secretary
K F Barclay

Parliamentary Draftsmen
G S Douglas QC
G Kowalski
J D Harkness

Assistant Solicitor
R Bland

Responsibilities

To keep under review with a view to its systematic development and reform, the law of Scotland

Founded

1965 under the provisions of the Law Commissions Act 1965

Scottish Legal Services Ombudsman

2 Greenside Lane, Edinburgh EH1 3AH
Tel 0131-556 5574

Officials
Scottish Legal Services Ombudsman
Garry S Watson

Responsibilities
To oversee the handling of complaints against legal practitioners. Members of the public first approach the relevant professional organisation, namely the Law Society of Scotland or the Faculty of Advocates. Complainers who are not satisfied that they have had a full and fair hearing may then raise the matter with the Ombudsman

Founded
1991 under the provisions of the Law Reform (Miscellaneous Provisions) (Scotland) Act 1990. The Ombudsman replaced the Lay Observer

Scottish Prisons Complaints Commission

Government Buildings, Broomhouse Drive, Edinburgh EH11 3XA
Tel 0131-244 8423 Fax 0131-244 8430

Officials

Commissioner
Dr Jim McManus

Deputy Commissioner
Alan Quinn

Secretary
Miss Janice Elvin

Responsibilities

The Commission is an independent body established to review prisoners' complaints which have not been resolved within the Scottish Prison Service (SPS). It has the powers to investigate complaints in whatever way it considers fit and to report its recommendations to the Chief Executive of SPS. An annual report is submitted to the Secretary of State for Scotland

Founded

1994 as a result of Government response to the Woolf Committee, SPS concern about the need for external reviews of complaints and commitments made in the Justice Charter

Securities and Investments Board

Gavrelle House, 2-14 Bunhill Row, London EC1Y 8RA
Tel 0171-638 1240 Fax 0171-382 5900

Board

Chairman
Andrew Large

Deputy Chairmen
Lord Alexander of Weedon QC
Viscount Runciman of Doxford CBE

Chief Executive
J R C Young CBE

Members
Mrs Rosalind Gilmore
Professor Robert Jack CBE
John Kennedy
Dr Oonagh McDonald
Lord Stewartby
Leonard Warwick
Brian Williamson CBE
Andrew S Winckler

Officials

Heads of Division
Head of Supervision
Andrew Winckler

Head of Enforcement
Jeremy Orme

Head of Policy and Legal Affairs
Michael Blair

Head of Operations
Brian Smith

Head of Public Affairs
Betty Powell

Adviser on International Affairs
Tim Shepheard-Walwyn

Head of Collective Investment Schemes
Richard Stocks

Responsibilities

The regulation of the financial services industry. Regulatory activity is then delegated to and exercised by recognised Self-Regulating Organisations (see below) and the Recognised Professional Bodies of the legal, accounting and insurance professions

SIB presents an annual report to Parliament

SIB's major aim is to achieve a high level of investor protection by promoting overall efficiency in the financial markets

Founded 1987 under the provisions of the Financial Services Act 1986

Self-Regulating Organisations

Investment Management Regulatory Organisation (IMRO)
Broadwalk House
5 Appold Street
London EC2A 2LL
Tel 0171-628 6022
Fax 0171-920 9285

Personal Investment Authority (PIA)
7th Floor
1 Canada Square
Canary Wharf
London E14 5AZ
Tel 0171-538 8860
Fax 0171-418 9300

Securities and Futures Authority (SFA)
Cottons Centre
Cottons Lane
London SE1 2QB
Tel 0171-378 9000
Fax 0171-357 7987

Security Commission

c/o Cabinet Office, 70 Whitehall, London SW1A 2AS
Tel 0171-270 0170

Officials

Chairman
The Rt Hon The Lord Lloyd of Berwick

Alternative Chairman
The Rt Hon Lady Justice Butler-Sloss DBE

Members
Sir John Blelloch KCB
Lieutenant-General Sir Derek Boorman KCB
Sir Christopher Curwen KCMG
Lord Tombs of Brailes
The Lord Wright of Richmond GCMG

Secretary
J K Barron

Responsibilities

On the Prime Minister's request, to investigate and report on the circumstances in which a breach of security has occurred in the public service, and on any related failure of departmental security arrangements or neglect of duty

In the light of any such investigation, to advise whether any change in security arrangements is necessary or desirable

Founded

1964

Security Service Tribunal

PO Box 18, London SE1 0TZ
Tel 0171-273 4095

Officials	*Commissioner* **The Rt Hon Lord Justice Stuart-Smith** *President* **The Right Hon Lord Justice (Simon) Brown** *Vice-President* **Sheriff John McInnes QC** *Member* **Sir Richard Gaskell**
Responsibilities	To investigate public complaints against the Security Service
Founded	1989 as a result of the Security Service Act 1989

Standing Advisory Commission on Human Rights

Temple Court, 39 North Street, Belfast BT1 1NA
Tel 01232 243987 Fax 01232 247844

Officials

Chairman
R Charles Hill QC

Secretary
E D Carson (7)

Responsibilities

To provide the Secretary of State for Northern Ireland with independent advice on the adequacy and effectiveness of the law as regards religious and political discrimination and on the full range of human rights safeguards in Northern Ireland. The advice provided by the Commission is contained in its annual reports, which are laid before Parliament

Founded

1973 under the provisions of the Northern Ireland Constitution Act 1973

Teacher Training Agency

Portland House, Stag Place, London SW1E 5TT
Tel 0171-925 3700 Fax 0171-925 3792

Board Members

Chairman
Geoffrey Parker

Chief Executive
Anthea Millett

Members
Lady Cox
Terry Creissen
Dr Dorian Edynbry
Prabhu Guptara
Jonathan Hewitt
Dr Peter Knight CBE
Ann Markham OBE
Professor Anthony O'Hear
Janet Trotter OBE
Dee Williams

CBI Observer
Brian Palmer

OFSTED Assessor
Michael Thomlinson

DFE Assessor
Nick Sanders

Head of Policy
Miss F Sulke

Secretary to the Board and Head of Administration
Stephen Hillier

Responsibilities

To fund teacher training; to accredit providers of initial training for school teachers; to provide information and advice about teacher training and teaching as a career and to carry out or commission research with a view to improving the standards of teaching and teacher training

Founded

September 1994 as a result of the Education Act 1994

UK Atomic Energy Authority (AEA Technology)

Harwell, Oxfordshire OX11 0RA
Tel 01235 821111 Fax 01235 832591

Members

Chairman
Sir Anthony Cleaver

Deputy Chairman
Dr B L Eyre CBE

Professor Michael Brady
J Bullock
Gordon A Campbell
R Sanderson OBE
Colin Sharman
Mrs S Shirley OBE

Chief Executive, Commercial Division
Dr P Watson

Chief Executive, Government Division
Dr D Pooley CBE

Managing Director, Services Division
A W Hills

Officials

Secretary
J R Bretherton

Executive Director, Finance
P G Daffern

Chief Press Officer
A Munn

Responsibilities

The United Kingdom Atomic Energy Authority (UKAEA) was set up in 1954 to develop the UK nuclear power programme. Since the mid-1980s, with the reduction in government funding of the UK's nuclear fission programme, UKAEA has successfully increased its income from private, non-nuclear and overseas sectors

In April 1994, UKAEA restructured to reflect its different responsibilities. The commercial division, known as **AEA Technology**, is being developed as a fully commercial science and engineering services business which solves technical and environmental problems for industries and governments around the world. It helps customers adopt and exploit technology so they can enhance products, develop and optimise plant and processes, meet safety requirements and manage environmental challenges. AEA Technology's markets include aerospace, defence, oil and gas, chemicals and pharmaceuticals, transport and public utilities. AEA Technology encompasses the new National Environmental Technology Centre, formed by the merger of AEA's and Warren Spring Laboratory's environmental capabilities

On 16 November 1994, it was announced in the Queen's Speech that AEA Technology is to be privatised during the next parliamentary term. Decisions on the form of privatisation will be taken in due course

UKAEA Government Division is responsible for the care of, and for dismantling, the UKAEA's radioactive facilities no longer in use and disposing of the radioactive wastes cost-effectively, safely and in an environmentally-acceptable way. As well as being charged with making the best use of the various UKAEA sites and operational facilities throughout the country, UKAEA Government Division provides the UK contribution to the international fusion programmes

Its main sites are Harwell and Culham in Oxfordshire; Winfrith (Dorset); Risley (Cheshire); Windscale (Cumbria); and Dounreay (Scotland)

UKAEA Government Division will remain in the public sector. A third, services division, will support the other divisions for an interim period

Founded

1954 under the provisions of the Atomic Energy Authority Act 1954, amended by the Atomic Energy Authority Acts of 1959 and 1971; UKAEA's functions were extended by the Science and Technology Act 1965.

Welsh Consumer Council/Cyngor Defnyddwyr Cymru

Castle Buildings, Womanby Street, Cardiff CF1 2BN
Tel 01222 396056 Fax 01222 238360

Members

Chairman
Beata Brookes

Members
Alan Barnish
R Ian Edge
Roger Warren Evans
William Evans
Gareth Jones
Jane Lloyd Hughes
Michael McEvoy
Elinor Patchell
Mair Stephens
Richard Thomas
Roderick Thurman
Mary Watkins

Officials

Director
Dr Nich Pearson

Responsibilities

To ensure that Welsh consumers are represented in central and local government decision-making, as well as commerce and industry, with particular attention being given to the disadvantaged

Founded

1975 as a result of a government White Paper

Welsh Development Agency

Pearl House, Greyfriars Road, Cardiff CF1 3XX
Tel 01345 775577 (English enquiries)
Tel 01345 775566 (Welsh enquiries)
+44 1443 845500 (International enquiries)
Fax: telephone numbers above and ask for appropriate fax number

Officials

Chairman
David S Rowe-Beddoe

Deputy Chairman
Dr Roy Bichan

Chief Executive
Barry Hartop

Members
Rhiannon Chapman
Robin Lewis OBE
David Malpas
Professor Garel Rhys OBE
George Wright MBE

Responsibilities

To further the regeneration of the economy and improve the environment of Wales

To help boost the growth, profitability and competitiveness of indigenous Welsh business

To build premises for industry and encourage private sector investment in property development

To fund land reclamation and environmental improvement throughout the Principality

To stimulate urban and rural regeneration and development

To promote Wales as a location for inward investment

Founded

1976 under the provisions of the Welsh Development Agency Act 1975

Abbreviations

A

ABRO	Army Base Repair Organisation
ABSDA	Army Base Storage and Distribution Agency
AC	Audit Commission for Local Authorities and the NHS in England and Wales
ACA	Associate, Institute of Chartered Accountants
ACAS	Advisory, Conciliation and Arbitration Service
ACBACS	Advisory Committee on Business Appointments of Crown Servants
ACCA	Associate, Association of Certified Accountants
ACGI	Associate, City and Guilds of London Institute
ACIArb	Associate, Chartered Institute of Arbitrators
ACIB	Associate, Chartered Institute of Bankers
ACIS	Associate, Chartered Institute of Secretaries
ACS	Assistant Chief Scientist
AD	Assistant Director; Allied Dunbar
ADAS	Agricultural Development and Advisory Service
ADC	Aide-de-Camp
ADC Gen	Aide-de-Camp General
ADS	Army Dental Service
AdvDip Crim	Advanced Diploma in Criminology
AE	Agricultural Economist
AFC	Air Force Cross
AFSA	Associate, Faculty of Secretaries and Administrators
AHSM	Associate, Institute of Health Services Management
AIQS	Associate Member, Institute of Quantity Surveyors
AKC	Associate, Kings College, London
ALA	Assistant Legal Adviser
AM	Master of Arts (United States of America)
AO	Actuarial Officer; Agricultural Officer
AOR	Assistant Official Receiver
AP	Assistant Principal
APC	Assistant Parliamentary Counsel
APS	Assistant Private Secretary
ARCS	Associate, Royal College of Science
ARCST	Associate, Royal College of Science and Technology, Glasgow
ARIAS	Associate, Royal Incorporation of Architects in Scotland
ARIBA	Associate, Royal Institute of British Architects
ARIC	Associate, Royal Institute of Chemistry
ARICS	Associate, Royal Institution of Chartered Surveyors
ARSM	Associate, Royal School of Mines
AS	Assistant Secretary; Assistant Solicitor
ASA	Advertising Standards Authority; Accounts Services Agency
ASWE	Admiralty Surface Weapons Establishment
ATS	Assistant Treasury Solicitor
AUS	Assistant Under Secretary

B

BA	Bachelor of Arts; The Buying Agency
BAOR	British Army of the Rhine
BBC	British Broadcasting Corporation
BCC	Broadcasting Complaints Commission
BCE	Boundary Commission for England
BCh or BChir	Bachelor of Surgery
BCL	Bachelor of Civil Law
BCNI	Boundary Commission for Northern Ireland
BCom	Bachelor of Commerce
BCS	Boundary Commission for Scotland
BCW	Boundary Commission for Wales
BDS	Bachelor of Dental Surgery
BE	Bank of England; Bachelor of Engineering
BJur	Bachelor of Jurisprudence
BL	Bachelor of Law
BM	Bachelor of Medicine
BOAC	British Overseas Airways Corporation
BP	British Petroleum
BPharm	Bachelor of Pharmacy
BPhil	Bachelor of Philosophy
BRE	Building Research Establishment
BRPB	British Rail Property Board
BS	Bachelor of Surgery; Bachelor of Science
BSc	Bachelor of Science
BSC	Broadcasting Standards Council
BScAgric	Bachelor of Science, Agriculture
BScEcon	Bachelor of Science, Economics

BScEng Bachelor of Science, Engineering
BScMet Bachelor of Science, Metallurgy
BSO Building Society Ombudsman
BSocSc Bachelor of Social Science
BTech Bachelor of Technology
BUPA British United Provident Association
BVetMed Bachelor of Veterinary Medicine
BVMS Bachelor of Veterinary Medicine and Surgery
BVSc Bachelor of Veterinary Science

C

C&E Customs and Excise
CA Chartered Accountant; Chartered Accountant (Scotland); Coastguard Agency
CAA Civil Aviation Authority
CADW Welsh Historic Monuments
CA(NI) Compensation Agency (NI)
CB Companion, Order of the Bath
CBC County Borough Council
CBE Commander, Order of the British Empire
CBIM Companion, British Institute of Management
CBiol Chartered Biologist
CC County Council; Chief Constable; Charity Commission
CCAP Citizen's Charter Advisory Panel
CCC Chessington Computer Centre
CChem Chartered Chemist
CDEP Central Directorate of Environmental Pollution
CDipAF Certified Diploma in Accounting and Finance
CEng Chartered Engineer
CEO Chief Executive Officer
CertEd Certificate of Education
CertHS Certificate in Historical Studies
CEst Crown Estate
CFE College of Further Education
CH Companies House
ChB Bachelor of Surgery
CICB Criminal Injuries Compensation Board
CICE Companion, Institution of Civil Engineers
CID Criminal Investigation Department
CIGs Current Intelligence Groups
CIMA Chartered Institute of Management Accountants
CIMgt Companion, Institute of Management
CinC Commander in Chief
CIPFA Chartered Institute of Public Finance and Accountancy
CIPM Companion, Institute of Personnel Management
CLAE Commission for Local Administration in England
CLAS Commission for Local Administration in Scotland
CLAW Commission for Local Administration in Wales
CMG Companion, Order of St Michael and St George
CMO Chief Medical Officer
CNO Chief Nursing Officer
CO Cabinet Office (Office of Public Service and Science); Commanding Officer
COI Central Office of Information
COMEDS Committee of the Chiefs of Military Medical Services in NATO
CPA Chartered Patent Agent
CPhys Chartered Physicist
CPMG Committee on Proprietary Medicinal Products
CPS Crown Prosecution Service
CQSW Certificate of Qualification in Social Work
CRE Commission for Racial Equality
CrO(S) Crown Office, Scotland
CS Court Service
CStat Chief Statistician
CSC Civil Service College
CSD Civil Service Department
CSF Civil Service Fellow
CSL Central Science Laboratory
CSM Medicines Commission, Committee on Safety of Medicines
CSMAA Civil Service Medical Aid Association
CSO Central Statistical Office
CSolO(NI) Crown Solicitor's Office (Northern Ireland)
CSPL Committee on Standards in Public Life
CST Council for Science and Technology
CStJ Commander, Most Venerable Order of the Hospital of St John of Jerusalem
CT Council on Tribunals
CTO Capital Taxes Office, Inland Revenue
CVL Central Veterinary Laboratory
CVO Companion, Victoria Order

D

DA Diploma in Anaesthesia
DAA Defence Accounts Agency
DAC Defence Animal Centre
DAFS Department of Agriculture and Fisheries for Scotland

DANC Defence, Press and Broadcasting Advisory (DA Notices) Committee
DANI Department of Agriculture for Northern Ireland
DAQMG Deputy Assistant Quartermaster General
DASA Defence Analytical Services Agency
DAvMed Diploma in Aviation Medicine
DBE Dame Commander, Order of the British Empire
DC Deputy Chairman
DCH Diploma in Child Health
DCL Doctor of Civil Law
DCTA Defence Clothing and Textiles Agency
DEA Department of Economic Affairs
DEDNI Department of Economic Development for Northern Ireland
DEmp Department of Employment
DENI Department of Education for Northern Ireland
DERA Defence Evaluation and Research Agency
DES Department of Education and Science (now Department for Education [DfE])
DfE Department for Education
DFPNI Department of Finance and Personnel, Northern Ireland
DG Director General
DH Department of Health
DHSS Department of Health and Social Security
DHSSNI Department of Health and Social Security Northern Ireland
DI District Inspector
DIC Diploma of the Imperial College
DIH Diploma in Industrial Health
DipArch Diploma in Architecture
DipBact Diploma in Bacteriology
DipCE Diploma in Civil Engineering
DipCrim Diploma in Criminology
DipEcon Diploma in Economics
DipEd Diploma in Education
DipHSM Diploma in Health Service Management
DipMan Diploma in Management
DipPE Diploma in Physical Education
DipSocSci Diploma in Social Science
DipStat Diploma in Statistics
DipTP Diploma in Town Planning
DIS Defence Intelligence Staff
DL Deputy Lieutenant
DLitt Doctor of Literature; Doctor of Letters
DMRT Diploma in Medical Radio Therapy
DNH Department of National Heritage
DNS Department for National Savings
DO Dental Officer
DObst RCOG Diploma of the Royal College of Obstetricians and Gynaecologists
DoE Department of the Environment
DoEDNI Department of Economic Development for Northern Ireland
DoENI Department for Education in Northern Ireland
DoEnvNI Department of the Environment for Northern Ireland
DoH Department of Health
DPCS Defence Postal and Courier Service
DPD Diploma in Public Dentistry
DPH Diploma in Public Health
DPhil Doctor of Philosophy
DPP Director of Public Prosecutions
DPP(NI) Department of the Director of Public Prosecutions (Northern Ireland)
Dr Doctor
DRCOG Diploma, Royal College of Obstetricians and Gynaecologists
DisSA Disposal Sales Agency
DS Deputy Secretary
DSA Driving Standards Agency
DSc Doctor of Science
DSC Distinguished Service Cross
DSO Companion of the Distinguished Service Order
DSS Department of Social Security; Director of Social Services
DTA Diploma of Tropical Medicine
DTI Department of Trade and Industry; District Tax Inspector
DTM&H Diploma in Tropical Medicine and Hygiene
DTMX Defence Transport and Movements Executive
DTp Department of Transport
DUniv Doctor of the University
DVLA Driver and Vehicle Licensing Agency
DVLA(NI) Driver and Vehicle Licensing Agency (Northern Ireland)
DVSM Diploma in Veterinary State Medicine
DVTA(NI) Driver and Vehicle Testing Agency (Northern Ireland)
DWI Drinking Water Inspectorate
DYRMS Duke of York's Royal Military School

E

EA Economic Adviser
EAD Exchequer and Audit Department (*now* National Audit Office)
EC European Commission
ECGD Export Credits Guarantee Department
Econ Economics
ED Education Department, Scottish Office

EDG Employment Department Group
EEB European Environmental Bureau
EEC European Economic Community
Eng Engineering
EOC Equal Opportunities Commission
EP English Partnerships
ES Employment Service
ESRC Economic and Social Research Council
EU European Union, formerly European Community
EurIng European Engineer

F

FAPS Fellow, American Physical Society
FAS Funding Agency for Schools
FBA Fellow, British Academy
FBCS Fellow, British Computer Society
FBIM Fellow, British Institute of Management
FBPsS Fellow, British Psychological Society
FC Forestry Commission
FCA Fellow, Institute of Chartered Accountants
FCAA Fellow, Chartered Association of Accountants
FCAM Fellow, CAM Foundation
FCCA Fellow, Chartered Association of Certified Accountants
FCGI Fellow, City and Guilds of London Institute
FCIA Fellow, Chartered Institute of Arbitrators
FCIB Fellow, Chartered Institute of Bankers
FCIBS Fellow, Chartered Institution of Building Services
FCIH Fellow, Chartered Institute of Housing
FCIPS Fellow, Chartered Institute of Purchasing and Supply (formerly FInstPS)
FCIS Fellow, Institute of Chartered Secretaries and Administrators
FCIT Fellow, Chartered Institute of Transport
FCMA Fellow, Chartered Institute of Management Accountants (formerly FICMA)
FCO Foreign and Commonwealth Office
FCS Fellow, Chemical Society (now absorbed into Royal Society of Chemistry)
FD Finance Director
FEFC Further Education Funding Council
FEng Fellow, Royal Academy of Engineering
FFA Fellow, Faculty of Actuaries
FFARCS Fellow, Faculty of Anaesthetists, Royal College of Surgeons of England
FFCM Fellow, Faculty of Community Medicine (*now see* FFPHM)
FFOM Fellow, Faculty of Occupational Medicine
FFPHM Fellow, Faculty of Public Health Medicine (formerly FFCM)
FFPM Fellow, Faculty of Pharmaceutical Medicine
FIA Fellow, Institute of Actuaries
FIBiol Fellow, Institute of Biology
FICE Fellow, Institution of Civil Engineers
FIChemE Fellow, Institution of Chemical Engineers
FICF Fellow, Institute of Chartered Foresters
FICFM Fellow, Institute of Charity Fundraising Managers
FICMA Fellow, Institute of Cost and Management Accountants
FIDPM Fellow, Institute of Data Processing Management
FIEE Fellow, Institution of Electrical Engineers
FIFireE Fellow, Institution of Fire Engineers
FIFST Fellow, Institute of Food Science and Technology
FIGeol Fellow, Institution of Geologists
FIHospE Fellow, Institute of Hospital Engineering
FIHT Fellow, Institution of Highways and Transportation
FIM Fellow, Institute of Materials
FIMarE Fellow, Institute of Marine Engineers
FIMechE Fellow, Institution of Mechanical Engineers
FIMgt Fellow, Institute of Management
FIMineE Fellow, Institution of Mining Engineers
FInstD Fellow, Institute of Directors
FInstE Fellow, Institute of Energy
FInstHSM Fellow, Institute of Health Service Managers
FInstM Fellow, Institute of Marketing
FInstP Fellow, Institute of Physics
FInstPS Fellow, Institute of Purchasing and Supply
FIOSH Fellow, Institution of Occupational Safety and Health
FIPM Fellow, Institute of Personnel Management
FIWEM Fellow, Institution of Water and Environmental Management
FIWES Fellow, Institution of Water Engineers and Scientists (*now see* FIWEM)
FIWO Fellow, Institution of Water Officers
FIWSC Fellow, Institute of Wood Science

FO Flag Officer
FOR Fellowship of Operational Research
FPRI Fellow, Plastics and Rubber Institute (*now see* FIM)
FRad Acad Fellow, Radio Academy
FRAeS Fellow, Royal Aeronautical Society
FRAS Fellow, Royal Astronomical Society
FRC Financial Reporting Council
FRC:ASB Financial Reporting Council, Accounting Standards Board
FRC:FRRP Financial Reporting Council, Financial Reporting Review Panel
FRCGP Fellow, Royal College of General Practitioners
FRCP Fellow, Royal College of Physicians, London
FRCPath Fellow, Royal College of Pathologists
FRCPEd Fellow, Royal College of Physicians, Edinburgh
FRCPGlas Fellow, Royal College of Physicians and Surgeons of Glasgow
FRCPsych Fellow, Royal College of Psychiatrists
FRCR Fellow, Royal College of Radiologists
FRCSGlas Fellow, Royal College of Physicians and Surgeons of Glasgow
FREconS Fellow, Royal Economic Society
FRGS Fellow, Royal Geographical Society
FRIC Fellow, Royal Institute of Chemistry (*now see* FRSC)
FRICS Fellow, Royal Institution of Chartered Surveyors
FRINA Fellow, Royal Institute of Naval Architects
FRInstB Fellow, Royal Institute of Biology
FRIPHH Fellow, Royal Institute of Public Health and Hygiene
FRPharmS Fellow, Royal Pharmaceutical Society
FRS Fellow, Royal Society
FRSA Fellow, Royal Society of Arts
FRSC Fellow, Royal Society of Chemistry (formerly FRIC)
FRSE Fellow, Royal Society of Edinburgh
FRSS Fellow, Royal Statistical Society
FS First Secretary
FSA Fellow, Society of Antiquaries
FSC Fire Service College
FSRP Fellow, Society for Radiological Protection
FSS Forensic Science Service

G

GAD Government Actuary's Department
GB Gaming Board for Great Britain
GBE Knight or Dame Grand Cross, Order of the British Empire
GCB Knight or Dame Grand Cross, Order of the Bath
GCHQ Government Communications Headquarters
GOR Government Offices for the Regions
GPL Government Property Lawyers
GRO(S) General Register Office (Scotland)

H

HA Health Authority; Highways Agency
HBLB Horserace Betting Levy Board
HC House of Commons
HD Health District
HEA Health Education Authority
HEFCE Higher Education Funding Council for England
HIE Highlands and Islands Enterprise
HL House of Lords
HMPS Her Majesty's Prison Service
HMLR HM Land Registry
HMS Her Majesty's Ship
HMSO Her Majesty's Stationery Office
HMT Her Majesty's Treasury
HMY Her Majesty's Yacht
HNC Higher National Certificate
HO Home Office
HQ Headquarters
HQSCS (NWE) HQ Service Children's Schools (NW Europe)
HRP Historic Royal Palaces
HS Historic Scotland
HSC Health and Safety Commission
HSE Health and Safety Commission: Health and Safety Executive
HyO Hydrographic Office

I

IA Immigration Appeals, The Appellate Authorities; Inspector of Accidents
IB Intervention Board
IBRD International Bank for Reconstruction and Development (World Bank)
ICA Institute of Chartered Accountants
ICR Institute of Cancer Research
IHQP Insolvency Headquarters, Policy
IMF International Monetary Fund
IND Immigration and Nationality Department, Home Office
INSEAD Institut Europeen d'Administration des Affaires
IOB Insurance Ombudsman Bureau

IPFA Member or Associate, Chartered Institute of Public Finance and Accountancy
IR Inland Revenue
IRRV Institute of Rating Revenues and Valuation
IRTU (NI) Industrial Research and Technology Unit (Northern Ireland)
IS Insolvency Service; Cabinet/Ministerial Committee on the Intelligence Services
ISO Imperial Service Order
IST Intelligence Service Tribunal
IT Information Technology
ITC Independent Television Commission
ITS Independent Tribunal Service

J

JIC Joint Intelligence Committee
JIS Joint Intelligence Secretariat
JNCC Joint Nature Conservation Committee
JP Justice of the Peace
jssc completed course at Joint Services Staff College

K

KBE Knight Commander, Order of the British Empire
KCB Knight Commander, Order of the Bath
KCMG Knight Commander, Order of St Michael and St George
KCVO Knight Commander, Royal Victorian Order
KG Knight, Order of the Garter
KSG Knight, Order of St Gregory the Great
KStJ Knight, Most Venerable Order of the Hospital of St John of Jerusalem
Kt Knight

L

LA Legal Assistant
LAD Lord Advocate's Department
LBS London Business School
LC Law Commission; Lancashire Constabulary
LCD Lord Chancellor's Department
LGC Laboratory of the Government Chemist
LGComm Local Government Commission
LGF Local Government Finance
LISA Logistic Information Systems Agency
LLB Bachelor of Laws
LLM Master of Laws
LRCP Licentiate, Royal College of Physicians, London
LSE London School of Economics
LSLO Legal Secretariat to the Law Officers
LTh Licentiate in Theology
LVO Lieutenant, Royal Victorian Order

M

MA Master of Arts; Ministry of Aviation
MAEcon Master of Arts, Economics
MAFF Ministry of Agriculture, Fisheries and Food
MB Bachelor of Medicine
MBA Master of Business Administration
MBCS Member of the British Computer Society
MBE Member, Order of the British Empire
MBIM Member, British Institute of Management
MC Medicines Commission; Military Cross
MCA Medicines Control Agency
MCC Marylebone Cricket Club
MCD Master of Civic Design
MCIBSE Member, Chartered Institution of Building Services Engineers
MCIPS Member, Chartered Institute of Purchasing and Supply
MCIT Member, Chartered Institute of Transport
MCSI Magistrates' Courts Services Inspectorate
MCrim Master of Criminology
MD Managing Director; Doctor of Medicine
MDA Medical Devices Agency
MEng Master of Engineering
Met Metallurgy
MFCM Member, Faculty of Community Medicine
MFOM Member, Faculty of Occupational Medicine
MFPHM Member, Faculty of Public Health Medicine
MFPM Member, Faculty of Pharmaceutical Medicine
MGDS RCS Member in General Dental Surgery, Royal College of Surgeons
MHS Meat Hygiene Service
MHSM Member, Institute of Health Services Management
MI5 Security Service
MI6 Secret Intelligence Service

MICE Member, Institution of Civil Engineers
MICGP Member, Irish College of General Practitioners
MICPS Member, Chartered Institute of Purchasing and Supply
MIEE Member, Institution of Electrical Engineers
MIFireE Member, Institution of Fire Engineers
MIFS Member, Institution of Fire Safety
MIGasE Member, Institution of Gas Engineers
MIHSM Member, Institute of Health Service Management
MIHT Member, Institution of Highways and Transportation
MIMarE Member, Institute of Marine Engineers
MIMC Member, Institute of Management Consultants
MIMechE Member, Institution of Mechanical Engineers
MInstAM Member, Institute of Administrative Management
MIOD Member, Institute of Directors
MIPD Member, Institute of Personnel Directors
MIProdE Member, Institution of Production Engineers (*now see* MIEE)
MIPM Member, Institute of Personnel Management
MIPS Member, Institute of Purchasing and Supply
MIS Member, Institute of Statistics
MIWEM Member, Institution of Water and Environmental Management
MMC Monopolies and Mergers Commission
MO Meteorological Office; Medical Officer
MoD Ministry of Defence
MoH Ministry of Health
MoT Ministry of Transport
MP Member of Parliament
MPA Master of Public Administration
MPhil Master of Philosophy
MPNI Ministry of Pensions and National Insurance
MPPS Master of Public Policy Studies
MRAeS Member, Royal Aeronautical Society
MRC Medical Research Council
MRCGP Member, Royal College of General Practitioners
MRCP Member, Royal College of Physicians, London
MRCPath Member, Royal College of Pathologists
MRCPsych Member, Royal College of Psychiatrists
MRCS Member, Royal College of Surgeons of England
MRCVS Member, Royal College of Veterinary Science
MRIN Member, Royal Institute of Navigation
MRTPI Member, Royal Town Planning Institute
MS Master of Science (US); Military Survey
MSA Marine Safety Agency
MSC Manpower Services Commission
MSc Master of Science
MScEcon Master of Science, Economics
MSI Member, Securities Institute
MSocSci Master of Social Sciences
MTh Master of Theology
MusB Bachelor of Music

N

NAA North Atlantic Assembly
NAB National Assistance Board
NAO National Audit Office
NARO Naval Aircraft Repair Organisation
NATO North Atlantic Treaty Organisation
NCC National Consumer Council
NCDN National Certificate of District Nursing
NCIS National Criminal Intelligence Service
ndc National Defence College; NATO Defence College
NEL National Engineering Laboratory
NERC Natural Environment Research Council
NHS National Health Service
NHSPA NHS Pensions Agency
NHSE NHS Estates
NIAO Northern Ireland Audit Office
NICS Northern Ireland Court Service
NICSA Northern Ireland Child Support Agency
NID Northern Ireland Departments
NIO Northern Ireland Office
NIPS Northern Ireland Prison Service
NPL National Physical Laboratory
NRA National Rivers Authority
NRI Natural Resources Institute
NRPB National Radiological Protection Board
NRTA Naval Recruiting and Training Agency
NWML National Weights and Measures Laboratory

O

OAIR Office of the Adjudicator for the Inland Revenue, Customs and Excise and the Contributions Agency

OBE	Officer, Order of the British Empire
OBO	Office of the Banking Ombudsman
OC	Officer Commanding
ODA	Overseas Development Administration
ODC(US)	Overseas Defence College (United States)
ODM	Ministry of Overseas Development
ODPR	Office of the Data Protection Registrar
OFFER	Office of Electricity Regulation
OFGAS	Office of Gas Supply
OFLOT	Office of the National Lottery
OFSTED	Office for Standards in Education
OFT	Office of Fair Trading
OFTEL	Office of Telecommunications
OFWAT	Office of Water Services
OHS	Occupational Health Service
OHSC	Office of the Health Service Commissioners (Ombudsman)
OLSO	Office of the Legal Services Ombudsman
OMCS	Office for the Minister for the Civil Service
OME	Office of Manpower Economics
O(NI)CC	Office of the NI Commissioner for Complaints (Ombudsman)
O(NI)PCA	Office of the NI Parliamentary Commissioner for Administration (Ombudsman)
OPB	Occupational Pensions Board
OPCA	Office of the Parliamentary Commissioner for Administration (Ombudsman)
OPCS	Office of Population Censuses and Surveys
OPRF	Office of Passenger Rail Franchising
OPSS	Office of Public Service and Science
OR	Operations Research
ORR	Office of the Rail Regulator
OS	Ordnance Survey
OS(NI)	Ordnance Survey (NI)
OSO	Office of Offshore Supplies
OStJ	Most Venerable Order of the Hospital of St John of Jerusalem
OUP	Oxford University Press

P

PA(NI)	Police Authority for NI
PB(EW)	Parole Board for England and Wales
PB(S)	Parole Board for Scotland
PC	Parliamentary Counsel; Privy Counsellor
PCA	Police Complaints Authority
PCC	Press Complaints Commission
PCO	Privy Council Office
PE	Principal Engineer Procurement Executive; Principal Examiner
PEFO	Principal Establishment and Finance Officer
PF	Procurator Fiscal
PGCE	Postgraduate Certificate in Education
PGO	Paymaster General's Office
PhB	Bachelor of Philosophy
PhD	Doctor of Philosophy
PHLS	Public Health Laboratory Service
PHSC	Political Honours Scrutiny Committee
PI	Planning Inspector
PIA	Planning Inspectorate Agency
PMO	Principal Medical Officer; Prime Minister's Office
PM	Prime Minister
PO	Patent Office(r); Probation Officer; Pensions Ombudsman
PPS	Principal Private Secretary; Parliamentary Private Secretary
PrisO	Prisons Ombudsman
PRO	Public Record Office
PRONI	Public Record Office Northern Ireland
PSA	Property Services Agency; PSA Services
psc	Graduate of Staff College († indicates Graduate of Senior Wing Staff College)
PSD	Pesticides Safety Directorate
PSIS	Permanent Secretaries' Committee on the Intelligence Services
psc(N)	Graduate of Staff College (Navy)
PS	Private Secretary
PTM	Panel on Takeovers and Mergers
PTO	Public Trust Office

Q

QC	Queen's Counsel
QCVSA	Queen's Commendation for Valuable Service in the Air
QECC	Queen Elizabeth II Conference Centre
QFSM	Queen's Fire Service Medal
QHDS	Queen's Honorary Dental Surgeon
QHP	Queen's Honorary Physician
QHS	Queen's Honorary Surgeon
QPM	Queen's Police Medal
QSM	Queen's Service Medal (NZ)
QVS	Queen Victoria School

R

RA	Radio Authority; Radiocommunications Agency; Royal Artillery

RADC	Royal Army Dental College
RAF	Royal Air Force
RAFMGDA	RAF Maintenance Group Defence Agency
RAFSEE	RAF Signals Engineering Establishment
RAFTGDA	RAF Training Group Defence Agency
RASA	Recruitment and Assessment Services Agency
RCA(NI)	Rate Collection Agency (NI)
rcds	completed a course, or served for a year on the staff of Royal College of Defence Studies
RCNC	Royal Corps of Naval Constructors
RCOG	Royal College of Obstetricians and Gynaecologists
RCP	Royal College of Physicians, London
RCP Edinburgh	Royal College of Physicians, Edinburgh
RFS	Registry of Friendly Societies
RGN	Registered General Nurse
RHA	Regional Health Authority
RHV	Registered Health Visitor
RIBA	Royal Institute of British Architects
RICS	Royal Institution of Chartered Surveyors
RINA	Royal Institution of Naval Architects
RM	Royal Mint; Registered Midwife
RMA	Royal Military Academy
RMCS	Royal Military College of Science
RMN	Registered Mental Nurse
RN	Royal Navy
RNAS	Royal Naval Air Service
RNH	Royal Naval Hospital
RP	Royal Parks
RS	Registers of Scotland

S

SAAS	Student Awards Agency for Scotland
SACHR	Standing Advisory Commission for Human Rights
SASA	Scottish Agricultural Science Agency
SC	Security Commission
SCA	Scottish Courts Administration
SCAA	School Curriculum and Assessment Authority
SCC	Scottish Consumer Council
ScD	Doctor of Science
SCS	Scottish Courts Service
SDD	Scottish Development Department
SE	Scottish Enterprise
SED	Scottish Education Department
SFE	Security Facilities Executive
SFO	Serious Fraud Office
SFPA	Scottish Fisheries Protection Agency
SHHD	Scottish Home and Health Department
SIB	Securities and Investments Board (inc FIMBRA, LAUTRO, IMRO, SFA and PIA)
SIS	Secret Intelligence Service; Security and Intelligence Services
SJD	Doctor of Juristic Science
SLC	Scottish Law Commission
SLSO	Scottish Legal Services Ombudsman
SO	Scientific Officer; Scottish Office; Staff Officer
SOPA	Scottish Office Pensions Agency
SoS	Secretary of State
SPCC	Scottish Prison Complaints Commission
SPO	Senior Patent Officer
SPS	Scottish Prison Service
SRM	State Registered Midwife
SRN	State Registered Nurse
SRO	Scottish Record Office
SS	Second Secretary; Steamship; Security Service
SSA(NI)	Social Security Agency (NI)
SSBA	Social Security Benefits Agency
SSC	Sea Systems Controllerate
SSCA	Social Security Contributions Agency
SSCSA	Social Security Child Support Agency
SSITSA	Social Security Information Technology Services Agency
SSRA	Social Security Resettlement Agency
SST	Security Service Tribunal
SSWPA	Social Security War Pensions Agency

T

TA	Territorial Army
TD	Territorial Efficiency Decoration
TEA(NI)	Training and Employment Agency (NI)
TI	Tax Inspector
TPA	Teachers' Pension Agency
TRL	Transport Research Laboratory
TS	Third Secretary
TSD	Treasury Solicitor's Department
tt	Tank Technology Course
TTA	Teacher Training Agency

U

UCLA	University of California, Los Angeles
UK	United Kingdom
UK Perm Rep	UK Permanent Representation, Brussels
UKAEA	UK Atomic Energy Authority
UKPA	UK Passport Agency

UN United Nations
US Under Secretary
USA United States of America

V

VAT Value Added Tax
VCA Vehicle Certification Agency
VI Vehicle Inspectorate
VLA(NI) Valuation and Lands Agency (NI)
VMD Veterinary Medicines Directorate
VO Veterinary Officer
VOA Valuation Office Agency
VRD Royal Naval Volunteer Reserve Officers' Decoration
VSO Voluntary Service Overseas

W

WCC Welsh Consumer Council
WDA Welsh Development Agency
WO Welsh Office
WPCC Wilton Park Conference Centre
WPSA World's Poultry Science Association
WS Writer to the Signet

Name Index

An alphabetical list of people whose names appear in *The Whitehall Companion*. See *Abbreviations* for full names of departments and other organisations.

Index